Complex Litigation

Complex Litigation

THIRD EDITION

E. Thomas Sullivan

President of the University of Vermont
Dean Emeritus, University of Minnesota Law School and
University of Arizona Rogers College of Law

Richard D. Freer

Charles Howard Candler Professor of Law
Emory University School of Law

Bradley G. Clary

Clinical Professor of Law
University of Minnesota
School of Law

Carolina Academic Press
Durham, North Carolina

ISBN 978-1-5310-1105-5
eISBN 978-1-5310-1106-2
LCCN 2018961309

Carolina Academic Press, LLC
700 Kent Street
Durham, North Carolina 27701
Telephone (919) 489-7486
Fax (919) 493-5668
www.cap-press.com

Printed in the United States of America

Each author can think of many people to whom we might dedicate this text. We appreciate the support of all of those persons over many years and in particular recognize these:

ETS: *To Leslie Black Sullivan.*

RDF: *To Louise, Courtney, and Collin.*

BGC: *To Leon Goodrich, Thomas Kane, and Donald Engle, my principal mentors in the trenches of complex litigation.*

Contents

Table of Cases

Preface

Litigation always has been a complicated undertaking. In the current age of multi-party, multi-claim, and overlapping multi-jurisdiction cases, lawsuits have assumed even higher levels of complexity. This text introduces in a comprehensive but compact way both fundamental and cutting-edge aspects of complex litigation.

In contrast to traditional casebooks, COMPLEX LITIGATION relies on a limited number of leading cases, coupled with extensive text and note material reviewing existing doctrine and exploring unanswered legal and policy issues. The reliance on text and notes to develop underlying legal doctrine minimizes the need for students to search for the necessary background based on fragments or inferences from principal cases.

The text comprehensively treats all aspects of the complex litigation process—from CAFA to the ALI Principles of the Law of Aggregate Litigation, from Internet personal jurisdiction to electronic discovery, and more. The text devotes attention to important and often neglected structural issues, including personal and subject matter jurisdiction, choice of law, mechanisms for coordinating overlapping federal and state litigation, and preclusion. It discusses the real world conduct, management, and control of the pre-trial and discovery process that characterizes complex cases, as well as trends and emerging legal doctrine that have promoted and facilitated the disposition of complex cases without trial.

Despite its broad coverage, COMPLEX LITIGATION is concise as a result of its primary use of text and note material to develop the implications of leading cases. It may easily be adopted for use in a two- or three-unit course.

Careful readers will notice our adoption of certain conventions. For example, in excerpted cases, we have deleted without notation various footnotes and citations. We have retained, however, selected footnotes within excerpted cases for teaching purposes. Those bear both consecutive numbering and, in brackets, the original note number from the opinion. We mostly have not included parallel case cites within excerpted opinions even if the original opinion did so. We have tried to eliminate most instances of boldface type even if excerpted opinions contained boldface headings.

President Sullivan and Professor Clary wish to acknowledge the support of the University of Minnesota, and the dedicated research assistance of the following law school students over the course of this project (in alphabetical order)—Hugh

Brown, Calvin Hoffman, David Klink, Anthony de Sam Lazaro, Ian Mccoy, Cicely Miltich, James Owens, and Nicholas Tymoczko. President Sullivan also wants to extend his appreciation to Worth Allen, law student at Vermont Law School, for his able research assistance.

Professor Freer acknowledges with gratitude the support of the administration and of his colleagues at Emory University School of Law. In particular, he is grateful to his Civil Procedure and Conflict of Laws colleagues Tom Arthur, Peter Hay, Jonathan Nash, Robert Schapiro, and George Shepherd for continuing (and patient) engagement.

Complex Litigation

Chapter 1

Territorial (Personal) Jurisdiction

A. Introduction

1. A Refresher as to Some Basic Principles

When a court has personal jurisdiction over the parties to a lawsuit, it has the power to bind the parties to the court's resolution of the issues. This power is grounded both in constitutional and statutory principles.

For a court to exercise personal jurisdiction, the following fundamentals need to be established. First, there must be some kind of validly-enacted statute or rule that enables the court to exercise the power over the parties. *E.g.*, Richard D. Freer, Civil Procedure 53–55 (4th ed. 2017). Second, the party who is initiating the exercise of the power (usually the plaintiff) must correctly comply with the provisions of the enabling statute or rule. *See Milliken v. Meyer*, 311 U.S. 457, 462–63 (1940). Third, the party invoking the power must inform the other interested parties of that invocation through a method for serving process under the statute or rule that is reasonably calculated to give notice to the interested parties under all the circumstances of the pendency of the proceeding and affords them an opportunity to appear. *E.g., Mullane v. Central Hanover Bank & Trust Co.*, 339 U.S. 306, 314–15 (1950). Fourth, the exercise of the power must satisfy constitutional due process in terms of substantial justice and fair play. *E.g., Int'l Shoe Co. v. Washington*, 326 U.S. 310, 316, 319 (1945). These due process roots are grounded in territorial principles—presence in a territory, contacts with a territory, or consent to be bound by the decisions of a particular territory's court.

There are, of course, validly enacted statutes and rules governing the powers of federal and state courts. For example, the United States Constitution (Article III) gives federal courts power to decide lawsuits of various types. The United States Congress has passed legislation enabling the exercise of power over subsets of those lawsuits. *E.g.*, 28 U.S.C. §§ 1331 and 1332 (2006) (providing for federal question and diversity jurisdiction). The United States Congress also has given the Supreme Court power to make rules for the conduct of court business, 28 U.S.C. § 2071 (2006), and has given the Supreme Court express power to prescribe rules of "practice and procedure," so long as the rules do not "abridge, enlarge, or modify any substantive right." 28 U.S.C. § 2072 (2006). Those procedural rules, particularly Fed. R. Civ. P. 4, enable courts to invoke power over the parties to the lawsuits and authorize complainants to serve process in various ways. The application of the rules, of course, still must comply with "due process." U.S. Const. amend. V. Similar state systems exist.

Let us assume that parties have complied with the relevant statutes and rules. Whether the court in that given case may exercise authority over the parties to the lawsuit now depends upon whether invocation of personal jurisdiction comports with constitutional due process. In analyzing constitutional due process, the court will look at several things: One is the level of contact between the defendant and the forum. Another is the relationship, if any, between the cause of action and the contact. Overall, the exercise of power must comport with "fair play and substantial justice." *E.g., Int'l Shoe Co.*, 326 U.S. at 319–20. Even a defendant's single contact with the forum may be sufficient to confer personal jurisdiction over the defendant where the plaintiff's cause of action relates to that contact. *McGee v. Int'l Life Ins. Co.*, 355 U.S. 220, 223 (1957). This is known as "specific personal jurisdiction."

To invoke specific personal jurisdiction the defendant must have "purposely avail[ed] itself of the privilege of conducting activities within the forum State, thus invoking the benefits and protections of its laws." *Hanson v. Denckla*, 357 U.S. 235, 253 (1958). Even then, the court should consider the factors of fair play and substantial justice. So, in a case where a defendant seems to have minimum contacts with the forum *related to* the cause of action, an assertion of personal jurisdiction over the defendant may still offend "fair play and substantial justice" in light of such factors as (1) the burdens on the defendant, (2) the slight interests of the forum state in the action, (3) the slight interests of the plaintiff in having the forum state exercise jurisdiction, and (4) the overall efficiencies. *Asahi Metal Industry Co. v. Superior Court*, 480 U.S. 102, 113–14 (1987). At the same time, one or more of these "fair play and substantial justice" factors may allow the exercise of personal jurisdiction, even when there is a relatively weak showing of minimum contacts. There must still be some showing of minimum contact to begin with; the "fairness" factors cannot of themselves invest the court with jurisdiction. *Stuart v. Spademan*, 772 F.2d 1185, 1191–92, 1194 n.7 (5th Cir. 1985).

One of the key factors in the personal jurisdiction analysis is "foreseeability." The defendant's contacts with the forum must be such that "he should reasonably anticipate being haled into court there." In this regard, it is not enough for assertion of personal jurisdiction that it was merely foreseeable for defendant's product by happenstance to wind up in the forum state through the actions of a consumer of defendant's product. *World-Wide Volkswagen Corp. v. Woodson*, 444 U.S. 286, 294–97 (1980).

The same essential principles apply in contract as opposed to tort cases. The decision in *Burger King Corp. v. Rudzewicz*, 471 U.S. 462 (1985), makes clear that the standard due process analysis applies in both. 471 U.S. at 479–80, citing *McGee*, 355 U.S. at 223.

2. Specific Jurisdiction/Stream of Commerce

Now that you have refreshed your recollection as to some of the key basic concepts, consider their application in a relatively complex setting.

Asahi Metal Industry Co., Ltd. v. Superior Court

Supreme Court of the United States
480 U.S. 102 (1987)

JUSTICE O'CONNOR announced the judgment of the Court and delivered the unanimous opinion of the Court with respect to Part I, the opinion of the Court with respect to Part II-B, in which THE CHIEF JUSTICE, JUSTICE BRENNAN, JUSTICE WHITE, JUSTICE MARSHALL, JUSTICE BLACKMUN, JUSTICE POWELL, and JUSTICE STEVENS join, and an opinion with respect to Parts II-A and III, in which THE CHIEF JUSTICE, JUSTICE POWELL, and JUSTICE SCALIA join.

This case presents the question whether the mere awareness on the part of a foreign defendant that the components it manufactured, sold, and delivered outside the United States would reach the forum State in the stream of commerce constitutes "minimum contacts" between the defendant and the forum State such that the exercise of jurisdiction "does not offend 'traditional notions of fair play and substantial justice.'" *International Shoe Co. v. Washington*, 326 U.S. 310, 316 (1945), quoting *Milliken v. Meyer*, 311 U.S. 457, 463 (1940).

I

On September 23, 1978, on Interstate Highway 80 in Solano County, California, Gary Zurcher lost control of his Honda motorcycle and collided with a tractor. Zurcher was severely injured, and his passenger and wife, Ruth Ann Moreno, was killed. In September 1979, Zurcher filed a product liability action in the Superior Court of the State of California in and for the County of Solano. Zurcher alleged that the 1978 accident was caused by a sudden loss of air and an explosion in the rear tire of the motorcycle, and alleged that the motorcycle tire, tube, and sealant were defective. Zurcher's complaint named, *inter alia*, Cheng Shin Rubber Industrial Co., Ltd. (Cheng Shin), the Taiwanese manufacturer of the tube. Cheng Shin in turn filed a cross-complaint seeking indemnification from its codefendants and from petitioner, Asahi Metal Industry Co., Ltd. (Asahi), the manufacturer of the tube's valve assembly. Zurcher's claims against Cheng Shin and the other defendants were eventually settled and dismissed, leaving only Cheng Shin's indemnity action against Asahi.

California's long-arm statute authorizes the exercise of jurisdiction "on any basis not inconsistent with the Constitution of this state or of the United States." Cal. Civ. Proc. Code Ann. §410.10 (West 1973). Asahi moved to quash Cheng Shin's service of summons, arguing the State could not exert jurisdiction over it consistent with the Due Process Clause of the Fourteenth Amendment.

In relation to the motion, the following information was submitted by Asahi and Cheng Shin. Asahi is a Japanese corporation. It manufactures tire valve assemblies in Japan and sells the assemblies to Cheng Shin, and to several other tire manufacturers, for use as components in finished tire tubes. Asahi's sales to Cheng Shin took place in Taiwan. The shipments from Asahi to Cheng Shin were sent from Japan to Taiwan. Cheng Shin bought and incorporated into its tire tubes 150,000 Asahi valve assemblies in 1978; 500,000 in 1979; 500,000 in 1980; 100,000 in 1981; and 100,000 in 1982. Sales to Cheng Shin accounted for 1.24 percent of Asahi's income in 1981 and 0.44 percent in 1982. Cheng Shin alleged that approximately 20 percent of its sales in the United States are in California. Cheng Shin purchases valve assemblies from other suppliers as well, and sells finished tubes throughout the world.

In 1983 an attorney for Cheng Shin conducted an informal examination of the valve stems of the tire tubes sold in one cycle store in Solano County. The attorney declared that of the approximately 115 tire tubes in the store, 97 were purportedly manufactured in Japan or Taiwan, and of those 97, 21 valve stems were marked with the circled letter "A", apparently Asahi's trademark. Of the 21 Asahi valve stems, 12 were incorporated into Cheng Shin tire tubes. The store contained 41 other Cheng Shin tubes that incorporated the valve assemblies of other manufacturers. Declaration of Kenneth B. Shepard in Opposition to Motion to Quash Subpoena, App. to Brief for Respondent 5–6. An affidavit of a manager of Cheng Shin whose duties included the purchasing of component parts stated: "'In discussions with Asahi regarding the purchase of valve stem assemblies the fact that my Company sells tubes throughout the world and specifically the United States has been discussed. I am informed and believe that Asahi was fully aware that valve stem assemblies sold to my Company and to others would end up throughout the United States and in California.'" 39 Cal. 3d 35, 48, n. 4, 702 P.2d 543, 549–550, n. 4 (1985). An affidavit of the president of Asahi, on the other hand, declared that Asahi "'has never contemplated that its limited sales of tire valves to Cheng Shin in Taiwan would subject it to lawsuits in California.'" *Ibid.* The record does not include any contract between Cheng Shin and Asahi. Tr. of Oral Arg. 24.

The Supreme Court of the State of California . . . observed: "Asahi has no offices, property or agents in California. It solicits no business in California and has made no direct sales [in California]." *Id.*, at 48, 702 P.2d, at 549. Moreover, "Asahi did not design or control the system of distribution that carried its valve assemblies into California." *Id.*, at 49, 702 P.2d, at 549. Nevertheless, the court found the exercise of jurisdiction over Asahi to be consistent with the Due Process Clause. It concluded that Asahi knew that some of the valve assemblies sold to Cheng Shin would be incorporated into tire tubes sold in California, and that Asahi benefited indirectly from the sale in California of products incorporating its components. The court considered Asahi's intentional act of placing its components into the stream of commerce—that is, by delivering the components to Cheng Shin in Taiwan—coupled with Asahi's awareness that some of the components would eventually find their way into California, sufficient to form the basis for state court jurisdiction under the Due Process Clause.

We granted certiorari . . . and now reverse.

II

A

The Due Process Clause of the Fourteenth Amendment limits the power of a state court to exert personal jurisdiction over a nonresident defendant. "[T]he constitutional touchstone" of the determination whether an exercise of personal jurisdiction comports with due process "remains whether the defendant purposefully established 'minimum contacts' in the forum State." *Burger King Corp. v. Rudzewicz*, 471 U.S. 462, 474 (1985), quoting *International Shoe Co. v. Washington*, 326 U.S., at 316. Most recently we have reaffirmed the oft-quoted reasoning of *Hanson v. Denckla*, 357 U.S. 235, 253 (1958), that minimum contacts must have a basis in "some act by which the defendant purposefully avails itself of the privilege of conducting activities within the forum State, thus invoking the benefits and protections of its laws." *Burger King*, 471 U.S., at 475. "Jurisdiction is proper . . . where the contacts proximately result from actions by the defendant *himself* that create a 'substantial connection' with the forum State." *Ibid.*, quoting *McGee v. International Life Insurance Co.*, 355 U.S. 220, 223 (1957) (emphasis in original).

Applying the principle that minimum contacts must be based on an act of the defendant, the Court in *World-Wide Volkswagen Corp. v. Woodson*, 444 U.S. 286 (1980), rejected the assertion that a *consumer's* unilateral act of bringing the defendant's product into the forum State was a sufficient constitutional basis for personal jurisdiction over the defendant. It had been argued in *World-Wide Volkswagen* that because an automobile retailer and its wholesale distributor sold a product mobile by design and purpose, they could foresee being haled into court in the distant States into which their customers might drive. The Court rejected this concept of foreseeability as an insufficient basis for jurisdiction under the Due Process Clause. *Id.*, at 295–296. The Court disclaimed, however, the idea that "foreseeability is wholly irrelevant" to personal jurisdiction, concluding that "[t]he forum State does not exceed its powers under the Due Process Clause if it asserts personal jurisdiction over a corporation that delivers its products into the stream of commerce with the expectation that they will be purchased by consumers in the forum State." *Id.*, at 297–298 (citation omitted). The Court reasoned:

> "When a corporation 'purposefully avails itself of the privilege of conducting activities within the forum State,' *Hanson v. Denckla*, 357 U.S. [235,] 253 [(1958)], it has clear notice that it is subject to suit there, and can act to alleviate the risk of burdensome litigation by procuring insurance, passing the expected costs on to customers, or, if the risks are too great, severing its connection with the State. Hence if the sale of a product of a manufacturer or distributor . . . is not simply an isolated occurrence, but arises from the efforts of the manufacturer or distributor to serve, directly or indirectly,

> the market for its product in other States, it is not unreasonable to subject it to suit in one of those States if its allegedly defective merchandise has there been the source of injury to its owners or to others."

Id., at 297.

The "substantial connection," *Burger King*, 471 U.S., at 475; *McGee*, 355 U.S., at 223, between the defendant and the forum State necessary for a finding of minimum contacts must come about by *an action of the defendant purposefully directed toward the forum State. Burger King, supra*, 471 U.S., at 476; *Keeton v. Hustler Magazine*, Inc., 465 U.S. 770, 774 (1984). The placement of a product into the stream of commerce, without more, is not an act of the defendant purposefully directed toward the forum State. Additional conduct of the defendant may indicate an intent or purpose to serve the market in the forum State, for example, designing the product for the market in the forum State, advertising in the forum State, establishing channels for providing regular advice to customers in the forum State, or marketing the product through a distributor who has agreed to serve as the sales agent in the forum State. But a defendant's awareness that the stream of commerce may or will sweep the product into the forum State does not convert the mere act of placing the product into the stream into an act purposefully directed toward the forum State.

Assuming, *arguendo*, that respondents have established Asahi's awareness that some of the valves sold to Cheng Shin would be incorporated into tire tubes sold in California, respondents have not demonstrated any action by Asahi to purposefully avail itself of the California market. Asahi does not do business in California. It has no office, agents, employees, or property in California. It does not advertise or otherwise solicit business in California. It did not create, control, or employ the distribution system that brought its valves to California. Cf. *Hicks v. Kawasaki Heavy Industries*, 452 F. Supp. 130 (MD Pa. 1978). There is no evidence that Asahi designed its product in anticipation of sales in California. Cf. *Rockwell International Corp. v. Costruzioni Aeronautiche Giovanni Agusta*, 553 F. Supp. 328 (ED Pa. 1982). On the basis of these facts, the exertion of personal jurisdiction over Asahi by the Superior Court of California[1] exceeds the limits of due process.

B

The strictures of the Due Process Clause forbid a state court to exercise personal jurisdiction over Asahi under circumstances that would offend "'traditional notions of fair play and substantial justice.'" *International Shoe Co. v. Washington*, 326 U.S., at 316, quoting *Milliken v. Meyer*, 311 U.S., at 463.

We have previously explained that the determination of the reasonableness of the exercise of jurisdiction in each case will depend on an evaluation of several factors.

---

1. [Court's footnote *] We have no occasion here to determine whether Congress could, consistent with the Due Process Clause of the Fifth Amendment, authorize federal court personal jurisdiction over alien defendants based on the aggregate of *national* contacts, rather than on the contacts between the defendant and the State in which the federal court sits. . . .

A court must consider the burden on the defendant, the interests of the forum State, and the plaintiff's interest in obtaining relief. It must also weigh in its determination "the interstate judicial system's interest in obtaining the most efficient resolution of controversies; and the shared interest of the several States in furthering fundamental substantive social policies." *World-Wide Volkswagen*, 444 U.S., at 292 (citations omitted).

A consideration of these factors in the present case clearly reveals the unreasonableness of the assertion of jurisdiction over Asahi, even apart from the question of the placement of goods in the stream of commerce.

Certainly the burden on the defendant in this case is severe. Asahi has been commanded by the Supreme Court of California not only to traverse the distance between Asahi's headquarters in Japan and the Superior Court of California in and for the County of Solano, but also to submit its dispute with Cheng Shin to a foreign nation's judicial system. The unique burdens placed upon one who must defend oneself in a foreign legal system should have significant weight in assessing the reasonableness of stretching the long arm of personal jurisdiction over national borders.

When minimum contacts have been established, often the interests of the plaintiff and the forum in the exercise of jurisdiction will justify even the serious burdens placed on the alien defendant. In the present case, however, the interests of the plaintiff and the forum in California's assertion of jurisdiction over Asahi are slight. All that remains is a claim for indemnification asserted by Cheng Shin, a Taiwanese corporation, against Asahi. The transaction on which the indemnification claim is based took place in Taiwan; Asahi's components were shipped from Japan to Taiwan. Cheng Shin has not demonstrated that it is more convenient for it to litigate its indemnification claim against Asahi in California rather than in Taiwan or Japan.

Because the plaintiff is not a California resident, California's legitimate interests in the dispute have considerably diminished. The Supreme Court of California argued that the State had an interest in "protecting its consumers by ensuring that foreign manufacturers comply with the state's safety standards." 39 Cal.3d, at 49. The State Supreme Court's definition of California's interest, however, was overly broad. The dispute between Cheng Shin and Asahi is primarily about indemnification rather than safety standards. Moreover, it is not at all clear at this point that California law should govern the question whether a Japanese corporation should indemnify a Taiwanese corporation on the basis of a sale made in Taiwan and a shipment of goods from Japan to Taiwan. *Phillips Petroleum Co. v. Shutts*, 472 U.S. 797, 821–822 (1985); *Allstate Insurance Co. v. Hague*, 449 U.S. 302, 312–313 (1981). The possibility of being haled into a California court as a result of an accident involving Asahi's components undoubtedly creates an additional deterrent to the manufacture of unsafe components; however, similar pressures will be placed on Asahi by the purchasers of its components as long as those who use Asahi components in their final products, and sell those products in California, are subject to the application of California tort law.

World-Wide Volkswagen also admonished courts to take into consideration the interests of the "several States," in addition to the forum State, in the efficient judicial resolution of the dispute and the advancement of substantive policies. In the present case, this advice calls for a court to consider the procedural and substantive policies of other *nations* whose interests are affected by the assertion of jurisdiction by the California court. The procedural and substantive interests of other nations in a state court's assertion of jurisdiction over an alien defendant will differ from case to case. In every case, however, those interests, as well as the Federal Government's interest in its foreign relations policies, will be best served by a careful inquiry into the reasonableness of the assertion of jurisdiction in the particular case, and an unwillingness to find the serious burdens on an alien defendant outweighed by minimal interests on the part of the plaintiff or the forum State. "Great care and reserve should be exercised when extending our notions of personal jurisdiction into the international field." *United States v. First National City Bank*, 379 U.S. 378, 404 (1965) (Harlan, J., dissenting). See Born, Reflections on Judicial Jurisdiction in International Cases, to be published in 17 Ga. J. Int'l & Comp. L. 1 (1987).

Considering the international context, the heavy burden on the alien defendant, and the slight interests of the plaintiff and the forum State, the exercise of personal jurisdiction by a California court over Asahi in this instance would be unreasonable and unfair.

III

Because the facts of this case do not establish minimum contacts such that the exercise of personal jurisdiction is consistent with fair play and substantial justice, the judgment of the Supreme Court of California is reversed, and the case is remanded for further proceedings not inconsistent with this opinion.

It is so ordered.

Notes and Questions

In concurrence, JUSTICE BRENNAN stated:

> Part II-A states that "a defendant's awareness that the stream of commerce may or will sweep the product into the forum State does not convert the mere act of placing the product into the stream into an act purposefully directed toward the forum State." *Ante*, at 112. Under this view, a plaintiff would be required to show "[a]dditional conduct" directed toward the forum before finding the exercise of jurisdiction over the defendant to be consistent with the Due Process Clause. *Ibid.* I see no need for such a showing, however. The stream of commerce refers not to unpredictable currents or eddies, but to the regular and anticipated flow of products from manufacture to distribution to retail sale. As long as a participant in this process is aware that the final product is being marketed in the forum State, the possibility of a lawsuit there cannot come as a surprise. Nor will the

> litigation present a burden for which there is no corresponding benefit. A defendant who has placed goods in the stream of commerce benefits economically from the retail sale of the final product in the forum State, and indirectly benefits from the State's laws that regulate and facilitate commercial activity. These benefits accrue regardless of whether that participant directly conducts business in the forum State, or engages in additional conduct directed toward that State. Accordingly, most courts and commentators have found that jurisdiction premised on the placement of a product into the stream of commerce is consistent with the Due Process Clause, and have not required a showing of additional conduct.

Asahi, 480 U.S. at 116.

Separately in concurrence Justice Stevens stated:

> The judgment of the Supreme Court of California should be reversed for the reasons stated in Part II-B of the Court's opinion. While I join Parts I and II-B, I do not join Part II-A for two reasons. First, it is not necessary to the Court's decision. An examination of minimum contacts is not always necessary to determine whether a state court's assertion of personal jurisdiction is constitutional. See *Burger King Corp. v. Rudzewicz*, 471 U.S. 462, 476–478 (1985). Part II-B establishes, after considering the factors set forth in *World-Wide Volkswagen Corp. v. Woodson*, 444 U.S. 286, 292 (1980), that California's exercise of jurisdiction over Asahi in this case would be "unreasonable and unfair." *Ante*, at 116. This finding alone requires reversal; this case fits within the rule that "minimum requirements inherent in the concept of 'fair play and substantial justice' may defeat the reasonableness of jurisdiction even if the defendant has purposefully engaged in forum activities." *Burger King*, 471 U.S., at 477–478 (quoting *International Shoe Co. v. Washington*, 326 U.S. 310, 320 (1945)). Accordingly, I see no reason in this case for the plurality to articulate "purposeful direction" or any other test as the nexus between an act of a defendant and the forum State that is necessary to establish minimum contacts.
>
> Second, even assuming that the test ought to be formulated here, Part II-A misapplies it to the facts of this case. The plurality seems to assume that an unwavering line can be drawn between "mere awareness" that a component will find its way into the forum State and "purposeful availment" of the forum's market. *Ante*, at 112. Over the course of its dealings with Cheng Shin, Asahi has arguably engaged in a higher quantum of conduct than "[t]he placement of a product into the stream of commerce, without more. . . ." *Ibid.* Whether or not this conduct rises to the level of purposeful availment requires a constitutional determination that is affected by the volume, the value, and the hazardous character of the components. In most circumstances I would be inclined to conclude that a regular course of dealing that results in deliveries of over 100,000 units annually over a period of several years would constitute "purposeful availment" even

> though the item delivered to the forum State was a standard product marketed throughout the world.

Asahi, 481 U.S. at 121–22.

How are courts to reconcile Justice Brennan's approach and Justice Stevens's comments with Justice O'Connor's? Notice that Justice Stevens's failure to adopt either Justice O'Connor's or Justice Brennan's view means that there is no majority opinion on what constitutes contact in the stream-of-commerce cases.

Now consider the Supreme Court's opinion in *McIntyre*.

J. McIntyre Machinery, Ltd. v. Nicastro

Supreme Court of the United States
131 S. Ct. 2780 (2011)

KENNEDY, J., announced the judgment of the Court and delivered an opinion, in which ROBERTS, C.J., and SCALIA and THOMAS, JJ., joined. BREYER, J., filed an opinion concurring in the judgment, in which ALITO, J., joined. GINSBURG, J., filed a dissenting opinion, in which SOTOMAYOR and KAGAN, JJ., joined.

KENNEDY, J.,

[Plaintiff Nicastro was injured while using a metal-shearing machine manufactured by defendant McIntyre. Nicastro sued in New Jersey, where the accident occurred. McIntyre was incorporated in England, operated there, and made the relevant machine there. An independent distributor sold McIntyre's machines in the United States and sold only one machine (the relevant one) in New Jersey. Effectively, McIntyre's only contact with New Jersey was its general desire that the independent American distributor sell McIntyre machines to anyone in the United States willing to buy them. The question presented, therefore, was whether a New Jersey state court could properly exercise personal jurisdiction over McIntyre, a foreign manufacturer, so long as McIntyre "[knew] or should know that its products are distributed through a nationwide distribution system that might lead to those products being sold in any of the fifty states." 131 S. Ct. at 2785 (quoting from the New Jersey Supreme Court decision).]

A court may subject a defendant to judgment only when the defendant has sufficient contacts with the sovereign "such that the maintenance of the suit does not offend 'traditional notions of fair play and substantial justice.'" *International Shoe Co. v. Washington*, 326 U.S. 310, 316 (1945) (quoting *Milliken v. Meyer*, 311 U.S. 457, 463 (1940)). Freeform notions of fundamental fairness divorced from traditional practice cannot transform a judgment rendered in the absence of authority into law. As a general rule, the sovereign's exercise of power requires some act by which the defendant "purposefully avails itself of the privilege of conducting activities within the forum State, thus invoking the benefits and protections of its laws," *Hanson*, 357 U.S. at 253, though in some cases, as with an intentional tort, the defendant might well fall within the State's authority by reason of his attempt to obstruct its laws. In products-liability cases like this one, it is the defendant's purposeful availment that makes jurisdiction consistent with "traditional notions of fair play and substantial justice."

. . .

The imprecision arising from *Asahi*, for the most part, results from its statement of the relation between jurisdiction and the "stream of commerce." The stream of commerce, like other metaphors, has its deficiencies as well as its utility. It refers to the movement of goods from manufacturers through distributors to consumers, yet beyond that descriptive purpose its meaning is far from exact. This Court has stated that a defendant's placing goods into the stream of commerce "with the expectation that they will be purchased by consumers within the forum State" may indicate purposeful availment. *World-Wide Volkswagen Corp. v. Woodson*, 444 U.S. 286, 298 (1980) (finding that expectation lacking). But that statement does not amend the general rule of personal jurisdiction. It merely observes that a defendant may in an appropriate case be subject to jurisdiction without entering the forum—itself an unexceptional proposition—as where manufacturers or distributors "seek to serve" a given State's market. *Id.* at 295. The principal inquiry in cases of this sort is whether the defendant's activities manifest an intention to submit to the power of a sovereign. In other words, the defendant must "purposefully avai[l] itself of the privilege of conducting activities within the forum State, thus invoking the benefits and protections of its laws." [*Hanson v. Denckla,* 357 U.S. 235, 253 (1958); *Insurance Corp. of Ireland, Ltd. v. Compagnie Des Bauxites de Guinea,* 456 U.S. 694, 704–705 (1982)] ("[A]ctions of the defendant may amount to a legal submission to the jurisdiction of the court"). Sometimes a defendant does so by sending its goods rather than its agents. The defendant's transmission of goods permits the exercise of jurisdiction only where the defendant can be said to have targeted the forum; as a general rule, it is not enough that the defendant might have predicted that its goods will reach the forum State.

In *Asahi*, an opinion by Justice Brennan for four Justices outlined a different approach. It discarded the central concept of sovereign authority in favor of considerations of fairness and foreseeability. As that concurrence contended, "jurisdiction premised on the placement of a product into the stream of commerce [without more] is consistent with the Due Process Clause," for "[a]s long as a participant in this process is aware that the final product is being marketed in the forum State, the possibility of a lawsuit there cannot come as a surprise." 480 U.S., at 117 (opinion concurring in part and concurring in judgment). It was the premise of the concurring opinion that the defendant's ability to anticipate suit renders the assertion of jurisdiction fair. In this way, the opinion made foreseeability the touchstone of jurisdiction.

The standard set forth in Justice Brennan's concurrence was rejected in an opinion written by Justice O'Connor; but the relevant part of that opinion, too, commanded the assent of only four Justices, not a majority of the Court. That opinion stated: "The 'substantial connection' between the defendant and the forum State necessary for a finding of minimum contacts must come about by an action of the defendant purposefully directed toward the forum State. The placement of a product into the stream of commerce, without more, is not an act of the defendant purposefully directed toward the forum State." *Id.*, at 112 (emphasis deleted; citations omitted).

Since *Asahi* was decided, the courts have sought to reconcile the competing opinions. But Justice Brennan's concurrence, advocating a rule based on general notions of fairness and foreseeability, is inconsistent with the premises of lawful judicial power. This Court's precedents make clear that it is the defendant's actions, not his expectations, that empower a State's courts to subject him to judgment.

Notes and Questions

1. Justices Breyer and Alito only concurred in the judgment in *McIntyre*, not in Justice Kennedy's reasoning. 131 S. Ct. at 2792–93. The two concurring Justices concluded that the New Jersey Supreme Court's articulated test was too automatic in favor of jurisdiction and that Justice Kennedy's plurality-opinion test was too strict. Justices Breyer and Alito instead reasoned that the plaintiff simply failed to prove that the single sale to New Jersey on the facts of the case supported an exercise of specific personal jurisdiction.

Justice Ginsburg then dissented, along with Justices Sotomayor and Kagan. These three Justices opined that McIntyre should not be able to escape personal jurisdiction in New Jersey merely by using an independent distributor. Instead, if McIntyre "targeted the United States (including all the States that constitute the Nation)," 131 S. Ct. at 2797, then McIntyre should be subject to suit in a specific state such as New Jersey. The three dissenters concluded that the effort to criticize Justice Brennan's concurring opinion in Asahi was effectively unnecessary, and that, in any event, Asahi was an easily distinguishable case. 131 S. Ct. at 2802–03.

2. What, then, does *McIntyre* mean? That is hard to say. It did not give the clear guidance on "stream of commerce" personal jurisdiction theory for which some readers hoped. Plainly, it is not enough for a plaintiff to assert personal jurisdiction in a particular state merely on the basis that the defendant introduced a product into commerce that conceivably could wind up in the state. But that is not new law. Beyond that, *McIntyre* will have to be construed narrowly in accordance with the *Marks* doctrine, i.e. when no single rationale commands a majority, "the holding of the Court may be viewed as that position taken by those Members who concurred in the judgmen[t] on the narrowest grounds." *Marks v. United States*, 430 U.S. 188, 193 (1977). Sweeping generalizations do not flow from the case.

3. Does the Supreme Court's subsequent opinion in *Bristol-Myers Squibb Co. v. Superior Court*, 137 S. Ct. 1773 (2017), shed light on what *McIntyre* means? In that case, non-residents of California sued Bristol-Myers Squibb (BMS) in state court in California. They alleged that the BMS drug Plavix caused personal injuries to them. BMS maintained certain research and laboratory facilities, certain sales

representatives, and a state-government advocacy office in California. BMS also sold Plavix in the state (almost 187 million pills generating more than 900 million dollars between 2006 and 2012).

But BMS "did not develop Plavix in California, did not create a marketing strategy for Plavix in California, and did not manufacture, label, package, or work on the regulatory approval of the product in California." *Id.* at 1778. None of the nonresidents were prescribed Plavix in California. None purchased Plavix there. None ingested Plavix there. And none were injured there.

BMS moved for dismissal on personal jurisdiction grounds. The California state courts denied the motion, but the Supreme Court reversed, holding that, "In order for a court to exercise specific jurisdiction over a claim, there must be an 'affiliation between the forum and the underlying controversy, principally, [an] activity or an occurrence that takes place in the forum state.' When there is no such connection, specific jurisdiction is lacking regardless of the extent of a defendant's unconnected activities in the State." *Id.* at 1781.

Justice Sotomayor dissented. Her view is that, "[T]here is nothing unfair about subjecting a massive corporation to suit in a State for a nationwide course of conduct that injures both forum residents and non-residents alike." *Id.* at 1784 (Sotomayor, J., dissenting). In other words, "[the nonresidents'] claims against Bristol-Myers concern conduct materially identical to acts the company took in California: its marketing and distribution of Plavix, which it undertook on a nationwide basis in all 50 States.... All of the plaintiffs—residents and nonresidents alike—allege that they were injured by the same essential acts. Our cases require no connection more direct than that." *Id.* at 1786. (Sotomayor, J., dissenting).

Do you agree? Would this be a form of "general" jurisdiction, i.e., if a company is engaged in nationwide commerce, it can be sued in any state where its business injured at least one resident plaintiff? What would the due process limit be on the exercise of this kind of jurisdiction?

3. General Jurisdiction

It is well settled that, if the defendant has sufficiently substantial systematic contacts with the forum to render the defendant "essentially at home" there, then the court may exercise personal jurisdiction over the parties on *any* cause of action. *E.g., Daimler AG v. Bauman*, 134 S. Ct. 746, 761 (2014); *Helicopteros Nacionales de Colombia, S.A. v. Hall*, 466 U.S. 408, 414 (1983); *see also Perkins v. Benguet Consolidated Mining Co.*, 342 U.S. 437, 438, 446 (1952). This concept is known as "general personal jurisdiction." Exactly what the concept means is the subject of the Supreme Court's opinions in *Goodyear Dunlop Tires Operations, S.A. v. Brown*, 131 S. Ct. 2846 (2011), in *Daimler*, and in *BNSF Railway Co. v. Tyrrell*, 137 S. Ct. 1549 (2017).

In *Goodyear*, a bus accident in France killed two boys from North Carolina. The boys' parents sued The Goodyear Tire and Rubber Company, an Ohio corporation, and three of that company's foreign subsidiaries, alleging that the accident was caused by a defective tire made in Turkey at the plant of one of the subsidiaries. The parents brought the action in North Carolina state court, and the three foreign subsidiaries challenged personal jurisdiction. A unanimous Supreme Court upheld the defense.

> Because the episode-in-suit, the bus accident, occurred in France, and the tire alleged to have caused the accident was manufactured and sold abroad, North Carolina courts lacked specific jurisdiction to adjudicate the controversy. . . . Were the foreign subsidiaries nonetheless amenable to general jurisdiction in North Carolina courts? Confusing or blending general and specific jurisdictional inquiries, the North Carolina courts answered yes. Some of the tires made abroad by Goodyear's foreign subsidiaries, the North Carolina Court of Appeals stressed, had reached North Carolina through "the stream of commerce"; that connection, the Court of Appeals believed, gave North Carolina courts the handle needed for the exercise of general jurisdiction over the foreign corporations. [Citation omitted]
>
> A connection so limited between the forum and the foreign corporation, we hold, is an inadequate basis for the exercise of general jurisdiction. Such a connection does not establish the "continuous and systematic" affiliation necessary to empower North Carolina courts to entertain claims unrelated to the foreign corporation's contacts with the State.

131 S. Ct. at 2851.

Said the Court: "For an individual, the paradigm forum for the exercise of general jurisdiction is the individual's domicile; for a corporation, it is an equivalent place, one in which the corporation is fairly regarded as at home." 131 S. Ct. at 2853–54.

Now consider the Supreme Court's opinion in the *Daimler* case.

Daimler AG v. Bauman

Supreme Court of the United States
134 S. Ct. 746 (2014)

GINSBURG, J.,

This case concerns the authority of a court in the United States to entertain a claim brought by foreign plaintiffs against a foreign defendant based on events occurring entirely outside the United States. The litigation commenced in 2004, when twenty-two Argentinian residents filed a complaint in the United States District Court for the Northern District of California against DaimlerChrysler Aktiengesellschaft (Daimler), a German public stock company, headquartered in Stuttgart, that manufactures Mercedes-Benz vehicles in Germany. The complaint alleged that during Argentina's 1976–1983 "Dirty War," Daimler's Argentinian subsidiary, Mercedes-Benz Argentina (MB Argentina) collaborated with state security forces to kidnap, detain, torture, and kill certain MB Argentina workers, among them, plaintiffs or persons closely related to plaintiffs. Damages for the alleged human-rights violations were sought from Daimler under the laws of the United States, California, and Argentina. Jurisdiction over the lawsuit was predicated on the California contacts of Mercedes-Benz USA, LLC (MBUSA), a subsidiary of Daimler incorporated in Delaware with its principal place of business in New Jersey. MBUSA distributes Daimler-manufactured vehicles to independent dealerships throughout the United States, including California.

The question presented is whether the Due Process Clause of the Fourteenth Amendment precludes the District Court from exercising jurisdiction over Daimler in this case, given the absence of any California connection to the atrocities, perpetrators, or victims described in the complaint. Plaintiffs invoked the court's general or all-purpose jurisdiction. . . .

In *Goodyear Dunlop Tires Operations, S.A. v. Brown*, 564 U.S. [915] (2011), we addressed the distinction between general or all-purpose jurisdiction, and specific or conduct-linked jurisdiction. As to the former, we held that a court may assert jurisdiction over a foreign corporation "to hear any and all claims against [it]" only when the corporation's affiliations with the State in which suit is brought are so constant and pervasive "as to render [it] essentially at home in the forum State." *Id.*, at [919]. Instructed by *Goodyear*, we conclude Daimler is not "at home" in California, and cannot be sued there for injuries plaintiffs attribute to MB Argentina's conduct in Argentina.

I

. . .

The incidents recounted in the complaint center on MB Argentina's plant in Gonzalez Catan, Argentina; no part of MB Argentina's alleged collaboration with Argentinian authorities took place in California or anywhere else in the United States.

Plaintiffs' operative complaint names only one corporate defendant: Daimler, the petitioner here. Plaintiffs seek to hold Daimler vicariously liable for MB Argentina's alleged malfeasance. Daimler is a German *Aktiengesellschaft* (public stock company) that manufactures Mercedes-Benz vehicles in Germany and has its headquarters in Stuttgart. At times relevant to this case, MB Argentina was a subsidiary wholly owned by Daimler's predecessor in interest.

Daimler moved to dismiss the action for want of personal jurisdiction. . . .

MBUSA, an indirect subsidiary of Daimler, is a Delaware limited liability corporation. MBUSA serves as Daimler's exclusive importer and distributor in the United States, purchasing Mercedes-Benz automobiles from Daimler in Germany, then importing those vehicles, and ultimately distributing them to independent dealerships located throughout the Nation. Although MBUSA's principal place of business is in New Jersey, MBUSA has multiple California-based facilities, including a regional office in Costa Mesa, a Vehicle Preparation Center in Carson, and a Classic

Center in Irvine. According to the record developed below, MBUSA is the largest supplier of luxury vehicles to the California market. In particular, over 10% of all sales of new vehicles in the United States take place in California, and MBUSA's California sales account for 2.4% of Daimler's worldwide sales.

The relationship between Daimler and MBUSA is delineated in a General Distributor Agreement, which sets forth requirements for MBUSA's distribution of Mercedes-Benz vehicles in the United States. That agreement established MBUSA as an "independent contracto[r]" that "buy[s] and sell[s] [vehicles] . . . as an independent business for [its] own account." App. 179a. The agreement "does not make [MBUSA] . . . a general or special agent, partner, joint venturer or employee of DAIMLERCHRYSLER or any DaimlerChrysler Group Company"; MBUSA "ha[s] no authority to make binding obligations for or act on behalf of DAIMLERCHRYSLER or any DaimlerChrysler Group Company." *Ibid.*

After allowing jurisdictional discovery on plaintiffs' agency allegations, the District Court granted Daimler's motion to dismiss. Daimler's own affiliations with California, the court first determined, were insufficient to support the exercise of all-purpose jurisdiction over the corporation. Next, the court declined to attribute MBUSA's California contacts to Daimler on an agency theory, concluding that plaintiffs failed to demonstrate that MBUSA acted as Daimler's agent.

[The Ninth Circuit in due course reversed.] . . .

We granted certiorari to decide whether, consistent with the Due Process Clause of the Fourteenth Amendment, Daimler is amenable to suit in California courts for claims involving only foreign plaintiffs and conduct occurring entirely abroad.

II

Federal courts ordinarily follow state law in determining the bounds of their jurisdiction over persons. See Fed. Rule Civ. Proc. 4(k)(1)(A) (service of process is effective to establish personal jurisdiction over a defendant "who is subject to the jurisdiction of a court of general jurisdiction in the state where the district court is located"). Under California's long-arm statute, California state courts may exercise personal jurisdiction "on any basis not inconsistent with the Constitution of this state or of the United States." Cal. Civ. Proc. Code Ann. § 410.10 (West 2004). California's long-arm statute allows the exercise of personal jurisdiction to the full extent permissible under the U.S. Constitution. We therefore inquire whether the Ninth Circuit's holding comports with the limits imposed by federal due process. See, *e.g.*, *Burger King Corp. v. Rudzewicz*, 471 U.S. 462, 464 (1985).

III

. . . .

Since *International Shoe*, "specific jurisdiction has become the centerpiece of modern jurisdiction theory, while general jurisdiction [has played] a reduced role." *Goodyear*, 564 U.S., at [925] (quoting Twitchell, The Myth of General Jurisdiction, 101 Harv. L. Rev. 610, 628 (1988)). *International Shoe*'s momentous departure from

Pennoyer's rigidly territorial focus, we have noted, unleashed a rapid expansion of tribunals' ability to hear claims against out-of-state defendants when the episode-in-suit occurred in the forum or the defendant purposefully availed itself of the forum. Our subsequent decisions have continued to bear out the prediction that "specific jurisdiction will come into sharper relief and form a considerably more significant part of the scene." von Mehren & Trautman 1164.

Our post-*International Shoe* opinions on general jurisdiction, by comparison, are few. "[The Court's] 1952 decision in *Perkins v. Benguet Consol. Mining Co.* remains the textbook case of general jurisdiction appropriately exercised over a foreign corporation that has not consented to suit in the forum." *Goodyear*, 564 U.S., at [928] (internal quotation marks and brackets omitted). The defendant in *Perkins*, Benguet, was a company incorporated under the laws of the Philippines, where it operated gold and silver mines. Benguet ceased its mining operations during the Japanese occupation of the Philippines in World War II; its president moved to Ohio, where he kept an office, maintained the company's files, and oversaw the company's activities. *Perkins v. Benguet Consol. Mining Co.*, 342 U.S. 437, 448 (1952). The plaintiff, an Ohio resident, sued Benguet on a claim that neither arose in Ohio nor related to the corporation's activities in that State. We held that the Ohio courts could exercise general jurisdiction over Benguet without offending due process. *Ibid.* That was so, we later noted, because "Ohio was the corporation's principal, if temporary, place of business." *Keeton v. Hustler Magazine, Inc.*, 465 U.S. 770, 780, n. 11 (1984).

The next case on point, *Helicopteros*, 466 U.S. 408, arose from a helicopter crash in Peru. Four U.S. citizens perished in that accident; their survivors and representatives brought suit in Texas state court against the helicopter's owner and operator, a Colombian corporation. That company's contacts with Texas were confined to "sending its chief executive officer to Houston for a contract-negotiation session; accepting into its New York bank account checks drawn on a Houston bank; purchasing helicopters, equipment, and training services from [a Texas-based helicopter company] for substantial sums; and sending personnel to [Texas] for training." *Id.* at 416. Notably, those contacts bore no apparent relationship to the accident that gave rise to the suit. We held that the company's Texas connections did not resemble the "continuous and systematic general business contacts . . . found to exist in *Perkins*." *Ibid.* "[M]ere purchases, even if occurring at regular intervals," we clarified, "are not enough to warrant a State's assertion of *in personam* jurisdiction over a nonresident corporation in a cause of action not related to those purchase transactions." *Id.*, at 418.

Most recently, in *Goodyear*, we answered the question: "Are foreign subsidiaries of a United States parent corporation amenable to suit in state court on claims unrelated to any activity of the subsidiaries in the forum State?" 564 U.S., at [918]. That case arose from a bus accident outside Paris that killed two boys from North Carolina. The boys' parents brought a wrongful-death suit in North Carolina state court alleging that the bus's tire was defectively manufactured. The complaint named as defendants not only The Goodyear Tire and Rubber Company (Goodyear), an

Ohio corporation, but also Goodyear's Turkish, French, and Luxembourgian subsidiaries. Those foreign subsidiaries, which manufactured tires for sale in Europe and Asia, lacked any affiliation with North Carolina. A small percentage of tires manufactured by the foreign subsidiaries were distributed in North Carolina, however, and on that ground, the North Carolina Court of Appeals held the subsidiaries amenable to the general jurisdiction of North Carolina courts.

We reversed, observing that the North Carolina court's analysis "elided the essential difference between case-specific and all-purpose (general) jurisdiction." *Id.*, at [927]. Although the placement of a product into the stream of commerce "may bolster an affiliation germane to *specific* jurisdiction," we explained, such contacts "do not warrant a determination that, based on those ties, the forum has *general* jurisdiction over a defendant." *Id.*, at [927]. As *International Shoe* itself teaches, a corporation's "continuous activity of some sorts within a state is not enough to support the demand that the corporation be amenable to suits unrelated to that activity." 326 U.S., at 318. Because Goodyear's foreign subsidiaries were "in no sense at home in North Carolina," we held, those subsidiaries could not be required to submit to the general jurisdiction of that State's courts. 564 U.S., at [929]. See also *J. McIntyre Machinery, Ltd. v. Nicastro*, 564 U.S. [873, 898–899] (2011) (Ginsburg, J., dissenting) (noting unanimous agreement that a foreign manufacturer, which engaged an independent U.S.-based distributor to sell its machines throughout the United States, could not be exposed to all-purpose jurisdiction in New Jersey courts based on those contacts).

As is evident from *Perkins, Helicopteros*, and *Goodyear*, general and specific jurisdiction have followed markedly different trajectories post- *International Shoe*. Specific jurisdiction has been cut loose from *Pennoyer*'s sway, but we have declined to stretch general jurisdiction beyond limits traditionally recognized As this Court has increasingly trained on the "relationship among the defendant, the forum, and the litigation," *Shaffer*, 433 U.S., at 204, *i.e.*, specific jurisdiction, general jurisdiction has come to occupy a less dominant place in the contemporary scheme.

IV

With this background, we turn directly to the question whether Daimler's affiliations with California are sufficient to subject it to the general (all-purpose) personal jurisdiction of that State's courts. In the proceedings below, the parties agreed on, or failed to contest, certain points we now take as given. Plaintiffs have never attempted to fit this case into the *specific* jurisdiction category. Nor did plaintiffs challenge on appeal the District Court's holding that Daimler's own contacts with California were, by themselves, too sporadic to justify the exercise of general jurisdiction. While plaintiffs ultimately persuaded the Ninth Circuit to impute MBUSA's California contacts to Daimler on an agency theory, at no point have they maintained that MBUSA is an alter ego of Daimler.

Daimler, on the other hand, failed to object below to plaintiffs' assertion that the California courts could exercise all-purpose jurisdiction over MBUSA. But see Brief for Petitioner 23, n. 4 (suggestion that in light of *Goodyear*, MBUSA may not be amenable to general jurisdiction in California); Brief for United States as *Amicus Curiae* 16, n. 5 (hereinafter U.S. Brief) (same). We will assume then, for purposes of this decision only, that MBUSA qualifies as at home in California.

A

In sustaining the exercise of general jurisdiction over Daimler, the Ninth Circuit relied on an agency theory, determining that MBUSA acted as Daimler's agent for jurisdictional purposes and then attributing MBUSA's California contacts to Daimler. The Ninth Circuit's agency analysis derived from Circuit precedent considering principally whether the subsidiary "performs services that are sufficiently important to the foreign corporation that if it did not have a representative to perform them, the corporation's own officials would undertake to perform substantially similar services." 644 F.3d, at 920 (quoting *Doe v. Unocal Corp.*, 248 F.3d 915, 928 (9th Cir. 2001); emphasis deleted).

This Court has not yet addressed whether a foreign corporation may be subjected to a court's general jurisdiction based on the contacts of its in-state subsidiary. Daimler argues, and several Courts of Appeals have held, that a subsidiary's jurisdictional contacts can be imputed to its parent only when the former is so dominated by the latter as to be its alter ego. The Ninth Circuit adopted a less rigorous test based on what it described as an "agency" relationship. Agencies, we note, come in many sizes and shapes: "One may be an agent for some business purposes and not others so that the fact that one may be an agent for one purpose does not make him or her an agent for every purpose." 2A C. J. S., Agency § 43, p. 367 (2013) (footnote omitted). A subsidiary, for example, might be its parent's agent for claims arising in the place where the subsidiary operates, yet not its agent regarding claims arising elsewhere. The Court of Appeals did not advert to that prospect. But we need not pass judgment on invocation of an agency theory in the context of general jurisdiction, for in no event can the appeals court's analysis be sustained.

The Ninth Circuit's agency finding rested primarily on its observation that MBUSA's services were "important" to Daimler, as gauged by Daimler's hypothetical readiness to perform those services itself if MBUSA did not exist. Formulated this way, the inquiry into importance stacks the deck, for it will always yield a pro-jurisdiction answer: "Anything a corporation does through an independent contractor, subsidiary, or distributor is presumably something that the corporation would do 'by other means' if the independent contractor, subsidiary, or distributor did not exist." 676 F.3d at 777 (O'Scannlain, J., dissenting from denial of rehearing en banc). The Ninth Circuit's agency theory thus appears to subject foreign corporations to general jurisdiction whenever they have an in-state subsidiary or affiliate, an outcome that would sweep beyond even the "sprawling view of general jurisdiction" we rejected in *Goodyear.* 564 U.S., at [929].

B

. . .

Goodyear made clear that only a limited set of affiliations with a forum will render a defendant amenable to all-purpose jurisdiction there. "For an individual, the paradigm forum for the exercise of general jurisdiction is the individual's domicile; for a corporation, it is an equivalent place, one in which the corporation is fairly regarded as at home." 564 U.S., at [924] (citing Brilmayer et al., A General Look at General Jurisdiction, 66 Texas L. Rev. 721, 728 (1988)). With respect to a corporation, the place of incorporation and principal place of business are "paradig[m] . . . bases for general jurisdiction." *Id.*, at 735. See also Twitchell, 101 Harv. L. Rev., at 633. Those affiliations have the virtue of being unique—that is, each ordinarily indicates only one place—as well as easily ascertainable. Cf. *Hertz Corp. v. Friend*, 559 U.S. 77, 94 (2010) ("Simple jurisdictional rules . . . promote greater predictability."). These bases afford plaintiffs recourse to at least one clear and certain forum in which a corporate defendant may be sued on any and all claims.

Goodyear did not hold that a corporation may be subject to general jurisdiction *only* in a forum where it is incorporated or has its principal place of business; it simply typed those places paradigm all-purpose forums. Plaintiffs would have us look beyond the exemplar bases *Goodyear* identified, and approve the exercise of general jurisdiction in every State in which a corporation "engages in a substantial, continuous, and systematic course of business." Brief for Respondents 16–17, and nn. 7–8. That formulation, we hold, is unacceptably grasping.

. . . [T]he inquiry under *Goodyear* is not whether a foreign corporation's in-forum contacts can be said to be in some sense "continuous and systematic," it is whether that corporation's "affiliations with the State are so 'continuous and systematic' as to render [it] essentially at home in the forum State." 564 U.S. at [919].

Here, neither Daimler nor MBUSA is incorporated in California, nor does either entity have its principal place of business there. If Daimler's California activities sufficed to allow adjudication of this Argentina-rooted case in California, the same global reach would presumably be available in every other State in which MBUSA's sales are sizable. Such exorbitant exercises of all-purpose jurisdiction would scarcely permit out-of-state defendants "to structure their primary conduct with some minimum assurance as to where that conduct will and will not render them liable to suit." *Burger King Corp.*, 471 U.S. at 472 (internal quotation marks omitted).

It was therefore error for the Ninth Circuit to conclude that Daimler, even with MBUSA's contacts attributed to it, was at home in California, and hence subject to suit there on claims by foreign plaintiffs having nothing to do with anything that occurred or had its principal impact in California.

Justice Sotomayor's proposal to import *Asahi*'s "reasonableness" check into the general jurisdiction determination, on the other hand, would indeed compound the jurisdictional inquiry. The reasonableness factors identified in *Asahi* include "the burden on the defendant," "the interests of the forum State," "the plaintiff's interest in obtaining relief," "the interstate judicial system's interest in obtaining the most efficient resolution of controversies," "the shared interest of the several States in furthering fundamental substantive social policies," and, in the international context, "the procedural and substantive policies of other *nations* whose interests are affected by the assertion of jurisdiction." 480 U.S. at 113–115 (some internal quotation marks omitted). Imposing such a checklist in cases of general jurisdiction would hardly promote the efficient disposition of an issue that should be resolved expeditiously at the outset of litigation.

C

Finally, the transnational context of this dispute bears attention. . . . The Ninth Circuit . . . paid little heed to the risks to international comity its expansive view of general jurisdiction posed. Other nations do not share the uninhibited approach to personal jurisdiction advanced by the Court of Appeals in this case. In the European Union, for example, a corporation may generally be sued in the nation in which it is "domiciled," a term defined to refer only to the location of the corporation's "statutory seat," "central administration," or "principal place of business." European Parliament and Council Reg. 1215/2012, Arts. 4(1), and 63(1), 2012 O.J. (L. 351) 7, 18. . . . Considerations of international rapport thus reinforce our determination that subjecting Daimler to the general jurisdiction of courts in California would not accord with the "fair play and substantial justice" due process demands. *International Shoe*, 326 U.S. at 316 (quoting *Milliken v. Meyer*, 311 U.S. 457, 463 (1940)).

For the reasons stated, the judgment of the United States Court of Appeals for the Ninth Circuit is

Reversed.

Notes and Questions

1. The Supreme Court in *Daimler* appears to have rejected a role for the fair play and substantial justice factors in the context of general jurisdiction.

2. Following the Supreme Court's decisions in *Goodyear, McIntyre*, and *Daimler*, how likely is it that a court may exercise general jurisdiction over a company based solely on a large volume of business conducted in the forum? The answer to that question is in part suggested by the Supreme Court's decision in *BNSF Railway Co. v. Tyrrell*, 137 S. Ct. 1549 (2017). In that case, plaintiff Nelson sued BNSF under the Federal Employers' Liability Act for alleged knee injuries sustained as an employee of the railroad. Plaintiff Tyrrell's estate sued BNSF under the FELA for Tyrrell's death from alleged exposure to carcinogens as a BNSF worker. Both suits were brought in Montana state courts. Neither plaintiff ever worked for BNSF in Montana.

BNSF is "incorporated in Delaware and has its principal place of business in Texas." *Id.* at 1554. It has "2061 miles of railroad track in Montana (about 6% of its total track mileage of 32,500), employs some 2100 workers there (less than 5% of its total work force of 43,300), generates less than 10% of its total revenue in the State, and maintains only one of its 24 automotive facilities in Montana (4%)." *Id.*

The Montana Supreme Court in relevant part ruled that Montana courts could exercise personal jurisdiction over BNSF because the company "does business" and can "be found in" Montana. The U.S. Supreme Court reversed. First, the Court ruled that there could not be specific personal jurisdiction over BNSF, because neither of the plaintiffs alleged that his injuries were from working in Montana. Second, the Court ruled that there could not be general personal jurisdiction over BNSF in Montana, because BNSF is not incorporated there, does not maintain its principal place of business there, and is not so active there as to "render [it] essentially at home." Third, the Court declined to reach the question whether BNSF had consented to personal jurisdiction, because the Montana Supreme Court had not ruled on that point.

Justice Sotomayor concurred in part and dissented in part, expressing the following concern: "The majority's approach grants a jurisdictional windfall to large multistate or multinational corporations that operate across many jurisdictions. Under its reasoning, it is virtually inconceivable that such corporations will ever be subject to general jurisdiction in any location other than their principal places of business or of incorporation." *Id.* at 1560. Do you agree with her conclusion? Suppose you do. Is the bottom line truly a "windfall" to defendants? How would a court know when a multistate corporation is doing enough business in a given state that the corporation should be susceptible to suit there on *any* cause of action regardless of the corporation's principal place of business or state of incorporation?

B. Consent or Waiver as a Basis for Jurisdiction

We are rarely concerned about personal jurisdiction over a plaintiff—by bringing a suit in a forum, the plaintiff has affirmatively indicated a willingness to be bound by the decision of the court in that forum. Therefore, the plaintiff does not require the protection that personal jurisdiction doctrine provides against unfair exercise of the court's power.

A defendant also may consent to or waive personal jurisdiction. The first significant consent case was *National Equipment Rental v. Szukhent*, 375 U.S. 311 (1964). The Szukhents, Michigan farmers, leased farm equipment from a New York company. On the back of the lease form was a clause saying that the Szukhents designated Florence Weinberg [at a New York City address] as an agent for the purpose of accepting service of process. The Szukhents defaulted on the lease, and the company sued in New York. The Supreme Court upheld jurisdiction, treating the lease clause as a valid consent to personal jurisdiction. This is an example of a consent which created jurisdiction that would not have existed without it.

The Supreme Court also has been receptive to forum selection clauses in the context of standard form, non-negotiable contracts. In *Carnival Cruise Lines v. Shute*, 499 U.S. 585 (1991), the Court reversed a lower court decision, refusing to enforce a forum selection clause. The clause stated, "all disputes and matters whatsoever arising under, in connection with or incident to this Contract shall be litigated, if at all, in and before a Court located in the State of Florida, U.S.A., to the exclusion of the Court of any other state or country." The Court ruled that such a clause is valid as long as the choice of forum is rational, there is no fraud or overreaching, and the defendant has notice of the clause at the time he enters the deal.

National Equipment Rental and *Carnival Cruise Lines* involved explicit consent. Implied consent as a basis for jurisdiction has essentially been supplanted by the *International Shoe* minimum contacts analysis, but implied consent nonetheless still has usefulness as a basis for jurisdiction. Consider for example *Hess v. Pawloski*, 274 U.S. 352 (1927), in which the Supreme Court upheld a state statute declaring that using the state's roads meant a person consents to specific personal jurisdiction in the state for matters arising out of the use.

In the years following *International Shoe*, courts have followed the doctrine that parties may consent to jurisdiction even in situations not covered by minimum contacts. *See McAninch v. Wintermute*, 491 F.3d 759, 766 (8th Cir. 2007) (plaintiff consents to personal jurisdiction by bringing suit in forum). Consent can be based on the designation of an in-state agent as required by state law. *R.R. Donnelly & Sons Co. v. Jet Messenger Servs., Inc.*, 2003 U.S. Dist. LEXIS 25421 (N.D. Ill. 2004) (corporation has consented to be sued in forum when it designates agent to receive service of process).

What about state registration-to-do-business statutes as a basis for consent? See the discussion in Freer, Civil Procedure 127–128 (4th ed. 2017). "The tenor of Supreme Court cases on personal jurisdiction since 2011 has been restrictive. *Goodyear, Daimler*, and *BNSF* rejected general jurisdiction. *J. McIntyre* and *Bristol-Myers Squibb* rejected specific jurisdiction. Discouraged by these precedents, some plaintiffs are attempting to get personal jurisdiction over businesses not on the basis of contacts but because of consent [based on state 'registration' statutes]." All states have "registration" statutes that require out-of-state businesses to "register," appoint an agent in-state, usually to maintain an office in-state, and to pay fees. The theory is that by adhering to the requirements of the registration statute, the company has consented to jurisdiction.

Whether the consent is to general or specific jurisdiction will depend on the terms of the statute. (Many are not clear on this score, and courts must interpret the legislation.) The more interesting question is whether a registration statute providing for general jurisdiction is constitutional. The Court upheld the validity of such a statute over a century ago. But today, in the "new era" of general jurisdiction, is this still true? Specifically, do *Goodyear, Daimler*, and *BNSF*—by appearing to permit general jurisdiction only where the defendant is "at home"—rule out general jurisdiction in other states based upon consent? The issue was raised in *BNSF*, but the Court did not address it because the state court had not done so. The issue is of increasing importance and a clear split of authority is emerging. *Compare, e.g., Hegna v. Smitty's Supply, Inc.*, 2017 WL 2563231 at *4 (E.D. Pa. 2017) (defendant "consented to general personal jurisdiction in Pennsylvania and . . . its consent is still valid under *Goodyear* and *Daimler*"), *with Famular v. Whirlpool Corp.*, 2017 WL 2470844 at *4 (S.D.N.Y.

2017) (defendant "is not subject to the general personal jurisdiction of the forum state merely by registering to do business with the state, whether that be through a theory of consent by registration or otherwise"). See *also AK Steel Corp. v. PAC Operating Limited Partnership*, 2018 WL 1536501 at *1 (D. Kan. March 29, 2018) (registration in Kansas results in general jurisdiction); *Gorton v. Air & Liquid Systems Corp.*, 2018 WL 1385531 (M.D. Pa. March 19, 2018) ("merely registering as a foreign corporation with a state—in the absence of specific statutory language providing otherwise—does not equate to being 'at home' in the state," but "if the relevant registration statute expressly says registration is a consent to general jurisdiction, and the business registered while that statute was in effect, and the relevant conduct at issue in the lawsuit occurred while that statute was in effect, that is a different matter").

Note that exercise of joinder devices can constitute consent to personal jurisdiction. For example, defendant can waive its defense of lack of personal jurisdiction by voluntarily filing third party claims. *Frank's Casing Crew & Rental Tools, Inc. v. PMR Technologies, Ltd.*, 292 F.3d 1363, 1372 (Fed. Cir. 2002). There is a split of authority on this point, however. *Bayou Steel Corp. v. M/V Amstelvoorn*, 809 F.2d 1147, 1149 (5th Cir. 1987). Similarly, an intervenor waives any personal jurisdiction objection by availing itself of the forum.

The Supreme Court has even ruled, in *Insurance Corp. of Ireland, LTD. v. Compagnie Des Bauxites De Guinea*, 456 U.S. 694 (1982), that a district court has discretion to conclude there is personal jurisdiction over a recalcitrant defendant as a discovery sanction when that defendant has failed to comply with jurisdictional discovery requests.

C. Personal Jurisdiction and the Internet

1. The Emergence of *Zippo*'s Sliding-Scale

Personal jurisdiction is grounded in historical concepts of territoriality as defined by state borders. The Internet, by contrast, is marked by its territorial indeterminacy. When a website infringes on a copyright or trademark, where does the infringement occur? Likewise, is a defamatory comment posted on someone's blog located in the state where the poster resides, where the comment is viewed, where the website's servers are located, or somewhere else altogether? The Internet thus forces courts to rethink how minimum contacts are assessed for the purposes of the exercise of personal jurisdiction.

In addition to the potential uncertainty over the location or even the existence of minimum contacts, the Internet is also easily, instantaneously, and continuously accessible from nearly anywhere by nearly anyone. It thus has the potential to subject people to jurisdiction in far off and unforeseen places. What is more, Internet users may not have reasonable expectations about the effects of their online activities or the jurisdictional consequences of such activities. How then should courts apply traditional notions of fair play and substantial justice to Internet cases? *Zippo Manufacturing Co. v. Zippo Dot Com, Inc.*, 952 F. Supp. 1119, 1124 (W.D. Pa. 1997) (internal citations omitted) announced the following test, which has gained widespread acceptance:

> [T]he likelihood that personal jurisdiction can be constitutionally exercised is directly proportionate to the nature and quality of commercial activity that an entity conducts over the Internet. This sliding scale is consistent with well developed personal jurisdiction principles. At one end of the spectrum are situations where a defendant clearly does business over the Internet. If the defendant enters into contracts with residents of a foreign jurisdiction that involve the knowing and repeated transmission of computer files over the Internet, personal jurisdiction is proper. At the opposite end are situations where a defendant has simply posted information on an Internet Web site which is accessible to users in foreign jurisdictions. A passive Web site that does little more than make information available to those who are interested in it is not grounds for the exercise of personal jurisdiction. The middle ground is occupied by interactive Web sites where a user can exchange information with the host computer. In these cases, the exercise of jurisdiction is determined by examining the level of interactivity and commercial nature of the exchange of information that occurs on the Web site.

Zippo Test

After formulating the test, the court concluded:

> [The defendant] Dot Com has done more than create an interactive Web site through which it exchanges information with Pennsylvania residents in hopes of using that information for commercial gain later. We are not being asked to determine whether Dot Com's Web site alone constitutes the purposeful availment of doing business in Pennsylvania. This is a "doing business over the Internet" case. . . . We are being asked to determine whether Dot Com's conducting of electronic commerce with Pennsylvania residents constitutes the purposeful availment of doing business in Pennsylvania. We conclude that it does. Dot Com has contracted with approximately 3,000 individuals and seven Internet access providers in Pennsylvania. The intended object of these transactions has been the downloading of the electronic messages that form the basis of this suit in Pennsylvania.

Id. at 1125–26.

Notes and Questions

1. If a single reinsurance certificate sent from Texas to California sufficed to confer personal jurisdiction in *McGee*, why does *Zippo* require "the knowing and repeated transmission of computer files?" Does this sound more like a test for general jurisdiction? It is not. Should it be?

2. Does a defendant who establishes an interactive website (one with links and, say, a message board) purposefully avail himself of the benefits and protections of doing business in other states in a way that a passive website (a single page advertisement, albeit a compelling one) does not? How? Suppose a passive website simply publishes information but has a wide readership, made possible by Google and the links of other websites. If the site benefits from these practices, which seem to hinge on interactivity and the interconnections of the internet, say through revenue generated by advertisements appearing on the site but over which it has no control, why should its operator be able to escape jurisdiction?

3. For that matter, how should a court determine a website's level of interactivity? There is widespread agreement that a website that posts information about available products or services, provides an order form, includes a mailing address, and offers an email link is no more than passive. *See, e.g.*, *Mink v. AAAA Dev. LLC*, 190 F.3d 333, 336–37 (5th Cir. 1999); *Cybersell, Inc. v. Cybersell, Inc.*, 130 F.3d 414 (9th Cir. 1997). *But see Christian Sci. Bd. of Dirs. of First Church of Christ, Scientist v. Nolan*, 259 F.3d 209, 218 n.11 (4th Cir. 2001) (describing such a website as "minimally interactive," and not just passive). Generally, bulletin board websites are treated as interactive, *see, e.g.*, *Revell v. Lidov*, 317 F.3d 467, 472 (5th Cir. 2002); so too are commercial websites that allow for the transaction of business online but that are not actually used to transact substantial amounts of business with the forum state, although the latter fact might help point to a conclusion of no jurisdiction. *See Millenium Enters., Inc. v. Millenium Music, LP*, 33 F. Supp. 2d 907, 920–21 (D. Ore. 1999); *GTE New Media Servs. Inc. v. BellSouth Corp.*, 199 F.3d 1343, 1350 (D.C. Cir. 2000). Do such websites amount to doing business online? Does the flexibility of the *Zippo* approach render it less rule-like and more descriptive, thereby creating potentially inconsistent results? *See, e.g.*, *Shamsuddin v. Vitamin Research Prods.*, 346 F. Supp. 2d 804, 810 (D. Md. 2004); *see also Hy Cite Corp. v. Badbusinessbureau.com, L.L.C.*, 297 F. Supp. 2d 1154, 1160 (W.D. Wis. 2004) ("I am reluctant to fall in line with these courts [applying *Zippo*]. . . . [I]t is not clear why a website's level of interactivity should be determinative on the issue of personal jurisdiction. . . .")

4. Despite some criticism, many courts have adopted the *Zippo* test, although it has been modified and applied in different ways. The following case is emblematic and widely cited. As you read it, think about the vast middle ground created by *Zippo's* sliding scale. What sorts of features make an interactive website a proper predicate for personal jurisdiction? Can a website be interactive for some persons and purposes but not others? If interactivity alone were insufficient for jurisdiction, what else would be needed?

2. Post-*Zippo* Developments as to Personal Jurisdiction and the Internet Today

Toys "R" Us, Inc. v. Step Two, S.A.

United States Court of Appeals, Third Circuit
318 F.3d 446 (2003)

Louis Oberdorfer, Senior District Judge, sitting by designation.

Toys "R" Us, Inc. and Geoffrey, Inc. ("Toys") brought this action against Step Two, S.A. and Imaginarium Net, S.L. ("Step Two"), alleging that Step Two used its Internet web sites to engage in trademark infringement, unfair competition, misuse of the trademark notice symbol, and unlawful "cybersquatting," in violation of the Lanham Act, 15 U.S.C. § 1501 *et seq*., and New Jersey state law. . . .

I

Toys, a Delaware corporation with its headquarters in New Jersey, owns retail stores worldwide where it sells toys, games, and numerous other products. In August 1999, Toys acquired Imaginarium Toy Centers, Inc., which owned and operated a network of "Imaginarium" stores for the sale of educational toys and games. As part of this acquisition, Toys acquired several Imaginarium trademarks, and subsequently filed applications for the registration of additional Imaginarium marks. Prior to Toys' acquisition, the owners of the Imaginarium mark had been marketing a line of educational toys and games since 1985 and had first registered the Imaginarium mark with the United States Patent and Trademark Office in 1989. Toys currently owns thirty-seven freestanding Imaginarium stores in the U.S., of which seven are located in New Jersey. In addition, there are Imaginarium shops within 175 of the Toys "R" Us stores in the U.S., including five New Jersey stores.

Step Two is a Spanish corporation that owns or has franchised toy stores operating under the name "Imaginarium" in Spain and nine other countries. It first registered the Imaginarium mark in Spain in 1991, and opened its first Imaginarium store in the Spanish city of Zaragoza in November 1992. Step Two began expanding its chain of Imaginarium stores by means of a franchise system in 1994. It has registered the Imaginarium mark in several other countries where its stores are located. There are now 165 Step Two Imaginarium stores. The stores have the same unique facade and logo as those owned by Toys, and sell the same types of merchandise as Toys sells in its Imaginarium stores. However, Step Two does not operate any stores, maintain any offices or bank accounts, or have any employees anywhere in the United States. Nor does it pay taxes to the U.S. or to any U.S. state. Step Two maintains that it has not directed any advertising or marketing efforts towards the United States. The record does, however, indicate some contacts between Step Two and the United States: for example, a portion of the merchandise sold at Step Two's Imaginarium stores is purchased from vendors in the

United States. Additionally, Felix Tena, President of Step Two, attends the New York Toy Fair once each year.

In the mid-1990s, both parties turned to the Internet to boost their sales. . . .

. . . .

II

. . . .

A. Personal Jurisdiction Based on the Operation of a Website

The advent of the Internet has required courts to fashion guidelines for when personal jurisdiction can be based on a defendant's operation of a web site. Courts have sought to articulate a standard that both embodies traditional rules and accounts for new factual scenarios created by the Internet. Under traditional jurisdictional analysis, the exercise of specific personal jurisdiction requires that the "plaintiff's cause of action is related to or arises out of the defendant's contacts with the forum." Pinker v. Roche Holdings Ltd., 292 F.3d 361, 368 (3d Cir. 2002). Beyond this basic nexus, for a finding of specific personal jurisdiction, the Due Process Clause of the Fifth Amendment requires (1) that the "defendant ha[ve] constitutionally sufficient 'minimum contacts' with the forum," *id.* (quoting Burger King Corp. v. Rudzewicz, 471 U.S. 462, 474 (1985)), and (2) that "subjecting the defendant to the court's jurisdiction comports with 'traditional notions of fair play and substantial justice,'" *id.* (quoting International Shoe Co. v. Washington, 326 U.S. 310, 316 (1945)). The first requirement, "minimum contacts," has been defined as "'some act by which the defendant purposefully avails itself of the privilege of conducting activities within the forum State, thus invoking the benefits and protections of its laws.'" Asahi Metal Indus. Co., Ltd. v. Superior Court of California, 480 U.S. 102, 109 (1987) (quoting Burger King Corp., 471 U.S. at 475). Second, jurisdiction exists only if its exercise "comports with traditional notions of fair play and substantial justice," *i.e.*, the defendant "should reasonably anticipate being haled into court" in that forum. World-Wide Volkswagen Corp. v. Woodson, 444 U.S. 286, 297 (1980).

The precise question raised by this case is whether the operation of a commercially interactive web site accessible in the forum state is sufficient to support specific personal jurisdiction, or whether there must be additional evidence that the defendant has "purposefully availed" itself of the privilege of engaging in activity in that state. Prior decisions indicate that such evidence *is* necessary, and that it should reflect intentional interaction with the forum state. If a defendant web site operator intentionally targets the site to the forum state, and/or knowingly conducts business with forum state residents via the site, then the "purposeful availment" requirement is satisfied. Below, we first review cases from this and other circuits that articulate this requirement. Next, we consider the role of related non-Internet contacts in demonstrating purposeful availment. We then assess whether the "purposeful availment" requirement has been satisfied in the present case.

1. The Purposeful Availment Requirement in Internet Cases

a. Third Circuit Cases

The opinion in *Zippo Manufacturing Co. v. Zippo Dot Com, Inc.*, 952 F. Supp. 1119 (W.D. Pa. 1997) has become a seminal authority regarding personal jurisdiction based upon the operation of an Internet web site. The court in *Zippo* stressed that the propriety of exercising jurisdiction depends on where on a sliding scale of commercial interactivity the web site falls. In cases where the defendant is clearly doing business through its web site in the forum state, and where the claim relates to or arises out of use of the web site, the *Zippo* court held that personal jurisdiction exists. *Id.* at 1124....

....

2. Non-Internet Contacts

In deciding whether to exercise jurisdiction over a cause of action arising from a defendant's operation of a web site, a court may consider the defendant's related non-Internet activities as part of the "purposeful availment" calculus....

[N]on-internet contacts such as serial business trips to the forum state, telephone and fax communications directed to the forum state, purchase contracts with forum state residents, contracts that apply the law of the forum state, and advertisements in local newspapers, may form part of the "something more" needed to establish personal jurisdiction. *See* Barrett v. Catacombs Press, 44 F. Supp. 2d 717, 726 (E.D. Pa. 1999), and cases there collected....

3. Personal Jurisdiction over Step Two

As *Zippo* ... indicate[s], the mere operation of a commercially interactive web site should not subject the operator to jurisdiction anywhere in the world. Rather, there must be evidence that the defendant "purposefully availed" itself of conducting activity in the forum state, by directly targeting its web site to the state, knowingly interacting with residents of the forum state via its web site, or through sufficient other related contacts.

Based on the facts established in this case thus far, Toys has failed to satisfy the purposeful availment requirement. Step Two's web sites, while commercial and interactive, do not appear to have been designed or intended to reach customers in New Jersey. Step Two's web sites are entirely in Spanish; prices for its merchandise are in pesetas or Euros, and merchandise can be shipped only to addresses within Spain. Most important, none of the portions of Step Two's web sites are designed to accommodate addresses within the United States. While it is possible to join Club Imaginarium and receive newsletters with only an email address, Step Two asks registrants to indicate their residence using fields that are not designed for addresses in the United States.

Moreover, the record may not now support a finding that Step Two knowingly conducted business with residents of New Jersey. The only documented sales to persons in the United States are the two contacts orchestrated by Toys, and it appears that Step Two scarcely recognized that sales with U.S. residents had been consummated.

At best, Toys has presented only inconclusive circumstantial evidence to suggest that Step Two targeted its web site to New Jersey residents, or that it purposefully availed itself of any effort to conduct activity in New Jersey. Many of the grounds for jurisdiction that Toys advanced below have been deemed insufficient by the courts. First, the two documented sales appear to be the kind of "fortuitous," "random," and "attenuated" contacts that the Supreme Court has held insufficient to warrant the exercise of jurisdiction. *See Burger King Corp.*, 471 U.S. at 475 (citations omitted). As for the electronic newsletters and other email correspondence, "telephone communication or mail sent by a defendant [do] not trigger personal jurisdiction if they 'do not show purposeful availment.'" *Barrett*, 44 F. Supp. 2d at 729 (quoting Mellon Bank (East) PSFS, N.A. v. DiVeronica Bros., Inc., 983 F.2d 551, 556 (3d Cir. 1993)). The court in *Barrett* found that the exchange of three emails between the plaintiff and defendant regarding the contents of the defendant's web site, without more, did not "amount to the level of purposeful targeting required under the minimum contacts analysis." *Id.* at 729; *see also* Machulsky v. Hall, 210 F. Supp. 2d 531, 542 (D.N.J. 2002) (minimal email correspondence, "by itself or even in conjunction with a single purchase, does not constitute sufficient minimum contacts."). Non-Internet contacts, such as Mr. Tena's visits to New York and the relationships with U.S. vendors, have not been explored sufficiently to determine whether they are related to Toys' cause of action, or whether they reflect "purposeful availment."

Absent further evidence showing purposeful availment, Toys cannot establish specific jurisdiction over Step Two. . . .

B. Jurisdictional Discovery

. . . .

Toys requested jurisdictional discovery for the purpose of establishing either specific personal jurisdiction, or jurisdiction under the federal long-arm statute, Fed. R. Civ. P. 4(k)(2).[2] The District Court denied Toys' request, explaining that "the clear focus of the Court is directed, as it should be, to the web site[,] [a]nd to the activity of the defendants related to that web site, which is making sales here, . . ." The court added that "the apparent contradictions, if such there will be in the Tena affidavit, [and] what else Mr. Tena might have been doing here, just have no relationship to where the eye is directed and should stay and that is, the web site activities of this defendant."

We are persuaded that the District Court erred when it denied Toys' request for jurisdictional discovery. The court's unwavering focus on the web site precluded

2. [Court's footnote #7] The federal long-arm statute sanctions personal jurisdiction over foreign defendants for claims arising under federal law when the defendant has sufficient contacts with the nation as a whole to justify the imposition of U.S. law, but without sufficient contacts to satisfy the due process concerns of the long-arm statute of any particular state.

consideration of other Internet and non-Internet contacts—indicated in various parts of the record—which, if explored, might provide the "something more" needed to bring Step Two within our jurisdiction. . . .

. . . .

CONCLUSION

For all of the reasons set forth above, we reverse the District Court's denial of Toys' request for jurisdictional discovery, vacate the District Court's dismissal of Toys' complaint, and remand the case for limited jurisdictional discovery guided by the foregoing analysis, and for reconsideration of jurisdiction with the benefit of the product of that discovery.

Notes and Questions

1. Does the Internet element of the tests used in *Zippo* and *Toys "R" Us* actually affect the jurisdictional calculus at all or is it simply a language for describing online activity? If it does not affect the calculus, why have a separate test for internet activity? Existing jurisdictional doctrine may be sufficiently expansive to encompass internet cases, for as the Court in *Hanson v. Denckla*, 357 U.S. 235, 250–51 (1958), explained:

> As technological progress has increased the flow of commerce between States, the need for jurisdiction over nonresidents has undergone a similar increase. At the same time, progress in communications and transportation has made the defense of a suit in a foreign tribunal less burdensome. In response to these changes, the requirements for personal jurisdiction over nonresidents have evolved from the rigid rule of *Pennoyer v. Neff*, 95 U.S. 714, to the flexible standard of *International Shoe Co. v. Washington*, 326 U.S. 310.

Numerous commentators have offered various proposals for reconciling *Zippo* and the internet personal jurisdiction analysis with the purposeful availment and aiming and effects tests. *See, e.g.*, C. Douglas Floyd & Shima Baradaran-Robison, *Toward a Unified Test of Personal Jurisdiction in an Era of Widely Diffused Wrongs: The Relevance of Purpose and Effects*, 81 Ind. L.J. 601 (2006) (arguing for a "unified approach" based not on problematic notions of the defendant's intent or purpose, but instead on "whether the defendant objectively should be held to be on notice that his conduct was substantially certain to" cause harm in the forum state).

2. What would it have taken for Step Two and its website to satisfy either the direct targeting or knowing interaction prongs of the "something more" than simply maintaining an interactive website requirement? In the full opinion, the court notes that inputting a U.S. shipping address was impossible given the website's configuration. Would the result have been different if blanks were provided so that users could input any shipping address or if the drop down menus included U.S. states? Could such a website be fairly described as targeting New Jersey, the U.S as a whole, or everywhere? What constitutes knowing interaction? In granting discovery on the

issue of jurisdiction, the court seemed receptive to the idea that even the possibility of knowledge of the purchasers' whereabouts would justify jurisdiction. Compare this approach with that taken in *Millenium Enterprises, Inc. v. Millenium Music, LP*, 33 F. Supp. 2d 907 (D. Ore. 1999).

Remember, we are dealing with specific jurisdiction. The claim for relief must arise out of the minimum contacts. That being the case, how closely does this "something more" have to be related to the Internet activity and the claim? How closely must the internet activity and the claim be related? Both *Zippo* and *Toys "R" Us* seem to accept the connection uncritically. Compare, for example, the opinions in *Dairy Farmers of America, Inc. v. Bassett & Walker Int'l, Inc.*, 702 F.3d 472 (8th Cir. 2012) (concluding that the defendant's communications with plaintiff in Missouri through phone, fax, and email did not constitute "transacting business" under the language of the Missouri long-arm statute) and in *MacDermid, Inc. v. Deiter*, 702 F.3d 725 (2d Cir. 2012) (concluding that the defendant's accessing of plaintiff's computer servers in Connecticut constituted "use of a computer" within the meaning of that state's long-arm statute).

3. *Defamation.* While *Toys "R" Us* examined a commercially interactive website, the direct targeting aspect of the analysis is useful in other contexts as well. Online defamation cases are common. Under a strict application of *Zippo*, however, might posters of defamatory material avoid jurisdiction simply because the website on which the offending comments appeared was passive? *See Atkinson v. McLaughlin*, 343 F. Supp. 2d 868, 872–74 (D.N.D. 2004). Does *Toys "R" Us* have the potential to remedy this gap?

Consider the potential applicability of *Calder v. Jones*, 465 U.S. 783 (1984), a defamation case, in which the Court focused the notion of minimum contacts on the defendant's purposeful conduct outside the forum state aimed at having effects in the forum state. In *Calder*, a reporter in Florida wrote an article about actress Shirley Jones. Jones sued the reporter, among others, in California where she resided. The Supreme Court held that California could exercise jurisdiction over the individual defendants "based on the effects of their Florida conduct in California." The court in a key passage stated that,

> petitioners are not charged with mere untargeted negligence. Rather, their intentional, and allegedly tortious, actions were expressly aimed at California. Petitioner South wrote and petitioner Calder edited an article that they knew would have a potentially devastating impact upon respondent. And they knew that the brunt of that injury would be felt by respondent in the State in which she lives and works and in which the National Enquirer has its largest circulation. Under the circumstances, petitioners must "reasonably anticipate being haled into court there" to answer for the truth of the statements made in their article. *Id.* at 789–90.

Note the importance of purposeful targeting within this "effects" test. "The 'effects test' theory of personal jurisdiction is typically invoked where 'the conduct that forms the basis for the controversy occurs entirely out of forum, and the only relevant jurisdictional contacts with the forum are therefore in-forum effects harmful to the plaintiff.' [citation omitted] Exercise of jurisdiction in such circumstances 'may be constitutional permissible if the defendant expressly aimed its conduct at the forum.' [citation omitted] The 'foreseeability of causing injury in another State,' however, will not suffice." *Charles Schwab Corp. v. Bank of America Corp.*, 883 F.3d 68, 87 (2d Cir. 2018).

Courts have struggled in internet jurisdiction cases to merge *Calder*'s aim and effects test with *Zippo*'s sliding scale. *See Young v. New Haven Advocate*, 315 F.3d 256 (4th Cir. 2002); *ALS Scan, Inc. v. Digital Serv. Consultants, Inc.*, 293 F.3d 707 (4th Cir. 2002); *Revell v. Lidov*, 317 F.3d 467 (5th Cir. 2002). Does *Zippo* play any role in determining whether electronic activity was directed into the forum? To what else might a court look? Apart from the constitutional analysis, why might a state want to limit its jurisdictional reach over claims of defamation against outstate defendants in such a way that jurisdiction is only proper if they are also transacting business in the state, online or otherwise? *See Best Van Lines, Inc. v. Walker*, 490 F.3d 239, 245 (2d Cir. 2007) ("[Drafters of the long-arm statute] intended to avoid unnecessary inhibitions on freedom of speech or the press. . . . [They] did not wish New York to force newspapers published in other states to defend themselves in states where they had no substantial interests. . . .").

4. What should be the effect of the Supreme Court's decision in *Walden v. Fiore*, 134 S. Ct. 1115 (2014)? There, a police agent in Georgia seized a large sum of cash from certain individuals. The agent knew of the individuals' "strong" connections with Nevada and could foresee that the individuals would suffer harm in Nevada. The Court rejected these factors as sufficient for the exercise of personal jurisdiction over the agent in Nevada, and said that, "[T]he plaintiff cannot be the only link between the defendant and the forum. Rather, it is the defendant's conduct that must form the necessary connection with the forum State that is the basis for its jurisdiction over him." The Court concluded that the *Calder* effects test is focused on the effects of a defendant's conduct on a forum at large, not simply on the effects of the conduct on the plaintiff. In footnote 9, the Court noted that, "Respondents warn that if [the agent] lacks minimum contacts in this case, it will bring about unfairness in cases where intentional torts are committed via the Internet or other electronic means. . . ." The Court, however, concluded that, "this case does not present the very different questions whether and how a defendant's virtual 'presence' and conduct translate into 'contacts' with a particular State . . . We leave questions about virtual contacts for another day." 134 S. Ct. at 1125.

5. *General jurisdiction and the Internet.* Would it have made any difference to the court's conclusion in *Toys "R" Us* if instead of two sales into New Jersey, Step Two had derived substantial revenue from online sales in New Jersey? Could the court then have asserted general personal jurisdiction? Could it have done so after *Daimler AG v. Bauman*, 134 S. Ct. 746 (2014)?

There is widespread agreement that the existence of a passive or even an interactive website is an insufficient stand-alone basis for the exercise of general jurisdiction. *See Soma Med. Int'l v. Standard Chartered Bank*, 196 F.3d 1292, 1296–97 (10th Cir. 1999) (applying *Zippo* and finding a passive website that offered information and solicited business, despite its continuous accessibility, insufficient for general jurisdiction); *Millennium Enters., Inc.*, 33 F. Supp. 2d at 908–10 (concluding that an interactive website through which one sale into the forum state had been made was insufficient for general jurisdiction; interaction via website alone was deemed insufficient, as holding otherwise would undermine personal jurisdiction requirements regarding purposeful availment). This should not be surprising. General jurisdiction is supposed to be hard to get.

But, consider *Gator.com Corp. v. L.L. Bean, Inc.*, 341 F.3d 1072 (9th Cir. 2003), in which the court concluded that, "[E]ven if the only contacts L.L. Bean [a Maine-based corporation] had with California were through its virtual store, a finding of general jurisdiction in the instant case would be consistent with the "sliding scale" test . . . Under the sliding-scale analysis, L.L. Bean's contacts with California are sufficient to confer general jurisdiction. L.L. Bean's website is highly interactive and very extensive." *Id.* at 1079–80.

After a rehearing *en banc* was granted, the parties settled, so *Gator* is of no precedential value. The sliding scale was announced as a test for specific jurisdiction. Does it make sense to extend it to apply where general jurisdiction is sought? This is not an issue to which the court in *Gator.com* gave much thought. That said, it is not alone in using *Zippo* in the general jurisdiction context. *See Mink v. AAAA Dev. LLC*, 190 F.3d 333 (5th Cir. 1999); *Gorman v. Ameritrade Holding Corp.*, 293 F.3d 506, 513 (D.C. Cir. 2002). *But see Revell v. Lidov*, 317 F.3d 467, 471 (5th Cir. 2002) (reasoning that *Zippo's* sliding scale "is not well adapted to the general jurisdiction inquiry, because even repeated contacts with forum residents by a foreign defendant may not constitute the requisite substantial, continuous and systematic contacts required for a finding of general jurisdiction"). Would use of a *Zippo* sliding scale after *Daimler AG v. Bauman* be viable for assessing general jurisdiction?

6. Where do blogs fall on *Zippo's* sliding scale? On many blogs, comments can be posted and may even need to be approved before they appear. This suggests that blogs are interactive. But blogs are often personal, and not business ventures. The interactivity is distinct from online commercial activity. Should the maintenance of a blog then subject its operator to jurisdiction where the blog is viewed? Would it matter if the blog had many readers and commenters in the forum state? What if the operator listed her blog on a forum state-based link aggregator/webpage with the aim of increasing web traffic? Consider *Healix Infusion Therapy, Inc. v. Helix Health*, 2008 U.S. Dist. LEXIS 34562 (S.D. Tex. Apr. 25, 2008) (rejecting exercise of personal jurisdiction based on a blog that was more than "passive" because the facts did not indicate that the blog was aimed at the residents of the Texas forum).

7. Where does a website that allows consumers to make hotel reservations fall on the sliding scale? Is it merely an advertisement? It would seem to be interactive.

Might it be doing business over the internet? Consider *Snowney v. Harrah's Entertainment, Inc.*, 112 P.3d 28 (Cal. 2005) (upholding the exercise of personal jurisdiction in California over Nevada hotels).

What counts as purposefully directing a website at a state's residents? Does providing directions from that state to the destination suffice? *Id.* at 35. What if the directions say "arriving from the west" and there is only one state to the west? What if the hotel provides a link to an online map site that allows the user to input her starting point but with the hotel marked as the destination? Would the result have been different if the hotels did not directly target California but derived substantial benefit from the state?

8. The cases discussed thus far concern websites that are the subject of the suit and at least in part the basis for asserting jurisdiction. In other cases, however, a defendant's website may not be essential to the plaintiff's claim and the injury suffered, but may nevertheless provide the grounds for personal jurisdiction. Consider *Brown v. Kerkhoff*, 504 F. Supp. 2d 464 (S.D. Ia. 2007) (analyzing a company's website contacts with the forum in conjunction with the company's more traditional contacts, and finding specific personal jurisdiction).

D. International Personal Jurisdiction

The tests for personal jurisdiction over foreign defendants in the United States are essentially the same as those for personal jurisdiction over domestic defendants. But for a foreign defendant there are occasions when the relevant "minimum contacts" are those of the defendant with the United States as a whole rather than with a specific state. This section is divided into two parts: (1) Same Tests, Similar Application; and (2) Nationwide Contacts Application.

1. Same Tests, Similar Application

First there are cases in which, when faced with a personal jurisdiction dispute over a foreign defendant in a state court, the Supreme Court essentially has treated the foreign defendant as if it were an out-of-state domestic defendant. Reconsider the Supreme Court's opinions in *Goodyear, McIntyre*, and *Daimler AG.* Does the personal jurisdiction analysis in those cases resemble the same analysis as would apply to a matter in which there is no international defendant? What do you make of the Court's international comity analysis in Part IVC of the *Daimler* opinion?

International Service. In the wake of *Asahi* came *Volkswagenwerk Aktiengesellschaft v. Schlunk*, 486 U.S. 694 (1988), where the Supreme Court considered whether international service through a domestic subsidiary was compatible with the Hague Service Convention.

Volkswagenwerk Aktiengesellschaft v. Schlunk

Supreme Court of the United States
486 U.S. 694 (1988)

JUSTICE O'CONNOR delivered the opinion of the Court.

This case involves an attempt to serve process on a foreign corporation by serving its domestic subsidiary which, under state law, is the foreign corporation's involuntary agent for service of process. We must decide whether such service is compatible with the Convention on Service Abroad of Judicial and Extrajudicial Documents in Civil and Commercial Matters, Nov. 15, 1965 (Hague Service Convention), [1969] 20 U.S.T. 361, T.I.A.S. No. 6638.

I

The parents of respondent Herwig Schlunk were killed in an automobile accident in 1983. Schlunk filed a wrongful death action on their behalf in the Circuit Court of Cook County, Illinois. Schlunk alleged that Volkswagen of America, Inc. (VWoA), had designed and sold the automobile that his parents were driving, and that defects in the automobile caused or contributed to their deaths. Schlunk also alleged that the driver of the other automobile involved in the collision was negligent; Schlunk has since obtained a default judgment against that person, who is no longer a party to this lawsuit. Schlunk successfully served his complaint on VWoA, and VWoA filed an answer denying that it had designed or assembled the automobile in question. Schlunk then amended the complaint to add as a defendant Volkswagen Aktiengesellschaft (VWAG), which is the petitioner here. VWAG, a corporation established under the laws of the Federal Republic of Germany, has its place of business in that country. VWoA is a wholly owned subsidiary of VWAG. Schlunk attempted to serve his amended complaint on VWAG by serving VWoA as VWAG's agent.

VWAG filed a special and limited appearance for the purpose of quashing service. VWAG asserted that it could be served only in accordance with the Hague Service Convention, and that Schlunk had not complied with the Convention's requirements....

....

We granted certiorari to address this issue which has given rise to disagreement among the lower courts....

II

The Hague Service Convention is a multilateral treaty that was formulated in 1964 by the Tenth Session of the Hague Conference of Private International Law. The Convention revised parts of the Hague Conventions on Civil Procedure of 1905 and 1954. The revision was intended to provide a simpler way to serve process abroad, to assure that defendants sued in foreign jurisdictions would receive actual and timely notice of suit, and to facilitate proof of service abroad....

The primary innovation of the Convention is that it requires each state to establish a central authority to receive requests for service of documents from other countries. 20 U.S.T. 362, T.I.A.S. 6638, Art. 2. Once a central authority receives a request in the proper form, it must serve the documents by a method prescribed by the internal law of the receiving state or by a method designated by the requester and compatible with that law. Art. 5. The central authority must then provide a certificate of service that conforms to a specified model. Art. 6. A state also may consent to methods of service within its boundaries other than a request to its central authority. Arts. 8–11, 19. The remaining provisions of the Convention that are relevant here limit the circumstances in which a default judgment may be entered against a defendant who had to be served abroad and did not appear, and provide some means for relief from such a judgment. Arts. 15, 16.

Article 1 defines the scope of the Convention, which is the subject of controversy in this case. It says: "The present Convention shall apply in all cases, in civil or commercial matters, where there is occasion to transmit a judicial or extrajudicial document for service abroad." . . .

The Convention does not specify the circumstances in which there is "occasion to transmit" a complaint "for service abroad." But at least the term "service of process" has a well-established technical meaning. Service of process refers to a formal delivery of documents that is legally sufficient to charge the defendant with notice of a pending action. 1 Ristau § 4–5(2), p. 123 (interpreting the Convention); Black's Law Dictionary 1227 (5th ed. 1979); see 4 C. Wright & A. Miller, Federal Practice and Procedure § 1063, p. 225 (2d ed. 1987). The legal sufficiency of a formal delivery of documents must be measured against some standard. The Convention does not prescribe a standard, so we almost necessarily must refer to the internal law of the forum state. If the internal law of the forum state defines the applicable method of serving process as requiring the transmittal of documents abroad, then the Hague Service Convention applies.

. . . .

VWAG protests that it is inconsistent with the purpose of the Convention to interpret it as applying only when the internal law of the forum requires service abroad. One of the two stated objectives of the Convention is "to create appropriate means to ensure that judicial and extrajudicial documents to be served abroad shall be brought to the notice of the addressee in sufficient time." 20 U.S.T., at 362. The Convention cannot assure adequate notice, VWAG argues, if the forum's internal law determines whether it applies. VWAG warns that countries could circumvent the Convention by defining methods of service of process that do not require transmission of documents abroad. . . .

VWAG correctly maintains that the Convention also aims to ensure that there will be adequate notice in cases in which there is occasion to serve process abroad. Thus compliance with the Convention is mandatory in all cases to which it applies, see *supra*, at 700–701, and Articles 15 and 16 provide an indirect sanction against those who ignore it, see 3 Actes et Documents, at 92, 363. Our interpretation of the Convention does not necessarily advance this particular objective, inasmuch as it makes recourse to the Convention's means of service dependent on the forum's internal law. But we do not think that this country, or any other country, will draft its internal laws deliberately so as to circumvent the Convention in cases in which it would be appropriate to transmit judicial documents for service abroad. . . .

Furthermore, nothing that we say today prevents compliance with the Convention even when the internal law of the forum does not so require. The Convention provides simple and certain means by which to serve process on a foreign national. Those who eschew its procedures risk discovering that the forum's internal law required transmittal of documents for service abroad, and that the Convention therefore provided the exclusive means of valid service. In addition, parties that comply with the Convention ultimately may find it easier to enforce their judgments abroad. See Westin, Enforcing Foreign Commercial Judgments and Arbitral Awards in the United States, West Germany, and England, Law & Policy Int'l Bus. 325, 340–341 (1987). For these reasons, we anticipate that parties may resort to the Convention voluntarily, even in cases that fall outside the scope of its mandatory application.

III

In this case, the Illinois long-arm statute authorized Schlunk to serve VWAG by substituted service on VWoA, without sending documents to Germany. See Ill. Rev. Stat., ch. 110, ¶ 2–209(a)(1) (1985). . . .

Where service on a domestic agent is valid and complete under both state law and the Due Process Clause, our inquiry ends and the Convention has no further implications. Whatever internal, private communications take place between the agent and a foreign principal are beyond the concerns of this case. The only transmittal to which the Convention applies is a transmittal abroad that is required as a necessary part of service. And, contrary to VWAG's assertion, the Due Process Clause does not require an official transmittal of documents abroad every time there is service on a foreign national. Applying this analysis, we conclude that this case does not present an occasion to transmit a judicial document for service abroad within the meaning of Article 1. Therefore, the Hague Service Convention does not apply, and service was proper. *The judgment of the Appellate Court is affirmed.*

Justice Brennan, with whom Justice Marshall and Justice Blackmun join, concurring in the judgment.

We acknowledged last Term, and the Court reiterates today that the terms of the Convention on Service Abroad of Judicial and Extrajudicial Documents in Civil or Commercial Matters, Nov. 15, 1965, [1969] 20 U.S.T. 361, T.I.A.S. No. 6638, are "mandatory," not "optional" with respect to any transmission that Article 1 covers. *Société Nationale Industrielle Aérospatiale v. United States District Court*, 482 U.S. 522, 534, and n. 15 (1987). Even so, the Court holds, and I agree, that a litigant may, consistent with the Convention, serve process on a foreign corporation by serving its wholly owned domestic subsidiary, because such process is not "service abroad" within the meaning of Article 1. The Court reaches that conclusion, however, by depriving the Convention of any mandatory effect, for in the Court's view the "forum's internal law" defines conclusively whether a particular process is "service abroad," which is covered by the Convention, or domestic service, which is not. I do not join the Court's opinion because I find it implausible that the Convention's framers intended to leave each contracting nation, and each of the 50 States within our Nation, free to decide for itself under what circumstances, if any, the Convention would control. Rather, in my view, the words "service abroad," read in light of the negotiating history, embody a substantive standard that limits a forum's latitude to deem service complete domestically.

. . . .

[But service] on a wholly owned, closely controlled subsidiary is reasonably calculated to reach the parent "in due time" as the Convention requires. See, *e.g.*, 9 W. Fletcher, Cyclopedia of Law of Private Corporations § 4412, p. 400 (rev. ed. 1985). That is, in fact, what our own Due Process Clause requires, see *Mullane v. Central Hanover Bank & Trust Co.*, 339 U.S. 306, 314–315 (1950), and since long before the Convention's implementation our law has permitted such service, see, *e.g., Perkins v. Benguet Consolidated Mining Co.*, 342 U.S. 437, 444–445 (1952); *Latimer v. S/A Industrias Reunidas F. Matarazzo*, 175 F.2d 184, 185 (CA2 1949) (L. Hand, J.). . . .

. . . .

Notes and Questions

One issue has been whether a summons and complaint may be served on a foreign defendant by a postal channel such as certified mail under Article 10(a) of the Hague Convention, which refers to "freedom to send judicial documents by postal channels directly to persons abroad." The Supreme Court resolved the debate in *Water Splash, Inc. v. Menon*, 137 S. Ct. 1504 (2017), holding that the Hague Service Convention does not bar service of a summons and complaint by mail. Article 10(a), referring to "the freedom to send judicial documents, by postal channels, directly to persons abroad" permits the sending of judicial documents for the purposes of service of process so long as two conditions are met: "first, the receiving state has not objected to service by mail; and second, service by mail is authorized under otherwise-applicable law." *Id.* at 1513.

2. Nationwide Contacts

What if a foreign defendant has contacts throughout the United States, but insufficient contacts in any one State to justify an exercise of jurisdiction? In such scenarios, federal courts have considered using a nationwide contacts test to exercise jurisdiction over the foreign entity.

An example is *Pinker v. Roche Holdings, Ltd.*, 292 F.3d 361 (3d Cir. 2002), in which the Third Circuit found jurisdiction over a Swiss company which "purposefully availed itself of the American securities market." As you read the opinion, consider the fairness of exercising jurisdiction in this manner.

Pinker v. Roche Holdings, Ltd.

United States Court of Appeals, Third Circuit
292 F.3d 361 (2002)

EDWARD BECKER, CHIEF JUDGE.

American Depositary Receipts ("ADRs") are financial instruments that allow investors in the United States to purchase and sell stock in foreign corporations in a simpler and more secure manner than trading in the underlying security in a foreign market. Harold Pinker, the plaintiff in this putative securities fraud class action, invested in ADRs of the defendant, Roche Holdings Ltd. ("Roche"), a Swiss corporation with its principal place of business in Switzerland. The gravamen of Pinker's action is that he purchased Roche ADRs at a price that was artificially inflated due to the company's misrepresentations about the competitiveness of the vitamin market when in fact its subsidiaries were engaged in a worldwide conspiracy to fix vitamin prices. As the truth about Roche's collusive activity began to emerge, Pinker alleges, the price of Roche ADRs dropped, and Pinker and other similarly situated investors suffered a loss. As a result, Pinker claims, Roche is liable for securities fraud in violation of Section 10(b) of the Securities Exchange Act, 15 U.S.C. § 78j(b), and Rule 10b–5, 17 C.F.R. § 240.10b–5, promulgated thereunder by the Securities and Exchange Commission ("SEC").

The District Court [in New Jersey] dismissed Pinker's complaint under both Fed. R. Civ. P. 12(b)(2) (for lack of personal jurisdiction) and Fed. R. Civ. P. 12(b)(6) (for failure to adequately plead reliance). In reviewing the District Court's dismissal of Pinker's complaint under Fed. R. Civ. P. 12(b)(2), we examine the extent of Roche's contacts with the United States as a whole. We think that by sponsoring ADRs that are actively traded by American investors, Roche purposely availed itself of the American securities market and thereby evidenced the requisite minimum contacts with the United States to support the exercise of personal jurisdiction by a federal court. Moreover, in light of the fact that Roche is alleged to have made affirmative misrepresentations that misled its ADR holders, we consider the exercise of personal jurisdiction over Roche consistent with "traditional notions of fair play and substantial justice." Int'l Shoe Co. v. Washington, 326 U.S. 310, 316 (1945) (quoting Milliken v. Meyer, 311 U.S. 457, 463 (1940)). Consequently, we conclude that the District Court had *in personam* jurisdiction over Roche and that dismissal under Rule 12(b)(2) was inappropriate.

. . . .

In a case such as this, where the plaintiff's claim is based on a federal statute authorizing nationwide service of process, *see* Section 27 of the 1934 Securities Act, 15 U.S.C. § 78aa, this Court has suggested in dicta that the relevant forum for analyzing the extent of the defendant's contacts is the United States as a whole. For instance, in *Max Daetwyler* [Max Daetwyler Corp. v. Meyer, 762 F.2d 290, 293 (3d Cir. 1985)], we recognized "[t]he constitutional validity of national contacts as a jurisdictional base" where a statute "provide[s] for nationwide service of process or service wherever defendant is 'doing business' or 'may be found.'" 762 F.2d at 294 n.3 (citations omitted). We considered the aggregation of the national contacts of an alien defendant "neither unfair nor unreasonable" under the Fifth Amendment in light of the fact that a federal court sits as a unit of the national government and, therefore, the territorial limitations that apply to the exercise of state court jurisdiction or, for that matter, federal jurisdiction in diversity cases, *see IMO Indus.*, [155 F.3d 254, 258–59 (3d Cir. 1998)]—are inapposite. *Max Daetwyler*, 762 F.2d at 294.

Where Congress has spoken by authorizing nationwide service of process, therefore, as it has in the Securities Act, the jurisdiction of a federal court need not be confined by the defendant's contacts with the state in which the federal court sits. *See* DeJames v. Magnificence Carriers, Inc., 654 F.2d 280, 284 (3d Cir. 1981). Following this reasoning, the district courts within this Circuit have repeatedly held that a "national contacts analysis" is appropriate "when appraising personal jurisdiction in a case arising under a federal statute that contains a nationwide service of process provision." We too are persuaded by the reasoning of our prior opinions on the subject, and, consistent with several of our sister courts of appeals, hold that a federal court's personal jurisdiction may be assessed on the basis of the defendant's national contacts when the plaintiff's claim rests on a federal statute authorizing nationwide service of process. *See* Republic of Panama v. BCCI Holdings (Luxembourg) S.A., 119 F.3d 935, 946–47 (11th Cir. 1997); Busch v. Buchman, Buchman & O'Brien Law Firm, 11 F.3d 1255, 1258 (5th Cir. 1994). . . .

. . . .

. . . In our view, by sponsoring an ADR facility, Roche "purposefully avail[ed] itself of the privilege of conducting activities" in the American securities market, and thereby established the requisite minimum contacts with the United States. Hanson v. Denckla, 357 US 235, 253 (1958). As discussed above, sponsored ADRs such as Roche's require the issuer to deposit shares with an American branch of a depositary and to enter a deposit agreement with the ADR holders defining the rights of ADR holders and the corresponding duties of the issuer. By sponsoring an ADR, therefore, Roche took affirmative steps purposefully directed at the American investing public. The aim of sponsoring an ADR, after all, is to allow American investors to trade equities of a foreign corporation domestically. Roche, therefore, clearly took "action"-sponsoring an ADR in a deliberate attempt to solicit American capital—"purposefully directed toward the [United States]." Asahi Metal Industry Co., Ltd. v. Superior Court of Cal., 480 U.S. 102, 112 (1987) (plurality opinion of O'Connor, J.).

Roche's sponsorship amounted to an active marketing of its equity interests to American investors. Just as solicitation of business in the forum state is generally sufficient to establish personal jurisdiction over the defendant for claims arising out of injuries to purchasers within the forum state, *see, e.g.*, McGee v. Int'l Life

Ins. Co., 355 U.S. 220 (1957) (upholding personal jurisdiction over a defendant who solicited in the forum state a reinsurance agreement that formed the basis for plaintiff's breach of contract claim), so too is personal jurisdiction appropriate where a foreign corporation has directly solicited investment from the American market. A foreign corporation that purposefully avails itself of the American securities market has adequate notice that it may be haled into an American court for fraudulently manipulating that market. Although the plaintiff's complaint does not allege that the fraudulent media releases and annual reports were specifically directed to American investors, a foreign corporation that has created an American market for its securities can fairly expect that that market will rely on reports and media releases issued by the corporation.

Roche argues that the exercise of personal jurisdiction in this case is inappropriate because its ADRs were not listed on any American exchanges. This factor, Roche contends, distinguishes this case from others in which federal courts have found the issuers of ADRs to be subject to personal jurisdiction. *See, e.g.*, Itoba Ltd. v. Lep Group PLC, 54 F.3d 118, 120 (2d Cir. 1995) (foreign issuer listed ADRs on the NASDAQ). We disagree. The mere fact that its ADRs were not listed on an American stock exchange does not demonstrate that Roche did not seek to avail itself of the American securities market, for even though Roche ADRs were not traded on an exchange, the complaint alleges that Roche ADRs were actively traded on the over-the-counter market and that the average daily trading volume of Roche ADRs was about 25,000.

....

Additionally, we believe that the national interest in furthering the policies of the American securities regulatory system militates in favor of exercising personal jurisdiction over Roche. As explained in Section I.B, ADRs are the preferred method for trading in foreign securities in the United States in part because they are a more secure investing option for Americans than purchasing the foreign corporation's stock directly due to the fact that they are subject to reporting and regulatory requirements under the Securities Act and the Exchange Act. Allowing Roche to escape the personal jurisdiction of the federal courts would in essence nullify the regulatory protection that American investors seek when they purchase ADRs. If ADRs are subject to the United States securities regulatory regime in theory, but are exempt in practice due to the inability of American courts to exercise personal jurisdiction over the foreign corporation issuer, one would expect them to be considered a less attractive option for American investors.

....

Notes and Questions

1. The Supreme Court has not yet ruled on the use of nationwide contacts for personal jurisdiction. In *Asahi* the Court noted: "We have no occasion here to

determine whether Congress could, consistent with the Due Process Clause of the Fifth Amendment, authorize federal court personal jurisdiction over alien defendants based on the aggregate of national contacts, rather than on the contacts between the defendant and the State in which the federal court sits." 480 U.S. at 113 n.*. Consider the following excerpt from Wendy Perdue, *Aliens, the Internet, and "Purposeful Availment": A Reassessment of Fifth Amendment Limits on Personal Jurisdiction*, 98 Nw. U. L. Rev. 455 (2004):

> The Supreme Court has never squarely considered what limits the Fifth Amendment imposes on assertions of personal jurisdiction in federal court. Commentators have, for the most part, assumed that the limits imposed by the Fifth Amendment are comparable to those imposed on the states by the Fourteenth Amendment. This Article examines that assumption and concludes that the limits imposed by the Fifth Amendment are not comparable to those imposed by the Fourteenth. Specifically, it argues that the Fifth Amendment should not be understood to include the requirement of purposeful availment and that jurisdiction should be constitutional on the basis of effects in the United States.

2. Consider also the separate but related issue of the territorial limits of service of process in "contacts with the United States as a whole" cases:

Rule 4(k) TERRITORIAL LIMITS OF EFFECTIVE SERVICE.

> . . . .
>
> (2) Federal Claim Outside State-Court Jurisdiction. For a claim that arises under federal law, serving a summons or filing a waiver of service establishes personal jurisdiction over a defendant if:
>
> (A) the defendant is not subject to jurisdiction in any state's courts of general jurisdiction; and
>
> (B) exercising jurisdiction is consistent with the United States Constitution and laws.

The Advisory Committee Notes to Rule 4(k)(2) as amended in 1993 reflect the following policy considerations:

> Paragraph (2) is new. It authorizes the exercise of territorial jurisdiction over the person of any defendant against whom is made a claim arising under any federal law if that person is subject to personal jurisdiction in no state. . . .
>
> This paragraph corrects a gap in the enforcement of federal law. Under the former rule, a problem was presented when the defendant was a non-resident of the United States having contacts with the United States sufficient to justify the application of United States law and to satisfy federal standards of forum selection, but having insufficient contact with any single state to support jurisdiction under state long-arm legislation or meet the requirements of the Fourteenth Amendment limitation on state court

territorial jurisdiction. In such cases, the defendant was shielded from the enforcement of federal law by the fortuity of a favorable limitation on the power of state courts, which was incorporated into the federal practice by the former rule. In this respect, the revision responds to the suggestion of the Supreme Court made in Omni Capital Int'l v. Rudolf Wolff & Co., Ltd., 484 U.S. 97, 111 (1987).

There remain constitutional limitations on the exercise of territorial jurisdiction by federal courts over persons outside the United States. These restrictions arise from the Fifth Amendment rather than from the Fourteenth Amendment, which limits state-court reach and which was incorporated into federal practice by the reference to state law in the text of the former subdivision (e) that is deleted by this revision. The Fifth Amendment requires that any defendant have affiliating contacts with the United States sufficient to justify the exercise of personal jurisdiction over that party. *Cf.* Wells Fargo & Co. v. Wells Fargo Express Co., 556 F.2d 406, 418 (9th Cir. 1977). There also may be a further Fifth Amendment constraint in that a plaintiff's forum selection might be so inconvenient to a defendant that it would be a denial of "fair play and substantial justice" required by the due process clause, even though the defendant had significant affiliating contacts with the United States. . . .

The district court should be especially scrupulous to protect aliens who reside in a foreign country from forum selections so onerous that injustice could result. "[G]reat care and reserve should be exercised when extending our notions of personal jurisdiction into the international field." Asahi Metal Indus. v. Superior Court of Cal., Solano County, 480 U.S. 102, 115 (1987), quoting United States v. First Nat'l City Bank, 379 U.S. 378, 404 (1965) (Harlan, J., dissenting).

This narrow extension of the federal reach applies only if a claim is made against the defendant under federal law. It does not establish personal jurisdiction if the only claims are those arising under state law or the law of another country. . . .

E. Nationwide Service of Process

When a federal statute authorizes nationwide service of process, it is really authorizing nationwide personal jurisdiction. According to Federal Rule of Civil Procedure 4, service is sufficient to confer personal jurisdiction over the served party when authorized by the statute (assuming of course that the statute is constitutional). Usually when dealing with a question of personal jurisdiction, the court will look to the forum state's long-arm statute, regardless of whether the case is based on federal question jurisdiction or diversity. And Rule 4 generally counsels that the federal court may exercise personal jurisdiction—that is, serve process outside the state in which it sits—when a state court could do so. When a statute authorizes nationwide service of process, however, the service of process is not extra-territorial; the court is not reaching for jurisdiction based on Rule 4(k)(1)(A), but rather Rule 4(k)(1)(C).

There is a circuit split on the matter of what the Due Process Clause requires. Some circuits use a "national contacts" approach, arguing that minimum contacts with the nation satisfy due process, while others require something more, invoking a "basic fairness standard" and looking for some contacts with the forum state. Generally, the fairness standard is expressed in terms of whether it is an undue burden on the defendant to litigate in the forum, although a minority of circuits requires contacts with the state in which the federal court sits.

Consider the following case where the Court concludes that there is simply no authorization for the service in the first place.

Omni Capital International, Ltd. v. Rudolf Wolff & Co., Ltd.

Supreme Court of the United States
484 U.S. 97 (1987)

Justice Blackmun delivered the opinion of the Court.

This case presents questions concerning the prerequisites to a federal court's exercise of *in personam* jurisdiction.

I

Petitioners Omni Capital International, Ltd., and Omni Capital Corporation (collectively Omni), New York corporations, marketed an investment program involving commodity-futures trades on the London Metals Exchange. Omni employed respondent Rudolf Wolff & Co., Ltd., a British corporation with its offices in London, as a broker to handle trades on that Exchange. Respondent James Gourlay, a citizen and resident of the United Kingdom, served as Wolff's representative in soliciting this business from Omni.

The United States Internal Revenue Service disallowed income tax deductions, claimed by the participants in Omni's investment program, and did so on the ground that the program's commodities trades on the London Metals Exchange were not bona fide arm's-length transactions. A number of corporate and individual investors who participated in Omni's program then sued Omni in four separate actions in the United States District Court for the Eastern District of Louisiana. The plaintiffs in each action charged that, by misrepresenting its tax benefits and future profits, Omni fraudulently induced them to participate in the investment program. Omni, in turn, impleaded Wolff and Gourlay, contending that its liability, if any, was caused by their improper trading activities.

The procedural history is complex. The original complaints, filed in 1980 and 1981, charged violations of the Securities Exchange Act of 1934, ch. 404, 48 Stat. 881, as amended, 15 U.S.C. § 78a *et seq.* (1982 ed. and Supp. IV); SEC Rule 10b–5, 17

CFR § 240.10b–5 (1987); and the Securities Act of 1933, 48 Stat. 74, as amended, 15 U.S.C. § 77a *et seq.* (1982 ed. and Supp. IV), and included pendent state-law claims. The four cases were consolidated in the District Court. While they were pending, this Court decided *Merrill Lynch, Pierce, Fenner & Smith, Inc. v. Curran*, 456 U.S. 353 (1982). In *Curran*, we recognized an implied private cause of action under the Commodity Exchange Act (CEA), 42 Stat. 998, as amended, 7 U.S.C. § 1 *et seq.* (1982 ed. and Supp. IV). The plaintiffs accordingly amended their complaints to allege violations of §§ 4b and 9(b) of the CEA, as amended, 7 U.S.C. §§ 6b and 13(b).

Wolff and Gourlay moved to dismiss the claims against them for lack of personal jurisdiction, and, as an additional ground, argued that the securities law claims failed to state causes of action. . . .

[W]e granted certiorari to decide whether, in this federal-question litigation arising under the CEA, the District Court may exercise personal jurisdiction over Wolff and Gourlay.

II

Omni's primary and fundamental contention is that in a suit under the CEA, the only limits on a district court's power to exercise personal jurisdiction derive from the Due Process Clause of the Fifth Amendment. The objection of the Court of Appeals, and of Wolff and Gourlay before this Court, is that, even if an exercise of personal jurisdiction would comport with that Due Process Clause,[3] the District Court cannot exercise personal jurisdiction over Wolff and Gourlay because they are not amenable to service of summons in the absence of a statute or rule authorizing such service. . . .

. . . .

Before a federal court may exercise personal jurisdiction over a defendant, the procedural requirement of service of summons must be satisfied. "[S]ervice of summons is the procedure by which a court having venue and jurisdiction of the subject matter of the suit asserts jurisdiction over the person of the party served." *Mississippi Publishing Corp. v. Murphree*, 326 U.S. 438, 444–445 (1946). Thus, before a court may exercise personal jurisdiction over a defendant, there must be more than notice to the defendant and a constitutionally sufficient relationship between the defendant and the forum. There also must be a basis for the defendant's amenability to service of summons. Absent consent, this means there must be authorization for service of summons on the defendant.

3. [Court's footnote #5] Under Omni's theory, a federal court could exercise personal jurisdiction, consistent with the Fifth Amendment, based on an aggregation of the defendant's contacts with the Nation as a whole, rather than on its contacts with the State in which the federal court sits. As was the case in *Asahi Metal Industry Co. v. Superior Court of Cal.*, 480 U.S. 102 (1987), "[w]e have no occasion" to consider the constitutional issues raised by this theory. *Id.*, at 113, n.

B

The next question, then, is whether there is authorization to serve summons in this litigation. Today, service of process in a federal action is covered generally by Rule 4 of the Federal Rules of Civil Procedure. . . . It authorizes service in the State in which the action is brought, or anywhere else authorized by a federal statute or by the Rules.

. . . .

[A] federal court normally looks either to a federal statute or to the long-arm statute of the State in which it sits to determine whether a defendant is amenable to service, a prerequisite to its exercise of personal jurisdiction. . . .

. . . .

Since the CEA does not authorize service of summons on Wolff and Gourlay, we look to the . . . long-arm statute of the State in which the District Court sits—here, Louisiana. The District Court held that the requirements of the Louisiana long-arm statute, were not met in this litigation. It noted that even the provision allowing a court to rely on the effects that the defendant causes within the State was "clearly not applicable" because it "applies only to a defendant who 'regularly does or solicits business, or engages in any other persistent course of conduct, or derives substantial revenue from goods used or consumed or services rendered, in this state.'" App. 22–23 (quoting La. Rev. Stat. Ann. § 13:3201(d) (West 1968)). Because the terms of the Louisiana statute were not met, the District Court considered a due process analysis unnecessary. Before us, Omni has not contended that Wolff and Gourlay may be reached under the Louisiana long-arm statute. Indeed, Omni has conceded that they may not. See Tr. of Oral Arg. 4. . . .

C

We would consider it unwise for a court to make its own rule authorizing service of summons. It seems likely that Congress has been acting on the assumption that federal courts cannot add to the scope of service of summons Congress has authorized. This Court in the past repeatedly has stated that a legislative grant of authority is necessary. . . .

We are not blind to the consequences of the inability to serve process on Wolff and Gourlay. A narrowly tailored service of process provision, authorizing service on an alien in a federal-question case when the alien is not amenable to service under the applicable state long-arm statute, might well serve the ends of the CEA and other federal statutes. It is not for the federal courts, however, to create such a rule as a matter of common law. That responsibility, in our view, better rests with those who propose the Federal Rules of Civil Procedure and with Congress.

Consider now one of the circuit court cases analyzing the due process issue involved in nationwide contacts analysis.

Republic of Panama v. BCCI Holdings (Luxembourg) S.A.

United States Court of Appeals, Eleventh Circuit
119 F.3d 935 (1997)

Phyllis Kravitch, Senior Circuit Judge:

The Republic of Panama filed this action in the Southern District of Florida asserting claims under the Racketeer Influenced and Corrupt Organizations Act ("RICO"), 18 U.S.C. §§ 1961 *et seq.*, and state law claims against several American and foreign banking entities. The complaint charged each of the defendants with participating in a scheme to assist former Panamanian military officer, Manuel Noriega, in illegally diverting Panamanian government funds for his personal use. The district court dismissed Panama's claims against First American Bank, N.A. and First American Bank of New York (the "First American defendants") for lack of personal jurisdiction and dismissed its claims with respect to the remaining defendants on the grounds of *forum non conveniens.* Panama appeals both rulings.

Addressing an issue that has divided district courts in this circuit, we conclude that the Due Process Clause of the Fifth Amendment provides an independent constitutional limitation on the court's exercise of personal jurisdiction over a domestic defendant served pursuant to a federal statute's nationwide service of process provision. On the facts of this case, we find no constitutional barrier to jurisdiction and therefore reverse the district court's order dismissing Panama's claims against the First American defendants for lack of personal jurisdiction.

Background

BCCI Holdings is the parent corporation of BCCI S.A. and BCCI Ltd. During the time period relevant to the complaint, these foreign defendants were the principal corporations in an international banking group operating in sixty-nine countries, including the United States. Collectively, they will be referred to as the "BCCI defendants" or as "BCCI." First American Bank, N.A. is an American bank with its principal place of business in the District of Columbia, and First American Bank of New York is a New York state bank with its principal place of business in New York City.

The complaint alleges that in 1981 the BCCI defendants "surreptitiously obtained control" of the First American defendants by demanding First American stock as security for loans. The complaint also alleges that the BCCI defendants actively misrepresented the nature of their control over the First American defendants and purposely concealed this ownership from federal regulators. Panama asserts that First American was the "alter ego" of BCCI and that the First American defendants were integrated into BCCI's worldwide legal and illegal banking operations with the "knowledge, agreement, and/or acquiescence" of Robert Altman. Altman served as a controlling officer of First American Bankshares, the parent company of the First American defendants, and as an officer and/or director of one of the conduit holding companies that BCCI used to control First American Bankshares.

The complaint further alleges that beginning in 1981 Manuel Noriega illegally diverted millions of dollars from the Panamanian government into secret BCCI accounts throughout the world. BCCI laundered the diverted funds, redistributed them to various accounts throughout the world, and made them available to Noriega and his family for their personal use. The BCCI defendants allegedly conducted these transfers to conceal Noriega's illegal activities from the Republic of Panama and from other lawful authorities.

From 1986 through 1987, the First American defendants allegedly assisted the BCCI defendants in transferring the money stolen by Noriega and in making these unlawful proceeds available to him and his family in this country. . . .

Panama alleged that the district court had jurisdiction over the First American defendants under RICO's nationwide service of process provision, 18 U.S.C. § 1965(d), which provides that process may be served "on any person in any judicial district in which such person resides, is found, has an agent, or transacts his affairs." The district court concluded that although Panama had satisfied the requirements of this section, Panama had not alleged sufficient contacts with Florida to satisfy the Due Process Clause of the Fifth Amendment. The court therefore granted the First American defendants' motion under Fed. R. Civ. P. 12(b)(2) to dismiss Panama's claims against them for lack of personal jurisdiction. . . .

In analyzing a motion to dismiss for lack of personal jurisdiction under Fed. R. Civ. P. 12(b)(2), we first determine whether the applicable statute potentially confers jurisdiction over the defendant, and then determine whether the exercise of jurisdiction comports with due process.

In this case, we need not pause long over the first question. Section 1965(d) of the RICO statute provides for service in any judicial district in which the defendant is found. When a federal statute provides for nationwide service of process, it becomes the statutory basis for personal jurisdiction. . . . Because the First American defendants are domestic corporations doing business in this country, the statutory basis for personal jurisdiction over these defendants is satisfied.

The constitutional question is considerably more involved. It is well established that when, as here, a federal statute provides the basis for jurisdiction, the constitutional limits of due process derive from the Fifth, rather than the Fourteenth, Amendment. There is considerable debate, however, over the scope of the limits imposed by the Fifth Amendment when jurisdiction is established over a domestic defendant via a nationwide service of process provision. Appellant urges us to adopt a "pure national contacts" approach. It asserts that the Fifth Amendment requires only that the defendant have "minimum contacts" with the United States as a whole. The First American appellees, on the other hand, contend that the "minimum contacts" inquiry is the same under the Fifth Amendment as it is under the Fourteenth Amendment. They therefore insist that under the Fifth Amendment courts must also focus on a defendant's contacts with the forum state rather than with the nation as a whole. The district court adopted yet a third approach-a "flexible minimum contacts" analysis that evaluates a defendant's contacts with the forum, but in a less demanding fashion than is required by the Fourteenth Amendment. . . .

Although the Supreme Court has never addressed the scope of due process protection under the Fifth Amendment in the jurisdictional context,[4] it often has discussed the due process protections afforded by the Fourteenth Amendment. Because the language and motivating policies of the due process clauses of these two amendments are substantially similar, opinions interpreting the Fourteenth Amendment due process clause provide important guidance for us in determining what due process requires in cases involving nationwide service of process In articulating the due process limits of the Fourteenth Amendment, the Supreme Court frequently has returned to the seminal case of *International Shoe Co. v. Washington*, in which it stated that due process requires that "the maintenance of the suit . . . not offend 'traditional notions of fair play and substantial justice.'" 326 U.S. 310, 316 (1945) (citation omitted). In its more recent opinions, the Court has clarified the meaning of this familiar phrase and increasingly emphasized that due process protects individual liberty interests by protecting parties from the unreasonable demands of litigating in a faraway forum. . . .

We discern no reason why these constitutional notions of "fairness" and "reasonableness," *see World-Wide Volkswagen* [World-Wide Volkswagen Corp. v. Woodson, 444 U.S. 286 (1980)], 444 U.S. at 291–92 should be discarded completely when jurisdiction is asserted under a federal statute rather than a state long-arm statute. The language of the Fifth Amendment is virtually identical to that of the Fourteenth Amendment, and both amendments were designed to protect individual liberties from the same types of government infringement. *See* Mathews v. Eldridge, 424 U.S. 319, 331–32 (1976) (relying on Fourteenth Amendment cases to define limits of the Fifth Amendment's procedural due process protections). Although the fact that the United States is the sovereign asserting its power undoubtedly must affect the way the constitutional balance is struck, the assertion of federal power should not cause courts to abandon completely their role as protectors of individual liberty and fundamental fairness.

Accordingly, several circuits have concluded that the Fifth Amendment, like the Fourteenth Amendment, protects individual litigants against the burdens of litigation in an unduly inconvenient forum. . . .

In determining whether the defendant has met his burden of establishing constitutionally significant inconvenience, courts should consider the factors used in

4. [Court's footnote #15] On two occasions, the Supreme Court has noted that the question of whether the Due Process Clause of the Fifth Amendment could be satisfied solely by reference to a defendant's contacts with the nation as a whole was not properly before it. *See Omni Capital Int'l v. Rudolf Wolff & Co., Ltd.*, 484 U.S. 97, 102 n.5 (1987); *Asahi Metal Industry v. Superior Court*, 480 U.S. 102, 113 n.* (1987) (plurality opinion).

determining fairness under the Fourteenth Amendment. Courts should not, however, apply these factors mechanically in cases involving federal statutes.

For example, a defendant's contacts with the forum state play no magical role in the Fifth Amendment analysis. . . . Thus, determining whether litigation imposes an undue burden on a litigant cannot be determined by evaluating only a defendant's contacts with the forum state. A court must therefore examine a defendant's aggregate contacts with the nation as a whole rather than his contacts with the forum state in conducting the Fifth Amendment analysis.

A defendant's "minimum contacts" with the United States do not, however, automatically satisfy the due process requirements of the Fifth Amendment. There are circumstances, although rare, in which a defendant may have sufficient contacts with the United States as a whole but still will be unduly burdened by the assertion of jurisdiction in a faraway and inconvenient forum. As the Court noted in *Burger King* [Burger King Corp. v. Rudzewicz, 471 U.S. 462 (1985)], "minimum requirements inherent in the concept of 'fair play and substantial justice' may defeat the reasonableness of jurisdiction even if the defendant has purposely engaged in forum activities." 471 U.S. at 477–78; *see also* Vermeulen v. Renault, U.S.A., Inc., 985 F.2d 1534, 1551 (11th Cir. 1993) (even though an alien defendant has purposely directed activities at the United States, Fifth Amendment requires that litigation in this country comport with traditional notions of fair play and substantial justice). Therefore, even when a defendant resides within the United States, courts must ensure that requiring a defendant to litigate in plaintiff's chosen forum is not unconstitutionally burdensome.

We emphasize that it is only in highly unusual cases that inconvenience will rise to a level of constitutional concern. *See Asahi*, [480 U.S. at 116] (Brennan, J., concurring in part and concurring in the judgment) (noting that only in "rare cases" will inconvenience become constitutionally unreasonable). . . . The burden is on the defendant to demonstrate that the assertion of jurisdiction in the forum will "make litigation 'so gravely difficult and inconvenient' that [he] unfairly is at a 'severe disadvantage' in comparison to his opponent." *Burger King*, [471 U.S. at 478] (citations omitted).

When a defendant makes a showing of constitutionally significant inconvenience, jurisdiction will comport with due process only if the federal interest in litigating the dispute in the chosen forum outweighs the burden imposed on the defendant. In evaluating the federal interest, courts should examine the federal policies advanced by the statute, the relationship between nationwide service of process and the advancement of these policies, the connection between the exercise of jurisdiction in the chosen forum and the plaintiff's vindication of his federal right, and concerns of judicial efficiency and economy. Where, as here, Congress has provided for nationwide service of process, courts should presume that nationwide personal jurisdiction is necessary to further congressional objectives.

d. Applying the Fifth Amendment Standards

Applying these standards in this case, we find no constitutional impediment to jurisdiction. First, we note that the First American defendants are large corporations providing banking services to customers in major metropolitan areas along the eastern seaboard. The fact that they may not have had significant contacts with Florida is insufficient to render Florida an unreasonably inconvenient forum. In addition, the fact that discovery for this litigation would be conducted throughout the world suggests that Florida is not significantly more inconvenient than other districts in this country. The First American defendants have presented no evidence that their ability to defend this lawsuit will be compromised significantly if they are required to litigate in Miami. In short, the First American defendants have failed to present a "compelling case" that litigating this action in the chosen forum will put them at a "severe disadvantage." *See Burger King*, 471 U.S. at 478.

Because we conclude that the First American defendants have not demonstrated any constitutionally significant inconvenience, we find no infringement of their individual liberty interests protected by the Due Process Clause of the Fifth Amendment. Therefore, we need not balance the federal interests at stake in this lawsuit. We hold that the district court erred in dismissing Panama's claims against the First American defendants for lack of personal jurisdiction. . . .

F. Personal Jurisdiction over Absent Defendants

1. Introduction

It has been possible to exercise personal jurisdiction over absent defendants ever since *International Shoe* replaced various legal fictions about presence with the minimum contacts analysis we know today. This section takes the analysis one step further to consider cases where jurisdiction exists even though the defendant lacks any contacts with the forum. Here, jurisdiction is based upon contacts of others, which are imputed to the defendant. Such imputation is possible when the parties are alter egos, in an agency relationship, or engaged in a conspiracy. These jurisdictional theories are useful in complex litigation because they have the potential to allow a plaintiff to bring a number of far-flung parties before a single court. As you consider the following cases ask yourself how they fit with the Supreme Court's statement that "[t]he requirements of *International Shoe* . . . must be met as to each defendant over whom a state court exercises jurisdiction." *Rush v. Savchuk*, 444 U.S. 320, 332 (1980). Also consider how they fit with the Supreme Court's view of agency theory expressed in the *Daimler AG v. Bauman* case.

2. Alter Ego and Agency Theories of Personal Jurisdiction

The general rule is that shareholders and their corporations are distinct and that neither liability nor jurisdictional contacts can be imputed from one to the other. Likewise, parent and subsidiary corporations are separate legal entities. Alter ego and agency theories of jurisdiction are exceptions to these general rules. Do the general rules make sense in a post-*International Shoe* world?

Doe v. Unocal Corp.

United States Court of Appeals, Ninth Circuit
248 F.3d 915 (2001)

PER CURIAM:

We affirm the district court's judgment and adopt the portions of its opinion, *Doe v. Unocal*, 27 F. Supp. 2d 1174 (C.D. Cal. 1998), appearing in the Appendix as our own. *See* Appendix *infra*.

Because appellants have failed to demonstrate by the "clearest showing that denial of discovery [has] result[ed] in actual and substantial prejudice," the district court did not abuse its discretion in denying discovery on the question of specific jurisdiction. *See* Butcher's Union Local No. 498 v. SDC Investment, Inc., 788 F.2d 535, 540 (9th Cir. 1986).

Affirmed.

APPENDIX

I

Doe plaintiffs, farmers from the Tenasserim region of Burma, bring this class action against defendants Unocal Corporation ("Unocal"), individuals John Imle and Roger C. Beach, who are, respectively, the President and Chairman/Chief Executive Officer of Unocal, and Total S.A. ("Total"), a French corporation. Plaintiffs allege that the State Law and Order Restoration Council ("SLORC") is a military junta that seized control in Burma (now known also as Myanmar) in 1988, and that the Myanmar Oil and Gas Enterprise ("MOGE") is a state-owned company controlled by SLORC that produces and sells energy products. Plaintiffs seek injunctive, declaratory and compensatory relief for alleged international human rights violations perpetrated by defendants in furtherance of defendants Unocal, Total and MOGE's joint venture, the Yadana gas pipeline project. . . .

Pending before the Court is the Motion of Defendant Total S.A. to Dismiss for Lack of Personal Jurisdiction. . . .

On August 28, 1998, the Court directed the parties to submit further briefing as to whether . . . Total's subsidiary holding companies in California, or Total's subsidiary holding companies in the United States with substantial California contacts, act as Total's agents by selectively acquiring and holding operating companies in specific niches in which Total has significant market share worldwide. . . .

II

B. Rule 12(b)(2) Motion to Dismiss

Fed. R. Civ. P. 12(b)(2) governs dismissal for lack of personal jurisdiction. In order to exercise personal jurisdiction over a nonresident defendant in a case presenting a federal question, the district court must first determine that "a rule or statute potentially confers jurisdiction over the defendant and then conclude that asserting jurisdiction does not offend the principles of Fifth Amendment due process." Go-Video, Inc. v. Akai Electric Co., Ltd., 885 F.2d 1406, 1413 (9th Cir. 1989). . . .

Total's motion to dismiss for lack of personal jurisdiction raises interesting questions regarding when a "national contacts" test is available under Fed. R. Civ. P. 4(k)(2) . . . and whether, with respect to general and specific personal jurisdiction under the forum state's long-arm statute, the alter ego and agency doctrines require the Court to attribute to a foreign national the contacts of its subsidiaries in the United States.

1. Rule 4(k)(2)

. . .

Rule 4(k)(2) provides no basis for jurisdiction based on Total's direct contacts. Total has no contacts of its own with the United States beyond listing its stock on various exchanges and promoting sales of stock in the United States. Plaintiffs have cited no authority for the proposition that such contacts suffice to establish personal jurisdiction, and the Court is not persuaded that Congress intended for the courts to assert jurisdiction under Rule 4(k)(2) whenever a corporation lists its stock on a United States exchange.

Total's remaining potential contacts with the United States are based on the activities of its subsidiaries. If Total's subsidiaries' contacts were imputed to Total, however, several states would have jurisdiction over Total, and Rule 4(k)(2) would not apply. In fact, plaintiffs' counsel stated at oral argument on August 18, 1998 that because they believe Total is subject to personal jurisdiction in several states under the alter ego and agency doctrines, they need not rely on their earlier contention that the Court should exercise personal jurisdiction over Total pursuant to Rule 4(k)(2).

. . .

(i) Attributing Contacts of Subsidiaries to the Parent Corporation

The existence of a relationship between a parent company and its subsidiaries is not sufficient to establish personal jurisdiction over the parent on the basis of the subsidiaries' minimum contacts with the forum. Transure, Inc. v. Marsh and McLennan, Inc., 766 F.2d 1297, 1299 (9th Cir. 1985). . . .

Nonetheless, "if the parent and subsidiary are not really separate entities, or one acts as an agent of the other, the local subsidiary's contacts with the forum may be imputed to the foreign parent corporation." El-Fadl v. Central Bank of Jordan,

75 F.3d 668, 676 (D.C. Cir. 1996). An alter ego or agency relationship is typified by parental control of the subsidiary's internal affairs or daily operations. *See* Kramer Motors, Inc. v. British Leyland, Ltd., 628 F.2d 1175, 1177 (9th Cir. 1980).[5]

(a) Alter Ego

To demonstrate that the parent and subsidiary are "not really separate entities" and satisfy the alter ego exception to the general rule that a subsidiary and the parent are separate entities, the plaintiff must make out a prima facie case "(1) that there is such unity of interest and ownership that the separate personalities [of the two entities] no longer exist and (2) that failure to disregard [their separate identities] would result in fraud or injustice." American Telephone & Telegraph Co. v. Compagnie Bruxelles Lambert, 94 F.3d 586, 591 (9th Cir. 1996) (citations omitted). The first prong of this test has alternately been stated as requiring a showing that the parent controls the subsidiary "to such a degree as to render the latter the mere instrumentality of the former." Calvert v. Huckins, 875 F. Supp. 674, 678 (E.D. Cal. 1995).

For example, where a parent corporation uses its subsidiary "as a marketing conduit" and attempts to shield itself from liability based on its subsidiaries' activities, piercing the corporate veil is appropriate and the alter-ego test is satisfied. *Cf.* United States v. Toyota Motor Corp., 561 F. Supp. 354, 359 (C.D. Cal. 1983). That test is also satisfied where the record indicates that the parent dictates "[e]very facet [of the subsidiary's] business-from broad policy decisions to routine matters of day-to-day operation [.]" Rollins Burdick Hunter of Southern California, Inc. v. Alexander & Alexander Services, Inc., 206 Cal. App. 3d 1, 11, 253 Cal. Rptr. 338 (2d Dist. 1988). Similarly, under California law, "inadequate capitalization of a subsidiary may alone be a basis for holding the parent corporation liable for the acts of the subsidiary." Slottow v. American Cas. Co. of Reading, Pennsylvania, 10 F.3d 1355, 1360 (9th Cir. 1993). . . .

[P]laintiffs argue that Total is the alter ego of several of its subsidiary holding companies based on Total's (1) involvement in its subsidiaries' acquisitions, divestments and capital expenditures; (2) formulation of general business policies and strategies applicable to its subsidiaries, including specialization in particular areas of commerce; (3) provision of loans and other types of financing to subsidiaries; (4) maintenance of overlapping directors and officers with its subsidiaries; and (5) alleged undercapitalization of holding company subsidiaries. A parent corporation may be directly involved in financing and macro-management of its subsidiaries, however, without exposing itself to a charge that each subsidiary is merely its alter ego. . . .

Plaintiffs' evidence here establishes only that Total is an active parent corporation involved directly in decision-making about its subsidiaries' holdings. Because

5. [Court's footnote #2] While the Court follows the alter ego and agency tests as articulated by the Ninth Circuit, the Court notes the useful discussion of alter ego as merger and agency as attribution in *In re Telectronics Pacing Systems, Inc.*, 953 F. Supp. 909 (S.D. Ohio 1997).

Total and its subsidiaries observe all of the corporate formalities necessary to maintain corporate separateness, the first prong of the alter ego test is not satisfied, and the Court need not address the equities.

(b) Agency

The agency test is satisfied by a showing that the subsidiary functions as the parent corporation's representative in that it performs services that are "sufficiently important to the foreign corporation that if it did not have a representative to perform them, the corporation's own officials would undertake to perform substantially similar services." Chan v. Society Expeditions, Inc., 39 F.3d 1398, 1405 (9th Cir. 1994) (quoting [Wells Fargo & Co. v. Wells Fargo Express Co., 556 F.2d 406, 423 (9th Cir. 1977]). . . .

Here, plaintiffs do not make out a prima facie case that Total's operational subsidiaries in California are its agents for purposes of personal jurisdiction. There is no evidence that in the absence of Total's California subsidiaries involved in petrochemical and chemical operations, Total would conduct and control those operations. . . .

[P]laintiffs argue that Total's world wide holdings and its stated corporate policy of investing in selected niche markets through acquisitions of businesses that further that strategy, show that Total is a "super-corporation" that conducts its energy related businesses through selectively acquired operating companies. By maintaining control of the operating companies through its subsidiary holding companies, plaintiffs argue that the subsidiary companies should be treated as Total's general agents in California for purposes of establishing personal jurisdiction over Total. As noted above, however, the record does not support plaintiffs' contention that Total directly controls the day-to-day activities of the California operating or holding companies. The fact that Total may indirectly control or supervise its subsidiaries, does not lead the Court to a different conclusion.

Notes and Questions

Recall that the Supreme Court in *Daimler AG*, supra, rejected *general* personal jurisdiction over Daimler under the plaintiff's agency theory and never reached an analysis of alter ego jurisdiction. How does the opinion in *Daimler* bear upon the analysis in *Doe v. Unocal*? The Court's opinion in *Daimler* seems to have expressly rejected the Ninth Circuit's view in *Unocal* that agency jurisdiction might be invoked where the "agent" is "important" to the principal's business. The Supreme Court concluded that the "inquiry into importance stacks the deck, for it will always yield a pro-jurisdiction answer." Note, though, that in *Unocal* the Ninth Circuit actually rejected personal jurisdiction based on agency theory on the facts of the case.

The following case addresses agency relations outside of the context of corporate structures as the basis for personal jurisdiction over absent defendants.

Daynard v. Ness, Motley, Loadholt, Richardson & Poole, P.A.

United States Court of Appeals, First Circuit
290 F.3d 42 (2002)

Sandra Lynch, Circuit Judge.

The issue on appeal is whether a federal district court sitting in Massachusetts has specific personal jurisdiction over a suit brought by Richard A. Daynard, a Massachusetts law professor, for fees in the tobacco litigation, against the Mississippi law firm of Scruggs, Millette, Bozeman & Dent, and Richard Scruggs, a senior partner ("Scruggs defendants"). At the heart of Daynard's claim is the argument that the court may reach the Scruggs defendants based in large part on contacts imputed from the South Carolina law firm of Ness, Motley, Loadholt, Richardson & Poole, and Ronald Motley ("Motley defendants"), all of whom purportedly acted on behalf of both firms in engaging Daynard to work on litigation against the tobacco industry. We conclude, contrary to the district court, that the Scruggs defendants are subject to specific personal jurisdiction based on their contacts with Massachusetts, particularly those contacts properly attributed to them from the Motley defendants, who are also defendants in this litigation.

Daynard is a law professor at Northeastern University specializing in litigation against the tobacco industry. He sued the Motley and Scruggs defendants, claiming that, pursuant to an oral agreement, he is entitled to a portion of the fees that these firms have received or will receive from their successful tobacco litigation.

The Motley defendants, based on their Massachusetts contacts, concede personal jurisdiction. . . .

Daynard argues that he need not show, for specific jurisdiction purposes, that the Scruggs defendants exerted substantial influence over the Motley defendants' in-forum activities in order to impute the Motley defendants' contacts to the Scruggs defendants. Daynard asserts that the defendants were engaged in a tobacco litigation joint venture and that, on this basis, attribution is proper.

We conclude that [the] substantial influence test is not controlling in this case, where Daynard alleges that the defendants were in a joint venture, or at least held themselves out to be in a type of agency relationship. We need not determine whether the defendants were actually engaged in a joint venture between themselves, however. The facts, as asserted by Daynard and construed in the light of whether he has made a prima facie jurisdictional showing, suffice to show a relationship between the two defendants sufficient to impute some of the Motley defendants' contacts to the Scruggs defendants. These same facts show that the Scruggs defendants held themselves out to be in some form of an agency relationship with the Motley defendants and, by accepting and encouraging Daynard's services, and agreeing to compensate him on the basis of a share of the fees, ratified the Motley defendants' in-forum activities giving rise to this lawsuit. . . .

. . . .

As to personal jurisdiction, Scruggs states that neither he nor his firm has ever had any offices, real estate, bank accounts, or other property in Massachusetts. Furthermore, none of the Scruggs defendants has ever practiced law in Massachusetts. Daynard does not deny this. In addition, Scruggs says that he has never traveled to Massachusetts in connection with any fee sharing arrangement with Daynard or in connection with any of Daynard's work under the alleged arrangement. He denies that he or his firm had any role in contacting or retaining Daynard in Massachusetts. He further states that the Scruggs defendants did not request, or even have knowledge of, the Motley defendants' meetings with Daynard. Scruggs also denies that the Scruggs defendants or the Mississippi joint venture, to the extent that it existed, ever gave the Motley defendants any directions with respect to Daynard. . . .

II

. . . .

C. Imputed Contacts

. . . .

2. Implied agency and ratification

For purposes of personal jurisdiction, the actions of an agent may be attributed to the principal. Whether or not an agent is initially authorized to act on behalf of a principal, the agent's actions may be attributed to the principal, for purposes of personal jurisdiction, if the principal later ratifies the agent's conduct. . . . First, we address whether the defendants were in any sort of agency relationship. Second, we discuss whether the Scruggs defendants initially authorized, or later ratified, the Motley defendants' actions. . . .

The facts as alleged by Daynard are sufficient to make the jurisdictional showing that, in Boston, Patrick of Ness Motley hired Daynard, that Daynard reasonably understood Patrick to be acting on behalf of a joint venture or other agency relationship between Ness Motley and Scruggs Millette, and that Daynard relied on this understanding by providing his services to both defendants.

Many of these same facts support the conclusion that the Scruggs defendants subsequently ratified the Motley defendants' conduct.

By knowingly accepting the benefits of the transaction initiated in Massachusetts, the Scruggs defendants ratified Patrick's act of hiring and retaining Daynard on behalf of both firms, which ultimately gave rise to this law suit. . . .

. . . .

D. The Remaining Constitutional Analysis

The easier question in the case is the remaining constitutional one. Given the Scruggs defendants' direct contacts with Massachusetts and their contacts imputed from the Motley defendants, do the Scruggs defendants have "minimum contacts" with Massachusetts "such that the maintenance of the suit does not offend 'traditional notions of fair play and substantial justice.'"? [*Int'l Shoe*, 326 U.S. at 316, (quoting *Milliken*, 311 U.S. at 463)]. The answer is yes. . . .

1. Relatedness.

As to the first requirement, that "the claim underlying the litigation must directly arise out of, or relate to, the defendant's forum-state activities," *Foster-Miller*, 46 F.3d at 144, the district court correctly concluded, based merely on the Scruggs defendants' direct contacts with the forum, that the alleged breach of contract in this case "arose" from a course of dealing between the parties. The contract was in the form of a working relationship—started in Massachusetts—that called for interaction between Massachusetts, South Carolina, and Mississippi. Drawing all inferences in favor of Daynard, he arguably meets the relatedness requirement. . . .

2. Purposeful availment.

. . . .

Combined with Patrick's physical presence in Massachusetts to negotiate the agreement which ultimately gave rise to this litigation, and the ongoing relationship between the Motley defendants and Daynard—properly attributed to the Scruggs defendants—we can properly say that the Scruggs defendants "engaged in . . . purposeful activity related to the forum that would make the exercise of jurisdiction fair, just, or reasonable." . . .

3. Reasonableness.

. . . .

The burden on the Scruggs defendants of appearing in Massachusetts, given that they routinely represent clients outside their home state, is not by any means unusual. In addition, Daynard's interest in bringing his action in this forum, given the traditional deference accorded to a plaintiff's choice of forum, weighs in favor of personal jurisdiction. This is particularly true in light of Massachusetts's stake in being able "to provide a convenient forum for its residents to redress injuries inflicted by out-of-forum actors." Massachusetts's adjudicatory interest is likely to weigh in favor of exercising personal jurisdiction because the district court has already decided that, as between Daynard and the Motley defendants, Massachusetts law governs the dispute over the oral fee-splitting arrangement. Finally, efficient administration of justice favors jurisdiction in Massachusetts, where this action is already proceeding against the Motley defendants. . . .

Notes and Questions

1. In agency theories of personal jurisdiction, as in alter ego theories, there is a two-part inquiry with regard to minimum contacts. (The same holds for conspiracy theories, as we shall see.) First, can the contacts of one party be imputed to the absent party? This, in turn, depends on two things: the applicable law governing jurisdiction and the facts on the ground. Second, are those contacts sufficient to

establish jurisdiction when applying the normal long-arm statute and due process analysis?

2. Must the party whose contacts are imputed to the absent defendant be a party to the litigation? *See Milligan v. Anderson*, 522 F.2d 1202 (10th Cir. 1975) (answering no). This is important because vicarious jurisdiction is often asserted in diversity cases and there is no reason to think that an agent and its principal will be citizens of the same state. The inclusion or exclusion of the agent can thus preserve or destroy subject matter jurisdiction. In *Milligan*, the agent's contacts provided personal jurisdiction over the absent principal while the agent's exclusion as a party preserved subject matter jurisdiction.

3. Conspiracy Theories of Jurisdiction

Conspiracy jurisdiction seeks to stretch the definition of "agent" appearing in state long-arm statutes to cover the actions of co-conspirators. The following case is typical. Consider the possible differences between the principal-agent relationship and the co-conspirator relationship and under what circumstances it makes sense to attribute the contacts of one co-conspirator to another.

FC Inv. Group LC v. IFX Markets, Ltd.

United States Court of Appeals, District of Columbia Circuit
529 F.3d 1087 (2008)

KAREN LECRAFT HENDERSON, CIRCUIT JUDGE.

FC Investment Group LC (FCIG) and Lawrence Jay Eisenberg (Eisenberg) sued IFX Markets, Ltd. (IFX), a London-based currency broker, alleging that IFX conspired with Titan Global Strategies, Ltd. (Titan), a now-defunct investment company, to defraud them of millions of dollars through a currency investment scheme. The district court denied their motion for jurisdictional discovery and ultimately dismissed their four-count complaint for lack of personal jurisdiction. FC Inv. Group LC v. IFX Markets, Ltd., 479 F. Supp. 2d 30, 44 (D.D.C. 2007). For the reasons set forth below, we affirm the district court.

I

FCIG, a Maryland limited liability company owned and managed by Eisenberg and with its principal place of business in the District of Columbia (District), and Eisenberg, a Maryland resident, allege that they lost several million dollars in a fraudulent investment scheme brokered by IFX and run by Titan....

In November 2004, Eisenberg and FCIG filed suit against IFX in district court. Their amended complaint contained four counts: (1) fraud/fraud in the inducement, (2) civil conspiracy, (3) civil aiding and abetting, and (4) conspiracy to violate the Racketeer Influenced and Corrupt Organizations Act (RICO), 18 U.S.C. §§ 1961 *et seq.*

In February 2005, IFX moved to dismiss the suit for lack of personal jurisdiction. In response, Eisenberg and FCIG asserted four bases for personal jurisdiction: (1) the district court had general personal jurisdiction over IFX based on its maintenance of an interactive website accessible—and used—in the District, (2) the court had specific personal jurisdiction over IFX based on Cruden's "regular" telephone calls to Eisenberg at Eisenberg's District office, (3) the court had personal jurisdiction over IFX based on the actions of IFX's coconspirator, Titan, in the District, and (4) the court had personal jurisdiction over IFX pursuant to RICO's nationwide service of process provisions. In February 2006, the district court rejected all four bases and dismissed their amended complaint. *FC Inv. Group*, 479 F. Supp. 2d at 44. It also denied the plaintiffs' request for jurisdictional discovery. Eisenberg and FCIG filed a timely appeal.

II

C. Conspiracy Jurisdiction

Eisenberg and FCIG argue further that specific jurisdiction exists "because IFX was a conspirator with Titan in wrongs that Titan perpetrated against FCIG through acts in the District." . . .

. . . .

In order "to establish jurisdiction under a theory of civil conspiracy, the plaintiff must plead with particularity overt acts within the forum taken in furtherance of the conspiracy." World Wide Minerals v. Republic of Kazakhstan, 296 F.3d 1154, 1168 (D.C. Cir. 2002). . . . We believe that Eisenberg and FCIG failed to plead the conspiracy with particularity. In support of their claim that IFX "had agreements and/or understandings with Titan . . . to commit fraud," they allege the following facts:

1. Lichtenstein [a member of Titan's board of directors] testified (apparently in a related case) that IFX was Titan's "business partner" and that his points of contact at IFX were Charles Cruden and senior sales executive Andy Demetriades.

2. Cruden [a Titan employee] sent Lichtenstein a fax inquiring when he would be available to meet with IFX employee Carole Napoliello.

3. "[N]umerous electronic-mail communications . . . between various IFX employees and Martinic, including a December 9, 2002 email . . . confirm[ ] IFX and Titan's 'close and effective working relationship.'"

4. Desiree Lichtman, [a Titan employee and assistant to Titan's "investment advisor" for FCIG], worked with Cruden and Napoliello to create a PowerPoint presentation that Eisenberg saw while visiting IFX's London offices. The PowerPoint presentation "indicated in no uncertain terms that Titan and IFX had established a joint venture with respect to foreign currency trading." The PowerPoint presentation "prominently displayed IFX's logo." It also discussed Titan's trading strategies and named several members of IFX's "Investment Committee."

5. "On December 10, 2002, Titan wired $100,000 to IFX from Titan's account at U.S. Bank."

6. "On March 10, 2003 Cruden sent a letter to Lichtenstein outlining further 'potential revenue streams' for Titan and IFX. . . ."

Even assuming the truth of these allegations, they fall short of the requirement that the plaintiff "plead with particularity 'the conspiracy as well as the overt acts within the forum taken in furtherance of the conspiracy.'" [*Jungquist v. Sheikh Sultan Bin Khalifa Al Nahyan*, 115 F.3d 1020, 1031 (D.C. Cir. 1997)] The allegations establish only the existence of an on-going business relationship between Titan and IFX. They do not demonstrate that IFX "had agreements and/or understandings with Titan and Martinic to commit fraud," or that IFX "acted with knowledge that it was [participating in a] fraudulent currency exchange scheme," and are therefore insufficient to establish a conspiracy theory of personal jurisdiction. *See* First Chicago Int'l v. United Exch. Co., 836 F.2d 1375, 1378–79 (D.C. Cir. 1988). . . .

D. RICO Jurisdiction

In Count IV of their amended complaint, Eisenberg and FCIG allege that IFX "violated the conspiracy section of RICO, 18 U.S.C. § 1962(d)." They argue that under RICO "the exercise of personal jurisdiction over IFX . . . was permissible, even in the absence of minimum contacts by IFX with the District," pursuant to RICO's "nationwide service of process provision, 18 U.S.C. § 1965(d)." But IFX counters that under RICO "at least one defendant must have minimum contacts with the District before jurisdiction will be had over the other, nonresident defendant in the alleged RICO conspiracy." . . .

Having considered the arguments of the parties, as well as the reasoning of our sister circuits on this question, we are persuaded to adopt the Second Circuit's reasoning. In *PT United Can Co. Ltd. v. Crown Cork & Seal Co.*, 138 F.3d 65, 70 (2d Cir. 1998), the Second Circuit explained that section "1965 must be read to give effect to all its sections in a way that renders a coherent whole." . . .

The Second Circuit endorsed the Ninth Circuit's holding in *Butcher's Union Local No. 498 v. SDC Inv. Inc.*, 788 F.2d 535, 538 (9th Cir. 1986), that "[f]or nationwide service to be imposed under section 1965(b), the court must have personal jurisdiction over at least one of the participants in the alleged multidistrict conspiracy and the plaintiff must show that there is no other district in which a court will have personal jurisdiction over all of the alleged co-conspirators." *Id., as cited in PT United Can*, 138 F.3d at 72 (adopting "the natural reading given to § 1965(b) by the 9th Circuit in *Butcher's Union*"). . . . Because the district court is otherwise without personal jurisdiction over IFX, the sole defendant, it is also without RICO jurisdiction over IFX.

For the foregoing reasons, the judgment of the district court is affirmed.

Notes and Questions

Does conspiracy as a basis for the exercise of personal jurisdiction raise due process problems not raised by agency theories of jurisdiction? *See* Ann Althouse, *The Use of Conspiracy Theory to Establish In Personam Jurisdiction: A Due Process Analysis*, 52

FORDHAM L. REV. 234 (1983) (arguing that "[t]he legal principle that co-conspirators act as each other's agents when they act in furtherance of a conspiracy should not, by automatic operation of law, permit the attribution of one party's forum contacts to another" because there is no guarantee that the due process requirements of personal jurisdiction will be satisfied). For this reason and others, some courts have either declined or been reluctant to recognize the theory. *See Chirila v. Conforte*, 47 Fed. Appx. 838, 842–43 (9th Cir. 2002); *Brown v. Kerkhoff*, 504 F. Supp. 2d 464, 513–18 (S.D. Iowa 2007). A District Court in the First Circuit has roundly rejected the existence of the theory. *In Re New Motor Vehicles Canadian Export Antitrust Litig.*, 307 F. Supp. 2d 145, 157–58 (D. Me. 2004). On the other side of the country, courts in Washington have decided that conspiracy jurisdiction does not comport with due process. *Silver Valley Partners, LLC v. De Motte*, 400 F. Supp. 2d 1262, 1268 (W.D. Wa. 2005); *Hewitt v. Hewitt*, 896 P.2d 1312, 1316 (Wash. Ct. App. 1995).

Against the line of reasoning embodied by these cases, the court in *Stauffacher v. Bennett*, 969 F.2d 455, 459 (7th Cir. 1992) (Posner, J.) (internal citations omitted) noted:

> Despite doubt . . . that the due process clause permits a state to assert extra-territorial jurisdiction over a person who did not foresee that the conspiracy which he joined would commit acts within that state, we have difficulty understanding why personal jurisdiction should be an exception. If through one of its members a conspiracy inflicts an actionable wrong in one jurisdiction, the other members should not be allowed to escape being sued there by hiding in another jurisdiction.

And the Second Circuit in *Charles Schwab Corp. v. Bank of America Corp.*, 883 F.3d 68 (2d Cir. 2018) has said that:

> Although neither this Court nor the Supreme Court has delineated when one conspirator's minimum contacts allow for personal jurisdiction over a co-conspirator, we have made clear that the mere existence of a conspiracy is not enough. . . . [P]laintiff must allege that (1) a conspiracy existed; (2) the defendant participated in the conspiracy; and (3) a co-conspirator's overt acts in furtherance of the conspiracy had sufficient contacts with a state to subject that co-conspirator to jurisdiction in that state.

Id. at 86–87. The Court then went on to give the plaintiff leave to amend its complaint to try to add allegations demonstrating overt acts in furtherance of the alleged conspiracy in the relevant state.

G. Personal Jurisdiction in Class Actions

Prior to *Phillips Petroleum Co. Inc, v. Shutts*, 472 U.S. 797 (1985), the Supreme Court rarely mentioned *plaintiffs'* due process rights in a personal jurisdiction context. *See* Linda S. Mullenix, *Class Actions, Personal Jurisdiction, and Plaintiff's Due*

Process: Implications for Mass Tort Litigation, 28 U.C. Davis L. Rev. 871, 887 (1995). Consider now the implications of the *Shutts* decision.

Phillips Petroleum Co. v. Shutts

Supreme Court of the United States
472 U.S. 797 (1985)

Justice Rehnquist delivered the opinion of the Court.

Petitioner is a Delaware corporation which has its principal place of business in Oklahoma. During the 1970's it produced or purchased natural gas from leased land located in 11 different States, and sold most of the gas in interstate commerce. Respondents are some 28,000 of the royalty owners possessing rights to the leases from which petitioner produced the gas; they reside in all 50 States, the District of Columbia, and several foreign countries. Respondents brought a class action against petitioner in the Kansas state court, seeking to recover interest on royalty payments which had been delayed by petitioner. They recovered judgment in the trial court, and the Supreme Court of Kansas affirmed the judgment over petitioner's contentions that the Due Process Clause of the Fourteenth Amendment prevented Kansas from adjudicating the claims of all the respondents, and that the Due Process Clause and the Full Faith and Credit Clause of Article IV of the Constitution prohibited the application of Kansas law to all of the transactions between petitioner and respondents. We granted certiorari to consider these claims. We reject petitioner's jurisdictional claim, but sustain its claim regarding the choice of law.

Because petitioner sold the gas to its customers in interstate commerce, it was required to secure approval for price increases from what was then the Federal Power Commission, and is now the Federal Energy Regulatory Commission. . . .

Although petitioner received higher gas prices pending review by the Commission, petitioner suspended any increase in royalties paid to the royalty owners because the higher price could be subject to recoupment by petitioner's customers. . . .

. . . .

Respondents Irl Shutts, Robert Anderson, and Betty Anderson filed suit against petitioner in Kansas state court, seeking interest payments on their suspended royalties which petitioner had possessed pending the Commission's approval of the price increases. Shutts is a resident of Kansas, and the Andersons live in Oklahoma. Shutts and the Andersons own gas leases in Oklahoma and Texas. Over petitioner's objection the Kansas trial court granted respondents' motion to certify the suit as a class action under Kansas law. The class as certified was comprised of 33,000 royalty owners who had royalties suspended by petitioner. The average claim of each royalty owner for interest on the suspended royalties was $100.

After the class was certified respondents provided each class member with notice through first-class mail. The notice described the action and informed each class member that he could appear in person or by counsel; otherwise each member would be represented by Shutts and the Andersons, the named plaintiffs. The notices also stated that class members would be included in the class and bound by the judgment unless they "opted out" of the lawsuit by executing and returning a "request for exclusion" that was included with the notice. The final class as certified contained 28,100 members; 3,400 had "opted out" of the class by returning the request for exclusion, and notice could not be delivered to another 1,500 members, who were also excluded. Less than 1,000 of the class members resided in Kansas. Only a minuscule amount, approximately one quarter of one percent, of the gas leases involved in the lawsuit were on Kansas land.

. . . .

II

Reduced to its essentials, petitioner's argument is that unless out-of-state plaintiffs affirmatively consent, the Kansas courts may not exert jurisdiction over their claims. Petitioner claims that failure to execute and return the "request for exclusion" provided with the class notice cannot constitute consent of the out-of-state plaintiffs; thus Kansas courts may exercise jurisdiction over these plaintiffs only if the plaintiffs possess the sufficient "minimum contacts" with Kansas as that term is used in cases involving personal jurisdiction over out-of-state defendants. . . .

. . . .

We think petitioner's premise is in error. The burdens placed by a State upon an absent class-action plaintiff are not of the same order or magnitude as those it places upon an absent defendant. An out-of-state defendant summoned by a plaintiff is faced with the full powers of the forum State to render judgment *against* it. The defendant must generally hire counsel and travel to the forum to defend itself from the plaintiff's claim, or suffer a default judgment. The defendant may be forced to participate in extended and often costly discovery, and will be forced to respond in damages or to comply with some other form of remedy imposed by the court should it lose the suit. The defendant may also face liability for court costs and attorney's fees. These burdens are substantial, and the minimum contacts requirement of the Due Process Clause prevents the forum State from unfairly imposing them upon the defendant.

A class-action plaintiff, however, is in quite a different posture. The Court noted this difference in *Hansberry v. Lee*, 311 U.S. 32, 40–41 (1940), which explained that a "class" or "representative" suit was an exception to the rule that one could not be bound by judgment *in personam* unless one was made fully a party in the traditional sense. As the Court pointed out in *Hansberry*, the class action was an invention of equity to enable it to proceed to a decree in suits where the number of those interested in the litigation was too great to permit joinder. The absent parties would be bound by the decree so long as the named parties adequately represented the absent class and the prosecution of the litigation was within the common interest.

Modern plaintiff class actions follow the same goals, permitting litigation of a suit involving common questions when there are too many plaintiffs for proper joinder. Class actions also may permit the plaintiffs to pool claims which would be uneconomical to litigate individually. For example, this lawsuit involves claims averaging about $100 per plaintiff; most of the plaintiffs would have no realistic day in court if a class action were not available.

In sharp contrast to the predicament of a defendant haled into an out-of-state forum, the plaintiffs in this suit were not haled anywhere to defend themselves upon pain of a default judgment. As commentators have noted, from the plaintiffs' point of view a class action resembles a "quasi-administrative proceeding, conducted by the judge." 3B J. Moore & J. Kennedy, Moore's Federal Practice ¶ 23.45[4–5] (1984); Kaplan, Continuing Work of the Civil Committee: *1966 Amendments to the Federal Rules of Civil Procedure (I)*, 81 Harv. L. Rev. 356, 398 (1967).

A plaintiff class in Kansas and numerous other jurisdictions cannot first be certified unless the judge, with the aid of the named plaintiffs and defendant, conducts an inquiry into the common nature of the named plaintiffs' and the absent plaintiffs' claims, the adequacy of representation, the jurisdiction possessed over the class, and any other matters that will bear upon proper representation of the absent plaintiffs' interest. Unlike a defendant in a civil suit, a class-action plaintiff is not required to fend for himself. The court and named plaintiffs protect his interests. Indeed, the class-action defendant itself has a great interest in ensuring that the absent plaintiff's claims are properly before the forum. In this case, for example, the defendant sought to avoid class certification by alleging that the absent plaintiffs would not be adequately represented and were not amenable to jurisdiction.

The concern of the typical class-action rules for the absent plaintiffs is manifested in other ways. Most jurisdictions, including Kansas, require that a class action, once certified, may not be dismissed or compromised without the approval of the court. In many jurisdictions such as Kansas the court may amend the pleadings to ensure that all sections of the class are represented adequately. . . .

Besides this continuing solicitude for their rights, absent plaintiff class members are not subject to other burdens imposed upon defendants. They need not hire counsel or appear. They are almost never subject to counterclaims or cross-claims, or liability for fees or costs. Absent plaintiff class members are not subject to coercive or punitive remedies. Nor will an adverse judgment typically bind an absent plaintiff for any damages, although a valid adverse judgment may extinguish any of the plaintiff's claims which were litigated.

Unlike a defendant in a normal civil suit, an absent class-action plaintiff is not required to do anything. He may sit back and allow the litigation to run its course, content in knowing that there are safeguards provided for his protection. In most class actions an absent plaintiff is provided at least with an opportunity to "opt out" of the class, and if he takes advantage of that opportunity he is removed from the litigation entirely. This was true of the Kansas proceedings in this case. . . .

Because States place fewer burdens upon absent class plaintiffs than they do upon absent defendants in nonclass suits, the Due Process Clause need not and does not afford the former as much protection from state-court jurisdiction as it does the latter. The Fourteenth Amendment does protect "persons," not "defendants," however, so absent plaintiffs as well as absent defendants are entitled to some protection from the jurisdiction of a forum State which seeks to adjudicate their claims. In this case we hold that a forum State may exercise jurisdiction over the claim of an absent class-action plaintiff, even though that plaintiff may not possess the minimum contacts with the forum which would support personal jurisdiction over a defendant. If the forum State wishes to bind an absent plaintiff concerning a claim for money damages or similar relief at law,[6] it must provide minimal procedural due process protection. The plaintiff must receive notice plus an opportunity to be heard and participate in the litigation, whether in person or through counsel. The notice must be the best practicable, "reasonably calculated, under all the circumstances, to apprise interested parties of the pendency of the action and afford them an opportunity to present their objections." *Mullane*, 339 U.S., at 314–315; cf. *Eisen v. Carlisle & Jacquelin*, [417 U.S. 156, 174–175] (1974). The notice should describe the action and the plaintiffs' rights in it. Additionally, we hold that due process requires at a minimum that an absent plaintiff be provided with an opportunity to remove himself from the class by executing and returning an "opt out" or "request for exclusion" form to the court. Finally, the Due Process Clause of course requires that the named plaintiff at all times adequately represent the interests of the absent class members.

We reject petitioner's contention that the Due Process Clause of the Fourteenth Amendment requires that absent plaintiffs affirmatively "opt in" to the class, rather than be deemed members of the class if they do not "opt out." We think that such a contention is supported by little, if any precedent, and that it ignores the differences between class-action plaintiffs, on the one hand, and defendants in nonclass civil suits on the other. Any plaintiff may consent to jurisdiction. *Keeton v. Hustler Magazine, Inc.*, 465 U.S. 770 (1984). The essential question, then, is how stringent the requirement for a showing of consent will be.

We think that the procedure followed by Kansas, where a fully descriptive notice is sent first-class mail to each class member, with an explanation of the right to "opt out," satisfies due process. . . .

. . . .

We therefore affirm the judgment of the Supreme Court of Kansas insofar as it upheld the jurisdiction of the Kansas courts over the plaintiff class members in this case, and reverse its judgment insofar as it held that Kansas law was applicable to all

6. [Court's footnote #3] Our holding today is limited to those class actions which seek to bind known plaintiffs concerning claims wholly or predominately for money judgments. We intimate no view concerning other types of class actions, such as those seeking equitable relief. Nor, of course, does our discussion of personal jurisdiction address class actions where the jurisdiction is asserted against a *defendant* class.

of the transactions which it sought to adjudicate. We remand the case to that court for further proceedings not inconsistent with this opinion.

It is so ordered.

Notes and Questions

1. *Shutts* examined opt-out classes. However, "it left open the more troubling question of due process requirements for equitable, hybrid mandatory class actions." Mullenix, 28 U.C. DAVIS L. REV. at 874. In general, says Professor Mullenix, "the courts have hewed to a general *Shutts* gloss that (b)(3) opt-out classes do not violate due process, extending this principle in many instances to include (b)(1) and (b)(2) mandatory non-opt-out classes. . . . [W]ith regard to hybrid class actions, these courts generally have reiterated the pre-*Shutts* principle that in cases where equitable or injunctive claims predominate, the mandatory non-opt-out class is proper. *See Williams v. Burlington N., Inc.*, 832 F.2d 100, 103–04 (7th Cir. 1987) (approving mandatory consent decree for employment discrimination settlement class; holding that use of equivalent due process protections satisfy fairness concerns for lack of opt-out provision)."

The Third and Ninth Circuits have a slightly different view. The Third Circuit held in *In re Real Estate Title*, 869 F.2d 760, 768 (3d Cir. 1989), that defendants must have minimum contacts with the forum when injunctive and monetary relief was involved:

> [W]e hold that, given that the absent member in this case loses more than the plaintiffs lost in *Shutts*, if the member has not been given the opportunity to opt out in a class action involving both important injunctive relief and damage claims, the member must either have minimum contacts with the forum or consent to jurisdiction in order to be enjoined by the district court that entertained the class action. Because neither factor is present, the injunction must be set aside.

2. *Shutts* rested jurisdiction on implied consent. Does the case have application where there are other bases for jurisdiction over absent plaintiff class members?

> The objectors contend that the district court erred in failing to apply the standard set forth by the Supreme Court in *Phillips Petroleum Co. v. Shutts*, which required that "an absent plaintiff be provided with an opportunity to remove himself from the class . . ." 472 U.S. 797 (1985). In the present case, however, there exists no absent plaintiff whose due process rights must be protected in this fashion. Rather, each of the objectors was subject to the jurisdiction of the district court. *See White v. NFL*, 836 F. Supp. at 1501–1504. . . . In the present case, each of the objectors either had minimum contacts with the forum or submitted himself to the jurisdiction of

> the district court by appearing through counsel to contest the merits of the settlement, offering testimony, cross-examining witnesses, and filing numerous memoranda of law regarding the settlement. [citation omitted] The district court's inclusion of the objectors in the mandatory class thus constituted a proper exercise of discretion.

White v. National Football League, 41 F.3d 402, 407–08 (8th Cir. 1994).

3. There is an important open question after the Supreme Court's opinion in *Bristol-Myers Squibb*: How does the case apply to members of a plaintiff class who are not residents of the forum state and have not suffered injury there? How does the opinion interact with the logic of *Shutts*? Does the logic of the *Squibb* opinion in effect end the concept of nationwide classes? Several courts have said no. *E.g., Swamy v. Title Source Inc.*, 2017 WL 5196780, at *2 (N.D. Cal. Nov. 10, 2017) (rejecting *B-M Squibb* challenge in FLSA collective action). In *Feller v. Transamerica Life Ins. Co.*, 2017 WL 6496803, at *17 (C.D. Cal. Dec. 11, 2017), the court said:

> Importantly, each plaintiff in a mass tort action is an actual named party in the litigation. *See Fitzhenry-Russell v. Dr. Pepper Snapple Grp., Inc.*, No. 17-CV-00564 NC, 2017 WL 4224723, at *5 (N.D. Cal. Sept. 22, 2017). Here, the proposed class representatives are the only plaintiffs actually named in the complaint. *See* Fed. R. Civ. P. 23. As the Supreme Court has found, "[n]on-named class members . . . may be parties for some purposes and not for others. The label 'party' does not indicate an absolute characteristic, but rather a conclusion about the applicability of various procedural rules that may differ based on context." *Devlin v. Scardelletti*, 536 U.S. 1, 9–10 (2002). The Supreme Court in *BMS* applied its reasoning to the narrower grounds of personal jurisdiction in the context of mass tort actions. Its reasoning does not reach so far as to bar the nonresident unnamed class members.

Others have said yes: *E.g., Wenokur v. AXA Equitable Life*, 2017 WL 4357916, at *4 n.4 (D. Ariz. Oct. 2, 2017) (refusing to certify nationwide class when class members have no connection to Arizona). The court in *In Re Dental Supplies Antitrust Litigation*, 2017 WL 4217115, at *9 (E.D.N.Y. Sept. 20, 2017), held:

> Plaintiffs attempt to side-step the due process holdings in *Bristol-Myers* by arguing that the case has no effect on the law in class actions because the case before the Supreme Court was not a class action. This argument is flawed. The constitutional requirement of due process does not wax and wane when the complaint is individual or on behalf of a class. Personal jurisdiction in class actions must comport with due process just the same as any other case. *See, e.g., King Cty. v. IKB Deutsche Industriebank AG*, 769 F. Supp. 2d 309, 315 (S.D.N.Y. 2011) (dismissing class action complaint against individual defendants for lack of personal jurisdiction because defendants' conduct lacked an articulable nexus to the plaintiffs' claims).

H. Personal Jurisdiction in MDL Cases

"When civil actions involving one or more common questions of fact are pending in different districts, such actions may be transferred to any district for coordinated or consolidated pre-trial proceedings." 28 U.S.C. § 1407 (1968). In that event, it is settled that the transferee district need not have personal jurisdiction over either plaintiffs or defendants, provided that personal jurisdiction was proper in the transferor court. 15 Wright & Miller, Federal Practice & Procedure § 3866 (4th ed. 2013). When such a scenario occurs, the parties to a case so transferred may potentially find themselves subject to the power of a jurisdiction with which they have no contact, and to which they have not consented. However, few, if any, cases have found that a transfer under the Multidistrict Litigation ("MDL") provision is unconstitutional for lack of personal jurisdiction of the transferee court over the parties.

The answer to this apparent discrepancy lies in the nature of 28 U.S.C. § 1407 itself. The following case illustrates how the MDL transfer provision allows transferee courts to assert personal jurisdiction over parties notwithstanding lack of minimum contacts or consent to jurisdiction.

In re Agent Orange Product Liability Litigation MDL No. 381

United States Court of Appeals, Second Circuit
818 F.2d 145 (1987)

Ralph Winter, Circuit Judge.

I

By any measure, this is an extraordinary piece of litigation. It concerns the liability of several major chemical companies and the United States government for injuries to members of the United States, Australian, and New Zealand armed forces and their families. These injuries were allegedly suffered as a result of the servicepersons' exposure to the herbicide Agent Orange while in Vietnam.

Agent Orange, which contains trace elements of the toxic by-product dioxin, was purchased by the United States government from the chemical companies and sprayed on various areas in South Vietnam on orders of United States military commanders. The spraying generally was intended to defoliate areas in order to reduce the military advantage afforded enemy forces by the jungle and to destroy enemy food supplies.

We are a court of law, and we must address and decide the issues raised as legal issues. We do take note, however, of the nationwide interest in this litigation and the strong emotions these proceedings have generated among Vietnam veterans and their families. The correspondence to the court, the extensive hearings held throughout the nation by the district court concerning the class settlement with the chemical companies, and even the arguments of counsel amply demonstrate that this litigation is viewed by many as something more than an action for damages for personal injuries. . . .

The procedural aspects of this litigation are also extraordinary. Chief Judge Weinstein certified it as a class action at the behest of most of the plaintiffs and over the objections of all of the defendants. Certain issues, such as the damage suffered by each plaintiff, were not, of course, to be determined in the class action. Instead, they were to be left to individual trials if the outcome of the class action proceedings was favorable to the plaintiffs. Some plaintiffs opted out of the class action, but their cases remained in the Eastern District of New York as part of a multidistrict referral.

The trial date set by Chief Judge Weinstein put the parties under great pressure, and just before the trial was to start, the defendants reached a $180 million settlement with the PMC. The size of the settlement seems extraordinary. However, given the serious nature of many of the various ailments and birth defects plaintiffs attributed to Agent Orange, the understandable sympathy a jury would have for the particular plaintiffs, and the large number of claimants, 240,000, the settlement was essentially a payment of nuisance value. Although the chances of the chemical companies' ultimately having to pay any damages may have been slim, they were exposed potentially to billions of dollars in damages if liability was established and millions in attorneys' fees merely to continue the litigation. . . .

II

. . . .

The Agent Orange litigation began in July 1978, with the filing of a lawsuit by Vietnam veteran Paul Reutershan, now deceased, in Supreme Court, New York County. The defendants were several chemical companies alleged to have manufactured Agent Orange. That case was removed to federal court and then transferred to the Eastern District of New York. On January 8, 1979, Reutershan's estate filed an amended complaint seeking relief on behalf of a class of veterans and their families injured by Agent Orange. Several other complaints alleging similar class claims were filed in late 1978 and early 1979. In March 1979, counsel for Reutershan's estate and for defendant Dow Chemical Co. jointly petitioned pursuant to 28 U.S.C. § 1407(c) (1982) for the establishment of a multidistrict litigation proceeding. The Judicial Panel on Multidistrict Litigation established In re "Agent Orange" Product Liability Litigation, MDL No. 381, in the Eastern District of New York. The first cases were transferred to the Eastern District on May 8, 1979, and nearly 600 cases have since been transferred. MDL No. 381 was assigned to then District Judge Pratt. . . .

Judge Pratt's duties as a newly-appointed member of this court precluded him from continuing as trial judge, and in October 1983, Chief Judge Weinstein assumed responsibility for MDL No. 381. . . .

III

Appellants contend that the district court was barred by the due process clause of the fifth amendment from exercising personal jurisdiction over class members who lack sufficient contacts with New York as defined in *International Shoe Co. v. Washington*, 326 U.S. 310 (1945), and its progeny. However, appellants concede, as they must, that Congress may, consistent with the due process clause, enact legislation authorizing the federal courts to exercise nationwide personal jurisdiction. See *Mississippi Publishing Corp. v. Murphree*, 326 U.S. 438, 442 (1946) ("Congress could provide for service of process anywhere in the United States"). One such piece of legislation is 28 U.S.C. § 1407 (1982), the multidistrict litigation statute. In the instant case, the district court was acting pursuant to a valid transfer order of the Judicial Panel on Multidistrict Litigation that was created by that statute. As the Panel has recognized,

Transfers under Section 1407 are simply not encumbered by considerations of in personam jurisdiction and venue.... Following a transfer, the transferee judge has all the jurisdiction and powers over pretrial proceedings in the actions transferred to him that the transferor judge would have had in the absence of transfer.

In re FMC Corp. Patent Litigation, 422 F.Supp. 1163, 1165 (J.P.M.D.L.1976) (citations omitted). *See also In re Sugar Industry Antitrust Litigation*, 399 F. Supp. 1397, 1400 (J.P.M.D.L.1975) (rejecting due process challenge similar to that raised by appellants in the instant case). Appellants' argument therefore fails....

Notes and Questions

28 U.S.C. § 1407 consistently has been held to "give the transferee district court control over any and all proceedings prior to trial." 4 WRIGHT & MILLER, FEDERAL PRACTICE & PROCEDURE § 1068.1 (4th ed. 2013). Therefore, the due process concern of preventing a court from inappropriately applying the law of a state with which the defendant has no minimum contacts is avoided, because the transferee court will apply the law of the transferor court. *See Ferens v. John Deere Co.*, 494 U.S. 516 (1990) ("In cases transferred from one federal judicial district to another pursuant to the federal change of venue statute, the transferee court shall apply the law of the transferor court, regardless of who initiates the transfer."). For a more detailed explanation of choice of law issues in MDL proceedings, see Chapter 4, *infra*. See also the general discussion of MDL proceedings in Chapter 3, section B.4, *infra*.

Chapter 2

Subject Matter Jurisdiction

A. Introduction

The preceding chapter addressed the need for a court to have personal jurisdiction, which can be thought of as power (or authority) over the *parties*. The court always has personal jurisdiction over the plaintiff, because she consents to the authority of the court by filing the case. The court will have personal jurisdiction over the defendant if she has engaged in some behavior that satisfies the requirements of the relevant statutes and of due process (or if she consents to jurisdiction or waives the defense by failing to assert it properly).

In this chapter, we address the court's power (or authority) over the *case itself.* Subject matter jurisdiction defines those types of disputes that a court may hear. To enter a valid judgment, a court must have both personal and subject matter jurisdiction, but the two doctrines are completely independent of one another.

State courts have general subject matter jurisdiction, which means that they can hear any type of dispute. The only exception is for a very limited number of cases in which federal courts have exclusive federal jurisdiction. These include bankruptcy, patent infringement, and some federal securities and antitrust cases. Outside this narrow group, however, state courts can hear any dispute, whether it arises under federal law, or the law of Nevada, or the law of Australia.

The federal courts are different. Reflecting the fact that the entire federal government is one of limited powers—of those ceded by the states and the people to the national government in the Constitution—Article III limits the types of disputes that can be heard in federal court. For our purposes (and those of your first-year course in Civil Procedure), there are two main bases of federal subject matter jurisdiction: federal question and diversity of citizenship. Section B reviews the basics of those types of jurisdiction.

Section C addresses the concept of supplemental jurisdiction, which allows federal courts to hear *claims* (not cases) that fail to invoke either federal question or diversity of citizenship jurisdiction. Finally, section D addresses congressional efforts to expand federal court jurisdiction over complex cases by overriding the most significant restriction on the invocation of diversity of citizenship jurisdiction—that is, the complete diversity rule.

Subject matter jurisdiction is to be contrasted with venue. Although subject matter jurisdiction tells us what kinds of cases and claims can be asserted in federal court, venue focuses on *which* federal court the case will proceed in. The entire country is divided into 94 federal districts, and a case should be filed in an appropriate district. The general venue provisions are found in § 1391(b), which allows the plaintiff to lay venue in any district in which all defendants "reside" or in any district in which a substantial part of the events underlying the claim arose. We deal with venue only in passing.

B. The Two Major Types of Federal Subject Matter Jurisdiction and the Concept Of Removal

Article III of the Constitution sets the outer boundary of federal subject matter jurisdiction. It contains nine types of cases. Of these, the two most frequently invoked are diversity of citizenship and federal question jurisdiction. The Constitution does not automatically grant jurisdiction to the federal courts of those cases. Rather, Congress must vest jurisdiction by statute. It has done so for diversity of citizenship jurisdiction consistently from the original Judiciary Act of 1789. It has done so for general federal question[1] cases since 1875.

Although you studied federal question and diversity of citizenship jurisdiction in Civil Procedure, we will review the basics. (For fuller review, *see* RICHARD D. FREER, CIVIL PROCEDURE 198–253 (4th ed. 2017).) As we do so, note how the restrictions of federal subject matter jurisdiction limit the federal courts' ability to entertain complex cases. This review will set up our discussion later in this chapter of congressional efforts to relax those restrictions to expand access to the federal courts for complex litigation.

1. Federal Question Jurisdiction

Federal question jurisdiction has never been controversial, and accounts for the clear majority of private civil filings in federal district courts. Because the governing law in federal question cases is federal, the purpose of such jurisdiction always has been clear: it provides a federal forum for the vindication of federally-created rights and for the expert, uniform, and sympathetic interpretation of federal law. It is worth remembering, however, that the Founders anticipated that such cases would also be filed and decided in state courts. Indeed, as noted above, Congress did not pass a statute granting federal courts power over "general" federal question

1. "General federal question" means that the court may hear a case arising under *any* federal law. Before 1875, Congress had granted federal question jurisdiction for cases arising under various *specific* federal laws.

cases until 1875. The Founders assumed that state courts would vindicate federal claims and apply federal law faithfully.[2]

Article III defines the judicial power of the federal courts to include "Cases . . . arising under this Constitution, the Laws of the United States, and Treaties made, or which shall be made, under their Authority." Section 1331 of the Judicial Code (28 U.S.C. § 1331) grants to the federal courts subject matter jurisdiction over "civil actions arising under the Constitution, laws, or treaties of the United States." The references to the Constitution, laws, and treaties are wordy ways of saying "federal law." Thus, the Constitution and § 1331 grant jurisdiction in identical operative terms: the federal courts may hear cases "arising under" federal law.

Interestingly, though, "arising under" does not mean the same thing in Article III as it does in § 1331. The Supreme Court has interpreted the statutory version of the phrase more narrowly than the identical constitutional phrase. As a policy matter, it makes sense that the constitutional grant would be broader than the statutory. This would give Congress great leeway in determining how much of the constitutional power to give to the federal courts. Congress must be careful not to swamp those tribunals by overzealous jurisdictional grants. As a practical matter, however, Congress did not draft the statutory grant in narrower terms than the constitutional. The courts have had to do the work, by interpreting the phrases to mean different things.

The constitutional phrase "arising under" is satisfied if any federal issue *might conceivably be raised at any point in the case*. The Supreme Court made this clear in *Osborn v. Bank of the United States*, 22 U.S. 738, 822–824 (1824), in which a bank formed by the federal government brought suit in federal court. In his opinion, Chief Justice John Marshall noted that in any case in which the bank was ever a party, a litigant might raise the question of whether the bank, as a creature of federal law, had the capacity to sue or be sued. Even though no one would seriously raise the question (because it was settled), the fact that a litigant *could do so* would satisfy "arising under" as used in Article III.

As a practical matter, if every case in which a federal issue might be raised could go to federal court, the federal judiciary would collapse. It simply could not handle the case overload. For example, every case involving land to which title at some point lay in the federal government could go to federal court. To avoid this debilitating caseload, it was important that the *statutory* grant of federal question jurisdiction be narrower than the *constitutional* grant.

Again, however, when Congress passed the general federal question statute in 1875, it used the same operative language—"arising under"—as that in Article III. It would be natural to assume that the same language would mean the same thing. In the *Pacific Railroad Removal Cases*, 115 U.S. 1 (1885), the Supreme Court interpreted

2. The Supremacy Clause of the Constitution (art. VI, para. 2) requires all courts—including state courts—to apply governing federal law.

the statutory grant as coextensive with the constitutional. It soon recognized that this reading could inundate federal courts, however, and imposed various "statutory" restrictions on federal question jurisdiction. We put "statutory" in quotation marks because the restriction is not found in the statutory language at all.

Through the years, the Court has imposed three restrictions on the statutory language. First, it insists that any federal question in the litigation be "substantial." *See, e.g., Gunn v. Minton*, 568 U.S. 251, 260 (2013). Second, it requires that the federal issue be sufficiently central to resolution of the dispute. *See, e.g., Grable & Sons Metal Products v. Darue Engineering & Manufacturing*, 545 U.S. 308, 312–315 (2005). And third, it requires that the federal law in the case be raised in a "well-pleaded complaint." This third requirement is the topic of the following classic case.

Louisville & Nashville Railroad Co. v. Mottley

Supreme Court of the United States
211 U.S. 149 (1908)

JUSTICE MOODY delivered the opinion of the Court.

[To settle an earlier tort claim, the railroad gave the Mottleys lifetime passes. The railroad honored the passes for many years, until a federal statute forbade railroads from honoring such passes. Because of this federal statute, the railroad refused to honor the Mottleys' pass. The Mottleys sued the railroad, seeking to enforce the agreement.]

Two questions of law were raised by the demurrer to the bill, were brought here by appeal, and have been argued before us. They are, first, whether that part of the act of Congress of June 29, 1906 (34 Stat. 584), which forbids the giving of free passes or the collection of any different compensation for transportation of passengers than that specified in the tariff filed, makes it unlawful to perform a contract for transportation of persons, who in good faith, before the passage of the act, had accepted such contract in satisfaction of a valid cause of action against the railroad; and, second, whether the statute, if it should be construed to render such a contract unlawful, is in violation of the Fifth Amendment of the Constitution of the United States. We do not deem it necessary, however, to consider either of these questions, because, in our opinion, the court below was without jurisdiction of the cause. Neither party has questioned that jurisdiction, but it is the duty of this court to see to it that the jurisdiction of the Circuit Court [which was the federal trial court at the time], which is defined and limited by statute, is not exceeded. This duty we have frequently performed of our own motion.

There was no diversity of citizenship and it is not and cannot be suggested that there was any ground of jurisdiction, except that the case was a "suit . . . arising under the Constitution and laws of the United States." It is the settled interpretation of these words, as used in this statute, conferring jurisdiction, that a suit arises under the Constitution and laws of the United States only when the plaintiff's statement of his own cause of action shows that it is based upon those laws or that

Constitution. It is not enough that the plaintiff alleges some anticipated defense to his cause of action and asserts that the defense is invalidated by some provision of the Constitution of the United States. Although such allegations show that very likely, in the course of the litigation, a question under the Constitution would arise, they do not show that the suit, that is, the plaintiff's original cause of action, arises under the Constitution. . . . [I]n Boston & Montana Consolidated Copper & Silver Mining Company v. Montana Ore Purchasing Company, 188 U.S. 632 [1903], the plaintiff brought suit . . . for the conversion of copper ore and for an injunction against its continuance. The plaintiff then alleged, for the purpose of showing jurisdiction, in substance, that the defendant would set up in defense certain laws of the United States. The cause was held to be beyond the jurisdiction of the Circuit Court, the court saying, by Mr. Justice Peckham.

> "It would be wholly unnecessary and improper in order to prove complainant's cause of action to go into any matters of defence which the defendants might possibly set up and then attempt to reply to such defence, and thus, if possible, to show that a Federal question might or probably would arise in the course of the trial of the case. To allege such defence and then make an answer to it before the defendant has the opportunity to itself plead or prove its own defence is inconsistent with any known rule of pleading so far as we are aware, and is improper.
>
> "The rule is a reasonable and just one that the complainant in the first instance shall be confined to a statement of its cause of action, leaving to the defendant to set up in his answer what his defence is and, if anything more than a denial of complainant's cause of action, imposing upon the defendant the burden of proving such defence.
>
> "Conforming itself to that rule the complainant would not, in the assertion or proof of its cause of action, bring up a single Federal question. The presentation of its cause of action would not show that it was one arising under the Constitution or laws of the United States.
>
> "The only way in which it might be claimed that a Federal question was presented would be in the complainant's statement of what the defence of defendants would be and complainant's answer to such defence. Under these circumstances the case is brought within the rule laid down in Tennessee v. Union & Planters' Bank. That case has been cited and approved many times since. . . ."

. . .

It is ordered that the judgment be reversed and the case remitted to the Circuit Court with instructions to dismiss the suit for want of jurisdiction.

Notes and Questions

1. The term "well-pleaded complaint" rule is somewhat misleading. It sounds as though the court should be concerned with syntax and grammar. In fact, the rule

means this: in assessing federal question jurisdiction, the court looks only at the plaintiff's *claim itself*; it ignores anything the defendant might say in her answer or counterclaim and it also ignores any extraneous material the plaintiff may have pleaded. In *Mottley*, the plaintiffs' complaint was, basically, "we have a contract with the defendant and the defendant is breaching it." The only federal issue would be the defendant's *excuse* for breaching the contract. In defense, the railroad would say "yes, we are breaching the contract, but we must do so because a federal law forbids us from honoring your free pass."

The Mottleys anticipated the defense and addressed it in their complaint, essentially saying "we have a contract with the defendant and the defendant is breaching it, and that federal law on which the defendant relies does not apply to us." There is nothing ethically or legally wrong with anticipating a defense (federal or otherwise). But such anticipated defenses are irrelevant in determining whether the case arises under federal law. The court considers only the claim itself. And here the claim—breach of contract—did not implicate federal law at all.

2. In *Mottley*, the effect of the well-pleaded complaint rule was to funnel to state courts disputes in which the adjudication actually will focus on federal law. The railroad did not dispute that it was breaching the contract. The only issue was whether the railroad had an excuse (the federal statute) for its breach. The only questions to be litigated were whether the federal law forbade the railroad from honoring the Mottleys' pass and, if so, whether the statute was constitutional. Yet, because the case did not invoke federal question (or diversity of citizenship) jurisdiction, the *Mottley* case had to be litigated in state court. This reminds us that state courts routinely interpret and apply federal law. And, as we will see in discussing diversity of citizenship jurisdiction, the converse is also true: federal courts routinely interpret and apply state law.

3. In *Mottley*, neither party nor the lower court raised the possibility that there was no federal subject matter jurisdiction. The Supreme Court raised the question on its own. This reminds of another important point: because federal courts have limited subject matter jurisdiction, they have the duty to assess—at any point in the litigation—whether the case is properly before them. In other words, subject matter jurisdiction is not a waivable defense. As soon as a federal court determines that it lacks subject matter jurisdiction—even if the court and parties have litigated for years in federal court—it must dismiss. (Or, if the case had been removed from state court—which we address in subsection 3 below—the federal court must remand the case to state court.)

2. Diversity of Citizenship Jurisdiction

The other major basis of federal subject matter jurisdiction is diversity of citizenship. These cases are placed in federal court not because federal law is implicated—it is not—but because of the citizenship of the parties and the amount in controversy of the dispute. Diversity jurisdiction always has been controversial. The underlying theory seems to be that federal courts should be available in disputes between citizens of different states to avoid the fear of local bias. As the Court has explained, "the purpose of the diversity requirement . . . is to provide a federal forum for important disputes where state courts might favor, or be perceived as favoring, home-state litigants." *Exxon Mobil Corp. v. Allapattah Services*, 545 U.S. 546, 553–554 (2005). *See also Bank of the United States v. Deveaux*, 9 U.S. 61. 87 (1809) (federal courts, "having no local attachments, will be likely to be impartial between the different States and their citizens").

This is the only explanation the Court has offered as justification for diversity of citizenship jurisdiction. Some have argued that the broader purpose of the diversity jurisdiction was to bring interstate matters of "national importance" into federal court. Indeed, as we will see in section C.4 of this chapter, that justification was employed to support the expansion of federal jurisdiction under the Class Action Fairness Act of 2005. Importantly, however, the Court has never expressly adopted or endorsed that justification for diversity jurisdiction. *See* C. Douglas Floyd, *The Inadequacy of the Interstate Commerce Justification for the Class Action Fairness Act of 2005*, 55 Emory L.J. 487, 500–507 (2006) (criticizing the "nationalizing" justification for the expansion of diversity-based jurisdiction).

As a practical matter, why would anyone fear local bias in a state court? One reason is that some state-court judges are elected, and thus have to run for re-election every few years. If such a judge ruled for citizens of other states—against local citizens—the local voters might vote the judge out of office. There are few data on whether such bias exists, but there certainly is fear of it, and it is hard to say that the fear of getting "hometowned" is baseless. In contrast, federal judges, you will recall, have the ultimate in job security. Under Article III, § 1 of the Constitution, they are appointed for life, never face an electorate, their pay cannot be reduced, and they can be removed from office only by impeachment. So federal judges, the theory goes, are less susceptible to local bias and therefore may rule against the local interest without fear of political reprisal. However one sides in the debate, it seems likely that Congress will never wholly abolish diversity of citizenship jurisdiction, because the organized bar likes the choice of forum it accords in many cases.

Interestingly, the current diversity statute is broader than its policy basis would require. That policy (avoidance of fear of local bias) would seem to require diversity jurisdiction only when a case involves one litigant who is a citizen of the state in which the case is filed. For instance, an Alabama litigant might fear getting "hometowned" by a New York court when litigating in New York against a New York citizen. But § 1332(a)(1) does not require a local litigant. Thus, a citizen of Pennsylvania may sue a citizen of Delaware under diversity jurisdiction in a federal court in Alaska.

As with federal question jurisdiction, the operative constitutional language and the operative statutory language is identical. Article III extends the federal judicial power to cases "between Citizens of different States." Section 1332(a)(1) of the Judicial Code (28 U.S.C. § 1332(a)(1)) uses the same language—granting jurisdiction over civil actions "between citizens of different States." But, as with federal question jurisdiction, the constitutional and statutory words mean different things. The statutory terminology is narrower, as it includes the "complete diversity rule," while the constitutional language does not. In addition, the statute (unlike Article III) imposes an amount-in-controversy requirement.

a. The Complete Diversity Rule

In *Strawbridge v. Curtiss*, 7 U.S. 267 (1806), the Court held that the diversity of citizenship statute requires that every plaintiff be of diverse citizenship from every defendant. The rule stands to this day, but applies only to cases brought under § 1332(a)(1), and not to the constitutional grant. Accordingly, Congress is free to override the complete diversity rule and permit jurisdiction based upon "minimal diversity"—that is, where one plaintiff is of diverse citizenship from one defendant. *State Farm Fire & Casualty Co. v. Tashire*, 386 U.S. 523, 531 (1967) ("Article III poses no obstacle to the legislative extension of federal jurisdiction, founded on diversity, so long as any two adverse parties are not co-citizens.").

In recent years, Congress has used minimal diversity to open the doors of the federal courthouse to certain types of complex disputes. We will study those efforts in section D of this chapter. For now, we focus on diversity under § 1332(a)(1).

> ***Example #1.*** Plaintiff, a citizen of New York, sues ten defendants. Nine of the defendants are citizens of Arizona and one is a citizen of New York. The case fails to invoke diversity jurisdiction, because the plaintiff is a co-citizen with one of the defendants.

Under Rule 21, the court might drop the non-diverse defendant and permit the case to proceed. Or, if inclusive joinder is important to Plaintiff, she may, presumably, sue all ten defendants in state court. Remember that state courts have general subject matter jurisdiction.

The courts have long used the "time of filing" rule, which holds that there must be complete diversity at the time the case is filed. A subsequent change in citizenship that would appear to defeat diversity is irrelevant. It is also irrelevant what the citizenships of the parties were when the claim arose. Complete diversity is assessed when the case is *filed*. This rule makes sense. A contrary rule would allow a person sued under diversity to destroy diversity by changing his citizenship to that of the other party.

> ***Example #2.*** P, a citizen of Nevada, sues D, a citizen of Utah, asserting diversity of citizenship jurisdiction. After the case is filed, D becomes a citizen of Nevada. Because the courts use the "time of filing" rule, diversity attached when the case was filed. D's subsequent machinations are irrelevant to jurisdiction.

How do we determine a litigant's citizenship? For a human who is a citizen of the United States, citizenship is the state of her domicile. Everyone is ascribed a domicile at birth (usually, the domicile of her parents). When she reaches the age of majority, one can change her domicile by (1) being physically present in another place and (2) forming the intent to make that place her home. A person may only have one domicile at a time, so is only a citizen of one state at a time. And everyone always has a domicile; there is no such thing as a person without a domicile. You retain your old domicile (even if you are no longer present there) until you obtain a new one. Note, also, that a United States citizen may be domiciled in a foreign country, in which case she is not a citizen of a state for diversity of citizenship purposes.

The citizenship of a corporation is defined by § 1332(c)(1), and consists of (1) the state[3] where the corporation is incorporated and (2) the one state in which the corporation has its principal place of business. Until 1958, courts generally treated corporations as citizens only of the state in which they were incorporated. Effective in that year, however, Congress passed what is now found in § 1332(c)(1), adding the state of the corporation's principal place of business as a state of the business's citizenship. Congress was motivated by the fact that many corporations incorporate in a state (often Delaware) in which they do little business. Considering only that state to be its citizenship allowed the corporation to invoke diversity jurisdiction in litigation against a citizen of the state of its principal place of business. Congress concluded that this permitted unnecessary access to federal courts, and expanded the definition of corporate citizenship.

So a corporation (unlike a human) might be a citizen of two states. Note that a corporation has only one principal place of business. It is impossible to have more than one. In *Hertz Corp. v. Friend*, 559 U.S. 77, 80 (2010), the Supreme Court defined the principal place of business as that place in which corporate managers "direct, control, and coordinate the corporation's activities." Courts refer to this place as the "nerve center." This corporate "nerve center" is usually the company's headquarters. For our purposes, we will simply assume that the principal place of business is in a particular state.

> ***Example #3.*** XYZ Corporation is incorporated in Delaware and has its principal place of business in California. It also has manufacturing plants in all 50 states. It is a citizen of Delaware and California only.

The world of business associations is divided into those that are corporations and those that are not. No statute addresses the citizenship of non-incorporated business forms, such as partnerships and limited liability companies. The courts have worked out clear rules in this regard, though. They conclude that a non-incorporated association is deemed a citizen of all states of which its members are citizens. This has long been understood for partnerships, as the Court confirmed in *Carden v. Arkoma Associates*, 494 U.S. 184, 195–196 (1990).

---

3. Technically, a corporation may incorporated in more than one state, and would be a citizen of each state in which it is incorporated. Although multi-state incorporation used to be common, today it is almost impossible to find a corporation incorporated in more than one state.

Example #4. Limited Partnership is formed under the law of California and has its principal place of business in Los Angeles. Its general and limited partners are citizens of California, Arizona, Nevada, and Oregon. It sues a corporation that is incorporated in Delaware and has its principal place of business in Oregon. There is no diversity of citizenship jurisdiction because both plaintiff and defendant are citizens of Oregon. The partnership's state of formation and principal place of business are irrelevant. It is a citizen of California, Arizona, Nevada, and Oregon.

The most important development in the law of business associations over the past generation is the limited liability company (LLC), which combines some favorable aspects of corporations with some favorable aspects of partnerships. After some uncertainty, courts have now agreed that LLCs are treated like partnerships. LLCs consist of "members" (not partners). They are thus ascribed the citizenship of all members. *See Belleville Catering Co. v. Champaign Market Place LLC*, 350 F.3d 691, 692 (7th Cir. 2003).

b. The Amount-in-Controversy Requirement

Congress always has imposed an amount-in-controversy requirement in diversity of citizenship cases. The requirement serves two purposes: it ensures that the federal courts not be burdened with small-claims matters and acts to control the docket of the federal bench. Presently, § 1332(a)(1) requires that the amount "exceed" $75,000. Thus, a claim for exactly $75,000 will not suffice.

The statute instructs the court to consider the amount of the claim "exclusive of interest and costs." Usually, one who wins a judgment is entitled to recover interest at the legal rate from the date of judgment. This interest is not included in the amount in controversy. Similarly, in most cases, the winning party recovers her costs from the loser. "Costs" in this sense refers to various expenses of litigation not including attorney's fees. (Under the "American rule," each party is expected to pay her own attorney's fees.) These "costs" of the litigation, which are usually determined after the case is concluded, are not included in the amount in controversy. It is worth noting, however, that sometimes parties are permitted by statute to recover their attorney's fees. In such cases, the fees may be included as damages, and thus would be included in the amount in controversy.[4]

Whatever amount the plaintiff claims is determinative unless it is "clear to a legal certainty" that she cannot recover more than $75,000. This might be true, for instance, if there were a statutory cap on recovery in a particular kind of case.

4. Moreover, sometimes the plaintiff's claim itself will be to recover interest. For example, plaintiff might sue because a financial institution failed to pay interest on investments. In such a case, the interest is the claim, and is included in the amount in controversy. When § 1332(a) excludes "interest," it means interest *on* the underlying claim. It does not rule out a claim to recover interest.

Courts use the "time of filing" rule in applying the amount-in-controversy requirement. So jurisdiction attaches when the plaintiff files a case making a good faith allegation that the claim exceeds $75,000.

> ***Example #5.*** Plaintiff sues for $100,000 and wins a judgment for $5,000. Defendant then claims that the court lacked subject matter jurisdiction because the amount-in-controversy, as shown by the judgment, was only $5,000. Defendant is wrong. Jurisdiction attached when the case was filed. The amount Plaintiff ultimately recovers is irrelevant to jurisdiction. (This makes sense; otherwise, jurisdiction would be in limbo until the litigation ended.)

Can a plaintiff aggregate (add) separate claims to meet the amount-in-controversy requirement? The answer is yes if the case is by one plaintiff against one defendant. But, as a general matter, claims cannot be aggregated if there are multiple parties on either side of the case.

> ***Example #6.*** P sues D and asserts four totally unrelated claims, each for $20,000. The amount-in-controversy requirement is satisfied. Because there is one plaintiff and one defendant, the claims are aggregated, and the amount is $80,000.

> ***Example #7.*** P-1 sues D for $60,000 and in the same case P-2 sues D for $30,000. This case cannot invoke diversity of citizenship jurisdiction because it fails to satisfy the amount-in-controversy requirement. Because there are multiple plaintiffs, aggregation is not permitted. (The same would be true if there were multiple defendants.)

If the case involves a joint claim, however, the amount in controversy is the value of the claim, regardless of the number of parties. So if P sued three alleged joint tortfeasors for $76,000, the requirement would be met. Because the claim is for joint liability, any of the three defendants could be held liable for the full amount of the claim. In such cases, there is nothing to aggregate—there is only one claim, and, here, it exceeded $75,000.

3. The Defendant's Prerogative: Removal Jurisdiction

The existence of federal subject matter jurisdiction gives the plaintiff's lawyer a choice of forum. Every diversity case and nearly every federal question case[5] may be brought either in federal or state court. The lawyer will make the choice based upon strategic considerations. Lawyers have definite ideas about the relative strengths of state and federal judges in given locales. In addition, the time from filing to trial may vary dramatically in the two systems. State courts may have less liberal (or less

---

5. The only exceptions, again, are those rare federal question cases that must be brought in federal court—including bankruptcy, patent infringement, and some securities and antitrust claims. Other federal question cases can be brought in either state or federal court.

onerous, depending on one's point of view) discovery rules. And the juries in the two systems are usually drawn from quite different geographic areas. State courts usually draw jurors from the county in which they sit. Federal courts draw from the entire federal district, which usually consists of many counties and, thus, a far wider cross-section of the populace.

If the plaintiff files the case in federal court, and the case indeed invokes federal subject matter jurisdiction, there is nothing the defendant can do to move the case into a state court. As we will see in Chapter 3, she may be able to have the case transferred to another federal court, but the case will be litigated in a federal forum.

On the other hand, if the plaintiff files the case in state court, the defendant may be able to *remove* it to the federal court system. Removal jurisdiction is not mentioned in Article III. It is wholly a product of Congress, and has been part of the jurisdictional statutes from the earliest days of the federal court system. Removal gives the defendant a voice in deciding which court system—state or federal—will adjudicate her case.

A case can only be removed if it invokes federal subject matter jurisdiction. That is, no defendant can remove a case to federal court unless the case "belongs" there—for example, because it invokes diversity of citizenship or federal question jurisdiction.

Removal of a general civil case[6] is governed by provisions found in 28 U.S.C. §§ 1441, 1446, and 1447. A defendant desiring to remove does not seek the federal court's permission. She simply removes the case by filing a notice of removal in federal court, accompanied by the documents served upon her in state court. The notice must be signed under Federal Rule 11 (with the concomitant certification that the document is not frivolous) and must establish a basis federal subject matter jurisdiction.

The defendant must remove the case no later than 30 days after she is *served* with the documents that first make the case removable. *Murphy Bros. v. Michetti Pipe Stringing, Inc.*, 526 U.S. 344 (1999). Ordinarily, these documents will be the process that was served on the defendant at the outset of the case. As we will see below, however, it is possible that a case not removable at the outset becomes removable later. The defendant always must remove within 30 days of service of the document that *first* makes the case removable.

Under the general removal statutes, the courts follow the "rule of unanimity," which requires that *all* defendants who have been served with a document that makes the case removable join in removing the case. If there are ten defendants and nine wish to remove but one does not, the case cannot be removed. Historically, courts did not agree on how to handle cases in which one defendant failed to remove within

6. The statutes permit removal of criminal cases in certain situations. In addition, there are special provisions concerning removal of certain types of civil rights disputes. We do not address these. We are concerned only with general civil removal.

30 days of service on her and then a second defendant was served with process. Congress resolved the matter with § 1446(b)(2)(B) and (C). These provide that the 30 days begin to run afresh when the second defendant is served. Accordingly, the first defendant's failure to remove within 30 days does not estop the second defendant from getting the first defendant to join her in removal.

If the plaintiff contests removal, she makes a motion to *remand* the case to state court. If this motion is based upon a procedural error by the defendant (for instance, if the defendant failed to sign her notice of removal under Rule 11), the plaintiff must move to remand no later than 30 days after removal. If the plaintiff fails to do this, she waives the procedural problem and the case stays in federal court (assuming there is federal subject matter jurisdiction). On the other hand, there is no time limit for a motion to remand if the federal court lacks subject matter jurisdiction. Indeed, the federal court should always assess its subject matter jurisdiction. If it finds there is none, it must remand the case to state court.[7]

Finally, there are two important limitations on removal, which apply only in diversity of citizenship cases. First, defendants cannot remove a diversity case if any defendant is a citizen of the forum. The rationale for this "in-state defendant" rule is that a citizen of the forum need not fear bias in the local courts and thus does not need access to the federal forum. Second, a diversity case cannot be removed more than one year after it was filed in state court. Because defendants must remove within *30 days* of service of the document that first made the case removable, this one-year rule comes into play in cases that are not removable when filed but become removable later. For example:

> ***Example #8.*** P, a citizen of Alabama, sues D-1, a citizen of New Jersey, and D-2, a citizen of Georgia, in a Georgia state court. The claims are based upon state law and meet the amount-in-controversy requirement for a diversity case. Even though P could have filed this case in federal court (because it satisfies the requirements for diversity), the defendants cannot remove the case. Why? Because D-2 is a citizen of the forum.
>
> ***Example #9.*** Suppose P voluntarily dismisses the claim against D-2. The case *now becomes removable*, because the in-state defendant has been dropped. So D-1 has 30 days from service of the dismissal of D-2 in which to remove.
>
> ***Example #10.*** But what if P had waited a year and a day after filing the case in state court to dismiss the claim against D-2? Then D-1 is probably out of luck. Under § 1446(c)(1), generally, a diversity case cannot be removed more than a year after it was filed in state court.

This one-year rule is subject to abuse. A plaintiff wanting to ensure litigation in state court can simply do what P did above—join an in-state defendant, wait a year

7. In a case filed originally in federal court (as opposed to removed from state court), anytime the court determines there is no federal subject matter jurisdiction, it must dismiss.

and dismiss the claim against the in-state defendant. Because of such possibilities, in 2011, Congress added an exception: removal can be effected more than a year after the case was filed if the district court finds that the plaintiff acted in bad faith to prevent removal. So if the court found that the plaintiff acted in bad faith by joining a defendant to defeat removal, the one-year limitation would not apply.

It is worth emphasizing: the in-state defendant rule and the one-year rule apply only if the defendant is removing on the basis of diversity of citizenship jurisdiction; they do not apply when a federal question case is removed.

C. Supplemental Jurisdiction

1. What It Does

Federal question and diversity of citizenship are examples of "independent" bases of federal subject matter jurisdiction. That means that they can be used to get a *case itself* into federal court. It is important to understand, however, that *every claim asserted in federal court* must be supported by federal subject matter jurisdiction. So not just the original claim by plaintiff against defendant, but *every* claim, must be assessed to see if it "belongs" in federal court.

For example, the plaintiff may have additional claims beyond that which invoked federal subject matter jurisdiction. The defendant may have a counterclaim against the plaintiff or a crossclaim against her co-defendants. And intervenors may assert claims or defend claims asserted against them. Even though the underlying claim by the plaintiff against the defendant got the case into federal court, each of these additional claims must also be supported by subject matter jurisdiction. If they are not, they cannot be heard in federal court. (Then what happens? Remember, the party asserting the particular claim may then assert the claim in state court, although the rest of the case stays in federal court.)

Often, such an additional claim will invoke an independent basis of federal subject matter jurisdiction. For example, the defendant's counterclaim against the plaintiff may invoke diversity of citizenship or federal question jurisdiction by itself. If so, it can be asserted in the pending case.

What happens, though, when a claim does not invoke an independent basis of federal subject matter jurisdiction? The federal court may nonetheless be able to hear the claim through *supplemental jurisdiction.* Supplemental jurisdiction cannot be used to get a *case* into federal court. Only an independent basis (such as diversity of citizenship and federal question) can do that. Once the case is in federal court, however, supplemental jurisdiction permits the federal court to hear claims that do not satisfy an independent basis of jurisdiction. In other words, supplemental jurisdiction allows a federal court to decide non-federal, non-diversity claims!

Given that federal courts are of limited subject matter jurisdiction—and that any improper exercise of jurisdiction by a federal court constitutes a usurpation of state judicial power—how can supplemental jurisdiction be justified? The reason: supplemental claims are so closely related to the claim that invoked federal subject matter jurisdiction (the "jurisdiction-invoking" claim) that they are part of the same "case or controversy" as that claim. When the plaintiff asserts a claim that gets the case into federal court, supplemental jurisdiction allows the court to hear non-federal, non-diversity claims that are part of the overall dispute as that jurisdiction-invoking claim. The theory is that the court takes jurisdiction over the *case as a whole*, and the case includes closely-related claims—even if those claims do not invoke an independent basis of subject matter jurisdiction.

How closely related do the claims have to be? In *United Mine Workers v. Gibbs*, 383 U.S. 715, 725–726 (1966), the Supreme Court held that federal courts have supplemental jurisdiction over claims that share a "common nucleus of operative fact" with the jurisdiction-invoking claim. The Court noted the practical convenience that the parties would ordinarily expect that such related claims would be tried in a single case. Of course, practical convenience is no basis for exercising federal jurisdiction. The point is that claims sharing a common nucleus of operative fact with the jurisdiction-invoking claim would comprise part of one case or controversy, over which the court could properly exercise power.

Most observers agree that the *Gibbs* "common nucleus" test is the constitutional limit of supplemental jurisdiction. And all agree that any claim arising from the same transaction or occurrence as the jurisdiction-invoking claim would satisfy the *Gibbs* test. This is handy, because many of the joinder provisions of the Federal Rules of Civil Procedure use "transaction or occurrence" as their operative test. For example, compulsory counterclaims under Rule 13(a) and crossclaims under Rule 13(g) must arise from the same transaction or occurrence as the underlying dispute.

Gibbs is broader than "transaction or occurrence." The proof comes from those cases in which courts have allowed supplemental jurisdiction over *permissive* counterclaims under Rule 13(b). These claims do *not* arise from the same transaction or occurrence as the underlying case. But sometimes they are sufficiently related to the jurisdiction-invoking claim to satisfy the *Gibbs* test. How can that be? Because, according to an emerging string of cases, *Gibbs* requires only that the supplemental claim and the jurisdiction-invoking claim share a "loose factual connection." *See Jones v. Ford Motor Credit Co.*, 358 F.3d 205, 210–215 (2d Cir. 2004) *quoting Channell v. Citicorp Nat'l Servs.*, 89 F.3d 379, 385–386 (7th Cir. 1996).[8]

In *Gibbs* and other cases, the federal courts spoke of "pendent"—as opposed to "supplemental" jurisdiction. Other cases spoke of "ancillary" jurisdiction. The

---

8. In these cases, the plaintiff sued a lender, claiming that the lender had engaged in improper discrimination. The defendant counterclaimed for the amount remaining on the loan. The courts held that the counterclaims did not arise from the same transaction or occurrence as the plaintiff's claim for discrimination, and thus were permissive counterclaims. Nonetheless, because of the "loose factual connection" with the plaintiff's claim, the counterclaim invoked supplemental jurisdiction.

distinctions, if any, between pendent and ancillary jurisdiction are of historical interest only, because Congress codified the entire area under the generic rubric "supplemental jurisdiction" in 28 U.S.C. § 1367. All of supplemental jurisdiction—that traditionally called pendent and that traditionally called ancillary—is dealt with by that statute, which became effective in 1990. Although the statute uses the generic label "supplemental," many courts continue to use the older terminology. There is no harm in that practice, so long as everyone realizes that the matter is governed by § 1367, to which we now turn.

2. Statutory Analysis

Section 1367 consists of four sections. We will focus in detail on the first two.

a. The Grant in § 1367(a)

Section 1367(a) grants supplemental jurisdiction to the full extent of Article III. It provides:

> Except as provided in subsections (b) and (c) or as expressly provided otherwise by Federal statute, in any civil action of which the district courts have original jurisdiction, the district courts shall have supplemental jurisdiction over all other claims that are so related to claims in the action within such original jurisdiction that they form part of the same case or controversy under Article III of the United States Constitution. Such supplemental jurisdiction shall include claims that involve the joinder or intervention of additional parties.

Courts agree that this language codified *Gibbs.* So subsection (a) will give supplemental jurisdiction over any claim that shares a common nucleus of operative fact with the claim that invoked federal subject matter jurisdiction in the first place. The facts of *Gibbs* provide an example:

> ***Problem #1.*** P, a citizen of Tennessee, sues D, also a citizen of Tennessee, for violation of federal labor laws. P joins a claim arising under state labor law, involving the same real-world event as the federal claim. The state law claim obviously does not invoke an independent basis of federal subject matter jurisdiction. First, it arises under state law, so it does not invoke federal question jurisdiction. Second, P and D are citizens of the same state, so there is no diversity of citizenship. Nonetheless, the state-law claim invokes supplemental jurisdiction. It arose from the same real-world event, so shares a common nucleus of operative fact with the jurisdiction-invoking claim.

The last sentence of § 1367(a) makes clear that the grant of supplemental jurisdiction operates even if it involves joinder of an additional party. To demonstrate the importance of this sentence, consider these facts:

> ***Problem #2.*** P, a citizen of California, sues the United States of America under the Federal Tort Claims Act, alleging that the Federal Aeronautical

Administration (FAA) was negligent in giving air traffic control advice to a private pilot. As a result, the plane crashed, killing P's husband and children, who were passengers in the plane. In the same case, P joins a claim against a separate defendant (a utility company), which is a citizen of California, alleging that it was at fault in the crash for maintaining power lines too close to the airfield. The claim against the United States invokes federal question jurisdiction. The claim against the utility company does not, because it is based upon state law. Neither does it invoke diversity of citizenship, because P and the utility company are co-citizens.

Notice how this case differs from Problem #1. Here, the non-federal, non-diversity claim is against a *separate defendant from the jurisdiction-invoking claim.* This was traditionally called "pendent parties" jurisdiction. The Supreme Court rejected it in *Finley v. United States*, 490 U.S. 545, 556 (1989), on which the facts of Problem #2 are based. The decision in *Finley* provided the impetus for passage of § 1367. And there is no question that the statute has overruled the result in *Finley.* First, the grant in § 1367(a) applies to the claim against the utility company, because it arose from a common nucleus of operative fact with the jurisdiction-invoking claim. Second, the last sentence of § 1367(a) makes it plain that this result applies even in the pendent parties scenario—in which the supplemental claim involves a different party from the jurisdiction-invoking claim.

b. The Limitations for Diversity Cases in § 1367(b)

Each of these examples involved federal question cases. That is, each case got into federal court on the basis of federal question jurisdiction. Interestingly, nothing in § 1367(a) limits its use to federal question cases. Accordingly, that section by itself would permit non-federal, non-diversity claims in diversity of citizenship cases. Doing so without limit, however, would imperil both the amount-in-controversy and complete diversity requirements in diversity cases. This Problem demonstrates that fact with regard to the amount-in-controversy requirement, and points out why Congress properly felt the need to provide limitations for the exercise of supplemental jurisdiction in § 1367(b).

Section 1367(b) provides:

> In any civil action of which the district courts have original jurisdiction founded solely on section 1332 of this title [diversity of citizenship and alienage], the district courts shall not have supplemental jurisdiction under subsection (a) over claims by plaintiffs against persons made parties under Rule 14, 19, 20, or 24 of the Federal Rules of Civil Procedure, or over claims by persons proposed to be joined as plaintiffs under Rule 19 of such rules or seeking to intervene as plaintiffs under Rule 24 of such rules, when exercising supplemental jurisdiction over such claims would be inconsistent with the jurisdictional requirements of section 1332.

Let's apply the provision.

> ***Problem #3.*** Two plaintiffs, P-1 and P-2, both citizens of New York, join in a single case to sue D, who is a citizen of Florida. The claims arise from the same nucleus of operative fact and arise under state law. P-1's claim against D exceeds \$75,000. P-2's claim against D, however, is for \$50,000. Right away we see that P-1's claim against D satisfies the requirements for diversity of citizenship. But P-2's claim against D does not. Although the parties are of diverse citizenship, that claim does not exceed \$75,000. Moreover, because the case is not brought by a single plaintiff against a single defendant, the two claims cannot be aggregated. And since the claim arises under state law, generally it will not invoke federal question jurisdiction.

So what happens to the claim by P-2? In *Clark v. Paul Gray, Inc.*, 306 U.S. 583, 589 (1939), the Supreme Court held that it could not be joined in the same case as P-1's claim. It concluded that *each* claim must meet the amount-in controversy requirement. Because P-2's claim does not, it must be dismissed. P-1's claim against D, however, can remain in federal court because it invoked diversity of citizenship jurisdiction.

But note how § 1367(a), by itself, would grant supplemental jurisdiction over the claim by P-2 against D. That claim shares a common nucleus of operative fact with the jurisdiction-invoking claim and the last sentence of § 1367(a) makes clear that the joinder of an additional party does not prohibit jurisdiction. Congress attempted to avoid such a result by limiting supplemental jurisdiction in diversity cases in § 1367(b). It is helpful to analyze § 1367(b) in three steps.

First, § 1367(b) applies only to cases in which the jurisdiction-invoking claim is based solely on diversity of citizenship. Thus, it would not apply in Problems 1 or 2 above. Why? Because, as noted, in each of those, the jurisdictional basis was federal question, not diversity. Section 1367(b) simply does not apply in federal question cases.

Second, § 1367(b) applies only to claims asserted "by plaintiffs." Again, Congress wanted to prevent plaintiffs from using supplemental jurisdiction to get around the complete diversity rule. The courts have never been worried about defendants' using supplemental jurisdiction in diversity cases. Two quick examples will suffice.

> ***Problem #4.*** P, a citizen of Pennsylvania, sues D, a citizen of Arizona, asserting a state-law claim of \$500,000. D files a compulsory counterclaim against P. By definition, the compulsory counterclaim arises from the same transaction or occurrence as plaintiff's claim. The claim is based upon state law but is for \$50,000. The counterclaim does not invoke federal question jurisdiction because it is based upon state law. It does not invoke diversity because does not exceed \$75,000.

What happens to the counterclaim? The federal courts have always permitted supplemental jurisdiction. Historically, they called this "ancillary" jurisdiction, and some courts still do. The test for ancillary is the same as for supplemental jurisdiction generally—whether the claim arises from a common nucleus of operative fact with the claim that invoked federal subject matter jurisdiction.

Does § 1367 change this result? No. First, § 1367(a) grants supplemental jurisdiction because the compulsory counterclaim satisfies *Gibbs.* Second, because § 1367(b) applies in diversity cases, it must be consulted. But third, § 1367(b) applies only to claims by plaintiffs. Because the counterclaim is asserted by the defendant, the section does not take away supplemental jurisdiction.

> ***Problem #5.*** P, a citizen of Minnesota, sues two defendants, D-1 and D-2, each of whom is a citizen of Wisconsin. P's claim against the two is based upon state law and is for $500,000. D-1 has a crossclaim against D-2, arising under state law, for $250,000. The crossclaim by D-1 against D-2 does not invoke federal question jurisdiction, because it is arises under state law. It also does not invoke diversity of citizenship, because D-1 and D-2 are citizens of Wisconsin.

What happens to the crossclaim? The federal courts have always permitted supplemental jurisdiction. Again, they tended to call it "ancillary" (and some still do). Because the crossclaim, by definition, arises from the same transaction or occurrence as the underlying dispute, it will always meet the "common nucleus" test of *Gibbs.*

Does § 1367 change this result? No. Again, § 1367(a) grants supplemental jurisdiction because the crossclaim meets *Gibbs.* And although § 1367(b) applies because this is a diversity case, it does not remove supplemental jurisdiction. Why? Because § 1367(b) only removes supplemental jurisdiction over claims by plaintiffs, and this (like the claim in Problem #4) is a claim by the defendant.

Third, § 1367(b) removes supplemental jurisdiction in diversity cases over certain claims *asserted by plaintiffs.* Specifically, these are (1) claims by plaintiffs against persons made parties under Rules 14, 19, 20, or 24, (2) claims by Rule 19 plaintiffs, and (3) claims by absentees seeking to intervene as plaintiffs under Rule 24. This part of the statute has created great difficulty. Note that while it prohibits supplemental jurisdiction over claims by plaintiffs *against* defendants joined under Rule 20, it does not remove supplemental jurisdiction over claims *by Rule 20 plaintiffs.*

Return to Problem #3. Section 1367(b), literally, does *not* apply to remove supplemental jurisdiction over the claim by P-2 against D. Although P-1 and P-2 are plaintiffs joined under Rule 20, *the statute does not remove supplemental jurisdiction over claims asserted by Rule 20 plaintiffs.* Rather, it applies to remove supplemental jurisdiction over claims by plaintiffs *against defendants joined under Rule 20.* So, on its face, § 1367(b) applies to defeat jurisdiction over claims by a single plaintiff against multiple defendants. But it does not apply to defeat jurisdiction over claims by multiple plaintiffs against a single defendant.

The same thing would happen in the class context.

> ***Problem #6.*** P, a citizen of Arkansas, is the representative of a class asserting a state-law claim against D, a citizen of Texas. P's claim exceeds $75,000, but the claims of the class members do not.

What happens to the class members' claims? Historically, the federal courts held that the class members could not proceed. The Supreme Court first held that the class members' claims cannot be aggregated (added) to meet the amount requirement. Then the Court held in *Zahn v. International Paper Co.*, 414 U.S. 291, 301 (1973), that *each class member's claim* must satisfy the amount-in-controversy requirement. Thus, each class member must assert a claim of over $75,000.

This result was inconsistent with the position taken by the Court concerning citizenship in the class action. Long ago, in *Supreme Tribe of Ben-Hur v. Cauble*, 255 U.S. 356, 365 (1921), the Court held that only the representative must be of diverse citizenship from the defendant. The fact that class members were co-citizens with the defendant was irrelevant. Against this background, the holding in *Zahn* made no sense. If the class members' citizenships were irrelevant, why should their amounts in controversy matter? After all, both the complete diversity rule and the amount-in-controversy requirements are statutory (not constitutional). So one would expect them to be treated the same.

But § 1367, on its face, changes the result in this example. Why? For exactly the same reasoning as in Problem #3. The claim by P against D invokes diversity of citizenship jurisdiction and the claims by class members invoke supplemental jurisdiction. They share a common nucleus of operative fact with P's claim, so § 1367(a) grants supplemental jurisdiction. Second, nothing in § 1367(b) removes that grant. Again, this is not a claim by a plaintiff against Rule 20 defendants. It is a claim by Rule 23 plaintiffs. And nothing in § 1367(b) addresses Rule 23 claims.

If that is true, however, it opens the door to an even greater change in existing law.

> ***Problem #7.*** P-1, a citizen of Ohio, and P-2, a citizen of Illinois, sue D, a citizen of Illinois, on a state-law claim for $500,000. The plaintiffs' claims arise from a common nucleus of operative fact. The claim by P-1 against D seems clearly to invoke diversity of citizenship jurisdiction. The claim by P-2 obviously does not, since it is by a citizen of Illinois against a co-citizen. The claim by P-2 would seem to invoke supplemental jurisdiction. It meets § 1367(a) because of its factual relatedness with the jurisdiction-invoking claim. And nothing in § 1367(b) appears to remove supplemental jurisdiction. After all, this is not a claim by a plaintiff against defendants joined under Rule 20.

Read literally, then, § 1367 seems to overrule *Clark, Zahn, and* the complete diversity rule. At least, it appears to do so in cases involving a single defendant. If there were multiple defendants, then any claim by the plaintiff would be against persons joined under Rule 20, for which supplemental jurisdiction in diversity cases is removed by § 1367(b).

Congress apparently understood that § 1367 would overrule *Zahn*, but did not intend that result. Buried in the legislative history of the statute is a single sentence addressing the matter. It says that nothing in § 1367 should be interpreted to change the result the courts had reached concerning the amount-in-controversy requirement in class actions. So at least someone tried to head off use of the statute to overrule *Zahn*. The note, however, did not address the possibility that the statute might overrule *Clark* or the complete diversity rule.

When the terms of a statute are inconsistent with the legislative history, it is not surprising that parties will litigate the question of which should prevail. For over a decade, the statute created considerable confusion. Six courts of appeals concluded that the statutory language prevailed, and thus that *Zahn* was overruled. Four courts of appeals reached the contrary conclusion. The Supreme Court finally addressed the matter in the following case. In it, the Court resolves what we have listed above as Problems 3 and 6. Its treatment of Problems 3 and 5 are the basis for its holding. Its discussion of Problem 6 is dictum.

As you read it, keep these questions in mind.

1. Why does the majority conclude that supplemental jurisdiction should apply in both the class and nonclass contexts concerning the amount-in-controversy requirement?

2. How does the majority justify treating citizenship and amount-in-controversy differently? After all, each is merely a statutory (not constitutional) requirement.

Exxon Mobil Corp. v. Allapattah Services

Supreme Court of the United States
545 U.S. 546 (2005)

Justice Kennedy delivered the opinion of the Court.

These consolidated cases [*Allapattah* from the Eleventh Circuit and *Ortiz* from the First Circuit] present the question whether a federal court in a diversity action may exercise supplemental jurisdiction over additional plaintiffs whose claims do not satisfy the minimum amount-in-controversy requirement, provided the claims are part of the same case or controversy as the claims of plaintiffs who do allege a sufficient amount in controversy. Our decision turns on the correct interpretation of 28 U.S.C. § 1367. The question has divided the Courts of Appeals, and we granted certiorari to resolve the conflict.

We hold that, where the other elements of jurisdiction are present and at least one named plaintiff in the action satisfies the amount-in-controversy requirement, § 1367 does authorize supplemental jurisdiction over the claims of other plaintiffs in the same Article III case or controversy, even if those claims are for less than the jurisdictional amount specified in the statute setting forth the requirements for diversity jurisdiction. . . .

I

In 1991, about 10,000 Exxon dealers filed a class-action suit against the Exxon Corporation in the United States District Court for the Northern District of Florida. The dealers alleged an intentional and systematic scheme by Exxon under which they were overcharged for fuel purchased from Exxon. The plaintiffs invoked the District Court's § 1332(a) diversity jurisdiction. After a unanimous jury verdict in favor of the plaintiffs, the District Court certified the case for interlocutory review, asking whether it had properly exercised § 1367 supplemental jurisdiction over the claims of class members who did not meet the jurisdictional minimum amount in controversy.

[In *Allapattah*], [t]he Court of Appeals for the Eleventh Circuit upheld the District Court's extension of supplemental jurisdiction to these class members. "We find," the court held, "that § 1367 clearly and unambiguously provides district courts with the authority in diversity class actions to exercise supplemental jurisdiction over the claims of class members who do not meet the minimum amount in controversy as long as the district court has original jurisdiction over the claims of at least one of the class representatives." This decision accords with the views of the Courts of Appeals for the Fourth, Sixth, and Seventh Circuits [citations omitted]. The Courts of Appeals for the Fifth and Ninth Circuits, adopting a similar analysis of the statute, have held that in a diversity class action the unnamed class members need not meet the amount-in-controversy requirement, provided the named class members do. These decisions, however, are unclear on whether all the named plaintiffs must satisfy this requirement [citations omitted].

In [*Ortiz*], the Court of Appeals for the First Circuit took a different position on the meaning of § 1367(a). In that case, a 9-year-old girl sued Star-Kist in a diversity action in the United States District Court for the District of Puerto Rico, seeking damages for unusually severe injuries she received when she sliced her finger on a tuna can. Her family joined in the suit, seeking damages for emotional distress and certain medical expenses. The District Court granted summary judgment to Star-Kist, finding that none of the plaintiffs met the minimum amount-in-controversy requirement. The Court of Appeals for the First Circuit, however, ruled that the injured girl, but not her family members, had made allegations of damages in the requisite amount.

The Court of Appeals then addressed whether, in light of the fact that one plaintiff met the requirements for original jurisdiction, supplemental jurisdiction over the remaining plaintiffs' claims was proper under § 1367. The court held that § 1367 authorizes supplemental jurisdiction only when the district court has original jurisdiction over the action, and that in a diversity case original jurisdiction is lacking if one plaintiff fails to satisfy the amount-in-controversy requirement. Although the

Court of Appeals claimed to "express no view" on whether the result would be the same in a class action, its analysis is inconsistent with that of the Court of Appeals for the Eleventh Circuit. The Court of Appeals for the First Circuit's view of § 1367 is, however, shared by the Courts of Appeal for the Third, Eighth, and Tenth Circuits, and the latter two Courts of Appeals have expressly applied this rule to class actions [citations omitted].

II

A

. . .

Although the district courts may not exercise jurisdiction absent a statutory basis, it is well established—in certain classes of cases—that, once a court has original jurisdiction over some claims in the action, it may exercise supplemental jurisdiction over additional claims that are part of the same case or controversy. The leading modern case for this principle is *Mine Workers v. Gibbs*, 383 U.S. 715 (1966). In *Gibbs*, the plaintiff alleged the defendant's conduct violated both federal and state law. The District Court, *Gibbs* held, had original jurisdiction over the action based on the federal claims. *Gibbs* confirmed that the District Court had the additional power (though not the obligation) to exercise supplemental jurisdiction over related state claims that arose from the same Article III case or controversy. ("The federal claim must have substance sufficient to confer subject matter jurisdiction on the court. . . . Assuming substantiality of the federal issues, there is *power* in federal courts to hear the whole").

. . .

We have not, however, applied *Gibbs*' expansive interpretive approach to other aspects of the jurisdictional statutes. For instance, we have consistently interpreted § 1332 as requiring complete diversity: In a case with multiple plaintiffs and multiple defendants, the presence in the action of a single plaintiff from the same State as a single defendant deprives the district court of original diversity jurisdiction over the entire action. The complete diversity requirement is not mandated by the Constitution, or by the plain text of § 1332(a). The Court, nonetheless, has adhered to the complete diversity rule in light of the purpose of the diversity requirement, which is to provide a federal forum for important disputes where state courts might favor, or be perceived as favoring, home-state litigants. The presence of parties from the same State on both sides of a case dispels this concern, eliminating a principal reason for conferring § 1332 jurisdiction over any of the claims in the action. The specific purpose of the complete diversity rule explains both why we have not adopted *Gibbs*' expansive interpretive approach to this aspect of the jurisdictional statute and why *Gibbs* does not undermine the complete diversity rule. In order for a federal court to invoke supplemental jurisdiction under *Gibbs*, it must first have original jurisdiction over at least one claim in the action. Incomplete diversity destroys original jurisdiction with respect to all claims, so there is nothing to which supplemental jurisdiction can adhere.

In contrast to the diversity requirement, most of the other statutory prerequisites for federal jurisdiction, including the federal-question and amount-in-controversy requirements, can be analyzed claim by claim. True, it does not follow by necessity from this that a district court has authority to exercise supplemental jurisdiction over all claims provided there is original jurisdiction over just one. Before the enactment of § 1367, the Court declined in contexts other than the pendent-claim instance to follow *Gibbs*' expansive approach to interpretation of the jurisdictional statutes. The Court took a more restrictive view of the proper interpretation of these statutes in so-called pendent-party cases involving supplemental jurisdiction over claims involving additional parties—plaintiffs or defendants—where the district courts would lack original jurisdiction over claims by each of the parties standing alone.

Thus, with respect to plaintiff-specific jurisdictional requirements, the Court held in *Clark v. Paul Gray, Inc.*, 306 U.S. 583 (1939), that every plaintiff must separately satisfy the amount-in-controversy requirement. Though *Clark* was a federal-question case, at that time federal-question jurisdiction had an amount-in-controversy requirement analogous to the amount-in-controversy requirement for diversity cases. "Proper practice," *Clark* held, "requires that where each of several plaintiffs is bound to establish the jurisdictional amount with respect to his own claim, the suit should be dismissed as to those who fail to show that the requisite amount is involved." The Court reaffirmed this rule, in the context of a class action brought invoking § 1332(a) diversity jurisdiction, in *Zahn v. International Paper Co.*, 414 U.S. 291 (1973). It follows "inescapably" from *Clark*, the Court held in *Zahn*, that "any plaintiff without the jurisdictional amount must be dismissed from the case, even though others allege jurisdictionally sufficient claims."

. . .

As the jurisdictional statutes existed in 1989, then, here is how matters stood: First, the diversity requirement in § 1332(a) required complete diversity; absent complete diversity, the district court lacked original jurisdiction over all of the claims in the action. Second, if the district court had original jurisdiction over at least one claim, the jurisdictional statutes implicitly authorized supplemental jurisdiction over all other claims between the same parties arising out of the same Article III case or controversy. Third, even when the district court had original jurisdiction over one or more claims between particular parties, the jurisdictional statutes did not authorize supplemental jurisdiction over additional claims involving other parties.

B

In *Finley* we emphasized that "whatever we say regarding the scope of jurisdiction conferred by a particular statute can of course be changed by Congress." In 1990, Congress accepted the invitation. It . . . enacted § 1367, the provision which controls these cases.

. . .

All parties to this litigation and all courts to consider the question agree that § 1367 overturned the result in *Finley*. There is no warrant, however, for assuming that § 1367 did no more than to overrule *Finley* and otherwise to codify the existing state of the law of supplemental jurisdiction. We must not give jurisdictional statutes a more expansive interpretation than their text warrants, but it is just as important not to adopt an artificial construction that is narrower than what the text provides. No sound canon of interpretation requires Congress to speak with extraordinary clarity in order to modify the rules of federal jurisdiction within appropriate constitutional bounds. Ordinary principles of statutory construction apply. In order to determine the scope of supplemental jurisdiction authorized by § 1367, then, we must examine the statute's text in light of context, structure, and related statutory provisions.

... The single question before us, therefore, is whether a diversity case in which the claims of some plaintiffs satisfy the amount-in-controversy requirement, but the claims of others plaintiffs do not, presents a "civil action of which the district courts have original jurisdiction." ...

We now conclude the answer must be yes. When the well-pleaded complaint contains at least one claim that satisfies the amount-in-controversy requirement, and there are no other relevant jurisdictional defects, the district court, beyond all question, has original jurisdiction over that claim. The presence of other claims in the complaint, over which the district court may lack original jurisdiction, is of no moment. If the court has original jurisdiction over a single claim in the complaint, it has original jurisdiction over a "civil action" within the meaning of § 1367(a), even if the civil action over which it has jurisdiction comprises fewer claims than were included in the complaint. Once the court determines it has original jurisdiction over the civil action, it can turn to the question whether it has a constitutional and statutory basis for exercising supplemental jurisdiction over the other claims in the action.

If § 1367(a) were the sum total of the relevant statutory language, our holding would rest on that language alone. The statute, of course, instructs us to examine § 1367(b) to determine if any of its exceptions apply, so we proceed to that section. While § 1367(b) qualifies the broad rule of § 1367(a), it does not withdraw supplemental jurisdiction over the claims of the additional parties at issue here. The specific exceptions to § 1367(a) contained in § 1367(b), moreover, provide additional support for our conclusion that § 1367(a) confers supplemental jurisdiction over these claims. Section 1367(b), which applies only to diversity cases, withholds supplemental jurisdiction over the claims of plaintiffs proposed to be joined as indispensable parties under Federal Rule of Civil Procedure 19, or who seek to intervene pursuant to Rule 24. Nothing in the text of § 1367(b), however, withholds supplemental jurisdiction over the claims of plaintiffs permissively joined under Rule 20 (like the additional plaintiffs in [*Ortiz*]) or certified as class-action members pursuant to Rule 23 (like the additional plaintiffs in [*Allapattah*]). The natural, indeed the necessary, inference is that § 1367 confers supplemental jurisdiction over claims by Rule 20 and Rule 23 plaintiffs. This inference, at least with respect to Rule 20 plaintiffs, is strengthened by the fact that § 1367(b) explicitly excludes supplemental jurisdiction over claims against defendants joined under Rule 20.

We cannot accept the view, urged by some of the parties, commentators, and Courts of Appeals, that a district court lacks original jurisdiction over a civil action unless the court has original jurisdiction over every claim in the complaint. As we understand this position, it requires assuming either that all claims in the complaint must stand or fall as a single, indivisible "civil action" as a matter of definitional necessity—what we will refer to as the "indivisibility theory"—or else that the inclusion of a claim or party falling outside the district court's original jurisdiction somehow contaminates every other claim in the complaint, depriving the court of original jurisdiction over any of these claims—what we will refer to as the "contamination theory."

The indivisibility theory is easily dismissed, as it is inconsistent with the whole notion of supplemental jurisdiction. If a district court must have original jurisdiction over every claim in the complaint in order to have "original jurisdiction" over a "civil action," then in *Gibbs* there was no civil action of which the district court could assume original jurisdiction under § 1331, and so no basis for exercising supplemental jurisdiction over any of the claims. The indivisibility theory is further belied by our practice—in both federal-question and diversity cases—of allowing federal courts to cure jurisdictional defects by dismissing the offending parties rather than dismissing the entire action. *Clark*, for example, makes clear that claims that are jurisdictionally defective as to amount in controversy do not destroy original jurisdiction over other claims. 306 U.S. at 590 (dismissing parties who failed to meet the amount-in-controversy requirement but retaining jurisdiction over the remaining party). If the presence of jurisdictionally problematic claims in the complaint meant the district court was without original jurisdiction over the single, indivisible civil action before it, then the district court would have to dismiss the whole action rather than particular parties.

We also find it unconvincing to say that the definitional indivisibility theory applies in the context of diversity cases but not in the context of federal-question cases. The broad and general language of the statute does not permit this result. The contention is premised on the notion that the phrase "original jurisdiction of all civil actions" means different things in § 1331 and § 1332. It is implausible, however, to say that the identical phrase means one thing (original jurisdiction in all actions where at least one claim in the complaint meets the following requirements) in § 1331 and something else (original jurisdiction in all actions where every claim in the complaint meets the following requirements) in § 1332.

The contamination theory, as we have noted, can make some sense in the special context of the complete diversity requirement because the presence of nondiverse parties on both sides of a lawsuit eliminates the justification for providing a federal forum. The theory, however, makes little sense with respect to the amount-in-controversy requirement, which is meant to ensure that a dispute is sufficiently important to warrant federal-court attention. The presence of a single nondiverse party may eliminate the fear of bias with respect to all claims, but the presence of a claim that falls short of the minimum amount in controversy does nothing to reduce the importance of the claims that do meet this requirement.

It is fallacious to suppose, simply from the proposition that § 1332 imposes both the diversity requirement and the amount-in-controversy requirement, that the contamination theory germane to the former is also relevant to the latter. There is no inherent logical connection between the amount-in-controversy requirement and § 1332 diversity jurisdiction. After all, federal-question jurisdiction once had an amount-in-controversy requirement as well. If such a requirement were revived under § 1331, it is clear beyond peradventure that § 1367(a) provides supplemental jurisdiction over federal-question cases where some, but not all, of the federal-law claims involve a sufficient amount in controversy. In other words, § 1367(a) unambiguously overrules the holding and the result in *Clark*. If that is so, however, it would be quite extraordinary to say that § 1367 did not also overrule *Zahn*, a case that was premised in substantial part on the holding in *Clark*.

. . .

Finally, it is suggested that our interpretation of § 1367(a) creates an anomaly regarding the exceptions listed in § 1367(b): It is not immediately obvious why Congress would withhold supplemental jurisdiction over plaintiffs joined as parties "needed for just adjudication" [Note: now called "a required party"] under Rule 19 but would allow supplemental jurisdiction over plaintiffs permissively joined under Rule 20. The omission of Rule 20 plaintiffs from the list of exceptions in § 1367(b) may have been an "unintentional drafting gap." If that is the case, it is up to Congress rather than the courts to fix it. The omission may seem odd, but it is not absurd. An alternative explanation for the different treatment of Rule 19 and Rule 20 is that Congress was concerned that extending supplemental jurisdiction to Rule 19 plaintiffs would allow circumvention of the complete diversity rule: A nondiverse plaintiff might be omitted intentionally from the original action, but joined later under Rule 19 as a necessary party. The contamination theory described above, if applicable, means this ruse would fail, but Congress may have wanted to make assurance double sure. More generally, Congress may have concluded that federal jurisdiction is only appropriate if the district court would have original jurisdiction over the claims of all those plaintiffs who are so essential to the action that they could be joined under Rule 19.

To the extent that the omission of Rule 20 plaintiffs from the list of § 1367(b) exceptions is anomalous, moreover, it is no more anomalous than the inclusion of Rule 19 plaintiffs in that list would be if the alternative view of § 1367(a) were to prevail. If the district court lacks original jurisdiction over a civil diversity action where any plaintiff's claims fail to comply with all the requirements of § 1332, there is no need for a special § 1367(b) exception for Rule 19 plaintiffs who do not meet these requirements. Though the omission of Rule 20 plaintiffs from § 1367(b) presents something of a puzzle on our view of the statute, the inclusion of Rule 19 plaintiffs in this section is at least as difficult to explain under the alternative view.

And so we circle back to the original question. When the well-pleaded complaint in district court includes multiple claims, all part of the same case or controversy, and some, but not all, of the claims are within the court's original jurisdiction, does the court have before it "any civil action of which the district courts have original jurisdiction"? It does. Under § 1367, the court has original jurisdiction over the civil action comprising the claims for which there is no jurisdictional defect. No other reading of § 1367 is plausible in light of the text and structure of the jurisdictional statute. Though the special nature and purpose of the diversity requirement mean that a single nondiverse party can contaminate every other claim in the lawsuit, the contamination does not occur with respect to jurisdictional defects that go only to the substantive importance of individual claims.

It follows from this conclusion that the threshold requirement of § 1367(a) is satisfied in cases, like those now before us, where some, but not all, of the plaintiffs in a diversity action allege a sufficient amount in controversy. We hold that § 1367 by its plain text overruled *Clark* and *Zahn* and authorized supplemental jurisdiction over all claims by diverse parties arising out of the same Article III case or controversy, subject only to enumerated exceptions not applicable in the cases now before us.

The proponents of the alternative view of § 1367 insist that the statute is at least ambiguous and that we should look to other interpretive tools, including the legislative history of § 1367, which supposedly demonstrate Congress did not intend § 1367 to overrule *Zahn*. We can reject this argument at the very outset simply because § 1367 is not ambiguous. For the reasons elaborated above, interpreting § 1367 to foreclose supplemental jurisdiction over plaintiffs in diversity cases who do not meet the minimum amount in controversy is inconsistent with the text, read in light of other statutory provisions and our established jurisprudence. Even if we were to stipulate, however, that the reading these proponents urge upon us is textually plausible, the legislative history cited to support it would not alter our view as to the best interpretation of § 1367.

. . .

As we have repeatedly held, the authoritative statement is the statutory text, not the legislative history or any other extrinsic material. Extrinsic materials have a role in statutory interpretation only to the extent they shed a reliable light on the enacting Legislature's understanding of otherwise ambiguous terms. Not all extrinsic materials are reliable sources of insight into legislative understandings, however, and legislative history in particular is vulnerable to two serious criticisms. First, legislative history is itself often murky, ambiguous, and contradictory. Judicial investigation of legislative history has a tendency to become, to borrow Judge Leventhal's memorable phrase, an exercise in "'looking over a crowd and picking out your friends.'" Second, judicial reliance on legislative materials like committee reports, which are not themselves subject to the requirements of Article I, may give unrepresentative committee members—or, worse yet, unelected staffers and lobbyists—both the power and the incentive to attempt strategic manipulations of legislative history to secure results they were unable to achieve through the statutory text. . . .

[The Court then concluded that the legislative history as a whole was not clear in indicating a congressional desire to maintain the *Zahn* and *Clark* rules.]

. . . [T]he worst fears of critics who argue legislative history will be used to circumvent the Article I process were realized in this case. The telltale evidence is the statement, by three law professors who participated in drafting § 1367, that § 1367 "on its face" permits "supplemental jurisdiction over claims of class members that do not satisfy section 1332's jurisdictional amount requirement, which would overrule [*Zahn*]. [There is] a disclaimer of intent to accomplish this result in the legislative history. . . . It would have been better had the statute dealt explicitly with this problem, and the legislative history was an attempt to correct the oversight." Rowe, Burbank, & Mengler, *Compounding or Creating Confusion About Supplemental Jurisdiction? A Reply to Professor Freer*, 40 Emory L.J. 943, 960, n.90 (1991). The professors were frank to concede that if one refuses to consider the legislative history, one has no choice but to "conclude that section 1367 has wiped *Zahn* off the books." *Ibid.* So there exists an acknowledgment . . . both that the plain text of § 1367 overruled *Zahn* and that language to the contrary in the House Report was a *post hoc* attempt to alter that result. One need not subscribe to the wholesale condemnation of legislative history to refuse to give any effect to such a deliberate effort to amend a statute through a committee report.

Shifting on leg history

In sum, even if we believed resort to legislative history were appropriate in these cases—a point we do not concede—we would not give significant weight to the House Report. . . .

The judgment of the Court of Appeals for the Eleventh Circuit [in *Allapattah*] is affirmed. The judgment of the Court of Appeals for the First Circuit [in *Ortiz*] is reversed, and the case is remanded for proceedings consistent with this opinion.

Justice Stevens, joined by Justice Breyer, dissenting.

. . .

The sweeping purpose that the Court's decision imputes to Congress bears no resemblance to the House Report's description of the statute. But this does not seem to trouble the Court, for its decision today treats statutory interpretation as a pedantic exercise, divorced from any serious attempt at ascertaining congressional intent. Of course, there are situations in which we do not honor Congress' apparent intent unless that intent is made "clear" in the text of a statute—in this way, we can be certain that Congress considered the issue and intended a disfavored outcome. . . . But that principle provides no basis for discounting the House Report, given that our cases have never recognized a presumption in *favor* of expansive diversity jurisdiction.

. . .

[Justice Ginsburg, in dissent, largely adopted the argument discussed by the majority as the "indivisibility theory."]

Notes and Questions

1. The majority opinion concludes that a federal court obtains subject matter jurisdiction differently in federal question and diversity cases. Specifically, federal question jurisdiction is invoked by a *claim*, to which the plaintiff may append other claims eligible for supplemental jurisdiction. In contrast, diversity jurisdiction is invoked by the *case*, so that the presence of any non-diverse opposing party prevents the federal court from taking jurisdiction over any part of the dispute. How does the Court justify the different treatment of these two bases of subject matter jurisdiction? How can any justification be reconciled with Federal Rule 21, which instructs federal district courts to dismiss non-diverse parties (rather than dismissing the entire suit)?

2. After *Allapattah*, supplemental jurisdiction is available to a plaintiff in a diversity case to overcome a lack of amount-in-controversy. It is not available, however, to a plaintiff in a diversity case to overcome a lack of complete diversity. Again, how does the Court justify this disparate treatment? Are you convinced? Do you think the Court was simply trying to engage in docket control? (Think of the onslaught of cases that could be brought in or removed to federal court if supplemental jurisdiction permitted plaintiffs to overcome the complete diversity rule.)

3. The Court in *Allapattah* employed a textual approach to statutory interpretation, and refused to look to legislative history when the statutory language was clear. But doesn't a textualist approach lead to a bizarre result in a case involving multiple defendants? Suppose the facts were exactly the same as in *Allapattah* except the plaintiffs asserted their claims against two defendants. As we see in Chapter 6, plaintiffs would join two or more defendants in a single case by using Rule 20. On its face, however, § 1367(b) prohibits the exercise of supplemental jurisdiction in a diversity case over claims "against persons made parties under Rule[] . . . 20." Literally, then, the statute appears to overrule *Zahn* and *Clark* if there is one defendant in the case (because then there is no claim against one joined under Rule 20), but not to overrule them if there are multiple defendants. *See* 4 MOORE'S FEDERAL PRACTICE § 20.07[3]. Does that make any sense? How could a court employing a textualist approach to statutory interpretation avoid such a result?

3. Ancillary Enforcement Jurisdiction

In contrast to supplemental jurisdiction, we now consider a concept that is still called "ancillary" jurisdiction, or "ancillary enforcement" jurisdiction. Unlike supplemental jurisdiction, which operates to get a claim into a case already in federal court, ancillary enforcement jurisdiction allows a federal court to entertain a separate *proceeding* that is closely related to a case over which the court had jurisdiction. Section 1367 does not apply to this branch of jurisdiction. *Garcia v. Teitler*, 443 F.3d 202, 207 (2d Cir. 2006). Rather, this doctrine is wholly judge-made.

This type of jurisdiction applies to proceedings that are so closely related to a case that was properly in federal court that it can be considered part of the same overall controversy. Jurisdiction over such ancillary or incidental proceedings is necessary "to enable a court to function successfully, that is, to manage its proceedings, vindicate its authority, and effectuate its decrees." *Kokkonen v. Guardian Life Ins. Co. of America*, 511 U.S. 375, 380 (1994). In 1934, the Court explained:

> That a federal court . . . has jurisdiction of a bill ancillary to an original case or proceeding in the same court, whether at law or in equity, to secure or preserve the fruits and advantages of a judgment or decree rendered therein, is well settled. And this, irrespective of whether the court would have jurisdiction if the proceeding were an original one. The proceeding being ancillary and dependent, the jurisdiction of the court follows that of the original cause, and may be maintained without regard to the citizenship of the parties or the amount involved.

Local Loan Co. v. Hunt, 292 U.S. 234, 239 (1934) (citations omitted).

For example, federal courts exercise ancillary jurisdiction over disputes about attorney's fees, even if that dispute does not assert a federal claim and would not invoke diversity of citizenship jurisdiction. In *Garcia v. Teitler*, 443 F.3d 202, 208–210 (2d Cir. 2006), a lawyer brought a civil action to recover fees for services allegedly rendered before he was discharged in a *criminal* case. Despite the lack of federal question or diversity jurisdiction, the court entertained the dispute.

Another common use of ancillary enforcement jurisdiction is for proceedings to enforce settlement agreements. Thus, if parties settle a case and dismiss the litigation, the court may be able to entertain a separate case for alleged breach of the agreement, even though there is nothing federal to the claim and the parties are not of diverse citizenship.

There are limits, however, to this doctrine. In *Kokkonen, supra*, 511 U.S. at 379–380 (1994), the parties settled their case and filed a stipulation of dismissal with prejudice under Federal Rule 41(a). The district judge signed the stipulation and the order of dismissal, but neither document referred to the settlement agreement itself. Later, after one party allegedly breached the terms of the settlement, the other requested that the district court enter an order enforcing the settlement agreement. The Supreme Court held that federal courts lacked ancillary enforcement jurisdiction. Because neither the stipulation nor the dismissal order incorporated the settlement itself, that agreement was not part of the record. Accordingly, the action to enforce it was "more than just a continuation or renewal of the dismissed suit, and hence requires its own basis for jurisdiction." 511 U.S. at 381.

D. Expansion of Jurisdiction Through Statutory Grants Based Upon Minimal Diversity

1. Background

The complete diversity rule is a significant restriction on federal subject matter jurisdiction under § 1332(a)(1). And as we just saw in *Allapattah*, even supplemental jurisdiction cannot overcome the complete diversity rule for claims asserted by a plaintiff. From time to time, Congress has attempted to expand federal subject matter jurisdiction by legislating around the complete diversity rule. We are primarily concerned with two modern efforts in this regard—the Multiparty, Multiforum Trial Jurisdiction Act of 2002 and the Class Action Fairness Act of 2005. Interestingly, however, the first effort to override the complete diversity rule by legislation dates back to 1917.

While reviewing these statutes, keep in mind that federal courts can be especially effective in promoting efficient joinder of all related parties. Why? Because federal courts (unlike state courts) can be permitted to exercise personal jurisdiction over parties based upon nationwide service of process. As you know from Chapter 1, under Federal Rule 4, federal courts generally will not exercise personal jurisdiction unless the state court in which it sits could do so. In other words, the federal court generally has no greater power to exercise personal jurisdiction than the state court of the state in which it sits. So if a potential defendant lacks minimum contacts with the forum, the court cannot join that person (unless she waives the personal jurisdiction defense).

But federal courts can be empowered to exercise personal jurisdiction based upon the potential party's contacts not with the state, but with the United States. This is usually done by enactment of a statute allowing the federal court to exercise nationwide service of process.

> ***Example #11.*** A case is pending in Maine. It would be desirable to join a potential defendant who is a citizen of Hawaii and who has never set foot off the island of Maui. Unless this person waives her personal jurisdiction defense, there is no way a state court in Maine can exercise personal jurisdiction over her, because she has no contacts with Maine. But a federal court in Maine may be permitted to exercise personal jurisdiction over her, because she does have minimum contacts with the United States. And federal courts, as a branch of the federal government, can be given power over people with such national contacts.

Congress can decide whether to grant the federal courts nationwide service of process. Of course, its doing so does not affect the requirements of subject matter jurisdiction. So even if personal jurisdiction were not a problem, the case could only invoke diversity of citizenship if the parties satisfied the complete diversity rule and the amount-in-controversy requirement. But these too can be changed by Congress. By combining legislation permitting nationwide service of process with legislation expanding federal subject matter jurisdiction (by overriding the complete diversity rule and amount-in-controversy requirements), Congress can create powerful magnets to focus complex litigation in the federal courts.

2. Interpleader

Interpleader is a specialized form of multiparty litigation, in which the focus of the dispute is ownership of money or tangible property. That property—called the stake or the *res*—is in the possession of the "stakeholder." The stakeholder is concerned that there are multiple claimants who argue that they, and not she, have the right to the property. Sometimes, the stakeholder will claim that she may be the rightful owner (the "interested stakeholder"), but sometimes she will not. In either event, she does not want to be sued about the ownership multiple times. Interpleader allows the stakeholder to join all the claimants in a single proceeding. It is a model of efficiency. It resolves all claims in a single case, thereby avoiding duplicative litigation. And because all interested persons are joined, they are bound by the judgment, and there is no risk of inconsistent results.

Many interpleader cases involve disputes over insurance proceeds.

> ***Example #12.*** After the insured under a life insurance policy dies, XYZ Insurance Co. holds $500,000 as the policy benefit. The decedent's spouse, son, daughter, and best friend all claim to be the sole beneficiary under the policy. XYZ does not want to be sued four times. Separate suits would be expensive and would open the possibility of multiple liability—one court might hold that one beneficiary gets the money and another might hold that another beneficiary gets the money. XYZ would thus be forced to pay the benefit twice. To avoid these problems, XYZ will use interpleader to force the four claimants into a single case. (In many instances, the insurance company will not claim an interest in the funds; it knows that someone is entitled to the money, and wants one court to determine who will get it.)

The efficacy of interpleader in federal court is limited in two significant ways. First, as a matter of personal jurisdiction, federal courts historically have taken the position that they can exercise personal jurisdiction over defendants only if the state court of the state in which they sit could do so. Interpleader is an *in personam* proceeding, so if a state court could not exercise personal jurisdiction over one of the claimants, the benefit of interpleader is largely lost. That one claimant will not be bound by the interpleader judgment and can sue the stakeholder in a separate proceeding. *New York Life Ins. Co. v. Dunlevy*, 241 U.S. 518, 522-523 (1916).

Second, restrictions on federal subject matter jurisdiction limit the availability of interpleader. Few, if any, interpleader claims will arise under federal law, so there will rarely be federal question jurisdiction. Instead, the interpleader case in federal court will almost always rely on diversity of citizenship jurisdiction. But if a single claimant is a citizen of the same state as the stakeholder, the case cannot invoke diversity of citizenship jurisdiction under § 1332(a)(1). Why? Because the complete diversity rule requires that the stakeholder be of diverse citizenship from every claimant.

Congress addressed both of these restrictions in the Federal Interpleader Act of 1917. The Act consists of three statutes in the Judicial Code: 28 U.S.C. §§ 1335, 1397, and 2361. Any case brought under this Act is called "statutory interpleader." Section 2361 extends personal jurisdiction to the constitutional maximum by permitting nationwide service of process on claimants. Accordingly, so long as the claimants have minimum contacts with the United States, there will be no personal jurisdiction problem. Section 1397 liberalizes venue for statutory interpleader cases.

Section 1335 is more interesting. It changes both statutory restrictions found on "regular" diversity jurisdiction in § 1332(a)(1). For one, the amount-in-controversy is a mere $500 or more, instead of the usual requirement that the amount exceed $75,000. For the other—and most significantly—it requires only "minimal" diversity. That is, under § 1335(a)(1), all that is required is "[t]wo or more adverse claimants, of diverse citizenship . . ." In other words, as long as one claimant is diverse from one other claimant, the statute is met. The claimants do not have to be of diverse citizenship from the stakeholder. In fact, the stakeholder's citizenship is irrelevant.

In the federal system today, there are two ways to invoke interpleader. One is under the Federal Interpleader Act, the key provisions of which we just discussed. This, as we said, is called "statutory interpleader." The other is to use Federal Rule 22, supported by "regular" diversity of citizenship jurisdiction under § 1332(a)(1) (which means the complete diversity rule applies—the stakeholder must be of diverse citizenship from every claimant). This is called "Rule interpleader."[9]

> ***Example #13.*** XYZ Insurance Co., a citizen of Connecticut, institutes interpleader under the Federal Interpleader Act. It joins four claimants—three of whom are citizens of New York and one of whom is a citizen of Connecticut. The case could not invoke diversity of citizenship jurisdiction under § 1332(a)(1), because the stakeholder is not diverse from every claimant. But subject matter jurisdiction is invoked under § 1335, because all that statute requires is that one claimant be diverse from one other claimant.

How can Congress simply run roughshod over the complete diversity rule? The answer lies in the fact that in *Strawbridge v. Curtiss*, the case that gave us the rule, the Court interpreted only the general diversity *statute* and not the *constitutional*

9. You may well ask why anyone would ever use Rule interpleader. After all, statutory interpleader offers the huge advantage of nationwide service of process. Rule interpleader does not. Thus, under Rule interpleader, the claimants must be subject to personal jurisdiction in the state in which the federal court sits. Given a choice, most stakeholders will use statutory interpleader. But consider this case: Stakeholder is a citizen of Arizona; all five claimants are citizens of California. Statutory interpleader is not available, because there is no claimant diverse from any other claimant. Rule interpleader might be the only way to get this case into federal court, assuming the amount in controversy exceeded $75,000.

grant of diversity of citizenship jurisdiction. Observers had long thought that to be true, based upon Chief Justice Marshall's rather cryptic language in that old case. In passing the Federal Interpleader Act, Congress obviously thought it to be true, basing jurisdiction on minimal diversity under the constitutional grant. It was not until 1967, however, that the Supreme Court confirmed that it was true. In *State Farm Fire & Casualty Co. v. Tashire*, 386 U.S. 523, 531 (1967), the Court upheld the grant of minimal diversity in § 1335. There, the Court said "Article III poses no obstacle to the legislative extension of federal jurisdiction, founded on diversity, so long as any two adverse parties are not co-citizens."

For generations, interpleader was the only example of the congressional extension of jurisdiction based upon minimal diversity. In the first decade of the new century, however, Congress used the power in an effort to empower federal courts to entertain complex litigation.

3. The Multiparty, Multiforum Trial Jurisdiction Act (MMTJA)

In 2002, Congress passed this Act, which is abbreviated MMTJA. Its provisions are spread throughout various sections of the Judicial Code. *See* 28 U.S.C. §§ 1369, 1697, 1785, 1391(g), and 1441(e). The key provisions are § 1369, which creates subject matter jurisdiction, and § 1441(e), which expands removal jurisdiction.

The basic idea behind this legislation is simple enough—in cases involving "a single accident" in which at least 75 people are killed, the federal courts will have jurisdiction based upon minimal diversity. The Act also permits nationwide service of process, and thereby avoids most personal jurisdiction problems, as was done with statutory interpleader.[10] Opening the federal courts to this extent would permit one court to handle the entire dispute. This would prevent overlapping and duplicative litigation in federal and state courts, avoid the resulting inefficiencies, and potentially inconsistent results, and permit a single judgment to bind all interested persons. The MMTJA can be seen as a powerful magnet to pull into one federal court all litigation relating to an accident in which at least 75 people were killed.

Lawyers must be adept at statutory interpretation. In dealing with statutes, there is no substitute for rolling up your sleeves and reading the provision with great care. Doing so with § 1369 will reveal some anomalies, as we will see in the Notes and Questions below. The statute provides:

> (a) In General.—The district courts shall have original jurisdiction of any civil action involving minimal diversity between adverse parties that arises from a single accident, where at least 75 natural persons have died in the accident at a discrete location, if—

10. Nationwide service of process is provided for in § 1697. Actually, MMTJA goes beyond statutory interpleader in one particular. Not only can parties be joined through nationwide service of process (as with statutory interpleader), but *witnesses* can be summoned to trial from anywhere in the country. 28 U.S.C. § 1785.

(1) a defendant resides in a State and a substantial part of the accident took place in another State or other location, regardless of whether that defendant is also a resident of the State where a substantial part of the accident took place;

(2) any two defendants reside in different States, regardless of whether such defendants are also residents of the same State or States; or

(3) substantial parts of the accident took place in different States.

(b) Limitation of Jurisdiction of District Courts.—The district court shall abstain from hearing any civil action described in subsection (a) in which—

(1) the substantial majority of all plaintiffs are citizens of a single State of which the primary defendants are also citizens; and

(2) the claims asserted will be governed primarily by the laws of that State.

(c) Special Rules and Definitions.—For purposes of this section—

(1) minimal diversity exists between adverse parties if any party is a citizen of State and any adverse party is a citizen of another State, a citizen or subject of a foreign state, or a foreign state as defined in section 1603(a) of this title;

(2) a corporation is deemed to be a citizen of any State, and a citizen or subject of any foreign state, in which it is incorporated or has its principal place of business, and is deemed to be a resident of any State in which it is incorporated or licensed to do business or is doing business;

(3) the term "injury" means—

(A) physical harm to a natural person; and

(B) physical damage to or destruction of tangible property, but only if physical harm described in subparagraph (A) exists;

(4) the term "accident" means a sudden accident, or a natural event culminating in an accident, that results in death incurred at a discrete location by at least 75 natural persons; and

(5) the term "State" includes the District of Columbia, the Commonwealth of Puerto Rico, and any territory or possession of the United States.

(d) Intervening Parties.—In any action in a district court which is or could have been brought, in whole or in part, under this section, any person with a claim arising from the accident described in subsection (a) shall be permitted to intervene as a party plaintiff in the action, even if that person could not have brought an action in a district court as an original matter.

(e) **Notification of Judicial Panel on Multidistrict Litigation.**— A district court in which an action under this section is pending shall promptly notify the judicial panel on multidistrict litigation of the pendency of the action.

Notes and Questions

Read § 1369 with care, and address the following questions.

1. In cases invoking the MMTJA, what is the amount-in-controversy requirement?

2. Note that jurisdiction is based upon "minimal diversity." Where in § 1369 is that defined? How is that defined?

3. Does the statute require the existence of a class action, or does it apply to individually-asserted claims?

4. The Act expressly applies to cases involving an accident in which at least 75 people are killed. Does it require that the claims asserted be for wrongful death?

In 2003, a fire broke out at a Rhode Island night club. A band was playing at the night club. Its pyrotechnics display ignited the ceiling tiles at the club, leading to a devastating conflagration. One hundred people were killed. Over two hundred others suffered personal injuries.

> ***Example #14.*** Suppose your client attended the night club and suffered personal injuries (but survived). She is a citizen of Rhode Island. Some of the defendants—such as the night club owner and operator and the city that approved the fire safety equipment—are citizens of Rhode Island. Other defendants—such as the band members and the manufacturers of the pyrotechnics and of the ceiling tiles—are not. Can your client sue in federal court under the MMTJA?

> ***Example #15.*** Suppose instead that your client did not attend the night club, but lent her car to someone who did. That person escaped injury in the fire. But your client's car was damaged by the fire. The damage is $150. Can your client sue in federal court under § 1369? If the answer is yes, why should federal courts be open for the assertion of such minor property claims?

5. Section 1369(a) creates jurisdiction for claims arising from an "accident." What is an accident? Notice that Congress defines "accident" in § 1369(c)(4) as "a sudden accident, or a natural event culminating in an accident, that results in death incurred at a discrete location by at least 75 natural persons." Black's Law Dictionary defines accident as "an unintended, unforeseen injurious occurrence."

Question: does "accident" include a natural event, such as an earthquake?

Question: would "accident" include a terrorist bombing?

6. As noted, § 1369(c)(4) defines "accident" in part as including "a sudden accident." What is a "sudden" accident?

> ***Example #16.*** Professional golfer Payne Stewart died when the private jet in which he was a passenger depressurized at high altitude. All aboard the plane died from hypoxia. More than an hour later, the plane ran out of fuel and plummeted to the ground. If such depressurization happened on an airliner with at least 75 persons aboard, would it constitute "a sudden accident"?

> ***Example #17.*** What if a small plane, such as Stewart's, depressurized at altitude, killing ten people, and the plane crashed an hour later, killing 65 persons on the ground. Would that constitute "a sudden accident"?

7. Section 1369(a) requires that something occur at a "discrete location." What is required—must the *accident* occur at a "discrete location" or must the 75 or more *people die* at a "discrete location"?

> ***Example #18.*** Suppose an explosion kills 50 people and injures 25 others in a single building. The injured are evacuated to a hospital 20 miles away. They later die in the hospital. Is the "discrete location" requirement satisfied?

8. Section 1369(c)(3) defines "injury." But the word "injury" does not appear anywhere else in the MMTJA.

9. Section 1369(c)(2) defines the *citizenship* of a corporation. Oddly, it is different from the definition of corporation Congress provided under the general diversity of citizenship statute at § 1332(c)(1). How does it differ? What possible reason would there be for this inconsistency?

10. Section 1369(c)(2) also defines the *residence* of a corporation. The definition is different from the definition of corporate residence in the general venue statute, § 1391(c)(2). How is it different? Nothing in the legislative history of the MMTJA suggests why these definitions should differ.

11. Under § 1369(a), the party invoking jurisdiction must show one of three additional factors, found at § 1369(a)(1), (2), and (3). The legislative history is sparse, but these factors apparently are intended to ensure that § 1369 applies only to cases in which multiple litigation in multiple states is likely. Only in such cases would the full reach of federal subject matter jurisdiction and personal jurisdiction be required.

The first possibility (in § 1369(a)(1)) is that any defendant "resides" in a state other than where the accident occurred. The presence of the word "resides" is surprising. Nowhere else in the Judicial Code is residence relevant to subject matter jurisdiction. It is relevant only to venue. Yet here Congress imports it to subject matter jurisdiction.

This requirement ought to be easy in most cases, especially given the breadth of the term "resides." Again, corporate residence is found at § 1369(c)(2).

The second possibility (in § 1369(a)(2)) also seems quite easy to meet—that any two defendants reside in different states. Because corporate defendants might have several residences, this is not much of a barrier.

The third possibility (in § 1369(a)(3)) is that "substantial parts of the accident took place in different states." How can this ever be met, however, if the accident that is the focus of the case must be "a sudden accident" at "a discrete location"?

12. Section 1369(b) is entitled "limitation of jurisdiction." But the provision itself requires that the district court "abstain" in certain circumstances. Abstention, however, is different from a limitation on jurisdiction. First, if the matter is one of subject matter jurisdiction, the party invoking jurisdiction has the burden of establishing that this subsection would not apply. If it's a doctrine of abstention, however, the party opposing jurisdiction would have the burden of demonstrating that the conditions are established. Second, if it's jurisdictional, the court has a duty to assess it at any time during the proceedings, and to dismiss whenever it is determined that there is no subject matter jurisdiction. On the other hand, abstention is typically addressed at the outset and there is no ongoing duty to assess it sua sponte. Third, jurisdictional issues are reviewed on appeal de novo, while a trial court's failure to abstain is generally reviewed by an abuse-of-discretion standard. We will study the classic abstention doctrines in Chapter 3(C)(2).

Consider the language concerning when a court should "abstain," set forth in § 1369(b)(1) and (2). The court abstains if the "substantial majority of all plaintiffs" are citizens of the same state as the "primary defendants," and if the claims are to be governed primarily by law of that same state.

> Does "substantial majority of all plaintiffs" refer to plaintiffs in the present case? Or potential plaintiffs? Or victims? How could Congress have expressed the idea more clearly?
>
> • In the Rhode Island night club fire case, discussed in Note 4 above, suppose the first case filed is by the representative of a Rhode Islander killed in the fire. He files in federal court under § 1369 and sues all the potential defendants—owners of the club, band members, the city, the manufacturer of ceiling tiles, the manufacturer of the pyrotechnics. Does that mean that the "substantial majority of all plaintiffs" are citizens of Rhode Island? So far, the sole plaintiff is a citizen of Rhode Island.
>
> Or, in contrast, is the court supposed to revisit the issue depending upon how many plaintiffs ultimately sue? That seems unwieldy, because the question of whether the case is properly in federal court would be a moving target. What should Congress have done to guide the courts here?
>
> Moreover, in determining the citizenship of a "substantial majority" of plaintiffs, does the court look at the number of plaintiffs or at the value of their claims? Suppose 74 plaintiffs claimed $1 each and the 75th plaintiff

sued for $1,000,000. Do the 74 with minimal claims constitute a "substantial majority"?

And what does "primary defendants" mean? Those with the deepest pockets? Those ultimately deemed most culpable? Those facing direct liability rather than derivative or vicarious liability through indemnity or contribution? When Congress uses unclear language, it creates more work for judges.

We have not completed our wrestling with MMTJA. We turn now to two provisions that drive home just how broad this Act is and how readily non-parties and defendants can override the plaintiff's initial choice of forum.

First, § 1369(d) allows intervention into a pending federal case brought under the MMTJA or that *could have been brought* under the Act, so long as the claim asserted arises from the accident. Apparently this was intended to create a statutory right to intervene without having to satisfy the requirements of the intervention provision of Federal Rule 24(a)(2). It also overrides the supplemental jurisdiction statute, which would not permit supplemental jurisdiction over a claim by a nondiverse intervenor plaintiff. So a person with any claim arising from the accident can intervene in federal court, regardless of citizenship and regardless of amount in controversy.

Second, § 1441(e) amends the removal statutes in interesting ways.

First, it abolishes the rule of unanimity. As we saw in the discussion of removal jurisdiction in § B.3, the general rule is that all defendants must agree to remove a case from state to federal court. Under the MMTJA, that is not true. Any defendant can remove the case from state to federal court. What part of the statute makes this clear?

Second, it abolishes the "in-state defendant" limitation. As we saw in § B.3, a diversity of citizenship case cannot be removed if any defendant is a citizen of the forum. That is not true under the MMTJA.

Third, the last sentence of § 1441(e)(1) abolishes the one-year limit on removal of diversity cases (which we saw in § B.3). It permits removal within 30 days of a defendant's becoming a party to a federal case under § 1369, just so it is before trial in the state court case.

Fourth, and most surprisingly, § 1441(e)(1)(B) allows removal of *cases in which there is not even minimal diversity.* This provision has come to be known as creating "piggy-back jurisdiction."

The following case applies § 1441(e). Before reading it, read the statute. In passing, note that § 1441(e)(2) makes a cross-reference to § 1407(j). Interestingly, there has never been a statute enumerated as § 1407(j).

Case v. ANPAC Louisiana Insurance Co. and In re Katrina Canal Breaches Consolidated Litigation

United States District Court for the Eastern District of Louisiana
466 F. Supp. 2d 781 (2006)

DUVAL, J.

Before the Court are two motions to remand in two separate actions. The first Motion to Remand is brought by Plaintiffs Gordon and Tanjha Case ("Cases") in their lawsuit against ANPAC Louisiana Insurance Company ("ANPAC"). Plaintiffs oppose removal, claiming that there is no subject matter jurisdiction over the proceeding under 28 U.S.C. §§ 1441(e)(1)(B) and 1369 ("Multiparty, Multiforum, Trial Jurisdiction Act" or "MMTJA").

The second Motion to Remand was filed by Plaintiffs Shirley and Robert Chamberlain ("Chamberlains") in their action against Louisiana Farm Bureau Mutual Insurance Company ("Farm Bureau"). Defendant also alleges jurisdiction and removal under the MMTJA. After reviewing the pleadings, memoranda, and relevant law as well as hearing oral argument, the Court finds that these actions were not properly removed under 28 U.S.C. § 1441(e)(1)(B), and thus, the Court remands these proceedings [to state court] for the reasons assigned below.

I. BACKGROUND

A. The Cases

The Cases instituted the state court action on August 22, 2006, against ANPAC Louisiana Insurance Company ("ANPAC") in Civil District Court, Parish of Orleans, Louisiana, seeking a declaratory judgment as well as damages in connection with destruction of their home during and in the aftermath of Hurricane Katrina. The parties are both [citizens of] Louisiana. . . .

Defendants, on the other hand, attribute the loss to the flooding that came as a result of the levee breaches.[11] This risk is allegedly not covered under the policy by virtue of the flood exclusion.

B. The Chamberlains

The Chamberlains also brought this action in Civil District Court in Orleans Parish, Louisiana, against their insurer Farm Bureau. The parties are both [citizens of] Louisiana. Plaintiffs purchased a homeowner's policy from Farm Bureau for, *inter alia*, hurricane wind coverage, and they allege that Farm Bureau failed to pay damages caused by wind. Plaintiffs also allege that their damages resulted from

11. [Court's footnote #5] The object of the *Chamberlain* litigation is the property located at 209 W. Brooks Street, New Orleans, Louisiana 70124. Defendants contend that the property flooded because of "breaks in the levees and floodwalls in St. Bernard, including, but not limited to, the failure of the levee and floodwall in the 17th Street and/or London Avenue Canals which caused flooding throughout New Orleans."

a covered peril under the State Farm policy, while Farm Bureau claims that such damages were caused by hurricane driven water, an excluded peril.

. . .

The Court analyzes these two cases together because both sets of Plaintiffs have allegations asserting coverage in their homeowner's policy for flood damage caused by levee breaches, and both Defendant insurers are attempting to remove these actions to federal court under the federal supplemental or piggy-back jurisdiction provided in Section 1441(e)(1)(B). In particular, both ANPAC and Farm Bureau assert jurisdiction under Section 1441(e)(1)(B) averring that they are both defendants in *Abadie et al. v. Aegis Security Ins. Co., et al.*, No. 06-5164 (E.D. La. filed Aug. 28, 2006), and the instant actions arise out of the same "accident" as in *Abadie*.

. . .

II. LEGAL STANDARD

A. Removal

"[A]ny civil action brought in a State court of which the district courts of the United States have original jurisdiction, may be removed by the defendant or the defendants, to the district court of the United States for the district and division embracing the place where such action is pending." 28 U.S.C. § 1441(a). The burden of proof for establishing federal jurisdiction is placed on the party seeking removal. . . .

B. Piggy-Back Jurisdiction under 28 U.S.C. § 1441(e)(1)(B)

Defendants contend that the Court has subject matter jurisdiction over this action pursuant to 28 U.S.C. § 1441(e)(1)(B). The statute provides:

> (e)(1) Notwithstanding the provisions of subsection (b) of this section, a defendant in a civil action in a State court may remove the action to the district court of the United States for the district and division embracing the place where the action is pending if—
>
> (A) the action could have been brought in a United States district court under section 1369 of this title; or
>
> (B) the defendant is a party to an action which is or could have been brought, in whole or in part, under section 1369 in a United States district court and arises from the same accident as the action in State court, even if the action to be removed could not have been brought in a district court as an original matter.

Under Section 1441(e)(1)(B), an action is removable if (1) the defendant in the action to be removed is also party to an action pending in a district court that could have been brought under 28 U.S.C. § 1369, and (2) the action to be removed arises from the same accident as that which is pending in the district court. Section 1441(e)(1) expands the scope of subject matter jurisdiction conferred by section 1369 . . .

. . . Section 1369 and its corresponding removal statute are meant to foster judicial economy in the resolution of actions involving certain mass disasters by circumventing conventional limitations on federal subject matter jurisdiction. Specifically, the drafters of the MMTJA sought to bypass the complete diversity rule and amount in controversy requirement of 28 U.S.C. § 1332 in order to prevent duplicative litigation in State and federal court, which potentially could lead to inconsistent results.... On the other hand, sidestepping traditional federal jurisdiction requirements, such as the complete diversity rule, and subsequently consolidating mass disaster litigation can potentially "impose a substantial burden on already overwhelmed courts."

With this backdrop in mind, the Fifth Circuit has indicated that section 1441(e)(1)(B) was intended to apply broadly in the context of mass disaster litigation....

While a broad interpretation of section 1441(e)(1)(B) is warranted, the statute must be read in tandem with section 1369, which has certain specific jurisdictional elements. In order to establish section 1441(e)(1)(B) piggy-back jurisdiction, the removing party must show that there is a pending action which is or could have been brought, in whole or in part, under section 1369. 28 U.S.C. § 1441(e)(1)(B).

The ... "in whole or in part" language in section 1441(e)(1)(B) may further broaden the scope of application of section 1369. Although section 1369 requires an action to arise from a "single accident, where at least 75 natural persons have died," section 1441(e)(1)(B) may slightly modify the test for establishing section 1369 jurisdiction for removal purposes, in that, only a *part* of the action pending need arise from a "single accident, where at least 75 natural persons have died." 28 U.S.C. §§ 1369 & 1441(e)(1)(B). In this way, though an action pending in federal district court to which the removing party is a defendant seeks recovery for damages caused by multiple accidents (e.g. multiple levee breaches), the removing party may need only establish that part of the pending action arises from a single accident for the purposes of removal, and the action to be removed arises from the same accident.

...

... For the purposes of this analysis, the Court will assume that the underlying pending action can contain claims arising from multiple accidents, and that the removing party need only show that the action to be removed arises from a "single accident," out of which arises part of the pending action.

...

III. ANALYSIS

The ultimate question presented to the Court is whether the actions brought by the Cases and Chamberlains can be removed under section 1441(e)(1)(B).... [T]he Court must decide 1) whether *Abadie* could have been brought under the MMTJA; and 2) whether the *Case* and *Chamberlain* actions arise out of the same "accident" as in *Abadie*.

A. Original Jurisdiction under 28 U.S.C. § 1369

i. The MMTJA

[The court here sets out § 1369.] . . .

Thus, . . . to establish original jurisdiction over *Abadie* under section 1369, the party asserting jurisdiction must show that: 1) there is minimal diversity between adverse parties in *Abadie;* 2) the action in *Abadie*, in whole or in part, arises from a single accident, where at least 75 natural persons have died in the accident at a discrete location; 3) a defendant in *Abadie* resides in a State and a substantial part of the accident took place in another State, or any two defendants in *Abadie* reside in different States, or substantial part of the accident took place in different states; and 4) the Court is not required to abstain from exercising its section 1369(a) jurisdiction under section 1369(b).

Because it is alleged that the plaintiffs in *Abadie* are "Citizens of a State that is different from the State where at least one of the Defendants is incorporated or doing business," the minimal diversity requirement is satisfied. Also, since a substantial part of the accident took place in Louisiana and several *Abadie* defendants are "foreign insurers domiciled in the various states," the third element is also satisfied.

Because the fourth prong only need be addressed if the second prong is satisfied, the Court must first consider whether the *Abadie* action arises, in whole or in part, from "a single accident, where at least 75 natural persons have died in the accident at a discrete location." 28 U.S.C. §§ 1369 & 1441(e)(1)(B).

ii. *The* Abadie *action*

. . .

[T]he relevant allegations made in the *Abadie* action can be summarized as claims against homeowner's insurers for coverage under the respective insurance policies for property damage to the plaintiffs' homes caused by flooding from the levee breaches. Defendants maintain that *Abadie* could have been brought originally under 28 U.S.C. § 1369, despite the fact that the *Abadie* Complaint contains no such allegation. Of course, the exercise of jurisdiction is permitted if Defendants can establish that *Abadie* could have been brought under section 1369. 28 U.S.C. § 1441(e)(1)(B).

Although many courts in this District have been presented with cases involving the MMTJA and its complementary piggy-back removal statute, no court has comprehensively confronted these statutes as [they relate] to the levee breaches. Overwhelmingly, the courts of this district have held that Hurricane Katrina itself was not an accident under section 1369. . . .

To the best of its knowledge, the Court knows of no other cases discussing whether a levee breach constitutes an "accident" under the MMTJA except that of *Carroll v. Lafayette Ins. Co.*, 2006 U.S. Dist. LEXIS 69334 (Sept. 14, 2006). In *Carroll*, Judge Lemelle held that there was no subject matter jurisdiction under sections 1369 or 1441(e)(1)(B) because plaintiffs' action "[arose] out of a series of events culminating in multiple accidents" as opposed to a single accident as is required by the MMTJA. Carroll, 2006 U.S. Dist. LEXIS 69334 at *3. Moreover, Judge Lemelle held that the "accident" did not occur at a "discrete location" because there were "multiple breaches at several locations not discrete."[12] *Id.* The facts plead in the instant cases require this Court to engage in a robust analysis of the MMTJA in order to clarify the role of the MMTJA in some of the litigation that has spawned from Hurricane Katrina.

iii. Interpretation of Federal Statutes

When interpreting a statute, courts must begin with an analysis of the statute's actual words because when "the language of the federal statute is plain and unambiguous, it begins and ends [the court's] inquiry." United States v. Osborne, 262 F.3d 486, 490 (5th Cir. 2001). The court may only refer to legislative history for congressional intent when the statute is unclear or ambiguous. . . .

iv. Single Accident

Section 1369(a) permits federal courts to exercise subject matter jurisdiction if it is established, *inter alia*, that the action "arises from a single accident . . ." 28 U.S.C. § 1369(a). The statute supplies its own definition of an accident as "a sudden accident, or a natural event culminating in an accident, that results in death incurred at a discrete location by at least 75 natural persons." 28 U.S.C. § 1369(c)(4). Needless to say, Hurricane Katrina was a natural event that resulted in massive damage to the metro New Orleans area as well as to much of the Gulf of Mexico region. Because the hurricane set in motion the events leading up to the devastation, however, does not make it appropriate to label the damage as a "single accident," as such would be a gross understatement.

The Court, thus, must look to the congressional intent to give content to the term "single accident." Sections 1369 and 1441(e)(1)(B) were enacted in 2002 with no debate. Prior [proposed] versions of the statute, however, were discussed on the House floor with remarks particularly focusing on the term accident, as is illustrated by the following comment:

> As defined in this section, "accident" must be sudden in nature, may include natural events culminating in accidents, and must occur in a discrete location. Thus, the bill is intended to apply to those events in which 25 or more persons are killed or injured together in a single, catastrophic accident, such as a hotel fire, a railroad, airplane or bus accident, or a bridge collapse. The reference to natural events is inserted to ensure that an accident

12. [Court's footnote #17] Another question that emanates from the gloss of the MMTJA relates to the degree of connexity between the "accident," the "discrete location," and the seventy-five deaths. The question is whether the "accident" must occur at a "discrete location" or whether the seventy-five deaths must occur at a "discrete location" or both. Judge Lemelle's conclusion that the "accident" must occur at a "discrete location" is reasonable, but the Court suggests that under the facts plead in these cases challenges to such an interpretation are not so easily dismissed.

> such as a bridge collapse qualifies as an accident within the scope of the bill, notwithstanding that the collapse was caused by long-term flooding, foundation shifting or other natural events that precipitate a sudden accident, but arguably are not "sudden" in and of themselves.
>
> Given this definition of accident, the bill does not apply to ordinary product liability actions, including failure to warn actions and design defect cases involving multiple, identically manufactured units, because the injuries in such actions do not usually occur in a large number together in a single accident. Therefore, the term "accident" does not include the act of or a decision relating to designing, manufacturing, labeling, packaging, testing or filing reports with Federal agencies with respect to any product. Of course, defectively manufactured, designed or labeled products may cause an "accident" within the meaning of the bill. For example, a defectively designed sprinkler system may fail to put out a hotel fire. To that limited extent the bill would reach suits raising product liability issues. The Committee has, however, strived to limit the scope of this bill so that it could be interpreted to apply to ordinary product liability actions, and believes that language of the bill is now sufficiently clear in that regard.

H.R. Rep. No. 102-373 (1991). There was concerted effort to limit the scope of the term "accident" so that the statute would apply to certain kinds of mass disasters, excluding, in particular, its application to products liability actions and toxic torts. . . .

The question, thus, is whether *Abadie* action arose out of, at least in part, a "single accident" for the purpose of establishing piggy-back jurisdiction. Here, it is certainly arguable that one levee breach is a single accident under the MMTJA. The natural event that culminated in the levee breaches was, of course, Hurricane Katrina, though the hurricane itself was not an accident. *Abadie* involves multiple levee breaches, all of which individually, may constitute "single accidents."

For the purposes of this analysis the Court will assume that section 1369 jurisdiction is available for the *Abadie* action despite it involving multiple accidents, and that a "single accident," that gives rise to part of the entire action may be piggybacked upon. Generally, section 1441(e)(1)(B) permits removal if the action to be removed arises out of the same accident as that pending in federal court for which there exists section 1369 jurisdiction. 28 U.S.C. § 1441(e)(1)(B). This requires the removing party to identify the "single accident," if such is not facially apparent, that gives rise both to the pending action and the action to be removed. If multiple accidents exists, as in *Abadie*, a removing party must 1) identify a "single accident;" 2) show that section 1369 jurisdiction exists with respect to the claims arising out of that "single accident;" and 3) show that the action to be removed also arises out of that identified "single accident."

Both Plaintiffs in the matters before the Court allege damages out of multiple levee breaches, which do not constitute a "single accident" under the MMTJA. The *Case* Defendant ANPAC argues that the breaches that occurred at various points of the New Orleans levee system constituted a single accident because the levees make up one system. The Chamberlains are more precise, alleging that their damages were caused by the single accident that was the breaches in the 17th Street Canal and/or the London Avenue Canal. Despite allegations of varying specificity, it is clear that both proceedings involve multiple levee breaches.

Interpreting the term "single accident" so broadly as providing for multiple levee breaches does not coincide with the purposes of the MMTJA. That is, section 1369 was meant to facilitate the consolidation of multiple actions that present identical issues of liability and causation of damages into one convenient forum. . . .

While the breaches occurred at several points along one levee system as the *Case* Defendant suggests, the causes for each of the failures involve separate and distinct factual inquiries, and the causation of individual damages presents unique questions of fact as to each claimant.

For example, the breach at the 17th Street Canal could have been a result of poor maintenance, while a breach elsewhere could have been because of poor construction or design. Further still, there might be a finding that the flooding overtopped the levees at a particular point and there was no negligence involved. Consolidation of cases where there exist such distinct issues of liability and causation of damages among the plaintiffs would not prevent duplicative litigation in State and federal court or otherwise foster judicial economy. In this way, the questions of fact presented by the multiple levee breaches are not identical, which justifies narrowly construing section 1369 so as to preclude labeling multiple levee breaches as a "single accident" for purposes of the MMTJA.

Because the *Case* Plaintiffs and *Chamberlain* Plaintiffs respectively bring actions arising out of multiple levee breaches, this precludes the possibility that these actions arose out of the same "single accident" that gives rise to part of the action in *Abadie.* There is no language in section 1441(e)(1)(B), which would suggest that only part of the action to be removed need arise from the "single accident" that triggers jurisdiction under the MMTJA. Rather, the requirement is that the removing party must show that the action pending in federal court "arises from the same accident as the action in State court." 28 U.S.C. § 1441(e)(1)(B). That is, the "single accident" must make up at least a part of the *Abadie* action, and the action to be removed must arise out of that same "single accident." Therefore, assuming that the *Abadie* action arises, in part, out of a "single accident," the Court finds here that the *Case* and *Chamberlain* actions do not respectively arise out of the same "single accident" that makes up a part of the *Abadie* action, which precludes the Court's exercise of removal subject matter jurisdiction under section 1441(e)(1)(B).

v. 75 Deaths at a Discrete Location

After considering whether the *Abadie* action arises, in whole or in part, out of a single accident, the Court must then determine whether the accident was such, "where at least 75 natural persons have died in the accident at a discrete location." 28 U.S.C. § 1369(a). This question requires the Court to engage in jurisdictional factfinding; however, the statute does not provide the legal standard for the burden of proof placed upon the removing party. The Court finds that the appropriate standard is that which is typically used in establishing facts when there has been no evidentiary hearing on the jurisdictional matter, to wit—the burdened party must make a *prima facie* showing that the facts exist making the exercise of subject matter jurisdiction appropriate. . . .

Applying this burden of proof . . . to the instant motion to remand, the Court finds that both ANPAC and Farm Bureau have not made a *prima facie* showing that seventy-five people have died at a discrete location due to a "single accident."

The term "discrete location" has no definition within the statute, and in fact, the statutory language is arguably ambiguous. In section 1369(a), the phrase "at a discrete location" grammatically modifies the word "accident" and/or the phrase "where at least 75 natural persons have died." 28 U.S.C. § 1369(a). This implies either that the accident must occur at a discrete location, or that the deaths must occur at a discrete location, or that both the accident and the deaths must occur at a discrete location. Whereas, in section 1369(c)(4), which defines the term accident, the phrase "incurred at a discrete location" clearly is intended to reference the deaths. In this way, "[w]hile the accident may not need to be localized, the plain language of the statute requires that the deaths resulting from the accident must occur at a discrete location." . . .

As with many other aspects of the MMTJA, there is a lack of jurisprudence that gives content to the term "discrete location. . . .

It is undisputed that more than seventy-five people died during and in the aftermath of Hurricane Katrina, but the Court cannot determine location or the cause of the deaths without what would be practically equivalent to a trial. Indeed, there may have been seventy-five deaths at a discrete location; however, the Court would have to determine that a single accident caused these deaths, and at a minimum, that the deaths occurred at a discrete location. Defendants can only speculate as to where the deaths occurred or what caused the deaths. Speculation is not sufficient in making a *prima facie* showing of section 1369 jurisdiction. Thus, the Court finds that Defendants have not made a *prima facie* showing that at least seventy-five deaths occurred at a discrete location in a single accident.

In order for a levee breach to be the kind of accident intended to fall within the scope of section 1369, there would have to be at least seventy-five deaths that occur at a discrete location due to the breach. The term discrete location would be bounded not physically, but by whether there exist common questions of fact among claimants as to liability and/or causation of damages. This limitation of what constitutes a "discrete location" would preclude the exercise of section 1369 jurisdiction over actions arising out of "single accidents" that have widespread damages, and deaths that occur in a number of places and for different reasons, though the accident might precipitate such deaths.

Moreover, for purposes of removal, the action to be removed would also need to arise out of the accident that caused the deaths at a discrete location, and not merely out of the "single accident" that causes diffuse damages, even if at least seventy-five people die. For example, the action to be removed would have to arise out of a levee breach that caused seventy-five deaths at a hospital in order to be removable under section 1441(e)(1)(B).

This proposition is further buttressed by the fact that section 1369(c)(4) defines an "accident" as "a natural event culminating in an accident, that results in *death incurred at a discrete location by at least 75 natural persons.*" 28 U.S.C. § 1369(c)(4) (emphasis added). The emphasized language is included as part of the definition of the term "accident," and thus, could be transplanted to section 1441(e)(1)(B) as well.[13] In other words, the statute contemplates that an "accident" is of a specific kind, and must result in seventy-five deaths at a discrete location in order to be an "accident" for the purposes of the MMTJA. A contrary holding would not serve judicial economy and would overburden a court with an array of actions presenting a multitude of wholly unrelated questions of fact.

. . .

The Court admits that the plain language of the statute is problematic, in that, it is not as narrowly crafted as intended by Congress. Fortunately, the Court need not resolve this dilemma with respect to the breadth of the word accident because it is clear that the Defendants have not met their burden of proof that seventy-five people have died at a discrete location due to a single accident. Even if they had, however, the Court finds that a levee breach causing widespread damage, including death, is not the kind of accident contemplated by the drafters of the MMTJA because the deaths do not occur at a discrete location.

The statute was clearly meant to foster judicial economy and provide jurisdiction in accidents such as an airplane crash, bridge collapses, hotel fires, and train wrecks, where fault is presumed just as in a *res ipsa loquitur* tort action. However, when there are multiple levee breaches, i.e. multiple accidents, where liability is not presumed and the question of causation of damages is not identical among claimants, judicial economy would not be served through consolidation of these actions. Accordingly,

13. [Court's footnote #25] The language "at a discrete location by at least 75 natural persons" is represented in section 1369(a), which is the substantive portion of the statute and in the definition of the word accident. At first glance, this might seem redundant; however, the Court finds that its inclusion is not mere surplusage and the language was meant to limit the word "accident" itself, even as used in section 1441(e)(1)(B).

IT IS ORDERED that Plaintiffs' Motion to Remand in Civil Action No. 06-7390 is hereby GRANTED and the proceeding is REMANDED to state court.

IT IS FURTHER ORDERED that Plaintiffs' Motion to Remand in Civil Action No. 05-4182 (pertaining to No. 06-5370) is hereby GRANTED and the proceeding is REMANDED to state court.

Notes and Questions

1. Section 1441(e) permits removal to a degree we have not seen before. It allows a party in a federal action brought under the Act (or that could have been brought under the Act) who is also a defendant in a state court case involving the same "accident" to remove the state case *even if there is no diversity.*

Let's consider the person whose car was damaged at the site of the Rhode Island night club fire. He is a Rhode Island citizen and asserts a claim against the owner of the club, also a Rhode Island citizen. The claim is for $150. This case could not be brought under § 1369 because there is not even minimal diversity. *But it can be removed* because the night club owner is also a defendant in a federal proceeding involving the same accident. So this $150 dispute between citizens of the same state can be dragged into federal court at the behest of a defendant who is already a party in a federal proceeding related to the accident.

2. Notice that § 1441(e) extends federal subject matter jurisdiction far beyond the grant of supplemental jurisdiction in § 1367(a). Supplemental jurisdiction allows a federal court to hear nondiverse claims *joined in a case that does invoke federal subject matter jurisdiction.* Here, Congress purports to vest federal jurisdiction for an entirely separate case, not merely a claim.

Moreover, § 1441(e) goes farther than MMTJA and the Federal Interpleader Act. Those statutes at least require minimal diversity between two adverse parties. Section 1441(e) purports to grant jurisdiction over disputes, such as those discussed in *Case,* in which all parties are co-citizens.

3. Congress envisioned that cases properly removed to federal court under MMTJA would be remanded after the federal court decided the question of liability. Section 1441(e)(2) provides that the federal court is to remand to state court for determination of damages. The section gives the federal court discretion to keep the case in the interest of convenience and interest of justice. But the presumption is that the case will be bifurcated, with the federal court determining liability and remanding to state court for determination of damages. In such a case, the federal court determines liability and certifies its intention to remand to state court for the damages determination. The losing party on the liability determination has a right to appeal that determination in the federal system. But the decision to remand itself is not subject to appellate review.

4. Congress did not try to justify the expansion of jurisdiction on the historic justification for diversity jurisdiction: to protect out-of-state defendants from fear of bias in state court. Rather, the congressional purpose was to foster the efficient resolution of complex litigation by concentrating it in federal court. Is this use of the diversity-jurisdiction power constitutional? Professor Floyd concludes that it is not. *See* C. Douglas Floyd, *The Limits of Minimal Diversity*, 55 Hastings L.J. 613 (2004).

Is this provision appropriately sensitive to the interests of state court systems? Does it make state courts mere factotums of the federal courts?

4. Class Action Fairness Act (CAFA)

a. Background

The final example of Congress's expansion of subject matter jurisdiction based upon minimal diversity is its most controversial: the Class Action Fairness Act, known as CAFA. Congress passed CAFA in 2005 in response to intense lobbying by business interests. Speaking very generally, there was then a widespread perception that it is more difficult for plaintiffs to pursue class actions in federal than in state court. Although many states have adopted Federal Rule 23 as their model for class actions, some plaintiffs prefer to bring class suits in state court. Why?

First, in various cases we will see in Chapter 6, the Supreme Court has been particularly strict in interpreting Rule 23. *See, e.g.*, *Wal-Mart Stores, Inc. v. Dukes*, 564 U.S. 338, 359–360 (2011) (rejecting nationwide class action for sex discrimination claims); *Ortiz v. Fibreboard Corp.*, 527 U.S. 815, 848, 864 (1999) (rejecting global settlement agreement under a "limited fund" theory); *Amchem Products, Inc. v. Windsor*, 521 U.S. 591, 622 (1997) (requiring that a class be certified before it can be settled).

Second, many lawyers believe that federal courts grant summary judgment more freely than some state courts.

Third, federal courts require that plaintiffs state facts supporting a "plausible" claim, which is more exacting than the "notice" pleading adopted by many state courts.[14]

Fourth, many lawyers also believe that federal courts impose particularly strict requirements concerning presentation of expert testimony, which may make it

14. The Supreme Court imposed plausibility pleading in *Ashcroft v. Iqbal*, 556 U.S. 662 (2009); *Bell Atlantic Corp. v. Twombly*, 550 U.S. 544 (2007), which are often referred to as "*Twiqbal*." Those cases interpreted Federal Rule 8(a)(2), which, on its face, requires only a "short and plain statement of the claim showing that the pleader is entitled to relief." Historically, the federal courts held that Rule 8(a)(2) required only that the plaintiff put the defendant "on notice" of the claim, without great detail. *Twiqbal*, in the opinion of many, imposes a stricter standard than notice pleading. Some states have adopted *Twiqbal*, and some have rejected it, leaving in place "notice" pleading. *See* Freer, Civil Procedure 353–365 (4th ed. 2017).

more difficult for plaintiffs to proceed. *See, e.g.*, *Kumho Tire Co. v. Carmichael*, 526 U.S. 137, 147–149 (1999) (expanding requirements for admission of scientific expert testimony to all experts).

Fifth, Rule 23(f) permits discretionary appellate review of class certification decisions. Empirical evidence suggests that this authority is used to review orders certifying classes more frequently than to review orders denying class certification. And in the majority of cases, it is used to reverse or vacate class certification. Richard D. Freer, *Interlocutory Review of Class Action Certification Decisions: A Preliminary Empirical Study of Federal and State Experience*, 35 W. St. L. Rev. 13 (2008). Very few states provide such a mechanism for interlocutory review of the certification decision.

In contrast, many corporate defendants complained that some state courts (focused in particular counties in some states) certified classes so readily that the practice amounted to "drive-by certification." As we will discuss in Chapter 6, certification of a class changes the settlement dynamics dramatically. A defendant facing a certified class often confronts enormous aggregate liability, which may impel it to settle, even if the underlying merits of the claims seem weak. *See, e.g.*, Janet Cooper Alexander, *Do the Merits Matter? A Study of Settlements in Securities Class Actions*, 43 Stan. L. Rev. 497 (1991); Richard A. Nagareda, *Aggregation and its Discontents: Class Settlement Pressure, Class-Wide Arbitration, and CAFA*, 106 Colum. L. Rev. 1872 (2006).

Whatever the accuracy of these perceptions, they were embraced by many. Based upon them, business interests lobbied Congress to expand access to federal court in class action and other complex cases. Congress responded. Proponents of CAFA argue that the legislation properly places in federal courts complex cases of truly national import and impact. Critics raise a host of problems—some of which are interpretational dilemmas created by CAFA's language. *See* Kevin M. Clermont & Theodore Eisenberg, *CAFA Judicata: A Tale of Waste and Politics*, 156 U. Pa. L. Rev. 1553, 1565 (2008) ("This sloppy drafting created a lot of unnecessary social friction and costly litigation. . . ."). More fundamentally, critics decry the Act's effect on federalism. CAFA, they assert, shifts state-law cases to the federal courts without justification in Article III. Indeed, some suggest that CAFA is essentially tort reform in jurisdictional guise—that the massive shift of cases to federal court is simply a backhand way to get rid of many class actions. *See generally* Stephen B. Burbank, *The Class Action Fairness Act of 2005 in Historical Context: A Preliminary View*, 156 U. Pa. L. Rev. 1439 (2008).

In passing CAFA, Congress was concerned in part about "coupon" class action settlements. These are cases in which plaintiff class counsel and the defendant agree to settle on terms that enrich the plaintiff's lawyers but provide only token benefits for class members. The classic token is a "coupon," which permits the class member to acquire merchandise or services from the defendant at a discount. Many times, such coupons go unredeemed. CAFA discourages such settlements by limiting attorney's fees to the value of coupons that are actually redeemed. *See* § 1712(a). We will discuss attorney's fee awards under CAFA at Chapter 6.

CAFA is not limited to cases denominated as class actions. It opens the federal courts to what it calls a "mass action." Section 1332(d)(11)(B)(i) defines this as a civil action "in which monetary relief claims of 100 or more persons are proposed to be tried jointly on the ground that the plaintiffs' claims involve common questions of law or fact . . ."[15] This broad definition permits application of CAFA to cases that would not be class actions in state court but which constitute similar aggregated litigation. *See* Robert H. Klonoff, Class Actions and Other Multi-Party Litigation 217 (2007) ("[O]ne of the states that concerned Congress was Mississippi, which permits mass actions but does not authorize class actions.").[16]

One interesting question is whether *parens patriae* actions brought by a state official to recover on behalf of members of the public qualify as a "mass action." In *Mississippi ex rel. Hood v. AU Optronics Corp.*, 571 U.S. 161, 168–169 (2014), the Supreme Court held that such a case is not a mass action under CAFA. Though the case resulted in relief for more than 100 persons, the state official constituted the sole plaintiff. Thus, the case was not brought by "100 or more persons."

The requirement that a mass action involve plaintiffs whose claims are "proposed to be tried jointly" does not mean that there must actually be a single trial. In *Bullard v. Burlington Northern Santa Fe Ry. Co.*, 535 F.3d 759 (7th Cir. 2008), 144 plaintiffs sued in state court, alleging claims arising from the same transaction or occurrence against the same defendant. After the defendant removed under CAFA, the plaintiffs moved to remand, arguing that they never asked for a single trial and that, indeed, there might be separate trials. The Seventh Circuit rejected the argument, with Judge Easterbrook concluding: "A trial of 10 exemplary plaintiffs, followed by application of issue or claim preclusion to 134 more plaintiffs without another trial, is one in which the claims of 100 or more persons are being tried jointly, and § 1332(d) thus brings the suits within federal jurisdiction." *Id.* at 762.

Congress based CAFA on some remarkable findings.

> (a) Findings. Congress finds the following:
>
> (1) Class action lawsuits are an important and valuable part of the legal system when they permit the fair and efficient resolution of

15. Plaintiffs may be able to avoid falling within the definition of mass action by failing to join at least 100 plaintiffs. In *Tanoh v. Dow Chemical Co.*, 561 F.3d 945 (9th Cir. 2009), plaintiffs filed seven separate cases against the chemical company, all alleging the same claims, but each joining fewer than 100 plaintiffs. Although in the aggregate there were 664 plaintiffs, the cases had not been consolidated, and they could not be removed to federal court as a mass action. *Id.* at 956.

16. Interestingly, however, Congress did not relax subject matter jurisdiction in mass actions to the extent it did in class actions. Although mass actions require only minimal diversity, as we will see below with class actions, the amount in controversy for each plaintiff must exceed $75,000; aggregation is not permitted.

legitimate claims of numerous parties by allowing the claims to be aggregated into a single action against a defendant that has allegedly caused harm.

(2) Over the past decade, there have been abuses of the class action device that have—

(A) harmed class members with legitimate claims and defendants that have acted responsibly;

(B) adversely affected interstate commerce; and

(C) undermined public respect for our judicial system.

(3) Class members often receive little or no benefit from class actions, and are sometimes harmed, such as where—

(A) counsel are awarded large fees, while leaving class members with coupons or other awards of little or no value;

(B) unjustified awards are made to certain plaintiffs at the expense of other class members; and

(C) confusing notices are published that prevent class members from being able to fully understand and effectively exercise their rights.

(4) Abuses in class actions undermine the national judicial system, the free flow of interstate commerce, and the concept of diversity jurisdiction as intended by the framers of the United States Constitution, in that State and local courts are—

(A) keeping cases of national importance out of Federal court;

(B) sometimes acting in ways that demonstrate bias against out-of-State defendants; and

(C) making judgments that impose their view of the law on other States and bind the rights of the residents of those States.

(b) Purposes. The purposes of this Act [adding 28 U.S.C. §§ 1453 and 1711 et seq., amending 28 U.S.C. §§ 1332, 1335, and 1603, and appearing in part as notes to 28 U.S.C. §§ 1332, 1711, 2071, and 2074] are to—

(1) assure fair and prompt recoveries for class members with legitimate claims;

(2) restore the intent of the framers of the United States Constitution by providing for Federal court consideration of interstate cases of national importance under diversity jurisdiction; and

(3) benefit society by encouraging innovation and lowering consumer prices.

28 U.S.C. § 1711 note, Act Feb. 18, 2005, P.L. 109-2, § 2, 119 Stat. 4.

b. Jurisdictional Provisions and Exceptions

We will see various CAFA provisions throughout the course, such as its limitation on attorney's fees in "coupon" settlement cases. Our focus here is on the Act's provisions for subject matter jurisdiction.

CAFA does not create a substantive claim, so cases brought under the Act do not invoke federal question jurisdiction. Rather, the legislation is based upon diversity of citizenship jurisdiction in Article III. Immediately above, in § (a)(4), we saw that Congress found that class action abuse undermined the "free flow of interstate commerce [and] the concept of diversity jurisdiction. . . ." In assessing the jurisdictional provisions, keep in mind that the purpose of diversity of citizenship jurisdiction (according to the Supreme Court) is to avoid local bias or the fear of local bias by providing an independent federal court to hear cases that arise under state law. Note also that Congress found that "cases of national importance" were being kept out of federal court. Throughout these materials, ask whether CAFA channels such cases into the federal courts.

CAFA's chief jurisdictional provisions are § 1332(d), which addresses original invocation of jurisdiction in federal court, and § 1453(b), which deals with removal. Read both with care. Several points stand out.

The CAFA Grants of Jurisdiction

First, § 1332(d)(2) predicates subject matter jurisdiction upon minimal diversity between *any* class member and *any* defendant. This is far broader than the grant under the regular diversity statute, § 1332(a)(1). There, as held in *Ben-Hur*, section B.3 above, the representative must be of diverse citizenship from every defendant. Even supplemental jurisdiction will not reach this far, as we saw in *Allapattah*, section C.2 above, because it relies on having the original claim satisfy *Ben-Hur.*

Second, § 1332(d)(2) requires that the amount in controversy exceed $5,000,000. Section 1332(d)(6) explains that "the claims of the individual class members shall be aggregated" to determine if that figure is satisfied. This is a vast change from practice under § 1332(a)(1), where aggregation of claims is not allowed. *Snyder v. Harris*, 394 U.S. 332, 339–340 (1969).

It also offers an advantage over supplemental jurisdiction. In *Allapattah*, we saw that class members' claims that do not exceed $75,000 may invoke supplemental jurisdiction, but the representative's claim *must exceed $75,000.* In many consumer class actions, no one—not even the representative—will have such a large claim. In that situation, § 1332(a)(1) and supplemental jurisdiction cannot be employed. But if all class claims add up to more than $5,000,000, the case meets the amount requirement for CAFA.

In § 1453(b), the CAFA removal provision repeals the "rule of unanimity," section B.3 above, that ordinarily applies in removal cases. Under CAFA, *a single defendant* can remove.

Section 1453(b) repeals the "in-state defendant" rule, section B.3 above, that applies in removal of "regular" diversity cases. That rule simply does not apply in CAFA removals.

Section 1453(b) also repeals the one-year limitation on removal of "regular" diversity cases, section B.3 above.

Sometimes, state-court plaintiffs wish to make their class actions "removal proof" to ensure that they remain in state court. In *Standard Fire Insurance Co. v. Knowles*, 568 U.S. 588 (2013), the representative filed a putative class action in state court. His lawyer attached an affidavit to the complaint stipulating that the class would not seek more than $5,000,000 in the suit. After the defendant removed to federal court under CAFA (minimal diversity was easily satisfied), the plaintiff moved to remand, based upon the stipulation. The district court conducted a hearing and concluded that the class claims in fact would exceed $5,000,000 but for the stipulation. The Supreme Court held that the case invoked CAFA jurisdiction. The stipulation did not divest the federal court of jurisdiction because it was not binding on class members. The class had not been certified, so the representative had no standing to bind the class members to the limitation on recovery. Jurisdiction is determined when the case is commenced, and at that point the representative spoke for no one but himself. 568 U.S. at 592–593.

Note that CAFA applies only if a class involves at least 100 members. *See* § 1332(d)(5)(B).

The "Carve-Outs" to CAFA Jurisdiction

The jurisdictional expansion wrought by CAFA could inundate the federal courts. Congress recognized this, and the need to trim the jurisdictional grant to its stated purpose. It undertook to ensure that class actions of truly local interest—in which there was no interstate or national interest—could stay in (or be remanded to) state court. Congress tried to limit the reach of CAFA in several provisions, three of which we address here.[17] Given the breadth of jurisdiction under CAFA, it is not surprising that a great deal of litigation has focused on the applicability of these three "carve-outs," or exceptions, to CAFA jurisdiction.

First, § 1332(d)(3) is known as the "discretionary" exception to jurisdiction under CAFA. It *permits* the court to decline to exercise jurisdiction "in the interests

---

17. Other exceptions include: § 1332(d)(5)(A) (cases in which states or state officials or other persons who are immune from suit (usually under the Eleventh Amendment) are the "primary defendants"); § 1332(d)(9) (securities law cases and those dealing with "internal affairs or governance" of a business arising under the law of the state in which the business was formed); and § 1332(d)(5)(B) (fewer than 100 class members or plaintiffs in a mass action).

of justice and looking at the totality of the circumstances." It may exercise this discretion, however, only if the following are citizens of the state in which the case was filed:

more than one-third but fewer than two-thirds of the members of the class *and*

"the primary defendants."

In such a case, this provision sets out six factors (§ 1332(d)(3)(A) through (F)) which the court must consider in determining whether to decline jurisdiction. Note how these factors attempt to ensure that only "appropriate" cases remain in federal court. Under § 1332(d)(3)(A), the judge is to assess, *inter alia*, whether the claims involve "matters of national or interstate interest." By implication, claims of local interest should proceed in state court. Similarly, § 1332(d)(3)(D) requires the judge to consider whether the forum has "a distinct nexus with the class members, the alleged harm, or the defendants." If so, presumably, it might be more appropriately handled in state court.

Second, § 1332(d)(4)(A) sets forth the "local controversy" exception to CAFA. It *requires* the district court to decline jurisdiction if the following are citizens of the state in which the case was filed:

more than two-thirds of the class members *and*

at least one defendant from whom "significant relief" is sought, whose "alleged conduct forms a significant basis" for the class claims.[18]

In addition, however, the "principal injuries resulting from the alleged conduct" must have been incurred in the forum state. And, during the past three years, no other class action has asserted similar allegations on behalf of the same persons against the defendant.

Third, § 1332(d)(4)(B) embodies the "home state" exception. It also *requires* the federal court to decline jurisdiction, but only if the following are citizens of the state in which the case was filed:

---

18. The Third Circuit has held that this requirement refers to defendants who are in the case at the time of the motion to remand. In other words, a defendant who would satisfy this criterion but who has been dismissed is irrelevant; remand cannot be based upon a dismissed defendant. *Kaufman v. Allstate New Jersey Ins. Co.*, 561 F.3d 144, 152–153 (3d Cir. 2009).

In addressing these factors, does the court limit itself to pleadings, or is it to look at evidence? First, regarding whether "significant relief is sought," the Ninth Circuit concludes that "sought" implies that the issue is assessed on the pleadings. Regarding whether defendant's "alleged conduct forms a significant basis for the claims asserted by the proposed plaintiff class," that court also concludes that a judge is limited to pleadings and may not look at evidence. But the third requirement is different. It is whether defendant "is a citizen of the [forum state]." The use of "is" here implies that a fact must be established by evidence, not merely asserted in pleadings. *See, e.g., Brinkley v. Monterey Fin. Servs., Inc.*, 873 F.3d 1118, 1121 (9th Cir. 2017); *Christmas v. Union Pac. R.R. Co.*, 698 F. App'x 887, 889–890, 892–893 (9th Cir. 2017); *Coleman v. Estes Express Lines, Inc.*, 631 F.3d 1010 (9th Cir. 2011).

two-thirds or more of the class members *and*

the "primary defendants."

Courts struggle with the terms from these exceptions. For example, what are "primary defendants," "principal injuries," and what constitutes "significant relief"? Moreover, how is a court to determine how many class members are citizens of a given state? Who has the burden of proof on the various issues? The following case addresses some of these questions.

In a typical case, plaintiff will file in state court, defendant will remove under CAFA, and plaintiff will move to remand to state court under one or more of the three exceptions to jurisdiction. Under CAFA, however, because removal can be effected by one defendant, any other *defendant* can move to remand to state court. That is what happens in this case.

Preston v. Tenet Healthsystems Memorial Medical Center, Inc.

United States Court of Appeals, Fifth Circuit
485 F.3d 804 (2007)

Stewart, Circuit Judge.

Tenet Health Systems Memorial Medical Center d/b/a Memorial Medical Center ("Memorial") moved to remand this class action lawsuit to state court under the "local controversy" exception of the Class Action Fairness Act of 2005 ("CAFA"), 28 U.S.C. § 1332(d). The district court granted the motion to remand, and LifeCare Management Services, L.L.C., and LifeCare Hospitals of New Orleans, L.L.C. (collectively "LifeCare"), timely appealed the order. We affirm the district court's judgment.

I. FACTUAL AND PROCEDURAL BACKGROUND

Preston represents a putative class of patients and the relatives of deceased and allegedly injured patients hospitalized at Memorial when Hurricane Katrina made landfall in New Orleans, Louisiana. Memorial owned and operated the hospital, and LifeCare leased the seventh floor of the facility for an acute care center. On October 6, 2005, Preston brought suit against Memorial in the Civil District Court for the Parish of Orleans. Preston asserted claims for negligence and intentional misconduct, "reverse patient dumping" under the Emergency Medical Treatment and Active Labor Act, 42 U.S.C. § 1395dd, and involuntary euthanization. Preston alleged that Memorial failed to design and maintain the premises in a manner that avoided loss of power in the building. Preston further alleged that Memorial and LifeCare failed to develop and implement an evacuation plan for the patients. According to the petition, Memorial's and LifeCare's failure to maintain the premises and timely evacuate the facility resulted in the deaths and injuries of hospitalized patients. Preston named LifeCare in the Fifth Supplemental Amended Petition for Damages, seeking to certify the following class of persons:

> All patients of Memorial and LifeCare who sustained injuries including death or personal injury as a result of the insufficient design, inspection and/or maintenance of LifeCare and/or Memorial's back-up electrical system, its failure to implement its evacuation plan and/or its emergency preparedness plan and/or its failure to have a plan which would have facilitated the safe transfer of patients out of harm's way, and its failure to have a plan of care for patients in the event of a power outage in the wake of Hurricane Katrina within the property owned by Memorial and leased and/or operated by LifeCare on or about the time period of August 26, 2005 through and including August 29, 2005 and thereafter, and all persons who sustained personal injury as a result of the deaths or personal injuries to patients of LifeCare and Memorial....

On June 26, 2006, LifeCare filed a timely notice of removal. Memorial never consented to removal from state court.... Preston filed a motion to remand under the local controversy exception of CAFA. On August 22, 2006, the district court conducted a non-evidentiary hearing on the remand motion. The court declined to rule on the motion at the hearing but instead ordered the parties to present additional evidence regarding the citizenship of the class members. Preston withdrew the motion to remand prior to the deadline for submitting additional proof. Nevertheless, on November 13, 2006, Memorial filed a memorandum supporting remand and adopting Preston's withdrawn motion.... On November 21, 2006, the district court remanded the lawsuit to state court under the local controversy exception, home state exception, and the discretionary jurisdiction provision.... LifeCare filed a timely petition for appeal pursuant to 28 U.S.C. § 1453 [(c)(1), which gives a court of appeals discretion to hear an appeal of an order granting or denying a motion to remand a CAFA case]. On February 5, 2007, this court granted permission to appeal. LifeCare only contests the district court's citizenship findings under CAFA's exceptions to federal jurisdiction.

II. STANDARD OF REVIEW

We review the district court's factual findings as to the citizenship of the parties for clear error.... A finding of fact is clearly erroneous only when "although there may be evidence to support it, the reviewing court on the entire [record] is left with the definite and firm conviction that a mistake has been committed." Campos v. City of Baytown, Tex., 840 F.2d 1240, 1243 (5th Cir. 1988) (*citing* Anderson v. City of Bessemer City, N.C., 470 U.S. 564, 573 (1985)).

The standard of review for a district court's remand under the discretionary provision [of CAFA] constitutes an issue of first impression. We review the district court's remand order for abuse of discretion. In determining the burden of proof to show citizenship under the local controversy exception, courts treating the question in the first instance looked to 28 U.S.C. § 1441(a), the general removal statute....

. . . [T]he local controversy and home state exceptions read that the "district courts *shall* decline to exercise jurisdiction," while the discretionary provision provides that the district court "*may* in the interests of justice and looking at the totality of the circumstances" decline to exercise jurisdiction. *Compare* §§ 1332(d)(2) & (4) with § 1332(d)(3). LifeCare cogently argues that the local controversy and home state exceptions should be construed narrowly and resolved in favor of federal jurisdiction based on the "shall decline to exercise jurisdiction" language, which represents the classic formulation for abstention. Under the discretionary jurisdiction provision, however, Congress permitted the district court greater latitude to remand class actions to state court. . . . [T]he district court does not wield unfettered discretion over whether to remand a case; instead Congress provided a list of factors to guide the district court's consideration.

III. DISCUSSION

A. Statutory Background

Congress enacted CAFA to expand federal jurisdiction over interstate class action lawsuits of national interest. CAFA contains a basic jurisdictional test for removal, which requires the removing defendant to prove minimal diversity and an aggregated amount in controversy of $5,000,000 or more. § 1332(d). CAFA eliminates the standard requirements of unanimous consent among the defendants and the one-year removal deadline. § 1453(b). The district court can decline jurisdiction under three provisions: (1) the home state exception, § 1332(d)(4)(B); (2) the local controversy exception, § 1332(d)(4)(A); and (3) discretionary jurisdiction, § 1332(d)(3).

. . .

Under the discretionary jurisdiction provision, a "district court may, in the interests of justice and looking at the totality of the circumstances, decline to exercise jurisdiction . . . over a class action in which greater than one-third but less than two-thirds of the members of all proposed plaintiff classes in the aggregate and the primary defendants are citizens of the State in which the action was originally filed. . . ." The district court must consider these factors:

(A) whether the claims asserted involve matters of national or interstate interest;

(B) whether the claims asserted will be governed by laws of the State in which the action was originally filed or by the laws of other States;

(C) whether the class action has been pleaded in a manner that seeks to avoid Federal jurisdiction;

(D) whether the action was brought in a forum with a distinct nexus with the class members, the alleged harm, or the defendants;

(E) whether the number of citizens of the State in which the action was originally filed in all proposed plaintiff classes in the aggregate is substantially larger than the number of citizens from any other State, and the

> citizenship of the other members of the proposed class is dispersed among a substantial number of States; and
>
> (F) whether, during the 3-year period preceding the filing of that class action, 1 or more other class actions asserting the same or similar claims on behalf of the same or other persons have been filed.

§ 1332(d)(3).

B. Discretionary Jurisdiction Provision

The district court remanded this class action lawsuit to state court under all three carve-outs to federal jurisdiction: the local controversy exception, the home state exception, and the discretionary jurisdiction provision. Each CAFA exception requires the court to make an objective factual finding regarding the percentage of class members that were citizens of Louisiana at the time of filing the class petition. . . .

. . . The movants must satisfy the citizenship requirement as a prerequisite to the district court weighing the additional statutory factors enumerated to guide the court's remand determination. The same legal principles apply to the discretionary jurisdiction provision as apply to the local controversy and home state exceptions. Despite the burden to prove a lesser percentage of class members were citizens of Louisiana, which party bears the burden of proof and the sufficiency of evidence necessary to satisfy the citizenship requirements remains consistent throughout either analysis.

Congress crafted CAFA to exclude only a narrow category of truly localized controversies, and § 1332(d)(3) provides a discretionary vehicle for district courts to ferret out the "controversy that uniquely affects a particular locality to the exclusion of all others." Evans [v. Walter Industries], 449 F.3d [1159], 1164 (11th Cir. 2006). After careful review of the record, the discretionary jurisdiction provision proves to be a particularly well-suited framework for considering the interconnections between the underlying facts giving rise to the alleged legal claims and the extenuating circumstances affecting this preliminary jurisdictional determination. The district court determined that a distinct nexus exists between the forum of Louisiana, the Defendants, and the proposed class. We observe, more specifically, that Preston alleges that LifeCare and Memorial, citizens of Louisiana, committed acts in Louisiana causing injuries and deaths to patients hospitalized in New Orleans . . . when Hurricane Katrina made landfall. The claims asserted in the petition involve issues of negligence governed by state law. Memorial does not contest that the instant lawsuit fulfills the threshold requirements for removal under CAFA, i.e. the requisite number of proposed class members, minimal diversity, and the necessary aggregate amount in controversy. Accordingly, we limit our review to whether Memorial presented sufficient evidence to show that a requisite percentage of the putative class members were citizens of Louisiana at the time that the suit was filed.

1. *Burden of Proof*

We now consider which party bears the burden of proof under the discretionary jurisdiction provision. Under CAFA, the moving party on the remand motion, not the defendant seeking federal jurisdiction, bears the burden to establish the [citizenship] of at least one-third of the class members at the time of filing the lawsuit. . . .

Under CAFA, . . . both plaintiffs and non-consenting defendants may move to remand the class action to state court because Congress eliminated the standard [removal] requirement that defendants must unanimously [seek removal].

Therefore, . . . we adopt the broader statement that "once federal jurisdiction has been established under [CAFA], the *objecting* party bears the burden of proof as to the applicability of any express statutory exception under §§ 1332(d)(4)(A) and (B) [the local controversy and home state exceptions]."

In *Frazier* [*v. Pioneer Americas LLC*, 455 F.3d 542 (5th Cir. 2006)], the court reasoned that the "longstanding § 1441(a) doctrine placing the burden on plaintiffs to show exceptions to jurisdiction buttresses the clear congressional intent to do the same with CAFA. This result is supported by the reality that plaintiffs are better positioned than defendants to carry this burden." . . . Accordingly, Memorial, the only party moving for remand, must show that the exceptions to federal jurisdiction apply in this class action despite its position as a named defendant.

2. *Evidentiary Standard for Proving Citizenship*

Memorial must prove that greater than one-third of the putative class members were citizens of Louisiana at the time of filing the class action petition. 28 U.S.C. § 1332(d)(7) ("Citizenship of the members of the proposed plaintiff classes shall be determined for purposes of paragraphs (2) through (6) as of the date of the filing of the complaint."). Preston filed this class action lawsuit on October 6, 2005; therefore, Memorial must prove citizenship as of this date. The parties contest the quantum of proof necessary to sustain the moving party's burden. Pursuant to well-settled principles of law, we hold that the party moving for remand under the CAFA exceptions to federal jurisdiction must prove the citizenship requirement by a preponderance of the evidence. This holding means that Memorial, as the movant, must demonstrate by a preponderance of the evidence that at least one-third of the putative class members were citizens of Louisiana.

. . .

In the context of diversity jurisdiction, once a person establishes his domicile in a particular state, he simultaneously establishes his citizenship in the same state. Someone acquires a "domicile of origin" at birth, and this domicile presumptively continues unless rebutted with sufficient evidence of change.

. . .

3. Evidence Adduced to Prove Citizenship Requirement

In an order dated August 22, 2006, the district court acknowledged that "limited discovery is required in order to determine whether it has jurisdiction, particularly in regards to Lifecare's claim that removal is proper under . . . [CAFA]." Accordingly, the district court ordered that Memorial "shall provide the Plaintiffs and Lifecare with patient information which will permit these parties to identify the patients who suffered personal injuries, including death, during the relevant period; these patients' addresses and phone numbers; as well as next of kin." In a second order, dated August 30, 2006, the district court required Memorial to "provide an affidavit of a Memorial representative attesting to the percentage of patients at issue, both deceased and living, with Louisiana addresses and percentage of those with addresses outside Louisiana." . . .

a. Residency: Medical Records and Current Addresses

Both Memorial and LifeCare submitted evidence in response to the district court's order. Memorial's Medical Records Supervisor, Hal Rome, submitted two affidavits averring to the residency of patients hospitalized when Hurricane Katrina made landfall. In the first affidavit, Rome avers to the following facts:

> That he has reviewed the complete list of all patients hospitalized at Memorial Medical Center at the time that Hurricane Katrina struck on August 29, 2005. That list contains a total of 256 patients. Of that total population of patients, the hospital's records show that 7 of those 256 patients, or 2.83% of the total, provided information to the hospital at the time they registered as patients indicating that they were residents of states other than Louisiana.

In his second affidavit, Rome produced a list showing that thirty-five patients died after the hurricane and records showing that two of the deceased patients gave out-of-state addresses. These same two patients were the only deceased persons that listed emergency contacts with telephone numbers outside of the New Orleans calling area.

LifeCare retained a private investigator, Robert Mazur, to trace the current mailing addresses of potential class members located throughout the country. LifeCare maintained that forty-nine of 146 persons identified as potential class members, more than one-third, currently reside outside of Louisiana. LifeCare's citizenship numbers include patients and surviving beneficiaries. In assessing these documents, the district court noted that "this information presents a valuable indication of the citizenship of the proposed class" but admonished LifeCare's failure to prove "residence and intent, both at the date the suit was filed." The district court reasoned that "LifeCare did not provide information regarding the length of time that these individuals have been residing outside of Louisiana. . . . Additionally, if these individuals were in fact displaced, LifeCare did not indicate whether these individuals intend to remain in their new state of residence."

We agree with the district court's treatment of LifeCare's rebuttal evidence. The pre-Katrina addresses in the medical records, however, only make a prima facie showing of domicile, and citizenship requires residency and the intent to return or remain in the state. . . . A party's residence alone does not establish domicile. We now turn to the evidence establishing intent, the second element of citizenship.

b. Intent: Statements from Potential Class Members

Memorial presented no evidence from its records to demonstrate that the hospitalized patients not only resided in Orleans Parish at the given addresses but also were domiciled in Louisiana at the time of Hurricane Katrina and at the time of filing suit. As the movant, it relies on the additional evidence filed by the plaintiffs. Preston submitted eight affidavits regarding the intent of potential class members to return to New Orleans, Louisiana, even though they currently resided in a different state. The named plaintiffs provided six of the eight affidavits. For example, the affidavit of Darlene Preston states her former address in New Orleans prior to Hurricane Katrina; her current address in Houston, Texas; and concludes by stating that "[s]he is planning on returning as soon as housing becomes available to her. She is a resident and domiciliary of and has always intended on returning to the City of New Orleans." The affidavit of Aster Abraham, currently residing in Dallas, Texas, states that she and her husband "completed repairs of the family home and she is returning July 2006." Similarly, Terry Gaines-Oden, currently residing in the Colony, Texas, avers that "she has every intention on returning as soon as her house is repaired." These affidavits unequivocally evince the intent of these plaintiffs to not change their domicile.

. . . In addition to the medical records and affidavits, LifeCare suggests that Memorial should adduce evidence of citizenship in accordance with traditional diversity cases involving one defendant. Prior to CAFA, the removing parties only needed to show citizenship with respect to the named plaintiffs. § 1332(d)(3)–(4). "The factors [considered by the district court] may include the places where the litigant exercises civil and political rights, pays taxes, owns real and personal property, has driver's and other licenses, maintains bank accounts, belongs to clubs and churches, has places of business or employment, and maintains a home for his family." This suggestion not only affects the moving party but suggests that at this threshold stage of the case, the district court must engage in the arduous task of examining the domicile of every proposed class member before ruling on the citizenship requirement. We decline to adopt such a heightened burden of proof considering the far greater number of plaintiffs involved in a class action as compared to the traditional diversity case. From a practical standpoint, class action lawsuits may become "totally unworkable in a diversity case if the citizenship of all members of the class, many of them unknown, had to be considered." CHARLES ALAN WRIGHT, THE LAW OF FEDERAL COURTS § 72, at 521 (5th ed. 1994). The requisite showing under CAFA prompts this court to reconcile congressional intent, our precedent for determining citizenship, and judicial economy. Thus, the evidentiary standard for establishing the domicile of more than one hundred plaintiffs must be based on practicality and reasonableness.

... Preston admitted the statements of eight potential class members. The district court concluded that the affidavits "suggest that at least some displaced proposed class members intend to return to New Orleans in the near future. Each of these individuals state that they lived in New Orleans at the time of the hurricane, but were forced to evacuate to another state. However, they continue to have every intention of returning to the New Orleans area."

In the wake of Hurricane Katrina, and the compounding effects of the breached levees, nearly eighty percent of New Orleans was engulfed in flood waters rising over twenty feet in lower-lying areas. These cataclysmic events damaged, destroyed, or rendered inaccessible approximately 850,000 housing units.[19] ... The sheer magnitude of this shared catalyst formed an adequate backdrop for the district court's extrapolation that the reasons offered by the affiants for not immediately returning home, i.e. repairing the family home, finding gainful employment, and waiting for the availability of housing units, were probably representative of many other proposed class members.

The [complaint] defines a circumscribed class that includes "all patients of Memorial and LifeCare who sustained injuries ... and all persons who sustained personal injury as a result of the deaths or personal injuries to patients of LifeCare and Memorial." The eight affidavits in and of themselves are not dispositive proof that at least one-third of the defined putative class were citizens of Louisiana at the time in which the suit was filed. The uncontroverted affidavits of eight beneficiaries stating an intent to return to New Orleans, the emergency contact phone numbers of the deceased patients, and the uncontroverted data gathered from the medical records, however, permitted the district court to make a reasonable assumption that at least one-third of the class members were citizens of Louisiana during the relevant time period regardless of the rebuttal evidence placed in the record....

Although the actual number of patients and beneficiaries remains an open question, the unequivocal affidavits of eight beneficiaries in conjunction with the residency information gleaned from the emergency contact data of the deceased patients gave the district court a reasonable indication as to the citizenship of these unaccounted for persons. LifeCare identified the current residences of only 146 potential class members to rebut the medical records and affiavits, but LifeCare's evidence fails to demonstrate an intent to change domicile by any of the identified persons. Even though eight affidavits may constitute a small number of statements outside the unique convergence of facts presented in this case, we find that here, the affidavits amplify the court's carefully reasoned conclusion about the probable

19. [Court's footnote #6] Pursuant to Fed. R. Evid. 201(b), this court may take judicial notice of facts "generally known within the territorial jurisdiction of the trial court" or "capable of accurate and ready determination by resort to sources whose accuracy cannot reasonably be questioned."

citizenship of the proposed class of hospitalized patients and their beneficiaries. Therefore, based on the record as a whole, the district court made a reasonable assumption that at least one-third of the class were Louisiana citizens at the time of filing the lawsuit on October 6, 2005, less than two months after the storm hit New Orleans. We do not find the district court's findings of fact clearly erroneous.

c. Presumption of Continuing Domicile

. . . "There is a presumption in favor of [a person's] continuing domicile which requires the party seeking to show a change in domicile to come forward with enough evidence to that effect. . . ." The law of continuing domicile gains special significance in light of the natural disaster forming the factual basis of this appeal. In a recent case analyzing the citizenship requirement of the local controversy exception, a district court recognized that "[g]iven the forced evacuation for several months from several south Louisiana parishes as a result of Katrina, it is reasonable to assume that residents of these parishes might change their addresses in the immediate aftermath of the storm without changing their domiciles." Caruso v. Allstate Ins. Co., 469 F. Supp. 2d 364, 469 F. Supp. 2d 364 (E.D. La. 2007) (denying the motion to remand on other grounds under the local controversy exception). The court described its conclusion as a "common-sense presumption" applied to a "closed-end class."

We agree with the notion that the damage and destruction wrought by Hurricane Katrina warrants the court's incorporation of common-sense as part of the calculus in determining the citizenship of the class members. While cognizant that the patient addresses provided by Memorial do not definitively reflect the patients' domicile at the time of filing suit, as required under traditional diversity standards, we also consider the common genesis of the historically unprecedented exodus from New Orleans in our assessment of the citizenship issue. In light of the vast post-Katrina diaspora and the undisputably slow revitalization in parts of New Orleans, it is unreasonable to demand precise empirical evidence of citizenship in a class action lawsuit filed less than sixty days after the hurricane and related flooding. Many Hurricane Katrina victims may intend to return home yet are still dispersed throughout Louisiana and other states for reasons beyond their control, such as not having shelter and employment in the New Orleans area. Therefore, we find the presumption of continuing domicile relevant in this case.

d. Population Survey Data

On appeal, LifeCare cites to a 2006 Louisiana Health and Population Survey Report, conducted by the Louisiana Public Health Institute on behalf of the Louisiana Department of Health and Hospitals. The survey estimated that the 2004 population of 444,515 persons living in Orleans Parish decreased dramatically to 191,139 persons after Hurricane Katrina. Based on surveys returned during June and October 2006, the Louisiana Department of Health and Hospitals published the report on January 17, 2007.

We find this survey to be much too broad to rebut the presumed citizenship of a class member. First, the survey data represents only an initial analysis conducted less than a year after Hurricane Katrina. Second, the published data only account for population decreases in the Orleans Parish area, while CAFA's citizenship requirement looks to citizenship in the state. Third, the submitted survey gives a disclaimer that "a comprehensive final report for all parishes will be produced when the project is completed and all parish specific reports are released." This statement clearly indicates that the project remains a work-in-progress and lends little insight into determining the number of class members no longer located in Louisiana due to the forced evacuation after Hurricane Katrina. Accordingly, we deem the census data as non-probative on whether one-third of the class members were domiciled in Louisiana at the time of filing suit.

4. *Determination of Class Size*

LifeCare argues that Memorial fails to establish the number of people composing the proposed class. Arguably, without knowing the number of persons in the class, the court cannot determine whether one-third of the class members are citizens of Louisiana. . . . LifeCare asserts that the statute requires concrete proof of the number of class members as a prerequisite to ruling on the citizenship requirement. . . .

. . .

At this preliminary stage, it is unnecessary for the district court to permit exhaustive discovery capable of determining the exact class size to an empirical certainty. Even though a party should take care in defining the putative class, the specificity argued for by LifeCare more appropriately occurs during class certification. Under Fed. R. Civ. P. 23, the district court must "evaluate with rigor the claims, defenses, relevant facts and applicable substantive law in order to make a meaningful determination of the certification issues." Unger v. Amedisys Inc., 401 F.3d 316, 321 (5th Cir. 2005). At the certification stage, the plaintiff must provide evidence or a reasonable estimate of purported class members. Then, the class size weighs in the district court's certification calculus. Moreover, we are not presented with a situation wherein the district court stymied the parties' efforts to marshal evidence and conduct discovery. Neither Memorial nor LifeCare contends that the district court thwarted their ability to gather relevant information by evidentiary rulings; to the contrary, the district court encouraged the introduction of evidence through two orders of the court.

. . .

. . . [T]he crux of this case revolves around a narrowly defined class and claims stemming from a localized chain of events. In aligning these circumstances and the adduced evidence, we are not in the position of having to put a square peg in a round hole. Instead, we are dealing with the congruence of fitted pieces. Keeping in mind the measurable bounds of the proposed class, we find that the district court made a reasonable inference regarding the temporary dual residency of the displaced Louisiana citizens at issue in this case. The record reflects that the plaintiffs defined a reasonably confined class and the district court, based on a preponderance of the evidence, made a credible estimate that at least one-third of the class were citizens of Louisiana at the time of filing suit.

5. *Statutory Factors for Determining the Interest of Justice*

a. Whether Claims Involve National or Interstate Interest

LifeCare argues that the evacuation of medical and other facilities during disasters such as Hurricane Katrina is an issue of national concern. This broad statement could swallow the rule, however, as many events isolated to one area at any particular time may reoccur in another geographic location in the future. Under CAFA, the terms local and national connote whether the interests of justice would be violated by a state court exercising jurisdiction over a large number of out-of-state citizens and applying the laws of other states. Just because the nation takes interest in Hurricane Katrina does not mean that the legal claims at issue in this class action lawsuit qualify as national or interstate interest. The factual scenario presented in this class action involves two Louisiana businesses operating a local hospital during a natural disaster destroying New Orleans and the compounded devastation of the local levee breach. The evacuation plans, building maintenance, and emergency care procedures are the work product and property of these local entities. Moreover, the district court denied any federal basis for jurisdiction after reviewing the class action petition, and neither party appealed this ruling. For these reasons, although the nation may still be watching the ever-evolving after effects of Hurricane Katrina, this class action lawsuit does not affect national interest as contemplated under the statute.

b. Whether Claims Are Governed by Louisiana Law and Whether the Class Action Was Pleaded to Avoid Federal Jurisdiction

The plaintiffs in this case assert a variety of negligence claims based on the delayed evacuation of patients from Memorial Medical Center after Hurricane Katrina made landfall. The majority of the claims asserted in the class petition involve negligence issues governed under Louisiana law. Specifically, Memorial and LifeCare argue that the Louisiana Medical Malpractice Act, L.S.A. R.S. 40:1299.41, et seq., governs the plaintiffs' causes of action.

... [T]he record does not indicate that the plaintiffs intentionally pleaded the case in a manner to avoid federal jurisdiction and neither defendant asserts such an allegation. Accordingly, the class action lawsuit as pleaded satisfies these two requirements.

c. Whether a Distinct Nexus Exists between the Forum and the Class Members, Alleged Harm, and the Defendants

The conduct alleged in the class action petition as causing the deaths and injuries of patients hospitalized at Memorial and LifeCare occurred at the defendants' medical facilities in New Orleans, Louisiana. Memorial owned and operated the hospital, and LifeCare leased one floor of the hospital for the operation of an acute care center.

Both Memorial and LifeCare are Louisiana corporations organized under the laws of the state, and based on the medical records, nearly ninety-seven percent of the patients permanently resided in Louisiana at the time of admission to these health centers. In light of the localized events giving rise to the alleged negligent conduct and the undisputed residency and citizenship information of the patients and the healthcare providers, we conclude that a distinct nexus exists between the forum of Louisiana and the class members, alleged harm, and the defendants.

d. State Citizenship of the Class Members

For the reasons thoroughly discussed in the citizenship analysis, we conclude that the "number of citizens of the State in which the action was originally filed in all proposed plaintiff classes in the aggregate is substantially larger than the number of citizens from any other State, and the citizenship of the other members of the proposed class is dispersed among a substantial number of States." Based on the record, an overwhelming number of patients permanently resided in New Orleans, Louisiana, and the vast majority of the emergency contact phone numbers listed for the deceased patients have the New Orleans area code. After the hurricane, many New Orleans residents were forced to relocate to surrounding areas in Louisiana and other states. As evinced through the affidavits, however, citizens of Louisiana are hindered from immediately acting on their desires to move back home due to employment, housing, and other related issues. Undoubtedly, some evacuees hold no intention of returning to Louisiana but surely are dispersed throughout the nation as opposed to one other state. For these reasons, we determine that the proposed class meets this requirement.

. . .

V. CONCLUSION

We recognize that Congress crafted CAFA to exclude only a narrow category of truly localized controversies, and the exceptions provide a statutory vehicle for the district courts to ferret out the "controversy that uniquely affects a particular locality to the exclusion of all others." This particular Hurricane Katrina case symbolizes a quintessential example of Congress' intent to carve-out exceptions to CAFA's expansive grant of federal jurisdiction when our courts confront a truly localized controversy. Based on the medical records, affidavits, and attending factual circumstances, we determine that the district court did not clearly err in finding that one-third of the class members were citizens of Louisiana at the time of filing suit. Accordingly, we affirm the district court's judgment. . . .

Notes and Questions

1. Ordinarily, the court recognized, the plaintiff should bear the burden of proof in a motion to remand to state court because "plaintiffs are better positioned than defendants to carry this burden [of showing an exception to jurisdiction]." In

Preston, however, the court put the burden on the defendant to show that one of the CAFA exceptions supported remand. Why?

2. In *Preston*, the parties went to considerable effort to discover facts relevant to whether an exception to CAFA should apply. The district court and the court of appeals spent considerable time assessing the facts and the arguments. Shouldn't jurisdictional rules be relatively easy to apply? Could the CAFA exceptions have been drafted to accomplish their goal without requiring so much time and effort? How? In the words of one scholar, "[w]orking with exceptions so complicated that even some academics have been unable to penetrate them ... Congress sacrificed transparency and accountability in the interests of preserving deniability." Burbank, *supra*, 156 U. Pa. L. Rev. at 1447.

3. In *Preston*, the court required the party moving for remand to show the underlying facts by a preponderance of the evidence, which is the normal standard in a civil case. As you recall from Civil Procedure, it requires the party to show that the fact is more likely than not. In *Preston*, the court concluded that nothing in CAFA required imposing a more rigorous burden.

4. In a companion opinion decided the same day as *Preston*, the Fifth Circuit reversed an order that would have remanded to state court under the "local controversy" exception. *Weems v. Tuoro Infirmary*, 485 F.3d 793 (5th Cir. 2007). The Fifth Circuit held that the plaintiffs—asserting slightly different claims against different defendants from those in *Preston*—had failed to satisfy the burden of showing that the case should be sent back to state court. In part, they failed to establish the requisite number of class members as citizens of Louisiana. The court explained:

> [One plaintiff] made no effort to provide citizenship data, stating in her motion that "plaintiffs *believe* that the majority of the members of this class, and certainly more than 2/3 of the members are from Louisiana." [Another plaintiff] submitted an affidavit from Sandy McCall, its director of medical records, stating that
>
> There were two hundred and ninety-nine (299) patients present on the premises of Touro Infirmary, immediately before, during and immediately after Hurricane Katrina made landfall in New Orleans on or about August 29, 2005. This number includes individuals who were patients of Specialty Hospital of New Orleans (SHONO, Inc.) and Kindred Hospital. Of the patients present on the Touro premises during and immediately after Hurricane Katrina, two hundred and forty-two (242) of those patients identified a Louisiana address as their primary billing address and residence.
>
> SHONO confirmed that 200 of the 242 patients listed in [plaintiff's] affidavit provided an Orleans Parish address as their primary residence. [The plaintiffs] presented no evidence, however, to demonstrate that these patients not only *resided* in Orleans Parish at the given addresses but also were *domiciled* in Louisiana at the time of Hurricane Katrina. A party's

> residence in a state alone does not establish domicile. Domicile requires residence in the state and an intent to remain in the state. Therefore, the medical records are not tantamount to sufficient proof of citizenship.

Id. at 798. Is this holding consistent with *Preston*?

Note on Burden of Proof on Removal

In *Preston*, the court was concerned, among other things, with which party bears the burden of proof on a motion to remand. A different question is who bears the burden of proof on removal. In non-CAFA cases, the rule is clear: the defendant, who is invoking federal jurisdiction, must show that the case is removable. *See* 13 Wright & Miller, Federal Practice and Procedure 103–105 (3d ed. 2018).

Does CAFA change things? The answer seems to be no. Courts have engaged the topic most interestingly regarding the amount in controversy requirement. The clear majority view is that the defendant removing a CAFA case must establish a "reasonable probability" that the aggregate amount in controversy exceeds $5,000,000. *See e.g., Sabrina Roppo v. Travelers Commercial Ins. Co.*, 869 F.3d 568, 578 n.23, 579 n.25 (7th Cir. 2017); *Scott v. Cricket Comms., LLC*, 865 F.3d 189, 197 (4th Cir. 2017); *Pazol v. Tough Mudder Inc.*, 819 F.3d 548, 552, 556–557 (1st Cir. 2016). As a practical matter, this standard is equivalent to the general civil standard of "preponderance of the evidence." *See, e.g, Frederico v. Home Depot*, 507 F.3d 188, 193–196 (3d Cir. 2007); *Smith v. Nationwide Prop. & Cas. Ins. Co.*, 505 F.3d 401, 404 (6th Cir. 2007).

In one influential case, *Amoche v. Guarantee Trust Life Ins. Co.*, 556 F.3d 41, 49–50 (1st Cir. 2009), the court addressed the question of burden:

> [Defendant] contends that a reasonable probability burden is too rigorous and that it should only be required to show, as if it were an initial plaintiff filing, that it is not a legal certainty that the amount in controversy is less than the jurisdictional minimum. This lesser burden, GTL argues, mirrors the burden on a plaintiff who initially files in federal court.
>
> The removing defendant's effort to liken its situation to cases in which the plaintiff has chosen to be in federal court and it is the defendant who seeks to defeat federal jurisdiction does not work. In CAFA, Congress expressly expanded federal jurisdiction largely for the benefit of defendants against a background of what it considered to be abusive class action practices in state courts. That did not mean, however, that Congress intended to place defendants in the same position as plaintiffs who originally choose a federal forum. Congress certainly did not use any statutory language adopting the analogy, and the policy considerations are very different in the two situations.
>
> Furthermore, placing a removing defendant in the same posture as a plaintiff who originally files in federal court would conflict with the general rule of deference to the plaintiff's chosen forum.

Ongoing Debate Over CAFA

The passage of CAFA in 2005 generated a great deal of commentary, almost all of it negative. *See, e.g.,* Symposium, *Fairness to Whom?: Perspectives on the Class Action Fairness Act of 2005*, 156 U. Pa. L. Rev. 1439 (2008); Symposium, *Developments in the Law—Class Action Fairness Act of 2005*, 39 Loy. L.A. L. Rev. 979 (2007). Despite arguments that CAFA should be repealed or amended significantly, the Act remains in force, which reflects the often frustrating reality that Congress rarely returns to amend a statute in light of academic criticism or judicial difficulty. CAFA is here to stay, and we close this chapter by noting some problems with the legislation on two levels.

As noted above, in passing CAFA, Congress relied on its power to base jurisdiction on minimal diversity. When the Supreme Court upheld the Federal Interpleader Act's grant of jurisdiction on that basis, it concluded that "Article III poses no obstacle to the legislative extension of federal jurisdiction, founded on diversity, so long as any two adverse parties are not co-citizens." *State Farm Fire & Casualty Co. v. Tashire*, 386 U.S. 523, 531 (1967).

Does this sentence justify the jurisdictional expansion in CAFA? Remember that Congress made various finding supporting the Act. Among them were: "Abuses in class actions undermine the national judicial system, the free flow of interstate commerce, and the concept of diversity jurisdiction as intended by the framers of the United States Constitution, in that State and local courts are ... keeping cases of national importance out of Federal court." Let us assess CAFA in light of these findings.

First, at a practical level, CAFA does a poor job of allocating cases of "national importance" to the federal courts. Consider this fact pattern:

> ***Example #19***. A class action is filed in state court of State X. The class consists entirely of citizens of State X. They allege harm sustained in State X, inflicted by a corporation incorporated in State Y with its principal place of business in State Z. The corporation does sufficient business in State X to be subject to personal jurisdiction there. The class claims, aggregated, exceed \$5,000,000. The defendant removes the case to federal court under CAFA.
>
> First, does the case invoke federal subject matter jurisdiction under CAFA? (The answer is yes; please articulate why.)
>
> Second, do any of the exceptions to CAFA apply? (The answer is no; please articulate why.)
>
> Third, as a matter of policy, what justifies placing this case in federal court? Is this a case of "national importance"? Does the policy underlying diversity of citizenship jurisdiction justify having this case in federal court?

Burbank, *supra*, 156 U. Pa. L. Rev. at 1527–1528 (criticizing jurisdictional overreach of CAFA to cases such as this). Professor Burbank concludes "the mere fact that a corporation is engaged in interstate commerce makes state law class action litigation against it (in all states but two) a matter of such strong 'national interest' as to trump the interests of the several states." Can you articulate support for this conclusion?

Second, at a more fundamental level, can the use of minimal diversity in CAFA be justified constitutionally? The knee-jerk reaction is simply to cite the *Tashire* case, quoted above, upholding jurisdiction as long as there are two adverse parties of different citizenship. Professor Floyd argues, however, that Congress's stated goals in CAFA do not fit the purposes for the grant of diversity jurisdiction, even as augmented by the necessary and proper clause. As we know, the Court has said that diversity jurisdiction serves to spare non-citizen litigants from the fear of local bias in local courts. The use of minimal diversity in CAFA, Floyd argues, is not based upon this rationale, but rests instead upon efficiency and avoidance of duplicative litigation. C. Douglas Floyd, *The Limits of Minimal Diversity*, 55 HASTINGS L.J. 613 (2004) (discussing the MMTJA and a proposed version of CAFA). He likewise concludes that the interstate commerce justification for CAFA is unimpressive. C. Douglas Floyd, *The Inadequacy of the Interstate Commerce Justification for the Class Action Fairness Act of 2005*, 55 EMORY L.J. 487, 500–507 (2006) (criticizing the "nationalizing" justification for the expansion of diversity-based jurisdiction).

Another scholar concludes that *Tashire*, in context, merely brought a modest extension of supplemental jurisdiction in interpleader cases. As such, it cannot justify the expansion to wholesale minimal diversity in CAFA. James F. Pfander, *Protective Jurisdiction, Aggregate Litigation, and the Limits of Article III*, 95 CAL. L. REV. 1423, 1453–1454 (2007).

It is rare to have such fundamental constitutional questions about a jurisdictional statute. So as the courts and litigants struggle with difficult interpretational issues, CAFA also forces us to consider the proper roles of the federal and state courts. And there is one lurking related thought—if Congress can wrest cases from the state courts as it has in CAFA, what is to stop it from decreeing the application of a single federal law to such cases? (We will address that topic in Chapter 4.)

Chapter 3

Coordination and Consolidation of Overlapping Litigation

A. Introduction

In this chapter, we deal with problems created by what we will call "overlapping litigation"—that is, multiple suits involving related events and parties. For simplicity, we can speak of Case 1 and Case 2 (although there may be hundreds of overlapping cases). Sometimes, overlapping cases present the same claims and parties. For instance, a plaintiff might file Case 1 and Case 2, asserting the same claim against the same defendant, in different courts. This might be a strategic effort to "shop"—to find whether one court would be more favorably disposed toward the plaintiff or the claim. Such "repetitive" litigation imposes duplication of effort on parties, and should be discouraged. Alan Vestal, *Repetitive Litigation*, 45 Iowa L. Rev. 525 (1960).

But how can it be avoided? One is tempted to say that claim or issue preclusion might limit the litigation in one of the fora. But claim and issue preclusion only flow from a valid final *judgment*, so neither can operate until a judgment is entered. Accordingly, we must look for other tools to avoid wasted effort caused by a plaintiff pursuing two cases at once.

"Reactive cases" are another example of overlapping litigation. Here, the defendant in Case 1 files Case 2, and asks the court in Case 2 either for an injunction stopping the plaintiff from proceeding in Case 1 or for a declaratory judgment that she should not be held liable in Case 1. Alan Vestal, *Reactive Litigation*, 47 Iowa L. Rev. 11 (1961). A good example involves patent law. In Case 1, a patent holder (the patentee) sues a manufacturer for alleged infringement of its patent. In Case 2, the manufacturer sues the patent holder, seeking a declaratory judgment that what it did did not constitute infringement (or perhaps that the patent is invalid). *See, e.g.*, *Kerotest Mfg. Co. v. C-O-Two Fire Equipment Co.*, 342 U.S. 180 (1952). Both cases present the same issues, and the overlapping litigation is wasteful. And again, claim and issue preclusion do nothing to prevent it—until a judgment is entered in one of the cases, claim and issue preclusion simply do not apply.

Much overlapping litigation involves different parties, so even ultimately (after entry of judgment) claim or issue preclusion might not apply.[1] For instance, if two

1. Claim and issue preclusion can only be asserted against one who was a party in a case in which a valid final judgment has been entered (or in privity with such a party). We discuss preclusion in Chapter 10.

passengers are injured in a taxicab crash (or if hundreds are injured in an airplane crash or by a toxic substance), they may sue separately. The judgment in Case 1 will not necessarily have a preclusive effect in Case 2.[2] The circumstances in which it may, based upon non-mutual assertion of preclusion, are discussed in Chapter 10.

What tools are available to avoid duplication of effort by the courts in Case 1 and Case 2? There are three general possibilities:

Option One: the cases might be transferred to a single court for coordinated or consolidated treatment there. It is important to remember, however, that transfer is only available between courts that are part of the same judicial system. Transfer is not possible from one judicial system to another. For example, a state court in Alabama cannot transfer a case to a state court in Colorado. A federal court in Washington cannot transfer a case to a state court in Oregon. The cases are in different judicial systems.

Option Two: one of the courts might *stay* (or dismiss) the case before it, and let the litigation proceed in the other forum. Dismissal might be ordered, for instance, under the doctrine of *forum non conveniens* or through some form of abstention.

Option Three: one of the courts may order the parties before it not to proceed in the other litigation; this is usually called an *anti-suit injunction*.

Overlapping litigation may arise in different ways, which affect the availability of these three options. Overlapping cases might (1) all be pending in federal courts, or (2) all be pending in state courts, or (3) be pending in both federal and state courts, or (4) be pending in both American and foreign courts.

When the overlapping cases are all in federal courts, Option One (transfer and coordination) is relatively easy. Because all cases are in the same judicial system, transfer to a single district is possible. Option One is not available in any of the other scenarios. Remember, transfer is impossible from one judicial system to another. (Review question: if Case 1 is in federal court and Case 2 is in state court, what might the defendant in Case 2 try to do to get that case into federal court? If she can get it into federal court, she might seek transfer and coordination.)

If transfer is not possible, Option Two may come into play. But is there something troublesome about a court simply eschewing its jurisdiction? If the plaintiff has properly invoked subject matter jurisdiction of her chosen court, what gives that

---

2. The judgment in Case 1 cannot have a claim preclusive effect in Case 2, because the cases involve different claimants. If the defendant wins a judgment in Case 1, it can have no issue preclusive effect in Case 2, because the plaintiff in Case 2 was not a party in Case 1. Thus, due process prohibits the use of issue preclusion. Only if the plaintiff won a judgment in Case 1, based upon a finding that the defendant was at fault, might there be room for issue preclusion in Case 2. And even here, it will be permitted only in the minority of states that permit non-mutual offensive issue preclusion (and only if the requirements of that doctrine are satisfied). Again, we will see all of this in Chapter 10.

court the right to refuse to hear the case? Is that an abdication of the court's constitutional or statutory responsibilities?

And consider Option Three. If the overlapping cases are in federal court, an anti-suit injunction generally is not seen as insulting to the court in which the other case is pending. Although the effect of the injunction is to halt litigation in that other court, that other court is in the same judicial system. Such an injunction does not ruffle feathers of a different sovereign. On the other hand, an anti-suit injunction by a federal court against litigation in a state court raises serious *federalism* concerns. With such an injunction, an arm of the federal government is essentially telling an arm of the state government that it cannot proceed with a case properly within its jurisdiction.[3] Because of the potential insult to the sovereignty of the state, Congress has limited the ability of federal courts to issue such injunctions. The same concerns are obvious in the international context—it is somewhat dicey for an American tribunal (federal or state) to enter an injunction essentially forbidding litigation in the courts of another country. Such orders raise delicate considerations of international relations.

Because the context of the overlapping litigation affects the manner in which courts may avoid redundancy, we divide this chapter into three further sections. Section B addresses overlapping cases that are all in federal courts, section C deals with overlapping cases pending in federal and state courts, and section D concerns overlapping cases pending in American and foreign courts.

B. Overlapping Federal Cases

It is possible that overlapping federal cases will be filed in the same federal district. If so, the court can coordinate proceedings through consolidation under Rule 42(a). It is more likely, however, that cases are pending in different federal districts. How does a court determine whether to proceed, to stay, or to enter an anti-suit injunction? The starting point is the aptly named first-filed rule.

1. The First-Filed Rule

The general rule is that the first case filed concerning related subject matter should take precedence. But there are exceptions to the rule. Moreover, there are different ways in which courts might vindicate the rule (remember Options One, Two, and Three above). Keep these points in mind in reading the next case.

---

3. Technically, as we will discuss below, an anti-suit injunction issues not to the other court, but to the parties. It tells them not to proceed with litigation in the other court. In effect, however, the injunction stops proceedings in the other court. When that other court is an arm of a different sovereign, the justice system must be concerned with avoiding insult by one system to the other.

Biolitec, Inc. v. Angiodynamics, Inc.

United States District Court for the District of Massachusetts
581 F. Supp. 2d 152 (2008)

[In this case, the district judge referred the defendant's motion to dismiss to a magistrate judge. A magistrate is not an Article III judge, but serves as an adjunct to the district court. A district judge can refer a motion to dismiss to a magistrate judge, who can hold a hearing and recommend final disposition to the district judge. As we will discuss in Chapter 5, the district judge must review the magistrate's recommendations, and may either adopt or reject them. Here, the district judge adopted the magistrate's findings, recommendations, and opinion.]

NEIMAN, CHIEF UNITED STATES MAGISTRATE JUDGE.

This is a declaratory judgment and breach of contract action in which Biolitec, Inc. ("Plaintiff") seeks to recover from AngioDynamics, Inc. ("Defendant") $1.6 million that it expended in helping defend Defendant in a patent infringement suit. Arguing that Plaintiff's complaint fails to state claims upon which relief may be granted, Defendant has moved to dismiss it pursuant to FED. R. CIV. P. 12(b)(6). Defendant also asserts that the complaint should be dismissed—or [the case should be] transferred to the United States District Court for the Northern District of New York—because there is a previously-filed action there involving the same parties and the same underlying transaction (hereinafter "the New York action"). . . .

I. FACTUAL BACKGROUND

. . . On April 1, 2002, Plaintiff and Defendant entered into a Supply and Distribution Agreement ("SDA"), pursuant to which Plaintiff agreed to sell Defendant certain laser and fiber products. In November of 2003, another company, Diomed, Inc. ("Diomed"), sued Defendant for patent infringement. One basis of that lawsuit involved Defendant's sale of certain products that incorporated and modified the products that Plaintiff had sold to Defendant.

Sections 7.2, 9.1 and 9.2 of the SDA discussed, as follows, the parties' obligations with respect to potential infringement allegations—such as those brought by Diomed—as well as the parties' indemnification rights:

> 7.2 *Infringement of Third Party Patents and Rights*. . . . If a third party asserts that a patent or other proprietary right owned by it is infringed by the manufacture, marketing, sale, distribution or use of a Product, the party against whom such a claim was asserted shall provide the other party with notice of such claim within fifteen (15) days. BIOLITEC agrees to undertake the sole and complete defense, at its sole cost and expense, of any such claim through counsel of its choice and control the settlement of any such claim. . . . If BIOLITEC fails to take such action, AngioDynamics shall be entitled to do so and BIOLITEC shall promptly reimburse AngioDynamics for pre-agreed upon expenses it incurs, including without limitation reasonable attorney's fees.

> 9.1 *Indemnification by BIOLITEC.* BIOLITEC agrees to indemnify and hold AngioDynamics harmless from and against any and all Loss that AngioDynamics may incur to the extent that such Loss arises out of or results from (i) a breach of any representation or warranty or agreement given in this Agreement by BIOLITEC, or (ii) the injury, illness or death of any person which arises out of or relates to the manufacture or the design of Products.
>
> 9.2 *Indemnification by AngioDynamics.* AngioDynamics agrees to indemnify and hold BIOLITEC harmless from and against any and all Loss that BIOLITEC may incur to the extent that such Loss arises out of or results from (i) the unlawful sale, promotion and distribution of the Products by AngioDynamics in the Territory, (ii) any unauthorized modification or alteration made by AngioDynamics to the Products, (iii) the improper sterilization or labeling of the Products, (iv) a breach of any representation made or warranty given in this Agreement by AngioDynamics, (v) mishandling of fibers during unpacking and repackaging of bulk fibers delivered to AngioDynamics for the purpose of putting into their kits, or (vi) the design of a product solely by AngioDynamics.

At or around the time that Diomed commenced its action, Defendant made a demand for indemnification upon Plaintiff. Although Plaintiff refused this demand, the parties entered into a Joint Defense Agreement ("JDA") dated November 24, 2003.

Alleging that it had reserved its rights with respect to its indemnity obligations, Plaintiff contributed \$1.6 million to Defendant's defense in the Diomed litigation.[4] On September 27, 2007, Plaintiff demanded that Defendant reimburse this \$1.6 million in defense costs, a demand Defendant has refused.

Plaintiff's complaint contains four counts. Count I seeks a judgment declaring, pursuant to 28 U.S.C. § 2201(a), that Defendant "is obligated . . . to reimburse Biolitec for the Defense Costs expended by Biolitec in defense of the [Diomed] Litigation." Count II, entitled breach of contract, alleges that Defendant breached both the SDA and the JDA and seeks damages of at least \$1.6 million. Count III, entitled quantum meruit/unjust enrichment, claims that Defendant has been unjustly enriched by at least \$1.6 million. And Count IV claims a violation of Mass. Gen. L. ch. 93A ("chapter 93A"), to wit, that Defendant's "intentional failure to render payment to Biolitec after demand, as well as its continued insistence that Biolitec owes an indemnity obligation under the [SDA]" constitutes "unfair and deceptive" conduct as well as "a willful effort to extort funds from [Plaintiff]."

. . .

4. [Court's footnote #1] Although it is not mentioned in the complaint, the parties have informed the court that, in March of 2007, a jury rendered a verdict against Defendant in the Diomed litigation in the amount of \$9,170,000.

II. PROCEDURAL BACKGROUND

Plaintiff commenced the instant action on January 11, 2008 and, on January 14, 2008, served Defendant with a copy of the summons and complaint. Meanwhile, on January 2, 2008, *Defendant* sued *Plaintiff* in the Northern District of New York, *i.e.*, the New York action. Plaintiff, however, was not served with a copy of the summons and complaint in the New York action until January 15, 2008. Plaintiff also points to the fact that the complaint was not delivered to its corporate office in East Longmeadow, Massachusetts, until January 27, 2008.

Defendant asserts five counts against Plaintiff in the New York action. Three of those counts involve the Diomed litigation: Plaintiff's alleged breach of [particular sections of the contract between them]. Two other counts in the New York action (Counts 2 and 4) involve similar allegations with respect to a pending patent infringement suit filed in July of 2005 against Defendant by another company, VNUS Technologies, Inc. ("VNUS").

Defendant filed its motion to dismiss in the instant action on February 4, 2008. . . . Plaintiff filed four counterclaims in the New York action on March 14, 2008. Those counterclaims assert that Defendant is obligated, pursuant to Section 9.2 of the [contract between them], to indemnify Plaintiff for the $1.6 million it expended in defense of the Diomed litigation (First Counterclaim); that Defendant has been unjustly enriched by $1.6 million (Second Counterclaim); that Plaintiff is entitled to a judgment declaring the parties' payment obligations with respect to both the Diomed and VNUS actions (Third Counterclaim); and that Plaintiff has suffered "loss" for which Defendant is obligated under Sections 1.13 and 9.2 of the [contract].

III. DISCUSSION . . .

1. Prior Pending Action Doctrine

Citing a footnote [in] . . . *Carmack v. Massachusetts Bay Transp. Auth.*, 465 F. Supp. 2d 18, 33 n.10 (D. Mass. 2006), Defendant asserts that something called the "prior pending action doctrine" calls for dismissal. As described by [the judge in *Carmack*], the court has an "inherent power to dismiss or stay an action in favor of prior litigation presenting the same claims and issues." *Id.* The doctrine applies here, Defendant argues, because there is a prior pending action between the same parties regarding the same claims and issues.

In opposition, Plaintiff originally asserted that dismissal under the prior pending action doctrine would be inappropriate because "[t]he vital issues in the present action, the payment of defense costs and the reasonable expectation of repayment, are not pending in the New York Action, as the New York Action is solely 'on the contract.'" That assertion, however, is no longer accurate given the counterclaims Plaintiff has since filed in the New York action, *i.e.*, that Defendant is obligated under the SDA to indemnify Plaintiff for the $1.6 million it expended in defense of the Diomed litigation (First Counterclaim), that Defendant has been unjustly enriched by $1.6 million (Second Counterclaim), that Plaintiff is entitled to a judgment declaring the parties' payment obligations with respect to both the Diomed and VNUS actions (Third Counterclaim), and that Plaintiff has suffered "loss" for which Defendant is obligated under Sections 1.13 and 9.2 of the SDA (Fourth Counterclaim). Aspects of these four counterclaims are quite similar, if not identical, to Plaintiff's claims here. (The only differences appear to be that Plaintiff's chapter 93A claim is not included in its counterclaims in the New York action and that the VNUS matter is mentioned in the New York action but not here.) Of course, the parties are identical in both lawsuits.

That being said, the court will not recommend dismissal based on the *Carmack* footnote inasmuch as the court's own research has not unearthed any decision within the First Circuit, not even *Carmack* itself, which actually dismissed a case based upon a "prior pending action doctrine." *But see Continental Time Corp. v. Swiss Credit Bank*, 543 F. Supp. 408, 410 (S.D.N.Y. 1982) (applying version of the doctrine in New York federal court); *Conant v. Sherwin L. Kantrovitz*, P.C., 29 Mass. App. Ct. 998, 563 N.E.2d 247, 249 (Mass. App. Ct. 1990) (similar in Massachusetts state court). More to the point, the court believes that the "first-filed rule"—discussed next—clearly calls for a transfer of this case to the Northern District of New York. . . .

2. First-Filed Rule

There is ample support within this circuit for transferring cases pursuant to the "first-filed rule," Defendant's second procedural argument. . . .

> [T]he "first-filed" rule . . . generally gives precedence to the first of two duplicative actions proceeding in different federal courts. "Where identical actions are proceeding concurrently in two federal courts, entailing duplicative litigation and a waste of judicial resources, the first filed action is generally preferred in a choice-of-venue decision." *Cianbro Corp. v. Curran-Lavoie, Inc.*, 814 F.2d 7, 11 (1st Cir. 1987); see *Gulf Oil Corp. v. Gilbert*, 330 U.S. 501, 508, 67 S. Ct. 839, 91 L. Ed. 1055 (1947) (the "plaintiff's choice of forum should rarely be disturbed").

Transcanada Power Mktg., Ltd. v. Narragansett Elec. Co., 402 F. Supp. 2d 343, 347 (D. Mass. 2005) (transferring case to forum where dispute was filed first). In other words, there is a "strong presumption" favoring the forum chosen first, against which the opposing party "must bear the burden of proving . . . that considerations of convenience and judicial efficiency strongly favor litigating the claim in the alternative forum." *Nowak v. Tak How Invs., Ltd.*, 94 F.3d 708, 719 (1st Cir. 1996). Indeed, as [the court in *Transcanada Power*] recognized, it is particularly appropriate to transfer a second case to the forum of the first case where, as here, "two sophisticated parties are negotiating at arm's length." *Transcanada Power*, 402 F. Supp. 2d at 350 (citations omitted).

To be sure, there are two generally-recognized exceptions to the first-filed rule: "The first is where there are 'special circumstances' justifying [having the cases heard in the second forum], such as where the party bringing the first-filed action engaged in misleading conduct in order to prevail in a pre-emptive 'race to the courthouse.' The second is where the balance of convenience substantially favors the second-filed action." *Id.* Here, however, Plaintiff does not contend that either of the exceptions applies. That is, Plaintiff neither argues that Defendant engaged in misleading conduct in order to prevail in a pre-emptive "race to the courthouse" nor that the balance of convenience substantially favors this lawsuit over the New York action. At most, Plaintiff, citing [*Transcanada Power*], argues that the vital issues to be determined are not "identical."

In the court's view, however, Plaintiff cannot distance itself from the first-filed rule, particularly given that its claims have now been filed as counterclaims in the New York action. True, the claims in the two cases are not mirror images of one another; for example, as indicated, the instant complaint, unlike the New York counterclaims, omits any reference to the VNUS suit and includes a chapter 93A cause of action. But the essence of Plaintiff's position in the two suits—particularly Plaintiff's emphasis on recovering its $1.6 million defense costs in the Diomed case as well as its request for a declaratory judgment—is identical. Accordingly, there are sufficient grounds for allowing Defendant's motion pursuant to the first-filed rule and transferring the case to the Northern District of New York.

Before moving on, the court adds one point. Plaintiff implies (but never really argues) that the present action was actually filed first since it was served on Defendant on January 14, 2008, i.e., one day prior to Defendant serving Plaintiff with the summons and complaint in the New York action, January 15, 2008, and nearly two weeks prior to the complaint in the New York action being delivered to Plaintiff's corporate office, January 27, 2008. In the court's view, this argument, if argument it is, is a red herring. Under the federal rules, the measuring date for present purposes is the date the complaint was filed in court, not the date of service. See Fed. R. Civ. P. 3 ("A civil action is commenced by filing a complaint with the court."). Cf. Fed. R. Civ. P. 4(m) (noting that a complaint will be dismissed if the defendant is not served within 120 days [changed in 2015 to 90 days] "after the complaint is filed"). Here, the New York action was filed on January 2, 2008, whereas the instant complaint was filed on January 11, 2008. Accordingly, there can be no question but that the New York action was filed first.

. . .

IV. CONCLUSION

For the reasons stated, the court recommends that Defendant's motion to dismiss be ALLOWED insofar as it requests that the case be transferred to the Northern District of New York, but otherwise DENIED.

Notes and Questions

1. The court in this case applied the first-filed rule. Did it explain, however, *why* the first-filed case should take precedence? In your view, *should* Case 1 take precedence? Why?

2. The case we read was filed on January 11, and the defendant (Angiodynamics) was served with process on January 14. Angiodynamics filed the New York case on January 2, but the defendant (Biolitec) was not served until January 15. Accordingly, Angiodynamics was aware that it had been sued (in the case we read) before Biolitec was aware that it had been sued (in the New York case). Why is that fact irrelevant under the first-filed rule? Should there instead be a "first-served" rule? Why should the act of filing be more important than the question of when the defendant became aware of the suit?

3. Would the court in the case we read have reached the same result if Biolitec had not filed the counterclaim in the New York litigation? If not, what would have happened—would this case and the New York case have proceeded simultaneously? What problems might that have created?

4. In the New York action, was Biolitec *required* by the compulsory counterclaim rule to assert the counterclaim it filed in March? Rule 13(a)(2)(A) provides an exception to the compulsory counterclaim rule. Would the exception have applied to Biolitec's counterclaim in the New York case?

5. How does the "prior pending action doctrine" (discussed in *Biolitec*) differ from the first-filed rule?

Note on Exceptions to the First-Filed Rule

The court in *Biolitec* recognized two exceptions to the first-filed rule. One, it said, is when "special circumstances" mandate that Case 2 should proceed. The example the court gave is that the plaintiff in Case 1 "engaged in misleading conduct" to win a "pre-emptive race to the courthouse." One instance of such behavior is *Sensient Colors, Inc. v. Allstate Ins. Co.*, 193 N.J. 373, 393–394 (2008), in which an insurance company caused its insured to believe that she would be covered for a claim, and then sued for a declaratory judgment that it was not obligated to cover it. Though the insurance company's case was filed before the insured's, the latter case was allowed to proceed.

Two, a court may refuse to defer to the first-filed case when the "balance of convenience substantially favors the second-filed action." In other words, if Case 2 is in a far more convenient place—the "center of gravity" of the litigation—it might proceed. Courts look to the same sorts of factors that govern motions to transfer, including residence of parties and witnesses, access to evidence, and what law will govern. We will discuss transfer in section B.2 below.

These two exceptions do not exhaust the list of occasions in which a court might not defer to the first-filed case. The issue often arises in patent litigation. As noted at the outset of this chapter, the holder of the patent may sue alleged infringers. Sometimes, however, a potential defendant—fearing that the patentee will sue it for infringement—may jump the gun and sue first, seeking a declaration that its product does not infringe the patentee's patent. These are often called "customer suits," because the party bringing the case is usually a customer of the patentee. Often, when the patentee then sues the infringer (maybe joining other infringers as well), courts will permit it to proceed, even though it was not the first filed.

While courts generally refer to such scenarios as raising "exceptions" to the first-filed rule, they should not be applied mechanically. In every situation, the question of whether to allow a later-filed case to take precedence is vested in the sound discretion of the judge. Every case is considered on its unique facts.

Note on Methods for Enforcing the First-Filed Rule

In *Biolitec*, the court vindicated the first-filed rule by transferring the case to the federal district in which the first-filed case was pending. (Though the court did not cite authority, it undoubtedly ordered transfer under 28 U.S.C. § 1404(a), which we discuss in section B.2 below.) The court enforced the first-filed rule by transferring to the court where Case 1 was pending.

But transfer is not the only vehicle for enforcing the first-filed rule. Instead, the court in which Case 2 is pending may *stay* the case. It would enter an order stating that it will not proceed further in the matter. *See, e.g.*, *Goldhammer v. Dunkin Donuts, Inc.*, 59 F.Supp.2d 248, 255–256 (D. Mass. 1999) (entering stay pending outcome of first-filed case). Later, after a final judgment is entered in Case 1, the court in Case 2 may then be able to dispose of all or part of Case 2 through claim or issue preclusion.

Another possibility is that the court in which Case 1 is pending may enter an anti-suit injunction, which would forbid the parties in Case 1 from litigating in Case 2. We will discuss the requirements of such orders in the context of overlapping federal and state litigation in Section C.2.

Problem

A sues Z in the United States District Court for the District of Arizona. One month later, Z files suit against A in the United States District Court for the District of Nevada. Assume that each court has personal and subject matter jurisdiction and that the cases assert claims arising from the same overall dispute. Assume also that each party files a compulsory counterclaim in the case in which she was sued. You represent A, who wants the litigation to proceed in the District of Arizona and not to be subject to the burden of overlapping litigation in the District of Nevada.

1. What motion(s) might A make in the federal court in Nevada?
2. What motion(s) might A make in the federal court in Arizona?

2. Transfer of Cases under §§ 1404(a) or 1406(a) (and a Refresher on Venue)

As we saw in *Biolitec*, one way to avoid duplication of effort in overlapping litigation is to transfer one case to the court in which related litigation is pending. Then the cases can be coordinated by that one court, perhaps (as we see in the next subsection) through consolidation. The court from which the case is transferred is the "transferor" and the court to which the case is transferred is the "transferee."

Transfer of civil cases from one federal district to another generally is governed by two statutes: 28 U.S.C. §§ 1404(a) and 1406(a). Why are there two transfer provisions? Section 1404(a) applies when the transferor district is a proper venue. Section 1406(a) applies when the transferor district is not a proper district. The former permits, but does not require, the original court to transfer the case to another district based upon considerations of convenience and the interest of justice. The latter, in contrast, permits the original court to transfer in the interest of justice or to dismiss. Dismissal would be based upon the fact that the present court is not a proper venue. A defendant might raise that defense by motion to dismiss under Federal Rule 12(b)(3) or by a motion to dismiss or transfer under § 1406(a).

Both statutes permit transfer even if the transferor district lacks personal jurisdiction over the defendant. The Supreme Court established this fact for § 1406(a) transfers in *Goldlawr, Inc. v. Heiman*, 369 U.S. 463, 466 (1962), and lower courts have extended the holding to § 1404(a) transfers.

On the other hand, both statutes require that the transferee district be one in which the action "might" or "could" have been brought. In *Hoffman v. Blaski*, 363 U.S. 335, 344 (1960), the Supreme Court held that this requires that the transferee district (1) be a proper venue and (2) have personal jurisdiction over the defendant. Indeed, these two things must be independently true, and not the result of waiver by the defendant. (Though *Hoffman* was a § 1404(a) case, every federal court to address the issue concludes that its holding applies to § 1406(a) transfers as well.)

> ***Example #1.*** P sues D in the District of Minnesota. D moves to transfer to the District of Hawaii. He admits that the District of Hawaii is not a proper venue and does not have personal jurisdiction over him, but says he will waive those defects. Transfer is not possible under either § 1404(a) or § 1406(a). Venue and personal jurisdiction must be proper in the transferee district independent of consent by D.[5]

How does one assess whether venue is proper (either in the original district or a proposed transferee district)? Though there are scores of specialized venue statutes throughout the United States Code, most cases are governed by the "general" venue provision in 28 U.S.C. § 1391(b). Stated generally, that provision permits venue in a district in which the defendant resides[6] (§ 1391(b)(1)) or in a district in which a

5. The Federal Jurisdiction and Venue Clarification Act of 2011 made one small inroad on the holding in *Hoffman*. That Act added a clause to § 1404(a) which permits transfer to any district at all, but only if transfer is justified under the standard prescribed in § 1404(a) and if *all* parties agree to the transferee district. It seems unlikely that many plaintiffs will to give up their chosen forum so readily.

6. If there are multiple defendants, they must all reside in the same district to satisfy § 1391(b)(1). The only exception is if all defendants reside in different districts of the forum state. Then, all

substantial part of the events underlying the case arose (§ 1391(b)(2)).[7] *See generally* 14D WRIGHT & MILLER, FEDERAL PRACTICE AND PROCEDURE § 3802 (3d ed. 2013). Where a defendant resides for venue purposes is defined in § 1391(c).

Before Congress enacted the transfer statutes in 1948, one federal court could not transfer to another. Instead, if litigation would be more convenient elsewhere (even in another federal district), a court could dismiss or stay the pending case under the common law doctrine of *forum non conveniens*. This would permit the parties to proceed with separate litigation in the more convenient forum. The idea underlying transfer and underlying *forum non conveniens* is the same—that while the present forum is proper, another is far more appropriate. Stated another way, while the original site may be fine, another court is the "center of gravity" where litigation ought to proceed.

Section 1404(a) permits transfer based upon "the convenience of parties and witnesses, in the interest of justice." In applying this provision (and, as we will see in section D of this chapter, in deciding whether to dismiss or stay under *forum non conveniens*), courts generally give some weight to the plaintiff's choice of forum. Thus, the burden is on the party seeking transfer (usually the defendant) to demonstrate that the plaintiff's choice ought to be overridden. District judges have very broad discretion in determining whether to order transfer.

Borrowing from the law of *forum non conveniens*, courts ruling on transfer under § 1404(a) look to a series of "public" and "private" factors. (These are sometimes called "*Gulf Oil* factors" after the Supreme Court decision in *Gulf Oil v. Gilbert*, 330 U.S. 501 (1947)). The public-interest considerations reflect the § 1404(a) provision for the "interest of justice." The private-interest considerations reflect the statute's reference to convenience of the parties and witnesses. As the Supreme Court summarized in *Atlantic Marine Construction Co. v. U.S. District Court*, 571 U.S. 49, 62 n.6 (2013):

> Factors relating to the parties' private interests include "relative ease of access to sources of proof; availability of compulsory process for attendance of unwilling, and the cost of obtaining attendance of willing, witnesses; possibility of view of premises, if view would be appropriate to the action; and all other practical problems that make trial of a case easy, expeditious and inexpensive." Piper Aircraft Co. v. Reyno, 454 U.S. 235, 241, n. 6, 102 S. Ct. 252, 70 L. Ed. 2d 419 (1981). Public-interest factors may include "the

---

defendants may be sued in a district in which any one resides. For example, if the only defendants reside, respectively, in the Southern District of California and the Central District of California, plaintiff may sue them as co-defendants in either of those districts.

7. Section 1391(b)(3)—the "fallback" venue provision—is very broad, as it permits venue in a district in which any defendant is subject to personal jurisdiction. But this provision almost never applies. It can be used only if no district *anywhere in the United States* will meet one of the choices in § 1391(b)(1) or § 1391(b)(2). If there is any district in the country in which the defendant resides or in which a substantial part of the claim arose, § 1391(b)(3) is inapplicable.

> administrative difficulties flowing from court congestion; the local interest in having localized controversies decided at home; [and] the interest in having the trial of a diversity case in a forum that is at home with the law." Ibid. The Court must also give some weight to the plaintiffs' choice of forum. See Norwood v. Kirkpatrick, 349 U.S. 29, 32, 75 S. Ct. 544, 99 L. Ed. 789 (1995).

One important issue in any case is choice of law. Choice-of-law rules are those that determine what substantive law will govern the dispute. Each state is free to create its own such rules. (One common standard, for instance, is that in tort cases, the court will apply the law of the state in which the injury was suffered.) In diversity of citizenship cases, the federal court must apply the choice-of-law rules of the forum state. *Klaxon v. Stentor Elec. Mfg. Co,* 313 U.S. 488 (1941).

> ***Example #2.*** A citizen of Idaho is involved in a car wreck with a citizen of New Hampshire while on vacation in Hawaii. She files a diversity of citizenship case in the District of New Hampshire. (Assume there is personal jurisdiction, subject matter jurisdiction, and that venue is proper.) The federal judge in that case will consult New Hampshire choice-of-law doctrine to determine what substantive tort law will govern in the case: the law of New Hampshire, or Idaho, or Hawaii. (It will probably be the law of Hawaii, but, as indicated, every state is free to determine its own choice-of-law rules, within limits we will see in Chapter 4.)

As we will see in Chapter 4, section C, in *Van Dusen v. Barrack*, 376 U.S. 612, 639 (1964), the Court held that when a diversity case is transferred under § 1404(a), the transferee district must apply the choice-of-law rules the transferor would have applied. Indeed, the Court even extended it to cases in which the *plaintiff* makes the motion to transfer. *Ferens v. John Deere Co.*, 494 U.S. 516, 523 (1990).

> ***Example #3.*** Let's say the District of New Hampshire transfers the diversity case to the District of Idaho under § 1404(a).[8] Under *Van Dusen*, the choice-of-law rules of New Hampshire are transferred with the case. So the federal judge to whom the case is assigned in Idaho must apply New Hampshire choice-of-law doctrine to determine what substantive law will govern the claims in the case. This fact can make life difficult for the transferee judge and may, depending on the facts, be a reason for declining to order transfer.

Courts agree that *Van Dusen* does not apply to transfers under § 1406(a). In such cases, the original district is an improper venue. It would be unfair to allow a plaintiff to sue in an improper forum and "capture" the choice-of-law rules (and thus, possibly, the governing law on the claims) of that forum.[9]

---

8. Remember that under *Hoffman*, the District of Idaho would have to be a proper venue and have personal jurisdiction over the defendant. For this hypothetical, we'll assume that it does.

9. For the same reason, *Van Dusen* does not apply when the transferor court lacks personal jurisdiction. Though the transferor's lack of personal jurisdiction will not impede its power to

We must consider one more thing before looking at an important case: the possibility that the parties entered into a valid forum selection clause. Many commercial contracts include these clauses, which provide that litigation among the parties will take place in a particular forum. Historically, such clauses were void (because they "ousted" courts of jurisdiction, and thereby violated the legislative prerogative of setting jurisdiction). Today, however, the overwhelming majority of states follow the lead of federal law in enforcing forum selection clauses, so long as they are not the product of overweening bargaining power. The leading case embracing these clauses is *M/S Bremen v. Zapata Off-Shore Co.*, 407 U.S. 1 (1972).

Suppose the parties to a contract agree to a valid forum selection clause. When a dispute arises, one of the parties sues in a different district. That district, while improper under the forum selection clause, is a proper venue under § 1391(b). Does the forum selection clause render venue improper? If the court orders transfer, is the transfer under § 1404(a) or § 1406(a)? If the court orders transfer, should *Van Dusen* apply? Lower courts failed to forge consensus on these and related questions, which prompted the Supreme Court to accept and decide the following case.

Atlantic Marine Construction Co. v. U.S. District Court

Supreme Court of the United States
571 U.S. 49 (2013)

Justice Alito delivered the opinion of the Court.

The question in this case concerns the procedure that is available for a defendant in a civil case who seeks to enforce a forum-selection clause. We reject petitioner's argument that such a clause may be enforced by a motion to dismiss under 28 U.S.C. § 1406(a) or Rule 12(b)(3) of the Federal Rules of Civil Procedure. Instead, a forum-selection clause may be enforced by a motion to transfer under § 1404(a), which provides that "[f]or the convenience of parties and witnesses, in the interest of justice, a district court may transfer any civil action to any other district or division where it might have been brought or to any district or division to which all parties have consented." When a defendant files such a motion, we conclude, a district court should transfer the case unless extraordinary circumstances unrelated to the convenience of the parties clearly disfavor a transfer. In the present case, both the District Court and the Court of Appeals misunderstood the standards to be applied in adjudicating a § 1404(a) motion in a case involving a forum-selection clause, and we therefore reverse the decision below.

---

order transfer under § 1404(a) or § 1406(a), the choice-of-law rules of that forum will not be transferred with the case.

I

Petitioner Atlantic Marine Construction Co., a Virginia corporation with its principal place of business in Virginia, entered into a contract with the United States Army Corps of Engineers to construct a child-development center at Fort Hood in the Western District of Texas. Atlantic Marine then entered into a subcontract with respondent J-Crew Management, Inc., a Texas corporation, for work on the project. This subcontract included a forum-selection clause, which stated that all disputes between the parties "shall be litigated in the Circuit Court for the City of Norfolk, Virginia, or the United States District Court for the Eastern District of Virginia, Norfolk Division."

When a dispute about payment under the subcontract arose, however, J-Crew sued Atlantic Marine in the Western District of Texas, invoking that court's diversity jurisdiction. Atlantic Marine moved to dismiss the suit, arguing that the forum-selection clause rendered venue in the Western District of Texas "wrong" under § 1406(a) and "improper" under Federal Rule of Civil Procedure 12(b)(3). In the alternative, Atlantic Marine moved to transfer the case to the Eastern District of Virginia under § 1404(a). J-Crew opposed these motions.

[After the district court denied the motions, Atlantic Marine petitioned the Court of Appeals for a writ of mandamus directing the District Court to dismiss the case under § 1406(a) or to transfer the case to the Eastern District of Virginia under § 1404(a). The Fifth Circuit denied the petition. There was no question that the forum selection clause was valid. There was also no question that venue was proper in the Western District of Texas under § 1391(b)(2) because a substantial part of the events underlying the claim arose there.]

II

Atlantic Marine contends that a party may enforce a forum-selection clause by seeking dismissal of the suit under § 1406(a) and Rule 12(b)(3). We disagree. Section 1406(a) and Rule 12(b)(3) allow dismissal only when venue is "wrong" or "improper." Whether venue is "wrong" or "improper" depends exclusively on whether the court in which the case was brought satisfies the requirements of federal venue laws, and those provisions say nothing about a forum-selection clause.

A

Section 1406(a) provides that "[t]he district court of a district in which is filed a case laying venue in the wrong division or district shall dismiss, or if it be in the interest of justice, transfer such case to any district or division in which it could have been brought." Rule 12(b)(3) states that a party may move to dismiss a case for "improper venue." These provisions therefore authorize dismissal only when venue is "wrong" or "improper" in the forum in which it was brought.

This question—whether venue is "wrong" or "improper"—is generally governed by 28 U. S. C. § 1391. That provision states that "[e]xcept as otherwise provided by law . . . this section shall govern the venue of all civil actions brought in district courts of the United States." . . . When venue is challenged, the court must determine whether the case falls within one of the three categories set out in § 1391(b). If it does, venue is proper; if it does not, venue is improper, and the case must be dismissed or transferred under § 1406(a). Whether the parties entered into a contract containing a forum-selection clause has no bearing on whether a case falls into one of the categories of cases listed in § 1391(b). As a result, a case filed in a district that falls within § 1391 may not be dismissed under § 1406(a) or Rule 12(b)(3).

. . .

The structure of the federal venue provisions confirms that they alone define whether venue exists in a given forum. In particular, the venue statutes reflect Congress' intent that venue should always lie in some federal court whenever federal courts have personal jurisdiction over the defendant. The first two paragraphs of § 1391(b) define the preferred judicial districts for venue in a typical case, but the third paragraph provides a fallback option: If no other venue is proper, then venue will lie in "any judicial district in which any defendant is subject to the court's personal jurisdiction" (emphasis added). The statute thereby ensures that so long as a federal court has personal jurisdiction over the defendant, venue will always lie somewhere. . . . Yet petitioner's approach would mean that in some number of cases—those in which the forum-selection clause points to a state or foreign court—venue would not lie in any federal district. That would not comport with the statute's design, which contemplates that venue will always exist in some federal court.

. . .

B

Although a forum-selection clause does not render venue in a court "wrong" or "improper" within the meaning of § 1406(a) or Rule 12(b)(3), the clause may be enforced through a motion to transfer under § 1404(a). That provision states that "[f]or the convenience of parties and witnesses, in the interest of justice, a district court may transfer any civil action to any other district or division where it might have been brought or to any district or division to which all parties have consented." Unlike § 1406(a), § 1404(a) does not condition transfer on the initial forum's being "wrong." And it permits transfer to any district where venue is also proper (i.e., "where [the case] might have been brought") or to any other district to which the parties have agreed by contract or stipulation.

Section 1404(a) therefore provides a mechanism for enforcement of forum-selection clauses that point to a particular federal district. And for the reasons we address in Part III, infra, a proper application of § 1404(a) requires that a forum-selection clause be "given controlling weight in all but the most exceptional cases."

Atlantic Marine argues that § 1404(a) is not a suitable mechanism to enforce forum-selection clauses because that provision cannot provide for transfer when a forum-selection clause specifies a state or foreign tribunal, and we agree with Atlantic Marine that the Court of Appeals failed to provide a sound answer to this problem.

The Court of Appeals opined that a forum-selection clause pointing to a nonfederal forum should be enforced through Rule 12(b)(3), which permits a party to move for dismissal of a case based on "improper venue." As Atlantic Marine persuasively argues, however, that conclusion cannot be reconciled with our construction of the term "improper venue" in § 1406 to refer only to a forum that does not satisfy federal venue laws. If venue is proper under federal venue rules, it does not matter for the purpose of Rule 12(b)(3) whether the forum-selection clause points to a federal or a nonfederal forum.

Instead, the appropriate way to enforce a forum-selection clause pointing to a state or foreign forum is through the doctrine of *forum non conveniens*. Section 1404(a) is merely a codification of the doctrine of *forum non conveniens* for the subset of cases in which the transferee forum is within the federal court system; in such cases, Congress has replaced the traditional remedy of outright dismissal with transfer. . . . For the remaining set of cases calling for a nonfederal forum, § 1404(a) has no application, but the residual doctrine of *forum non conveniens* "has continuing application in federal courts." And because both § 1404(a) and the *forum non conveniens* doctrine from which it derives entail the same balancing-of-interests standard, courts should evaluate a forum-selection clause pointing to a nonfederal forum in the same way that they evaluate a forum-selection clause pointing to a federal forum. . . .

C

[The Court here declined to rule on whether a forum selection clause may be enforced through a motion to dismiss for failure to state a claim under Federal Rule 12(b)(6), as some courts have permitted. The issue was pressed in an amicus curiae brief, but because the parties did not raise it, the Court refused to resolve it.]

III

Although the Court of Appeals correctly identified § 1404(a) as the appropriate provision to enforce the forum-selection clause in this case, the Court of Appeals erred in failing to make the adjustments required in a § 1404(a) analysis when the transfer motion is premised on a forum-selection clause. When the parties have agreed to a valid forum-selection clause, a district court should ordinarily transfer the case to the forum specified in that clause. Only under extraordinary circumstances unrelated to the convenience of the parties should a § 1404(a) motion be denied. And no such exceptional factors appear to be present in this case.

A

In the typical case not involving a forum-selection clause, a district court considering a § 1404(a) motion (or a forum non conveniens motion) must evaluate both the convenience of the parties and various public-interest considerations. [In a footnote here, the Court listed the public and private factors, which were set forth in the text preceding this case.] Ordinarily, the district court would weigh the relevant factors and decide whether, on balance, a transfer would serve "the convenience of parties and witnesses" and otherwise promote "the interest of justice."

The calculus changes, however, when the parties' contract contains a valid forum-selection clause, which "represents the parties' agreement as to the most proper forum." The "enforcement of valid forum-selection clauses, bargained for by the parties, protects their legitimate expectations and furthers vital interests of the justice system." For that reason, and because the overarching consideration under § 1404(a) is whether a transfer would promote "the interest of justice," "a valid forum-selection clause [should be] given controlling weight in all but the most exceptional cases." The presence of a valid forum-selection clause requires district courts to adjust their usual § 1404(a) analysis in three ways.

First, the plaintiff's choice of forum merits no weight. Rather, as the party defying the forum-selection clause, the plaintiff bears the burden of establishing that transfer to the forum for which the parties bargained is unwarranted. Because plaintiffs are ordinarily allowed to select whatever forum they consider most advantageous (consistent with jurisdictional and venue limitations), we have termed their selection the "plaintiff's venue privilege." But when a plaintiff agrees by contract to bring suit only in a specified forum—presumably in exchange for other binding promises by the defendant—the plaintiff has effectively exercised its "venue privilege" before a dispute arises. Only that initial choice deserves deference, and the plaintiff must bear the burden of showing why the court should not transfer the case to the forum to which the parties agreed.

Second, a court evaluating a defendant's § 1404(a) motion to transfer based on a forum-selection clause should not consider arguments about the parties' private interests. When parties agree to a forum-selection clause, they waive the right to challenge the preselected forum as inconvenient or less convenient for themselves or their witnesses, or for their pursuit of the litigation. A court accordingly must deem the private-interest factors to weigh entirely in favor of the preselected forum. As we have explained in a different but "'instructive'" context, "[w]hatever 'inconvenience' [the parties] would suffer by being forced to litigate in the contractual forum as [they] agreed to do was clearly foreseeable at the time of contracting." The Bremen v. Zapata Off-Shore Co., 407 U.S. 1, 17–18, 92 S. Ct. 1907, 32 L. Ed. 2d 513 (1972).

As a consequence, a district court may consider arguments about public-interest factors only. Because those factors will rarely defeat a transfer motion, the practical result is that forum-selection clauses should control except in unusual cases. Although it is "conceivable in a particular case" that the district court "would refuse to transfer a case notwithstanding the counterweight of a forum-selection clause," such cases will not be common.

Third, when a party bound by a forum-selection clause flouts its contractual obligation and files suit in a different forum, a § 1404(a) transfer of venue will not carry with it the original venue's choice-of-law rules—a factor that in some circumstances may affect public-interest considerations. See Piper Aircraft Co. v. Reyno, 454 U.S. 235, 241, n. 6, 102 S. Ct. 252, 70 L. Ed. 2d 419 (1981) (listing a court's familiarity with the "law that must govern the action" as a potential factor). A federal court sitting in diversity ordinarily must follow the choice-of-law rules of the State in which it sits. See Klaxon Co. v. Stentor Elec. Mfg. Co., 313 U.S. 487, 494–496, 61 S. Ct. 1020, 85 L. Ed. 1477 (1941). However, we previously identified an exception to that principle for § 1404(a) transfers, requiring that the state law applicable in the original court also apply in the transferee court. We deemed that exception necessary to prevent "defendants, properly subjected to suit in the transferor State," from "invok[ing] § 1404(a) to gain the benefits of the laws of another jurisdiction . . . ."

The policies motivating our exception to the *Klaxon* rule for § 1404(a) transfers, however, do not support an extension to cases where a defendant's motion is premised on enforcement of a valid forum-selection clause. To the contrary, those considerations lead us to reject the rule that the law of the court in which the plaintiff inappropriately filed suit should follow the case to the forum contractually selected by the parties. In *Van Dusen*, we were concerned that, through a § 1404(a) transfer, a defendant could "defeat the state-law advantages that might accrue from the exercise of [the plaintiff's] venue privilege." But as discussed above, a plaintiff who files suit in violation of a forum-selection clause enjoys no such "privilege" with respect to its choice of forum, and therefore it is entitled to no concomitant "state-law advantages." Not only would it be inequitable to allow the plaintiff to fasten its choice of substantive law to the venue transfer, but it would also encourage gamesmanship. Because "§ 1404(a) should not create or multiply opportunities for forum shopping," we will not apply the *Van Dusen* rule when a transfer stems from enforcement of a forum-selection clause: The court in the contractually selected venue should not apply the law of the transferor venue to which the parties waived their right.[10]

When parties have contracted in advance to litigate disputes in a particular forum, courts should not unnecessarily disrupt the parties' settled expectations. A forum-selection clause, after all, may have figured centrally in the parties' negotiations and may have affected how they set monetary and other contractual terms; it may, in fact, have been a critical factor in their agreement to do business together in

---

10. [Court's footnote #8] For the reasons detailed above, see Part II-B, supra, the same standards should apply to motions to dismiss for forum non conveniens in cases involving valid forum-selection clauses pointing to state or foreign forums. We have noted in contexts unrelated to forum-selection clauses that a defendant "invoking forum non conveniens ordinarily bears a heavy burden in opposing the plaintiff's chosen forum." *Sinochem Int'l Co. v. Malaysia Int'l Shipping Co.*, 549 U.S. 422, 430, 127 S. Ct. 1184, 167 L. Ed. 2d 15 (2007). That is because of the "hars[h] result" of that doctrine: Unlike a § 1404(a) motion, a successful motion under forum non conveniens requires dismissal of the case. That inconveniences plaintiffs in several respects and even "makes it possible for [plaintiffs] to lose out completely, through the running of the statute of limitations in the forum finally deemed appropriate." Such caution is not warranted, however, when the plaintiff has violated a contractual obligation by filing suit in a forum other than the one specified in a valid forum-selection clause. In such a case, dismissal would work no injustice on the plaintiff.

the first place. In all but the most unusual cases, therefore, "the interest of justice" is served by holding parties to their bargain.

The District Court's application of § 1404(a) in this case did not comport with these principles. The District Court improperly placed the burden on Atlantic Marine to prove that transfer to the parties' contractually preselected forum was appropriate. As the party acting in violation of the forum-selection clause, J-Crew must bear the burden of showing that public-interest factors overwhelmingly disfavor a transfer.

The District Court also erred in giving weight to arguments about the parties' private interests, given that all private interests, as expressed in the forum-selection clause, weigh in favor of the transfer. The District Court stated that the private-interest factors "militat[e] against a transfer to Virginia" because "compulsory process will not be available for the majority of J-Crew's witnesses" and there will be "significant expense for those willing witnesses." But when J-Crew entered into a contract to litigate all disputes in Virginia, it knew that a distant forum might hinder its ability to call certain witnesses and might impose other burdens on its litigation efforts. It nevertheless promised to resolve its disputes in Virginia, and the District Court should not have given any weight to J-Crew's current claims of inconvenience.

The District Court also held that the public-interest factors weighed in favor of keeping the case in Texas because Texas contract law is more familiar to federal judges in Texas than to their federal colleagues in Virginia. That ruling, however, rested in part on the District Court's belief that the federal court sitting in Virginia would have been required to apply Texas' choice-of-law rules, which in this case pointed to Texas contract law. But for the reasons we have explained, the transferee court would apply Virginia choice-of-law rules. It is true that even these Virginia rules may point to the contract law of Texas, as the State in which the contract was formed. But at minimum, the fact that the Virginia court will not be required to apply Texas choice-of-law rules reduces whatever weight the District Court might have given to the public-interest factor that looks to the familiarity of the transferee court with the applicable law. And, in any event, federal judges routinely apply the law of a State other than the State in which they sit. We are not aware of any exceptionally arcane features of Texas contract law that are likely to defy comprehension by a federal judge sitting in Virginia.

. . .

We reverse the judgment of the Court of Appeals for the Fifth Circuit. Although no public-interest factors that might support the denial of Atlantic Marine's motion to transfer are apparent on the record before us, we remand the case for the courts below to decide that question.

It is so ordered.

Notes and Questions

1. When a party seeks to enforce a valid forum selection clause by transfer under § 1404(a), why are the private-interest factors and the plaintiff's choice of forum entitled to no consideration?

2. If the forum selection clause in *Atlantic Marine* had prescribed litigation in a state court in Virginia, why would § 1404(a) be irrelevant? What doctrine could the court have used to impel the plaintiff to pursue the case in state court in Virginia?

3. In *Atlantic Marine*, the plaintiff sued in a district that was a proper venue under § 1391(b). Suppose the plaintiff had sued in an improper venue. Would the forum selection clause in favor of the Eastern District of Virginia nonetheless be enforced through transfer? How?

4. Suppose a valid forum selection clause calls for litigation in a district that is not a proper venue under § 1391(b). Can a court transfer to that district under § 1404(a) or § 1406(a)?

5. As seen above, in *Van Dusen*, the Court held that in a § 1404(a) transfer, the choice-of-law rules of the transferor are transferred with the case. The transfer in *Atlantic Marine* was ordered under § 1404(a). Why did *Van Dusen* not apply?

6. In an earlier case, *Stewart Organization, Inc. v. Ricoh Corp.*, 487 U.S. 22, 29 (1988), the Court said that though the existence of a valid forum selection clause was not dispositive in ruling on a transfer motion, it will be "a significant factor that figures centrally in the district court's calculus." Does *Atlantic Marine* replace that analysis with a directive to enforce such clauses? Can you imagine a scenario in which a court would refuse to order transfer to a district prescribed by a valid forum selection clause?

7. In *Atlantic Marine*, the forum selection clause clearly applied to the dispute between the parties and prescribed venue in a specific federal district. Sometimes, however, there is a significant question about whether the clause covers the dispute at hand. For instance, a clause referring only to contract claims might not apply to tort claims, even if the alleged tort arose from the contractual relationship. On the other hand, courts will not allow a plaintiff to defeat a forum selection clause by "artful pleading"—that is, making a contract case "sound" like a tort case.

In *Vangura Kitchen Tops, Inc. v. C&C North America, Inc.*, 2008 U.S. Dist. LEXIS 79360 at *2 (W.D. Pa. 2008), two parties entered into a contract that required "any claim or action for breach of this Agreement" to be pursued in a particular federal district. Plaintiff, one of the parties to the contract, sued the other party and additional defendants and alleged, inter alia, that the defendants conspired to interfere with the plaintiff's rights under the contract. The court concluded that the clause did not govern: "Where, as here, a forum selection clause is only applicable to claims against one of multiple parties, by its terms such clause does not [apply to] claims . . . in tort against third parties. . . . However, claims against third parties that are 'closely related' to the claims for breach of contract containing the forum selection clause may afford venue over such closely related claims, but this is a narrow rule." *Id.* at *5.

3. Consolidation and "Low Numbering"

Case 1 is filed in the Central District of California and Case 2 is filed in the District of Maine. The federal court in Maine orders transfer under § 1404(a) to the Central District of California. This fact does not ensure, however, that the treatment of Cases 1 and 2 will be coordinated. Indeed, it does not even ensure that the cases will be assigned to the same judge in the Central District of California.

For each district, Congress sets the number of district judgeships. The number ranges from two judges in each of four districts to 28 in the Central District of California and in the Southern District of New York. When a case is filed in any district, it is assigned at random to one of the judges.

Each district has a system through which it attempts to guide related litigation to the same judge. The system is set up by Local Rule[11] and is usually called "low numbering." This refers to the fact that cases are assigned docket numbers when they are filed, and the earliest case has the lowest docket number. For instance, the first case filed in a district in 2019 would be numbered "19-0001," and the four hundredth case will be "19-0400," and so forth. Let's say the latter case is related to the former—say, because they arise from the same bus crash. By Local Rule, the latter case will be "low numbered" to the judge to whom the earlier case was assigned. The MANUAL FOR COMPLEX LITIGATION (FOURTH)[12] § 20.11 provides: "All related civil cases pending in the same court should initially be assigned to a single judge to determine whether consolidation, or at least coordination of pretrial proceedings, is feasible and is likely to reduce conflicts and duplication."

More important, however, is Federal Rule 42(a), which permits *consolidation* of separate cases. Read that Rule before addressing the following Notes and Questions. As a practical matter, whether cases are formally consolidated under Rule 42(a) or simply coordinated before a single judge, the MANUAL FOR COMPLEX LITIGATION instructs that "the court should enter an order establishing a master file for the litigation in the clerk's office, relieving the parties from multiple filings of the same [documents], and providing that documents need not be filed separately in an individual case file unless uniquely applicable to that particular case." Such action, which should be taken only if it promotes convenience for the parties and lawyers, is

11. Every federal district has its own Local Rules. While these are not supposed to contradict the Federal Rules of Civil Procedure, they often supplement them in significant (and occasionally onerous) ways. Every time you are engaged in litigation in federal court, be sure to consult that district's Local Rules.

12. The MANUAL is produced by the Federal Judicial Center, which is the research and educational arm of the federal judiciary. The MANUAL contains very helpful discussions of virtually every aspect of complex litigation. The fourth edition was published in 2004.

part of the judge's ongoing case management responsibility, which we will consider in detail in Chapter 5.

Consolidation can be ordered for all purposes or for discrete aspects of litigation, in the court's discretion. It is not uncommon, for example, to have cases consolidated for discovery, for motions, or for trial. Consolidating for discovery might save a party or witness from the burden of being deposed multiple times. Complex litigation often features consolidated pleadings. For example, suppose scores of related cases are pending in the same district—perhaps involving personal injury claims arising from use of a product. The judge may order all plaintiffs to file a consolidated complaint or all defendants to join a consolidated answer. The consolidated pleading might streamline proceedings by operating in lieu of (and, indeed, superseding) the scores of earlier individual pleadings. *See* 8 MOORE'S FEDERAL PRACTICE §8.13[5] (3d ed. 2018) ("As a management tool for complex litigation, the consolidated complaint has been found to have significant advantages.").

Consolidation for any purpose usually requires that the court appoint "lead" or "liaison" counsel to coordinate and represent one or both sides of the litigation. Lawyers will covet the appointment as lead or liaison counsel for at least two reasons. First, that lawyer then enjoys a measure of control in the litigation. Second, it likely ensures compensation for these efforts on behalf of the plaintiff or defendant "team." We will discuss the appointment and compensation of lead and liaison counsel in Chapter 9.

At some point, consolidated litigation with lead counsel can start to look like class action litigation. Instead of viewing each party's contentions, the court seems more concerned with processing the case with a "point person" on one or both sides of the disputes. In class litigation, however, as we will see in Chapter 6, Rule 23 includes procedures to protect individual interest. In Rule 23(b)(3) classes, for example, members can opt out and pursue litigation on their own.

There is a black-letter principle, cited in nearly every case under Rule 42(a), that an order of consolidation does not "merge" the cases; they do not become a single case. Courts routinely cite *Johnson v. Manhattan Ry. Co.*, 289 U.S. 479 (1933), to this effect. While it is true that each case retains its separate docket number and that a separate judgment will be entered for each, consolidation does in fact run the risk of merging matters de facto. MOORE'S FEDERAL PRACTICE, *supra,* §8.13 (despite *Johnson*, "there has been an inclination . . . to treat consolidated cases as having been merged into a new case"). The fact that consolidated cases are not merged is demonstrated by *Hall v. Hall*, 138 S. Ct. 1118, 1124–1125 (2018). There, the Court held that a final judgment in a consolidated case is immediately appealable, even though another consolidated case remains pending at the district court.

Even though consolidation does not merge the cases, courts must be aware of potential risks. For one, consolidating cases always involves a loss of control for individual parties and their lawyers. Before consolidation, you might be the sole lawyer representing a sole plaintiff in a case. After consolidation, you might find your case consolidated with scores of others, in which a different lawyer is the lead counsel. This is undoubtedly frustrating for the lawyer cut out of the role of running her client's case. It is probably more frustrating—and potentially more damaging—however, for the client. Once the center of attention in her own case, this client may now feel that she has become part of the faceless crowd, robbed of a meaningful voice.

Consolidation also raises the problem of "bystander" litigants. For example, suppose Corporation is one of several defendants sued by one plaintiff in one case arising from a mass disaster. There are scores of other cases by different plaintiffs against the other defendants, but none of the other plaintiffs has sued Corporation. An order consolidating the cases raises two significant problems for Corporation. First, other plaintiffs may now decide to sue Corporation. Second, even if no other plaintiff sues Corporation, it is now a party to much more involved and expensive litigation. Among other things, should Corporation monitor discovery by or against other defendants to protect its own interests? If so, the case will become more expensive for it.

Notes and Questions

1. Suppose Case 1 and Case 2 are pending in different federal districts. Why can they not be consolidated?

2. What is the standard for consolidating cases? If the standard is met, *must* the court consolidate?

3. Consolidation is to be distinguished from an order of separate trials under Rule 42(b) or Rule 20(b). With the latter, in the context of a single case, the court decides that certain issues or claims should be tried separately. For example, if the plaintiff asserted unrelated claims against the defendant (or if the defendant asserted a permissive counterclaim against the plaintiff), the court might conclude that the disparate claims would confuse the jury. It could order separate trials of the claims. The case remains, however, a single action. There is one docket number and one judgment.

4. Multidistrict Litigation (MDL) Under § 1407

Congress passed § 1407 in 1968 in the wake of a huge number of overlapping cases growing out of alleged antitrust violations in a particular industry. For the most part, Congress was concerned about redundant discovery requests in the overlapping cases, and sought to facilitate the coordination of discovery across the related litigation. As we will see, however, § 1407 is not limited to the coordination of discovery.

Section 1407 is entitled "Multidistrict Litigation," and everyone refers to it by the shorthand "MDL." It is a transfer statute, but differs in several significant ways from §§ 1404(a) and 1406(a).

First, the transfer is not ordered by the transferor court. Rather, it is ordered by the Judicial Panel on Multidistrict Litigation (JPML, or Panel), membership of which is prescribed in § 1407(d). That section provides that the Panel consist of "seven circuit and district judges designated from time to time by the Chief Justice of the United States." No two judges may be from the same circuit. Federal judges appointed to the JPML do this work in addition to their regular caseload in the court of appeals or district court. The JPML does not have a courthouse. It convenes as necessary and where convenient to consider whether cases ought to be transferred under § 1407(a). As with transfers under §§ 1404(a) and 1406(a), we refer to the original court as the "transferor" and the one to which the case is sent as the "transferee." The JPML orders transfer not only to the transferee district, but to a particular judge there.

Second, transfer under § 1407(a) is intended to facilitate only "coordinated or consolidated *pretrial* proceedings." Transfers under §§ 1404(a) and 1406(a), in contrast, result in transfer for all purposes; a case transferred under one of those statutes is not expected to come back to the transferor court. The opposite is true with MDL.[13]

Third, § 1407(a) provides: "Each action so transferred shall be remanded by the panel at or before the conclusion of such pretrial proceedings to the district from which it was transferred unless it shall have been previously terminated." In other words, MDL transfer is not made for all purposes. Rather, the pretrial matters are litigated in the transferee district, after which they are remanded to the districts whence they came.

Fourth, we saw in section B.2 of this chapter that the transferee district for transfer under either § 1404(a) or § 1406(a) must be a proper venue and must have personal jurisdiction over the defendant. The leading case for this proposition, discussed above, was *Hoffman v. Blaski*, 363 U.S. 335 (1960). *Hoffman* was based upon the provisions in §§ 1404(a) and 1406(a) that transfer is permissible only to a district in which the action "could" or "might" have been brought. Section 1407(a) contains no such limitation. It permits MDL transfer to *any* district. *Hoffman* does not apply to MDL transfers. That means that the JPML may transfer cases to a district in which venue would not be proper under § 1391(b) and which lacks personal jurisdiction over the defendant. The harshness of this provision is tempered, at least in theory, by the fact that MDL transfers are solely for "pretrial" purposes.

MDL transfer and coordination is proper only when the JPML determines "that transfers for such proceedings will be for the convenience of parties and witnesses and will promote the just and efficient conduct of such actions." The Panel rarely provides much guidance in its opinions as to what these considerations entail. Most of its opinions recite facts and the JPML's conclusion that transfer and consolidated proceedings will serve goals of convenience, justice, and efficiency.

---

13. There is an exception, found in § 1407(h). It provides that certain antitrust cases can be transferred for all purposes. We assume throughout these materials that § 1407(h) does not apply.

Manual for Complex Litigation (Fourth)

§ 20.131: Requests for Transfer

Transfer proceedings may be initiated by one of the parties or by the Panel itself, although the latter procedure is ordinarily used only for "tag-along" cases (transfer on the request of a person not a party in one or more of the cases). The Panel evaluates each group of cases proposed for multidistrict treatment on the cases' own facts in light of the statutory criteria. The objective of transfer is to eliminate duplication in discovery, avoid conflicting rulings and schedules, reduce litigation cost, and save the time and effort of the parties, the attorneys, the witnesses, and the courts. As few as two cases may warrant multidistrict treatment, although those advocating transfer bear a heavy burden of persuasion when there are only a few actions, particularly those involving the same parties and counsel.

... Section 1407(a) authorizes the panel to transfer only "civil actions," not claims; however, section 1407(a) also empowers the Panel to accomplish "partial" transfer by (1) transferring an action in its entirety to the transferee district, and (2) simultaneously remanding to the transferor district any claims for which transfer was not deemed appropriate, such as cross-claims, counterclaims, or third-party claims.

A transfer under section 1407 becomes effective when the order granting the transfer is filed in the office of the clerk of the transferee court. At that point, the jurisdiction of the transferor court ceases and the transferee court has exclusive jurisdiction.

... The Panel has sometimes delayed ruling on transfer to permit the court in which the case is pending to decide critical, fully briefed and argued motions....

More often, however, the Panel has held that the pendency of potentially dispositive motions is not an impediment to transfer of actions, because such motions can be addressed to the transferee judge for resolution after transfer. Furthermore, the pendency of motions raising questions common to related actions can itself be an additional justification for transfer.

The Panel uses no single factor to select the transferee district, but the Panel does consider where the largest number of cases is pending, where discovery has occurred, where cases have progressed furthest, the site of the occurrence of common facts, where the cost and inconvenience will be minimized, and the experience, skill, and caseloads of the available judges. Based on these factors, the Panel will designate a judge (on rare occasions, two judges) to whom the cases are then transferred for pretrial proceedings. The judge is usually a member of the transferee court, but occasionally the Panel selects a judge designated to sit specially in the transferee district on an intracircuit or intercircuit assignment.

Remember that MDL transfer is for "pretrial" purposes only. Pretrial entails far more, however, than the conduct of discovery.

In re Donald J. Trump Casino Securities Litigation

United States Court of Appeals, Third Circuit
7 F.3d 357 (1993)

Becker, Circuit Judge.

. . .

. . . [T]he JPML transferred a number of complaints that different plaintiffs had filed in the Southern and Eastern Districts of New York to the District of New Jersey for consolidated pre-trial proceedings pursuant to 28 U.S.C. § 1407. At oral argument, the question arose whether the district court possessed the authority to terminate the transferred cases under Rule 12(b)(6). Surprisingly, no judicial precedent addresses this point, so we take this opportunity to make clear that § 1407 empowers transferee courts to enter a dispositive pre-trial order terminating a case.

Section 1407 authorizes the consolidation and transfer of civil actions containing common questions of fact "for coordinated or consolidated pretrial proceedings." 28 U.S.C. § 1407(a). The section further directs that the transferee court should remand the case to the transferor court "unless it shall have been previously terminated," which suggests that Congress contemplated that transferee courts would dismiss cases in response to dispositive motions. The dismissal of a complaint under Rule 12(b)(6) constitutes such a pre-trial proceeding.

Apparently, transferee courts frequently terminate consolidated cases in practice. *See* In re Korean Air Lines Disaster, 829 F.2d 1171, 1176, 265 U.S. App. D.C. 39 n.9 (D.C. Cir. 1987) (noting that as of 1986 transferee courts had terminated over two-thirds of all cases subject to § 1407 proceedings), aff'd sub nom. Chan v. Korean Air Lines, Ltd., 490 U.S. 122 (1989). Moreover, the practice comports with the rules the JPML promulgated pursuant to § 1407, see Rule 14(a) ("Actions terminated in the transferee district court by valid judgment, including . . . judgment of dismissal . . . , shall not be remanded . . . and shall be dismissed by the transferee district court."), as well as the views of commentators. *See* Manual for Complex Litigation, Second, § 31.122, at 254 (1985) (stating "the transferee judge has the power to terminate actions by rulings on motions under Fed. R. Civ. P. 12"); Stanley A. Weigel, *The Judicial Panel on Multidistrict Litigation, Transferor Courts and Transferee Courts*, 78 F.R.D. 575, 582–83 (1978).

In sum, we are satisfied that § 1407 empowered the district court to dismiss the plaintiffs' complaint under Rule 12(b)(6).[14]

---

14. [Court's footnote #8] The transfer of the complaints filed in the Southern and Eastern Districts of New York to the District of New Jersey presents a potential choice of law issue in terms of

---

Notes and Questions

1. Though § 1407 limits the MDL transferee court to "pretrial" matters, these include dispositive motions. Thus, for example, the transferee court can enter summary judgment, voluntary or involuntary dismissal on any grounds, and default judgment. It can rule on non-dispositive pretrial matters as well, such as motions to certify class actions, to transfer under § 1404(a) and § 1406(a). It can also oversee pretrial settlement and rule on associated awards of costs and attorneys' fees. Because of these broad powers, the clear majority of cases transferred for MDL treatment are never remanded to their transferor courts. They are concluded—by motion, settlement, or otherwise—in the transferee court. *See* 15 Wright & Miller, Federal Practice and Procedure § 3866 (3d ed. 2013).

2. Suppose one of several cases that are transferred under § 1407 is resolved finally in the transferee district. That is, assume the transferee enters a dispositive order in one of several MDL cases. The Supreme Court has held that the final judgment in that case is appealable immediately, without awaiting the outcome of the other cases. *Gelboim v. Bank of Am. Corp.*, 135 S. Ct. 897, 904 (2015). Thus, as with consolidation under Rule 42(a), the MDL cases retain their separate character and are not merged into a single proceeding.

3. The footnote in the *Trump* case raises an interesting issue. We saw in Section B.2 above that in a § 1404(a) transfer diversity of citizenship cases, the transferee court will generally apply the choice-of-law rules that would have been applied by the transferor court. This is required by *Van Dusen v. Barrack*, 376 U.S. 612, 639 (1964). What happens in MDL cases? By and large, the issue is handled as it is under § 1404(a). Thus, if the case invoked diversity of citizenship jurisdiction, courts apply the holding of *Van Dusen*. In federal question cases, however, there is a split of authority. The majority view, as noted in footnote 8 of *Trump*, is that the transferee court applies its own interpretation of federal law. *See*, e.g., *Murphy v. FDIC*, 208 F.3d 959, 964 (11th Cir. 2000); *Campos v. Ticketmaster Corp.*, 140 F.3d 1166, 1171 n.4 (8th Cir. 1998). Why should federal question and diversity cases be treated differently in this regard? In Chapter 4 we will return to these potentially thorny questions of choice of law.

---

whether Second or Third Circuit precedent controls. The district court followed the approach the D.C. Circuit adopted in the leading case on choice of law in multidistrict transfers, *see In re Korean Air Lines Disaster*, 829 F.2d at 1176. Consequently, the district court held that while only this court's precedent would control, the Second Circuit's precedent would merit close consideration. Because neither party has challenged the district court's holding on this point, we assume without deciding that it was correct.

Note on Global Settlements and the "Quasi-Class Action"

Most civil cases are settled—almost always in the pretrial phase of litigation. By placing multiple related cases before a single judge, MDL facilitates coordinated settlement of all the cases—so-called "global" settlement. "One of the values of multidistrict proceedings is that they bring before a single judge all of the federal cases, parties, and counsel comprising the litigation. They therefore afford a unique opportunity for the negotiation of a global settlement. Few cases are remanded [to their original courts] for trial; most multidistrict litigation is settled in the transferee court." MANUAL FOR COMPLEX LITIGATION (FOURTH) § 20.132.

As cases such as *Wal-Mart* make it more difficult to certify class actions in federal court, there seems to be a trend, at least in tort cases, to pursue aggregate litigation through MDL consolidation of non-class cases. Once cases are transferred under § 1407, the parties seek to negotiate a "non-class aggregate contractual settlement" which, if successfully implemented,[15] results in the transferee judge's dismissing the cases. MDL courts maintain the authority to oversee implementation of the settlement. *In re Patenaude*, 210 F.3d 135, 142–146 (3d Cir. 2000).

This trend is complemented by the emergence of the "quasi-class action," which was pioneered in *In re Zyprexa Products Liability Litigation*, 233 F.R.D. 122, 122 (E.D. N.Y. 2006). There, the transferee judge in MDL cases seized the authority to determine attorneys' fee awards in individual cases. The move was surprising because the plaintiffs' lawyers had entered into contracts with their clients providing what the fees would be. The transferee judge concluded that the fees were too high and simply cut them. While it is clear that courts have the authority to approve attorneys' fees in class actions, *In re Zyprexa* involved no class actions. The court claimed the authority, however, because the MDL cases were a "quasi-class action" over which it could oversee fee awards. We will address the issue when we discuss attorneys' fees in Chapter 7, section A.3.

Global non-class aggregate settlement of MDL matters and the "quasi-class action" raise significant issues of fairness. While the defendants in such cases undoubtedly value the ability to determine their aggregate liability once and for all, the worry is whether claimants are treated unfairly. Because these cases are not class actions, none of the procedural protections accorded by Federal Rule 23—including fairness hearings for settlements—applies. Commentators have voiced such concerns. *See, e.g.*, Linda Mullenix, *Aggregate Litigation and the Death of Democratic Dispute Resolution*, 107 Nw. U. L. Rev. 511 (2013); Charles Silver & Geoffrey Miller, *The Quasi-Class Action Method of Managing Multi-District Litigations: Problems and a Proposal*, 63 VAND. L. REV. 107 (2010).

---

15. The agreements usually require that the settlement becomes effective only if a specified percentage of plaintiffs agree to its terms. The percentage needs to be high enough to ensure the defendants that they will be exposed to litigation in a manageable minority of cases.

Note on the Lexecon *Case*

What if a case is not settled or otherwise disposed of at the pretrial stage? As noted, § 1407 envisions that the JPML will transfer cases back to their transferor courts after pretrial proceedings. As a practical matter, however, returning cases to their original courts for trial may be wasteful. Through the MDL proceedings, the transferee judge has developed expertise and familiarity with the cases and will often be in the best position to preside at trial. Sending the cases back to their original courts will impose burdens on those judges, who have not overseen the litigation in the interim. Recognizing these practical considerations, MDL transferee courts routinely invoked § 1404(a) to order transfer of the MDL cases to themselves for all purposes. The practice, which went on for decades, was so widespread that the JPML adopted a rule expressly permitting an MDL transferee court to transfer the MDL cases to itself under § 1404(a).

To the surprise of many, the Supreme Court unanimously rejected the practice, and invalidated the JPML rule on the matter, in *Lexecon Inc. v. Milberg Weiss Bershad Hynes & Lerach*, 523 U.S. 26, 27 (1998). The Court concluded that self-transfer under § 1404(a) was inconsistent with the statutory command that cases be remanded to the transferor courts after pretrial had run its course.

In *Lexecon*, a prominent New York law firm, which specialized in representing plaintiffs in federal class actions, was engaged in MDL cases involving failed savings and loan associations in the District of Arizona. The law firm filed a claim in that litigation against a law and economics consulting firm and one of its principals (a law professor) regarding expert opinions they had expressed on behalf of defendants in the litigation. The consultants sued the law firm for defamation and related torts in the Northern District of Illinois. The JPML transferred that case to the District of Arizona, where the MDL proceedings were still pending. That court transferred the case to itself under § 1404(a). It presided at trial, which resulted in judgment for the law firm on the claims against it. Because the Supreme Court held that the District of Arizona had no authority to transfer the case to itself, the case had to be returned to its transferee district, the Northern District of Illinois, for trial. The jury returned a verdict of $45,000,000 in favor of the plaintiffs against the law firm. The case was settled before the jury determined whether to assess punitive damages.[16]

The decision in *Lexecon* has had many critics. Indeed, the Court recognized that self-transfer under § 1404(a) might be a preferable policy choice, but concluded that the matter was one for Congress, and not the judiciary, to decide. Congress undertook to obviate the *Lexecon* holding by statute. Somehow, though, the result was the

16. Things got much worse for that law firm in later years. The firm and some partners were indicted on federal charges, including racketeering and mail fraud, arising from use of legal fees to induce plaintiffs to sue. Four partners pleaded guilty, served prison sentences, and made restitution of millions of dollars.

Multiparty, Multiforum Trial Jurisdiction Act of 2002. That Act, which we considered in detail in Chapter 2, section D.3, expands federal subject matter jurisdiction in some cases and does nothing to address the *Lexecon* issue.

The Manual for Complex Litigation (Fourth) § 20.132, counsels courts on four ways to avoid the strictures of *Lexecon*:

1. The transferee court could conduct a "bellwether" trial of one of the cases originally filed in that district. The parties in other cases could consent to be bound by the outcome of this "test case." Or, at the least, the result of that trial could inform a global settlement.
2. Parties may dismiss their cases after MDL transfer and refile in the transferee court or otherwise waive venue objections to trial there.
3. After pretrial proceedings are completed and the case is remanded to the transferor court, that court could transfer the case to the transferee under § 1404(a) or 1406(a).
4. The transferee judge, after completing pretrial matters, could be assigned as a judge in the transferor court and try the case there.

C. Overlapping Litigation in Federal and State Courts

In section A above, we saw three options to avoid problems caused by overlapping litigation. As we saw in section B, all three options are available when the overlapping litigation was in federal courts. In this section, we deal with the thornier problem of overlapping litigation in state and federal court. Why is this scenario more difficult?

For starters, the cases here are pending in different judicial systems, so Option One—transfer from one court to another—is not available. The only thing that comes close is *removal*, which allows the defendant in a state-court case to have the case moved from a state trial court to a federal trial court. From there, it might be transferred to another federal court for coordination or consolidation with other cases. With the Multiparty, Multiforum Trial Jurisdiction Act of 2002 and the Class Action Fairness Act—which we discussed in Chapter 2, sections D.3 and D.4, and will see again below—Congress expanded the availability of removal in certain types of complex cases. Removal, however, is a one-way street: It permits moving a case from the state to the federal judicial system, but no mechanism allows litigants to transfer a case properly filed in a federal court to a state court.

Second, Option Two—an injunction against litigation in state court—raises federalism concerns. State courts, of course, constitute the judicial branch of a sovereign government. An injunction from a federal court that has the effect of halting state court litigation is a slap in the face of that sovereign—something to be avoided if possible.

Finally, Option Three—in which a federal court abstains in favor of pending state litigation—raises serious questions about abdication of that court's jurisdiction. The justifications for such action are, and should be, quite limited.

1. Anti-Suit Injunctions Issued by the Federal Court

An injunction is "[a] court order commanding or preventing an action." LAW DICTIONARY 855 (9th ed. 2009). It is the archetypal equitable—as opposed to legal—remedy. As you recall from Civil Procedure, separate law and equity courts developed in England, and the equity courts offered a panoply of remedies not available at law. The typical remedy in a law court was and is damages—that is, money to compensate the plaintiff for harm inflicted by the defendant. Equity courts, in contrast, developed "specific" remedies, such as the injunction, declaratory judgment, rescission, and reformation. As a general rule, equitable remedies are available only if the legal remedy—damages—will not make one whole.

There are many kinds of injunctions, issued for many purposes. We are concerned with the anti-suit injunction, by which one court commands persons over whom it has personal jurisdiction not to proceed with litigation in another case. The anti-suit injunction does not issue to the other court. That is, the federal court in which Case 1 is pending does not issue an injunction to the state court presiding over Case 2 prohibiting the latter court to proceed. Instead, anti-suit injunctions issue to the persons involved both in Case 1 and Case 2, and orders them not to engage further in Case 2. Anyone who violates the injunction can be punished by the court that issued the injunction—potentially by fine or even incarceration until the person agrees to desist.

a. Can State Courts Enjoin Federal Litigation?

As discussed below, a federal court can enjoin parties from pursuing litigation in a state court, but only in narrow circumstances, with sensitivity to the principle of federalism. What about the converse? Can a state court issue an injunction against parties' proceeding with litigation in a federal court?

Donovan v. City of Dallas

Supreme Court of the United States
377 U.S. 408 (1964)

JUSTICE BLACK delivered the opinion of the Court.

The question presented here is whether a state court can validly enjoin a person from prosecuting an action *in personam* in a district or appellate court of the United States which has jurisdiction both of the parties and of the subject matter.

The City of Dallas, Texas, owns Love Field, a municipal airport. In 1961, 46 Dallas citizens who owned or had interests in property near the airport filed a class suit in a Texas court to restrain the city from building an additional runway and from issuing and selling municipal bonds for that purpose. The complaint alleged many damages that would occur to the plaintiffs if the runway should be built and charged that issuance of the bonds would be illegal for many reasons. The case was tried, summary judgment was given for the city, the Texas Court of Civil Appeals affirmed, the Supreme Court of Texas denied review, and we denied certiorari. Later 120 Dallas citizens, including 27 of the plaintiffs in the earlier action, filed another action in the United States District Court for the Northern District of Texas seeking similar relief. A number of new defendants were named in addition to the City of Dallas, all the defendants being charged with taking part in plans to construct the runway and to issue and sell bonds in violation of state and federal laws. The complaint sought an injunction against construction of the runway, issuance of bonds, payment on bonds already issued, and circulation of false information about the bond issue, as well as a declaration that all the bonds were illegal and void. None of the bonds would be approved, and therefore under Texas law none could be issued, so long as there was pending litigation challenging their validity. The city filed a motion to dismiss and an answer to the complaint in the federal court. But at the same time the city applied to the Texas Court of Civil Appeals for a writ of prohibition to bar all the plaintiffs in the case in the United States District Court from prosecuting their case there. The Texas Court of Civil Appeals denied relief, holding that it was without power to enjoin litigants from prosecuting an action in a federal court and that the defense of *res judicata* on which the city relied could be raised and adjudicated in the United States District Court. On petition for mandamus the Supreme Court of Texas took a different view, however, held it the duty of the Court of Civil Appeals to prohibit the litigants from further prosecuting the United States District Court case, and stated that a writ of mandamus would issue should the Court of Civil Appeals fail to perform this duty. The Court of Civil Appeals promptly issued a writ prohibiting all the plaintiffs in the United States District Court case from any further prosecution of that case.... The United States District Court in an unreported opinion dismissed the case pending there. Counsel Donovan, who is one of the petitioners here, excepted to the dismissal and then filed an appeal from that dismissal in the United States Court of Appeals for the Fifth Circuit. The Texas Court of Civil Appeals thereupon cited Donovan and the other United States District Court claimants for contempt and convicted 87 of them on a finding that they had violated its "valid order." . . .

. . . We think the Texas Court of Civil Appeals was right in its first holding that it was without power to enjoin these litigants from prosecuting their federal-court action, and we therefore reverse the State Supreme Court's judgment upsetting that of the Court of Appeals. We vacate the later contempt judgment of the Court of Civil Appeals, which rested on the mistaken belief that the writ prohibiting litigation by the federal plaintiffs was "valid."

Early in the history of our country a general rule was established that state and federal courts would not interfere with or try to restrain each other's proceedings. That rule has continued substantially unchanged to this time. An exception has been made in cases where a court has custody of property, that is, proceedings *in rem* or *quasi in rem*. In such cases this Court has said that the state or federal court having custody of such property has exclusive jurisdiction to proceed. Princess Lida v. Thompson, 305 U.S. 456, 465–468 [1939]. In *Princess Lida* this Court said "where the judgment sought is strictly *in personam*, both the state court and the federal court, having concurrent jurisdiction, may proceed with the litigation at least until judgment is obtained in one of them which may be set up as res judicata in the other." *Id.*, at 466. See also Kline v. Burke Construction Co., 260 U.S. 226 [1922]. It may be that a full hearing in an appropriate court would justify a finding that the state-court judgment in favor of Dallas in the first suit barred the issues raised in the second suit, a question as to which we express no opinion. But plaintiffs in the second suit chose to file that case in the federal court. They had a right to do this, a right which is theirs by reason of congressional enactments passed pursuant to congressional policy. And whether . . . a plea of *res judicata* in the second suit would be good is a question for the federal court to decide. While Congress has seen fit to authorize courts of the United States to restrain state-court proceedings in some special circumstances, it has in no way relaxed the old and well-established judicially declared rule that state courts are completely without power to restrain federal-court proceedings in *in personam* actions like the one here. And it does not matter that the prohibition here was addressed to the parties rather than to the federal court itself. For the heart of the rule as declared by this Court is that:

> . . . where the jurisdiction of a court, and the right of a plaintiff to prosecute his suit in it, have once attached, that right cannot be arrested or taken away by proceedings in another court. . . . The fact, therefore, that an injunction issues only to the parties before the court, and not to the court, is no evasion of the difficulties that are the necessary result of an attempt to exercise that power over a party who is a litigant in another and independent forum.

Petitioners being properly in the federal court had a right granted by Congress to have the court decide the issues they presented, and to appeal to the Court of Appeals from the District Court's dismissal. They have been punished both for prosecuting their federal-court case and for appealing it. They dismissed their appeal because of threats to punish them more if they did not do so. The legal effect of such a coerced dismissal on their appeal is not now before us, but the propriety of a state court's punishment of a federal-court litigant for pursuing his right to federal-court remedies is. That right was granted by Congress and cannot be taken away by the State. The Texas courts were without power to take away this federal right by contempt proceedings or otherwise.

. . .

The judgment of the Texas Supreme Court is reversed, the judgment of the Texas Court of Civil Appeals is vacated, and the case is remanded to the Court of Civil Appeals for further proceedings not inconsistent with this opinion.

It is so ordered.

Justice Harlan, with whom Justices Clark and Stewart join, dissenting.

The question presented by this case is not the general one stated by the Court at the outset of its opinion, but a much narrower one: May a state court enjoin resident state-court suitors from prosecuting in the federal courts vexatious, duplicative litigation which has the effect of thwarting a state-court judgment already rendered against them? Given the Texas Supreme Court's finding, amply supported by the record and in no way challenged by this Court, that this controversy "has reached the point of vexatious and harassing litigation," I consider both the state injunction and the ensuing contempt adjudication to have been perfectly proper.

. . .

None of the cases on which the Court relies deals with, or in any way negatives, the power of a state court to enjoin federal litigation in circumstances such as those involved here. None of them was concerned with vexatious litigation. [The dissenters then discussed the cases.]

Kline v. Burke Construction Co., 260 U.S. 226, 230 held, with respect to state and federal courts, that "where the action first brought is *in personam* and seeks only a personal judgment, another action for the same cause in another jurisdiction is not precluded." The *dictum* from *Princess Lida v. Thompson*, 305 U.S. 456, 466, which the Court quotes, is to the same effect. In neither case is there any discussion of a court's power in equity to prevent persons subject to its jurisdiction from maintaining vexatious and harassing suits elsewhere. Moreover, the opinions in both cases explain the rule permitting state and federal courts to issue injunctions protective of their jurisdiction in *in rem* actions—a rule which the Court here does not question . . . —on the ground that the rule is necessary to permit the court which first acquires jurisdiction over the subject matter of a controversy "effectively [to] exercise the jurisdiction vested in it . . . ," Princess Lida, *supra*, at 467. That reasoning is fully applicable here, since maintenance of the suit in the federal court has the automatic effect of nullifying the Texas court's decree.

. . .

In short, today's decision rests upon confusion between two distinct lines of authority in this Court, one involving vexatious litigation and the other not.

I would affirm.

Notes and Questions

1. In *in personam* litigation, as we will see below, it is *possible* (within limits) for a federal court to enjoin litigation in state court. Why, then, should a state court be unable to enjoin litigation in federal court?

2. Why should *in rem* or *quasi in rem* cases be treated differently?

3. Recall from section B.1 above that when overlapping cases are pending in the federal courts, the first-filed rule counsels that only one of the two should proceed. Why does the first-filed rule mean less in the federal-state context?

4. Do the dissenting justices explain how a court is to know when litigation is "vexatious"? Which court is supposed to make that determination?

5. Was the Court's majority opinion influenced by the fact that it was dealing with federal court power in 1964?

b. The All Writs Act and the Anti-Injunction Act

The All Writs Act, 28 U.S.C. § 1651(a), provides: "The Supreme Court and all courts established by Act of Congress may issue all writs necessary or appropriate in aid of their respective jurisdictions and agreeable to the usages and principles of law."

The Act applies only to federal courts and preserves their rights to issue writs and remedies that courts had at common law. A "writ" is simply an order, and includes all manner of injunctions—including the anti-suit injunction. The most important limitation in the Act is that any order be "in aid" of the court's jurisdiction.

In the context of the anti-suit injunction, the "in aid of jurisdiction" requirement will rarely present a problem. The federal court will be one in which an action is already pending, and the injunction will be necessary to avoid intrusion into its authority by another case.

The Anti-Injunction Act, 28 U.S.C. § 2283, is an important statement of federalism. Some version of it has been included in federal law since the Judiciary Act of 1791. The present version was passed in 1948. It applies only when there is overlapping litigation in federal and state court, and provides: "A court of the United States may not grant an injunction to stay proceedings in a State court except as expressly authorized by Act of Congress, or where necessary in aid of its jurisdiction, or to protect or effectuate its judgments."

This statute establishes the starting point that a federal court cannot issue an anti-suit injunction against "proceedings in a State court." But it provides three exceptions: (1) if Congress "expressly authorized" such an order, (2) if an injunction would be "necessary in aid of [the federal] court's jurisdiction," or (3) if an injunction is necessary to protect or effectuate a federal court judgment.

Before getting to the three exceptions, however, the first question in any case in which a party seeks a federal injunction against state-court proceedings is whether the Anti-Injunction Act applies at all. If it does not, there is no statutory impediment to an injunction.

Dombrowski v. Pfister

Supreme Court of the United States
380 U.S. 479 (1965)

JUSTICE BRENNAN delivered the opinion of the Court.

[For our purposes, the importance of this case consists of footnote 2, which set forth the text of the Anti-Injunction Act and then explained:]

The District Court did not suggest that this statute denied power to issue the injunctions sought. This statute and its predecessors do not preclude injunctions against the institution of state court proceedings, but only bar stays of suits already instituted. See Ex parte Young, [209 U.S. 123 (1908)]. *See generally* Warren, *Federal and State Court Interference*, 43 HARV. L. REV. 345, 366–378 (1930); Note, *Federal Power to Enjoin State Court Proceedings*, 74 HARV. L. REV. 726, 728–729 (1961). Since the grand jury was not convened and indictments were not obtained until after the filing of the complaint, which sought interlocutory as well as permanent relief, no state "proceedings" were pending within the intendment of § 2283. To hold otherwise would mean that any threat of prosecution sufficient to justify equitable intervention would also be a "proceeding" for § 2283. Nor are the subsequently obtained indictments "proceedings" against which injunctive relief is precluded by § 2283. The indictments were obtained only because the District Court erroneously dismissed the complaint and dissolved the temporary restraining order issued by Judge Wisdom in aid of the jurisdiction of the District Court properly invoked by the complaint. We therefore find it unnecessary to resolve the question whether suits under 42 U. S. C. § 1983 (1958 ed.) come under the "expressly authorized" exception to § 2283. . . .

Notes and Questions

1. Some courts and commentators refer to the *Dombrowski* "exception." That terminology is misleading. If the federal court issues an anti-suit injunction before the state case is filed, the Anti-Injunction Act simply does not apply, so there is no need for an "exception."

2. *Dombrowski* raises another important issue of timing. Consider this timetable:

> ***Example #4.*** On February 1, Case 1 is filed in federal court, properly invoking federal subject matter jurisdiction. On February 4, Plaintiff in Case 1 asks the federal court to issue an injunction prohibiting Defendant from instituting a related case in state court. The federal court hears oral argument on the issue and takes the matter under advisement. On February 5, Defendant in Case 1 files Case 2 in state court.

Does the Anti-Injunction Act apply? *Dombrowski* is not on point, because the federal court did not *actually issue an anti-suit injunction before the state case was filed*. On the other hand, unlike *Dombrowski*, the federal court had been asked to issue an injunction before the state case was filed.

In *Barancik v. Investors Funding Corp.*, 489 F.2d 933, 936–937 (7th Cir. 1973), the Seventh Circuit held that the Anti-Injunction Act does not apply in this circumstance. The court was swayed by the fact that a party had moved in federal court for an injunction before the state case was filed. In its view, the federal court's "injunctive power" had been engaged before state litigation was initiated. In other words, *Barancik* equated a request for a federal injunction with the actual issuance of a federal injunction. *Barancik* is still the law in the Seventh Circuit and has been cited with approval in two other courts of appeals. As the following case makes clear, however, it is no longer the majority view.

Denny's, Inc. v. Cake

United States Court of Appeals, Fourth Circuit
364 F.3d 521 (2004)

Motz, Circuit Judge.

Upon notification from California officials that its vacation pay practices violated state labor law, Denny's, Inc. brought this action in federal court in South Carolina. Denny's asked the court to declare that the Employee Retirement Income Security Act (ERISA) preempted these state-law claims, and enjoin the California Labor Commissioner from applying the state law against Denny's. Shortly thereafter, the Commissioner sued Denny's in state court in California seeking to enforce the state law. Several months later, the district court dismissed this action, finding it lacked personal jurisdiction over the Commissioner. We believe that the court did have jurisdiction, but conclude that the Anti-Injunction Act bars all of the relief that Denny's seeks. Accordingly, we vacate the judgment of the district court and remand for entry of an order dismissing the complaint for failure to state a claim upon which relief can be granted.

I

Denny's, a restaurant chain with its principal place of business in South Carolina, maintains the Denny's, Inc. Vacation Plan ("the Plan") and the Denny's, Inc. Employee Benefits Trust ("the Trust") for the stated purpose of providing vacation benefits to eligible employees. The Plan provides that salaried and hourly employees cannot use vacation benefit days and will not be paid any vacation benefits upon termination of their employment until and unless they have completed, respectively, six months or one year of continuous employment with Denny's.

On July 11, 2002, Denny's received a letter from an attorney at the California Department of Industrial Relations. The purpose of the letter was "to come to a global resolution" of issues raised by claims of former Denny's employees filed with the California Labor Commissioner. The attorney explained that Denny's policy requiring forfeiture of vacation benefits when employees leave prior to six months or one year of employment violated Cal. Lab. Code § 227.3. That statute provides that when "an employee is terminated without having taken off his vested vacation time, all vested vacation shall be paid to him as wages" and, further, "that an employment contract or employer policy shall not provide for forfeiture of vested vacation time upon termination." § 227.3.

The California attorney noted that the Department had concluded that "Denny's method of funding its vacation pay plan constituted a payroll practice and the plan is not therefore an ERISA plan which preempts state enforcement laws." The attorney recounted prior discussions and litigation between the parties on this issue, including a state court's refusal to grant summary judgment to Denny's on its preemption defense. Given the numerous claims filed with the Department, the attorney proposed that Denny's meet with the Commissioner and discuss an "amicable resolution" to avoid "the time and expense of litigation." Otherwise, the Department would have "to file an action against Denny's to finally resolve this issue."

In response, on September 6, 2002, Denny's filed this action for declaratory and injunctive relief in federal court in South Carolina against the Commissioner and the director of the Department of Industrial Relations (collectively, "Commissioner"). Denny's sought: (1) a declaration that the Plan and Trust constitute an ERISA plan; (2) a declaration that "ERISA preempts the California statutes, regulations, and any action or decision" of the Commissioner "having the effect of law that [the Commissioner] seeks to enforce against [Denny's] based upon California law"; and (3) "preliminary and permanent injunctions barring [the Commissioner] from taking any action to enforce California law against [Denny's] with regard to the Plan and the Trust."

Three weeks later, the Commissioner filed a complaint against Denny's in California state court, for damages and injunctive relief. The Commissioner asked the state court to award it unpaid vacation wages and waiting time penalties pursuant to Cal. Lab. Code § 203, and to order Denny's to "cease and desist from violating" all provisions of the state labor code. In its answer to the Commissioner's state court lawsuit, Denny's alleged ERISA preemption as an affirmative defense.

The Commissioner then moved to dismiss the present action, contending that a federal district court in South Carolina lacked personal jurisdiction over the California officials, notwithstanding ERISA's nationwide service of process provision, 29 U.S.C. § 1132 (e)(2) (2000). Alternatively, the Commissioner contended that the Anti-Injunction Act, 28 U.S.C. § 2283 (2000) and abstention based on *Younger v. Harris*, 401 U.S. 37, 91 S. Ct. 746, 27 L. Ed. 2d 669 (1971), compelled dismissal. [T]he district court granted the Commissioner's motion, concluding that it had no personal jurisdiction over the Commissioner.

II

[The court here concluded that the lower court had personal jurisdiction over the Commissioner.]

III

Because the district court found it lacked personal jurisdiction over the Commissioner, it did not address the Commissioner's alternative Anti-Injunction Act (hereinafter "the Act") argument. The Commissioner reiterates on appeal that the Act bars a federal court from granting the relief requested by Denny's and so requires dismissal of the case * * *. The Act provides:

> A court of the United States may not grant an injunction to stay proceedings in a State court except as expressly authorized by Act of Congress, or where necessary in aid of its jurisdiction, or to protect or effectuate its judgments.

28 U.S.C. § 2283.[17]

The Act serves as a "necessary concomitant of the Framers' decision to authorize, and Congress' decision to implement, a dual system of federal and state courts" and "represents Congress' considered judgment as to how to balance the tensions inherent in such a system." Chick Kam Choo v. Exxon Corp., 486 U.S. 140, 146 (1988). Accordingly, "we take seriously the mandate in the Anti-Injunction Act and recognize that for over two hundred years, the Act has helped to define our nation's system of federalism." Employers Res. Mgmt. Co. v. Shannon, 65 F.3d 1126, 1130 (4th Cir. 1995).

The Act constitutes "an absolute prohibition against any injunction of any state-court proceedings, unless the injunction falls within one of the three specifically defined exceptions in the Act." Vendo Co. v. Lektro-Vend Corp., 433 U.S. 623, 630 (1977)....

Notwithstanding the inapplicability of the only exceptions to the Act recognized by Congress, Denny's contends that the Act does not bar its suit because of a judicial exception created by one of our sister circuits and followed by two others. Specifically, Denny's contends that the Act's prohibition on enjoining "proceedings in state court" does not apply because *when it filed this action requesting injunctive relief* in early September 2002, "there were no pending state proceedings, within the meaning of the [Act] or otherwise."

---

17. [Court's footnote #8] Although Denny's does not specifically request an "injunction to stay proceedings in State court," it does seek to enjoin state officials "from taking any action to enforce California law against it." If granted, this relief amounts to a "stay of proceedings in a State court." *See, e.g., Atlantic C. L. R. Co. v. Brotherhood of Locomotive Engineers*, 398 U.S. 281, 287 (1970) (finding that the Act "cannot be evaded" by framing an injunction as a restraint on a party rather than directly on the state court). Moreover, when the Act bars an injunction it "also bars the issuance of a declaratory judgment that would have the same effect as an injunction." *Texas Employers' Ins. Ass'n v. Jackson*, 862 F.2d 491, 506 (5th Cir. 1988) (en banc) (internal quotation marks and citation omitted). This is clearly the case here: Denny's request for a declaration that ERISA preempts the enforcement of a California labor law against the Plan has "the same effect" as its request for an injunction to prevent enforcement of that state law against the Plan; both "result in precisely the same interference with and disruption of state proceedings that the long-standing policy limiting injunctions was designed to avoid." *Samuels v. Mackell*, 401 U.S. 66, 72 (1971). Thus, if the Act bars the injunction Denny's has sought, it also bars the declaratory relief it has sought.

The Seventh Circuit so held in *Barancik v. Investors Funding Corp.*, 489 F.2d 933, 937 (7th Cir. 1973); see also Hyde Park Partners, L.P. v. Connolly, 839 F.2d 837, 842 n. 6 (1st Cir. 1988) (dicta); Nat'l City Lines, Inc. v. LLC Corp., 687 F.2d 1122, 1127 (8th Cir. 1982). Other circuits, however, have rejected this judicial exception. Royal Ins. Co. of Am. v. Quinn-L Capital Corp., 3 F.3d 877, 885 (5th Cir. 1993) (holding that the Act does apply even if the request for federal injunctive relief is filed first); Roth v. Bank of the Commonwealth, 583 F.2d 527, 533 (6th Cir. 1978) (same); see also Standard Microsystems Corp. v. Texas Instruments, 916 F.2d 58, 61–62 (2d Cir. 1990) (criticizing the reasoning in *Barancik* and stating that the court had "considerable doubt [about] whether the *Barancik* rule should be adopted in this circuit"); Nat'l City Lines, 687 F.2d at 1135 (Arnold, J., dissenting) (explaining that "the mere filing of a motion in a federal court seeking to enjoin state-court proceedings should [not] in and of itself deprive later filed state-court action of the protection of § 2283").

As always, we turn first to the plain language of the statute to determine its meaning. The plain language of the Act clearly and unequivocally prohibits a federal court from granting "an injunction to stay proceedings in a State court." Of course, . . . for the Act's bar to apply, proceedings in state court must have begun. *See* Dombrowski v. Pfister, 380 U.S. 479, 484 n. 2 (1965) (the Act does "not preclude injunctions against the institution of state court proceedings, but only bars stays of suits already instituted"). But nothing in the Act confines its bar to situations in which the federal plaintiff requests injunctive relief *after* the state suit has been filed.

. . . A court may not disregard the plain language of a statute unless a literal application of the statutory language "would lead to absurd results . . . or would thwart the obvious purpose of the statute." In re Trans Alaska Pipeline Rate Cases, 436 U.S. 631, 643 (1978) (internal quotation marks and citation omitted). Here literal application of the Act's language would neither thwart its purpose nor produce an absurd result. Quite the contrary, abiding by the statutory language clearly furthers the Act's purpose of avoiding "unseemly conflict between the state and the federal courts." N.L.R.B. v. Nash-Finch Co., 404 U.S. 138, 146 (1971).

Moreover, the Supreme Court has directed that the Act, in particular, "is not a statute conveying a broad general policy for appropriate ad hoc application" but rather is "expressed in a clear-cut prohibition qualified only by specifically defined exceptions." Amalgamated Clothing Workers v. Richman Bros., 348 U.S. 511, 515–16 (1955). Courts are not to "enlarge[]" these "exceptions . . . by loose statutory construction." Atlantic C.L.R. Co., 398 U.S. at 287. Instead, "any doubts as to the propriety of a federal injunction against state court proceedings should be resolved in favor of permitting the state courts to proceed . . . to finally determine the controversy." *Id.* at 297.

The *Barancik* court acknowledged the Supreme Court directive that the Act "imposes an absolute ban, circumscribing the federal court's power to act unless a case falls within one of the explicit exceptions from its command." 489 F.2d at 937. It also recognized that "the mere fact that the federal complaint was filed before the state proceeding was commenced is not sufficient to avoid the statutory bar." *Id.* at

936 (citing Kline v. Burke Construction Co., 260 U.S. 226, 232 (1922)). But see Nat'l City Lines, 687 F.2d at 1127 (stating that the Act "is inapplicable when a federal court has first obtained jurisdiction of a matter in controversy by the institution of suit"). Nevertheless, the *Barancik* court concluded that "the mandatory prohibition in § 2283 against injunctions staying state court proceedings does not apply to state actions commenced after a motion for injunctive relief is filed in the federal court." 489 F.2d at 938.

The *Barancik* court advanced several policy concerns in support of its holding. For example, it worried that "unless the applicability of the statutory bar is determined by the state of the record at the time the motion for an injunction is made, a litigant would have an absolute right to defeat a well-founded motion by taking the very step the federal court was being urged to enjoin." *Id.* at 937. But a federal court can eliminate this problem by issuing a temporary restraining order against the filing of a state court suit while considering a motion for a preliminary injunction seeking such relief. The *Barancik* court feared that such reliance on temporary restraining orders "might encourage the liberal granting of the kind of protective orders the statute was intended to prevent." 489 F.2d at 938. However, the basic harm the statute was intended to prevent was not the liberal granting of protective orders, *per se*, but the "needless friction between state and federal courts." Mitchum v. Foster, 407 U.S. 225, 233(1972) (internal quotation marks and citation omitted). Temporarily staying a potential state suit before it is filed so that an anti-suit injunction can be considered would seemingly create significantly less friction than allowing a state suit to be commenced, only to enjoin it after it is filed.

The *Barancik* court also suggested that its ruling had "the salutary advantage of discouraging the unseemly race to the state courthouse . . . while the federal court had under consideration a motion for a status quo order." 489 F.2d at 935 n. 5. But by hinging the applicability of § 2283 on whether the state or federal suit is commenced first, the *Barancik* rule creates a race to the courthouse of its own. *See* Roth, 583 F.2d at 533 (noting that the *Barancik* rule "merely moves the finish line"). Even worse, following *Barancik* would permit a federal court plaintiff who wins this race, to "unilaterally . . . nullify the effectiveness of" the Act with the "mere application for injunctive relief." Standard Microsystems, 916 F.2d at 62; *see also* Diane P. Wood, *Fine-Tuning Judicial Federalism: A Proposal for Reform of the Anti-Injunction Act*, 1990 B.Y.U. L. Rev. 289, 312 (1990) (arguing that the *Barancik* court's result does not seem "in line with the statute" because the "Act would become too easy to evade in many cases if the timing of the request for the injunction became the dispositive factor").

Although we recognize the legitimacy of the concerns raised by the Seventh Circuit in *Barancik*, the exception it created to meet these concerns poses its own problems. Moreover, even if application of the *Barancik* holding would result in better policy in the eyes of some, this is not the course Congress has chosen in the Act; views as to good policy cannot overcome a clear statutory directive. Therefore, we hold that the Act's prohibition on enjoining state court proceedings applies to any such proceeding pending at the time the federal court *acts* on the request for injunctive relief, regardless of when the state court action was filed. Since the California proceeding was clearly pending at the time the district court acted on Denny's request for injunctive relief, the Act bars the relief Denny's requested.

Because the Act rendered the district court powerless to issue any of the relief Denny's requested, *see supra* n. 8, its complaint should have been dismissed for failure to state a claim upon which relief can be granted. Fed. R. Civ. P. 12(b)(6). Accordingly, we vacate the judgment of the district court dismissing for lack of personal jurisdiction and remand with instructions to enter an order dismissing the case for failure to state a claim upon which relief can be granted.

IV

For the foregoing reasons, the judgment of the district court is *VACATED AND REMANDED.*

WILLIAMS, CIRCUIT JUDGE, concurring in part.

At the outset, I concur completely in the majority's [personal] jurisdictional analysis. . . . I write separately to highlight some of my concerns * * *.

. . . The plain language of the Anti-Injunction Act [AIA] prohibits injunctions "to stay proceedings in a State court." Nothing in this language limits the prohibition to state actions filed before the federal action is filed. Moreover, interpreting a predecessor statute to the AIA, the Supreme Court held in *Kline v. Burke Construction Co.*, 260 U.S. 226 (1922), that the predecessor statute barred the federal court from enjoining a state court action that was filed *after* the commencement of the federal court action. . . . Although I agree with many of the concerns expressed . . . in *Barancik* [,] especially the fear that our holding will pressure federal courts to grant temporary restraining orders, . . . I agree with my colleagues that we are bound by the plain language of the statute and that the plain language of the AIA bars an injunction in this case, unless one of its exceptions applies.[18]

. . .

Notes and Questions

1. What policies support the holding in *Barancik*? Does the court in *Denny's* reject those policy bases?

2. What language of the Anti-Injunction Act is inconsistent with the holding in *Barancik*?

---

18. [Court's footnote *] I note that the facts of this case suggest a particularly troubling scenario. For example, even had Denny's requested a temporary restraining order against the filing of state court proceedings, the district court likely would have denied it based on the erroneous belief that it lacked personal jurisdiction. If so, the California state officials still would have been able to file their state court action, which we now hold cannot be enjoined by the federal court. In such a circumstance, the applicability of the AIA hinges entirely on the fortuity of the district court's erroneous procedural ruling.

3. Consider footnote 8 in the *Denny's* opinion. The court makes it clear that a party cannot seek to avoid the Anti-Injunction Act by refusing to use the word "injunction." If the *effect* of the relief sought is to enjoin the parties from litigating in state court, the Anti-Injunction Act may prohibit it—no matter what the party may have called it. Thus, for instance, the Anti-Injunction Act prohibited a "declaratory judgment" that would have had the effect of an anti-suit injunction. *Texas Employers' Ins. Assn. v. Jackson*, 862 F.2d 491, 504–508.

4. After the decision in *Denny's*, one more court of appeals took a position on the issue. In *Monster Beverage Corp. v. Herrera*, 650 F. App'x 344, 346–347 (9th Cir. 2016), the Ninth Circuit adopted the reasoning in *Denny's* and rejected *Barancik*. Although the Tenth Circuit has not addressed the issue, a district court in that circuit has also sided with *Denny's* and rejected *Barancik*. *RadioShack Corp. v. Ruffin*, 2012 WL 589283 at *2–6 (D. Kan. 2012). On the other hand, the District of Columbia Circuit has not addressed the issue, but the district court there adopted *Barancik*. *Lattimore v. Nw. Co-Op Homes Ass'n*, 1990 WL 10521534 at *3–5 (D.D.C. 1990).

Dombrowski, Barancik, and *Denny's* all addressed whether the Anti-Injunction Act applies at all. If it does not, then the federal court is free, under the All Writs Act, to issue an anti-suit injunction (This assumes, of course, that the circumstances satisfy the equitable requirements for an injunction).

What happens, though, if the Anti-Injunction Act does apply? The Act prohibits the federal court from issuing an injunction *unless* the case falls within one of its three exceptions. We turn now to those exceptions.

First, the federal court can issue an injunction when "expressly authorized by Act of Congress." Thus, Congress can remove the ban on anti-suit injunctions against state-court proceedings whenever it considers such a move appropriate. It has done so rarely—for example, with regard to bankruptcy proceedings. Interestingly, the Supreme Court has held injunctions "expressly authorized" even when Congress was silent. In *Mitchum v. Foster*, 407 U.S. 225, 242–243 (1972), it held that 42 U.S.C. § 1983—which allows suit for deprivation of federal civil rights under color of state law—expressly authorizes anti-suit injunctions against state-court proceedings. The Court concluded that § 1983 created a federal right that could "be given its intended scope" only if the federal court could enjoin overlapping state-court cases. *Id.* at 238.

Let's jump to the third exception, and then focus on the second one. Under the third exception, a federal court may enjoin state litigation "to protect or effectuate its judgments." This "relitigation" provision is "founded in the well recognized concepts of res judicata and collateral estoppel." *Chick Kam Choo v. Exxon Corp.*, 486 U.S. 140, 147 (1988). This means that a state court will not be permitted to undo something that was established by a valid final federal court judgment. It can apply, then, only after entry of a final judgment in federal court.

In *Smith v. Bayer Corp.*, 564 U.S. 299 (2011), Case 1 was a state-court product liability class action against Bayer. Case 2 was a federal-court class action brought by a different representative on behalf of largely the same class, asserting the same claims against Bayer. The federal court in Case 2 denied class certification and entered final judgment dismissing plaintiff's claims on the merits. To stop the state court from proceeding with a class action on the same basic claims for the largely the same class, the federal court issued an anti-suit injunction against the representative in Case 1, barring him from proceeding. According to the federal court, an injunction was necessary under the "relitigation" exception to stop the representative in Case 2 (who was a member of the putative class in Case 1) from relitigating the question of class certification.

The Supreme Court reversed. Though it emphasized that the exceptions to the Anti-Injunction Act are to be interpreted narrowly, the Court's opinion was based upon the law of issue preclusion, which we address in Chapter 10. *Id.* at 306–307. The relitigation exception provision applies only when (1) the issue decided by the federal court is the same as that presented to the state court and (2) the parties in the two cases are the same or fall within "a few discrete exceptions to the general rule against binding nonparties." *Id.* at 307–308. The facts in *Smith* failed to satisfy either criterion. First, though the state had adopted Federal Rule 23, its courts interpreted it differently from the federal courts. Thus, any issues decided by the federal court were not the same as those pending in the state court. Second, the representative in Case 1 was not a party to the Case 2, and thus could not be bound by the judgment in Case 2. Though a nonparty may be bound if he was a member of a class, the federal court's denial of class certification meant that members of the putative class could not be bound by the federal court's rejection of class certification.

We focus on the second exception to the Anti-Injunction Act, which allows an anti-suit order when it is "necessary in aid of [the federal court's] jurisdiction." This provision undoubtedly applies in *in rem* and *quasi in rem* cases in which the federal court has seized the property. *Kline v. Burke Constr. Co.*, 260 U.S. 226, 230 (1922). In recent years, some courts applied it to *in personam* cases in an effort to facilitate federal court management of complex litigation. The next case is a leading example of this trend. While reading it, focus on how the court justifies its conclusion, and how it limits the effect of its holding.

In re Diet Drugs Products Liability Litigation

United States Court of Appeals, Third Circuit
282 F.3d 220 (2002)

Scirica, Circuit Judge.

In this matter involving competing mass tort class actions in federal and state courts, we address an interlocutory appeal in a complex multidistrict federal class action comprising six million members from an order enjoining a mass opt out of a state class. We will affirm.

I

[American Home Products manufactured and marketed two popular appetite suppressants in the 1990s. Over 4,000,000 people took one of these (Pondimin) and over 2,000,000 used the other (Redux). In 1997, the Food and Drug Administration issued a public health advisory alert concerning the drugs, after which the American Home Products removed them from the market. Subsequent studies supported the conclusion that the drugs might cause heart damage.

Approximately 18,000 individual cases and over 100 putative class actions were filed in federal and state courts concerning these diet drugs. The Judicial Panel on Multidistrict Litigation transferred all federal cases to the Eastern District of Pennsylvania for coordinated pretrial proceedings as MDL case 1203. One of the first cases filed in the matter was a state-court class action in Hidalgo County, Texas, on behalf of all purchasers of the drug in Texas. This case—*Gonzalez*—was filed several months before the MDL case.

The parties reached a tentative global settlement in the MDL case—called the *Brown* class—proposing to include all persons in the United States who had ingested either of the diet drugs. The settlement would have resolved all claims, even those pending in state court. Members of the *Gonzalez* class were a subset of members of the *Brown* class. The federal court in the MDL case issued a pretrial order—PTO 1227—that did two things: (1) it enjoined counsel for the plaintiffs in *Gonzalez* from attempting to have the *Gonzalez* class members "opt out" (withdraw) from the *Brown* settlement, and (2) declared "null and void" a state-court order in *Gonzalez* permitting members of that class to opt out of *Brown*.

Because *Gonzalez* was filed before *Brown*, the Anti-Injunction Act applied. Thus, PTO 1227 could be upheld only if supported by an exception to the Anti-Injunction Act.]

. . .

IV

a. Anti-Injunction Act/All Writs Act

The District Court issued PTO 1227 under the All Writs Act, which provides "all courts established by Act of Congress may issue all writs necessary or appropriate in aid of their respective jurisdictions and agreeable to the usages and principles of law." 28 U.S.C. § 1651. The power granted by the All Writs Act is limited by the Anti-Injunction Act, 28 U.S.C. § 2283, which prohibits, with certain specified exceptions, injunctions by federal courts that have the effect of staying a state court proceeding. Appellants contend the District Court's order was prohibited by the Anti-Injunction Act. American Home Products and the *Brown* plaintiffs claim the injunction falls under one of the Act's exceptions. We hold the District Court's order was not barred by the Anti-Injunction Act and was a valid exercise of its power under the All Writs Act.

The Anti-Injunction Act prohibits most injunctions "to stay proceedings in a State court." 28 U.S.C. § 2283. Insofar as PTO 1227 enjoined *Gonzalez* class counsel, and those working in concert, from pursuing the opt out contemplated by the Texas opt-out order, it operated to stay the proceedings in the Hidalgo County court, if only indirectly. An order directed at the parties and their representatives, but not at the court itself, does not remove it from the scope of the Anti-Injunction Act. "It is settled that the prohibition of § 2283 cannot be evaded by addressing the order to the parties. . . ." Atl. Coast Line R.R. Co. v. Bhd. of Locomotive Eng'rs, 398 U.S. 281, 287 (1970). Therefore, to the extent PTO 1227 had the effect of staying the Hidalgo County court's proceedings, it was prohibited by the Anti-Injunction Act, unless it fell within one of the Act's exceptions.

[The only exception arguably applicable was that for injunctions "necessary in aid of [the federal court's] jurisdiction."]

In *Atlantic Coast*, the Court . . . elaborated: an injunction is necessary in aid of a court's jurisdiction only if "some federal injunctive relief may be necessary to prevent a state court from so interfering with a federal court's consideration or disposition of a case as to seriously impair the federal court's flexibility and authority to decide that case."

Without more, it may not be sufficient that prior resolution of a state court action will deprive a federal court of the opportunity to resolve the merits of a parallel action in federal court. "The traditional notion is that *in personam* actions in federal and state court may proceed concurrently, without interference from either court, and there is no evidence that the exception to § 2283 was intended to alter this balance." Vendo Co. v. Lektro-Vend Corp., 433 U.S. 623, 642 (1977). In ordinary actions *in personam*, "each court is free to proceed in its own way and in its own time, without reference to the proceedings in the other court. Whenever a judgment is rendered in one of the courts and pleaded in the other, the effect of that judgment is to be determined by the application of the principle of *res adjudicata* by the court in which the action is still pending. . . ." Kline v. Burke Constr. Co., 260 U.S. 226, 230 (1922). Therefore, it may not be sufficient that state actions risk some measure of inconvenience or duplicative litigation. An injunction may issue, however, where "the state court action threatens to frustrate proceedings and disrupt the orderly resolution of the federal litigation." Winkler v. Eli Lilly & Co., 101 F.3d 1196, 1202 (7th Cir. 1996). In other words, the state action must not simply threaten to reach judgment first, it must interfere with the federal court's own path to judgment.

Several factors are relevant to determine whether sufficient interference is threatened to justify an injunction otherwise prohibited by the Anti-Injunction Act. First, we look to the nature of the federal action to determine what kinds of state court interference would sufficiently impair the federal proceeding. Second, we assess the state court's actions, in order to determine whether they present a sufficient threat to the federal action. And finally, we consider principles of federalism and comity, for a primary aim of the Anti-Injunction Act is "to prevent needless friction between the state and federal courts." Okla. Packing Co. v. Okla. Gas & Elec. Co., 309 U.S. 4, 9 (1940).

We turn first to the nature of the federal action. While, as noted, the "necessary in aid of jurisdiction" exception does not ordinarily permit injunctions merely to prevent duplicative actions *in personam*, federal courts are permitted to stay later-initiated state court proceedings over the same res in actions *in rem*, because "the exercise by the state court of jurisdiction over the same res necessarily impairs, and may defeat, the jurisdiction of the federal court already attached." Kline, 260 U.S. at 229; see also In re Gen. Motors Corp. Pick-Up Truck Fuel Tank Prods. Liab. Litig., 134 F.3d 133, 145 (3d Cir. 1998) ("GM Trucks II"). Federal courts may also issue such injunctions to protect exclusive federal jurisdiction of a case that has been removed from state court.

We have recognized another category of federal cases for which state court actions present a special threat to the jurisdiction of the federal court. Under an appropriate set of facts, a federal court entertaining complex litigation, especially when it involves a substantial class of persons from multiple states, or represents a consolidation of cases from multiple districts, may appropriately enjoin state court proceedings in order to protect its jurisdiction. Carlough v. Amchem Prods., Inc., 10 F.3d 189, 202–04 (3d Cir. 1993). *Carlough* involved a nationwide class of plaintiffs and several defendants—primarily manufacturers of asbestos-related products—and third-party defendants—primarily insurance providers. We found the complexity of the case to be a substantial factor in justifying the injunction imposed.

Implicit in *Carlough* is the recognition that maintaining "the federal court's flexibility and authority to decide" such complex nationwide cases makes special demands on the court that may justify an injunction otherwise prohibited by the Anti-Injunction Act. Several other courts have concurred.[19] See, e.g., Hanlon v. Chrysler Corp., 150 F.3d 1011 (9th Cir. 1998); *Winkler*, 101 F.3d at 1203 ("The Anti-Injunction Act does not bar courts with jurisdiction over complex multidistrict litigation from issuing injunctions to protect the integrity of their rulings."); . . . In re Corrugated Container Antitrust Litig., 659 F.2d 1332, 1334–35 (5th Cir. Unit A 1981) (approving injunction in a "complicated antitrust action [that] has required a great deal of the district court's time and has necessitated that it maintain a flexible approach in resolving the various claims of the many parties.");. . . .

19. [Court's footnote #12] In several cases, courts have analogized complex litigation cases to actions in rem. As one court reasoned, "the district court had before it a class action proceeding so far advanced that it was the virtual equivalent of a res over which the district judge required full control." *Baldwin-United*, 770 F.2d at 337;. . . . The *in rem* analogy may help to bring into focus what makes these cases stand apart. In cases *in rem*, "the jurisdiction over the same res necessarily impairs, and may defeat, the jurisdiction of the federal court already attached." *Kline*, 260 U.S. at 229. Similarly, where complex cases are sufficiently developed, mere exercise of parallel jurisdiction by the state court may present enough of a threat to the jurisdiction of the federal court to justify issuance of an injunction. What is ultimately important, in any event, is that in both kinds of cases state actions over the same subject matter have the potential to "so interfere with a federal court's consideration or disposition of a case as to seriously impair the federal court's flexibility and authority to decide the case." *Atl. Coast*, 398 U.S. at 295.

This is not to say that class actions are, by virtue of that categorization alone, exempt from the general rule that *in personam* cases must be permitted to proceed in parallel. Federal courts ordinarily refrain from enjoining a state action even where the state court is asked to approve a settlement substantially similar to one the federal court has already rejected. That a state court may resolve an issue first (which may operate as *res judicata*), is not by itself a sufficient threat to the federal court's jurisdiction that justifies an injunction, unless the proceedings in state courts threaten to "frustrate proceedings and disrupt the orderly resolution of the federal litigation." Winkler, 101 F.3d at 1202. Still, while the potentially preclusive effects of the state action may not themselves justify an injunction, they might do so indirectly. If, for example, the possibility of an earlier state court judgment is disruptive to settlement negotiations in federal court, the existence of the state court action might sufficiently interfere with the federal court's flexibility to justify an injunction.

The threat to the federal court's jurisdiction posed by parallel state actions is particularly significant where there are conditional class certifications and impending settlements in federal actions. Many—though not all—of the cases permitting injunctions in complex litigation cases involve injunctions issued as the parties approached settlement. . . . Complex cases in the later stages—where, for instance, settlement negotiations are underway—embody an enormous amount of time and expenditure of resources. It is in the nature of complex litigation that the parties often seek complicated, comprehensive settlements to resolve as many claims as possible in one proceeding. These cases are especially vulnerable to parallel state actions that may "frustrate the district court's efforts to craft a settlement in the multi-district litigation before it," *Carlough*, 10 F.3d at 203, thereby destroying the ability to achieve the benefits of consolidation. In complex cases where certification or settlement has received conditional approval, or perhaps even where settlement is pending, the challenges facing the overseeing court are such that it is likely that almost any parallel litigation in other fora presents a genuine threat to the jurisdiction of the federal court.

This case amply highlights these concerns. MDL 1203 represented the consolidation of over two thousand cases that had been filed in or removed to federal court. The *Brown* class finally certified comprised six million members. The District Court entered well over one thousand orders in the case. This massive consolidation enabled the possibility of a global resolution that promised to minimize the various difficulties associated with duplicative and competing lawsuits. The central events in this dispute occurred after two years of exhaustive work by the parties and the District Court, and after a conditional class certification and preliminary settlement had been negotiated and approved by the District Court. There can be no doubt that keeping this enormously complicated settlement process on track required careful management by the District Court. Any state court action that might interfere with the District Court's oversight of the settlement at that time, given the careful balancing it embodied, was a serious threat to the District Court's ability to manage the final stages of this complex litigation.[20] Duplicative and competing actions were substantially more likely to "frustrate proceedings and disrupt the orderly resolution" of this dispute at the time PTO 1227 was issued than they would be in ordinary actions *in personam*. This is especially true where, as here, the litigants in state court have the ability to tailor their state actions to the terms of the pending federal settlement.

Determining the applicability of the *Carlough* rule also requires assessment of the character of the state court action, for we must assess the level of interference with the federal action actually threatened by the state court proceeding. In *Carlough*, our approval of the injunction was supported by the direct threat to the federal action the state court action represented. After the district court had provisionally certified the *Carlough* class, and after a preliminary settlement had been negotiated and presented to the court, a parallel action was filed in West Virginia. As here, the plaintiffs in that case . . . sought an order of the state court opting out the members of the West Virginia class from the federal class. They also sought a declaration that *Carlough* would not be binding on the members of the West Virginia class.

We viewed the filing of the West Virginia action as an intentional "preemptive strike" against the federal action. The purpose of the West Virginia filing was "to challenge the propriety of the federal class action." We found "it difficult to imagine a more detrimental effect upon the district court's ability to effectuate the settlement of this complex and far-reaching matter then would occur if the West Virginia state court was permitted to make a determination regarding the validity of the federal settlement."

Also significant in *Carlough* was the threat posed by the attempt to secure a mass opt out. We noted that permitting a state court to issue such an order "would be disruptive to the district court's ongoing settlement management and would jeopardize the settlement's fruition." Additionally, we noted the confusion that would likely result among West Virginia residents as to their status in the "dueling lawsuits." All of this amounted to direct interference with the district court's ability to manage the federal action effectively.

The interference that would have been caused by the Hidalgo County court's order implicates the same concerns that animated our decision in *Carlough*. The Texas court's order directly affected the identity of the parties to MDL 1203 and did so contrary to a previous District Court order. It sought to "declare what the federal court should and should not do with respect to the federal settlement." Furthermore,

20. [Court's footnote #13] Among other vulnerabilities, it is worth highlighting one example. The settlement agreement in this case expressly permitted American Home Products to terminate the settlement agreement, at its discretion, based on the number of opt outs. That provision was, of course, created with the complicated opt-out provisions crafted specifically for MDL 1203 in mind. External actions that would disturb that balance, by altering the number of opt outs through a different mechanism, clearly would substantially interfere with MDL 1203.

as in *Carlough*, the Texas order would have created confusion among those who were members of both the federal and the state classes. It would be difficult to discern which, if any, action one was a party to, especially since the Texas order was entered during, and shortly before the end of, the MDL 1203 opt-out period.

Attempting to distinguish their case from *Carlough*, appellants contend their action cannot be characterized as a preemptive strike against the federal action because the *Gonzalez* action was filed before the creation of MDL 1203. Yet we do not believe a state court action must necessarily be a preemptive strike before meriting the *Carlough* exception. The test, as always, is whether the state court proceeding "so interferes with a federal court's consideration or disposition of a case as to seriously impair the federal court's flexibility and authority to decide that case." *Atl. Coast*, 398 U.S. at 295. Of course, where a state court proceeding amounts to an attack on a federal action, we are more likely to find significant interference. We are also less likely to find that comity demands deference to the state court action. But there are any number of factors that may play a role, and we do not understand either *Carlough* or *GM Trucks II* to hold that this element is necessary, in all cases, for application of the exception.

In any event, appellants' attempt to distinguish *Carlough* on this ground fails. While the relative timing of the filing of the actions makes clear that *Gonzalez* was not filed as a preemptive strike on MDL 1203, there is no doubt the motion requesting the Texas court to opt *Gonzalez* class members out of the *Brown* class was a preemptive strike. The District Court found it necessary to enjoin only the part of the action that directly—and by design—interfered with the federal action.[21]

Because an injunction must be necessary in aid of jurisdiction to fall under this application to the Anti-Injunction Act, it is important to carefully tailor such injunctions to meet the needs of the case. Notably, the relief we approved in *Carlough* was substantially broader than the relief granted by the District Court here. The federal order in *Carlough* enjoined the West Virginia plaintiffs, as well as their attorneys and representatives, from pursuing the [state-court] action or initiating similar litigation in any other forum. The injunction in *Carlough* effectively stayed the entire parallel state action, not only the attempted opt out, or other portions directed squarely at the federal action. Here, by contrast, the District Court's order enjoined only the pursuit of the attempted mass opt out—the part of *Gonzalez* that unquestionably interfered with the management of MDL 1203. It did not prevent the *Gonzalez* plaintiffs from individually opting out. Furthermore, the injunction

21. [Court's footnote #14] Even if the District Court had, as in *Carlough*, enjoined the state court action *in toto*, it is far from clear that the fact that *Gonzalez* was filed before the creation of MDL 1203 would be dispositive. It is conceivable that an earlier filed state court action might present just as great an interference with the federal proceeding as a later filed state action. While the prior filing of a state action will generally be a factor, and may, in certain circumstances, be dispositive, there is no apparent value in adopting a rigid rule to that effect.

was not directed at a proceeding in which plaintiffs had merely requested relief that threatened to interfere with the federal action, it was directed at a proceeding in which the state court had actually granted such a request, making the interference substantially more manifest. Under these circumstances, we find the District Court's injunction to be well within its "sound discretion."

The propriety of an injunction directed at the Texas order is also consistent with considerations of federalism and comity. The Texas plaintiffs who wished to opt out of the *Brown* class were given an adequate opportunity to individually opt out of the federal action, a factor we found significant in *Carlough*. As such, Texas residents retained the option to commence lawsuits in the forum of their choice. Furthermore, the injunction only prevented application of a particular order that was directed squarely at the federal action. *Cf. Baldwin-United*, 770 F.2d at 337 ("To the extent that the impending state court suits were vexatious and harassing, our interest in preserving federalism and comity with the state courts is not significantly disturbed by the issuance of injunctive relief."). It did not so much interfere with the state court proceeding as prevent state court interference with the federal proceeding. Failing to act on the Hidalgo County order threatened to "create the very 'needless friction between state and federal courts' which the Anti-Injunction Act was designed to prevent." *Winkler*, 101 F.3d at 1203 (quoting *Okla. Packing Co.*, 309 U.S. at 9). "While the Anti-Injunction Act is designed to avoid disharmony between federal and state systems, the exception in § 2283 reflects congressional recognition that injunctions may sometimes be necessary in order to avoid that disharmony." Amalgamated Sugar Co. v. NL Indus., Inc., 825 F.2d 634, 639 (2d Cir. 1987).

The District Court's order clearly falls under the "necessary in aid of its jurisdiction" exception to the Anti-Injunction Act. The complexity of this multidistrict class action in its mature stages—with a provisionally certified class and preliminarily approved settlement—entailed that the District Court required flexibility to bring the case to judgment. The nature of the Texas order was such that the required flexibility and eventual resolution were directly threatened. Finally, the principle embodied in the Anti-Injunction Act that federal courts maintain respect for state court proceedings is not undermined by the issuance of the injunction.

Our holding that PTO 1227 was necessary in aid of the District Court's jurisdiction for purposes of the Anti-Injunction Act necessarily implies it was authorized under the All Writs Act as well. For the All Writs Act grants federal courts the authority to issue all writs "necessary or appropriate in aid" of a court's jurisdiction. 28 U.S.C. § 1651(a). Insofar as it also permits writs "appropriate in aid" of jurisdiction, the court's authority to issue writs is, if anything, broader than the exception contained in the Anti-Injunction Act. But since "the parallel 'necessary in aid of jurisdiction' language is construed similarly in both the All-Writs Act and the Anti-Injunction Act," a finding that an injunction is "necessary in aid" of jurisdiction for purposes of one these statutes implies its necessity for purposes of the other. Accordingly, the District Court was empowered to issue PTO 1227 under the All Writs Act, and was not prevented from doing so by the Anti-Injunction Act.

. . .

For the foregoing reasons, we will affirm the order issued by the District Court.

Notes and Questions

1. Will the court's opinion support an injunction "in aid of" a federal court's jurisdiction only in class action cases? Only in MDL cases?

2. According to the court, is there any difference in the meaning of "necessary in aid of [a federal court's] jurisdiction" as used in the Anti-Injunction Act and "necessary or appropriate in aid of [a federal court's] jurisdiction" in the All Writs Act?

3. Also according to the court, what sorts of "interference" will support an injunction? Suppose there are conflicting discovery orders, in which the state court orders discovery that the federal court prohibits (or vice versa). Would such orders justify an injunction?

4. The usual rule (as we saw in *Donovan*, in section C.1.b. above) is that parallel *in personam* cases may proceed simultaneously. Of course, a judgment entered in one might have preclusive effect in the other, but, generally, before a judgment is entered the two cases proceed without interference from the other court. In *Donovan*, the Court noted an exception for *in rem* and *quasi in rem* cases. In such cases, the court with possession of the property has sole jurisdiction to proceed. At least one court has likened the administration of complex litigation to possession of property, so the court may enjoin state-court litigation that interferes with that administration. *Battle v. Liberty National Life Ins. Co.*, 877 F.2d 877, 882 (11th Cir. 1989). Consider, for example, a nationwide class action on the verge of global settlement. Could the settlement itself be seen as property for this purpose?

5. The *Diet Drugs* case was decided before passage of the Class Action Fairness Act (CAFA), discussed in Chapter 2.D.4. Do you think CAFA affects the number of cases in which anti-suit injunctions against state-court proceedings are necessary?

6. As we have seen, a court can issue an injunction against a party; the party is already before the jurisdiction of the court and would be bound by the injunction. But can a court legitimately enjoin a non-litigant? The Supreme Court approved such an injunction under the All Writs Act in *United States v. New York Telephone Co.*, 434 U.S. 159 (1977) (injunction against telephone company to permit federal law enforcement officers to install pen registers, which records the number dialed but not the conversations, on specified telephones). Such injunctions are rare.

Problem

P-1 filed a federal-court class action on behalf of similarly situated persons, alleging that Defendant's product—a composite siding for houses—was defective. The court certified the case to proceed as a class action and ultimately approved settlement, by which each member of the plaintiff class was entitled to various damages.

They were not entitled, however, to cost-of-repair damages, because those were not recoverable under applicable state law. The federal court approved the settlement and entered final judgment. It retained ancillary enforcement jurisdiction to enforce terms of the settlement agreement.

P-2 then brought a wholly separate case—on behalf of different plaintiffs—against Defendant. The suit was filed in state court, and the court held that cost-of-repair damages were available. Defendant then moved in the federal court for an injunction prohibiting the state court from permitting recovery of cost-of-repair damages in P-2 case. The federal court held that such an injunction was proper, "in aid of its jurisdiction."

Was the federal court correct? *See Sandpiper Village Condominium Assn. v. Louisiana-Pacific Corp.*, 428 F.3d 831, 843–846 (9th Cir. 2005).

Note on the Rooker-Feldman *Doctrine*

The *Rooker-Feldman* doctrine stands for the proposition that a federal court cannot review judicial proceedings of a state court. Judgments of state trial courts can only be appealed to state appellate courts. The only federal appellate review of state-court judgments is when the Supreme Court reviews the ruling of the highest state court on matters of federal law. Accordingly, a case in federal district court that would have the effect of reviewing what a state court did is barred. The federal court cannot relitigate an issue actually decided in the state courts or "inextricably intertwined" with such an issue. The doctrine takes its name from two cases: *Rooker v. Fidelity Trust Co.*, 263 U.S. 413 (1923) and *District of Columbia Court of Appeals v. Feldman*, 460 U.S. 462 (1983).

> ***Example #5.*** Graduates of non-accredited law schools sue state authorities in state court to challenge the rule that only graduates of accredited law schools can become members of the state bar. The case is litigated and the plaintiffs lose. Then they sue in federal court, asserting that the exclusion from the bar violates the Constitution. This case is barred under the *Rooker-Feldman* doctrine. The only avenue for federal-court review would have been to appeal through the state-court system and from the highest state court seek review at the Supreme Court of the United States.

In *In re Diet Drugs*, plaintiffs in the *Gonzalez* case challenged the federal district court order that declared the Texas ruling "null and void." They argued that that order violated *Rooker-Feldman.* The Third Circuit rejected the argument. It explained that the federal district court:

> ... did not review the Texas opt-out order, [but] simply applied its indisputable authority to determine the opt-out rules for the plaintiff class before it, and to determine who had properly opted out under those rules. Making determinations concerning the identity of the parties to a case before it is at the core of the District Court's authority. The Texas opt-out order purported to make a determination with respect to the parties to the federal

> action. It was, in other words, effectively an attempt to make an interlocutory procedural ruling in a case pending before another court. . . . The *Rooker-Feldman* doctrine does not work to defeat a district court's authority over the management of its own case.

228 F.3d at 241.

The Supreme Court has limited *Rooker-Feldman* to cases in which the state-court losing party then files suit in federal court, seeking review of the state-court judgment. *Exxon Mobil Corp. v. Saudi Basic Industries Corp.*, 544 U.S. 280, 284 (2005).

2. Abstention by the Federal Court

Instead of entering an anti-suit injunction, a federal court might avoid overlapping litigation by abstaining—that is, by refusing to exercise its jurisdiction, thereby letting the state-court case take precedence.

a. Background on the Types of Abstention

We deal here with a series of judge-made doctrines by which a federal court declines to exercise jurisdiction it clearly has. Some scholars have argued that abstention violates principles of separation of powers. Specifically, the legislative branch is responsible for setting federal subject matter jurisdiction (within the boundaries of Article III). For the judiciary simply to eschew its determination, the argument goes, usurps a function that should be performed by Congress. Despite the argument, abstention is well established.

There are several abstention doctrines, most of which have limited potential for obviating problems of overlapping litigation. Indeed, we will look at only one of these doctrines in detail. We summarize the other forms of abstention as background and to demonstrate their limited usefulness in addressing complex litigation.

Pullman Abstention. The Texas Railroad Commission (TRC) entered an order which, if interpreted one way, would violate equal protection and due process by discriminating on the basis of race. Plaintiffs with standing sued in federal court, invoking federal question jurisdiction, to challenge the order. The Supreme Court held that the federal courts should abstain and not entertain the case. *Railroad Commission of Texas v. Pullman*, 312 U.S. 296 (1941). The TRC order was ambiguous, and might be interpreted in a way that would not be discriminatory. If so, the federal constitutional challenge would be avoided. Moreover, the ambiguous state law concerned the regulation of rail transport, which is an important state function.

Pullman abstention is proper only when there is a federal constitutional challenge to an ambiguous state law. The federal court does not dismiss, but stays the proceeding to allow the state mechanism to interpret the ambiguous state law. If the state mechanism interprets it one way, the federal constitutional challenge disappears. If the state mechanism interprets it the other way, the parties can return to the federal court for a ruling on the resultant constitutional challenge. As a practical matter, *Pullman* will not play a role in most complex litigation for the simple reason that such cases rarely present constitutional challenges to ambiguous state law.

***Burford* Abstention.** This form of abstention also arose from a challenge to an order of the Texas Railroad Commission (TRC). That body not only regulates the operation of railroads, but has authority to allocate drilling rights for oil and gas. The TRC entered an order granting Burford the right to drill in certain areas. Sun Oil Company challenged the order by filing suit in federal court. The case invoked both diversity of citizenship and federal question jurisdiction. Basically, Sun Oil claimed that the TRC order violated a variety of its rights.

The Supreme Court held that the federal court should have abstained and dismissed Sun Oil's case. *Burford v. Sun Oil Co.*, 319 U.S. 315, 333–334 (1943). It noted that Texas had established a complex scheme by which orders of this type were reviewed administratively and then by a particular state court. The state legislature expressly stated the need for such a system to avoid having various state courts become involved in reviewing TRC orders. *Burford* abstention is proper only when a federal court decision might "disrupt[t] . . . state efforts to establish a coherent policy with respect to a matter of substantial public concern." *Colorado River Water Conservation Dist. v. United States*, 424 U.S. 800, 814 (1976). It is of limited use in most complex cases, since most cases do not challenge state administrative regulation.

***Thibodaux* Abstention.** This is a particularly confused area, having its genesis in *Louisiana Power & Light Co. v. City of Thibodaux*, 360 U.S. 25 (1959). The case involved a challenge—brought under diversity jurisdiction—to state condemnation of real property through the power of eminent domain. Its ultimate reach is unclear, but the doctrine is of limited utility to the types of private civil litigation ordinarily involved in this course.

***Younger* "Abstention."** In *Younger v. Harris*, 401 U.S. 37 (1971), the plaintiff was indicted by California authorities and charged with violation of a syndicalism statute. (Syndicalism is the advocacy of illegal methods to change political control.) He sued in federal court under federal question jurisdiction, arguing that his prosecution violated federal constitutional rights. He sought an injunction against the prosecution. The Supreme Court held that the federal court could not issue the injunction. *Id.* at 53–54. Instead, the plaintiff could raise his constitutional objections in the state criminal prosecution. Accordingly, the Court concluded, he had an adequate remedy at law and could not qualify for equitable relief. Federal restraint was important to "our federalism," to allow the state courts to apply federal constitutional law. *Id.* at 43–44.

Some observers do not consider *Younger* an "abstention" doctrine. Rather, it falls under the rubric "equitable restraint" because no court will issue equitable relief (such as an injunction) when a legal remedy (such as damages or the right to defend against a criminal charge) is adequate. There are exceptions to *Younger* and serious questions about whether it applies to claims for other forms of equitable relief.

Younger is only occasionally relevant in private civil litigation. An example is *Pennzoil Co. v. Texaco, Inc.* 481 U.S. 1 (1987), which involved a challenge in federal court to an allegedly prohibitive bond requirement employed in Texas state courts to prevent execution of a judgment prior to appeal. Although the dispute was between private parties, the Court concluded that federalism concerns "mandate[ ] application of *Younger* abstention not only when the pending proceedings are criminal, but also when certain civil proceedings are pending, if the State's interests in the proceeding are so important that the exercise of the federal judicial power would disregard the comity between the States and the National Government." *Id.* at 11.

b. Abstention to Avoid Overlapping Litigation: Colorado River *Abstention*

There is one abstention doctrine that holds especial promise for the avoidance of overlapping litigation in federal and state court. In *Colorado River Water Conservation Dist. v. United States*, 424 U.S. 800 (1976), the United States sued about 1000 water users in Colorado. It sought a declaration as to its rights and the rights of Indian tribes to water in a certain part of the state. The suit was filed in the federal district court for the District of Colorado, in Denver. Earlier, a proceeding had been filed in state court in the area affected, about 300 miles from Denver. The United States had been joined in that case, which was ongoing. The Supreme Court noted that none of the abstention doctrines discussed above applied. It also emphasized that abstention of any type is exceptional, and that ordinarily federal courts have "a virtually unflagging obligation . . . to exercise the jurisdiction given them." 424 U.S. at 817.

Nonetheless, the Court held that the federal court should have abstained (through dismissal) in the interest of "wise judicial administration." *Id.* In other words, the Court justified abstention in an effort to avoid overlapping litigation. On its face, it is difficult to square this result with the presumption, stated in *Donovan* in section C.1.b. above, that the judicial system will tolerate parallel *in personam* cases in federal and state courts.

The Court identified four factors for deciding whether "wise judicial administration" counseled dismissal. *Id.* at 818. First, whether either the federal or state court had seized property; on the facts of *Colorado River*, neither court had done so. Second, the relative inconvenience of the federal forum; on the facts of the case, the federal forum was 300 miles from the affected area, which imposed a burden on some of the litigants. Third, the desirability of avoiding piecemeal litigation; the Court noted federal legislation permitting the United States to be joined in state water proceedings, which demonstrated a federal desire to avoid overlapping litigation. Fourth, the order in which the cases were filed; the state case, as noted, was filed first. Although no factor is determinative, the Court concluded that in the aggregate they presented "extraordinary" circumstances that supported abstention. Academics have largely criticized the opinion. *See, e.g.*, Linda Mullenix, *A Branch Too Far: Pruning the Abstention Doctrine*, 75 Geo. L.J. 99 (1986).

The Court has revisited *Colorado River* from time to time, and seems to have drawn back from liberal application of this brand of abstention. *See, e.g., Moses H. Cone Memorial Hospital v. Mercury Construction Corp.*, 460 U.S. 1, 19, 23 (1983) (rejecting application of *Colorado River* while emphasizing the extraordinary nature of abstention; presentation of a federal substantive issue in the case also counseled against abstention). Lower courts, however, continue to find circumstances in which to use it.

Ingalls v. The AES Corporation

United States Court of Appeals, Seventh Circuit
2008 U.S. App. LEXIS 7717

In January 2007 Dwane Ingalls brought this diversity action against The AES Corporation, claiming that AES breached a contract for the sale and purchase of stock options and committed fraud in relation to that contract. AES moved to dismiss or stay these proceedings in favor of parallel state proceedings. The district court granted the motion to stay the federal suit, finding that a state suit Ingalls had filed against AES in July 2004 was parallel and that abstention was proper under the doctrine established in *Colorado River Water Conservation Dist. v. United States*, 424 U.S. 800 (1976). We affirm.

Ingalls began his career at AES in 1990. In January 2001 Ingalls accepted a transfer to work for the Indianapolis Power and Light Company (IPL), which AES was in the process of acquiring, as a vice president and business unit leader. At about the same time, AES began having financial problems. In late 2001 AES asked its officers, including those working at its subsidiaries, to voluntarily give up their 2001 cash bonuses and accept reduced base salaries for 2002 in exchange for AES stock options that would vest in 10 years. Ingalls allegedly accepted this offer, giving up his $50,000 bonus for 2001 and $55,000 of his $125,000 base salary for 2002.

In the spring of 2003, Ingalls became concerned about the leadership at IPL as well as the effect of AES's financial problems on IPL and IPALCO Enterprises, Inc. (IPALCO), IPL's holding company. After voicing these concerns to IPL's Chief Executive Officer, Ann Murtlow, and to others, Murtlow fired Ingalls in March 2004, allegedly because Ingalls had lost faith in the company's leadership. When Ingalls was formally terminated, he refused to sign the separation agreement that AES proposed, losing any severance pay and stock options to which he would have otherwise been entitled.

In November 2004 Ingalls contacted AES to request that the stock options he had purchased at the end of 2001 be issued to him. He was told that these options were subject to AES's general stock option policy under which all rights to options terminate 180 days after an employee leaves the company. Ingalls alleges that this was the first time he heard that the options offered for purchase in 2001 were subject to the general stock option policies.

Meanwhile, in July 2004 Ingalls filed suit against AES, IPALCO, IPL, and Murtlow in Indiana state court. His amended complaint alleged four causes of action, two of which are relevant here. First, he claimed that when the defendants terminated him they breached an implied 10-year employment contract that was supposedly created when he accepted the 2001 stock option offer because, he argued, he had to be employed with AES for the options to vest, which took 10 years. Second, he claimed the defendants failed to pay him all of the wages owed him, including the stock options he bought as part of the 2001 offer. In November 2006 the state court granted partial summary judgment to the defendants on the wages claim because Ingalls had not first filed an administrative grievance as required by law.

In January 2007 Ingalls filed this suit in federal district court, alleging three causes of action based on the 2001 stock option offer: (1) breach of contract for the purchase of stock options, (2) fraud, and (3) state securities fraud. The district court granted the defendant's motion to stay the federal court proceedings. The court first held that the two suits were parallel because two of the state claims and all of the federal claims "revolve around the same transactions involving the ten year stock options" and Ingalls had "simply asserted some new theories for relief" stemming from events central to his state case. The court then applied the 10-factor test we have established for determining whether *Colorado River* abstention is appropriate, concluding that most of the factors weighed in favor of abstention.

On appeal Ingalls argues that the district court abused its discretion in holding that the state and federal cases are parallel. He contends that the two suits are not parallel because he is seeking redress in the state case for different stock options than those at stake in the federal case. He also disputes whether the district court applied the proper rules for determining if cases are parallel. Finally, Ingalls frivolously contends that AES conceded in a discovery letter that the stock options in the federal case are not part of the state case.

Abstention under the *Colorado River* doctrine is reserved for exceptional circumstances in which a stay of federal court proceedings in favor of concurrent state court proceedings would promote "wise judicial administration" out of recognition that federal courts have a "virtually unflagging obligation" to exercise the jurisdiction given them. Colorado River, 424 U.S. at 817 (internal quotation marks and citation omitted) . . . District courts must conduct a two-part inquiry to determine if abstention is appropriate. Tyrer v. City of South Beloit, 456 F.3d 744, 751 (7th Cir. 2006). First, the court considers whether the state and federal suits are parallel. If the court concludes that the suits are parallel, the court then considers several non-exclusive factors to determine if exceptional circumstances exist to justify abstention.

Whether the two suits are parallel is a legal issue that we review de novo. Two suits are parallel "when substantially the same parties are contemporaneously litigating substantially the same issues in another forum." The suits need not be identical. Rather, contrary to Ingalls's argument that similar facts are irrelevant, the district court should determine whether the suits "arise out of the same facts and raise similar factual and legal issues." *Tyrer*, 456 F.3d at 752.

We agree with the district court that the state and federal proceedings here are parallel. The two suits involve the same parties—Ingalls and AES. The addition of IPALCO, IPL, and Murtlow as defendants in the state case does not destroy the parallel nature of the cases. Importantly, the two suits arise out of the same facts and raise similar factual and legal issues. Although Ingalls argues that his state case focuses on stock options granted to him as incentive compensation while his federal case centers on the stock options he purchased, his amended complaint in the state case and his deposition testimony show that the stock options relevant to the federal claim are central to two of the state court claims. Although the state court disposed of the wages claim, the claim for breach of his employment contract remains. The factual and legal analyses for that claim and the claims in the federal case would be substantially similar. Both courts would have to determine the terms of the offer, whether Ingalls accepted the offer, and what, if any, obligations each party incurred. In the course of discovery in the state case, any fraudulent behavior would likely be uncovered, thus reaching the fraud claims in the federal suit. The state court litigation will likely dispose of all claims presented in the federal case, which indicates that the cases are parallel. *See* . . . Day v. Union Mines, Inc., 862 F.2d 652, 656 (7th Cir. 1988) (state and federal cases parallel when state court would inevitably reach federal case issues even though specific issue not raised in state complaint).

Ingalls's argument that the cases are not parallel because he is seeking different remedies in each case is unpersuasive. His state and federal complaints show that he is actually seeking substantially the same remedies—to be made whole and placed in the same position he would have held but for the breach of employment contract (state case) and breach of the option offer (federal case) plus reimbursement for all financial losses due to AES's alleged misconduct. The similarity in the remedies Ingalls seeks suggests that Ingalls has merely repackaged his state complaints in this federal action.

Turning to the second step of the abstention analysis, we review for an abuse of discretion whether the district court appropriately applied the 10-factor test to determine if abstention is appropriate. On appeal Ingalls does not address the district court's application of the 10-factor test. Because he did not present an argument, let alone develop one, any challenge to the district court's application of the 10-factor test is waived.

Regardless, our review of the record convinces us that the district court did not abuse its discretion in holding that abstention was proper. The court must apply the non-exclusive factors on a case-by-case basis. No factor is "necessarily determinative." *Colorado River*, 424 U.S. at 818. . . . In this case, most factors applicable to the situation weigh in favor of abstention. First, the desirability of avoiding piecemeal litigation weighs in favor of abstention. The two courts would be considering the same issues in relation to the 2001 stock option offer and likely hear similar pretrial motions, evidence, and witnesses. Therefore the possibility exists that the courts will come to conflicting decisions in the interpretation of the same transaction. Second, the state court obtained jurisdiction more than two years before the federal court, and the state case has progressed further than the federal case. Substantial discovery has been conducted in the state case, and the state court has already made a substantive ruling on one claim. In contrast, the federal case has not moved beyond the abstention issue. These factors therefore weigh in favor of abstention. Third, state law governs all of Ingalls's claims. *See Day*, 862 F.2d at 660 ("[S]tate court's expertise in applying its own law favors a *Colorado River* stay."). Fourth, because all claims stem from state law, the state court will adequately protect Ingalls's rights. Fifth, the state and federal courts have concurrent jurisdiction. *See id.* at 702–03. Finally, Ingalls filed his federal suit just two months after the state court granted partial summary judgment to AES on the wages claim, which suggests that the federal suit may be vexatious and contrived. The other factors are either inapplicable or neutral.

AFFIRMED.

Notes and Questions

1. The court relies in part on its decision in *Tyrer v. City of South Beloit*, 456 F.3d 744, 754 (7th. 2006). There, it listed the ten discretionary factors as: (1) whether the state has assumed jurisdiction over property; (2) the inconvenience of the federal forum; (3) the desirability of avoiding piecemeal litigation; (4) the order in which jurisdiction was obtained by the concurrent forums; (5) the source of governing law, state or federal; (6) the adequacy of state-court action to protect the federal plaintiff's rights; (7) the relative progress of state and federal proceedings; (8) the presence or absence of concurrent jurisdiction; (9) the availability of removal; and (10) the vexatious or contrived nature of the federal claim.

2. In *Tyrer*, the court of appeals affirmed the invocation of *Colorado River* abstention, but disagreed on the remedy. The district court had dismissed the case, which the court of appeals found improper. Instead, the federal action should merely be stayed to allow the state case to proceed. Interestingly, as noted, the Court in *Colorado River* itself held that the federal case should be dismissed.

3. The court in *Ingalls* noted that the dispute was governed by state law, which augured in favor of abstention. Could *Colorado River* be used to abstain in any diversity of citizenship case in which there is an overlapping state-court case? After all, under the *Erie* Doctrine, state law will govern in every diversity case.

4. Most courts to address the issue conclude that *Colorado River* abstention is appropriate not only in the federal-state court context, but when parallel litigation is filed in courts in other countries. *See, e.g., Answers in Genesis of Kentucky, Inc. v. Creation Ministries Int'l, Ltd.*, 566 F.3d 459, 466–469 (6th Cir. 2009); *Ingersoll Milling Mach. Co v. Granger*, 833 F.3d 680, 683 (7th Cir. 1987). Some observers consider this extension problematic. After all, when an American court abstains in favor of proceedings in another American court, it is deferring to a tribunal that is part of the same federal union. This is not the case, however, when the court to which deference is paid is in another country.

Reflecting this concern and others, the Eleventh Circuit has refused to accept *Colorado River* uncritically in the international context. It adopts what it calls "international abstention," in which the American court must balance (1) interests of international comity, (2) fairness to litigants, and (3) the efficient use of scarce judicial resources. The leading case is *Turner Entertainment Co. v. Degeto Film GmbH*, 25 F.3d 1512, 1518 (11th Cir. 1994). For an interesting discussion of the topic, see Gaspard Curioni, Note, *Interest Balancing and International Abstention*, 93 Boston U. L. Rev. 621 (2013).

5. In one context, abstention does not require a showing of "extraordinary" or "exceptional" circumstances. Specifically, if the federal-court claimant seeks declaratory relief, as opposed to damages or some other form of coercive relief, the Declaratory Judgment Act gives the federal judge greater discretion than she has under *Colorado River* to decline to declare the rights of the parties. *Wilton v. Seven Falls Co.*, 515 U.S. 277, 286–288 (1995). Stated another way, it is easier to get abstention in a declaratory judgment case than in other actions.

3. Removal from State to Federal Court

As discussed above, overlapping litigation in federal and state courts cannot be remedied by transfer. Absent federal legislation—which does not yet exist—there is simply no mechanism for transferring cases between different judicial systems. But there is removal. This, as we discussed in Chapter 2, section B.3, permits the defendant to have a case filed in a state trial court "removed" to the federal trial court that geographically embraces the state court. Removal does nothing to coordinate that case with pending federal litigation. It does, however, get the case into federal court. This means, of course, that it might be transferred to another federal court under § 1404(a) or included in multidistrict proceedings under § 1407.

Removal only works, however, if the case "belongs" in federal court. As a general matter, that means it must invoke diversity of citizenship or federal question jurisdiction. Even then, in diversity cases, there are statutory impediments—discussed in Chapter 2—including the rule that the case cannot be removed if any defendant is a citizen of the forum.

The Supreme Court closed a door that lower courts had opened for removal. Through the years, some lower courts used the All Writs Act, 28 U.S.C. § 1651(a) as a bootstrap to remove cases from state court. That statute, which we discussed in section C.1.c above, provides that federal courts "may issue all writs necessary or appropriate in aid of their respective jurisdictions. . . ." According to some lower courts, this statute gave federal courts removal jurisdiction over cases when necessary to prevent frustration of orders already entered by the federal court. In other words, if a pending state case threatened to undo something a federal court had done, the defendant could remove the case to federal court under the All Writs Act. *See, e.g., Xiong v. Minnesota*, 195 F.3d 424, 426 (8th Cir. 1999); *Bylinski v. Allen Park*, 169 F.3d

1001, 1003 (6th Cir. 1999). Other lower courts disagreed. *See, e.g.*, *Hillman v. Webley*, 115 F.3d 1461, 1469 (10th Cir. 1997).

In 2002, the Court held that § 1651(a) does not support removal. *Syngenta Crop Protection, Inc. v. Henson*, 537 U.S. 28, 31 (2002). Under § 1441(a), a case can be removed only if it would invoke federal subject matter jurisdiction. The All Writs Act does not grant subject matter jurisdiction. *Id.* at 33–34.

On the other hand, Congress has expanded the right to remove in this century. In Chapter 2.D.4, we considered the extraordinary expansion of federal subject matter jurisdiction wrought by the Multiparty, Multiforum Trial Jurisdiction Act (MMTJA) and the Class Action Fairness Act (CAFA). Each is based upon the constitutional power over disputes between citizens of different states.

As we saw, however, each pushed this power to the constitutional maximum (and, in the eyes of some, beyond). All that is required is that a single plaintiff (or member of a plaintiff class) be of diverse citizenship from a single defendant. Under the MMTJA, there is no amount-in-controversy requirement. Under CAFA, the class claims, in the aggregate, must exceed $5,000,000. Moreover, each Act also repeals the in-state defendant rule and the one-year limitation on removal of diversity cases. So it is easier to remove cases under these Acts than ever before.

On the other hand, each Act has detailed and confusing provisions for remand to state court of cases in which the litigation is deemed by statutory factors to be localized.

D. Overlapping Litigation in American and Foreign Courts

Only two options are available for avoiding overlapping litigation pending in American courts (either federal or state) on the one hand, and a foreign tribunal on the other. Transfer is out of the question. Removal is also meaningless. To avoid duplication of effort in the two courts, the American court may either (1) enjoin parties from litigating in the foreign court or (2) dismiss or stay the pending litigation. The abstention doctrines discussed at section C.2.a. above will rarely be proper when the overlapping litigation is in another country. Rather, the dismissal or stay will be based upon *forum non conveniens.*

1. Anti-Suit Injunctions by the American Court

The federal or state court in the United States may, in proper circumstances, enjoin persons from engaging in litigation in the other country. If the litigation is in federal court, the Anti-Injunction Act does not apply. It applies, as we saw in section C.1.b. above only when the injunction will prohibit litigation in a state court. Instead, the All Writs Act will apply, and will provide the authorization for an anti-suit injunction. Federal Rule 65 provides for preliminary injunctions (which maintain the status quo until trial) and temporary restraining orders (TROs) (which maintain the status quo until the court can rule on the motion for preliminary injunction).

Goss International Corporation v. Tokyo Kikai Seisakusho, Ltd.

United States District Court for the Northern District of Iowa
435 F. Supp. 2d 919 (2006)

READE, DISTRICT JUDGE.

I. INTRODUCTION

Before the court is the Motion for Preliminary and Permanent Injunctions ("Motion"), filed by Plaintiff Goss International Corporation ("Goss") (docket no. 512).

II. BACKGROUND

On December 3, 2003, a jury returned a verdict in favor of Goss on its claims that Defendants Tokyo Kikai Seisakusho, Ltd. and TKS (U.S.A.), Inc. (collectively "TKS") engaged in dumping in violation of the Antidumping Act of 1916, 15 U.S.C. § 72 (1994) ("1916 Act"). [This refers to alleged predatory pricing—the defendant "dumped" products into the United States market at unfair prices.] The jury awarded damages to Goss totaling $10,539,949.00. On December 4, 2003, pursuant to the 1916 Act's provision for treble damages, the court entered judgment in favor of Goss against TKS in the amount of $31,619,847.00, with interest thereon at the rate provided in 28 U.S.C. § 1961, and costs. On June 2, 2004, the court awarded Goss attorneys' fees and expenses in the amount of $3,484,158.00 and taxed costs against TKS in the amount of $681,475.05.

On June 23, 2004, TKS filed a Notice of Appeal, in which it challenged all adverse rulings by the court.

On December 3, 2004, Congress repealed the 1916 Act. Miscellaneous Trade & Technical Corrections Act of 2004. However, Congress excluded all pending actions from the repeal. Therefore, the repeal does not affect this case.

On December 8, 2004, a new law came into force in Japan. Law No. 162 is entitled . . . "Special Measures Law Concerning the Obligation of Return of the Benefits and the Like under the United States Antidumping Act of 1916" ("Japanese Special Measures Law"). The law, a so-called "clawback statute,"[22] authorizes Japanese parties, against whom a U.S. judgment has been rendered under the 1916 Act, to sue in Japan to recover the full amount of the judgment, interest and expenses, including attorney fees. It renders all wholly-owned parent companies and subsidiaries of

---

22. [Court's footnote #1] Generally speaking, a clawback statute is a statute that enables a defendant who has paid judgment damages in an overseas country to recover that judgment from the successful plaintiff in the defendant's home country. . . .

the prevailing plaintiff in the U.S. action jointly and severally liable for the clawback judgment.[23]

Pursuant to a stipulation filed by the parties ("2004 Stipulation"), in late 2004 the court ordered that (1) "TKS shall not file suit or assert or attempt to assert any rights or remedies under the [Japanese Special Measures Law] . . . before all appeals, including without limitation any motion for rehearing or petition for certiorari, in this case are exhausted" and (2) "TKS shall provide Goss' counsel of record with fourteen (14) days' prior written notice before filing suit or asserting or attempting to assert any rights or remedies under the [Japanese Special Measures Law]. . . ."

On January 23, 2006, the Eighth Circuit Court of Appeals affirmed the court's judgment in all respects. . . . On June 5, 2006, the Supreme Court denied TKS's Petition for a Writ of Certiorari.

On June 5, 2006, hours after the Supreme Court denied TKS's petition for a writ of certiorari, TKS gave Goss notice that it intended to file suit and assert its rights under the Japanese Special Measures Law. Pursuant to the 2004 Stipulation and the court's order enforcing it, under the *status quo*, TKS may file suit in Japan under the Japanese Special Measures Law on June 19, 2006.

On June 8, 2006, Goss filed the instant Motion. On June 12, 2006, TKS filed a Resistance. On June 14, 2006, the court held a hearing ("Hearing") on the Motion, insofar as it requests a preliminary injunction.[24] . . . The Motion is fully submitted, and thus the court turns to consider it.

III. THE MERITS

A. Summary of Argument

In the Motion, Goss asks the court for a foreign anti-suit injunction. That is, Goss requests a

> preliminary . . . injunction[] enjoining [TKS] and their representatives, officers, directors, agents, attorneys, employees, and shareholders, and anyone acting in concert with them, from asserting or attempting to assert or pursue any rights or remedies granted under [the Japanese Special Measures Law] against Goss or any of its affiliates or subsidiaries.

Goss contends that the Japanese Special Measures Law "directly attacks the [c]ourt's final jurisdiction and judgment." Goss points out that "the sole basis for Goss's liability under the Japanese [Special Measures Law] is Goss's receipt of damages awarded by this [c]ourt."

---

23. [Court's footnote #2] The clawback statute is not unique to Japan. The European Union has a similar provision. On December 15, 2003, the European Council promulgated a similar clawback regulation. . . .

24. [Court's footnote #3] At the Hearing, it became clear that, at this time, only the preliminary injunction is at issue. The court shall reserve ruling on the Motion insofar as Goss requests a permanent injunction. In due course, the court shall set a briefing schedule on the permanent injunction request.

Goss contends an injunction is necessary to protect the court's jurisdiction and its judgment from "imminent danger of being invalidated and undone." Goss contends that it is fundamentally unfair for a company, like TKS, to do business in the United States for decades, intentionally violate the laws of the United States, litigate in the United States' federal courts for more than six years, and then "thumb its nose at this [c]ourt and the federal judiciary by taking advantage of special legislation in Japan...." Goss points out that TKS recently announced its plans to continue to do business in the United States "for years to come" and to "compete vigorously for new business and services in the United States."

... TKS contends that Goss has not demonstrated that the court should grant a preliminary injunction....

B. Foreign Anti-Suit Injunctions Generally

The parties agree that the court has the equitable power to issue a foreign anti-suit injunction. "It is beyond question that a federal court may enjoin a party before it from pursuing litigation in a foreign forum." *Paramedics Electromedicina Comercial, Ltda. v. GE Med. Sys. Info. Techs., Inc.*, 369 F.3d 645, 652 (2d Cir. 2004)....

The parties also agree that the All Writs Act, 28 U.S.C. § 1651, empowers the court to issue an injunction barring TKS from filing suit under the Japanese Special Measures Law. The All Writs Act grants the court the power to "issue all writs necessary or appropriate in aid of their respective jurisdictions and agreeable to the usages and principles of law." 28 U.S.C. § 1651(a)....

Even though a federal district court has the power to issue a foreign anti-suit injunction, it is not a power the court should exercise lightly or with abandon.... "[P]rinciples of comity counsel that injunctions restraining foreign litigation be 'used sparingly' and 'granted only with care and great restraint.'" *Paramedics*, 369 F.3d at 652 (quoting *China Trade* [*& Dev. Corp. v. M.V. Choong Yong*], 837 F.2d at 36 [(2d Cir. 1987)])....Clearly, a federal district court should not lightly interfere with judicial proceedings in other sovereign nations. The foreseen and unforeseen consequences of the court's actions are potentially myriad and may manifest themselves at an international level. *See* George A. Bermann, *The Use of Anti-Suit Injunctions in International Litigation*, 28 COLUM. J. TRANSNAT'L L. 589, 604 (1990) ("Judicial interference with a foreign country's exercise of adjudicatory authority has a potential for embarrassing the political branches of government and disturbing our relations with that country.")

In sum, the court is cognizant that it must proceed with great caution before issuing a foreign anti-suit injunction—even if the injunction is issued only on a preliminary basis. A court must avoid a modern-day Scylla and Charybdis and "find a way to accommodate conflicting, mutually inconsistent national policies without unduly interfering with the judicial processes of a foreign sovereign." *Quaak* [*v. Klynveld Peat Marwick Goerdeler Bedrijfsrevisoren*], 361 F.3d 11, 16....As the First Circuit Court of Appeals recently recognized, this difficult task is "particularly formidable given the absence of guidance from the Supreme Court," "the paucity of precedent"[25] and an apparent circuit-split. In this case, the court must navigate these troubled waters in just two days.

C. Standards for Granting a Preliminary Injunction: *Dataphase* factors

In the Eighth Circuit, applications for preliminary injunctions are generally measured against the standards set forth in *Dataphase Systems, Inc. v. C L Systems, Inc.*, 640 F.2d 109, 114 (8th Cir. 1981) (en banc).[26] The party moving for a preliminary injunction has the burden of establishing entitlement to such relief. The court must consider four factors: (1) the movant's likelihood of success on the merits; (2) the threat of irreparable harm to the moving party; (3) the balance between this harm and the injury that granting the injunction will inflict on other interested parties; and (4) whether the grant of a preliminary injunction is in the public interest. *Dataphase*, 640 F.2d at 114. "None of these factors by itself is determinative; rather, in each case the four factors must be balanced to determine whether they tilt toward or away from granting a preliminary injunction." *West Pub. Co. v. Mead Data Cent., Inc.*, 799 F.2d 1219, 1222 (8th Cir. 1986). A party moving for a preliminary injunction is required to establish a sufficient threat of irreparable harm. The district court has broad discretion when ruling on requests for preliminary injunctions . . . .

The court now turns to consider the four *Dataphase* factors.

1. Likelihood of success on the merits

The first factor . . . under *Dataphase* is the likelihood or probability of success on the merits. In considering this factor, the court need not decide whether Goss ultimately will succeed on the movant's claims. Rather, the movant's success on

---

25. [Court's footnote #5] Although the *Quaack* court was referring to the fact that there are few First Circuit Court of Appeals cases on point, matters are worse in the Eighth Circuit. The parties cite no on-point Eighth Circuit Court of Appeals cases; it appears the Eighth Circuit Court of Appeals has never had the occasion to discuss the standards for issuing a preliminary foreign anti-suit injunction. But see *Medtronic* [*v. Catalyst Research Corp.*], 664 F.2d at 661–66 [(8th Cir. 1981)] (affirming grant of foreign anti-suit injunction).

26. [Court's footnote #7] A number of other circuit courts of appeals have rejected the usual standards for measuring the merits of an application for a preliminary injunction in the context of an application for a foreign anti-suit injunction. *See, e.g., Karaha Bodas Co. v. Negara*, 335 F.3d 357, 364 (5th Cir. 2003) ("Although both the district court and the parties discussed all four prerequisites to the issuance of a traditional preliminary injunction, the suitability of such relief ultimately depends on considerations unique to antisuit injunctions."); *see also E&J Gallo Winery v. Andina Licores, S.A.*, 446 F.3d 984, 990–91 (9th Cir. 2006) (adopting Fifth Circuit approach and holding that movant "need not meet our usual test of a likelihood of success on the merits of the underlying claim" but instead "need only demonstrate the factors specific to an anti-suit injunction weigh in favor of granting the injunction"). These courts have narrowed the inquiry to whether the movant is likely to succeed on the merits, considering a number of factors specific to the propriety of anti-suit injunctions. *Karaha*, 335 F.3d at 364 n.19. Because the Eighth Circuit Court of Appeals has not yet carved out such an exception to *Dataphase*, the court shall consider all four *Dataphase* factors. This decision is immaterial in the present case, however, because the court shall find that all four *Dataphase* factors weigh in favor of the issuance of a preliminary injunction.

the merits must be "at least . . . sufficiently likely to support the kind of relief it requests." *Sanborn Mfg. v. Campbell Hausfeld/Scott Fetzer Co.*, 997 F.2d 484, 488 (8th Cir. 1993). Thus, a showing of likelihood of success on the merits requires simply that the moving party find support for its position in the governing law.

a. Preliminary considerations

Goss contends that because it has prevailed on the merits of its claims under the 1916 Act, it has "already prevailed on the merits," and thus the first *Dataphase* factor weighs in favor of granting a preliminary injunction. The court cannot accept this argument. Goss's request for a permanent injunction and its original Complaint alleging a violation of the 1916 Act are separate legal issues—indeed, the latter was resolved at all levels of the federal judiciary days before the former was even filed. The court agrees with TKS that the correct question before the court on this *Dataphase* factor is "whether Goss is likely to prevail on its motion for an anti-suit injunction." . . . The court shall thus consider the traditional standards by which courts have determined whether to grant foreign anti-suit injunctions. *See Karaha Bodas Co. v. Negara*, 335 F.3d 357, 364 (5th Cir. 2003) (equating likelihood of success on merits standard with traditional standards by which courts have decided to grant foreign anti-suit injunctions); *see also Dataphase*, 640 F.2d at 113 ("At base, the question is whether the balance of equities so favors the movant that justice requires the court to intervene to preserve the status quo until the merits are determined.").

The Eighth Circuit Court of Appeals has not had the opportunity to indicate what standards apply for the issuance of foreign anti-suit injunctions. It is settled, however, that a foreign anti-suit injunction is only appropriate if the foreign litigation involves the same issues and parties as the federal action and if the federal action is dispositive of the foreign litigation. . . In this case, the issues are the same and the United States action is dispositive of the foreign litigation. As Goss points out, the sole basis for Goss's liability under the Japanese Special Measures Law is Goss's receipt of damages awarded by this court. The judgment and jurisdiction of this court is thus intimately tied to any future action TKS might file under the Japanese Special Measures Law. The court also finds that the parties are the same. It is immaterial that the target of TKS's suit in Japan would in the first instance be Goss Japan, because Goss Japan is a subsidiary of Goss.

b. Circuit split

Beyond this threshold question, there is presently a circuit split as to what factors a court must consider before issuing an anti-suit injunction. *See Quaak*, 361 F.3d at 17 (discussing differences between the so-called "liberal approach," which the Fifth and Ninth Circuit Courts of Appeals have adopted, and the so-called "conservative approach," which the First, Second, Third, Sixth and D.C. Circuit Courts of Appeals have adopted). . . . The difference between the two approaches concerns how much weight the court should give to considerations of international comity.

See id. Compare Kaepa, Inc. v. Achilles Corp., 76 F.3d 624, 627 (5th Cir. 1996) (inquiring as to whether international anti-suit injunction would "actually threaten relations" between nations), *with Quaak*, 361 F.3d at 18–19 (holding that courts must consider "the totality of the circumstances" and determine whether there is sufficient evidence to overcome a "rebuttable presumption" against international anti-suit injunctions). The Supreme Court has defined comity as "the recognition which one nation allows within its territory to the legislative, executive or judicial acts of another nation, having due regard both to international duty and convenience, and to the rights of its own citizens or of other persons who are under the protection of its laws." *Hilton v. Guyot*, 159 U.S. 113, 164, 16 S. Ct. 139, 40 L. Ed. 95 (1895).

c. Analysis

The court finds that, under either the liberal or the conservative approach, Goss has met its burden. Even among those courts that afford international comity the greatest respect, it is settled that considerations of comity have diminished force when, as here, one court has already reached judgment. . . . As the D.C. Circuit explained:

> Courts have a duty to protect their legitimately conferred jurisdiction to the extent necessary to provide full justice to litigants. Thus, when the action of a litigant in another forum threatens to paralyze the jurisdiction of the court, the court may consider the effectiveness and propriety of issuing an injunction against the litigant's participation in the foreign proceedings.
>
> These situations may arise either before or after a judgment has been entered. The policies that guide the exercise of discretion vary slightly in each situation. When the injunction is requested after a previous judgment on the merits, there is little interference with the rule favoring parallel proceedings in matters subject to concurrent jurisdiction. Thus, a court may freely protect the integrity of its judgments by preventing their evasion through vexatious or oppressive relitigation.

Laker Airways Ltd. v. Sabena, Belgian World Airlines, 731 F.2d 909, 927–928, 235 U.S. App. D.C. 207 (D.C. Cir. 1984) (footnotes omitted).

. . .

The court finds that TKS's intended invocation of the Japanese Special Measures Law is a direct attack on this court's judgment in favor of Goss and a frontal assault on the jurisdiction of this court and the federal judiciary as a whole. "[A] direct interference with the jurisdiction of [a] United States court justifie[s] the defensive issuance of an antisuit injunction . . ." *Gau Shan* [*v. Bankers Trust Co.*], 956 F.2d at 1356 [(6th Cir. 1992)] (citing *Laker Airways*, 731 F.2d at 915). In effect, TKS seeks to institute a lawsuit "for the sole purpose of terminating" this court's judgment in Goss's favor, thereby in a single filing attempting to undo six years of federal court litigation. *See id.* (discussing *Laker Airways*). The court finds TKS's proposed litigation in Japan, after six years of litigation in the United States, is clearly vexatious and oppressive.

... The court is aware that the issuance of a preliminary injunction in this case may have international repercussions. Weighing all the factors and looking at this case in its procedural context, however, the court finds that its interest in protecting the integrity of its judgments and jurisdiction outweighs concerns over international comity.

Accordingly, the court finds the first *Dataphase* factor, likelihood of success on the merits, weighs in favor of granting a preliminary injunction in this case.

2. Threat of irreparable harm

...

The court finds that Goss would suffer great harm if the court does not grant the preliminary injunction. This harm is not limited to TKS's ability to clawback the judgment at issue from Goss's Japanese subsidiary, Goss Japan. At the Hearing, Goss's executive vice-president, chief financial officer and secretary, Joseph Patrick Gaynor, III, testified. Mr. Gaynor is a member of the Board of Directors of Goss Japan. Mr. Gaynor testified that Goss Japan is currently running a "break even operation." If TKS sues Goss Japan under the Japanese Special Measures Law, lenders might balk at loaning Goss Japan money. Goss Japan's customers—in essence its unsecured creditors—would be wary to advance money for Goss Japan's products. Based on Mr. Gaynor's testimony and the court's own common sense, the court finds that the Japanese Special Measures Law poses a threat to the survival of Goss Japan and would thus harm Goss.

Accordingly, the court finds the second *Dataphase* factor, the threat of irreparable harm, weighs in favor of granting a preliminary injunction in this case.

3. Balance of harms

The court finds the threat of irreparable harm to Goss in this case outweighs the harm to TKS that may be occasioned by its inability to avail itself of the Japanese Special Measures Law while the court considers Goss's Motion for Permanent Injunction. The court will rule upon the Motion for Permanent Injunction expeditiously. This factor, therefore, weighs in favor of the issuance of the requested preliminary injunction.

4. Public interest

The final factor the court must consider in determining whether to issue the requested preliminary injunction is whether public interest favors preventing TKS from availing itself of the Japanese Special Measures Law while the court considers Goss's Motion for Permanent Injunction. The court finds that it does. The court incorporates by reference its discussion and findings regarding Congress's repeal of the 1916 Act in its analysis of the first *Dataphase* factor. It is clear that the public has an interest in preserving the jurisdiction of the federal judiciary. Moreover, the legislative and executive branches, acting in the public interest, have determined that the court's judgment should be enforced. This factor therefore weighs in favor of the issuance of the requested preliminary injunction.

5. Conclusion

Because all four *Dataphase* factors weigh in favor of the issuance of a preliminary injunction, the court shall grant Goss's Motion. The court stresses, however, that it does not purport to enjoin the government of Japan or the Japanese judiciary; rather, it is enjoining TKS from availing itself of the Japanese Special Measures Law. Even so, the court does not enjoin a party from availing itself of a foreign remedy lightly. The court also stresses that this is only a "preliminary assessment" pending consideration of Goss's request for a permanent injunction. The court recognizes that "[t]he equities of this situation . . . may change." *Id.* The court finds, however, that, at this moment, justice requires it to intervene to preserve the *status quo* until the merits of Goss's request for a permanent injunction are determined after fuller consideration.

IV. DISPOSITION

Goss's Motion for Preliminary and Permanent Injunctions is GRANTED IN PART. The court grants Goss's Motion insofar as it requests a preliminary injunction. The court enjoins TKS and their representatives, officers, directors, agents, attorneys, employees, and shareholders, and anyone acting in concert with them, from asserting or attempting to assert or pursue any rights or remedies granted under the Japanese Special Measures Law against Goss or any of its affiliates or subsidiaries. The court RESERVES RULING on Goss's Motion insofar as it requests a permanent injunction. The court shall establish an orderly briefing schedule on the Motion in the near future.

Notes and Questions

1. This opinion addressed the propriety of a *preliminary* injunction, which will maintain the status quo pending the ultimate resolution of the plaintiff's request for a *permanent* injunction. One requirement for the preliminary injunction, as the court made clear, was "likelihood" of success on the merits. To prevail on its claim for a permanent injunction, the plaintiff must actually win on the merits. "The standard for a preliminary injunction is essentially the same as for a permanent injunction with the exception that the plaintiff must show a likelihood of success on the merits rather than actual success." *Amoco Prod. Co. v. Village of Gambell*, 480 U.S. 531, 546 n.12 (1987).

Thus, the result of this opinion is *not* that the defendant can *never* sue under the new Japanese law in the Japanese courts. That question is presented by the plaintiff's request for a permanent injunction, and will be decided after plenary proceedings in the Northern District of Iowa. The court is not in a position to rule on that request here. The preliminary injunction maintains the status quo (meaning that TKS cannot sue in Japan) until the litigation runs its course on the request for the permanent injunction.

2. Why was the court required to rule on the preliminary injunction "in just two days"? What would have happened if the court had not entered a preliminary injunction within two days?

3. According to the court, to what does "on the merits" refer? In other words, why was the plaintiff's victory in the underlying suit irrelevant to the injunction?

4. Why was the plaintiff's success on the underlying suit relevant to the assessment of comity? Why should that success be relevant to that injunctive factor but not to the "success on the merits" factor?

5. What special interests are at play in an anti-suit injunction against foreign litigation? How do these interests compare to those implicated by an anti-suit injunction against state-court litigation?

6. On appeal of the decision we read, the Eighth Circuit vacated the injunction. At that point, because TKS had paid the judgment, there was no tension between the foreign and American court systems. While the clawback statute was an affront to the American judgment, the court explained, that was a problem to be addressed (if at all) by the political branches, and not by the federal courts. Accordingly, the Eighth Circuit remanded to the district court with instructions to dismiss the case. *Goss International Corp. v. Man Roland Druckmaschinen Aktiengesellschaft*, 491 F.3d 355, 359–368 (8th Cir. 2007). The parties ultimately settled the dispute on undisclosed terms.

7. In *Winter v. NRDC*, 555 U.S. 7 (2008), the Supreme Court considered whether the mere "possibility" of success on the merits was sufficient to justify an injunction. It concluded that, in any event, the applicant must show that irreparable harm is likely, and not merely possible.

In *Winter*, the Ninth Circuit had granted a preliminary injunction to stop the Navy from conducting antisubmarine drills that allegedly harmed marine mammals. The Ninth Circuit entered the injunction based on mere "possibility" of irreparable harm because, it concluded, the plaintiffs (environmental groups) had shown a strong likelihood of success on the merits. The Supreme Court vacated the injunction and reiterated the four-step balancing test we read in *Goss*.

2. Dismissal or Stay for *Forum Non Conveniens*

Forum non conveniens is a doctrine by which a court *dismisses* or *stays* a case that is properly within its jurisdiction. It may be seen as a form of abstention—exercised because there is another court in which the litigation is far more convenient and sensible. Why, though, would a court dismiss or stay? Because that other court—the more convenient court—is in a *different judicial system*. Thus, transfer is impossible. In 1991, the National Conference of Commissioners on Uniform State Laws proposed the "Uniform Transfer of Litigation Act," which would permit a state court to transfer a case to a state court in another state (if both states had adopted the Act). The Act has not been adopted by any state. Accordingly, transfer from a state court in one state to a state court in another state remains impossible.

> ***Example #6.*** Case 1 is filed in state court in Florida. Case 2, involving the same parties and same real-world events, is filed in state court in Wyoming. If the Wyoming court determines that the Florida court is far more convenient, it cannot transfer the case to Florida. It may, however, dismiss or stay under the doctrine of *forum non conveniens.* The parties would then proceed to litigate in Florida.
>
> Recall, however, that a federal court in Wyoming could transfer the case to a federal court in Florida. Why? How (what statute(s) could it use)?

While *forum non conveniens* can arise when overlapping litigation is pending in state courts, it is usually encountered when the center-of-gravity court is in a foreign country. The leading case—which you probably read in Civil Procedure—is *Piper Aircraft Co. v. Reyno*, 454 U.S. 235 (1981). There, the Supreme Court upheld dismissal of a case pending in federal court in Pennsylvania in favor of litigation in Scotland. The case concerned the crash of an aircraft manufactured in the United States, but which crashed in Scotland. The plane was owned and operated by a British corporation and maintained by another British entity. All victims, including the pilot, were Scottish, as were their next-of-kin.

The Court in *Piper* set forth a series of public and private factors for determining whether to apply *forum non conveniens.* These factors were taken from the old case of *Gulf Oil Corp. v. Gilbert*, 330 U.S. 501, 508–509 (1947), which we discussed in section B.2 of this chapter. *Gulf Oil* concerned overlapping litigation in federal courts, and led to the enactment of 28 U.S.C. § 1404. Accordingly, overlapping cases in federal courts today are handled by transfer, not by *forum non conveniens* dismissal or stay.

The following case applies *Piper.* In reading it, consider whether the court was correct to make its order *sua sponte.* Moreover, consider what the defendant "wins" by getting the case in the United States dismissed. It is more than simply getting a case dismissed. What else does the defendant "win"?

Estate of Thomson v. Toyota Motor Corporation Worldwide

United States Court of Appeals, Sixth Circuit
545 F.3d 357 (2008)

COHN, DISTRICT JUDGE, sitting by designation.

This is a tort case. Plaintiffs-Appellants, the Estate of Dorothy Thomson ("the Estate") and Colleen Miller sued Defendants-Appellees, Toyota Motor Corporation Worldwide ("TMC") and Thrifty Rent-A-Car Systems, Inc. ("Thrifty") in the Northern District of Ohio following a car accident in South Africa in which Colleen Miller and Dorothy Thomson were injured. Thomson subsequently died from her injuries. The district court granted TMC's motion to dismiss for lack of personal jurisdiction and *sua sponte* dismissed plaintiffs' claims against Thrifty under the doctrine of *forum non conveniens.* For the reasons that follow, we affirm.

I. BACKGROUND

In late September 2005, Miller and Thomson, her mother, went on vacation to South Africa. They were joined by Rita Miller, Colleen Miller's daughter-in-law. On September 28, 2005, Rita Miller rented a Toyota Condor from a "Thrifty Car Rentals" at the airport in Port Elizabeth, South Africa.

On October 3, 2005, Rita Miller's husband was driving the car. Thomson, Colleen Miller, and Rita Miller were passengers. Plaintiffs allege that the brakes "malfunctioned and seized." They further allege that the bonded brake lining of the brake shoe came unglued and then wedged between the brake shoe and the brake drum. Plaintiffs say that this caused the car to become uncontrollable and resulted in a crash. Thomson and Colleen Miller were seriously injured, and Thomson died on October 9, 2005, due to complications from her injuries.

Colleen Miller and the Estate, citizens of Ohio, sued TMC and Thrifty in the district court for the Northern District of Ohio. TMC filed a motion to dismiss under Fed. R. Civ. P. 12(b)(2) for lack of personal jurisdiction and under Fed. R. Civ. P. 12(b)(3) for improper venue, or in the alternative for *forum non conveniens*. Thrifty filed a motion to dismiss under Fed. R. Civ. P. 12(b)(6) for failure to state a claim. The district court granted TMC's motion for lack of personal jurisdiction and *sua sponte* dismissed Thrifty on the grounds of *forum non conveniens*. Plaintiffs appeal.

II. ANALYSIS

A. Dismissal of TMC—Lack of Personal Jurisdiction

. . .

The district court determined that TMC did not have sufficient contacts with Ohio to support general jurisdiction under Ohio's long-arm statute or comport with due process. We agree. TMC is a Japanese corporation headquartered in Japan. It does not conduct any business, have any employees, or own property in Ohio. It does not market or ship any vehicles into the United States, much less into Ohio.

[The court rejected the argument that TMC was the "alter ego" of Toyota Motor Sales, U.S.A., Inc.] . . . .

B. Dismissal of Thrifty—*Forum Non Conveniens*

1. Legal Standards

The district court dismissed Thrifty on the grounds of *forum non conveniens*. We review the district court's decision for an abuse of discretion.

The Supreme Court has explained that the common law doctrine of *forum non conveniens* reflects a court's assessment of a "range of considerations, most notably the convenience to the parties and the practical difficulties that can attend the adjudication of a dispute in a certain locality." *Quackenbush v. Allstate Ins. Co.*, 517 U.S. 706, 723 (1996) (citations omitted). The Supreme Court has further explained that the doctrine is essentially "a supervening venue provision, permitting displacement of the ordinary rules of venue when, in light of certain conditions, the trial court thinks that jurisdiction ought to be declined." *American Dredging Co. v. Miller*, 510 U.S. 443, 453 (1994). The doctrine is a flexible one, requiring the court to weigh multiple factors relating to fairness and convenience based on the particular facts of the case. See *Piper Aircraft Co. v. Reyno*, 454 U.S. 235, 249–50 (1981). Thus, where a district court "has considered the relevant public and private interest factors, and where its balancing of these factors is reasonable, its decision deserves substantial deference." Id. at 257.

The first step in the *forum non conveniens* analysis is establishing an adequate alternative forum. The second step requires a balance of private and public factors listed in *Gulf Oil Corp. v. Gilbert*, 330 U.S. 501, 508–09 (1947), superceded on other grounds by 28 U.S.C. § 1404, to determine whether a trial in plaintiffs' chosen forum would be unnecessarily burdensome for the defendant or the court. Private factors include the

> relative ease of access to sources of proof; availability of compulsory process for attendance of unwilling, and the cost of obtaining attendance of willing, witnesses; possibility of view of premises, if view would be appropriate to the action; and all other practical problems that make trial of a case easy, expeditious and inexpensive.

Gulf Oil, 330 U.S. at 508. The public factors include

> court congestion; the 'local interest in having localized controversies decided at home;' the interest in having the trial of a diversity case in a forum that is at home with the law that must govern the action; the avoidance of unnecessary problems in conflict of laws, or in the application of foreign law; and the unfairness of burdening citizens in an unrelated forum with jury duty.

Piper Aircraft, 454 U.S. at 241 n.6 (quoting *Gulf Oil*, 330 U.S. at 509).

2. *Sua Sponte* Dismissal

As an initial matter, the district court's decision to *sua sponte* dismiss was not improper. *See Chambers v. NASCO, Inc.*, 501 U.S. 32 (1991). In *Chambers*, the Supreme Court listed a number of judicial acts as within a court's inherent authority, including dismissal on the grounds of *forum non conveniens.*

Moreover, plaintiffs' argument that the district court's decision was improper because Thrifty presented no evidence in support [of the dismissal] is not well-taken. Although Thrifty did not move for dismissal on the grounds of *forum non conveniens*, and consequently did not present any argument on this issue, it joined in TMC's motion on these grounds and TMC's motion contained arguments and documents relevant to the issue that applied to Thrifty. . . .

3. Adequate Alternative Forum

Plaintiffs first argue that the district court erred in determining that an adequate alternative forum exists in South Africa. . . . Plaintiffs say that because Thrifty has denied that it is the proper defendant in this action, there has not been a showing of an adequate alternative forum.

This argument misses the point. While Thrifty asserts it is not a proper defendant, it has not asserted that plaintiffs are unable to sue any entity connected with them. Indeed, the record shows that Thrifty entered into a License Agreement with an entity called the Safy Group ("Safy") and Safy conducts business in South Africa using Thrifty's name. Thrifty also notes that the contract signed by Rita Miller not only contains the name "Thrifty," but also "Dollar," "Buzz Car Rental," and "Sani Van Rentals." It also indicates that the vehicle was rented from "South African Licensee, Spring Car Wholesaler CC." Thrifty further explains that Safy is a substantial corporation present in South Africa that operates, using the Thrifty and Dollar names under the license agreement, Buzz Car Rental, a trading entity within Spring Car Wholesalers, CC, a division of Safy. Thrifty also says that in addition to Safy, other entities known as the Safy Trust, Buzz Car Rental, and Spring Car Wholesaler CC are South African corporations. Thus, Thrifty is not, as plaintiffs contend, trying to hide its corporate identity, but rather makes clear that Safy, or its affiliates listed above, is the entity with whom plaintiffs contracted. Thus, an adequate forum exists in South Africa and there are corporate entities, indeed the proper entities, in South Africa which are amenable to service.

4. Plaintiffs' Choice of Forum

Plaintiffs argue that the district court did not give due deference to their choice of forum. In general, the deference due a plaintiff's choice of a home forum permits dismissal only when the defendant "establish[es] such oppressiveness and vexation to a defendant as to be out of all proportion to plaintiff's convenience, which may be shown to be slight or nonexistent." *Koster v. Am. Lumbermens Mut. Cas. Co.*, 330 U.S. 518, 524 (1947). . . .

Here the district court did not specifically state that it was giving heightened deference to plaintiffs' chosen forum; however, it did acknowledge that a plaintiff's choice of forum is ordinarily not to be disturbed. It is also clear that the district court considered all of the *Gulf Oil* factors and found that they weighed in favor of a South African forum. Given this, it follows that the district court concluded that plaintiffs' chosen forum was simply outweighed by the many factors favoring South Africa. . . .

5. *Gulf Oil* Factors

Plaintiffs next contend that the district court did not properly balance the *Gulf Oil* private and public interest factors. We disagree.

As to the private interest factors, it is clear that they weigh in favor of South Africa. The vehicle involved in the accident was purchased, kept, maintained, and rented in South Africa. The accident occurred in South Africa. Plaintiffs were treated in South Africa. Documents related to the vehicle, the accident investigation, and plaintiffs' medical records are all located in South Africa. Witnesses, other than family members of plaintiffs, are located in South Africa. Such witnesses include those involved in the sale, maintenance, and rental of the vehicle, law enforcement who investigated the accident, and medical personnel involved in plaintiffs' treatment.

Plaintiffs say that they are in possession of many of the relevant documents and therefore there is no need to obtain documents from South Africa. Even assuming this was the case, although Thrifty vigorously contends otherwise, plaintiffs have not adequately shown the availability of relevant witnesses from South Africa. Plaintiffs cite the Hague Convention, noting that the United States and South Africa are signatories. However, as the district court noted, South Africa specifically declared in its Reservations and Declarations that "Letters of Request issued for the purpose of obtaining pre-trial discovery of documents as known in common law countries, will not be executed." The district court noted that it may lack the power to compel documents or witnesses because of this reservation. Even assuming compulsory process may be obtained, the cost of procuring evidence and willing witnesses from South Africa would be prohibitively expensive. The fact that witnesses were not specifically identified is not fatal to a finding that a dismissal on *forum non conveniens* grounds is proper.

As to the public interest factors, the district court explained:

> The result of this trial will have a greater impact on the residents of South Africa; the car was manufactured to the requirements of vehicles operated in South Africa, not those that govern vehicles in the United States. Any outcome might alter those requirements for vehicles in South Africa. If the case continued in this court, American jurors would be burdened by a case whose resolution will be felt the greatest in South Africa, while South African citizens would be deprived of hearing a case regarding the safety of a vehicle marketed, sold, and used in their country.

While plaintiffs say that the Estate is administered by two Ohio citizens, and Colleen Miller is an Ohio citizen who continues to see doctors in Ohio these facts are not sufficient to tip the balance in favor of plaintiffs' choice of forum.

Moreover, the district court considered the choice of law issue, concluding that under Ohio choice of law rules, South African law would likely apply. Apparently, the parties did not brief the choice of law issue extensively before the district court. Nevertheless, the district court engaged in a rather detailed analysis. On appeal, plaintiffs challenge the district court's conclusion, stating that the district court failed to first find a conflict between Ohio law and South African law. Thrifty suggests that Ohio choice of law rules do not first require the existence of a conflict and says that the district court's view is correct. We need not reach this issue because the factors discussed above so clearly point in favor of adjudication of this case in South Africa.

The difficulties occasioned upon plaintiffs in having to litigate their case in South Africa are not unappreciated. However, this is a products liability action in which the product at issue—a Toyota Condor—was designed in Japan and manufactured, marketed, sold, and rented in South Africa. It is not sold in the United States. The

Holding

majority of the evidence, other than what plaintiffs have procured, is located in South Africa. The witnesses, with the exception of Colleen Miller and plaintiffs' family, are in South Africa. South Africa has a greater overall interest in the outcome of this ligation than the United States. The district court was correct in determining that South Africa is the most convenient and proper forum.

III. CONCLUSION

For the reasons stated above, the decision of the district court is AFFIRMED.

Notes and Questions

1. By winning under *forum non conveniens*, the defendant has ensured that any litigation against it will take place in South Africa. What advantages does that give the defendant? What disadvantages does that impose on the plaintiffs? Is the court appropriately concerned with those disadvantages?

2. What if South African law does not recognize recovery for certain claims that are commonplace in the United States? In *Piper*, for example, it was clear that the courts in Great Britain would not permit recovery for anguish in a wrongful death case and would not apply American product liability theories. As a result, the invocation of *forum non conveniens* often means that the plaintiff will have a more difficult time imposing liability on the defendant and—even if successful—will recover less in the foreign tribunal.

Do these facts counsel an American court not to invoke *forum non conveniens*? In *Piper*, the Court said that the change in law (resulting from having the litigation proceed in a foreign tribunal) "ordinarily" should *not* be given "substantial weight." 454 U.S. at 254. Only if the remedy in the foreign court is so inadequate that it amounts to "no remedy at all" might a court decline to enter a *forum non conveniens* order on this basis. *Id.* at 241 n.6.

There are few data, but those that exist paint a stark picture. A survey of 85 cases dismissed under *forum non conveniens* in favor of a foreign court demonstrated that *every case* was ultimately abandoned or settled for minimal amounts. David W. Robertson, Forum Non Conveniens *in America and England: "A Rather Fantastic Fiction,"* 103 L.Q. Rev. 398, 418–420 (1987). In *Piper*, after the case was dismissed in the United States, apparently no lawyer in the United Kingdom found it worthwhile to pursue litigation there. Richard D. Freer, *Refracting Domestic and Global Choice-of-Forum Doctrine Through the Lens of a Single Case*, 2007 B.Y.U. L. Rev. 959, 972 n.50.

In practice, then, it is often true that dismissal under *forum non conveniens* is tantamount to a dismissal on the merits. The defendant may never face meaningful litigation in the foreign tribunal. Given what is at stake, should a court ever invoke *forum non conveniens sua sponte*?

3. If the American court were to apply South African substantive law in deciding the case, would the result be different? Is *forum non conveniens* a doctrine based

upon a lack of faith in the ability of American courts to apply the law of another country?

4. As we saw in *Estate of Thomson*, the *Piper* factors are numerous and not arranged hierarchically. A court is directed to be flexible and pragmatic and to weigh the various factors according to the facts of the case. This means that the outcome of a *forum non conveniens* motion is difficult to predict. It also means that an order invoking *forum non conveniens* is difficult to reverse on appeal. This is especially so because the appellate court can reverse only if the trial judge committed an "abuse of discretion"—which is a very deferential review standard.

The unpredictable nature of *forum non conveniens* doctrine is shown in a companion case to *Estate of Thomson*. One of the plaintiffs in *Estate of Thomson* was Colleen Miller. Her husband sued Toyota and Thrifty in a separate suit, seeking loss of consortium because of his wife's injuries. His case was transferred from federal court in Ohio to federal court in Florida. That court then denied Thrifty's motion to dismiss for forum non conveniens. According to that court, although South African courts were *available*, they were not adequate. *Miller v. Toyota Motor Corp.*, 594 F. Supp. 2d 1254 (M.D. Fla. 2008). Hence, in these closely related cases—involving spouses—different federal courts came to different conclusions.

5. A court invoking *forum non conveniens* usually has discretion to dismiss or to stay the pending case. What advantage might there be to either course?

6. In *Piper*, the plaintiffs were Scottish. (The person appointed as executrix to represent the victims of the plane crash was an American, but she sued on behalf of citizens of Great Britain.) In such a case, we might ask why American courts should be made available—with American remedies and procedures—to aliens.

> [I]f American courts are open to such cases, foreign plaintiffs are afforded substantive and procedural advantages unavailable to similarly situated compatriots who are injured by non-American defendants.... Other nations are certainly free to give their citizens modern tools of procedure, including wide-ranging discovery, to provide for jury trials, cutting-edge theories of liability, and expansive remedies. If they do not, should American courts provide these things for the foreign citizen?

Freer, *supra*, 2007 B.Y.U. L. Rev. at 975. In *Estate of Thomson*, is a different question raised? Specifically, if citizens of the United States choose to interact with foreigners who harm them, do they forego access to American courts?

7. Orders of *forum non conveniens* are often conditional. That is, the court grants a motion to dismiss or stay, conditioned upon the defendant's agreeing to something when the litigation proceeds in the foreign court. Typically, the defendant is asked to waive any objection to personal jurisdiction there, or perhaps to waive a statute of limitations defense.

8. Suppose the plaintiffs in *Estate of Thomson* had filed the case in state court in Ohio, instead of federal court. Would the state court have been free to reject

forum non conveniens and keep the case? In other words, while *Piper* clearly sets forth the federal law on *forum non conveniens*, are states free to set forth their own rules on *forum non conveniens*? We will discuss choice-of-law matters in detail in Chapter 4, but the answer seems to be that states are free to determine their own law of *forum non conveniens. See generally*, Allan Stein, Erie *and Court Access*, 100 Yale L.J. 1935 (1991).

9. Most, but not all, states recognize the doctrine of *forum non conveniens*. In most of these it is a common law doctrine. In California, however, it is codified. Cal. Code Civ. Pro. § 418.10(a)(2) permits a defendant to move "[t]o stay or dismiss the action on the ground of inconvenient forum."

E. The American Law Institute Proposal

Throughout this chapter, we have seen that there are serious limitations on the ability of one court to "gather" and coordinate overlapping cases. Particularly when the cases are pending in state and federal courts, the options are quite restricted. Once related cases are in the federal system, there are helpful mechanisms for transfer and coordination, but, under existing law, unless someone removes state litigation to federal court, there is no device by which overlapping cases in state systems can be gathered along with pending federal cases into a single federal court.

In 1993, the American Law Institute (ALI) approved a set of Statutory Recommendations, which emanated from its Project on Complex Litigation. ALI, Complex Litigation: Statutory Recommendations and Analysis (1994). The project included detailed provisions for consolidating complex litigation—involving numerous claimants in tort or contract—in a single court, either state or federal. Perhaps even more ambitious was the ALI's proposal for a federal statute on choice of law in complex cases, which we will see in Chapter 4, section D.4.

The gathering function of the ALI proposal would be overseen by a to-be-created Complex Litigation Panel. Significantly, this panel would be permitted to "order the removal to federal court and consolidation of one or more civil actions pending in one or more state courts." Proposal § 5.01(a). The cases would have to arise from the same transaction or occurrence, or series of transactions or occurrences, and present a common question of law or fact. (This is the basic standard for joinder of parties under Federal Rule 20(a).) The ALI also proposed the less radical step of transferring and consolidating actions pending in different federal courts, on the same standard. The transfer and consolidation of all cases—those initially filed in federal court and those removed from state court—would be for all purposes, and not (as under § 1407) for pretrial stages only.

The proposal was particularly strong medicine, and essentially allowed the federal system to reach into the state courts and pluck cases that would then be subject to combined treatment in a federal district court. Removal from state court could be blocked if *all* parties and the state-court judge objected. Proposal § 5.01(b). Although the panel would be instructed to weigh state interests in determining whether to order removal and transfer, it is clear that the proposal would fundamentally restructure the allocation of judicial power in the United States.

This conclusion is especially obvious when we realize that the ALI proposed removal without regard to whether the state court cases would have invoked federal subject matter jurisdiction. Rather, the ALI proposed that such cases would fall within the supplemental jurisdiction of the federal courts, because they involve the same transaction or occurrence as cases that already invoked federal jurisdiction. Accordingly, as Professor Floyd concluded, "[t]he range of potentially removable state law cases in which there is no, or incomplete, diversity of citizenship between the parties is vast. Thousands of . . . product liability and mass tort cases now litigated exclusively in state court, subject to state substantive and choice of law rules will, under the ALI proposal, become subject to removal and transfer to a potentially distant federal district court for disposition by a federal judge and jury." C. Douglas Floyd, *The ALI, Supplemental Jurisdiction, and the Federal Constitutional Case*, 1995 B.Y.U. L. Rev. 819, 821.

The ALI proposal failed to garner support, and was never introduced at Congress. In your view, was the removal provision constitutional? Could Congress have passed such legislation under its commerce power without regard to Article III?

Chapter 4

Choice of Law Issues in Complex Litigation

A. Introduction

Choice of law questions can arise in any case. They present especially difficult problems in complex litigation—whether that litigation involves joinder of multiple claims or parties in a single case, a class action, or overlapping cases. By "choice of law" (also called "conflict of laws"), we refer to that doctrine by which a court decides what law will apply in a dispute. For example:

> ***Example #1.*** P, a citizen of Pennsylvania, buys a ticket from an airline to fly from Philadelphia to Phoenix; the flight is to have one stop on the way, in Denver. On approach to land in Denver, the plane crashes, killing P. The executor of P's estate sues the airline in state court in Pennsylvania, seeking damages for wrongful death. Under Pennsylvania law, the plaintiff in such a case can recover for lost earnings over what would have been the expected lifespan of the decedent. Under Colorado law, however, such a case cannot include recovery for lost earnings of the decedent.[1]

Which law applies—Pennsylvania or Colorado? As an intuitive matter, most people probably assume that a Pennsylvania court will apply Pennsylvania law, and that a Colorado court will apply Colorado law. But that is not necessarily the case. Rather, each court will apply principles of choice of law to determine whether the law of Pennsylvania or Colorado (or possibly some other state or country) will govern the question of proper remedy for the wrongful death claim.

Every state is free to develop its own conflict of laws rules, subject to limitations imposed by the due process and full faith and credit clauses of the Constitution. In most states, this doctrine is developed in common law, though a few states have legislated on the topic. Regardless of source, however, it is important to understand that states have adopted different choice of law rules. The traditional approach, still followed in some states, is *lex loci*, which counsels application of the law of the place where the key underlying event took place—in our hypothetical, Colorado. More modern theories emphasize less determinate factors, such as what

1. The facts are from *Griffith v. United Air Lines, Inc.*, 416 Pa. 1 (1964). (The court held that Pennsylvania applies the law of the state with the most significant relationship to the dispute, which, it held, was Pennsylvania. *Id.* at 10–21.)

jurisdiction has the most significant relationship to the dispute. In our example, which involves the distribution of the Pennsylvania decedent's assets, this would probably be Pennsylvania.

The point is not to learn the various choice of law approaches; you can study those in the course on Conflict of Laws. Our goal is to appreciate that there are different views on how choice of law analysis is done and that they may lead to the application of different substantive law in related litigation. In our federal republic—with a national government and 50 separate sovereign states—we frequently face the application of different laws to related cases (or of different laws even as to different parties or claims within a single case). This abiding characteristic of American litigation presents a challenging hurdle to effective coordination of overlapping litigation.

In our example above, suppose citizens of 15 states died in the plane crash. It is theoretically possible that the claim on behalf of each victim would be governed by the law of the state of her citizenship. In other words, it is theoretically possible that 15 substantive laws might govern the merits of the claims. This, in turn, may balkanize the litigation and thwart a court's efforts to manage overlapping disputes through the tools we saw in Chapter 3. For example, it might make little sense to transfer and consolidate separate cases if each ultimately will be judged by a different law. Similarly, perhaps it is difficult to certify a class action (at least under Rule 23(b)(3)) if different law will govern the claims of different class members; in such a case, it may be impossible to find that common questions predominate. Or consider cases transferred and consolidated for pretrial purposes under the multidistrict litigation statute, § 1407. The fact that different laws may ultimately govern in these cases creates obvious logistical problems.

We avoid most conflict of laws problem in cases arising under federal law. In such cases—whether filed in state or federal court—federal law creates the rule of decision, on which there is no competing state law. (Although there can be disagreements among federal courts on the interpretation of federal law; we saw how this was handled under § 1407 in Chapter 3, section B.4.) The more serious problems—our focus here—arise with the assertion of state-created claims. Those may be filed in state court or, if the requirements for diversity of citizenship jurisdiction are met, in federal court. Does a federal court sitting in diversity fashion federal conflict of laws rules or must it apply state choice of law doctrine? If the latter, which state's law governs? These questions implicate the *Erie* Doctrine—born, of course, of the famous case of *Erie Railroad Co. v. Tompkins*, 304 U.S. 64 (1938).

Section B of this chapter reviews *Erie* and discusses how it applies to choice of law doctrine. As we will see, federal courts in diversity of citizenship cases must use *state* conflict of laws rules. In section C, we consider the effect that transfer of a case might have on the application of choice of law rules. As a general matter, in diversity cases, choice of law rules transfer with the case, which means that the transferee court may be required to apply the substantive laws of different states in cases consolidated there. This fact can be frustrating for judges, who, as discussed in Chapters 3 and 6, face increasing pressure to manage cases efficiently. In section D, then, we will explore paths by which a judge might try to apply a single state's law to related cases. For instance, the court might simply apply forum law to all related claims, or apply the choice of law rules creatively to find that a single law governs across the dispute, or to fashion federal common law to apply to the dispute. Some courts go too far, and undermine the federalism interests embodied in *Erie*. We will conclude by addressing what Congress might do concerning choice of law rules in complex litigation, and the impact on conflict of laws of its expansion of federal jurisdiction in the first decade of the twenty-first century.

B. *Erie* and *Klaxon*

What most people call "the *Erie* Doctrine" is actually two doctrines, as the Supreme Court made clear in *Hanna v. Plumer*, 380 U.S. 460 (1965). Each is concerned with what is often called "vertical choice of law"—that is, whether a federal court is to apply federal law or state law to decide a particular issue. The question is vertical because federal law—if applicable—will trump state law because of the Supremacy Clause of the Constitution, art. VI, § 1, clause 2. If, on the other hand, the court determines that it must follow state law on the issue, the federal court then faces a "horizontal choice of law" issue. Specifically, the question is: which state's law governs? The question is horizontal because the conflict is between sovereigns of equal dignity. *See generally* Richard D. Freer, Civil Procedure § 10.2 (4th ed. 2017). The example at the beginning of this chapter raised such a horizontal question—does the federal judge follow the law of Pennsylvania or of Colorado?

The first inquiry in vertical choice of law analysis is whether there is a federal directive on point. If so, it controls. It trumps any contrary state law as long as it (the federal directive) is valid. This is the holding in *Hanna*, in which Federal Rule 4, which permits substituted service of process, governed in a diversity case filed in a state that did not recognize substituted service on the facts presented. The Rule was on point and validly enacted under the Rules Enabling Act, 28 U.S.C. § 2072, which permits the Supreme Court to promulgate rules that govern the procedure of the federal courts. While the federal directive in *Hanna* was a Federal Rule, the directive may be found in the Constitution, federal statutes, regulations, or even in federal common law. The point for present purposes is simple: If there is a valid federal directive that covers the issue being considered, it "wins." Because of the supremacy clause, there is no role for state law to play.

If there is no valid federal directive on point, the federal court faces a true *Erie* (as opposed to *Hanna*) question. Here, the resolution is guided in part by the Rules of Decision Act, which provides that state law "shall be regarded as rules of decision in civil actions" in federal courts, "in cases where they apply." 28 U.S.C. § 1652. This circular language has been the source of much vexation and a great deal of academic writing. Virtually every commentator agrees that the Court has not given consistent guidance in this area. Speaking generally, however, a federal court in a diversity of citizenship case *must* apply state law on matters that are "substantive" or "bound up" with substance. *Byrd v. Blue Ridge Electrical Cooperative, Inc.*, 356 U.S. 525, 535 (1958) (federal court "must . . . first examine the [state law] to determine whether it is bound up with these rights and obligations in such a way that its application in the federal court is required."). This result is commanded by § 1652.

While the terms "substantive" and "bound up" are not self-defining (indeed, the Court has never tried to define "bound up"), there are some clear examples. The elements of a claim or defense are clearly substantive, since they define when one party is liable to another. The example at the outset of this chapter—dealing with what remedies can be recovered in a wrongful death case—is clearly something on which state law governs. In *Guaranty Trust Co. v. York*, 326 U.S. 99, 109 (1945), the Court held that the statute of limitations is a "substantive" matter for *Erie* purposes. Thus, a federal court in a diversity case must apply the state statute of limitations. (We will see in section D of this chapter, however, that statutes of limitations may be considered "procedural" for other purposes.)

What happens, though, if the state law under consideration is not "substantive," but instead raises what the Court has called a matter of "form and mode" of enforcing a claim? Here, the Court has indicated that if ignoring state law would result in a different outcome in federal court than in state court, the federal court generally will follow state law. It is not absolutely required to do so, however. It may ignore state law if some federal interest outweighs the interest the state has in its rule.

For example, in *Byrd v. Blue Ridge Electrical Cooperative, supra*, state law required that a particular issue be decided by a judge, not a jury. The state expressed no reason for this rule—that is just how the issue was handled. Federal courts, however, "under the influence—if not the command—of the Seventh Amendment,"[2] 356 U.S. at 537, would prefer to have juries decide the question. Because the state did not have any stated interest in (or reason for) its rule, and because the federal interest in allocating authority between judge and jury is substantial, the federal court was free to ignore state law. Similarly, in *Gasperini v. Center for Humanities, Inc.*, 518 U.S. 415, 418 (1996), state law provided that appellate courts were to apply a test for motions for new trial *de novo*, rather than affirming trial court decisions that were not "clearly erroneous." In the federal courts, appellate courts would prefer not to apply the rule *de novo*, in part because it might implicate that part of the Seventh Amendment that prohibits reexamination of jury verdicts. The Court held that federal courts were free to ignore state law on this point. *Id.* at 439. Again, its interest in allocating authority as an independent system of justice outweighed the contrary state interest.

In the following case, the Court addresses what law must be followed concerning conflict of laws in a diversity of citizenship case. In other words, in a diversity

2. If the Seventh Amendment (which preserves the right to jury trial in civil actions at law in federal court) had actually been on point, it would have trumped state law under the supremacy clause. In other words, it would have presented a *Hanna* issue, and not an *Erie* issue. For whatever reason, the Court in *Byrd* refused to hold that the Seventh Amendment was on point.

case governed by state substantive law, is there a federal directive that would specify which of several potentially applicable state laws should apply? If not, does the choice of law rule of the state in which the federal court sits govern?

Klaxon Company v. Stentor Electric Manufacturing Co., Inc.

Supreme Court of the United States
313 U.S. 487 (1941)

Justice Reed delivered the opinion of the Court.

The principal question in this case is whether in diversity cases the federal courts must follow conflict of laws rules prevailing in the states in which they sit. We left this open in *Ruhlin v. New York Life Insurance Co.*, 304 U.S. 202, 208, n. 2 [1938]. The frequent recurrence of the problem, as well as the conflict of approach to the problem between the Third Circuit's opinion here and that of the First Circuit in *Sampson v. Channell*, 110 F.2d 754, 759–62 [1940], led us to grant certiorari.

[Stentor, a New York corporation, entered into a contract with Klaxon, a Delaware corporation. The contract was entered in New York and to be performed principally in New York. Stentor sued Klaxon under diversity jurisdiction in the federal district court in Delaware and won a jury verdict and judgment of $100,000. Under §480 of the New York Civil Practice Act, a successful claimant was entitled to recover interest on its judgment, payable from the date the case was filed. (A more typical provision would have been to permit recovery of interest on the judgment, payable from the date of the judgment.) Stentor moved to amend the judgment to include interest under §480.]

... The District Court granted the motion, taking the view that the rights of the parties were governed by New York law and that under New York law the addition of such interest was mandatory. The Circuit Court of Appeals affirmed, and we granted certiorari, limited to the question whether §480 of the New York Civil Practice Act is applicable to an action in the federal court in Delaware.

The Circuit Court of Appeals was of the view that under New York law the right to interest before verdict under §480 went to the substance of the obligation, and that proper construction of the contract in suit fixed New York as the place of performance. It then concluded that §480 was applicable to the case because "it is clear by what we think is undoubtedly the better view of the law that the rules for ascertaining the measure of damages are not a matter of procedure at all, but are matters of substance which should be settled by reference to the law of the appropriate state according to the type of case being tried in the forum. The measure of damages for breach of a contract is determined by the law of the place of performance; Restatement, Conflict of Laws §413." The court referred also to §418 of the Restatement, which makes interest part of the damages to be determined by the law of the place of performance. Application of the New York statute apparently followed from the court's independent determination of the "better view" without regard to Delaware law, for no Delaware decision or statute was cited or discussed.

We are of opinion that the prohibition declared in *Erie R. Co. v. Tompkins*, 304 U.S. 64 [1938], against such independent determinations by the federal courts, extends to the field of conflict of laws. The conflict of laws rules to be applied by the federal court in Delaware must conform to those prevailing in Delaware's state courts. Otherwise, the accident of diversity of citizenship would constantly disturb equal administration of justice in coordinate state and federal courts sitting side by side. Any other ruling would do violence to the principle of uniformity within a state, upon which the *Tompkins* decision is based. Whatever lack of uniformity this may produce between federal courts in different states is attributable to our federal system, which leaves to a state, within the limits permitted by the Constitution, the right to pursue local policies diverging from those of its neighbors. It is not for the federal courts to thwart such local policies by enforcing an independent "general law" of conflict of laws. Subject only to review by this Court on any federal question that may arise, Delaware is free to determine whether a given matter is to be governed by the law of the forum or some other law. This Court's views are not the decisive factor in determining the applicable conflicts rule. And the proper function of the Delaware federal court is to ascertain what the [Delaware] state law is, not what it ought to be.

. . .

Looking then to the Delaware cases, petitioner relies on one group to support his contention that the Delaware state courts would refuse to apply § 480 of the New York Civil Practice Act, and respondent on another to prove the contrary. We make no analysis of these Delaware decisions, but leave this for the Circuit Court of Appeals when the case is remanded.

Respondent makes the further argument that the judgment must be affirmed because, under the full faith and credit clause of the Constitution, the state courts of Delaware would be obliged to give effect to the New York statute. The argument rests mainly on the decision of this Court in *John Hancock Mutual Life Ins. Co. v. Yates*, 299 U.S. 178 [1936], where a New York statute was held such an integral part of a contract of insurance, that Georgia was compelled to sustain the contract under the full faith and credit clause. Here, however, § 480 of the New York Civil Practice Act is in no way related to the validity of the contract in suit, but merely to an incidental item of damages, interest, with respect to which courts at the forum have commonly been free to apply their own or some other law as they see fit. Nothing in the Constitution ensures unlimited extraterritorial recognition of all statutes or of any statute under all circumstances. The full faith and credit clause does not go so far as to compel Delaware to apply § 480 if such application would interfere with its local policy.

Accordingly, the judgment is reversed and the case remanded to the Circuit Court of Appeals for decision in conformity with the law of Delaware.

Reversed.

Notes and Questions

1. The Court seemed from its opening sentence to see this as a horizontal choice of law case, presenting only the question of which state's law to apply. Is there any plausible argument for application of federal law?

2. The Court concludes that choice of law doctrine presents a matter on which state law *must* govern in a diversity case—that is, that state choice of law rules are "substantive" for *Erie* purposes. How, then, is choice of law doctrine "substantive"? Is it more or less "substantive" than statute of limitations?

3. The Court did not hold that Delaware *substantive law of contracts* would govern the dispute. Rather, it held that the federal court in Delaware must apply Delaware choice of law doctrine. Application of that doctrine might lead the court to apply the substantive contract law of Delaware, New York, or Switzerland. Again, we are not concerned with how one undertakes that horizontal choice of law analysis—whether to apply the law of Delaware, New York, or Switzerland. We simply need to know that a federal court sitting in diversity must use the conflicts rules of the state in which it sits.

Interestingly, the Court presaged the holding in *Klaxon* in *Erie* itself. There, the case was filed in federal court in New York, but ultimately applied the tort law of Pennsylvania. Why? Because New York choice of law doctrine dictated that the state where the injury occurred—Pennsylvania—would govern on the merits. Once the Court decided in *Erie* that state (as opposed to federal) law governed, everyone seemed to agree that it would be the law of Pennsylvania. By implication, this conclusion was supported by using the choice of law rules of the state in which the federal court sat.

4. *Klaxon* can be criticized because it permits a plaintiff to "capture" the choice of law rules of a state that might counsel application of the law of a state with a relatively minor connection with the dispute. In *Klaxon* itself, for example, it is not clear that Delaware choice of law rules will result in application of Delaware law of contracts to the dispute, but they might. And if they do, the critics point out, the *Klaxon* rule will have facilitated the adoption of the law of a state with minimal connection to the dispute. Despite the criticism, the Court has reaffirmed the holding in *Klaxon*, and there is no doubt that it remains good law. *Day & Zimmerman, Inc. v. Challoner*, 423 U.S. 3, 4 (1975); *Nolan v. Transocean Air Lines*, 365 U.S. 293 (1961).

C. Choice of Law in Transferred Cases

We discussed transfer of cases in Chapter 3, section B.2. The main transfer statute, § 1404(a), permits transfer from one federal district court to another based upon convenience of the parties and witnesses and the "interest of justice." Recall that under § 1404(a), the transferor court must be a proper venue and the transferee court must also be a proper venue and have personal jurisdiction over the defendant.

> ***Example #2***. P, a citizen of Louisiana, sues D, a citizen of Illinois, in federal court in Illinois, invoking diversity of citizenship jurisdiction. Suppose the federal judge in Illinois transfers the case to federal court in California, which, we will say, is a proper venue and has personal jurisdiction over D. What choice of law rules does the federal judge in California apply?

In *Van Dusen v. Barrack*, 376 U.S. 612, 639 (1964), the Court held that the transferee court must apply the choice of law doctrine the transferor court would have applied. Under *Klaxon*, that means it would apply the conflict of laws rules of the state in which the case was initially filed. In our example, the federal judge in California would apply Illinois choice of law rules.

Although under § 1404(a) any party may move for transfer, it is usually the defendant who does so. Suppose, however, the *plaintiff* seeks transfer under § 1404(a). Should *Van Dusen* apply then? If so, couldn't the plaintiff choose a forum with choice of law rules that would allow her to "capture" a favorable substantive law, which would apply after transfer to a more convenient venue? Is there anything wrong with that? The next cases address these questions.

Ferens v. John Deere Co.

Supreme Court of the United States
494 U.S. 516 (1990)

JUSTICE KENNEDY delivered the opinion of the Court.

... In *Van Dusen* v. *Barrack*, 376 U.S. 612 (1964), we held that, following a transfer under § 1404(a) initiated by a defendant, the transferee court must follow the choice-of-law rules that prevailed in the transferor court. We now decide that, when a plaintiff moves for the transfer, the same rule applies.

I

[Albert Ferens lost his right hand while operating a harvester manufactured by John Deere, which is a large manufacturer of farm equipment. The injury was suffered at Ferens's home in Pennsylvania. For some reason, Ferens and his wife did not sue Deere until more than two years after the accident. They filed a diversity case in the Western District of Pennsylvania, asserting contract and warranty claims, which were not barred by the statute of limitations. But they could not bring a tort claim in that court, because Pennsylvania had a two-year statute of limitations on tort claims.

But Mississippi had a six-year statute of limitations for tort cases. So the Ferenses brought their tort case against Deere under diversity jurisdiction in the Southern District of Mississippi. Though the Ferenses had no contact with Mississippi, and the claim in no way implicated that state, Deere was subject to general personal jurisdiction there. This is because, at the time, corporations were subject to general personal jurisdiction (and thus could be sued on a claim arising anywhere) in all states in which they had continuous and systematic contacts; Deere certainly had such contacts with Mississippi. (By the way, today, Deere would not be subject to general personal jurisdiction in Mississippi. Today, as we saw in Chapter 1, general jurisdiction over a corporation is appropriate only where it "at home," which means where it is incorporated and where it has its principal place of business. Deere had neither such tie with Mississippi.)

Now the Ferenses moved to transfer their tort case from the federal court in Mississippi to the Western District of Pennsylvania. The court in Mississippi granted the motion under § 1404(a), and the tort case, after transfer, was then consolidated with the pending contract/warranty case in federal court in Pennsylvania. The question then became whether *Van Dusen* should apply where, as in this case, the plaintiff (not the defendant) moved to transfer. If so, then the federal court in Pennsylvania would be required to apply Mississippi choice of law doctrine. That doctrine dictated that Mississippi's six-year tort statute of limitations would govern. The Third Circuit held that *Van Dusen* did not apply. Here, the Supreme Court reverses.]

II

Section 1404(a) states only that a district court may transfer venue for the convenience of the parties and witnesses when in the interest of justice. It says nothing about choice of law and nothing about affording plaintiffs different treatment from defendants. We touched upon these issues in *Van Dusen*, but left open the question presented in this case. . . . [In *Van Dusen*, we] held that the law applicable to a diversity case does not change upon a transfer initiated by a defendant.

III

. . . *Van Dusen* reveals three independent reasons for our decision. First, § 1404(a) should not deprive parties of state-law advantages that exist absent diversity jurisdiction. Second, § 1404(a) should not create or multiply opportunities for forum shopping. Third, the decision to transfer venue under § 1404(a) should turn on considerations of convenience and the interest of justice rather than on the possible prejudice resulting from a change of law. Although commentators have questioned whether the scant legislative history of § 1404(a) compels reliance on these three policies, we find it prudent to consider them in deciding whether the rule in *Van Dusen* applies to transfers initiated by plaintiffs. We decide that, in addition to other considerations, these policies require a transferee forum to apply the law of the transferor court, regardless of who initiates the transfer. . . .

A

The policy that § 1404(a) should not deprive parties of state-law advantages, although perhaps discernible in the legislative history, has its real foundation in *Erie R. Co. v. Tompkins*, 304 U.S. 64 (1938). The *Erie* rule remains a vital expression of the federal system and the concomitant integrity of the separate States. We explained *Erie* in *Guaranty Trust Co. v. York*, 326 U.S. 99, 109 (1945), as follows:

> "In essence, the intent of [the *Erie*] decision was to insure that, in all cases where a federal court is exercising jurisdiction solely because of the diversity

of citizenship of the parties, the outcome of the litigation in the federal court should be substantially the same, so far as legal rules determine the outcome of a litigation, as it would be if tried in a State court. The nub of the policy that underlies *Erie R. Co.* v. *Tompkins* is that for the same transaction the accident of a suit by a non-resident litigant in a federal court instead of in a State court a block away should not lead to a substantially different result."

. . .

The *Erie* policy had a clear implication for *Van Dusen*. The existence of diversity jurisdiction gave the defendants the opportunity to make a motion to transfer venue under § 1404(a), and if the applicable law were to change after transfer, the plaintiff's venue privilege and resulting state-law advantages could be defeated at the defendant's option. To allow the transfer and at the same time preserve the plaintiff's state-law advantages, we held that the choice-of-law rules should not change following a transfer initiated by a defendant.

Transfers initiated by a plaintiff involve some different considerations, but lead to the same result. Applying the transferor law, of course, will not deprive the plaintiff of any state-law advantages. A defendant, in one sense, also will lose no legal advantage if the transferor law controls after a transfer initiated by the plaintiff; the same law, after all, would have applied if the plaintiff had not made the motion. In another sense, however, a defendant may lose a nonlegal advantage. Deere, for example, would lose whatever advantage inheres in not having to litigate in Pennsylvania, or, put another way, in forcing the Ferenses to litigate in Mississippi or not at all.

We, nonetheless, find the advantage that the defendant loses slight. A plaintiff always can sue in the favorable state court or sue in diversity and not seek a transfer. By asking for application of the Mississippi statute of limitations following a transfer to Pennsylvania on grounds of convenience, the Ferenses are seeking to deprive Deere only of the advantage of using against them the inconvenience of litigating in Mississippi. . . .

Applying the transferee law, by contrast, would undermine the *Erie* rule in a serious way. It would mean that initiating a transfer under § 1404(a) changes the state law applicable to a diversity case. We have held, in an isolated circumstance, that § 1404(a) may pre-empt state law. See *Stewart Organization, Inc. v. Ricoh Corp.*, 487 U.S. 22 (1988) (holding that federal law determines the validity of a forum selection clause). In general, however, we have seen § 1404(a) as a housekeeping measure that should not alter the state law governing a case under *Erie*. The Mississippi statute of limitations, which everyone agrees would have applied if the Ferenses had not moved for a transfer, should continue to apply in this case.

In any event, defendants in the position of Deere would not fare much better if we required application of the transferee law instead of the transferor law. True, if the transferee law were to apply, some plaintiffs would not sue these defendants for fear that they would have no choice but to litigate in an inconvenient forum. But applying the transferee law would not discourage all plaintiffs from suing. Some plaintiffs would prefer to litigate in an inconvenient forum with favorable law than to litigate in a convenient forum with unfavorable law or not to litigate at all. The Ferenses, no doubt, would have abided by their initial choice of the District Court in Mississippi had they known that the District Court in Pennsylvania would dismiss their action. If we were to rule for Deere in this case, we would accomplish little more than discouraging the occasional motions by plaintiffs to transfer inconvenient cases. Other plaintiffs would sue in an inconvenient forum with the expectation that the defendants themselves would seek transfer to a convenient forum, resulting in application of the transferor law under *Van Dusen*. In this case, for example, Deere might have moved for a transfer if the Ferenses had not.

B

... [E]ven without § 1404(a), a plaintiff already has the option of shopping for a forum with the most favorable law. The Ferenses, for example, had an opportunity for forum shopping in the state courts because both the Mississippi and Pennsylvania courts had jurisdiction and because they each would have applied a different statute of limitations. Diversity jurisdiction did not eliminate these forum shopping opportunities; instead, under *Erie*, the federal courts had to replicate them. ... Applying the transferor law would not give a plaintiff an opportunity to use a transfer to obtain a law that he could not obtain through his initial forum selection. If it does make selection of the most favorable law more convenient, it does no more than recognize a forum shopping choice that already exists. This fact does not require us to apply the transferee law. Section 1404(a), to reiterate, exists to make venue convenient and should not allow the defendant to use inconvenience to discourage plaintiffs from exercising the opportunities that they already have.

Applying the transferee law, by contrast, might create opportunities for forum shopping in an indirect way. The advantage to Mississippi's personal injury lawyers that resulted from the State's then applicable 6-year statute of limitations has not escaped us; Mississippi's long limitation period no doubt drew plaintiffs to the State. Although *Sun Oil* held that the federal courts have little interest in a State's decision to create a long statute of limitations or to apply its statute of limitations to claims governed by foreign law, we should recognize the consequences of our interpretation of § 1404(a). Applying the transferee law, to the extent that it discourages plaintiff-initiated transfers, might give States incentives to enact similar laws to bring in out-of-state business that would not be moved at the instance of the plaintiff.

C

Van Dusen also made clear that the decision to transfer venue under § 1404(a) should turn on considerations of convenience rather than on the possibility of prejudice resulting from a change in the applicable law. We reasoned in *Van Dusen* that, if the law changed following a transfer initiated by the defendant, a district court "would at least be reluctant to grant transfers, despite considerations of convenience, if to do so might conceivably prejudice the claim of a plaintiff." The court, to determine the prejudice, might have to make an elaborate survey of the law, including statutes of limitations, burdens of proof, presumptions, and the like. This would turn what is supposed to be a statute for convenience of the courts into one expending extensive judicial time and resources. Because this difficult task is contrary to the purpose of the statute, in *Van Dusen* we made it unnecessary by ruling that a transfer of venue by the defendant does not result in a change of law. This same policy requires application of the transferor law when a plaintiff initiates a transfer.

If the law were to change following a transfer initiated by a plaintiff, a district court in a similar fashion would be at least reluctant to grant a transfer that would prejudice the defendant. Hardship might occur because plaintiffs may find as many opportunities to exploit application of the transferee law as they would find opportunities for exploiting application of the transferor law. If the transferee law were to apply, moreover, the plaintiff simply would not move to transfer unless the benefits of convenience outweighed the loss of favorable law.

. . .

IV

Some may object that a district court in Pennsylvania should not have to apply a Mississippi statute of limitations to a Pennsylvania cause of action. This point, although understandable, should have little to do with the outcome of this case. Congress gave the Ferenses the power to seek a transfer in § 1404(a), and our decision in *Van Dusen* already could require a district court in Pennsylvania to apply the Mississippi statute of limitations to Pennsylvania claims. Our rule may seem too generous because it allows the Ferenses to have both their choice of law and their choice of forum, or even to reward the Ferenses for conduct that seems manipulative. We nonetheless see no alternative rule that would produce a more acceptable result. Deciding that the transferee law should apply, in effect, would tell the Ferenses that they should have continued to litigate their warranty action in Pennsylvania and their tort action in Mississippi. Some might find this preferable, but we do not. . . . From a substantive standpoint, two further objections give us pause but do not persuade us to change our rule. First, one might ask why we require the Ferenses to file in the District Court in Mississippi at all. Efficiency might seem to dictate a rule allowing plaintiffs in the Ferenses' position not to file in an inconvenient forum and then to return to a convenient forum though a transfer of venue, but instead simply to file in the convenient forum and ask for the law of the inconvenient forum to apply. Although our rule may invoke certain formality, one must remember that § 1404(a) does not provide for an automatic transfer of venue. The section, instead, permits a transfer only when convenient and "in the interest of justice." Plaintiffs in the position of the Ferenses must go to the distant forum because they have no guarantee, until the court there examines the facts, that they may obtain a transfer. . . .

Second, one might contend that, because no *per se* rule requiring a court to apply either the transferor law or the transferee law will seem appropriate in all circumstances, we should develop more sophisticated federal choice-of-law rules for diversity actions involving transfers. To a large extent, however, state conflicts-of-law rules already ensure that appropriate laws will apply to diversity cases. Federal law, as a general matter, does not interfere with these rules. In addition, even if more elaborate federal choice-of-law rules would not run afoul of *Klaxon* and *Erie*, we believe that applying the law of the transferor forum effects the appropriate balance between fairness and simplicity. Cf. R. Leflar, American Conflicts Law § 143, p. 293 (3d ed. 1977) (arguing against a federal common law of conflicts).

For the foregoing reasons, we conclude that Mississippi's statute of limitations should govern the Ferenses' action. We reverse and remand for proceedings consistent with this opinion.

It is so ordered.

Justice Scalia, with whom Justices Brennan, Marshall and Blackmun join, dissenting.

. . .

We left open in *Van Dusen* the question presented today, viz., whether "the same considerations would govern" if a plaintiff sought a § 1404(a) transfer. In my view, neither of those considerations is served—and indeed both are positively defeated—by a departure from *Klaxon* in that context. First, just as it is unlikely that Congress, in enacting § 1404(a), meant to provide the defendant with a vehicle by which to manipulate in his favor the substantive law to be applied in a diversity case, so too is it unlikely that Congress meant to provide the *plaintiff* with a vehicle by which to appropriate the law of a distant and inconvenient forum in which he does not intend to litigate, and to carry that prize back to the State in which he wishes to try the case. Second, application of the transferor court's law in this context would encourage forum shopping between federal and state courts in the same jurisdiction on the basis of differential substantive law. It is true, of course, that the plaintiffs here did not select the *Mississippi* federal court in preference to the Mississippi state courts because of any differential substantive law; the former, like the latter, would have applied Mississippi choice-of-law rules and thus the Mississippi statute of limitations. But one must be blind to reality to say that it is the *Mississippi* federal court in which these plaintiffs have chosen to sue. That was merely a way station en route to suit in the *Pennsylvania* federal court. The plaintiffs were seeking to achieve exactly what *Klaxon* was designed to prevent: the use of a Pennsylvania federal court instead of a Pennsylvania state court in order to obtain application of a different substantive law. Our decision in *Van Dusen* compromised "the principle of uniformity within a state," *Klaxon*, only in the abstract, but today's decision compromises it precisely in the respect that matters—*i. e.*, insofar as it bears upon the plaintiff's choice between a state and a federal forum. The significant federal judicial policy expressed in *Erie* and *Klaxon* is reduced to a laughingstock if it can so readily be evaded through filing-and-transfer.

. . .

. . . [I]t seems to me that a proper calculation of systemic costs would go as follows: Saved by the Court's rule will be the incremental cost of trying in forums that are inconvenient (but not so inconvenient as to prompt the court's *sua sponte* transfer) those suits that are now filed in such forums for choice-of-law purposes. But incurred by the Court's rule will be the costs of considering and effecting transfer, not only in those suits but in the indeterminate number of additional suits that will be filed in inconvenient forums now that filing-and-transfer is an approved form of shopping for law; plus the costs attending the necessity for transferee courts to figure out the choice-of-law rules (and probably the substantive law) of distant States much more often than our *Van Dusen* decision would require. It should be noted that the file-and-transfer ploy sanctioned by the Court today will be available not merely to achieve the relatively rare (and generally unneeded) benefit of a longer statute of limitations, but also to bring home to the desired state of litigation all sorts of favorable choice-of-law rules regarding substantive liability—in an era when the diversity among the States in choice-of-law principles has become kaleidoscopic.[3]

. . .

For the foregoing reasons, I respectfully dissent.

Notes and Questions

1. The result in this case is a win-win situation for the Ferenses. Not only do they get the advantage of the long Mississippi statute of limitations, but they get to litigate at home in Pennsylvania, too. Could they have achieved this in state court in Pennsylvania? If not, what does *Ferens* do to the *Erie* notion that cases ought to be treated alike in state and federal court?

2. The majority opinion asserts that applying the choice of law rules of the transferee court would dissuade plaintiffs from making transfer motions. Is that a bad thing? Why should a plaintiff, who choses the venue when filing the action, be permitted to transfer? In cases such as *Ferens* it would ensure the litigation would go forward in an inconvenient forum (after all, Mississippi, though a proper venue [because the defendant resided there], had no connection to the dispute). In such a case, the majority asserts, the defendant may well then move to transfer. If you were Deere's lawyer, would you have moved to transfer to federal court in Pennsylvania? Why?

3. Given that Mississippi was not a convenient forum, and that the Ferenses' contract claims were pending in federal court in Pennsylvania, the Mississippi federal court might have ordered transfer *sua sponte* under § 1404(a). After *Ferens*, would *Van Dusen* apply when a court does so? Do we know? Should *Van Dusen* apply?

---

3. [Dissent's footnote #2] The current edition of Professor Leflar's treatise on American Conflicts Law lists 10 separate theories of choice of law that are applied, individually or in various combinations, by the 50 States. See R. Leflar, L. McDougall III, & R. Felix, American Conflicts Law §§ 86–91, 93–96 (4th ed. 1986). See also Kay, *Theory into Practice: Choice of Law in the Courts*, 34 Mercer L. Rev. 521, 525–584, 591–592 (1983).

4. *Ferens* illustrates the operation of the transfer statute to coordinate and consolidate overlapping cases in federal courts. First, the cases can be put in the same district through transfer. Second, once there, they can be consolidated. Here, the overlapping litigation was created by the plaintiffs, who filed in different fora. Why should the judicial system be so solicitous of such plaintiffs?

5. In *Atlantic Marine Construction Co. v. United States District Court*, 571 U.S. 49, 62 (2013), which we read in Chapter 3 section B.2, the Court held that a forum selection clause may be enforced by transfer to the agreed-upon district under § 1404(a). If venue was proper under the applicable venue statutes in the transferor district, the appropriate transfer vehicle is § 1404(a). Interestingly, however, the Court concluded that *Van Dusen* does not apply in such a case. *Id.* at 65–66. The Court reasoned that a plaintiff who sues in a district that violates a valid forum selection clause should not be permitted to capture the choice of law rules that district would have applied. The Ferenses were able to capture the choice of law rules of a place with no connection to the dispute.

6. *Ferens* involved transfer under § 1404(a), which, as we saw in Chapter 3, applies only if the original (transferor) federal court is a proper venue. The other major transfer statute, § 1406(a), permits transfer if the original federal court is an improper venue. Should *Van Dusen* apply in transfers under § 1406(a)? The clear majority opinion is that it should not, because it would be improper to let a plaintiff file in an *improper* venue and capture the choice of law rules of that venue. *See* Richard D. Freer, Civil Procedure 303–304 (4th ed. 2017). Similarly, *Van Dusen* does not apply in a § 1404(a) transfer if the transferor district lacked personal jurisdiction over the defendant. This makes sense: it would be untenable to allow the plaintiff to sue in a forum that lacked personal jurisdiction and to capture the choice of law doctrine of that forum.

Note on Choice of Law in Federal Question and Multidistrict Cases

Van Dusen applies to transfers of diversity of citizenship cases. *Klaxon* held that a federal court exercising diversity jurisdiction must apply the state choice of law rules of the state in which the federal court sits. It is those choice of law rules that transfer with the diversity case under most § 1404(a) transfers (except, as discussed in Notes 5 and 6 immediately above, those based upon a forum selection clause or when the transferor lacked personal jurisdiction).

In federal question cases, *Van Dusen* should not apply. First, the federalism concerns of *Erie* are not implicated in federal question cases. Second, federal law (in theory, at least) is intended to be uniform—a single national law, rather than two sets of law competing for application. *See* 15 Wright & Miller, Federal Practice and Procedure § 3846 (3d ed. 2018). Accordingly, courts readily conclude that, after transfer, the transferee district is to apply its own interpretation of federal law. *See, e.g., Hooper v. Lockheed Martin Corp.*, 688 F.3d 1037, 1046 (9th Cir. 2012).

Sections 1404(a) and 1406(a) permit transfer of cases for all purposes. Recall from Chapter 3, section B.4, however, that under § 1407 (the multidistrict litigation

(MDL) statute), the Judicial Panel on Multidistrict Litigation orders transfer from transferee courts to a transferor court for consolidated *pretrial* litigation. After pretrial proceedings are concluded, the cases are to be remanded to their transferor districts. In MDL transfers, does *Van Dusen* apply? Most courts have reached the same conclusions under § 1407 as they have under § 1404(a) and § 1406(a). Thus, *Van Dusen* does apply to MDL cases that invoke diversity of citizenship jurisdiction, and does not apply to MDL cases that invoke federal question jurisdiction. *See* 15 WRIGHT & MILLER, *supra,* § 3867 (3d ed. 2013).

Because MDL involves the possibility of remand to the transferor court, we can encounter an interesting permutation regarding applicable law.

> ***Example #3.*** The JPML orders § 1407 transfer of a federal question case from the Northern District of Iowa (which is in the Eighth Circuit) to the District of South Carolina (which is in the Fourth Circuit). In pretrial proceedings, the District of South Carolina rules on a matter of federal law by applying Fourth Circuit law. After completion of pretrial matters, the case is remanded to the Northern District of Iowa. Is that court "stuck" with the ruling on the federal issue, or can it now revisit the question under the law of the Eighth Circuit?

The transferor court is usually deemed bound by the transferee court's ruling under the doctrine of "law of the case." As we will see in Chapter 10, there is no role here for claim or issue preclusion, because no case has yet gone to judgment (claim and issue preclusion flow only from certain valid final judgments). Law of the case applies before entry of judgment, and provides that a decision made in a case generally will bind throughout the proceedings. *See* 17 MOORE'S FEDERAL PRACTICE § 112.07[2][c] (3d ed. 2018) ("an interpretation of federal law made by a transferee court may bind the transferor courts as the 'law of the case' ... even though their interpretation of the applicable federal law might be different from that of the transferee court.").

Let's wrestle with one last choice of law issue. Some federal statutes dictate that state law will apply to particular issues. For example, for certain claims under federal securities law, a statute (15 U.S.C. § 78aa-1) adopts as the statute of limitations "the limitations period provided by the laws applicable in the jurisdiction." In other words, it requires application of the statute of limitations set for similar claims by state law of the state in which the federal court sits. When such a case is transferred under § 1407, should *Van Dusen* apply? Here the courts have not forged consensus. The Seventh Circuit concludes that it should, and held that "when the law of the United States is geographically non-uniform, a transferee court should use the rule of the transferor court ... to implement the central conclusion of ... *Van Dusen* ..." *Eckstein v. Balcor Film Investors,* 8 F.3d 1121, 1127 (7th Cir. 1993). The Second Circuit reached the opposite conclusion, however, and held that *Van Dusen* is limited to diversity cases. *Menowitz v. Brown,* 991 F.3d 36, 40–41 (2d Cir. 1993). The Supreme Court has yet to weigh in on the matter. Which approach do you find most persuasive?

D. Efforts to Ensure a Single Governing Law

One upshot of *Erie, Klaxon*, and *Ferens* is that related claims may be governed by different substantive laws. And this, as we noted, may render it more difficult for a court to manage the litigation. As discussed in Chapter 6, this problem is particularly acute in class actions under Rule 23(b)(3), where common questions must predominate over individual questions. As Professor Silberman explains, "attempts to structure nationwide classes involving state law claims—such as damage actions for consumer fraud or misrepresentation, overcharges in contract and insurance cases, personal injury and breach of warranty claims for defective products, punitive damage classes, and claims for medical monitoring—often turn on whether the law of a single state or multiple states is to be applied." Linda Silberman, *The Role of Choice of Law in National Class Actions*, 156 U. Pa. L. Rev. 2001, 2002 (2008).

Even in non-class cases, tools of judicial management such as consolidation can be hampered by application of divergent laws. Life is simpler if a single substantive law governs related litigation—or even if a single choice of law rule might be employed for related cases. But multiple laws are a fact of life in our federal system, and state sovereignty trumps the systemic desire for efficient handling of related litigation.

Nonetheless, as we explore in this section, there are four ways in which related litigation may be adjudicated under a single governing law. First, the forum state may seek to apply its own law to all related claims. Second, in some instances, courts may fashion federal common law, vindication of which will invoke federal question jurisdiction. Third, courts may attempt to fashion a uniform federal common law choice of law rule in deciding what governing law to apply; this uniform rule might make it easier to conclude that all claims should be adjudicated under a single law. Finally, Congress might impose a uniform choice of law doctrine in some complex cases.

1. Application of Forum Law

One salutary possibility might be that the forum state (or a federal court in a diversity case) applies its substantive law to all related claims. There are constitutional limits, however, on a court's ability to do this, imposed by the due process and full faith and credit clauses. The following cases address those limits.

Phillips Petroleum Co. v. Shutts

Supreme Court of the United States
472 U.S. 797 (1985)

[We studied this case in Chapter 1, concerning personal jurisdiction. Here, we address a different part of the opinion, dealing with choice of law. The plaintiff class consisted of 33,000 owners of royalty interests in gas wells, to whom the defendant owed royalty payments. The defendant delayed paying the royalties, and plaintiffs brought this class action to recover interest for the delay. The average claim per class member was approximately $100. The Kansas trial court certified the class under its equivalent of Federal Rule 23(b)(3) and gave notice to class members, as required by that provision. About 3,400 members opted out, leaving a class of more than 29,000. Of these, however, only about 1,000 were citizens of Kansas. The others were citizens of various other states, including Texas, Oklahoma, and Louisiana.

The Kansas Supreme Court held that all class members were subject to personal jurisdiction in Kansas and thus bound by the class judgment. The Court reasoned that by not exercising a right (under the applicable class action rule) to opt out of the class proceeding, the class members had consented to personal jurisdiction in Kansas. (We saw that part of the opinion in Chapter 1.) In addition, the Kansas court held that Kansas law applied to all members' claims for interest. In this part of the opinion, the Supreme Court reverses that aspect of the Kansas decision.]

JUSTICE REHNQUIST delivered the opinion of the Court.

. . .

III

The Kansas courts applied Kansas contract and Kansas equity law to every claim in this case, notwithstanding that over 99% of the gas leases and some 97% of the plaintiffs in the case had no apparent connection to the State of Kansas except for this lawsuit. Petitioner protested that the Kansas courts should apply the laws of the States where the leases were located, or at least apply Texas and Oklahoma law because so many of the leases came from those States. The Kansas courts disregarded this contention and found petitioner liable for interest on the suspended royalties as a matter of Kansas law, and set the interest rates under Kansas equity principles.

Petitioner contends that total application of Kansas substantive law violated the constitutional limitations on choice of law mandated by the Due Process Clause of the Fourteenth Amendment and the Full Faith and Credit Clause of Article IV, § 1. We must first determine whether Kansas law conflicts in any material way with any other law which could apply. There can be no injury in applying Kansas law if it is not in conflict with that of any other jurisdiction connected to this suit.

Petitioner claims that Kansas law conflicts with that of a number of States connected to this litigation, especially Texas and Oklahoma. These putative conflicts range from the direct to the tangential, and may be addressed by the Supreme Court of Kansas on remand under the correct constitutional standard. For example, there is no recorded Oklahoma decision dealing with interest liability for suspended royalties: whether Oklahoma is likely to impose liability would require a survey of Oklahoma oil and gas law. Even if Oklahoma found such liability, petitioner shows that Oklahoma would most likely apply its constitutional and statutory 6% interest rate rather than the much higher Kansas rates applied in this litigation.

Additionally, petitioner points to an Oklahoma statute which excuses liability for interest if a creditor accepts payment of the full principal without a claim for interest, Okla. Stat., Tit. 23, § 8 (1951). Petitioner contends that by ignoring this statute the Kansas courts created liability that does not exist in Oklahoma.

Petitioner also points out several conflicts between Kansas and Texas law. Although Texas recognizes interest liability for suspended royalties, Texas has never awarded any such interest at a rate greater than 6%, which corresponds with the Texas constitutional and statutory rate.[4] Moreover, at least one court interpreting Texas law appears to have held that Texas excuses interest liability once the gas company offers to take an indemnity from the royalty owner and pay him the suspended royalty while the price increase is still tentative. Such a rule is contrary to Kansas law as applied below, but if applied to the Texas plaintiffs or leases in this case, would vastly reduce petitioner's liability.

The conflicts on the applicable interest rates, alone . . . certainly amounted to millions of dollars in liability. We think that the Supreme Court of Kansas erred in deciding on the basis that it did that the application of its laws to all claims would be constitutional.

Four Terms ago we addressed a similar situation in *Allstate Ins. Co. v. Hague*, 449 U.S. 302 (1981). In that case we were confronted with two conflicting rules of state insurance law. Minnesota permitted the "stacking" of separate uninsured motorist policies while Wisconsin did not. Although the decedent lived in Wisconsin, took out insurance policies and was killed there, he was employed in Minnesota, and after his death his widow moved to Minnesota for reasons unrelated to the litigation, and was appointed personal representative of his estate. She filed suit in Minnesota courts, which applied the Minnesota stacking rule.

The plurality in *Allstate* noted that a particular set of facts giving rise to litigation could justify, constitutionally, the application of more than one jurisdiction's laws. The plurality recognized, however, that the Due Process Clause and the Full Faith and Credit Clause provided modest restrictions on the application of forum law. These restrictions required "that for a State's substantive law to be selected in a constitutionally permissible manner, that State must have a significant contact or significant aggregation of contacts, creating state interests, such that choice of its law is neither arbitrary nor fundamentally unfair." *Id.*, at 312–313. The dissenting Justices were in substantial agreement with this principle. *Id.*, at 332. The dissent stressed that the Due Process Clause prohibited the application of law which was only casually or slightly related to the litigation, while the Full Faith and Credit Clause required the forum to respect the laws and judgments of other States, subject to the forum's own interests in furthering its public policy.

4. [Court's footnote #7] The Kansas interest rate also conflicts with the rate which is applicable in Louisiana. At the time this suit was filed that rate was 7%.

The plurality in *Allstate* affirmed the application of Minnesota law because of the forum's significant contacts to the litigation which supported the State's interest in applying its law. Kansas' contacts to this litigation, as explained by the Kansas Supreme Court, can be gleaned from the opinion below.

Petitioner owns property and conducts substantial business in the State, so Kansas certainly has an interest in regulating petitioner's conduct in Kansas. Moreover, oil and gas extraction is an important business to Kansas, and although only a few leases in issue are located in Kansas, hundreds of Kansas plaintiffs were affected by petitioner's suspension of royalties; thus the court held that the State has a real interest in protecting "the rights of these royalty owners both as individual residents of [Kansas] and as members of this particular class of plaintiffs." The Kansas Supreme Court pointed out that Kansas courts are quite familiar with this type of lawsuit, and "[the] plaintiff class members have indicated their desire to have this action determined under the laws of Kansas." Finally, the Kansas court buttressed its use of Kansas law by stating that this lawsuit was analogous to a suit against a "common fund" located in Kansas.

We do not lightly discount this description of Kansas' contacts with this litigation and its interest in applying its law. There is, however, no "common fund" located in Kansas that would require or support the application of only Kansas law to all these claims. See, *e.g.*, *Hartford Life Ins. Co. v. Ibs*, 237 U.S. 662 (1915). As the Kansas court noted, petitioner commingled the suspended royalties with its general corporate accounts. There is no specific identifiable res in Kansas, nor is there any limited amount which may be depleted before every plaintiff is compensated. Only by somehow aggregating all the separate claims in this case could a "common fund" in any sense be created, and the term becomes all but meaningless when used in such an expansive sense.

We also give little credence to the idea that Kansas law should apply to all claims because the plaintiffs, by failing to opt out, evinced their desire to be bound by Kansas law. Even if one could say that the plaintiffs "consented" to the application of Kansas law by not opting out, plaintiff's desire for forum law is rarely, if ever controlling. In most cases the plaintiff shows his obvious wish for forum law by filing there. "If a plaintiff could choose the substantive rules to be applied to an action . . . the invitation to forum shopping would be irresistible." *Allstate*, *supra*, at 337 (opinion of Powell, J.). Even if a plaintiff evidences his desire for forum law by moving to the forum, we have generally accorded such a move little or no significance. *John Hancock Mut. Life Ins. Co. v. Yates*, 299 U.S. 178, 182 (1936); *Home Ins. Co. v. Dick*, 281 U.S. 397, 408 (1930). In *Allstate* the plaintiff's move to the forum was only relevant because it was unrelated and prior to the litigation. Thus the plaintiffs' desire for Kansas law, manifested by their participation in this Kansas lawsuit, bears little relevance.

The Supreme Court of Kansas in its opinion in this case expressed the view that by reason of the fact that it was adjudicating a nationwide class action, it had much greater latitude in applying its own law to the transactions in question than might otherwise be the case . . . .

We think that this is something of a "bootstrap" argument. The Kansas class-action statute, like those of most other jurisdictions, requires that there be "common issues of law or fact." But while a State may, for the reasons we have previously stated, assume jurisdiction over the claims of plaintiffs whose principal contacts are with other States, it may not use this assumption of jurisdiction as an added weight in the scale when considering the permissible constitutional limits on choice of substantive law. It may not take a transaction with little or no relationship to the forum and apply the law of the forum in order to satisfy the procedural requirement that there be a "common question of law." The issue of personal jurisdiction over plaintiffs in a class action is entirely distinct from the question of the constitutional limitations on choice of law; the latter calculus is not altered by the fact that it may be more difficult or more burdensome to comply with the constitutional limitations because of the large number of transactions which the State proposes to adjudicate and which have little connection with the forum.

Kansas must have a "significant contact or significant aggregation of contacts" to the claims asserted by each member of the plaintiff class, contacts "creating state interests," in order to ensure that the choice of Kansas law is not arbitrary or unfair. *Allstate*, 449 U.S., at 312–313. Given Kansas' lack of "interest" in claims unrelated to that State, and the substantive conflict with jurisdictions such as Texas, we conclude that application of Kansas law to every claim in this case is sufficiently arbitrary and unfair as to exceed constitutional limits.[5]

When considering fairness in this context, an important element is the expectation of the parties. There is no indication that when the leases involving land and royalty owners outside of Kansas were executed, the parties had any idea that Kansas law would control. Neither the Due Process Clause nor the Full Faith and Credit Clause requires Kansas "to substitute for its own [laws], applicable to persons and events within it, the conflicting statute of another state," *Pacific Employers Ins. Co. v.*

5. [Court's footnote #8] In this case the Kansas Supreme Court held that "[the] trial court did not determine whether any difference existed between the laws of Kansas and other states or whether another state's law should be applied." 235 Kan. 195, 221, 679 P. 2d 1159, 1180 (1984). Respondents contend that the trial court and the Supreme Court actually incorporated by reference the opinion in *Shutts, Executor*, 222 Kan. 527, 567 P. 2d 1292 (1977), where the court looked to the Texas and Oklahoma interest rate statutes and found them inapplicable. We do not think that the Kansas Supreme Court fully adopted the choice-of-law discussion in *Shutts, Executor* as its holding in this case. But even if we agreed that *Shutts, Executor* was somehow incorporated below, that would be insufficient. *Shutts, Executor* was a pre-*Allstate* case involving only 2 other States, rather than the 10 present here. Moreover, the gas region involved in *Shutts, Executor* was primarily within Kansas borders. *Shutts, Executor* only considered the conflict involving interest rate liability and state statutes, and in finding the 6% Texas rate inapplicable it cited but did not follow contrary Texas precedent. 222 Kan., at 562–565, 567 P. 2d, at 1317–1319.

Industrial Accident Comm'n, 306 U.S. 493, 502 (1939), but Kansas "may not abrogate the rights of parties beyond its borders having no relation to anything done or to be done within them." *Home Ins. Co. v. Dick, supra*, at 410.

Here the Supreme Court of Kansas took the view that in a nationwide class action where procedural due process guarantees of notice and adequate representation were met, "the law of the forum should be applied unless compelling reasons exist for applying a different law." 235 Kan., at 221, 679 P. 2d, at 1181. Whatever practical reasons may have commended this rule to the Supreme Court of Kansas, for the reasons already stated we do not believe that it is consistent with the decisions of this Court. We make no effort to determine for ourselves which law must apply to the various transactions involved in this lawsuit, and we reaffirm our observation in *Allstate* that in many situations a state court may be free to apply one of several choices of law. But the constitutional limitations laid down in cases such as *Allstate* and *Home Ins. Co.* v. *Dick, supra*, must be respected even in a nationwide class action.

We therefore affirm the judgment of the Supreme Court of Kansas insofar as it upheld the jurisdiction of the Kansas courts over the plaintiff class members in this case, and reverse its judgment insofar as it held that Kansas law was applicable to all of the transactions which it sought to adjudicate. We remand the case to that court for further proceedings not inconsistent with this opinion.

It is so ordered.

[Separate opinion of Justice Stevens, concurring and dissenting, is omitted.]

Notes and Questions

1. As to what claims may a Kansas court apply Kansas law? What law will apply to the other claims in this class action?

2. Do you find it inconsistent that class members were subject to personal jurisdiction in Kansas courts but that Kansas law could not apply to them? After all, the class members had enough connection with Kansas for a court of that state to issue orders that bind them. Why are those connections insufficient to warrant the application of the same state's law?

3. Was the Court's holding based upon due process or full faith and credit? Did the Court give any hint that the standards under those two provisions might differ?

Shutts was not the only class action filed in Kansas concerning late payments of royalties. Another class action, substantially similar but against a different oil company, made its way to the Supreme Court three years later. It is our next case, *Sun Oil Co. v. Wortman*, 486 U.S. 717 (1988). After remand in *Shutts*, the Kansas courts in *Wortman* decided two key issues. First, they held that the Kansas statute of limitations applied to all class members, even those whose claims for interest were based upon the substantive law of another state, and even though the statute of limitations of the other state would bar the claim. Second, on the merits, the Kansas courts concluded that the laws of the other states would charge interest on the delayed royalties at a rate set by *federal* regulation. At the Supreme Court, the defendant argued that each of these rulings violated due process and full faith and credit protections.

Sun Oil Co. v. Wortman

Supreme Court of the United States
486 U.S. 717 (1988)

Justice Scalia delivered the opinion of the Court.

. . .

II

This Court has long and repeatedly held that the Constitution does not bar application of the forum State's statute of limitations to claims that in their substance are and must be governed by the law of a different State. See, *e.g.*, *Wells v. Simonds Abrasive Co.*, 345 U.S. 514, 516–518 (1953); *Townsend v. Jemison*, 50 U.S. 407, 413–420 (1850); *McElmoyle v. Cohen*, 13 Pet. 312, 327–328 (1839). We granted certiorari to reexamine this issue. We conclude that our prior holdings are sound.

A

The Full Faith and Credit Clause provides:

> "Full Faith and Credit shall be given in each State to the public Acts, Records, and judicial Proceedings of every other State. And the Congress may by general Laws prescribe the Manner in which such Acts, Records and Proceedings shall be proved, and the Effect thereof."

The Full Faith and Credit Clause does not compel "a state to substitute the statutes of other states for its own statutes dealing with a subject matter concerning which it is competent to legislate." *Pacific Employers Ins. Co. v. Industrial Accident Comm'n*, 306 U.S. 493, 501 (1939). Since the procedural rules of its courts are surely matters on which a State is competent to legislate, it follows that a State may apply its own procedural rules to actions litigated in its courts. The issue here, then, can be characterized as whether a statute of limitations may be considered as a procedural matter for purposes of the Full Faith and Credit Clause.

. . .

The historical record shows conclusively, we think, that the society which adopted the Constitution did not regard statutes of limitations as substantive provisions, akin to the rules governing the validity and effect of contracts, but rather as procedural restrictions fashioned by each jurisdiction for its own courts. As Chancellor Kent explained in his landmark work, 2 J. Kent, Commentaries on American Law 462–463 (2d ed. 1832): "The period sufficient to constitute a bar to the litigation of sta[l]e demands, is a question of municipal policy and regulation, and one which belongs to the discretion of every government, consulting its own interest and convenience."

Unable to sustain the contention that under the original understanding of the Full Faith and Credit Clause statutes of limitations would have been considered substantive, petitioner argues that we should apply the modern understanding that they are so. It is now agreed, petitioner argues, that the primary function of a statute of limitations is to balance the competing substantive values of repose and vindication of the underlying right; and we should apply that understanding here, as we have applied it in the area of choice of law for purposes of federal diversity jurisdiction, where we have held that statutes of limitations are substantive, see *Guaranty Trust Co. v. York*, 326 U.S. 99 (1945).

To address the last point first: *Guaranty Trust* itself rejects the notion that there is an equivalence between what is substantive under the *Erie* doctrine and what is substantive for purposes of conflict of laws. Except at the extremes, the terms "substance" and "procedure" precisely describe very little except a dichotomy, and what they mean in a particular context is largely determined by the purposes for which the dichotomy is drawn. In the context of our *Erie* jurisprudence, that purpose is to establish (within the limits of applicable federal law, including the prescribed Rules of Federal Procedure) substantial uniformity of predictable outcome between cases tried in a federal court and cases tried in the courts of the State in which the federal court sits. The purpose of the substance/procedure dichotomy in the context of the Full Faith and Credit Clause, by contrast, is not to establish uniformity but to delimit spheres of state legislative competence. How different the two purposes (and hence the appropriate meanings) are is suggested by this: It is never the case under *Erie* that either federal *or* state law—if the two differ—can properly be applied to a particular issue, but since the legislative jurisdictions of the States overlap, it is frequently the case under the Full Faith and Credit Clause that a court can lawfully apply either the law of one State or the contrary law of another. Today, for example, we do not hold that Kansas must apply its own statute of limitations to a claim governed in its substance by another State's law, but only that it may.

But to address petitioner's broader point of which the *Erie* argument is only a part—that we should update our notion of what is sufficiently "substantive" to require full faith and credit: We cannot imagine what would be the basis for such an updating. As we have just observed, the words "substantive" and "procedural" themselves (besides not appearing in the Full Faith and Credit Clause) do not have a precise content, even (indeed especially) as their usage has evolved. And if one consults the purpose of their usage in the full-faith-and-credit context, that purpose is quite simply to give both the forum State and other interested States the legislative jurisdiction to which they are entitled. If we abandon the currently applied, traditional notions of such entitlement we would embark upon the enterprise of constitutionalizing choice-of-law rules, with no compass to guide us beyond our own perceptions of what seems desirable. There is no more reason to consider recharacterizing statutes of limitation as substantive under the Full Faith and Credit Clause than there is to consider recharacterizing a host of other matters generally treated as procedural under conflicts law, and hence generally regarded as within the forum

State's legislative jurisdiction. See, *e.g.*, Restatement (Second) of Conflict of Laws § 131 (remedies available), § 133 (placement of burden of proof), § 134 (burden of production), § 135 (sufficiency of the evidence), § 139 (privileges) (1971).

In sum, long established and still subsisting choice-of-law practices that come to be thought, by modern scholars, unwise, do not thereby become unconstitutional. If current conditions render it desirable that forum States no longer treat a particular issue as procedural for conflict of laws purposes, those States can themselves adopt a rule to that effect, *e.g.*, *Heavner v. Uniroyal, Inc.*, 305 A.2d 412, 415–418 (N.J. 1973) (statute of limitations), or it can be proposed that Congress legislate to that effect under the second sentence of the Full Faith and Credit Clause, cf. *Mills v. Duryee*, 11 U.S. 481, 485 (1813); *Pacific Employers Ins. Co. v. Industrial Accident Comm'n*, 306 U.S. at 502. It is not the function of this Court, however, to make departures from established choice-of-law precedent and practice constitutionally mandatory. We hold, therefore, that Kansas did not violate the Full Faith and Credit Clause when it applied its own statute of limitations.

B

Petitioner also makes a due process attack upon the Kansas court's application of its own statute of limitations. Here again neither the tradition in place when the constitutional provision was adopted nor subsequent practice supports the contention. At the time the Fourteenth Amendment was adopted, this Court had not only explicitly approved (under the Full Faith and Credit Clause) forum-state application of its own statute of limitations, but the practice had gone essentially unchallenged. And it has gone essentially unchallenged since. "If a thing has been practised for two hundred years by common consent, it will need a strong case for the Fourteenth Amendment to affect it." *Jackman v. Rosenbaum Co.*, 260 U.S. 22, 31 (1922).

A State's interest in regulating the workload of its courts and determining when a claim is too stale to be adjudicated certainly suffices to give it legislative jurisdiction to control the remedies available in its courts by imposing statutes of limitations. Moreover, petitioner could in no way have been unfairly surprised by the application to it of a rule that is as old as the Republic. There is, in short, nothing in Kansas' action here that is "arbitrary or unfair," and the due process challenge is entirely without substance.

III

In *Shutts* . . . we held that Kansas could not apply its own law to claims for interest by nonresidents concerning royalties from property located in other States. The Kansas Supreme Court has complied with that ruling, but petitioner claims that it has unconstitutionally distorted Texas [and] Oklahoma . . . law. . . .

To constitute a violation of the Full Faith and Credit Clause or the Due Process Clause, it is not enough that a state court misconstrue the law of another State. Rather, our cases make plain that the misconstruction must contradict law of the other State that is clearly established and that has been brought to the court's attention. See, *e.g.*, *Pennsylvania Fire Ins. Co. v. Gold Issue Mining & Milling Co.*, 243 U.S.

93, 96, (1917); *Western Life Indemnity Co. v. Rupp*, 235 U.S. 261, 275 (1914); *Louisville & Nashville R. Co. v. Melton*, 218 U.S. 36, 51–52 (1910); *Banholzer v. New York Life Ins. Co.*, 178 U.S. 402, 408 (1900). We cannot conclude that any of the interpretations at issue here runs afoul of this standard.

1. *Texas:* Petitioner contests the Kansas Supreme Court's interpretation of Texas law on the interest rate. Texas' statutory rate of 6% does not apply when a "specified rate of interest is agreed upon by the parties." Tex. Rev. Civ. Stat. Ann., Art. 5069-1.03 (Vernon 1987). Such an agreement need not be express, but can be inferred from conduct. See *Preston Farm & Ranch Supply, Inc. v. Bio-Zyme Enterprises*, 625 S.W.2d 295, 298, 300 (Tex. 1981). The Kansas court held an agreement to pay interest at a higher rate was implied by petitioner's undertaking with the [Federal Power Commission (FPC)] to comply with federal regulations setting forth the applicable rates of interest for refundable moneys held in suspense. [This refers to the fact that the FPC permitted the oil company to increase rates charged for gas before the new rate was formally approved; in case the rate was not formally approved, the oil company was required to refund overcharges and interest set by federal regulations. It is that interest rate set by federal regulation that the state courts in this case applied to Texas and Oklahoma claims.]

Petitioner brought to the Kansas court's attention no Texas decision clearly indicating that an agreement to pay interest at a specified rate would not be implied in these circumstances. Petitioner's reliance on *Phillips Petroleum Co. v. Stahl Petroleum Co.*, 569 S.W.2d 480 (Tex. 1978), is misplaced. Although that case was similar to the present one on its facts, the point at issue here was neither raised nor decided. In *Stahl*, the intermediate Texas court had ordered interest paid at the statutory 6% rate. There is nothing to indicate, however, that the royalty owner had requested anything else, and only the lessee and not the royalty owner appealed. Thus, the Texas Supreme Court's holding that 6% interest was payable is in no way a holding that more than 6% was not. It is far from unconstitutional for the Kansas Supreme Court to anticipate that the Texas Supreme Court would distinguish the case on the eminently reasonable ground that no rate of interest based on an implied agreement was at issue.

2. *Oklahoma:* Petitioner contests the Kansas Supreme Court's interpretations of Oklahoma law as to both liability for interest and the rate to be paid. Concerning liability, petitioner relies on a statute providing that "accepting payment of the whole principal, as such, waives all claim to interest." Okla. Stat., Tit. 23, § 8 (1981). But the Oklahoma Supreme Court has held that this statute does not bar a claim for interest based on an implied agreement to pay interest, since in that event the interest becomes, for purposes of the statute, part of the "principal" owed. See *Webster Drilling Co. v. Sterling Oil of Oklahoma, Inc.*, 376 P.2d 236, 238 (1962). Regarding the rate of interest, Oklahoma law provides for 6% only "in the absence of any contract as to the rate of interest, and by contract the parties may agree to any rate as may be authorized by law." Okla. Stat., Tit. 15, § 266 (1981). Thus, for Oklahoma as for Texas, petitioner's contention founders on the fact that it pointed to no decision

indicating that an agreement to pay more than 6% interest would not be implied in circumstances such as those of the present case.

. . .

For the reasons stated, the judgment of the Kansas Supreme Court is *Affirmed.*

[Separate opinions of BRENNAN, J., concurring in part and concurring in the judgment and O'CONNOR, J., concurring in part and dissenting in part, are omitted.]

Notes and Questions

1. Under *Shutts*, Kansas cannot apply Kansas contract law to claims asserted by Texans for delayed royalty payments on Texas wells. But under *Wortman*, Kansas can apply its statute of limitations to such claims asserted under Texas law. Why the difference?

2. Before *Wortman*, there was widespread agreement that the forum state could apply its own statute of limitations if it were shorter than the limitations period prescribed by the law of the state that created the claim. There was significant debate, however, about the propriety of a forum state's applying its statute of limitations if that period were *longer* than that of the other state. In *Wortman*, the Court permitted exactly that. Assuming that Kansas had no connection to the dispute other than the pendency of suit, how can it effectively lengthen the lifespan of a claim arising in another state?

3. The Kansas courts' machinations concerning the applicable substantive law were rather remarkable. In the face of state statutes prescribing different interest rates, the courts concluded that the statutory rates were waivable and that as a matter of industry practice everyone agreed that they would employ the highest interest rate approved by the Federal Power Commission. Interestingly, the result under that rate turned out exactly the same as it would have under Kansas law. Under *Shutts*, Kansas cannot apply its substantive law to claims unconnected with Kansas. But the courts' consideration of other states' laws resulted (rather conveniently, some would say) in application of law that was functionally identical to that of Kansas. (Ultimately, the same thing happened on the merits in *Shutts* as well.)

Realistically, though, how effective can the Supreme Court be in reviewing one state court's interpretation of another state's law? In her separate opinion in *Wortman*, Justice O'Connor (who had been a state trial and appellate judge before her appointment to the Supreme Court) argued that a state court could "invent a legal theory so novel or strange that the other State has never had an opportunity to reject it; then, on the basis of nothing but unsupported speculation, 'predict' that the other State would adopt the theory if it had the chance." 486 U.S. at 749 (O'Connor, J., concurring and dissenting). Is she right? Would such an effort survive the scrutiny employed in *Wortman*?

4. The Supreme Court can only review state-court decisions on matters of federal law. After *Erie*, and the demise of "general" federal common law, the Court has no

role telling state courts what state law means. Notice, though, how the defendant's challenge to the Kansas courts' interpretation of Texas and Oklahoma law required the Supreme Court to engage in an assessment of state law. Does the assessment in section III of *Wortman* violate the principles of *Erie*?

2. Use of Choice of Law Doctrine to Support Application of a Single Law

We have seen that a forum cannot simply decree that its substantive law will govern all claims in related litigation. There must be sufficient contact between the claimant, the claim, and the forum. We have also seen, though, that it is difficult to police how one state applies the law of another state. The same is true about reviewing the application of choice of law rules. Indeed, modern conflicts law—with its focus on the interests of various affected states, as we noted in section A above—is inherently indeterminate. One scholar summarizes: "Doubts about the coherence and intellectual integrity of modern conflicts theory are rampant.... In short, it has become increasingly difficult to find a consensus about what conflicts law is or ought to be." Gene Shreve, *Reform Aspirations of the Complex Litigation Project*, 54 La. L. Rev. 1139, 1147 (1994).

Some courts have used this indeterminacy to find that the conflicts rules mandate the application of the law of a single state to complex proceedings involving the citizens of (and events taking place in) many states, thereby simplifying aggregate management of the related litigation.

In *Powers v. Lycoming Engines*, 245 F.R.D. 226 (E.D. Pa. 2006), the court certified a nationwide class of airplane owners who sued Lycoming, which manufactured their planes' engines. They alleged that the crankshafts were defective and that the manufacturer knowingly concealed the defect. The court applied Pennsylvania choice of law rules to conclude that all claims would be governed by Pennsylvania law. *Id.* at 235. That holding facilitated certification of the class; had different state laws applied, it is doubtful the court could have found that common questions predominated.

One claim was for breach of implied warranty. The court canvassed the laws of the various states of which class members were citizens and concluded that 14 states required a showing of privity for such a claim; others, however, did not. Nonetheless, flexible choice of law doctrine permitted the court to apply a single law:

> In light of these policy reasons, there is a real conflict between the application of Pennsylvania law and the laws of the fourteen states that require privity. Allowing the plaintiffs to sue a manufacturer with whom they did not deal directly will frustrate the interests of those states that do not permit it. On the other hand, insulating Lycoming from suit will frustrate Pennsylvania's interest in bypassing privity. Therefore, there is a real conflict, requiring a balancing of the respective interests of the states.

> The balancing test results in the application of Pennsylvania law. The manufacturer is located in Pennsylvania, the interest of the fourteen privity states in protecting a resident manufacturer is absent, the manufacturer's right to disclaim a warranty will be preserved, and the goal of saving costs will not be thwarted by the application of Pennsylvania law. At the same time, Pennsylvania's interest in avoiding a needless multiplicity of actions where each buyer would have to sue his own seller and those up the distribution chain until the actual manufacturer is reached will be advanced by applying its state law. Application of Pennsylvania law will not impinge on the interests of states that retain the privity requirement in the interest of reducing litigation and costs. The litigation and its attendant costs will take place in Pennsylvania at one time, not many times in those other states. Therefore, Pennsylvania law will apply to the breach of implied warranty claims of the residents of the fourteen states that require privity of contract.

Id. at 234. Elsewhere in the opinion, the court noted that class members' contacts with the defendant, and any false representations by the defendant, would have taken place in the class members' home states. Because a customer buys an airplane, however, and not simply an engine, "it is unlikely" that any class members relied upon a misrepresentation by the engine manufacturer. "Consequently, the place where the false representations were received is not a factor" in the choice of law assessment. *Id.* at 232.

It is easy to sympathize with what the court did in *Powers*. After all, courts are under great pressure to process cases. They understandably look for shortcuts to manage complex litigation. But what the court did in *Powers* is difficult to justify under *Shutts*.

Dean Kramer has written about the "consensus . . . that ordinary choice-of-law principles should yield in suits consolidating large numbers of claims and that courts should apply a single law in such cases." Larry Kramer, *Choice of Law in Complex Litigation*, 71 N.Y.U. L. Rev. 547, 547 (1996). He finds that consensus indefensible, however, in view of the dictates of *Erie* and *Klaxon*. Because "choice of law is part of the process of defining the parties' rights," *id.* at 548, he argues, it should not be pushed aside simply because the courts have procedural tools fostering efficient handling of related cases.

There is an interesting irony here. In *Wortman*, the Court adamantly refused to "constitutionaliz[e]" choice of law doctrine, establishing state hegemony over conflicts law. At the same time, however, the flexibility of modern conflicts law often permits federal courts to apply a single state's substantive law to all related claims, thereby possibly undermining other states' interests in having their substantive law applied.

Is there any recourse against overly creative use of choice of law doctrine in this way? How likely is meaningful appellate scrutiny on a question of state choice of law rules?

3. Application of Federal Common Law

If plaintiffs sue to vindicate a right created by federal legislation, their claims will invoke federal question jurisdiction under § 1331. Remember, too, that such cases might instead be brought in state court. In either scenario, the federal law creating the claim will be the rule of decision and generally there will be no conflict of laws problem.

In this subsection we address the possibility that litigation may be governed by federal *common* law—that is, judge-made (non-legislative) law. Invocation of federal common law is rare, as we will see. When it is appropriate, however, the plaintiff's vindication of the claim created by that judge-made law will invoke federal question jurisdiction under § 1331. *Illinois v. City of Milwaukee*, 406 U.S. 91, 99–100 (1972).

At this point, you may be tempted to say "but wait—I thought *Erie* got rid of federal common law." No. *Erie* only got rid of "general" federal common law. Federal common law still exists, but only in limited situations. The starting point is the Rules of Decision Act, § 2072, which we mentioned in section B above but now set forth in full:

> The laws of the several states, except where the Constitution or treaties of the United States or Acts of Congress otherwise require or provide, shall be regarded as rules of decision in civil actions in the courts of the United States, in cases where they apply.

In *Swift v. Tyson*, 41 U.S. 1, 12 (1842), the Court held that the "laws of the several states," as used in the statute, included only state *statutory* law and common law of a "local" nature. It did not include common law of a *general* nature. (By the way, the courts had a very difficult time telling local from general.) Thus, federal courts in diversity cases were not required to follow state law if it was judge-made law about a general topic. Because most of the basic law we study in the first year of law school—contracts, property, and torts—evolved through general common law, federal courts were free to ignore a great deal of state law. *Swift* reflected a nineteenth-century conviction that there was only one true "law"—and the federal courts aggrandized to themselves the job of discovering that true law.

State courts were not required to accept the federal court's divination of the general common law. This fact led to "vertical disuniformity"—that is, different law applied depending upon whether the parties litigated in federal or state court. In *Swift* itself, the Court embraced as general federal common law that discharge of a debt constituted valid consideration for a contract; state courts in New York, however, held that it was not. So, the law on consideration for the citizens of New York depended upon whether the litigation was in state court (where discharge of a debt would not support a bargain) or federal court (where it would).

This state of affairs was untenable. It was also unconstitutional. *Erie* overruled *Swift* in dramatic terms. It could have held simply that "laws" in the Rules of Decision Act included state common law of a general nature. The Court went beyond this, however, and held that nothing in the Constitution gave the federal judiciary the authority to prescribe common law of general application. The federal courts had seized this common law-making function from the state courts in violation of the Tenth Amendment.

Erie did not end federal common law—just *general* federal common law. Indeed, the day the Court decided *Erie*, it also decided *Hinderlider v. La Plata River & Cherry Creek Ditch Co.*, 304 U.S. 92 (1938). There, the Court held that federal common law governs the apportionment of an interstate stream between two states. *Id.* at 110. Upon reflection, there *must* be federal common law on this issue. In a dispute between two states, how could a court ever decide which state's law to apply? The matter—an interstate dispute—cries out for decision under federal law; otherwise, selection of one state's law would be unfair to the other. Because there was no federal constitutional or statutory provision on point, the only federal law available would be judge-made—that is, federal common law.

In a different case, Justice Jackson explained:

> The federal courts have no *general* common law, as in a sense they have no general or comprehensive jurisprudence of any kind, because many subjects of private law which bulk large in the traditional common law are ordinarily within the province of the states and not of the federal government. But this is not to say that wherever we have occasion to decide a federal question which cannot be answered from federal statutes alone we may not resort to all of the source materials of the common law, or that when we have fashioned an answer it does not become a part of the federal non-statutory or common law.

D'Oench, Duhme & Co. v. Federal Deposit Ins. Corp., 315 U.S. 447, 469 (1942) (Jackson, J., concurring) (emphasis original).

The Court has not always been clear in defining when federal courts may make federal common law. (You may study the issue in detail in a course on Federal Courts.) Suffice to say for our purposes that the Court has allowed federal common law when cases implicate "unique federal interests." For example, in *Clearfield Trust Co. v. United States*, 318 U.S. 363, 366–367 (1943), the government issued a check, which was stolen and negotiated. In litigation over liability for the stolen funds, the Court concluded that federal common law should govern. Disbursing funds from the treasury is a governmental activity, and a uniform federal standard was desirable, to ensure that the government's position was treated uniformly, without variation from state-to-state. In the next case, the Court upholds federal common law in a case in which the federal government was not a litigant.

Boyle v. United Technologies Corporation

Supreme Court of the United States
487 U.S. 500 (1988)

Justice Scalia delivered the opinion of the Court.

This case requires us to decide when a contractor providing military equipment to the Federal Government can be held liable under state tort law for injury caused by a design defect.

[Lieutenant Boyle, a Marine helicopter pilot, was killed when the craft he was flying crashed into the ocean off Virginia Beach; he was trapped inside and drowned. His father sued the manufacturer of the helicopter, invoking diversity of citizenship jurisdiction and alleging, *inter alia*, that the emergency hatch system design was defective because the hatch opened inwardly instead of outwardly. He won a judgment of $725,000. On appeal, the Fourth Circuit reversed and remanded with instructions to dismiss the suit. With regard to the escape hatch design, it held that the defendant could not be liable, because it had satisfied the requirements of the "military contractor defense" that the Fourth Circuit had recently recognized as a matter of federal common law. The part of the opinion reproduced is the Supreme Court's treatment of the federal common law issue.]

II

Petitioner's broadest contention is that, in the absence of legislation specifically immunizing Government contractors from liability for design defects, there is no basis for judicial recognition of such a defense. We disagree. In most fields of activity, to be sure, this Court has refused to find federal pre-emption of state law in the absence of either a clear statutory prescription, or a direct conflict between federal and state law. But we have held that a few areas, involving "uniquely federal interests," *Texas Industries, Inc. v. Radcliff Materials, Inc.*, 451 U.S. 630, 640 (1981), are so committed by the Constitution and laws of the United States to federal control that state law is pre-empted and replaced, where necessary, by federal law of a content prescribed (absent explicit statutory directive) by the courts—so-called "federal common law." See, *e.g., United States v. Kimbell Foods, Inc.*, 440 U.S. 715, 726–729 (1979); *Banco Nacional v. Sabbatino*, 376 U.S. 398, 426–427 (1964); *Clearfield Trust Co. v. United States*, 318 U.S. 363, 366–367 (1943); *D'Oench, Duhme & Co. v. FDIC*, 315 U.S. 447, 457–458 (1942).

The dispute in the present case borders upon two areas that we have found to involve such "uniquely federal interests." We have held that obligations to and rights of the United States under its contracts are governed exclusively by federal law. See, *e.g., United States v. Little Lake Misere Land Co.*, 412 U.S. 580, 592–594 (1973); *Clearfield Trust, supra*. The present case does not involve an obligation to the United States under its contract, but rather liability to third persons. That liability may be styled one in tort, but it arises out of performance of the contract—and traditionally has been regarded as sufficiently related to the contract that until 1962 Virginia would generally allow design defect suits only by the purchaser and those in privity with the seller. See *General Bronze Corp. v. Kostopulos*, 203 Va. 66, 69–70, 122 S. E. 2d 548, 551 (1961); see also Va. Code § 8.2-318 (1965) (eliminating privity requirement).

Another area that we have found to be of peculiarly federal concern, warranting the displacement of state law, is the civil liability of federal officials for actions taken in the course of their duty. We have held in many contexts that the scope of that liability is controlled by federal law. See, *e.g.*, *Westfall v. Erwin*, 484 U.S. 292, 295 (1988); *Howard v. Lyons*, [360 U.S. 593 (1959),] *supra*, at 597; *Bradley v. Fisher*, 13 Wall. 335 (1872). The present case involves an independent contractor performing its obligation under a procurement contract, rather than an official performing his duty as a federal employee, but there is obviously implicated the same interest in getting the Government's work done.

[T]he reasons for considering these closely related areas to be of "uniquely federal" interest apply as well to the civil liabilities arising out of the performance of federal procurement contracts. . . .

[I]t is plain that the Federal Government's interest in the procurement of equipment is implicated by suits such as the present one—even though the dispute is one between private parties. It is true that where "litigation is purely between private parties and does not touch the rights and duties of the United States," *Bank of America Nat. Trust & Sav. Assn. v. Parnell*, 352 U.S. 29, 33 (1956), federal law does not govern. Thus, for example, in *Miree v. DeKalb County*, 433 U.S. 25, 30 (1977), which involved the question whether certain private parties could sue as third-party beneficiaries to an agreement between a municipality and the Federal Aviation Administration, we found that state law was not displaced because "the operations of the United States in connection with FAA grants such as these . . . would [not] be burdened" by allowing state law to determine whether third-party beneficiaries could sue, and because "any federal interest in the outcome of the [dispute] before us '[was] far too speculative, far too remote a possibility to justify the application of federal law to transactions essentially of local concern.'" But the same is not true here. The imposition of liability on Government contractors will directly affect the terms of Government contracts: either the contractor will decline to manufacture the design specified by the Government, or it will raise its price. Either way, the interests of the United States will be directly affected.

That the procurement of equipment by the United States is an area of uniquely federal interest does not, however, end the inquiry. That merely establishes a necessary, not a sufficient, condition for the displacement of state law. Displacement will occur only where, as we have variously described, a "significant conflict" exists between an identifiable "federal policy or interest and the [operation] of state law," *Wallis* [*v. Pan American Petroleum Corp.*, 384 U.S. 63 (1966)], *supra*, or the application of state law would "frustrate specific objectives" of federal legislation, *Kimbell Foods*, 440 U.S., at 728. The conflict with federal policy need not be as sharp as that which must exist for ordinary pre-emption when Congress legislates "in a field which the States have traditionally occupied." . . . But conflict there must be. In some cases, for example where the federal interest requires a uniform rule, the entire body of state law applicable to the area conflicts and is replaced by federal rules. See, *e.g.*, *Clearfield Trust* (rights and obligations of United States with respect to commercial paper must be governed by uniform federal rule). In others, the conflict is more narrow, and only particular elements of state law are superseded. See, *e.g.*, *Little Lake Misere Land Co.* (even assuming state law should generally govern federal land acquisitions, particular state law at issue may not); *Howard v. Lyons* (state defamation law generally applicable to federal official, but federal privilege governs for statements made in the course of federal official's duties).

In *Miree*, the suit was not seeking to impose upon the person contracting with the Government a duty contrary to the duty imposed by the Government contract. Rather, it was the contractual duty *itself* that the private plaintiff (as third-party beneficiary) sought to enforce. Between *Miree* and the present case, it is easy to conceive of an intermediate situation, in which the duty sought to be imposed on the contractor is not identical to one assumed under the contract, but is also not contrary to any assumed. If, for example, the United States contracts for the purchase and installation of an air-conditioning unit, specifying the cooling capacity but not the precise manner of construction, a state law imposing upon the manufacturer of such units a duty of care to include a certain safety feature would not be a duty identical to anything promised [to] the Government, but neither would it be contrary. The contractor could comply with both its contractual obligations and the state-prescribed duty of care. No one suggests that state law would generally be preempted in this context.

The present case, however, is at the opposite extreme from *Miree*. Here the state-imposed duty of care that is the asserted basis of the contractor's liability (specifically, the duty to equip helicopters with the sort of escape-hatch mechanism petitioner claims was necessary) is precisely contrary to the duty imposed by the Government contract (the duty to manufacture and deliver helicopters with the sort of escape-hatch mechanism shown by the specifications). Even in this sort of situation, it would be unreasonable to say that there is always a "significant conflict" between the state law and a federal policy or interest. If, for example, a federal procurement officer orders, by model number, a quantity of stock helicopters that happen to be equipped with escape hatches opening outward, it is impossible to say that the Government has a significant interest in that particular feature. That would be scarcely more reasonable than saying that a private individual who orders such a craft by model number cannot sue for the manufacturer's negligence because he got precisely what he ordered.

. . .

There is . . . a statutory provision that demonstrates the potential for, and suggests the outlines of, "significant conflict" between federal interests and state law in the context of Government procurement. In the FTCA [Federal Tort Claims Act], Congress authorized damages to be recovered against the United States for harm caused by the negligent or wrongful conduct of Government employees, to the extent that a private person would be liable under the law of the place where the conduct occurred. 28 U.S.C. § 1346(b). It excepted from this consent to suit, however,

> "[a]ny claim . . . based upon the exercise or performance or the failure to exercise or perform a discretionary function or duty on the part of a federal agency or an employee of the Government, whether or not the discretion involved be abused." 28 U.S.C. § 2680(a).

We think that the selection of the appropriate design for military equipment to be used by our Armed Forces is assuredly a discretionary function within the meaning of this provision. It often involves not merely engineering analysis but judgment as to the balancing of many technical, military, and even social considerations, including specifically the trade-off between greater safety and greater combat effectiveness. And we are further of the view that permitting "second-guessing" of these judgments, through state tort suits against contractors would produce the same effect sought to be avoided by the FTCA exemption. The financial burden of judgments against the contractors would ultimately be passed through, substantially if not totally, to the United States itself, since defense contractors will predictably raise their prices to cover, or to insure against, contingent liability for the Government-ordered designs. To put the point differently: It makes little sense to insulate the Government against financial liability for the judgment that a particular feature of military equipment is necessary when the Government produces the equipment itself, but not when it contracts for the production. In sum, we are of the view that state law which holds Government contractors liable for design defects in military equipment does in some circumstances present a "significant conflict" with federal policy and must be displaced.

We agree with the scope of displacement adopted by the Fourth Circuit here, which is also that adopted by the Ninth Circuit [in an earlier case]. Liability for design defects in military equipment cannot be imposed, pursuant to state law, when (1) the United States approved reasonably precise specifications; (2) the equipment conformed to those specifications; and (3) the supplier warned the United States about the dangers in the use of the equipment that were known to the supplier but not to the United States. The first two of these conditions assure that the suit is within the area where the policy of the "discretionary function" would be frustrated—*i.e.*, they assure that the design feature in question was considered by a Government officer, and not merely by the contractor itself. The third condition is necessary because, in its absence, the displacement of state tort law would create some incentive for the manufacturer to withhold knowledge of risks, since conveying that knowledge might disrupt the contract but withholding it would produce no liability. We adopt this provision lest our effort to protect discretionary functions perversely impede them by cutting off information highly relevant to the discretionary decision.

. . .

[The Court vacated the judgment and remanded the case to the Fourth Circuit to consider whether the case should proceed to jury trial on the government contractor defense.]

JUSTICE BRENNAN, with whom JUSTICES MARSHALL and BLACKMUN join, dissenting.

. . .

. . . The Court—unelected and unaccountable to the people—has unabashedly stepped into the breach to legislate a rule denying Lt. Boyle's family the compensation that state law assures them. This time the injustice is of this Court's own making.

Worse yet, the injustice will extend far beyond the facts of this case, for the Court's newly discovered Government contractor defense is breathtakingly sweeping. It applies not only to military equipment like the CH-53D helicopter, but (so far as I can tell) to any made-to-order gadget that the Federal Government might purchase after previewing plans—from NASA's Challenger space shuttle to the Postal Service's old mail cars. The contractor may invoke the defense in suits brought not only by military personnel like Lt. Boyle, or Government employees, but by anyone injured by a Government contractor's negligent design, including, for example, the children who might have died had respondent's helicopter crashed on the beach. It applies even if the Government has not intentionally sacrificed safety for other interests like speed or efficiency, and, indeed, even if the equipment is not of a type that is typically considered dangerous; thus, the contractor who designs a Government building can invoke the defense when the elevator cable snaps or the walls collapse. And the defense is invocable regardless of how blatant or easily remedied the defect, so long as the contractor missed it and the specifications approved by the Government, however unreasonably dangerous, were "reasonably precise."

In my view, this Court lacks both authority and expertise to fashion such a rule, whether to protect the Treasury of the United States or the coffers of industry. Because I would leave that exercise of legislative power to Congress, where our Constitution places it, I would reverse the Court of Appeals and reinstate petitioner's jury award.

. . .

Here, as in *Miree*, *Parnell*, and *Wallis*, a Government contract governed by federal common law looms in the background. But here, too, the United States is not a party to the suit and the suit neither "touch[es] the rights and duties of the United States," nor has a "direct effect upon the United States or its Treasury." The relationship at issue is at best collateral to the Government contract. We have no greater power to displace state law governing the collateral relationship in the Government procurement realm than we had to dictate federal rules governing equally collateral relationships in the areas of aviation, Government-issued commercial paper, or federal lands.

That the Government might have to pay higher prices for what it orders if delivery in accordance with the contract exposes the seller to potential liability, does not distinguish this case. Each of the cases just discussed declined to extend the reach of federal common law despite the assertion of comparable interests that would have affected the terms of the Government contract—whether its price or its substance—just as "directly" (or indirectly). Third-party beneficiaries can sue under a county's contract with the FAA, for example, even though—as the Court's focus on the absence of "*direct* effect on the United States or its Treasury," (emphasis added), suggests—counties will likely pass on the costs to the Government in future contract negotiations. Similarly, we held that state law may govern the circumstances under which stolen federal bonds can be recovered, notwithstanding Parnell's argument that "the value of bonds to the first purchaser and hence their salability by the Government would be materially affected." As in each of the cases declining to extend the traditional reach of federal law of contracts beyond the rights and duties of the *Federal Government*, "any federal interest in the outcome of the question before us 'is far too speculative, far too remote a possibility to justify the application of federal law to transactions essentially of local concern.'"

[The opinion of JUSTICE STEVENS, dissenting, is omitted.]

Notes and Questions

1. Does *Boyle* stand for the proposition that federal common law may be employed whenever tort liability will be indirectly absorbed by the federal government? If not, when does *Boyle* permit federal common law?

2. What interest of the United States is harmed by imposing tort liability on a private contractor that provides equipment to the military? How is that interest harmed?

3. Of what significance to the Court was the Federal Tort Claims Act? In other words, why was that legislation relevant to the decision to adopt federal common law?

4. Under *Boyle*, what factors are assessed in determining whether to apply federal common law? How are the factors weighed?

In the following case, the Eastern District of New York applied federal common law to massive litigation arising from exposure of military personnel to a defoliant. Doing so allowed the court to process the sprawling litigation under a single substantive law. In the opinion below, the Second Circuit reversed, and held that federal common law did not apply. Note that the Second Circuit's decision was made 18 years *before* the Supreme Court's opinion in *Boyle*. It is nonetheless worthwhile because it discusses other relevant cases, including *Miree*. In reading it, consider whether *Boyle* strengthens the Second Circuit's rejection of federal common law.

In re "Agent Orange" Product Liability Litigation

United States Court of Appeals, Second Circuit
635 F.2d 987 (1980)

KEARSE, CIRCUIT JUDGE.

This appeal presents the question whether claims asserted by veterans of the United States armed forces against companies which supplied the United States government with chemicals that are alleged to have been contaminated and to have injured the veterans and their families, are governed by federal common law. Defendants-appellants Diamond Shamrock Corporation, Monsanto Company, Thompson-Hayward Chemical Company, Hercules Incorporated and the Dow Chemical Company were the manufacturers of various herbicides including "Agent Orange" (hereinafter collectively referred to as "Agent Orange") for use by the military as defoliants in the Vietnam War. The plaintiffs, veterans of that war and their families, allege that they have sustained various physical injuries by reason of the veterans' exposure to Agent Orange. Plaintiffs seek redress of those injuries under federal common law, and have invoked the "federal question" jurisdiction of the district court. 28 U.S.C. § 1331(a) (1976). Defendants contest the existence of a federal common law cause of action, and moved below to dismiss for lack of subject matter jurisdiction. The United States District Court for the Eastern District of New York, George C. Pratt, Judge, denied their motion. [The order was approved for interlocutory appellate review.]

We agree with defendants that there is no federal common law right of action under the circumstances of this litigation. Accordingly, we reverse.

I

The present litigation began in late 1978 and early 1979, when several individual veterans and their families commenced actions in the Northern District of Illinois and the Southern and Eastern Districts of New York, claiming injury from the veterans' exposure to Agent Orange and purporting to represent several classes of injured persons and persons allegedly "at risk" of injury. The plaintiffs in most of these actions were represented by the same attorney, who filed substantially identical complaints in all actions, naming the same defendant manufacturers. By order of the Judicial Panel on Multidistrict Litigation, thirteen such actions, involving thirty named plaintiffs, were transferred to the Eastern District of New York and assigned to Judge Pratt for coordinated or consolidated pretrial proceedings pursuant to 28 U.S.C. § 1407 (1976). Subsequently, additional actions were filed and were transferred to the Eastern District. It appears that there are presently more than 800 named plaintiffs in these proceedings.

[After various motions, the district judge entered his ruling on the third amended complaint, which is the subject of the appeal.]

A. The Third Amended Complaint

The basic thrust of the Complaint is relatively simple: defendants manufactured a "phenoxy herbicide," Agent Orange, for use by the military in Vietnam. The herbicide was allegedly contaminated with certain toxic organic chemicals, including 2,3,7,8-tetrachlorodibenzo-p-dioxin ("dioxin"), which plaintiffs describe as "one of the most toxic substances ever developed by man." The plaintiff veterans assert that they were exposed to Agent Orange, and thus to the dioxin it contained, while serving in Vietnam. They claim to have sustained various physical injuries, or to be "at risk" of such injuries, by reason of that exposure. Plaintiffs seek relief on a number of theories, including strict product liability, negligence, and breach of warranty.

What marks these proceedings as somewhat extraordinary are the size of the plaintiff class and the scope of the relief that is sought. Plaintiffs purport to represent the 2.4 million veterans who served as combat soldiers in Southeast Asia from 1962 through 1971, as well as most of the families or survivors of those veterans. Fifteen plaintiff subclasses are identified; many of these subclasses consist of persons who are "at risk" of, but have yet to sustain, various physical injuries. Plaintiffs have alleged that "the combined liquid assets of the "corporate defendants' will be insufficient to fully compensate the entire class of plaintiffs." Plaintiffs therefore seek, in addition to unspecified damages, a decree requiring defendants, upon a determination of liability, to establish

> a trust fund out of the current earnings of the defendants in the nature of a reserve against the claims of all the individual members of the plaintiff class to insure that the compensation of any group of individual plaintiffs will not impair the rights of those not before the Court at that time.

Plaintiffs also seek a permanent injunction against further manufacture of Agent Orange.

Defendants deny that there is any causal connection between exposure to Agent Orange and the injuries that plaintiffs claim to have sustained, and vigorously contest the propriety of the various remedial measures that plaintiffs seek to impose on them. This case, however, is still at the pleading stage, and for purposes of deciding the jurisdictional question before us, plaintiffs' factual allegations must be accepted as true.

B. The Decision of the District Court

Plaintiffs argue that federal common law should be applied to their claims principally because of the unique federal nature of the relationship between the soldier and his government, relying chiefly on *United States v. Standard Oil Co.*, 332 U.S. 301, 305 (1947) ("Perhaps no relation between the Government and a citizen is more distinctively federal in character than that between it and members of its armed forces."). They contend that this interest brings the case within the doctrine of *Clearfield Trust Co. v. United States*, 318 U.S. 363, 366 (1943), which held that, in order to ensure uniformity and certainty, "(t)he rights and duties of the United States on commercial paper which it issues are governed by federal rather than local law." Plaintiffs argue that the government similarly has an interest in having all of its veterans compensated by government contractors who manufactured or marketed Agent Orange, and that application of the respective state laws would impede recovery on a uniform basis.

The district court rejected the contention that *Clearfield Trust* stated the controlling principle, recognizing that the United States, a party to *Clearfield Trust*, is not party to the plaintiffs' claims here. Rather, the court recognized that since the present action involves only private parties, the federal common law issue is controlled by the principles set forth in *Miree v. DeKalb County*, 433 U.S. 25 (1977), and *Wallis v. Pan American Petroleum Corp.*, 384 U.S. 63 (1966). After reviewing the latter decisions, the district court applied a three-factor test to determine whether federal common law governs plaintiffs' claims:

> (1) the existence of a substantial federal interest in the outcome of a litigation; (2) the effect on this federal interest should state law be applied; and (3) the effect on state interests should state law be displaced by federal common law.

With respect to the first factor, the district court recognized two principal federal interests that may be affected by the present lawsuits: the federal government's interest in its relations with members of the armed forces, and its interest in its relations with suppliers of war materiel. As to the government's interest in the welfare of its veterans, the court stated that:

> Soldiers serving in the armed forces are government charges, entitled to government protection. Torts committed by war contractors against soldiers in action constitute "harms inflicted" on the soldiers and "interference" with the relationship between soldiers and the government. Such harms and interferences implicate federal interests identified in (*United States v. Standard Oil, supra*).

The court rejected defendants' contention that these interests were already protected by the Congressionally-enacted scheme of veterans' benefits, 38 U.S.C. § 310 et seq. (1976) . . . .

Finally, the court reasoned that because of the large number of veterans claiming injury, and the large potential liability of the five defendants, the foregoing federal interests were "substantial" for purposes of the federal common law analysis:

> The estimated number of involved veterans ranges from thousands to millions, and the estimated potential liability of the five war contractors ranges from millions to billions of dollars. As the number of veterans and the size of the claims against the war contractors increase so the federal interest in this litigation expands.

As to the government's interest in its relations with its military suppliers, the court referred to a number of "speculative" ways in which lawsuits such as the present ones might adversely affect that interest, pointing out that in response to any increase in their potential liability, military suppliers might raise their prices, attach conditions to the use of their products, or stop dealing with the government altogether.[6] The court concluded that

> government relations with war contractors might well be drastically altered by changes in the rules governing liability of war contractors to soldiers for injuries caused by inherently "dangerous" war materials.

Turning to the second part of its test, the court found that the federal interest it had identified would be adversely affected if the issues in these lawsuits were adjudicated under state law:

> Application of varying state laws would burden federal interests by creating uncertainty as to the rights of both veterans and war contractors. It would also be unfair in that essentially similar claims, involving veterans and war contractors identically situated in all relevant respects, would be treated differently under different state laws.

Finally, as to the third part of its test, the court determined that application of federal common law would not have any significant adverse impact on state interests. While noting that "(t)ort claims are traditionally matters for state law, which has developed comprehensive substantive and procedural rules to govern them," the court distinguished the instant tort actions, finding that

> state law has not considered the complex question of a war contractor's liability to soldiers injured by toxic chemicals subject to federal regulation while engaged in combat and serving abroad.

The court concluded:

> Because state law is no more or less developed as to such claims than federal common law, application of federal common law thereto would not significantly displace state law.

Having found substantial federal interests that would be adversely affected by application of state law to the instant claims, and having determined that there were no substantial state interests in having state law applied, the district court ruled that plaintiffs had stated valid causes of action under the federal common law. The court therefore held that it had subject matter jurisdiction over the case, and denied defendants' motion to dismiss. This appeal followed.

II

Both plaintiffs and defendants accept the three-part test that the district court applied to the federal common law issue, and for purposes of discussion we accept that framework. But, focusing our consideration chiefly on the first factor of the test, i.e., "the existence of a substantial federal interest in the outcome of the litigation,"

---

6. [Court's footnote #8] The court also noted that if defendants are eventually held liable for massive damages awards, the resulting blow to their financial health could have serious repercussions in the national economy.

we disagree with the district court's analysis and conclude that the court gave insufficient weight to the Supreme Court's repeated admonition that

> in deciding whether rules of federal common law should be fashioned, normally the guiding principle is that a significant conflict between some federal policy or interest and the use of state law in the premises must first be specifically shown. . . .

Wallis v. Pan American Petroleum Corp., supra, 384 U.S. at 68, *quoted with emphasis in Miree v. DeKalb County, supra*, 433 U.S. at 31, 97 S. Ct. at 2494. Principally we reject the district court's conclusion that there is an identifiable federal policy at stake in this litigation that warrants the creation of federal common law rules.[7]

In considering plaintiffs' contentions, it is essential to delineate precisely the relation of the United States to the claims here at issue. These claims are brought by former servicemen and their families against private manufacturers; they are not asserted by or against the United States, and they do not directly implicate the rights and duties of the United States. They are thus unlike the claims in *United States v. Standard Oil Co., supra*, in which the government brought suit to recover for its payments to a soldier injured as a result of the defendant's negligence, and *Clearfield Trust Co. v. United States, supra*, in which the government brought suit to enforce its rights in commercial paper issued by it. In each of those cases the government was a party seeking to enforce its own asserted rights, and analysis reveals two federal concerns which are inherent in such cases. First, the government has an interest in having uniform rules govern its rights and obligations. Second, the government has a substantive interest in the contents of those uniform rules. The first interest prizes uniformity for its own sake and is content-neutral; it does not dictate the substance of the federal common law rule to be applied. Thus, in *United States v. Standard Oil Co., supra*, the Court applied federal common law, recognizing the government's interest in uniformity, but refused to impose the liability argued for by the United States as the substance of that law.

The present litigation is fundamentally different from *Standard Oil* and *Clearfield Trust* with respect to both uniformity interest and substantive interest in the content of the rules to be applied. Since this litigation is between private parties and no substantial rights or duties of the government hinge on its outcome, there is no federal interest in uniformity for its own sake.[8] The fact that application of state law may produce a variety of results is of no moment. It is in the nature of a federal

7. [Court's footnote #11] Since we conclude that there is not now an identifiable federal policy, we need not reach the second and third factors of the test and speculate as to how state law, if it were already developed, would affect the federal policy if it were identifiable-or vice versa.

8. [Court's footnote #12] Compare *Bank of America Nat'l Trust & Sav. Ass'n v. Parnell*, 352 U.S. 29, 32–34 (1956), private litigation involving the issues of whether certain government bonds were "overdue" and whether the defendant had taken title to the bonds in good faith. The Court observed that the question of when a government bond is overdue is a matter of federal law, but held that questions as to a party's good faith are left to local law.

system that different states will apply different rules of law, based on their individual perceptions of what is in the best interests of their citizens. That alone is not grounds in private litigation for judicially creating an overriding federal law. Indeed, even where a federal statutory program governs the rights of private litigants and Congress has left gaps to be filled by the courts, uniformity is not prized for its own sake. For example, in *Auto Workers v. Hoosier Corp.*, 383 U.S. 696, 701–05 (1966), the Court dealt with a suit under § 301 of the National Labor Relations Act, to which federal common law applied. Yet in determining the timeliness of such suits, the Court ruled that the appropriate state statutes of limitations should apply, and refused to impose a uniform federal period of limitations....

The second fundamental difference between the present litigation and the *Clearfield Trust* type of case is that in the latter, the government's substantive interest in the litigation is essentially monothetic, in that it is concerned only with preserving the federal fisc, whereas here the government has two interests; and here the two interests have been placed in sharp contrast with one another. Thus, the government has an interest in the welfare of its veterans; they have given of themselves in the most fundamental way possible in the national interest. But the government also has an interest in the suppliers of its materiel; imposition, for example, of strict liability as contended for by plaintiffs would affect the government's ability to procure materiel without the exaction of significantly higher prices, or the attachment of onerous conditions, or the demand of indemnification or the like. As plaintiffs' counsel has observed, "this litigation will have a direct and lasting impact on the relationship between the federal government and war contractors... and between the federal government and veterans." (Letter dated October 21, 1980, V.J. Yannacone, Jr. to A. D. Fusaro.) It is obvious that the government is interested. But unlike a simple uniformity interest, neither the government's interest in its veterans nor its interest in its suppliers is content-neutral. Each interest will be furthered only if the federal rule of law to be applied favors that particular group.

The extent to which either group should be favored, and its welfare deemed "paramount," is preeminently a policy determination of the sort reserved in the first instance for Congress. The welfare of veterans and that of military suppliers are clearly federal concerns which Congress should appropriately consider in setting policy for the governance of the nation, and it is properly left to Congress in the first instance to strike the balance between the conflicting interests of the veterans and the contractors, and thereby identify federal policy. Although Congress has turned its attention to the Agent Orange problem,[9] it has not determined what the federal policy is with respect to the reconciliation of these two competing interests....

9. [Court's footnote #13] Congress has directed the Administrator of Veterans' Affairs to design and conduct an epidemiological study of veterans who were exposed to Agent Orange, and to report periodically to Congress until the study is completed. See Pub. L. No. 96–151, 96th Cong., 1st Sess. (1979); 38 U.S.C. § 219 note (Supp. 1980).

We conclude that in the present case, while the federal government has obvious interests in the welfare of the parties to the litigation, its interest in the outcome of the litigation, *i.e.*, in how the parties' welfares should be balanced, is as yet undetermined. The teaching of *Wallis* and *Miree* is that before federal common law rules should be fashioned, the use of state law must pose a threat to an "identifiable" federal policy. In the present litigation the federal policy is not yet identifiable. We conclude, therefore, that the district court erred in ruling that plaintiffs' claims were governed by federal common law. The order denying defendants' motion to dismiss for lack of subject matter jurisdiction is accordingly

Reversed.

FEINBERG, CHIEF JUDGE, dissenting.

This case presents us with a unique set of facts, parties, and pleadings. Many aspects of plaintiffs' case are troublesome, because plaintiffs seek unusual relief, both procedural and substantive, as to which I express no view. But the issue now before us is far narrower, and raises more familiar considerations. . . .

. . . [A]ll involved in this case . . . appear to agree that federal question jurisdiction depends upon whether a federal common law rule of product liability should be applied.

Looking . . . to *Miree* and *Wallis*, the first question we must answer is whether the federal government has a "substantial interest" in the outcome of this litigation. It is plain that this question must be answered affirmatively. As the Supreme Court observed in *United States v. Standard Oil Company*, 332 U.S. 301 (1947),

> Perhaps no relation between the Government and a citizen is more distinctively federal in character than that between it and members of its armed forces. To whatever extent state law may apply to govern the relations between soldiers or others in the armed forces and persons outside them or non-federal governmental agencies, the scope, nature, legal incidents and consequences of the relation between persons in service and the government are fundamentally derived from federal sources and governed by federal authority. So also we think are interferences with that relationship such as the facts of this case involve. For, as the Federal Government has the exclusive power to establish and define the relationship by virtue of its military and other powers, equally clearly it has power in execution of the same functions to protect the relation once formed from harms inflicted by others.

332 U.S. at 305–06 (footnotes omitted). This obviously federal relationship does not depend primarily upon any particular statute, but rather inheres in the federal government's exclusive capacity to wage war. . . .

The majority . . . concludes that because the government has arguably conflicting substantive interests in the outcome of the litigation, "the federal policy is not yet identifiable." The allegedly conflicting federal interests are in the welfare of veterans and in the welfare of suppliers of war materiel. But that the plaintiff veterans and the defendant contractors have opposing interests in this litigation hardly means that the paramount federal interest is somehow divided or self-contradictory. The United States has a clear interest in the protection of its soldiers from harm caused by defective war materiel. What other interests does the United States arguably have that might conflict with this clear interest? One such interest might be in seeing that defendants, as suppliers of war materiel, are treated fairly. But that interest cannot be said to conflict with the government's interest in the safety of its soldiers. Another such interest might be in preventing defendants from being driven to bankruptcy by large damage awards to Agent Orange plaintiffs, who have already made claims assertedly greater than defendants' combined liquid assets. This, I take it, is what the majority means by its reference to the federal interest in the "welfare" of defendants. But this interest lies in the future, and in the realm of speculation. . . .

Because I conclude that the district court does have jurisdiction over the case before us, I dissent from the opinion of the majority.

Notes and Questions

1. As noted before the opinion, *Agent Orange* was decided before the Supreme Court decided *Boyle*. Would *Boyle* have changed the result in *Agent Orange*?

2. One of the factors for determining whether to apply federal common law is the interest of the federal government in the outcome of the case. Can a relevant interest be shown when the United States is not a party to the case?

3. According to the dissent in *Agent Orange*, what interest did the United States have in the outcome of the litigation? Why did it justify the application of federal common law?

4. Some litigation, like *Agent Orange*, is truly national in scope: claimants are citizens of a substantial number of states and a judgment may well effect the national economy. Would these facts permit Congress to create a federal claim and prescribe the elements of that claim? The answer seems to be "yes" under the commerce power and the necessary and proper clause of the Constitution. *See, e.g.*, Kramer, *supra*, 71 N.Y.U. L. Rev. at 550 ("There is . . . a decent argument that the national character of the problems that give rise to complex litigation justifies preempting state law with uniform federal tort or contract law.") Yet the same characteristics will not justify a federal court's creation of federal common law. Why?

5. In *Kohr v. Allegheny Airlines, Inc.*, 504 F.2d 400, 403 (7th Cir. 1974), the Seventh Circuit held that the federal interest in regulating national airspace justified the creation of a federal common law rule of indemnity or contribution. If the court was right, why wouldn't the national interest in railroads have justified federal common law in *Erie* itself?

4. Federal Legislation and its Impact

We have noted the tension between the underlying premise that state law governs the choice of law inquiry and the desire to facilitate efficient packaging by finding that a single law governs related litigation. We also noted immediately above that Congress undoubtedly has broad power to legislate substantively concerning topics that often spawn complex litigation. It rarely has done so. By and large, it has left the fields of mass torts, contract, and fraud to the states. That being so, cases involving these fields historically may get into federal court only through diversity of citizenship jurisdiction under § 1332(a)(1).

Congress has, however, shown an interest in passing jurisdictional statutes aimed at complex litigation. In Chapter 2, sections C.3 and C.4, we saw that Congress has expanded access to the federal courts by permitting jurisdiction based upon "minimal" diversity with the Multiparty, Multiforum Trial Jurisdiction Act of 2002 (MMTJA) and the Class Action Fairness Act of 2005 (CAFA). So, while Congress shows little interest in creating substantive law that will affect complex litigation generally, it is willing to expand jurisdiction to facilitate it.

But what about choice of law doctrine? Could Congress impose a federal choice of law rule? Stated another way, could Congress obviate *Klaxon* by providing that in defined cases, the federal court will follow a prescribed standard for determining which state's law (or states' laws) will govern related litigation?

In 1994, the American Law Institute (ALI) proposed a series of statutes, which emanated from its Project on Complex Litigation. ALI, COMPLEX LITIGATION: STATUTORY RECOMMENDATIONS AND ANALYSIS (1994). The project included detailed provisions for consolidating complex litigation—involving numerous claimants in tort or contract—in a single court, either state or federal. Most noteworthy for present purposes was a proposal for a federal statute on choice of law in complex cases.[10] The underlying premise was "the driving intention of the Project to ensure

---

10. One example should suffice. Section 6.01 concerned choice of law in mass torts, and provided: (a) Except as provided in 6.04 through 6.06, in actions consolidated under 5.01 in which the parties assert the application of laws that are in material conflict, the transferee court shall choose the law governing the rights, liabilities, and defenses of the parties with respect to a tort claim by applying the criteria set forth in the following subsections with the objective of applying, to the extent feasible, a single state's law to all similar tort claims being asserted against a defendant. (b) In determining the governing law under subsection (a), the court shall consider the following factors for purposes of identifying each state having a policy that would be furthered by the application of its laws: (1) the place or places of injury; (2) the pace or places of the conduct causing the injury; and (3) the primary places of business or habitual residences of the plaintiffs and defendants. (c) If, in analyzing the factors set forth in subsection (b), the court finds that only one state has a policy that would be furthered by the application of its law, that state's law shall govern. If more than one state has a policy that would be furthered by the application of its law, the court shall choose the applicable law from among the laws of the interested states under the following rules: (1) If the place of injury and the place of the conduct causing the injury are in the same state, that's state's law governs. (2) If subsection (c)(1) does not apply but all the plaintiffs habitually reside or their primary places of business in the same state, and a defendant has its primary place

that one state's law will apply to common issues, notwithstanding the fact that the involved litigants may hail from all fifty states as well as foreign nations, and regardless of the fact that many litigants may have no contact at all with the state whose law would apply. . . ." Fred I. Williams, *The Complex Litigation Project's Choice of Law Rules for Mass Torts and How to Escape Them*, 1995 B.Y.U. L. REV. 1081, 1082.

The ALI proposal on choice of law generally was not well received. On the specifics, one scholar concluded that the principal provision "lays out a sequence of mechanical, territorial rules that tell submissive judges who wins and how to write the opinion. This part of the section reads like assembly instructions for a moderately complicated child's toy. It is so rule-bound that it should delight a judge too busy or too lazy to think about the conflicts issue in his case." Shreve, *supra*, 54 LA. L. REV. at 1147. More broadly, another leading commentator lamented, "the Institute's proposals are troubling because they subvert basic *Erie* doctrine in garden-variety diversity cases, blithely endorse vertical forum shopping, and inadequately justify a federalized regime in mass-tort cases." Linda S. Mullenix, *Federalizing Choice of Law for Mass-Tort Litigation*, 70 TEX. L. REV. 1623, 1630 (1992) (Professor Mullenix reviewed an earlier draft of the ALI proposal).

Although the ALI Complex Litigation Project had its supporters and its choice of law provisions represented a valiant effort to wrestle with a thorny problem, ultimately it had no impact. Congress never seriously considered enacting any part of the Project.

---

of business or habitually resides in that state that state's law governs the claims with the respect to that defendant. Plaintiffs shall be considered as sharing a common habitual residence or primary place of business if they are located in states whose laws are not in material conflict. (3) If neither subsection (c)(1) nor (c)(2) applies, but all of the plaintiffs habitually reside or have their primary places of business in the same state, and that state also is the place of injury, then that state's law governs. Plaintiffs shall be considered as sharing a common habitual residence or primary place of business if they are located in states whose laws are not in material conflict. (4) In all other cases, the law of the state were the conduct causing the injury occurred governs. When conduct occurred in more than one state, the court shall choose the law of the conduct state that has the most significant relationship to the occurrence. (d) When necessary to avoid unfair surprise or arbitrary results, the transferee court may choose the applicable law on the basis of additional factors that reflect the regulatory policies and legitimate interests of a particular state not otherwise identified under subsection (b), or it may depart from the order of preferences for selecting the governing law prescribed by subsection (c). (e) If the court determines that the application of a single state's law to all elements of the claims pending against a defendant would be inappropriate, it may divide the actions into subgroups of claims, issues, or parties to foster consolidated treatment under 3.01, and allow more that one state's law to be applied. The court also may determine that only certain claims or issues involving one or more of the parties should be governed by the law chosen by the application of the rules in subsection (c), and that other claims or parties should be remanded to the transferor courts for individual treatment under the laws normally applicable in those courts, in either instance, the court may exercise its authority under 3.06 (c) to sever, transfer, or remand issues or claims for treatment consistent with its determination. The proposal included similarly detailed provisions for mass contract cases in which the parties had executed a law selection clause (§ 6.02), mass contract cases in which the parties had not agreed on applicable law (§ 6.03), statute of limitations (§ 6.04), recovery of monetary relief (§ 6.05), and punitive damages (§ 6.06).

Perhaps the difficulties encountered by the ALI project in drafting a choice of law provision dissuaded Congress from the effort. Although there were efforts to include such a provision in both the MMTJA and CAFA, neither Act includes such a statute. *See* David Marcus, Erie, *the Class Action Fairness Act, and Some Federalism Implications of Diversity Jurisdiction*, 48 Wm. & Mary L. Rev. 1247, 1308–1310 (2007) (discussing effort to include choice of law provision in CAFA).

Indeed, legislative history of CAFA makes plain that "[t]he Act does not change the application of the *Erie* Doctrine, which requires federal courts to apply the substantive law dictated by applicable choice-of-law principles in actions arising under diversity jurisdiction." S.Rep. No. 109–14, at 49 (2005), *reprinted at* 2005 U.S.C.C.A.N. 3, 46. Thus, "[i]n entrusting class action litigation to the federal courts without accompanying federal substantive law or federal choice of law principles, Congress has allowed the choice of law consequences to fall where they may." Silberman, *supra*, 156 U. Pa. L. Rev. at 2031.

Despite the seeming clarity on this point, two scholars have argued that federal courts are free to ignore *Klaxon* in some instances in cases brought under CAFA. First, Professor Issacharoff concluded that in CAFA cases involving a "national market," courts are not required to apply *Klaxon*. Samuel Issacharoff, *Settled Expectations in a World of Unsettled Law: Choice of Law After the Class Action Fairness* Act, 106 Colum. L. Rev. 1839 (2006). He concluded that *Klaxon* is not constitutionally mandated, but was based upon policy considerations from *Erie*. *Id.* at 1851–1857.[11]

With *Klaxon* disarmed to this extent, Professor Issacharoff continued: "Building on the jurisdictional basis of CAFA, it is possible to fashion a presumptive baseline rule for national market conduct that transcends the regulatory reach of any particular state. The underlying principle is extraordinarily simple: Any actor who engages in nationwide economic activity must be accountable to one single rule of readily discernible substantive law when challenged on the basis of its nationwide activity." *Id.* at 1867. His default rule is the choice of law doctrine of the defendant's home state.

Professor Nagareda argued that CAFA has essentially placed all nationwide class actions in federal court. If that is so, he asked, why would the federal courts, despite CAFA, not develop distinctively federal choice of law rules? After all, ignoring *Klaxon* and forging a different choice of law doctrine will not create a lack of uniformity between federal and state courts—for the simple reason that state courts do not hear nationwide class actions. Richard A. Nagareda, *Bootstrapping in Choice of Law After the Class Action Fairness Act*, 74 U.M.K.C. L. Rev. 661, 683–684 (2006). *See also* Richard A. Nagareda, *Class Settlement Pressure, Class-Wide Arbitration, and CAFA*, 106 Colum. L. Rev. 1872 (2006) (CAFA "might exercise 'influence' [as the Seventh

11. Professor Burbank agrees that the issue of whether *Klaxon* is based in the Constitution should at least be reassessed. Stephen B. Burbank, *Aggregation on the Couch: The Strategic Use of Ambiguity and Hypocrisy*, 106 Colum. L. Rev. 1924, 1938 (2006).

Amendment did in *Byrd*] here in such a way as to make divergence on grounds of aggregation, rather than forum, the thing to be avoided."); Linda Silberman, *supra*, 156 U. Pa. L. Rev. 2001 (suggesting jettisoning of *Klaxon* in favor of a federal choice of law rule).

While we are thinking of legislative solutions, why should Congress not pass substantive tort laws for use in "national market" and other interstate cases? *See* Mullenix, *supra*, 70 Tex. L. Rev. at 1629 ("although every law reform group that has considered the problems of mass-tort litigation has characterized this litigation as constituting a set of legal problems of national scope, the reformers uniformly have stopped short of federalizing substantive tort law."). Such legislation could undoubtedly be based upon Congress's power over interstate commerce. Would that power include authority to prescribe choice of law rules for interstate tort cases? Presumably, the answer is yes. After all, if it has the greater power to prescribe rules of decisions, it must have the lesser power to direct a court to apply the law of a particular jurisdiction.

Remember, though, that MMTJA and CAFA were not passed on the basis of the commerce power, but under the grant of diversity of citizenship jurisdiction in Article III. Does the constitutional grant of diversity of citizenship jurisdiction in Article III empower Congress to enact laws like MMTJA and CAFA? Professor Floyd has argued that the underlying justification of diversity jurisdiction—avoiding the fear of local bias in state courts—cannot be used "to achieve judicial and litigant economy and consistent outcome between federal and state litigation arising from the same events or transactions." C. Douglas Floyd, *The Limits of Minimal Diversity*, 55 Hastings L.J. 613, 616 (2004). Would a federal choice of law statute for interstate tort cases serve the purpose of diversity jurisdiction?

Chapter 5

Judicial Management and Control of the Pretrial Procedure

A. Introduction

The litigation process can be long and expensive. Although movies and television shows focus on trial because it holds great potential for drama, trial is the tip of the litigation iceberg. In the real world, very few cases go to trial. Most of the work litigators do is pretrial litigation. (This is why law firms that once had "trial" departments now have "litigation" departments.) Indeed, issues we have already addressed in this book—whether the case is in the right court, how many parties and claims are asserted, whether overlapping cases can be coordinated—are usually determined long before a case goes to trial. Similarly, several topics to be addressed in succeeding chapters deal with pretrial events, including appointment of lead counsel, discovery, and disposition on motion.

In this chapter, we focus on the role of the court in pretrial litigation. This role has changed over time. You will remember from Civil Procedure that American courts embrace the "adversary system." Under this model, each litigant presents its case vigorously, on the theory that this clash of self-interested combatants will hone the issues, enhance the possibility of finding the truth, and reach a just result. The adversary system envisions a largely passive judge. The parties, and not the court, are responsible for initiating and developing the case, framing the issues, discovering the evidence and presenting it at trial. In theory, the judge is *reactive*. She is a neutral umpire, called into action when a party asks her to make an order, such as a motion to dismiss, to transfer a case to another venue, or to strike a pleading.[1]

While American courts probably have never been *wholly* reactive, there is no question today that judges have assumed an active role in *managing cases*, rather than simply reacting to the parties' requests. "The once prevalent view that the only appropriate role for judges is essentially passive has been largely replaced by the belief that the judiciary must assume a major responsibility both for the fairness and the efficiency of all stages of civil litigation, and that in many cases courts can

---

1. Not all judicial systems envision such a passive judge. In most of continental Europe, for example, the courts follow an "inquisitorial" model, in which the judge is expected to make an independent investigation into the merits of the case. She routinely takes charge of the case in a way that American lawyers traditionally would have found overly intrusive.

meet this responsibility only by dynamic, active involvement in the pretrial process from shortly after its inception." 3 MOORE'S FEDERAL PRACTICE § 16.03 (3d ed. 2018). This chapter addresses the tools of judicial case management and some of its ramifications.

What spawned this modern view of judicial engagement and oversight of litigation? One factor is an increase in the number of cases. There is a general sense that there was a "litigation explosion" in the latter part of the twentieth century, driven by various factors. In the 1960s, the Supreme Court and Congress recognized new civil rights and embraced the notion that private civil litigation was an appropriate way to enforce the law. Increased centralization of the economy meant that a single defective product or fraudulent statement could affect thousands of people. Into the new century, the number of cases filed per federal district judge has tended to increase year after year.

In addition, Congress has expanded federal subject matter jurisdiction both on the civil and criminal sides. Remember from Chapter 3, for example, that Congress passed the Multiparty, Multiforum Trial Jurisdiction Act in 2002 and the Class Action Fairness Act in 2005. At the same time, Congress has been reluctant to increase the number of federal judges. One reason for increased judicial control, then, is to achieve efficiency: hands-on management by the judge may keep the case moving and avoid backlog.

Another catalyst is the role courts have been required to play in some complex litigation, particularly the class action. As discussed in Chapters 6 and 7, every class case presents potential conflicts of interest between class counsel and the class members. The reaction to this potential conflict was to put the judge in the position of ensuring that class members' interests are protected. Under Rule 23(e), as we saw, the court must assess whether a proposed settlement or dismissal of class claims is fair.

Whatever the causes, there is no doubt that we are in an era of what Professor Resnik has called "managerial judging." Judith Resnik, *Managerial Judges*, 96 HARV. L. REV. 374 (1982). The Administrative Office of the United States Courts requires federal judges to file detailed reports on cases and their resolution, which may foster the perception that judges' jobs have become bureaucratic, increasingly aimed at keeping the cases moving through the system. This managerial role might "be teaching judges to value their statistics, such as the number of case dispositions, more than they value the quality of their dispositions." *Id.* at 380.

In section B, we will discuss the principal mechanisms by which federal district judges manage the pretrial phase of litigation. The focus will be on Rule 16, which requires early court involvement and imposes significant burdens on the parties in the first months of a case. Until 1983, there was debate over whether courts might use their oversight function to facilitate settlement. Since then, however, it has become clear they may, which raises the question of how far a judge can go in urging compromise. Sections C and D address two ramifications of increased judicial management. First, to what extent can federal judges delegate judicial functions? The pressure to dispose of cases creates an incentive to delegate judicial tasks to magistrate judges and masters. At some point, however, delegation can become abdication, so the courts must ensure that they retain ultimate decision-making authority. Second, judges who are actively engaged in case management may be exposed to matters not filtered by the rules of evidence. This may increase the possibility of claims that they have lost their impartiality, and thus should be disqualified from the case. Finally, section E reviews a panoply of sanctions available to enforce court orders regarding case management.

B. Overview of Pretrial Judicial Management, Including Alternative Dispute Resolution and Fostering Settlement

Various Federal Rules envision active judicial pretrial management. Rule 23(g), as we will see in Chapter 6, requires the judge to appoint qualified class counsel for a certified class action. Rule 37 calls on the judge to enforce the discovery provisions. The principal tool for present purposes, however, is Rule 16. Before addressing it in detail, consider the following discussion of it.

> The current version of Rule 16 clearly reflects the view that in most cases judges cannot leave all of the responsibility for the timing and content of the case development process with the lawyers and litigants. Instead, the Rule is based on the premise that the judiciary must serve as the critical source of discipline in the system. After considering the inputs and needs of the parties, it is the court's responsibility to ensure that each case is positioned as quickly and as efficiently as possible for disposition. Toward this end, it is the court's responsibility to fix the deadlines for all the major pretrial events and for the trial, just as it is the court's responsibility to fix the fundamental shape and direction of pretrial activity. This philosophy is manifest in the key phrases through which the objectives of Rule 16 are articulated in its first paragraph: "expediting disposition," "establishing early and continuing control," "discouraging wasteful pretrial activities," "improving the quality of the trial," and "facilitating settlement."
>
> Two major underpinnings appear to support this philosophy. The first is the notion that, if the judiciary does not establish early and continuing control of the pretrial process, at least in most mainstream cases, several negative consequences are likely: instead of being well-focused and efficient, the case development process will meander, communication across party lines will be slow and oblique, unnecessary work will be done and unnecessary costs will be incurred, adversarial friction will intensify, opportunities for early settlement will be missed, the time that elapses before disposition is reached will be considerably and unjustifiably extended, and justice (meaning the product of reliable application of the law to all the truly pertinent

> evidence) will be threatened or compromised. Thus, one of the fundamental premises of the modern version of Rule 16 is that if the pretrial system that is established through the other rules (pleading, discovery, motions) is left to adversarial self-execution, that pretrial system too often will fail.
>
> Although unnecessary cost and unjustifiable delay are the forms of system failure that Rule 16 is most commonly associated with attacking, many of the Rule's provisions and much of its administration are informed by the overriding goal of securing justice on the merits. Since 1938, one of the principal purposes of the Rule has been to reduce the likelihood that the outcome of civil litigation would turn on procedural subtlety or tactical advantage. The Rule as originally crafted was designed, in part, to encourage better preparation for and to reduce surprise at trial, as well as to thwart the practice of filing motions at the last pretrial minute, either to cause delay or to distract and confuse an opponent or the court. One reason the current version of Rule 16 encourages intellectually assertive intervention by judges *throughout the pretrial period* is to reduce the room for parties to gain unfair advantage by obscuring issues, blocking efficient access to the most important evidence, trying to catch an opponent by surprise with new theories or information unveiled at the last minute, or forcing an opponent to spend time and resources on unproductive, distracting undertakings. Thus, a key goal of modern case management is to promote justice by controlling the ill-effects of adversarial excesses.
>
> The second major underpinning of the current version of Rule 16 is the assumption that precious judicial resources are more effectively spent in active case management than in the more passive traditional forms of presiding at trial and ruling on motions. By expending a modest amount of time on management activity in the earlier stages of litigation, judges will save greater time that they would otherwise be forced to spend ruling on motions and presiding over trials. Under this theory, a judge who is intellectually active and wise can help parties identify early what really separates them—and can then steer the parties toward efficient, relatively frictionless acquisition of the information that will enable them either to settle their case or to present it promptly for disposition by motion.

3 Moore's Federal Practice § 16.03 (3d ed. 2018).

Rule 16 does not operate in a vacuum. Much of its timing dovetails with events addressed by Rule 26. Rule 26(a)(1) requires parties to disclose certain information to the other parties, and Rule 26(f) requires parties or their lawyers to confer very early in the case. It is important to understand the system set up by Rules 16 and 26 for early and vigorous action by the parties and oversight by the court.

The driving factor is Rule 16(b)(2), which requires the court to enter a scheduling order, generally within 90 days after the defendants are served with process.

Under Rule 16(b)(3)(A), this order must set time limits for joinder of other parties, amending pleadings, filing motions, and—importantly—for the completion of discovery. It is a roadmap of the litigation—of how the parties will spend the months or years that pass between now and trial. In other words, the parties and the court must be in a position to set these cut-offs within three or four months after the case is filed.

Now look at Rule 26(f)(1). It requires that the parties confer at least 21 days before the scheduling order is due. Rule 26(f)(2) imposes significant responsibilities for that conference. The purpose of the meeting is to "consider the nature and basis of their claims and defenses and the possibilities for a prompt settling or resolving of the case; make or arrange for the disclosures required by Rule 26(a)(1); discuss any issues about preserving discoverable information; and develop a proposed discovery plan." Notice the early engagement of settlement discussions.

Notice also the need to develop a discovery plan. Within 14 days after the Rule 26(f) conference, the parties must do two more things. First, they file with the court a detailed written discovery plan. The discussion of discovery started at the Rule 26(f) conference must result in a written product for the judge within two weeks. She will use this to set discovery cut-offs in her scheduling order. Second, each party must serve on all other parties their required disclosures under Rule 26(a)(1).

This is a rigorous schedule. Not only is the court actively involved early in the case, but the parties are required to "front-load" the case, meaning that the parties and counsel have a great deal to do early in the case. The days of filing a case and sitting around waiting for something to happen are long gone.

The original version of Rule 16, promulgated in 1938, was based upon the assumption that there would be only one pretrial conference. It would take place shortly before the start of trial—certainly after completion of discovery—and was aimed at streamlining trial itself. (That purpose is now reflected in Rule 16(e).) Today, however, Rule 16 permits the court to hold multiple pretrial conferences, for any of the purposes set forth in Rule 16(a). Rule 16(c)(2) lists no fewer than 16 topics which may be considered at any pretrial conference. Multiple conferences are commonplace in complex cases.

Notably, Rule 16(a)(5) allows conferences to "facilitat[e] settlement" and Rule 16(c)(2)(I) states that "settling the case" is a proper topic. Until 1983, there was substantial debate about whether the court should be engaged actively in facilitating settlement. The issue is now settled, though the debate is not. Professor Molot has questioned the propriety of case management as a judicial goal at all, noting that it is not a traditional judicial role and that it is thus a relatively standardless exercise. Particularly when it comes to fostering settlement, he notes "[w]hen a judge calls parties into his or her chambers to urge a settlement, his or her actions bear almost no resemblance to the traditional judicial role. . . . There are no legal standards to govern judicial conduct in settlement negotiations. And there generally is no appellate review either of the judge's tactics or the judge's views regarding the merits of the case." Jonathan Molot, *An Old Judicial Role for a New Litigation Era*, 113 YALE L.J. 27, 43 (2003).

Read Rule 16(a), (b), (c), and (f) and Rules 26(a) and (f), and address the following.

Notes and Questions

1. To what extent is Rule 16 based upon lack of faith in lawyers? Or is it lack of faith in the adversary system? Or is it both?

2. Rule 16(a) addresses pretrial conferences. Rule 16(b) addresses scheduling orders. Which, if either, is required in most cases? In what types of cases is it (or are they) not required?

3. Does Rule 16 give the judge flexibility to treat cases differently, or does it impose a one-size-fits-all mentality? What provisions of Rule 16 convince you of your view?

4. Rules 16 and 26 impose great burdens on counsel in the early months of a case. Defense lawyers generally bill by the hour. The early activity can result in significant bills to the client, which may lead the client to consider settlement. Plaintiffs' lawyers generally bill on a contingent fee basis. As they invest more time in the case (without payment), they may have an incentive to consider settlement, and the realization of some recovery for the hard work.

5. Litigating in federal court requires more than mastery of the Federal Rules of Civil Procedure. Each federal district has its own set of Local Rules, which complement the Federal Rules. Local Rules differ from court to court. In some districts, the Local Rules may exceed 100 pages; in others, they may comprise a fraction of that. Moreover, each individual judge within a district may promulgate her own provisions for litigation in her court. In theory, Local Rules and an individual judge's rules do not contradict the Federal Rules. Usually, they add specific requirements not addressed by the Federal Rules.

6. One thing to watch for in Local Rules is a provision for alternative dispute resolution (ADR). In the 1990s, Congress invited districts to experiment with provisions that might engage ADR. The principal forms of ADR are arbitration and mediation. Detailed consideration of these is beyond our scope, but we should understand the basics. What we are discussing here is "court annexed" ADR—that is, ADR implemented by Local Rules. Beyond this, parties generally are free to enter arbitration agreements, which are contractual provisions to submit disputes to arbitration. The Federal Arbitration Act, aspects of which we discuss in Chapters 6 and 9, expresses a strong national policy of enforcing such arbitration agreements.

Arbitration (whether contractual or court-annexed), like litigation, is usually a zero-sum game, so there will be a winner and a loser. The parties present their evidence before an arbitrator (or panel of arbitrators), and the rules of evidence do not apply (unless the parties agree that they do). As usually addressed in Local Rules in federal courts, the arbitration decision will become a final judgment unless one of the parties rejects it, in which case the dispute goes to trial. (This is quite different from contractual arbitration, in which the parties generally are not free to go to trial, and in which there is limited judicial review of the arbitration decision.) The arbitration decision may be a "reality check" that the parties may accept or use as the basis for settlement talks.

Mediation, in contrast, is not a zero-sum game. Here, a third party tries to help the parties reach a resolution, usually requiring a little give and take from all sides. Local Rules may funnel certain types of cases into arbitration or mediation. Again, there is great variety from district to district.

It has always been true that the majority of cases will be settled without going to trial. The percentage of such cases has been on the rise in recent years, so that now fewer than two percent of cases filed in federal court will go to trial. Sometimes the parties reach settlement terms on their own. (Remember that the Rule 26(f) conference expressly requires the parties to consider the prospect of settlement.) But we have seen that Rule 16 supports the court's facilitation of settlement. What happens if a party or lawyer fails to appear or to participate meaningfully in such efforts (or, for that matter, anything the court orders under Rule 16)? Read Rule 16(f) closely. Notice the broad range of sanctions available for enforcing case management orders. These include not just monetary sanctions but "merits" sanctions: orders that may (or will) affect the outcome of the case itself. Rule 16(f) incorporates merits sanctions found in Rule 37(d), which involves failure to abide by discovery provisions. The following case involves Local Rules, ADR, merits sanctions, and a Hall of Fame football coach.

Switzer v. Much, Shelist, Freed, Denenberg, Ament, Bell & Rubenstein, P.C.

United States District Court for the Western District of Oklahoma
214 F.R.D. 682 (2003)

HEATON, DISTRICT JUDGE.

Following the nonappearance of representatives of the defendant and its insurer at the court-ordered settlement conference in this case, Magistrate Judge Argo conducted a hearing addressing potential sanctions. [Reference of matters to magistrate judges is addressed in section C of this chapter.] On December 20, 2002, Judge Argo submitted his Report and Recommendation, finding that defendant had violated the local rules and the prior orders of this Court and that significant sanctions were warranted, and recommending that, as an appropriate sanction, defendant be precluded from defending against plaintiffs' claims on the issue of liability other than through cross-examination of plaintiffs' witnesses. Defendant would, however, be allowed to present witnesses regarding damages. Defendant has filed its objection to the Report ("Defendant's Objection" hereafter) and plaintiffs have responded. [Here, the district judge reviews the Report and Recommendation of the magistrate judge; we will discuss this procedure in section C below.]

. . . [T]he Court concurs in the Magistrate Judge's conclusion that defendant's conduct violated Court rules and orders and that substantial sanctions are warranted. However, the Court also concludes that sanctions different from those proposed by Judge Argo best fit the circumstances presented here.

BACKGROUND

. . .

At the March 5, 2002, scheduling conference, the Court ordered this case to mediation. The scheduling order directed that the mediation occur by June 1, 2002. That date was subsequently extended to August 1, 2002 [and then again to November 15, 2002.] When . . . the Court granted various extensions of the deadlines, including that for the mediation, [it] included the following language in the revised scheduling order:

> This case was ordered to mediation by August 1, 2002. Both parties are admonished that an order for mediation is just that—an order. It is not a suggestion to be ignored at will.

. . . Judge Argo heard testimony as to the circumstances surrounding the missed deadline and concluded it was principally defendant's lack of diligence which led to noncompliance with the order.

On November 21, 2002, the Court directed the parties to file a report as to the mediation, stating its date, the identity of the mediator and the results. From the information included in plaintiffs' response, the Court learned the mediation had occurred, but also concluded defendant might have violated the applicable rules regarding attendance. [Local Rule] 16.3 Supp. § 3.3(a). The Court ordered defendant to show cause why it should not be sanctioned for noncompliance with those requirements. The defendant's response made clear it had violated the rules in that it did not have a client representative present, did not have the insurer present, and its lead counsel did not attend. In its subsequent order, the Court explained at some length the basis for the attendance requirements at mediation conferences and sanctioned defendant for its noncompliance, imposing monetary sanctions of $1120.

The Court had previously ordered the case to a judicial settlement conference pursuant to the local court rules. [Local Rule] 16.2. That conference was to occur on December 18, 2002. Again, defendant failed to appear. . . .

DISCUSSION

It is clear that defendant violated the applicable rules and this Court's order. The local rules require the attendance of the lead attorney who will try the case, the parties or, in the case of a corporation, a representative of the party having full settlement authority, and "other interested entities" such as insurers. [Local Rule] 16.2(c). Here, no one but counsel appeared for defendant.

Defendant argues that the local rule is ambiguous and should be interpreted as defendant's counsel apparently interpreted it, to the effect that the insurer's representative may also represent the corporate party. That interpretation is incorrect. Both the structure and express terms of the rule make clear that both a representative of the party and a representative of any insurer involved are expected to attend. The order referring the case to settlement conference is even more explicit in its requirements for party presence, involvement, and settlement authority, separate from those requiring the attendance of an insurer representative with full settlement authority. Of course the discussion is somewhat academic in the present context, as defendant had neither a party representative nor an insurer representative present.

. . .

Defendant argues that the Court's local rules are invalid insofar as they purport to direct the attendance of a non-party—here, the insurer—at a settlement conference. If the present circumstances involved an effort to hold the insurer in contempt or to otherwise impose monetary liability directly on the insurer, defendant's argument might have both application and merit. In the present circumstances, it does not. The matter now before the Court involves sanctions against defendant, a party to the action. While the insurer has an unmistakable financial interest in minimizing the exposure of its insured to liability, and hence has a strong incentive to attend and otherwise comply with orders regarding settlement conferences, the question of whether the Court might directly order a non-party insurer to do something or mete out penalties for its failure to comply is simply not before the Court. Defendant's argument therefore has no application to the present controversy.

Defendant also argues the Court's settlement procedures may be invalid due to inconsistency with the provisions of Fed. R. Civ. P. 16(c)[(1)]. It is unclear whether defendant is suggesting Rule 16(c)[(1)] authorizes a court to require only a represented party's lawyer to be present (i.e. not the party itself) or whether it is suggesting Rule 16(c)[(1)] confers a right on the party to elect to participate in person or by phone. Neither suggestion has merit. The rule explicitly states the court may, where appropriate, order "a party or its representative" to be present. That result does not appear to be different from what a court has the inherent power to do anyway. Further, the plain import of the rule is to give the court, not the party, the option of requiring attendance either by phone or in person.

In short, there is no question the Court's orders and the local rules were violated. The question thus becomes whether Judge Argo properly recommended sanctions and, if so, what the appropriate sanctions are.

The Court fully concurs in Judge Argo's conclusion that sanctions are warranted and that they should be severe and substantial. The described pattern of events—repetitive violations of the Court's rules and orders—warrants a substantial sanction. If this case involved merely an isolated instance of someone forgetting a meeting or misinterpreting a rule, the result would be different. However, that is not what these facts present. Here, defendant was warned via admonishment to observe the Court's orders. It was warned again, by way of monetary sanctions, about its noncompliance with the attendance rules. Against that backdrop, it violated substantially the same rules yet again.

Magistrate Judge Argo concluded, and the Court concurs, that the facts reflect that "Defendant has consistently displayed an arrogant attitude and disregard for this Court's scheduling orders." It is apparent from (among other things) counsel's comments at the sanctions hearing that it viewed settlement discussions in this case as useless and was uninterested in participating in them. Its repetitive violations reflect the same attitude. The defendant's Objection to Judge Argo's recommendations does nothing to dispel, and indeed continues, the pattern of arrogance.

Although the Court views Judge Argo's Report as a measured and thorough analysis of, and reaction to, the circumstances, defendant elects to characterize Judge Argo as "incensed," acting with "rancor," "acute indignation," "wrath," "fury," and as being "intolerant of minor inconveniences."[2] Further, defendant couples its hyperbolic characterizations with thinly veiled suggestions of bias and partiality on the Judge's part. Defendant's characterizations of Judge Argo's conduct and Report are plainly inconsistent with what the record reflects.

. . .

In sum, the Magistrate Judge's conclusion that defendant's conduct warrants substantial sanctions is fully supported by the record and one with which the Court is in full accord.

NATURE OF THE SANCTIONS

. . .

In determining the appropriate sanction, a number of factors guide the court's exercise of discretion. In deciding whether dismissal with prejudice is warranted, the Tenth Circuit has identified these factors as guiding a court's discretion: (1) the degree of actual prejudice to the opposing party, (2) the amount of interference with the judicial process, and (3) the culpability of the litigant. *Hancock v. City of Oklahoma City*, 857 F.2d 1394 (10th Cir. 1988); *Meade v. Grubbs*, 841 F.2d 1512 (10th Cir. 1988). Later cases identify additional factors to consider, including whether the court warned the party in advance that sanctions for noncompliance would result and the efficacy of lesser sanctions. *Jones v. Thompson*, 996 F.2d 261 (10th Cir. 1993); *Ehrenhaus v. Reynolds*, 965 F.2d 916 (10th Cir. 1992). These standards are generally applicable here, though applied to a defendant and hence involve something other than dismissal of the case. Of course, these standards must be considered in the context of

2. [Court's footnote #11] The latter phrase appears in connection with perhaps the most obvious manifestation of arrogance in Defendant's Objection. Judge Argo noted Mr. King, lead counsel for defendant, was twenty minutes late for the conference and had not called to advise he would be late or state the reason therefore, and that the conference was delayed as a result. Defendant chooses to characterize the Judge's reaction as intolerance of the inconveniences occasioned by the needs of a sick child, which of course misses the point entirely, and sarcastically suggests the need for a rule to forewarn others of this policy of intolerance. Such an argument is beneath the level of professionalism the Court would expect from counsel of the caliber of those representing defendant.

the "judicial system's strong predisposition to resolve cases on their merits." *Hancock*, 857 F.2d at 1396.

Applying these considerations to the current circumstances, the Court concludes there was some measure of prejudice to the opposing party in preparing for and appearing at mediation or settlement conferences which may have been unsuccessful due to defendant's noncompliance with the rules.[3] Were that the most pertinent consideration, the Court could remedy the situation with a sanction awarding plaintiffs their costs, as was done with the prior sanctions order. However, prejudice to the plaintiffs is not the most relevant factor applicable here.

The most pertinent considerations include the defendant's repeated violations of the rules and orders of this Court. Defendant had been warned of the seriousness with which this Court viewed violation of its orders related to settlement, and had been sanctioned for conduct substantially similar to that now at issue. Notwithstanding that background, defendant nonetheless violated the attendance requirements again. Such circumstances plainly dictate the imposition of substantial sanctions.

Like the Magistrate Judge, the Court concludes entry of default judgment against defendant is too extreme a sanction. The Court also agrees with Judge Argo that, given defendant's track record, the imposition of monetary sanctions based on plaintiffs' costs of attending the abortive settlement conference is inadequate. Striking the appropriate balance between those extremes is difficult, but in doing so the Court attaches substantial weight to the need to resolve cases on their merits. Sanctions which prevent a determination on the merits, such as a dismissal with prejudice or entry of a default judgment, are properly reserved for cases where extreme sanctions are warranted.

Here, Judge Argo did not recommend the entry of default judgment against defendant. He correctly noted and considered the need to impose lesser sanctions and concluded a sanction precluding the presentation of defense witnesses and evidence was appropriate. Defendant argues that, in the context of this case, that result is tantamount to entry of default judgment. Though the sanction recommended by Judge Argo was less than default judgment, and may or may not be "tantamount" to it, it is evident the recommended sanction would have a significant impact on the substantive disposition of plaintiffs' claims. The malpractice claim potentially seeks over four million dollars, plus punitive damages. Defendant's ability to offer witnesses or other evidence relating to the firm's representation of the plaintiffs has, potentially, huge economic consequences to the parties. The Court concludes that, while a substantial and severe sanction is warranted, a sanction with less impact on the substantive disposition of the case is more appropriate.

3. [Court's footnote #14] There is, of course, no way to know whether this case might have settled had defendant complied with the various rules and orders, nor does the Court mean to suggest that this case necessarily should have settled.

Accordingly, with the qualifications noted herein, the Court adopts the [Magistrate Judge's] Report insofar as it establishes the need for substantial sanctions against defendant. In lieu of the sanctions recommended by the Magistrate Judge, the Court imposes the following as sanctions for defendant's conduct:

1. Defendant shall pay to the Clerk of the Court for the benefit of the General Court Fund, within thirty (30) days of this Order, the sum of $1000, attributable to the time the Magistrate Judge and his staff spent in conjunction with the settlement conference.

2. Defendant's statute of limitations defense and any similar defenses which, if prevailing, would prevent the disposition of plaintiffs' claims on their substantive merits (i.e. waiver, estoppel or similar defenses) are stricken.

3. Defendant shall pay the plaintiffs' reasonable attorney's fees and costs incurred in pursuit of this case, the amount to be determined by the Court in the ordinary fashion at its conclusion. Defendant will pay plaintiffs' reasonable attorney's fees and costs—win, lose or draw—regardless of whether attorney's fees would otherwise be assessable against the opposing party.

4. Counsel for defendant shall forward a copy of this Order to [defendant and defendant's insurance company] immediately upon its receipt.

Additionally, the Court orders a further settlement conference on Friday, January 17, 2003, at 9:00 a.m., before U.S. Magistrate Judge Robert Bachrach.[4] The parties shall submit, not later than 12:00 noon on Wednesday, January 15, 2003, a settlement conference statement conforming to the local rules. The provisions of this Court's November 14, 2002, referral order, to the extent not modified by this Order, shall be applicable to this referral and are deemed incorporated herein.

. . .

This Court has neither the authority nor the desire to force the parties to settle this case. It may well be one in which settlement is not feasible or appropriate and, if so, a trial should occur. That is what the Court is here for. However, in the interest of managing its resources and minimizing cost and delay to the parties, the Court does have both the specific and inherent authority to require attendance at, and good faith participation in, a settlement conference. FED. R. CIV. P. 16(a)(5);

4. [Court's footnote #17] Subsequent to the docket call in this case, the parties jointly advised the Court of their view that, in light of the contentious nature of this sanctions dispute, a different magistrate than Judge Argo might be more successful in exploring settlement possibilities if the Court directed another conference. Both took pains to assure the Court they did not question Judge Argo's impartiality or otherwise object to him, but felt assignment to a different Judge not involved with the sanctions dispute might enhance the prospects for a successful conference. The Court defers to the parties in that regard, but certainly has full confidence in Judge Argo's continuing ability to conduct a proper settlement conference in this case.

Schwartzman, Inc. v. ACF Industries, Inc., 167 F.R.D. 694, 697–98 (D.N.M. 1996). The Court expects, and will accept, nothing less.

Notes and Questions

1. What did Defendant do wrong? What sanctions did the court impose for each infraction?

2. What provision(s) of Rule 16(f) gave the court the authority to strike Defendant's defenses? And what provision(s) of Rule 16(f) gave the court the authority to enter the other sanctions?

3. In the court's view, what is the purpose of sanctions in this case? Why did it deem monetary sanctions insufficient for that purpose? Would the sanctions entered have been proper upon the Defendant's *first* failure to attend a court-ordered conference? How can we tell?

4. If you were Plaintiff's lawyer, how would the sanctions entered here affect your settlement demands?

5. Does a court have the authority to order the insurance carrier for the defendant—which is not a party—to attend a settlement conference? What does Rule 16 say about that? Could a Local Rule require it?

6. In the last paragraph of the opinion, the court says that it does not have the authority to "force the parties to settle" the case. Why, then, should it have the authority to force the parties to attend a settlement conference, particularly when the lawyers for one side determine that such a conference would be a waste of time?

7. Does the court's last footnote weaken its conclusion that the magistrate judge did not demonstrate partiality?

We are tempted to ask whether the recent efforts at case management have been successful. But that begs a more fundamental question: How would we know? In other words, what would we look to as signs of success?

One result of increased case management may be an increased ability to resolve disputes without trial. Professor Arthur Miller laments this trend: "Rule 16 conferences . . . often clarify what factual or legal issues may be in dispute, thus permitting focused discovery and identification of claims and defenses suitable for summary resolution. In addition, a judge who actively participates throughout the pretrial phase and is familiar with the dispute's facts and theories may be more inclined to believe that having the same evidence presented at trial is unnecessary and to resolve the case on summary judgment." Arthur Miller, *The Pretrial Rush to Judgment: Are the "Litigation Explosion," "Liability Crisis," and Efficiency Cliches Eroding Our Day in Court and Jury Trial Commitments?*, 78 N.Y.U. L. Rev. 982, 1006 (2003).

If Professor Miller is right, and hands-on judicial management has led to increased use of summary judgment, why is that not a sign of success?

C. Judicial Adjuncts: Magistrate Judges and Masters

It is not surprising that federal judges would seek to cope with increased case filings, expanded federal subject matter jurisdiction, and the demands of complex litigation by seeking to delegate some judicial functions. But delegation is potentially alarming. Federal district judges, court of appeals judges, and Justices of the Supreme Court are nominated by the President and must be confirmed by the Senate. Article III, § 1, of the Constitution gives these "Article III" judges extraordinary job security: they never face an electorate, they have life tenure, meaning they can be removed from office only by impeachment (which has happened only eight times in the nation's history). Not only that, but Congress cannot reduce their compensation. This political insulation makes the judges free to rule as the law requires without fear of retaliation by Congress or reprisal from the public.

Article III of the Constitution requires that the "judicial power of the United States" be exercised by Article III judges. Magistrate judges, who are salaried federal judicial officers, are not Article III judges. Masters, who are not federal employees but may be appointed to serve on a case-by-case basis, also are not Article III judges. That does not mean that matters cannot be delegated to them, but the delegation must be carefully circumscribed, to ensure that the federal "judicial power" remains in the district judge.[5]

Suffice to say that delegation to magistrate judges and masters must be so tailored that the ultimate decision in the case rests with the district judge. Magistrate judges and masters are appointed in different ways and their authority is different. Throughout, keep in mind the mechanisms by which the judicial system seeks to ensure that these adjuncts do not exercise ultimate decision-making power. Also keep in mind that parties may waive their right to have an Article III judge make the ultimate determination in their case. Thus, as we will see, litigants can consent to decision-making by an adjunct. (Indeed, one example of eschewing an Article III forum is when the plaintiff who could invoke diversity of citizenship or federal question jurisdiction chooses instead to file in state court.)

It is worth noting that Article III judges comprise a modest percentage (approximately three percent) of all the employees of the federal judicial branch. That branch

5. Similar problems arise with the creation of "Article I" courts by Congress (such as the tax court, bankruptcy court, and Territorial courts) and with adjudicatory functions before administrative agencies. For instance, the Supreme Court declared part of the Bankruptcy Reform Act of 1978 unconstitutional because it permitted bankruptcy judges (who are not Article III judges) to decide "inherently judicial" matters. *Northern Pipeline Construction Co. v. Marathon Pipe Line Co.*, 458 U.S. 50, 71 (1982). Specifically, it allowed them to decide disputes between private parties. In contrast, public rights disputes (those "between the Government and persons subject to its authority in connection with the performance of the constitutional functions of the executive or legislative departments") are not inherently judicial. *Id.* at 68. In *Stern v. Marshall*, 564 U.S. 462 (2011), the Court concluded that federal bankruptcy judges lack power under Article III to hear a claim by Anna Nicole Smith concerning alleged efforts to prohibit her from inheriting from her husband's estate.

employs over 30,000 persons. Of that number, only 855 are Article III judges (there are 667 authorized district court judgeships, 179 authorized court of appeals judgeships, and nine Justices of the Supreme Court). Each Article III judge has multiple law clerks and other support staff, and there are thousands of employees engaged in administrative, clerical, and security services for the federal court system.

1. Delegation to Magistrate Judges

In 1968, Congress created the position of United States Magistrate, for the express purpose of serving as adjunct judicial officers to federal district courts. In 1993, the name was officially changed to "magistrate judge." They are important players in the federal judicial system. Indeed, it is likely that the federal court system could not function effectively without them, a fact bolstered by the numbers. In 2018, there were 667 authorized district judgeships and 559 magistrates judges.

Magistrate judges, as noted, are not appointed under Article III. They do not have life tenure and are not nominated by the President and confirmed by the Senate. Rather, by statute, they serve eight-year terms and are appointed by the district judges for the district in which they serve. 28 U.S.C. § 631(a).

What do magistrate judges do? Various duties under 28 U.S.C. § 636(a) are not particularly relevant for our purposes, such as those dealing with criminal cases. Under § 636(c), magistrate judges may conduct civil trials, but only if the parties consent. In such a case, the parties waive their right to an Article III judge, so having the magistrate judge conduct trial is acceptable. For us, the most significant provision is § 636(b)(1), which concerns delegation of various *pretrial* issues from the district judge. This authority is often used to have the magistrate preside over discovery matters; the *Switzer* case was an example.

Section 636(b)(1) provides:

> Notwithstanding any provision of law to the contrary—
>
> (A) a [district] judge may designate a magistrate judge to hear and determine any pretrial matter pending before the court, except a motion for injunctive relief, for judgment on the pleadings, for summary judgment, to dismiss or quash an indictment or information made by the defendant, to suppress evidence in a criminal case, to dismiss or to permit maintenance of a class action, to dismiss for failure to state a claim upon which relief can be granted, and to involuntarily dismiss an action. A judge of the court may reconsider any pretrial matter under this subparagraph (A) where it has been shown that the magistrate judge's order is clearly erroneous or contrary to law.
>
> (B) a [district] judge may also designate a magistrate judge to conduct hearings, including evidentiary hearings, and to submit to a judge of the court proposed findings of fact and recommendations for the disposition, by a judge of the court, of any motion excepted in subparagraph (A), of

applications for post-trial relief made by individuals convicted of criminal offenses and of prisoner petitions challenging conditions of confinement.

(C) the magistrate judge shall file his proposed findings and recommendations under subparagraph (B) with the court and a copy shall forthwith be mailed to all parties.

Within 14 days after being served with a copy, any party may serve and file written objections to such proposed findings and recommendations as provided by rules of court. A judge of the court shall make a de novo determination of those portions of the report or specified proposed findings or recommendations to which objection is made. A judge of the court may accept, reject, or modify, in whole or in part, the findings or recommendations made by the magistrate judge. The judge may also receive further evidence or recommit the matter to the magistrate judge with instructions.[6]

Federal Rule 72, which applies to proceedings before magistrate judges, mirrors § 636(b)(1), and makes the distinction between what it calls "dispositive" and "nondispositive" matters. Compare Rule 72 with § 636(b)(1). The matters excepted from § 636(b)(1)(A) are considered "dispositive" under Rule 72. It is important to note the different levels of potential review by the district judge on the two types of matters.

Notes and Questions

1. On nondispositive matters, the magistrate is permitted to "hear and determine" (in § 636(b)(1)(A)) or "hear and decide" (in Rule 72(a)). Under what standard does the district judge review such decisions by a magistrate judge?

2. On dispositive matters under and § 636(b)(1)(B) and Rule 72(b), however, the magistrate does not "determine." Rather, what does she do? Assuming timely objection, what level of review is required by the district judge on these matters?

3. Why is there more searching district court review on dispositive matters? Is this fact of constitutional importance?

4. May a district judge refer to a magistrate for decision on a motion to certify a class action? Is such a motion "dispositive"? Why?

5. Is the list of matters on which a magistrate judge can merely make recommendations exhaustive? Or can courts add to the list by requiring *de novo* review for motions that are *functionally* dispositive? The next case addresses this question.

6. Section 636(b)(3) provides that magistrates "may be assigned such additional duties as are not inconsistent with the Constitution and laws of the United States." For example, it was proper to refer to a magistrate the task of determining damages after the district court entered default judgment. *Callier v. Gray*, 167 F.3d 977, 982–983 (6th Cir. 1999) (noting that magistrate judge's determination was subject to review by district judge).

Williams v. Beemiller, Inc.

United States Court of Appeals for the Second Circuit
527 F.3d 259 (2008)

Straub, Circuit Judge.

... This appeal raises the issues of whether we have jurisdiction to review a magistrate judge's order remanding a case to state court and whether a magistrate judge's authority to hear and determine pretrial matters under the Federal Magistrates Act includes the power to decide a motion to remand a case to state court. *See* 28 U.S.C. § 636(b)(1)(A); *see also* Fed. R. Civ. P. 72(a) & Advisory Committee Notes, 1983 Addition (noting that Rule 72(a) addressing district court-ordered referrals of non-dispositive matters under § 636(b)(1)(A)). For the reasons set forth below, we conclude that it does not. Accordingly, we vacate the District Court's order and remand the case to the District Court for proceedings consistent with this opinion.

FACTUAL AND PROCEDURAL BACKGROUND

This case arises from a drive-by shooting that occurred on August 16, 2003. While playing basketball in his neighborhood, Plaintiff-Appellee Daniel Williams was shot and injured by Defendant Cornell Caldwell. The police soon apprehended Caldwell, who eventually pleaded guilty to attempted assault in the first degree in Erie County Court in the State of New York. On July 28, 2005, Daniel Williams and his father commenced this action in New York State Supreme Court for the County of Erie. Plaintiffs alleged that [several defendants, including Beemiller, Inc., Charles Brown, MKS, and Gun-A-Rama] had negligently sold or distributed the firearm used by Caldwell to shoot Williams and thus contributed to his injuries.

Claiming diversity jurisdiction ..., [two of the defendants,] Beemiller and Brown[,] removed the case to federal court on November 23, 2005. Shortly thereafter, written consents to removal were filed on behalf of [two other defendants,] MKS and Gun-A-Rama. Written consents were never filed on behalf of the remaining defendants. Citing defendants' failure to obtain the requisite consent to removal from all defendants, Plaintiffs moved for remand of the action to state court and for the award of costs and expenses, pursuant to 28 U.S.C. § 1447(c).

On January 4, 2006, the District Court referred all non-dispositive pretrial matters to the Magistrate Judge pursuant to 28 U.S.C. § 636(b)(1)(A). On June 29, 2006, the Magistrate Judge entered a decision and order granting Plaintiffs' motion for remand and determining that the Plaintiffs were entitled to an award of costs. In doing so, the Magistrate Judge concluded that "a motion for remand [is] not dispositive as it resolves only the question of whether there is a proper basis for federal jurisdiction to support removal and does not reach a determination of either the merits of a plaintiff's claims or defendant's defenses or counterclaims." However, the Magistrate Judge also acknowledged contrary authority on the issue and invited the District Court to treat the decision and order as a report and recommendation, if the District Court deemed it appropriate. On July 14, 2006, Defendants-Appellants timely submitted objections to the Magistrate Judge's order. In relevant part, Defendants-Appellants argued that the District Court should review the order *de novo* as a report and recommendation on a dispositive motion.

On September 26, 2006, the District Court entered an order denying Defendants-Appellants' objections. Upon finding that a motion for remand is considered non-dispositive, the District Court reviewed the decision and order of the Magistrate Judge and concluded that it was neither "clearly erroneous [nor] contrary to law" under Federal Rule of Civil Procedure 72(a).

On October 26, 2006, Defendants-Appellants timely filed a notice of appeal with this Court. On January 23, 2007, Plaintiffs-Appellees moved, *inter alia*, to dismiss the appeal pursuant to 28 U.S.C. § 1447(d), which prohibits appellate review of an order remanding a case to state court. On April 12, 2007, a panel of this Court denied the motion and directed the parties to further brief the following issues: "1) whether, under 28 U.S.C. § 636(b)(1)(A) and Fed. R. Civ. P. 72, a motion to remand a case to state court is a dispositive matter upon which a magistrate judge is unauthorized to rule without *de novo* review by the district court; 2) whether 28 U.S.C. § 1447(d) bars an appeal of a district court's order reviewing a magistrate judge's remand order under a clear-error-and-contrary-to-law standard of review; and 3) whether resolution of either of these two questions is dependent on resolution of the other." We now consider these issues.

DISCUSSION

I. Jurisdiction to Review Remand Order

[The court here concluded that 28 U.S.C. § 1447(d) did not bar appellate jurisdiction. That subsection provides that an "order remanding a case to the State court from which it was removed is not reviewable on appeal or otherwise. . . ." Case law makes it clear, however, that § 1447(d) applies only when the remand order is based upon factors not present in this case.]

Having concluded that we have jurisdiction to consider the issue raised by this appeal, we now turn to the question of whether a magistrate judge has the authority to remand a previously removed case to state court.

II. Authority of a Magistrate Judge to Order Remand

Defendants-Appellants argue that the District Court erred in failing to consider the Magistrate Judge's remand order as a report and recommendation and, thus, in failing to review the order *de novo*. In advancing this argument, Defendants-Appellants contend that a remand order cannot reasonably be considered a mere "pretrial matter" within the meaning of 28 U.S.C. § 636(b)(1)(A) or a "nondispositive matter" under Federal Rule of Civil Procedure because such an order effectively terminates all proceedings in federal court. . . . We review *de novo* questions of statutory interpretation, as well as a district court's interpretation of the Federal Rules of Civil Procedure. Given the possible constitutional implications of delegating Article III judges' duties to magistrate judges, we have generally "avoided constitutional issues in this area by construing the Federal Magistrates Act narrowly 'in light of its structure and purpose,'" *In re United States*, 10 F.3d 931, 934 n.4 (2d Cir. 1993). Where, as here, a party argues that a district court erroneously treated a matter referred to a magistrate judge as "not dispositive" and thus failed to review *de novo* the decision by a magistrate judge in that matter, our sister circuits have analyzed the practical effect of the challenged action on the instant litigation. *See, e.g., Phinney v. Wentworth Douglas Hosp.*, 199 F.3d 1, 5–6 (1st Cir. 1999) (stating, in dicta, that a magistrate judge's imposition of discovery sanctions should be considered dispositive where such sanctions "fully dispose[] of a claim or defense" and thus fall within the "same genre as the enumerated motions" of § 636(b)(1)(A)); *Rajaratnam v. Moyer*, 47 F.3d 922, 923–24 (7th Cir. 1995) (holding that the denial of an application for attorney's fees should be considered dispositive for purposes of § 636(b)(1)(A) and reviewed *de novo* by the district court). In reaching these conclusions, these courts considered the dispositive orders listed explicitly in § 636(b)(1)(A) to be non-exhaustive. *See, e.g., Phinney*, 199 F.3d at 5–6 (concluding that "the terms dispositive and nondispositive as used in Rule 72 must be construed in harmony with the classification limned in section 636(b)(1)" and rejecting the proposition that "dispositive motions are those excepted motions specifically enumerated in section 636(b)(1)(A) . . . and no others"); *see also Gomez* [*v. United States*], 490 U.S. 858, 873–74 (concluding that jury selection in a felony trial is dispositive for purposes of § 636(b)(1)(B), despite its absence from that provision, because it is "more akin to those precisely defined, 'dispositive' matters" enumerated therein than the "'nondispositive,' pretrial matter[s] governed by § 636(b)(1)(A)"). We agree that the list is non-exhaustive.

The question of whether a magistrate judge may order a case remanded to state court under § 1447(c) is one of first impression in this Circuit. All three of our sister circuits that have considered the matter have concluded that such orders are dispositive because they are "functionally equivalent" to an order of dismissal for the purposes of § 636(b)(1)(A) and Rule 72(a). *See Vogel* [*v. United States Office Prods. Co.*], 258 F.3d at 514–17 [(6th Cir. 2001)]; *First Union Mortgage Corp. v. Smith*, 229 F.3d 992, 994–97 (10th Cir. 2000); *In re U.S. Healthcare*, 159 F.3d at 145–46 [(3d Cir. 1998)]. In *U.S. Healthcare*, the Third Circuit stated that "a remand order is dispositive insofar as proceedings in the federal court are concerned" and is thus "the functional equivalent of an order of dismissal" for the purpose of § 636(b)(1)(A). . . . The Sixth and Tenth Circuits agreed with the reasoning of the Third Circuit. *See* Vogel, 258 F.3d at 517 (concluding that "a remand order is the functional equivalent of an order to dismiss" and thus is "dispositive . . . and can only be entered by district courts"); *First Union Mortgage Corp.*, 229 F.3d at 996 (concluding that "[s]ection 636 and Rule 72 must be read, where possible, so as to avoid constitutional problems" and holding that remand order is "a final decision or dispositive motion that must ultimately be made by the district court in order to survive Article III scrutiny"). We now join them.

Because a § 1447(c) remand order "determine[s] the fundamental question of whether a case could proceed in a federal court," *U.S. Healthcare*, 159 F.3d at 146, it is indistinguishable from a motion to dismiss the action from federal court based on a lack of subject matter jurisdiction for the purpose of § 636(b)(1)(A). A motion to remand is not a "pretrial matter" under § 636(b)(1)(A), and a magistrate judge presented with such a motion should provide a report and recommendation to the district court that is subject to *de novo* review under Rule 72. The Defendants-Appellants here are entitled to the District Court's *de novo* review of the Magistrate Judge's report and recommendation regarding Plaintiffs-Appellants' motion to remand.

CONCLUSION

For the foregoing reasons, we vacate the order of the District Court overruling the Defendants-Appellants' objections and remand the case for proceedings consistent with this opinion. We express no view as to the merits of Plaintiffs-Appellants' motion to remand under § 1447(c).

Notes and Questions

1. Why was the motion to remand to state court "dispositive"? What about the fact that a motion to remand is not listed in § 636(b)(1)(A) as a topic on which there must be *de novo* review? Should that matter?

2. A district court's review under the "clearly erroneous or contrary to law" is deferential. (Again, as to what magistrate decisions is this the appropriate standard of review?) This standard is similar to that applied on several matters by appellate courts when reviewing trial courts. Because such review is done "on the record" on appeal, there is usually no reason the district judge cannot discharge this level of review without holding a hearing; she reviews the record generated by the magistrate.

3. Under § 636(b)(1)(C) and Rule 72(b)(3), the district judge must "determine" the matter *de novo*. The district judge may also "receive further evidence." Does *de novo* require that the district judge hold a hearing? Or can she simply review the record generated by the magistrate *de novo*?

In *United States v. Raddatz*, 447 U.S. 667 (1980), the magistrate based his findings and recommendations in a criminal motion to suppress on contested testimony. The Court held that the district judge was not required to hold an evidentiary hearing to make its *de novo* determination on which testimony was more believable. It emphasized that the statute requires a "*de novo* determination, not a *de novo* hearing." *Id.* at 674. On the other hand, the lower courts seem to agree that a district judge cannot *reject* a magistrate's finding on credibility without hearing the witness testify. *See, e.g., Jackson v. United States*, 859 F.3d 495, 499 (7th Cir. 2017).

4. Courts have not agreed on whether a motion for sanctions under Federal Rule 11 is "dispositive." Some courts hold that it is, which means, of course, that the magistrate judge may only make a recommendation to the district court. *See, e.g.,*

Alpern v. Lieb, 38 F.3d 933, 936 (7th Cir. 1994); *Bennett v. General Caster Serv. of N. Gordon Co.,* 976 F.2d 995, 998 (6th Cir. 1992). There is authority, however, that the issue is non-dispositive. *See, e.g., Maisonvill v. F2 America, Inc.,* 902 F.2d 746, 748 (9th Cir. 1990). A panel of the Second Circuit was unable to reach a majority opinion on the question. *Kiobel v. Millson,* 592 F.3d 78 (2d Cir. 2010).

2. Delegation to Masters

As we just saw, a magistrate judge is an employee of the federal judicial branch of government (although not an Article III judge). We now look at a different kind of adjunct to the court—masters. These people are *not* employed by the federal judiciary. They are appointed by the court for a particular case or series of related cases. The court sets their fee, which is usually paid by the parties.[7]

Federal Rule 53 deals with masters. Historically, district courts maintained a list of "general" or "standing" masters, from whom the judge could select for delegation of tasks. A master appointed not from the list, but for a particular case, was called a "special" master. With the creation of magistrate judges in 1968, there was no longer a need for "standing" masters, so Rule 53 was amended in 1983 to delete reference to "standing" masters. Technically, then, all masters today are "special" masters and it would seem pointless to put the adjective in their title. But old habits die hard.

Remember that magistrate judges can conduct civil trials only if the parties consent. We would expect at least as much of a limitation with masters. *See* Fed. R. Civ. P. 53(a)(1)(A) (allowing masters to act with consent of parties). Indeed, with the creation of so many magistrate positions, one wonders what masters are supposed to do. On the other hand, there may be times when there are not enough district and magistrate judges to keep up with the case load.

Moreover, district and magistrate judges are generalists—they are not expected to be expert in any particular field. Maybe a court would find it helpful to delegate some functions to an expert. For example, it might be helpful to have an economist or accountant do complex damages calculations. Keep these points in mind when you read Rule 53 and address the following.

Notes and Questions

1. Rule 53(a)(1) emphasizes that the listed tasks are the "only" ones for which a master can be used. Under what circumstances and for what purposes can a master be used at trial? Does it matter if it is a case in which there is a right to jury trial?

2. Must there be an "exceptional" condition to appoint a master to resolve damages computations that the judge found difficult?

---

7. Under § 636(b)(2), a magistrate judge can be appointed as master, in which case she simply draws her salary and is not paid an additional amount for her service as master.

3. Under what circumstances and for what purposes can a master be used in pretrial? Does that part of the rule require an "exceptional" condition for such appointment? On the other hand, are the conditions imposed by this part of the rule in fact exceptional?

4. Rule 53(b) requires great detail and clarity in any order appointing a master. It also ensures that there is no conflict of interest between the master and a party. How does it do this?

5. How and when may the parties respond to the master's action or proposed action? How do the parties know what that action or proposed action is?

6. Assuming that a party objects to a master's findings of fact, what level of review does the district judge apply? How does this compare to review of nondispositive findings by magistrate judges?

7. What level of review does the district judge apply to a master's conclusions (or recommended conclusions) of law? How does this compare to review of proposed dispositive rulings by magistrate judges?

8. What level of review does the district judge apply to a master's procedural rulings?

9. How is compensation of the master set? Do the parties end up paying this equally? Rule 53(a)(3) requires the court to "consider the fairness of imposing the likely expenses on the parties" and must avoid "unreasonable expense or delay."

In *La Buy v. Howes Leather Co., Inc.*, 352 U.S. 249 (1957), a district judge had two complex antitrust cases before him. In one, there were 87 plaintiffs and six defendants. In the other, there were six plaintiffs and six defendants. Over 50 depositions had been taken and there were numerous motions concerning discovery and the merits. Indeed, the docket sheet simply listing the hearings and filings was over 27 pages long. The parties estimated that trials would take several weeks.

The district judge *sua sponte* ordered that a special master "take evidence and . . . report the same to this Court, together with his findings of fact and conclusions of law." *Id.* at 253. All parties objected. Rule 53 then—as today—requires an "exceptional" condition to use a master in this way. The district judge purported to find such a condition in the fact that he was "confronted with an extremely congested calendar." *Id.*

The Supreme Court concluded that the district judge erred. *Id.* at 256. A crowded docket does not justify this use of a master. But the Court faced a jurisdictional hurdle. Under 28 U.S.C. § 1291, one has a right to appeal only "final decisions of the district courts of the United States. . . ." As interpreted, "final decisions" means "final judgments," which is the trial court's resolution of the entire case on the merits. An order referring matters to a master is not a final judgment and cannot be reviewed by an appellate court unless some exception to the final judgment rule can be invoked.

In Chapter 3, section C.1.c., we considered the All Writs Act, 28 U.S.C. § 1651. Among other orders, that statute permits an appellate court to issue an extraordinary writ of prohibition or of mandamus to a district court. Such a writ cannot be used, however, as a substitute for appeal. Rather, it is permissible only when the district court's action is so lacking in basis—so devoid of merit—as to constitute an abdication of duty. This is a rigorous standard, and is not routinely invoked.

In *La Buy*, the Court concluded that an extraordinary writ was appropriate, because the district court's reference to a master constituted an improper relinquishment of its jurisdiction and responsibility. 352 U.S. at 258–259. Though extraordinary writs constitute appellate review, they are not technically "appeals" of a case. Instead, the petition for a writ constitutes a new legal proceeding, one filed initially in the court of appeals. The petition names the district court as the respondent. An example was *Atlantic Marine Construction Co. v. U.S. District Court,* which we read in Chapter 3 Section B.2. In earlier times, as when *La Buy* was decided, the district judge was named as respondent personally. La Buy was the judge against whom the writ was sought. The Court explained:

> . . . It is true that mandamus should be resorted to only in extreme cases, since it places trial judges in the anomalous position of being litigants without counsel other than uncompensated volunteers. However, there is an end of patience and it clearly appears that the Court of Appeals has for years admonished the trial judges of the Seventh Circuit that the practice of making references "does not commend itself" and ". . . should seldom be made, and if at all only when unusual circumstances exist." Again, in 1942, it pointed out that the words "exception" and "exceptional" as used in [Rule 53] are not elastic terms with the trial court the sole judge of their elasticity. "Litigants are entitled to a trial by the court, in every suit, save where exceptional circumstances are shown." . . . The record does not show to what extent references are made by the full bench of the District Court in the Northern District; however, it does reveal that [the judge in this case] has referred 11 cases to masters in the past 6 years. But even "a little cloud may bring a flood's downpour" if we approve the practice here indulged, particularly in the face of presently congested dockets, increased filings, and more extended trials. This is not to say that we are neither aware of nor fully appreciative of the unfortunate congestion of the court calendar in many of our District Courts. . . . But . . . congestion in itself is not such an exceptional circumstance as to warrant a reference to a master. If such were the test, present congestion would make references the rule rather than the exception. . . . We agree that the detailed accounting required . . . to determine the damages suffered by each plaintiff might be referred to a master after the court has determined the over-all liability of defendants, provided the circumstances indicate that the use of the court's time is not warranted in receiving the proof and making the tabulation.

352 U.S. at 256–259. In other words, the writ was issued not because Judge La Buy was wrong to assign the trial duties to the master. It was issued because Judge La Buy was *so* wrong that his action constituted an "abdication of the judicial function depriving the parties of a trial before the court on the basic issues involved in the litigation." *Id.* at 256.

The limitations on use of masters at trial in Rule 53(a)(1)(B) reflect the concerns of the Court in *La Buy*. They do not provide that masters can *never* be used to make findings of fact at trial, but impose strict limits.

The last two sentences of the excerpt from *La Buy* recognized a classic use of masters—so classic, in fact, that it does not require a showing of "extraordinary" condition. Specifically, a master might be used "to perform an accounting or resolve a difficult computation of damages." FED. R. CIV. P. 53(a)(1)(B)(ii). This is, of course, usually a *post-trial* activity and arises only when the court has determined the merits of liability and decided that it desires the assistance of a master. The Rules Advisory Committee Notes to Rule 53 said that a master can thus be used when calculations involve "ministerial determinations" not involving credibility of witnesses.

The following case discusses the proper use of masters and the district judge's authority to oversee and remove them. Notice the tasks assigned to the master and his team. Judges, who are generalists, would have neither the expertise nor the time to undertake the tasks. Rule 53 permitted the court to engage people with relevant experience. (By the way, note how much this master was paid.)

Cordoza v. Pacific States Steel Corporation

United States Court of Appeals, Ninth Circuit
320 F.3d 989 (2003)

MCKEOWN, CIRCUIT JUDGE.

This appeal comes to us from the midst of lengthy post-judgment proceedings in an Employee Retirement Income Security Act case. For nearly two decades, the district court has overseen efforts by a series of special masters to transform an insolvent company's contaminated steel plant site into a means of funding the former steelworkers' medical plan. After other parties accused the special master of serious misconduct, the district court launched an investigation, held a hearing, and finally relieved the special master of his duties, requiring him to disgorge a portion of the considerable sum he had already retained as compensation.

The terminated special master now appeals these orders, although development of the steel plant site continues under a new special master. As a threshold matter, we address whether we have jurisdiction over this interlocutory appeal. . . . We . . . treat the appeal as a petition for a writ of mandamus. Having reviewed the considerable record and the district court's lengthy and careful findings, we conclude that a writ is not appropriate because the district court did not make a clear error or exceed its authority under Federal Rule of Civil Procedure 53 in supervising the special master and setting his compensation.

BACKGROUND AND PROCEDURAL HISTORY

The Pacific States Steel Corporation ("PSSC") operated a plant in Union City, California, that shut down in 1978, leaving a parcel of contaminated land and a bankrupt medical plan for retired steelworkers and their dependents. These pensioners filed a class action in the United States District Court for the Northern District of California with now-Chief Judge Marilyn Hall Patel presiding over the case. Judge Patel ordered PSSC to continue paying the pensioners' medical benefits, but the company had few assets from which to obtain the necessary funding. Judge Patel and the parties decided that the best way to fund the medical plan was to clean up and develop the toxic land on which the plant had been located.

Little did Judge Patel know that these post-judgment proceedings would become a miniature *Jarndyce v. Jarndyce*, grinding on for more than two decades after the steel plant had closed its doors.[8] The first special master, appointed in 1984 to determine the assets and liabilities of PSSC, tried unsuccessfully to develop the plant site. He was then replaced in 1990 by the appellants, Bruce Train and his associates, Theodore Sorensen and Hans Lemcke (collectively referred to as "Train" or "the Special Master").

In 1995, Train proposed, and Judge Patel adopted, an Amended Plan under which Train would form two companies, PASSCO Administrative Services and PASSCO Development Company, to obtain funding, develop the plant site, and use the resulting profits to pay the medical benefits. Services were to be billed on an hourly basis. In a somewhat unusual arrangement, Train was to receive other kinds of compensation, including an interest in the developed land. But the Amended Plan's terms, including Train's compensation, were always subject to further modification by the district court.

Train reached agreements in 1994 and 1995 with the Redevelopment Agency for the City of Union City ("RDA") for funding that resulted in the development of a small part of the plant site, where homes have now been built. Train also persuaded Rust Remedial Services, Inc. ("Rust") to perform clean-up work on the site for deferred compensation.

By 1996, negotiations between Train and all of the other parties involved in developing the rest of the plant site had bogged down amid mutual antagonism. A major sticking point seemed to be the amount of Train's compensation. Three years later, after the parties failed to reach a compromise in settlement conferences before

8. [Court's footnote #1] *See generally* Charles Dickens, Bleak House (1853); *see also* David I. Levine, *Calculating Fees of Special Masters*, 37 Hastings L.J. 141, 147 n.23 (1985) (discussing the accuracy of Dickens' account of the dismal state of English Chancery proceedings, including the role played by special masters).

a magistrate, Judge Patel conducted a settlement conference herself. Upon observing the parties during the conference, she began to have "grave concerns" about Train's motivations and "whether he could in fact accomplish the task assigned him—development of the property for the benefit of the pensioners."

Judge Patel then started an investigation, consulting with outside real estate experts, ordering Train to produce his books and records, directing him not to spend any more of PSSC's money, and appointing an independent auditor. She also suspended Train pending the outcome of the investigation and appointed court overseers to manage PSSC. After learning that Train was still speaking to potential developers, the district court again issued an order reminding Train that he had been suspended.

In August 2000, after the auditor's report was released, RDA filed a motion requesting that the district court set the Special Master's final compensation at $3 million and order disgorgement of all compensation received in excess of that amount. Although determined to avoid having "satellite litigation spawned" over the compensation issue, Judge Patel permitted limited discovery. . . . Train was finally terminated as Special Master on December 1, 2000. . . .

After four days of hearings, in early 2001, the district court entered a lengthy order, complete with detailed findings, examples, and record references. While acknowledging that Train had resolved some of the infrastructure problems and had initially obtained some funding from the RDA for the site, Judge Patel found that, in the end, Train had not accomplished the primary tasks for which he was appointed—the development of the plant site and the funding of the medical plan.

In the meantime, Judge Patel concluded, Train had (1) rejected valid offers from the RDA in order to hold out for more compensation for himself, (2) misappropriated creditors' funds by forming a $1 million litigation war chest, (3) paid for personal tax advice with PSSC funds, and (4) overbilled for a legal assistant. Judge Patel also noted that Train had failed to keep records or attempt to track down the medical fund recipients, preventing the pensioners from being identified even when there were funds to pay them.

In the final order setting the Special Master's compensation, Judge Patel accepted that the Special Master's work could be valued at $3.6 million ($1.2 million already received by each of the individual appellants Train, Lemcke, and Sorensen), but ordered Train personally to disgorge $48,035 for personal legal services he charged to PSSC and $65,034 for overbilling the services of the legal assistant. Judge Patel later awarded $24,634 in attorney's fees. Train appeals the termination, compensation, and attorney's fees orders. . . .

DISCUSSION

. . . Although we may consider [Train's] notice of appeal as a petition for a writ of mandamus, we decline to issue the writ because the district court's orders were not "a clear abuse of discretion." *See Bankers Life & Cas. Co. v. Holland*, 346 U.S. 379, 383 (1953).

I. A SPECIAL MASTER'S RIGHT TO APPEAL

This is the rare situation in which an officer of the court is appealing from an order of the court. Federal Rule of Civil Procedure 53 gives the district court authority to appoint a special master, to "specify or limit" his powers, and to fix his compensation. Fed. R. Civ. P. 53(a)(c). Rule 53 is derived from Equity Rules regulating "masters in chancery," officers "appointed by the court to assist it in various proceedings incidental to the progress of a cause before it."

The moniker of "special" master underscores the unique nature of the master's role. A special master is a "surrogate" of the court "and in that sense the service performed is an important public duty of high order in much the same way as is serving in the Judiciary." *Louisiana v. Mississippi*, 466 U.S. 921, 921 (1984) (Burger, C.J., dissenting in part from the allowance of the Special Master's expenses); See *In re Gilbert*, 276 U.S. 6, 9 (1928) (observing that accepting appointment as a special master means assuming "the duties and obligations of a judicial officer"); *York Int'l Bldg., Inc. v. Chaney*, 527 F.2d 1061, 1068 (9th Cir. 1975) (noting the "well established principle" that special masters administering bankruptcy estates "are not acting as private persons, but as officers of the court."). Indeed, in this era of complex litigation, special masters may, subject to judicial review, be called upon to perform a broad range of judicial functions—supervising discovery, issuing stipulations of fact, and in exceptional circumstances, hearing and making recommendations with regard to motions to dismiss and for summary judgment.

Judge Patel's appointment of special masters to develop the plant site and fund the medical plan continues a long tradition, with its roots in equity, of using special masters in post-judgment proceedings. Linda J. Silberman, *Masters and Magistrates Part II: The American Analogue*, 50 N.Y.U. L. Rev. 1297, 1321–1323 (1975); *Hilao v. Estate of Marcos*, 103 F.3d 767, 782 (9th Cir. 1996) (special master appointed to supervise taking of depositions of randomly-selected class members to determine distribution of compensatory damages award); *New York State Ass'n for Retarded Children v. Carey*, 706 F.2d 956, 962–965 (2d Cir. 1983) (approving the appointment of a special master to monitor compliance with a consent decree). In light of this tradition, it might seem strange to suggest that a special master can suddenly shift roles from surrogate of the court to quasi-party with the right to challenge that court's order setting his compensation. *See Devlin v. Scardelletti*, 536 U.S. 1 (2002) ("Only parties to a lawsuit, or those that properly become parties, may appeal an adverse judgment.").

Nonetheless, the right of a special master to appeal is also part of that tradition. In *Hinckley v. Gilman, Clinton, and Springfield Ry. Co.*, the Supreme Court permitted a receiver to appeal an order "relating to the settlement of his accounts," reasoning that "for this purpose he occupies the position of a party to the suit, although an officer of the court." 94 U.S. 467, 469 (1876). The order setting his compensation made the receiver "subject[] to the jurisdiction of the court," and so he had the "corresponding right to contend against all claims made against him." *Id.* A review of cases confirms that appeals by special masters are indeed rare and few in number.

Lest we be tempted by the parties' suggestion that *Hinckley's* advanced age renders it obsolete, the Supreme Court reaffirmed *Hinckley*'s continuing vitality just last year when holding that a non-class member who did not successfully intervene in the district court could still appeal a class settlement. *See Devlin*, 536 U.S. 1. As the Supreme Court recognized, the receiver in *Hinckley* could appeal because he was a party in the limited sense that he was bound by the order setting his compensation. *See also Williams v. Morgan*, 111 U.S. 684, 698–99 (1884) (referring to litigants such as the receiver in *Hinckley* as "quasi-parties"). Train is similarly bound, and because *Hinckley* remains good law, Train has the right to appeal.

II. FINAL AND COLLATERAL ORDERS

Although Train has the right to appeal, he can only do so from orders constituting a final judgment under 28 U.S.C. § 1291 or fitting [an exception like the "collateral order" doctrine, which, the court concludes, does not apply here. Accordingly, Train may appeal, but only after the court enters final judgment on the merits of the entire case.]

III. WRIT OF MANDAMUS

Although Train has not filed a petition for a writ of mandamus, a notice of appeal from an otherwise nonappealable order can be considered as a mandamus petition, "an extraordinary remedy that may be obtained 'only to confine an inferior court to a lawful exercise of its prescribed jurisdiction or to compel it to exercise its authority when it is its duty to do so.'" *Executive Software N. Am., Inc. v. United States Dist. Court*, 24 F.3d 1545, 1550 (9th Cir. 1994). . . . [W]e will only issue the writ for usurpation of judicial power or a clear abuse of discretion. *Id.* Five "objective principles" guide the inquiry: whether (1) Train has no other adequate means, such as direct appeal, to attain the relief, (2) he will be damaged or prejudiced in a way not correctable on appeal, (3) the district court's order is clearly erroneous as a matter of law, (4) the district court's order is an oft-repeated error, or manifests a persistent disregard of the federal rules, or (5) the district court's order raises new and important problems, or issues of law of first impression. *Id.*

We address the third factor first, because the others are irrelevant if the district court's conclusions were legally correct. Here, nothing in the record supports issuing a writ of mandamus because Judge Patel did not abuse her discretion, much less make a clear error. . . .

. . .

We . . . hold that Judge Patel did not make a clear error worthy of mandamus in issuing the other orders regarding Train. In a comprehensive and detailed forty-page order, Judge Patel catalogued abundant evidence in support of both her earlier orders limiting, and eventually terminating, Train's authority as Special Master, as well as the final orders setting the amount of his ultimate compensation and awarding attorney's fees.

Judge Patel concluded that Train's early efforts from 1990–1995 warranted his keeping much of the money he already received. Against this favorable finding she weighed numerous improprieties—breaches of fiduciary duty, unethical behavior, failure to keep records, lying and disloyalty to the court, alienating the only source of funding, and a general failure to accomplish the task for which he was appointed. Facing the difficulty of quantifying the damage from Train's behavior, Judge Patel ordered Train to disgorge only the amount spent on legal services for himself and the amount improperly billed for the services of a legal assistant.

. . .

Train argues that Judge Patel's findings are not supported by the evidence. This attack at best raises a factual dispute, not the prospect that the district court made a clear error requiring a writ of mandamus. Although we do not endeavor to analyze each of the factual findings at this stage of the litigation, we note that the findings are detailed and backed by specific examples and citation to documentary evidence. If Judge Patel abused her discretion, the matter can be considered on direct appeal, and Train's compensation can be adjusted accordingly. Similarly, we see no clear error in the awarding of attorney's fees to the parties for the cost of exposing Train's alleged misconduct. That award, too, can be appealed at the conclusion of the current proceedings.

The notice of appeal is construed as a petition for a writ of mandamus, which is denied.

Notes and Questions

1. Under what part of Rule 53 would the district court's use of masters in this case be justified?

2. The masters in *Cordoza* were asked to do something extraordinary: find a use for contaminated property that would generate money to fund a retirement plan. It makes sense that a judge would appoint a master with expertise in the particular area. But is there any danger in this practice? Wayne Brazil, who served as a magistrate judge, believes that "generalist judges may be tempted to rely too heavily on the master's expertise." Wayne Brazil, *Special Masters in Complex Cases: Extending the Judiciary or Reshaping Adjudication?*, 53 U. Chi. L. Rev. 394, 419 (1986). What is wrong with relying on someone hired for her expertise?

3. *Cordoza* is a good example of "institutional" or "structural" litigation. In these cases, the court enters an order or decree commanding reform, and appoints a master to get it done. Examples include school desegregation orders or changes in the operation of a facility for the handicapped. For instance, in *Ruiz v. Estelle*, 679 F.2d 1115 (5th Cir. 1982), the court ordered reform of a state prison system. It engaged a master to implement the court order and oversee compliance. The court gave the master "unlimited access" to the prison premises and records and allowed him to hold confidential interviews with staff members and inmates. The Fifth Circuit upheld the delegation, which it characterized as "report[ing] on compliance with the district court's decrees and . . . help[ing] to implement the decree." *Id.* at 1161.

It is imperative in such cases, however, that the master actually undertake to enforce a court order. In *Cobell v. Norton*, 334 F.3d 1128 (9th Cir. 2003), the district judge, over the objection of the defendant, appointed a "court monitor" in a case against the United States concerning its failure to account for government trust benefits to Indians. The "monitor" was given sweeping powers to investigate a wide range of activities by the Department of the Interior. After the investigation, the court held the Department of the Interior in contempt.

The Ninth Circuit rejected this use of Rule 53 and held that the district court had no inherent power to impose such a "monitor." First, the "Monitor could [not] have been limited to enforcing a decree, for there was no decree to enforce, let alone the sort of specific and detailed decreed issued in *Ruiz* and typical of such cases." *Id.* at 1143. Second, the authority given was far too sweeping: "The Monitor's portfolio was truly extraordinary; instead of resolving disputes brought to him by the parties, he became something like a party himself. The Monitor was charged with an investigative, quasi-inquisitorial, quasi-prosecutorial role that is unknown to our adversarial legal system." *Id.* at 1142.

Could the "monitor" have been given these powers in this case if the parties consented? Apparently so. The court said: "When the parties consent to such an arrangement, we have no occasion to inject ourselves into their affairs." *Id.* What part of Rule 53 makes that clear?

4. Masters are profitably employed to oversee the pretrial phase of complex litigation, including discovery. "Special masters can successfully oversee discovery, particularly where there are numerous issues—such as claims of privilege—to resolve or where the parties are extraordinarily contentious." MANUAL FOR COMPLEX LITIGATION (FOURTH) § 11.424 (2004). Although often this is a task the judge certainly could do, use of masters to oversee progress of the case through pretrial may be especially efficient. In addition, the court can call on masters with expertise as needed. For instance, cases involving discovery of electronically generated and stored information might benefit from the appointment of a master well versed in such matters.

5. Masters are frequently engaged in active promotion of settlement. This is a task the district judge should avoid. Why? It often involves blunt talk with parties individually—including *ex parte* communication—which is always problematic for the court. Moreover, it would expose the judge to information that would not be admissible at trial, and on which an ultimate decision cannot be based. The worry is that the judge, once exposed to such information, will not be able to ignore it. To avoid such problems, courts may appoint a master (or magistrate). Because this adjunct will not be presiding if there is a trial, she has far greater freedom to engage in such discussions and in (figurative) arm-twisting to get the parties to work out their differences.

Note on Court Appointment of Expert Witnesses

Magistrate judges and special masters are adjuncts to a federal judge: they perform judicial functions, but, as we just saw, under carefully limited circumstances.

Here we address a different issue: the authority of the district judge to appoint an expert witness. Many complex cases feature expert testimony. In fact, it is common for the parties to retain experts—both to consult generally on the case and to give testimony at trial (and, of course, in discovery). Regardless of what the parties do, the court has the authority to appoint an expert witness. This is done to aid the court, not one of the parties, and the expert so appointed must be impartial. One problem, of course, is that once the expert runs her tests or executes her studies and comes to a conclusion, that conclusion will probably favor one party over the other.

The federal court's authority to appoint an expert witness is embodied in Federal Rule of Evidence 706, which provides:

> (a) Appointment. The court may on its own motion or on the motion of any party enter an order to show cause why expert witnesses should not be appointed, and may request the parties to submit nominations. The court may appoint any expert witnesses agreed upon by the parties, and may appoint expert witnesses of its own selection. An expert witness shall not be appointed by the court unless the witness consents to act. A witness so appointed shall be informed of the witness' duties by the court in writing, a copy of which shall be filed with the clerk, or at a conference in which the parties shall have opportunity to participate. A witness so appointed shall advise the parties of the witness' findings, if any; the witness' deposition may be taken by any party; and the witness may be called to testify by the court or any party. The witness shall be subject to cross-examination by each party, including a party calling the witness.
>
> (b) Compensation.—Expert witnesses so appointed are entitled to reasonable compensation in whatever sum the court may allow. The compensation thus fixed is payable from funds which may be provided by law in criminal cases and civil actions and proceedings involving just compensation under the fifth amendment. In other civil actions and proceedings the compensation shall be paid by the parties in such proportion and at such time as the court directs, and thereafter charged in like manner as other costs.

Under this provision, the court in *In re Breast Implant Cases*, 942 F. Supp. 958, 960–961 (S.D.N.Y. 1996), appointed experts to determine the relevance of proposed scientific evidence. In another case, after the parties' medical experts disagreed on whether the plaintiff was totally disabled by a disease, the court appointed an independent medical expert to help analyze the expert evidence. *Walker v. American Home Shield Long Term Disability Plan*, 180 F.3d 1065, 1071 (9th Cir. 1999). In a case involving prison conditions, the court appointed experts from different professions to analyze the prison. *Alexander S. v. Boyd*, 876 F.Supp. 773, 782 (D.S.C. 1995).

Court appointment of expert witnesses is fraught with problems, and the practice remains relatively rare. Consider the following discussion, which is written by

Judge Jack Weinstein of the Eastern District of New York (a former Civil Procedure professor). Note his reliance on the adversarial model of litigation.

> Rule 706 codifies the judge's inherent power to appoint expert witnesses—a specific instance of the court's general power to call witnesses . . . in civil and criminal cases. The appointment may be initiated by motion of the court or the motion of any party. In practice, this is a rare occurrence in both state and federal courts. There are several reasons for this rarity.
>
> Perhaps most basically, it is against the common-law tradition for the court to get involved in the process of actually digging out evidence. That occurs more often in the Continental or inquisitorial system than in the adversarial process of the English common-law. . . .
>
> Also arising from our respect for the adversarial process is the fear of ex parte communications between the court and its expert. . . .
>
> Then there is the expense. Court-appointed experts are entitled to "reasonable compensation in whatever sum the court may allow." While there are limited funds available for this purpose in criminal cases, there are virtually none in civil cases where the parties must share the cost "in such proportion . . . as the court directs." . . .
>
> A court-appointed expert may be called as a trial witness "by the court or any party." This prospect complicates the task of getting an expert who is willing to serve. . . .
>
> Whatever its cause, it is indisputable that court appointment of experts is a rarity. This is unfortunate, since it tends to sacrifice truth on the altar of expediency. . . .

WEINSTEIN'S FEDERAL EVIDENCE § 706.02.

Judges have occasionally engaged experts outside Rule 706. In the complex and complicated antitrust litigation against Microsoft, the district judge asked a distinguished economist to file an *amicus curiae* brief in the case. The expert did so, and the court ultimately relied upon the brief as authority for its decision. *United States v. Microsoft Corp.*, 253 F.3d 34, 47, 89 (D.C. Cir. 2001). One scholar reacted: "this option is uncommon and usually is unattractive. If a judge is to go to the effort of identifying and arranging for the involvement of some expert, usually the judge will want input more flexible and interactive than the formality of a brief permits. In this situation, the judge should consider appointing a court expert under Federal Rule of Evidence 706." John Shepard Wiley, Jr., *Taming Patent: Six Steps for Surviving Scary Patent Cases*, 50 UCLA L. REV. 1413, 1425 (2003).

An older complex antitrust case, which pre-dated the adoption of the Federal Rules of Evidence, involves a more creative engagement of an expert. After two years of pretrial activity in *United States v. United Shoe Machinery Corp.*, 110 F. Supp. 295 (D. Mass. 1953), Judge Charles Wyzanski decided he needed more grounding in economics. He appointed as his law clerk an economist who did not have a law degree. The law clerk retained his position as assistant professor at Harvard while working for the judge. Carl Kaysen, *In Memoriam: Charles E. Wyzanski, Jr.*, 100 HARV. L. REV. 713, 714 (1987).

Judge Wyzanski likened his employment of the economics professor to consulting a book on economics. Just as no party had the right to object to the judge's reading, so no party should object to consulting an expert. *Id.* Interestingly, the judge later changed his mind, and concluded that he should have made Dr. Kaysen's report available to them for review and comment. *Id.* at 715.

Finally, in the excerpt above, note that Judge Weinstein worries about the risk of *ex parte* communications—that is, communications directly with the court outside the hearing of one or more of the parties. One consequence of increased judicial managerial responsibility is exposure to such communications. It raises a possibility to which we now turn—that a party will move to have the judge disqualified.

D. Motions to Disqualify (or "Recuse")

In federal court, cases are assigned to a single district judge for all purposes. The assignment is made at random by the clerk's office when the case is filed. The same judge who handles pretrial conferences will handle motions, discovery, and eventually trial itself.[9] (A magistrate judge may be assigned at the outset as well; she will handle all matters the district judge refers to her.) Over the span of the case, the judge usually gets to know the parties and the lawyers and, because of pretrial management, soon learns the basic contentions in the case. This is an advantage in that the parties do not have to educate a new judge for each aspect of the case. It is a disadvantage, however, if you conclude that the judge doesn't like you.

And with increased case management, there are increased possibilities that the judge might form an impression, pro or con, of a party or a lawyer. One of the significant worries about judicial oversight of cases and increased numbers of pretrial conferences is that the judge may lose her impartiality. As Professor Resnik observed: "[J]udges are in close contact with attorneys during the course of management. Such interactions may become occasions for the development of intense feelings—admiration, friendship, or antipathy. Therefore, management becomes a fertile field for the growth of personal bias." Judith Resnik, *Managerial Judges, supra*, 96 HARV. L. REV. at 427.

Two statutes govern disqualification of judges in federal court. Although they use the term "disqualification," courts and lawyers frequently refer to the process of removing a judge from a case as "recusal." There was some historical distinction

9. There are some exceptions. For instance, in Chapter 3, section B.3, we saw that a case may be assigned through "low numbering" to a judge who is already handling related litigation.

between the terms, but now they are interchangeable. While some state court systems give a peremptory right to have a judge removed from a case, the federal system has never adopted such a rule.

The two federal statutes are 28 U.S.C. §§ 144 and 455. Section 144 is flawed and should be of little consequence. First, it applies only to district judges, while § 455 applies to all Article III judges and magistrate judges (and even, through Rule 53, to masters). Second, § 144 permits recusal on only a single basis: actual bias or prejudice. Section 455 also includes this basis, along with several others. Third, § 144 requires a party to move for recusal, and imposes a cumbersome affidavit and certification requirement. Under § 455, in contrast, the judge is under a duty to recuse herself; parties need not make motions, although they may do so if they desire simply by calling the court's attention to the basis for recusal, without an affidavit or certification.

With these distinctions in mind, study the two provisions. Section 144 provides:

> Whenever a party to any proceeding in a district court makes and files a timely and sufficient affidavit that the judge before whom the matter is pending has a personal bias or prejudice either against him or in favor of any adverse party, such judge shall proceed no further therein, but another judge shall be assigned to hear such proceeding.
>
> The affidavit shall state the facts and the reasons for the belief that bias or prejudice exists and shall be filed not less than ten days before the beginning of the term at which the proceeding is to be heard, or good cause shall be shown for failure to file it within such time. A party may file only one such affidavit in any case. It shall be accompanied by a certificate of counsel of record stating that it is made in good faith.

Section 455 provides in relevant part:

> (a) Any justice, judge, or magistrate [judge] of the United States shall disqualify himself in any proceeding in which his impartiality might reasonably be questioned.
>
> (b) He shall also disqualify himself in the following circumstances:
>
> > (1) Where he has a personal bias or prejudice concerning a party, or personal knowledge of disputed evidentiary facts concerning the proceeding;
> >
> > (2) Where in private practice he served as lawyer in the matter in controversy, or a lawyer with whom he previously practiced law served during such association as a lawyer concerning the matter, or the judge or such lawyer has been a material witness concerning it;
> >
> > (3) Where he has served in governmental employment and in such capacity participated as counsel, adviser or material witness concerning the proceeding or expressed an opinion concerning the merits of the particular case in controversy;

(4) He knows that he, individually or as a fiduciary, or his spouse or minor child residing in his household, has a financial interest in the subject matter in controversy or in a party to the proceeding, or any other interest that could be substantially affected by the outcome of the proceeding;

(5) He or his spouse, or a person within the third degree of relationship to either of them, or the spouse of such a person:

(i) Is a party to the proceeding, or an officer, director, or trustee of a party;

(ii) Is acting as a lawyer in the proceeding;

(iii) Is known by the judge to have an interest that could be substantially affected by the outcome of the proceeding;

(iv) Is to the judge's knowledge likely to be a material witness in the proceeding.

Section 455(b)(1) contains two bases for recusal. The first—"a personal bias or prejudice concerning a party"—is precisely the same as the sole basis for disqualification under § 144—that is, actual bias or prejudice. Importantly, though, bias or prejudice will only disqualify a judge under either of these provisions if its source is "extrajudicial." We will see this concept below, but it requires that the judge's disfavor must arise from outside the litigation. This is a significant restriction on recusal.

The second basis in § 455(b)(1) is that the judge has "personal knowledge of disputed evidentiary facts concerning the proceeding." The remaining provisions of § 455(b) are relatively specific. If any applies, the judge must recuse. The most significant provision in recusal law is § 455(a), which requires the judge to recuse when her "impartiality might reasonably be questioned." Here, a judge who harbors no actual bias may have to admit that her conduct might appear to reflect bias.

Who rules on a motion to recuse? Though it is acceptable to have the challenged judge ask a colleague to rule on the motion, that practice is rare. In almost all instances, the judge will rule on the question of whether she should be disqualified.

Notes and Questions

1. Section 455(b) deals with a judge's previous association with a case now before him. It distinguishes, however, between a judge who was previously in private practice (in § 455(b)(2)) and one who was previously in government service (in § 455(b)(3)). What difference does it make?

2. Suppose a judge is assigned to work on a case involving XYZ Corp, which is publicly traded, with millions of shares of stock owned by thousands of shareholders. The judge owns one share of stock in XYZ Corp. Must she recuse under § 455(b)(4)? Compare the language concerning financial interest with that dealing

with other (non-financial) interests. While she is disqualified for any direct financial interest, a non-financial interest is disqualifying only if that interest "could be substantially affected by the outcome of the proceeding." So there is a degree of discretion concerning non-financial interests that is not present with regard to financial interests.

Section 455(f) is a salutary provision. It applies when a judge discovers that she has a financial interest in a party "after substantial judicial time has been devoted to the matter." In such a case, if the interest is not substantial, she may simply divest the interest and avoid recusal. What policy supports this provision?

3. Although § 455 on its face applies to more judicial officers than § 144, it says nothing about masters. But Rule 53(a)(2) provides: "A master must not have a relationship to the parties, attorneys, action, or court that would require disqualification of a judge under 28 U.S.C. § 455, unless the parties, with the court's approval, consent to the appointment after the master discloses any potential grounds for disqualification." Moreover, under Rule 53(b)(3)(A), a master cannot be appointed until she "files an affidavit disclosing whether there is any ground for disqualification under 28 U.S.C. § 455."

4. As noted, bias or prejudice generally will only disqualify a judge if it is "extrajudicial." And even if a judge has no actual bias or prejudice, § 455(a) imposes a duty to recuse based upon the appearance that she has lost her impartiality. The following case deals with these issues in the context of the court's active engagement in pretrial management, including settlement discussions.

Fairley v. Andrews

United States District Court for the Northern District of Illinois
423 F. Supp. 2d 800 (2006)

Castillo, District Judge.

This hotly-contested lawsuit—in which two former guards at the Cook County jail have alleged a conspiracy by defendants [who include the county and the sheriff and other corrections officials] to cover up inmate abuse—has been pending before this Court for over two and a half years. It is the oldest lawsuit presently pending on this Court's docket. During the course of this litigation, this Court has resolved 146 contested motions, mainly concerning discovery disputes between the parties. That number does not include either the instant motion for recusal or the twelve motions for summary judgment which this Court was actively considering at the time Defendants filed the instant motions.

On February 17, 2006—only two months before trial was scheduled to begin in this case—defendants [filed a recusal motion under § 144 and § 455]. . . . In what can only be described as a kitchen-sink approach to this matter, Defendants' . . .

motion[s] contain a broad slew of allegations which purport to demonstrate this Court's bias against them. In light of the extremely contentious and protracted proceedings in this case, this Court considers this to be a very serious motion which warrants close scrutiny. This Court has carefully considered each of Defendants' arguments and allegations and will address them all below.

LEGAL STANDARDS

... Under section 455(a), a judge must recuse himself "in any proceeding in which his impartiality might reasonably be questioned." 28 U.S.C. § 455(a). This is an objective standard that asks if a reasonable observer would perceive "a significant risk that the judge will resolve the case on a basis other than the merits." *Hook v. McDade*, 89 F.3d 350, 354 (7th Cir. 1996). Section 455(a) only applies if a judge's impartiality would be questioned by a "well-informed, thoughtful observer rather than ... a hypersensitive or unduly suspicious observer." *Hook*, 89 F.3d at 354.

[R]ecusal statutes require bias to "stem from an extrajudicial source." *Liteky v. United States*, 510 U.S. 540, 544, 554 (1994). The Supreme Court, however, has held that the extrajudicial source doctrine is not absolute, and in some rare cases recusal is warranted where a judge's "favorable or unfavorable predisposition ... even though it springs from the facts adduced or events occurring at trial ... is so extreme as to display the clear inability to render fair judgment." Consequently, this Court will address each of Defendants' arguments for recusal, even though the vast majority of their arguments are based on judicial sources.

ANALYSIS

I. No Actual Bias Exists Under 28 U.S.C. § 144

This Court has no conceivable actual bias in this case. Pursuant to section 144, Defendants have submitted affidavits purporting to demonstrate this Court's actual bias against them personally and against their case generally. These affidavits contain self-serving, broad allegations of this Court's partiality. Defendants argue that this Court is biased because it: (1) has entered numerous adverse rulings against Defendants; (2) has allegedly threatened to communicate with potential jurors regarding defense counsel's conduct in this case; [and] (3) has made comments in the course of settlement discussions and on the record indicating the Court's disapproval of defense counsel's refusal to settle in light of the perceived merits of Plaintiffs' case.... Despite the far-fetched nature of some of the assertions put forth in Defendants' motion and accompanying affidavits, this Court will fully address each of the arguments below to ensure that there is no lingering doubt regarding this Court's lack of actual interest or bias in this case.

A. Judicial Rulings

... Defendant Sheahan's counsel made clear that at the heart of this motion lie "rulings that the Court has made to motions, some of the procedures that were put in place through the discovery process." The Supreme Court has held, however, that "judicial rulings alone almost never constitute a valid basis for a bias or partiality motion." *Liteky*, 510 U.S. at 555. In the absence of evidence of extrajudical bias, adverse rulings "can only in the rarest circumstances evidence the degree of favoritism or antagonism required[.]" The Seventh Circuit has acknowledged that rather than demonstrating judicial bias, numerous rulings in favor of one party "may show nothing more than that [party] had the better case or the abler lawyer."

. . .

B. Communication with Prospective Jury

Defendants' allegation that this Judge intends to tell the jury that the defense of this case is a waste of taxpayer dollars is simply untrue. This Court intends to do nothing of the sort, and nothing in any comments this Court has made justifies an inference to the contrary. The comment that Defendants rely on is:

> I will tell you, I think what is going on here is a travesty in terms of a misexpenditure of public funds, that somebody should be held accountable. And if I go through this trial with a bunch of jurors, if I go through this trial, I will be very vocal about that on a public record; and if there is a verdict for the plaintiff, I will not end my criticism of the decisions that were made in this case, and I intend to make every defense counsel bare their records as to how much money has been paid by the taxpayers in this county. That's where I intend to go with this.

This Court stated and meant that "if I go through this trial" and "if there is a verdict for the plaintiff," *then* "I will be very vocal" and "I will not end my criticism of the decisions that were made in this case" about the misexpenditure of public funds. Defendants' strained reading of this passage and inflammatory accusation that this Court would commit an ethical violation belie not only the record but common sense, as such a comment to the jury would necessarily result in a mistrial. In every trial before this Court, this Court admonishes jurors not to read anything about the case in the media or elsewhere nor to discuss this case with anyone. Nothing in this Court's statements justify Defendants' insinuation that any other procedure would be followed in this case.

C. Comments Made in the Context of Settlement Discussions and Referencing the Cost of this Litigation

It is no secret among members of the federal bar that this Court strongly encourages an early and constant assessment of settlement possibilities in order to avoid the "winner take all" outcome that litigation often presents. In fact, in certain instances after both parties have devoted significant resources to a lawsuit, it is difficult to distinguish the winner from the loser. This lawsuit clearly falls into that category.

This Court has personally held three lengthy settlement conferences in this case and has repeatedly made additional offers to hold more conferences in chambers which Defendants have rejected. None of the comments made or matters discussed in the course of these settlement conferences have been publicized. All such comments are covered by the settlement privilege. *See* Fed. R. Evid. 408. This Court has never breached that privilege during the public proceedings on this lawsuit.[10]

Defendants assert that comments this Court made during the course of settlement discussions or in referencing those conferences should be the basis for recusal. For the reasons set forth below, this Court strongly disagrees.

1. Admonishments of Defense Counsel and Litigation Subcommittee

Defendants claim that this Court has "baselessly" accused Defendants' counsel of improper motives in their defense of this case. This Court, rather than "accusing" Defendants of anything "baseless," has repeatedly noted that the parties' unwillingness to heed the Court's reasonable recommendations in the context of settlement negotiations has contributed to the astronomical cost of the present litigation. These recommendations were supported by this Court's even-handed analysis of the facts presented by the parties in those settlement conferences, the risks to the parties of trying this case before a jury, and this Court's twelve years of experience in presiding over civil rights cases. Only after spending hours presiding over fruitless settlement discussions in which Defendants' counsel repeatedly cited the Litigation Subcommittee's unwillingness to accept this Court's recommendations did this Court form a well-founded concern that:

> Well, I think the Litigation Subcommittee is good at rejecting things, but what they're not good at is evaluating litigation, and that's unfortunate. So if they want to take the position, which I think is probably not the unanimous view, but the problem is I have defense attorneys who have a self-interest, their own pocketbook, and they're lining their pocketbook with taxpayer money at this point, and I'm wondering if the Litigation Subcommittee has considered that.

This statement represents an informed observation by this Court that the Litigation Subcommittee had not fully considered the benefits of settlement given the risks incumbent in trying this case.

. . .

---

10. [Court's footnote #13] This Court is concerned, however, that the rules of this Court have been breached by the publication of Plaintiffs' specific settlement demand in the media. *See* Abdon M. Pallasch, *Sheriff: Biased Judge Should Quit Jail Beating Case*, CHI. SUN TIMES, Feb. 27, 2006. At a status hearing held on March 14, 2006, all counsel with one glaring exception—defense attorney John T. Roache of the law firm of Bell, Boyd & Lloyd, LLC—denied disclosing Plaintiffs' specific settlement demand to the media. All settlement discussions and demands in this case are inadmissible at trial pursuant to FED. R. EVID. 408. Local Rule 83.53.6 prohibits any extrajudicial statements to the public media that a lawyer knows or reasonably should know would be inadmissible as evidence in a trial. . . . The dissemination of Plaintiffs' specific demand to a member of the media can only serve to prejudice Plaintiffs by setting a numeric "cap" on their damages or by seeking to depict Plaintiffs as being driven solely by monetary concerns. Therefore, this Court has no choice but to refer this matter to this Court's Executive Committee for appropriate potential disciplinary proceedings against any member of this Court's bar who violated [Local Rule] 83.53.6(b)(6).

Defendants' suggestion that this Court's admonishment of their attorneys' conduct justifies recusal is also erroneous. Ordinarily, an allegation of judicial bias relates to bias against a party, not a party's attorney. *Charron v. U.S.*, 200 F.3d 785, 788–89 (Fed. Cir. 1999). A judicial bias against the lawyer only warrants recusal where it becomes so pervasive that the client's rights are likely to be affected. . . .

2. Comment Regarding the Misexpenditure of Taxpayer Money

One serious problem posed by this hotly-disputed litigation is that both sides may be paid by the Cook County taxpayers. Plaintiffs' attorneys will, of course, only receive fees if they prevail. In that circumstance, those fees and any judgment for Plaintiffs would be paid by the taxpayers of Cook County. Defendants' private counsel are all being paid with public funds. The cost of defending this litigation has already significantly exceeded early possibilities for a cost-effective settlement. Any such possibility was rejected by Defendants' attorneys. Given that reality, this Court has expressed its concern that taxpayer dollars are being misappropriated in this case. Specifically, this Court has stated that:

> "It's the opinion, very strong opinion, on my part that this is going to lead to a waste of taxpayers' money, and it already has, with no insult to defense counsel. But the fact that I've paid for you all to be here in this courtroom and that, more importantly, a lot of other people that don't make as much money as I do have paid, I think it's very sad to me."
>
> "I'm also concerned, I will tell you this, just as a Cook County taxpayer, about the amount of money that is being spent in this case. You know, all the taxpayers in Cook County paid their property tax bills on November 1st. How much have the defendants spent in attorneys fees in this case? I think we could have had the case settled already."
>
> "I think there should be some public accounting of how this money is being spent at this point, and I really call on the sheriff to take a look at this and the County board to take a look at this because this is a misexpenditure of public funds. This is not like a company just spending money."

Defendants assert that this Court's statements demonstrate bias because: (1) this Court seeks to encourage settlement in this purportedly "meritless" case; and (2) this Court's pecuniary interest in this litigation as a taxpayer of Cook County "is the reason for" his opposition to Defendants' defense of this case. None of these statements indicate that this Court has a pecuniary interest in this litigation. A pecuniary interest, such as that of a taxpayer, "which a judge has in common with many others in a public matter is not sufficient to disqualify him." [citations omitted]

[T]here is no support for Defendants' accusation that this Court's comments regarding expenditure of taxpayers' money is linked to any pecuniary interest that might warrant recusal. The Court acknowledges that it probably pushed too hard to settle this lawsuit because of its general concerns for the Cook County taxpayers. The Court's expressed concerns, however, do not require its recusal.

. . .

4. Comments Regarding the Merits of Case

. . .

Defendants also object to this Court's comments during a settlement conference that took place on December 13, 2005. Defendants assert that during that conference this Court likened the continued defense of this case to Vietnam and informed the parties that he believes Plaintiffs will likely prevail at trial and the County will be forced to pay Plaintiffs' attorneys' fees. This Court is more than entitled to assess the merits of the parties' cases in the course of settlement discussions, and this Court's analogy to Vietnam simply conveyed its opinion—proven true over the course of this litigation—that often there is no winner in a case like this when parties refuse to consider reasonable settlement offers and litigation drags on.

. . . Numerous Circuits agree that these kinds of comments do not necessitate judicial recusal.[11] As the Supreme Court has held, "opinions formed by the judge on the basis of facts introduced or events occurring in the course of the current proceedings, or of prior proceedings, do not constitute a basis for a bias or partiality motion unless they display a deep-seated favoritism or antagonism that would make fair judgment impossible."[12] *Liteky*, 510 U.S. at 555. Nothing this Court said

11. [Court's footnote #14] *See, e.g., U.S. v. Wallace*, 250 F.3d 738 (5th Cir. 2001) (finding that a district judge's statements made in chambers to attorneys and outside the presence of the jury, expressing concern regarding the parties' and attorneys' conduct "were within the ambit of opinions formed by the judge on the basis of facts introduced or events occurring in the course of the current proceedings" and did not raise a serious question of impartiality); *West v. Johnson*, 92 F.3d 1385, 1411 (5th Cir. 1996) (noting that judge's statement that "the only action this Court would like to be involved in the future with regard to [plaintiff] would be to see the motherf****r fried," was "obviously based on matters learned at trial and, though inappropriate, does not reveal such a high degree of favoritism or antagonism as to make fair judgment impossible") (internal quotation omitted); *Price v. Kramer*, 200 F.3d 1237, 1253 (9th Cir. 2000) (holding that a statement which simply conveys the court's evaluation of which side had the better case does not indicate bias); *PeopleHelpers Found, Inc. v. City of Richmond*, 12 F.3d 1321, 1325–26 (4th Cir. 1993) (finding that a judge's comments about his perception of a defendant's conduct, "while perhaps caustic," were "made in an effort to further the settlement process;" and accordingly, "we cannot conclude that a reasonable person would question his impartiality."); *In re Martinez-Catala*, 129 F.3d 213, 219 (1st Cir. 1997) (stating that "in pressing each side to take a reasonable view of its situation, judges often give the parties the court's impression of apparent strengths and weaknesses. There are dangers in this practice, of course, but clients are often well served by settlements, and settlements often result from realistic appraisals of strengths and weaknesses."); *see also U.S. v. Larson*, 110 F.3d 620, 623 (8th Cir. 1997) (finding that a trial judge who admitted that his comments expressing disapproval of plea agreement were contrary to Federal Rule of Criminal Procedure 11(e) did not display such a "deep-seated favoritism or antagonism that fair judgment is impossible") (quoting *Liteky*, 510 U.S. at 555).

12. [Court's footnote #15] The Supreme Court used as an example of such a high degree of antagonism the statements by the District Judge in *Berger v. United States*, 255 U.S. 22, 28, 41 S. Ct. 230, 65 L. Ed. 481 (1921), who stated that "one must have a very judicial mind, indeed, not [to be] prejudiced against the German Americans" because their "hearts are reeking with disloyalty." *Liteky*, 510 U.S. at 555.

regarding the strength of Plaintiffs' case displays the "deep seated antagonism" toward Defendants or favoritism toward Plaintiffs that could indicate an actual bias.

. . .

II. Appearance of Bias Pursuant to 28 U.S.C. § 455(a)

. . . [T]hough this Court can state without hesitation that nothing in Defendants' briefs or affidavits sufficiently demonstrates this Court's actual bias, after a careful evaluation of the record and transcripts in this case, this Court finds that reasonable minds may disagree as to whether recusal is appropriate in this matter under section 455(a). As explained above, 28 U.S.C. § 455(a) requires a district judge to recuse himself if a reasonable person would perceive a significant risk that the judge will resolve the case on a basis other than the merits. In applying this standard, the Court must bear in mind that these "outside observers are less inclined to credit judges' impartiality and mental discipline than the judiciary itself will be." *Matter of Hatcher*, 150 F.3d 631, 637 (7th Cir. 1998) (citations omitted). Whether a "reasonable person," rather than a "hypersensitive or unduly suspicious person," would perceive a significant risk that this Court will resolve the case on a basis other than the merits is a difficult question in light of these circumstances. This Court reluctantly concludes that recusal is the most prudent course in this matter pursuant to 28 U.S.C. § 455(a).

In this case, none of this Court's individual statements, when viewed in their proper context, warrant recusal under section 455(a). However, in doing the required self-evaluation under this section, this Court finds that all of this Court's statements and interactions with Defendants in this case, taken together, may give pause to a non-legal observer, not versed in the ways of the courtroom and the risks of litigation. This Court candidly admits that its statements on February 1, 2006, regarding public corruption and Defendants' obstinate refusal to consider settlement were a mistake in judgment by this Court. Perhaps because this status hearing occurred shortly after this Court had issued a public corruption sentencing opinion, this Court had the general topic of public corruption on its mind when it made the unfortunate statements. This Court tried to make it clear that it was not accusing Defendants of public corruption. Instead, the Court's primary concern was the continued, seemingly mindless expenditure of public funds in Defendants' draconian defense of this lawsuit. In hindsight, a good argument could be made that this Court should have referred the difficult discovery proceedings to the capable Magistrate Judge assigned to this lawsuit instead of following its usual "hands-on" approach and becoming frustrated by Defendants' attorneys' ill-advised decision to contest almost every issue in this lawsuit while absolutely refusing to consider any type of reasonable settlement. This Court admits in retrospect that it may have pushed too hard to reach a compromise settlement in this lawsuit. The Court did not intend to have its colorful statements coerce a settlement between the parties. The Court will avoid these types of statements in the future.

After careful evaluation of this Court's unfortunate public corruption statements—especially in the wider context of the Court's negative interactions with Defendants' counsel during the contested and extended pretrial proceedings—this Court ultimately concludes the reasonable person standard under section 455(a) has been satisfied and that this Court's recusal is required. This Court feels it must find in the affirmative, using the utmost caution so that Plaintiffs will not be prejudiced by any imagined, contrived, or perceived grounds for appeal that Defendants might use if they ultimately lose at trial. In addition, this Court recuses itself out of utmost caution for the judicial system as a whole because "if a judge proceeds in a case when there is (only) an appearance of impropriety in his doing so, the injury is to the judicial system as a whole and not to the substantial rights of the parties." *U.S. v. Troxell*, 887 F.2d 830, 833 (7th Cir. 1989). "Judges may choose to step aside in close cases; the 'duty to sit' concept has been modified by amended section 455." *Martinez-Catala*, 129 F.3d at 221.

CONCLUSION

This Court recuses itself reluctantly because it is mindful that a sister or brother Judge will be left with this hotly contested piece of litigation, its remaining contested motions, and the possibility of a full-blown trial that unfortunately may mirror the hostile nature of pre-trial proceedings. . . .

Notes and Questions

1. The judge in *Fairley* finally recused under § 455(a) because a reasonable person could conclude that he had lost his impartiality. He did so, however, only after publishing many pages (omitted here) reviewing his individual rulings in the case and attempting to establish that he had no bias or prejudice in fact. Why did he not simply rule on the basis of § 455(a)?

2. The judge in *Fairley* said, among other things: "And if this case goes all the way to verdict and the verdict comes out as I think it's going to be, there will be a price to be paid, I think, in the public where this should be debated, and it's a huge price." 423 F. Supp. 2d. at 816. He concluded that this and similar statements were not cause for alarm because *jurors* would be screened to ensure they had not heard such remarks. Doesn't the judge miss the point? The worry here is not prejudice of jurors, but of the judge.

3. According to the judge in *Fairley*, when would bias against a lawyer (and not her client) mandate recusal?

4. Should the judge in *Fairley* have assigned the settlement discussion aspect of the case to a magistrate or master? Why do you suppose he did not?

5. The Supreme Court has clarified a good deal about the operation of § 455(a). *Liteky v. United States*, which the court in *Fairley* cited several times, is a leading case. Among other things, it established that the "extrajudicial source" doctrine, which applies to disqualification under 28 U.S.C.A. § 144 and § 455(b)(1), also applies to

an assertion under §455(a) that the judge's impartiality could reasonably be questioned. 510 U.S. at 554. The Court discussed what this "doctrine" means.

> ... As we have described it, however, there is not much doctrine to the doctrine. The fact that an opinion held by a judge derives from a source outside judicial proceedings is not a *necessary* condition for "bias or prejudice" recusal, since predispositions developed during the course of a trial will sometimes (albeit rarely) suffice. Nor is it a *sufficient* condition for "bias or prejudice" recusal, since *some* opinions acquired outside the conduct of judicial proceedings (for example, the judge's view of the law acquired in scholarly reading) will *not* suffice. Since neither the presence of an extrajudicial source necessarily establishes bias, nor the absence of an extrajudicial source necessarily precludes bias, it would be better to speak of the presence of a significant (and often determinative) "extrajudicial source" *factor*, than of an "extrajudicial source" *doctrine*, in recusal jurisprudence.

Id. at 554–555.

Earlier in the *Liteky* opinion the Court had said that "the origin of the 'extrajudicial source' doctrine, and the key to understanding its flexible scope (or the so-called 'exceptions' to it), is simply the pejorative connotation of the words 'bias or prejudice.'" 510 U.S. at 510. The words "connote a favorable or unfavorable disposition or opinion that is somehow *wrongful* or *inappropriate*." *Id.* (emphasis original). The opinion can be wrongful or inappropriate either because it is undeserved, or because it rests upon knowledge that the subject ought not to possess, or because it is excessive in degree.

6. The Court has made clear that scienter is not required for recusal under §455(a). In other words, "[t]he judge's lack of knowledge of a disqualifying circumstance may bear on the question of remedy, but does not eliminate the risk that 'his impartiality might reasonably be questioned' by other persons." *Liljeberg v. Health Services Acquisition Corp.*, 486 U.S. 847, 859 (1988).

7. A wooden application of the extrajudicial source rule would create a Catch-22. We may share Professor Resnik's concern that the judge's increased exposure to the parties in case management increases the chances that she will become biased. But if bias is caused by exposure to matters involved in the litigation, it is not "extrajudicial," and would not support recusal. By the way, what examples can you think of for "extrajudicial" sources of bias or prejudice?

8. Some well publicized recusal orders involve judges who were overseeing complex litigation. The district judge presiding over the government's case against Microsoft made his views of the merits clear to the press, at an antitrust seminar, and in a speech at a college. He apparently gave secret interviews to some members of the press long before the judgment was entered, in which he opined on the merits. Canon 3A(6) of the Code of Conduct for federal judges requires them to "avoid public comment on the merits of . . . pending or impending" cases. Canon 2 reflects language of §455(a) and mandates that judges avoid impropriety and the

appearance of impropriety. In ordering the judge's recusal, the court of appeals concluded "that the District Judge violated each of these ethical precepts by talking about the case with reporters. The violations were deliberate, repeated, egregious, and flagrant." *United States v. Microsoft Corp.*, 253 F.3d 34, 107–117 (D.C. Cir. 2001).

The case presented an interesting question of what can be done to "fix" a wrongful refusal to recuse. Should recusal be prospective, or should the recusal order result in vacating all that had been decided in the case (which could result in substantial relitigation)? The court of appeals took a middle course, ordering recusal and vacating only the district court's ruling on remedy. This result left the liability determination intact. *Id.* at 117.

Some complex cases stay in the judicial system for many years, which may lead to a strained relationship between the judge and a party or lawyer. A good example is the government's civil antitrust case against International Business Machines Corp. (IBM) in the Southern District of New York. Judge Edelstein presided over this truly mammoth litigation. Eleven years after it was filed, and in *the fifth year of trial*, IBM sought recusal on the basis of bias and appearance of bias. Judge Edelstein refused to step down, and the Second Circuit refused to issue mandamus to compel him to do so. It noted that the judge's "asperity and incivility" toward witnesses did not demonstrate bias. Likewise, statistics could not show bias, even though the judge had interrupted IBM's witnesses more than he had the government's witnesses. In sum, any rancor in the relationship did not come from an extrajudicial source and would not support recusal. *In re IBM Corp.*, 618 F.2d 923, 928–931 (2d Cir. 1980).

Eventually, however, Judge Edelstein went too far. In 1982, in the eighth year of trial, the government concluded that there was "little prospect of victory or meaningful recovery," and entered a stipulation with IBM to dismiss the case. The judge refused to recognize the stipulation and made statements to the press questioning whether the government was acting in the public's interest. The behavior became so egregious that the Second Circuit took the extraordinary step of issuing mandamus to require Judge Edelstein to conclude the litigation. *In re IBM Corp.*, 687 F.2d 591, 594 (2d Cir. 1982).

E. Judicial Control Through Sanctions

A court must have authority to enforce its orders. In this section, we review a panoply of tools by which the court can compel compliance or punish non-compliance with orders related to pretrial procedure. We should distinguish between a "merits" sanction and a "monetary" sanction. The former affects the underlying dispute—for example, as by striking a claim or a defense. A monetary sanction requires one party or lawyer write a check to cover costs (and possibly attorneys' fees) incurred by the other party or lawyer. This money may be paid to the other party or to the court. We saw the distinction between merits and monetary sanctions in *Switzer* in section B of this chapter.

In discussing monetary orders, it is important to distinguish between costs and attorneys' fees. Costs are the expenses of litigation: things like filing fees, service of process fees, costs of discovery, witness fees, costs of giving notice to class members, etc. Under Rule 54(d)(1) such costs "should be allowed to the prevailing party" unless the court directs otherwise. In other words, generally, the losing party pays the winning party's costs. Such costs are "taxed" by the court clerk to the losing party and are included in the judgment.

But costs do not include attorney's fees. And in most cases, the attorney's fees will amount to more than the costs. On attorney's fees, the American Rule is that each party bears her own. In other words, the general rule is that the loser does *not* pay the winner's attorneys' fees. This rule is controversial, and many argue that the United States should adopt a "loser pays" rule on attorney's fees. Those supporting the American rule argue that the contrary position would chill meritorious litigation. That is, a person with a legitimate claim that is close on the merits will not take the chance of incurring liability for the defendant's attorneys' fees should she lose. The American rule is subject to exceptions, which permit "fee shifting." We see some examples below and will see more in Chapter 7. As we address the various potential sanctions, keep in mind the distinctions between merits sanctions and monetary awards, including awards of attorney's fees.

1. Federal Rules

Various Federal Rules give the court power to enforce pretrial orders. In *Switzer*, in section B of this chapter, we saw Rule 16(f). The court used it to impose both a merits and a monetary sanction. Another possibility is Rule 41(b), which permits a court to dismiss claims involuntarily when the plaintiff fails to prosecute the action with sufficient diligence or fails to comply with the Federal Rules or a court order. The leading Rule 41(b) case, *Link v. Wabash Railroad Co.*, 370 U.S. 626 (1962), upheld involuntary dismissal for various dilatory acts by the plaintiff's lawyer. The straw that broke the camel's back was his failure to attend a pretrial conference!

Rule 26(g) imposes on counsel a certification requirement regarding discovery documents. That is, signing such a document constitutes a certification that it is not interposed for delay or burden and is otherwise appropriate. We will discuss the discovery phase of litigation in Chapter 8, but note here that Rule 37 provides sanctions for enforcing discovery rules and orders. (Indeed, Rule 16(f) incorporates sanctions from Rule 37, as also seen in *Switzer.*)

A lynchpin of professionalism is Federal Rule 11, which you studied in Civil Procedure. It requires counsel to sign all documents other than those relating to discovery (which, as we saw, are certified under Rule 26(g)). Under Rule 11(b), the signature is a certification to the court of several important things. The provision requires that the person certify "to the best of the person's knowledge, information, and belief, formed after an inquiry reasonable under the circumstances" that four specific items are true. Importantly, Rule 11(b) imposes a continuing certification.

Specifically, the certification under Rule 11(b) is made not just when the lawyer signs the document, but every time she *presents* a document to the court. The first sentence indicates that "presenting" includes "signing, filing, submitting, or later advocating" something asserted in the document. Before 1993, the certification was simply as of the time of signing.

In the aggregate, the certification requirement is intended to ensure that there are reasonable bases for the version of the facts and law asserted.

- First, under Rule 11(b)(1), the signer certifies that the document is not presented for an improper purpose, such as delay or harassment.
- Second, under Rule 11(b)(2), she certifies that the legal contentions are warranted by law or "by a nonfrivolous argument for extending, modifying, or reversing existing law or for establishing new law." This is intended to protect creative lawyering and the assertion of novel theories of the law; the only limitation is that they not be frivolous.
- Third, under Rule 11(b)(3), the signer certifies that the factual contentions "have evidentiary support or, if specifically so identified, will likely have evidentiary support after a reasonable opportunity for further investigation or discovery." This is good language and protects the lawyer who believes that evidence will be found to support a factual assertion.
- Finally, Rule 11(b)(4) provides in like terms for the *denials* of factual allegations. Obviously, then, Rule 11(b)(3) is aimed at parties asserting a claim and Rule 11(b)(4) is aimed at parties defending against a claim.

Purported violations of Rule 11 may be raised in two ways. First, of course, the court may raise them on its own. Under Rule 11(c)(3), the court will enter an order to show cause requiring a party, attorney, or law firm to show cause why specified behavior did not violate Rule 11(b). Second, a party may move for sanctions against another party or her attorney or law firm under Rule 11(c)(2). The motion must state specifically what conduct allegedly violated Rule 11(b) and must be brought separately from any other motions. It is important to note, however, that Rule 11(c)(2) has a "safe harbor" of 21 days for the party allegedly violating Rule 11.

Regardless of how the matter gets to the court—on the court's initiative or by motion after the safe harbor period—what sanctions are available?

First, sanctions under Rule 11 are not required (they once were), but are to be imposed in the discretion of the court.

Second, the purpose of sanctions is not to punish wrongful behavior, but to deter such behavior in the future. As Rule 11(c)(4) states, "A sanction imposed under this rule must be limited to what suffices to deter repetition of the conduct or comparable conduct by others similarly situated." Rule 11(c)(4) suggests that nonmonetary sanctions are appropriate. These can include directives to the person violating the Rule to do some act. The court may order the offender to "pay a penalty into court." Also, if imposed on motion and "warranted for effective deterrence," the court may require the offender to pay all or part of the expenses—expressly including attorneys' fees—incurred by the moving party as a direct result of the violation of Rule 11. Note that under Rule 11(c)(5)(A), a party represented by counsel cannot be held liable for a monetary sanction for violating Rule 11(b)(2). This makes sense, because that certification relates to the legal contentions; a party represented by a lawyer cannot be presumed to know the law sufficiently to satisfy that certification item.

2. Statutory Fee Shifting

In Chapter 7, we will study the court's authority to appoint class or lead counsel and to provide for payment of attorney's fees in complex litigation. Congress has passed various statutes to allow recovery of attorney's fees in certain substantive areas. Of more general interest is 28 U.S.C. § 1927. That statute permits fee-shifting against a lawyer who has acted inappropriately in creating unnecessary litigation.

Dixon v. Clem

United States Court of Appeals, Sixth Circuit
492 F.3d 665 (2007)

[A high school carpentry teacher, Dixon, was fired for taking topless photographs of a female student. He hired a lawyer named Blum, who filed suit for Dixon under 42 U.S.C. § 1983, which creates a claim for deprivation of one's federal civil rights under color of state law. Dixon sued a variety of school officials, alleging *inter alia* that they had violated his right of due process. Dixon lost on the merits, after which the defendants sought to recover attorneys' fees under 42 U.S.C. § 1988(b). That statute permits an award of attorney's fees to the "prevailing party" in a § 1983 case.]

Following the dismissal of Dixon's claims against them, the defendants filed a motion for attorney fees pursuant to 42 U.S.C. § 1988. They argued that, as the prevailing parties in Dixon's § 1983 action, they were entitled to such fees. *See* 42 U.S.C. § 1988(b) (providing that, in a civil-rights action, "the court, in its discretion, may allow the prevailing party . . . a reasonable attorney's fee as part of the costs").

The district court denied the defendants' motion, concluding that Dixon's claims, although "extremely close to the line," were not frivolous. . . . "Before a defendant may recover attorney's fees under 42 U.S.C. § 1988, the plaintiff's claim must have been 'frivolous, unreasonable, or groundless,' or 'the plaintiff continued to litigate after it clearly became so.'" . . . *Christiansburg Garment Co. v. EEOC*, 434 U.S. 412, 422 (1978).

But the district court did not leave the defendants entirely without a remedy. Instead, it sua sponte imposed sanctions directly on Blum as Dixon's attorney pursuant to 28 U.S.C. § 1927, which provides that

> [a]ny attorney or other person admitted to conduct cases in any court of the United States or any Territory thereof who so multiplies the proceedings

> in any case unreasonably and vexatiously may be required by the court *to satisfy personally* the excess costs, expenses, and attorneys' fees reasonably incurred because of such conduct.

The district court set forth a laundry list of "improper conduct by the Plaintiff's counsel," which included

> the pressing of specious legal claims and filings in this case which either contained inappropriate language, claims and assertions (requiring unnecessary responses) or which were inappropriate *en toto*. Indeed, despite being warned by the Court that his actions were improper, Mr. Blum continued to make personal attacks. Additionally, he continued to instruct opposing counsel and the Court as to the "proper procedures" that each should follow.

Some of Blum's arguments were inappropriate, moreover, because they were "directly contradictory to the explicit language of the [Kentucky] state court of appeals." The district court said that although it "is reluctant to hold Dixon responsible [for] the conduct set out above, it has no reluctance toward holding Mr. Blum responsible." It concluded that the "total effect" of Blum's misconduct was "to cause needless delay to the Court and unnecessary expense to the Defendants." *Id.* The sanctions imposed totaled $6,938.00.

...

Simply put, the record in this case fully supports the district court's decision to impose sanctions on Blum. The briefing in the present appeal hints at why. In response to [a defendant's] qualified-immunity argument, Blum states as follows:

> [Defendant's] attempt to claim quasi-judicial immunity is likewise devoid of supporting materials. All he has established so far is that he called the historical docudrama exercise "a hearing," generated a "final order" after it, and that it was conducted indoors. This is insufficient. If a judge or hearing officer calls a plaintiff into his chambers saying, "your trial is about to begin" and then rapes her and states that she has "prevailed," the fact that he calls it "a trial" will hardly allow him to invoke quasi-judicial immunity. The historical docudrama exercise in this case occupies a position about halfway between a bona fide tribunal hearing and a rape.

If this is the type of language that Blum believes will persuade us to reverse a ruling against both him and his client, we can understand why his conduct before the district court got him into trouble in the first place. Nor are we surprised to discover that other courts have been displeased with his conduct in the past. He has been reprimanded and/or sanctioned on at least three separate occasions by three separate federal courts, including this one....

We would be wrong, of course, to presume that Blum misbehaved in this case simply because he has misbehaved in previous cases. Such a presumption would violate the principles that underlie the innocent-until-proven-guilty maxim in criminal cases as well as the general prohibition against the admission of propensity evidence in federal cases. *See* Fed. R. Evid. 404(b) ("Evidence of other crimes, wrongs, or acts is not admissible to prove the character of a person in order to show action in conformity therewith.").

But where, as here, we must resolve the less-probing question of whether the district court abused its discretion in concluding that Blum had misbehaved, Blum's prior conduct is telling. *Cf. id.* (noting that, as an exception to the general rule, evidence of past wrongdoing may be admissible, among other reasons, to prove the "absence of mistake or accident"). This was, moreover, "a lengthy and complex case with which the district court was closely familiar." *See Bridgeport Music, Inc. v. London Music, U.K.*, Nos. 05-5045-5058, 226 Fed. Appx. 491, 2007 U.S. App. LEXIS 7847, at *7 (6th Cir. Mar. 28, 2007) (concluding that, in a "lengthy and complex" case where the "court employs the proper legal standard and specifically and thoroughly states the reasons for its decision, that decision is entitled to considerable deference").

. . .

We therefore affirm the district court's decision to impose sanctions on Blum. In addition, we cannot emphasize enough that Blum needs to learn his lesson at some point: His behavior, whether motivated by bad faith or not, not only reflects poorly on himself and his profession, but, far more importantly, is of no benefit to his clients.

Notes and Questions

1. Under § 1927, a sanction is permitted only if: (1) the attorney sanctioned engaged in "unreasonable and vexatious" conduct and (2) the conduct "multiplie[d] the proceedings." Beyond this, courts must tailor the sanction to the extra litigation incurred because of the behavior. In other words, "the dollar amount of the sanction must bear a financial nexus to the excess proceedings, i.e., the sanction may not exceed the 'costs, expenses, and attorneys' fees reasonably incurred because of such conduct.'" *Peterson v. BMI Refractories*, 124 F.3d 1386, 1396 (11th Cir. 1997). How should a court determine the attorney's fees reasonably incurred by the other party? We will discuss attorney's fee awards in a different context in Chapter 7, and see how courts might assess what fee is reasonable.

2. The clear majority of the courts of appeals conclude that § 1927 does not require a showing that the attorney sanctioned acted with subjective intent. In *Amlong & Amlong, P.A. v. Denny's, Inc.*, 500 F.3d 1230, 1239–1241 (11th Cir. 2006), the court surveyed the case law:

> We have consistently held that an attorney multiplies proceedings "unreasonably and vexatiously" within the meaning of the statute only when the attorney's conduct is so egregious that it is "tantamount to bad faith." Avirgan v. Hull, 932 F.2d 1572, 1582 (11th Cir. 1991); see also Schwartz v. Millon Air, Inc., 341 F.3d 1220, 1225 (11th Cir. 2003) ("'Bad faith' is the touchstone.").

The [lawyers sanctioned] argue, however, that "bad faith" in this context means subjective bad faith—that is, deliberate wrongdoing, such as proceeding with claims the attorney knows for a fact are false or frivolous. In other legal contexts, the term "bad faith" usually refers to deliberate fraud or misconduct. See BLACK'S LAW DICTIONARY 149 (8th ed. 2004) (defining "bad faith" as "[d]ishonesty of belief or purpose"). But it is clear from the statutory language and the case law that for purposes of § 1927, bad faith turns not on the attorney's subjective intent, but on the attorney's objective conduct. The term "unreasonably" necessarily connotes that the district court must compare the attorney's conduct against the conduct of a "reasonable" attorney and make a judgment about whether the conduct was acceptable according to some objective standard. The term "vexatiously" similarly requires an evaluation of the attorney's objective conduct.

Indeed, other circuits, too, have found that the phrase "unreasonably and vexatiously" demands an objective analysis and that § 1927 does not require a malicious intent or a bad purpose. For example, in Cruz v. Savage, 896 F.2d 626 (1st Cir. 1990), the First Circuit stated, "The attorney need not intend to harass or annoy by his conduct nor be guilty of conscious impropriety to be sanctioned. It is enough that an attorney acts in disregard of whether his conduct constitutes harassment or vexation. . . ." Similarly, in Knorr Brake Corp. v. Harbil, Inc., 738 F.2d 223 (7th Cir. 1984), the Seventh Circuit noted that a court "need not find that the attorney acted because of malice" to issue sanctions against the attorney. The Tenth Circuit in Braley v. Campbell, 832 F.2d 1504 (10th Cir. 1987), explicitly said that the statute demands an objective analysis (holding that "the proper standard under . . . § 1927 is that excess costs, expenses, or attorney's fees are imposable against an attorney personally for conduct that, viewed objectively, manifests either intentional or reckless disregard of the attorney's duties to the court."). The Sixth Circuit in Jones v. Continental Corp., 789 F.2d 1225 (6th Cir. 1986), observed that "28 U.S.C. § 1927 authorizes a court to assess fees against an attorney for 'unreasonable and vexatious' multiplication of litigation despite the absence of any conscious impropriety." But see, e.g., Oliveri v. Thompson, 803 F.2d 1265, 1273 (2d Cir. 1986) (holding that sanctions are appropriate under § 1927 only if "the attorney's actions are so completely without merit as to require the conclusion that they must have been undertaken for some improper purpose").

Other courts also have determined that "reckless" conduct is sufficient to justify sanctions under § 1927. See, e.g., Estate of Blas ex rel. Chargualaf v. Winkler, 792 F.2d 858, 860 (9th Cir. 1989) (stating that sanctions under § 1927 require a finding of bad faith, but a showing of either "recklessness or bad faith" is adequate to support such a finding); Manax v. McNamara, 842 F.2d 808, 814 (5th Cir. 1988) (holding that "recklessness, bad faith, or improper motive" can support a finding of unreasonable and vexatious conduct). These observations also prescribe an objective analysis, because reckless conduct simply means conduct that grossly deviates from reasonable conduct. See Schwartz, 341 F.3d at 1227 (describing recklessness as "a gross deviation from conduct that might be reasonable in the circumstances"). Determining whether conduct is reckless necessarily involves comparing the conduct objectively against the conduct of a reasonable attorney.

. . .

In short, a district court may impose sanctions for egregious conduct by an attorney even if the attorney acted without the specific purpose or intent to multiply the proceedings. That is not to say the attorney's purpose or intent is irrelevant. Although the attorney's objective conduct is the focus of the analysis, the attorney's subjective state of mind is frequently an important piece of the calculus, because a given act is more likely to fall outside the bounds of acceptable conduct and therefore be "unreasonabl[e] and vexatious[ ]" if it is done with a malicious purpose or intent.

3. Inherent Authority

Federal courts have "inherent power" to sanction bad faith litigation conduct by lawyers or litigants. The leading reminder of this power is *Chambers v. NASCO, Inc.*, 501 U.S. 32 (1991), in which the Supreme Court upheld a district court order requiring the losing party to pay nearly $1,000,000 in attorneys' fees to the plaintiff. It was the defendant, and not its attorney, who acted inappropriately in the conduct of the litigation. Some of the sanctioned conduct did not violate Rule 11 or § 1927. Nonetheless, the Court upheld the entire award, invoking the "inherent authority" of courts to punish inappropriate litigation behavior. *Id.* at 55.

In *Goodyear Tire & Rubber Co. v. Haeger*, 137 S. Ct. 1178, 1186 (2017), the Court held that an award of attorneys' fees under a court's inherent authority must be compensatory, and not punitive. The party moving for sanctions must show a "causal link—between the litigant's misbehavior and legal fees paid by the opposing party." *Id.* The Court reversed a judgment of $2,700,000 in attorneys' fees and remanded the case for application of the "but for" causation test: the moving party may recover only that portion of her fees that she would not have paid but for the misconduct of the other party. *Id.* at 1187.

In *Belleville Catering Co. v. Champaign Market Place LLC*, 350 F.3d 691 (7th Cir. 2003), lawyers failed to assess whether there was subject matter jurisdiction over the dispute. The district court also failed to address the issue, and the case went through trial, resulting in a judgment for the plaintiff. On appeal, the Seventh Circuit vacated the judgment, because the case failed to invoke federal question, diversity of citizenship, or any other basis of federal jurisdiction. Despite this lack of subject matter jurisdiction, the Seventh Circuit required the lawyers to re-litigate the case in state court without charging their clients. The court explained:

> The costs of a doomed foray into federal court should fall on the lawyers who failed to do their homework, not on the hapless clients. Although we lack jurisdiction to resolve the merits, we have ample authority to govern the practice of counsel in the litigation. . . . The best way for counsel to make the litigants whole is to perform, without additional fees, any further services that are necessary to bring this suit to a conclusion in state court, or via settlement. That way the clients will pay just once for the litigation. This is intended not as a sanction, but simply to ensure that clients need not pay for lawyers' time that has been wasted for reasons beyond the clients' control.

Id. at 694.

4. Contempt

A provision in the federal criminal code permits a federal court "to punish by fine or imprisonment, or both, at its discretion . . . disobedience or resistance to its lawful writ, process, order, rule, decree, or command." 18 U.S.C. § 401(3). To be convicted of criminal contempt, the order violated must be clear and definite. This could include orders regarding pretrial management in a civil case. And given the scope of pretrial authority exercised by the court under Rule 16, there will be few, if any, orders that exceed the district judge's power. But if counsel thinks the judge has gone too far, may she simply ignore the order? The answer is clear: "If a person to whom a court directs an order believes that the order is incorrect, the remedy is to appeal, but, absent a stay, he must comply promptly with the order pending appeal. Persons who make private determinations of the law and refuse to obey an order generally risk criminal contempt even if the order is ultimately ruled incorrect." *Maness v. Meyers*, 419 U.S. 449, 458 (1975).

Federal Rule of Criminal (not Civil) Procedure 42(a) establishes procedures for criminal contempt, and requires that the contemnor be given notice and a trial or hearing, usually with a government lawyer as prosecutor. If the contempt involves disrespect to that judge, she must not preside at the trial or hearing, unless the defendant consents. Under Rule 42(b), what is often called "direct" contempt—that is, "if the judge saw or heard the contemptuous conduct and so certifies"—may be handled in a summary proceeding.

Civil contempt may also be employed to enforce court orders. One example is the use of a fine for each day the party does not comply with the order. As the late Professor Fyr said, with such orders, the court "is into behavior modification." It is often very difficult to determine where civil contempt ends and criminal contempt begins. One dramatic difference is that civil contempt is not deemed a separate proceeding from the case in which it arises. Accordingly, the person cited cannot appeal until final judgment. In contrast, a criminal contempt conviction is deemed separate from the underlying case, and is therefore immediately appealable.

Chapter 6

Aggregate Litigation: Party and Claim Joinder in the Context of a Single Case

A. Introduction

There is no single definition of "complex litigation." Sometimes the term connotes that the litigation involves big stakes or important issues, such as product safety or massive fraud. Sometimes it refers to the fact that the legal issues presented are complicated. Usually, the term seems to be invoked because there are numerous related cases or a single case with numerous parties and claims.

For our purposes, it is helpful to distinguish between (1) complexity arising within a single case and (2) complexity that arises because there are multiple overlapping cases that address the same problem. The latter scenario is addressed in Chapter 3, including such doctrines as consolidation, transfer, multidistrict litigation (MDL), anti-suit injunctions, and *forum non conveniens*. That chapter deals not only with how to coordinate separate cases but with issues of federalism and comity—because sometimes the overlapping litigation will be filed in the courts of different sovereigns—federal courts, state courts, and courts of foreign countries.

Our present task involves the joinder provisions of the Federal Rules of Civil Procedure. Those rules define the scope of litigation: how many parties may be joined and how many claims may be asserted in a single case in federal court.[1] Chapter 3 was concerned with multiple suits pending at the same time, usually in different courts. The joinder provisions are intended to permit efficient "packaging" of litigation, so that all related claims may be asserted in a single case, and all interested parties may be bound by a single judgment.

Remember, however, something we learned in Chapter 2: each claim asserted in federal court must be supported by federal subject matter jurisdiction. So, after determining that a joinder rule permits the assertion of a claim, we must assess whether that claim is supported by diversity of citizenship or federal question jurisdiction. If neither of those is invoked, we consider whether the claim will invoke supplemental jurisdiction. If the claim invokes any of these bases of subject matter

1. The case could be in state court, in which instance, the state rules of procedure would apply. Most states have adopted the Federal Rules, including, of course, their joinder provisions.

jurisdiction, it may be asserted in the pending federal case. If it does not, it cannot be joined in the pending case—and must be pursued in state court.

In section B, we discuss the basic joinder provisions of Federal Rules 13, 14, 18, 19, 20, and 24. This may be a review of material covered in first-year Civil Procedure. Sections C, D, E, and F all deal with the class action under Federal Rule 23, which is the primary focus of this chapter. Section C concerns the requirements for having a class action "certified." Section D addresses major issues in the litigation of a class case. Section E focuses on settlement of class actions, and section F on jurisdictional and related matters. Section H considers the bankruptcy "alternative" to joinder or class litigation. Section G discusses the significant threat to class litigation posed by recent developments in the law of arbitration. Finally, section I addresses special statutory provisions addressing aggregate litigation.

B. Joinder Provisions Other Than The Class Action

1. Party Joinder: Rules 20, 19, 24, and 14

a. Permissive Party Joinder (Rule 20)

Many cases are brought by a single plaintiff against a single defendant. Rule 20(a), however, empowers the plaintiff (who is responsible initially for structuring the suit) to join multiple plaintiffs or multiple defendants. Rule 20 is permissive: the plaintiff *may* join multiple parties, but is not required to do so.

Rule 20(a)(1) permits joinder of multiple plaintiffs if their claims:

(A) "aris[e] out of the same transaction, occurrence or series of transactions or occurrences," and

(B) will raise "any question of law or fact common to all plaintiffs."

Rule 20(a)(2) permits multiple defendants based upon the same test: the claims *against those defendants*:

(A) arise from the same transaction or occurrence (or series) and

(B) will raise any common question of law or fact.

> ***Example #1.*** A, B, and C are passengers in a taxicab. They are injured when the cab crashes. A, B, and C may join as co-plaintiffs, because their claims arise from the same transaction or occurrence and will raise the common question of whether the driver was at fault. Moreover, the plaintiffs may sue two defendants—the driver and the company for which the driver was working. Why? Because the claims against those two arose from the same transaction and raise the common question of whether the driver was at fault (in which case the company would likely be liable).

This simple fact pattern, then, could generate one case with three plaintiffs suing two defendants. Sometimes the facts are not so simple. Courts emphasize that Rule 20's "same transaction" standard is flexible and fact specific; it is designed to permit the joinder of parties asserting "logically related" claims to promote judicial economy. In *Mosley v. General Motors Corp.*, 497 F.2d 1330, 1332–1334 (8th Cir. 1974), the court held that allegations that General Motors had engaged in a company-wide policy of racial discrimination satisfied the "same transaction or occurrence" standard of Rule 20 despite the fact that the effects of that policy may have varied from employee to employee. The court explained.

> The purpose of the rule is to promote trial convenience and expedite the final determination of disputes, thereby preventing multiple lawsuits.... Single trials generally tend to lessen the delay, expense and inconvenience to all concerned....
>
> Here ... the plaintiffs have asserted a right to relief arising out of the same transactions or occurrences. Each of the ten plaintiffs alleged that he had been injured by the same general policy of discrimination on the part of General Motors and the Union.... Thus the plaintiffs meet the first requisite for joinder under Rule 20(a).
>
> The second requisite necessary to sustain a permissive joinder under the rule is that a question of law or fact common to all the parties will arise in the action. The rule does not require that all questions of law and fact raised by the dispute be common.

Remember: rules do not affect jurisdictional doctrines. Thus, the plaintiffs would need to assess whether the two defendants would be subject to personal jurisdiction in the forum. And if the case is to be filed in federal court, they must assess whether the case, as structured, would invoke diversity of citizenship or federal question jurisdiction (it is unlikely that there would be federal question jurisdiction, because there is nothing federal about most car crashes).

b. Compulsory Party Joinder (Rule 19)

Rule 19 becomes relevant after a case is filed. The plaintiff has structured the case as she desired, and has left out someone who could have been joined initially. Here, that non-party ("Absentee") must be joined if feasible. Why? Because Absentee is "required." Though Rule 19(a) uses that term, most judges and lawyers use the term "necessary."

In other words, Rule 19 overrides the plaintiff's structuring of the case. Our system values litigant autonomy—plaintiffs generally should be allowed to join whomever they wish under Rule 20(a). In the Rule 19 situation, however, other policies trump that interest in autonomy. There are three such policies.

- First, Rule 19(a)(1)(A) provides for joinder because, without Absentee, the court cannot accord complete relief among the parties. The policy here is that the court requires joinder to avoid multiple litigation: if Absentee is not joined in the present case, there will be a second case involving Absentee, which may be wasteful of our limited judicial resources.

Historically, Rule 19(a)(1)(A) has had very little independent significance. The other two bases of compulsory joinder have proved far more important.

- Second, under Rule 19(a)(1)(B)(i), Absentee has an interest in the pending case. Her joinder is required to avoid "practical" harm to that interest.

The policy is compelling and arises in a good many cases: if Absentee is not joined, her interest may suffer practical impairment.

- Third, under Rule 19(a)(1)(B)(ii), Absentee again has an interest in the pending case. Here, however, we focus not on Absentee, but on the defendant. If Absentee is not joined, the defendant may be subjected to "double, multiple, or otherwise inconsistent obligations."

The latter two provisions are called the "prejudice" prongs of Rule 19. In each, the court (usually on motion of a party) orders joinder of Absentee to avoid harm (prejudice) to someone. In Rule 19(a)(1)(B)(i), we are avoiding practical impairment of Absentee's interest. In Rule 19(a)(1)(B)(ii), we are avoiding harm to the defendant that could result from judgments in separate cases. This concept of overriding the plaintiff's structuring of the case to avoid prejudice is a recurring theme: it is the basis for Rule 23(b)(1) class actions.

Often, a single case will raise concerns under both Rule 19(a)(1)(B)(i) and 19(a)(1)(B)(ii).

> ***Example #2***. Absentee holds a stock certificate for ownership of 100 shares of Corporation. It is worth a great deal of money. P sues Corporation, asserting that P and Absentee bought the stock jointly. P asks the court to cancel Absentee's stock and reissue the stock in the joint name of P and Absentee.

Absentee is necessary under Rule 19(a)(1)(B)(i), because her interest in the stock may be harmed if the suit goes forward without her; if P wins, Absentee's stock will be canceled. Absentee is also necessary under Rule 19(a)(1)(B)(ii) because, if Absentee is not joined, Corporation could be subjected to inconsistent obligations. For instance, if P wins the present case, the court will order Corporation to cancel the stock and reissue it in the joint names of P and Absentee. Then Absentee may sue Corporation and win, in which case there will be an inconsistent court order, instructing Corporation not to cancel the stock. The way to avoid both of these potential harms—to Absentee and to Corporation—is to compel the joinder of Absentee in the present case.

Again, though, joinder rules do not affect jurisdiction. So, the court can order the joinder of Absentee only if it would have personal jurisdiction over Absentee. Remember, too, that Absentee will be joined either to assert or to defend against a claim. In federal court, we must assess whether *that claim* will invoke subject matter jurisdiction. If it does—because it meets the requirements for diversity of citizenship or federal question or supplemental jurisdiction—joinder is proper. If the claim does not invoke subject matter jurisdiction, Absentee cannot be joined.

Suppose Absentee is "necessary" under Rule 19(a) but cannot be joined, either because of lack of personal jurisdiction or subject matter jurisdiction. Then the court must apply the balancing test of Rule 19(b) to determine whether it will (1) proceed without Absentee or (2) dismiss the entire case. This decision is made on the specific facts of the case, guided by the court's assessment of the likelihood of harm and other factors listed in Rule 19(b). If the court decides, based upon those factors, to dismiss the case, Absentee is labeled "indispensable."

c. Intervention (Rule 24)

Intervention, like Rule 19, involves a case in which we are concerned about the interest of a non-party, whom we again call Absentee. Here, however, Absentee protects her interest by voluntarily joining the case. The overlap with Rule 19 is most obvious in "intervention of right" under Rule 24(a)(2). It is proper when Absentee claims an "interest relating to the property or transaction that is the subject of the action, and is so situated that disposing of the action may as a practical matter impair or impede the movant's ability to protect its interest, unless existing parties adequately represent that interest." This test is tantamount to Rule 19(a)(1)(B)(i), in which the court orders joinder to avoid practical impairment of Absentee's interest.

Return to Example #2. Absentee would have the right to intervene into the case for the same reason that she was necessary under Rule 19(a)(1)(B)(i): to avoid practical harm to her interest in the stock. Interestingly, the Federal Rules provide two mechanisms for protecting the rights of a non-party when the litigation threatens practical harm to her interest: the court can order her joinder under Rule 19 or she can protect herself by intervening.

There is also "permissive intervention" under Rule 24(b)(2), which allows Absentee to join if she has "a claim or defense that shares with the main action a common question of law or fact." Whether to permit intervention is in the court's discretion.

An absentee who intervenes waives any objection she may have had to personal jurisdiction, because she voluntarily joins the case. But subject matter jurisdiction, of course, cannot be waived. So, the court must assess the claim by the intervenor-plaintiff or against the intervenor-defendant for subject matter jurisdiction.[2] If it invokes diversity of citizenship or federal question or supplemental jurisdiction, intervention is allowed. If it does not, intervention is denied.

---

2. One might ask why anyone would intervene as a *defendant*. After all, why open oneself to being sued? The intervenor must assess which side of the litigation best represents her interest. Consider Example #2. Absentee's interest—maintaining the status quo, in which she is the owner of all 100 shares of stock—is shared by Corporation. It is being attacked by P. So, Absentee would likely intervene as a defendant.

d. Impleader (Rule 14)

Rule 14(a)(1), though denominated "third-party practice," is usually called "impleader." It permits a *defending party* to join a new party, called the third-party defendant (TPD) to the case. So, as with Rule 19 and intervention, the plaintiff structured the case in such a way as to leave someone out. Here, the defendant joins the Absentee by asserting a claim against her. Impleader is rather narrow—in practice, it permits joinder of the TPD for claims of indemnity or contribution.

> ***Example #3.*** P sues General Contractor for damage to P's building. The damage was caused by Subcontractor, whom General Contractor had hired to do a specific task. General Contractor is vicariously liable for Subcontractor's negligence. General Contractor may implead Subcontractor for indemnification. Thus, if P wins, General Contractor's impleader claim will shift ultimate liability to Subcontractor.

Again, joinder rules do not affect jurisdiction. Impleader is possible only if the court will have personal jurisdiction over TPD and if the claim by the defendant against TPD invokes federal subject matter jurisdiction—diversity of citizenship or federal question or supplemental jurisdiction.

Notes and Questions

1. The Rule 20(a)(1) test is easy to apply in cases involving a single event, such as a bridge collapse or an explosion. In such cases, the plaintiffs' claims clearly arise from the same transaction or occurrence. Courts have more difficulty applying Rule 20 in product defect and toxic tort actions. There, though all plaintiffs used the same product, they did so at different times and in different places (and possibly in different amounts). Does the "logical relationship" test from *Mosley* (quoted in section 1(a) above) help resolve such cases? How about the language from Rule 20(a)(1) permitting joinder if (inter alia) the claims arise from a "series of transactions or occurrences"?

In *Abraham v. Volkswagen of America, Inc.*, 795 F.2d 238 (2d Cir. 1986), the plaintiffs claimed that a defect in the valve stem seals of their vehicles caused excessive oil consumption, engine damage and failure, and decreased the resale value of their cars. Even though some cars needed repairs earlier than others, and though the driving and maintenance history of each car differed, the Second Circuit upheld joinder. It held that the allegedly faulty valve stem seal was a single defect that caused the various damages. This satisfied the same transaction or occurrence (or series thereof) requirement. The court concluded: "All plaintiffs now allege as the basis for their claims the purchase of a Volkswagen Rabbit with a valve stem seal made of defective material that will cause it to harden and break over time. We think that amply satisfies the requirement of a series of logically related transactions." *Id.* at 251.

Abdullah v. Acands, Inc., 30 F.3d 264, 269 n.5 (1st Cir. 1994), reflects a more restrictive view. There, 1000 plaintiffs sued 93 defendants. The plaintiffs had been crew members on different vessels. They alleged that the defendants designed, manufactured, or supplied asbestos-containing machinery that was placed on their ships.[3] They alleged personal injuries from their resulting exposure to asbestos. The First Circuit held that the complaint failed to satisfy Rule 20(a)(1):

> The Complaint is bereft of factual allegations indicating why 1000 plaintiffs and 93 defendants belong in the same action. It gives no indication of whether plaintiffs were injured while serving on the same vessels or during the same time periods; no indication of whether they were injured by exposure to the same asbestos-containing products or equipment, nor any specification of the products or equipment to which they were exposed.

These cases reflect different views on the requirement of transactional relatedness. In *Abraham*, the court was willing to focus on the single product involved and not on the separate harms it caused. In *Abdullah*, the court did not do this, but focused on each episode of harm.

2. Some courts have been remarkably aggressive in stretching the concept of transactional relatedness in Rule 20(a)—none more so than *Hall v. E.I DuPont de Nemours Co.*, 345 F. Supp. 353 (E.D.N.Y. 1972). In that case, 13 children were injured while playing with blasting caps. The caps in each case could have been manufactured by any of six companies. The children were not related to each other. Indeed, they were injured in separate explosions in ten states over four years. The parents of the children sued on their behalves as co-plaintiffs. They alleged that the manufacturers were liable, *inter alia*, for failure to warn on the dangers of blasting caps.

The court upheld joinder. It did so by focusing on the plaintiffs' theories of tort liability. The plaintiffs alleged "enterprise liability"—that the entire industry was liable for its practice. This focus allowed the court to shift attention away from the separate transactions toward the overall alleged culpability of the blasting cap industry. The court concluded: "[t]he allegations in this case suggest that the entire blasting cap industry and its trade association provide the logical locus at which precautions should be taken and liability imposed." *Id.* at 378. By focusing on the legal theory, the court was able to conclude, in essence, that the case was not about separate explosions in different places, but about the single practice of an industry. The approach is an especially bold application of the Second Circuit approach in *Abraham*.

---

3. Asbestos is a fire-resistant material that was used widely in ships, buildings, and appliances throughout most of the twentieth century. It became clear that exposure to asbestos could cause cancer. Innumerable plaintiffs filed personal injury and wrongful death claims. There were also thousands of cases regarding insurance coverage for asbestos claims and thousands more concerning the financial responsibility for the federally-mandated abatement of asbestos from buildings. Asbestos is responsible for more litigation than any other single product, and we will see several asbestos cases throughout the book. The Report of an ad hoc Judicial Conference Committee in 1991 characterized asbestos as "a tale of danger known in the 1930s, exposure inflicted upon millions of Americans in the 1940s and 1950s, injuries that began to take their toll in the 1960s, and a flood of lawsuits beginning in the 1970s."

3. Joinder of defendants presents the same issue, because Rule 20(a)(2) adopts the same operative language as Rule 20(a)(1). Again, the plaintiff's legal theory may affect whether the standard is satisfied. In *Poster v. Central Gulf Steamship Corp.*, 25 F.R.D. 18, 20 (E.D. Pa. 1960), the plaintiff sued two steamship companies. He had served as a crew member for each company, but several months apart. On his first voyage, for Company 1, he contracted amebiasis (a painful gastrointestinal ailment), allegedly because Company 1 had created an unsanitary food preparation area. On his second voyage, for Company 2, the same thing happened. He sued both companies in a single case.

> The court upheld joinder, focusing on the plaintiff's allegation that the actions of Company 2 *aggravated the injuries suffered when he was sailing for Company 1*. It concluded: "[w]e think that the joinder of the two steamship companies here complied with Rule 20(a) since plaintiff-libellant's claim for relief is based upon two occurrences, the same in nature, and the second of which might result in concurrent liability of both companies." The plaintiff's theory of *concurrent liability*—that each defendant was responsible for the plaintiff's present state of suffering—allowed the court to treat separate events as arising from a series of related transactions under Rule 20(a)(2).

4. Joinder assessments reflect competing values and goals. On the one hand, inclusive joinder permits courts to decide entire disputes—related claims of related parties—in a single case. On the other hand, though, courts do not want to create an unmanageable or confusing jumble.

Rule 20(b) ameliorates the tension of these competing values by permitting the court to order separate trials of individual claims. This is usually done to avoid confusing the jury if vastly different claims involving different times and places are involved. When the court orders separate trials, the case remains a single action. The results of the separate trials are reflected in a single judgment. Rule 42(a) also provides authority for ordering separate trials.

5. If the trial court concludes that joinder is not proper under Rule 20(a), the remedy is to "sever" under Federal Rule 21. To sever means to divide what was one case into more than one case. Assume that two plaintiffs, A and B, sue D in a single case. The court finds that A and B cannot be joined as co-plaintiffs under Rule 20(a)(1). It will order severance, which will result in dropping B from the case. B will then sue D in a separate suit. After severance, then, there will be two cases.

2. Claim Joinder: Rules 18 and 13

In section 1, we determined how many parties will be joined in one case. Now we switch to determine what claims those parties may assert.

a. Claim Joinder by the Plaintiff (Rule 18(a))

Rule 18(a) permits the plaintiff to "assert . . . as many claims as it has against an opposing party." The claims need not be related in any way. Plaintiff could join in one case a contract claim, an unrelated tort claim, and an unrelated statutory claim. If the plaintiff asserts unrelated claims, the court may order separate trials under Rule 20(b) or Rule 42(b) to avoid confusion.

Rule 18(a) is not limited to plaintiffs, but applies to any party asserting a claim. Accordingly, a defendant who impleads a third-party defendant (TPD) under Rule 14(a), which we discussed above in section 1(d), may join any other claim she may have against the TPD.

We continue to say: the joinder rules do not affect jurisdiction. Thus, once a case is in federal court, the court must assess each individual claim for federal subject matter jurisdiction. If the claim is supported by diversity of citizenship, federal question, or supplemental jurisdiction, it may be asserted in the pending case. If not, it may not be asserted in the pending case (but may be asserted state court).

b. Claim Joinder by Defending Parties (Rule 13)

A defending party may assert a claim in the pending case. (We have seen an example: impleader, by which a defending party asserts a claim for indemnity or contribution against an absentee, who becomes the third-party defendant.) Here we address claims that may be asserted against parties who have already been joined in the case.

Counterclaim (Rules 13(a) and (b)). A counterclaim is asserted against an "opposing party." Almost always, the counterclaim is asserted by a defendant (D) against a plaintiff (P). They are "opposing parties," because P has asserted a claim against D.

If D's counterclaim against P arises from the same transaction or occurrence as P's claim, it is a "compulsory counterclaim" under Rule 13(a)(1) and must (subject to some exceptions we need not address) be asserted in the pending case. If D does not assert the compulsory counterclaim in the pending case, she will be barred—by "rule preclusion"—from filing a separate case to pursue the claim.

On the other hand, if D's counterclaim against P does not arise from the same transaction or occurrence as P's claim, it is a "permissive counterclaim" under Rule 13(b). D has the option to assert the permissive counterclaim in the pending case or to sue on it in a separate action.

And, again, each claim in federal court must invoke federal subject matter jurisdiction. So, the court will assess whether the counterclaim, whether compulsory or permissive, invokes diversity of citizenship, federal question, or supplemental jurisdiction.

Crossclaim (Rule 13(g)). A crossclaim is asserted against a "co-party," not against an opposing party. Rule 13(g) requires that this claim arise from the same transaction or occurrence as the underlying case. Despite that requirement, the crossclaim is never compulsory. So a party may assert the claim in the pending case, but is not required to do so. She may assert it in a separate action.

Crossclaims will be relevant only when the plaintiff used Rule 20(a) to structure the case with multiple plaintiffs or multiple defendants. Though a plaintiff may file a crossclaim against a co-plaintiff, such claims are rare. The vast majority of crossclaims are by one defendant against a co-defendant.

And (for the last time) the federal court must assess whether the crossclaim invokes federal subject matter jurisdiction—diversity of citizenship, federal question, or supplemental jurisdiction. Only if it does can it be joined in the pending case.

Problem

P, driving her car, collides with a car driven by D-1 but owned by D-2. D-2 was not in the car at the time of the collision. D-2, as owner, is vicariously liable for the acts of D-1. P sues D-1 and D-2.

(a) Are D-1 and D-2 properly joined as co-defendants?

D-2 knows that her car has been damaged but does not know who was at fault in the collision.

(b) What claim may D-2 file against P in the pending case? What happens if she does not file it?

(c) What claim may D-2 file against D-1 in the pending case? What happens if she does not file it.

(d) Assume D-2 files the claim you noted in (c). If D-2 has an unrelated claim against D-1 (let's say a contract claim from a business venture), may she join that in the pending case as well?

D-1 believes that her insurance company owes her indemnification for the claim against her.

(e) Can D-1 join the insurance company in the pending case? If so, how?

This Problem implicated Rule 20(a)(1), Rule 13(a), Rule 13(g), Rule 18(a), and Rule 14(a). And this was a simple fender-bender. We turn now to the most complex of joinder provisions.

C. The Class Action: Certification Under Rule 23(a) and Rule 23(b)

1. Introduction and Background

The party joinder provisions we have studied (Rules 20, 19, 24, and 14) are just that: *party* joinder. The persons or entities joined will be full-fledged litigants in the case. They are brought before the jurisdiction of the court—either voluntarily (by asserting a claim) or by service of process. Because they are parties, they are bound by the judgment in the case.

The class action is different. Here, a party (the "representative" or "named representative") sues on behalf of others (the "class members"). (There can be multiple representatives, but for simplicity we will speak of "the representative.") The representative is a party. The class members are not. In many cases, then, the court refers to the representative as the "named plaintiff"—she is a full-fledged litigant. They refer to class members as "absentee class members"—to drive home the point that they are not joined as parties. Throughout the book, we will simply talk of the "representative" and of "class members."

Here is the genius of the class action: if it is done correctly, the judgment in a class action will bind the class members—even though they are not parties. This fact raises a profound question of due process: how can non-parties (who are never formally brought before the jurisdiction of the court) be bound by a judgment? The answer, discussed in section C.2.c.iv below, is that the interests of the class members are *adequately represented* by the representative.

Thus, due process can be satisfied (and therefore render a judgment valid) either because a person or entity was either joined as a litigant or adequately represented by a litigant. One question to keep in mind throughout our study is whether representation alone is sufficient to bind class members even if the class members receive no notification that someone is litigating on their behalf. (We will see that the answer is yes in some cases but not in others.)

The benefit of the class action is that it binds the class members. The claims of dozens or hundreds or thousands (or millions?) are determined in one case. The class members sink or swim together. Accordingly, one of the underlying rationales for class practice is efficiency—the court system decides one case (albeit a complicated case) rather than numerous individual suits.

But efficiency is not the only goal of procedure. Litigant autonomy is another, and in the class suit, the class members sacrifice their autonomy. The fate of their claims rests with how well the representative and the class lawyer do. Should the class members be allowed to decide for themselves whether to do this? We will see that the answer depends upon which "type" of class action we use.

Also, consider the defendant's position. Without the class action, potentially, it faces numerous individual suits. If all were litigated, it might win some and might lose some. With the class action, however, it is all or nothing—the defendant either escapes liability for all claims or gets hit with potentially devastating liability on the basis of one suit. This fact often increases the defendant's willingness to settle the case—even if the class claims are substantively weak. Settlement in such cases has been called "legalized blackmail," because the defendant simply cannot afford to risk such stunning liability as the result of a single case.

Considering the defendant's position also raises a paradox, at least with "negative-value" claims.

> ***Example #4.*** Retailer violated a consumer protection law by overcharging customers. The average customer was overcharged by $30.

The customers have negative-value claims; they are not economically viable if they must be asserted individually. In the famous phrase of Judge Posner, "only a lunatic or a fanatic sues for $30." *Carnegie v. Household Int'l, Inc.*, 376 F.3d 656, 661 (7th Cir. 2004).[4] No lawyer will take your case, and no normal person would go to the trouble of litigating over $30. With the class action, however, the case can become economically viable. If 100,000 consumers were affected, this is now a $3,000,000 case. Here, then, is the paradox: we (often) justify the class action as efficient, because it substitutes one case for many; but in cases involving negative-value claims, the class action actually creates litigation that otherwise would not have been filed.

Usually, our society does not favor the creation of litigation. We also honor the maxim *de minimus non curat lex*—that the law does not remedy minor harms; in this life, we are expected occasionally to take our lumps for $30. In this instance, however, there are countervailing policies. If the class device is not available (and assuming the state does not act against the retailer either criminally or administratively), the retailer who overcharged consumers will "get away" with the bad behavior. There will be no *compensation* to victims and there will be no *deterrence* of wrongdoers—both of which are important policies in law.

The class action is an important tool for the private enforcement of our public laws, such as consumer protection laws. In an era when government enforcement resources are strained, private enforcement becomes increasingly important. Indeed, one of the express purposes of the drafters of the federal class action rule was to facilitate the private enforcement of civil rights laws. Throughout our study, let's keep in mind whether class litigation is intended to serve the compensatory function of the law, the deterrent function of the law, or both.

Also, throughout our study, we will see that the class action is rife with potential conflicts of interest. We worry that the interests of the representative—whose actions will bind the class members—align with those class members. The class action provisions insist on such alignment, as we will see. Another potential conflict is between the class lawyer and the class members.

> ***Example #5.*** Let's say the fact pattern in Example #4 leads to filing a class action on behalf of 100,000 customers. The aggregate class claim is $3,000,000. Retailer wants to settle the case. It approaches Class Lawyer and offers to settle by giving customers coupons for a nominal credit at Retailer stores, by paying the representative an "incentive fee" of $10,000, and by paying Class Lawyer a fee of $500,000.

---

4. Not all negative value claims are small. For instance, in *Italian Colors Restaurant v. American Express Travel Related Servs. Co.*, 133 S. Ct. 2304 (2013), each class member had an antitrust claim for tens of thousands of dollars. They were negative value claims, however, because the expense of getting an expert to testify on relevant economic issues would exceed the value of the claim.

> This is a very good deal for Retailer, who "buys peace" for $510,000 plus coupons that are unlikely to be redeemed. It is a very good deal for the representative, whose $30 claim has been parlayed into $10,000. And it is a very good deal for Class Lawyer, who makes $500,000 for relatively little effort.

The haunting question: is it a good deal for the class members? Example #5 points out the need to have someone—in addition to the representative and the laywer—looking out for the interests of the class members. The person thrust into this role is the judge. Concerns about potential conflicts of interest put the judge in this fiduciary position, which is reflected by the fact that Rule 23(e) requires the court to approve settlement or voluntary dismissal of a class action. We consider those rules in section E.

Class practice in federal court is governed by Federal Rule 23. Most (but not all) states have adopted the Federal Rules, so most states have a class action provision modeled on Rule 23. Those states are free, however, to interpret their rule as they see fit, and are not bound by federal court interpretations of Rule 23. Rule 23 was drafted in its present basic form in the 1966 amendments to the Federal Rules.

Before turning to Rule 23, we make three points. First, though there can be defendant classes, the overwhelming majority of class actions involve plaintiff classes. Throughout the materials, except in section C.5 below (which is expressly about defendant class actions), we will assume a plaintiff class.

Second, a class action is commenced like any other case—by filing a complaint. Here, the complaint will state that the representative sues "on behalf of those similarly situated." At that point the case is a "putative" class action. It does not become a true class action until it is "certified." Usually, the parties engage in discovery between the time the case is filed and the time the representative brings the motion to certify the class. At that motion, the burden is on the representative to demonstrate that the case satisfies the requirements of Rule 23(a) and Rule 23(b). It is routine to have a lapse of several months between filing the case and the motion to certify. During that time, as we discuss in section D.4, the parties may engage in discovery regarding whether the class should be certified.

Third, the ruling on the class certification motion is a watershed event. If certification is denied, the case proceeds with the representative as the sole plaintiff. (If there were multiple representatives, the case would proceed with them as the plaintiffs.) If certification is granted, the stakes change dramatically for the defendant. It now faces potentially devastating liability based upon the outcome of a single case, which increases its incentive to settle the case. Certification is decided before adjudication on the merits, so it is possible that the class claims are not strong on the merits. Nonetheless, the defendant may have no practical choice but to settle.

Because the ruling on certification is usually a make-or-break moment, the parties spare no expense or effort. The focus on certification is whether the representative can show compliance with the requirements of Rule 23(a) and Rule 23(b). This section focuses on those requirements. We will see that the certification decision is based upon evidence, not merely upon pleadings. One of the important recent trends is "front-loading" class litigation—that is, requiring the representative to be prepared to *demonstrate*—including, where applicable, with properly qualified expert witness testimony—compliance with the requirements of certification.

2. Rule 23(a): Prerequisites for All Class Actions

a. Overview

Rule 23(a) prescribes the prerequisites for all class actions. There are no options here: the representative must demonstrate that *all* of the requirements of Rule 23(a) are satisfied.

> **Rule 23(a) Prerequisites.** One or more members of a class may sue or be sued as representative parties on behalf of all members only if:
>
> (1) the class is so numerous that joinder of all members is impracticable;
>
> (2) there are questions of law or fact common to the class;
>
> (3) the claims or defenses of the representative parties are typical of the claims or defenses of the class; and
>
> (4) the representative parties will fairly and adequately protect the interests of the class.

Though the Rule expressly prescribes four prerequisites, all courts agree that there is a fifth requirement: the existence of a class. This requirement is implicit from the first phrase of the Rule, that one or more members "of a class" may bring a class action.

b. Implicit Requirement of a Class: Ascertainability and Manageability

The wise class lawyer understands that she must convince the court that the class action she proposes will be manageable. She thinks of the complaint, and the later motion to certify the class, as opportunities to assure the judge that the litigation will be administratively feasible. She starts this process with her class definition. We list some of the guideposts that can be gleaned from case law.

First, avoid defining the class in open-ended terms or by subjective intent of the class members. The lawyer must remember that if the class proceeds and wins a judgment or settlement, the court must administer the relief—must determine who benefits from the judgment or settlement. Class definitions such as "people interested in peaceful political discussion" or that include persons based upon their subjective intent are unlikely to be enforceable. After all, nearly everyone is "interested in peaceful political discussion," and it is likely impossible for a court to determine which members of a putative class had a specific subjective intent without having a trial for each class member, which defeats the efficiency of the class action.[5]

Second, it is wise to include temporal and geographic limitations on class membership. Temporally, it makes sense to limit the class to the appropriate statute of limitations. Doing so will impress the judge that counsel is not overreaching. Geographically, though it is possible to have multistate (and even nationwide) classes, they may present significant administrative problems, such as choice of law and personal jurisdiction over class members.

Third, the degree of detail required in defining the class is affected by the type of class asserted. As discussed in section C.3, there are different types of classes. One type—under Rule 23(b)(3)—requires the court to give individual notice to all reasonably identifiable class members. The other types—under Rule 23(b)(1) and 23(b)(2)—do not. It stands to reason, then, that courts insist on more detail regarding the Rule 23(b)(3) class. Moreover, the Rule 23(b)(3) class almost always seeks monetary relief. Thus, if the class wins a judgment or settlement, the court likely will need to identify who is in the class. Such precision is not necessarily required, for example, in Rule 23(b)(2) cases, in which the class seeks injunctive or declaratory relief.

In recent years, the Third Circuit has imposed a requirement of "ascertainability," which consists of two prongs: (1) the class must be "defined with reference to objective criteria" and (2) the representative must show that "there is a reliable and administratively feasible mechanism for determining whether putative class members fall within the class definition." *Carrera v. Bayer Corp.*, 727 F.3d 300, 305 (3d Cir. 2013).

The first prong of this requirement is not controversial. All courts are leery of class definitions that depend upon subjective intent. The more objective the class definition, the greater the chance of certification.

The second prong—administrative feasibility—is controversial. Importantly, the Third Circuit applies that prong only in Rule 23(b)(3) classes. It appears to require that the representative demonstrate—*at the class certification stage*—that there will be a feasible way to identify individual class members who will be entitled to recover if the class prevails. Other courts, while embracing the notion of administrative feasibility in Rule 23(b)(3) classes, seem to allow certification if they are convinced that *ultimately* (not necessarily at the certification stage) they will be able to determine who is in the class.

---

5. An example is *Simer v. Rios*, 661 F.2d 655, 669 (7th Cir. 1981), which rejected a class of "all low income persons otherwise eligible for participation in the 1979 CIP who were denied 1979 CIP assistance . . . or discouraged from applying for assistance." Even if one can identify "low income persons," the court noted "the difficulty of identifying class members whose membership in the class depends on each individual's state of mind."

> ***Example #6.*** Thousands of people purchase a dietary supplement. They claim that the product did not do what it was supposed to do. Representative files a Rule 23(b)(3) class action against the manufacturer, seeking refunds of the purchase price. Because the purchases were made over-the-counter, without prescription, no one will have a record of who bought the product.

The Third Circuit might deny certification here because the class is not administratively feasible. In that court's view, the fact that we cannot identify—at the certification stage—who is in the class would defeat certification. On similar facts, though, other courts likely would certify the class (assuming, of course, that the other requirements are satisfied). To them, it is sufficient that ultimately, through public notice and filing of claim forms, the court will be able to determine who purchased the product during the relevant time. *See, e.g., Rikos v. Proctor & Gamble Co.*, 799 F.3d 497, 525–526 (6th Cir. 2015) (upholding certification on facts similar to those in Example #6).

Several circuits expressly reject the second prong of the Third Circuit's concept of ascertainability. *See, e.g., In re Petrobras Securities,* 862 F.3d 250, 266 (2d Cir. 2017); *Briseno v. ConAgra Foods, Inc.*, 844 F.3d 1121, 1126 (9th Cir. 2017); *Sandusky Wellness Ctr., LLC v. Medtox Sci., Inc.*, 821 F.3d 992, 995–996 (8th Cir. 2016); *Rikos v. Procter & Gamble Co., supra,* 799 F.3d at 525–526; *Mullins v. Direct Digital, LLC,* 795 F.3d 654, 657–658 (7th Cir. 2015).

Accordingly, these courts require a form of ascertainability—all courts do. They part company with the Third Circuit over its insistence that members of a Rule 23(b)(3) class be identifiable (apparently with 100 percent accuracy)[6] at the certification stage.[7] To the other courts, certification is proper if the class definition is based upon "objective criteria that establish a membership with definite boundaries," *Petrobras, supra,* 862 F.3d at 264, and that membership can be determined "with reasonable accuracy" at an appropriate time, which might be after discovery and notice have brought the claimants forward. *Rikos, supra,* 799 F.3d at 525.

Ultimately, this concern boils down to *manageability.* The representative must convince the court that the class action, if certified and litigated, will be administratively feasible.

---

6. The Sixth Circuit in *Rikos* characterized the Third Circuit as requiring "100 percent accuracy" in identifying individual members of a Rule 23(b)(3) class.

7. One Third Circuit judge has urged that court to eliminate the strict administrative feasibility requirement in Rule 23(b)(3) classes. *Byrd v. Aaron's Inc.*, 784 F.3d 154, 177 (3d Cir. 2015) (Rendell, J., concurring). Another, in dissenting from the denial of *en banc* review in *Carrera,* said that the strict test "gives the impression to many that we now carry [the ascertainability requirement] too far." *Carrera*, 2014 WL 3887938 at *1 (Ambro, J.).

c. The Four Express Requirements and the Need for Proof

We turn now to the four express requirements of Rule 23(a). Before considering them, we note two things. First, the requirements of Rule 23(a) are not hermetically sealed. That is, evidence supporting one requirement might well support another as well. In particular, the requirement that the representative's claim be "typical" of claims of the class in Rule 23(a)(3) overlaps a good deal with whether the representative will be adequate under Rule 23(a)(4).

Second, as we will see in *Wal-Mart,* the representative must be prepared to *prove*—and not merely to allege—that the requirements of Rule 23(a) (and, as we will see Rule 23(b)) are satisfied. Accordingly, at the class certification stage, the representative must have evidence demonstrating satisfaction of the requirements. As we discuss each requirement, consider how the representative might obtain such evidence.

i. Rule 23(a)(1): Numerosity

Rule 23(a)'s requirement that "the class is so numerous that joinder of all members is impracticable" is not as simple as it seems. The idea underlying the requirement is easily understood: if the number of class members is so low that joinder as co-plaintiffs under Rule 20(a)(1) is feasible, a class action is not necessary. The determination of whether there are so many claimants that joinder is impracticable is made on a case-by-case basis. *See* Alexandra Lahav, *The Curse of Bigness and the Optimal Size of Class Actions,* 63 Vand. L. Rev. 117 (2010).

The analysis starts with numbers—how many class members are there? Although no specific numerical guidelines have been established, it seems safe to conclude that classes comprising of hundreds or thousands of members normally will meet the "numerosity" requirement, while classes in the teens and twenties usually will not. Some courts espouse a rule of thumb: more than 40 is sufficient, fewer than 21 is insufficient, and the cases in between depend on other factors. *Cox v. American Cast Iron Pipe Co.,* 784 F.2d 1546, 1553 (11th Cir. 1986). But such statements are merely generalizations; there is no "magic number" for satisfying Rule 23(a)(1).

The number of claimants is only the starting point. Courts look to other factors, including geographic dispersion and the relationship among the putative class members.

- One court rejected class certification in a case with 350 claimants. All were political subdivisions of a state. The court noted that the putative class members were not geographically dispersed and could join as co-plaintiffs in a single suit, represented by the same state attorney. *Utah v. American Pipe & Constr. Co.,* 49 F.R.D. 17, 19 (C.D. Cal. 1969). *See also Liberty Lincoln Mercury, Inc. v. Ford Mktg. Corp.*, 149 F.R.D. 65, 74 (D.N.J. 1993) (class of 123 automobile dealerships not certified in action challenging violations of state franchise practices act; joinder was practicable because all were easily identifiable and were located in the same state).

Another factor is whether the claimants would be able or willing to sue individually. In negative-value cases, individual claims may be so small that potential claimants would not sue individually. In such a case, the Supreme Court has noted that "most of the plaintiffs would have no realistic day in court if a class action were not available." *Phillips Petroleum Co. v. Shutts,* 472 U.S. 797, 809 (1985).

- One court upheld a class of 19 members in part because the claimants were so intimidated by the defendant that they would not sue individually. *Arkansas Educ. Ass'n v. Board of Educ.,* 446 F.2d 763, 765–766 (8th Cir. 1971).
- Similarly, one court certified a class of low-income claimants, in part because they were unlikely to file individual suits. *Jackson v. Foley,* 156 F.R.D. 538, 542 (E.D.N.Y. 1994) ("The requirement that joinder be impracticable depends not only on numbers, but on the totality of the circumstances of a case.").
- Another court noted that the claimants' inability to speak English and lack of understanding of the legal system made it unlikely that they would sue individually. *Rodriguez v. Berrymore Farms, Inc.,* 672 F. Supp. 1009, 1013 (W.D. Mich. 1987).
- In *Dale Electronics v. R.C.L. Electronics, Inc.,* 53 F.R.D. 531, 534 (D.N.H. 1971), the court certified a *defendant* class of 13. It explained:

> While it must be conceded that thirteen defendants are not a numerous class judged by normal class action standards, it is not numbers alone, but whether . . . the numbers make joinder impracticable that is the test. Professor Wright has pointed out: "For the class to be large enough to permit a class suit, impossibility of joinder is not required. Extreme difficulty or impracticability of joinder is sufficient. One court has referred to 'the numbers game aspect of Rule 23,' *but it is clear that no numerical test is possible.*" Wright, Law of Federal Courts, page 308 (2nd Ed. 1970). [Emphasis added.]

The court concluded that joinder was impracticable because some of the defendants would not be subject to personal jurisdiction. We discuss the due process implications of this holding in section C.5, which addresses defendant class actions. For present purposes, *Dale Electronics* is notable for its numerosity analysis.

Question

We will see in section F.1 that a class action can invoke diversity of citizenship jurisdiction if the representative is of diverse citizenship from all defendants. In other words, the citizenships of class members other than the representative are irrelevant. In a non-class case, in contrast, diversity jurisdiction requires that all plaintiffs be of diverse citizenship from all defendants. Suppose joinder of co-plaintiffs under Rule 20(a)(1) would include a citizen of the same state as the defendant. This would make it impossible for the individuals to invoke diversity of citizenship. Would this fact support certification of a class because individual joinder is impracticable?

ii. Rule 23(a)(2): Commonality

Rule 23(a)(2) requires that there be "questions of law or fact common to the class."

As one court observed, "[t]he significance of commonality is self-evident: it provides the necessary glue among class members to make adjudicating the case as a class worthwhile." *Newton v. Merrill Lynch, Pierce, Fenner & Smith, Inc.*, 259 F.3d 154, 182 (3d Cir. 2001).

Before reading the most important commonality case, we make three quick points. First, although the Rule refers to "questions," plural, it has long been clear that a single common question will suffice. 7A Wright & Miller § 1763.

Second, the requirement of Rule 23(a)(2) must be distinguished from one of the requirements of Rule 23(b)(3). All that is required here is that a common question *exist.* It need not be the most important question in the case. It must simply exist. If the representative seeks certification under Rule 23(b)(3), however, the common questions in the case must predominate over the individual questions in the case. (Keep this distinction in mind as you read the next case; the dissent makes much of it.)

Third, historically, satisfying Rule 23(a)(2) was not difficult. Few opinions gave it more than passive treatment. That changed dramatically with the following case. By the way, *Wal-Mart* decided two issues, so we have divided the opinion into two parts in this book. First is the part in which the Court held that Rule 23(a)(2) was not satisfied. On this point, the Court split, five Justices to four. In section C.3.b, we will read the other part of the opinion, in which the Justices unanimously agreed that the case did not satisfy a different part of Rule 23.

Wal-Mart Stores, Inc. v. Dukes

Supreme Court of the United States
564 U.S. 338 (2011)

Justice Scalia delivered the opinion of the Court.

We are presented with one of the most expansive class actions ever. The District Court and the Court of Appeals approved the certification of a class comprising about one and a half million plaintiffs, current and former female employees of petitioner Wal-Mart who allege that the discretion exercised by their local supervisors over pay and promotion matters violates Title VII by discriminating against women. In addition to injunctive and declaratory relief, the plaintiffs seek an award of backpay. We consider whether the certification of the plaintiff class was consistent with Federal Rules of Civil Procedure 23(a) and (b)(2).

I

A

Petitioner Wal-Mart is the Nation's largest private employer. It operates four types of retail stores throughout the country: Discount Stores, Supercenters, Neighborhood Markets, and Sam's Clubs. Those stores are divided into seven nationwide divisions, which in turn comprise 41 regions of 80 to 85 stores apiece. Each store has between 40 and 53 separate departments and 80 to 500 staff positions. In all, Wal-Mart operates approximately 3,400 stores and employs more than one million people.

Pay and promotion decisions at Wal-Mart are generally committed to local managers' broad discretion, which is exercised "in a largely subjective manner." Local store managers may increase the wages of hourly employees (within limits) with only limited corporate oversight. As for salaried employees, such as store managers and their deputies, higher corporate authorities have discretion to set their pay within preestablished ranges.

Promotions work in a similar fashion. Wal-Mart permits store managers to apply their own subjective criteria when selecting candidates as "support managers," which is the first step on the path to management. Admission to Wal-Mart's management training program, however, does require that a candidate meet certain objective criteria, including an above-average performance rating, at least one year's tenure in the applicant's current position, and a willingness to relocate. But except for those requirements, regional and district managers have discretion to use their own judgment when selecting candidates for management training. Promotion to higher office—*e.g.*, assistant manager, co-manager, or store manager—is similarly at the discretion of the employee's superiors after prescribed objective factors are satisfied.

B

The named plaintiffs in this lawsuit, representing the 1.5 million members of the certified class, are three current or former Wal-Mart employees who allege that the company discriminated against them on the basis of their sex by denying them equal pay or promotions, in violation of Title VII of the Civil Rights Act of 1964, 78 Stat. 253, as amended, 42 U.S.C. § 2000e–1 *et seq.*

. . .

These plaintiffs, respondents here, do not allege that Wal-Mart has any express corporate policy against the advancement of women. Rather, they claim that their local managers' discretion over pay and promotions is exercised disproportionately in favor of men, leading to an unlawful disparate impact on female employees, see 42 U.S.C. § 2000e–2(k). And, respondents say, because Wal-Mart is aware of this effect, its refusal to cabin its managers' authority amounts to disparate treatment, see § 2000e–2(a). Their complaint seeks injunctive and declaratory relief, punitive damages, and backpay. It does not ask for compensatory damages.

Importantly for our purposes, respondents claim that the discrimination to which they have been subjected is common to *all* Wal-Mart's female employees. The basic theory of their case is that a strong and uniform "corporate culture" permits bias against women to infect, perhaps subconsciously, the discretionary decisionmaking of each one of Wal-Mart's thousands of managers—thereby making every woman at the company the victim of one common discriminatory practice. Respondents therefore wish to litigate the Title VII claims of all female employees at Wal-Mart's stores in a nationwide class action.

C

. . . .

. . . [R]espondents moved the District Court to certify a plaintiff class consisting of "'[a]ll women employed at any Wal-Mart domestic retail store at any time since December 26, 1998, who have been or may be subjected to Wal-Mart's challenged pay and management track promotions policies and practices.'" As evidence that there were indeed "questions of law or fact common to" all the women of Wal-Mart, as Rule 23(a)(2) requires, respondents relied chiefly on three forms of proof: statistical evidence about pay and promotion disparities between men and women at the company, anecdotal reports of discrimination from about 120 of Wal-Mart's female employees, and the testimony of a sociologist, Dr. William Bielby, who conducted a "social framework analysis" of Wal-Mart's "culture" and personnel practices, and concluded that the company was "vulnerable" to gender discrimination. . . .

D

A divided en banc Court of Appeals substantially affirmed the District Court's certification order. The majority concluded that respondents' evidence of commonality was sufficient to "raise the common question whether Wal-Mart's female employees nationwide were subjected to a single set of corporate policies (not merely a number of independent discriminatory acts) that may have worked to unlawfully discriminate against them in violation of Title VII." It also agreed with the District Court that the named plaintiffs' claims were sufficiently typical of the class as a whole to satisfy Rule 23(a)(3), and that they could serve as adequate class representatives, see Rule 23(a)(4). With respect to the Rule 23(b)(2) question, the Ninth Circuit held that respondents' backpay claims could be certified as part of a (b)(2) class because they did not "predominat[e]" over the requests for declaratory and injunctive relief, meaning they were not "superior in strength, influence, or authority" to the nonmonetary claims.[8] . . .

---

8. [Court's footnote #4] To enable that result, the Court of Appeals trimmed the (b)(2) class in two ways: First, it remanded that part of the certification order which included respondents' punitive-damages claim in the (b)(2) class, so that the District Court might consider whether that might cause the monetary relief to predominate. Second, it accepted in part Wal-Mart's argument that since class members whom it no longer employed had no standing to seek injunctive or declaratory relief, as to them monetary claims must predominate. It excluded from the certified class "those putative class members who were no longer Wal-Mart employees *at the time Plaintiffs' complaint was filed*" (emphasis added).

II

A

The crux of this case is commonality—the rule requiring a plaintiff to show that "there are questions of law or fact common to the class." Rule 23(a)(2).[9] That language is easy to misread, since "[a]ny competently crafted class complaint literally raises common 'questions.'" Nagareda, *Class Certification in the Age of Aggregate Proof*, 84 N.Y.U. L. Rev. 97, 131–132 (2009). For example: Do all of us plaintiffs indeed work for Wal-Mart? Do our managers have discretion over pay? Is that an unlawful employment practice? What remedies should we get? Reciting these questions is not sufficient to obtain class certification. Commonality requires the plaintiff to demonstrate that the class members "have suffered the same injury," [*General Telephone Co. v.*] *Falcon*, [457 U.S. 147 (1982),] *supra*, at 157. This does not mean merely that they have all suffered a violation of the same provision of law. Title VII, for example, can be violated in many ways—by intentional discrimination, or by hiring and promotion criteria that result in disparate impact, and by the use of these practices on the part of many different superiors in a single company. Quite obviously, the mere claim by employees of the same company that they have suffered a Title VII injury, or even a disparate-impact Title VII injury, gives no cause to believe that all their claims can productively be litigated at once. Their claims must depend upon a common contention—for example, the assertion of discriminatory bias on the part of the same supervisor. That common contention, moreover, must be of such a nature that it is capable of classwide resolution—which means that determination of its truth or falsity will resolve an issue that is central to the validity of each one of the claims in one stroke.

> "What matters to class certification . . . is not the raising of common 'questions'—even in droves—but, rather the capacity of a classwide proceeding to generate common *answers* apt to drive the resolution of the litigation. Dissimilarities within the proposed class are what have the potential to impede the generation of common answers." Nagareda, *supra*, at 132.

Rule 23 does not set forth a mere pleading standard. A party seeking class certification must affirmatively demonstrate his compliance with the Rule—that is, he must be prepared to prove that there are *in fact* sufficiently numerous parties, common questions of law or fact, etc. We recognized in *Falcon* that "sometimes it may be necessary for the court to probe behind the pleadings before coming to rest on the certification question," 457 U.S., at 160, and that certification is proper only if "the trial court is satisfied, after a rigorous analysis, that the prerequisites of Rule 23(a) have been satisfied," *id.*, at 161; see *id.*, at 160 ("[A]ctual, not presumed, conformance with Rule 23(a) remains . . . indispensable"). Frequently that "rigorous

9. [Court's footnote #5] In light of our disposition of the commonality question, however, it is unnecessary to resolve whether respondents have satisfied the typicality and adequate-representation requirements of Rule 23(a).

analysis" will entail some overlap with the merits of the plaintiff's underlying claim. That cannot be helped. "'[T]he class determination generally involves considerations that are enmeshed in the factual and legal issues comprising the plaintiff's cause of action.'"[10]

. . .

In this case, proof of commonality necessarily overlaps with respondents' merits contention that Wal-Mart engages in a *pattern or practice* of discrimination. That is so because, in resolving an individual's Title VII claim, the crux of the inquiry is "the reason for a particular employment decision," *Cooper* v. *Federal Reserve Bank of Richmond*, 467 U.S. 867, 876 (1984). Here respondents wish to sue about literally millions of employment decisions at once. Without some glue holding the alleged *reasons* for all those decisions together, it will be impossible to say that examination of all the class members' claims for relief will produce a common answer to the crucial question *why was I disfavored*.

B

This Court's opinion in *Falcon* describes how the commonality issue must be approached. There an employee who claimed that he was deliberately denied a promotion on account of race obtained certification of a class comprising all employees wrongfully denied promotions and all applicants wrongfully denied jobs. . . . We rejected that composite class for lack of commonality and typicality, explaining:

> "Conceptually, there is a wide gap between (a) an individual's claim that he has been denied a promotion [or higher pay] on discriminatory grounds, and his otherwise unsupported allegation that the company has a policy of discrimination, and (b) the existence of a class of persons who have suffered the same injury as that individual, such that the individual's claim and the class claim will share common questions of law or fact and that the individual's claim will be typical of the class claims."

Falcon suggested two ways in which that conceptual gap might be bridged. First, if the employer "used a biased testing procedure to evaluate both applicants for employment and incumbent employees, a class action on behalf of every applicant or employee who might have been prejudiced by the test clearly would satisfy the commonality and typicality requirements of Rule 23(a)." *Id.*, at 159, n. 15. Second, "[s]ignificant proof that an employer operated under a general policy of

10. [Court's footnote #6] A statement in one of our prior cases, *Eisen v. Carlisle & Jacquelin*, 417 U.S. 156, 177 (1974), is sometimes mistakenly cited to the contrary: "We find nothing in either the language or history of Rule 23 that gives a court any authority to conduct a preliminary inquiry into the merits of a suit in order to determine whether it may be maintained as a class action." But in that case, the judge had conducted a preliminary inquiry into the merits of a suit, not in order to determine the propriety of certification under Rules 23(a) and (b) (he had already done that), but in order to shift the cost of notice required by Rule 23(c)(2) from the plaintiff to the defendants. To the extent the quoted statement goes beyond the permissibility of a merits inquiry for any other pretrial purpose, it is the purest dictum and is contradicted by our other cases.

discrimination conceivably could justify a class of both applicants and employees if the discrimination manifested itself in hiring and promotion practices in the same general fashion, such as through entirely subjective decisionmaking processes." *Ibid.* We think that statement precisely describes respondents' burden in this case. The first manner of bridging the gap obviously has no application here; Wal-Mart has no testing procedure or other companywide evaluation method that can be charged with bias. The whole point of permitting discretionary decisionmaking is to avoid evaluating employees under a common standard.

The second manner of bridging the gap requires "significant proof" that Wal-Mart "operated under a general policy of discrimination." That is entirely absent here. Wal-Mart's announced policy forbids sex discrimination, and as the District Court recognized the company imposes penalties for denials of equal employment opportunity. The only evidence of a "general policy of discrimination" respondents produced was the testimony of Dr. William Bielby, their sociological expert. Relying on "social framework" analysis, Bielby testified that Wal-Mart has a "strong corporate culture," that makes it "'vulnerable'" to "gender bias." He could not, however, "determine with any specificity how regularly stereotypes play a meaningful role in employment decisions at Wal-Mart. At his deposition . . . Dr. Bielby conceded that he could not calculate whether 0.5 percent or 95 percent of the employment decisions at Wal-Mart might be determined by stereotyped thinking." 222 F.R.D. 189, 192 (ND Cal. 2004). The parties dispute whether Bielby's testimony even met the standards for the admission of expert testimony under Federal Rule of Civil Procedure 702 and our *Daubert* case, see *Daubert v. Merrell Dow Pharmaceuticals, Inc.*, 509 U.S. 579 (1993). The District Court concluded that *Daubert* did not apply to expert testimony at the certification stage of class-action proceedings. We doubt that is so, but even if properly considered, Bielby's testimony does nothing to advance respondents' case. "[W]hether 0.5 percent or 95 percent of the employment decisions at Wal-Mart might be determined by stereotyped thinking" is the essential question on which respondents' theory of commonality depends. If Bielby admittedly has no answer to that question, we can safely disregard what he has to say. It is worlds away from "significant proof" that Wal-Mart "operated under a general policy of discrimination."

C

The only corporate policy that the plaintiffs' evidence convincingly establishes is Wal-Mart's "policy" of *allowing discretion* by local supervisors over employment matters. On its face, of course, that is just the opposite of a uniform employment practice that would provide the commonality needed for a class action; it is a policy *against having* uniform employment practices. It is also a very common and presumptively reasonable way of doing business—one that we have said "should itself raise no inference of discriminatory conduct," *Watson v. Fort Worth Bank & Trust*, 487 U.S. 977, 990 (1988).

To be sure, we have recognized that, "in appropriate cases," giving discretion to lower-level supervisors can be the basis of Title VII liability under a disparate-impact theory—since "an employer's undisciplined system of subjective decisionmaking [can have] precisely the same effects as a system pervaded by impermissible intentional discrimination." *Id.*, at 990–991. But the recognition that this type of Title VII claim "can" exist does not lead to the conclusion that every employee in a company using a system of discretion has such a claim in common. To the contrary, left to their own devices most managers in any corporation—and surely most managers in a corporation that forbids sex discrimination—would select sex-neutral, performance-based criteria for hiring and promotion that produce no actionable disparity at all. Others may choose to reward various attributes that produce disparate impact—such as scores on general aptitude tests or educational achievements. And still other managers may be guilty of intentional discrimination that produces a sex-based disparity. In such a company, demonstrating the invalidity of one manager's use of discretion will do nothing to demonstrate the invalidity of another's. A party seeking to certify a nationwide class will be unable to show that all the employees' Title VII claims will in fact depend on the answers to common questions.

Respondents have not identified a common mode of exercising discretion that pervades the entire company—aside from their reliance on Dr. Bielby's social frameworks analysis that we have rejected. In a company of Wal-Mart's size and geographical scope, it is quite unbelievable that all managers would exercise their discretion in a common way without some common direction. Respondents attempt to make that showing by means of statistical and anecdotal evidence, but their evidence falls well short.

The statistical evidence consists primarily of regression analyses performed by Dr. Richard Drogin, a statistician, and Dr. Marc Bendick, a labor economist. Drogin conducted his analysis region-by-region, comparing the number of women promoted into management positions with the percentage of women in the available pool of hourly workers. After considering regional and national data, Drogin concluded that "there are statistically significant disparities between men and women at Wal-Mart . . . [and] these disparities . . . can be explained only by gender discrimination." Bendick compared work-force data from Wal-Mart and competitive retailers and concluded that Wal-Mart "promotes a lower percentage of women than its competitors."

Even if they are taken at face value, these studies are insufficient to establish that respondents' theory can be proved on a classwide basis. . . . As [Ninth Circuit] Judge Ikuta observed in her dissent, "[i]nformation about disparities at the regional and national level does not establish the existence of disparities at individual stores, let alone raise the inference that a company-wide policy of discrimination is implemented by discretionary decisions at the store and district level." A regional pay disparity, for example, may be attributable to only a small set of Wal-Mart stores, and cannot by itself establish the uniform, store-by-store disparity upon which the plaintiffs' theory of commonality depends.

There is another, more fundamental, respect in which respondents' statistical proof fails. Even if it established (as it does not) a pay or promotion pattern that differs from the nationwide figures or the regional figures in *all* of Wal-Mart's 3,400 stores, that would still not demonstrate that commonality of issue exists. Some managers will claim that the availability of women, or qualified women, or interested women, in their stores' area does not mirror the national or regional statistics. And almost all of them will claim to have been applying some sex-neutral, performance-based criteria—whose nature and effects will differ from store to store. In the landmark case of ours which held that giving discretion to lower-level supervisors can be the basis of Title VII liability under a disparate-impact theory, the plurality opinion *conditioned* that holding on the corollary that merely proving that the discretionary system has produced a racial or sexual disparity *is not enough.* "[T]he plaintiff must begin by identifying the specific employment practice that is challenged." *Watson*, 487 U.S., at 994 . . . . That is all the more necessary when a class of plaintiffs is sought to be certified. Other than the bare existence of delegated discretion, respondents have identified no "specific employment practice"—much less one that ties all their 1.5 million claims together. Merely showing that Wal-Mart's policy of discretion has produced an overall sex-based disparity does not suffice.

Respondents' anecdotal evidence suffers from the same defects, and in addition is too weak to raise any inference that all the individual, discretionary personnel decisions are discriminatory. . . . [R]espondents filed some 120 affidavits reporting experiences of discrimination—about 1 for every 12,500 class members—relating to only some 235 out of Wal-Mart's 3,400 stores. Even if every single one of these accounts is true, that would not demonstrate that the entire company "operate[s] under a general policy of discrimination," which is what respondents must show to certify a companywide class.

The dissent misunderstands the nature of the foregoing analysis. It criticizes our focus on the dissimilarities between the putative class members on the ground that we have "blend[ed]" Rule 23(a)(2)'s commonality requirement with Rule 23(b)(3)'s inquiry into whether common questions "predominate" over individual ones. That is not so. We quite agree that for purposes of Rule 23(a)(2) "'[e]ven a single [common] question'" will do. We consider dissimilarities not in order to determine (as Rule 23(b)(3) requires) whether common questions *predominate*, but in order to determine (as Rule 23(a)(2) requires) whether there *is* "[e]ven a single [common] question." And there is not here. Because respondents provide no convincing proof of a companywide discriminatory pay and promotion policy, we have concluded that they have not established the existence of any common question.

In sum, we agree with [Ninth Circuit] Chief Judge Kozinski that the members of the class:

> "held a multitude of different jobs, at different levels of Wal-Mart's hierarchy, for variable lengths of time, in 3,400 stores, sprinkled across 50 states, with a kaleidoscope of supervisors (male and female), subject to a variety of regional policies that all differed . . . . Some thrived while others did poorly. They have little in common but their sex and this lawsuit." (dissenting opinion).

....

Reversed.

JUSTICE GINSBURG, with whom JUSTICE BREYER, JUSTICE SOTOMAYOR, and JUSTICE KAGAN join, concurring in part and dissenting in part.

....

Whether the class the plaintiffs describe meets the specific requirements of Rule 23(b)(3) is not before the Court, and I would reserve that matter for consideration and decision on remand. The Court, however, disqualifies the class at the starting gate, holding that the plaintiffs cannot cross the "commonality" line set by Rule 23(a)(2). In so ruling, the Court imports into the Rule 23(a) determination concerns properly addressed in a Rule 23(b)(3) assessment.

I

....

B

The District Court, recognizing that "one significant issue common to the class may be sufficient to warrant certification," ... found that the plaintiffs easily met that test....

... The named plaintiffs, led by Betty Dukes, propose to litigate, on behalf of the class, allegations that Wal-Mart discriminates on the basis of gender in pay and promotions. They allege that the company "[r]eli[es] on gender stereotypes in making employment decisions such as ... promotion[s] [and] pay." Wal-Mart permits those prejudices to infect personnel decisions, the plaintiffs contend, by leaving pay and promotions in the hands of "a nearly all male managerial workforce" using "arbitrary and subjective criteria." ...

Women fill 70 percent of the hourly jobs in the retailer's stores but make up only "33 percent of management employees." 222 F.R.D., at 146. The plaintiffs' "largely uncontested descriptive statistics" also show that women working in the company's stores "are paid less than men in every region" and "that the salary gap widens over time even for men and women hired into the same jobs at the same time."

...

Wal-Mart's supervisors do not make their discretionary decisions in a vacuum. The District Court reviewed means Wal-Mart used to maintain a "carefully constructed ... corporate culture," such as frequent meetings to re-inforce the common way of thinking, regular transfers of managers between stores to ensure uniformity throughout the company, monitoring of stores "on a close and constant basis," and "Wal-Mart TV," "broadcas[t] ... into all stores."

The plaintiffs' evidence, including class members' tales of their own experiences, suggests that gender bias suffused Wal-Mart's company culture. Among illustrations, senior management often refer to female associates as "little Janie Qs." One manager told an employee that "[m]en are here to make a career and women aren't."

A committee of female Wal-Mart executives concluded that "[s]tereotypes limit the opportunities offered to women."

. . . .

C

The District Court's identification of a common question, whether Wal-Mart's pay and promotions policies gave rise to unlawful discrimination, was hardly infirm. The practice of delegating to supervisors large discretion to make personnel decisions, uncontrolled by formal standards, has long been known to have the potential to produce disparate effects. Managers, like all humankind, may be prey to biases of which they are unaware. The risk of discrimination is heightened when those managers are predominantly of one sex, and are steeped in a corporate culture that perpetuates gender stereotypes.

. . . .

II

A

The Court gives no credence to the key dispute common to the class: whether Wal-Mart's discretionary pay and promotion policies are discriminatory. . . . "What matters," the Court asserts, "is not the raising of common 'questions,'" but whether there are "[d]issimilarities within the proposed class" that "have the potential to impede the generation of common answers."

The Court blends Rule 23(a)(2)'s threshold criterion with the more demanding criteria of Rule 23(b)(3), and thereby elevates the (a)(2) inquiry so that it is no longer "easily satisfied," 5 J. Moore et al., Moore's Federal Practice § 23.23[2], p. 23–72 (3d ed. 2011). Rule 23(b)(3) certification requires, in addition to the four 23(a) findings, determinations that "questions of law or fact common to class members predominate over any questions affecting only individual members" and that "a class action is superior to other available methods for . . . adjudicating the controversy."

The Court's emphasis on differences between class members mimics the Rule 23(b)(3) inquiry into whether common questions "predominate" over individual issues. And by asking whether the individual differences "impede" common adjudication, the Court duplicates 23(b)(3)'s question whether "a class action is superior" to other modes of adjudication. Indeed, Professor Nagareda, whose "dissimilarities" inquiry the Court endorses, developed his position in the context of Rule 23(b)(3). See 84 N.Y.U. L. Rev., at 131 (Rule 23(b)(3) requires "some decisive degree of similarity across the proposed class" because it "speaks of common 'questions' that 'predominate' over individual ones"). . . . If courts must conduct a "dissimilarities" analysis at the Rule 23(a)(2) stage, no mission remains for Rule 23(b)(3).

Because Rule 23(a) is also a prerequisite for Rule 23(b)(1) and Rule 23(b)(2) classes, the Court's "dissimilarities" position is far reaching. Individual differences should not bar a Rule 23(b)(1) or Rule 23(b)(2) class, so long as the Rule 23(a) threshold is met. . . .

D

. . . .

Wal-Mart's delegation of discretion over pay and promotions is a policy uniform throughout all stores. The very nature of discretion is that people will exercise it in various ways. A system of delegated discretion . . . is a practice actionable under Title VII when it produces discriminatory outcomes. A finding that Wal-Mart's pay and promotions practices in fact violate the law would be the first step in the usual order of proof for plaintiffs seeking individual remedies for company-wide discrimination. . . . That each individual employee's unique circumstances will ultimately determine whether she is entitled to backpay or damages, § 2000e–5(g)(2)(A) (barring backpay if a plaintiff "was refused . . . advancement . . . for any reason other than discrimination"), should not factor into the Rule 23(a)(2) determination.

. . . .

Notes and Questions

1. In Part II(C) of its opinion, the majority recognized that the existence of a single common question will satisfy Rule 23(a)(2). It holds that there is none. The allegation that all claimants suffered from a violation of federal labor law was insufficient, because that law may be violated in a variety of ways. The majority concludes that each class member must have suffered "the same injury." Because Wal-Mart store managers exercise independent judgment concerning pay and promotion, the majority concluded, an employee in Fresno could not have suffered the same harm as an employee in Buffalo.

After *Wal-Mart*, lower courts have concluded that class members can suffer "the same injury" by showing a common instance of injurious conduct, even though members' harms may vary substantially. *See, e.g., In re Deepwater Horizon*, 739 F.3d 790, 810–811 (5th Cir. 2014). Thus, *Wal-Mart* does not require that every question be common—there may be individual questions, for example, as to the damages suffered by different class members. But the underlying harm suffered must be uniform for all class members.

2. In Part II(A) of it opinion, the majority holds that Rule 23(a)(2) requires class litigation generate "common answers" for all class members. In applying the "common answers" standard, the Court provides this guidance: the common issue "must be of such a nature that it is capable of classwide resolution—which means that determination of its truth or falsity will resolve an issue that is central to the validity of each one of the claims in one stroke."

Accordingly, there must be some issue, shared by all class members, which, when adjudicated, will generate *answers* for all class members. But Rule 23(a)(2) requires "common questions," not "common answers." Did the majority re-write the Rule?

3. It is impossible to quantify how much more rigorous the *Wal-Mart* approach is to previous practice. Without doubt, though, the focus on generating common *answers* and on resolving claims in "one stroke" rather than the mere existence of

common *questions* is important, and has resulted in denials of certification for failure to satisfy Rule 23(a)(2). *See, e.g., DL v. District of Columbia*, 713 F.3d 120, 127 (D.C. Cir. 2013) ("the harms alleged . . . involve different policies and practices at different stages of the District's Child Find and FAPE process; the district court identified no single or uniform policy or practice that bridges all their claims").

4. According to the majority, in Part II(B) of its opinion, why was Dr. Bielby's "social framework analysis" insufficient to demonstrate commonality?

5. According to the majority, in Part II(C) of its opinion, why was plaintiffs' statistical proof of discriminatory impact insufficient? In the same section, why was plaintiffs' anecdotal evidence insufficient to demonstrate commonality?

6. Was the dissent correct in charging that the majority imported the stricter requirement of Rule 23(b)(3) into the analysis of Rule 23(a)(2)? Notice what was at stake here. In the second part of the *Wal-Mart* opinion, which we will read in section C.3.b, the Court unanimously held that the plaintiffs could not proceed with a class action under Rule 23(b)(2). If the Court had concluded that the class satisfied Rule 23(a)(2), on remand, the claimants could have pursued a Rule 23(b)(3) class action. The holding that commonality is not satisfied precludes any class action.

7. After *Wal-Mart*, how could the plaintiffs' lawyers restructure their case so that a number of more limited class actions may proceed? How would you define those classes?

8. Many consider the *Wal-Mart* definition of commonality to raise a significant hurdle to class certification in federal court. Professor Sherry argues that plaintiffs' lawyers in that case (and the Ninth Circuit) contributed to that development by overreaching in seeking (and allowing) certification of a nationwide class. Suzanna Sherry, *Hogs Get Slaughtered at the Supreme Court*, 2011 Sup. Ct. Rev. 1.

Note on Front-Loading and Consideration of the Merits

Wal-Mart did much more than change the standard for commonality. The majority made other significant points:

- In Part II(A), the majority said: "Rule 23 does not set forth a mere pleading standard. A party seeking class certification must affirmatively demonstrate his compliance with the Rule—that is, he must be prepared to prove that there are *in fact* sufficiently numerous parties, common questions of law or fact, etc." There must be "rigorous analysis," "significant proof," and "actual, not presumed, conformance with Rule 23."[11]
- In Part II(B), the majority noted that the district court considered expert testimony at certification without requiring that the expert be qualified under Federal Rule of Evidence 702 and *Daubert v. Merrell Dow Pharmaceuticals,*

11. For these points, the Court cited *General Telephone Co. of Southwest v. Falcon*, 457 U.S. 147, 156 (1982). We will see the *Falcon* case when we discuss typicality under Rule 23(a)(3).

Inc., 509 U.S. 579 (1993). The majority expressed doubt about whether that practice was proper. Lower courts appear to have taken the hint. *See, e.g., Messner v. Northshore Univ. Healthsystem*, 669 F.3d, 806 (7th Cir. 2012) ("If a district court has doubts about whether an expert's opinion may be critical for a class certification decision, the court should make an explicit *Daubert* ruling.").

These developments reflect significant "front-loading" of the litigation for the representative. At the certification stage, she must present *evidence* that proves satisfaction of the requirements of Rule 23. To the extent she will be relying on expert testimony to do so, she must qualify the witness under *Daubert*. Marshaling that evidence may be expensive and time-consuming.

In assessing evidence on certification, courts had long been vexed by a statement in *Eisen v. Carlisle & Jacquelin*, 417 U.S. 156, 177 (1974). That opinion implied, to some at least, that a court considering class certification should not decide facts that overlap with the underlying merits. In footnote 6, *Wal-Mart* happily put this concern to rest, calling it the "purest dictum." It is now clear that courts, in ruling on class certification, may consider and even rule upon factual issues that implicate the merits of the case. The court should not, however, decide merits-based issues that are not related to certification. "Merits questions may be considered to the extent—but only to the extent—that they are relevant to determining whether the Rule 23 prerequisites . . . are satisfied." *Amgen, Inc. v. Connecticut Ret. Plans & Trust Funds*, 133 S. Ct. 1184, 1194–1195 (2013).

iii. Rule 23(a)(3): Typicality

Rule 23(a)(3) requires that the claims of the plaintiff representative be "typical of the claims . . . of the class." This factor is closely related to Rule 23(a)(4), which requires that the representative fairly and adequately protect the interests of the class. Both focus on the relationship between the representative and the class members. The requirement that the representative's claim be typical of the claims of class members helps to ensure that the representative will be adequate. If the representative "feels the same pain" as the class members, she may have the appropriate incentive to litigate vigorously.

Typicality is also closely related to commonality under Rule 23(a)(2). If the representative's claim does not share commonality with those of the class members (as was the case in *Wal-Mart*), her claim will not be typical of those of the class. Moreover, she will not be an adequate representative. As we said at the outset: the Rule 23(a) requirements are not hermetically sealed.

The representative's claims need not be identical to those of the class members. There is no single test for whether the claims are too divergent to satisfy the requirement. Courts look to whether the "essential characteristics" of the claims are the same, and recognize that some factual differences—for instance, as to damages—will not preclude class treatment. If class members' claims will require a great deal of individualized litigation, the benefit of the class action is lost, and certification should be denied. We focus now on two famous cases that raise related typicality issues.

The* Falcon *Issue. In *General Telephone Co. v. Falcon*, 457 U.S. 147 (1982), the representative sued on behalf of a class of Mexican-Americans, charging that the defendant had discriminated against them on the basis of national origin. There were two groups of class members: one consisted of persons employed by the defendant but denied promotion; the second consisted of persons whom the defendant had refused to hire. Both groups claimed that the defendant discriminated against them because of national origin.

Falcon, the representative, was a member of the first group in the class: he was employed by the defendant but was denied promotion. The Court held that he could not represent the other group in the class. Why? Falcon had suffered the harm of not being promoted. He was trying to represent a group whose harm was not being hired. Thus, Falcon's claim was not typical of those of the second group in the class.

Note four things about *Falcon*. First, *Wal-Mart* quoted extensively from *Falcon*, which emphasizes the similarity between commonality and typicality. The *Falcon* Court expressly noted that the two "tend to merge" and serve as "guideposts for determining whether under the particular circumstances maintenance of a class action is economical . . . ." 457 U.S. at 157, n. 13.

Second, *Wal-Mart* and *Falcon* are consistent. In each case, class members claimed discrimination on a particular basis—sex in one and national origin in the other. But Rule 23(a) requires a more refined sense of the harm suffered. It is not enough to say, "I suffered because of my national origin." The representative must show that she suffered *the same harm*—for example, lack of promotion—because of national origin.

Third, there was potential conflict of interest between Falcon and some members of the putative class. Falcon and one group in the class have already been hired; they want promotions. Potentially, Falcon does not want the group that was not hired to prevail. If they do, they will create more competition for the promotion Falcon seeks.

Fourth, the *Falcon* problem is fixable. The case might be divided in to subclasses—one for those employees denied promotion and another for those who were not hired. A new representative will be required for the latter group. Instead of subclasses in the same case, a separate class action could be filed for those who were not hired.

The* LaMar *Issue. In addition to suffering the same harm as the class, the representative must have suffered at the hands of the same defendants. In *LaMar v. H&B Novelty & Loan Co.*, 489 F.2d 461 (9th Cir. 1973), a class of persons who did business with pawn shops sued for alleged violation of federal truth-in-lending laws. There were several defendants, joined under Rule 20(a)(2). The representative, however, had done business with only one of the defendants. The fact that he was not harmed by the other defendants meant that his claim was not typical of those of class members who dealt with the other defendants.

There are ways to fix the *LaMar* problem. The case can be restructured with multiple representatives—Representative 1 representing those class members who did business with Defendant 1, Representative 2 for those members who dealt with Defendant 2, and so forth.

If the defendants engaged in a conspiracy, it is likely that a single representative could act on behalf of all class members. The theory is that each member was harmed not by a single defendant but by the concerted efforts of the conspiracy.

Other potential issues. Though the mere existence of individual questions involving the representative will not preclude class certification, sometimes individual defenses unique to the representative do defeat typicality. For instance, in *Gary Plastic Packaging Corp. v. Merrill Lynch, Pierce, Fenner & Smith, Inc.*, 903 F.2d 176, 179–80 (2d Cir. 1990), the fact that the representative bought certificates of deposit from the defendant after the defendant's alleged fraud was known subjected it to unique defenses (such as assumption of the risk) and defeated typicality. In another case, the representative was subject to deportation, while other class members were not. The court rejected class certification. *Hagan v. City of Winnemucca*, 108 F.R.D. 61, 65-66 (D. Nev. 1985). The concern in these cases is that the defense against the representative will become the focus of the litigation or that the representative will be distracted or preoccupied in a way that may compromise her ability to serve as representative. The problem may be seen either as one of lack of typicality or of failure to provide adequate representation, to which we now turn.

iv. Rule 23(a)(4): Fair and Adequate Representation

Rule 23(a)(4) requires that "the representative parties will fairly and adequately protect the interests of the class." The drafters of the 1966 amendments to Rule 23 intended this provision to meet the requirements of due process articulated by the Supreme Court in *Hansberry v. Lee*, 311 U.S. 32 (1940).

Hansberry: Constitutional Underpinnings

Rule 23 raises a profound issue of due process. The representative is a party to the litigation, as are the defendants. They will be bound by the judgment—win or lose—because they are clearly subject to the personal jurisdiction of the court. The plaintiff is bound, because she voluntarily invoked the judicial machinery by filing suit. The defendants are bound, because they were served with process, which constitutes the court's exercise of authority over them.

But class members are not parties. They did not bring the suit. They have not been served with process. How, then, can they be bound by the judgment in the case? The answer lies in the fact that they were represented by the plaintiff. As the Court explained in *Hansberry*, 311 U.S. at 41:

> It is a principle of general application in Anglo-American jurisprudence that one is not bound by a judgment in personam in a litigation in which

> he is not designated as a party or to which he has not been made a party by service of process. . . .
>
> To these general rules there is a recognized exception that, to an extent not precisely defined by judicial opinion, the judgment in a "class" or "representative" suit, to which some members of the class are parties, may bind members of the class or those represented who were not made parties to it. . . .

As a matter of constitutional law, then, class members are entitled to fair and adequate representation. *Hansberry* remains the leading case on what due process requires in this regard. *Hansberry* concerned the enforcement of a racially restrictive covenant in a subdivision in Chicago. The covenant prohibited homeowners, who were white, from renting or selling to non-whites. The case was decided before *Shelley v. Kramer,* 334 U.S. 1 (1948), which declared such restrictions unconstitutional. The covenant provided that it would go into effect only if 95 percent of the owners in the subdivision signed it.

Hansberry hinged on the validity of a judgment in an earlier case, *Burke v. Kleiman*, 277 Ill. App. 519 (1934). In that case, a white homeowner, who did not favor the restrictive covenant, rented his property in the subdivision to a black family. Other owners in the subdivision sued to enforce the covenant and sought an injunction to stop the rental. They sued in a class action, and purported to represent all homeowners in the subdivision.

At trial in *Burke*, the parties stipulated that 95 percent of the owners had signed the covenant, making it effective. (In fact, barely half the homeowners had actually signed, and the covenant should never have gone into effect.) The Illinois trial court upheld the covenant and forbade the homeowner from renting to the black family. The Illinois Court of Appeals affirmed the judgment.

Years later, a different white homeowner in the subdivision contracted to sell his house to a black family, the Hansberrys. Another white homeowner then sued in state court to stop the sale. That plaintiff relied on the judgment in *Burke* and argued that because *Burke* was a class action, the judgment bound all homeowners in the subdivision, including the one trying to sell to the Hansberrys. The Illinois courts held that *Burke* bound the parties, enforced the restrictive covenant, and refused to allow the sale to the Hansberrys.

The Supreme Court reversed. It held that the homeowners selling to the Hansberrys were not bound by the judgment in *Burke*. Why? Because they were not members of the class that sued in *Burke*. The class in *Burke* sought to *enforce* the restrictive covenant. The judgment in that case would bind all homeowners who agreed with that position. But it could not bind homeowners who *opposed* enforcement of the covenant. Those in favor of the covenant and those opposed to it are not members of the same class, and a representative from one group cannot bind someone in the other group. The Court, 311 U.S. at 45–46, explained:

> Those who sought to secure its benefits by enforcing it could not be said to be in the same class with or represent those whose interest was in resisting performance .... If those who thus seek to secure the benefits of the agreement were rightly regarded by the state Supreme Court as constituting a class, it is evident that those signers or their successors who are interested in challenging the validity of the agreement and resisting its performance are not of the same class in the sense that their interests are identical so that any group who had elected to enforce rights conferred by the agreement could be said to be acting in the interest of any others who were free to deny its obligation....
>
> [A] selection of representatives for purposes of litigation, whose substantial interests are not necessarily or even probably the same as those whom they are deemed to represent, does not afford that protection to absent parties which due process requires....

Thus, a judgment in a class action cannot, consistent with due process of law, bind members of the class whose interests directly conflict with those of the representative who purports to stand in judgment for them. On the other hand, if the representative and the class members are on the same page, with no conflict on the central goal of the case, a judgment in the class action will bind the class members. According to *Hansberry*, the binding effect comes from the adequate representation.

But do the class members need to be given notice that they are in the class? *Hansberry* said nothing about this. We will have something to say about this when we get to the Rule 23(b)(3) class action, in section C.3.c. Just keep that question in the back of your mind until then.

We turn now from constitutional considerations of adequate representation to the application of Rule 23(a)(4). One of the goals of the drafters of Rule 23 was to provide factors to assess before certifying a class. Conscientious application of Rule 23 will avoid the possibility that a class judgment, like that in *Burke v. Kleiman*, might be found in a separate case to have been faulty.

Applying Rule 23(a)(4)

The conflict in *Burke v. Kleiman* could not have been starker: the representative said "yes" on the basic issue in the case, and purported to bind people who said "no" on the same issue. Such conflict on the basic purpose of the suit is rare. More commonly, issues of adequate representation will not rise to the level of a due process violation. Our question is when disagreement on lesser issues might preclude certification under Rule 23(a)(4).

We are concerned here with whether the representative is adequate. Rule 23(g), which we address in section D.1 also requires the class lawyer to represent the interests of the class fairly and adequately. So, both the representative and the class lawyer are fiduciaries, acting in the interest of others.

Rule 23(a)(4) does not require that the representative be "the best" one available. She must simply be "adequate." As noted, challenges to adequacy often overlap with challenges regarding typicality. For instance, the representative who is subject to a unique defense may be rejected either because her claim is not typical or because she will not be an adequate representative. Challenges to a representative under Rule 23(a)(4) generally fall into one of several categories.

Interests Antagonistic to the Class.

It would be unrealistic to require that the representative never disagree with class members. There may be heated disagreements and even conflicts of interest. The question is when these become so profound as to disqualify the representative. (Again, the problem could as readily be said to be one of typicality.)

- Disagreements regarding litigation strategy or remedies usually will not violate Rule 23(a)(4). This fact can be frustrating for class members who disagree with decisions by the representative. Sometimes, such class members will attempt to intervene into the class action under Rule 24. Doing so gives them party status.
- The existence of a material, non-speculative disagreement on core issues, however, will raise serious problems under Rule 23(a)(4) even if they do not rise to the level of due process violations. In *Amchem Products, Inc. v. Windsor*, 521 U.S. 592, 610–611 (1997),[12] the parties asked the court to approve their global settlement of thousands of claims arising from exposure to asbestos.[13] Some members of the class had already manifested personal injuries, and sought compensation for those injuries. Others, however, had been exposed to asbestos but had not yet manifested symptoms ("exposure-only" claims). One reason for rejecting the settlement was the conflict between those who had already suffered harm and those who, because of exposure, might in the future suffer personal injuries. The Court explained: "[F]or the currently injured, the critical goal is generous immediate payments. That goal tugs against the interest of exposure-only plaintiffs in ensuring an ample, inflation-protected fund for the future."
- Similarly, a representative is not adequate when the putative class consists of some members who benefited from the acts claimed to have hurt other class members. In *Pickett v. Iowa Beef Processors,* 209 F.3d 1276, 1280 (11th Cir. 2000), a class action alleging harm from marketing agreements, some class members benefitted from the agreements; the internal conflict precluded certification. (The issue, again, could just as readily be said to raise a problem with typicality.)

Relationship with Class Lawyer.

Courts have found the representative inadequate if she has a close business or personal relationship with the class lawyer. The concern here is that the representative

12. We will see this case in detail in section 6.E, on class settlement.

13. *See* footnote 3 *supra.*

has a conflict of interest: she might be tempted to approve a settlement on terms that enrich the lawyer and do not fairly compensate the class. The court in *Kramer v. Scientific Control Corp.*, 534 F.2d 1085, 1093 (3d Cir. 1976), adopted a per se rule that "no member of the bar . . . maintaining an employment relationship, including a partnership . . . or sharing office or suite space with an attorney class representative during the preparation or pendency of a Rule 23(b)(3) class action may serve as counsel to the class if the action might result in the creation of a fund from which an attorneys' fee award would be appropriate."

Knowledge, Engagement of, and Financial Wherewithal of the Representative.

The representative is a fiduciary and must take the job seriously. But the representative is probably not a lawyer, so cannot be expected to bring legal expertise to the job. And she likely has a real-world job, so cannot be expected to spend all waking hours working on the case. Thus, there is a tendency to say that the class lawyer can do all the heavy lifting, and the representative is more or less "along for the ride." At some point, though, this becomes problematic. If the representative is clueless about the case and thoroughly disengaged, the class is essentially "headless." It is run entirely by a lawyer, who lacks standing to bring the claim.

Courts endeavor to find a happy medium. The representative should have some rudimentary understanding of the dispute and her role in it. The goal is to have a representative who is sufficiently engaged and savvy that she will be able to provide a brake on any attempt by the class lawyer to do something that would not be in the best interests of the class.

That said, one can find cases that seem to give the lawyer *carte blanche.* For example, in *Kirkpatrick v. J.C. Bradford & Co.*, 827 F.2d 718, 727–728 (11th Cir. 1987), the court explained:

> Although the interests of the plaintiff class certainly would be better served if the named plaintiffs fully participate in the litigation . . . the economics of the class action suit often are such that counsel have a greater financial incentive for obtaining a successful resolution of a class suit than do the individual class members. . . . It is not surprising, then, that the subjective desire to vigorously prosecute a class action . . . quite often is supplied more by counsel than by the class members themselves. Obviously this creates a potential for abuse. Yet the financial incentives offered by the class suit serve both the public interests in the private enforcement of various regulatory schemes, particularly those governing the securities markets, and the private interests of the class members in obtaining redress of legal grievances that might not feasibly be remedied within the framework of a multiplicity of small individual suits for damages.

In contrast, in *Berger v. Compaq Computer Corp.*, 257 F.3d 475, 478 (5th Cir. 2001), the court held that a representative must show that she is "willing and able to take an active role in and control the litigation and to protect the interests of [the class members]." In *Baffa v. Donaldson, Lufkin & Jenrette Securities Corp.*, 222 F.3d 52,

60–61 (2d Cir. 2000), a securities fraud case, the Second Circuit explained that the representative, though only eighteen years old, "understood the nature of his proposed role in the litigation and demonstrated his willingness to carry it forward." The court noted that the representative "understood that he and others had sustained a loss due to the alleged fraud."

Defendants sometimes challenge the representative by alleging that she lacks the financial ability to prosecute the case. Most lawyers take class actions on a contingent fee basis, so there is no need for the representative to pay those. She will be responsible, however, for various costs of litigation as they are incurred—filing fees, expenses of discovery and, in Rule 23(b)(3) classes, the cost of giving required notice to the class members.

Historically, lawyers could advance money to the representative to pay these expenses—but only if the representative was required to reimburse the lawyer if the class lost the case. There is a trend, however, sparked by Rule 1.8(e) of the American Bar Association Model Rules of Professional Responsibility, to permit attorneys to advance expenses on a contingent basis. Under such provisions, the client repays the lawyer only if the class recovers some remedy. This trend makes it easier for class lawyers to enlist representatives, but raises a concern that it allows the lawyer to "buy" a class claim.

3. Rule 23(b): The Types of Class Actions

After the party seeking class certification demonstrates that the case satisfies all the prerequisites of Rule 23(a), that party must then show—again, based upon evidence, not pleadings—that the case fits within one of the types, or categories, of class actions recognized by Rule 23(b). Under Rule 23(b), then, there is a choice: the party seeking certification must satisfy only one of the types of classes recognized. Nothing precludes the representative from seeking certification under more than one type of class action. A class certified under more than one ground of Rule 23(b) is a "hybrid" class action.

The Advisory Committee revised Rule 23 substantially in 1966. One principal goal was to define the types of class actions in practical, functional terms. Rule 23 practice before 1966 was rarely used, and was based upon difficult legal concepts concerning the relationships among the class members and the defendant. The 1966 version (the core of which remains intact) was intended to "describe[] in more practical terms the occasions for maintaining class actions" and "provide[] that all class actions maintained to the end as such will result in judgments including those whom the court finds to be members of the class, whether or not the judgment is favorable to the class...." The drafters intended to invigorate class action practice in the federal courts.

Before looking at the individual provisions, we note that Rule 23(b)(1) and 23(b)(2) provide for "mandatory" class actions. That means that the class members have no right to opt out of the class. If the class is certified and the case goes to judgment, they are bound by that judgment. Moreover, those class members are not entitled to notice that they are members of a class action. They are bound, even if they did not know about the case.

In contrast, the Rule 23(b)(3) class action is not mandatory. Members of a Rule 23(b)(3) class have a right to "opt out" of the class, in which case they will not be bound by the class judgment. The Rule recognizes that the right to opt out is worthless if the class member is unaware of the action, and thus requires the court to notify members that they are in the class. We will discuss this notice and the opt out in section C.3.c.

a. Rule 23(b)(1): The "Prejudice" Class Actions

Rule 23(b)(1) provides that "[a] class action may be maintained if . . . prosecuting separate actions by or against individual class members would create a risk of:

> (A) inconsistent or varying adjudications with respect to individual class members that would establish incompatible standards of conduct for the party opposing the class; or
>
> (B) adjudications with respect to individual class members that, as a practical matter, would be dispositive of the interests of the other members not parties to the individual adjudications or would substantially impair or impede their ability to protect their interests."

Two points are immediately apparent. First, Rule 23(b)(1) recognizes two forms of class, routinely referred to as "23(b)(1)(A)" and "23(b)(1)(B)" classes.

Second, the language of the Rule mirrors language of Rule 19, governing necessary parties (which we studied in section B.1.b of this chapter). The Advisory Committee amended Rule 23 and Rule 19 together, expressly to emphasize their similarity. Just as Rule 19 compelled the joinder of a non-party to avoid prejudice (either to the non-party or to the defendant), so too Rule 23(b)(1) is based upon the same concerns.

Rule 19 permits a court to order joinder of a non-party (absentee) because the structure of the case threatens either the absentee or the defendant. Specifically, joinder would be compelled either because (1) nonjoinder might subject the absentee's interest to practical impairment or (2) nonjoinder might subject the defendant to the risk of incurring multiple or inconsistent obligations. Rule 23(b)(1) does the same thing, but when the number of absentees is so great that their individual joinder is impracticable. Rule 23(b)(1) classes are often called "prejudice" classes.

Rule 23(b)(1)(A). This provision is the class equivalent of Rule 19(a)(1)(B)(ii). In the Rule 19 context, the worry is that not joining the absentee will subject the defendant to multiple or inconsistent obligations. In the class context, the absentees are the potential class members. The concern is that if they sue individually (and are not bound by a single class judgment), the defendant may be subjected to judgments that require it to act in inconsistent ways—it would be subjected to contradictory orders requiring "incompatible standards of conduct."

> ***Example #7.*** To raise money to expand an airport, City issues bonds. Many citizens of City oppose the bond issuance, and argue that it is improper. If the citizens sue individually, one case might result in a judgment instructing City to terminate the project. Another might result in a judgment instructing City to proceed with the project in part. Yet another might result in a judgment approving the project fully. City would be left in an untenable situation—abiding by one judgment would violate another.

To avoid subjecting City to this dilemma, the citizens may sue as a class. The judgment will bind them all, and City will not be subjected to uncertainty about how to proceed.

Because the concern is with inflicting on the defendant "incompatible standards of conduct," Rule 23(b)(1)(A) is implicated when the prospective suits by potential class members are for declaratory or injunctive relief. It is not implicated when the claims are for damages—because different results in damages cases do not establish "incompatible standards of conduct."

> ***Example #8.*** More than 100 passengers were injured when an airplane operated by Airline crashes on landing. If the passengers sue Airline individually, some may win, and some may lose. This means, in turn, that Airline will be required to pay some passengers (those who win) but not to pay the others (those who lose). As Rule 23(b)(1)(A) (and, for that matter, Rule 19(a)(1)(B)(ii)) is interpreted, Airline would not be subjected to incompatible "standards of conduct." No incompatible standard of conduct is implicated when a defendant must write a check to one passenger but not to another.

Rule 23(b)(1)(B). This provision is the class equivalent of Rule 19(a)(1)(B)(i). In the Rule 19 context, the worry is that not joining the absentee may subject the absentee's interest to practical harm. In the class context, the absentees are the potential class members. The concern is that if they sue individually (and are not bound by a single class judgment), some of the potential class members will suffer practical impairment of their interest.

Most efforts to employ Rule 23(b)(1)(B) are based upon the "limited fund" theory. The theory is implicated when the defendant faces liability for monetary relief that vastly exceeds the funds available. An example is based upon the facts of *Coburn v. 4-R Corp.*, 77 F.R.D. 43 (E.D. Ky. 1977):

> ***Example #9.*** More than 100 people were killed when a fire engulfed a theater. Based upon litigated wrongful death cases in the area, the court estimated that the potential liability for the operator of the theater exceeded \$16,000,000. The defendant's assets, including insurance coverage, totaled \$3,000,000. If the wrongful death claims were asserted individually, the assets of the defendant would be exhausted before many of the claimants could win a judgment. There would be a rush to the courthouse, in which

the first group of successful claimants would exhaust the funds available for others. That would prejudice those plaintiffs who were later in the litigation queue.

A Rule 23(b)(1)(A) class avoids leaving the later litigants with no recovery. If the class is certified and wins, each class member will recover a like percentage of her damages. No one will be fully compensated, but no one will be left out.

Courts accept the theory behind the "limited fund" class action. But courts have taken different approaches to the degree of proof required. In the *Coburn* case, on which Example #9 is based, the court certified the class because it found "good reason to believe" from the estimates of the value of the claims and of the defendant's resources, "that total judgments might substantially exceed the ability of defendants to respond." *Coburn*, 77 F.R.D. at 45. Other courts have been more demanding. The Ninth Circuit held that a Rule 23(b)(1)(B) is proper only if there is a showing that individual judgments "inescapably will alter the substance of the rights of those having similar claims." The Second Circuit seemed to take a middle course, requiring only a "substantial probability—that is, less than a preponderance but more than a mere possibility . . . ." *In re Agent Orange Product Liability Litigation*, 100 F.R.D. 718, 726 (E.D.N.Y. 1983), *aff'd*, 818 F.2d 145 (2d Cir. 1987).

The Supreme Court addressed the issue in *Ortiz v. Fibreboard Corp.*, 527 U.S. 815 (1999). There, one of the principal manufacturers of asbestos,[14] Fibreboard faced billions of dollars in liability for personal injuries caused by exposure to asbestos. It entered into a "Global Settlement Agreement" by which its insurance companies, and Fibreboard created a fund of about $1,535,000,000 to settle the class claims. Almost all the money in the fund was contributed by the insurers. Fibreboard contributed only about $10,000,000, even though it had a net worth of over $230,000,000. The parties stipulated that the class claims exceeded the fund they had created, and the plaintiffs sought certification under Rule 23(b)(1)(B).

The Court rejected certification, based upon its understanding of the "historical use" of the limited class action. That historical use had three features, none of which was satisfied in *Ortiz*.

- **First.** The inadequacy of the funds to cover the numerous claims must be *demonstrated.* The court must make an independent determination on this point. In *Ortiz*, there was no proof; the parties had stipulated about the amount of money available, without any effort to demonstrate, for instance, how much insurance money would be available.
- **Second.** The "whole of the inadequate fund" must be devoted to paying off all the claims. In the "historical use" of the theory, the defendant is essentially wiped out financially. The court was troubled that Fibreboard would come out

14. *See* footnote 3 *supra*.

of the settlement unscathed, with almost all its wealth intact. Again, the parties simply stipulated as to how much money was available. Litigation could have resulted in a finding that more insurance money was available and likely would have allowed recovery of greater amounts from Fibreboard.

- **Third.** The proposed distribution of funds must be equitable. In *Ortiz,* there were three major problems with the proposed settlement.
  - **One.** The class definition excluded many people with claims, including those who had settled with Fibreboard but retained the right to sue upon manifestation of malignancy. By excluding these people, the class created the very prejudice that Rule 23(b)(1)(B) is intended to avoid: these claimants might be unable to recover because all available funds would already have gone to compensate others.
  - **Two.** The proposed distribution was unfair because it treated claimants as having claims of equal value. Specifically, if there were individual litigation, those members whose claims arose while the defendant had applicable insurance would be worth far more than those whose claims arose when there was no insurance. Yet the proposed settlement distribution treated them alike.
  - **Three.** There was an inherent conflict among members of the class. Some had already manifested injury while others had been exposed but had not yet manifested symptoms ("exposure-only" claims). These groups had conflicting interests: those currently injured want immediate payment, while those having suffered exposure want the establishment of an ample fund for future claims. (This concern could be raised in challenging adequacy of representation under Rule 23(a)(4).)

The Court urged caution in the use of Rule 23(b)(1) classes for the distribution of money. As noted, Rule 23(b)(1) is a mandatory class—the members have no right to opt out, and are bound by the judgment in the case. Traditionally, damages claims have been brought under Rule 23(b)(3), which provides class members with notice and a right to opt out of the case. The limited fund class action robs individuals of control over their damages claim. The Court was concerned that overzealous use of Rule 23(b)(1)(B) would raise potential problems under the Rules Enabling Act (which provides that the Federal Rule may not modify substantive rights) and due process. We will see shortly (in the next subsection) that the Court has returned to the due process point in the context of the other type of mandatory class, the Rule 23(b)(2).

Notes and Questions

1. We reflexively assume that defendants will always oppose motions to certify a plaintiff class. Often, though, as in *Ortiz,* the defendants want the class certified

because they have worked out a settlement on favorable terms. *Ortiz* was filed after the class lawyer and lawyers for Fibreboard and the insurance companies had hammered out the terms of the settlement. All parties were "on board" to have the case filed and settled on the terms stated. As we will see in section E, certified class actions can be settled or voluntarily dismissed only with court approval.

2. Assuming that the net assets of the defendant can be ascertained with certainty, the amount of available insurance will frequently be disputed. *Ortiz* contemplates an evidentiary hearing on that issue, with the court making findings of fact regarding the aggregate value of the claims and the total assets available to satisfy them. In this regard, *Ortiz* may have presaged *Wal-Mart*, with its insistence that certification be based on evidentiary proof, and not merely on pleadings.

3. The Court in *Ortiz* expressly refused to adopt a standard of proof for showing that the available funds are insufficient. It noted the Ninth Circuit's "inescapably" language and the Second Circuit's "substantial probability" language, both quoted above. It concluded that neither standard would have been satisfied on the facts, so refused to take a position.

Note on the "Limited Generosity" Class

Rule 23(b)(1)(B) has occasionally been used to certify classes involving claims for punitive (or "exemplary") damages. Those damages are intended to punish the defendant for egregious conduct. Suppose hundreds of people have a punitive damages claim against Defendant. If they sue individually, at some point—after several have recovered—a court may refuse to allow further punitive damages awards. It would do so on the theory that it is unfair to impose multiple punishments for a single bad act. That ruling might preclude other plaintiffs from recovering punitive damages. The argument for Rule 23(b)(1)(B) is that these later claimants should not be left out. A class action would allow all of them to recover a portion of the punitive award.

Some courts, at least before *Ortiz*, accepted the theory. *See, e.g., In re School Asbestos Litigation*, 789 F.3d 996, 1003–1004 (3d Cir. 1986). The theory was rekindled in the tobacco litigation. *See* Elizabeth J. Cabraser, *Unfinished Business: Reaching the Due Process Limits of Punitive Damages in Tobacco Litigation Through Unitary Classwide Adjudication*, 36 Wake Forest L. Rev. 979 (2001) (Ms. Cabraser is a leading plaintiffs' attorney).

The theory, however, assumes that there is some right to punitive damages or to the equitable allocation of punitive damages awards. *See* Richard A. Nagareda, *Punitive Damages Class Actions and the Baseline of Tort,* 36 Wake Forest L. Rev. 943 (2001) (expressing this and other concerns). The Second Circuit rejected the limited generosity theory in *In re Simon II Litigation,* 407 F.3d 125, 134–138 (2d Cir. 2005). It concluded that the notion that a court might preclude recovery of punitive damages was merely "theoretical."

b. Rule 23(b)(2): Injunctive or Declaratory Relief

Rule 23(b)(2) provides for a class action when:

> the party opposing the class has acted or refused to act on grounds that apply generally to the class, so that final injunctive relief or corresponding declaratory relief is appropriate respecting the class as a whole.

There are two requirements: (1) the defendant[15] must have acted or failed to act similarly toward all class members and (2) the class must seek injunctive or declaratory relief to remedy the harm inflicted by the defendant. Rule 23(b)(2) classes (like Rule 23(b)(1) classes) are "mandatory": class members do not have the right to opt out of the case and will be bound by the judgment.

When restructuring Rule 23 in 1966, the Advisory Committee made clear that Rule 23(b)(2) was intended to facilitate suits to desegregate public schools. For an interesting discussion of the drafters' goals, see David Marcus, *Flawed but Noble: Desegregation Litigation and its Implications for the Modern Class Action,* 63 FLA. L. REV. 657 (2011). Of course, other claims may be asserted under the provision; it is commonly used, for example, in employment discrimination.

One interesting question stands out: because the case seeks injunctive or declaratory relief against a course of conduct by the defendant that affects an entire class, why file a class action at all? In other words, why not simply have one person sue? If she wins, the court will enter an injunction or declaration telling the defendant to modify its behavior. The problem is that those other claimants likely would not be able to enforce the injunction or declaration.

> ***Example #10.*** Company discriminates against employees on the basis of age. Employee-1 sues individually seeking an injunction. She wins. The court enters an order commanding Company to stop discriminating on the basis of age. Now Company continues to discriminate against other employees on the basis of age. Those employees likely cannot use the injunction won by Employee-1. They were not parties to the case brought by Employee-1 and she did not purport to represent them, so they cannot enforce the judgment.[16]

If Employee-1's case were a Rule 23(b)(2) class, however, and were successful, the other employees could enforce the judgment. If Company discriminated against any one of them, that person could ask the court to have Company held in contempt for violating the judgment. So, one purpose of a class action here is to obtain a judgment that will inure to the benefit of the entire class. Similarly, if the defendant

---

15. If, as we are assuming, the case involves a plaintiff class, the "party opposing the class" will be the defendant.

16. Even if the employees could use nonmutual offensive issue preclusion, which we will discuss in Chapter 10, they would need to file suit to do so. Thus, enforcing the injunction won by Employee-1 would require filing subsequent cases.

wins the class action, the judgment binds all class members. So, the defendant is protected from a constant parade of separate suits by different employees.

Can a Rule 23(b)(2) Class Seek Monetary Relief?

Rule 23(b)(2) expressly provides that the class seek injunctive or declaratory relief. Does this provision rule out the possibility of recovering monetary relief in a Rule 23(b)(2) class? The issue is important because in many cases, claimants will want both *prospective* relief (an injunction or declaration) to stop the defendant's improper behavior in the future and *retrospective* relief (restitution or damages) to compensate for injuries already inflicted. This likelihood was enhanced in discrimination cases by the passage of the Civil Rights Act of 1991, which for the first time authorized plaintiffs in Title VII actions, alleging intentional discrimination, to recover compensatory and punitive damages. 42 U.S.C. § 1981a(a)(1) (2000). Before the 1991 Act, recovery in such actions was limited to reinstatement and other equitable relief, with or without back pay.

Courts developed three theories for permitting recovery of monetary relief (in addition to injunctive or declaratory relief) in Rule 23(b)(2) actions.

- One, some courts upheld the recovery of money if it could be characterized as "equitable," as opposed to "legal," relief.[17]
- Two, some courts upheld monetary relief as long as the demand for injunctive or declaratory relief "predominated" over the monetary claim.
- Three, some courts permitted recovery of money if it was "incidental" to the equitable relief and would "flow directly" from liability to the class.

The Supreme Court addressed the issue in *Wal-Mart*, one part of which we have already read. As you study this portion of the opinion, consider whether any of the three theories just listed survived.

Wal-Mart Stores, Inc. v. Dukes

Supreme Court of the United States
564 U.S. 338 (2011)

[In the portion of this opinion we saw in section C.2.c.ii, a majority of five Justices held that the class failed to satisfy commonality under Rule 23(a)(2). In this portion of the opinion, all nine Justices agree that the case should not have been certified as a Rule 23(b)(2) class action.]

---

17. The archetypal "legal" remedy is damages, which seek to compensate the plaintiff for harm inflicted by the defendant. Not all monetary relief is "legal," however. For example, restitution, which seeks to disgorge from the defendant an unjust gain, is an equitable remedy. Among other things, the distinction between legal and equitable claims is important for determining whether there is a right to jury trial under the Seventh Amendment.

III

We also conclude that respondents' claims for backpay were improperly certified under Federal Rule of Civil Procedure 23(b)(2). Our opinion in *Ticor Title Ins. Co. v. Brown*, 511 U.S. 117, 121 (1994) *(per curiam)* expressed serious doubt about whether claims for monetary relief may be certified under that provision. We now hold that they may not, at least where (as here) the monetary relief is not incidental to the injunctive or declaratory relief.

A

Rule 23(b)(2) allows class treatment when "the party opposing the class has acted or refused to act on grounds that apply generally to the class, so that final injunctive relief or corresponding declaratory relief is appropriate respecting the class as a whole." One possible reading of this provision is that it applies *only* to requests for such injunctive or declaratory relief and does not authorize the class certification of monetary claims at all. We need not reach that broader question in this case, because we think that, at a minimum, claims for *individualized* relief (like the backpay at issue here) do not satisfy the Rule. The key to the (b)(2) class is "the indivisible nature of the injunctive or declaratory remedy warranted—the notion that the conduct is such that it can be enjoined or declared unlawful only as to all of the class members or as to none of them." Nagareda, 84 N.Y.U. L. Rev., at 132. In other words, Rule 23(b)(2) applies only when a single injunction or declaratory judgment would provide relief to each member of the class. It does not authorize class certification when each individual class member would be entitled to a *different* injunction or declaratory judgment against the defendant. Similarly, it does not authorize class certification when each class member would be entitled to an individualized award of monetary damages.

That interpretation accords with the history of the Rule. Because Rule 23 "stems from equity practice" that predated its codification, *Amchem Products, Inc. v. Windsor*, 521 U.S. 591, 613 (1997), in determining its meaning we have previously looked to the historical models on which the Rule was based, *Ortiz v. Fibreboard Corp.*, 527 U.S. 815, 841–845 (1999). As we observed in *Amchem*, "[c]ivil rights cases against parties charged with unlawful, class-based discrimination are prime examples" of what (b)(2) is meant to capture. 521 U.S., at 614. In particular, the Rule reflects a series of decisions involving challenges to racial segregation—conduct that was remedied by a single classwide order. In none of the cases cited by the Advisory Committee as examples of (b)(2)'s antecedents did the plaintiffs combine any claim for individualized relief with their classwide injunction. . . .

Permitting the combination of individualized and classwide relief in a (b)(2) class is also inconsistent with the structure of Rule 23(b). Classes certified under (b)(1) and (b)(2) share the most traditional justifications for class treatment—that individual adjudications would be impossible or unworkable, as in a (b)(1) class, or that the relief sought must perforce affect the entire class at once, as in a (b)(2) class.

For that reason these are also mandatory classes: The Rule provides no opportunity for (b)(1) or (b)(2) class members to opt out, and does not even oblige the District Court to afford them notice of the action. [Rule 23(b)(3), by contrast,] allows class certification in a much wider set of circumstances but with greater procedural protections. Its only prerequisites are that "the questions of law or fact common to class members predominate over any questions affecting only individual members, and that a class action is superior to other available methods for fairly and efficiently adjudicating the controversy." Rule 23(b)(3). And unlike (b)(1) and (b)(2) classes, the (b)(3) class is not mandatory; class members are entitled to receive "the best notice that is practicable under the circumstances" and to withdraw from the class at their option. *See* Rule 23(c)(2)(B).

Given that structure, we think it clear that individualized monetary claims belong in Rule 23(b)(3). The procedural protections attending the (b)(3) class—predominance, superiority, mandatory notice, and the right to opt out—are missing from (b)(2) not because the Rule considers them unnecessary, but because it considers them unnecessary *to a (b)(2) class.* When a class seeks an indivisible injunction benefitting all its members at once, there is no reason to undertake a case-specific inquiry into whether class issues predominate or whether class action is a superior method of adjudicating the dispute. Predominance and superiority are self-evident. But with respect to each class member's individualized claim for money, that is not so—which is precisely why (b)(3) requires the judge to make findings about predominance and superiority before allowing the class. Similarly, (b)(2) does not require that class members be given notice and opt-out rights, presumably because it is thought (rightly or wrongly) that notice has no purpose when the class is mandatory, and that depriving people of their right to sue in this manner complies with the Due Process Clause. In the context of a class action predominantly for money damages we have held that absence of notice and opt-out violates due process. See *Phillips Petroleum Co. v. Shutts*, 472 U.S. 797, 812 (1985). While we have never held that to be so where the monetary claims do not predominate, the serious possibility that it may be so provides an additional reason not to read Rule 23(b)(2) to include the monetary claims here.

B

Against that conclusion, respondents argue that their claims for backpay were appropriately certified as part of a class under Rule 23(b)(2) because those claims do not "predominate" over their requests for injunctive and declaratory relief. They rely upon the Advisory Committee's statement that Rule 23(b)(2) "does not extend to cases in which the appropriate final relief relates *exclusively or predominantly* to money damages." 39 F.R.D., at 102 (emphasis added). The negative implication, they argue, is that it *does* extend to cases in which the appropriate final relief relates only partially and nonpredominantly to money damages. Of course it is the Rule itself, not the Advisory Committee's description of it, that governs. And a mere negative inference does not in our view suffice to establish a disposition that has no basis in the Rule's text, and that does obvious violence to the Rule's structural features. The mere "predominance" of a proper (b)(2) injunctive claim does nothing to justify elimination of Rule 23(b)(3)'s procedural protections: It neither establishes the superiority of *class* adjudication over *individual* adjudication nor cures the notice and opt-out problems. We fail to see why the Rule should be read to nullify these protections whenever a plaintiff class, at its option, combines its monetary claims with a request—even a "predominating request"—for an injunction.

Respondents' predominance test, moreover, creates perverse incentives for class representatives to place at risk potentially valid claims for monetary relief. In this case, for example, the named plaintiffs declined to include employees' claims for compensatory damages in their complaint. That strategy of including only backpay claims made it more likely that monetary relief would not "predominate." But it also created the possibility (if the predominance test were correct) that individual class members' compensatory-damages claims would be *precluded* by litigation they had no power to hold themselves apart from. . . .

. . . .

Finally, respondents argue that their backpay claims are appropriate for a (b)(2) class action because a backpay award is equitable in nature. The latter may be true, but it is irrelevant. The Rule does not speak of "equitable" remedies generally but of injunctions and declaratory judgments. As Title VII itself makes pellucidly clear, backpay is neither. See 42 U.S.C. § 2000e–5(g)(2)(B)(i) and (ii) (distinguishing between declaratory and injunctive relief and the payment of "backpay," see § 2000e–5(g)(2)(A)).

C

In *Allison v. Citgo Petroleum Corp.*, 151 F.3d 402, 415 (CA5 1998), the Fifth Circuit held that a (b)(2) class would permit the certification of monetary relief that is "incidental to requested injunctive or declaratory relief," which it defined as "damages that flow directly from liability to the class *as a whole* on the claims forming the basis of the injunctive or declaratory relief." In that court's view, such "incidental damage should not require additional hearings to resolve the disparate merits of each individual's case; it should neither introduce new substantial legal or factual issues, nor entail complex individualized determinations." We need not decide in this case whether there are any forms of "incidental" monetary relief that are consistent with the interpretation of Rule 23(b)(2) we have announced and that comply with the Due Process Clause. Respondents do not argue that they can satisfy this standard, and in any event they cannot.

Contrary to the Ninth Circuit's view, Wal-Mart is entitled to individualized determinations of each employee's eligibility for backpay. Title VII includes a detailed remedial scheme. If a plaintiff prevails in showing that an employer has discriminated against him in violation of the statute, the court "may enjoin the respondent from engaging in such unlawful employment practice, and order such affirmative action as may be appropriate, [including] reinstatement or hiring of employees, with or without backpay . . . or any other equitable relief as the court deems appropriate." § 2000e–5(g)(1). But if the employer can show that it took an adverse employment action against an employee for any reason other than discrimination, the court cannot order the "hiring, reinstatement, or promotion of an individual as an employee, or the payment to him of any backpay." § 2000e–5(g)(2)(A).

We have established a procedure for trying pattern-or-practice cases that gives effect to these statutory requirements. When the plaintiff seeks individual relief such as reinstatement or backpay after establishing a pattern or practice of discrimination, "a district court must usually conduct additional proceedings . . . to determine the scope of individual relief." *Teamsters*, [*Int'l Bhd. of Teamsters v. United States*, 431 U.S. 324 (1977)], at 361. At this phase, the burden of proof will shift to the company, but it will have the right to raise any individual affirmative defenses it may have, and to "demonstrate that the individual applicant was denied an employment opportunity for lawful reasons."

The Court of Appeals believed that it was possible to replace such proceedings with Trial by Formula. A sample set of the class members would be selected, as to whom liability for sex discrimination and the backpay owing as a result would be determined in depositions supervised by a master. The percentage of claims determined to be valid would then be applied to the entire remaining class, and the number of (presumptively) valid claims thus derived would be multiplied by the average backpay award in the sample set to arrive at the entire class recovery—without further individualized proceedings. . . . We disapprove that novel project. Because the Rules Enabling Act forbids interpreting Rule 23 to "abridge, enlarge or modify any substantive right," 28 U.S.C. § 2072(b) . . . , a class cannot be certified on the premise that Wal-Mart will not be entitled to litigate its statutory defenses to individual claims. And because the necessity of that litigation will prevent backpay from being "incidental" to the classwide injunction, respondents' class could not be certified even assuming, *arguendo*, that "incidental" monetary relief can be awarded to a 23(b)(2) class.

Notes and Questions

1. The Court did not say that monetary relief can *never* be recovered in a Rule 23(b)(2) class. The problem in *Wal-Mart* was that the monetary relief sought on the facts of the case required individualized adjudication: it was not clear that any two employees were in the same position in terms of how much backpay would be awarded or how it would be calculated. Accordingly, an injunction (or declaration) would not have resolved the case for all class members. The result in a Rule 23(b)(2) judgment must be to validate or to reject the claim for all class members. A single order must deny or provide relief for the entire class.

2. Revisit this passage from Part III(A) of the opinion:

> Classes certified under (b)(1) and (b)(2) share the most traditional justifications for class treatment—that individual adjudications would be impossible or unworkable, as in a (b)(1) class, or that the relief sought must perforce affect the entire class at once, as in a (b)(2) class. For that reason these are also mandatory classes: The Rule provides no opportunity for (b)(1) or (b)(2) class members to opt out, and does not even oblige the District Court to afford them notice of the action.

(a) Why would individual adjudications be impossible or unworkable in the Rule 23(b)(1) situation?

(b) After *Wal-Mart*, must the relief sought in a Rule 23(b)(2) class "perforce affect the entire class at once"? Would that effect be undermined by allowing individualized monetary relief?

3. Before the *Wal-Mart* opinion, we listed three theories that lower courts had used to justify monetary recovery in a Rule 23(b)(2) class.

(a) Why did the Court reject the first theory?

(b) Why did the Court reject the second theory?

(c) Did the Court embrace the third theory? If so, in what circumstances?

4. In the discussion of the *Ortiz* case in section C.3.a, we noted that the Court was concerned that allowing recovery of damages in a mandatory class action (there, a Rule 23(b)(1) class) implicates due process—the implication being that someone with a damages claim should have the right to notice and opt out, so she may pursue that claim on her own (rather than as part of a class). In *Wal-Mart*, Justice Scalia (for the unanimous Court) returns to the point:

> In the context of a class action predominantly for money damages we have held that absence of notice and opt-out violates due process. [Citing *Phillips Petroleum Corp. v. Shutts*, 472 U.S. 797, 812 (1985), which we discuss in another context in section F(2).] While we have never held that to be so where the monetary claims do not predominate, the serious possibility that it may be so provides an additional reason not to read Rule 23(b)(2) to include the monetary claims here.

Does this passage undermine your (possible) conclusion in Note 3 that *Wal-Mart* embraces at least one theory for the recovery of money in a Rule 23(b)(3) class?

5. *Wal-Mart* leaves open the possibility, on appropriate facts, for a "hybrid" class action—Rule 23(b)(2) to pursue the injunctive or declaratory relief and Rule 23(b)(3) to pursue individualized monetary relief. The representative in such a case would need to convince the court that the requirements for each are satisfied.

c. Rule 23(b)(3): The "Damages" Class Action

Though Rule 23(b)(3) does not separate its two requirements into different sections, we do so for clarity. Rule 23(b)(3) authorizes a class action when the court finds:

> [1] that the questions of law or fact common to class members predominate over any questions affecting only individual members, and
>
> [2] that a class action is superior to other available methods for fairly and efficiently adjudicating the controversy. The matters pertinent to these findings [of superiority] include:
>
> > (A) the class members' interests in individually controlling the prosecution or defense of separate actions;
> >
> > (B) the extent and nature of any litigation concerning the controversy already begun by or against class members;
> >
> > (C) the desirability or undesirability of concentrating the litigation of the claims in the particular forum; and
> >
> > (D) the likely difficulties in managing a class action.

Though the Rule does not specify relief, Rule 23(b)(3) classes usually seek damages. This is so common that many people call a Rule 23(b)(3) class a "damages" class.

Rule 23(b)(3) was the most controversial development to emerge from the 1966 restructuring of the Rule. In *Wal-Mart*, as we just saw, the Court explained that class members in Rule 23(b)(1) and (b)(2) classes are likely to be cohesive groups. Members of a 23(b)(1) class are so closely related that separate adjudication creates the risk of harm to the defendant or to other claimants. Members of a 23(b)(2) class have been treated in a common way by the defendant and, certainly after *Wal-Mart*, seek a single, unitary remedy.

But members of a Rule 23(b)(3) class are bound together merely by common facts—they happened to be on the same ill-fated flight, or to have used the same tainted product, or to have invested based upon the same fraudulent pitch. Because of this lack of cohesiveness, and because the members usually are seeking damages, the Rule provides two important procedural protections that are not required in the mandatory classes: (1) members of a 23(b)(3) class must be given notice that they are in the class and (2) they may choose to opt out of the class and thereby avoid being bound by the class judgment. The two protections are obviously related: the right to opt out would be worthless without notice of the fact that one is a member of the class.

As we saw in Note 4 in the preceding subsection, the Court has held that due process requires these protections when the case is "predominantly" for the recovery of damages. *Phillips Petroleum Corp. v. Shutts*, 472 U.S. 797, 812 (1985). And it hinted in *Wal-Mart* that they probably are required even in cases in which the claims for damages are not "predominant." After the decisions in *Ortiz* and *Wal-Mart*, it seems likely most class actions seeking damages will proceed under Rule 23(b)(3). *Ortiz* made it relatively more difficult (though arguably not impossible) to seek damages in a "limited fund" case under Rule 23(b)(1). *Wal-Mart* made it more difficult (though arguably not impossible) to recover money in a Rule 23(b)(2) class.

The Advisory Committee thought the Rule 23(b)(3) class action would be especially useful for the assertion of "negative value" claims—those that are not economically feasible to pursue individually. For instance, imagine a consumer fraud case in which each member of the class suffers a $30 harm. On the other hand, the Committee opined that the Rule 23(b)(3) class would rarely be used in mass tort cases. Keep this prediction in mind as we explore the two requirements of the Rule.

i. Whether Common Questions "Predominate"

Rule 23(b)(3) does not define "predominate," and courts have not developed any definitive qualitative or quantitative test for deciding whether the requirement is met. 7AA Wright & Miller, Federal Practice and Procedure § 1778 (3d ed. 2018). Clearly, this requirement is more demanding than the Rule 23(a)(2) requirement of commonality. Rule 23(a) merely requires that commonality exist. Rule 23(b)(3) requires that common questions *predominate* over individual questions.

From the case law, we can glean some general guidance. For starters, the inquiry is pragmatic and made on a case-by-case basis. Further, no court requires that *every* issue in the case be common to each class member. Even in cases involving common causation and harm, there will often be individual questions of damages, as when people are injured in a train derailment. Indeed, the common issues need not be dispositive of the case. It is enough if the "central" or "core" issues of liability may be determined by proof common to the class, even though individual damages issues or affirmative defenses remain to be determined. Thus, we may have class treatment of liability or causation, and leave the determination of individual damages to subsequent resolution. On the other hand, if the core issues of the case require individual adjudication, the predominance requirement is not met.

As noted, the Advisory Committee in 1966 expressed doubt that mass tort cases would be susceptible to Rule 23(b)(3) treatment. It reasoned that "the likelihood that significant questions, not only of damages but of liability and defenses to liability, would be present, affecting the individuals in different ways. In these circumstances an action conducted nominally as a class action would degenerate in practice into multiple lawsuits separately tried." For a decade or so, courts were reluctant to apply the Rule to mass torts. In the 1980s, however, when courts started to deal with a "litigation explosion"—caused in part by development of cutting-edge tort theories of product liability—courts started being more adventurous.

Indeed, it seems that Rule 23(b)(3) would readily apply to a mass tort resulting from a single event, such as a plane crash, explosion, or bridge collapse. There, the questions of liability, including causation, usually will be subject to proof *en masse*.

And, as noted, the courts could provide separate hearings to determine individual damages. The aggregate litigation of core issues of liability would be salutary—a court would be required to litigate these questions only once, and all class members would be bound by the outcome.[18]

The bigger problem came in trying to apply Rule 23(b)(3) to toxic torts and other "dispersed" claims arising from exposure to a harmful substance or product. In *In re Northern Dist. of Cal., Dalkon Shield IUD Products Liability Litigation.*, 693 F.2d 847, 852–53 (9th Cir. 1982), the court noted: "[i]n products liability actions, . . . individual issues may outnumber common issues," because the harm does not arise from single accident or occurrence.

But the docket pressure of an increasing caseload was relentless, and courts adapted. For example, in *In re "Agent Orange" Product Liability Litigation*, 100 F.R.D. 718 (E.D.N.Y. 1983), the district court certified a Rule 23(b)(3) class of military veterans who were exposed, during service in Southeast Asia, to a chemical compound called Agent Orange. The compound was a defoliant. Dropped from aircraft on thickly forested areas during the Vietnam War, it was intended to kill vegetation to allow surveillance of enemy activity. We read a decision in this case in Chapter 4.D.3 on federal common law.

Sadly, the compound caused cancer and other illnesses for many of the servicepeople who were exposed to it. The result was a staggering case load, including claims for personal injuries, wrongful death, and loss of consortium. They were asserted by service personnel, their representatives, and family members. The cases involved innumerable individual questions. But every case against manufacturers of Agent Orange presented one common question: whether the civilian companies that made the compound for the military could claim immunity under the "military contractor defense." If so, they would be immune from liability.

The entire tragedy involving Agent Orange cried out for a legislative solution. When Congress failed to rise to the task, however, the labyrinth of issues fell to the courts. The district court certified a Rule 23(b)(3) class to determine a single issue: whether the defendants were protected by the military contractor defense. That one issue predominated over the thousands of individual questions, such as severity of exposure and harm suffered. The court also noted that resolution of that issue might promote settlement. *Id.* at 720–24. After rejecting the military contractor defense,

18. Even in such cases, Rule 23(b)(3) certification is not always appropriate. In *Steering Comm. v. Exxon Mobil Corp.*, 461 F.3d 598, 602 (5th Cir. 2006), the class sought damages for injuries suffered from inhalation of smoke from a fire at a chemical plant. Though the harms resulted from a single event, the court concluded that individual issues predominated: "each individual plaintiff suffered different alleged periods and magnitudes of exposure and suffered different alleged symptoms as a result."

the district judge was able to facilitate (some would say coerce) settlement,[19] as we will see in section E.

No product has caused more litigation than asbestos.[20] After the product had been in common use for decades, it became clear that exposure to it (by breathing its fibers) could cause cancer. Innumerable people were exposed to the product. Hundreds of thousands of claims were asserted for personal injuries and wrongful death. These led to another round of extensive litigation concerning insurance liability for the claims. The federal government mandated the removal of asbestos from buildings, which led to more litigation concerning liability for the expense of abatement. Asbestos claims are still being prosecuted, more than 40 years after the danger became apparent.

Certification under Rule 23(b)(3) for personal injury cases arising from exposure to asbestos seems problematic. After all, people were exposed at different times and places to different amounts of the product, manufactured by different companies, and suffered different levels of harm. Despite this, some courts proceeded. One important example is *Jenkins v. Raymark Industries, Inc.*, 782 F.2d 468 (5th Cir. 1986). The district court certified a class of about 900 members. It focused the class litigation on specific questions, such as whether asbestos-containing insulation products were capable of producing dust sufficient to cause harm, whether the defendants' products were defective as marketed, and whether the defendants should have known about the risk. This latter point was the "state-of-the-art" defense, which, if applicable, would defeat the class claims (note the similarity of this defense to the military contractor defense in *Agent Orange*).

The Fifth Circuit affirmed the certification, and noted: "[i]t is difficult to imagine that class jury findings on the class questions will not significantly advance the resolution of the underlying hundreds of cases." *Id.* at 472–73. This phrase—about advancing resolution of the class cases—has been repeated in many decisions since. The Fifth Circuit also recognized the need for innovation: "the courts are now being forced to rethink the alternatives and priorities by the current volume of litigation and more frequent mass disasters." *Id.* at 473. In its view, the district court's "plan is clearly superior to the alternative of repeating, hundreds of times over, the litigation of the state of the art issues with . . . days of the same witnesses, exhibits and issues from trial to trial. . . . Necessity moves us to change and invent." *Id.*

---

19. On appeal from the district court's approval of the settlement, the Second Circuit affirmed the Rule 23(b)(3) certification, although without enthusiasm. (The opinion is said to "damn with faint praise.") *In re Agent Orange Prod. Liability Litigation*, 818 F.2d 145 (2d Cir. 1987). The Second Circuit "share[d] the prevalent skepticism about the usefulness of the class action device in mass tort litigation," but concluded that "its use was justified here in light of the centrality of the military contractor defense to the claims of all plaintiffs." *Id.* at 151.

20. *See* note 3 *supra*.

ii. Whether the Class Action Is "Superior"

In addition to predominance of common questions, the representative in a Rule 23(b)(3) class action must demonstrate that the class action is superior to other methods of resolving the dispute. Like predominance, this requirement is fact-specific and highly discretionary with the trial court. In determining whether a class action is superior, the Rule counsels the court to consider:

- A class member's interest in individually controlling the assertion of her claim;
- Whether other litigation already presents the issues;
- Desirability of concentrating litigation in one forum; and
- Difficulties of managing a class action.

Superiority Factors

The most obvious alternative is the conduct of individual litigation, either separately or by using the joinder rules discussed in section B. But what about negative value cases? By definition, plaintiffs with a negative value claim will not sue individually. Without the class action, there would be no litigation at all.

On the other hand, what if the class claims are so substantial that people will want to sue individually? Does that mean that no Rule 23(b)(3) class is possible? If the court certifies a class with large individual claims, we may worry that members will opt out. If enough do, it may mean that the class should be de-certified for failure to satisfy numerosity under Rule 23(a)(1).

One possible alternative to the class action is the "test case." Here, one or more cases proceed through trial. The parties agree to abide by the results of those cases to resolve the remaining claims. Or, if the plaintiffs win those cases, the remaining claimants may sue and attempt to use non-mutual offensive issue preclusion, which we discuss in Chapter 10. Or judgments in the test cases might be used to provide data to assist in settlement of the remaining cases. In general, the test case has not proved as useful as hoped.

Other alternatives to the class action are explored in Chapter 4. They include consolidation of cases in the same district and multidistrict litigation (MDL) under 28 U.S.C. § 1407. The latter permits transfer of a large number of related cases to a single federal district for coordinated pretrial proceedings. Under that process, however, cases that are not resolved in the pretrial phase are remanded to their original districts for trial. In contrast, the class action can bind all class members to a single judgment.

Another factor in the superiority analysis is "the extent and nature of any litigation concerning the controversy already begun by or against class members." If other actions are pending, does this indicate that class members have a strong interest in individually controlling their own actions and having their own day in court? Or does the existence of other actions suggest that a class action should be certified to avoid inconsistent judgments and prevent further repetitive litigation?

The final express factor is "the likely difficulties in managing a class action." Several of those difficulties are encountered in the following case. As you read it, consider which aspects of the district court's ruling related to the predominance requirement and which related to the superiority requirement.

Castano v. American Tobacco Company

United States Court of Appeals, Fifth Circuit
84 F.3d 734 (1996)

JERRY E. SMITH, CIRCUIT JUDGE:

In what may be the largest class action ever attempted in federal court, the district court in this case embarked "on a road certainly less traveled, if ever taken at all," *Castano v. American Tobacco Co.*, 160 F.R.D. 544, 560 (E.D.La.1995) (citing EDWARD C. LATHAM, *THE POETRY OF ROBERT FROST*, "The Road Not Taken" 105 (1969)), and entered a class certification order. The court defined the class as:

> (a) All nicotine-dependent persons in the United States . . . who have purchased and smoked cigarettes manufactured by the defendants;
>
> (b) the estates, representatives, and administrators of these nicotine-dependent cigarette smokers; and
>
> (c) the spouses, children, relatives and "significant others" of these nicotine-dependent cigarette smokers as their heirs or survivors.

The plaintiffs limit the claims to years since 1943.

This matter comes before us on interlocutory appeal, under 28 U.S.C. § 1292(b), of the class certification order. Concluding that the district court abused its discretion in certifying the class, we reverse.

I

A. The Class Complaint

The plaintiffs filed this class complaint against the defendant tobacco companies and the Tobacco Institute, Inc., seeking compensation solely for the injury of nicotine addiction. The gravamen of their complaint is the novel and wholly untested theory that the defendants fraudulently failed to inform consumers that nicotine is addictive and manipulated the level of nicotine in cigarettes to sustain their addictive nature. The class complaint alleges nine causes of action: fraud and deceit, negligent misrepresentation, intentional infliction of emotional distress, negligence and negligent infliction of emotional distress, violation of state consumer protection statutes, breach of express warranty, breach of implied warranty, strict product liability, and redhibition pursuant to the Louisiana Civil Code.

The plaintiffs seek compensatory and punitive damages and attorneys' fees. In addition, the plaintiffs seek equitable relief for fraud and deceit, negligent misrepresentation, violation of consumer protection statutes, and breach of express and implied warranty. The equitable remedies include a declaration that defendants are financially responsible for notifying all class members of nicotine's addictive nature, a declaration that the defendants manipulated nicotine levels with the intent to sustain the addiction of plaintiffs and the class members, an order that the defendants disgorge any profits made from the sale of cigarettes, restitution for sums paid for cigarettes, and the establishment of a medical monitoring fund. [As the name implies, this is a fund, created at the defendant's expense, to provide periodic testing. We discuss it further in section D.6.]

The plaintiffs initially defined the class as "all nicotine dependent persons in the United States," including current, former and deceased smokers since 1943. Plaintiffs conceded that addiction would have to be proven by each class member; the defendants argued that proving class membership will require individual mini-trials to determine whether addiction actually exists.

. . . .

B. The Class Certification Order

Following extensive briefing, the district court granted, in part, plaintiffs' motion for class certification, concluding that the prerequisites of Fed. R. Civ. P. 23(a) had been met. The court rejected certification, under Fed. R. Civ. P. 23(b)(2), of the plaintiffs' claim for equitable relief, including the claim for medical monitoring. . . .

The court did grant the plaintiffs' motion to certify the class under Fed. R. Civ. P. 23(b)(3), organizing the class action issues into four categories: (1) core liability; (2) injury-in-fact, proximate cause, reliance and affirmative defenses; (3) compensatory damages; and (4) punitive damages. *Id.* at 553–58. It then analyzed each category to determine whether it met the predominance and superiority requirements of rule 23(b)(3). Using its power to sever issues for certification under Fed. R. Civ. P. 23(c)(4), the court certified the class on core liability and punitive damages, and certified the class conditionally pursuant to Fed. R. Civ. P. 23(c)(1).

1. Core Liability Issues

The court defined core liability issues as "common factual issues [of] whether defendants knew cigarette smoking was addictive, failed to inform cigarette smokers of such, and took actions to addict cigarette smokers. Common legal issues include fraud, negligence, breach of warranty (express or implied), strict liability, and violation of consumer protection statutes. . . ."

The court found that the predominance requirement of rule 23(b)(3) was satisfied for the core liability issues. Without any specific analysis regarding the multitude of issues that make up "core liability," the court found that under *Jenkins v. Raymark Indus.*, 782 F.2d 468 (5th Cir. 1986), common issues predominate because resolution of core liability issues would significantly advance the individual cases. The court did not discuss why "core liability" issues would be a significant, rather than just common, part of each individual trial, nor why the individual issues in the remaining categories did not predominate over the common "core liability" issues.

The only specific analysis on predominance analysis was on the plaintiffs' fraud claim. The court determined that it would be premature to hold that individual reliance issues predominate over common issues. Relying on *Eisen v. Carlisle & Jacquelin*, 417 U.S. 156 (1974), the court stated that it could not inquire into the merits of the plaintiffs' claim to determine whether reliance would be an issue in individual trials. . . .

The court also deferred substantial consideration of how variations in state law would affect predominance. Relying on two district court opinions, the court concluded that issues of fraud, breach of warranty, negligence, intentional tort, and strict liability do not vary so much from state to state as to cause individual issues to predominate. . . .

The court also concluded that a class action is superior to other methods for adjudication of the core liability issues. Relying heavily on *Jenkins*, the court noted that having this common issue litigated in a class action was superior to repeated trials of the same evidence. . . .

2. Injury-in-fact, Proximate Cause, Reliance, Affirmative Defenses, and Compensatory Damages

Using the same methodology as it did for the core liability issues, the district court refused to certify the issues of injury-in-fact, proximate cause, reliance, affirmative defenses, and compensatory damages, concluding that the "issues are so overwhelmingly replete with individual circumstances that they quickly outweigh predominance and superiority." . . .

3. Punitive Damages

In certifying punitive damages for class treatment, the court adopted the plaintiffs' trial plan for punitive damages: The class jury would develop a ratio of punitive damages to actual damages, and the court would apply that ratio in individual cases. As it did with the core liability issues, the court determined that variations in state law, including differing burdens of proof, did not preclude certification. . . .

II

. . . .

The district court erred in its analysis in two distinct ways. First, it failed to consider how variations in state law affect predominance and superiority. Second, its predominance inquiry did not include consideration of how a trial on the merits would be conducted.

Each of these defects mandates reversal. Moreover, at this time, while the tort is immature, the class complaint must be dismissed, as class certification cannot be found to be a superior method of adjudication.

A. Variations in State Law

. . . .

In a multi-state class action, variations in state law may swamp any common issues and defeat predominance. *See Georgine v. Amchem Prods.*, 83 F.3d 610, 618 (3d Cir. 1996) (decertifying class because legal and factual differences in the plaintiffs' claims "when exponentially magnified by choice of law considerations, eclipse any common issues in this case"). . . .

. . . .

A district court's duty to determine whether the plaintiff has borne its burden on class certification requires that a court consider variations in state law when a class action involves multiple jurisdictions. . . .

A requirement that a court know which law will apply before making a predominance determination is especially important when there may be differences in state law. *See In the Matter of Rhone-Poulenc Rorer, Inc.* ("*Rhone-Poulenc*"), 51 F.3d 1293, 1299–1302 (7th Cir. 1995) (mandamus) (comparing differing state pattern instructions on negligence and differing formulations of the meaning of negligence); *In re "Agent Orange" Prod. Liability Litigation*, 818 F.2d 145, 165 (2d Cir. 1987) (noting possibility of differences in state products liability law). Given the plaintiffs' burden, a court cannot rely on assurances of counsel that any problems with predominance or superiority can be overcome. . . .

The able opinion in *School Asbestos* [*In re School Asbestos Litigation*, 789 F.2d 996 (3d Cir. 1986)] demonstrates what is required from a district court when variations in state law exist. There, the court affirmed class certification, despite variations in state law, because:

> To meet the problem of diversity in applicable state law, class plaintiffs have undertaken an extensive analysis of the variances in products liability among the jurisdictions. That review separates the law into four categories. Even assuming additional permutations and combinations, plaintiffs have made a creditable showing, which apparently satisfied the district court, that class certification does not present insuperable obstacles. Although we have some doubt on this score, the effort may nonetheless prove successful.

789 F.2d at 1010. . . .

A thorough review of the record demonstrates that, in this case, the district court did not properly consider how variations in state law affect predominance. The court acknowledged as much in its order granting class certification, for, in declining to make a choice of law determination, it noted that "[t]he parties have only briefly addressed the conflict of laws issue in this matter." Similarly, the court stated that "there has been no showing that the consumer protection statutes differ so much as to make individual issues predominate."

The district court's review of state law variances can hardly be considered extensive; it conducted a cursory review of state law variations and gave short shrift to the defendants' arguments concerning variations. In response to the defendants' extensive analysis of how state law varied on fraud, products liability, affirmative defenses, negligent infliction of emotional distress, consumer protection statutes, and punitive damages, the court examined a sample phase 1 jury interrogatory and verdict form, a survey of medical monitoring decisions, a survey of consumer fraud class actions, and a survey of punitive damages law in the defendants' home states. The court also relied on two district court opinions granting certification in multi-state class actions.

The district court's consideration of state law variations was inadequate. The surveys provided by the plaintiffs failed to discuss, in any meaningful way, how the court could deal with variations in state law. The consumer fraud survey simply quoted a few state courts that had certified state class actions. The survey of punitive damages was limited to the defendants' home states. Moreover, the two district court opinions on which the court relied did not support the proposition that variations in state law could be ignored. Nothing in the record demonstrates that the court critically analyzed how variations in state law would affect predominance.

The court also failed to perform its duty to determine whether the class action would be manageable in light of state law variations. The court's only discussion of manageability is a citation to *Jenkins* and the claim that "[w]hile manageability of the liability issues in this case may well prove to be difficult, the Court finds that any such difficulties pale in comparison to the specter of thousands, if not millions, of similar trials of liability proceeding in thousands of courtrooms around the nation."

The problem with this approach is that it substitutes case-specific analysis with a generalized reference to *Jenkins*. The *Jenkins* court, however, was not faced with managing a novel claim involving eight causes of action, multiple jurisdictions, millions of plaintiffs, eight defendants, and over fifty years of alleged wrongful conduct. Instead, Jenkins involved only 893 personal injury asbestos cases, the law of only one state, and the prospect of trial occurring in only one district. Accordingly, for purposes of the instant case, *Jenkins* is largely inapposite.

. . . .

B. Predominance

The district court's second error was that it failed to consider how the plaintiffs' addiction claims would be tried, individually or on a class basis. . . .

A district court certainly may look past the pleadings to determine whether the requirements of rule 23 have been met. Going beyond the pleadings is necessary, as a court must understand the claims, defenses, relevant facts, and applicable substantive law in order to make a meaningful determination of the certification issues. *See* Manual for Complex Litigation § 30.11 (3d ed. 1995).

The district court's predominance inquiry demonstrates why such an understanding is necessary. The premise of the court's opinion is a citation to *Jenkins* and a conclusion that class treatment of common issues would significantly advance the individual trials. Absent knowledge of how addiction-as-injury cases would actually be tried, however, it was impossible for the court to know whether the common issues would be a "significant" portion of the individual trials. The court just assumed that because the common issues would play a part in every trial, they must be significant. The court's synthesis of *Jenkins* and *Eisen* would write the predominance requirement out of the rule, and any common issue would predominate if it were common to all the individual trials.

The court's treatment of the fraud claim also demonstrates the error inherent in its approach. According to both the advisory committee's notes to Rule 23(b)(3) and this court's decision in *Simon v. Merrill Lynch, Pierce, Fenner & Smith, Inc.*, 482 F.2d 880 (5th Cir. 1973), a fraud class action cannot be certified when individual reliance will be an issue. The district court avoided the reach of this court's decision in *Simon* by an erroneous reading of *Eisen*; the court refused to consider whether reliance would be an issue in individual trials.

The problem with the district court's approach is that after the class trial, it might have decided that reliance must be proven in individual trials. The court then would have been faced with the difficult choice of decertifying the class after phase 1 and wasting judicial resources, or continuing with a class action that would have failed the predominance requirement of rule 23(b)(3).[21]

III

In addition to the reasons given above, regarding the district court's procedural errors, this class must be decertified because it independently fails the superiority requirement of rule 23(b)(3). In the context of mass tort class actions, certification dramatically affects the stakes for defendants. Class certification magnifies and strengthens the number of unmeritorious claims.... Aggregation of claims also makes it more likely that a defendant will be found liable and results in significantly higher damage awards....

In addition to skewing trial outcomes, class certification creates insurmountable pressure on defendants to settle, whereas individual trials would not.... The risk of facing an all-or-nothing verdict presents too high a risk, even when the probability of an adverse judgment is low. *In the Matter of Rhone-Poulenc*, 51 F.3d at 1298. These settlements have been referred to as judicial blackmail.

21. [Court's footnote #21] Severing the defendants' conduct from reliance under rule 23(c)(4) does not save the class action. A district court cannot manufacture predominance through the nimble use of subdivision (c)(4). The proper interpretation of the interaction between subdivisions (b)(3) and (c)(4) is that a cause of action, as a whole, must satisfy the predominance requirement of (b)(3) and that (c)(4) is a housekeeping rule that allows courts to sever the common issues for a class trial.... Reading rule 23(c)(4) as allowing a court to sever issues until the remaining common issue predominates over the remaining individual issues would eviscerate the predominance requirement of rule 23(b)(3); the result would be automatic certification in every case where there is a common issue, a result that could not have been intended.

It is no surprise then, that historically, certification of mass tort litigation classes has been disfavored. The traditional concern over the rights of defendants in mass tort class actions is magnified in the instant case. Our specific concern is that a mass tort cannot be properly certified without a prior track record of trials from which the district court can draw the information necessary to make the predominance and superiority analysis required by rule 23. This is because certification of an immature tort results in a higher than normal risk that the class action may not be superior to individual adjudication.

. . . The court acknowledged the extensive manageability problems with this class. Such problems include difficult choice of law determinations, subclassing of eight claims with variations in state law, *Erie* guesses, notice to millions of class members, further subclassing to take account of transient plaintiffs, and the difficult procedure for determining who is nicotine-dependent. Cases with far fewer manageability problems have given courts pause. . . .

The district court's rationale for certification in spite of such problems—i.e., that a class trial would preserve judicial resources in the millions of inevitable individual trials—is based on pure speculation. Not every mass tort is asbestos, and not every mass tort will result in the same judicial crises. The judicial crisis to which the district court referred is only theoretical.

What the district court failed to consider, and what no court can determine at this time, is the very real possibility that the judicial crisis may fail to materialize. The plaintiffs' claims are based on a new theory of liability and the existence of new evidence. Until plaintiffs decide to file individual claims, a court cannot, from the existence of injury, presume that all or even any plaintiffs will pursue legal remedies. Nor can a court make a superiority determination based on such speculation. . . .

Severe manageability problems and the lack of a judicial crisis are not the only reasons why superiority is lacking. The most compelling rationale for finding superiority in a class action—the existence of a negative value suit—is missing in this case. *Accord Phillips Petroleum Co. v. Shutts*, 472 U.S. 797, 809 (1985); *In the Matter of Rhone-Poulenc*, 51 F.3d at 1299.

. . . .

In a case such as this one, where each plaintiff may receive a large award, and fee shifting often is available, we find Chief Judge Posner's analysis of superiority to be persuasive:

> For this consensus or maturing of judgment the district judge proposes to substitute a single trial before a single jury. . . . One jury . . . will hold the fate of an industry in the palm of its hand. . . . That kind of thing can happen in our system of civil justice. . . . But it need not be tolerated when the alternative exists of submitting an issue to multiple juries constituting in the aggregate a much larger and more diverse sample of decision-makers. That would not be a feasible option if the stakes to each class member were too slight to repay the cost of suit. . . . But this is not the case. . . . Each

> plaintiff if successful is apt to receive a judgment in the millions. With the aggregate stakes in the tens or hundreds of millions of dollars, or even in the billions, it is not a waste of judicial resources to conduct more than one trial, before more than six jurors, to determine whether a major segment of the international pharmaceutical industry is to follow the asbestos manufacturers into Chapter 11.

In the Matter of Rhone-Poulenc, 51 F.3d at 1300. So too here, we cannot say that it would be a waste to allow individual trials to proceed, before a district court engages in the complicated predominance and superiority analysis necessary to certify a class.

> Fairness may demand that mass torts with few prior verdicts or judgments be litigated first in smaller units—even single-plaintiff, single-defendant trials—until general causation, typical injuries, and levels of damages become established. Thus, "mature" mass torts like asbestos or Dalkon Shield may call for procedures that are not appropriate for incipient mass tort cases, such as those involving injuries arising from new products, chemical substances, or pharmaceuticals.

Manual for Complex Litigation § 33.26.

The remaining rationale for superiority—judicial efficiency—is also lacking. In the context of an immature tort, any savings in judicial resources is speculative, and any imagined savings would be overwhelmed by the procedural problems that certification of a *sui generis* cause of action brings with it.

Even assuming *arguendo* that the tort system will see many more addiction-as-injury claims, a conclusion that certification will save judicial resources is premature at this stage of the litigation. Take for example the district court's plan to divide core liability from other issues such as comparative negligence and reliance. The assumption is that after a class verdict, the common issues will not be a part of follow-up trials. The court has no basis for that assumption.

It may be that comparative negligence will be raised in the individual trials, and the evidence presented at the class trial will have to be repeated. The same may be true for reliance. The net result may be a waste, not a savings, in judicial resources. Only after the courts have more experience with this type of case can a court certify issues in a way that preserves judicial resources. . . .

. . . .

The plaintiffs' final retort is that individual trials are inadequate because time is running out for many of the plaintiffs. They point out that prior litigation against the tobacco companies has taken up to ten years to wind through the legal system. While a compelling rhetorical argument, it is ultimately inconsistent with the plaintiffs' own arguments and ignores the realities of the legal system. First, the plaintiffs' reliance on prior personal injury cases is unpersuasive, as they admit that they have new evidence and are pursuing a claim entirely different from that of past plaintiffs.

Second, the plaintiffs' claim that time is running out ignores the reality of the class action device. In a complicated case involving multiple jurisdictions, the conflict of law question itself could take decades to work its way through the courts. Once that issue has been resolved, discovery, subclassing, and ultimately the class trial would take place. Next would come the appellate process. After the class trial, the individual trials and appeals on comparative negligence and damages would have to take place. The net result could be that the class action device would lengthen, not shorten, the time it takes for the plaintiffs to reach final judgment.

IV

. . . .

We have once before stated that "traditional ways of proceeding reflect far more than habit. They reflect the very culture of the jury trial. . . ." *In re Fibreboard Corp.*, 893 F.2d 706, 711 (5th Cir. 1990). The collective wisdom of individual juries is necessary before this court commits the fate of an entire industry or, indeed, the fate of a class of millions, to a single jury. For the forgoing reasons, we REVERSE and REMAND with instructions that the district court dismiss the class complaint.

Notes and Questions

1. Why was the claim for nicotine dependence in *Castano* an "immature" tort?

2. Why did it matter that the claim for nicotine dependence was an "immature" tort?

3. Why would certifying the class in *Castano* have run the risk of "judicial blackmail"?

4. In Part II(B) of its opinion, the court noted the propriety of a court's considering (in a class certification motion) facts that relate to the merits of the case. The Supreme Court made this point in *Wal-Mart*, as we discussed in Note on Front-Loading and Consideration of the Merits in section C.2.c.ii, in this chapter.

5. The court's opinion turned in significant measure on its conclusion that the district court had not sufficiently analyzed "how variations in state law would affect predominance." In cases invoking diversity of citizenship jurisdiction, state law governs on the substantive issues, including the elements of claims and defenses. This is the thrust of the *Erie* Doctrine, which we addressed in Chapter 4.B.

But variations in state law are not always fatal to a Rule 23(b)(3) class. One way to handle them is to limit the class to residents of a particular state. Another is to have subclasses for claimants from the various states. Still another is to follow the example of *In re School Asbestos Litigation*, 789 F.2d 996 (3d Cir. 1986), on which the *Castano* court relied. There, the court certified a nationwide class. Though the applicable law varied from state to state, the plaintiffs showed that all states fell into one of four approaches. The court could use four "grids" to match each claimant with the appropriate law.

Maybe variations in state law do not matter if the case settles. In *In re Warfarin Sodium Antitrust Litigation*, 391 F.3d 516, 529 (3d Cir. 2004), the court concluded: "when dealing with variations in state laws, the same concerns with regards to case manageability that arise with litigation classes are not present with settlement classes, and thus those variations are irrelevant to certification of a settlement class." Does this conclusion strike you as correct? (Can't parties agree to settle on any terms, regardless of the governing law?)

6. Re-read footnote 21 of *Castano*. It sets up the following discussion.

iii. "Issue Certification"

Rule 23(c)(4)–(5) provide:

> (4) *Particular Issues.* When appropriate, an action may be brought or maintained as a class action with respect to particular issues.
>
> (5) *Subclasses.* When appropriate, a class may be divided into subclasses that are each treated as a class under this rule.

Rule 23(c)(5) is the authority for creating subclasses. In section C.2.c, we discussed the use of subclasses as a way to avoid a *Falcon* or *LaMar* problem. We also discussed it in Note 5 after *Castano*. Each subclass must be headed by its own representative, who must satisfy the requirements of Rule 23(a) and (b).

Our focus here is on Rule 23(c)(4), which raises the idea of "issue certification"—certifying a class to determine one or more issues, but not the entire case. The question is not whether this can be done—clearly, as Rule 23(c)(4) says and as discussed above in cases like *Jenkins*—it can. The question is: can it be used as a way to satisfy the predominance requirement of Rule 23(b)(3)?

> ***Example #11.*** A class action raises ten issues, two of which are common to all class members and eight of which vary with individual class members. In determining whether common questions predominate, does the court consider all ten issues? If so, it seems unlikely that Rule 23(b)(3) can be met, because 80 percent of the issues are not common. Or can the court assess predominance by considering only the two common issues? If so, predominance will clearly be met, because those two issues—our focus—are common to all class members.

In footnote 21 of *Castano,* the Fifth Circuit rejected the latter approach. It said:

> The proper interpretation of the interaction between subdivisions (b)(3) and (c)(4) is that a cause of action, as a whole, must satisfy the predominance requirement of (b)(3) and that (c)(4) is a housekeeping rule that allows courts to sever the common issues for a class trial. . . . Reading rule 23(c)(4) as allowing a court to sever issues until the remaining common issue predominates over the remaining individual issues would eviscerate the predominance requirement of rule 23(b)(3); the result would be automatic certification in every case where there is a common issue, a result that could not have been intended.

The quoted statement seems hard to reconcile with the result of the Fifth Circuit's earlier opinion in *Jenkins*. There, that court affirmed the district court's plan to hold class litigation of specific issues, including the state-of-the-art defense. The court noted: "[i]t is difficult to imagine that class jury findings on the class questions will not significantly advance the resolution of the underlying hundreds of cases." 782 F.2d at 472–73.

Be that as it may, the Fifth Circuit jettisoned the approach of footnote 21 and embraced "issue certification." *In re Deepwater Horizon*, 739 F.3d 790, 806 (5th Cir. 2014). In doing so, the Fifth Circuit joined the overwhelming majority view. One scholar notes that the Fifth Circuit thus joins "[t]he First, Second, Third, Fourth, Sixth, Seventh, Ninth, and Eleventh Circuits . . . each [of which has] taken various approaches to facilitate issue classes to different degrees." Elizabeth Chamblee Burch, *Constructing Issue Classes*, 101 VA. L. REV. 1855, 1892 (2015) (footnotes omitted).[22]

The commonest approach appears to be that suggested by the American Law Institute's PRINCIPLES OF AGGREGATE LITIGATION § 2.02(a)(1): issue certification is proper when resolving the issue will "materially advance the resolution of multiple civil claims by addressing the core of the dispute in a manner superior to other realistic procedural alternatives, so as to generate significant judicial efficiencies." This view is reminiscent of *Jenkins*. It is also consistent with what the court did in *Agent Orange*.

More support for the practice comes from the Advisory Committee in its 1966 amendments to Rule 23, when it explained that "an action may be maintained as a class action as to particular issues only. For example, in a fraud or similar case the action may retain its 'class' character only through the adjudication of liability to the class; the members of the class may thereafter be required to come in individually and prove the amounts of their respective claims." The MANUAL FOR COMPLEX LITIGATION, which is published by the Federal Judicial Center, has also long encouraged the use of issue certification where it will "materially advance the disposition of the litigation as a whole." MANUAL FOR COMPLEX LITIGATION (4TH) § 21.24.

iv. Rule 23(b)(3) Cases in Other Contexts

Any substantive claim may be the basis of a Rule 23(b)(3) class action. In this section, we note a few areas in which there has been considerable Rule 23(b)(3) litigation over the decades.

---

22. Among the courts adopting issue certification are: *Gates v. Rohm & Haas Co.*, 655 F.3d 255, 273 (3d Cir. 2011) (adopting PRINCIPLES OF AGGREGATE LITIGATION quoted below in text); *In re Nassau Cnty. Strip Search Cases*, 461 F.3d 219, 227 (2d Cir. 2006) ("a court may employ subsection (c)(4) to certify a class as to liability regardless of whether the claim as a whole satisfies Rule 23(b)(3)'s predominance requirement."); and *Gunnells v. Healthplan Servs., Inc.*, 348 F.3d 417, 438–439 (4th Cir. 2003) ("According to the dissent, a district court must first 'determine that' an entire lawsuit 'as [a] whole' . . . satisfies . . . 23(b)(3) and only if the entire lawsuit does satisfy those requirements may a court 'manage[] through orders authorized by 23(c).' The dissent's argument finds no support in the law—not in Rule 23 itself nor in any case or treatise.").

Antitrust. In many antitrust cases, the core issue of liability will often be whether the defendants conspired to restrain trade—for example, by fixing prices. Proof of conspiracy is often the predominant issue, because it supports recovery by all class members. The fact that individual proof of damages may be required does not necessarily defeat certification. *See, e.g., In re Visa Check/MasterMoney Antitrust Litigation*, 280 F.3d 124, 139–140 (2d Cir. 2001).

In some antitrust cases, common questions do not predominate, and certification is denied. Proof of antitrust liability requires that the plaintiff show not only that the defendants engaged in unlawful conduct, but that the conduct had an impact on each plaintiff. In *Windham v. American Brands, Inc.*, 565 F.2d 59, 65 (4th Cir. 1977), the markets in which the plaintiffs purchased tobacco were so complicated, each involving different grades of tobacco and different purchasers, that aggregate proof of impact was impossible; individual questions overwhelmed any commonality.

The Supreme Court rejected a Rule 23(b)(3) class in *Comcast Corp. v. Behrend*, 133 S. Ct. 1426 (2013), because of proof problems at the class certification stage. Plaintiffs alleged that Comcast had "clustered" cable television providers in Philadelphia in an effort to exclude from that market companies that could have provided cheaper alternatives to cable service. At the certification stage, the question was whether the plaintiffs could show that injury and damages could be demonstrated on a class-wide basis. They were not required to prove injury and damages—those would be questions for trial. They needed to convince the court that when the case went to trial, there would be a way to demonstrate those things on a class-wide basis. If they were unable to do that, common questions could not predominate, and certification would be denied.

The plaintiffs tried to make the showings by presenting expert witness testimony at the certification hearing. That testimony demonstrated that injury and damages could be proved *en masse*. But they encountered a problem: their experts had prepared their testimony based upon four theories of antitrust impact—all of which the plaintiff had alleged. The district judge, however, rejected three of these theories, and permitted the plaintiffs to proceed only on something called the "overbuilder" theory (we don't care what that means). Thus, the expert testimony (based upon four theories) did not match the single damages model on which the plaintiffs were permitted to proceed. The Court held that the disconnect between the theory and the expert testimony was fatal.

Comcast is consistent with the increased "front-loading" of class litigation we discussed in section C.2.c. Antitrust plaintiffs must be prepared to demonstrate at certification that, when the issue arises at trial, they will be able to prove antitrust impact and damages on a group-wide basis. Moreover, the Court held, the defendant must be permitted to present evidence at the certification stage to rebut the plaintiffs' damages model.

Fraud (and Securities Fraud). One element in a claim for fraud is that the defendant made a misrepresentation of fact. If the defendant interacted individually with each claimant, and allegedly made the misrepresentation orally, it may be difficult to show that common questions predominate; the representations to each member will be unique. Suppose, however, that the defendant had read from a standard "pitch" statement in inducing each claimant to buy a product. There, the misrepresentations may have been identical, even though some aspects of the interactions differed. On facts similar to these, the California Supreme Court upheld class certification in *Vasquez v. Superior Court,* 484 P.2d 964, 966–967 (Cal. 1971).

Another element of fraud is that the plaintiff reasonably relied upon the defendant's misrepresentation. This element also raises the possibility that individual questions will overwhelm common questions. In *Castano,* the Fifth Circuit laid down a blanket precept: "a fraud class action cannot be certified [under Rule 23(b)(3)] when individual reliance will be an issue." 84 F.3d at 745. It is possible, though, on the facts of a case, that "common issues do not necessarily fail to predominate simply because reliance must be shown [individually]." *Jensen v. Fiserv Trust Co.,* 256 F. Appx. 924, 926 (9th Cir. 2007). In *Jensen,* the court concluded that reliance could be assumed, or inferred, because the defendant told the plaintiffs that they would realize substantial profits from the proposed deal.

The Supreme Court has adopted a presumption of reliance in "fraud on the market" cases under Rule 10b-5. The doctrine applies only regarding publicly-traded securities. It provides that when a corporation makes a materially misleading public statement about the value of the securities, there is a rebuttable presumption that people who bought or sold securities did so in reliance on that misrepresentation. *Basic, Inc. v. Levinson,,* 485 U.S. 224, 246–250 (1988). Without that holding, Rule 10b-5 public misrepresentation cases could not be certified under Rule 23(b)(3). Each claimant would be required to demonstrate that she relied on the misrepresentation, which would flood the case with individual issues.

In *Halliburton Co. v. Erica P. John Fund, Inc.,* 124 S. Ct. 2398, 2413–2414 (2014), the Court reaffirmed the presumption. It emphasized, however, that the defendants have a right to attempt to rebut the presumption at the certification stage. Indeed, the defendants in *Halliburton* attempted to do so, by showing that the alleged misstatement had no impact on the price of the company's stock.

Employment. *Wal-Mart* was not a Rule 23(b)(3) case (it was filed under Rule 23(b)(2)). And in light of the holding that the class failed to demonstrate commonality under Rule 23(a)(2), it could not have been certified under Rule 23(b)(3). On appropriate facts, however, employment discrimination cases may proceed under Rule 23(b)(3), and the Court discussed an issue that might come up in such cases. You recall that in *Wal-Mart,* the lower courts permitted the class to proceed to recover back pay. The problem, as we saw, was that each class member's back pay issue was unique, meaning that common questions could not predominate. The Ninth Circuit attempted to avoid the need for individual litigation of back pay. It held that a subset of individual cases would go to trial, and that other members' back pay would be extrapolated from those results.

The Supreme Court rejected the plan, which it called "Trial by Formula." The Ninth Circuit approach would have denied Wal-Mart the right to present defenses to individual's claims — a right it had under the relevant employment law. Thus, the Ninth Circuit's plan threatened to modify substantive law, which would violate the Rules Enabling Act.

Wal-Mart does not stand for the proposition that a class can never use representative evidence to prove class members' monetary recovery. *See* Alexandra D. Lahav, *The Case For "Trial by Formula,"* 90 Texas L. Rev. 571 (2012). Indeed, the Court upheld a classwide demonstration of damages in *Tyson Foods, Inc. v. Bouaphakeo*, 136 S. Ct. 1036 (2016). In that case, employees of a meat-packing plant sued under state law and the Fair Labor Standards Act. They claimed that the defendant employer wrongfully denied them compensation for time donning and doffing protective gear that they were required to wear while working in the plant. The claims related to overtime work, which required that each employee show that she had worked more than 40 hours per week, including time spent donning and doffing. Because the defendant failed to keep records, the class presented representative evidence based upon videotaped observations of an expert. The expert used the observations to average the times spent by various groups of employees putting on and taking off the protective garb.

The Court refused to adopt a blanket rule that representative evidence cannot be used in class actions. The question was not whether there should be special rules for class actions, but whether — in an individual suit — a plaintiff could have relied on the expert's averages. The answer was yes. The Court, 136 S. Ct. at 1048, explained:

> The Court's holding in the instant case is in accord with *Wal-Mart*. The underlying question in *Wal-Mart*, as here, was whether the sample at issue could have been used to establish liability in an individual action. Since the Court [in *Wal-Mart*] held that the employees were not similarly situated, none of them could have prevailed in an individual suit by relying on depositions detailing the ways in which other employees were discriminated against by their particular store managers. By extension, if the employees had brought 1½ million individual suits, there would be little or no role for representative evidence. Permitting the use of that sample in a class action, therefore, would have violated the Rules Enabling Act by giving plaintiffs and defendants different rights in a class proceeding than they could have asserted in an individual action.
>
> In contrast, the study here could have been sufficient to sustain a jury finding as to hours worked if it were introduced in each employee's individual action. While the experiences of the employees in *Wal-Mart* bore little relationship to one another, in this case each employee worked in the same facility, did similar work, and was paid under the same policy.

4. Can a Class Include Future Claims or Members?

Toxic torts raise the possibility of inflicting present harm and of putting the persons exposed at risk of future manifestation of illness. Those presently harmed have claims for personal injuries. Those exposed but not yet ill have "exposure-only" claims.

Do "exposure-only" claimants have a present claim? The answer depends upon the governing law. Some states do not recognize a separate claim for exposure; some states require proof of some substantial likelihood of contracting an illness; still others appear to require an accompanying physical injury. Beyond this, even if the applicable law recognizes a claim, there is a significant issue about whether exposure-only claimants have suffered "concrete" harm or "injury in fact" required to have standing under Article III. The Supreme Court has not decided the question. We discuss it in section F.3.b.

Beyond this, can a class include people who have not yet suffered harm? For example, if a faulty product remains on the market and will harm people in the future, can a class action today include those people? Even if the answer is yes, the inclusion raises two significant issues. First, there is likely a significant conflict between those presently injured (who want compensation now) and those who will be injured in the future (who will want a sufficient fund established now to compensate them when they are hurt); a representative who is presently injured probably cannot adequately represent those harmed in the future. Second, if the class is brought under Rule 23(b)(3), how can they possibly be given the required notice and right to opt out? We will return to that problem in discussing *Amchem* in section E.4.

Occasionally, courts have certified classes with future members. In *Robertson v. National Basketball Association*, 389 F. Supp. 867 (S.D.N.Y. 1975), a class of professional basketball players sued the National Basketball Association (NBA) for alleged violations of antitrust laws. The class alleged that the NBA had imposed anticompetitive intra-league rules (such as the college draft) and inter-league rules (merger with a rival league) that restrained players' ability to have teams bid for their services. The district court certified a Rule 23(b)(1)(A) class consisting of present and future NBA players affected and to be affected by the challenged practices. Concerning future members, the court, 389 F. Supp. at 897 (footnotes omitted), explained:

> The class is neither amorphous, nor imprecise; at the present time there are three hundred and sixty-five class members.... The fact that fifty to a hundred more members may be joining the class does not make it unmanageable.... This court can determine at any time whether a particular individual is a member of the class, for it will be composed of "a well-defined, discrete and limited number of NBA basketball players all of whom are well known and will be readily identifiable by exact name at all stages of this action." This factor makes this case distinguishable from [a case involving] (all past and future purchasers of tickets from

> Pan American [Airways]') and from [a case involving] ('all past, present and future ticketholders of the Buffalo Bills).
>
> Courts have approved classes which included future members. . . . In view of the size of the class and that plaintiffs have agreed to give notice of the proceedings to all present and future members, the notice requirement does not raise a serious issue.

Robertson is one of the rare cases in which a class may contain persons who have not yet been harmed. In *Robertson*, the group of future members was small, because only about 50 new people per year join the NBA. Moreover, they are well known and easily found. As the court noted, at any one time, it will be able to identify exactly who is in the class, because it will consist of that finite group of players in the NBA. Note also that *Robertson* was not certified under Rule 23(b)(3), so the court was not required to deal with the problem of giving notice to persons who have not yet been harmed.

5. Defendant Class Actions

Rule 23(a) contemplates that actions may be maintained against a class of defendants, as well as on behalf of a class of plaintiffs. It provides "[o]ne or more members of a class may *sue or be sued* as representative parties on behalf of all members" if the requirements of Rule 23(a) are satisfied (emphasis added). Indeed, there can be "bilateral" classes—in which a plaintiff class sues a defendant class.

That said, defendant classes are rare, and there are many unanswered questions concerning them. For example, is there a constitutional problem with binding defendant class members in a mandatory class? The stakes for a defendant class are far different from a plaintiff class. If a plaintiff class loses, members' claims are extinguished. But if a defendant class loses, liability is imposed upon those defendants. Can that be done without notice? Without the right to opt out? Without personal jurisdiction over the defendants by serving process on all of them?

In *Dale Electronics v. R.C.L. Electronics, Inc.*, 53 F.R.D. 531, 536 (D.N.H. 1971), the court certified a defendant class of only 13 members. The case was brought by a patent holder against alleged infringers, and sought a declaration that the plaintiff's five patents were valid. The court certified five classes—one for each of the patents. It held that joinder was impracticable because it would not have personal jurisdiction over several of the defendants:

> In the instant case, with the exception of Sprague which does business in New Hampshire, the locations of the defendants range from California to New York, and from North Carolina to Nebraska. Joinder is not only impracticable, but impossible.

The court failed to address the obvious implication: how can a court enter a judgment that purports to bind someone over whom it has no personal jurisdiction? Can personal jurisdiction over the representative suffice to satisfy the due process rights of class members for this purpose? This is a significant question, which the court in *Dale Electronics* simply ignored. We will have more to say about personal jurisdiction over class members in section F.2. One of the courts to discuss the problem of personal jurisdiction over defendant class members most meaningfully was not required to decide the matter, because it held that certification was properly denied. *Henson v. E. Lincoln Twp.*, 814 F.2d 410, 415–417 (7th Cir. 1987).

Issues under Rule 23(a). In a plaintiff class action, the representative stepped up voluntarily to lead the class. In contrast, the representative of a defendant class has had that honor forced upon her. Courts agree, though, as the Second Circuit colorfully says, that Rule 23(a)(4) requires an adequate representative, and not a willing one. *Consol. Rail Corp. v. Town of Hyde Park*, 47 F.3d 473, 483–84 (2d Cir. 1995). At the same time, courts are especially rigorous in assessing whether a defendant class representative is adequate. They seek to guard against the possibility that the plaintiff will select a weak opponent as the named class representative. 7A WRIGHT & MILLER, FEDERAL PRACTICE AND PROCEDURE § 1770 (3d ed. 2018).

Issues under Rule 23(b). Though Rule 23(b)(3) does not exclude defendant classes, and some cases address them, *see, e.g.*, *Consolidated Rail Corp. v. Town of Hyde Park*, 47 F.3d 473, 484–85 (2d Cir. 1995), they seem like a non-starter. One assumes that every member of such a class would exercise the right to opt out. Assuming most (if not all) members opt out, the class might be de-certified for lack of numerosity or because the class action is no longer the superior method for adjudicating the dispute.

The language of Rule 23(b)(1) seems to contemplate defendant classes. It speaks of the risk caused by "prosecuting by *or against* individual class members." Nonetheless, it is difficult to envision a Rule 23(b)(1)(A) defendant class. That subdivision provides for a class to avoid the imposition of "incompatible standards of conduct for the party opposing the class." As Dean Klonoff explains: "In a defendant class, the focus is on whether the plaintiff (who is opposing the class) would be subject to incompatible standards. But a plaintiff who simply recovers against some, but not all, defendants is not thereby subjected to incompatible standards." Robert H. Klonoff, CLASS ACTIONS AND OTHER MULTI-PARTY LITIGATION 379 (4th ed. 2012).

There may be a role for defendant classes under Rule 23(b)(1)(B). This class is aimed at avoiding impairment of individual interests if aggregate litigation is not allowed. One possibility is a defendant class of partners, who are jointly and severally liable for partnership debts. Arguably, a judgment against one of them might impair the other partners' interests.

The language of Rule 23(b)(2) is especially problematic when it comes to defendant class actions. It requires that "the party opposing the class" have acted or refused to act on grounds that apply generally to the class. When a plaintiff sues a defendant class, it is the defendant class members, and not the plaintiff (who is the party "opposing the class") who are alleged to have taken the actions that give rise to the suit. Not surprisingly, then, the Advisory Committee that drafted the Rule discussed Rule 23(b)(2) only in the context of plaintiff class actions.

The language and history of the Rule have led some courts to conclude that defendant class actions simply are not authorized by the language of Rule 23(b)(2). *See, e.g.*, *Tilley v. TSX Cos., Inc.*, 345 F.3d 34 (1st Cir. 2003); *Thompson v. Bd. of Educ. of Romeo Cmty. Schs.*, 709 F.2d 1200 (6th Cir. 1983); *Paxman v. Campbell*, 612 F.2d 848 (4th Cir. 1980).

The leading case on defendant Rule 23(b)(2) classes is *Henson v. E. Lincoln Twp.*, 814 F.2d 410, 416 (7th Cir. 1987). The court held that a defendant class usually is not allowed under Rule 23(b)(2). It noted, however, that the language of the Rule might encompass declaratory judgment actions against a defendant class. *Id.* at 414. This is because in declaratory judgment, the normal role of plaintiff and defendant is often reversed.

For example, a plaintiff may seek declaratory relief that it is not liable to a class of defendants. As *Henson* acknowledges, the availability of declaratory relief in effect converts what would be a plaintiff class action against the declaratory judgment plaintiff into a defendant class action against potential suitors. Other examples could be when a debtor seeks a declaration of non-liability to a class of creditors.

Question

In *Dale Electronics*, as noted at the outset of this subsection, a patent holder sought declaratory judgment against a defendant class. Specifically, it sought a declaration that its patents, which the defendants were allegedly infringing, were valid. The court certified the class under Rule 23(b)(1)(A) and Rule 23(b)(1)(B) and Rule 23(b)(2). Which, if any, of these Rules was properly invoked?

D. Issues in Class Litigation

In this section, we assume that the court has held a hearing on the motion to certify the class and has granted the motion. Now we address issues that commonly arise in the litigation of the class action.

1. Definition of the Class and Appointment of Class Counsel

Under Rule 23(c)(1)(B), a district court that grants a motion to certify must enter an order to "define the class and the class claims, issues, or defenses and must appoint class counsel under Rule 23(g)." The certification order is not cast in stone. Rule 23(c)(1)(C) provides that a certification order "may be altered or amended before final judgment." As the case progresses, things may change: a representative may withdraw for personal reasons or her claim may become moot, discovery may show that the case requires subclasses with different representatives. While a district court should not issue what used to be called "conditional certification," after the class is certified, the court must monitor the case and adapt to new evidence and change as warranted. Occasionally, courts will de-certify a class based upon changed conditions.

When a lawyer files a class action complaint, she represents the representative; the representative is her client. If the class is certified, the lawyer would like to become "class counsel," in which case the class itself becomes her client. Historically, courts were not intimately engaged with the selection of class counsel. When related classes were filed, and one was certified, the lawyers in the cases generally agreed on who would serve as class counsel. Courts undertook to ensure that class counsel was competent, but rarely second-guessed the group choice.

Today, Rule 23(c)(1)(B) requires the court to select class counsel. In most cases, there will be competition for the appointment. After all, class counsel gets to make the key decisions in the case and will hope, if successful, to recover a handsome fee. When there are multiple applicants, "the court must appoint the applicant best able to represent the interests of the class." Fed. R. Civ. P. 23(g)(2)(B). If there is only one applicant, the court must ensure that she satisfies the criteria listed in Rule 23(g)(1) and that she will, in the words of Rule 23(g)(4), "fairly and adequately represent the interests of the class."

Among other things, Rule 23(g)(1)(A) requires the court to consider the lawyer's "experience in handling class actions." Critics believe that this focus makes it too difficult for new lawyers to "break in" as class attorneys. In fact, there is a small group of well-known plaintiff class action firms involved in many cases around the country. We will consider Rule 23(g) in detail in Chapter 7.A.3.b.

2. Interlocutory Appeal of the Certification Decision

Decisions on motions to certify a class action are watershed events. The ruling determines whether the case will go forward with a single (or a few) plaintiffs or as aggregate litigation. If the case involves negative-value claims, denial of a motion to certify may be seen, *de facto*, as the "death knell" of the case; with one or a few such claims, the plaintiff side has no incentive to litigate. If the court grants certification, the defendant may face colossal aggregate liability, so its incentive to settle increases dramatically. Either way, the party that loses on the certification motion often would like to seek appellate review.

The problem for that litigant is that rulings on certification motions are not final judgments, and therefore are not automatically appealable under 28 U.S.C. § 1291. They are interlocutory (non-final) rulings and historically could be appealed only if the losing party could fit the case within one of the narrow exceptions to the final judgment rule. This is difficult to do. For instance, interlocutory review under 28 U.S.C. § 1292(b) requires the district judge to certify that there is a "controlling question of law" that justifies immediate appeal, and further requires the court of appeals to agree to hear the issue. Class certification can rarely be said to involve a "controlling question of law," although some courts used § 1291(b)(2), particularly in cases of egregious certification orders. For example, in *Castano*, the Fifth Circuit reviewed certification under § 1291(b)(2).

Against this background, Rule 23(f) was promulgated in 1998. As amended in 2018, it provides:

> **(f) Appeals.** A court of appeals may permit an appeal from an order granting or denying class-action certification under this rule, but not from an order under Rule 23(e)(1). A party may petition for permission to appeal with the circuit clerk within 14 days after the order is entered, or within 45 days after the order is entered if any party is the United States, a United States agency, or a United States officer or employee sued for an act or omission occurring in connection with duties performed on the United States' behalf. An appeal does not stay proceedings in the district court unless the district judge or the court of appeals so orders.

One early study concluded that Rule 23(f) increased the number of interlocutory appeals of certification decisions four-fold. Brian Anderson & Patrick McLain, *A Progress Report on Rule 23(f): Five Years of Immediate Class Certification Appeals*, Legal Backgrounder, Mar. 19, 2004, at 1.

Notes and Questions

1. Does Rule 23(f) require the court of appeals to hear the appeal?

2. When and where does the party seeking to appeal under Rule 23(f) file its petition? The language allowing 45 days in certain cases involving the United States or its agencies or employees was added effective December 1, 2018.

3. Also added in 2018 is the provision that one may not seek appeal "from an order under Rule 23(e)(1)." That Rule, as we discuss in section E, deals with the courts' giving notice to class members in connection with possible settlement of a certified class action.

4. Rule 23(f) gives no guidance to courts of appeals regarding whether they should grant a petition for appeal. The matter is left to the discretion of each court. The Advisory Committee that drafted the provision stated that this discretion is "akin to the discretion exercised by the Supreme Court in acting on a petition for certiorari." It suggested, however, that appeals might be appropriate when the ruling is the "death knell" of claimants' case, or when granting certification creates significant settlement pressure on the defendant, as well as when "the certification decision turns on a novel or unsettled question of law." Several circuits have looked to these factors, and have added others, such as whether the district court's certification ruling is questionable.

5. Although Rule 23(f) is neutral on its face, one empirical study—though a bit dated now—found that the provision had been used primarily to reverse orders granting class certification. Through 2007, in 52.5 percent of all Rule 23(f) decisions, the courts of appeals reversed or vacated an order of class certification. Only

ten percent of the opinions reversed a denial of class certification. Richard D. Freer, *Interlocutory Review of Class Action Certification Decisions: A Preliminary Empirical Study of Federal and State Experience*, 35 W. St. L. Rev. 13, 19 (2008). Such statistics support the general perception, noted in Chapter 2.D.4.a, that class plaintiffs may prefer litigating in state court to federal court. As we noted there, many plaintiffs' lawyers criticize the Class Action Fairness Act (CAFA) because it channels more class actions into federal court.

3. Communicating with Class Members

Attorneys or parties in a putative or certified class action will want to communicate with class members for a variety of reasons and at various stages in the action. Before filing, the plaintiffs' lawyer will want to talk to potential class members to gather information relevant to the case. After the case is filed, the plaintiff's lawyer may want to communicate with class members for a variety of reasons, including:

- to inform putative members of the case
- to explain how a class action works
- to obtain information to help prosecute the action
- to rebut any misinformation provided by the defendant
- to discourage putative members from accepting offers of settlement from the defendant or (in a Rule 23(b)(3) case) to opt out of the class
- if the original representative is inappropriate for some reason or withdraws from the case, to obtain a new representative
- to obtain new representatives to satisfy a *Falcon* or *LaMar* problem[23]
- to obtain new representatives to represent subclasses.

On the other side of the case, defense counsel may want to communicate with class members for a variety of reasons, including:

- to provide them with the defense view of the case
- to obtain information necessary to the defense
- to rebut any misinformation provided by the plaintiff
- to encourage class members to settle their claims or (in a Rule 23(b)(3) case) to opt out of the class.

These communications, from either side, might be made in person, by email, or telephone, by a web posting, or publication (print, internet, or broadcast). Whatever their format, such communications raise the potential for abuse and coercion.

---

23. As we saw in section C.2.c.iv of this chapter, dealing with adequacy of representation, *Falcon* requires that the representative have suffered the same harm as class members. *LaMar* requires (generally) that the representative have dealt with each defendant.

Rules of professional conduct impose restrictions on contact. In addition, courts in certain instances may enter orders limiting contact with class members.

a. Limits Imposed by Professionalism

Each state has rules of professional conduct, including rules relating to communications between lawyers, their clients, and represented and unrepresented parties. We will refer to the American Bar Association's Model Rules of Professional Conduct. For us, the most pertinent are:

> Model Rule 1.4 provides that a lawyer shall inform the client of any decision requiring the client's informed consent, shall keep the client reasonably informed, shall promptly respond to reasonable requests for information, and shall consult with the client about how the objects of the representation are to be achieved.
>
> Rule 4.2 prohibits a lawyer representing a client from communicating about the case with a person whom the lawyer knows *is represented by another lawyer* in the matter (absent the consent of the other lawyer or a court order).
>
> Rule 4.3 provides that in dealing, on behalf of a client, with a person who is *not represented* by counsel, the lawyer shall not imply that she is disinterested and, generally, shall not give that person legal advice (other than the advice to obtain counsel).
>
> Rule 7.1 prohibits a lawyer from making false or misleading statements regarding the lawyer or her services.
>
> Model Rule 7.2 permits a lawyer to advertise her services by written, recorded, or electronic communications, including communications by newspaper, television, and the internet, provided a responsible lawyer or law firm is identified. Such advertising is justified to inform the public regarding the availability of legal services. It may include services offered, the basis for fees, references, and, with consent, the names of clients currently represented.
>
> Rule 7.3 prohibits a lawyer from soliciting employment from prospective clients through in-person, telephone, or real-time electronic communication, unless the lawyer has a family, close personal, or previous professional relationship with the person. This Rule reflects concern that such personal contacts involve the potential for abuse of untrained lay persons by undue influence.

Notes and Questions

1. Assume a plaintiff's lawyer is interested in filing a class action on behalf of condomium owners, based upon credible information that there are structural problems that affect all units and are apparently the fault of the builder. There are 400 condominium units in the development.

(a) Would it be proper for the lawyer to appear at a monthly meeting of the homeowners' association and inform them of the potential suit?

(b) Would it be proper for her to describe how a class action works?

(c) Would it be proper for her to ask people in the audience if they would like to serve as class representative in the case?

2. Assume a class action has been filed against Defendant, but has not been certified.

(a) Would it be proper for Defendant's lawyer to contact the representative to give her the "Defendant's side" of the case?

(b) Would it be proper for Defendant's lawyer to contact putative class members to give them the "Defendant's side" of the case?

(c) Would it be proper for Defendant's lawyer to contact putative class members to urge them to opt out of the class action if it proceeds?

(d) Would it be proper for Defendant's lawyer to contact putative class members to get information relevant to the case?

3. Assume that the court, in the case discussed in Question 2, grants the motion to certify the case as a class action.

(a) Would it be proper for Defendant's lawyer to contact the class members for any of the purposes listed in Question 2 (b), (c), and (d)?

(b) What is different here—about class members—than in Question 2? (Hint: did class certification change the situation from one involving Model Rule 4.3 to Model Rule 4.2?)[24]

4. Assume that after the filing of a class action, but before certification, the claim of the representative becomes moot. We will see in section F.3 that the class action might continue if another claimant—with a live claim—is substituted as representative.

(a) Would it be proper for the lawyer who filed the case to contact putative class members to find a new representative?

(b) If so, what can she say to accomplish her goal?

---

24. The majority view is that, before a class is certified, counsel for defendant may contact putative class members without notice to or approval by opposing counsel or the court. This contact can be for the purpose of providing information to the putative class members, obtaining information from them, or encouraging them to opt out of the action or to settle their individual claims. Of course, the communications cannot be misleading, coercive, or otherwise abusive. *See, e.g., Great Rivers Coop. of Southeastern Iowa v. Farmland Indus.*, 59 F.3d 764, 766 (8th Cir. 1995); *Beasley v. Custom Commc'ns, Inc*, 2016 WL 6684206, at *3–4 (E.D.N.C. 2016) (insufficient evidence of misconduct to justify plaintiffs' requested restriction of defendant's communication with putative class members).

5. Assume the same facts as in Question 4, but the class is certified. Now the representative's claim becomes moot and the plaintiff-side lawyer wants to find a new representative. Can the class lawyer communicate with class members to do so?

6. Sometimes, members of a certified class will continue to have routine business or social interaction with the defendant. Suppose a class action is filed on behalf of people who borrowed money from Bank. The case alleges that Bank overcharged these customers in violation of applicable law. The class is certified. The customers and Bank have an ongoing business relationship——the customers still owe balances on their loans and may have checking accounts at Bank. Accordingly, there will be communications between Bank and the class members—but it will be about business as usual. Now suppose Bank's lawyers tell Bank to have Bank employees telephone the customers and urge them to opt out of the class action.

(a) Which Model Rule(s) has/have the lawyers violated?

(b) Believe it or not, this actually happened. *See Kleiner v. First National Bank of Atlanta*, 751 F.2d 1193 (11th Cir. 1993).

b. The Court's Authority Under Rule 23 to Limit Communications (and Constitutional Limits on that Authority)

In 1977, the Supreme Court opened the door to lawyer advertising. In *Bates v. State Bar of Arizona*, 433 U.S. 350, 365, 382 (1977), it held that Arizona's ban on lawyer advertising violated the First Amendment. It emphasized, however, that false or misleading advertising is subject to restraint. *Id.* at 383. In *Ohralik v. Ohio State Bar Ass'n*, 436 U.S. 447, 457–458 (1978), it held that the First Amendment does not prohibit a state from disciplining a lawyer for in-person solicitation.

As we explored in the preceding subsection, once a class is certified, the class members generally are treated as "represented" parties under Model Rule 4.2, meaning that the defendant's lawyer cannot contact them without consent or a court order. Pre-certification, however, the class members are not "represented" parties, and Model Rule 4.3 applies. Despite the advent of lawyer advertising, courts remained wary of permitting counsel for either side to contact members of a putative class. Thus, it was common for courts to enter blanket orders forbidding such contact. So common, in fact, that the MANUAL FOR COMPLEX LITIGATION recommended such orders and district courts promulgated Local Rules recommending such orders.

The authority for issuing restrictions on party and lawyer contact with putative class members is Federal Rule 23(d), which gives the court wide latitude in overseeing class actions. It provides:

Rule 23(d). Conducting the Action.

(1) *In General.* In conducting an action under this rule, the court may issue orders that:

(A) determine the course of proceedings or prescribe measures to prevent undue repetition or complication in presenting evidence or argument;

(B) require—to protect class members and fairly conduct the action—giving appropriate notice to some or all class members of:

(i) any step in the action;

(ii) the proposed extent of the judgment; or

(iii) the members' opportunity to signify whether they consider the representation fair and adequate, to intervene and present claims or defenses, or to otherwise come into the action;

(C) impose conditions on the representative parties or on intervenors;

(D) require that the pleadings be amended to eliminate allegations about representation of absent persons and that the action proceed accordingly; or

(E) deal with similar procedural matters.

(2) *Combining and Amending Orders.* An order under Rule 23(d)(1) may be altered or amended from time to time and may be combined with an order under Rule 16.

The leading case addressing the scope of court's authority to limit class communications under Rule 23(d) is *Gulf Oil Co. v. Bernard*, 452 U.S. 89 (1981). There, a class of present and future black employees at a Gulf Oil refinery sued, alleging racial discrimination. The case was filed after the Equal Employment Opportunity Commission (EEOC) had brought an administrative proceeding against Gulf. The EEOC and Gulf entered into a "conciliation agreement" that required Gulf to cease various practices, to undertake an affirmative action program, and to offer back pay to alleged victims, based upon a formula.

Before the class action was filed, Gulf began mailing notices to employees, advising them of the conciliation agreement with the EEOC and informing them of the amount of back pay to which the agreement entitled them. Gulf asked the employees to accept that amount and to sign releases, which would settle their claims and remove them from the class.

After the class action was filed, Gulf asked the court to enter an order banning plaintiffs' lawyer from communicating with the class members about the case. (Presumably, Gulf wanted to stop plaintiffs' lawyer from urging class members to reject the conciliation agreement and remain in the class.) The district court "imposed a complete ban on all communications concerning the class action between parties or their counsel and any actual or potential class member who was not a formal party, without the prior approval of the court." Moreover, the order exempted Gulf's communications about the EEOC conciliation agreement. The court entered the order without making findings of fact or issuing an opinion. Thereafter, it denied plaintiffs' request to send notice to class members to urge them to talk to a lawyer before signing the releases sent by Gulf.

The Supreme Court held that the district court exceeded its authority under Rule 23(d). (It refused to address the question of whether the order violated the First Amendment.) After noting that the order constituted a significant restriction on speech—one that interfered with plaintiff's efforts to inform putative class members of the suit—the Court set standards for when Rule 23(d) may be used to restrict communications to putative class members. A district court entering a restriction on contact:

- Must base the order "on a clear record"
- Must base the order on "specific findings" and
- The findings must reflect a "weighing of the need for a limitation and the potential interferences with the rights of the parties"

Moreover, the "mere possibility of abuses" does not justify "routine adoption of a communications ban that interferes with the formation of a class or the prosecution of a class action in accordance with the Rules." 432 U.S. at 104.

Notes and Questions

1. *Gulf Oil* has had a profound impact. Before the decision, courts routinely issued blanket orders prohibiting contact with putative class members. After the decision, such blanket orders have disappeared. Local Rules recommending such blanket orders have disappeared. Today, "[m]ost judges are reluctant to restrict communications between parties or their counsel and potential class members, except when necessary to prevent serious misconduct." Manual for Complex Litigation § 21.12.

2. After a class is certified, the class lawyer's client is the class itself. Generally, a court has no business limiting communications between a lawyer and her clients. Before certification, however, that lawyer's client is the representative, not the class members. Nonetheless, "an attorney acting on behalf of a putative class must act in the best interests of the class as a whole." Manual for Complex Litigation § 21.12. The best interests of the class may require the class lawyer to obtain and to provide information relevant to the case and to respond to questions. The court can intervene, under *Gulf Oil*, if the contact involves misleading, abusive, or coercive conduct.

3. *Gulf Oil* involved a restriction on the plaintiff class's lawyer. Should the holding apply to restrictions on *defendant's* lawyer's contact with putative class members? Clearly, the defendant's lawyer cannot contact the representative (without permission), since the representative is represented by counsel. But putative class members are not represented. Defense counsel might wish to obtain and to provide information and to discuss possible settlement. Most courts appear to conclude that

Gulf Oil applies to defense communications as well as plaintiff communications. *See In re School Asbestos Litigation*, 842 F.2d 671 (3d Cir. 1988); *Bonanno v. Quiznos Masters LLC*, 2007 WL 1089779, at *3 (D. Colo. 2007) (*Gulf Oil* has been found to apply to defense communications). Thus, defense counsel may be permitted such contact absent misleading, abusive, or coercive conduct.

---

4. Discovery from Class Members

The discovery phase of complex litigation raises so many topics that we devote Chapter 8 to it. We focus here on an overview of discovery in class cases.

Generally, there are two phases of discovery in a class action: (1) that regarding whether certification should be granted and, if it is granted, (2) discovery relating to the merits of the case. In some cases, the court may be able to rule on certification without discovery. "Discovery may not be necessary when claims for relief rest on readily available and undisputed facts or raise only issues of law (such as a challenge to the legality of a statute or regulation)." Manual for Complex Litigation § 21.14. In most instances, however, the court will permit pre-certification discovery—aimed at whether the requirements of Rule 23(a) and 23(b) are satisfied. Thus, discovery will focus on evidence bearing on numerosity, typicality, adequacy of representation, whether the defendant treated potential class members alike, whether common questions predominate, and the like.

Often, plaintiffs will move for certification based upon evidence gathered without formal discovery—such as expert witness reports, declarations from potential class members, and information about how many claimants may be in the class. Likewise, defendants often oppose certification with evidence gleaned from outside the formal discovery process.

It may be increasingly difficult for courts to draw the line between "certification discovery" and "merits discovery." *Wal-Mart* made it clear that a court, in ruling on a certification motion, should not hesitate to consider evidence relating to the underlying merits of the case. Judges must be diligent to allow enough discovery to facilitate the certification decision without allowing it to wander into merits issues that are extraneous to that decision. Once the class is certified, the court will permit discovery on the merits, as in any case.

In either phase, are class members subject to discovery? Before certification, they are not represented by counsel, so, generally, the defendant and its lawyer may contact putative class members, subject to court restriction for abusive contact. After certification, however, class members are treated as represented by counsel, so the defendant and its lawyer may not approach them without permission. Here is the problem: though class members are treated as represented for purposes of professional responsibility, they are not parties. And the discovery tools most useful for getting information from class members—interrogatories under Rule 33 and requests to produce under Rule 34[25]—may, by the express terms of those Rules, only be sent to parties.

Despite this fact, courts may allow such discovery from class members of a certified class. The authority for doing so is the court's general power to manage class actions, reflected in Rule 23(d). The leading case remains *Brennan v. Midwestern United Life Insurance Co.*, 450 F.2d 999, 1005 (7th Cir. 1971). There, the court recognized that discovery from class members is not the norm, and that a court must be careful to weigh the need for the information against the burden imposed on the members. In any such effort, the court must be alert to the possibility that discovery might be used as a tool of harassment—aimed at forcing class members to settle their individual claims or to opt out of a Rule 23(b)(3) class.

The court explained:

> It is true that an absent class member is given a "free ride" under Rule 23 and has no duty to actively engage in the prosecution of the action. Yet the absent class member's interests are identical with those of the named plaintiff and his rights . . . are adjudicated in the principal suit. If discovery from the absent member is necessary or helpful to the proper presentation and correct adjudication of the principal suit, we see no reason why it should not allowed so long as adequate precautionary measures are taken to insure that the absent member is not misled or confused. . . .

In *Brennan*, the district court directed the class lawyer to send interrogatories and a request to produce documents to each class member, indicating that the court had approved this action and setting a deadline for response. The court, after holding a hearing on the matter, dismissed—with prejudice—the claims of class members who did not respond to the discovery requests. The Seventh Circuit affirmed, and noted that even though class members are not parties, thy do not have the right to ignore court notices that warned them of the consequence of ignoring the requests for discovery.

5. Notice of Class Membership, Opting Out, and Intervention into Class Action

a. The Provisions

We focus here on Rule 23(c)(2). It purpose is to notify class members that they are members of a certified class filed on their behalf. We need to distinguish this from Rule 23(e)(1), which deals with notice to class members about the possible

25. Depositions under Rule 30 or 31 may be used to get information from non-parties. So, the defendant presumably could notice depositions of class members and have them subpoenaed to compel their attendance. But depositions are expensive and time-consuming, and it is unlikely that the defendant would want to spend its resources in this way—except to depose class representatives and any class members who will be witnesses at trial.

settlement or voluntary dismissal of the case. As amended in part effective December 1, 2018, Rule 23(c)(2) provides:

Rule 23(c)(2) Notice.

(A) *For (b)(1) or (b)(2) Classes.* For any class certified under Rule 23(b)(1) or (b)(2), the court may direct appropriate notice to the class.

(B) *For (b)(3) Classes.* For any class certified under Rule 23(b)(3)—or upon ordering notice under Rule 23(e)(1) to a class proposed to be certified for purposes of settlement under Rule 23(b)(3)—the court must direct to class members the best notice that is practicable under the circumstances, including individual notice to all members who can be identified through reasonable effort. The notice may be by one of the following: United States mail, electronic means, or other appropriate means. The notice must clearly and concisely state in plain, easily understood language:

(i) the nature of the action;

(ii) the definition of the class certified;

(iii) the class claims, issues, or defenses;

(iv) that a class member may enter an appearance through an attorney if the member so desires;

(v) that the court will exclude from the class any member who requests exclusion;

(vi) the time and manner for requesting exclusion; and

(vii) the binding effect of a class judgment on members under Rule 23(c)(3).

Notes and Questions

1. Regarding Rule 23(b)(1) and 23(b)(2) classes:

(a) Must notice be given to class members?

(b) If notice is given, must it be given to each member individually?

(c) If notice is not given individually, how might it be given?

(d) If notice is given, who gives it?

(e) If notice is given, what does it say?

2. Regarding Rule 23(b)(3) classes:

(a) Must notice be given to class members?

(b) Must it be given to each member individually?

(c) What if there are class members who cannot be identified individually?

(d) Who gives the notice?

(e) What does the notice say?

3. If a member of a Rule 23(b)(3) class receives notice and takes no action, will she be bound by the judgment in the case?

4. The 2018 amendment to Rule 23(c)(2) added the provision permitting notice to be made by mail, electronic, or other appropriate means. Historically, courts have used mail to give individual notice. In recent years, courts have permitted electronic methods, and the amendment recognizes that development.

5. *Hansberry v. Lee*, 311 U.S. 32 (1940), held that a non-party can be bound by a judgment based upon adequate representation of her interest. In the Rule 23(b)(3) class, though, we see that Rule 23 *also requires notice.*

(a) Why should notice be required in these cases and not in Rule 23(b)(1) or 23(b)(2) cases?

(b) Suppose the Rule provided notice to members of a Rule 23(b)(3) class but no right to opt out of the class? Would such a provision accord with due process? The answer must be no. Reconsider this passage from *Wal-Mart*:

> [Rule 23](b)(2) [like Rule 23(b)(1)] does not require that class members be given notice and opt-out rights, presumably because it is thought (rightly or wrongly) that notice has no purpose when the class is mandatory, and that depriving people of their right to sue in this manner complies with the Due Process Clause. In the context of a class action predominantly for money damages we have held that absence of notice and opt-out violates due process. See *Phillips Petroleum Co.* v. *Shutts*, 472 U.S. 797, 812 (1985). While we have never held that to be so where the monetary claims do not predominate, the serious possibility that it may be so provides an additional reason not to read Rule 23(b)(2) to include the monetary claims here.

Wal-Mart, 564 U.S. at 363.[26]

Rule 23(b)(3) classes almost always are "predominantly for money damages," so class members must be given notice and a chance to opt out. For such claims, the individual must be in control—to have the option to go along with the class action or to sue individually or with others (or not to sue at all). Given the importance of individual autonomy on these claims, should we re-think our answer to Question 3 and provide that the class member will be bound by the class judgment only if she opts in?

6. The notice in a Rule 23(b)(3) class action must include the specifics listed in Rule 23(c)(2)(B)(i) through (vii). These specifics are intended to give the member enough information to make a wise decision about how to pursue her interest.

26. *See also Eisen v. Carlisle & Jacquelin*, 417 U.S. 156, 176 (1974) ("Petitioner further contends that adequate representation, rather than notice, is the touchstone of due process in a class action and therefore satisfies Rule 23. We think this view has little to commend it.").

7. Rule 23(c)(2)(B) says that the required notice must be stated "in plain, easily understood language." This is an aspiration, but often not a reality—because of the way the notice evolves. The notice is a court document, sent from the court itself. And the final version of the notice is the judge's decision. But the court invariably has the parties submit drafts of the notice. Each side, predictably, attempts subtly to put itself in the most favorable light. The judge makes the final decision, but the result is usually a legalistic document that laypeople find difficult to decipher. Nonetheless, the fact that it comes from the court presumably commands people's attention, even in an era of junk mail and spam.

8. An example of discretionary notice that may be given in a mandatory class action is notice to members of a "limited fund" class to make their claims after the defendant's liability and the limited fund are established. In addition, as part of its broad supervisory power, under Rule 23(d)(1)(B), a court may give notice to class members as appropriate throughout the case. For instance, if the representative withdraws, the court might notify class members to enable one or more of them to intervene as a representative.

b. "Best Notice Practicable . . ." and Who Pays to Give It

For Rule 23(b)(3) classes, Rule 23(c)(2) requires "the best notice that is practicable under the circumstances, including individual notice to all members who can be identified through reasonable effort." FED. R. CIV. P. 23(c)(2)(B). The clear intent of the provision is to satisfy the due process requirement of notice established in *Mullane v. Central Hanover Bank & Trust Co.*, 339 U.S. 306, 318 (1950): notice "reasonably calculated, under all the circumstances, to apprise the parties of the pendency of the action . . . ." In *Mullane* (which was not a class action), the Court did not require individual notice to everyone whose interest could have been affected by a judgment in the case, even if they could be identified with reasonable effort. Rule 23(c)(2)(B), by requiring individual notice of all who can be reasonably identified, may afford more protection than due process requires.

At any rate, the Rule is read literally, as the Court made clear in *Eisen v. Carlisle & Jacquelin*, 417 U.S. 156, 176 (1974). The Rule says individual notice to those who can be identified with reasonable effort, and that is what it means. Courts may not decide to give notice to some percentage of those who are reasonably identifiable.

Eisen was a federal question case for securities fraud. The representative's personal claim was worth around $70. The class was huge, and thousands of members could be identified through reasonable effort (from brokerage records, for example). The cost of mailing notice to those individuals was $225,000. The lower courts allocated that expense between the representative and the defendant, based upon their assessment of the likelihood that the class would prevail. The Supreme Court reversed and imposed a categorical rule: the representative pays to give the notice. Period. The theory was straightforward: the representative seeks to pursue the class action, and should pay for it.

Obviously, no representative with a $70 claim is going to spend $225,000 to prosecute the class action. Increasingly today, the class lawyer can advance this expense in hope of winning a favorable judgment or settlement. And, as a general rule, the prevailing party in litigation recovers its costs (not attorney's fees) from the loser. So if the plaintiff class wins, it may recover the cost of giving notice from the defendant. In the meantime, however, the plaintiff must bear the cost. By imposing this expense on the representative, however, *Eisen* imposes a hurdle to large-scale classes.

Can the defendant be required to bear the expense of identifying class members? In *Oppenheimer Fund, Inc. v. Sanders,* 437 US. 340, 350 (1978), the lower courts ordered the defendant to do so, and noted that (1) the expanse was relatively small, (2) the defendant had full control of the computer tapes that contained the names and addresses, and (3) the defendant was charged with violating fiduciary duties to the class. The Supreme Court reversed. First, the information was not discoverable under the discovery rules (which would have required the defendant to bear the cost). Second, the matter fell within Rule 23(d)—the provision giving the court broad managerial power over class actions. Once Rule 23 applied, the Court concluded, *Eisen* applied, and the representative was required to bear the expense.

The Court in *Oppenheimer* left open this possibility: "it may be appropriate to leave the cost where it falls [when] the task ordered is one that the defendant must perform in any event in the ordinary course of business." 437 U.S. at 358. For instance, in a class action against a retailer or utility provider, the court might require the defendant to include class notice with its periodic billing statement.

Finally, if class members cannot be identified individually with reasonable effort, published notice will be "the best notice practicable" and will satisfy Rule 23(c)(2). As noted above, publication is a broader notion than it was when *Eisen* was decided. Print media were largely the only option. In the 1980s, courts started permitting publication on television and radio. Now, of course, the internet opens more possibilities.

c. Opting Out or Entering an "Appearance" in a Rule 23(b)(3) Class

The class notice given to members of a Rule 23(b)(3) class will inform them of what they must do to be excluded from the class. Everyone calls this "opting out" of the class, though Rule 23 does not use that term. The court will set a date by which the member must notify the court in a specified way—traditionally by mail, but now permissibly by internet. If the class member opts out in time, she will not be bound by the judgment in the class action. If she does not opt out within the time set by the court, she will be bound by that judgment.

Another option, in Rule 23(c)(2)(B)(iv) is to "enter an appearance through an attorney." This is done is by moving to intervene under Rule 24, which we discussed in B.1.c. Upon intervening, the person becomes a party. There is some question whether the "enter an appearance" language creates an automatic right to intervene.

Even if it does, the court has broad authority under Rule 23(d) to manage the case, and thus to determine the role intervenors will play in the case.

d. Intervening into Any Class Action

Indeed, in any class action, any class member may seek to intervene under Rule 24. She would do this to gain party status. For example, a class member frustrated by acts taken by the representative may seek to intervene to have her voice heard or her interest represented individually. Intervention into a class action works as it does in any case.

6. Class Remedies

Classes may seek the full panoply of remedies available under the substantive law. In addition, there are remedial possibilities unique to class practice. We list some of the more common remedies. They may be awarded as part of final judgment or may constitute part of a class settlement.

- **Injunctive or declaratory relief.** Of course, this is the focus of the Rule 23(b)(2) class. Final judgment will spell out the terms of the injunction or declaration, and any class member can seek to have the defendant held in contempt for violating the order.
- **Damages or other monetary relief.** General damages are intended to compensate class members for harm inflicted by the defendant. Not all monetary relief constitutes damages. For example, restitution seeks to recover sums unjustly retained by the defendant.
  - If the judgment or settlement creates a fund of money, individual class members may establish the amount to which they are entitled in a variety of ways:
    - By trial, with or without a jury.
    - By arbitration.
    - By administrative mechanism involving members' submission of a "claim form." These proceedings are often overseen by masters, whom the court appoints under Rule 53, which is discussed in Chapter 5.C.2.
    - By mathematical or other formula. Expert witnesses may establish a formula that can be applied to determine individual recoveries. In *Tyson Foods v. Bouaphakeo*, 136 S. Ct. 1036 (2016), the Supreme Court permitted representative proof, derived from sampling, to demonstrate that common questions predominated in a Rule 23(b)(3) class. The Court concluded that a class may rely on representational proof if an individual plaintiff could have done so.
- **Fluid recovery.**

  Example #12. Taxi Co. wrongfully set its meters to charge passengers more than it was permitted to charge under applicable regulations. This resulted in overcharging passengers in Los Angeles for, say, six months, at which point the problem was corrected. All people who rode in Taxi's cabs in Los Angeles over that period were overcharged a certain amount per mile travelled. P files a class action on behalf of those passengers. Taxi has a record of all trips made by its cabs, but has no record of who the passengers were.

(a) Can a class action be maintained?

(b) If so, how can the court provide a remedy—and for whom?

These are the basic facts of *Daar v. Yellow Cab Co.*, 433 P.2d 732 (Cal. 1967). The California Supreme Court, applying the California class action rule (which differs significantly from Rule 23, though possibly not in ways that affect this issue), held that the class could be certified. It seemed to foresee creation of a fund from which individual passengers could make claims (perhaps by affidavit): after the court determined "the total amount of the . . . overcharges, . . . no one may recover his separate damages until he comes forward, identifies himself and proves the amount thereof." *Id.* at 740.

But that is not how the case ended. The parties agreed to settle the case by having Taxi set its meters below the authorized fare for the same period (in our example, six months). There was no need to create a fund from which individuals would make claims. This form of relief is often called "fluid recovery." It does not provide a remedy for exactly the group that was harmed, but "to individuals similarly situated to the class (and hence often encompass[ing] many class members." 4 Newberg on Class Actions § 12:27 (5th ed. 2018).

Fluid recovery raises fundamental questions about the purpose of the class action. If the purpose is to compensate those people who were harmed by the defendant's acts, the class in *Daar* was not wholly successful: surely there was some overlap between the group that was overcharged and the group that was undercharged, but it was not 100 percent. On the other hand, if (as the California Supreme Court emphasized) the purpose is to deter the defendant from such behavior, the settlement in *Daar* worked—Taxi did not "get away" with the overcharging. Moreover, fluid recovery saves the cost and burden of collecting a fund and having individuals make claims. The cost of having each person come forward with proof of how many times she rode in a taxicab during the relevant period would not be worth the effort.

A quick aside: notice the difference technology might make. Suppose a case like *Daar* involved a ride-sharing business such as Uber. Given that each transaction generates an electronic record and a charge against a credit card, identifying class members would be much easier than in the faceless, often cash-paid, world of taxicabs. In such a case, would there be a role for fluid recovery?

- *Cy pres.* This phrase is part of a longer Norman French phrase that means "as near as [possible]," and is often used in administering wills and trusts to permit distributions to charitable causes when the exact terms of the will or trust cannot be carried out. In class practice, *cy pres* usually arises when a class judgment or settlement has resulted in a fund of money. Individual claimants have made their claims from the fund, and have not exhausted the funds. What happens to the money that is left over?

  Possibilities include (1) returning the money to the defendant, (2) having it escheat to the state, or (3) distributing it to appropriate charitable organizations. *Cy pres* is the term used for this latter option. Again, we see the policies of compensation and deterrence. If the purpose of the litigation is to compensate those harmed, arguably, that has been achieved (because all the claims have been paid). So, the money might be returned to the defendant. On the other hand, if the purpose is to deter, then escheat or *cy pres* make more sense. *Cy pres* can target the cause benefited. For example, in litigation against tobacco companies, a *cy pres* award might give money to non-profit organizations dedicated to wellness. This may be better than escheat, which simply gives the money to the state treasury.

  Cy pres has its critics, but "[c]ourts in every circuit, and appellate courts in most, have approved the use of cy pres for unclaimed class action awards." *Id.* We will have more to say about *cy pres* when discussing class settlement in section E.[27]

  Some courts and lawyers use "fluid recovery" and "*cy pres*" interchangeably. We follow the terminology suggested by the authors of the Newberg treatise: fluid recovery means directing a remedy toward a group that is similar (indeed, overlaps with) the group that was harmed. *Cy pres*, in contrast,

---

27. *In re Google Referrer Header Privacy Litigation*, 869 F.3d 737 (9th Cir. 2017), *cert. granted sub nom. Frank v. Gaos*, 138 S. Ct. 1697 (April 30, 2018), is a class action brought on behalf of 129 million people who used Google Search over nine years. The complaint alleged that Google violated class members' privacy rights under the Stored Communications Act and various state laws by disclosing their Internet search terms to third-party websites. It sought statutory and punitive damages as well as injunctive and declaratory relief. The terms of the settlement reached by the parties called for Google to pay $8.5 million, of which $3.5 million went to class counsel and incentive payments to representatives. The remaining $5 million was distributed in a *cy pres* arrangement to six institutions that "devote the funds to promote public awareness and education . . . related to protecting privacy on the Internet." The Ninth Circuit held that the district court did not abuse its discretion by approving the settlement. (The dissenting judge pointed out that 47 percent of the *cy pres* funds were being donated to class counsels' alma maters.)

The Supreme Court has granted certiorari in the case on the following issue: "Whether, or in what circumstances, a cy pres award of class action proceeds that provides no direct relief to class members supports class certification and comports with the requirement that a settlement binding class members must be 'fair, reasonable, and adequate.'" The case will be argued sometime during the October 2018 Term of the Supreme Court.

directs a remedy toward third parties who were not harmed by the defendant. 4 Newberg on Class Actions §§ 12:26, 12:27 (5th ed. 2018).

- **Incentive payments to the representative.** The representative is a member of the class and, as such, will be entitled to recover her share of any class recovery. Though Rule 23 does not refer to the practice, many courts permit an "incentive award" or "bonus" to the representative. They reason that the representative shouldered burdens and responsibilities on behalf of the class, and should be compensated for doing so. There is a good bit of case law about the details of these awards: the source of funding, eligibility, judicial review, and the size of the award.

  For our purposes, it is sufficient to note the potential conflict of interest caused by such a payment. Suppose the defendant offers to settle a class action by agreeing to pay the class lawyer a huge fee and the representative a large bonus, while doing very little for class members. We worry that the lawyer and the representative may be swayed by these sums, and not by their fiduciary duty to the class. This concern underlies the requirements, discussed in section E, that the court approve any settlement of a certified class action and that any "side deals" be made known. Depending upon the facts, courts seem to be comfortable with incentive payments in the $10,000–$15,000 range, but these are by no means routine. Higher payments tend to raise judicial eyebrows.

- **Medical Monitoring.** In "exposure-only" cases, one possible remedy is a court order for medical monitoring. Some states recognize a claim for medical monitoring, while others consider it a remedy "which must be supplemental to another cause of action." Edward Sherman, *No-Injury Plaintiffs and Standing*, 82 Geo. Wash. L. Rev. 834, 939 (2014). Though details vary, the idea is to have the defendant provide periodic testing for class members to determine whether they have manifested symptoms.

Questions

1. Would an order to set up a medical monitoring system be appropriate under Rule 23(b)(1), 23(b)(2), or 23(b)(3)?

2. Would the answer to Question 1 differ depending upon whether the court order:

   (a) Required the defendant to set up such a system, by arranging the engagement of doctors and laboratories or

   (b) Required the defendant to pay to set up such a system?

E. Settlement, Voluntary Dismissal, or Compromise of a (Certified) Class Action

1. The Need for Court Engagement; Rule 23(e)

Most class actions, like most lawsuits, are resolved by settlement rather than adjudication on the merits. In the non-class context, the parties generally are free to settle the case on whatever terms they agree to; after entering the settlement agreement, the plaintiff usually dismisses the case voluntarily. In the class action, however, the court must approve any settlement or voluntary dismissal of a certified class action. In addition, it must give notice to class members—in an effort to get their feedback on whether to approve a proposed settlement. (Though Rule 23(e) addresses voluntary dismissal and compromise as well as settlement, for simplicity we refer to settlement.)

This court engagement reflects the reality that class practice is filled with inherent potential conflicts of interest. Return to Example #5 from earlier in the chapter. It involves a consumer class action against Retailer with 100,000 class members, each having an average claim of $30.

> The aggregate class claim is $3,000,000. Retailer wants to settle the case. It approaches Class Lawyer and offers to settle by giving customers coupons for a nominal credit at Retailer stores, by paying the representative an "incentive fee" of $10,000, and by paying Class Lawyer a fee of $500,000.
>
> This is a very good deal for Retailer, who "buys peace" for $510,000 plus coupons that are unlikely to be redeemed. It is a very good deal for the representative, whose $30 claim has been parlayed into $10,000. And it is a very good deal for Class Lawyer, who makes $500,000 for relatively little effort.

But the central question is whether this is a good deal for the class members. And the only person in position to review the terms of the settlement objectively is the judge. As Judge Posner stated pointedly:

> ... The problem in the class-action setting, and the reason that judicial approval of the settlement of such an action is required, is that the negotiator on the plaintiffs' side, that is, the lawyer for the class, is potentially an unreliable agent of his principals.... Ordinarily the named plaintiffs are nominees, indeed pawns, of the lawyer, and ordinarily the unnamed class members have individually too little at stake to spend time monitoring the lawyer—and their only coordination is through him.... The danger of collusive settlements ... makes it imperative that the district judge conduct a careful inquiry into the fairness of a settlement to the class members before allowing it to go into effect and extinguish, by the operation of res judicata, the claims of the class members who do not opt out of the settlement....

Mars Steel Corp. v. Continental Illinois National Bank & Trust Co. of Chicago, 834 F.2d 677, 681–682 (7th Cir. 1987).

One problem for the judge, however, is that she can only know what the parties tell her. Accordingly, the procedural rules relating to judicial review of settlements must include some mechanism for disclosure to the court of the relevant facts and terms of the agreement. Rule 23(e) governs the process of court approval. It was amended effective December 1, 2018 (in ways that will be discussed).

Rule 23(e). Settlement, Voluntary Dismissal, or Compromise.

The claims, issues, or defenses of a certified class—or a class proposed to be certified for purposes of settlement—may be settled, voluntarily dismissed, or compromised only with the court's approval. The following procedures apply to a proposed settlement, voluntary dismissal, or compromise:

(1) **Notice to the Class.**

(A) *Information That Parties Must Provide to the Court.* The parties must provide the court with information sufficient to enable it to determine whether to give notice of the proposal to the class.

(B) *Grounds for a Decision to Give Notice.* The court must direct notice in a reasonable manner to all class members who would be bound by the proposal if giving notice is justified by the parties' showing that the court will likely be able to:

(i) approve the proposal under Rule 23(e)(2); and

(ii) certify the class for purposes of judgment on the proposal.

(2) **Approval of the Proposal.** If the proposal would bind class members, the court may approve it only after a hearing and only on finding that it is fair, reasonable, and adequate after considering whether:

(A) the class representatives and class counsel have adequately represented the class;

(B) the proposal was negotiated at arm's length;

(C) the relief provided for the class is adequate, taking into account:

(i) the costs, risks, and delay of trial and appeal;

(ii) the effectiveness of any proposed method of distributing relief to the class, including the method of processing class-member claims;

(iii) the terms of any proposed award of attorney's fees, including timing of payment; and

(iv) any agreement required to be identified under Rule 23(e)(3); and

(D) the proposal treats class members equitably relative to each other.

(3) **Identifying Agreements.** The parties seeking approval must file a statement identifying any agreement made in connection with the proposal.

(4) **New Opportunity to Be Excluded.** If the class action was previously certified under Rule 23(b)(3), the court may refuse to approve a settlement unless it affords a new opportunity to request exclusion to individual class members who had an earlier opportunity to request exclusion but did not do so.

(5) **Class-Member Objections.**

(A) *In General.* Any class member may object to the proposal if it requires court approval under this subdivision. The objection must state whether it applies only to the objector, to a specific subset of the class, or to the entire class, and also state with specificity the grounds for the objection.

(B) *Court Approval Required for Payment in Connection with an Objection.* Unless approved by the court after a hearing, no payment or other consideration may be provided in connection with:

(i) forgoing or withdrawing an objection, or

(ii) forgoing, dismissing, or abandoning an appeal from a judgment approving the proposal. . . .

[Subsection (C) is omitted.]

Notes and Questions

1. Rule 23(e) prescribes a process for assessing whether the court should approve a proposed settlement. Suppose a class action has been filed but not certified.

(a) Can the representative and the defendant agree to settle the representative's claim without going through this process (and, therefore, without court approval)?

(b) Can the defendant settle claims of individual class members without going through this process (and, therefore, without court approval)?

(c) For many years, it was not clear whether Rule 23(e) applied both to putative and certified classes. Courts reached inconsistent answers. What part of Rule 23(e) resolves that issue?

2. What information about the settlement must the parties provide to the court? When do they do so?

3. Rule 23(e)(2) was amended in 2018 to set out some factors for the court to consider in determining whether to approve a proposed settlement. Courts have developed factors over many years before that, as we will see below. Whatever the factors may be, what is the ultimate test for determining whether the court should approve the settlement?

4. Can the court approve a settlement without holding a hearing?

5. How does Rule 23(e) give class members a chance to voice their opinions of the proposed settlement?

2. Overview of the Process

When the lawyers for the parties have reached a settlement of a certified class, intended to bind class members, they present it to the court and request approval under Rule 23(e). The court undertakes a two-step assessment. First, the court considers whether to give "preliminary approval" to the settlement. This step is to determine whether the settlement is sufficiently promising to justify giving notice to the class members. If the court rejects preliminary approval, the lawyers go back to the bargaining table.

If the court grants preliminary (or "conditional") settlement, the next step is to send notice to the class members. The point of this notice, which comes from the court, is to allow class members to object to the proposed settlement. Notice under Rule 23(e)(1) must be given in "a reasonable manner to all class members who would be bound by the proposal." This provision applies in all three types of class action, so must be given to settle a Rule 23(b)(1) or 23(b)(2) or 23(b)(3) class action. This differs from notice of pendency of the class action, which, as we saw in section C.3.c, was required only in Rule 23(b)(3) classes.

Historically, "reasonable manner" has included mail and publication. Today, electronic means of notice may be used. Unlike the notice given to Rule 23(b)(3) class members under Rule 23(c)(2), there is no requirement that the notice be the best practicable under the circumstances. Neither is there a requirement of individual notice to class members who can be identified with reasonable effort. On the other hand, the Advisory Committee noted that individual notice might be appropriate if class members will be required to take some action, such as filing a claim, to participate in distribution of a settlement fund.

Rule 23(e) says nothing about the content of the notice. Clearly, it should include appropriate detail regarding the terms of the proposal, information on how to voice objections, and information about the fairness hearing. One important piece of information will be the terms concerning attorney's fees to be paid to class counsel.

The court then holds the "fairness hearing" to determine whether the settlement should be approved. The court determines that the settlement is fair, reasonable, and adequate, it will give the settlement "final approval" and it will be carried out according to its terms. If the court denies final approval, the case will proceed in litigation, or the court may postpone trial to allow the parties and lawyers to try again to settle the case.

This two-step approach is implicit in Rule 23(e)(1), which provides for notice to class members only if the parties demonstrate that the court is "likely" to approve the settlement and enter final judgment based upon it. If the court gives notice, it will schedule the fairness hearing. At that hearing, the sole question before the judge is whether the settlement is fair, reasonable, and adequate. The judge may not rewrite the parties' agreement. She may of course ask questions but ultimately either approves or rejects the proposed settlement.

Class members who object to the settlement—called "objectors"—may be heard at the hearing or otherwise, as the court decides. It is common to have objections stated in writing. The class members' reaction to the proposed settlement is not binding on the judge, but can be an important factor in determining whether to approve the agreement. We will see this point in the *General Motors* case below.

Rule 23(e)(4) is an interesting provision. It applies in Rule 23(b)(3) classes only. It envisions that the class members have received notice under Rule 23(c)(2) and have not opted out. Now they receive notice of the proposed settlement. Remember that the court cannot re-write the terms of the settlement. But the court may reject the settlement if it fails to give class members a second chance to opt out. This provision will not apply routinely. It is intended to protect class members when the terms of the settlement may be quite different from what was envisioned when the class was certified.

3. Getting Information to the Court

One goal of Rule 23(e) is to put the judge in a position to know whether the settlement is fair, reasonable, and adequate. To that end, Rule 23(e)(1)(A) instructs the parties to provide sufficient evidence from which the judge can determine whether to give notice to the class. Rule 23(e)(1)(B) provides that the court will only give notice if it is "likely" that the settlement will be approved. Thus, the parties must provide sufficient evidence to show whether the settlement is fair, reasonable, and adequate.

This language, added in 2018, is further evidence of front-loading of class litigation, because it "calls for the parties to present details bearing on the proposed settlement up front." Marcus, *supra*, 96 N.C. L. REV. at 933. In this regard, Rule 23(e)(2)(B)(ii) requires the court to assess "the effectiveness of any proposed method of distributing relief to the class, including the method of processing class-member claims." Thus, counsel should provide the court with details, for example, about how class members will make claims from any fund created by the settlement and, importantly, about what should be done with funds left over, if any, after class members make their claims. This latter point raises the possible use of *cy pres*, which, as we saw in section D.6, awards such funds to charitable groups. Professor Marcus notes that "addressing [*cy pres*] in a way that is accessible to class members could support arguments that they had in a sense assented to this disposition of unclaimed funds. If one regards the funds as the property of the class members, that could be important." Marcus, *supra*, 96 N.C. L. REV. at 934.

Other information to be provided to the court early, as reflected in Rule 23(e)(2)(B)(iii), are "the terms of any proposed award of attorney's fees, including timing of payment." The reference to timing of payment suggests the possibility that lawyer's fees may be deferred. For example, is the fee set as a percentage of the total fund contributed by the defendant—or of the fund that is actually distributed to class members? The answer to this question tells us a great deal about the lawyer's incentive to ensure payment to claimants. Marcus, *supra*, 96 N.C. L. Rev. at 934–935.

Thus, the Rule urges the lawyers to share with the court as much information as they can about the settlement—and early in the proceedings. This fact, in turn, enhances the notice given to class members: the more the court knows, the more it can share in the notice to the class. Presumably, this information leads to better decision-making by class members, including better assessments of whether the proposed settlement makes sense.

The Rule funnels more information to the court. Under Rule 23(e)(3), the parties must "file a statement identifying any agreement made in connection with the proposal." This provision deals with "side agreements"—deals that, while technically separate from the class settlement, may have influenced that settlement.

> ***Example #13.*** Representative and Defendant enter into an agreement which has nothing to do with the class recovery but which provides a huge benefit to the representative. The court should know about this "side agreement" because it may have been made to purchase the representative's acquiescence in the terms of the class settlement.

Rule 23(e) also provides the court with information about objections made by class members, which may provide an important perspective for the court. Sometimes, objections lead to denials of motions to certify. Sometimes they lead to redefinition of the class or the settlement. Sometimes, however, objectors do not act in the best interests of the class: "Many objectors inject themselves into class-action settlement proceedings primarily to obstruct or delay those proceedings, thereby inducing other counsel to give them a special recovery in return for dropping their objections." 7B Wright & Miller, Federal Practice and Procedure 169 (3d ed. 2018).

Section 23(e)(5) deals with these problems in two ways. First, Rule 23(e)(5)(A) requires that the class member's objection be stated with specificity and state whether it is made on behalf of the objector herself or on behalf of the class or a subset thereof. Second, Rule 23(e)(5)(B) forbids payments to objectors unless the court approves. The goal is to allow the court to ferret out whether the defendant paid off an objector to get her to withdraw what could be a legitimate objection.

4. "Settlement Classes"—*Amchem Products, Inc. v. Windsor*

A "settlement" class is one in which the parties never really intended to go to trial. (It is distinguished from a "litigation" class, which the parties intend to adjudicate.) In some cases, the parties work out a settlement before the case is even filed. Starting in the 1980s, an increasing number of settlement classes were filed in which the plaintiff sought class certification and approval of settlement simultaneously. Nothing in Rule 23 prohibits this "one-stop shopping," and, over time, courts frequently dealt with such cases. Some courts concluded that they could approve settlement under Rule 23(e) without assessing whether the class should be certified under Rules 23(a) and (b).

The Supreme Court rejected the practice in *Amchem Products, Inc. v. Windsor*, 521 U.S. 591 (1997). The Court made clear that Rule 23(e) does not supersede Rules 23(a) and (b). Rather, it is to be applied only *after* the court determines that certification is appropriate. The fact that a proposed settlement may be fair did not justify ignoring Rules 23(a) and (b). A case that purported to be a class action but did not satisfy the requirements simply cannot be said to be a legitimate, recognized form of litigation. Satisfying the certification requirements ensured that the court was dealing with a "case" and not some administrative creation.

However, the fact that a class was destined to be settled will affect the certification decision in one way (and only one way). Specifically, when the case is brought under Rule 23(b)(3), the factor in Rule 23(b)(3)(D)—"likely difficulties in managing a class action"—need not be addressed. If the case is to settle, there will be no trial and no intractable management problems.

Outside that, however, the certification requirements of Rule 23(a) and (b) must be satisfied. Indeed, the Court said, because of the concern with overly broad settlement certifications, those factors "demand undiluted—even heightened, attention in the settlement context." 521 U.S. at 620.

In the Rule 23(b)(3) context, simultaneous certification and settlement envisions that class members will receive unitary notice—one document that informs them that they are members of a Rule 23(b)(3) class and have the right to opt out while at the same time telling them that the court is considering whether to allow settlement on terms that are also set out in the notice.

Note on Settling Future Claims (More Amchem*)*

In section C.4, we discussed the "futures" problem—whether a class can include future members or present members who later manifest harm. The problem arises readily in toxic tort cases. The archetypal example concerned exposure to asbestos. The exposure caused physical injuries for thousands of people; their claim was for personal injuries. But thousands of others were exposed and had not yet manifested illness; indeed, hopefully, they never will. Some jurisdictions recognize an exposure-only claim, so people exposed can sue even before any manifestation of illness. But many people exposed to the toxin will not sue until they get sick.

Amchem involved thousands of claims against manufacturers of asbestos. The case as finally structured was a settlement class action—no one expected the case to be tried. The key driver to the settlement was the defendants' desire for "global peace." They wanted to settle not only the pending personal injury and exposure cases, but wanted reasonable assurance against claims to be filed in the future. (It is not irrational for defendants to want global peace; the question is whether the class action is a proper vehicle for achieving it.) Thus, the plaintiffs' lawyers were under pressure to find a way to settle present and future claims—literally, claims that had not yet been filed.

The result was a stunning labyrinth worthy of an administrative agency. We need not get trapped in the details—suffice it to say that the agreement purported to settle present and future claims. The Supreme Court refused to answer the fundamental question of whether exposure-only and future claimants had standing. It ruled based upon Rule 23, and held that the class failed to satisfy Rule 23(a)(4), because the representatives were not adequate, and Rule 23(b)(3), because common questions did not predominate over individual questions.

- *Adequacy of representation*. The Court focused on the stark conflict of interest between those presently injured and future claimants. The former want money now; the latter want money set aside in an inflation-proof fund to compensate them when and if they need it. The district court failed to establish subclasses, so the same representatives purported to represent everyone in the class. The Court, 521 U.S. at 626, explained:

  > The settling parties, in sum, achieved a global compromise with no structural assurance of fair and adequate representation for the diverse groups and individuals affected. Although the named parties alleged a range of complaints, each served generally as representative for the whole, not for a separate constituency.

  We saw the same problem in another significant asbestos case, *Ortiz v. Fibreboard Corp.*, which we discussed in section C.2.iv, concerning adequacy of representation.

Question

How could subclasses have alleviated the concern expressed in the quote above?

- *Notice*. *Amchem* was a Rule 23(b)(3) class, which requires that class members be provided the "best notice practicable" informing them of the class and of their right to opt out. The Court, 521 U.S. at 628, cast significant doubt on how such notice can be given in the futures situation:

  > . . . Many persons in the exposure-only category . . . may not even know of their exposure, or realize the extent of the harm they may incur. Even if they fully appreciate the significance of class notice, those without current afflictions may not have the information or foresight needed to decide, intelligently, whether to stay in or opt out.
  >
  > Family members of asbestos-exposed individuals may themselves fall prey to disease or may ultimately have ripe claims for loss of consortium. Yet large numbers of people in this category—future spouses and children of asbestos victims—could not be alerted to their class membership. And current spouses and children of [those] . . . exposed may know nothing of that exposure.

> Because we have concluded that the class in this case cannot satisfy the requirements of common issue predominance and adequacy of representation, we need not rule, definitively, on the notice given here.... [W]e recognize the gravity of the question whether class action notice sufficient under the Constitution and Rule 23 could ever be given to legions so unselfconscious and amorphous.

Question

Would such problems be irrelevant if the class were certified under Rule 23(b)(1) or (b)(2)?

5. Factors for Assessing Whether to Approve the Proposed Settlement

Under Rule 23(e)(2), the court may approve the proposed settlement only if it is "fair, reasonable, and adequate." Until 2018, the Rule did not include any factors for making this assessment. In 2018, it added a rather minimalist list: the court must "consider whether":

(A) the class representatives and class counsel have adequately represented the class;

(B) the proposal was negotiated at arm's length;

(C) the relief provided for the class is adequate, taking into account:

  (i) the costs, risks, and delay of trial and appeal;

  (ii) the effectiveness of any proposed method of distributing relief to the class, including the method of processing class-member claims;

  (iii) the terms of any proposed award of attorney's fees, including timing of payment; and

  (iv) any agreement required to be identified under Rule 23(e)(3); and

(D) the proposal treats class members equitably relative to each other.

Through the years, courts have generated considerable case law regarding factors to be considered in deciding whether a proposal should be approved. The general guidance now provided in Rule 23(e)(2) does not replace that case law, but may be said to structure the court's approach. It is impossible to catalogue every factor that comes into play, but some general observations are possible:

- the determination is made on a case-by-case basis
- the court will consider anything that bears on the ultimate question: whether the settlement is fair, reasonable, and adequate for class members; such things include—
  - the nature of claims and defenses
  - the thoroughness of the settlement process

- likelihood of success on the merits of both sides
- whether there are serious questions of law or fact
- whether the outcome, if litigated, is in doubt
- comparison of the settlement terms against what the class likely could win through trial
- whether the allocation of settlement remedies is fair
- remedial issues, such as fund distribution, fluid recovery, medical monitoring, or *cy pres*
- problems with giving notice to class members under Rule 23(e)
- whether future claims are waived
- whether the representative is receiving an unusually high "incentive award" or "bonus"
- the provision for attorney's fees to the class lawyer
- issues raised by objectors

It is important to understand the momentum faced by the judge. She knows only what the parties have told her. The parties and their lawyers are now unified—they all favor the settlement—so the judge will not receive the benefit of an adversarial presentation on any of the relevant issues. Lawyers the judge may know and respect have decided that the terms are just. Against all this momentum, the judge stands as the protector of class members' interests. She will want to know (but is not bound by) what objecting class members say—not only in terms of percentages for and against, but in their particular objections to the proposal. The 2018 amendment to Rule 23(e)(1)(A)—requiring the parties to provide information underlying the proposal early in the proceedings—is aimed at putting the judge in position to discharge her responsibility.

As you read the following case, consider whether the district court made its decision with too little information? If so, what information would have been helpful? Or did the district court simply fail to appreciate the importance of the information it had?

In re General Motors Pick-Up Truck Fuel Tank Product Liability Litigation

United States Court of Appeals, Third Circuit
55 F.3d 768 (1995)

BECKER, CIRCUIT JUDGE:

This is an appeal from an order of the District Court for the Eastern District of Pennsylvania approving the settlement of a large class action following its certification of a so-called settlement class. Numerous objectors challenge the fairness and reasonableness of the settlement. . . .

The class members are purchasers, over a 15 year period, of mid- and full-sized General Motors pick-up trucks with model C, K, R, or V chassis, which, it was subsequently determined, may have had a design defect in their location of the fuel tank. Objectors claim that the side-saddle tanks rendered the trucks especially vulnerable to fuel fires in side collisions. Many of the class members are individual owners (i.e., own a single truck), while others are "fleet owners," who own a number of trucks. Many of the fleet owners are governmental agencies. As will become apparent, the negotiated settlement treats fleet owners quite differently from individual owners, a fact with serious implications for the fairness of the settlement and the adequacy of representation of the class. . . .

. . . We . . . conclude that the settlement is not fair and adequate; more precisely, we hold that the district court abused its discretion in determining that it was, primarily because the district court erred in accepting plaintiffs' unreasonably high estimate of the settlement's worth, in over-estimating the risk of maintaining class status and of establishing liability and damages, and in misinterpreting the reaction of the class. . . .

I. Facts, Procedural History, and Standard of Review

A. General Background

Between 1973 and 1987, General Motors sold over 6.3 million C/K pickup trucks with side-mounted fuel tanks. In late October 1992, after the public announcement of previously undisclosed information regarding the safety of the fuel tank placement in GM pickups, consumer class action lawsuits were filed in several jurisdictions. The National Highway Traffic Safety Administration ("NHTSA") commenced an investigation of the alleged defects relating to side-impact fires on these trucks, and consumer advocacy groups sought a recall.

. . . Ultimately, dozens of actions were filed in various courts throughout the United States on behalf of consumer classes; the federal cases were dismissed, remanded to state court, or transferred to the Eastern District of Pennsylvania.

. . . [P]laintiffs filed a Consolidated Amended Class Action Complaint . . . that consolidated all of the actions . . . and listed nearly 300 representative plaintiffs, including both individual and fleet owners. The Complaint alleged violations of two federal statutes, the Magnuson-Moss Act and the Lanham Trademark Act; [and a variety of state-law claims]. The complaint sought, inter alia, an order . . . requiring GM to recall the trucks or pay for their repair. GM answered this complaint, denying all substantive allegations and raising numerous affirmative defenses.

[On the same day,] plaintiffs filed a consolidated motion for nationwide class certification. [The court allowed discovery focused on class certification issues, during which the parties reach a settlement in principle and informed the district judge.] For purposes of settlement only and without prejudice to GM's substantial opposition to class certification, the named parties agreed to the certification of a settlement class of C/K pickup owners, described below.

B. The Settlement Agreement

[T]he settlement agreement provides for members of the settlement class to receive $1,000 coupons redeemable toward the purchase of any new GMC Truck or Chevrolet light duty truck. Settlement certificates are transferable with the vehicle. They are redeemable by the then current owner of the 1973–86 C/K and 1987–91 R/V light duty pickup trucks or chassis cabs at any authorized Chevrolet or GMC Truck dealer for a fifteen month period. Settlement class members do not have to trade in their current vehicle to use the certificate, and the certificates can be used in conjunction with GM and GMAC incentive programs.

The class members can freely transfer the certificate to an immediate family member who resides with the class member. Class members can also transfer the $1000 certificate to a family member who does not reside with the class member by designating the transferee family member within sixty days, running from the date that GM mailed notice of the proposed settlement. Additionally, the $1000 certificate can be transferred with the title to the settlement class vehicle, that is, to a third party who purchases the class member's vehicle.

In lieu of a $1,000 certificate, and without transferring title to the settlement class vehicle, a class member may instead request that a nontransferable $500 certificate (counterintuitively known as the "transfer certificate") be issued to any third party except a GMC dealer or its affiliates. This $500 certificate is redeemable with the purchase of a new C or K series GMC or Chevrolet full-size pickup truck or its replacement model. The $500 certificate cannot be used in conjunction with any GMC or GMAC marketing incentive, must be used on the more expensive full size models, and is subject to the same fifteen-month redemption period as the $1,000 certificates....

Under the terms of the agreement, the approval of the settlement and corresponding entry of final judgment would have no effect upon any accrued or future claims for personal injury or death ...

The settlement agreement before us also provides that plaintiffs' counsel would apply to the district court for an award of reasonable attorneys' fees and reimbursement of expenses, both to be paid by GM.... Plaintiffs' counsel filed their fee applications ... [which] remained in the files of the clerk of the district court where class members could theoretically review them, but no information about attorneys' fees other than the fact that a fee application would be made was included in the class notice. GM did not file any formal objections to the fee applications.

C. Approval of the Settlement and Fees

The district court reviewed the substantive terms of the settlement on July 12, 1993 and made the preliminary determination ... that the proposed settlement appeared reasonable. Also ... the court "provisionally" certified the class of GM truck owners as a settlement class (i.e., for settlement purposes only) pursuant to Rule 23(b)(3) .... The court approved the form of and dissemination to putative class members of the combined notice of the pendency of the action and the proposed settlement pursuant to Rules 23(c)(2) and 23(e). . . .

In response to the notice, over 5,200 truck owners elected to opt out of the class, and approximately 6,500 truck owners (a number which includes fleet owners who own as many as 1,000 vehicles each) objected to the settlement. . . .

A settlement fairness hearing was held . . . during which the objectors who submitted written briefs were permitted to speak. The district court approved the settlement in a Memorandum and Order . . . In that order, the court confirmed its [previous order] which had provisionally certified the settlement class. [It also] set forth findings of fact and conclusions of law to justify its approval of the settlement as fair, reasonable and adequate . . . .

. . . .

II. Anatomy of the Class Claims

. . . The case did not involve any pickup trucks that had actually experienced fuel tank fires caused by side-impact collisions. Moreover, personal injury or death claims were expressly omitted from the complaint as well as from the settlement—class members remain free to pursue such claims if any should accrue.

The aggregated treatment of these claims was potentially complicated by the differences in underlying facts. The trucks at issue had nineteen different fuel tank systems; proof might thus be required for each design on relevant issues. Furthermore, unlike the federal securities laws where there is a presumption of reliance on a material misrepresentation . . . plaintiffs would likely have had to prove individual reliance on the allegedly misleading materials under the various state laws applicable to most of these claims. More fundamentally, the complaint itself invoked state laws that implicated different legal standards on, for example, the warranty claims (the laws contain various privity requirements or the need for an allegedly defective product to fail in service before a warranty claim can be sustained), negligent misrepresentation, negligence, and strict products liability. . . .

III. Rule 23—Relevant Fundamental Principles

. . . .

. . . [T]his court has adopted a nine-factor test to help district courts structure their final decisions to approve settlements as fair, reasonable, and adequate as required by Rule 23(e). *See Girsh v. Jepson*, 521 F.2d 153, 157 (3d Cir. 1975). Those factors are: (1) the complexity and duration of the litigation; (2) the reaction of the class to the settlement; (3) the stage of the proceedings; (4) the risks of establishing liability; (5) the risks of establishing damages; (6) the risks of maintaining a class action; (7) the ability of the defendants to withstand a greater judgment; (8) the range of reasonableness of the settlement in light of the best recovery; and (9) the range of reasonableness of the settlement in light of all the attendant risks of litigation. The proponents of the settlement bear the burden of proving that these factors weigh in favor of approval. . . .

VI. Is the Settlement Fair, Reasonable, and Adequate?

Invoking the correct standard of review under *Girsh v. Jepson*, . . . the objectors . . . argue that the district court abused its discretion when it approved the settlement as fair, reasonable, and adequate. . . . Rule 23(e) imposes on the trial judge the duty of protecting absentees, which is executed by the court's assuring that the settlement represents adequate compensation for the release of the class claims. . . . Some courts have described their duty under Rule 23(e) as the "fiduciary responsibility" of ensuring that the settlement is fair and not a product of collusion. . . .

There are certain basic questions that courts can ask to detect those cases settled in the absence of sustained effort by class representatives sufficient to protect the interests of the absentees. For instance: Is the relief afforded by the settlement *significantly* less than what appears appropriate in light of the preliminary discovery? Have major causes of action or types of relief sought in the complaint been omitted by the settlement? Did the parties achieve the settlement after little or no discovery? Does it appear that the parties negotiated simultaneously on attorneys' fees and class relief? . . . [T]hese questions raise a red flag in this case.

. . . .

A. Adequacy of Settlement—General Principles

This inquiry measures the value of the settlement itself to determine whether the decision to settle represents a good value for a relatively weak case or a sell-out of an otherwise strong case. The *Girsh* test calls upon courts to make this evaluation from two slightly different vantage points. According to *Girsh*, courts approving settlements should determine a range of reasonable settlements in light of the best possible recovery (the eighth *Girsh* factor) and a range in light of all the attendant risks of litigation (the ninth factor). . . .

In formulaic terms we agree that "in cases primarily seeking monetary relief, the present value of the damages plaintiffs would likely recover if successful, appropriately discounted for the risk of not prevailing, should be compared with the amount of the proposed settlement." [Manual for Complex Litigation] 2d § 30.44, at 252. This figure should generate a range of reasonableness (based on size of the proposed award and the uncertainty inherent in these estimates) within which a district court approving (or rejecting) a settlement will not be set aside. . . . The evaluating court must, of course, guard against demanding too large a settlement based on its view of the merits of the litigation; after all, settlement is a compromise, a yielding of the highest hopes in exchange for certainty and resolution. . . . The primary touchstone of this inquiry is the economic valuation of the proposed settlement.

. . . .

1. Valuation of the Settlement—Introduction

The value of the $1,000 certificates is sharply disputed. GM argues that the certificates are worth close to their face value since they can be redeemed for a broad array of GM trucks and can be used in combination with dealer incentives. For those unable or unwilling to purchase another GM truck, GM argues, cash can be realized from transferring the certificate within the household for full value or selling the certificate for $500. Plaintiffs presented an expert, Dr. Itmar Simonsen, who placed the value of the certificates between $1.98 and $2.18 billion, based on an estimate that 34% to 38% of the class would redeem the certificate in purchasing a new truck and an additional 11% of the class would sell their certificates for $500. Objectors contest these estimates and many of the assumptions used to generate them.

We therefore analyze several of the foundations for the district court's evaluation. . . . [Doing so] lead[s] ineluctably to the conclusion that the district court overvalued this settlement, which in turn gives credence to the contention of the objectors that the proffered settlement was, in reality, a sophisticated GM marketing program.

a. Plaintiffs' Witness Dr. Itmar Simonsen

Dr. Simonsen's methods and assumptions raise serious doubts about the reliability of the valuations they generated. Although Simonsen's conclusion was based on his estimate that between 34% and 38% of the class members would use the certificate, his own telephone survey revealed that only 14% of the class reported that they would "definitely" or "probably" buy a new truck. Apparently Simonsen only excluded those who responded that they would "definitely not buy" or "probably not buy" a new truck, a methodological choice which is questionable. Furthermore, Simonsen discounted the statistics by seemingly arbitrary factors in an effort to be "conservative," but without some basis or explanation for the derivation of those factors, we have no way of judging whether they were conservative or aggressive.

Even more importantly, the raw survey data probably overstate the prospects that the certificates will be used since there are substantial obstacles to obtaining and transferring the certificates, none of which Simonsen deals with. Finally, Simonsen supposed that a higher percentage of fleet owners than individual owners would redeem the certificates, but this seems to disregard the statutory and regulatory constraints that often restrict fleet buyers' purchase decisions. Indubitably all of these concerns reduce the value of the settlement, yet Simonsen appears simply to have multiplied his estimated number of users by the coupon amount or transfer value.

. . . .

b. Inability of Class Members to Use Certificates

The district court also erred by not adequately accounting for the different abilities (not inclinations) of class members to use the settlement. One sign that a settlement may not be fair is that some segments of the class are treated differently from others. . . . Consequently, the fact that the coupon settlement benefits certain groups of the class more than others suggests that the district court did not adequately discharge its duties to safeguard the interests of the absentees. . . .

People of lesser financial means will be unable to benefit comparably from the settlement. GM cites a number of other judicially approved class action settlements that awarded coupons and argues that, since this coupon provides far more consideration, it necessarily merits approval. . . .

These cases, however, differ dramatically in the amount of money required to purchase the good—i.e. to realize the certificate's value—and in the frequency with which a typical consumer might expect to purchase the good. Whether a new truck costs between $20,000 and $33,000 . . . this purchase is not comparable to buying a new food processor or even an airline ticket. As the district court acknowledged, "a substantial number of class members" would not be able to afford a new truck within the fifteen month coupon period. . . .

Even where class members do manage to use the certificates, we are concerned about their real value. It may not be the case that the certificates saved those class members $1,000 on something they would have otherwise bought; those class members may only have purchased new GM trucks because they felt beholden to use the certificates. Thus, rather than providing substantial value to the class, the certificate settlement might be little more than a sales promotion for GM. . . .

We turn then to the fleet buyers, who constitute a readily identifiable category of plaintiffs arguably disadvantaged by the settlement. Budgetary constraints prevent some of them from replacing their entire fleets within the fifteen month redemption period. . . .

. . . .

c. Value of the Transfer Option

In order to support its conclusion that the settlement was reasonable and fair, the district court cited the ability of fleet buyers and those consumers with budget constraints to realize value from the certificates by transferring them. We believe that the value of the transfer option is dubious, and consequently that the settlement was unfair to substantial portions of the class.

. . . .

d. GM's Implicit Valuation of the Claim

Our concerns about the adequacy of the settlement are complicated by the generous attorneys' fees GM agreed to pay in this case. Although originally GM vigorously contested the viability of the class claims and the class, the company, in view of its willingness to pay attorneys' fees of $9.5 million, may, at the time of settlement, have valued the claims at some substantial multiple of the fee award.[28] This $9.5 million attorney's fee award seems unusually large in light of the fact that the settlement

---

28. [Court's footnote #27] GM was apparently so eager to have this $9.5 million fee approved that its counsel did not even object when the district court applied a multiplier notwithstanding clear Supreme Court precedent invalidating the use of multipliers. *See City of Burlington v. Dague*, [505 U.S. 557]. In our view, the fact that counsel to this large multinational corporation did not

itself offered no cash outlay to the class. GM's apparent willingness to pay plaintiffs' counsel close to $9.5 million indicates that the party in perhaps the best position to evaluate the claim may have thought the action, which both plaintiffs' counsel and the defense contend was not worth much, posed a significant enough threat to cause GM to strike a lucrative deal with plaintiffs' counsel.

. . . .

2. Valuing This Settlement Relative to the Relief Requested

The ninth *Girsh* factor also undermines the district court's decision. In the class action context, "the relief sought in the complaint" serves as a useful benchmark in deciding the reasonableness of a settlement. . . . The coupons offered by GM simply do not address the safety defect that formed the central basis of the amended complaint filed barely four months before the settlement.[29] . . .

. . . .

B. Complexity of the Suit

This factor is intended to capture "the probable costs, in both time and money, of continued litigation." . . . By measuring the costs of continuing on the adversarial path, a court can gauge the benefit of settling the claim amicably. The district court here concluded that the litigation "would be mammoth" and would have resulted in a "substantial delay in . . . recovery."

[Trial of] the action would . . . involve a complex web of state and federal warranty, tort, and consumer protection claims even if the class had been subdivided and some of the legal issues simplified. Had the case not been settled, both plaintiffs and GM would have had to conduct discovery into the background of the six million vehicles owned by class members, including any representations allegedly made to plaintiffs. Each side would also have needed to hire or produce a retinue of experts to testify on a variety of complex issues. Undoubtedly, GM would have ardently contested the action at every step, leading to a plethora of pretrial motions. In contrast, this settlement made its remedies immediately available and avoided the substantial delay and expense that would have accompanied the pursuit of this litigation. The district court thus correctly concluded that the complexity factor weighed in favor of approving the settlement.

C. Reaction of the Class

. . . [C]ourts look to the number and vociferousness of the objectors. Courts have generally assumed that "silence constitutes tacit consent to the agreement." . . .

---

object to this clear error raises a smoking gun signaling GM's awareness of the questionable settlement it made. [We will discuss multipliers in Chapter 7.]

29. [Court's footnote #28] In the amended consolidated complaint, class counsel described the trucks as "rolling firebombs" and estimated that an additional 200 deaths would occur unless GM took prompt corrective action.

In a class action case involving securities litigation, this court has recognized the possibility that the assumption that silence constitutes tacit consent "understates potential objectors since many shareholders have small holdings or diversified portfolios, . . . and thus have an insufficient incentive to contest an unpalatable settlement agreement because the cost of contesting exceeds the objector's pro rata benefit." . . . Although this is not a securities class action and the amounts at stake could be significant, the absentees may not fully appreciate the size of their potential claims since, by excluding those owners whose trucks have already experienced some mishap related to the fuel tank design, the class may include only those who have no reason (outside of media coverage) to know of the latent defect or the claim based on the alleged existence of that defect.

Even where there are no incentives or informational barriers to class opposition, the inference of approval drawn from silence may be unwarranted. As we noted earlier, Judge Posner has explained that "where notice of the class action is . . . sent simultaneously with the notice of the settlement itself, the class members are presented with what looks like a fait accompli." . . . In this case especially, the combined notice largely defeats the potential for objection since the notice did not inform the class that the original complaint had sought a retrofit.[30] Without information about the original complaint, absentees lacked any basis for comparing the settlement offered to them to the original prayer. It is instructive that many of the better-informed absentees, the fleet owners, did object.

. . . .

Although the absolute number of objectors was relatively low,[31] there are other indications that the class reaction to the suit was quite negative: The seemingly low number of objectors includes some fleet owners who each own as many as 1,000 trucks, and those who did object did so quite vociferously. In conjunction with the already-noted problems associated with assuming that the class members possessed adequate interest and information to voice objections, the appeals of those who actually objected demonstrate that the reaction of the class was actually negative, and not supported by the "vast majority of the class members" as the district court concluded. The class reaction factor plainly does not, contrary to the district court's conclusion, weigh in favor of approving the settlement.

D. Stage of Proceedings

The stage-of-proceedings facet of the *Girsh* test captures the degree of case development that class counsel have accomplished prior to settlement. Through this lens,

---

30. [Court's footnote #31] There may also have been other deficiencies in the notice. The fact that the notice did not disclose the attorneys fees that the class counsel and defendants agreed to, and the fact that the notice suggested that class members could also have a recall remedy from NHTSA (though many of the trucks were so old that NHTSA lacked the power to recall them), may also have helped suppress potential objection.

31. [Court's footnote #32] Of approximately 5.7 million class members, 6,450 owners objected and 5,203 opted out.

courts can determine whether counsel had an adequate appreciation of the merits of the case before negotiating. The district court found that this factor favored settlement approval, relying on the fact that settlement was presented for approval less than six months prior to the scheduled trial date.

. . . .

The relevant period of time this case was in litigation was quite brief; approximately four months elapsed from the filing of the consolidated complaint to the reaching of the settlement agreement. To be sure, we cannot measure the extent of counsel's effort from the time of the litigation alone; class counsel in this case are known to be quite industrious, and the district court properly considered class counsel's review of the materials from prior product liability proceedings . . . However, mere access to the materials from other proceedings does not establish that counsel developed the merits, particularly where the other cases were premised on different theories of recovery. [N]othing in the record demonstrates that [counsel] had conducted significant independent discovery or investigations to develop the merits of their case (as opposed to supporting the value of the settlement), that they had retained their own experts, or that they had deposed a significant number of the individuals implicated in the materials from these other proceedings. . . .

At all events, the inchoate stage of case development reduces our confidence that the proceedings had advanced to the point that counsel could fairly, safely, and appropriately decide to settle the action. . . .

Beyond the incipient stage of the case and the modest indications of substantive development, there is little basis for presuming vigorous prosecution of the case from the fact that settlement negotiations occurred. In ordinary class action settlements (i.e., where the court certifies the class before settlement negotiations commence) courts can presume that the negotiations occurred at arm's length because they have already determined that the counsel negotiating on behalf of the class adequately represents the class's interests. . . . In cases such as this one, however, where there has been no determination by the court that a proper class exists, the mere fact that negotiations transpired does not tend to prove that the class's interests were pursued. . . .

Furthermore, to the extent that this stage-of-proceedings factor also aims to assure that courts have enough exposure to the merits of the case to enable them to make these evaluations, it cannot support settlement approval here. With little adversarial briefing on either class status or the substantive legal claims, the district court had virtually nothing to aid its evaluation of the settlement terms. We therefore conclude that the district court clearly erred in finding that this factor weighed in favor of settlement approval.

E. Risks of Establishing Liability

By evaluating the risks of establishing liability, the district court can examine what the potential rewards (or downside) of litigation might have been had class counsel elected to litigate the claims rather than settle them. . . . The district court here concluded that this factor also weighed in favor of approving the settlement since "there appear[ed] to be a substantial risk in establishing liability because of the complexity and size of the case along with the legal and factual problems raised by GM." While we agree with the district court that, on balance, the prospective difficulty faced by a nationwide class of establishing liability favored settlement, we believe the question is much closer than it thought, and thus the factor does not weigh heavily in favor of settlement as the district court believed.

. . . .

F. Risks of Establishing Damages

. . . .

. . . In assessing this *Girsh* factor, the district court relied on its belief that the class could not demonstrate any diminution of the trucks' value relative to Ford and Dodge trucks by referring to the Kelley Blue Book.

We do not, however, believe that this is the only permissible approach to measuring the value of the defect. According to the Uniform Commercial Code, "the measure of damages for breach of warranty is the difference at the time and place of acceptance between the value of the goods accepted and the value they would have had if they had been as warranted, unless special circumstances show proximate damages of a different amount." Although diminished resale value might represent one method of measuring the damage suffered by owners from the publicity about the fuel tanks, it does not fully measure the difference between the value the defect-free truck would have had at delivery and the actual value of the truck as delivered. Measuring damages with a focus on resale value confounds the effects of varying rates of depreciation with the effect of the defect on the market value. . . .

The cost of a retrofit, which effectively puts the truck in the condition in which it allegedly should have been delivered, may constitute an alternative measure of the damages arising from the breach of warranty. . . .

Because the district court based its appraisal of this factor on its exclusive reference to the Kelley Blue Book and refused to consider alternative measures that appear to provide concrete (and substantial) damage figures, we believe that the court erred in finding that the risks of proving damages were so great that they strongly favored settlement approval.

G. Risks of Maintaining Class Status

. . . .

The district court found that this factor favored settlement . . . . The Court cited the "myriad factual and legal issues" and the vigorous contest waged by GM prior to settlement negotiations as the basis for this finding. Two observations, which the district court appeared to ignore, weaken the basis for its finding that the risk involved in maintaining class status favored settlement.

First, Rule 23(a) does not require that class members share every factual and legal predicate to meet the commonality and typicality standards. . . . Indeed, a number of mass tort class actions have been certified notwithstanding individual issues of causation, reliance, and damages. . . .

. . . .

Second, even if the action could not be certified as it was originally filed, the district court disregarded the possibility that there were other ways to aggregate the litigation and/or adjudication of these claims. The court might have considered dividing the class into geographic or model-year sub-classes or allowing the case to continue as a multi-district litigation for the remainder of pre-trial discovery. Each of those alternatives could have surmounted some of the individual issues while retaining some of the substantive advantages of the class action as framed here. Thus, the court's conclusion that this factor favored settlement may have reflected its mistaken all-or-nothing approach to certifying this national class.

. . . .

H. Ability to Withstand Greater Judgment

We find no error in the district court's resolution of this final *Girsh* factor—whether the defendant has the ability to withstand a greater judgment. The district court determined that GM "could withstand a judgment greater than the proposed settlement," although it did not attribute any significance to this finding "under these facts. . . ."

I. Summary

[W]e hold that the settlement is not fair, reasonable, or adequate under the nine factor *Girsh* test of this circuit. . . .

Notes and Questions

1. Was the district court's error the result of:

a. its having insufficient information or

b. its failure to appreciate the information it had?

2. In some cases, the district judge oversees the settlement process directly, interacting with the lawyers as they attempt to forge agreement. There is a risk that the judge may become so invested in the settlement that she finds it difficult to determine whether the settlement is "fair, reasonable, and adequate."

A vivid example is the role taken by the district judge in engineering the settlement of the *Agent Orange* cases. Despite what some assert was the judge's strong suspicion that the plaintiffs would not likely prevail on the merits if the case were tried, the judge cajoled a settlement by setting an inflexible trial date, hiring a consultant to develop a settlement strategy, appointing a special master to handle negotiations, advising the parties of how he would likely rule on certain issues, and convening a negotiating marathon the weekend before trial was to begin. *See* PETER H. SCHUCK, AGENT ORANGE ON TRIAL: MASS TOXIC DISASTERS IN THE COURTS 143–67 (1986). Some conclude that the judge's hands-on engagement made it difficult, if not impossible, to perform the task of determining whether the settlement that he himself largely had crafted and pressed upon the parties was "fair, reasonable, and adequate" as required by Rule 23. Peter H. Schuck, *The Role of Judges in Settling Complex Cases: The Agent Orange Example*, 53 U. Chi. L. Rev. 337, 361–362 (1986).

In Chapter 3.C, we saw that a district judge might rely on adjuncts—particularly on magistrate judges—to oversee the settlement process, thus retaining her objectivity when it comes time to assess whether the settlement should be approved.

3. In *In re Prudential Insurance Company America Sales Practice Litigation Agent Actions*, 148 F.3d 283, 323–324 (3d Cir. 1998), the Third Circuit employed the "*Girsh* factors" that were used in the *General Motors* case, but added the following:

> it may be useful to expand the traditional *Girsh* factors to include, when appropriate, these factors among others: the maturity of the underlying substantive issues, as measured by experience in adjudicating individual actions, the development of scientific knowledge, the extent of discovery on the merits, and other factors that bear on the ability to assess the probable outcome of a trial on the merits of liability and individual damages; the existence and probable outcome of claims by other classes and subclasses; the comparison between the results achieved by the settlement for individual class or subclass members and the results achieved—or likely to be achieved—for other claimants; whether class or subclass members are accorded the right to opt out of the settlement; whether any provisions for attorneys' fees are reasonable; and whether the procedure for processing individual claims under the settlement is fair and reasonable.

As we said at the outset, there is no magic formula. The court must assess all available information relevant to the task of determining whether the proposed settlement is "fair, reasonable, and adequate" for the class members.

F. The Class Action: Jurisdiction and Related Issues

1. Subject Matter Jurisdiction

Like any case in federal court, a class action must invoke a basis of federal subject matter jurisdiction. We reviewed the two principal bases of such jurisdiction—federal question under 28 U.S.C. § 1331 and diversity of citizenship under 28 U.S.C. § 1332(a)(1)—in Chapter 2.B.

A class might invoke federal question jurisdiction under 28 U.S.C. § 1331 by asserting a claim that arises under federal law. Examples include classes for violations of federal securities, antitrust, employment, and civil rights laws.

In the non-class context, a case invokes diversity of citizenship jurisdiction, as we reviewed in Chapter 2, (1) if all plaintiffs are of diverse citizenship from all defendants and (2) the amount in controversy exceeds $75,000. In the class action, since class members are not parties to the case, do we include their citizenships or amounts in controversy?

The law developed oddly in this area. As to citizenship, the Court held in 1921 the representative had to be of diverse citizenship from every defendant. The citizenship of other class members was irrelevant. *Supreme Tribe of Ben-Hur v. Cauble*, 255 U.S. 356, 366–367 (1921).[32] This remains the law.

> ***Example #14.*** Representative (a citizen of California) brings a class action on behalf of a class of citizens of California and Arizona. Defendant is a citizen of Arizona. Citizenship is satisfied, because Representative is of diverse citizenship from Defendant. (If there were multiple representatives, each must be of diverse citizenship from all defendants.)

As to amount in controversy, however, the Court did just the opposite: it held that each class member's claim must meet the statutory requirement. *Zahn v. International Paper*, 414 U.S. 291, 301 (1973). Under *Zahn*, then, each member of the class must have a claim that exceeds $75,000.

This result was abrogated, however, by the supplemental jurisdiction statute, 28 U.S.C. § 1367. As we saw in *Exxon Mobil Corp. v. Allapattah Services*, 545 U.S. 546, 559–567 (2005), which we read in Chapter 2.C.2.b, the Court held that class members' claims not exceeding $75,000 will invoke supplemental jurisdiction. It is imperative, however, that the representative's claim exceed $75,000 (so the case will invoke diversity of citizenship).

> ***Example #15.*** Representative's claim exceeds $75,000, but class members' claims are capped at $20,000 apiece. The claim by Representative against Defendant invokes diversity of citizenship jurisdiction: as we saw in Example #14, it is asserted by a citizen of California against a citizen of Arizona and, as we see here, it exceeds $75,000. The court will have supplemental jurisdiction over the claims asserted by the class members.

At the end of the day, then, citizenship and amount in controversy are reckoned in the same way: the court looks to the representative. *Allapattah* made it easier for a class to invoke diversity of citizenship. On the other hand, it requires that the representative's claim exceed $75,000. That will rarely be the true with negative-value claims, such as most consumer cases. As we saw in Chapter 2.D.4, however, the Class Action Fairness Act (CAFA) vastly expanded federal subject matter jurisdiction for class actions. As we saw in detail there, a case invokes CAFA jurisdiction if *any* class member is of diverse citizenship from *any* defendant and if the class claims, in the aggregate, exceed $5,000,000.

---

32. The Court might have based this holding on supplemental jurisdiction, but did not. It simply treated the representative as the only party on the plaintiff side. Moreover, the term "supplemental jurisdiction" did not become part of the lexicon until 1990, with passage of the supplemental jurisdiction statute, 28 U.S.C. § 1367.

2. Personal Jurisdiction

Phillips Petroleum Co. v. Shutts, 472 U.S. 797 (1985), was a Rule 23(b)(3) class action in state court in Kansas (the Kansas rule mirrored Rule 23). The class consisted of 33,000 holders of royalty interests in oil and gas wells situated in several states, including Kansas, Texas, and Oklahoma. The defendant delayed making royalty payments to class members. When it finally made the payments, it failed to pay interest for the period of the delay. The class sued to recover the interest claims. Most claims were for around $100. After opt outs, the class consisted of roughly 28,000 members. The Kansas courts held that they had personal jurisdiction over all class members and that Kansas law governed on the substantive issues concerning the defendant's liability.

In *Shutts*, the Supreme Court held that Kansas erred by applying Kansas law to the claims of non-Kansas class members. We read that portion of the opinion in Chapter 4.D.1. Now we focus on the personal jurisdiction aspect of the case. The Court held that all members of the class, *even those who had no contacts with Kansas*, were bound by the judgment. Though an adverse judgment would extinguish the claims of class members, plaintiff class members are in a significantly different position from defendants. The defendant must hire a lawyer in the forum, participate in discovery, and faces the imposition of liability. Because these burdens are so substantial, the law requires that the defendant have minimum contacts with the forum and be served with process.

Plaintiff class members, in contrast, are not required to hire lawyers, are generally not subject to discovery, and do not face the imposition of liability. "A class-action plaintiff is not required to do anything. He may sit back and allow the litigation to run its course, content in knowing that there are safeguards provided for his protection." 472 U.S. at 808. In light of these differences, due process rights of plaintiff class members are protected by affording them notice and the opportunity to opt out. The fact that they did not opt out means that they are subject to personal jurisdiction in Kansas.

Questions

1. How can a court in a state with which a class member has no contacts require her to take an affirmative act (opt out) to avoid being bound by a judgment?

2. In *Shutts*, the Court expressly limited its holding to Rule 23(b)(3) plaintiff classes. Should the holding in *Shutts* apply in Rule 23(b)(1) and (b)(2) classes? Perhaps not, because those class members do not have the opportunity to opt out. On the other hand, they, like Rule 23(b)(3) plaintiff class members, are "along for the ride."

3. Should *Shutts* apply to defendant classes?

4. Can plaintiff class members always "sit back and allow the litigation to run its course"? Suppose the defendant asserts a counterclaim against the class. Or

suppose the defendant, if it prevails, would be entitled to recover attorneys' fees from the plaintiff side. Can class members be required to pay a counterclaim judgment or attorney's fees even if they have no minimum contacts with the forum state?

5. In section D(4), we saw that a court might require class members to respond to discovery requests. Can it do so with regard to members who lack minimum contacts with the forum state?

6. One upshot of *Shutts* is that a state court may have personal jurisdiction over class members but lack the power to impose state substantive law for adjudicating their claims. Should it be easier for a state to exercise personal jurisdiction than to apply its substantive law? We addressed that and related questions in Chapter 4.D.

3. Mootness and Standing

Under Article III of the Constitution, federal courts may only hear "cases" or "controversies." They may not, for example, issue advisory opinions. Various doctrines of "justiciability" determine whether an action constitutes a case or controversy, and you study them in detail in Constitutional Law. We focus on two that have special class action wrinkles: mootness and standing.

a. Mootness

Mootness requires that the claimant have a "live" claim—a harm that will be remedied if she wins a judgment. In the class context, we worry about what happens to the class action if the representative's claim becomes moot. We address three scenarios.

> ***Scenario 1.*** Representative files a class action. The court certifies the class, after which Representative's claim becomes moot. As long as some class member has a "live" claim, the case will not be dismissed as moot. Moreover, depending on the facts, Representative may remain an appropriate representative.

This scenario is based upon *Sosna v. Iowa*, 419 U.S. 393 (1975), in which a woman sued to challenge a state residency requirement. The law provided that no one could seek a divorce in Iowa unless she had lived there for at least one year. Plaintiff's class argued that the requirement was unconstitutional. In upholding standing, the Court emphasized the importance of class certification. When the class is certified, we essentially consider the class itself to be the plaintiff. As long as (1) Representative's claim was live when the class was certified and (2) some class members have live claims after Representative's claim becomes moot, the case survives.

> ***Scenario 2.*** Representative files a class action. *Before the court rules on certification,* Representative's claim becomes moot. Here, the case becomes moot. However, most courts will allow the case to continue if a class member with a live claim intervenes and qualifies as the new class representative.

Here, because the class was not certified, the court will not consider the class to be the plaintiff. The sole plaintiff was Representative, and her claim is moot. But "the fact that certification has not taken place before the representative's individual claim is lost does not necessarily mean that the suit is not a proper class action." 7AA Wright & Miller, Federal Practice and Procedure 419 (3d ed. 2018). Accordingly, a member with a live claim can intervene under Rule 24 and qualify as the representative. Courts addressing this situation say that the certification with the new representative would "relate back" to filing and thus avoid dismissal. *Id.*

> ***Scenario 3.*** Representative files a class action. The court *denies* the motion to certify the class. At this point, Representative can seek appellate review of the denial of certification because her claim is still live. But suppose Representative's claim now becomes moot. May Representative seek appellate review of the denial of certification?

In *United States Parole Commission v. Geraghty*, 445 U.S. 388, 403 (1980), the Court said yes. It distinguished two issues in any class action: the propriety of certification and the merits. The fact that the representative's claim on the merits was moot did not rob him of the personal stake he had in the class-certification issue.

For years, some defendants attempted to create mootness by making an offer of judgment under Rule 68 to the representative. The offer would satisfy the representative's claim fully. If the representative accepted the offer, her claim would become moot. What if she rejected the offer? Some defendants then would move to dismiss, arguing that the representative's claim was moot because an offer of full compensation was pending—the representative did not have to litigate her claim.

Some lower courts agreed with the argument that the defendant could "pick off" representatives in this way. The Supreme Court, however, rejected it. The Court held that an unaccepted settlement offer has no effect and does not create mootness. "Like other unaccepted contract offers, it creates no lasting right or obligation. With the offer off the table, and the defendant's continuing denial of liability, adversity between the parties persists." *Campbell-Ewald Co. v. Gomex*, 136 S. Ct. 663, 666 (2016).

Questions

1. In Scenario 2, could the lawyer representing Representative have contacted putative class members to inquire into their interest to serve as representative? Remember our discussion of communicating with class members in section D.3.

2. In Scenario 1, there is no doubt that the class lawyer could have contacted class members to make that inquiry. Why? (After certification, who is the lawyer's client?)

b. Standing, "Exposure-Only" Claims, and the Problem of the "No-Injury Class"

Standing requires that the claimant have suffered actual harm. In the class context, "the court must be able to find that both the class and the representatives have suffered some injury requiring court intervention." 7AA WRIGHT & MILLER, FEDERAL PRACTICE AND PROCEDURE 390 (3d ed. 2018).

"Exposure-only" claims, in which claimants have been exposed to a toxic material but have not yet manifested symptoms, raise significant issues of standing. Some states do not recognize a separate claim for exposure; some states require proof of some likelihood of contracting an illness; still others appear to require an accompanying physical injury. Beyond that is the question of whether an exposure claim satisfies the "concreteness" or "injury in fact" requirements for constitutional standing. Professor Sherman summarizes:

> In mass tort cases involving exposure to toxic substances like asbestos, many courts have found the injury in fact requirement for standing satisfied only by an increased risk of a medical condition at a later time. This rationale has also been extended to delayed manifestation in pharmaceutical and medical device litigation where the plaintiff's condition due to exposure can be viewed as a "ticking time bomb" for possible future injury.

Edward Sherman, *No-Injury Plaintiffs and Standing, supra*, 82 GEO. WASH. L. REV. at 937–838.

We shift focus to the emergence of another set of claims that raise standing issues: "no-injury" claims. There are various laws that make it unlawful to do certain things but that do not necessarily result in much, if any, harm. They address things like receiving robo-calls or unwanted faxes, or having an organization retain your data for longer than it should. They provide for nominal "statutory damages" (usually $100 to $1000), which, when multiplied by the number of class members, can impose significant liability.

In *Spokeo, Inc. v. Robins*, 136 S. Ct. 1540, 1550 (2016), the plaintiff sued for violation of the Fair Credit Reporting Act (FCRA). He alleged that the defendant had posted inaccurate information about him on its website. The inaccurate information, however, did not hurt the plaintiff—indeed, it placed him in a more favorable light than an accurate posting would have. He brought a class action in federal court, seeking statutory damages on behalf of an enormous class. Though the representative clearly had standing under the statute, the Supreme Court concluded that he might lack standing as a constitutional matter:

> Robins cannot satisfy the demands of Article III by alleging a bare procedural violation. A violation of one of the FCRA's procedural requirements may result in no harm. For example, even if a consumer reporting agency fails to provide the required notice to a user of the agency's consumer information, that information regardless may be entirely accurate. In addition, not all inaccuracies cause harm or present any material risk of harm. An example that comes readily to mind is an incorrect zip code. It is difficult to imagine how the dissemination of an incorrect zip code, without more, could work any concrete harm.

The Court remanded the case for determination of whether the plaintiff suffered "concrete harm," which is required for Article III standing.

No-injury class actions are big business. One study concluded that they resulted in defendant settlement liability of $4,000,000,000 over the decade 2005–2015. More than one-third of that sum went to class counsel. Joanna Shepherd, *An Empirical Survey of No-Injury Class Actions*, Emory Univ. Sch. Law, Legal Studies Research Paper Series No. 16-402 (2016). Such data raise a familiar issue: is the class action intended to foster compensation or deterrence? Arguing that no-injury classes overdeter and undercompensate, some urged the Advisory Committee "to revise Rule 23 to put an end to the 'no injury' class action." Richard L. Marcus, *Revolution v. Evolution in Class Action Reform*, 96 N.C. L. Rev. 903, 931 (2018). The Committee declined to do so. *Id.* at 933.

4. Statute of Limitations

Statutes of limitations are intended to ensure timely assertion of claims. They provide that the plaintiff must commence her action (usually, "commence" means "file") before a given period—two years, five years, whatever—has elapsed. Generally, commencing the action "tolls" the statute of limitations. That means it stops the statute from running.

> ***Example #16.*** Representative commences a class action on April 1. The statute of limitations for the claim asserted would run on April 11. In September, the court denies the motion to certify the class. Representative has no problems. The denial of certification means that his claim will continue as an individual claim. And because he commenced the case before the statute of limitations ran, his claim is not barred. But what about claims of the would-be class members?

For most purposes, as we have seen, a case is not treated as a class action until it is certified. Here, the situation is different. In *American Pipe and Construction Co. v. State of Utah*, 414 U.S. 538, 550–556 (1974), the Supreme Court held that filing the class action as such—even without certification—operates to toll the statute of limitations for all putative class members. Because Representative filed that case with 10 days left on the statute of limitations (she filed on April 1 and the statute would have run on April 11), the would-be class members have 10 days in which to assert their claims. They might do so by filing their own cases or by intervening in Representative's case. If they fail to assert the claim within 10 days after the denial of class certification, their claims will be barred.

In *American Pipe*, certification was denied for lack of numerosity. Some people were concerned that tolling might not apply if certification were denied for lack of adequacy. They asked: how can an inadequate representative take an act that would benefit a class she is not qualified to represent? As it turns out, this concern was not justified. In *Crown, Cork & Seal Co v. Parker*, 462 U.S. 345 (1983), the Court applied the *American Pipe* rule even though the class representative had been held inadequate.

The result is a black-letter rule that is easy to apply: filing a putative class action tolls the statute of limitations for the individual claims of class members, regardless of why class certification is rejected. The rule is supported by common sense. If tolling did not apply, each putative class member would be required to file an individual suit before the statute ran. This unnecessary filing of numerous suits would be a waste of time.

Can the *American Pipe* rule be used by successive class actions? Lower courts split on the question, which the Supreme Court resolved in 2018. In *China Agritech, Inc. v. Resh*, 138 S. Ct. 1800, 1808–1809 (2018), the Court rejected sequential tolling in this situation, explaining: "Respondents' proposed reading would allow the statute of limitations to be extended time and again; as each class is denied certification, a new named plaintiff could file a class complaint that resuscitate the litigation. . . . Endless tolling of a statute of limitations is not a result envisioned by *American Pipe*." Thus, the filing of a putative class action tolls the statute of limitations for claims later asserted by class members in a *non-class* case.

Notes and Questions

1. One potential problem with applying *American Pipe* is how closely the class claim and the later individual claims must be. Tolling is based on the principle that the defendant is put on notice of what claims it must defend. It is not fair to toll claims that are quite distinct from the ones asserted on behalf of the putative class. A concurring opinion in *Crown, Cork & Seal* expressed the concern well: "[W]hen a plaintiff invokes *American Pipe* in support of a separate lawsuit, the district court should take care to ensure that the suit raises claims that 'concern the same evidence, memories, and witnesses as the subject matter of the original class suit,' so that 'the defendant will not be prejudiced.' Claims as to which the defendant was not fairly placed on notice by the class suit are not protected under *American Pipe* and are barred by the statute of limitations." 462 U.S. at 354–355.

2. Suppose a class is certified under Rule 23(b)(3) and a member opts out. Does *American Pipe* apply to toll her claim? Should it matter that she affirmatively rejected the representation offered to her?

3. A statute of repose is different from a statute of limitations. As noted, the latter is to ensure diligent commencement of a case. The former is intended to provide the defendant with an absolute bar beyond which it cannot be sued. Statutes of repose are rather rare. Suppose a state has a medical malpractice statute of limitations of two years and statute of repose of six years. Usually, the statute of limitations for any claim is tolled while the plaintiff is a minor.

Suppose a doctor commits malpractice and injures a 10-year-old child. Because the statute of limitations is tolled during minority, the two-year statute will not start to run until the plaintiff reaches age 18. Thus, under the statute of limitations, she could sue until she turns 20 years old. But the statute of repose provides the doctor could not be sued more than six years after the negligence. So, the statute of repose would cut off the child's right to sue at age 16. Thus, a statute of repose can cut short but can never extend a statute of limitations.

The Supreme Court held in *California Public Employees' Retirement System v. ANZ Securities, Inc.*, 137 S. Ct. 2042, 2051–2052 (2017), that the *American Pipe* tolling rule does not apply to statutes of repose.

G. Trends in Aggregate Litigation and the Arbitration Threat

The class action is a powerful tool for dealing with widespread harm, but it is not the only one. Another, which we mention briefly, is the "victim compensation fund" (VCF), which creates a source for compensating those who have been hurt by a product or mass disaster. After the terrorist attacks of September 11, 2001, Congress created a VCF to compensate victims; the top award under that VCF was $8.5 million. Another VCF compensated victims of the BP oil spill in the Gulf of Mexico. Others have provided for victims of mass shootings.

The goal of a VCF is to provide relief for victims without requiring them to demonstrate tort liability. Some VCF programs, such as that arising from 9/11, require claimants to waive their right to sue. Others augment the right to sue in tort. There is considerable debate about whether victims prefer VCFs over tort litigation. Professor Hensler found that victims of the 9/11 attacks preferred the tort system, which focuses on economic loss, to the VCF, which was based more upon need. Deborah R. Hensler, *Money Talks: Searching for Justice Through Compensation for Personal Injury and Death,* 53 DePaul L. Rev. 417, 432–451 (2003).

Another means for addressing widespread harm is "multidistrict litigation" (MDL) under § 1407. We discussed MDL in Chapter 3.B.4. As we will see, § 1407 permits transfer of related federal cases to a single district for coordinated proceedings. The transfer is for pretrial purposes only, however, so the transferee judge may not try the cases. Today, over one-third of the federal civil docket—and the overwhelming majority of federal tort cases—are subject to coordinated oversight under the MDL statute. *See* Thomas Metzloff, *The MDL Vortex Reconsidered*, 99 Judicature 37 (2015).

Increasingly, as discussed in Chapter 3, the transferee judge in MDL attempts to get the parties to enter into a "global settlement" to resolve as many of the cases as possible. Though the cases retain their status as separate suits, MDL practice can look a great deal like class litigation. The MDL judge routinely appoints lead counsel to speak for the plaintiffs' side. That counsel controls matters much the way class counsel does under Rule 23. Plaintiffs in the other cases start to look a bit like class members (even though they filed individual cases): in the MDL global settlement, they are now "along for the ride," with the lead counsel making the meaningful decisions.

Some courts have come to refer to MDL matters as "quasi-class actions." *See, e.g., In re Vioxx,* 650 F. Supp. 2d 549, 553–554 (E.D. La. 2009). Global settlement in the MDL context raises significant questions of fairness, however, because (unless the MDL cases are certified as class actions) none of the Rule 23 protections, such as judicial review of settlements, applies. *See* Jaime L. Dodge, *Behind the Curtain of Multi-District Litigation,* 64 EMORY L.J. 329 (2015); Myriam Gilles, *Tribal Rituals of the MDL,* 5 J. OF TORT LAW 173 (2014); Linda S. Mullenix, *Aggregate Litigation and the Death of Democratic Dispute Resolution,* 107 NW. U. L. REV. 511 (2013).

In view of alternatives such as VCF and MDL global settlement, some question the future of the class action. Ken Feinberg, who administered the 9/11 VCF, is quoted as saying "class actions are dead." *Id.* Many disagree. *See* Georgene Vairo, *Is the Class Action Really Dead? Is That Good or Bad for Class Members?,* 64 EMORY L.J. 477 (2014).

In some substantive areas, however, many are coming to agree that recent developments bode ill for class actions. Specifically, developments under the Federal Arbitration Act (FAA), 9 U.S.C. § 1 et seq., are affecting the availability of class actions in consumer and employment cases. *See* Brian T. Fitzpatrick, *The End of Class Actions?,* 57 ARIZ. L. REV. 161 (2015). We will see in Chapter 9 that there are two types of arbitration: contractual and court-ordered.

The FAA addresses only contractual arbitration, in which the parties to a contract agree that a dispute arising from the contract will be submitted to arbitration. Arbitration is adversarial, with the presentation of evidence by both sides, but is less formal than court litigation. There is no formal discovery, proceedings are private, with no public access, there is no jury, and the decision by the arbitrator (or, commonly, a panel of three arbitrators) is generally final, with very limited judicial review.

Historically, courts were reluctant to enforce arbitration agreements. Congress passed the FAA in 1925 to require courts to enforce valid arbitration provisions. At that time, arbitration provisions were found only in agreements between businesses, and thus did not raise an issue of imbalance in bargaining position. In the past generation, however, the Supreme Court has applied the FAA to "contracts of adhesion," in which one party, with superior bargaining power, offers to provide a product or service on a "take-it-or-leave-it" basis; the contract contains an arbitration clause, by which the consumer agrees to submit a dispute to arbitration. With the Court's application of the FAA to adhesion contracts, arbitration clauses have become nearly ubiquitous in consumer contracts with cellphone companies, wireless providers, credit card companies, investment services, and many others.

The Court has also applied the FAA to the vindication of various federal statutory claims. Historically, the Court refused to permit parties to arbitrate certain federal claims, on the theory that such cases required the formal adjudication process of court litigation. The Court in recent years has rejected this theory, and seems to envision arbitration as being of equal dignity with court litigation for the vindication of federal claims. Thus, for example, a claim that the terms of one's contract with a credit card company violate federal antitrust law may be submitted to arbitration if the consumer's contract provides for it.

In recent years, many companies have added another clause to their adhesion contracts: The "class action waiver" or "aggregation waiver." These provisions require the consumer to arbitrate alone; they forbid her from joining in arbitration with others. Such provisions do not create a problem when the claims are sizeable. In those cases, an individual consumer will be able to find a lawyer to represent her in the arbitration; the size of the claim makes it worth the lawyer's time. The problem arises in negative-value claims—those which are not worth pursuing, either in court or in arbitration. No lawyer will take a negative-value arbitration unless the claims of many persons can be aggregated in a single case. Yet that aggregation is forbidden by these class action waiver clauses.

The aggregation waiver raises a fundamental clash between the policy of enforcing contracts and the policy of access to the courts. The Court in recent years has sided with the former policy interest. In *AT&T Mobility LLC v. Concepcion*, 563 U.S. 333 (2011), consumers agreed to a cellular telephone plan that offered each customer a free phone. The provider shipped the phones to the customers, but then billed each for the sales tax on the phone ($30.22 per unit). Although the agreement contained an arbitration clause and a class waiver provision, consumers filed a diversity of citizenship class action in federal court, asserting that charging for the sales tax on the phones violated California consumer protection law. The defendant moved to compel arbitration, but the lower federal courts refused. They relied upon California case law that prohibited class waivers of arbitration. *Discover Bank v. Superior Court*, 113 P.3d 1100 (Cal. 2005).

The Supreme Court held that the FAA pre-empted the California law. Section 2 of the FAA provides for enforcement of arbitration clauses "save upon such grounds as exist at law or in equity for revocation of any contract." According to the Court, this clause permits invalidation of arbitration clauses on state-law grounds that apply to contracts generally, but not on grounds that apply only to arbitration clauses. 563 U.S. at 339–341. Because the California rule singled out arbitration clauses, it stood as "an obstacle to the accomplishment of the FAA's objectives" and was preempted. *Id.* at 343.

On the facts of *Concepcion*, the Court found that arbitration provided meaningful redress for consumers. The clause required arbitration in the customer's home county and provided that the defendant would pay all arbitration costs; if the arbitration award was higher than the defendant had offered in settlement, the customer would receive liquidated damages of $7,500 plus double attorney's fees. To the Court, these provisions made individual arbitration realistic; thus, individual arbitration would provide "effective vindication" of the plaintiffs' claims. *See* Myriam Gilles, *Killing Them with Kindness: Examining "Consumer-Friendly" Arbitration Clauses After* AT&T Mobility v. Concepcion, 88 Notre Dame L. Rev. 805 (2013).

Not all arbitration provisions are as generous. *Concepcion* left open the possibility that less generous clauses might not provide "effective vindication." Such a case was *Italian Colors Restaurant v. American Express Travel Related Services Co.*, 133 S. Ct. 2304 (2013). In that case, a class of restaurant owners sued a credit card company for alleged violations of federal antitrust laws. Specifically, the class alleged that the defendant had used its monopoly power to force them to accept higher credit card interest rates than those charged by competitors. The agreement required arbitration and forbade aggregation. (Though the claims amounted to tens of thousands of dollars, they were negative-value, because prosecuting a case required retaining expert witnesses whose fees likely would exceed any recovery.) The Second Circuit concluded that individual pursuit of the claims was not feasible, and thus, that aggregate assertion was the "only economically feasible means" for plaintiffs to pursue their federal claim. *See In re American Express Merchs. Litigation*, 667 F.3d 204, 213–14 (2d Cir. 2012).

The Supreme Court reversed. The Court was willing to assume that individual litigation would be economically infeasible (because of the expense of expert testimony). *Concepcion* nonetheless governed. According to the Court, nothing in the FAA, the antitrust laws, or in Rule 23 demonstrates an intention to prohibit parties from foregoing their right to assert class claims. Thus, "the antitrust laws do not guarantee an affordable procedural path to the vindication of every claim," and the fact that it is not economically worth pursuing the claim "does not constitute the elimination of the right to pursue that remedy." *Italian Colors,* 133 S. Ct. at 2306, 2311.

The Court has continued in its FAA decisions to elevate the policy of contract over various substantive policies. For example, in *Epic Systems Corp. v. Lewis,* 138 S. Ct. 1612 (2018), employees whose contracts required arbitration of employment disputes asserted wage and hour claims under the Fair Labor Standards Act and related state-law claims. They argued that enforcing the class action waiver in their contracts would violate the National Labor Relations Act (NLRA), because it would interfere with their right to engage in "concerted activities for the purpose of collective bargaining or other mutual aid or protection." The Court concluded that the quoted language from the NLRA referred only to collective action in unionization and bargaining, and not to litigation. The NLRA was passed ten years after the FAA, and did not purport to override its policy of enforcing arbitration clauses as drafted. *See, e.g., Kindred Nursing Ctrs. Ltd. v. Clark*, 137 S. Ct. 1421, 1426–1429 (2017) (Kentucky rule requiring that power of attorney expressly state that a representative may waive litigation rights is preempted by FAA; wrongful death claims against nursing home must be pursued in arbitration); *DirecTV v. Imburgia*, 136 S. Ct. 463, 467–471 (2015) (provision that arbitration clause would be unenforceable if the "law of your state" made class arbitration waivers unenforceable is preempted by FAA; state-law claim regarding early termination fees must be pursued in arbitration).

The upshot of these cases is clear: If the plaintiffs enter into a contract—even a contract of adhesion—that agrees to individual arbitration, they will be bound by their contract. Though Congress may provide that aggregate assertion of claims is necessary for vindication of particular claims, it has rarely done so. When it does not, the contract reigns supreme.

Of course, the parties remain free to provide in the contract for group or class arbitration. When they do, the provision will be enforced. *See, e.g., Oxford Health Plans LLC v. Sutter*, 133 S. Ct. 2064 (2013) (upholding arbitrator's decision that parties agreed to class arbitration). Rule 23 does not apply in arbitration, but the leading arbitration services do have class action rules.

Such cases will be rare, however, because so many companies place class waivers into their arbitration provisions. Unless Congress intervenes, companies can, in some cases at least, effectively close the door to the enforcement of some laws.

H. The Bankruptcy "Alternative" to Class Litigation

Companies faced with mass tort liability to large numbers of current and future claimants might seek reorganization under Chapter 11 of the Bankruptcy Code, which provides a means of discharging those liabilities while preserving their ongoing economic viability. Bankruptcy proceedings provide an important alternative to Rule 23 as a means for aggregating and resolving mass claims.

The initiation of Chapter 11 reorganization proceedings does not require the debtor to demonstrate that it is actually or potentially insolvent. *See, e.g., United States v. Huebner*, 48 F.3d 376, 379 (9th Cir. 1994). The potential attractiveness of bankruptcy reorganization derives from a number of unique attributes of bankruptcy procedure. Federal district courts exercise exclusive jurisdiction over bankruptcy cases (although they most often refer them to the bankruptcy court, which is an Article I rather than an Article III tribunal). Additionally, federal courts possess concurrent jurisdiction over "proceedings arising in or related to" bankruptcy cases. 28 U.S.C. § 1334(b).

When a debtor files a Chapter 11 petition, all proceedings against the debtor or significantly related to the bankruptcy estate are automatically stayed, whether they are pending in federal or state court. *See* 11 U.S.C. § 362(a). This stay freezes both state and federal actions against the debtor, and essentially requires those plaintiffs to assert their claims in the bankruptcy proceeding. Additionally, the Bankruptcy Rules authorize nationwide service of process. FED. R. BANKR. P. 7004(d). Section 1452(a) of the Judicial Code authorizes a "party" to remove from state court any claim over which the federal court would have jurisdiction under section 1334, including any proceedings arising in or related to the bankruptcy case, even in the absence of diversity or federal question jurisdiction. 28 U.S.C. § 1452(a).

Further, the Bankruptcy Code authorizes a district court to transfer unliquidated tort claims related to bankruptcy to the district in which the bankruptcy proceeding is pending or to the district in which the claims arose. 11 U.S.C. § 157(b)

(5). A court may also transfer other bankruptcy-related claims to any district "in the interest of justice or for the convenience of the parties." 28 U.S.C. § 1412. Such transfers may be for all purposes, including trial. These provisions provide a powerful mechanism for consolidating all claims against the debtor and related proceedings for resolution by the Bankruptcy Court.

Lawyers and commentators debate the advantages of bankruptcy versus Rule 23 for achieving disposition of mass torts. Those preferring bankruptcy point to the Supreme Court's decisions in *Amchem* and *Ortiz* as making the class action alternative unavailable as a practical matter in most contexts. They also point out the more powerful aggregative tools available in bankruptcy in comparison with normal class litigation, including the fact that claimants have no "opt out" rights and the ability of the bankruptcy court to "bring a halt to individual collection efforts and to oversee the orderly liquidation or reorganization of the debtor for the benefit of all creditors." S. Elizabeth Gibson, *A Response to Professor Resnick: Will This Vehicle Pass Inspection?*, 148 U. PA. L. REV. 2095 (2000). They argue that bankruptcy is more equitable, because it requires all stakeholders (including other creditors and shareholders) in the company to sacrifice in achieving an approved reorganization plan. Moreover, bankruptcy reorganization preserves the company as an ongoing entity, potentially making additional assets available to claimants as a result of its future operations, whereas the *Ortiz* standard may effectively require the liquidation of the company.

Further, bankruptcy requires the members of each impaired class to approve the plan of reorganization by specified percentages, and imposes substantive protections for non-consenting classes. It also provides additional protections to creditors, including the appointment of a future claims representative. Proponents argue that the compensation of creditors' committees is not dependent on receiving a share of the "settlement," and that such committees are accordingly less likely to have conflicts of interest with the claimants. Further, they tout the ability of bankruptcy to ensure sufficient funds to compensate future claimants.

On other side of the debate, commentators have expressed concern that the provisions of the Bankruptcy Code were not drafted with the problems presented by mass torts involving future claims in mind, as illustrated by an unresolved controversy over whether such claims are dischargeable "claims" in bankruptcy. The process of "claims estimation" for the purpose of disclosure, determining whether a plan of reorganization is "feasible" and allocating voting rights has proved difficult and imprecise. Moreover, bankruptcy proceedings may lump creditors together so long as their claims are "substantially similar," as determined primarily by their priority in distribution. This may place tort claimants having significant differences in the strength, nature, and timing of their claims in the same class.

The adequacy of the "representation" by appointed creditors' committees in bankruptcy typically receives little scrutiny—less than is demanded by Rule 23(a). Further, in class actions, a court must approve settlements as fair, adequate, and reasonable, in contrast to the more limited scrutiny provided to reorganization plans. Additionally, the delay and transaction costs of bankruptcy proceedings for claimants are argued to be significantly greater than those of the typical settlement class action. As a result of delay, the extension of the automatic stay, and the inclusion of third parties in the bankruptcy proceedings, critics argue that tort claimants have little leverage to force an adequate settlement in bankruptcy.

In *Ortiz*, 527 U.S. at 860 n.34, the Court observed:

> While there is no inherent conflict between a limited fund class action under Rule 23(b)(1)(B) and the Bankruptcy Code, . . . it is worth noting that if limited fund certification is allowed in a situation where a company provides only a *de minimis* contribution to the ultimate settlement fund, the incentives such a resolution would provide to companies facing tort liability to engineer settlements similar to the one negotiated in this case would, in all likelihood, significantly undermine protections for creditors built into the Bankruptcy Code.

I. Special Statutory Provisions: CAFA, PSLRA, ALI Principles

We have focused on Rule 23. Various statutes, however, may have an impact on class practice, including settlement. We discussed the motivation behind and the jurisdictional provisions of the Class Action Fairness Act (CAFA) in Chapter 2.D.4. CAFA was intended to open the doors to federal court for interstate class actions, based upon a perception that state courts were being too lenient in certifying class actions.

Among the principal concerns was the "coupon settlement"—settlement of a class action under which the defendant "provides" to class members coupons or other rebates of dubious actual value. We saw an example in *General Motors Pick-Up Truck*, in which class members received coupons that most would never use. On the other hand, the settlement bestowed generous fees on the class attorneys.

CAFA contains several provisions concerning settlement of class actions that invoke its jurisdictional grant. These include:

- 28 U.S.C. § 1712 provides that when a class settlement distributes coupons to class members, the attorney's fee must be based upon the actual value of the coupons to the class members. This precludes the parties' attempting to base class counsel's fee on an inflated estimate of the value of the coupons.
- 28 U.S.C. § 1713 addresses settlements that call for class members to contribute to paying class counsel's attorney's fee, resulting in a net loss to the class member. These settlements are allowed "only if the court makes a written finding that nonmonetary benefits to the class member substantially outweigh the monetary loss."

- 28 U.S.C. § 1714 prohibits approval of a settlement that favors class members geographically situated closer to the court than others.
- 28 U.S.C. § 1715 is a particularly detailed provision requiring that a federal official and a state official be notified of a class action settlement. The court cannot approve the settlement fewer than 90 days after this notice is given. The purpose is to allow governmental input on the appropriateness of the settlement.

The Private Securities Litigation Reform Act (PSLRA) was designed to limit frivolous securities fraud cases. It is not limited to class actions. Among other things, PSLRA imposes heightened pleading requirements in all cases. The plaintiff must state her claim with detail, including identification of each misleading statement and explanation of why it was misleading. 15 U.S.C. § 78u-4(b)(1).

The PSLRA affects class practice in several ways. Most interesting is the requirement that any plaintiff filing a class action must publish a notice telling putative members of the case and stating that any member may move to serve as "lead plaintiff." The court is to presume that the lead plaintiff is the one with the largest financial stake in the suit. The lead plaintiff (usually it will be an institutional investor, like a mutual fund) is free to retain its own counsel to serve as class counsel. Unlike practice under Rule 23(g), then, the court does not appoint class counsel. 15 U.S.C. § 78u-4(a)(3)(B)(v).

In addition, the PSLRA generally forbids incentive awards to representatives. It provides that class representatives cannot be "treated unequally" from other class members. The one exception is that the representative may recover "reasonable costs and expenses (including lost wages) directly relating to the representation of the class." The PSLRA also contains a very detailed list of information that must be included in "[a]ny proposed or final settlement agreement that is published or otherwise disseminated to the class. . . ." The full list is beyond our scope, but includes detailed disclosure on the parties' agreement or disagreement on the average damages per share of stock and on any application that will be made for attorney's fees. 15 U.S.C. § 77z-a(7) & § 78u-4(a)(7).

The American Law Institute (ALI) promulgated PRINCIPLES OF THE LAW OF AGGREGATE LITIGATION in 2010. The study does not have the force of a statute, but constituted an ambitious effort to state guiding principles underlying aggregate litigation, including class actions. Among its recommendations concerning class actions generally were:

- *Structural safeguards regarding representation.* The ALI suggests a focus on structural safeguards designed to assure the protection of represented parties, rather than an analysis of interest alignment alone. Among the methods suggested for judges to assure such adequate representation are giving control of the litigation to named parties with "sizeable stakes," appointing counsel, using fee awards and incentive bonuses to reward good performance, requiring notice to and communications with class members and permitting them to opt-out, and using case management techniques such as severance, consolidation, and use of sub-classes. ALI § 1.05(c).

- *Conflicts of interest.* The study provides that the court must determine that there are no "structural conflicts of interest" between the claimants and the lawyers representing them or among the claimants themselves. "Structural" conflicts are those that create a significant risk that the lawyers will "skew systematically" the conduct of the litigation to favor some claimants over others on grounds unrelated to a reasoned evaluation of their claims, or to favor the lawyers over the claimants. ALI § 2.07(a)(1)(A), (B).
- *A fundamental reconceptualization of the types of class actions.* Instead of the three-part structure of Rule 23(b)(3), the ALI proposed distinguishing class actions in terms of their procedural consequences and binding effect according to whether an action seeks "indivisible" or "divisible" remedies. ALI § 2.04(a), (b). A right to opt out is accorded only in class actions seeking "divisible" relief on behalf of the class.
- *A lack of focus on whether common questions predominate.* Rather than inquire whether common questions "predominate" in the action taken as a whole, the proposal suggests that a court may accord class action treatment to a common issue if it would "materially advance" the resolution of multiple claims by "addressing the core of the dispute" in a way superior to alternative procedures, provided the issue is otherwise appropriate for class treatment and its resolution would not compromise the fair resolution of the remaining issues. ALI § 2.02(a)(1)–(3).

Regarding settlement of aggregate litigation, the ALI:

- Rejected the notion that Rule 23(e) should apply only to certified classes. It expressed the view that settlement of the representative's individual claim before certification warranted at least "limited judicial oversight" to protect against the use of leverage by the class representative to exact a premium in settlement. ALI § 3.02(b).
- Rejected wide-ranging multi-factor approaches (such as that used in *General Motors*) for approval of settlements. Instead, the court approving a settlement should enter findings and conclusions regarding whether (1) the class was adequately represented, (2) the relief provided is fair and reasonable in light of the probability of success and the costs, risks, and delays of litigation, (3) the class members are treated equitably among themselves, and (4) the settlement was negotiated at arm's length. An adverse finding on any one of these factors would require disapproval of the settlement. ALI § 3.05(a) & (b).
- Rejected the notion that a settlement class must satisfy all requirements for certification and that the court should be required to determine that common questions predominate over individual issues. It asserts that the focus should be shifted away from factors that are relevant if there were to be a trial to whether representation was adequate and the terms of the settlement fair. § 3.06(a), (b).

Chapter 7

Appointment, Organization, and Compensation of Lead, Liaison, and Class Counsel

A. Appointment of Class and Lead Counsel

1. Introduction

In complex cases, and particularly in cases transferred for coordinated and consolidated pretrial proceedings under 28 U.S.C. § 1407, multiple counsel representing individual clients and multiple, sometimes overlapping, classes and subclasses, typically are involved. In the class action context, the filing of a putative class action requires the court "at an early practicable time" to determine whether a class action will be certified and to appoint counsel for the class. *See* Fed. R. Civ. P. 23(c)(1)(A), (g). The lawyer appointed by the court to represent the class is designated as "class counsel." As discussed in more depth in Chapter 6, section C, the "client" of class counsel is the "class as a whole," rather than any individual named class representative or member of the class. For example, class counsel may negotiate and accept a settlement on behalf of the class, which the court may approve over the objections of a majority of the class and even of all or most of the named class representatives, if it determines the settlement to be fair, reasonable, and adequate for the class as a whole.

Where multiple individual or class actions are filed by different counsel, some means must be found to coordinate and rationalize the proceedings to avoid duplicative and redundant motions, discovery, and other proceedings, and to achieve judicial and litigant economy. It has long been settled that, both in the exercise of its inherent powers to manage the proceedings before it, and pursuant to Rule 42(a) of the Federal Rules of Civil Procedure (which authorizes federal district courts in consolidated proceedings to issue "orders to avoid unnecessary cost or delay"), a federal district court has the authority to appoint "lead counsel" to coordinate the efforts of multiple counsel during the pre-trial process and, if necessary, for trial. *See MacAlister v. Guterma*, 263 F.2d 65 (2d Cir. 1958) (rejecting the argument that such appointments impermissibly interfere with a litigant's right to choose his or her own counsel).

Where multiple actions on behalf of the same class are pending before the same court, the appointment of class counsel is synonymous with the appointment of lead counsel, and vice versa. (In that context, the appointed counsel might more appropriately be described as "lead class counsel.") With some frequency, however, consolidated proceedings involve both individual actions and class actions on behalf of differing classes or subclasses. If the plaintiffs in the individual actions are members of one or more classes or subclasses, they may be able to opt out and pursue their own actions through their own counsel. In that context, the appointment of lead counsel to coordinate the pre-trial or trial activities of multiple individual plaintiffs or classes who are separately represented by their own counsel is conceptually distinct from the appointment of class counsel to represent the various classes involved in the action. Put another way, a "class counsel" designation defines the relationship between the lawyer for the class and the members of the class. A "lead counsel" designation defines the relationship and powers of the attorney so designated to those of other attorneys separately representing individual litigants or differing classes or subclasses. In practice, however, the concepts are frequently lumped together, and the appointment of "lead counsel" in consolidated proceedings carries with it the responsibilities and powers of both designations.

2. Note on the Traditional Model of Designating Class or Lead Counsel: Effective Self-Appointment and Routine Court Approval

Chapter 5 discussed several ways managerial judging guides the flow of litigation. Judicial oversight also plays a major role in appointment of counsel. In the past, courts routinely accepted private designations of both class and lead counsel without searching examination. Many courts followed the "first to file" rule under which the first lawsuit filed determined the lead plaintiff and counsel. *See In re Cendant Corp. Litig.*, 264 F.3d 201, 255 (3d Cir. 2001):

> Although some courts have played an active role with regard to selecting lead counsel in securities cases, most have traditionally appointed the person who filed the first suit as lead plaintiff, and generally selected that person's lawyer to serve as lead counsel (assuming, of course, that the lawyer possessed sufficient competence and experience) . . . .

Id.

Other courts allowed a private ordering process of logrolling and patronage, under which competing counsel would agree upon a counsel structure. That structure frequently involved the appointment of an "executive committee" of counsel in addition to the designation of lead and liaison counsel, and various committees to perform designated functions. These plaintiff steering committees are usually referred to as PSCs. Committee assignments were given to attorneys who supported the arrangement. The agreed upon structure would then be presented as a fait accompli to the court for its approval, which normally ensued as a matter of course.

This system, ripe for abuse from the outset, fell into disfavor after becoming known to better serve the interests of counsel than client. The *Fine Paper* line of cases documented a series of exorbitant abuses, leading that court to conclude: "It was inevitable that this type of structure would generate wasted hours on useless tasks, propagate duplication and mask outright padding." *In re Fine Paper Antitrust Litigation* ("*Fine Paper I*"), 98 F.R.D. 48, 75 (E.D. Pa. 1983). While the Third Circuit found it necessary to remand the case for reconsideration in certain respects, that court emphasized that it "found more in the trial court's opinion of which we wholeheartedly approve than we have found necessary to reverse." *In re Fine Paper Antitrust Litigation*, 751 F.2d 562, 601 (3d Cir. 1984).

3. The Emergence of Active Judicial Involvement in the Selection and Appointment of Class and Lead Counsel

Mounting objections to the traditional approach of deference to private choice and minimal judicial review in the selection of class and lead counsel have led to dramatic changes in the current approach. The MANUAL FOR COMPLEX LITIGATION and the Federal Rules of Civil Procedure encourage active judicial involvement in the scrutiny and selection of class and lead counsel, and courts of appeal have approved the appointment of lead counsel to conduct trial as well as pretrial proceedings. *See In re Air Crash Disaster at Fla. Everglades on Dec. 29, 1972*, 549 F.3d 1006 (5th Cir. 1977); *Farber v. Riker-Maxson Corp.*, 442 F.2d 457 (2d Cir. 1971).

Some courts have endorsed a "free market" approach to the process by inviting "competitive bids" for the position of class counsel. And, in one of the most important areas characterized by complex, class action litigation, Congress adopted special provisions for the selection of "lead plaintiff" and lead counsel in class action litigation under the Securities Act of 1933 and the Securities and Exchange Act of 1934. We describe each of these interrelated developments in turn.

a. Appointment and Powers of Lead and Liaison Counsel

The MANUAL FOR COMPLEX LITIGATION §§ 10.22, 10.221, 10.222, 10.224, 10.225, 40.22 (4th ed. 2004), contains the following discussion of the court's role in appointing lead and "liaison" counsel in complex litigation, as well as the functions of such counsel:

> **§ 10.22 Coordination in Multiparty Litigation — Lead/Liaison Counsel and Committees**
>
> Complex litigation often involves numerous parties with common or similar interests but separate counsel. Traditional procedures in which all papers and documents are served on all attorneys, and each attorney files motions, presents arguments, and examines witnesses, may waste time and money, confuse and misdirect the litigation, and burden the court unnecessarily. Instituting special procedures for coordination of counsel early in the litigation will help to avoid these problems.

In some cases the attorneys coordinate their activities without the court's assistance, and such efforts should be encouraged. More often, however, the court will need to institute procedures under which one or more attorneys are selected and authorized to act on behalf of other counsel and their clients with respect to specified aspects of the litigation. To do so, invite submissions and suggestions from all counsel and conduct an independent review (usually a hearing is advisable) to ensure that counsel appointed to leading roles are qualified and responsible, that they will fairly and adequately represent all of the parties on their side, and that their charges will be reasonable. Counsel designated by the court also assume a responsibility to the court and an obligation to act fairly, efficiently, and economically in the interests of all parties and parties' counsel.

§ 10.221 Organizational Structures

Attorneys designated by the court to act on behalf of other counsel and parties in addition to their own clients (referred to collectively as "designated counsel") generally fall into one of the following categories:

- *Liaison counsel.* Charged with essentially administrative matters, such as communications between the court and other counsel (including receiving and distributing notices, orders, motions, and briefs on behalf of the group), convening meetings of counsel, advising parties of developments, and otherwise assisting in the coordination of activities and positions. . . .
- *Lead counsel.* Charged with formulating (in consultation with other counsel) and presenting positions on substantive and procedural issues during the litigation. Typically they act for the group—either personally or by coordinating the efforts of others—in presenting written and oral arguments and suggestions to the court, working with opposing counsel in developing and implementing a litigation plan, initiating and organizing discovery requests and responses, conducting the principal examination of deponents, employing experts, arranging for support services, and seeing that schedules are met.
- *Trial counsel.* Serve as principal attorneys at trial for the group and organize and coordinate the work of the other attorneys on the trial team.
- *Committees of counsel.* Often called steering committees, coordinating committees, management committees, executive committees, discovery committees, or trial teams. Committees are most commonly needed when group members' interests and positions are sufficiently dissimilar to justify giving them representation in decision making. The court or lead counsel may task committees with preparing briefs or conducting portions of the discovery program if one lawyer cannot

do so adequately. Committees of counsel can sometimes lead to substantially increased costs, and they should try to avoid unnecessary duplication of efforts and control fees and expenses. . . .

§ 10.222 Powers and Responsibilities

The functions of lead, liaison, and trial counsel, and of each committee, should be stated in either a court order or a separate document drafted by counsel for judicial review and approval. This document will inform other counsel and parties of the scope of designated counsel's authority and define responsibilities within the group. . . .

Counsel in leadership positions should keep the other attorneys in the group advised of the progress of the litigation and consult them about decisions significantly affecting their clients. Counsel must use their judgment about limits on this communication; too much communication may defeat the objectives of efficiency and economy, while too little may prejudice the interests of the parties. . . .

§ 10.224 Court's Responsibilities

Few decisions by the court in complex litigation are as difficult and sensitive as the appointment of designated counsel. There is often intense competition for appointment by the court as designated counsel, an appointment that may implicitly promise large fees and a prominent role in the litigation. Side agreements among attorneys also may have a significant effect on positions taken in the proceedings. At the same time, because appointment of designated counsel will alter the usual dynamics of client representation in important ways, attorneys will have legitimate concerns that their clients' interests be adequately represented.

For these reasons, the judge is advised to take an active part in the decision on the appointment of counsel. Deferring to proposals by counsel without independent examination, even those that seem to have the concurrence of a majority of those affected, invites problems down the road if designated counsel turn out to be unwilling or unable to discharge their responsibilities satisfactorily or if they incur excessive costs. It is important to assess the following factors:

- qualifications, functions, organization, and compensation of designated counsel;
- whether there has been full disclosure of all agreements and understandings among counsel;
- would-be designated attorneys' competence for assignments;
- whether there are clear and satisfactory guidelines for compensation and reimbursement, and whether the arrangements for coordination among counsel are fair, reasonable, and efficient;

- whether designated counsel fairly represent the various interests in the litigation—where diverse interests exist among the parties, the court may designate a committee of counsel representing different interests;
- the attorneys' resources, commitment, and qualifications to accomplish the assigned tasks; and
- the attorneys' ability to command the respect of their colleagues and work cooperatively with opposing counsel and the court—experience in similar roles in other litigation may be useful, but an attorney may have generated personal antagonisms during prior proceedings that will undermine his or her effectiveness in the present case.

. . . .

§ 40.22 Sample Order: Responsibilities of Designated Counsel

It is ORDERED:

1. *Plaintiffs' Lead Counsel.* Plaintiffs' lead counsel shall be generally responsible for coordinating the activities of plaintiffs during pretrial proceedings and shall:

(a) determine (after such consultation with other members of Plaintiffs' Steering Committee and other cocounsel as may be appropriate) and present (in briefs, oral argument, or such other fashion as may be appropriate, personally or by a designee) to the court and opposing parties the position of the plaintiffs on all matters arising during pretrial proceedings;

(b) coordinate the initiation and conduct of discovery on behalf of plaintiffs consistent with the requirements of Fed. R. Civ. P. 26(b)(1), 26(2), and 26(g), including the preparation of joint interrogatories and requests for production of documents and the examination of witnesses in depositions;

(c) conduct settlement negotiations on behalf of plaintiffs, but not enter binding agreements except to the extent expressly authorized;

(d) delegate specific tasks to other counsel or committees of counsel, as authorized by the court, in a manner to ensure that pretrial preparation for the plaintiffs is conducted efficiently and effectively;

(e) enter into stipulations with opposing counsel as necessary for the conduct of the litigation;

(f) prepare and distribute periodic status reports to the parties;

(g) maintain adequate time and disbursement records covering services as lead counsel;

(h) monitor the activities of cocounsel to ensure that schedules are met and unnecessary expenditures of time and funds are avoided; and

(i) perform such other duties as may be incidental to proper coordination of plaintiffs' pretrial activities or authorized by further order of the court.

2. *Plaintiffs' Liaison Counsel.* Plaintiffs' liaison counsel shall:

(a) maintain and distribute to cocounsel and to defendants' liaison counsel an up-to-date service list;

(b) receive and, as appropriate, distribute to cocounsel orders from the court [and documents from opposing parties and counsel];

(c) maintain and make available to cocounsel at reasonable hours a complete file of all documents served by or upon each party [except such documents as may be available at a document depository]; and

(d) establish and maintain a document depository.

3. *Plaintiffs' Steering Committee.* The other members of plaintiffs' steering committee shall from time to time consult with plaintiffs' lead and liaison counsel in coordinating the plaintiffs' pretrial activities and in planning for trial.

. . . .

5. *Privileges Preserved.* No communication among plaintiffs' counsel or among defendants' counsel shall be taken as a waiver of any privilege or protection to which they would otherwise be entitled.

Dated: ____________ ________________________

United States District Judge

Notes and Questions

1. Is this approach superior to the private ordering approach exemplified in *Fine Paper*? Do you see any difficulties/shortcomings in the MANUAL's suggested approach?

2. Does the role contemplated for lead counsel by the MANUAL raise any concerns about impermissible or unwarranted interference with a litigant's right to individual representation by counsel of his or her own choice? Courts regularly have rejected such claims. *See Farber v. Riker-Maxson Corp.*, 442 F.2d 457, 458 (2d Cir. 1971) (Appellant was denied the opportunity to file a motion because the court-appointed lead counsel did not agree that it needed to be filed. The court held that deference to the appointed lead counsel did not "deny appellants an appropriate opportunity to participate in the litigation." The court said that individual plaintiffs and lawyers must not be "permitted to do what [they please] in litigation as complex as this, and . . . behave in total disregard of the interest of the other litigants and of the class."); *In re Federal Skywalk Cases*, 680 F.2d 1175, 1191 (8th Cir. 1982) ("Indeed, the very nature of a class action requires that the class representative, and his or her attorney, represent the class and that members of the class cannot continue to file motions as they might in an individual action.").

3. Are some of the specific powers and responsibilities that the MANUAL contemplates for lead counsel more problematic than others? Although the MANUAL's

Sample Order appointing designated counsel does not explicitly do so, such orders in practice commonly restrict a litigant's right to initiate discovery, make motions, and take other significant steps in the litigation without the approval of lead counsel or the court. Consider the following order entered in *In re Worldcom, Inc. Sec. Litig.*, 2003 U.S. Dist. LEXIS 8979 (S.D.N.Y. May 28, 2003):

> 17. No attorney for any plaintiff in an Individual Action may contact defense counsel regarding discovery without the consent of Lead Counsel or, in the absence of such permission, leave of the Court. No attorney for any plaintiff in an Individual Action other than Liaison Counsel may contact Lead Counsel regarding discovery without being advised by Liaison Counsel that Lead Counsel has consented to the contact, or in the absence of such consent, leave of the Court.
>
> 18. Counsel may seek relief from these restrictions and from any of the provisions of this Order by application to the Court upon a showing of good cause. A showing of good cause regarding discovery issues includes a showing that the discovery issue is unique to an Individual Action.

See also, e.g., In re Flight Safety Technologies, Inc. Sec. Litig., 231 F.R.D. 124, 133 (D. Conn. 2005) ("No pleadings or other papers shall be filed or discovery conducted by any plaintiff excepted [sic] as directed or undertaken by Lead Counsel"); *Crawford v. Onyx Software Corp.*, 2002 U.S. Dist. LEXIS 1101 (W.D. Wash. Jan. 10, 2002) ("No motion, discovery request, or other pretrial proceedings shall be initiated or filed by any plaintiff without the approval of lead counsel, so as to prevent duplicative pleadings or discovery by plaintiffs. No settlement negotiations shall be conducted without the approval of lead counsel.").

4. To the extent such orders prevent individually represented plaintiffs (as opposed to members of a certified class represented by class counsel) from conducting or participating in settlement negotiations, are they valid?

5. The issue of "aggregate settlement" of non-class proceedings has generated considerable controversy in light of the American Law Institute's Principles of the Law of Aggregate Litigation (2010). The Principles address perceived impediments to settlement arising from state rules similar to section 1.8(g) of the ABA Model Rules of Professional Conduct, which provides that "A lawyer who represents two or more clients shall not participate in making an aggregate settlement of claims of or against the clients . . . unless each client gives informed consent, in a writing signed by the client. The lawyer's disclosure shall include the existence and nature of all the claims . . . involved and of the participation of each person in the settlement." Under existing interpretations, a client cannot grant a valid advance waiver of the protection of section 1.8(g) by agreeing to be bound by the decision of counsel or a majority vote of the group of clients. PRINCIPLES, *supra*, § 3.17, cmt. a.

This issue has assumed considerable importance, not only in the context of multidistrict and consolidated proceedings in which lead counsel attempts to negotiate a settlement on behalf of all claimants, but also with respect to individually retained attorneys who have amassed large "inventories" of claims based on injuries to multiple clients caused by the same events or products. In such circumstances, defendants frequently condition settlement on the attorney's ability to obtain the consent of all or a specified percentage of the consolidated or inventory claims, and require that all claims be settled on the basis of a formula or "grid" which does not take account of the individual circumstances of each plaintiff.

The ALI proposal is based on the concern that, by prohibiting advance waivers of individual client settlement approval, current law improperly permits one or a small number of claimants to block a settlement that would be beneficial to the group as a whole, and to demand special compensation for their approval. *Id.*, § 3.17, cmt. b. Section 3.17(b) of the Principles attempts to address this problem by providing that before the receipt of a proposed settlement offer, individual claimants may "enter into an agreement in writing through shared counsel allowing each participating claimant to be bound by a substantial-majority vote of all claimants" (or of each "category" of claimants created by the settlement). However, before obtaining such consent, the lawyer must provide the claimants with the information they need to make an informed decision, *id.* § 3.17(b)(2), and certain other conditions must be met. The power to approve the settlement must remain with the claimants, and cannot be assigned to the lawyers. Before entering such an agreement, claimants must be advised that they may elect to follow the traditional rule, and cannot be denied representation for that reason. *Id.* § 3.17(b)(4). The proposal is limited to cases involving a substantial amount in controversy and a large number of claimants. *Id.*, § 3.17(c). The agreement is not enforceable unless it is "fair and reasonable from a procedural standpoint." *Id.*, § 3.17(d). What objections might be raised to this proposal? Are they outweighed by its benefits?

b. Appointment of "Class Counsel" under Rule 23(g)

Federal Rule 23(g) encourages active judicial involvement in the appointment of designated counsel. The Rule represents how critically important the selection of class counsel is to successful class action proceedings. Rule 23(g) complements Rule 23(a)(4), which "will continue to call for scrutiny of the proposed class representative, while [Rule 23(g)] will guide the court in assessing proposed class counsel as part of the certification decision." 2003 Advisory Committee Note. Rule 23(g) also enables courts to address the structure of potential fee awards at the outset of a case.

Rule 23(g)'s full text provides:

> (g) Class Counsel.
>
> (1) *Appointing Class Counsel.* Unless a statute provides otherwise, a court that certifies a class must appoint class counsel. In appointing class counsel, the court:
>
> (A) must consider:
>
> (i) the work counsel has done in identifying or investigating potential claims in the action;

(ii) counsel's experience in handling class actions, other complex litigation, and the types of claims asserted in the action;

(iii) counsel's knowledge of the applicable law; and

(iv) the resources that counsel will commit to representing the class;

(B) may consider any other matter pertinent to counsel's ability to fairly and adequately represent the interests of the class;

(C) may order potential class counsel to provide information on any subject pertinent to the appointment and to propose terms for attorney's fees and nontaxable costs;

(D) may include in the appointing order provisions about the award of attorney's fees or nontaxable costs under Rule 23(h); and

(E) may make further orders in connection with the appointment.

(2) *Standard for Appointing Class Counsel.* When one applicant seeks appointment as class counsel, the court may appoint that applicant only if the applicant is adequate under Rule 23(g)(1) and (4). If more than one adequate applicant seeks appointment, the court must appoint the applicant best able to represent the interests of the class.

(3) *Interim Counsel.* The court may designate interim counsel to act on behalf of a putative class before determining whether to certify the action as a class action.

(4) *Duty of Class Counsel.* Class counsel must fairly and adequately represent the interests of the class.

Notes and Questions

1. Rule 23(g) ended the practice of deferring to private choice in the selection of class counsel, in favor of active judicial management and control. Were there any advantages to the system of private arrangements? Does the current rule, favoring judicial management, impact the willingness of private attorneys to investigate and initiate class actions on behalf of large numbers of injured persons who may lack the incentive and resources to maintain individual actions?

2. Are the criteria specified in Rule 23(g) sufficiently definitive to guide trial judges in their application and to achieve a consistent approach from judge to judge?

3. Rule 23(g)(1)(C) permits but does not require the court to direct potential class counsel to provide "information on any subject pertinent to the appointment and to propose terms for attorney's fees and nontaxable costs." Is there any reason why the court should not require counsel to propose a basis for an award of fees and costs before appointing class counsel in every case, rather than waiting until the conclusion of the litigation to determine the amount of any fees award? (Reconsider this question after you have read the material on fee awards at the end of this chapter.)

4. In addition to the work, experience, knowledge and resources of an attorney, Rule 23(g) provides that the court "may consider any other matter pertinent to counsel's ability to fairly and adequately represent the interests of the class." What "other matters" might be relevant?

5. Note the similarity of many of the factors listed in the MANUAL FOR COMPLEX LITIGATION bearing on the appointment of lead counsel, and those enumerated in Rule 23(g) with respect to the appointment of class counsel.

c. Selection of Class or Lead Counsel Based on the Submission of Bids

In the past, some courts used a "bidding" process for the selection of class or lead counsel. Counsel wishing to be designated were required to submit, in addition to information regarding such matters as their experience, conduct of similar cases, competence, resources, and the work they had done in investigating and preparing the case, their "bid" on the fees and costs they would seek from any recovery if the action were successful. Typically, the "request" for bids would include a "fee bid schedule" or "grid" requiring information regarding the percentage of recovery that the attorney would seek for various ranges of recovery and stages at which the action was settled or resolved. Commentators have debated the advantages and disadvantages of lead counsel auctions. For an instructive judicial analysis of the auction approach, see *In re Auction Houses Antitrust Litig.*, 197 F.R.D. 71 (S.D.N.Y. 2000).

Notes and Questions

1. Do you think the bidding process is consistent with Rule 23(g)?

2. Rule 23(g)(2) contemplates that the court may select among competing applicants for the position of class counsel. The clear implication of the Advisory Committee note is that the court may invite applications for the position of class counsel by lawyers who previously had no involvement in any pending action and no attorney-client relationship with the putative class representative. When would it be appropriate to do so? Would a lawyer selected in this way, and having no previous attorney-client relationship with any named class representative, likely be subject to the control of the "client"?

3. In *In re Cendant Corp. Litig.*, 264 F.3d 201 (3d Cir. 2001), the Third Circuit summarized the arguments for and against the "bidding" process for selecting lead or class counsel as follows:

> The auction method offers several potential advantages. First, unlike all of the methods previously discussed, it deals with counsel selection in addition to counsel retention. When an auction is used, counsel are no longer "selected" by the race-to-the-courthouse method, and this means that courts can exercise greater control over counsel quality. Second, auctions may lead to lower-priced representation. Under the traditional method, lead counsel (who has already been appointed) tries to get as much as it can

> from the court in terms of fees. Under the auction method, in contrast, prospective lead counsel compete to submit the lowest reasonable bid. Third, assuming a sufficiently large number of bidders, an auction will likely better approximate a market transaction than having a judge set attorneys fees after the fact. Fourth, auctions may provide a way for new firms to enter the market for plaintiff-side securities class action lawyers, thus rendering the overall market more competitive. Fifth, the auction method may require a smaller investment of judicial time than the time-consuming lodestar method, and could minimize the dangers of hindsight biases associated with the traditional, after-the-fact approach to determining fees. . . .
>
> Auctions may not be a panacea, however. One persistent criticism is that courts generally identify the "lowest" bid submitted by an "adequate" bidder and appoint that bidder as lead counsel, without performing the cost/quality weighing in the way that a real client would. Another fear is that because auctions do not reward the attorneys who discover legal violations, they may reduce lawyers' incentives to seek out and disclose illegality (because unless they are selected as lead counsel, they may not be compensated for the time they spent doing so). Moreover, bids in large, potentially high-recovery, cases are likely to be quite complex and it may be difficult for courts to assess their relative costs to the class. This risk is especially strong in cases where the bids consist of a complicated set of alternate fees that vary depending on the size of the recovery and the stage of the proceedings at which the recovery is obtained. In such situations, a court cannot assess which bid is the cheapest without first assessing the likely amount of recovery. Additionally, if there are too few bidders, the degree to which an auction will actually simulate the market is questionable. Finally, there is a risk that auctions could result in a "winner's curse," systematically selecting bidders who overestimate the odds or amount of a likely recovery. Such a "winning" bidder might then find itself litigating an unprofitable case, which may then give it an incentive to settle early and cheaply. No consensus has yet emerged about the relative efficacy of the auction technique. . . .

Id. at 258–260. Do the arguments in favor of the bidding process outweigh those against it?

4. Note on the Organization of Defense Counsel in Complex Cases

In consolidated actions, the court may appoint lead and liaison counsel to organize the defense of the case as well as its prosecution. Just as courts have the power to compel plaintiff-counsel coordination, courts have the power to order joint defense groups. §§ 10.22, 10.221, 10.222, 10.224, and 10.225 of the MANUAL FOR COMPLEX LITIGATION, set out above, clearly contemplate that such appointments may be made with respect to both plaintiffs and defendants. (For example, section 10.221 of the

MANUAL states, "depending on the number and complexity of different interests represented, both lead and liaison counsel may be appointed for one side, with only liaison counsel appointed for the other.")

Nevertheless, in practice, courts rarely make such designations with respect to multiple defendants in complex cases. One reason may be that even though multiple defendants may be involved in consolidated cases, they tend to be common to most of the consolidated actions. As a consequence, their number may not be large enough to require such designations. Another is that, perhaps for the same reason, multiple defendants in consolidated or other complex cases routinely voluntarily organize themselves to reduce costs and promote the efficient preparation of their defenses. Do other considerations also suggest that the appointment of designated counsel for the defense should be approached more cautiously than for plaintiffs?

Typically, a voluntary defense organization structure would consist of an "executive committee" of lawyers for the various defendants charged with overall policy direction and division of assignments, "liaison" counsel to coordinate the activities of the various attorneys, and various committees and subcommittees drawn from the lawyers and firms involved to perform particular tasks, such as fact investigation; discovery; development, supervision and operation of litigation support systems and document depositories; retention and preparation of experts on various issues; identification of witnesses and preparation of testimony for trial; legal analysis and briefing, and so on. Each of the tasks may be further subdivided to focus on particular issues, witnesses, evidence, or other tasks.

Such voluntary coordination—which may also take place among counsel for both plaintiffs and defendants in related cases that have not been formally aggregated through class or consolidated proceedings—has become increasingly common. *See generally* Howard M. Erichson, *Informal Aggregation: Procedural and Ethical Implications of Coordination Among Counsel in Related Lawsuits*, 50 DUKE L.J. 381 (2000). Professor Erichson points out that informal cooperation among lawyers raises a host of issues regarding such matters as confidentiality of exchanged information, duties owed by counsel for one cooperating party to other parties and their counsel, and liability for malpractice. *See id.* at 418–448. Counsel for defendants (and plaintiffs) seeking to coordinate their activities voluntarily may seek to specify and resolve these issues by entering into "joint defense" or "cooperation" agreements, which set out confidentiality obligations, duties of cooperation and loyalty, basis for cost sharing, and scope of indemnification or other liability among the cooperating parties. *Id.* at 404–05.

B. Award of Attorney's Fees in Complex Litigation

1. Basis for Fee Awards

In *Alyeska Pipeline Service Co. v. Wilderness Society*, 421 U.S. 240 (1975), the Supreme Court strongly reaffirmed the "American Rule" that, absent statutory authorization or contractual provision, a prevailing party is not entitled to recover its attorneys' fees from its opponent. The Court accordingly rejected the fee award in that case, which had been based on a "private attorney general" theory:

> ... [Congress has not] extended any roving authority to the Judiciary to allow counsel fees as costs or otherwise whenever the courts might deem them warranted. What Congress has done, however, while fully recognizing and accepting the general rule, is to make specific and explicit provisions for the allowance of attorneys' fees under selected statutes granting or protecting various federal rights. These statutory allowances are now available in a variety of circumstances, but they also differ considerably among themselves. Under the antitrust laws, for instance, allowance of attorneys' fees to a plaintiff awarded treble damages is mandatory. In patent litigation, in contrast, "[t]he court in *exceptional* cases may award reasonable attorney fees to the prevailing party." 35 U.S.C. § 285 (emphasis added). Under Title II of the Civil Rights Act of 1964, 42 U.S.C. § 2000a-3(b), the prevailing party is entitled to attorneys' fees, at the discretion of the court, but we have held that Congress intended that the award should be made to the successful plaintiff absent exceptional circumstances. *Newman v. Piggie Park Enterprises, Inc.*, 390 U.S. 400, 402 (1968). Under this scheme of things, it is apparent that the circumstances under which attorneys' fees are to be awarded and the range of discretion of the courts in making those awards are matters for Congress to determine.
>
> It is true that under some, if not most, of the statutes providing for the allowance of reasonable fees, Congress has opted to rely heavily on private enforcement to implement public policy and to allow counsel fees so as to encourage private litigation. Fee shifting in connection with treble-damages awards under the antitrust laws is a prime example ... and we have noted that Title II of the Civil Rights Act of 1964 was intended "not simply to penalize litigants who deliberately advance arguments they know to be untenable but, more broadly, to encourage individuals injured by racial discrimination to seek judicial relief under Title II. ..." But congressional utilization of the private-attorney-general concept can in no sense be construed as a grant of authority to the Judiciary to jettison the traditional rule against nonstatutory allowances to the prevailing party and to award attorneys' fees whenever the courts deem the public policy furthered by a particular statute important enough to warrant the award.

Id. at 254–70.

2. Fee Awards in Complex Litigation

a. Background

In ordinary litigation, litigants may hire their lawyers on an hourly basis under retainer agreements. More commonly, plaintiffs, particularly in personal injury and civil rights actions, may obtain representation by entering contingent fee agreements, under which their attorneys are compensated by a percentage of recovery (usually about one-third) in the event they prevail, and receive no fee if they lose. Although such contingency agreements are widely disapproved of in other countries, they have the advantage of providing litigants who lack the resources necessary to hire an attorney an avenue for rectifying wrongs and obtaining compensation for injuries that otherwise might go unredressed and uncompensated.

On the other hand, contingency agreements have been criticized on the ground that they may generate unnecessary litigation, provide incentives to lawyers to stir up litigation, and result in "windfall" fees in cases where the percentage of recovery far exceeds the amount of time and effort that the attorney has devoted to the case. Lester Brickman, *Contingent Fees Without Contingencies: Hamlet Without the Prince of Denmark?*, 37 UCLA L. Rev. 29, 47 (1989). They may also create a conflict of interest between attorney and client, as the attorney may have an incentive to strike a quick settlement generating a generous fee, even if the amount of recovery received by the client is less than might have resulted had the case been fully litigated.

In many cases, however, such private fee arrangements may be insufficient to ensure that rights will be vindicated and wrongdoers held accountable for their actions in individual litigation. This particularly is true where, as is often the case in antitrust, securities, consumer protection, and civil rights actions, the financial injuries suffered by an individual plaintiff are small. In such circumstances, the fees that would be incurred in litigating individual cases would far exceed the amount that any individual plaintiff would be willing to pay, and a percentage of such small recoveries would not be sufficient to induce an attorney to take the case on contingency.

Accordingly, the possibility that claims may be aggregated through such devices as multidistrict consolidation and class actions, and that a substantial award of attorneys fees may be obtained under the auspices of the court if the action is successful, or as part of a negotiated settlement, truly provides the "engine" that drives the pursuit of most complex litigation. Understanding this reality, and the basis for such awards—as well as the benefits and disadvantages that they may entail—is therefore pivotal to understanding complex litigation itself.

The Supreme Court's opinion in *Alyeska* sets the stage by its endorsement of the American rule that a prevailing party may not ordinarily recover its attorneys' fees as part of costs or otherwise. Despite this general rule, however, fee shifting in favor of plaintiffs is a signal characteristic of modern complex litigation. In the wake of *Alyeska*, Congress has passed many statutes in the areas of antitrust, securities, and civil rights containing explicit fee shifting authorizations designed to encourage enforcement of the statutes by "private attorneys general." These statutes, which are in addition to the "common fund" doctrine discussed later in this chapter, generally limit the award of fees to parties who have "prevailed in the underlying litigation." The Supreme Court has held that under such statutes, fees routinely should be awarded to prevailing plaintiffs absent special circumstances making the award unjust. *Christianburg Garment Co. v. Equal Employment Opportunity Commission*, 434 U.S. 412, 417 (1978). The fees award under such statutes belongs to the plaintiff not to the attorney, but retainer agreements in such cases customarily assign any recovery of statutory fees to the attorney.[1]

b. Who Is a "Prevailing Party"?

As illustrated by the next case, whether a party should be held to have "prevailed" and therefore be entitled to a statutory fee award sometimes proves to be a difficult inquiry.

Buckhannon Bd. & Care Home, Inc. v. W. Va. Dep't of Health and Human Res.

Supreme Court of the United States
532 U.S. 598 (2001)

Chief Justice Rehnquist delivered the opinion of the Court.

Numerous federal statutes allow courts to award attorney's fees and costs to the "prevailing party." The question presented here is whether this term includes a party that has failed to secure a judgment on the merits or a court-ordered consent decree, but has nonetheless achieved the desired result because the lawsuit brought about a voluntary change in the defendant's conduct. We hold that it does not.

Buckhannon Board and Care Home, Inc., which operates care homes that provide assisted living to their residents, failed an inspection by the West Virginia Office of the State Fire Marshal because some of the residents were incapable of "self-preservation" as defined under state law.... On October 28, 1997, after receiving cease and desist orders requiring the closure of its residential care facilities within 30 days, Buckhannon Board and Care Home, Inc., on behalf of itself and other similarly situated homes and residents (hereinafter petitioners), brought suit in the United States District Court for the Northern District of West Virginia against the State of West Virginia, two of its agencies, and 18 individuals (hereinafter respondents), seeking declaratory and injunctive relief that the "self-preservation" requirement violated the Fair Housing Amendments Act of 1988 (FHAA), 102 Stat. 1619, 42 U.S.C. § 3601 et seq., and the Americans with Disabilities Act of 1990 (ADA), 104 Stat. 327, 42 U.S.C. § 12101 et seq.

---

1. The Supreme Court has made clear that the privately negotiated fee arrangement between a plaintiff and its attorney is separate from any entitlement that the plaintiff may have to a statutory fees award if it prevails, and that a statutory fee award establishes neither a ceiling nor a floor on the privately negotiated fee. *See, e.g.*, *Venegas v. Mitchell*, 495 U.S. 82 (1990) (private contingency agreement not unenforceable because it provided for a fee in excess of the statutory award; suggesting that in cases where the statutory fee exceeds the privately negotiated fee, the excess may be retained by the plaintiff); *Blanchard v. Bergeron*, 489 U.S. 87 (1989) (contingent fee agreement does not impose a ceiling on the amount of the statutory fee).

Respondents agreed to stay enforcement of the cease-and-desist orders pending resolution of the case and the parties began discovery. In 1998, the West Virginia Legislature enacted two bills eliminating the "self-preservation" requirement, and respondents moved to dismiss the case as moot. The District Court granted the motion, finding that the 1998 legislation had eliminated the allegedly offensive provisions and that there was no indication that the West Virginia Legislature would repeal the amendments.

Petitioners requested attorney's fees as the "prevailing party" under the FHAA, 42 U.S.C. §3613(c)(2) ("[T]he court, in its discretion, may allow the prevailing party . . . a reasonable attorney's fee and costs"), and ADA, 42 U.S.C. §12205 ("[T]he court . . . , in its discretion, may allow the prevailing party . . . a reasonable attorney's fee, including litigation expenses, and costs"). Petitioners argued that they were entitled to attorney's fees under the "catalyst theory," which posits that a plaintiff is a "prevailing party" if it achieves the desired result because the lawsuit brought about a voluntary change in the defendant's conduct. Although most Courts of Appeals recognize the "catalyst theory," the Court of Appeals for the Fourth Circuit rejected it in *S-1 and S-2 v. State Bd. of Ed. of N. C.*, 21 F.3d 49, 51 (C.A.4 1994) (en banc) . . . .

To resolve the disagreement amongst the Courts of Appeals, we granted certiorari . . . and now affirm.

In the United States, parties are ordinarily required to bear their own attorney's fees—the prevailing party is not entitled to collect from the loser. See *Alyeska Pipeline Service Co. v. Wilderness Society*, 421 U.S. 240, 247 (1975). . . . Congress, however, has authorized the award of attorney's fees to the "prevailing party" in numerous statutes in addition to those at issue here, such as the Civil Rights Act of 1964, 78 Stat. 259, 42 U.S.C. §2000e-5(k), the Voting Rights Act Amendments of 1975, 89 Stat. 402, 42 U.S.C. §1973l(e), and the Civil Rights Attorney's Fees Awards Act of 1976, 90 Stat. 2641, 42 U.S.C. §1988.

In designating those parties eligible for an award of litigation costs, Congress employed the term "prevailing party," a legal term of art. Black's Law Dictionary 1145 (7th ed. 1999) defines "prevailing party" as "[a] party in whose favor a judgment is rendered, regardless of the amount of damages awarded <in certain cases, the court will award attorney's fees to the prevailing party>.—Also termed *successful party*." This view that a "prevailing party" is one who has been awarded some relief by the court can be distilled from our prior cases.

. . . .

In addition to judgments on the merits, we have held that settlement agreements enforced through a consent decree may serve as the basis for an award of attorney's fees. See *Maher v. Gagne*, 448 U.S. 122 (1980). Although a consent decree does not always include an admission of liability by the defendant . . . it nonetheless is a court-ordered "chang[e][in] the legal relationship between [the plaintiff] and the defendant." *Texas State Teachers Assn. v. Garland Independent School Dist.*, 489

U.S. 782, 792 (1989).[2] . . . These decisions, taken together, establish that enforceable judgments on the merits and court-ordered consent decrees create the "material alteration of the legal relationship of the parties" necessary to permit an award of attorney's fees. . . .

We think, however, the "catalyst theory" falls on the other side of the line from these examples. It allows an award where there is no judicially sanctioned change in the legal relationship of the parties. Even under a limited form of the "catalyst theory," a plaintiff could recover attorney's fees if it established that the "complaint had sufficient merit to withstand a motion to dismiss for lack of jurisdiction or failure to state a claim on which relief may be granted." This is not the type of legal merit that our prior decisions, based upon plain language and congressional intent, have found necessary. . . . A defendant's voluntary change in conduct, although perhaps accomplishing what the plaintiff sought to achieve by the lawsuit, lacks the necessary judicial *imprimatur* on the change. Our precedents thus counsel against holding that the term "prevailing party" authorizes an award of attorney's fees *without* a corresponding alteration in the legal relationship of the parties.

. . . [S]everal Courts of Appeals have relied upon dicta in our prior cases in approving the "catalyst theory. . . ." Now that the issue is squarely presented, it behooves us to reconcile the plain language of the statutes with our prior *holdings*. We have only awarded attorney's fees where the plaintiff has received a judgment on the merits . . . or obtained a court-ordered consent decree . . . [W]e have not awarded attorney's fees where the plaintiff has secured the reversal of a directed verdict . . . or acquired a judicial pronouncement that the defendant has violated the Constitution unaccompanied by "*judicial* relief". . . . Never have we awarded attorney's fees for a nonjudicial "alteration of actual circumstances. . . ." While urging an expansion of our precedents on this front, the dissenters would simultaneously abrogate the "merit" requirement of our prior cases and award attorney's fees where the plaintiff's claim "was at least colorable" and "not . . . groundless. . . ." We cannot agree that the term "prevailing party" authorizes federal courts to award attorney's fees to a plaintiff who, by simply filing a nonfrivolous but nonetheless potentially meritless lawsuit (it will never be determined), has reached the "sought-after destination" without obtaining any judicial relief. . . .

. . . .

---

2. [Court's footnote #7] We have subsequently characterized the *Maher* opinion as also allowing for an award of attorney's fees for private settlements. See *Farrar v. Hobby*, [506 U.S. 103, 111 (1992)]. . . . But this dictum ignores that *Maher* only "held that fees *may* be assessed . . . after a case has been settled by the entry of a consent decree." *Evans v. Jeff D.*, 475 U.S. 717 (1986). Private settlements do not entail the judicial approval and oversight involved in consent decrees. And federal jurisdiction to enforce a private contractual settlement will often be lacking unless the terms of the agreement are incorporated into the order of dismissal. See *Kokkonen v. Guardian Life Ins. Co. of America*, 511 U.S. 375 (1994).

Petitioners finally assert that the "catalyst theory" is necessary to prevent defendants from unilaterally mooting an action before judgment in an effort to avoid an award of attorney's fees. They also claim that the rejection of the "catalyst theory" will deter plaintiffs with meritorious but expensive cases from bringing suit. We are skeptical of these assertions, which are entirely speculative and unsupported by any empirical evidence (*e.g.*, whether the number of suits brought in the Fourth Circuit has declined, in relation to other Circuits, since the decision in *S-1 and S-2*).

Petitioners discount the disincentive that the "catalyst theory" may have upon a defendant's decision to voluntarily change its conduct, conduct that may not be illegal. "The defendants' potential liability for fees in this kind of litigation can be as significant as, and sometimes even more significant than, their potential liability on the merits," *Evans v. Jeff D.*, 475 U.S. 717, 734 (1986), and the possibility of being assessed attorney's fees may well deter a defendant from altering its conduct.

And petitioners' fear of mischievous defendants only materializes in claims for equitable relief, for so long as the plaintiff has a cause of action for damages, a defendant's change in conduct will not moot the case. Even then, it is not clear how often courts will find a case mooted: "It is well settled that a defendant's voluntary cessation of a challenged practice does not deprive a federal court of its power to determine the legality of the practice" unless it is "absolutely clear that the allegedly wrongful behavior could not reasonably be expected to recur." *Friends of Earth, Inc. v. Laidlaw Environmental Services (TOC), Inc.*, 528 U.S. 167, 189 (2000). . . .

We have also stated that "[a] request for attorney's fees should not result in a second major litigation," *Hensley v. Eckerhart*, 461 U.S. 424, 437 (1983), and have accordingly avoided an interpretation of the fee-shifting statutes that would have "spawn[ed] a second litigation of significant dimension. . . ." Among other things, a "catalyst theory" hearing would require analysis of the defendant's subjective motivations in changing its conduct, an analysis that "will likely depend on a highly factbound inquiry and may turn on reasonable inferences from the nature and timing of the defendant's change in conduct." Brief for United States as *Amicus Curiae* 28. . . .

[F]or the reasons stated above, we hold that the "catalyst theory" is not a permissible basis for the award of attorney's fees under the FHAA, 42 U.S.C. § 3613(c)(2), and ADA, 42 U.S.C. § 12205.

[The concurring opinion of Justice Scalia is omitted.]

JUSTICE GINSBURG, with whom JUSTICE STEVENS, JUSTICE SOUTER, and JUSTICE BREYER join, dissenting.

. . . .

The Court's insistence that there be a document filed in court—a litigated judgment or court-endorsed settlement—upsets long-prevailing Circuit precedent applicable to scores of federal fee-shifting statutes. The decision allows a defendant to escape a statutory obligation to pay a plaintiff's counsel fees, even though the suit's merit led the defendant to abandon the fray, to switch rather than fight on, to accord plaintiff sooner rather than later the principal redress sought in the complaint. Concomitantly, the Court's constricted definition of "prevailing party," and consequent rejection of the "catalyst theory," impede access to court for the less well heeled, and shrink the incentive Congress created for the enforcement of federal law by private attorneys general.

....

I

....

The array of federal-court decisions applying the catalyst rule suggested three conditions necessary to a party's qualification as "prevailing" short of a favorable final judgment or consent decree. A plaintiff first had to show that the defendant provided "some of the benefit sought" by the lawsuit.... Under most Circuits' precedents, a plaintiff had to demonstrate as well that the suit stated a genuine claim, *i.e.*, one that was at least "colorable," not "frivolous, unreasonable, or groundless...." Plaintiff finally had to establish that her suit was a "substantial" or "significant" cause of defendant's action providing relief.... In some Circuits, to make this causation showing, plaintiff had to satisfy the trial court that the suit achieved results "by threat of victory," not "by dint of nuisance and threat of expense...." One who crossed these three thresholds would be recognized as a "prevailing party" to whom the district court, "in its discretion," could award attorney's fees.

Developed over decades and in legions of federal-court decisions, the catalyst rule and these implementing standards deserve this Court's respect and approbation.

II

....

C

....

A lawsuit's ultimate purpose is to achieve actual relief from an opponent. Favorable judgment may be instrumental in gaining that relief. Generally, however, "the judicial decree is not the end but the means. At the end of the rainbow lies not a judgment, but some action (or cessation of action) by the defendant...." *Hewitt v. Helms*, 482 U.S. 755, 761 (1987). On this common understanding, if a party reaches the "sought-after destination," then the party "prevails" regardless of the "route taken...."

Under a fair reading of the FHAA and ADA provisions in point, I would hold that a party "prevails" in "a true and proper sense..." when she achieves, by instituting litigation, the practical relief sought in her complaint. The Court misreads Congress, as I see it, by insisting that, invariably, relief must be displayed in a judgment, and correspondingly that a defendant's voluntary action never suffices....

III

As the Courts of Appeals have long recognized, the catalyst rule suitably advances Congress' endeavor to place private actions, in civil rights and other legislatively defined areas, securely within the federal law enforcement arsenal.

. . . .

. . . Congress enacted § 1988 to ensure that nonaffluent plaintiffs would have "effective access" to the Nation's courts to enforce civil rights laws. That objective accounts for the fee-shifting provisions before the Court in this case, prescriptions of the FHAA and the ADA modeled on § 1988.

Under the catalyst rule that held sway until today, plaintiffs who obtained the relief they sought through suit on genuine claims ordinarily qualified as "prevailing parties," so that courts had discretion to award them their costs and fees. Persons with limited resources were not impelled to "wage total law" in order to assure that their counsel fees would be paid. They could accept relief, in money or of another kind, voluntarily proffered by a defendant who sought to avoid a recorded decree. And they could rely on a judge then to determine, in her equitable discretion, whether counsel fees were warranted and, if so, in what amount.[3]

Congress appears to have envisioned that very prospect. The Senate Report on the 1976 Civil Rights Attorney's Fees Awards Act states: "[F]or purposes of the award of counsel fees, parties may be considered to have prevailed when they vindicate rights through a consent judgment *or without formally obtaining relief*." S.Rep. No. 94-1011, at 5, U.S.Code Cong. & Admin. News 1976, pp. 5908, 5912 (emphasis added). In support, the Report cites cases in which parties recovered fees in the absence of any court-conferred relief. The House Report corroborates: "[A]fter a complaint is filed, a defendant might voluntarily cease the unlawful practice. *A court should still award fees* even though it might conclude, as a matter of equity, that *no formal relief*, such as an injunction, is needed." H.R.Rep. No. 94-1558, at 7 (emphases added). . . .

. . . .

Notes and Questions

1. The Court in *Buckhannon* did not write on a clean slate. In *Hensley v. Eckerhart*, 461 U.S. 424 (1983), a leading case interpreting the Civil Rights Attorney's Fee Awards Act of 1976, and excerpted *infra*, Section B(3) of this chapter, the Court had stated that "a typical formulation is that 'plaintiffs may be considered "prevailing parties" for attorney's fees purposes if they succeed on any significant issue in litigation which achieves some of the benefit the parties sought in bringing suit.'" *Id.* at

---

3. [Court's footnote #10] Given the protection furnished by the catalyst rule, aggrieved individuals were not left to worry, and wrongdoers were not led to believe, that strategic maneuvers by defendants might succeed in averting a fee award. . . .

433. In *Farrar v. Hobby*, 506 U.S. 103 (1992), the Court stated that "a plaintiff 'prevails' when actual relief on the merits of his claim materially alters the legal relationship between the parties by modifying the defendant's behavior in a way that directly benefits the plaintiff." *Id.* at 111–12.[4] In *Hewit v. Helms*, 482 U.S. 755 (1987), the Court stated that the plaintiff must "receive at least some relief on the merits of his claim before he can be said to prevail." *Id.* at 760. In *Texas State Teachers Ass'n v. Garland Indep. Sch. Dist.*, 489 U.S. 782 (1989), the Court had held that a consent decree could support a "prevailing party" fee award because, although it might not include an admission of liability by the defendant, it involved a court ordered change in the legal relationship of the parties. "The touchstone of the prevailing party inquiry must be the material alteration of the legal relationship of the parties. . . ." *Id.* at 792–93. In that case, the plaintiff prevailed on a secondary issue, but not on the central issue in the case. The Court ruled the secondary success was enough to allow the plaintiff to seek attorneys' fees. It suggested the fees could be pro-rated based on the level of success the plaintiff achieved: "The *degree* of the plaintiff's success in relation to the other goals of the lawsuit is a factor critical to the determination of the size of a reasonable fee, not to eligibility for a fee award at all." *Id.* at 790.

2. In *Buckhannon*, the Supreme Court interpreted these decisions as establishing "that enforceable judgments on the merits and court-ordered consent decrees create the 'material alteration of the legal relationship of the parties' necessary to permit an award of attorney's fees." 532 U.S. at 604 (quoting *Texas State*, 489 U.S. at 792–93).

The majority recognized that not only a litigated decree, but also a consent decree entered without any admission of liability, could supply the necessary "judicial imprimatur." On the other hand, footnote 7 of the Court's opinion seems clearly to rule out a settlement not incorporated into a consent decree as a basis for a fee award: "Private settlements do not entail the judicial approval and oversight involved in consent decrees." *Id.* at n.7.

3. In *Sole v. Wyner*, 551 U.S. 74, 83, 86 (2007), the Court held that the granting of a preliminary injunction did not automatically qualify the plaintiff as a prevailing party. "Prevailing party status, we hold, does not attend achievement of a preliminary injunction that is reversed, dissolved, or otherwise undone by the final decision in the same case." The Court continued, "[w]e express no view on whether, in the absence of a final decision on the merits of a claim for permanent injunctive relief, success in gaining a preliminary injunction may sometimes warrant an award of counsel fees. We decide only that a plaintiff who gains a preliminary injunction does not qualify for an award of counsel fees under § 1988(b) if the merits of the case are ultimately decided against her." *Id.* at 2196. *Compare Dearmore v. City of Garland*,

---

4. As discussed below, the fact that the plaintiff achieved only partial success was to be taken into account in determining the amount of the fee to be awarded, rather than by completely denying fees. For example, in *Farrar*, the Court held that a civil rights plaintiff who recovered only $1 in nominal damages on a $17 million claim, and no declaratory or injunctive relief, was entitled to no fee award.

519 F.3d 517 (5th Cir. 2008) (a plaintiff who obtains a preliminary injunction followed by defendant's action mooting the case is entitled to fees if (1) the preliminary injunction is based on an unambiguous indication of probable success on the merits as opposed to a balancing of equities; and (2) the injunction caused the defendant to moot the action preventing the plaintiff from obtaining final relief on the merits). More recently, the Supreme Court has clarified that the bar for earning attorney fees is actually rather low. The "fee claimant need not be a 'prevailing party' to be eligible for attorney fees" under a general fee-shifting statute, rather, the claimant is only required to "show 'some degree of success on the merits' before a court may award attorney fees." *Hardt v. Reliance Standard Life Ins. Co.*, 560 U.S. 242, 242, 254 (2010).

c. Fee Awards Based on the "Common Fund" Doctrine

Alyeska affirmed that prevailing parties are generally not owed attorney's fees from losing parties unless a statute or contract provides for such fees. However, to a considerable degree, *Alyeska*'s restrictive holding is irrelevant to complex cases involving the aggregation of claims through class actions, or where many actions involving the same subject matter have been transferred for coordinated or consolidated pre-trial proceedings under 28 U.S.C. § 1407. (Multidistrict Litigation, or MDL, was covered in depth in Chapter 3(B)(4).) That is because most such actions are settled, not tried, and because, regardless of the presence of a fee statute, an award of fees to class or lead counsel is proper under the long-standing equitable "common fund" doctrine in cases where the settlement creates a monetary fund for the benefit of all. In *Alyeska*, the Supreme Court refused to expand this concept to permit fees to be awarded to counsel on a "public policy" or "private attorney general" theory. In doing so, however, it specifically recognized and endorsed the "historic power of equity to permit the trustee of a fund or property, or a party preserving or recovering a fund for the benefit of others in addition to himself, to recover his costs, including his attorney's fees, from the fund or property itself or directly from the other parties enjoying the benefit." 421 U.S. at 257 (1975). The purpose of such awards is to prevent unjust enrichment by the class members or plaintiffs who have benefited from the efforts of class or lead counsel. As stated in *Mills v. Electric Auto-Lite Co.*, 396 U.S. 375 (1970), "to allow the others to obtain full benefit from the plaintiff's efforts without contributing equally to the litigation expenses would be to enrich the others unjustly at the plaintiff's expense." *Id.* at 392.

3. The "Lodestar" Method of Determining Fee Awards

Hensley v. Eckerhart

Supreme Court of the United States
461 U.S. 424 (1983)

Justice Powell delivered the opinion of the Court.

Title 42 U.S.C. § 1988 provides that in federal civil rights actions "the court, in its discretion, may allow the prevailing party, other than the United States, a reasonable attorney's fee as part of the costs." The issue in this case is whether a partially prevailing plaintiff may recover an attorney's fee for legal services on unsuccessful claims.

I

A

[In August 1977 respondents filed an amended one-count complaint specifying the conditions that allegedly violated their constitutional right to treatment in the Forensic Unit of a state hospital.]

In August 1979, following a three-week trial, the District Court held that an involuntarily committed patient has a constitutional right to minimally adequate treatment. . . . The court then found constitutional violations in five of six general areas: physical environment; individual treatment plans; least restrictive environment; visitation, telephone, and mail privileges; and seclusion and restraint. With respect to staffing, the sixth general area, the District Court found that the Forensic Unit's staffing levels, which had increased during the litigation, were minimally adequate. Petitioners did not appeal the District Court's decision on the merits.

B

In February 1980 respondents filed a request for attorney's fees for the period from January 1975 through the end of the litigation. Their four attorneys claimed 2,985 hours worked and sought payment at rates varying from $40 to $65 per hour. This amounted to approximately $150,000. Respondents also requested that the fee be enhanced by thirty to fifty percent, for a total award of somewhere between $195,000 and $225,000. Petitioners opposed the request on numerous grounds, including inclusion of hours spent in pursuit of unsuccessful claims.

The District Court first determined that respondents were prevailing parties under 42 U.S.C. § 1988 even though they had not succeeded on every claim. It then refused to eliminate from the award hours spent on unsuccessful claims[.] . . . Finding that respondents "have obtained relief of significant import," the District Court awarded a fee of $133,332.25. This award differed from the fee request in two respects. First, the court reduced the number of hours claimed by one attorney by thirty percent to account for his inexperience and failure to keep contemporaneous records. Second, the court declined to adopt an enhancement factor to increase the award.

The Court of Appeals for the Eighth Circuit affirmed on the basis of the District Court's memorandum opinion and order. We granted certiorari, and now vacate and remand for further proceedings.

II

The amount of the fee, of course, must be determined on the facts of each case. On this issue the House Report simply refers to twelve factors set forth in *Johnson v. Georgia Highway Express, Inc.*, 488 F.2d 714 (CA5 1974).[5] The Senate Report cites to *Johnson* as well . . . . One of the factors in *Johnson*, "the amount involved and the results obtained," indicates that the level of a plaintiff's success is relevant to the amount of fees to be awarded. The importance of this relationship is confirmed in varying degrees by the other cases cited approvingly in the Senate Report.

. . . .

In this case petitioners contend that "an award of attorney's fees must be proportioned to be consistent with the extent to which a plaintiff has prevailed, and only time reasonably expended in support of successful claims should be compensated." Respondents agree that a plaintiff's success is relevant, but propose a less stringent standard focusing on "whether the time spent prosecuting [an unsuccessful] claim in any way contributed to the results achieved." Both parties acknowledge the discretion of the district court in this area. We take this opportunity to clarify the proper relationship of the results obtained to an award of attorney's fees.

III

A

A plaintiff must be a "prevailing party" to recover an attorney's fee under § 1988. The standard for making this threshold determination has been framed in various ways. A typical formulation is that "plaintiffs may be considered 'prevailing parties' for attorney's fees purposes if they succeed on any significant issue in litigation which achieves some of the benefit the parties sought in bringing suit." *Nadeau v. Helgemoe*, 581 F.2d 275, 278–279 (1st Cir. 1978). This is a generous formulation that brings the plaintiff only across the statutory threshold. It remains for the district court to determine what fee is "reasonable."

The most useful starting point for determining the amount of a reasonable fee is the number of hours reasonably expended on the litigation . . . by a reasonable hourly rate. This calculation provides an objective basis on which to make an initial estimate of the value of a lawyer's services. The party seeking an award of fees should submit evidence supporting the hours worked and rates claimed. Where the documentation of hours is inadequate, the district court may reduce the award accordingly.

---

5. [Court's footnote #3] The twelve factors are: (1) the time and labor required; (2) the novelty and difficulty of the questions; (3) the skill requisite to perform the legal service properly; (4) the preclusion of employment by the attorney due to acceptance of the case; (5) the customary fee; (6) whether the fee is fixed or contingent; (7) time limitations imposed by the client or the circumstances; (8) the amount involved and the results obtained; (9) the experience, reputation, and ability of the attorneys; (10) the "undesirability" of the case; (11) the nature and length of the professional relationship with the client; and (12) awards in similar cases. 488 F.2d, at 717–719. These factors derive directly from the American Bar Association Code of Professional Responsibility, Disciplinary Rule 2-106.

The district court also should exclude from this initial fee calculation hours that were not "reasonably expended." Cases may be overstaffed, and the skill and experience of lawyers vary widely. Counsel for the prevailing party should make a good faith effort to exclude from a fee request hours that are excessive, redundant, or otherwise unnecessary, just as a lawyer in private practice ethically is obligated to exclude such hours from his fee submission. "In the private sector, 'billing judgment' is an important component in fee setting. It is no less important here. Hours that are not properly billed to one's client also are not properly billed to one's *adversary* pursuant to statutory authority." *Copeland v. Marshall*, 641 F.2d 880, 891 (1980) (en banc) (emphasis in original).

B

The product of reasonable hours times a reasonable rate does not end the inquiry. There remain other considerations that may lead the district court to adjust the fee upward or downward, including the important factor of the "results obtained." This factor is particularly crucial where a plaintiff is deemed "prevailing" even though he succeeded on only some of his claims for relief. In this situation two questions must be addressed. First, did the plaintiff fail to prevail on claims that were unrelated to the claims on which he succeeded? Second, did the plaintiff achieve a level of success that makes the hours reasonably expended a satisfactory basis for making a fee award?

In some cases a plaintiff may present in one lawsuit distinctly different claims for relief that are based on different facts and legal theories. In such a suit, even where the claims are brought against the same defendants—often an institution and its officers, as in this case—counsel's work on one claim will be unrelated to his work on another claim. Accordingly, work on an unsuccessful claim cannot be deemed to have been "expended in pursuit of the ultimate result achieved. . . ." The congressional intent to limit awards to prevailing parties requires that these unrelated claims be treated as if they had been raised in separate lawsuits, and therefore no fee may be awarded for services on the unsuccessful claim.

It may well be that cases involving such unrelated claims are unlikely to arise with great frequency. Many civil rights cases will present only a single claim. In other cases the plaintiff's claims for relief will involve a common core of facts or will be based on related legal theories. Much of counsel's time will be devoted generally to the litigation as a whole, making it difficult to divide the hours expended on a claim-by-claim basis. Such a lawsuit cannot be viewed as a series of discrete claims. Instead the district court should focus on the significance of the overall relief obtained by the plaintiff in relation to the hours reasonably expended on the litigation.

Where a plaintiff has obtained excellent results, his attorney should recover a fully compensatory fee. Normally this will encompass all hours reasonably expended on the litigation, and indeed in some cases of exceptional success an enhanced award may be justified. In these circumstances the fee award should not be reduced simply because the plaintiff failed to prevail on every contention raised in the lawsuit. Litigants in good faith may raise alternative legal grounds for a desired outcome, and the court's rejection of or failure to reach certain grounds is not a sufficient reason for reducing a fee. The result is what matters.[6]

If, on the other hand, a plaintiff has achieved only partial or limited success, the product of hours reasonably expended on the litigation as a whole times a reasonable hourly rate may be an excessive amount. This will be true even where the plaintiff's claims were interrelated, nonfrivolous, and raised in good faith. Congress has not authorized an award of fees whenever it was reasonable for a plaintiff to bring a lawsuit or whenever conscientious counsel tried the case with devotion and skill. Again, the most critical factor is the degree of success obtained.

Application of this principle is particularly important in complex civil rights litigation involving numerous challenges to institutional practices or conditions. This type of litigation is lengthy and demands many hours of lawyers' services. Although the plaintiff often may succeed in identifying some unlawful practices or conditions, the range of possible success is vast. That the plaintiff is a "prevailing party" therefore may say little about whether the expenditure of counsel's time was reasonable in relation to the success achieved. In this case, for example, the District Court's award of fees based on 2,557 hours worked may have been reasonable in light of the substantial relief obtained. But had respondents prevailed on only one of their six general claims, for example the claim that petitioners' visitation, mail, and telephone policies were overly restrictive . . . a fee award based on the claimed hours clearly would have been excessive.

There is no precise rule or formula for making these determinations. The district court may attempt to identify specific hours that should be eliminated, or it may simply reduce the award to account for the limited success. The court necessarily has discretion in making this equitable judgment. This discretion, however, must be exercised in light of the considerations we have identified.

C

A request for attorney's fees should not result in a second major litigation. Ideally, of course, litigants will settle the amount of a fee. Where settlement is not possible, the fee applicant bears the burden of establishing entitlement to an award and documenting the appropriate hours expended and hourly rates. The applicant should exercise "billing judgment" with respect to hours worked, and should maintain

6. [Court's footnote #11] We agree with the District Court's rejection of "a mathematical approach comparing the total number of issues in the case with those actually prevailed upon." Such a ratio provides little aid in determining what is a reasonable fee in light of all the relevant factors. Nor is it necessarily significant that a prevailing plaintiff did not receive all the relief requested. For example, a plaintiff who failed to recover damages but obtained injunctive relief, or vice versa, may recover a fee award based on all hours reasonably expended if the relief obtained justified that expenditure of attorney time.

billing time records in a manner that will enable a reviewing court to identify distinct claims.[7]

We reemphasize that the district court has discretion in determining the amount of a fee award. This is appropriate in view of the district court's superior understanding of the litigation and the desirability of avoiding frequent appellate review of what essentially are factual matters. It remains important, however, for the district court to provide a concise but clear explanation of its reasons for the fee award. When an adjustment is requested on the basis of either the exceptional or limited nature of the relief obtained by the plaintiff, the district court should make clear that it has considered the relationship between the amount of the fee awarded and the results obtained.

IV

In this case the District Court began by finding that "[t]he relief [respondents] obtained at trial was substantial and certainly entitles them to be considered prevailing . . . , without the need of examining those issues disposed of prior to trial in order to determine which went in [respondents'] favor." It then declined to divide the hours worked between winning and losing claims, stating that this fails to consider "the relative importance of various issues, the interrelation of the issues, the difficulty in identifying issues, or the extent to which a party prevails on various issues." Finally, the court assessed the "amount involved/results obtained" and declared: "Not only should [respondents] be considered prevailing parties, they are parties who have obtained relief of significant import. [Respondents'] relief affects not only them, but also numerous other institutionalized patients similarly situated. The extent of this relief clearly justifies the award of a reasonable attorney's fee."

These findings represent a commendable effort to explain the fee award. Given the interrelated nature of the facts and legal theories in this case, the District Court did not err in refusing to apportion the fee award mechanically on the basis of respondents' success or failure on particular issues. And given the findings with respect to the level of respondents' success, the District Court's award may be consistent with our holding today.

We are unable to affirm the decisions below, however, because the District Court's opinion did not properly consider the relationship between the extent of success

---

7. [Court's footnote #12] We recognize that there is no certain method of determining when claims are "related" or "unrelated." Plaintiff's counsel, of course, is not required to record in great detail how each minute of his time was expended. But at least counsel should identify the general subject matter of his time expenditures. See *Nadeau v. Helgemoe*, 581 F.2d 275, 279 (1st Cir. 1978) ("As for the future, we would not view with sympathy any claim that a district court abused its discretion in awarding unreasonably low attorney's fees in a suit in which plaintiffs were only partially successful if counsel's records do not provide a proper basis for determining how much time was spent on particular claims.").

and the amount of the fee award. The court's finding that "the [significant] extent of the relief clearly justifies the award of a reasonable attorney's fee" does not answer the question of what is "reasonable" in light of that level of success. We emphasize that the inquiry does not end with a finding that the plaintiff obtained significant relief. A reduced fee award is appropriate if the relief, however significant, is limited in comparison to the scope of the litigation as a whole.

V

We hold that the extent of a plaintiff's success is a crucial factor in determining the proper amount of an award of attorney's fees under 42 U.S.C. § 1988. Where the plaintiff has failed to prevail on a claim that is distinct in all respects from his successful claims, the hours spent on the unsuccessful claim should be excluded in considering the amount of a reasonable fee. Where a lawsuit consists of related claims, a plaintiff who has won substantial relief should not have his attorney's fee reduced simply because the district court did not adopt each contention raised. But where the plaintiff achieved only limited success, the district court should award only that amount of fees that is reasonable in relation to the results obtained. On remand the District Court should determine the proper amount of the attorney's fee award in light of these standards.

. . . .

[The concurring opinion of Chief Justice Burger and the opinion of Justice Brennan, concurring in part in dissenting in part, are omitted.]

Notes and Questions

1. *Hensley* endorses what is commonly termed a "lodestar" calculation as the starting point for all statutory fee awards. The lodestar equals "the number of hours reasonably expended on the litigation multiplied by a reasonable hourly rate." *Hensley*, 461 U.S. at 433. This deceptively simple formulation actually masks a host of difficulties. The system has a potential to discourage early settlement and provides a temptation for lawyers to overstaff and overwork cases. Further, the number of billing records that a court must sort through to determine whether the hours are reasonable for the task at hand can be overwhelming, and many courts shy away from using the lodestar method for this reason.

2. Historically, courts used multipliers to adjust the lodestar amount upwards or downwards based on factors such as the complexity of a case, the quality of representation, or the contingency of non-recovery. These multipliers were arguably justified to achieve the "private attorney general" purpose of fee statutes and motivate attorneys to aggressively pursue cases when they know there will be no compensation if they are not successful.

The Supreme Court has expressed skepticism regarding the use of multipliers in all but the most extraordinary circumstances. *See City of Burlington v. Dague,* 505

U.S. 557 (1992); *Perdue v. Kenny*, 559 U.S. 542 (2010). This has not stopped at least five states from passing state laws approving their use. The Florida Supreme Court has been the most explicit, declaring ". . . with all due deference to the United States Supreme Court, we do not accept the *Dague* majority's rationale for rejecting contingency fee multipliers," and "[w]e also reject Justice Scalia's reasoning in *Dague* that enhancement for contingency 'would likely duplicate in substantial part factors already subsumed in the lodestar.'" *Joyce v. Federated Nat'l Ins. Co.*, 228 So. 3d 1122, 1132, 1133 (Fla. 2017).

3. In *City of Burlington v. Dague*, 505 U.S. 557 (1992), the Court dropped the other shoe by ruling that contingency of success enhancements also are improper in determining statutory fee awards (in that case, under the Solid Waste Disposal Act and the Clean Water Act). The Court reasoned that such an enhancement might duplicate factors already taken into account in the lodestar (in other words, it would enable "double counting"), might encourage non-meritorious claims (because fee enhancements take into account the amount of risk the attorney assumed in taking on a case, and so the greater the risk, the greater the fee enhancement), would be difficult to apply, and would have the effect of compensating an attorney for time spent on unsuccessful cases, contrary to Congress' intent that defendants be required to pay fees only to plaintiffs who had "prevailed." *Burlington*, 505 U.S. at 563. Justice Blackmun dissented, arguing that the statutory fee is designed to be consistent with fees one would obtain in private practice, which customarily allow additional compensation for the risk of non-payment in the form of contingent fee agreements. He also argued that the majority's decision would weaken statutes containing fee shifting provisions (for example civil rights laws and environmental laws) because fewer meritorious claims would be brought under these statutes and less competent counsel would bring them. *Id.* at 568. Justice O'Connor also dissented on the ground that contingency enhancements were necessary to "attract competent counsel." *Id.* at 575.

Who had the better of this argument?

4. The "Percentage of Recovery" Method of Determining Fee Awards

The impact of the Court's decisions on statutory fees awards has been significantly blunted by increasing use of the "percentage of recovery" method of determining fees awards, particularly in "common fund" cases. Because most complex cases are settled by the creation of a fund to be shared by class members, the "common benefit" theory permits the court to award fees to lead, class or other counsel who have contributed to the creation of the fund regardless of any statutory fee authorization. Such "common fund" fees awards could be and have been calculated using the "lodestar" method, but that approach has fallen into disfavor. Encouraged by a footnote in *Blum v. Stenson*, 465 U.S. 886, 900 n.16 (1984) ("[u]nder the 'common fund doctrine,' . . . a reasonable fee is based on a percentage of the fund bestowed on the class") which seemed to endorse percentage awards in common fund cases, courts of appeals have increasingly mandated use of the percentage of recovery method in common fund cases, or concluded that district courts have discretion to employ the percentage method rather than conduct a lodestar calculation. The trend toward percentage rather than lodestar fee awards has been driven by perceived problems with the lodestar approach mentioned *infra*, Note 1, Section B(3) of this chapter.

Notes and Questions

1. Is the percentage of recovery method really as simple as its proponents contend? For example, how should the court determine what percentage should be awarded? In *Paul, Johnson, Alston & Hunt v. Graulty*, 886 F.2d 268 (9th Cir. 1989), the Ninth Circuit recognized that percentage fee awards generally range between 20 and 30 percent, and adopted a "benchmark" award of 25 percent, which could be adjusted upward or downward to take account of unusual circumstances. Courts still find 25 percent to be an appropriate benchmark. *See Stanger v. China Electric Motor, Inc.*, 812 F.3d 734 (9th Cir. 2016); *Moyle v. Liberty Mutual Ret. Benefit Plan*, 2018 WL 1141499 (S.D. Cal. Mar. 2, 2018); *Good v. West Virginia-American Water Company*, 2017 WL 2884535 (S.D. W. Va. July 6, 2017). How easy will it be to determine whether such adjustments should be made? What factors should be taken into account?

2. In *Gunter v. Ridgewood Energy Corp.*, 223 F.3d 190 (3d Cir. 2000), the Third Circuit stated that in applying the percentage of recovery method to determining attorney's fees in complex cases, the court should consider a number of factors including (1) the size of the fund and the number of persons benefited; (2) the presence or absence of substantial objections by class members; (3) the skill and efficiency of the attorneys involved; (4) the complexity and duration of the litigation; (5) the risk of nonpayment; (6) the amount of time devoted by plaintiffs' counsel; and (7) awards in similar cases. In that case, plaintiff's attorneys had requested a fees award of 33% of the $9.5 million settlement fund after several years of difficult litigation in which the defendants had initially indicated that they lacked resources to fund a settlement of more than $1 million. The district court provided only a conclusory explanation of its decision to reduce the award to 18 percent of the fund. The court of appeals reversed on the ground that the trial court had failed adequately to explain the reduction and to the extent it referenced the relevant factors, failed to apply them properly. The court of appeals also faulted the district court for failing to "cross-check" the final percentage award with the fees that would have been awarded under the lodestar method. *See also Goldberger v. Integrated Resources, Inc.*, 209 F.3d 43 (2d Cir. 2000) (adopting a multi-factor approach). How easy will it be to determine the proper percentage fee award under such a "multifactor" approach?

As illustrated by *Gunter*, courts applying the percentage of recovery method increasingly have concluded that the percentage award should be cross checked against the lodestar fee. If such cross-checks are routinely conducted or required, are any savings from use of the percentage of recovery method illusory?

3. Other complexities arise when the settlement becomes very large. Such cases are commonly referred to as "megafund" cases. In *In re Synthroid Marketing Litig.*, 264 F.3d 712 (7th Cir. 2001), the Seventh Circuit reversed the district court's decision that fees in "megafund" cases should be capped at 10% of the fund, in favor of a "market-based" approach. However, most courts have recognized that the percentage of the fee award should decline as the size of the fund becomes larger, because the very large amount of the fund turns more on the sheer size of the class than on the efforts of the attorneys, and to ensure that the amount of the fee is reasonably taking account of the time and effort devoted to the case. *See, e.g., In re Prudential Insurance Co. America Sales Practice Litig.*, 148 F.3d 283 (3d Cir. 1998) (remanding fee award negotiated as part of class action settlement of 6.7% of the settlement fund for reconsideration on the ground that the potential $1 billion recovery suggested that a lower percentage would produce a reasonable fee); *In re Cendant Corp. PRIDES Litig.*, 243 F.3d 722 (3d Cir. 2001) (reversing fee award of 5.7% of $340 million settlement; noting fee awards should normally decrease on a sliding scale as the amount of recovery increases). How easy will it be to determine what the appropriate "sliding scale" should be?

4. As mentioned in Section B(3), Note 2, the Supreme Court has disapproved "multipliers" for statutory fee awards determined by applying the lodestar approach. Nevertheless, those courts that continue to use the lodestar approach in common fund fees cases have permitted the use of multipliers, particularly to take account of the contingency of success. *See, e.g., In re Wash. Pub. Power Supply System Sec. Litig.*, 19 F.3d 1291 (9th Cir. 1994); *In re Prudential Insurance Co. America Sales Practice Litigation*, 148 F.3d 283 (3d Cir. 1998). On what grounds can the Court's decision in *Dague* be argued to be inapplicable to lodestar calculations in common fund fee cases?

5. Determining Attorneys' Fees in Cases Where the Relief Obtained is Difficult to Value

When the relief obtained in the action is predominately injunctive or declaratory in nature, or is difficult to value, a percentage common fund fee award is inappropriate, because there is no fund to which a percentage may be applied. In such cases, the lodestar method is commonly employed to make an initial fee determination.

Similar problems arise in cases whose settlements do not directly award money damages, but rather compensate class members with coupons, discounts, or rebates on subsequent purchases of the defendant's products. Such settlements have become increasingly common and have been frequently disapproved by the courts based on a concern that the class is being shortchanged while class counsel receives generous compensation in exchange for global peace for the defendant. *See Synfuel Technologies, Inc. v. DHL Express, Inc.*, 463 F.3d 646, 654 (7th Cir. 2006); *Davis v. Carl Cannon Chevrolet-Olds, Inc.*, 182 F.3d 792, 798 (11th Cir. 1999).

Courts are divided on how fees should be awarded in these cases. Some prefer the lodestar method, but have adjusted the award to take account of the actual benefit to the class as reflected by the coupons actually redeemed. *See Strong v. BellSouth Telecommunications Inc.*, 137 F.3d 844 (5th Cir. 1998). Others have applied the percentage of recovery method, but have noted that valuation of the settlement turns on factors such as the expected redemption rate and may be difficult to determine. *See, e.g., In re Compact Disc Minimum Advertised Price Antitrust Litig.*, 216 F.R.D. 197, 217 (D. Me. 2003).

Federal Rule of Civil Procedure 23(h) allows courts to use either the lodestar or percentage of recovery method to determine fees, while cautioning courts to give extra attention to these settlements that are difficult to value.

The Class Action Fairness Act of 2005 also addresses coupon settlements in the actions to which it applies (*see supra*, Chapter 2). 28 U.S.C. § 1712(a) provides that "If a proposed settlement in a class action provides for a recovery of coupons to a class member, the portion of any attorney's fee award to class counsel that is attributable to the award of the coupons shall be based on the value to class members of the coupons that are redeemed." The Act also makes complicated provisions regarding determination of fees in settlements involving both equitable relief and coupons, providing generally that the portion of the fee award based on a portion of the recovery of coupons shall be based on the value of the coupons redeemed, and the portion of the fee award not based on a portion of the coupon recovery shall be calculated using the lodestar method. *Id.* § 1712(b), (c). These provisions are models of ambiguity, and their meaning remains uncertain. *See, e.g., In re HP Inkjet Printer Litig.*, 716 F.3d 1173 (9th Cir. 2013).

A separate challenge arises when courts must determine fee amounts in cases involving conventional funds, portions of which remain unclaimed and subject to reversion to the defendant. The Supreme Court has held that these fee awards must be based on the entire amount of the fund, regardless of what portion remains unclaimed. *Boeing Co. v. Van Gemert*, 444 U.S. 472 (1980). The Court reasoned that because "each member of a certified class has an undisputed and mathematically ascertainable claim to part of a lump-sum judgment recovered on his behalf... a fee awarded against the entire judgment fund will shift the costs of litigation to each absentee in the exact proportion that the value of his claim bears to the total recovery." *Id.* at 472, 479. The American Law Institute's Principles of the Law of Aggregate Litigation (§ 3.13(a)) supports this opinion, asserting that fees in class actions should be based on "the actual value of the judgment or settlement to the class."

6. Court Authority Over Negotiated Fees

Staton v. Boeing Co.

United States Court of Appeals, Ninth Circuit
327 F.3d 938 (2003)

BERZON, CIRCUIT JUDGE.

This case involves a consent decree in an employment discrimination class lawsuit. The action was brought in 1998 by a class of approximately 15,000 African-American employees of the Boeing Company ("Boeing" or "the Company") against the Company. The decree requires Boeing to pay $7.3 million in monetary relief to the class, less reversions and an opt-out credit,[8] and releases Boeing from race discrimination-related and other claims. It further provides for certain injunctive relief, although much of this relief appears to be largely precatory in nature. Finally, the decree awards to the lawyers for the class ("class counsel") $4.05 million in attorneys' fees.[9]

. . . .

We hold that the district court acted within its discretion in certifying the case as a class action pursuant to Rule 23(a). We agree with the objectors, however, that the district court should not have approved the settlement agreement under Rule 23(e), because of several considerations relating to the award of attorneys' fees and because of the structure of the damages payments established by the decree.

The parties negotiated the amount of attorneys' fees as part of the settlement between the class and the Company. They included as a term of the proposed decree the amount of attorneys' fees that class counsel would receive. The action falls under the terms of two fee-shifting statutes. By negotiating fees as an integral part of the settlement rather than applying to the district court to award fees from the fund created, Boeing and class counsel employed a procedure permissible if fees can be justified as statutory fees payable by the defendant.

Boeing and class counsel did not, however, seek to justify the attorneys' fees on this basis but instead made a hybrid argument: They maintained that the award is an appropriate percentage of a putative "common fund" created by the decree even though common funds, as opposed to statutory fee-shifting agreements, usually do not isolate attorneys' fees from the class award before an application is made to the court. The district court approved the fees on that common fund basis.

The incorporation of an amount of fees calculated as if there were a common fund as an integral part of the settlement agreement allows too much leeway for

8. [Court's footnote #1] After applying the reversion and opt-out provisions, the damages awarded by the decree amount to approximately $6.5 million.

9. [Court's footnote #2] This amount includes $3.85 million in fees and costs to class counsel and $200,000 to objectors' counsel.

lawyers representing a class to spurn a fair, adequate and reasonable settlement for their clients in favor of inflated attorneys' fees. We hold, therefore, that the parties to a class action may not include in a settlement agreement an amount of attorneys' fees measured as a percentage of an actual or putative common fund created for the benefit of the class. Instead, in order to obtain fees justified on a common fund basis, the class's lawyers must ordinarily petition the court for an award of fees, separate from and subsequent to settlement.

. . . .

[II.B.3.] *Attorneys' Fees*

a. *Necessity of Scrutiny:* Attorneys' fees provisions included in proposed class action settlement agreements are, like every other aspect of such agreements, subject to the determination whether the settlement is "fundamentally fair, adequate, and reasonable." Fed. R. Civ. P. 23(e). There is no exception in Rule 23(e) for fees provisions contained in proposed class action settlement agreements. Thus, to avoid abdicating its responsibility to review the agreement for the protection of the class, a district court must carefully assess the reasonableness of a fee amount spelled out in a class action settlement agreement. . . .

That the defendant in form agrees to pay the fees independently of any monetary award or injunctive relief provided to the class in the agreement does not detract from the need carefully to scrutinize the fee award. Ordinarily, "a defendant is interested only in disposing of the total claim asserted against it . . . the allocation between the class payment and the attorneys' fees is of little or no interest to the defense. . . ."

Given these economic realities, the assumption in scrutinizing a class action settlement agreement must be, and has always been, that the members of the class retain an interest in assuring that the fees to be paid class counsel are not unreasonably high. If fees are unreasonably high, the likelihood is that the defendant obtained an economically beneficial concession with regard to the merits provisions, in the form of lower monetary payments to class members or less injunctive relief for the class than could otherwise have obtained. . . . In other words, the negotiation of class counsel's attorneys' fees is not exempt from the truism that there is no such thing as a free lunch.

. . . .

The district court was therefore obligated to assure itself that the fees awarded in the agreement were not unreasonably high, so as to ensure that the class members' interests were not compromised in favor of those of class counsel.

b. *Substantive Scrutiny of Statutory Fees:* Generally, litigants in the United States pay their own attorneys' fees, regardless of the outcome of the proceedings. In order to encourage private enforcement of the law, however, Congress has legislated that in certain cases prevailing parties may recover their attorneys' fees from the opposing side.

Both Title VII, § 2000e, et seq., and § 1981—the two federal statutes under which this suit was brought—have fee-shifting provisions.... The parties therefore could have negotiated an award of fees under § 2000e-5(k) and § 1988. Had they done so, the district court's review would have focused on the reasonableness of the fee request under the lodestar calculation method. Were the amount of fees Boeing agreed to pay in the settlement agreement distinctly higher than the fees class counsel could have been awarded by the district court using the lodestar method, the court would almost surely have had to find the fees unreasonable. Absent some unusual explanation, a defendant would not agree in a class action settlement to pay out of its own pocket fees measurably higher than it could conceivably have to pay were the fee amount litigated, unless there was some non-fee benefit the defendant received thereby.

In fact, no lodestar-based scrutiny of the fees awarded class counsel in the settlement agreement ever took place. Boeing and class counsel did not attempt to explain the award of fees provided in the consent decree as negotiated under the applicable fee-shifting statutes. Further, the record as it stands would not have been sufficient for such an inquiry, as it contains only the barest estimate of hours expended, with no detail. Not even a summary of the billing records was submitted.

We are therefore in no position to determine whether the fees Boeing agreed to pay are reasonable lodestar fees under the applicable fee-shifting statutes and do not do so. On remand, the parties are free to attempt such justification, based on the principles outlined in this opinion and in the extensive lodestar fees case law.

c. *The Common Fund Justification:* Rather than justifying the attorneys' fees provisions of the settlement agreement on the statutory fee-shifting basis that would properly have applied, the parties sought to justify the fee amount according to the principles applicable to common funds. They did so by constructing a hypothetical "fund" by adding together the amount of money Boeing would pay in damages to members of the class under the agreement, the amount of fees provided to various counsel, the cost of the class action notices paid for by Boeing, and a gross amount of money ascribed to all the injunctive relief contained in the agreement. For clarity, we will call the total of all those monetary amounts the "putative fund," for, as we shall see, it is not properly viewed as a common fund as that term is used in attorneys' fees law. (We will continue, also for clarity, to call the doctrine by its usual name, "common fund.") The parties portrayed the total fee award as 28% of the putative fund, and maintained that such a percentage is well within the percentage permitted under our common fund fee cases. The district court viewed the fee award as the parties requested and approved it, and the consent decree as a whole, on that basis. For several reasons, that approval was not appropriate.

i. *Availability of common fund fees*

Before we can decide whether the attempted common fund justification in this case was adequate, we must resolve whether the existence of potentially applicable fee-shifting statutory provisions precludes class counsel from recovering attorneys' fees under the common fund doctrine. We conclude, as have the two other circuits that have addressed the issue, that there is no preclusion on recovery of common fund fees where a fee-shifting statute applies.

... [T]he common fund doctrine ensures that each member of the winning party contributes proportionately to the payment of attorneys' fees. In contrast to fee-shifting statutes, which enable a prevailing party to recover attorneys' fees from the vanquished party, the common fund doctrine permits the court to award attorneys' fees from monetary payments that the prevailing party recovered in the lawsuit. Put another way, in common fund cases, a variant of the usual rule applies and the winning party pays his or her own attorneys' fees; in fee-shifting cases, the usual rule is rejected and the losing party covers the bill. . . .

The procedures used to determine the amount of reasonable attorneys' fees differ concomitantly in cases involving a common fund from those in which attorneys' fees are sought under a fee-shifting statute. As in a statutory fee-shifting case, a district court in a common fund case can apply the lodestar method to determine the amount of attorneys' fees. In common fund cases, however, the court can apply a risk multiplier when using the lodestar approach. . . .[10]

Alternatively, in a common fund case, the district court can determine the amount of attorneys' fees to be drawn from the fund by employing a "percentage" method. . . . As its name suggests, under the percentage method, "the court simply awards the attorneys a percentage of the fund. . . ." "This circuit has established 25% of the common fund as a benchmark award for attorney fees."

. . . .

Application of the common fund doctrine to class action settlements does not compromise the purposes underlying fee-shifting statutes. In settlement negotiations, the defendant's determination of the amount it will pay into a common fund will necessarily be informed by the magnitude of its potential liability for fees under the fee-shifting statute, as those fees will have to be paid after successful litigation and could be treated at that point as part of a common fund against which the attorneys' fees are measured. Conversely, the prevailing party will expect that part of any aggregate fund will go toward attorneys' fees and so can insist as a condition of settlement that the defendants contribute a higher amount to the settlement than if the defendants were to pay the fees separately under a fee-shifting statute.

The district court did not, therefore, err in treating this case as one that *could* fall under the common fund doctrine rather than under the potentially applicable fee-shifting provisions, *if* the parties properly so agreed, the resulting fee was reasonable, and other requisites applicable to common fund fees were met.

---

10. The Supreme Court has since shunned multipliers, holding that "there is a strong presumption that the lodestar is sufficient." *Perdue v. Kenny A. ex rel. Winn*, 559 U.S. 542, 546 (2010).—Eds.

The possibility that a prevailing party could recover fees either under the court's equitable powers or under its statutory authority does not, however, give the parties or the court free rein once either the common fund or the statutory rubric is selected. Fees sought or awarded under a fee-shifting statute require the application of the standards and procedures crafted for such statutes, discussed above. Similarly, if the parties invoke common fund principles, they must follow common fund procedures and standards, designed to protect class members when common fund fees are awarded. We turn next to the specific procedure employed in the negotiation and award of the attorneys' fees in this case.

ii. *Inclusion in the settlement of the attorneys' fees*

The parties negotiated the amount of attorneys' fees awarded class counsel as a term of the settlement agreement and thus conditioned the merits settlement upon judicial approval of the agreed-upon fees. . . . By proceeding in this fashion with respect to attorneys' fees and then attempting to justify the fees not as statutory fees but as common fund fees, the parties followed an irregular and, as we hold below, improper procedure.

Under regular common fund procedure, the parties settle for the total amount of the common fund and shift the fund to the court's supervision. The plaintiffs' lawyers then apply to the court for a fee award from the fund. . . .

In setting the amount of common fund fees, the district court has a special duty to protect the interests of the class. On this issue, the class's lawyers occupy a position adversarial to the interests of their clients. . . .

When the ordinary procedure is not followed and instead the parties explicitly condition the merits settlement on a fee award justified on a common fund basis, the obvious risk arises that plaintiffs' lawyers will be induced to forego a fair settlement for their clients in order to gain a higher award of attorneys' fees. That risk is, if anything, exacerbated where, as here, the agreement provides for payment of fees by the defendant, as in a statutory fee-shifting situation, but the parties choose to justify the fee as coming from a putative common fund. Where that is the case, courts have to be alert to the possibility that the parties have adopted this hybrid course precisely because the fee award is in fact higher than could be supported on a statutory fee-shifting basis, yet the deal is so dependent upon class counsel receiving a greater-than-lodestar amount of fees that the parties were not willing to give the court supervisory discretion to determine the distribution of the total settlement package between counsel and the class.

We recognize that in *Evans*, 475 U.S. at 720, 106 S. Ct. 1531, the Court held that the parties to a class action may simultaneously negotiate merits relief and an award of attorneys' fees under a fee-shifting statute, and may condition the entire settlement upon a waiver of fees.

We hold, therefore, that in a class action involving both a statutory fee-shifting provision and an actual or putative common fund, the parties may negotiate and settle the amount of statutory fees along with the merits of the case, as permitted by *Evans*. In the course of judicial review, the amount of such attorneys' fees can be approved if they meet the reasonableness standard when measured against statutory fee principles. Alternatively, the parties may negotiate and agree to the value of a common fund (which will ordinarily include an amount representing an estimated hypothetical award of statutory fees) and provide that, subsequently, class counsel will apply to the court for an award from the fund, using common fund fee principles. In those circumstances, the agreement as a whole does not stand or fall on the amount of fees. Instead, after the court determines the reasonable amount of attorneys' fees, all the remaining value of the fund belongs to the class rather than reverting to the defendant.

The parties in this case did not follow either of these procedures, or any other that adequately protected the class from the possibility that class counsel were accepting an excessive fee at the expense of the class. The district court therefore erred in approving the consent decree.

iii. *Injunctive relief as part of the district court's putative fund*

Even if the fee award had been determined in a procedurally proper way, approval of the amount of the attorneys' fees on common fund principles would still have been mistaken as a matter of law, because the actual percentage award was much higher than the 28% the district court recognized.

. . . .

. . . The court found that the fees constituted 28% of the putative fund, just above the 25% benchmark. To make this calculation, however, the court included in the amount of the putative fund an estimated value of $3.65 million for injunctive relief, the amount that the decree required Boeing to spend on approval and implementation of this component.

. . . [W]e have no difficulty here deciding that the district court abused its discretion in counting the parties' estimated value of that relief towards the putative fund.

The injunctive relief included in the consent decree requires Boeing only to "meet and confer" with class counsel or to discuss certain issues. Although Boeing must participate in such conferences and discussions, there is no requirement that Boeing take any action with respect to what the Company learns. The conferences and discussions may not result in tangible relief to class members. . . .

Additionally, while the injunctive relief (along with the cost of obtaining approval of the decree) is to cost Boeing a fixed minimum amount, $3.65 million, some of the injunctive relief described in the consent decree consists of steps Boeing had apparently decided to take on its own, even before it entered the settlement. The decree also permits Boeing to credit expenditures towards the injunctive relief amount without regard to whether such expenditures are in addition to the cost of Boeing's prior outlays for administering similar programs. Thus, the true cost of the injunction to the defendant—and the true benefit to the plaintiff class—is a matter of speculation and may be far less than $3.65 million. That amount of money cannot be accurately traced to the decree, let alone to the beneficiaries making up the class. Without the estimated value of the injunctive relief, the fund is reduced to only $10.55 million, and the fee award of $4.05 million constitutes 38%—well above the 25% benchmark—of the putative fund.

We do not hold that a district court can never consider the value of injunctive relief in determining the reasonableness of a common fund fee. For instance, in *Hanlon* [*v. Chrysler Corp.*, 150 F.3d 1011, 1029 (9th Cir. 1998)], we upheld the use of the common fund doctrine to award attorneys' fees after the parties reached a settlement agreement under which Chrysler would replace defective latches on minivans that it had manufactured. Although the replacement of latches is injunctive in nature, the agreement bestowed upon each beneficiary a clearly measurable benefit: one replacement latch for each minivan owned. The court could therefore, with some degree of accuracy, value the benefits conferred. Even so, in *Hanlon* the district court used its valuation of the fund only as a cross-check of the lodestar amount, "reject[ing] the idea of a straight percentage recovery because of its uncertainty as to the valuation of the settlement," and it was on that basis that we affirmed the fee award.

Precisely because the value of injunctive relief is difficult to quantify, its value is also easily manipulable by overreaching lawyers seeking to increase the value assigned to a common fund. We hold, therefore, that only in the unusual instance where the value to individual class members of benefits deriving from injunctive relief can be accurately ascertained may courts include such relief as part of the value of a common fund for purposes of applying the percentage method of determining fees. . . . When this is not the case, courts should consider the value of the injunctive relief obtained as a "relevant circumstance" in determining what percentage of the common fund class counsel should receive as attorneys' fees, rather than as part of the fund itself. Alternatively, particularly where obtaining injunctive relief likely accounted for a significant part of the fees expended, courts can use the common fund version of the lodestar method either to set the fee award or as a cross-check to assist in the determination of how the "relevant circumstance" of the injunctive relief should affect a percentage award. . . .

The district court did not employ either of these procedures here. Nor can we determine on the record before us that considering the injunctive relief as a "relevant circumstance" or employing the common fund lodestar method would have justified the award of $4.05 million as a reasonable fee. On this ground, also, the district court erred in approving the proposed attorneys' fees award.

. . . .

III. CONCLUSION

. . . .

On remand, the parties will have a choice concerning whether to attempt to justify the present proposed agreement under the principles outlined above or, instead, to renegotiate the aspects of the agreement we have indicated are questionable. If they choose the former course and are able to justify the damages distribution (which on the present record appears quite unlikely), they will then also have to substantiate the fee award using a lodestar calculation under the applicable fee-shifting statutes rather than on a common fund basis. For the reasons stated, the fee as it stands cannot be justified on a common fund basis, and the court can only approve or disapprove the present agreement in its entirety. Thus, if the fee cannot be justified on the fee-shifting statutory basis, the entire agreement will have to be renegotiated.

. . . .

[The dissenting opinion of Judge Trott is omitted.]

Notes and Questions

1. As the Court notes, in *Staton*, in *Evans v. Jeff D.*, 475 U.S. 717 (1986), the Supreme Court approved the practice of simultaneous negotiation for an attorneys' fee award as part of an overall settlement package. That practice is controversial because it raises the prospect that the defendant may have agreed to a generous fee award to induce plaintiffs' counsel to accept an inadequate settlement of the merits. In *Evans* itself, however, which involved individual litigation, the defendant made a settlement offer which required the plaintiff to waive any entitlement to fees under the Civil Rights Fees Act. The Court upheld the practice on the ground that unless defendants can be assured of the extent of their overall potential liability including fees in the settlement agreement, desirable settlements often might be deterred. On the other hand, it could be argued that permitting such a practice will discourage civil rights enforcement by permitting defendants to pit the interests of the client against those of their attorneys, contrary to the purpose of the Fees Act to encourage attorneys to undertake such cases.

In class actions and other aggregated litigation, fee waivers are not a significant issue. In that context, defendants have a strong motivation to provide class counsel with adequate incentive to reach a comprehensive settlement of the aggregated claims. Indeed, in that context, the danger is not that a fee waiver will be demanded, but that overly generous provisions for fees may induce class or lead counsel to accept an inadequate settlement on the merits. It is this danger that underlies the Ninth Circuit's analysis in *Staton*.

2. *Staton* clearly assumes that if fees are claimed under a statutory fee shifting provision, any fees award agreed to by settlement is subject to review by the trial court applying lodestar principles. But it then asserts that where the amount of fees is settled, rather than litigated, "the court need not inquire into the reasonableness of fees even at the high end [of the amount that would be awarded by the court under the lodestar method] with precisely the same level of scrutiny as when the fee amount is litigated." What does this mean?

3. Further, *Staton* makes clear that in the statutory fee context, the parties can condition the settlement on the court's approval of the negotiated fee. Why shouldn't the same be true in a common fund case?

4. What about the Supreme Court's conclusion in *Evans* that the defendant must be able to predict its aggregate liability including attorneys' fees to provide an adequate incentive for settlement? Could the defendants in *Staton* have served that goal without negotiating the amount of the fee? On the other hand, does the restrictive approach adopted by the *Staton* majority provide adequate incentive for plaintiffs' counsel to reach a settlement?

5. "Clear sailing agreements" can be reached during settlement negotiations and involve a defendant agreeing not to protest a plaintiff's fee request as long as the request is below a certain amount. Do such agreements pose any dangers? How do such agreements contrast with the issue presented in *Staton*? *See Malchman v. Davis*, 761 F.2d 893, 906 (2d Cir. 1985) (Newman, J., concurring); *compare In re Prudential Insurance Co. Am. Sales Practice Litig.*, 148 F.3d 283 (3d Cir. 1998) (declining to hold clear sailing agreements improper, but remanding on other grounds).

7. Note on the Allocation of Fee Awards Among Counsel

In a complex case, numerous counsel may participate in the preparation and presentation of the plaintiffs' case. Typically, this results from work assignments under the supervision of class or lead counsel. If the plaintiffs "prevail" under a statutory fee shifting provision, or succeed in creating a "common fund" by settlement or litigation, court approval of the overall amount of the fee award does not, in itself, determine how the award should be allocated among counsel who have contributed to the result.

A ready means of allocation exists if the fee award is determined using the lodestar method. In that event, the hours and hourly rate spent by each lawyer contributing to the overall result are known and fees can be apportioned accordingly. Common fund cases present greater difficulties, because calculation of the overall award does not suggest how it should be allocated among counsel. In general, courts have encouraged counsel to attempt to agree among themselves on the allocation of the award, subject to the supervision of the court (which may employ a special master to assist in the resolution of remaining disputes). *See, e.g., In re Warfarin Sodium Antitrust Litig.*, 212 F.R.D. 231 (D. Del. 2002). *See also In re Agent Orange Product Liability Litig.*, 818 F.2d 216 (2d Cir. 1987). Although counsel are encouraged to agree on the allocation of the award, the court retains ultimate authority to disapprove the agreement if it concludes that it is not fairly reflective of the respective contributions of counsel. *In re FPI/Agretech Securities Litig.*, 105 F.3d 469 (9th Cir. 1997).

Class members in class action or consolidated litigation frequently retain their own attorneys. Courts generally disapprove efforts by these class members to avoid contributing to the common fund fee award established to compensate the class and lead counsel. Standard practice is for all class members of a successful suit to contribute an equal share to the common fund, regardless of private retainers. *See In re Fine Paper Antitrust Litig.*, 98 F.R.D. 48 (E.D. Pa. 1983).

However, many decisions have recognized that an additional fee assessment beyond that imposed by private agreement may be appropriate to take account of the greater contributions of class or lead counsel. *See Vincent v. Hughes Air West, Inc.*, 557 F.2d 759, 772 (9th Cir. 1977) (assessing fees for lead counsel of 5% of entire judgment or settlement and ordering that the assessment come from any contingent fee of individual counsel in excess of 20%). In theory, the allocation of the common fund or statutory fee award should turn on the relative contributions of counsel to the result. *Accord, In re Air Crash Disaster at Fla. Everglades* on Dec. 29, 1972, 549 F.2d 1006 (5th Cir. 1977) (upholding power of district court to order payment of the fees of plaintiffs' committee out of fees to which other plaintiffs' counsel otherwise would be entitled, but remanding for a proper hearing).

In class actions, Rule 23 expressly confers upon courts authority to approve attorneys' fees and settlement terms. There is no such explicit authority for courts handling multidistrict litigation (MDL). Courts get around this by labeling MDL proceedings as quasi-class actions and exerting authority in the same way as they would in a traditional class action. *See, e.g., In re Zyprexa Prods. Liab. Litig.*, 424 F. Supp. 2d 488 and 433 F. Supp. 2d 268 (E.D.N.Y. 2006); *In re Vioxx Prods. Liab. Litig.*, 574 F. Supp. 2d 606 (E.D. La. 2008). Refer to Chapter 3(B)(4) for more on MDL proceedings.

In Charles Silver and Geoffrey P. Miller, *The Quasi-Class Action Method of Managing Multi-District Litigations: Problems and a Proposal*, 63 VAND. L. REV. 107 (2010), Professors Silver and Miller advance a wide-ranging critique of the prevailing "quasi-class action" approach to MDL management. They contend that the common practice of judicial appointment of lead attorneys and control of their compensation through contingent fee caps and forced transfers from non-lead lawyers has serious disadvantages, including compromising judicial independence, requiring judges to make decisions without adequate information and standards, lack of transparency, overcompensating some lawyers while undercompensating others, and often producing a suboptimal level of "common benefit" work. They further contend that such forced taxation of fees is not justified by the common fund doctrine.

8. Note on Expert Witness Fees and Litigation Expenses

Complex litigation involves very substantial costs, beyond attorneys' fees, such as expert witness fees (which can rival attorneys' fees in magnitude), and substantial out-of-pocket expenses for travel, depositions, telephone, document review, computerized legal research, consultants, and a variety of other expenses. Are these expenses recoverable by a prevailing party?

Complex cases often involve two types of expert witnesses: testifying experts and consulting experts. Testifying experts are hired to testify at trial, while consulting experts are hired to advise counsel without testifying. Both are expensive, and neither are recoverable costs. The Supreme Court has held that recoverable costs included in Federal Rule of Civil Procedure 54(d) are limited to those specified by 28 U.S.C. § 1920, which includes "Compensation of court appointed experts." § 1920(6). The Court has ruled that because the statute specifies "court appointed," it does not intend to cover experts retained directly by litigants. *Crawford Fitting Co. v. J.T. Gibbons, Inc.*, 482 U.S. 437 (1987). Courts have not distinguished between testifying experts and consulting experts when it comes to fee recovery.

In *West Virginia University Hospitals, Inc. v. Casey*, 499 U.S. 83 (1991), the Court took the next step, holding that a party's expert witness expenses could not be recovered under a statute such as the Civil Rights Fees Act providing for recovery of costs and attorneys' fees by the prevailing party. The court held that the reference to "costs" in such statutes should be understood to refer to the same costs as recoverable under Rule 54(d). It further reasoned that statutory usage clearly distinguished between attorneys' fees and expert witness fees, which Congress had long regarded as "distinct items of expense." *Id.* at 92.

The impact of these decisions has been somewhat blunted by Congress' subsequent enactment of express statutory authorizations for the recovery of expert witness fees by prevailing parties. For example, Congress quickly reacted to *Casey* by amending the Civil Rights Fees Act just a few months after the decision, to provide that "[i]n awarding an attorney's fee under subsection (b) of this section in any action or proceeding to enforce a provision of section 1981 or 1981a of this title, the court, in its discretion, may include expert fees as part of the attorney's fee." 42 U.S.C. § 1988(c). Similarly the attorney's fee provision of Title VII of the 1964 Civil Rights Act now provides that "[i]n any action or proceeding under this subchapter the court, in its discretion, may allow the prevailing party, other than the Commission or the United States, a reasonable attorney's fee (including expert fees) as part of the costs, and the Commission and the United States shall be liable for costs the same as a private person." 42 U.S.C.A. § 2000e-5 (West 2007).

Moreover, expert witness fees in complex litigation routinely are recovered as part of "common fund" fee awards on the ground that they contributed to the benefit achieved for the class, as are other costs that typify complex cases such as those for travel, telephone, paralegals, litigation and trial support services, computerized legal research, consultants, document copying and imaging, etc. (Another, increasingly important topic in complex litigation is the recoverability of the costs of e-discovery by a prevailing party. That subject is addressed in Chapter 8.C, *infra*.)

Chapter 8

Discovery

A. Introduction

Discovery in complex litigation always has been a daunting task. In the United States' antitrust case against IBM during the 1970s, over 50 million documents and 500 witnesses were involved. Discovery took six years, and the sheer complexity of the case led some to speculate that it could lead to the end of litigation in antitrust cases. *The Monster Case*, TIME, June 2, 1975, at 1.

Electronic data storage, which began in the 1970s and today is the dominant form of record keeping, makes storing, cataloging, and searching data a massive challenge for law firms of all sizes. Courts have compounded the challenge in a litigation context by increasing the amount of electronic data that litigants are expected to retain and produce if requested. For example, in *Aguilar v. U.S. Immigration and Customs Enforcement Div.*, 255 F.R.D. 350 (S.D.N.Y. 2008), the court ruled that companies need to be *ready* to produce *metadata* (discussed in section B(6) *infra*) in litigation.

Even more hazardous is the problem of information technology used by a company's employees without a company's knowledge, such as portable hard drives, and internet based storage. Such information may be discoverable, but at least initially may be unknown to the company. *See* Deborah H. Juhnke, *Under the Radar* 29 NAT'L L. J., Aug. 20, 2007, at 1.

The consequences of failing to retain, and if necessary, produce such information are significant. Litigants face sanctions, and their lawyers face disciplinary measures for failing to retain and produce electronic information. *See* Sanctions, *infra*. The "broad array of pitfalls and the ability to reveal mistakes and outright gamesmanship through the often inerasable trail of electronic evidence" make shortfalls in this area even more dangerous. *See* John J. Coughlin, *Learning from the E-Discovery Mistakes of Others*, 30 NAT'L L.J., Dec. 10, 2007, at 4. As a result, companies and their lawyers are spending substantial amounts in an attempt to retain, sort, and produce such information.

This expense is taking a heavy toll. For many cases, litigants are simply being priced out of the litigation system. "[Justice] Stephen Breyer . . . [has] expressed concern that, with ordinary cases costing millions just in e-discovery work, 'you're going to drive out of the litigation system a lot of people who ought to be there; so that justice is determined by wealth, not by the merits of the case.'" *Id.* According to a joint survey by the American College of Trial Lawyers and the Institute for the

Advancement of the American Legal System, "[t]here is a serious concern that the costs and burdens of discovery are driving litigation away from the court system and forcing settlements based on the costs, as opposed to the merits, of cases." American College of Trial Lawyers & Institute for the Advancement of the American Legal System, *Interim Report & 2008 Litigation Survey of the Fellows of the American College of Trial Lawyers*, Sept. 9, 2008, at 1 [hereinafter Litigation Survey].

Solutions so far have been of doubtful effectiveness. Arbitration, once a solution to the time and cost of litigation, is itself becoming bogged down by many of litigation's problems. "Today . . . the experience of massive, uncontrolled document discovery, particularly with regard to electronic documents, has eviscerated most of the benefits of arbitration." Thomas L. Aldrich, *Arbitration's E-Discovery Conundrum*, 31 NAT'L L. J., Dec. 15, 2008, at 1.

The Federal Rules of Civil Procedure encourage a collaborative approach among parties to e-discovery issues. Federal Rule of Evidence 502 attempts to reduce the number of privilege-related disputes by maintaining privilege for inadvertently disclosed information. As long as the party has taken reasonable steps to prevent disclosure, and takes reasonable steps to rectify the error after inadvertent disclosure, privilege is maintained. Fed. R. Evid. 502(b). Further, even if privilege is waived, it is only waived for the particular document in question, and not for the entire subject matter of the communications. Fed. R. Evid. 502(a).

Federal Rule of Civil Procedure 26 provides a limited privilege for draft reports and communications by experts. This in theory removes the need to retain two sets of experts; one set to prepare reports and to testify concerning their content, and another set to give behind-the-scenes advice to counsel and to insulate much of the report preparation from discovery.

Moreover, even to the extent that the past 15 years' updates to the rules have been successful, the Joint Report suggests that many lawyers would like to see a much more thorough overhaul of the discovery system. Litigation Survey, *supra*, at 5. The report refers to the changes effected to date as "tinkering around the edges" that has not had a substantive effect on the problems associated with discovery today. *Id.*

Ultimately, even a major re-working of the discovery process will be unlikely to make discovery problems go away. Discovery always will be a balance between a desire to locate full information about a dispute and to prevent trial by ambush on the one hand, and a desire to prevent abuse, litigation by attrition, and costs out of proportion to benefits on the other. Any legislative approach to the current problems of discovery will have to leave room for those on the ground to strike this balance. This responsibility, primarily, will fall on lawyers and judges.

B. The Discovery Process in Complex Litigation

1. Discovery Plans

Discovery plans are formulated by the parties and the court. They provide a blueprint for the conduct of discovery. Each plan has its roots in the Rule 26(f) conference of the parties early in the litigation. According to Rule 26(f), the plan should do the following.

> [S]tate the parties' views and proposals on: (A) what changes should be made in the timing, form, or requirement for disclosures under Rule 26(a) . . . (B) the subjects on which discovery may be needed, when discovery should be completed, and whether discovery should be conducted in phases or be limited to or focused on particular issues; (C) any issues about disclosure, discovery, or preservation of electronically stored information, including the form or forms in which it should be produced; (D) any issues about claims of privilege . . . (E) What changes should be made in the limitations on discovery imposed under these rules or by local rule, and what other limitations should be imposed; and (F) any other orders that the court should issue under Rule 26(c) or under Rule 16(b) and (c).

FED. R. CIV. P. 26(f)(3). The discovery conference between the parties is intended to provide the basis for the actual Rule 16(b) scheduling order. Rule 16(b)(3) provides for inclusion of the results of the discovery conference in the scheduling order. Therefore, the parties themselves have primary responsibility for mapping out a discovery plan for the litigation, subject of course to judicial intervention at the Rule 16(b) conference. The parties are obligated to attempt to agree. "If a party or its attorney fails to participate in good faith in developing and submitting a proposed discovery plan as required by Rule 26(f)," Rule 37(f) provides for the possibility of sanctions. Courts have imposed sanctions for failure to participate in formulating a discovery plan. *See United States v. Knudson*, 959 F. Supp. 1180 (D. Neb. 1997).

Complex litigation is particularly susceptible to discovery problems, given the potentially large volume of material involved. Accordingly, in complex cases, judges need to exercise greater control than in cases involving smaller discovery.

The Federal Judicial Center's MANUAL FOR COMPLEX LITIGATION (FOURTH) (2004) (hereafter the MANUAL) provides a useful guide for dealing with discovery in complex cases. The central thrust of the MANUAL anticipates a large role for judicial management of the discovery plan:

> The judge should ask the lawyers initially to propose a plan, but should not accept joint recommendations uncritically. Limits may be necessary even regarding discovery on which counsel agree. The judge's role is to oversee the plan and provide guidance and control. In performing that role, even with limited familiarity with the case, the judge must retain responsibility

> for control of discovery. The judge should not hesitate to ask why particular discovery is needed and whether information can be obtained more efficiently and economically by other means. Regular contact with counsel through periodic conferences will enable the judge to monitor the progress of the plan, ensure that it is operating fairly and effectively, and adjust it as needed.

Id. § 11.42. The MANUAL contemplates close judicial supervision during and after the formation of the discovery plan. It suggests several specific steps that judges should take to obtain the best blend of efficiency and truth. *See id.* § 11.421. Judges should, for example, carefully scrutinize proposed discovery to make sure that it is not cumulative or duplicative, and that it is not less convenient, burdensome, or expensive than other sources. *Id.* Judges should also direct disclosure of core information to save the expense of formal discovery when eventual production is inevitable. *Id.* Finally, judges should balance carefully cost against benefit when considering both subject matter and format of discovery. *Id.*

Note

For a particularly instructive case regarding the trial court's discretion to manage discovery in complex cases, see *B.F. Goodrich v. Betkoski*, 99 F.3d 505, 523–24 (2d Cir. 1996). In the course of this litigation, the district court placed certain restrictions on discovery. The appellants contended that these discovery limitations were so severe as to be an abuse of the trial court's discretion and to constitute reversible error. The Second Circuit ruled that:

> A trial court necessarily has wide discretion in managing pre-trial discovery, *see Cruden v. Bank of New York*, 957 F.2d 961, 972 (2d Cir. 1992), and we will not disturb its orders absent a clear abuse of its discretion, *id.*; *Robertson v. National Basketball Ass'n*, 622 F.2d 34, 35–36 (2d Cir. 1980). Reversal of a judgment because of an improper order denying or curtailing discovery is "unusual." 8 Charles Alan Wright, Arthur R. Miller & Richard L. Marcus, *Federal Practice and Procedure* § 2006, at 92 (2d ed. 1994).
>
> We find no abuse of discretion in the district court's management of discovery. In complex multi-party litigation, a trial court often needs to use its broad authority to control discovery. Some of the measures adopted here, such as time limits, schedules for discovery, and limitations on deposition discovery, have been specifically recommended as acceptable options. *See Manual For Complex Litigation (Third)* § 21.422 (1995); H.R.Rep. No. 253(I), 99th Cong., 2d Sess. 80 (1985), *reprinted in* 1986 U.S.C.C.A.N. 2835, 2862 (supporting the enactment of amendments to CERCLA and urging district courts to "carefully manage" CERCLA cases "to insure that the litigation is conducted in an expeditious manner" through, *inter alia*, the "exercise of strict judicial control over multi-party proceedings . . . as well as use of the procedures set forth in the Manual For Complex Litigation").

The district court sought to guard against what it thought might be a wildfire of unwarranted discovery, recognizing that unduly extensive use of discovery could make the litigation expense disproportionate to the cost of cleaning up the landfills. In order to have orderly and reasonable discovery, the trial judge required that a high standard of good cause be met before discovery beyond that provided in the uniform orders would be permitted. Its orders were tailored appropriately to meet this need.

Appellants also strongly challenge the denial of their requests for additional discovery under Fed. R. Civ. P. 56(f). Rule 56(f) allows a party faced with a motion for summary judgment to request additional discovery, and the Supreme Court has suggested that such a request be granted when "the nonmoving party has not had an opportunity to make full discovery." Celotex, 477 U.S. at 326. Here too we will reverse only if there was an abuse of discretion. *Paddington Partners v. Bouchard*, 34 F.3d 1132, 1137 (2d Cir. 1994). Doubtless, more discovery might have been helpful, but in a case this complex the information falling within the broad purview of federal discovery is almost without limit. In this light it is hard to fault the district court for placing limitations on discovery. Given the circumstances of this case, we see no abuse of discretion either in its discovery orders or its decision rejecting the appellants' Rule 56(f) motions.

2. Document Depositories

A document depository (i.e., a centrally located, searchable electronic database of documents that is accessible by parties relevant to a particular action) can be useful in all forms of litigation. The cost of establishing a document depository can be prohibitive, and one is therefore typically only used in instances of complex litigation.

More specifically, document depositories are most commonly used in multidistrict litigation. The procedural framework for multidistrict litigation grew out of the electrical equipment antitrust cases of the 1960s, in which more than 1,800 separate damage actions were filed in 33 federal district courts. *See* Reports of the Proceedings of the Judicial Conference of the United States, Washington, D.C., Mar. 10–11, 1966, 25 (1966). Due to the high volume of cases, coordinated measures were required to ensure that this massive wave of litigation would not overwhelm completely the federal court system. Ultimately, as discussed in Chapter 3(B)(4), these efforts at pretrial consolidation and coordination were codified in 28 U.S.C. § 1407.

Under § 1407, a panel of seven federal judges determines which cases qualify for multidistrict litigation treatment, as well as to which district courts to transfer and consolidate such cases in. The only requirement for such a transfer is that it will result in the convenience of the parties and witnesses and will promote the just and efficient conduct of the cases.

Document depositories are common in the context of multidistrict litigation because, first, there are often many concurrent claims. Second, such claims are consolidated in a single court, which may be remote geographically for many of the parties, making physical access to the documents difficult. Thus, once established, a document depository not only allows fast and convenient access to a voluminous amount of documents, but the format that the documents are archived in is easily searchable and without geographic limitation.

Although many courts have implemented some form of a document depository system, the decisions resulting from such cases usually provide little insight into the creation of the depositories themselves. This is largely due to the fact that document depositories are created out of a need for expediency. The precise manner in which they are created is accomplished through the mutual agreement of the parties and the judge. The creation and implementation of such systems, while certainly a vital part of any trial that requires their use, are thus rarely memorialized in the final disposition of a particular court.

3. Document Retention Policies

> Prior to 2015, the rules of civil procedure were silent about any duty to preserve evidence for use in discovery; litigants were left to the not-always-clear common law articulation of that duty. The 2015 amendments to federal rules, however, explicitly, if not comprehensively, address the duty to preserve . . . "electronically stored information" and provide important guidance on the sanctions that may be imposed for the failure to preserve electronic evidence.

Haydock & Herr, Discovery Practice § 28.02 (8th ed. 2017). There is a duty to preserve evidence for litigation. However, this duty is not well defined. The duty clearly exists when a lawsuit has been filed. *See id.* (citing *In re Napster, Inc., Copyright Litig.*, 462 F. Supp. 2d 1060 (N.D. Cal. 2006)). But a standard formulation states that "[t]he duty to preserve material evidence arises not only during litigation but also extends to that period before the litigation when a party reasonably should know that the evidence may be relevant to anticipated litigation." *See, e.g., Velez v. Marriott PR Management, Inc.*, 590 F. Supp. 2d 235, 258 (D.P.R. 2008). This formulation is less than clear. But counsel need to proceed cautiously because, if a retention duty has arisen, the consequences for breaching that duty are potentially very serious. How serious depends on the answers to such questions as: 1) What evidence was destroyed? 2) What relationship did the evidence bear to the issues in litigation? 3) Is the evidence still obtainable elsewhere? 4) What was the state of mind of the party who destroyed the evidence? 5) How much prejudice has been done to the opposing party? Haydock & Herr, *supra*, § 28.02 (4th ed. 2008).

Sanctions are discussed later in this chapter. They may range from monetary sanctions to reimburse the other party for expenses incurred because of misconduct, to "merits" sanctions, which may affect the outcome of the case. Indeed, in extreme cases, discovery abuse can result in dismissal or entry of default judgment. Document retention protocols, therefore, should be on every lawyer's checklist even before the formal commencement of threatened litigation. A document retention policy is a continuous system put in place by an organization designed to keep documents available for as long as they are needed, and to destroy them as soon as they are no longer required.

The primary responsibility for guiding a party's document retention will rest initially with lawyers, as judges only have control after litigation begins.

> In terms of legal requirements for record retention . . . a good general rule is to retain documents for the period of the statute of limitations for each area of law that might be implicated by that particular document. . . . Once possible litigation over the product is time-barred, however, there is probably no longer a business or legal need to keep the documents, and they should be destroyed.

John P. Hutchins & J. Timothy Mast, Document Retention Basics, 907 PLI/PAT 657, 661–68 (2008).

In the wake of the Enron scandal, document retention policies began to receive heavy scrutiny, as "testimony in court confirmed what outside observers had long suspected—that instructions to 'follow the document retention policy' were simply coded orders to 'shred 'em.'" Wright & Graham, Federal Practice & Procedure § 5178. As a result, calls for a closer judicial scrutiny have been growing. *See id. See also* Christopher R. Egan, *Arthur Andersen's Evidence Destruction Policy: Why Current Spoliation Standards Do Not Adequately Protect Investors*, 34 Tex. Tech. L. Rev. 61 (2002).

Once litigation is anticipated, a party's burden increases. Even adhering to a well defined document retention policy may not be sufficient. A party must suspend its routine document destruction policies, and put in place a "litigation hold." *See, e.g., Samsung Electronics Co., Ltd. v. Rambus, Inc.*, 439 F. Supp. 2d 524 (E.D. Va. 2007) (vacated on unrelated grounds); *Zubulake v. UBS Warburg, LLC*, 220 F.R.D. 212 (S.D.N.Y. 2003). A well-designed and implemented routine document retention policy, however, should make it easier for the party to know what it is "holding" when the need for a "hold" arises.

Although the primary responsibility for document retention lies with lawyers, judges also have a part to play in ensuring that evidence is preserved. Judges may do so by enforcing common law duties to preserve evidence, but they may also issue a document preservation order "requiring the parties to preserve and retain documents, files, data, and records that may be relevant to the litigation." Manual, *supra*, § 11.442. Parties, of course, are already under a common law duty to do this, but a court order also may be necessary. A document retention order in a complex case will ensure that there is no doubt about the scope of the duty to preserve evidence. In complex cases, where there is a large amount of potentially relevant material, a document retention order may focus attention on the difficulties of preserving such a large amount of information and of identifying things that need not be preserved. The order may provide an incentive to "define the scope of contemplated discovery narrowly" to minimize the intrusion occasioned by preservation of information on complex, frequently used computer systems. *Id.* A sample document preservation order from the MANUAL is recreated below.

Preservation of Documents, Data, and Tangible Things
Interim Order Regarding Preservation

[The primary purpose of this order is to have the parties meet and confer to develop their own preservation plan. If the court determines that such a conference is unnecessary or undesirable, paragraph 3, Duty to Preserve, may be modified to serve as a stand-alone preservation order.]

1. Order to Meet and Confer

To further the just, speedy, and economical management of discovery, the parties are ORDERED to meet and confer as soon as practicable, no later than 30 days after the date of this order, to develop a plan for the preservation of documents, data, and tangible things reasonably anticipated to be subject to discovery in this action. The parties may conduct this conference as part of the Rule 26(f) conference if it is scheduled to take place within 30 days of the date of this order. The resulting preservation plan may be submitted to this Court as a proposed order under Rule 16(e).

2. Subjects for Consideration

The parties should attempt to reach agreement on all issues regarding the preservation of documents, data, and tangible things. These issues include, but are not necessarily limited to:

(a) the extent of the preservation obligation, identifying the types of material to be preserved, the subject matter, time frame, the authors and addressees, and key words to be used in identifying responsive materials;

(b) the identification of persons responsible for carrying out preservation obligations on behalf of each party;

(c) the form and method of providing notice of the duty to preserve to persons identified as custodians of documents, data, and tangible things;

(d) mechanisms for monitoring, certifying, or auditing custodian compliance with preservation obligations;

(e) whether preservation will require suspending or modifying any routine business processes or procedures, with special attention to document-management programs and the recycling of computer data storage media;

(f) the methods to preserve any volatile but potentially discoverable material, such as voicemail, active data in databases, or electronic messages;

(g) the anticipated costs of preservation and ways to reduce or share these costs; and

(h) a mechanism to review and modify the preservation obligation as discovery proceeds, eliminating or adding particular categories of documents, data, and tangible things.

3. Duty to Preserve

(a) Until the parties reach agreement on a preservation plan, all parties and their counsel are reminded of their duty to preserve evidence that may be relevant to this action. . . .

(b) "Documents, data, and tangible things" is to be interpreted broadly. . . .

(c) "Preservation" is to be interpreted broadly to accomplish the goal of maintaining the integrity of all documents, data, and tangible things reasonably anticipated to be subject to discovery under FED. R. CIV. P. 26, 45, and 56(e) in this action. . . .

(d) If the business practices of any party involve the routine destruction, recycling, relocation, or mutation of such materials, the party must . . . either

(1) halt such business processes;

(2) sequester or remove such material from the business process; or

(3) arrange for the preservation of complete and accurate duplicates or copies of such material, suitable for later discovery if requested.

(e) Before the conference to develop a preservation plan, a party may apply to the court for further instructions regarding the duty to preserve specific categories of documents, data, or tangible things. A party may seek permission to resume routine business processes relating to the storage or destruction of specific categories of documents, data, or tangible things, upon a showing of undue cost, burden, or overbreadth.

4. Procedure in the Event No Agreement Is Reached

If, after conferring to develop a preservation plan, counsel do not reach agreement on the subjects listed under paragraph 2 of this order or on other material aspects of preservation, the parties are to submit to the court within three days of the conference a statement of the unresolved issues together with each party's proposal for their resolution of the issues. . . .

MANUAL, *supra*, § 40.25.

Notes and Questions

1. Each side in a dispute has a duty to preserve relevant evidence. Each side also needs to be active in enforcing the other side's duty. *See Mathis v. John Morden Buick, Inc.*, 136 F.3d 1153, 1156 (7th Cir. 1998) ("Judges must be vigilant to prevent destruction of evidence, but litigants who are not diligent in defense of their own interests cannot expect rescue by appellate courts.").

2. There also are professional responsibility implications to destroying evidence. *See* Model Rule of Professional Conduct 3.4(a), which states that a lawyer shall not "unlawfully obstruct another party's access to evidence or unlawfully alter, destroy or conceal a document or other material having potential evidentiary value. A lawyer shall not counsel or assist another person to do any such act." *See 1st Technology, LLC v. Rational Enterprises Ltd.*, 2008 U.S. Dist. LEXIS 106101 (D. Nev. July 15, 2008) (ordering defense counsel to produce relevant documents in their custody, prohibiting them from destroying these documents, and rejecting the argument that the lawyers' professional responsibility to their clients prohibited them from producing the documents). Keep in mind that the lawyer may find herself personally responsible for the wrongdoing of a client. While documents may be nominally in control of the client, this does not prevent the lawyer from having any responsibility in the event of wrongdoing. *See Mosel Vitelic Corp. v. Micron Technology, Inc.*, 162 F. Supp. 2d 307 (D. Del. 2000).

3. While a document preservation order may appear to be a good routine judicial practice, some courts have ruled them inappropriate absent circumstances which specifically justify them. *See Hester v. Bayer Corp.*, 206 F.R.D. 683 (M.D. Ala. 2001). In *Pueblo of Laguna v. United States*, 60 Fed. Cl. 133, 138 (Fed. Cl. 2004), the court held that

> the proponent [of a document preservation order] ordinarily must show that absent a court order, there is significant risk that relevant evidence will be lost or destroyed—a burden often met by demonstrating that the opposing party has lost or destroyed evidence in the past or has inadequate retention procedures in place. *See* In re Potash, 1994 WL 1108312, at *8 (D. Minn. Dec. 5, 1994). More than that, the proponent must show that the particular steps to be adopted will be effective, but not overbroad—the court will neither lightly exercise its inherent power to protect evidence nor indulge in an exercise in futility.

4. Judicial Management Techniques

In addition to careful scrutiny of discovery plans, document depositories, and document preservation orders, judges have other devices for managing discovery in complex litigation. Protective orders, described below, are a valuable tool for preventing discovery from becoming unmanageable. They may be used to limit the topics of discovery, the types of discovery that may be taken, and may prevent disputes by reassuring parties that the damage done by producing certain types of documents will be limited. Prompt resolution of discovery disputes is also important. Manual, *supra*, § 11.423 ("Discovery disputes, with their potential for breeding satellite litigation, are a major source of cost and delay. Few aspects of litigation management are more important than the prompt and inexpensive resolution of [discovery disputes].")

The Manual suggests six other methods for limiting discovery. *Id.* § 11.422.

- *Time limits and schedules.* The discovery plan should include a schedule for the completion of specified discovery, affording a basis for judicial monitoring of progress. Setting a discovery cutoff date is an important objective, but may not be feasible at the initial conference in complex litigation. The discovery cutoff should not be so far in advance of the anticipated trial date that the product of discovery becomes stale and the parties' preparation outdated. Time limits impose valuable discipline on attorneys, forcing them to be selective and helping to move the case expeditiously, but standing alone they may be insufficient to control discovery costs. Unless time limits are complemented by other limitations, attorneys may simply conduct multi-track discovery, thereby increasing expense and prejudicing parties with limited resources. To prevent time limits from being frustrated, the judge should rule promptly on disputes so that further discovery is not delayed or hampered while a ruling is pending. Although attorneys will sometimes argue over "priorities," the rules provide for no such presumptive standing.
- *Limits on quantity.* Time limits may be complemented by limits on the number and length of depositions, on the number of interrogatories, and on the volume of requests for production. Imposing such limitations only after hearing from the attorneys makes possible a reasonably informed judgment about the needs of the case. Limitations are best applied sequentially to particular phases of the litigation, rather than as aggregate limitations. When limits are placed on discovery of voluminous transactions or other events, consider using statistical sampling techniques to measure whether the results of the discovery fairly represent what unrestricted discovery would have been expected to produce (section 11.493 discusses statistical sampling).
- *Phased, sequenced, or targeted discovery.* Counsel and the judge will rarely be able to determine conclusively early in the litigation what discovery will be necessary; some discovery of potential relevance at the outset may be rendered irrelevant as the litigation proceeds, and the need for other discovery may become known only through later developments. For effective discovery control, initial discovery should focus on matters—witnesses, documents, information—that appear pivotal. As the litigation proceeds, this initial discovery may render other discovery unnecessary or provide leads for further necessary discovery. Initial discovery may also be targeted at information that might facilitate settlement negotiations or provide the foundation for a dispositive motion; a discovery plan may call for limited discovery to lay the foundation for early settlement discussions. Targeted discovery may be non-exhaustive, conducted to produce critical information rapidly on one or more specific issues. In permitting this kind of discovery, it is important to balance the potential savings against the risk of later duplicative discovery should it be necessary to resume the deposition of a witness or the production of documents. Targeted discovery may in some cases be appropriate in connection with a motion for class certification; however, matters relevant to such a motion may be so intertwined with

the merits that targeting discovery would be inefficient. *See* sections 11.41 and 21.2.

- *Subject-matter priorities.* Where the scope of the litigation is in doubt at the outset—as, for example, in antitrust litigation—the court should consider limiting discovery to particular time periods or geographical areas, until the relevance of expanded discovery has been established. *See* section 11.41.
- *Sequencing by parties.* Although discovery by all parties ordinarily proceeds concurrently, sometimes one or more parties should be allowed to proceed first. For example, if a party needs discovery to respond to an early summary judgment motion, that party may be given priority. Some judges establish periods in which particular parties have exclusive or preferential rights to take depositions, and in multiple litigation, those judges direct that discovery be conducted in some cases before others. Sometimes judges order "common" discovery to proceed in a specified sequence, without similarly limiting "individual" discovery in the various cases.
- *Forms of discovery.* Some judges prescribe a sequence for particular types of discovery—for example, interrogatories may be used to identify needed discovery and documents, followed by requests for production of documents, depositions, and finally requests for admission. If the court directs that discovery be conducted in a specified sequence, it should grant leave to vary the order for good cause, as when emergency depositions are needed for witnesses in ill health or about to leave the country.

Id. § 11.422.

However, the Seventh Circuit has pointed out,

> [a]lthough the effective management of complex litigation requires that the district judge be allowed broad discretion in guiding the discovery process and therefore in exercising his powers under Rules 26(c) and (d), *Chrysler Corp. v. Fedders Corp.*, 643 F.2d 1229, 1240 (6th Cir. 1981), his discretion is not unlimited, and if we have a firm conviction that he has made a mistake we must reverse, *Silkwood v. Kerr-McGee Corp.*, 563 F.2d 433, 436 (10th Cir. 1977).

Marrese v. American Academy of Orthopedic Surgeons, 706 F.2d 1488, 1493 (7th Cir. 1983).

Policy considerations can also limit judicial discretion concerning discovery. In *Morales v. Turman*, 59 F.R.D. 157, 159 (E.D. Tex. 1972), the court held that,

> [w]hen important civil rights are in issue in complex litigation of widespread concern, a court must make every effort to enhance the fact-finding process available to counsel for both sides. The trial court's discretion must be guided by "considerations of policy and of necessity, propriety and expediency in the particular case at hand." *United States v. Kohler*, 9 F.R.D. 289, 291 (D. Pa. 1949).

For an illustration of a staged approach to discovery, see *Klein v. King*, 132 F.R.D. 525, 529 (D. Mass. 1991):

> The plan the Court hereby imposes contemplates dividing discovery into two or three stages (the parties, at a juncture to be described, will have a great deal to say about whether there are two or three stages). The purpose of the first stage will be to get as efficiently on the table as possible the core information that the parties need in order to value the case sensibly for settlement purposes. In this stage we will focus primarily on documents, and on those documents that shed the most light on the most important facts. After core document production, and a limited number of depositions, the parties will participate in Court-ordered settlement negotiations, hosted by a special master or team of special masters of their choosing (assuming they can agree on nominees in whom the Court has confidence). The Court expects the parties to make a very hard run at settlement at this juncture. If that hard run fails, they will have two options. The first option would be to conduct limited additional discovery, for about two months, for the purpose of explicating matters that surfaced as obstacles to settlement in the negotiations held at the end of the first stage. That discovery would make up stage two of the pretrial process. It would be followed by another, final round of settlement negotiations, again hosted by the special master(s). If settlement could not be achieved, the parties would move into stage three of the pretrial period, during which they would be permitted to complete the document, deposition, and other discovery necessary to prepare the case for trial. If the parties, with inputs from the special master, conclude after the settlement negotiations at the end of stage one that there is no point in returning after two months or so of additional discovery for further settlement negotiations, they would skip what we are labeling stage two and move directly into the broader additional discovery necessary to dispose of the case by trial (what we are calling the final discovery stage).

5. Traditional Discovery Techniques in Complex Cases

It is costly to collect large volumes of documents, and costly to manage them once collected. To reduce costs, the MANUAL suggests that the court should seek to prevent overly broad document requests, and "direct counsel to frame requests for production of the fewest documents possible." MANUAL, *supra*, § 11.443. This approach reduces the number of documents that must be identified, copied, transported, and reviewed, and will also tend to reduce discovery disputes, as parties may be less inclined to object to narrower requests on the grounds of burden.

Judges also have tools available to mitigate the time and expense involved with the other main discovery tools available to litigants. Depositions "are often overused and conducted inefficiently, and thus tend to be the most costly and time-consuming activity in complex litigation." *Id.* § 11.45. The MANUAL suggests that courts should use their Rule 26(b)(2) authority to limit the number of depositions to which parties stipulate, to cut down on the number of depositions taken. *Id.* § 11.451. The court in *Schwab v. Philip Morris*, 449 F. Supp. 2d 992 (E.D.N.Y. 2006) (reversed on unrelated grounds), upheld a magistrate judge's decision to limit a cigarette manufacturer to forty depositions of smokers in preparation for class certification, despite the manufacturer's request for over 600.

Interrogatories also have the potential to consume resources. *See Id.* § 11.46. Interrogatories can be streamlined by "requiring similarly situated parties to confer and develop a single or master set of interrogatories to be served on an opposing party." *Id.* § 11.464. This will reduce duplicative responses. The MANUAL also suggests mandatory use of interrogatories from other litigation where possible. *Id.* Finally, parties may name organizations as deponents, reducing the need for lengthy interrogatories which require opposing parties to name everyone fulfilling a relevant role within their organization. *Id.*

Stipulations and requests for admission also can be used to narrow the issues, and therefore the scope of discovery. As far as stipulations are concerned, the MANUAL suggests that courts can "[stress] the distinction between conceding the truth of some fact . . . and conceding its admissibility or weight." *Id.* § 11.471. Parties may be willing to admit a fact, thus eliminating the need for discovery, while still planning to contest its relevance. Requests for admission under Rule 36 are much narrower. They are only usable against the party who made them, in the action in which they were made. Still, the MANUAL does suggest a simple request for renewal of admissions made in previous litigation. *Id.* § 11.472. And even though requests for admission may be less useful than stipulations, narrowly tailored requests can produce similarly narrowly tailored responses that reduce the effort needed to prove a relevant fact.

The Federal Rules Committee adopted limitations on interrogatories and depositions in 2015. These limits are still viewed as inadequate for complex litigation.

6. Electronic Discovery

More than 93% of information is now created electronically and email has become the primary means of communication within and without the business world. Richard K. Herrmann et al., *Managing Discovery in the Digital Age: A Guide to Electronic Discovery in the District of Delaware*, 8 DEL. L. REV. 75, 75 (2005). The amount of potentially discoverable information has increased dramatically. Because the procedural system created by the Federal Rules relies on discovery to uncover the relevant facts, as well as to narrow and define the issues, abundant and liberal discovery mechanisms are needed.

Liberal discovery, however, is expensive. The expense increases as the scope of discovery increases—a problem made acute by both complex litigation and the abundance of electronically stored information (ESI). Indeed, in one survey of trial lawyers, more than 75% agreed that "discovery costs, as a share of total litigation costs, have increased disproportionately due to the advent of e-discovery." The American College of Trial Lawyers Task Force on Discovery and The Institute for the Advancement of the American Legal System, Interim Report & 2008 Litigation Survey of the Fellows of the American College of Trial Lawyers, Sept. 9, 2008.

According to one estimate, Fortune 1000 corporations are budgeting $5 million to $10 million annually for e-discovery, with some companies spending much more. THE RISE OF ANALYTICS IN E-DISCOVERY, http://www.ftijournal.com/article/the-rise-of-analytics-in-e-discovery. This is in part because traditional electronic search methods, such as using keywords, have proven inadequate for effective document review.

> For example, in the famous Enron data set . . . executives used many code words (often "Star Wars" references) to disguise illegal activities. These code words would have provided attorneys with a whole armory of smoking guns that could have been used to reveal a host of crimes and misdemeanors; that is if the attorneys knew what those words were. What reasonable attorney would have thought to use "Millennium Falcon" or "Chewbacca" in a keyword search of an energy company's transactions. New e-discovery tools, however, can recognize patterns and alert attorneys to the occurrence of seemingly inexplicable (and, therefore, attention worthy) words and phrases.

Id.

The following cases address one way to deal with potentially expensive discovery requests for ESI. As you read them, ask whether other approaches might work better. Does the proposed solution solve other discovery problems as well?

Zubulake v. UBS Warburg LLC a/k/a *Zubulake I*

United States District Court for the Southern District of New York
217 F.R.D. 309 (2003)

SCHEINDLIN, DISTRICT JUDGE.

I. INTRODUCTION

The Supreme Court recently reiterated that our "simplified notice pleading standard relies on liberal discovery rules and summary judgment motions to define disputed facts and issues and to dispose of unmeritorious claims."[1] Thus, it is now beyond dispute that "[b]road discovery is a cornerstone of the litigation process contemplated by the Federal Rules of Civil Procedure."[2]

In one context, however, the reliance on broad discovery has hit a roadblock. As individuals and corporations increasingly do business electronically—using

---

1. [Court's footnote #2] *Swierkiewicz v. Sorema, N.A.*, 534 U.S. 506, 512 (2002).
2. [Court's footnote #3] *Jones v. Goord*, No. 95 Civ. 8026, 2002 U.S. Dist. LEXIS 8707, at *1 (S.D.N.Y. May 16, 2002).

computers to create and store documents, make deals, and exchange e-mails—the universe of discoverable material has expanded exponentially. The more information there is to discover, the more expensive it is to discover all the relevant information until, in the end, "discovery is not just about uncovering the truth, but also about how much of the truth the parties can afford to disinter."

This case provides a textbook example of the difficulty of balancing the competing needs of broad discovery and manageable costs. Laura Zubulake is suing UBS Warburg LLC, UBS Warburg, and UBS AG (collectively, "UBS" or the "Firm") under Federal, State and City law for gender discrimination and illegal retaliation. Zubulake's case is certainly not frivolous and if she prevails, her damages may be substantial. She contends that key evidence is located in various e-mails exchanged among UBS employees that now exist only on backup tapes and perhaps other archived media. According to UBS, restoring those e-mails would cost approximately $175,000.00, exclusive of attorney time in reviewing the e-mails. Zubulake now moves for an order compelling UBS to produce those e-mails at its expense.

II. BACKGROUND

A. Zubulake's Lawsuit

UBS hired Zubulake on August 23, 1999, as a director and senior salesperson on its U.S. Asian Equities Sales Desk (the "Desk"), where she reported to Dominic Vail, the Desk's manager. At the time she was hired, Zubulake was told that she would be considered for Vail's position if and when it became vacant.

In December 2000, Vail indeed left his position to move to the Firm's London office. But Zubulake was not considered for his position, and the Firm instead hired Matthew Chapin as director of the Desk. Zubulake alleges that from the outset Chapin treated her differently than the other members of the Desk, all of whom were male. In particular, Chapin "undermined Ms. Zubulake's ability to perform her job by, *inter alia:* (a) ridiculing and belittling her in front of co-workers; (b) excluding her from work-related outings with male co-workers and clients; (c) making sexist remarks in her presence; and (d) isolating her from the other senior salespersons on the Desk by seating her apart from them." No such actions were taken against any of Zubulake's male co-workers.

Zubulake ultimately responded by filing a Charge of (gender) Discrimination with the EEOC on August 16, 2001. On October 9, 2001, Zubulake was fired with two weeks' notice. On February 15, 2002, Zubulake filed the instant action, suing for sex discrimination and retaliation under Title VII, the New York State Human Rights Law, and the Administrative Code of the City of New York. UBS timely answered on March 12, 2002, denying the allegations. UBS's argument is, in essence, that Chapin's conduct was not unlawfully discriminatory because he treated everyone equally badly. On the one hand, UBS points to evidence that Chapin's anti-social behavior was not limited to women: a former employee made allegations of national origin discrimination against Chapin, and a number of male employees on the Desk also complained about him. On the other hand, Chapin was responsible for hiring three new female employees to the Desk.

B. The Discovery Dispute

Discovery in this action commenced on or about June 3, 2002, when Zubulake served UBS with her first document request. At issue here is request number twenty-eight, for "[a]ll documents concerning any communication by or between UBS employees concerning Plaintiff." The term document in Zubulake's request "includ[es], without limitation, electronic or computerized data compilations." On July 8, 2002, UBS responded by producing approximately 350 pages of documents, including approximately 100 pages of e-mails. UBS also objected to a substantial portion of Zubulake's requests.

On September 12, 2002—after an exchange of angry letters and a conference before United States Magistrate Judge Gabriel W. Gorenstein—the parties reached an agreement (the "9/12/02 Agreement"). With respect to document request twenty-eight, the parties reached the following agreement, in relevant part:

> Defendants will [] ask UBS about how to retrieve e-mails that are saved in the firm's computer system *and will produce responsive e-mails if retrieval is possible* and Plaintiff names a few individuals.

Pursuant to the 9/12/02 Agreement, UBS agreed unconditionally to produce responsive e-mails from the accounts of five individuals named by Zubulake: Matthew Chapin, Rose Tong (a human relations representation who was assigned to handle issues concerning Zubulake), Vinay Datta (a co-worker on the Desk), Andrew Clarke (another co-worker on the Desk), and Jeremy Hardisty (Chapin's supervisor and the individual to whom Zubulake originally complained about Chapin). UBS was to produce such e-mails sent between August 1999 (when Zubulake was hired) and December 2001 (one month after her termination), to the extent possible.

UBS, however, produced no additional e-mails and insisted that its initial production (the 100 pages of e-mails) was complete. As UBS's opposition to the instant motion makes clear—although it remains unsaid—UBS never searched for responsive e-mails on any of its backup tapes. To the contrary, UBS informed Zubulake that the cost of producing e-mails on backup tapes would be prohibitive (estimated at the time at approximately $300,000.00).

Zubulake, believing that the 9/12/02 Agreement included production of e-mails from backup tapes, objected to UBS's non-production. In fact, Zubulake *knew* that there were additional responsive e-mails that UBS had failed to produce because she herself had produced approximately 450 pages of e-mail correspondence. Clearly, numerous responsive e-mails had been created and deleted at UBS, and Zubulake wanted them.

On December 2, 2002, the parties again appeared before Judge Gorenstein, who ordered UBS to produce for deposition a person with knowledge of UBS's e-mail retention policies in an effort to determine whether the backup tapes contained the deleted e-mails and the burden of producing them. In response, UBS produced Christopher Behny, Manager of Global Messaging, who was deposed on January 14, 2003. Mr. Behny testified to UBS's e-mail backup protocol, and also to the cost of restoring the relevant data.

III. LEGAL STANDARD

Federal Rules of Civil Procedure 26 through 37 govern discovery in all civil actions. . . .

The application of these various discovery rules is particularly complicated where electronic data is sought because otherwise discoverable evidence is often only available from expensive-to-restore backup media. That being so, courts have devised creative solutions for balancing the broad scope of discovery prescribed in Rule 26(b)(1) with the cost-consciousness of Rule 26(b)(2). By and large, the solution has been to consider cost-shifting: forcing the requesting party, rather than the answering party, to bear the cost of discovery.

By far, the most influential response to the problem of cost-shifting relating to the discovery of electronic data was given by United States Magistrate Judge James C. Francis IV of this district in *Rowe Entertainment*. Judge Francis utilized an eight-factor test to determine whether discovery costs should be shifted. Those eight factors are:

> (1) the specificity of the discovery requests; (2) the likelihood of discovering critical information; (3) the availability of such information from other sources; (4) the purposes for which the responding party maintains the requested data; (5) the relative benefits to the parties of obtaining the information; (6) the total cost associated with production; (7) the relative ability of each party to control costs and its incentive to do so; and (8) the resources available to each party.

Both Zubulake and UBS agree that the eight-factor *Rowe* test should be used to determine whether cost-shifting is appropriate.

IV. DISCUSSION

A. Should Discovery of UBS's Electronic Data Be Permitted?

Under Rule 34, a party may request discovery of any document, "including writings, drawings, graphs, charts, photographs, phonorecords, and other data compilations. . . ." The "inclusive description" of the term document "accord[s] with changing technology."[3] "It makes clear that Rule 34 applies to *electronics* [sic] data compilations." Thus, "[e]lectronic documents are no less subject to disclosure than paper records."[4] This is true not only of electronic documents that are currently

---

3. [Court's footnote #36] Advisory Committee Note to Fed. R. Civ. P. 34.

4. [Court's footnote #37] *Rowe v. William Morris Agency, Inc.*, 205 F.R.D. 421, 428 (S.D.N.Y.) (collecting cases).

in use, but also of documents that may have been deleted and now reside only on backup disks.[5]

That being so, Zubulake is entitled to discovery of the requested e-mails so long as they are relevant to her claims, which they clearly are. As noted, e-mail constituted a substantial means of communication among UBS employees. To that end, UBS has already produced approximately 100 pages of e-mails, the contents of which are unquestionably relevant.

Nonetheless, UBS argues that Zubulake is not entitled to any further discovery because it already produced all responsive documents, to wit, the 100 pages of e-mails. This argument is unpersuasive for two reasons. *First*, because of the way that UBS backs up its e-mail files, it clearly could not have searched all of its e-mails without restoring the ninety-four backup tapes (which UBS admits that it has not done). [UBS determined that all emails responsive to Zubulake's request were found on 94 back-up tapes.] UBS therefore cannot represent that it has produced all responsive e-mails. *Second*, Zubulake herself has produced over 450 pages of relevant e-mails, including e-mails that would have been responsive to her discovery requests but were never produced by UBS. These two facts strongly suggest that there are e-mails that Zubulake has not received that reside on UBS's backup media.

B. Should Cost-Shifting Be Considered?

Because it apparently recognizes that Zubulake is entitled to the requested discovery, UBS expends most of its efforts urging the court to shift the cost of production to "protect [it] . . . from undue burden or expense."[6] Faced with similar applications, courts generally engage in some sort of cost-shifting analysis, whether the refined eight-factor *Rowe* test or a cruder application of Rule 34's proportionality test, or something in between.

The first question, however, is whether cost-shifting must be considered in every case involving the discovery of electronic data, which—in today's world—includes virtually all cases. In light of the accepted principle, stated above, that electronic evidence is no less discoverable than paper evidence, the answer is, "No." The Supreme Court has instructed that "the presumption is that the responding party must bear the expense of complying with discovery requests. . . ."[7] Any principled approach to electronic evidence must respect this presumption.

Courts must remember that cost-shifting may effectively end discovery, especially when private parties are engaged in litigation with large corporations. As large

5. [Court's footnote #38] *See Antioch Co. v. Scrapbook Borders, Inc.*, 210 F.R.D. 645, 652 (D. Minn. 2002) ("[I]t is a well accepted proposition that deleted computer files, whether they be e-mails or otherwise, are discoverable."); *Simon Property Group L.P. v. mySimon, Inc.*, 194 F.R.D. 639, 640 (S.D. Ind. 2000) ("First, computer records, including records that have been 'deleted,' are documents discoverable under Fed. R. Civ. P. 34.").

6. [Court's footnote #42] Def. Mem. at 9 (quoting Fed. R. Civ. P. 26(c)).

7. [Court's footnote #44] *Oppenheimer Fund*, 437 U.S. at 358 (1978).

companies increasingly move to entirely paper-free environments, the frequent use of cost-shifting will have the effect of crippling discovery in discrimination and retaliation cases. This will both undermine the "strong public policy favor[ing] resolving disputes on their merits,"[8] and may ultimately deter the filing of potentially meritorious claims.

Thus, cost-shifting should be considered *only* when electronic discovery imposes an "undue burden or expense" on the responding party. The burden or expense of discovery is, in turn, "undue" when it "outweighs its likely benefit, taking into account the needs of the case, the amount in controversy, the parties' resources, the importance of the issues at stake in the litigation, and the importance of the proposed discovery in resolving the issues."

Many courts have automatically assumed that an undue burden or expense may arise simply because electronic evidence is involved. This makes no sense. Electronic evidence is frequently cheaper and easier to produce than paper evidence because it can be searched automatically, key words can be run for privilege checks, and the production can be made in electronic form obviating the need for mass photocopying.

In fact, whether production of documents is unduly burdensome or expensive turns primarily on whether it is kept in an *accessible or inaccessible* format (a distinction that corresponds closely to the expense of production). In the world of paper documents, for example, a document is accessible if it is readily available in a usable format and reasonably indexed. Examples of inaccessible paper documents could include (a) documents in storage in a difficult to reach place; (b) documents converted to microfiche and not easily readable; or (c) documents kept haphazardly, with no indexing system, in quantities that make page-by-page searches impracticable. But in the world of electronic data, thanks to search engines, any data that is retained in a machine readable format is typically accessible.

Whether electronic data is accessible or inaccessible turns largely on the media on which it is stored. Five categories of data, listed in order from most accessible to least accessible, are described in the literature on electronic data storage:

> 1. *Active, online data:* "On-line storage is generally provided by magnetic disk. It is used in the very active stages of an electronic records [sic] life—when it is being created or received and processed, as well as when the access frequency is high and the required speed of access is very fast, *i.e.*, milliseconds." Examples of online data include hard drives.
>
> 2. *Near-line data:* "This typically consists of a robotic storage device (robotic library) that houses removable media, uses robotic arms to access the media, and uses multiple read/write devices to store and retrieve records. Access speeds can range from as low as milliseconds if the media is already in a read device, up to 10–30 seconds for optical disk technology, and between 20–120

8. [Court's footnote #45] *Pecarsky v. Galaxiworld.com, Inc.*, 249 F.3d 167, 172 (2d Cir. 2001).

seconds for sequentially searched media, such as magnetic tape." Examples include optical disks.

3. *Offline storage/archives:* "This is removable optical disk or magnetic tape media, which can be labeled and stored in a shelf or rack. Off-line storage of electronic records is traditionally used for making disaster copies of records and also for records considered 'archival' in that their likelihood of retrieval is minimal. Accessibility to off-line media involves manual intervention and is much slower than on-line or near-line storage. Access speed may be minutes, hours, or even days, depending on the access-effectiveness of the storage facility." The principled difference between nearline data and offline data is that offline data lacks "the coordinated control of an intelligent disk subsystem," and is, in the lingo, JBOD ("Just a Bunch Of Disks").

4. *Backup tapes:* "A device, like a tape recorder, that reads data from and writes it onto a tape. Tape drives have data capacities of anywhere from a few hundred kilobytes to several gigabytes. Their transfer speeds also vary considerably . . . The disadvantage of tape drives is that they are sequential-access devices, which means that to read any particular block of data, you need to read all the preceding blocks." As a result, "[t]he data on a backup tape are not organized for retrieval of individual documents or files [because] . . . the organization of the data mirrors the computer's structure, not the human records management structure." Backup tapes also typically employ some sort of data compression, permitting more data to be stored on each tape, but also making restoration more time-consuming and expensive, especially given the lack of uniform standard governing data compression.

5. *Erased, fragmented or damaged data:* "When a file is first created and saved, it is laid down on the [storage media] in contiguous clusters . . . As files are erased, their clusters are made available again as free space. Eventually, some newly created files become larger than the remaining contiguous free space. These files are then broken up and randomly placed throughout the disk." Such broken-up files are said to be "fragmented," and along with damaged and erased data can only be accessed after significant processing.

. . .

C. What Is the Proper Cost-Shifting Analysis?

In the year since *Rowe* was decided, its eight factor test has unquestionably become the gold standard for courts resolving electronic discovery disputes. But there is little doubt that the *Rowe* factors will generally favor cost-shifting. Indeed, of the handful of reported opinions that apply *Rowe* or some modification thereof, *all of them* have ordered the cost of discovery to be shifted to the requesting party.

In order to maintain the presumption that the responding party pays, the cost-shifting analysis must be neutral; close calls should be resolved in favor of the presumption. The *Rowe* factors, as applied, undercut that presumption for three reasons. *First*, the Rowe test is incomplete. *Second*, courts have given equal weight to all of the factors, when certain factors should predominate. *Third*, courts applying the *Rowe* test have not always developed a full factual record.

1. The *Rowe* Test Is Incomplete

a. A Modification of *Rowe*: Additional Factors

Certain factors specifically identified in the Rules are omitted from *Rowe*'s eight factors. In particular, Rule 26 [now Rule 26(b)(1)] requires consideration of "the amount in controversy, the parties' resources, the importance of the issues at stake in the litigation, and the importance of the proposed discovery in resolving the issues." Yet *Rowe* makes no mention of either the amount in controversy or the importance of the issues at stake in the litigation. These factors should be added. Doing so would balance the *Rowe* factor that typically weighs most heavily in favor of cost-shifting, "the total cost associated with production." The cost of production is almost always an objectively large number in cases where litigating cost-shifting is worthwhile. But the cost of production when compared to "the amount in controversy" may tell a different story. A response to a discovery request costing $100,000 sounds (and is) costly, but in a case potentially worth millions of dollars, the cost of responding may not be unduly burdensome.

Rowe also contemplates "the resources available to each party." But here too—although this consideration may be implicit in the *Rowe* test—the absolute wealth of the parties is not the relevant factor. More important than comparing the relative ability of a party to pay for discovery, the focus should be on the total cost of production as compared to the resources available to each party. Thus, discovery that would be too expensive for one defendant to bear would be a drop in the bucket for another.

Last, "the importance of the issues at stake in the litigation" is a critical consideration, even if it is one that will rarely be invoked. For example, if a case has the potential for broad public impact, then public policy weighs heavily in favor of permitting extensive discovery. Cases of this ilk might include toxic tort class actions, environmental actions, so-called "impact" or social reform litigation, cases involving criminal conduct, or cases implicating important legal or constitutional questions.

b. A Modification of *Rowe*: Eliminating Two Factors

Two of the *Rowe* factors should be eliminated:

First, the *Rowe* test includes "the specificity of the discovery request." Specificity is surely the touchstone of any good discovery request, requiring a party to frame a request broadly enough to obtain relevant evidence, yet narrowly enough to control costs. But relevance and cost are already two of the *Rowe* factors (the second and sixth). Because the first and second factors are duplicative, they can be combined. Thus, the first factor should be: the extent to which the request is specifically tailored to discover relevant information.

Second, the fourth factor, "the purposes for which the responding party maintains the requested data" is typically unimportant. Whether the data is kept for a business purpose or for disaster recovery does not affect its *accessibility*, which is the practical basis for calculating the cost of production. Although a business purpose will often coincide with accessibility—data that is inaccessible is unlikely to be used or needed in the ordinary course of business—the concepts are not coterminous. In particular, a good deal of accessible data may be retained, though not in the ordinary course of business. For example, data that should rightly have been erased pursuant to a document retention/destruction policy may be inadvertently retained. If so, the fact that it should have been erased in no way shields that data from discovery. As long as the data is accessible, it must be produced.

. . .

c. A New Seven-Factor Test

Set forth below is a new seven-factor test based on the modifications to *Rowe* discussed in the preceding sections.

1. The extent to which the request is specifically tailored to discover relevant information;
2. The availability of such information from other sources;
3. The total cost of production, compared to the amount in controversy;
4. The total cost of production, compared to the resources available to each party;
5. The relative ability of each party to control costs and its incentive to do so;
6. The importance of the issues at stake in the litigation; and
7. The relative benefits to the parties of obtaining the information.

2. The Seven Factors Should Not Be Weighted Equally

Whenever a court applies a multi-factor test, there is a temptation to treat the factors as a check-list,[9] resolving the issue in favor of whichever column has the most checks. But "we do not just add up the factors."[10] When evaluating cost-shifting, the central question must be, does the request impose an "undue burden or expense" on the responding party?[11] Put another way, "how important is the sought-after evidence in comparison to the cost of production?" The seven-factor test articulated above provides some guidance in answering this question, but the test cannot be mechanically applied at the risk of losing sight of its purpose.

Weighting the factors in descending order of importance may solve the problem and avoid a mechanistic application of the test. The first two factors—comprising the marginal utility test—are the most important. These factors include: (1) The

9. [Court's footnote #71] *See, e.g., Big O Tires, Inc. v. Bigfoot 4X4, Inc.*, 167 F. Supp. 2d 1216, 1227 (D. Colo. 2001) ("A majority of factors in the likelihood of confusion test weigh in favor of Big O. I therefore conclude that Big O has shown a likelihood of success on the merits.").

10. [Court's footnote #72] *Noble v. United States*, 231 F.3d 352, 359 (7th Cir. 2000).

11. [Court's footnote #73] Fed. R. Civ. P. 26(b)(iii).

extent to which the request is specifically tailored to discover relevant information and (2) the availability of such information from other sources. The substance of the marginal utility test was well described in *McPeek v. Ashcroft:*

> The more likely it is that the backup tape contains information that is relevant to a claim or defense, the fairer it is that the [responding party] search at its own expense. The less likely it is, the more unjust it would be to make the [responding party] search at its own expense. The difference is "at the margin."

The second group of factors addresses cost issues: "How expensive will this production be?" and, "Who can handle that expense?" These factors include: (3) the total cost of production compared to the amount in controversy, (4) the total cost of production compared to the resources available to each party and (5) the relative ability of each party to control costs and its incentive to do so. The third "group"—(6) the importance of the litigation itself—stands alone, and as noted earlier will only rarely come into play. But where it does, this factor has the potential to predominate over the others. Collectively, the first three groups correspond to the three explicit considerations of Rule 26(b)(2)(iii) [now Rule 26(b)(2)(C)]. Finally, the last factor (7) the relative benefits of production as between the requesting and producing parties is the least important because it is fair to presume that the response to a discovery request generally benefits the requesting party. But in the unusual case where production will also provide a tangible or strategic benefit to the responding party, that fact may weigh *against* shifting costs.

D. A Factual Basis Is Required to Support the Analysis

. . .

Requiring the responding party to restore and produce responsive documents from a small sample of backup tapes will inform the cost-shifting analysis laid out above. When based on an actual sample, the marginal utility test will not be an exercise in speculation—there will be tangible evidence of what the backup tapes may have to offer. There will also be tangible evidence of the time and cost required to restore the backup tapes, which in turn will inform the second group of cost-shifting factors. Thus, by requiring a sample restoration of backup tapes, the entire cost-shifting analysis can be grounded in fact rather than guesswork.

IV. CONCLUSION AND ORDER

. . .

Accordingly, UBS is ordered to produce *all* responsive e-mails that exist on its optical disks or on its active servers (*i.e.*, in HP OpenMail files) at its own expense. UBS is also ordered to produce, at its expense, responsive e-mails from any *five* backup tapes selected *by Zubulake.* UBS should then prepare an affidavit detailing the results of its search, as well as the time and money spent. After reviewing the contents of the backup tapes and UBS's certification, the Court will conduct the appropriate cost-shifting analysis.

Zubulake v. UBS Warburg LLC a/k/a *Zubulake III*

United States District Court for the Southern District of New York
216 F.R.D. 280 (2003)

OPINION AND ORDER

SCHEINDLIN, DISTRICT JUDGE.

On May 13, 2003, I ordered defendants UBS Warburg LLC, UBS Warburg, and UBS AG (collectively "UBS") to restore and produce certain e-mails from a small group of backup tapes. Having reviewed the results of this sample restoration, Laura Zubulake now moves for an order compelling UBS to produce all remaining backup e-mails at its expense. UBS argues that based on the sampling, the costs should be shifted to Zubulake.

For the reasons fully explained below, Zubulake must share in the costs of restoration, although UBS must bear the bulk of that expense. In addition, UBS must pay for any costs incurred in reviewing the restored documents for privilege.

I. BACKGROUND

The question presented in this dispute is which party should pay for the costs incurred in restoring and producing [the backup tapes containing email files responsive to Zubulake's discovery request].

In order to obtain a factual basis to support the cost-shifting analysis, I ordered UBS to restore and produce e-mails from five of the ninety-four backup tapes that UBS had then identified as containing responsive documents; Zubulake was permitted to select the five tapes to be restored. UBS now reports, however, that there are only seventy-seven backup tapes that contain responsive data, including the five already restored. I further ordered UBS to "prepare an affidavit detailing the results of its search, as well as the time and money spent." UBS has complied by submitting counsel's declaration.

According to the declaration, Zubulake selected the backup tapes corresponding to Matthew Chapin's e-mails from May, June, July, August, and September 2001. That period includes the time from Zubulake's initial EEOC charge of discrimination (August 2001) until just before her termination (in the first week of October 2001). UBS hired an outside vendor, Pinkerton Consulting & Investigations, to perform the restoration.

Pinkerton was able to restore each of the backup tapes. UBS deemed approximately 600 [of the emails on these tapes] to be responsive to Zubulake's document request and they were produced. UBS also produced, under the terms of the May 13 Order, fewer than twenty e-mails extracted from UBS's optical disk storage system.

Pinkerton billed UBS 31.5 hours for its restoration services at an hourly rate of $245, six hours for the development, refinement and execution of a search script at $245 an hour, and 101.5 hours of "CPU Bench Utilization" time for use of Pinkerton's computer systems at a rate of $18.50 per hour. Pinkerton also included a five percent "administrative overhead fee" of $459.38. Thus, the total cost of restoration and search was $11,524.63. In addition, UBS incurred the following costs: $4,633 in attorney time for the document review (11.3 hours at $410 per hour) and $2,845.80 in paralegal time for tasks related to document production (16.74 hours at $170 per hour). UBS also paid $432.60 in photocopying costs, which, of course, will be paid by Zubulake and is not part of this cost-shifting analysis. The total cost of restoration and production from the five backup tapes was $19,003.43.

UBS now asks that the cost of any further production—estimated to be $273,649.39, based on the cost incurred in restoring five tapes and producing responsive documents from those tapes—be shifted to Zubulake. The total figure includes $165,954.67 to restore and search the tapes and $107,694.72 in attorney and paralegal review costs. These costs will be addressed separately below.

II. LEGAL STANDARD

. . .

Although "the presumption is that the responding party must bear the expense of complying with discovery requests," requests that run afoul of the Rule 26(b)(2) [now 26(b)(1)] proportionality test may subject the requesting party to protective orders under Rule 26(c), "including orders conditioning discovery on the requesting party's payment of the costs of discovery."[12] A court will order such a cost-shifting protective order only upon motion of the responding party to a discovery request, and "for good cause shown." Thus, the responding party has the burden of proof on a motion for cost-shifting.

III. DISCUSSION

A. Cost-shifting Generally

In *Zubulake I*, I considered plaintiff's request for information contained only on backup tapes and determined that cost-shifting *might* be appropriate. It is worth emphasizing again that cost-shifting is potentially appropriate only when *inaccessible* data is sought. When a discovery request seeks accessible data—for example, active on-line or near-line data—it is typically inappropriate to consider cost-shifting. . . .

B. Application of the Seven Factor Test

1. Factors One and Two

These two factors should be weighted the most heavily in the cost-shifting analysis. . . .

a. The Extent to Which the Request Is Specifically Tailored to Discover Relevant Information

The document request at issue asks for "[a]ll documents concerning any communication by or between UBS employees concerning Plaintiff," and was subsequently narrowed to pertain to only five employees (Chapin, Hardisty, Tong, Datta,

12. [Court's footnote #28] *Oppenheimer Fund, Inc. v. Sanders*, 437 U.S. 340, 358 (1978).

and Clarke) and to the period from August 1999 to December 2001. This is a relatively limited and targeted request, a fact borne out by the e-mails UBS actually produced, both initially and as a result of the sample restoration.

At oral argument, Zubulake presented the court with sixty-eight e-mails (of the 600 she received) that she claims are "highly relevant to the issues in this case" and thus require, in her view, that UBS bear the cost of production. And indeed, a review of these e-mails reveals that they are relevant. Taken together, they tell a compelling story of the dysfunctional atmosphere surrounding UBS's U.S. Asian Equities Sales Desk (the "Desk"). Presumably, these sixty-eight e-mails are reasonably representative of the seventy-seven backup tapes. . . .

While all of these e-mails are likely to have some "tendency to make the existence of any fact that is of consequence to the determination of the action more probable or less probable than it would be without the evidence," *none* of them provide any direct evidence of discrimination. To be sure, the e-mails reveal a hostile relationship between Chapin and Zubulake—UBS does not contest this. But nowhere (in the sixty-eight e-mails produced to the Court) is there evidence that Chapin's dislike of Zubulake related to her gender.

b. The Availability of Such Information from Other Sources

The other half of the marginal utility test is the availability of the relevant data from other sources. Neither party seemed to know how many of the 600 e-mails produced in response to the May 13 Order had been previously produced. UBS argues that "nearly all of the restored e-mails that relate to plaintiff's allegations in this matter or to the merits of her case were already produced." This statement is perhaps too careful, because UBS goes on to observe that "the vast majority of the restored e-mails that were produced do *not* relate at all to plaintiff's allegations in this matter or to the merits of her case." But this determination is not for UBS to make; as the saying goes, "one man's trash is another man's treasure."

It is axiomatic that a requesting party may obtain "any matter, not privileged, that is relevant to the claim or defense of any party." The simple fact is that UBS previously produced only 100 pages of e-mails, but has now produced 853 pages (comprising the 600 responsive e-mails) from the five selected backup tapes alone. UBS itself decided that it was obliged to provide these 853 pages of e-mail pursuant to the requirements of Rule 26. Having done so, these numbers lead to the unavoidable conclusion that there are a significant number of responsive e-mails that now exist only on backup tapes.

. . .

In sum, hundreds of the e-mails produced from the five backup tapes were not previously produced, and so were only available from the tapes. The contents of these e-mails are also new. Although some of the substance is available from other sources (*e.g.*, evidence of the sour relationship between Chapin and Zubulake), a good deal of it is only found on the backup tapes (*e.g.*, inconsistencies with UBS's EEOC filing and Chapin's deposition testimony). Moreover, an e-mail contains the precise words used by the author. Because of that, it is a particularly powerful form of proof at trial when offered as an admission of a party opponent.

c. Weighing Factors One and Two

The sample restoration, which resulted in the production of relevant e-mail, has demonstrated that Zubulake's discovery request was narrowly tailored to discover relevant information. And while the subject matter of some of those e-mails was addressed in other documents, these particular e-mails are only available from the backup tapes. Thus, direct evidence of discrimination may only be available through restoration. As a result, the marginal utility of this additional discovery may be quite high.

While restoration may be the only means for obtaining direct evidence of discrimination, the existence of that evidence is still speculative. The best that can be said is that Zubulake has demonstrated that the marginal utility is *potentially* high. All-in-all, because UBS bears the burden of proving that cost-shifting is warranted, the marginal utility test tips slightly against cost-shifting.

2. Factors Three, Four and Five

"The second group of factors addresses cost issues: 'How expensive will this production be?' and, 'Who can handle that expense?'"

a. The Total Cost of Production Compared to the Amount in Controversy

UBS spent $11,524.63, or $2,304.93 per tape, to restore the five back-up tapes. Thus, the total cost of restoring the remaining seventy-two tapes extrapolates to $165,954.67.

In order to assess the amount in controversy, I posed the following question to the parties: Assuming that a jury returns a verdict in favor of plaintiff, what economic damages can the plaintiff reasonably expect to recover? Plaintiff answered that reasonable damages are between $15,271,361 and $19,227,361, depending upon how front pay is calculated. UBS answered that damages could be as high as $1,265,000.

Obviously, this is a significant disparity. At this early stage, I cannot assess the accuracy of either estimate. Plaintiff had every incentive to high-ball the figure and UBS had every incentive to low-ball it. It is clear, however, that this case has the potential for a multi-million dollar recovery. Whatever else might be said, this is not a nuisance value case, a small case or a frivolous case. Most people do not earn $650,000 a year. If Zubulake prevails, her damages award undoubtedly will be higher than that of the vast majority of Title VII plaintiffs.

In an ordinary case, a responding party should not be required to pay for the restoration of inaccessible data if the cost of that restoration is significantly disproportionate to the value of the case. Assuming this to be a multi-million dollar case, the cost of restoration is surely not "significantly disproportionate" to the projected value of this case. This factor weighs against cost-shifting.

b. The Total Cost of Production Compared to the Resources Available to Each Party

There is no question that UBS has exponentially more resources available to it than Zubulake. While Zubulake is an accomplished equities trader, she has now been unemployed for close to two years. Given the difficulties in the equities market and the fact that she is suing her former employer, she may not be particularly marketable. On the other hand, she asserts that she has a $19 million claim against UBS. So while UBS's resources clearly dwarf Zubulake's, she may have the financial wherewithal to cover at least some of the cost of restoration. In addition, it is not unheard of for plaintiff's firms to front huge expenses when multi-million dollar recoveries are in sight. Thus, while this factor weighs against cost shifting, it does not rule it out.

c. The Relative Ability of Each Party to Control Costs and Its Incentive to Do So

Restoration of backup tapes must generally be done by an outside vendor. Here, UBS had complete control over the selection of the vendor. It is entirely possible that a less-expensive vendor could have been found. However, once that vendor is selected, costs are not within the control of either party. In addition, because these backup tapes are relatively well-organized—meaning that UBS knows what e-mails can be found on each tape—there is nothing more that Zubulake can do to focus her discovery request or reduce its cost. Zubulake has already made a targeted discovery request and the restoration of the sample tapes has not enabled her to cut back on that request. Thus, this factor is neutral.

3. Factor Six: The Importance of the Issues at Stake in the Litigation

As noted in *Zubulake I*, this factor "will only rarely come into play." Although this case revolves around a weighty issue—discrimination in the workplace—it is hardly unique. Claims of discrimination are common, and while discrimination is an important problem, this litigation does not present a particularly novel issue. If I were to consider the issues in this discrimination case sufficiently important to weigh in the cost-shifting analysis, then this factor would be virtually meaningless. Accordingly, this factor is neutral.

4. Factor Seven: The Relative Benefits to the Parties of Obtaining the Information

Although Zubulake argues that there are potential benefits to UBS in undertaking the restoration of these backup tapes—in particular, the opportunity to obtain evidence that may be useful at summary judgment or trial—there can be no question that Zubulake stands to gain far more than does UBS, as will typically be the case. Certainly, absent an order, UBS would not restore any of this data of its own volition. Accordingly, this factor weighs in favor of cost-shifting.

5. Summary and Conclusion

Factors one through four tip against cost-shifting (although factor two only slightly so). Factors five and six are neutral, and factor seven favors cost-shifting. As noted in my earlier opinion in this case, however, a list of factors is not merely a matter of counting and adding; it is only a guide. Because some of the factors cut against cost shifting, but only *slightly so*—in particular, the possibility that the continued production will produce valuable new information—some cost-shifting is appropriate in this case, although UBS should pay the majority of the costs. There is plainly relevant evidence that is only available on UBS's backup tapes. At the same time, Zubulake has not been able to show that there is indispensable evidence on those backup tapes (although the fact that Chapin apparently deleted certain e-mails indicates that such evidence may exist).

The next question is how much of the cost should be shifted. It is beyond cavil that the precise allocation is a matter of judgment and fairness rather than a mathematical consequence of the seven factors discussed above. Nonetheless, the analysis of those factors does inform the exercise of discretion. Because the seven factor test requires that UBS pay the lion's share, the percentage assigned to Zubulake must be less than fifty percent. A share that is too costly may chill the rights of litigants to pursue meritorious claims. However, because the success of this search is somewhat speculative, any cost that fairly can be assigned to Zubulake is appropriate and ensures that UBS's expenses will not be unduly burdensome. A twenty-five percent assignment to Zubulake meets these goals.

C. Other Costs

The final question is whether this result should apply to the entire cost of the production, or only to the cost of restoring the backup tapes. The difference is not academic—the estimated cost of *restoring and searching* the remaining backup tapes is $165,954.67, while the estimated cost of *producing* them (restoration and searching costs plus attorney and paralegal costs) is $273,649.39 ($19,003.43 for the five sample tapes, or $3,800.69 per tape, times seventy-two un-restored tapes), a difference of $107,694.72.

As a general rule, where cost-shifting is appropriate, only the costs of restoration and searching should be shifted. Restoration, of course, is the act of making inaccessible material accessible. That "special purpose" or "extraordinary step" should be the subject of cost-shifting. Search costs should also be shifted because they are so intertwined with the restoration process; a vendor like Pinkerton will not only develop and refine the search script, but also necessarily execute the search as it conducts the restoration. However, the responding party should *always* bear the cost of reviewing and producing electronic data once it has been converted to an accessible form. This is so for two reasons.

First, the producing party has the exclusive ability to control the cost of reviewing the documents. In this case, UBS decided—as is its right—to have a senior associate at a top New York City law firm conduct the privilege review at a cost of $410 per hour. But the job could just as easily have been done (while perhaps not as well) by a first-year associate or contract attorney at a far lower rate. UBS could similarly have obtained paralegal assistance for far less than $170 per hour.

Moreover, the producing party unilaterally decides on the review protocol. When reviewing electronic data, that review may range from reading every word of every document to conducting a series of targeted key word searches. Indeed, many parties to document-intensive litigation enter into so-called "claw-back" agreements that allow the parties to forego privilege review altogether in favor of an agreement to return inadvertently produced privileged documents. The parties here can still reach such an agreement with respect to the remaining seventy-two tapes and thereby avoid any cost of reviewing these tapes for privilege.

Second, the argument that *all* costs related to the production of restored data should be shifted misapprehends the nature of the cost-shifting inquiry. Recalling that cost-shifting is only appropriate for inaccessible—*but otherwise discoverable*—data, it necessarily follows that once the data has been restored to an accessible format and responsive documents located, cost-shifting is no longer appropriate. Had it always been accessible, there is no question that UBS would have had to produce the data at its own cost. Indeed, this is precisely what I ordered in *Zubulake I* with respect to certain e-mails kept on UBS's optical disk system.

Documents stored on backup tapes can be likened to paper records locked inside a sophisticated safe to which no one has the key or combination. The cost of accessing those documents may be onerous, and in some cases the parties should split the cost of breaking into the safe. But once the safe is opened, the production of the documents found inside is the sole responsibility of the responding party. The point is simple: technology may increasingly permit litigants to reconstruct lost or inaccessible information, but once restored to an accessible form, the usual rules of discovery apply.

IV. CONCLUSION

For the reasons set forth above, the costs of restoring any backup tapes are allocated between UBS and Zubulake seventy-five percent and twenty-five percent, respectively. All other costs are to be borne exclusively by UBS. Notwithstanding this ruling, UBS can potentially impose a shift of all of its costs, attorney's fees included, by making an offer to the plaintiff under Rule 68.

Notes and Questions

1. A jury ultimately awarded Zubulake a $29.5 million verdict. UBS appealed, and the parties settled for an undisclosed amount before the case reached an appellate court. Victor Li, *Looking back on Zubulake, 10 years later*, ABA J., Sept. 2014, http://www.abajournal.com/magazine/article/looking_back_on_zubulake_10_years_later.

2. *Zubulake* opinions I and III address three issues. (There was an intervening *Zubulake II* opinion not excerpted for this text.) The first is whether the requested emails, regardless of storage method, are discoverable. That is, are they relevant under Rule 26 and do they fit within Rule 34's definition of "documents"? The answer here, clearly, is yes. (Since *Zubulake* was decided, Rule 34 has been amended several times specifically to cover ESI.) Second, the court asks whether compliance

with the request is unduly burdensome or expensive for the responding party. Remember, the costs of responding to discovery normally fall to the responding party. The answer turns largely on the accessibility of the data. The court identifies five categories of data and characterizes their relative accessibility. Why would a company—UBS for instance—bother to store presumably important data in an inaccessible manner? *See, e.g., Semsroth v. City of Wichita*, 239 F.R.D. 630, 632 (D. Kan. 2006) ("Defendants store information only on (1) their active user e-mail files and (2) on back-up tapes. . . . [Defendant] keeps back-up tapes for disaster recovery purposes only, and not to retrieve information."). Only if the data are inaccessible should the court turn to the third issue: whether cost-shifting is appropriate and how to determine this. *Zubulake I* provides the method; *Zubulake III* the answer. Consider, however, that the second and third issues are really part of Rule 26(b)(1)'s proportionality analysis, which is warranted here because producing inaccessibly stored electronic information is so expensive.

3. Section IV(C)(1)(c) is the most important part of *Zubulake I*. This is where the court set forth a new test to determine whether cost-shifting is appropriate. Emphasizing that these factors should not be weighted equally in all situations, the court identified the following seven factors to be considered in any cost shifting analysis:

1. The extent to which the request is specifically tailored to discover relevant information;
2. The availability of such information from other sources;
3. The total cost of production, compared to the amount in controversy;
4. The total cost of production, compared to the resources available to each party;
5. The relative ability of each party to control costs and its incentive to do so;
6. The importance of the issues at stake in the litigation; and
7. The relative benefits to the parties of obtaining the information.

Zubulake I is devoted largely to developing the appropriate framework within which to carry out the cost-shifting analysis. *Zubulake I* purports to refine *Rowe*, which itself purports to refine Rule 26(b)(2) for electronic discovery. Compare the *Zubulake* and *Rowe* tests. How different do you think they actually are? Take one example: *Zubulake I* combines *Rowe*'s first two factors into one. But does this one factor still have two parts?

4. If you conclude that the tests differ in important ways, does one offer advantages over the others? *See Hagemeyer N. Am., Inc. v. Gateway Data Sci. Corp.*, 222 F.R.D. 594, 602 (E.D. Wis. 2004) ("*Zubulake* brought the cost-shifting analysis closer to the Rule 26(b)(2) proportionality test by adding two factors that *Rowe* had omitted and made the analysis dependent on the facts of the case."); *but see* Panel Discussion, *Managing Electronic Discovery: Views from the Judges*, 76 FORDHAM L. REV 1, 24 (2007) (Judge Francis, who formulated the *Rowe* test, saying "I am

resistant to the hierarchy approach [of *Zubulake*] because my fear is that the factor at the top of the hierarchy will almost always wash out the other factors.").

5. Fed. R. Civ. P. 26(b)(1) was adjusted in 2015 to include a proportionality provision regarding the scope and limits of discovery. Discovery requests must be "proportional to the needs of the case, the parties' relative access to relevant information, the importance of the issues at stake in the action considering the amount in controversy, the parties' resources, the importance of discovery in resolving the issues, and whether the burden or expense of the proposed discovery outweighs its likely benefit." These conditions were more generally urged in prior Rule 26(b)(2)(c)(iii). For a history of the proportionality approach, see generally E. Thomas Sullivan & Richard S. Frase, Proportionality Principles in American Law (2009).

Chief Justice Roberts has characterized the 2015 amendments to the Federal Rules of Civil Procedure as a "big deal." John Roberts, *2015 Year-End Report on the Federal Judiciary* at 5. The amendments "address the most serious impediments to just, speedy, and efficient resolution of civil disputes." *Id.* at 4. Accordingly, the amendments "1) encourage greater cooperation among counsel; 2) focus discovery . . . on what is truly necessary to resolve the case; 3) engage judges in early and active case management; and 4) address serious new problems associated with vast amounts of electronically stored information." *Id.* at 5.

The revisions to Rule 26(b)(1), according to Chief Justice Roberts, "crystalize the concept of reasonable limits on discovery through increased reliance on the common-sense concept of proportionality . . . ." *Id.* at 6. In determining whether a discovery request is proportional, one should consider:

> [T]he importance of the issues at stake in the action, the amount in controversy, the parties' relative access to the relevant information, the parties' resources, the importance of the discovery in resolving the issues, and whether the burden or expense of the proposed discovery outweighs its likely benefit.

Fed. R. Civ. P. 26(B)(1).

6. In practice, it is helpful to put a plan into place when creating proportional preservation. By understanding the issues of the case, cooperating with the opposing party, having awareness of what data can be found, and knowing the difference between data that needs to be preserved and data that needs to be compiled will make the process of creating proportional preservation more efficient and help avoid the possibility of sanctions. Michael Hamilton, *Proportionality in Preservation*, 85 U.S.L.W. 1139 (Feb. 23, 2017).

7. You might also try to match *Zubulake*'s seven factors with Rule 26(b)(1) & (2). Does Rule 26(b)(1) & (2) contain anything that *Zubulake* doesn't? *See Wiginton v. CB Richard Ellis, Inc.*, 229 F.R.D. 568, 572–73 (N.D. Ill. 2004) ("[W]e find that the proportionality test set forth in [Rule 26(b)(2)] must shape the test. Thus,

we modify the *Zubulake* rules by adding a factor that considers the importance of the requested discovery in resolving the issues of the litigation."). If the goal is to accurately reflect Rule 26, why not stick with Rule 26? *See Thompson v. U.S. Dep't of Hous. & Urban Dev.*, 219 F.R.D. 93, 98 (D. Md. 2003) ("In addition to the tests fashioned by these courts, it also can be argued with some force that the Rule 26(b)(2) balancing factors are all that is needed to allow a court to reach a fair result when considering the scope of electronic records.").

8. Apart from Rule 26, there are now at least four tests for cost-shifting: *Rowe, Zubulake, Wiginton*, and the marginal utility analysis, which is incorporated into the previous three tests and is generally agreed to be the most important. Under the marginal utility test, "[t]he more likely it is that the backup tape contains" relevant information, "the fairer it is that the" responding party bear the cost; "the less likely it is, the more unjust it would be to make the [responding party] search at its own expense. The difference is 'at the margin.'" *McPeek v. Ashcroft*, 202 F.R.D. 31, 34 (D.D.C. 2001).

9. How should the probability and the relevance be assessed? In *Zubulake III*, once duplicates were eliminated, roughly 56% of the emails were responsive and 6% were characterized as "highly relevant to the issues in this case" by the plaintiff. UBS disputed this and, as the Court noted, "nowhere is there evidence that Chapin's dislike of Zubulake related to her gender." Ultimately, though, the test "tips slightly against cost-shifting." Is there a percentage of relevant emails that would have tipped the test the other way, and how would a court know that? What if of the thousands of emails only one was at all relevant, but it was a smoking gun, that is, *really* relevant? Are courts well-equipped to make these calculations? *Wiginton*, 229 F.R.D. at 573–75 provides another point of comparison when answering these questions.

10. In framing its analysis, the Court in *Zubulake I* notes "that cost-shifting may effectively end discovery, especially when private parties are engaged in litigation with large corporations." Given the presumption that the responding party must bear the costs and the fact that large corporations can afford to generate and store potentially relevant information, why shouldn't they have to pay for it when requested in discovery? Why consider cost-shifting at all? Doesn't it have the potential to prevent resolution on the merits? As the quotation above suggests, traditionally issues of e-discovery and cost-shifting have arisen in asymmetrical contexts, where a resource-poor plaintiff seeks e-discovery from a resource-rich defendant, but that is changing. *See, e.g., Smith v. Cafe Asia*, 246 F.R.D. 19 (D.D.C. 2007) (ordering e-discovery of images kept on the plaintiff's cell phone in a sexual harassment case); Richard L. Marcus, *E-Discovery Beyond the Federal Rules*, 37 U. Balt. L. Rev. 321, 344 (2008).

11. What if UBS had sued Zubulake? Would she have a stronger case for discovering UBS's ESI and against cost-shifting? If so, why? If not, why not? If you think policy considerations matter, do you think our procedural rules should apply differently to different parties? Where would that leave our procedural system?

12. An emerging issue of contention between the Circuits is a prevailing party's ability to recover costs accrued in producing electronic discovery. As the prevalence of e-discovery and the sheer amount of accessible relevant data grow, litigation costs associated with data searching, processing, and production have also increased. Under the terms of 28 U.S.C. § 1920(4) recoverable costs include "exemplification and the cost of making copies of any materials where the copies are necessarily obtained for use in the case." Congress had amended Section 1920(4) in 2008 to replace "copies of papers" with the "any materials" language.

Courts recognize a strong presumption in favor of awarding costs that fit within the categories of 28 U.S.C. § 1920, but they also retain wide discretion in how to interpret the statute. Disagreement now exists regarding which aspects of e-discovery constitute "making copies." The Third and Fourth Circuits have held that the statute does not cover ESI processing costs, while the Sixth Circuit has held the opposite.[13]

The Federal Circuit, however, has held that costs associated with collecting, processing, and producing ESI are modern equivalents of activities that the statute embraced.[14] Courts upholding taxation for services leading up to copying regard these services as an indispensable part of the copying process.[15]

The Third Circuit's decision in *Race Tires America*,[16] exhibits the range of difference in recovery between a broad and narrow interpretation of the amended statute. The district court had awarded the defendant $370,000 to cover the costs of its data extraction, processing, and production only to have the award reduced on appeal to a mere $30,370.42.

> The question presented here is whether § 1920(4) authorizes the taxation of an electronic discovery consultant's charges for data collection, preservation, searching, culling, conversion, and production as either the "exemplification [or] the . . . making [of] copies of any materials where the copies are necessarily obtained for use in the case."
>
> . . .
>
> The decisions that allow taxation of all, or essentially all, electronic discovery consultant charges, such as the District Court's ruling in this case, are untethered from the statutory mooring. Section 1920(4) does not state that all steps that lead up to the production of copies of materials are taxable. It does not authorize taxation merely because today's technology requires technical expertise not ordinarily possessed by the typical legal

---

13. *See Race Tires America, Inc. v. Hoosier Racing Tire Corp.*, 674 F.3d 158 (3d Cir. 2012); *Country Vintner of N.C., LLC v. E. & J. Gallo Winery, Inc.*, 2013 U.S. App. LEXIS 8629 (4th Cir. 2013) (taxing only the costs of converting electronic files to non-editable formats, and transferring files onto CDs); *Colosi v. Jones Lang LaSalle Americas, Inc.*, 781 F.3d 293 (6th Cir. 2015) (§ 1920 is broad enough to provide courts discretion to tax costs of copying related to ESI).

14. *See CBT Flint Partners, LLC v. Return Path, Inc.*, 501 Fed. Appx. 980 (Fed. Cir. 2013).

15. *See Race Tires*, 674 F.3d at 168.

16. 674 F.3d 158 (3d Cir. 2012).

> professional. It does not say that activities that encourage cost savings may be taxed. Section 1920(4) authorizes awarding only the cost of making copies.
>
> . . .
>
> It may be that extensive "processing" of ESI is essential to make a comprehensive and intelligible production . . . . But that does not mean that the services leading up to the actual production constitute "making copies." . . . None of the steps that preceded the actual act of making copies in the pre-digital era would have been considered taxable. And that is because Congress did not authorize taxation of charges necessarily incurred to discharge discovery obligations. It allowed only for the taxation of the costs of making copies.
>
> . . .
>
> In sum, we conclude that of the numerous services the vendors performed, only the scanning of hard copy documents, the conversion of native files to TIFF, and the transfer of VHS tapes to DVD involved "copying," and that the costs attributable to only those activities are recoverable under § 1920(4)'s allowance for the "costs of making copies of any materials." Those costs total $30,370.42.

Through cost-shifting, *Zubulake* addresses the expense of e-discovery that results from the volume of ESI created and the formats in which it is stored. But e-discovery creates other issues as well. These include the preservation and retrieval of ESI, its location (ESI can be found on computers, networks, backup tapes, PDAs, flashdrives, and cell phone text messages, among other places), the mechanics of searching through such information (relevant email must be distinguished from spam, for instance), the format in which ESI is to be produced, and the privilege and work product review that precedes production.

Dealing with these issues within the framework of a party-driven but adversarial process leads to frustration. Almost 77% of surveyed trial lawyers said "that courts do not understand the difficulties in providing e-discovery" and 63% said "e-discovery is being abused by counsel." The American College of Trial Lawyers Task Force on Discovery and The Institute for the Advancement of the American Legal System, Interim Report & 2008 Litigation Survey of the Fellows of the American College of Trial Lawyers, Sept. 9, 2008. Courts are no happier than the lawyers. One study found that 25% of e-discovery opinions impose sanctions. Kroll Ontrack, Year in Review: Courts Unsympathetic to Electronic Discovery Ignorance or Misconduct (press release), http://www.krollontrack.com/news-releases/?getPressRelease=61208 (Dec. 2, 2008).

In response, courts have formulated specific procedures to control e-discovery. According to one estimate, 41 district courts now have such procedures. Electronic

Discovery Law, http://www.ediscoverylaw.com/2008/10/articles/resources/updated-list-local-rules-forms-and-guidelines-of-united-states-district-courts-addressing-ediscovery-issues/. Many of these procedures were adopted prior to the passage of the e-discovery amendments to the Federal Rules, which are discussed below. They remain relevant because they can provide both a level of detail and specificity missing from the Rules and a key to how individual courts approach e-discovery. These procedures vary in scope and specificity. Federal District Courts in Delaware, Kansas, and Maryland have all adopted comprehensive and influential procedures that involve the imposition of sanctions. Kroll Ontrack, Year In Rs, which serve as useful guides for the conduct of e-discovery in complex cases. These procedures can be found respectively at:

http://www.ded.uscourts.gov/SLR/Misc/EDiscov.pdf

http://www.ksd.uscourts.gov/guidelines/electronicdiscoveryguidelines.pdf

http://www.mdd.uscourts.gov/news/news/ESIProtocol.pdf

The goal of these guidelines is to facilitate e-discovery and to ensure that it is a cooperative process carried out in compliance with the Federal Rules to the extent that they cover ESI. Despite their common goal, these procedures take different approaches to reach it. The Federal Courts in Maryland and Kansas provide suggested procedures and identify relevant issues. The District Court of Kansas concludes its suggested procedures with 50 questions concerning ESI that counsel should be prepared to ask and answer at the 26(f) conference. The District Court of Delaware, by contrast, provides a set of "default standards" that apply unless the parties formulate their own plan.

The broad outlines of the plans in the Districts of Delaware, Kansas, and Maryland are similar. Generally, the first steps prescribed are for counsel (1) to learn of the existence and extent of the client's ESI, including who controls such information; (2) to determine what ESI will be requested; and (3) to communicate this information to opposing counsel. Throughout, the emphasis is on preparation, communication, and cooperation. Pursuant to Rule 26(f), the parties then meet. The guidelines for each court specify appropriate issues to be addressed at that time. After all of this, a formal discovery plan is created.

While the specific provisions of these rules and guidelines cover much of the same ground, in places they adopt different approaches. As the discussion of metadata, *infra*, should make clear, the format in which ESI is produced is important. In the District of Kansas, "Counsel should attempt to agree on the format and media to be used in the production of ESI." Going a step further, the Districts of Delaware and Maryland provide that if the parties cannot agree, "text searchable image files (e.g., PDF or TIFF)" shall be provided and the producing party shall maintain the ESI in its original format.

Apart from the format in which ESI is produced, the order in which it is produced is also important. The Districts of Delaware and Maryland provide for phased discovery. The District of Maryland rule is illustrative:

> [The parties should discuss] the need for two-tier or staged discovery of ESI, considering whether ESI initially can be produced in a manner that is more cost-effective, while reserving the right to request or to oppose additional more comprehensive production in a latter stage or stages. Absent agreement or good cause shown, discovery of ESI should proceed in the following sequence: 1) after receiving requests for production of ESI, the parties should search their ESI, other than that identified as not reasonably accessible without undue burden or cost, and produce responsive ESI within the parameters of Fed. R. Civ. P. 26(b)(2)(C) [and 26(b)(2)(B)]; 2) searches of or for ESI identified as not reasonably accessible should not be conducted until the prior step has been completed; and, 3) requests for information expected to be found in or among ESI that was identified as not reasonably accessible should be narrowly focused, with a factual basis supporting each request.

Judge Paul W. Grimm et al., Suggested Protocol for Discovery of Electronically Stored Information ("ESI"), ¶ 8. M, at 23. The steps of phased discovery are dictated by the accessibility of the ESI.

By contrast, without discussing phased discovery, the District of Kansas provides:

> If the requesting party intends to seek discovery of ESI from sources identified as not reasonably accessible, the parties should discuss: (1) the burdens and costs of accessing and retrieving the information, (2) the needs that may establish good cause for requiring production of all or part of the information, even if the information sought is not reasonably accessible, and (3) conditions on obtaining and producing this information such as scope, time, and allocation of cost.

U.S. District Court for the District of Kansas, Guidelines for Discovery of Electronically Stored Information (ESI), ¶ 4(g), at 2.

Given the volume of information that must be produced in e-discovery, the risk of disclosing privileged information or work product is great. The District of Kansas allows for "quick peek" and "clawback agreements," under which information can be produced either without waiving "privilege or protection" or without waiving the right to have the information returned, but cautions that "[t]he parties should be aware that there is an issue of whether such agreements bind third parties who are not parties to the agreements." *Id.* ¶ 4(h), at 3. In federal court in Maryland, such agreements are subject to the standard announced in *Hopson v. Mayor and City Council of Baltimore*, 232 F.R.D. 228 (D. Md. 2005) (discussing the importance of clawback and other waiver protection agreements, noting the uncertainty with regard to governing law, and formulating a cautious approach). Grimm et al., *supra*, ¶ 4B, at 4.

The District of Delaware is unique in creating an e-discovery liaison through whom "all requests and responses shall be made." The liaison must be familiar with its party's information systems, knowledgeable about the technical specifics of ESI, and prepared to participate in the discovery proceedings. Additionally, that court provides for "retention coordinators," who ensure that ESI susceptible to deletion or modification is preserved and unaltered, and available for discovery. Even apart from court requirements, why might a prudent legal team want a conscientious retention coordinator? To avoid the risk of a spoliation of evidence allegation?

Having seen some of the differences in the approaches adopted by Federal Courts in Delaware, Kansas, and Maryland, do you think one is preferable to the others? *Cf. O'Bar v. Lowe's Home Centers, Inc.*, 2007 U.S. Dist. LEXIS 32497, *10–24 (W.D.N.C. May 2, 2007) (adopting the District of Maryland's e-discovery procedures for a pre-certification discovery plan in a putative class action). In creating such guidelines, courts are already playing a more active part in what was initially conceived as a party-driven process. Would it be better if their role were to increase even more, such that they were formulating mandatory protocols of greater specificity?

When the Federal Rules were revised in 2006, several provisions were added specifically to address e-discovery.[17] Beyond simply acknowledging e-discovery, the amendments address five major issues relevant to the discovery of ESI: privilege/waiver, preservation duties, form of production, inaccessible information, and sanctions. Rule 26(a)(1) now specifically includes "electronically stored information" among the materials that must be disclosed by a party if the ESI may be used by the party to support a claim or defense. Rule 34 makes clear that a party may request ESI as it would other discoverable material and governs the form of production. The request "may specify the form or forms in which electronically stored information is to be produced." In response, the producing party "may state an objection to a requested form. . . . If the responding party objects to a requested form—or if no form was specified in the request—the party must state the form or forms it intends to use." Finally, absent agreement or court order, Rule 34(b)(2)(E) provides a set of default procedures:

(i) A party must produce documents as they are kept in the usual course of business or must organize and label them to correspond to the categories in the request;

(ii) If a request does not specify a form for producing electronically stored information, a party must produce it in a form or forms in which it is ordinarily maintained or in a reasonably usable form or forms; and

(iii) A party need not produce the same electronically stored information in more than one form.

Although it does not mention ESI, Rule 26(b)(5)(B) was added to address the problem—made especially acute by the volume of ESI and the formats in which it is

---

17. This discussion draws on the Notes of Advisory Committee on 2006 amendments.

stored—of inadvertent disclosure and thus waiver of potentially privileged materials. It provides:

> If information produced in discovery is subject to a claim of privilege or of protection as trial-preparation material, the party making the claim may notify any party that received the information of the claim and the basis for it. After being notified, a party must promptly return, sequester, or destroy the specified information and any copies it has; must not use or disclose the information until the claim is resolved; must take reasonable steps to retrieve the information if the party disclosed it before being notified; and may promptly present the information to the court under seal for a determination of the claim. The producing party must preserve the information until the claim is resolved.

Fed. R. Civ. P. 26(b)(5)(B).

Note that the rule is entirely procedural. It does not help a court determine whether waiver has actually occurred. This question is answered by the substantive law of waiver applicable in a given case. *See* section E, *infra*, for a discussion of Federal Rule of Evidence 502. If data is to be produced, it must first be preserved, which can be challenging given the amount of data created by most companies.

When litigation is reasonably anticipated, parties must preserve relevant information. Routine document and ESI destruction or recycling programs must be overridden to ensure that information that may be relevant in the litigation is preserved. When evidence is destroyed or lost during a litigation hold, the party may be subject to significant sanctions (and possibly tort liability) for spoliation.

In 2006, the Federal Rules Advisory Committee adopted an initial version of Rule 37(e) that was meant to provide litigants protection from court sanctions when electronically stored information is lost despite the parties' routine, good-faith efforts towards preservation. Recognize that the rule addresses ESI that is lost, rather than the *Zubulake* situation in which ESI is not lost but can only be retrieved at enormous expense. By 2015, it had become apparent that this rule had "not adequately addressed the serious problems resulting from the continued exponential growth in the volume of such information." The Committee found that Federal Circuits were establishing inconsistent standards for when sanctions would be imposed, resulting in litigants having "to expend excessive effort and money on preservation in order to avoid the risk of severe sanctions if a court finds they did not do enough." The rule adopted in 2015 provides courts with more specific guidelines:

> (e) If electronically stored information that should have been preserved in the anticipation or conduct of litigation is lost because a party failed to take reasonable steps to preserve it, and it cannot be restored or replaced through additional discovery, the court:
>
> > (1) upon finding prejudice to another party from loss of the information, may order measures no greater than necessary to cure the prejudice; or

(2) only upon finding that the party acted with the intent to deprive another party of the information's use in the litigation may:

(A) presume that the lost information was unfavorable to the party;

(B) instruct the jury that it may or must presume the information was unfavorable to the party; or

(C) dismiss the action or enter a default judgment.

Fed. R. Civ. P. 37

This updated rule was tested in *Mathew Enterprise, Inc. v. Chrysler Group, LLC*, 2016 U.S. Dist. LEXIS (N.D. Cal. 2016), a case involving a motion for non-intentional spoliation sanctions. The plaintiff, a Chrysler dealer, sued Chrysler for price discrimination under the Robinson-Patman Act (RPA). For nearly a year after first threatening Chrysler with litigation, and during the period in which Chrysler allegedly continued to violate RPA, the plaintiff "made no effort to preserve communications from customers or internal emails." *Id.* at *2. The outside vendor that stored the plaintiff's emails was not notified of a litigation hold and continued to automatically delete emails. Additionally, the plaintiff switched email providers during this period and lost all its old emails in the process. The data could not be recovered.

The court granted relief heavily favoring Chrysler, including allowing Chrysler to rebut any testimony offered by plaintiff's witnesses with the spoliation argument. Nonetheless, the court pointed out that it had "take[n] care . . . 'to ensure that curative measures under (e)(1) do not have the effect of measures that are permitted under subdivision (e)(2) only on a finding of intent to deprive another party of the lost information's use in the litigation.'" *Id.* at *10.

Two further changes warrant extended discussion. First, Rule 26(b)(2)(B) puts specific limitations on the discovery of electronically stored information. Second, e-discovery is made a focal point of both the Rule 26(f) and Rule 16 conferences. Rule 26(b)(2)(B) was adopted "to address issues raised by difficulties in locating, retrieving, and providing discovery of some electronically stored information." Notes of the Advisory Committee on 2006 amendments. It provides:

> A party need not provide discovery of electronically stored information from sources that the party identifies as not reasonably accessible because of undue burden or cost. On motion to compel discovery or for a protective order, the party from whom discovery is sought must show that the information is not reasonably accessible because of undue burden or cost. If that showing is made, the court may nonetheless order discovery from such sources if the requesting party shows good cause, considering the limitations of Rule 26(b)(2)(C). The court may specify conditions for the discovery.

This creates a two-tiered procedure for dealing with discovery requests for ESI. The first is party-driven and concerns reasonably accessible responsive ESI. Lee H. Rosenthal, *A Few Thoughts on Electronic Discovery after December 1, 2006*, 116 YALE

L.J. Pocket Part 167, 168 (Nov. 30, 2006). A producing party can, however, decline to turn over potentially responsive ESI that it identifies as not reasonably accessible. Such identification "does not relieve the party of its common-law or statutory duties to preserve evidence." Notes of the Advisory Committee on 2006 amendments. To determine whether ESI is not reasonably accessible, a responding party must first determine where and how it is stored. *See Peskoff v. Faber*, 2006 U.S. Dist. LEXIS 46372 (D.D.C. July 11, 2006) (identifying five potential locations of varying accessibility where requested email might be found and ordering the responding party to provide an affidavit addressing its location). How is the requesting party to know if the responding party is correct that the requested information is not reasonably accessible? The Advisory Committee notes that "[t]he requesting party may need discovery to test this assertion." What form should such discovery take?

The second tier of discovery under 26(b)(2)(B) is court supervised and is initiated by motion, either to compel production or for a protective order. *Rosenthal, supra*, at 171. Initially, the producing party bears the burden of establishing that the requested material is not reasonably accessible. After such a showing, the court proceeds to the good cause analysis, under which the moving party bears the burden.

How is the accessibility of ESI to be assessed? The rule frames the issue of accessibility in terms of burden or cost, and not various technological features of the ESI or even ease of access (the traditional definition of accessibility). Why might the drafters have defined accessibility in this way? *See W.E. Aubuchon, Inc. v. Benefirst*, 245 F.R.D. 38, 42–43 (D. Mass. 2007) ("[T]he records sought by the Plaintiffs are stored on a server used by BeneFirst in Pembroke Massachusetts, which is clearly an accessible format [under the categories announced in *Zubulake* above]. However, because of BeneFirst's method of storage and lack of an indexing system, it will be extremely costly to retrieve the requested data"); *see also Best Buy Stores, L.P. v. Developers Diversified Realty Corp.*, DDR GLH, LLC, 247 F.R.D. 567, 569–70 (D. Minn. 2007) (reversing magistrate judge's order that requested information was "reasonably accessible because $124,000 is a reasonable cost considering the potential breach of contract damages in excess of $800,000." The court went on to find that "[b]ecause of the high cost to restore and maintain the database and the fact that it would have to be restored from original sources," the requested information was not reasonably accessible.).

Suppose that a party to pending litigation fails to preserve accessible ESI known to be relevant. As a result the discovery request can only be satisfied by restoring not reasonably accessible backup tapes. Should a party in such a situation be able to benefit from Rule 26(b)(2)'s limit? *Compare Id.* at 570–71 *with Disability Rights Council of Greater Wash. v. Wash. Metro. Area Transit Auth.*, 242 F.R.D. 139, 147–48 (D.D.C. 2007) ("I am anything but certain that I should permit a party who has failed to preserve accessible information without cause to then complain about the inaccessibility of the only electronically stored information that remains. It reminds me too much of Leo Kosten's definition of chutzpah: 'that quality enshrined in a man who, having killed his mother and his father, throws himself on the mercy of the court because he is an orphan.'"). Ultimately, that dicta did not decide the case in *Disability Rights Council*. The court continued on to the good cause analysis and granted the motion to compel.

Assuming that the responding party has shown that the requested information is not reasonably accessible, how is a court to determine whether the requesting party has good cause for nevertheless compelling disclosure? The advisory committee identifies a non-exhaustive list of seven relevant considerations: "(1) the specificity of the discovery request; (2) the quantity of information available from other and more easily accessed sources; (3) the failure to produce relevant information that seems likely to have existed but is no longer available on more easily accessed sources; (4) the likelihood of finding relevant, responsive information that cannot be obtained from other, more easily accessed sources; (5) predictions as to the importance and usefulness of the further information; (6) the importance of the issues at stake in the litigation; and (7) the parties' resources." Notes of the Advisory Committee on 2006 Amendments. These factors overlap with those in *Zubulake*, but at least by their terms the issue here is the appropriateness of production and not cost-shifting. Should that be a separate analysis? For an example of the good cause analysis, which resulted in granting the motion to compel and a detailed order governing the search protocol, see *Disability Rights Council*, 242 F.R.D. at 148.

Because the good cause inquiry concerns information that by definition has not been searched, how are factors (2), (4), and (5) to be assessed? The Advisory Committee says, "the parties may need some focused discovery, which may include sampling of the sources, to learn more about what burdens and costs are involved in accessing the information, what the information consists of, and how valuable it is for the litigation in light of information that can be obtained by exhausting other opportunities for discovery." Notes of the Advisory Committee on 2006 Amendments. This approach mirrors that taken in the *Zubulake* opinions above. You might now ask yourself how discovery about discovery can simplify an already expensive and cumbersome process.

Rule 26(f) has undergone three changes related to the discovery of ESI. First, the discovery plan created by the parties must now address "any issues about disclosure or discovery of electronically stored information, including the form or forms in which it should be produced." Form of production is a frequent issue of contention among parties. *See In re Priceline.com Inc. Securities Litig.*, 233 F.R.D. 88 (D. Conn. 2005) (discussing the relevant issues and crafting a detailed discovery order). Do you think an obligation to discuss these issues will actually lead to their resolution? Second, at the discovery conference the parties should "discuss any issues about preserving discoverable information; and develop a proposed discovery plan." Third, the parties should discuss "any issues about claims of privilege or of protection as trial-preparation materials, including—if the parties agree on a procedure to assert these claims after production—whether to ask the court to include their agreement in an order."

Neither the second nor the third change mentions ESI, and both apply to all discoverable material, but both are especially important in the context of e-discovery. In what ways does ESI differ from other information, thus necessitating an increased emphasis on preservation? *See, e.g.*, *Rosenthal, supra*, at 168–69 ("[E]lectronically stored information is dynamic, unlike static words on paper, which complicates decisions about what has to be retained and how. Affirmative steps are necessary to preserve electronically stored information; passivity often leads to alteration, deletion, or destruction of information. By contrast, passivity preserves paper; affirmative steps are necessary to destroy a paper or similar physical record of information."). Given the often precarious nature of ESI and the importance of preservation, should the amendments have provided more guidance? When is the obligation to preserve triggered and how far does it extend? Note that each party is not left to address these issues alone, as had been the case before. Instead, they are forced to act in concert to determine the appropriateness of different approaches to preservation.

As has been suggested already, the focus of the 2006 amendments generally, and the meet and confer obligations particularly, is to foster the "open and forthright sharing of information by all parties to a case with the aim of expediting case progress, minimizing burden and expense, and removing contentiousness as much as possible." *Bd. of Regents of the Univ. of Nebraska v. BASP Corp.*, 2007 U.S. Dist. LEXIS 82492, at *5 (D. Neb. Nov. 5, 2007). In many respects this returns discovery to its roots, but it is not without risks. As one commentator and judge put it:

> The amendments increase the demands on lawyers early in litigation, reflecting the complexity of electronic discovery as compared to conventional discovery. . . . To manage these increased demands without unduly front-loading a case and delaying attention to the merits, judges must be simultaneously demanding and patient. Judges should not relax the emerging standard for a meaningful meet-and-confer exchange on electronic discovery issues. But at the same time, judges must understand the difficulties lawyers face in trying to learn their clients' information systems as well as the other disclosure and meet-and-confer subjects early in the case. Judges' patience need not mean significant delays in lawyers' meeting the meet-and-confer obligations. Rather than postpone compliance, which inevitably delays all other steps in the litigation, judges should be alert to the need to engage in the process, even in this very early stage of a case.

Rosenthal, supra, at 176–77.

A Note on Metadata

Metadata is increasingly important. More and more information is stored and transferred electronically. Metadata is information about a document's history that a computer stores automatically. Information such as the amount of time a document was open, when it was created, who created it, who has looked at it and what edits and changes have been made to the document can be retrieved and reviewed later. There may be different obligations as to the handling of metadata depending on the absence or presence of litigation. Keep in mind the discussion above regarding litigation holds and the risk of spoliation.

Metadata absent litigation. Even absent imminent litigation, an attorney should consider how to handle metadata when engaged in electronic correspondence. From both a lawyering and ethical standpoint, one may want to "scrub" documents to remove metadata from communications prior to sending. Since metadata can contain changes made to a document in so-called "red-line" or "track-changes" functions, it is vital that one not send more information than she intends. Revisions and draft history of a document can disclose privileged information or work product. Metadata can end up exhibiting text that was removed to protect information not intended or required to be disclosed. Inadvertent disclosures could be devastating to a later (hypothetical) case. Privilege can be deemed to have been waived not just as to the information disclosed, but also as to related information as well.

The converse of a drafter scrubbing metadata in the absence of litigation is the recipient of documents "mining" those documents for metadata in search of information that could be advantageous. Although through this simple tactic one can gain an advantage, there are ethical implications. Jurisdictions vary as to the ethical propriety of such mining, so it is important that you ascertain the rules that apply before engaging in such mining.

The first to address the issue formally was the New York Committee on Professional Ethics. The New York Committee concluded that the rules of professional conduct (modeled after the ABA Model Rules) precluded such a practice. Finding such practice "prejudicial to the administration of justice," the Committee stated that lawyers may not exploit embedded metadata. Alabama, Arizona, the District of Columbia, Florida, Maine, Mississippi, New Hampshire, and North Carolina have all accepted approaches similar to the New York Committee. In these jurisdictions, mining for metadata is a violation of the standards for professional conduct.

The American Bar Association came down on the other side. In Formal Opinion 06-442 (2006), the ABA rejected the New York approach. It decided that under Rule 4.4, receipt of an inadvertently sent document requires only that the receiving attorney notify the sender; it does not require that the document be returned unread. Relating this same standard to metadata, the ABA concluded that there was no duty to refrain from looking at metadata. The ABA placed the onus to protect metadata on the transmitting lawyers, arguing that there were several methods available to limit the creation and transmission of metadata, an issue which was not considered by the New York Committee's decision issued five years earlier. Although it has received some criticism from legal scholars, and has been rejected by each of the states who have followed New York's lead, the ABA's opinion has significant weight. It has been adopted generally by Colorado, Pennsylvania, and Wisconsin.

The Minnesota Professional Responsibility Board, for example, ruled in 2010 that an attorney, under the professional conduct rules, has a professional duty to avoid revealing a client's secrets in metadata when sending electronic documents. The Board noted in its opinion that metadata can be "scrubbed" from the electronic material before being sent, and that under the duty of competence "steps can be taken to prevent or minimize the transmission of metadata." The Board did comment, though, that in some contexts, such as litigation, "it may be impermissible or illegal" to remove metadata "from evidentiary documents in the context of litigation." Lawyer's Professional Responsibility Board, Opinion 22 (Mar. 26, 2010).

The Board also observed that the receiving lawyer who discovers the metadata must promptly notify the supplier of the metadata. But, "[w]hether the lawyer [who must notify a sender under the rule] is required to take additional steps, such as returning the original document, is a matter of law. . . ." *Id.*

The Vermont Bar Association follows the Minnesota approach on the sender scrubbing the metadata before it is electronically sent, but implies that the receiving lawyers can and perhaps should search for metadata under a duty of diligence. The Association goes on to say "whether inadvertent disclosure of privileged information constitutes a waiver of the document's privileged status is a question of substantive law." However, "Vermont lawyers are subject to the obligation to notify opposing counsel if they receive documents that they know or reasonably should know were inadvertently disclosed," the opinion concludes. Vermont Bar Association Professional Responsibility Section, Ethics Opinion 2009-1.

American Bar Association Model Rule 1.1, regarding an attorney's duty of competence, was amended in 2012 to reflect advancing technologies. The Rule itself requires that a lawyer provide "competent representation" to a client. In Comment 8 to the Model Rule, attorneys must "keep abreast of changes in the law and its practice, including the benefits and risks associated with relevant technology," as well as complying with continuing education requirements. The Comment does not affirm any new obligations on lawyers, but it is a reminder that lawyers should be mindful of new technology and their own proficiency.

The Seventh Circuit and the Southern District of New York agree on the need for mindfulness and proficiency. Under the Seventh Circuit's Electronic Discovery Pilot Program, introduced in 2009, attorneys must designate e-discovery liaisons if they are not sufficiently competent in their client's data storage technology. The Pilot Program received immediate acceptance, and after Phase One, "over ninety percent of the judges thought the Principle 'increased' or 'greatly increased' counsels' level of attention to the technologies affecting the discovery process and the demonstrated familiarity counsel had with their clients' electronic data and data systems."[18] Phase 2 of the Program expanded the number of participating judges and lawyers and continued to receive nearly unanimous positive feedback. "One hundred percent of the

18. Phase I report: https://www.discoverypilot.com/sites/default/files/phase1report.pdf.

responding judges . . . agreed or strongly agreed that the program 'has contributed to a more efficient discovery process.'" Ninety-six percent of responding attorneys felt that the program either had no effect or increased their ability to zealously represent their clients, and many attorneys felt that the program improved levels of communication during litigation.[19]

Judge Shira Scheindlin, author of the famous *Zubulake* decisions, chaired the Judicial Improvements Committee of the Southern District of New York in 2011 when the Committee created its own duty of competence of electronic discovery. The Southern District's program lasted for three years, from 2011 to 2014. One of the central tenets of this program was a requirement that counsel for both parties certify either that they have sufficient knowledge regarding their clients' technological systems or that they will designate a competent person to address the issues. While adoption of this and other elements of the pilot became voluntary after the program's cessation, the Judicial Improvements Committee urged members of the bench and bar "to consider the provisions of the pilot program as the best practices and to use them in particular cases as they see fit."[20]

Metadata in anticipation of litigation. But how should a lawyer handle existing metadata embedded in documents that are known to be relevant to pending or anticipated litigation? The rules now raise additional complexities. Once litigation is actually commenced or reasonably anticipated, "scrubbing" metadata out of documents that might be produced in discovery could amount to spoliation of evidence. Rule 34 states that the scope of discovery for electronically stored information is broad, including "writings, drawings, graphs, charts, photographs, sound recordings, images, and other data or data compilations—stored in any medium from which information can be obtained either directly or, if necessary, after translation by the responding party into a reasonably usable form." Although metadata is not mentioned in the rules, courts might infer that metadata is subject to a preservation obligation, or included within the scope of a document request, even if it is not explicitly mentioned.

The following cases demonstrate various approaches to the question of how to handle metadata. As you read them, try to determine what each court had in mind as an objective when choosing that approach.

---

19. Phase II report: https://www.discoverypilot.com/sites/default/files/Phase-Two-Final-Report-Appendix.pdf.

20. http://www.nysd.uscourts.gov/rules/Complex_Civil_Rules_Pilot_14.11.14.pdf.

Williams v. Sprint/United Management Co.

United States District Court for the District of Kansas
230 F.R.D. 640 (2005)

MEMORANDUM AND ORDER

WAXSE, UNITED STATES MAGISTRATE JUDGE.

Plaintiff Shirley Williams filed this suit on behalf of herself and others similarly situated, asserting that her age was a determining factor in Defendant's decision to terminate her employment during a reduction-in-force (RIF).... The parties are presently engaged in discovery concerning the merits of Plaintiffs' pattern and practice allegations. This matter is presently before the Court on Defendant's Response to the Court's July 12, 2005 Order (doc. 3037), which ordered Defendant to show cause why it should not produce electronic Microsoft Excel spreadsheets in the manner in which they were maintained and why it should not be sanctioned for "scrubbing" the metadata and locking certain data on the electronic spreadsheets prior to producing them to Plaintiffs without either the agreement of the parties or the approval of the Court.

II. Discussion

....

B. Metadata

....

1. Emerging standards of electronic discovery with regard to metadata

c. Application to this case

The narrow issue currently before the Court is whether, under emerging standards of electronic discovery, the Court's Order directing Defendant to produce electronic spreadsheets as they are kept in the ordinary course of business requires Defendant to produce those documents with the metadata intact.

...

Based on these emerging standards, the Court holds that when a party is ordered to produce electronic documents as they are maintained in the ordinary course of business,[21] the producing party should produce the electronic documents with their metadata intact, unless that party timely objects to production of metadata, the parties agree that the metadata should not be produced, or the producing party requests a protective order. The initial burden with regard to the disclosure of the metadata would therefore be placed on the party to whom the request or order to

21. [Court's footnote #69] The same principle may apply when a party *requests* electronic documents be produced as they are maintained in the ordinary course of business, as an "active file," or in their "native format."

produce is directed. The burden to object to the disclosure of metadata is appropriately placed on the party ordered to produce its electronic documents as they are ordinarily maintained because that party already has access to the metadata and is in the best position to determine whether producing it is objectionable. Placing the burden on the producing party is further supported by the fact that metadata is an inherent part of an electronic document, and its removal ordinarily requires an affirmative act by the producing party that alters the electronic document.

i. Relevancy

Defendant maintains that the metadata it removed from its electronic spreadsheets has absolutely no evidentiary value and is completely irrelevant. It argues that Plaintiffs' suggestion that the metadata may identify the computers used to create or modify the spreadsheets or reveal titles of documents that may assist in efforts to piece together the facts of the RIFs at issue in this case has no relevance to Plaintiffs' claim that Defendant maintained discriminatory policies or practices used to effectuate a pattern and practice of age discrimination. Defendant likewise argues that the metadata is not necessary because the titles of documents can be gleaned from the subject spreadsheets, and these titles adequately describe the data included in such spreadsheets.

The Court agrees with Defendant that certain metadata from the spreadsheets may be irrelevant to the claims and defenses in this case. The Court, however, does not find that all of the spreadsheets' metadata is irrelevant. In light of Plaintiffs' allegations that Defendant reworked pools of employees in order to improve distribution to pass its adverse impact analysis, the Court finds that some of the metadata is relevant and likely to lead to the discovery of admissible evidence. While the Court cannot fashion an exhaustive list of the spreadsheet metadata that may be relevant, the Court does find that metadata associated with any changes to the spreadsheets, the dates of any changes, the identification of the individuals making any changes, and other metadata from which Plaintiffs could determine the final versus draft version of the spreadsheets appear relevant. Plaintiffs' allegation that Defendant reworked the pools is not a new allegation. Thus, Defendant should reasonably have known that Plaintiffs were expecting the electronic spreadsheets to contain their metadata intact. Furthermore, if Defendant believed the metadata to be irrelevant, it should have asserted a relevancy objection instead of making the unilateral decision to produce the spreadsheets with the metadata removed.

ii. Reliability

Defendant also argues that the metadata removed from the electronic spreadsheets may be inaccurate and therefore has no evidentiary value. The Court finds that this is not sufficient justification for removing the metadata absent agreement of the parties or the Court's approval. If Defendant had any concerns regarding the accuracy or reliability of the metadata, it should have communicated those concerns to the Court before it scrubbed the metadata.

iii. Privilege

Defendant also argues that production of certain metadata removed by Defendant would facilitate the revelation of information that is attorney-client privileged and/or attorney work product. Defendant claims that through the use of easily accessible technology, metadata may reveal information extracted from a document, such as the items redacted by Defendant's counsel, as well as other protected or privileged matters. It further claims that metadata may create a data trail that reveals changes to prior drafts or edits.

The Court agrees with Defendant that it should not be required to produce metadata directly corresponding to the information that it was permitted to redact, namely the adverse impact analyses and social security numbers. The Court is cognizant that all or some of the metadata may reveal the redacted information. The Court will therefore permit Defendant to remove metadata directly corresponding to Defendant's adverse impact analyses and social security number information.

For any other metadata Defendant claims is protected by the attorney-client privilege or as attorney work product, the Court finds that Defendant should have raised this issue prior to its unilateral decision to produce the spreadsheets with the metadata removed. Fed. R. Civ. P. 26(b)(5) requires a party withholding otherwise discoverable information on the basis of privilege to make the claim expressly and to describe the nature of the documents, communications, or things not produced or disclosed in a manner that, without revealing the privileged information, will enable the other parties to assess the applicability of the privilege. Normally, this is accomplished by objecting and providing a privilege log for "documents, communications, or tangible things" not produced.

In this case, Defendant has failed to object and has not provided a privilege log identifying the electronic documents that it claims contain privileged metadata. Defendant has not provided the Court with even a general description of the purportedly privileged metadata that was scrubbed from the spreadsheets. As Defendant has failed to provide any privilege log for the electronic documents it claims contain metadata that will reveal privileged communications or attorney work product, the Court holds that Defendant has waived any attorney-client privilege or work product protection with regard to the spreadsheets' metadata except for metadata directly corresponding to the adverse impact analyses and social security number information, which the Court has permitted Defendant to remove from the spreadsheets.

2. Plaintiffs never requested the production of metadata

Defendant also argues that Plaintiffs never requested the metadata and that metadata was never mentioned during any of the discovery conferences. While metadata was never mentioned during any of the discovery conferences or in any of the Court's orders, the Court finds that Defendant should reasonably have been aware that the spreadsheets' metadata was encompassed within the Court's directive that it produce the electronic Excel spreadsheets as they are maintained in the regular course of business. Defendant is correct in asserting that Plaintiffs never expressly requested metadata and that the Court never expressly ordered Defendant to produce the electronic spreadsheets' metadata. However, taken in the context of Plaintiffs' stated reasons for requesting the Excel spreadsheets in their native electronic format and the Court's repeated statements that the spreadsheets should be produced in the electronic form in which they are maintained, the Court finds that Defendant should have reasonably understood that the Court expected and intended for Defendant to produce the spreadsheets' metadata along with the Excel spreadsheets. If Defendant did not understand the Court's ruling, it should have requested clarification of the Court's order. As the Sedona Working Group on Electronic Document Production observed: "Of course, if the producing party knows or should reasonably know that particular metadata is relevant to the dispute, it should be produced."[22] Here, the Court finds that Defendant should have reasonably known that the metadata was relevant to the dispute and therefore should have either been produced or an appropriate objection made or motion filed.

. . .

C. Locked Spreadsheet Cells and Data

The Court next addresses whether Defendant has shown cause for the locking of certain data and cells on the Excel spreadsheets produced to Plaintiffs. Defendant states that it locked the value of the cells in the spreadsheets to ensure the integrity of the data regarding RIFs, i.e., to ensure that the data could not be accidentally or intentionally altered. Defendant claims its purpose was not to preclude Plaintiffs from sorting or filtering the data, a task it claims Plaintiffs could easily accomplish by copying the data to another spreadsheet. Instead, Defendant claims it locked the data to preclude inadvertent or intentional modification of the data it produced. It argues that because electronic data is not ordinarily static, locking the data was essential to ensure that Defendant could demonstrate data subsequently used in the case was identical to data it produced electronically. It asserts that no malicious intent was associated with Defendant's efforts to preserve the integrity of the data it produced.

The Court finds that Defendant has failed to show sufficient cause for its unannounced and unilateral actions in locking certain data and cells on the Excel spreadsheets the Court ordered it to produce to Plaintiffs in the manner in which they were maintained. . . .

Defendant's concerns regarding maintaining the integrity of the spreadsheet's values and data could have been addressed by the less intrusive and more efficient use of "hash marks." For example, Defendant could have run the data through a mathematical process to generate a shorter symbolic reference to the original file, called

22. [Court's footnote #73] *The Sedona Principles*, Cmt. 12.

a "hash mark" or "hash value," that is unique to that particular file.[23] This "digital fingerprint" akin to a tamper-evident seal on a software package would have shown if the electronic spreadsheets were altered. When an electronic file is sent with a hash mark, others can read it, but the file cannot be altered without a change also occurring in the hash mark.[24] The producing party can be certain that the file was not altered by running the creator's hash mark algorithm to verify that the original hash mark is generated.[25] This method allows a large amount of data to be self-authenticating with a rather small hash mark, efficiently assuring that the original image has not been manipulated. . . .[26]

IT IS THEREFORE ORDERED that Defendant has failed to show cause why it should not produce the electronic spreadsheets in the manner in which they were maintained. Defendant therefore shall produce the electronic spreadsheets in the manner in which they were maintained, which includes the spreadsheets' metadata. Defendant may, however, redact its adverse impact analyses and any social security numbers from the spreadsheets prior to producing them to Plaintiffs. Defendant may also remove the metadata directly corresponding to the redacted information. . . .

Kentucky Speedway, LLC v. National Association of Stock Car Auto Racing, Inc.

United States District Court for the Eastern District of Kentucky
2006 U.S. Dist. LEXIS 92028 (Dec. 18, 2006)

J. Gregory Wehrman, United States Magistrate Judge.

On October 12, 2006, this court denied plaintiff's motion to compel defendant to produce certain highly confidential financial documents, but without prejudice to renew that motion upon full compliance with the order. Plaintiff Speedway subsequently renewed the motion orally. . . .

III. Plaintiff's Sealed Motion to Compel Certain Categories of Documents

Plaintiff Speedway seeks to compel four categories of documents which NASCAR and ISC [International Speedway] have refused to produce [including] 3) metadata concerning author and document creation information from ISC. . . .

---

23. [Court's footnote #74] Dean M. Harts, *Reel to Real: Should You Believe What You See? Keeping the Good and Eliminating the Bad of Computer-Generated Evidence Will Be Accomplished Through Methods of Self-Authentication and Vigilance*, 66 Def. Couns. J. 514, 522 (1999).

24. [Court's footnote #75] *Id.*

25. [Court's footnote #76] *Id.*

26. [Court's footnote #77] *Id.*

A. Pre-1997 Documents

Speedway alleges that defendants NASCAR and ISC have monopolized markets for premier stock car racing and premier stock car racetracks over a prolonged period of time.

. . .

C. Metadata

Metadata has been defined as "information about a particular data set which describes how, when, and by whom it was collected, created, accessed, or modified and how it was formatted." *Williams v. Sprint/United Management Co.*, 230 F.R.D. 640, 646 (D. Kan. 2005) (quoting Appendix F to *The Sedona Guidelines: Best Practice Guidelines and Commentary for Managing Information & Records in the Electronic Age)*. Relying chiefly on the *Williams* case, plaintiff seeks metadata for virtually all records maintained in electronic form which have been produced to date.

Rule 34 specifically includes the term "data compilations" as documents that must be produced, but does not define that term to necessarily include metadata. Rule 34 provides that where a request does not specify the form of production, information must be produced "either in a form or forms in which it is ordinarily maintained, or in a reasonably usable form or forms." [Rule 34(b)(2)(E)(ii), Fed. R. Civ. P.] The Advisory Committee Notes to the newly amended rule make clear that if the information is maintained in a way that makes it "searchable by electronic means," then "the information should not be produced in a form that removes or significantly degrades this feature." However, as one commentator has observed, "[n]either default form is intended to mandate production of metadata or embedded data." Allman, T., The Impact of the Proposed Federal E-Discovery Rules, 7 Sedona Conf. J. 31 (Fall 2006). *The Sedona Principles for Electronic Document Production* also suggests that a party should not be required to produce metadata absent a clear agreement or court order. Principle 12, *The Sedona Principles.*

In the rapidly evolving world of electronic discovery, the holding of the *Williams* case is not persuasive. Having the benefit of the newly amended rules, advisory notes, and commentary of scholars, I respectfully disagree with its conclusion that a producing party "should produce the electronic documents with their metadata intact, unless that party timely objects . . . , the parties agree that the metadata should not be produced, or the producing party requests a protective order." As noted in *Wyeth v. Impax laboratories*, Inc., 2006 WL 3091331 (D. Del. 2006), "'[e]merging standards of electronic discovery appear to articulate a general presumption against the production of metadata.'" Although plaintiff may protest that Delaware has adopted local standards which provide a "default standard" against the production of metadata, this court is convinced—at least on the facts of this case—that the production of metadata is not warranted.

The issue of whether metadata is relevant or should be produced is one which ordinarily should be addressed by the parties in a Rule 26(f) conference. Here, the parties clearly had no agreement that the electronic files would be produced in any particular format. Plaintiff did not notify defendant ISC that it sought metadata until seven months after ISC had produced both hard copy and electronic copies of its documents.

Plaintiff has not made any showing of a particularized need for the metadata.[27] Although plaintiff argues generally that it "needs document custodian information for the prosecution of its case" because "Kentucky Speedway has *no idea* of the origin of many of the documents" plaintiff does not identify any specific document or documents for which such information would be relevant and is not obtainable through other means. DE #139, at p. 4. In most cases and for most documents, metadata does not provide relevant information. Metadata may or may not provide the information plaintiff seeks concerning specific documents in this case. Depending on the format, the metadata may identify the typist but not the document's author, or even just a specific computer from which the document originated or was generated.

To the extent that plaintiff seeks metadata for a specific document or documents where date and authorship information is unknown but relevant, plaintiff should identify that document or documents by Bates Number or by other reasonably identifying features. Responding to a request for additional information concerning specific documents would be far less burdensome to defendant and far more likely to produce relevant information. Should the parties be unable to resolve any dispute concerning any limited requests by plaintiff for metadata on a specific document or documents, the parties may contact the court by telephone for assistance.

Notes and Questions

1. What recourse does a requesting party have if she believes that there is relevant metadata, when the producing party denies the metadata's existence? Should the court adopt a *Zubulake I* approach to such situations?

2. What is "particularized need"? Can it be a way to get at the desired metadata short of convincing the court to adopt a *Zubulake I* approach?

3. Why does the *Williams* case focus on viewability? What is the relationship between viewability and discoverability?

4. In practice, a data retention policy is important. Although metadata sometimes can be useful in the general course of business, the regular deletion or "scrubbing" of metadata can help eliminate some discovery issues. However, in anticipation of litigation, discoverable documents must be placed on a "hold" and not altered. To scrub

---

27. [Court's footnote #4] In its reply memorandum, Kentucky Speedway offers to stipulate that to the extent ISC identifies date, authorship, and custodial information, plaintiff will not seek metadata. To the extent that plaintiff seeks this information for every document thus far produced by ISC, the request is overbroad and unduly burdensome for the same reasons as indicated for the metadata request.

metadata at such a time could amount to spoliation, akin to shredding paper drafts of discoverable documents.

5. Treatment of metadata in the context of public records requests is a developing area. The Arizona Supreme Court delivered the first decisive ruling on the subject in 2009. "We today hold that if a public entity maintains a public record in an electronic format, then the electronic version, including any embedded metadata, is subject to disclosure under our public records laws." *Lake v. City of Phoenix*, 222 Ariz. 547, 548 (2009). The Washington Supreme Court and a New York appellate court soon came to the same conclusion. *See O'Neill v. City of Shoreline*, 170 Wash. 2d 138, 138 (2010) ("metadata associated with public records is subject to disclosure"); *Irwin v. Onondaga Cty. Res. Recovery Agency*, 72 A.D.3d 314, 322 (N.Y. App. 2010) ("metadata . . . constitutes a 'record' subject to disclosure").

C. Protective Orders

1. Introduction

Federal Rule 26(c) provides that "A party or any person from whom discovery is sought may move for a protective order in the court where the action is pending. . . . The court may, for good cause, issue an order to protect a party or person from annoyance, embarrassment, oppression, or undue burden or expense." The Rule goes on to specify the purposes for which courts may issue a protective order. The list, however, is not exhaustive. Rather, the rule is only limited by the requirement, as noted above, that it must "protect a party or person from annoyance, embarrassment, oppression, or undue burden or expense." Also, a proposed rule change to Rule 26(c) includes an express approval of protective orders specifying terms, including time and place or the allocation of expenses, for the disclosure or discovery.

Discovery allowed by the federal rules is extremely broad. This serves an important purpose. As the Supreme Court said in *Hickman v. Taylor*, 329 U.S. 495 (1947),

> The . . . rules . . . restrict the pleadings to the task of general notice-giving and invest the deposition-discovery process with a vital role in the preparation for trial. The various instruments of discovery now serve (1) as a device, along with the pre-trial hearing under Rule 16, to narrow and clarify the basic issues between the parties, and (2) as a device for ascertaining the facts, or information as to the existence or whereabouts of facts, relative to those issues. Thus civil trials in the federal courts no longer need be carried on in the dark. The way is now clear, consistent with recognized privileges, for the parties to obtain the fullest possible knowledge of the issues and facts before trial.

Id. at 501. This broad potential scope for discovery has its costs. Discovery can be expensive, imposing a substantial burden on parties. "The total judicial system may be better off because of the greater amount of information before the court, but it may have acquired these gains at additional net costs in work and money." WILLIAM A. GLASER, PRETRIAL DISCOVERY AND THE ADVERSARY SYSTEM 234 (1968). Without a limit on the broad discovery regime, a party could simply flood its adversaries with requests for documents, electronic files, and depositions, making the litigation too costly to continue. This danger is particularly acute in complex cases involving high stakes and multiple parties. Rule 26(c) gives courts the ability to regulate this behavior.

The potential for discovery to reveal sensitive information is also a significant concern. Without adequate protections for sensitive trade secrets, business information, or personal information, parties could either a) force their opponents to settle or abandon meritorious cases just to avoid revealing such information, or b) sue to gain this information through discovery. Rule 26(c) was adopted to mitigate these situations. "Because of liberal discovery and the potential for abuse, the federal rules confer broad discretion on the district court to decide when a protective order is appropriate, and what degree of protection is required." *Miscellaneous Docket Matter #1 v. Miscellaneous Docket Matter #2*, 197 F.3d 922 (8th Cir. 1999).

2. Protective Orders and the First Amendment

Rule 26(c) Protective Orders involve government restriction on public access to information. The First Amendment provides that "Congress shall make no law . . . abridging the freedom of speech." There is a strong presumption of public access to trials and to materials used in trials. Of course, discovery is a pre-trial procedure, and may require a party to produce information that ultimately will not be admissible at trial. Can a court issue a protective order essentially denying public access to discovery materials? Keep that question in mind as you read the following case.

Seattle Times Co. v. Rhinehart

Supreme Court of the United States
467 U.S. 20 (1984)

JUSTICE POWELL delivered the opinion of the Court.

This case presents the issue whether parties to civil litigation have a First Amendment right to disseminate, in advance of trial, information gained through the pretrial discovery process.

I

Respondent Rhinehart is the spiritual leader of a religious group, the Aquarian Foundation. The Foundation has fewer than 1,000 members, most of whom live in the State of Washington. Aquarian beliefs include life after death and the ability to communicate with the dead through a medium. Rhinehart is the primary Aquarian medium.

In recent years, the Seattle Times and the Walla Walla Union-Bulletin have published stories about Rhinehart and the Foundation. . . .

II

Rhinehart brought this action in the Washington Superior Court on behalf of himself and the Foundation against the Seattle Times, the Walla Walla Union-Bulletin, the authors of the articles, and the spouses of the authors. . . . The complaint alleges that the articles contained statements that were "fictional and untrue," and that the defendants—petitioners here—knew, or should have known, they were false. . . .

Petitioners filed an answer, denying many of the allegations of the complaint and asserting affirmative defenses. Petitioners promptly initiated extensive discovery. They deposed Rhinehart, requested production of documents pertaining to the financial affairs of Rhinehart and the Foundation, and served extensive interrogatories on Rhinehart and the other respondents. Respondents turned over a number of financial documents, including several of Rhinehart's income tax returns. Respondents refused, however, to disclose certain financial information, the identity of the Foundation's donors during the preceding 10 years, and a list of its members during that period.

Petitioners filed a motion under the State's Civil Rule 37 requesting an order compelling discovery. In their supporting memorandum, petitioners recognized that the principal issue as to discovery was respondents' "refusa[l] to permit any effective inquiry into their financial affairs, such as the source of their donations, their financial transactions, uses of their wealth and assets, and their financial condition in general." Respondents opposed the motion, arguing in particular that compelled production of the identities of the Foundation's donors and members would violate the First Amendment rights of members and donors to privacy, freedom of religion, and freedom of association. Respondents also moved for a protective order preventing petitioners from disseminating any information gained through discovery. Respondents noted that petitioners had stated their intention to continue publishing articles about respondents and this litigation, and their intent to use information gained through discovery in future articles.

In a lengthy ruling, the trial court initially granted the motion to compel and ordered respondents to identify all donors who made contributions during the five years preceding the date of the complaint, along with the amounts donated. The court also required respondents to divulge enough membership information to substantiate any claims of diminished membership.

Respondents filed a motion for reconsideration in which they renewed their motion for a protective order. They submitted affidavits of several Foundation members to support their request. The affidavits detailed a series of letters and telephone calls defaming the Foundation, its members, and Rhinehart—including several that threatened physical harm to those associated with the Foundation. The affiants also described incidents at the Foundation's headquarters involving attacks, threats, and assaults directed at Foundation members by anonymous individuals and groups. In general, the affidavits averred that public release of the donor lists would adversely affect Foundation membership and income and would subject its members to additional harassment and reprisals.

Persuaded by these affidavits, the trial court issued a protective order covering all information obtained through the discovery process that pertained to "the financial affairs of the various plaintiffs, the names and addresses of Aquarian Foundation members, contributors, or clients, and the names and addresses of those who have been contributors, clients, or donors to any of the various plaintiffs." The order prohibited petitioners from publishing, disseminating, or using the information in any way except where necessary to prepare for and try the case. By its terms, the order did not apply to information gained by means other than the discovery process. In an accompanying opinion, the trial court recognized that the protective order would restrict petitioners' right to publish information obtained by discovery, but the court reasoned that the restriction was necessary to avoid the "chilling effect" that dissemination would have on "a party's willingness to bring his case to court."

Respondents appealed from the trial court's production order, and petitioners appealed from the protective order. The Supreme Court of Washington affirmed both. . . .

III

Most States, including Washington, have adopted discovery provisions modeled on Rules 26 through 37 of the Federal Rules of Civil Procedure. F. James & G. Hazard, Civil Procedure 179 (1977). Rule 26(b)(1) provides that a party "may obtain discovery regarding any matter, not privileged, which is relevant to the subject matter involved in the pending action." It further provides that discovery is not limited to matters that will be admissible at trial so long as the information sought "appears reasonably calculated to lead to the discovery of admissible evidence." Wash. Super. Ct. Civil Rule 26(b)(1) [since amended to include proportionality requirement].

The Rules do not differentiate between information that is private or intimate and that to which no privacy interests attach. Under the Rules, the only express limitations are that the information sought is not privileged, and is relevant to the subject matter of the pending action. Thus, the Rules often allow extensive intrusion into the affairs of both litigants and third parties. If a litigant fails to comply with a request for discovery, the court may issue an order directing compliance that is enforceable by the court's contempt powers. Wash. Super. Ct. Civil Rule 37(b).

Petitioners argue that the First Amendment imposes strict limits on the availability of any judicial order that has the effect of restricting expression. They contend that civil discovery is not different from other sources of information, and that therefore the information is "protected speech" for First Amendment purposes. Petitioners assert the right in this case to disseminate any information gained through discovery. They do recognize that in limited circumstances, not thought to be present here, some information may be restrained. They submit, however:

> When a protective order seeks to limit expression, it may do so only if the proponent shows a compelling governmental interest. Mere speculation and conjecture are insufficient. Any restraining order, moreover, must be narrowly drawn and precise. Finally, before issuing such an order a court must determine that there are no alternatives which intrude less directly on expression.

Brief for Petitioners 10.

We think the rule urged by petitioners would impose an unwarranted restriction on the duty and discretion of a trial court to oversee the discovery process.

IV

It is, of course, clear that information obtained through civil discovery authorized by modern rules of civil procedure would rarely, if ever, fall within the classes of unprotected speech identified by decisions of this Court. In this case, as petitioners argue, there certainly is a public interest in knowing more about respondents. This interest may well include most—and possibly all—of what has been discovered as a result of the court's order under Rule 26(b)(1). It does not necessarily follow, however, that a litigant has an unrestrained right to disseminate information that has been obtained through pretrial discovery. For even though the broad sweep of the First Amendment seems to prohibit all restraints on free expression, this Court has observed that "[f]reedom of speech . . . does not comprehend the right to speak on any subject at any time." American Communications Assn. v. Douds, 339 U.S. 382, 394–395 (1950).

The critical question that this case presents is whether a litigant's freedom comprehends the right to disseminate information that he has obtained pursuant to a court order that both granted him access to that information and placed restraints on the way in which the information might be used. In addressing that question it is necessary to consider whether the "practice in question [furthers] an important or substantial governmental interest unrelated to the suppression of expression" and whether "the limitation of First Amendment freedoms [is] no greater than is necessary or essential to the protection of the particular governmental interest involved." Procunier v. Martinez, 416 U.S. 396, 413 (1974); see Brown v. Glines, 444 U.S. 348, 354–355 (1980); Buckley v. Valeo, 424 U.S. 1, 25 (1976).

A

At the outset, it is important to recognize the extent of the impairment of First Amendment rights that a protective order, such as the one at issue here, may cause. As in all civil litigation, petitioners gained the information they wish to disseminate only by virtue of the trial court's discovery processes. As the Rules authorizing discovery were adopted by the state legislature, the processes thereunder are a matter of legislative grace. A litigant has no First Amendment right of access to information made available only for purposes of trying his suit. Zemel v. Rusk, 381 U.S. 1, 16–17 (1965) ("The right to speak and publish does not carry with it the unrestrained right to gather information"). Thus, continued court control over the discovered information does not raise the same specter of government censorship that such control might suggest in other situations. See In re Halkin, 598 F.2d at 206–207 (Wilkey, J., dissenting).

Moreover, pretrial depositions and interrogatories are not public components of a civil trial.[28] Such proceedings were not open to the public at common law, Gannett Co. v. DePasquale, 443 U.S. 368, 389 (1979), and, in general, they are conducted in private as a matter of modern practice. See id., at 396 (BURGER, C.J., concurring); Marcus, *Myth and Reality in Protective Order Litigation*, 69 CORNELL L.REV. 1 (1983). Much of the information that surfaces during pretrial discovery may be unrelated, or only tangentially related, to the underlying cause of action. Therefore, restraints placed on discovered, but not yet admitted, information are not a restriction on a traditionally public source of information.

Finally, it is significant to note that an order prohibiting dissemination of discovered information before trial is not the kind of classic prior restraint that requires exacting First Amendment scrutiny. See Gannett Co. v. DePasquale, supra, at 399 (POWELL, J., concurring). As in this case, such a protective order prevents a party from disseminating only that information obtained through use of the discovery process. Thus, the party may disseminate the identical information covered by the protective order as long as the information is gained through means independent of the court's processes. In sum, judicial limitations on a party's ability to disseminate information discovered in advance of trial implicates the First Amendment rights of the restricted party to a far lesser extent than would restraints on dissemination of information in a different context. Therefore, our consideration of the provision for protective orders contained in the Washington Civil Rules takes into account the unique position that such orders occupy in relation to the First Amendment.

B

Rule 26(c) furthers a substantial governmental interest unrelated to the suppression of expression. Procunier, supra, at 413. . . . Liberal discovery is provided for the sole purpose of assisting in the preparation and trial, or the settlement, of litigated disputes. Because of the liberality of pretrial discovery permitted by Rule 26(b)(1), it is necessary for the trial court to have the authority to issue protective orders conferred by Rule 26(c). It is clear from experience that pretrial discovery by depositions and interrogatories has a significant potential for abuse. This abuse is not limited to

---

28. [Court's footnote #19] Discovery rarely takes place in public. Depositions are scheduled at times and places most convenient to those involved. Interrogatories are answered in private. Rules of Civil Procedure may require parties to file with the clerk of the court interrogatory answers, responses to requests for admissions, and deposition transcripts. See FED. RULE CIV. PROC. 5(D). Jurisdictions that require filing of discovery materials customarily provide that trial courts may order that the materials not be filed or that they be filed under seal. See *id.*; Wash. Super. Ct. Civil Rule 26(c). Federal district courts may adopt local rules providing that the fruits of discovery are not to be filed except on order of the court. *See, e.g.*, C.D. Cal. Rule 8.3; S.D.N.Y. Civ. Rule 19. Thus, to the extent that courthouse records could serve as a source of public information, access to that source customarily is subject to the control of the trial court.

matters of delay and expense; discovery also may seriously implicate privacy interests of litigants and third parties. The Rules do not distinguish between public and private information. Nor do they apply only to parties to the litigation, as relevant information in the hands of third parties may be subject to discovery.

There is an opportunity, therefore, for litigants to obtain—incidentally or purposefully—information that not only is irrelevant but if publicly released could be damaging to reputation and privacy. The government clearly has a substantial interest in preventing this sort of abuse of its processes. . . . The prevention of the abuse that can attend the coerced production of information under a State's discovery rule is sufficient justification for the authorization of protective orders.

C

We also find that the provision for protective orders in the Washington Rules requires, in itself, no heightened First Amendment scrutiny. To be sure, Rule 26(c) confers broad discretion on the trial court to decide when a protective order is appropriate and what degree of protection is required. The Legislature of the State of Washington, following the example of the Congress in its approval of the Federal Rules of Civil Procedure, has determined that such discretion is necessary, and we find no reason to disagree. The trial court is in the best position to weigh fairly the competing needs and interests of parties affected by discovery. The unique character of the discovery process requires that the trial court have substantial latitude to fashion protective orders.

V

The facts in this case illustrate the concerns that justifiably may prompt a court to issue a protective order. As we have noted, the trial court's order allowing discovery was extremely broad. It compelled respondents—among other things—to identify all persons who had made donations over a 5-year period to Rhinehart and the Aquarian Foundation, together with the amounts donated. In effect the order would compel disclosure of membership as well as sources of financial support. The Supreme Court of Washington found that dissemination of this information would "result in annoyance, embarrassment and even oppression." It is sufficient for purposes of our decision that the highest court in the State found no abuse of discretion in the trial court's decision to issue a protective order pursuant to a constitutional state law. We therefore hold that where, as in this case, a protective order is entered on a showing of good cause as required by Rule 26(c), is limited to the context of pretrial civil discovery, and does not restrict the dissemination of the information if gained from other sources, it does not offend the First Amendment.

The judgment accordingly is affirmed.

Notes and Questions

1. To what extent may courts consider the purposes of the First Amendment in deciding whether to issue a protective order? In *Cipollone Co. v. Liggett Group, Inc.*,

785 F.2d 1108 (3d Cir. 1986), the Third Circuit held that the district court had erred in applying a "least restrictive means test," as opposed to a "good cause" test. Consistent with its holding in *New York v. United States Metal Refining*, 771 F.2d 796 (3d Cir. 1985), the court held:

> In the first place, the Supreme Court's holding in *Seattle Times* was peremptory: "a protective order . . . entered on a showing of good cause as required by Rule 26(c) . . . does not offend the First Amendment." This statement leaves no room for lower courts to consider first amendment factors in fashioning or reviewing Rule 26(c) orders. The unequivocal nature of the Court's holding supersedes any ambiguity in its earlier discussion.
>
> Second, the rest of the Supreme Court's opinion, which emphasized that the discovery process was not a forum traditionally open to the public, and that the process was "a matter of legislative grace," to which no first amendment rights attached is consistent with the position that the first amendment is simply irrelevant to protective orders in civil discovery; it does not comport with the district court's insistence on a less restrictive means test in protective order determinations. . . .
>
> *Seattle Times* required the district court merely to inquire whether the defendants had demonstrated good cause for the protective order. . . .

Id. at 1119.

2. Is there a good rationale for considering the First Amendment basis for Rule 26(c) when deciding whether to allow public dissemination of discovery materials, but not when deciding whether to allow discovery of the materials in the first place?

3. It is clear that the First Amendment does not require materials to be made public simply because they are produced during discovery. Does this hold true when the materials are filed as exhibits during trial or in support of a dispositive motion? There is a strong presumption of access to materials used during trial, based on the common law right of access to court records, and the First Amendment right to attend trials and judicial proceedings. *See Wilson v. American Motors Corp.*, 759 F.2d 1568 (11th Cir. 1985). Most circuits have found that this right extends to materials filed in connection with dispositive motions. In *Rushford v. New Yorker Magazine*, 846 F.2d 249 (4th Cir. 1988), the court held "to limit . . . access to the documents submitted in connection with the summary judgment motion, there must be a showing, in the first instance by the district court, that the denial serves an important governmental interest and that there is no less restrictive way to serve that governmental interest." *Id.* at 253. *See also Va. Dept. of State Police v. Washington Post*, 386 F.3d 567, 573 (4th Cir. 2004); *Anderson v. Cryovac, Inc.*, 805 F.2d 1, 13 (1st Cir. 1986). There is disagreement, however, on whether the common law presumption applies to motions that do not go to the merits of a case. For example, *Brown & Williamson Tobacco Corp. v. FTC*, 710 F.2d 1165 (6th Cir. 1983), held that all documents filed for the court's consideration in a civil case were subject to presumptive access. On the other hand, *Anderson*, 805 F.2d at 13, held:

> [A] request to compel or protect the disclosure of information in the discovery process is not a request for the disposition of substantive rights. Materials submitted to the court for its consideration of a discovery motion are actually one step further removed in public concern from the trial process than the discovery materials themselves.

---

3. The Outer Boundaries: Protective Orders

Trial courts have wide discretion to enter protective orders. Moreover, just as courts have broad power to issue protective orders, they also have the power to change them, even after the action in which they are filed has been dismissed or resolved. *United Nuclear Corp. v. Cranford*, 905 F.2d 1424 (10th Cir. 1990). Motions to modify protective orders may be made either by the parties themselves, or by third parties. Modifications tend to be made in complex litigation for two reasons. First, protective orders in complex litigation frequently take the form of "umbrella" protective orders (*see infra*) which are entered in advance of discovery, and apply to all materials deemed confidential by the opposing party. Wright, Miller & Marcus, Federal Practice & Procedure § 2044.1 (3d ed. 2008). The broad scope of such orders arguably calls for correspondingly broad court discretion to modify them. *Id.* Secondly, complex litigation typically involves complex discovery efforts. Plaintiffs in one case may hope to avoid a portion of their discovery costs by gaining access to discovery already conducted in a different, similar case. A protective order in the different case, however, may block the access, *id.*, and thus require modification.

A modification request in this second scenario presents a court with a choice between competing values. On one hand, it is arguably inefficient from a systemic perspective to force a party to one case to commence from scratch discovery already conducted in a similar case. On the other hand, the protective order in the first case may have speeded discovery in that litigation by enabling parties to produce sensitive material without lengthy dispute, in confidence that the material would not be disseminated to third persons. If a court were to develop a reputation for modifying protective orders to allow new persons to review sensitive information produced in discovery, then the parties to any given litigation might be much less forthcoming in voluntarily producing documents at all. Courts have adopted two different views of the "free-rider" problem.

The Seventh Circuit has expressed sensitivity to the concern of efficiency. In *Wilk v. Am. Med. Ass'n*, 635 F.2d 1295 (7th Cir. 1980), the court allowed intervenors, who were plaintiffs in a similar suit against the same defendant, to use materials discovered by the plaintiffs in an antitrust action against the American Medical Association.

> Federal Rule of Civil Procedure 26(c) permits protective orders to be issued "for good cause shown" to protect litigants from burdensome or oppressive discovery. Yet, "(a)s a general proposition, pre-trial discovery must take

> place in the (*sic*) public unless compelling reasons exist for denying the public access to the proceedings." This presumption should operate with all the more force when litigants seek to use discovery in aid of collateral litigation on similar issues, for in addition to the abstract virtues of sunlight as a disinfectant, access in such cases materially eases the tasks of courts and litigants and speeds up what may otherwise be a lengthy process. Particularly in litigation of this magnitude, we . . . are impressed with the wastefulness of requiring the State of New York to duplicate discovery already made. Rule 1 of the Federal Rules requires the Rules to be construed "to secure the just, speedy, and inexpensive determination of every action." We therefore agree with the result reached by every other appellate court which has considered the issue, and hold that where an appropriate modification of a protective order can place private litigants in a position they would otherwise reach only after repetition of another's discovery, such modification can be denied only where it would tangibly prejudice substantial rights of the party opposing modification. *Olympic Refining Co. v. Carter*, 332 F.2d 260, 265–66 (9th Cir.), cert. denied, 379 U.S. 900, 85 S. Ct. 186, 13 L. Ed. 2d 175 (1964). Once such prejudice is demonstrated, however, the district court has broad discretion in judging whether that injury outweighs the benefits of any possible modification of the protective order.

Id. at 1299. The *Wilk* view remains the dominant one in the Seventh Circuit, and the majority of other circuits.

The Second Circuit, however, established a different approach one year earlier in *Martindell v. Int'l Tel. & Tel. Corp.*, 594 F.2d 291 (2d Cir. 1979). In *Martindell*, the government sought access to deposition transcripts taken in a stockholders derivative action against ITT. The government sought to use the transcripts in its investigations of ITT for perjury, obstruction of justice and conspiracy related to the company's actions in relation to the election in Chile. The Second Circuit strongly disagreed with the district court's decision to allow the government to intervene at all ("[t]he government may not, however, simply by picking up the telephone or writing a letter to the court (as was the case here) insinuate itself into a private civil lawsuit between others."). However, given that the government *had* intervened, and the decision had not been appealed the court was forced to decide whether modification of the protective order was appropriate. It stated:

> [A] vital function of a protective order issued under Rule 26(c) . . . is to "secure the just, speedy, and inexpensive determination" of civil disputes, Rule 1, by encouraging full disclosure of all evidence which might be relevant. This objective represents the cornerstone of our administration of civil justice. Unless a valid Rule 26(c) protective order is to be fully and fairly enforceable, witnesses relying upon such orders will be inhibited from giving essential testimony in civil litigation, thus undermining a procedural system that has been successfully developed over the years for disposition of civil differences. In short, witnesses might be expected frequently

> to refuse to testify pursuant to protective orders if their testimony were to be made available to the Government for criminal investigatory purposes in disregard of those orders.

Id. at 95–96. The court went on to hold that "absent a showing of improvidence in the grant of a protective order or some extraordinary circumstance, or compelling need . . . a witness should be entitled to rely upon the enforceability of the protective order in a case."

Notes and Questions

1. The *Wilk* court attempted to distinguish *Martindell.* "[*Martindell* is] distinguishable in that the party seeking access . . . was the federal government, which in each case had at its disposal special investigatory powers not available to private litigants." *Wilk*, 635 F.2d at 1299–1300. Based on the extracts above, do you find this distinction compelling?

2. So-called "Umbrella Orders" are especially prevalent in complex litigation because of the extent of documents at stake. Such orders apply from the outset to large numbers of documents, without the need for individual scrutiny. Such orders typically apply to "trade secrets, special formulas, company security matters, customer lists, financial data, projected sales data, production data, [and] matters relating to mergers and acquisitions, and data which touch upon the topic of price." Manual § 40.27. This is why "[c]ourts may choose to utilize an 'umbrella approach' when a large number of confidential documents are at issue." *Uniroyal Chemical Co., Inc. v. Syngenta Crop Protection*, 224 F.R.D. 53 (D. Conn. 2004). Notice, though, that:

> First, a party must make some threshold showing of good cause to believe that discovery will involve confidential or protected information . . . . After receiving documents, the opposing party has the right to contest those documents which it believes not to be confidential. At this stage, the party seeking the protection shoulders the burden of proof in justifying retaining the confidentiality designation.

Gillard v. Boulder Valley School District Re-2, 196 F.R.D. 382, 386 (D. Col. 2000). In *Makar-Wellborn v. Sony Electronics, Inc.*, 187 F.R.D. 576, 577 (E.D. Wis. 1999), the court held that the parties had failed to make a good cause showing for a protective order. "Their stipulation merely states that they seek to protect information 'pertaining to personnel files or confidential personnel-related documents' . . . the parties proposed order could cover a lion's share of the material produced. . . ." *Id.* But such orders are routinely granted when they contribute to efficiency. *See Bayer AG & Miles, Inc. v. Barr Labs., Inc.*, 162 F.R.D. 456 (S.D.N.Y. 1995).

The Manual describes the advantages and disadvantages of such orders:

> When the volume of potentially protected materials is larger, an umbrella order will expedite production, reduce costs, and avoid the burden on the court of document by document adjudication. Umbrella orders provide that

> all assertedly confidential material disclosed (and appropriately identified, usually by stamp) is presumptively protected unless challenged. The orders are made without a particularized showing to support the claim for protection, but such a showing must be made whenever a claim under an order is challenged. Some courts have therefore found that umbrella orders simply postpone, rather than eliminate, the need for the court to closely scrutinize discovery material to determine whether protection is justified, thereby delaying rather than expediting the litigation.[29]

MANUAL § 11.432.

3. Note that "blanket orders are inherently subject to challenge and modification, as the party resisting disclosure generally has not made a particularized showing of good cause with respect to any individual document." *San Jose Mercury News, Inc. v. U.S. District Court*, 187 F.3d 1096, 1103 (9th Cir. 1999).

D. Attorney-Client Privilege, Joint Defense Privilege, and the Work Product Doctrine

An attorney's advice is most valuable when it is given in light of full and candid disclosure. Clients will be unwilling to be open with their attorneys if those conversations could later be used against them in court. To avoid this chilling effect, courts have interpreted broadly this privilege to protect communications between clients and their lawyers.

The attorney-client privilege is classically defined as "(1) Where legal advice of any kind is sought (2) from a professional legal adviser in their capacity as such, (3) the communications related to that purpose (4) made in confidence (5) by the client, (6) are at [the client's] instance permanently protected (7) from disclosure by [the client] or by the legal adviser, (8) except the protection can be waived." 8 WIGMORE ON EVIDENCE § 2292 (4th ed. 1995).

The Supreme Court has defined a client, for purposes of federal privilege law, to include all corporate employees whom a lawyer interviews for the purpose of the

29. *See John Does I-VI v. Yogi*, 110 F.R.D. 629, 632 (D.D.C. 1986). The problems of preserving protection for documents produced under umbrella orders are aggravated by the understandable tendency of counsel to err on the side of caution by designating any possibly sensitive documents as confidential under the order. The time saved by excessive designations, however, may be more than offset by the difficulties of later opposing some request for access or disclosure. Although the judge, in the interest of reducing the time and expense of the discovery process, should be somewhat tolerant of this practice, counsel should not mark documents as protected under the order without a good-faith belief that they are entitled to protection. Counsel should also be cautioned against objecting to document requests without first ascertaining that the requested documents exist. The designation of a document as confidential should be viewed as equivalent to a motion for a protective order and subject to the sanctions of Federal Rule of Civil Procedure 37(a)(4), as provided by Rule 26(c).

lawyer giving the company legal advice. This extends to any employee who is acting within their ordinary corporate duties, regardless of their status as an entry level employee, a manager, or anywhere in between. *Upjohn Co. v. United States*, 449 U.S. 383, 390 (1981).

Federal Rule of Evidence 501, however, makes clear that "state law governs privilege regarding a claim or defense for which state law supplies the rule of decision." Some states still define an entity client in terms of the "control group" of senior managers, typically those corporate officers who are authorized to act on behalf of the company.

In complex cases with multiple parties on each side of the litigation, a critical question often arises as to the scope of privilege among each party. Attorney-client privilege usually doesn't apply when "strangers" are present during a communication between a lawyer and a client. So, what happens when the parties and their lawyers on the same general side of a complex dispute (the plaintiffs generally or the defendants generally) want to share strategy communications among each other? Does a discussion among parties ostensibly on the same side of the litigation waive any claims of attorney-client privilege to those matters discussed? A doctrine of Joint Defense Privilege or The Joint Interest Doctrine has emerged in response to these kinds of questions.

Consider the following observation from the Fourth Circuit:

> The concept of a joint defense privilege first arose in the context of criminal co-defendants whose attorneys shared information in the course of devising a joint strategy for their clients' defense. An exception to the general rule that disclosure to a third party of privileged information thereby waives the privilege, a joint defense privilege cannot be waived without the consent of all parties who share the privilege.... Because "[t]he need to protect the free flow of information from client to attorney logically exists whenever multiple clients share a common interest about a legal matter," courts have extended the joint defense privilege to civil co-defendants; companies that had been individually summoned before a grand jury who shared information before any indictment was returned; potential co-parties to prospective litigation; plaintiffs who were pursuing separate actions in different states; and civil defendants who were sued in separate actions.

In re Grand Jury Subpoenas 89-3 and 89-4, John Doe 89-129, 902 F.2d 244, 248–49 (4th Cir. 1990).

But what is the scope of this protection? What if while both parties are defendants, there are matters on which their interests diverge? Must the communication be in anticipation of litigation, or can it be simply a general strategy communication to discuss potential liability? Consider these questions while you read the following case:

United States ex rel. Burroughs v. Denardi

United States District Court for the Southern District of California
167 F.R.D. 680 (1996)

PAPAS, UNITED STATES MAGISTRATE JUDGE.

On November 14, 1995, defendant DeNardi Corp., DeNardi Equip. Co., Inc., Harold DeNardi, Robert Wood, Jr. and Rodney Furuya (hereafter defendants or "DeNardi") moved this court to compel plaintiff George Burroughs (hereafter plaintiff or "Burroughs") to produce certain documents which Burroughs claimed were privileged.

I. OVERVIEW

This case arises under the False Claims Act, 31 U.S.C. § 3729 et seq. Burroughs alleges that defendants engaged in fraud against the U.S. Government by making inflated claims for payment on various government contracts.

On August 8, 1995, DeNardi served on plaintiff its First Request for Production of Documents. Plaintiff responded by producing a privilege log, dated September 14, 1995. The privilege log contained entries for the documents that are the subject of this motion:

(1) Letter from P. Stillman to U.S. Attorney Alan Bersin, dated February 10, 1994. Plaintiff later disclosed to defendants that the February 10, 1994 letter from P. Stillman to Alan Bersin was the formal "Disclosure Statement" required by 31 U.S.C. § 3730(b)(2).[30]

(2) Letter from P. Stillman to NCIS Gabrielle Corruth, dated June 13, 1994;

(3) Letter from P. Stillman to AUSA Jack Robinson, dated April 5, 1994; (4) Letter from P. Stillman to DOD Attorney Richard Vartain, dated April 7, 1994; (5) Letter from Y. Hanchett to AUSA Jack Robinson, dated June 13, 1994.

Plaintiff claims that these documents are protected from disclosure by the attorney-client privilege, work-product doctrine, joint-prosecution privilege and the law enforcement evidentiary/investigatory files privilege. Defendant disagrees and seeks an order compelling plaintiff to produce the documents.

II. ATTORNEY-CLIENT PRIVILEGE

Plaintiff argues that the documents are protected from disclosure by the attorney-client privilege. He asserts that the documents are a compilation of communications from himself to his attorneys for the purpose of obtaining legal advice. He also asserts that while he expected that factual information referred to in the documents might be discoverable the actual documents themselves are protected from discovery.

30. [Court's footnote #1] Pursuant to 31 U.S.C. § 3730(b)(2), plaintiff must submit to the Department of Justice, in connection with filing a false claims action, a statement which constitutes a "written disclosure of substantially all material evidence and information" the plaintiff has in his possession.

Defendants argue that the documents are not protected by the attorney-client privilege. They cite *U.S. ex rel. Stone v. Rockwell*, 144 F.R.D. 396, 398–400 (D. Colo. 1992); *U.S. ex rel. Robinson v. Northrop Corp.*, 824 F. Supp. 830, 838–9 (N.D. Ill.1993); and *U.S. ex rel. Grand v. Northrop*, 811 F. Supp. 333, 337 (S.D. Ohio 1992) to support their position. In *Stone*, the court held that the Disclosure Statement in that case did not enjoy the protection of the attorney-client privilege. The *Stone* court reasoned that the document was a recitation of facts and allegations communicated by the plaintiff to the government for the purposes of complying with the statutory conditions precedent to bringing suit against the defendants. It also noted that the communications by plaintiff were not made for the purpose of seeking legal advice, nor were they intended to be confidential. *Robinson, supra* and *Grand, supra* are generally in accord with the *Stone* court's analysis.

Pursuant to Fed. R. Evid. 501, federal law governs the availability and scope of the attorney-client privilege in non-diversity actions. Under federal law the attorney-client privilege applies:

(1) where legal advice of any kind is sought,

(2) from a professional legal adviser in his capacity as such,

(3) the communications relating to that purpose,

(4) made in confidence,

(5) by the client,

(6) are at that instance permanently protected,

(7) from disclosure by himself or by the legal adviser,

(8) unless the protection is waived.

In this case, the communications by plaintiff to Attorney Stillman were designed to give Attorney Stillman the percipient facts and evidence within plaintiff's knowledge so Attorney Stillman could comply with 31 U.S.C. § 3730(b)(2) on plaintiff's behalf. The communications contained in the documents were not made for the purpose of seeking legal advice. Percipient facts cannot achieve the protected status under the attorney-client privilege by merely repeating them to an attorney. *Matter of Grand Jury Subpoenas*, 959 F.2d 1158, 1166 (2d Cir. 1992); *In re Grand Jury Proceedings*, 896 F.2d 1267, 1270 (11th Cir. 1990). Moreover, the communications were not made in confidence. They were the facts underlying the events, told to Attorney Stillman by plaintiff to permit Attorney Stillman to assemble the information in a way to apprise the government of all the material evidence and information plaintiff had in his possession at the time. As a result, plaintiff has failed to show that the documents are protected by the attorney-client privilege.

III. WORK-PRODUCT IMMUNITY

Defendants argue that the documents are not entitled to protection from discovery by the work-product doctrine. Their argument is twofold. First, the documents should not contain plaintiff's counsel's opinions. Second, because they have been disclosed to the government, the documents lose their work product protection. In support of their position, defendants cite *Robinson*, 824 F. Supp. at 830. In *Robinson*, the court held the Disclosure Statement in that case did not enjoy protection from discovery by virtue of the work-product immunity.

Plaintiff, on the other hand, asserts that the documents sought, and in particular the Disclosure Statement, are the product of numerous meetings between plaintiff and his attorneys. After the meetings, plaintiff's attorneys selected, from all of the information imparted by plaintiff, those facts and documents that they deemed "material" to proving violations of the False Claims Act, 31 U.S.C. § 3729, et seq. This process, it is argued, necessarily required plaintiff's attorneys to organize the facts and evidence presented to them into a written disclosure to the government in order to indicate how defendants committed fraud on the U.S. government. Plaintiff therefore contends that the process of selection and organization of facts and evidence, and writing the statement for the government's review, required his attorneys to assess the weight and organization of the evidence to prove his claims. Consequently, plaintiff asserts that the documents at issue contain plaintiff's counsel's mental impressions, theories and opinions regarding plaintiff's claims and are, therefore, protected from disclosure by the work-product immunity. . . .

While trial preparation materials may be discoverable upon an appropriate showing, the materials containing mental impressions, conclusions, opinions, and legal theories of an attorney are discoverable only in rare and extraordinary circumstances. *Connolly Data Systems v. Victor Technologies*, 114 F.R.D. 89 (S.D. Cal. 1987). *See In re Doe*, 662 F.2d 1073 (4th Cir. 1981) (holding discovery of opinion-work product only in extraordinary circumstances); *In re Murphy*, 560 F.2d 326, 336 (8th Cir. 1977) ("Opinion-work product enjoys a nearly absolute immunity and can be discovered only in rare and extraordinary circumstances"); *Handgards, Inc. v. Johnson & Johnson*, 413 F. Supp. 926 (N.D. Cal. 1976).

The Supreme Court in *Hickman v. Taylor*, 329 U.S. 495 (1947), noted the importance of protecting the thought processes of attorneys:

> Historically, a lawyer is an officer of the court and is bound to work for the advancement of justice while faithfully protecting the rightful interests of his clients. In performing his various duties . . . it is essential that a lawyer work with a certain degree of privacy, free from unnecessary intrusion by opposing parties and their counsel. Proper preparation of client's case demands that he assemble information, sift what he considers to be relevant from the irrelevant facts, prepare his legal theories and plan his strategy without undue and needless interference. That is the historical and necessary way in which lawyers act within the framework of our system of jurisprudence to promote justice and to protect their client's interests.

Plaintiff asserts that the documents sought by defendants reveal the facts and evidence his attorneys felt were important to prove his claims. Moreover, he contends that the organization and characterization of the facts and evidence presented reveal the attorneys' assessment of the strength of such facts and evidence. Without more, it would be difficult for the court to see how the documents could be characterized as anything other than "opinion-work product," specifically protected from disclosure to opposing counsel, because the disclosure would potentially reveal plaintiff's counsel's mental impressions, opinions and theories about the case.

Rule 26(b)(3) also makes clear that materials prepared in anticipation of litigation, or in preparation for trial, may be discoverable upon a proper showing. Therefore, if the documents do not qualify as "opinion-work product" as discussed above, they may still be discoverable if defendants show that they (a) have substantial need for the documents; and (b) they are unable without undue hardship to obtain the substantial equivalent of the documents by other means.

In this instance, defendants have not and cannot establish both substantial need for the documents and undue hardship in obtaining by other means the substantial equivalent of the documents . . . [P]laintiff's counsel has provided defendants with access to all the information they themselves used to prepare plaintiff's communications to the government. Shortly after the plaintiff's deposition began, plaintiff's counsel provided defendants with a 97 page memorandum written by plaintiff which exhaustively discusses all of his claims. The memorandum contains the names of witnesses and lists the relevant documents for each claim. This memorandum appears to be a comprehensive recitation of the facts that support each of plaintiff's claims along with a cross-reference to relevant documents to support plaintiff's theories of liability. Moreover, the court has been made aware that, while the 97 page memorandum may not be the original memorandum prepared by plaintiff, plaintiff's counsel has endeavored, or is endeavoring, to provide defendants with a computer disk containing the original memorandum written by plaintiff.

The documents sought by defendants have not been provided to the court for review. Since the court has not reviewed the documents in question it is difficult, if not impossible, to ascertain whether the organization and characterization of the facts and evidence presented would indeed reveal plaintiff's counsel's assessment of the strength of such facts and evidence (which would, in turn, reveal plaintiff's counsel's mental impressions, opinions and theories about the case). Therefore, plaintiff is directed to provide the court with copies of all the documents in question, on or before February 28, 1996, so that the court can perform an in camera review of the documents.

IV. WAIVER OF WORK-PRODUCT IMMUNITY

If the court's review of the documents in question indeed reveals that the documents are protected from discovery by the work-product immunity, then the court must decide whether plaintiff waived the work-product protection by disclosing the information contained in the documents to the government, a third party that has not intervened in the action.

One of the primary functions of the work-product doctrine is to prevent a current or potential adversary in litigation from gaining access to the fruits of counsel's investigative and analytical effort, and strategies for developing and presenting the client's case. Therefore, analysis of issues of waiver of the work-product protection must focus on whether the disclosures in issue increased the likelihood that a current or potential opponent in the litigation would gain access to the documents in question. *Bank of the West v. Valley National Bank*, 132 F.R.D. 250, 262 (N.D. Cal. 1990); *In re Subpoenas Duces Tecum*, 738 F.2d 1367, 1374–1375 (D.C. Cir. 1984).

Plaintiff argues that any work product protection afforded the documents in question was not waived by disclosure of the information to the government. Plaintiff asserts that he and the government share common interests against the defendants. Consequently, plaintiff asserts that he and the government share a joint prosecution privilege which protects the documents from disclosure to the defendants. Defendants, on the other hand, argue that the joint prosecution privilege does not apply when, as here, the government chooses not to intervene in the case, nor is a party to the litigation. Defendants further assert that the government's rights and interests are limited after it makes the decision not to intervene in the case. Therefore, it cannot be seen to share with plaintiff the requisite common interests that give rise to a joint prosecution privilege.

The court's inquiry therefore focuses on the joint prosecution privilege and its application to whether plaintiff can claim such a privilege when he discloses information to the government, pursuant to requirements of the False Claims Act. The privilege, originally called the "joint defense privilege," protects communications between an individual and an attorney for another when the communications are part of an on-going and joint effort to set up a common defense strategy. To establish the existence of a joint defense privilege, the party asserting the privilege must show that (1) the communications were made in the course of a joint defense effort, (2) the statements were designed to further the joint defense effort, and (3) the privilege has not been waived. *United States v. Bay State Ambulance & Hosp. Rental Serv.*, 874 F.2d 20, 28 (1st Cir. 1989) citing *In re Bevill, Bresler & Schulman Asset Management Corp.*, 805 F.2d 120, 126 (3d Cir. 1986); see also *Waller v. Financial Corp. of America*, 828 F.2d 579 (9th Cir. 1987). Courts have held that while the joint defense privilege is an extension of the attorney-client privilege, it also applies to the work-product doctrine. *Western Fuels Assn. v. Burlington Northern R.R.*, 102 F.R.D. 201, 203 (D. Wyo. 1984); *Haines v. Liggett Group*, 975 F.2d 81 (3d Cir. 1992). Courts have also held that the privilege does not solely apply to cooperating defendants. It also applies to cooperating plaintiffs. *Sedlacek v. Morgan Whitney Trading Group*, 795 F. Supp. 329, 331 (C.D. Cal. 1992); *Loustalet v. Refco*, 154 F.R.D. 243, 247 (C.D. Cal. 1992); *In re Grand Jury Subpoenas*, 902 F.2d 244 (4th Cir. 1990). Further, the privilege is not limited to co-parties. *Loustalet, supra*, at 247, *In re Grand Jury Subpoenas, supra*, at 249. Therefore, whether the jointly interested persons are defendants or plaintiffs, and whether the litigation or potential litigation is civil or criminal, the rationale for the privilege is clear: Persons who share a common interest in litigation should be able to communicate confidentially with their respective attorneys, and with each other, to more effectively prosecute or defend their claims. *In re Grand Jury Subpoenas, supra*, at 249.

In light of the foregoing, this court must examine the extent of the common interests between plaintiff and the government to decide whether plaintiff's disclosure of his attorney's work product is consistent with the nature of the work product doctrine.

In this action, the False Claims Act, 31 U.S.C. § 3729 et seq., itself provides ample support that plaintiff and the government share sufficient common interests, as against the defendants. 31 U.S.C. § 3730(b)(1) provides that (a) person may bring a civil action for violation of section 3729 for the person and for the United States Government. The action shall be brought in the name of the Government. . . . This section makes clear that plaintiff and the government essentially stand in the same shoes as against the defendants. . . . For all practical purposes, plaintiff and the government are essentially the same party. All of plaintiff's claims, litigation strategies, and ultimate goals, are all asserted on behalf of the government. Consequently, the court concludes that plaintiff and the government have sufficient commonality of interests such that they can successfully assert the joint prosecution privilege. As a result, plaintiff's disclosure of the documents to the government did not result in a waiver of the work-product immunity, if that protection applies.

Notes and Questions

1. Suppose there have been communications between co-defendants, one of whom has now pleaded guilty. Is there a joint defense privilege for new communications? Is there a joint defense privilege for previous communications? Would it matter to the analysis whether each defendant knew that the co-defendant was pleading guilty?

2. Suppose there have been communications among co-defendants, and the communications devolve into a discussion limited to how only one of those parties might avoid liability in the lawsuit. Would a joint defense privilege apply to those communications?

3. What is the true scope of the joint defense privilege? You should be certain to stipulate with other attorneys what your understanding of the privilege is with regard to any discussion between parties. Short of a signed agreement between the parties, a note for your own files is better than nothing.

4. Counsel should be mindful of individual and corporate representation. When an employee of a corporation has interests that might be at odds with the defense of the corporation, the extent of privilege can be difficult to ascertain. *See In re Bevill, Bresler & Schulman Mgmt. Corp.*, 805 F.2d 120 (3d Cir. 1986). The timing or currency of this litigation also is relevant to the privilege.

5. When parties that had been on the same side of litigation later enter into litigation against one another, what happens to previously privileged materials? *See In re Grand Jury Subpoena*, 274 F.3d 563 (1st Cir. 2001) (holding that the privilege does

not apply in subsequent civil litigation between former joint clients because in such a situation, one client's interest in the privilege is counterbalanced by the other's interest in being able to waive it).

Note on Experts and Privilege

Changes to Federal Rule of Civil Procedure 26 have had a significant impact upon discovery of expert witnesses. An amendment extended attorney-client privilege and work-product protection to reports and communications with expert witnesses.

Experts are people with specialized training or knowledge who often bring that expertise to bear in litigation. Experts are used in two ways in litigation. First is the "consulting expert," who is hired to assist the lawyer in preparing and monitoring a case. For example, in a medical malpractice case, both sides might find it helpful to have a medical expert behind the scenes with whom to consult as the case unfolds. Second is the "expert witness," who will testify at trial on behalf of the party. Experts witnesses, unlike lay witnesses, are entitled to testify as to their opinions. Expert witnesses are hired to give their professional opinions.

> Discovery concerning expert witnesses is handled by required disclosure under Rule 26(a)(2).... [E]xpert witnesses ... retained specially for this case must provide a detailed report. [In addition,] Rule 26(b)(4) does four things.
>
> First, Rule 26(b)(4)(A) gives parties a right to take the deposition of any expert witness identified through Rule 26(a)(2) (assuming she has produced the written report (if required)).
>
> 
>
> Second, Rule 26(b)(4)(E) provides that the party seeking discovery of an expert witness (most commonly, taking her deposition) generally must pay a reasonable fee to the expert for her time spent responding to the discovery request.
>
> Third, Rule 26(b)(4)(D) addresses experts "retained or specially employed ... in anticipation of litigation or to prepare for trial" but who are not expected to testify at trial—in other words, the consulting expert. The Rule states a longstanding general rule that there will be no discovery of "facts known or opinions held" by such a person. This makes great sense. Because this expert is not going to testify, and therefore cannot influence the jury, it is not clear why the other party should be concerned with her opinions....
>
> Fourth, and most importantly, Rule 26(b)(4)(B) and (C) extend work product protection to two things: (1) drafts of reports and disclosures under Rule 26(a)(2) and (2) communication between a party's lawyer and

> an expert witness who was required to produce a written report under Rule 26(a)(2)(B).
>
> Before Rule 26(b)(4)(B) and (C) extended work product protection, drafts of an expert witness's Rule 26(a)(2) report and communications between her and the party's lawyer generally were discoverable. So the lawyer would be less likely to share facts with the expert witness that might be risky to the party's position. That is where consulting experts came in. Because generally there is no discovery of facts known or opinions held by consulting experts, a lawyer would hire such a person and could talk freely. The lawyer could relate hypotheticals to the consultant and ask for opinions, even on risky scenarios, without fear of discovery. Then, having mapped out the exact contours of her position, the lawyer would retain a separate expert—the expert witness—who would testify at trial. And the lawyer would relate to the expert witness only a narrow, non-risky, set of facts.
>
> Now, things are different. Because Rule 26(b)(4)(B) and (C) extend work product protection to drafts by expert witnesses and to communications between such witnesses and the party's lawyer, there is no need to hire a separate consulting expert. The lawyer can run through all scenarios with the expert, knowing that their communications and the drafts of the expert's report are protected.

Richard D. Freer, Civil Procedure 455–56 (4th ed. 2017).

The goal of the rule change is to reduce the costs of discovery. The prior version of Rule 26 required disclosure of all information relied upon by retained expert witnesses who will testify at trial. Such information included communications with the experts by the lawyers retaining them. This Rule led to the common practice for attorneys to retain two experts; one to testify at trial based on non-privileged information, and one for consultation on matters including privileged matters which might be risky if disclosed. By protecting communications between expert witnesses and the lawyers who have retained them, even if the experts will be testifying in the litigation, the new rule effectively halves expert retention costs.

The amended rule still allows matter of course discovery of such information as expert compensation, identification of the facts or data provided for the basis of the expert's opinion, and assumptions made by the expert. Critics argue that the new rule limits opposing parties' chances of exploring an expert's partisan relationship with an attorney.

The rules advisory committee noted that many lawyers already stipulate out of discovery of communications between experts and the retaining lawyers. Thus, codifying the practice in the rules balances effective trial preparation and cost-savings.

For a case considering the difficulties of balancing the work product doctrine and the discovery of the basis of experts' opinions, see *Bogosian v. Gulf Oil Corp.*, 738 F.2d 587 (3d Cir. 1984) (holding that "the marginal value in the revelation on cross-examination that the expert's view may have originated with an attorney's opinion or theory does not warrant overriding the strong policy against disclosure of documents consisting of core attorney's work product.").

E. Discovery Sanctions

Unlike a civil law jurisdiction and more than almost any other aspect of our procedural system, discovery is left to the litigants. It requires some measure of cooperation, especially among the professionals involved. By their very nature, however, litigants are adversaries, and adversaries may be tempted to take advantage in unfair ways of each other. Not surprisingly, it is still true that "[a]buse of the judicial process occurs most often in connection with discovery." Charles B. Renfrew, *Discovery Sanctions: A Judicial Perspective*, 67 Cal. L. Rev. 264, 264 (1979). Indeed, cries of discovery abuse are a common refrain, especially in complex litigation, where the stakes are high and the issues difficult. Sanctions are one way of addressing these problems.

Discovery sanctions are imposed for procedural violations. Nevertheless the sanctions may have substantive consequences. As you read the materials that follow, consider the foundational premise of our procedural system: that disputes should be resolved on the merits. Are sanctions a necessary compromise?

National Hockey League v. Metropolitan Hockey Club

Supreme Court of the United States
427 U.S. 639 (1976)

PER CURIAM.

This case arises out of the dismissal, under Fed. R. Civ. Proc. 37, of respondents' antitrust action against petitioners for failure to timely answer written interrogatories as ordered by the District Court. The Court of Appeals for the Third Circuit reversed the judgment of dismissal, finding that the District Court had abused its discretion. The question presented is whether the Court of Appeals was correct in so concluding. Rule 37 provides in pertinent part as follows:

> If a party ... fails to obey an order to provide or permit discovery ... the court in which the action is pending may make such orders in regard to the failure as are just, and among others the following:
>
> (C) An order striking out pleadings or parts thereof, or staying further proceedings until the order is obeyed, or dismissing the action or proceeding or any part thereof, or rendering a judgment by default against the disobedient party.

This Court held in *Societe Internationale v. Rogers*, 357 U.S. 197, 212 (1958), that Rule 37 "should not be construed to authorize dismissal of (a) complaint because of petitioner's noncompliance with a pretrial production order when it has been established that failure to comply has been due to inability, and not to willfulness, bad faith, or any fault of petitioner."

While there have been amendments to the Rule since the decision in *Rogers*, neither the parties, the District Court, nor the Court of Appeals suggested that the changes would affect the teachings of the quoted language from that decision.

The District Court, in its memorandum opinion directing that respondents' complaint be dismissed, summarized the factual history of the discovery proceeding in these words:

> After seventeen months where crucial interrogatories remained substantially unanswered despite numerous extensions granted at the eleventh hour and, in many instances, beyond the eleventh hour, and notwithstanding several admonitions by the Court and promises and commitments by the plaintiffs, the Court must and does conclude that the conduct of the plaintiffs demonstrates the callous disregard of responsibilities counsel owe to the Court and to their opponents. The practices of the plaintiffs exemplify flagrant bad faith when after being expressly directed to perform an act by a date certain, Viz., June 14, 1974, they failed to perform and compounded that noncompliance by waiting until five days afterwards before they filed any motions. Moreover, this action was taken in the face of warnings that their failure to provide certain information could result in the imposition of sanctions under Fed. R. Civ. P. 37. If the sanction of dismissal is not warranted by the circumstances of this case, then the Court can envisage no set of facts whereby that sanction should ever be applied.

63 F.R.D. 641, 656 (1974).

The Court of Appeals, in reversing the order of the District Court by a divided vote stated:

> After carefully reviewing the record, we conclude that there is insufficient evidence to support a finding that M-GB's failure to file supplemental answers by June 14, 1974 was in flagrant bad faith, willful or intentional. 531 F.2d 1188, 1195 (1976).

The Court of Appeals did not question any of the findings of historical fact which had been made by the District Court, but simply concluded that there was in the record evidence of "extenuating factors." The Court of Appeals emphasized that none of the parties had really pressed discovery until after a consent decree was entered between petitioners and all of the other original plaintiffs except the respondents approximately one year after the commencement of the litigation. It also noted that respondents' counsel took over the litigation, which previously had been managed by another attorney, after the entry of the consent decree, and that respondents' counsel encountered difficulties in obtaining some of the requested information. The Court of Appeals also referred to a colloquy during the oral argument on petitioners' motion to dismiss in which respondents' lead counsel assured the District Court that he would not knowingly and willfully disregard the final deadline.

While the Court of Appeals stated that the District Court was required to consider the full record in determining whether to dismiss for failure to comply with discovery orders, see *Link v. Wabash R. Co.,* 370 U.S. 626, 633–634 (1962), we think that the comprehensive memorandum of the District Court supporting its order of dismissal indicates that the court did just that. That record shows that the District Court was extremely patient in its efforts to allow the respondents ample time to comply with its discovery orders. Not only did respondents fail to file their responses on time, but the responses which they ultimately did file were found by the District Court to be grossly inadequate.

The question, of course, is not whether this Court, or whether the Court of Appeals, would as an original matter have dismissed the action; it is whether the District Court abused its discretion in so doing. *E.g.,* C. Wright & A. Miller, Federal Practice and Procedure: Civil § 2284, p. 765 (1970); *General Dynamics Corp. v. Selb Mfg. Co.,* 481 F.2d 1204, 1211 (CA81973); *Baker v. F & F Investment,* 470 F.2d 778, 781 (CA2 1972). Certainly the findings contained in the memorandum opinion of the District Court quoted earlier in this opinion are fully supported by the record. We think that the lenity evidenced in the opinion of the Court of Appeals, while certainly a significant factor in considering the imposition of sanctions under Rule 37, cannot be allowed to wholly supplant other and equally necessary considerations embodied in that Rule.

There is a natural tendency on the part of reviewing courts, properly employing the benefit of hindsight, to be heavily influenced by the severity of outright dismissal as a sanction for failure to comply with a discovery order. It is quite reasonable to conclude that a party who has been subjected to such an order will feel duly chastened, so that even though he succeeds in having the order reversed on appeal he will nonetheless comply promptly with future discovery orders of the district court.

But here, as in other areas of the law, the most severe in the spectrum of sanctions provided by statute or rule must be available to the district court in appropriate cases, not merely to penalize those whose conduct may be deemed to warrant such a sanction, but to deter those who might be tempted to such conduct in the absence of such a deterrent. If the decision of the Court of Appeals remained undisturbed in this case, it might well be that these respondents would faithfully comply with all future discovery orders entered by the District Court in this case. But other parties to other lawsuits would feel freer than we think Rule 37 contemplates they should feel to flout other discovery orders of other district courts. Under the circumstances of this case, we hold that the District Judge did not abuse his discretion in finding bad faith on the part of these respondents, and concluding that the extreme sanction of dismissal was appropriate in this case by reason of respondents' "flagrant bad faith" and their counsel's "callous disregard" of their responsibilities. Therefore, the petition for a writ of certiorari is granted and the judgment of the Court of Appeals is reversed.

So ordered.

MR. JUSTICE BRENNAN and MR. JUSTICE WHITE dissent.

MR. JUSTICE STEVENS took no part in the consideration or decision of this case.

Notes and Questions

1. Despite trends toward case management and increased judicial involvement, discovery remains largely a party-driven process. As the Court notes, while the defendant's interrogatories went unanswered for seventeen months, neither party "pressed discovery" for at least the first twelve months, at which point a consent decree was entered and plaintiffs obtained new counsel. That being the case, how blameworthy, and thus punishable, do you find the plaintiffs' behavior? Was the defendant harmed by it? Was the court harmed by it? Do you find the reasoning of the Supreme Court and District Court more persuasive than that of the Appellate Court? Why? In *National Hockey League*, the party bringing the claim was sanctioned. In effect it was forced to forfeit a claim they elected to bring. Should the factors that go into the imposition of litigation-ending sanctions differ when the party against whom a claim is brought is sanctioned? Are the rights of the defendant somehow more impaired by such sanctions?

2. In *National Hockey League*, the Court noted that "[t]here is a natural tendency on the part of reviewing courts, properly employing the benefit of hindsight, to be heavily influenced by the severity of outright dismissal as a sanction for failure to comply with a discovery order," 427 U.S. at 642, and so to prefer lesser sanctions. Nevertheless, and with an eye to deterring others "who might be tempted to such conduct in the absence of such deterrent," the Court upheld dismissal. Should a court consider such external factors when resolving a dispute that above all else is between the parties before it? One might think that such an attitude not only compromises the goal of resolution on the merits, but also does so not for the benefit of the involved parties, but for courts and future litigants. Is that fair? As a matter of fact, courts disfavor both litigation-ending sanctions and severe sanctions generally. *See Webb v. District of Columbia*, 146 F.3d 964 (D.C. Cir. 1998) (reversing default judgment entered in plaintiff's favor as sanction for defendant's destruction of files because plaintiff was not unduly prejudiced and neither deterrence nor respect for the judicial system warranted such severe action); *Bonds v. District of Columbia*, 93 F.3d 801 (D.C. Cir. 1996) (reversing an order precluding the defendant from

offering any fact witnesses after it failed to respond to an interrogatory, which had the effect of ending the litigation).

3. In the wake of *National Hockey League*, one judge wrote:

> The most serious abuse of the judicial process occurs in discovery, and rule 37, together with the inherent power of the courts to punish those who interfere with the administration of justice, gives courts the means to deal with the problem.... What judges sometimes tend to overlook is that deterrence, which is an achievable goal, requires a readiness to impose relatively severe sanctions.... Abuse of the judicial process is difficult to detect and prove, and that difficulty means that abuse that is detected and proven must be dealt with severely.

Renfrew, 67 CAL. L. REV. at 271, 275. On the whole, Judge Renfrew's statement expresses optimism about the utility of sanctions. Do you think such optimism is warranted today?

4. Rule 37 gives the judge the authority to impose a variety of sanctions of varying severity for a party's failure to comply with discovery. *Coleman (Parent) Holdings, Inc. v. Morgan Stanley & Co.*, 2005 WL 679071 (Fla. Cir. Ct. Mar. 1, 2005), illustrates the extent to which discovery can break down, the array of sanctions available to the judge to impose order, and the problems such sanctions can create for the noncompliant party. After a transaction with Sunbeam Corporation, Coleman sued Morgan Stanley, Sunbeam's investment banker, alleging fraud. For more than two years Coleman sought access to various emails and electronic files. Throughout discovery, Morgan Stanley allegedly engaged in systematic misconduct.

The court concluded:

> 31. Given the history of the discovery, there is no way to know if all potentially responsive backup tapes have been located.
>
> 32. In sum, despite MS & Co.'s affirmative duty arising out of the litigation to produce its e-mails, and contrary to federal law requiring it to preserve the e-mails, MS & Co. failed to preserve many e-mails and failed to produce all e-mails required by the Agreed Order. The failings include overwriting e-mails after 12 months; failing to conduct proper searches for tapes that may contain e-mails; providing a certificate of compliance known to be false when made and only recently withdrawn; failing to timely notify CPH when additional tapes were located; failing to use reasonable efforts to search the newly discovered tapes; failing to timely process and search data held in the staging area or notify CPH of the deficiency; failing to write software scripts consistent with the Agreed Order; and discovering the deficiencies only after CPH was given the opportunity to check MS & Co.'s work and the MS & Co.'s attorneys were required to certify the completeness of the prior searches. Many of these failings were done knowingly, deliberately, and in bad faith.

> . . .
>
> The failures outlined in this Order are of two types. First, by overwriting e-mails contrary to its legal obligation to maintain them in readily accessible form for two years and with knowledge that legal action was threatened, MS & Co. has spoiled evidence, justifying sanctions. . . . Second, MS & Co.'s willful disobedience of the Agreed Order justifies sanctions. . . . The conclusion is inescapable that MS & Co. sought to thwart discovery *in this specific case.*
>
> Sanctions in this context are not meant to be punitive. They are intended, though, to level the playing field.

Despite the limited purpose sanctions were to serve, the judge proceeded to order: (1) an adverse inference with regard to the destroyed emails and files that were not produced and (2) a statement of facts to be read into the record explaining Morgan Stanley's violation of federal regulations regarding document retention and detailing its discovery failures. The order also (3) shifted to Morgan Stanley the burden of proving that it did not participate in the fraud and (4) allowed Coleman to argue that Morgan Stanley's concealment of its actions was "evidence of malice or evil intent, going to the issue of punitive damages." 2005 WL 679071, at *7. Finally, (5) further compliance with past discovery orders was required and (6) Morgan Stanley was ordered to pay Coleman's costs and fees associated with the motion leading to this order.

The case then proceeded to trial, where a jury awarded Coleman $1.58 billion dollars in compensatory and punitive damages. On appeal, the trial court was reversed on grounds unrelated to the sanctions. *Morgan Stanley & Co. v. Coleman (Parent) Holdings Inc.*, 955 So. 2d 1124 (Fl. Dist. Ct. App. 2007). The majority opinion did not address the use of sanctions, but in a footnote, the dissent wrote that "the trial court did not abuse its discretion in the sanction imposed on Morgan Stanley for substantial violations of court orders." Id. at 1133 n. 4.

How does the sanctions result strike you? Is there a point where procedural abuse becomes so bad that it is worth cutting short resolution of a case, or at least some aspect of a case, on the merits? Keeping in mind that the 2015 amendments to Rule 37 limited imposition of the most severe sanctions to instances of intentional noncompliance, do you think the *Coleman* sanctions would be upheld today?

The sanctions ordered in *Coleman (Parent) Holdings* have their analogues in Rule 37. At the lower end of the spectrum, if a party successfully moves for compelled disclosure or a protective order, the court may force the losing party to bear the costs associated with the motion. Fed. R. Civ. P. 37(a)(4). For failure to obey a court order, including a discovery order, the court may, among other options, treat certain facts as established, prohibit the sanctioned party from supporting or opposing claims, strike pleadings in whole or in part, dismiss the action, render default judgment, or hold the sanctioned party in contempt. *See* Fed. R. Civ. P. 37(b)(2). A number of the 37(b)(2) sanctions are also available when a party fails to provide the information required by Rule 26(a), to admit what is requested under Rule 36, to attend its own depositions, to answer interrogatories, or to respond to requests for inspection.

What consequences follow from the fact that a party must ordinarily disobey a court order before being sanctioned under Rule 37(b)(2)(A)–(E)? Remember that most of these orders will be discovery orders granted after one party has moved either to compel or for a protective order.

5. In *Qualcomm Inc. v. Broadcom Corp.*, 2008 U.S. Dist. LEXIS 911 (S.D. Cal. Jan. 7, 2008), a lengthy and acrimonious patent dispute, the district court had found that Qualcomm, the plaintiff, had

> actively organized and/or participated in a plan to profit heavily by (1) wrongfully concealing the patents-in-suit while participating in the JVT and then (2) actively hiding this concealment from the Court, the jury, and opposing counsel during the present litigation.... [Further, Qualcomm's] counsel participated in an organized program of litigation misconduct and concealment throughout discovery, trial, and post-trial.

Upon referral from the district court, the magistrate judge imposed sanctions on both Qualcomm and its outside counsel. Qualcomm managed to produce 1.2 million pages of marginally relevant documents while allegedly hiding 46,000 critical documents. As a result, they were ordered to pay $8.5 million. Additionally, the court sanctioned attorneys directly involved in discovery for allegedly allowing Qualcomm to withhold

> tens of thousands of emails showing that it actively participated in the JVT in 2002 and 2003 and then utilized Broadcom's lack of access to the suppressed evidence to repeatedly and falsely aver that there was "no evidence" that it had participated in the JVT prior to September 2003. Qualcomm's misconduct in hiding the emails and electronic documents prevented Broadcom from correcting the false statements and countering the misleading arguments.

2008 U.S. Dist. LEXIS 911, at *23–24.

The attorneys were referred to the California State Bar Association for potential ethics investigations.[31] However, before imposing sanctions, the court had to confront Qualcomm's argument that Broadcom was also at fault for not filing a motion to compel.

> Qualcomm attempts to capitalize on [Broadcom's failure to file a motion to compel], arguing "Broadcom never raised any concern regarding the scope of documents Qualcomm agreed to produce in response to Request No. 50, and never filed a motion to compel concerning this request. Accordingly, there is no order compelling Qualcomm to respond more fully to it."

---

31. This particular sanction was reversed as to six attorneys. *See Qualcomm Inc. v. Broadcom Corp.*, 2008 U.S. Dist. LEXIS 16897, at *8–10 (S.D. Cal. Mar. 5, 2008).

> Qualcomm made the same argument with regard to its other discovery responses.

2008 U.S. Dist. LEXIS 911, at *29–30 n.4.

The court noted,

> This argument is indicative of the gamesmanship Qualcomm engaged in throughout this litigation. Why should Broadcom file a motion to compel when Qualcomm agreed to produce the documents? What would the court have compelled: Qualcomm to do what it already said it would do? Should all parties file motions to compel to preserve their rights in case the other side hides documents?

2008 U.S. Dist. LEXIS 911, at *30 n.4.

> This dilemma highlights another problem with Qualcomm's conduct in this case. The Federal Rules of Civil Procedure require parties to respond to discovery in good faith; the rules do not require or anticipate judicial involvement unless or until an actual dispute is discovered. As the Advisory Committee explained, "[i]f primary responsibility for conducting discovery is to continue to rest with the litigants, they must be obliged to act responsibly and avoid abuse." FED. R. CIV. P. 26(g) Advisory Committee Notes (1983 Amendment).

2008 U.S. Dist. LEXIS 911, at *30–31.

Having read the foregoing, what is your prediction as to how opposing parties in complex cases are likely to behave in the future? In complex litigation, the stakes are high and historically severe sanctions rarely have been upheld. From a purely pragmatic standpoint, cooperation may not have made sense. *See* John S. Beckerman, *Confronting Civil Discovery's Fatal Flaws*, 84 MINN. L. REV. 505 (2000). Do you think that will change?

Discovery requires not only cooperation, but the continued existence of discoverable material. This much is obvious. The following two cases explore the duty to preserve discoverable material and the consequences that follow from failing to do so, either intentionally or unintentionally.

Arthur Andersen LLP v. United States

Supreme Court of the United States
544 U.S. 696 (2005)

CHIEF JUSTICE REHNQUIST delivered the opinion of the Court.

As Enron Corporation's financial difficulties became public in 2001, petitioner Arthur Andersen LLP, Enron's auditor, instructed its employees to destroy documents pursuant to its document retention policy. A jury found that this action made petitioner guilty of violating 18 U.S.C. §§ 1512(b)(2)(A) and (B). These sections make it a crime to "knowingly us[e] intimidation or physical force, threate[n], or corruptly persuad[e] another person . . . with intent to . . . cause" that person to "withhold" documents from, or "alter" documents for use in, an "official proceeding." The Court of Appeals for the Fifth Circuit affirmed. We hold that the jury instructions failed to convey properly the elements of a "corrup[t] persua[sion]" conviction under § 1512(b), and therefore reverse.

Enron Corporation, during the 1990's, switched its business from operation of natural gas pipelines to an energy conglomerate, a move that was accompanied by aggressive accounting practices and rapid growth. Petitioner audited Enron's publicly filed financial statements and provided internal audit and consulting services to it. Petitioner's "engagement team" for Enron was headed by David Duncan. Beginning in 2000, Enron's financial performance began to suffer, and, as 2001 wore on, worsened. On August 14, 2001, Jeffrey Skilling, Enron's Chief Executive Officer (CEO), unexpectedly resigned. Within days, Sherron Watkins, a senior accountant at Enron, warned Kenneth Lay, Enron's newly reappointed CEO, that Enron could "implode in a wave of accounting scandals." She likewise informed Duncan and Michael Odom, one of petitioner's partners who had supervisory responsibility over Duncan, of the looming problems.

On August 28, an article in the Wall Street Journal suggested improprieties at Enron, and the SEC opened an informal investigation. By early September, petitioner had formed an Enron "crisis-response" team, which included Nancy Temple, an in-house counsel. On October 8, petitioner retained outside counsel to represent it in any litigation that might arise from the Enron matter. The next day, Temple discussed Enron with other in-house counsel. Her notes from that meeting reflect that "some SEC investigation" is "highly probable." Id., at 3.

On October 10, Odom spoke at a general training meeting attended by 89 employees, including 10 from the Enron engagement team. Odom urged everyone to comply with the firm's document retention policy.[32] He added: "'[I]f it's destroyed in the course of [the] normal policy and litigation is filed the next day, that's great. . . . [W]e've followed our own policy, and whatever there was that might have been of interest to somebody is gone and irretrievable.'" On October 12, Temple entered the

---

32. [Court's footnote #4] The firm's policy called for a single central engagement file, which "should contain only that information which is relevant to supporting our work." App. JA-45. The policy stated that, "[i]n cases of threatened litigation, . . . no related information will be destroyed." *Id.*, at JA-44. It also separately provided that, if petitioner is "advised of litigation or subpoenas regarding a particular engagement, the related information should not be destroyed. *See* Policy Statement No. 780-Notification of Litigation." *Id.*, at JA-65 (emphasis deleted). Policy Statement No. 780 set forth "notification" procedures for whenever "professional practice litigation against [petitioner] or any of its personnel has been commenced, has been threatened or is judged likely to occur, or when governmental or professional investigations that may involve [petitioner] or any of its personnel have been commenced or are judged likely." *Id.*, at JA-29 to JA-30.

Enron matter into her computer, designating the "Type of Potential Claim" as "Professional Practice-Government/Regulatory Inv[estigation]." Temple also e-mailed Odom, suggesting that he "'remin[d] the engagement team of our documentation and retention policy.'"

On October 16, Enron announced its third quarter results. That release disclosed a $1.01 billion charge to earnings. The following day, the SEC notified Enron by letter that it had opened an investigation in August and requested certain information and documents. On October 19, Enron forwarded a copy of that letter to petitioner.

On the same day, Temple also sent an e-mail to a member of petitioner's internal team of accounting experts and attached a copy of the document policy. On October 20, the Enron crisis-response team held a conference call, during which Temple instructed everyone to "[m]ake sure to follow the [document] policy." On October 23, Enron CEO Lay declined to answer questions during a call with analysts because of "potential lawsuits, as well as the SEC inquiry." After the call, Duncan met with other Andersen partners on the Enron engagement team and told them that they should ensure team members were complying with the document policy. Another meeting for all team members followed, during which Duncan distributed the policy and told everyone to comply. These, and other smaller meetings, were followed by substantial destruction of paper and electronic documents.

On October 26, one of petitioner's senior partners circulated a New York Times article discussing the SEC's response to Enron. His e-mail commented that "the problems are just beginning and we will be in the cross hairs. The marketplace is going to keep the pressure on this and is going to force the SEC to be tough." On October 30, the SEC opened a formal investigation and sent Enron a letter that requested accounting documents.

Throughout this time period, the document destruction continued, despite reservations by some of petitioner's managers.[33] On November 8, Enron announced that it would issue a comprehensive restatement of its earnings and assets. Also on November 8, the SEC served Enron and petitioner with subpoenas for records. On November 9, Duncan's secretary sent an e-mail that stated: "Per Dave—No more shredding.... We have been officially served for our documents." Enron filed for bankruptcy less than a month later. Duncan was fired and later pleaded guilty to witness tampering.

In March 2002, petitioner was indicted in the Southern District of Texas on one count of violating §§ 1512(b)(2)(A) and (B). The indictment alleged that, between

33. [Court's footnote #6] For example, on October 26, John Riley, another partner with petitioner, saw Duncan shredding documents and told him "this wouldn't be the best time in the world for you guys to be shredding a bunch of stuff." On October 31, David Stulb, a forensics investigator for petitioner, met with Duncan. During the meeting, Duncan picked up a document with the words "smoking gun" written on it and began to destroy it, adding "we don't need this." Stulb cautioned Duncan on the need to maintain documents and later informed Temple that Duncan needed advice on the document retention policy.

October 10 and November 9, 2001, petitioner "did knowingly, intentionally and corruptly persuade . . . other persons, to wit: [petitioner's] employees, with intent to cause" them to withhold documents from, and alter documents for use in, "official proceedings, namely: regulatory and criminal proceedings and investigations." A jury trial followed. When the case went to the jury, that body deliberated for seven days and then declared that it was deadlocked. The District Court delivered an "*Allen* charge," *Allen v. United States*, 164 U.S. 492 (1896), and, after three more days of deliberation, the jury returned a guilty verdict. The District Court denied petitioner's motion for a judgment of acquittal.

The Court of Appeals for the Fifth Circuit affirmed. It held that the jury instructions properly conveyed the meaning of "corruptly persuades" and "official proceeding"; that the jury need not find any consciousness of wrongdoing; and that there was no reversible error. Because of a split of authority regarding the meaning of § 1512(b), we granted certiorari.

Chapter 73 of Title 18 of the United States Code provides criminal sanctions for those who obstruct justice. Sections 1512(b)(2)(A) and (B), part of the witness tampering provisions, provide in relevant part:

> Whoever knowingly uses intimidation or physical force, threatens, or corruptly persuades another person, or attempts to do so, or engages in misleading conduct toward another person, with intent to . . . cause or induce any person to . . . withhold testimony, or withhold a record, document, or other object, from an official proceeding [or] alter, destroy, mutilate, or conceal an object with intent to impair the object's integrity or availability for use in an official proceeding . . . shall be fined under this title or imprisoned not more than ten years, or both.

In this case, our attention is focused on what it means to "knowingly . . . corruptly persuad[e]" another person "with intent to . . . cause" that person to "withhold" documents from, or "alter" documents for use in, an "official proceeding."

"We have traditionally exercised restraint in assessing the reach of a federal criminal statute, both out of deference to the prerogatives of Congress, *Dowling v. United States*, 473 U.S. 207 (1985), and out of concern that 'a fair warning should be given to the world in language that the common world will understand, of what the law intends to do if a certain line is passed,' *McBoyle v. United States*, 283 U.S. 25, 27 (1931)." *United States v. Aguilar*, 515 U.S. 593, 600 (1995).

Such restraint is particularly appropriate here, where the act underlying the conviction—"persua[sion]"—is by itself innocuous. Indeed, "persuad[ing]" a person "with intent to . . . cause" that person to "withhold" testimony or documents from a Government proceeding or Government official is not inherently malign. Consider a mother who suggests to her son that he invoke his right against compelled self-incrimination, see U.S. Const., Amdt. 5, or a wife who persuades her husband not to disclose marital confidences, see *Trammel v. United States*, 445 U.S. 40 (1980).

Nor is it necessarily corrupt for an attorney to "persuad[e]" a client "with intent to . . . cause" that client to "withhold" documents from the Government. In *Upjohn Co. v. United States*, 449 U.S. 383 (1981), for example, we held that Upjohn was justified in withholding documents that were covered by the attorney-client privilege from the Internal Revenue Service (IRS). *See id.*, at 395. No one would suggest that an attorney who "persuade[d]" Upjohn to take that step acted wrongfully, even though he surely intended that his client keep those documents out of the IRS' hands.

"Document retention policies," which are created in part to keep certain information from getting into the hands of others, including the Government, are common in business. See generally Chase, *To Shred or Not to Shred: Document Retention Policies and Federal Obstruction of Justice Statutes*, 8 Ford. J. Corp. & Fin. L. 721 (2003). It is, of course, not wrongful for a manager to instruct his employees to comply with a valid document retention policy under ordinary circumstances.

Acknowledging this point, the parties have largely focused their attention on the word "corruptly" as the key to what may or may not lawfully be done in the situation presented here. Section 1512(b) punishes not just "corruptly persuad[ing]" another, but "*knowingly* (3)27 corruptly persuad[ing]" another. (Emphasis added.) The Government suggests that "knowingly" does not modify "corruptly persuades," but that is not how the statute most naturally reads. It provides the *mens rea*—"knowingly"—and then a list of acts—"uses intimidation or physical force, threatens, or corruptly persuades." We have recognized with regard to similar statutory language that the *mens rea* at least applies to the acts that immediately follow, if not to other elements down the statutory chain. *See United States v. X-Citement Video*, Inc., 513 U.S. 64, 68 (1994) (recognizing that the "most natural grammatical reading" of 18 U.S.C. §§ 2252(a)(1) and (2) "suggests that the term 'knowingly' modifies only the surrounding verbs: transports, ships, receives, distributes, or reproduces"); *see also Liparota v. United States*, 471 U.S. 419 (1985). The Government suggests that it is "questionable whether Congress would employ such an inelegant formulation as 'knowingly . . . corruptly persuades.'" Long experience has not taught us to share the Government's doubts on this score, and we must simply interpret the statute as written.

The parties have not pointed us to another interpretation of "knowingly . . . corruptly" to guide us here. In any event, the natural meaning of these terms provides a clear answer. *See Bailey v. United States,* 516 U.S. 137, 144–145. "[K]nowledge" and "knowingly" are normally associated with awareness, understanding, or consciousness. *See* Black's Law Dictionary 888 (8th ed. 2004) (hereinafter Black's); Webster's Third New International Dictionary 1252–1253 (1993) (hereinafter Webster's 3d); American Heritage Dictionary of the English Language 725 (1981) (hereinafter Am. Hert.). "Corrupt" and "corruptly" are normally associated with wrongful, immoral, depraved, or evil. See Black's 371; Webster's 3d 512; Am. Hert. 299–300. Joining these meanings together here makes sense both linguistically and in the statutory scheme. Only persons conscious of wrongdoing can be said to "knowingly . . . corruptly persuad[e]." And limiting criminality to persuaders conscious of their wrongdoing sensibly allows § 1512(b) to reach only those with the level of "culpability . . . we usually require in order to impose criminal liability." *United States v. Aguilar*, 515 U.S. at 602; *see also Liparota v. United States, supra*, at 426.

The outer limits of this element need not be explored here because the jury instructions at issue simply failed to convey the requisite consciousness of wrongdoing. Indeed, it is striking how little culpability the instructions required. For example, the jury was told that, "even if [petitioner] honestly and sincerely believed that its conduct was lawful, you may find [petitioner] guilty." The instructions also diluted the meaning of "corruptly" so that it covered innocent conduct.

The parties vigorously disputed how the jury would be instructed on "corruptly." The District Court based its instruction on the definition of that term found in the Fifth Circuit Pattern Jury Instruction for § 1503. This pattern instruction defined "corruptly" as "'knowingly and dishonestly, with the specific intent to subvert or undermine the integrity'" of a proceeding. The Government, however, insisted on excluding "dishonestly" and adding the term "impede" to the phrase "subvert or undermine." The District Court agreed over petitioner's objections, and the jury was told to convict if it found petitioner intended to "subvert, undermine, or impede" governmental factfinding by suggesting to its employees that they enforce the document retention policy.

These changes were significant. No longer was any type of "dishonest[y]" necessary to a finding of guilt, and it was enough for petitioner to have simply "impede[d]" the Government's factfinding ability. . . .

The instructions also were infirm for another reason. They led the jury to believe that it did not have to find *any* nexus between the "persua[sion]" to destroy documents and any particular proceeding. In resisting any type of nexus element, the Government relies heavily on § 1512(e)(1), which states that an official proceeding "need not be pending or about to be instituted at the time of the offense." It is, however, one thing to say that a proceeding "need not be pending or about to be instituted at the time of the offense," and quite another to say a proceeding need not even be foreseen. A "knowingly . . . corrup[t] persuade[r]" cannot be someone who persuades others to shred documents under a document retention policy when he does not have in contemplation any particular official proceeding in which those documents might be material. . . .

For these reasons, the jury instructions here were flawed in important respects. The judgment of the Court of Appeals is reversed, and the case is remanded for further proceedings consistent with this opinion.

It is so ordered.

West v. Goodyear Tire & Rubber Co.

United States Court of Appeals, Second Circuit
167 F.3d 776 (1999)

McLaughlin, Circuit Judge:

BACKGROUND

Ronald West owned and operated West Indies Auto Body in Poughkeepsie, New York for over 16 years. While West specialized in auto body repair, he also performed tire and rim work and owned a tire mounting machine and an air compressor that are central to this case.

In January 1991, Aston Weir brought two tires that had been manufactured by The Goodyear Tire & Rubber Company ("Goodyear") into West's shop. Weir asked West to find some rims to fit the tires, mount the tires on the rims, and put the assembled wheels on Weir's truck.

As fate would have it, West already had two used rims that he had purchased from a junkyard. West knew that the used rims were 16.5 inches in diameter because, upon examination, he saw that "[i]t said 16.5 on the rim." The rims had been manufactured by The Budd Company ("Budd").

West never tried to determine the diameter of the two tires—he simply assumed (incorrectly) that both were 16.5 inches in diameter. Had West read the information printed on the tires, he would have seen that they had a diameter of only 16 inches. He would also have seen Goodyear's "Safety warning" that instructed the user to "MOUNT ONLY ON 16 INCH RIMS." West admitted at a deposition that if he had read the safety warning he would not have tried to mount Weir's tires onto the 16.5 inch rims.

On January 5, 1991, West undertook to mount the 16 inch tires onto the 16.5 inch rims. Despite the fact that they were mismatched, the mounting of the first tire and rim went smoothly. West was able to inflate the tire, and the beads of the tire (the bands at the bottom of the sidewall that fit within the rim) fit within the rim. West put to one side this first inflated tire/rim combination (which the parties refer to as the "exemplar wheel") and turned his attention to the second tire.

West placed the second rim on his tire changing machine, lubricated the second tire, placed it on the changing machine, and engaged the machine's safety lock. West could not, however, get the second tire/rim combination to hold air. Removing the tire and rim from the tire mounting machine, he noticed that the beads of the tire were not seating properly within the rim. West bounced the tire on the ground several times to get the beads to seat properly. West then set the tire on the ground, and started to add air using a hand-held air nozzle that was connected to an air compressor. The compressor was set at an astronomical pressure of 160 pounds per square inch. West added air for a period between one and five minutes, but never checked the inflation pressure of the tire. At some point, the tire exploded, injuring West.

West did not return to his shop for about two weeks after the accident. When he returned, he noticed that the first tire and rim that he successfully mounted, the "exemplar wheel," was still fully inflated, but he did nothing in particular with the exemplar wheel. West retained an attorney, and in late January 1991, the attorney's investigator removed both the exemplar wheel and the tattered remains of the second wheel. The exemplar wheel was still fully inflated at that time.

West's counsel kept the exemplar wheel for about 10 months. During this period, West's lawyer retained Risjord & James, a law firm, based in Kansas, that specializes in tire explosion cases. On November 7, 1991, West's attorney sent all the accident related materials, including the exemplar wheel, to Risjord & James in Kansas. When the exemplar wheel was received, Randy James of Risjord & James took photos of it and then ordered that it be deflated. James claims that he was afraid that the wheel might explode and cause serious injury. James did not notify the manufacturer of the tire (Goodyear) or the rim (Budd) before he deflated the exemplar wheel.

On February 26, 1992, West and his wife filed suit in the United States District Court for the Southern District of New York (Owen, Judge), alleging that the negligence of Goodyear and Budd had caused his injuries. The Wests sought compensatory and punitive damages for Mr. West's injuries and Mrs. West's loss of consortium.

After discovery began, the defendants asked to inspect West's shop, and especially his tire mounting machine and air compressor. An inspection was scheduled for June 1993. However, in May 1993, with no notice to the defendants, West went ahead and sold the tire changing machine and air compressor. Although the defendants eventually located the tire mounting machine and compressor, they had been left outside and exposed to the elements for some time, and their condition had deteriorated.

On January 2, 1996, Budd moved for dismissal of the complaint based on spoliation of the exemplar wheel, the tire changing machine and the air compressor. At the same time, Goodyear moved for an order excluding the spoliated evidence, but did not seek dismissal. Both defendants also moved for summary judgment on West's punitive damage claims.

Mr. West died on November 19, 1996, and Mrs. West, as executrix of Mr. West's estate, was substituted as party-plaintiff for her late husband.

On May 2, 1997, Judge Owen held a hearing on all the pending motions, and on July 18, 1997, he granted partial summary judgment to the defendants on the punitive damage claims. On February 13, 1998, Judge Owen dismissed the complaint in its entirety as a sanction for spoliation of the evidence. Mrs. West now appeals both orders.

DISCUSSION

I. Spoliation of Evidence

Mrs. West contends that Judge Owen abused his discretion by dismissing the complaint as a sanction for spoliation. Essentially, Mrs. West claims that, in this case, dismissal was a Draconian remedy for spoliation. We agree, and vacate and remand the judgment of the district court for consideration of a lesser sanction.

A. Standard of Review

Dismissal of a case as a sanction for spoliation of evidence is reviewed under an abuse of discretion standard. We will reject the district court's factual findings in support of its imposition of sanctions only if they are clearly erroneous.

B. Governing Law

Spoliation is the destruction or significant alteration of evidence, or the failure to preserve property for another's use as evidence in pending or reasonably foreseeable litigation. *See generally Black's Law Dictionary* 1401 (6th ed. 1990). It has long been the rule that spoliators should not benefit from their wrongdoing, as illustrated by "that favourite maxim of the law, *omnia presumuntur contra spoliatorem.*" 1 Sir T. Willes Chitty, et al., *Smith's Leading Cases 404* (13th ed. 1929); *see Kronisch v. United States*, 150 F.3d 112, 126 (2d Cir. 1998).

A federal district court may impose sanctions under Fed. R. Civ. P. 37(b) when a party spoliates evidence in violation of a court order. See Fed. R. Civ. P. 37(b)(2); *John B. Hull, Inc. v. Waterbury Petroleum Prods., Inc.*, 845 F.2d 1172, 1176 (2d Cir. 1988). Even without a discovery order, a district court may impose sanctions for spoliation, exercising its inherent power to control litigation. *See Chambers v. NASCO, Inc.*, [501 U.S. 32, 43–45] (1991); *Sassower v. Field*, 973 F.2d 75, 80–81 (2d Cir. 1992); see also P.L. McGlynn, Note, *Spoliation in the Product Liability Context*, 27 U. Mem. L.Rev. 663 (1997).

Although a district court has broad discretion in crafting a proper sanction for spoliation, we have explained that the applicable sanction should be molded to serve the prophylactic, punitive, and remedial rationales underlying the spoliation doctrine. *See Kronisch*, 150 F.3d at 126. The sanction should be designed to: (1) deter parties from engaging in spoliation; (2) place the risk of an erroneous judgment on the party who wrongfully created the risk; and (3) restore "the prejudiced party to the same position he would have been in absent the wrongful destruction of evidence by the opposing party." *Id.; see Update Art, Inc. v. Modiin Pub., Ltd.*, 843 F.2d 67, 71 (2d Cir. 1988); 7 James Wm. Moore, *Moore's Federal Practice* § 37.50[1][a], at 37–72, 37–73 (1998); Jamie S. Gorelick et al., *Destruction of Evidence* § 3.14, at 111 (1989).

"[O]utright dismissal of a lawsuit . . . is within the court's discretion." *Chambers*, [501 U.S. at 45]; *see* Fed. R. Civ. P. 37(b)(2)(C). Dismissal is appropriate if there is a showing of willfulness, bad faith, or fault on the part of the sanctioned party. *See Jones v. NFTA*, 836 F.2d 731, 734 (2d Cir. 1987). However, because dismissal is a "drastic remedy," it "should be imposed only in extreme circumstances, usually after consideration of alternative, less drastic sanctions." *John B. Hull, Inc.*, 845 F.2d at 1176 (citation and internal quotation omitted); *see Valentine v. Museum of Modern Art,* 29 F.3d 47, 49–50 (2d Cir. 1994) (per curiam).

Defendants maintain that dismissal was appropriate in this case because the spoliated evidence was essential to their central defense: that West grossly over-inflated the tires to fit them on mismatched rims. They argue that if the exemplar wheel had been preserved in its inflated state, it would have been over-inflated and would have provided highly probative evidence of their theory of the case. In essence, defendants believe that by deflating the exemplar wheel, West's lawyers deflated their case.

Similarly, defendants hoped to use the tire mounting machine and air compressor to prove that West did indeed over-inflate the tires. When the defendants located the mounting machine and air compressor, their experts examined them and concluded that, due to poor maintenance, they malfunctioned and could have caused over-inflation. However, because West sold these items and the purchaser left them outside over the winter, defendants' experts had no way to determine the condition of the machines when they were in West's shop at the time of the accident. This problem, they assert, seriously damaged the defense case.

Judge Owen found that the disabilities that defendants would suffer at trial could not be redressed by any sanction short of dismissal. He concluded that:

> Merely excluding all reference to the exemplar tire or parts would be inadequate: defendants are entitled to have the opportunity to show that plaintiff should have been on notice that he was mismatching. Instructing the jury that it may draw adverse inferences from plaintiff's spoliation is also wholly inadequate and fails in effecting fairness, considering that evidence which defendants are now unable to offer might have been dispositive.

We disagree with Judge Owen's conclusion that dismissal constituted the only adequate sanction. It was not necessary to dismiss the complaint in order to vindicate the trifold aims of: (1) deterring future spoliation of evidence; (2) protecting the defendants' interests; and (3) remedying the prejudice defendants suffered as a result of West's actions. *See Kronisch*, 150 F.3d at 126. Judge Owen could have combined alternative sanctions in a way that would fully protect Goodyear and Budd from prejudice. For example, the trial judge could: (1) instruct the jury to presume that the exemplar tire was overinflated; (2) instruct the jury to presume that the tire mounting machine and air compressor malfunctioned; and (3) preclude Mrs. West from offering evidence on these issues. We have previously endorsed use of these alternative sanctions, and in this case, conclude that they will suffice to protect the defendants.[34] *See, e.g., id.* (adverse presumption instruction); *Daval*

34. [Court's footnote #1] It is noteworthy that Goodyear did not move for dismissal as a sanction for spoliation; it only sought to have evidence relating to the spoliated materials excluded at trial. Only Budd moved to dismiss the complaint on the ground of spoliation. Obviously, Goodyear

Steel Prods. v. M/V Fakredine, 951 F.2d 1357, 1366 (2d Cir. 1991) (barring party from presenting evidence opposing claim); *see also Konstantopoulos v. Westvaco Corp.*, 112 F.3d 710, 719–21 (3d Cir. 1997) (preventing spoliator's expert witness from testifying about spoliated evidence); *Dillon v. Nissan Motor Co.*, 986 F.2d 263, 267 (8th Cir. 1993) (same).

Although we cite some examples of alternative sanctions, we decline to prescribe precisely which remedial measures Judge Owen should adopt on remand. We leave this question to the sound discretion of Judge Owen, confident that he will arrive at an appropriate sanction, short of dismissal, which will serve the punitive, remedial, and prophylactic aims of the spoliation rules. . . .

CONCLUSION

Dismissal of the complaint was too harsh a sanction under the circumstances of this case. The judgment of the district court is therefore VACATED and REMANDED with instructions to fashion an appropriate, but less severe, sanction for plaintiffs' spoliation.

Notes and Questions

1. *Arthur Andersen* is an extreme case. Instructional error aside, was there a basis for conviction? Regardless, the case shows how spoliation can shade into obstruction of justice charges. *West* better exemplifies the more common issues surrounding spoliation and the context in which these issues normally arise. That said, motions for adverse inferences are common anytime a party has large amounts of potentially relevant materials and the duty to preserve that material.

2. Willfulness, bad faith, or fault is required to impose litigation-ending sanctions. Should the same be true when imposing an adverse inference for spoliation? *See Reilly v. NatWest Mkts. Group, Inc.*, 181 F.3d 253, 267–68 (2d Cir. 1999) (noting first that the issue is unresolved and holding "that a finding of bad faith or intentional misconduct is not the sine qua non to sanctioning a spoliator with an adverse inference"). The spoliator in *Reilly* "exhibited at least gross negligence." *Id.* at 268. What about simple negligence? Updates to the Federal Rules of Civil Procedure in 2015 included a new Rule 37(e). The advisory committee decided that the rules should "preserve a broad range of measures to cure prejudice caused by [negligence], but to limit the most severe measures to instances of intentional loss or destruction." Fed. R. Civ. P. 37(e). Here is how one court differentiated the new rule from the old:

> Generally, a party bringing a spoliation motion must demonstrate that: (1) the party charged with destroying the evidence had an obligation to preserve it; (2) the records were destroyed with a "culpable state of mind";

---

believed that lesser sanctions, like exclusion of spoliated evidence, would protect its interests, although Goodyear would now benefit from the district court's dismissal.

> and, (3) the destroyed evidence was relevant to the party's claim or defense. *Residential Funding Corp. v. DeGeorge Fin. Corp.*, 306 F.3d 99, 107 (2d Cir. 2002). This general rule applied to the destruction of both tangible and electronic evidence until December 1, 2015, at which time Rule 37 of the Federal Rules of Civil Procedure was amended to provide a different standard for destruction of electronically stored information. This new rule "rejects cases such as *Residential Funding Corp. v. DeGeorge Financial Corp.*, 306 F.3d 99 (2d Cir. 2002), that authorize the giving of adverse-inference instructions on a finding of negligence or gross negligence." *McIntosh v. United States*, 2016 WL 1274585, *31 (S.D.N.Y. 2016).

Moody v. CSX Transp., Inc., 271 F. Supp. 3d 410, 425 (W.D.N.Y. 2017).

3. In *Arthur Andersen*, the defendants continued to shred documents until proceedings were actually initiated. When should a company institute a litigation hold? *See* Matthew P. McGuire, *Document Management and E-Discovery in Class Actions: Avoiding the Spoliation Trap*, Pratt's Privacy & Data Security L.J. (2006) ("The dilemma for financial institutions is when to institute 'litigation holds' on the routine destruction of documents and data pursuant to existing retention policies. Failing to retain documents and electronic data that could be relevant to future litigation could result in draconian spoliation sanctions down the road. However, retaining vast quantities of documents and electronic data imposes severe burdens from both a time and cost perspective.").

4. Keep in mind that Rule 37(e) would not affect the outcome in *West*, as the rule applies only to ESI, whereas *West* involved physical evidence.

5. How might spoliation sanctions affect the development of a case? *See United States v. Kitsap Physicians Serv.*, 314 F.3d 995 (9th Cir. 2002) (noting that a showing of spoliation justifying an adverse inference might be sufficient to defeat summary judgment). Once a plaintiff gets past summary judgment, the incentives to settle increase. *See* Stephen D. Whetstone & Michael S. Simon, *The Stakes Have Never Been Higher: Recent Court Rulings Have Turned Electronic Data Discovery into a High-Stakes Game of 'Gotcha,'* Nat'l L.J., July 17, 2006.

6. Might a court reach a different conclusion from the court in the *West* case? For comparison purposes, review the Fourth Circuit's opinion in *Silvestri v. Gen. Motors Corp.*, 271 F.3d 583, 594–95 (4th Cir. 2001) (upholding dismissal of plaintiff's case for failure to preserve an automobile after a crash: "Thus, not only was the evidence lost to General Motors, but the evidence that was preserved was incomplete and indefinite. To require General Motors to rely on the evidence collected by Silvestri's experts in lieu of what it could have collected would result in irreparable prejudice. Short of dismissal, the district court would have been left to formulate an order that created facts as established or that created presumptions. But when Silvestri presents vehicle data as his only evidence of a product defect and that data is incomplete and perhaps inaccurate, the court would have no basis for determining what

facts should be taken as established. On the other hand, if the court denied Silvestri's experts from testifying, as would be an alternative, then Silvestri would have no case at all. In short, we conclude that the district court's finding that General Motors was 'highly prejudiced' was not clearly erroneous and that in the peculiar circumstances of this case, the court's order dismissing this case, although severe, was not an abuse of discretion.").

7. The subject of spoliation is likely to remain a hot topic for the indefinite future. There is a growing body of case law addressing the question of the appropriate sanction for willful, grossly negligent, or negligent destruction of discoverable material, especially in this electronic age. Consider, for example, the opinion below:

The Pension Committee of the University of Montreal Pension Plan v. Banc of America Securities, LLC

United States District Court for the Southern District of New York
2010 U.S. Dist. LEXIS 4546 (Jan. 15, 2010, as amended May 28, 2010)

Scheindlin, United States District Judge. Amended Opinion and Order

Zubulake Revisited: Six Years Later

I. INTRODUCTION

In an era where vast amounts of electronic information is available for review, discovery in certain cases has become increasingly complex and expensive. Courts cannot and do not expect that any party can meet a standard of perfection. Nonetheless, the courts have a right to expect that litigants and counsel will take the necessary steps to ensure that relevant records are preserved when litigation is reasonably anticipated, and that such records are collected, reviewed, and produced to the opposing party.

In February, 2004, a group of investors brought this action to recover losses of 550 million dollars stemming from the liquidation of two British Virgin Islands based hedge funds in which they held shares: Lancer Offshore, Inc. and OmniFund Ltd. (the "Funds"). Plaintiffs have asserted claims under the federal securities laws and under New York law against former directors, administrators, the auditor, and the prime broker and custodian of the Funds.

In October, 2007, during the discovery process, Citco NV, its parent company, the Citco Group Limited, and former Lancer Offshore directors who were Citco officers (collectively with Citco NV, the "Citco Defendants") claimed that substantial gaps were found in plaintiffs' document productions. As a result, depositions were held and declarations were submitted. This occurred from October, 2007 through June, 2008. Following the close of this discovery, the Citco Defendants moved for sanctions, alleging that each plaintiff failed to preserve and produce documents—including those stored electronically—and submitted false and misleading declarations regarding their document collection and preservation efforts. The Citco

Defendants seek dismissal of the Complaint—or any lesser sanction the Court deems appropriate—based on plaintiffs' alleged misconduct.

Based on my review of the evidence, I conclude that all of these plaintiffs were either negligent or grossly negligent in meeting their discovery obligations. As a result, sanctions are required.

II. AN ANALYTICAL FRAMEWORK AND APPLICABLE LAW

From the outset, it is important to recognize what this case involves and what it does not. This case does not present any egregious examples of litigants purposefully destroying evidence. This is a case where plaintiffs failed to timely institute written litigation holds and engaged in careless and indifferent collection efforts after the duty to preserve arose. As a result, there can be little doubt that some documents were lost or destroyed.

The question, then, is whether plaintiffs' conduct requires this Court to impose a sanction for the spoliation of evidence. To answer this question, there are several concepts that must be carefully reviewed and analyzed. The first is plaintiffs' level of culpability—that is, was their conduct of discovery acceptable or was it negligent, grossly negligent, or willful. The second is the interplay between the duty to preserve evidence and the spoliation of evidence. The third is which party should bear the burden of proving that evidence has been lost or destroyed and the consequences resulting from that loss. And the fourth is the appropriate remedy for the harm caused by the spoliation.

A. Defining Negligence, Gross Negligence, and Willfulness in the Discovery Context

While many treatises and cases routinely define negligence, gross negligence, and willfulness in the context of tortious conduct, I have found no clear definition of these terms in the context of discovery misconduct. It is apparent to me that these terms simply describe a continuum. Conduct is either acceptable or unacceptable. Once it is unacceptable the only question is how bad is the conduct.

[Negligence] is conduct "which falls below the standard established by law for the protection of others against unreasonable risk of harm." [Negligence] is caused by heedlessness or inadvertence, by which the negligent party is unaware of the results which may follow from [its] act. But it may also arise where the negligent party has considered the possible consequences carefully, and has exercised [its] own best judgment.[35]

"Gross negligence has been described as a failure to exercise even that care which a careless person would use." According to a leading treatise—Prosser & Keeton on Torts—most courts find that gross negligence is something more than negligence "and differs from ordinary negligence only in degree, and not in kind."

---

35. [Court's footnote #10] Prosser & Keeton on Torts § 31 at 169 (5th ed. 1984) (quoting Restatement (Second) of Torts § 282) (citations omitted).

The same treatise groups willful, wanton, and reckless into one category that requires "that the actor has intentionally done an act of an unreasonable character in disregard of a known or obvious risk that was so great as to make it highly probable that harm would follow, and which thus is usually accompanied by a conscious indifference to the consequences."[36]

A failure to preserve evidence resulting in the loss or destruction of relevant information is surely negligent, and, depending on the circumstances, may be grossly negligent or willful. For example, the intentional destruction of relevant records, either paper or electronic, after the duty to preserve has attached, is willful. Possibly after October, 2003, when *Zubulake IV* was issued, and definitely after July, 2004, when the final relevant *Zubulake* opinion was issued, the failure to issue a written litigation hold constitutes gross negligence because that failure is likely to result in the destruction of relevant information.

The next step in the discovery process is collection and review. Once again, depending on the extent of the failure to collect evidence, or the sloppiness of the review, the resulting loss or destruction of evidence is surely negligent, and, depending on the circumstances may be grossly negligent or willful. For example, the failure to collect records—either paper or electronic—from key players constitutes gross negligence or willfulness as does the destruction of email or certain backup tapes after the duty to preserve has attached. By contrast, the failure to obtain records from all those employees who had any involvement with the issues raised in the litigation or anticipated litigation, as opposed to just the key players, could constitute negligence. Similarly, the failure to take all appropriate measures to preserve ESI likely falls in the negligence category.

B. The Duty to Preserve and Spoliation

Spoliation refers to the destruction or material alteration of evidence or to the failure to preserve property for another's use as evidence in pending or reasonably foreseeable litigation. The right to impose sanctions for spoliation arises from a court's inherent power to control the judicial process and litigation, but the power is limited to that necessary to redress conduct "which abuses the judicial process." The policy underlying this inherent power of the courts is the need to preserve the integrity of the judicial process in order to retain confidence that the process works to uncover the truth.... The courts must protect the integrity of the judicial process because, "[a]s soon as the process falters ... the people are then justified in abandoning support for the system."[37]

---

36. [Court's footnote #13] Id. at 213 (citing Restatement (Second) of Torts § 500 and collecting cases).

37. [Court's footnote #22] *Silvestri v. General Motors*, 271 F.3d 583, 589 (4th Cir. 2001) (quoting Chambers v. NASCO, Inc., 501 U.S. 32, 45–46, 111 S. Ct. 2123, 115 L. Ed. 2d 27 (1991), and *United States v. Shaffer Equip. Co.*, 11 F.3d 450, 457 (4th Cir. 1993)) (citations omitted).

The common law duty to preserve evidence relevant to litigation is well recognized. The case law makes crystal clear that the breach of the duty to preserve, and the resulting spoliation of evidence, may result in the imposition of sanctions by a court because the court has the obligation to ensure that the judicial process is not abused.

It is well established that the duty to preserve evidence arises when a party reasonably anticipates litigation. "'[O]nce a party reasonably anticipates litigation, it must suspend its routine document retention/destruction policy and put in place a 'litigation hold' to ensure the preservation of relevant documents.'"[38] A plaintiff's duty is more often triggered before litigation commences, in large part because plaintiffs control the timing of litigation.

C. Burdens of Proof

The third preliminary matter that must be analyzed is what can be done when documents are no longer available. This is not an easy question. It is often impossible to know what lost documents would have contained. At best, their content can be inferred from existing documents or recalled during depositions. But this is not always possible. Who then should bear the burden of establishing the relevance of evidence that can no longer be found? And, an even more difficult question is who should be required to prove that the absence of the missing material has caused prejudice to the innocent party.

The burden of proof question differs depending on the severity of the sanction. For less severe sanctions—such as fines and cost-shifting—the inquiry focuses more on the conduct of the spoliating party than on whether documents were lost, and, if so, whether those documents were relevant and resulted in prejudice to the innocent party. As explained more thoroughly below, for more severe sanctions—such as dismissal, preclusion, or the imposition of an adverse inference—the court must consider, in addition to the conduct of the spoliating party, whether any missing evidence was relevant and whether the innocent party has suffered prejudice as a result of the loss of evidence.

On the question of what is "relevant," the Second Circuit has provided the following guidance:

[O]ur cases make clear that "relevant" in this context means something more than sufficiently probative to satisfy Rule 401 of the Federal Rules of Evidence. Rather, the party seeking an adverse inference must adduce sufficient evidence from which a reasonable trier of fact could infer that "the destroyed or unavailable evidence would have been of the nature alleged by the party affected by its destruction."[39]

---

38. [Court's footnote #26] *Treppel*, 249 F.R.D. at 118 (quoting *Zubulake IV*, 220 F.R.D. at 218).

39. [Court's footnote #29] Residential Funding Corp. v. DeGeorge Fin. Corp., 306 F.3d 99, 108–09 (2d Cir. 2002) (quoting Kronisch, 150 F.3d at 127) (emphasis added).

It is not enough for the innocent party to show that the destroyed evidence would have been responsive to a document request. The innocent party must also show that the evidence would have been helpful in proving its claims or defenses—i.e., that the innocent party is prejudiced without that evidence. Proof of relevance does not necessarily equal proof of prejudice.

In short, the innocent party must prove the following three elements: that the spoliating party (1) had control over the evidence and an obligation to preserve it at the time of destruction or loss; (2) acted with a culpable state of mind upon destroying or losing the evidence; and that (3) the missing evidence is relevant to the innocent party's claim or defense.

Relevance and prejudice may be presumed when the spoliating party acted in bad faith or in a grossly negligent manner. . . . Although many courts in this district presume relevance where there is a finding of gross negligence, application of the presumption is not required. However, when the spoliating party was merely negligent, the innocent party must prove both relevance and prejudice in order to justify the imposition of a severe sanction. . . .

No matter what level of culpability is found, any presumption is rebuttable and the spoliating party should have the opportunity to demonstrate that the innocent party has not been prejudiced by the absence of the missing information. If the spoliating party offers proof that there has been no prejudice, the innocent party, of course, may offer evidence to counter that proof. While requiring the innocent party to demonstrate the relevance of information that it can never review may seem unfair, the party seeking relief has some obligation to make a showing of relevance and eventually prejudice, lest litigation become a "gotcha" game rather than a full and fair opportunity to air the merits of a dispute. If a presumption of relevance and prejudice were awarded to every party who can show that an adversary failed to produce any document, even if such failure is completely inadvertent, the incentive to find such error and capitalize on it would be overwhelming. This would not be a good thing.

To ensure that no party's task is too onerous or too lenient, I am employing the following burden shifting test: When the spoliating party's conduct is sufficiently egregious to justify a court's imposition of a presumption of relevance and prejudice, or when the spoliating party's conduct warrants permitting the jury to make such a presumption, the burden then shifts to the spoliating party to rebut that presumption. The spoliating party can do so, for example, by demonstrating that the innocent party had access to the evidence alleged to have been destroyed or that the evidence would not support the innocent party's claims or defenses. If the spoliating party demonstrates to a court's satisfaction that there could not have been any prejudice to the innocent party, then no jury instruction will be warranted, although a lesser sanction might still be required.

D. Remedies

The remaining question is what remedy should the court impose. . . . Where the breach of a discovery obligation is the non-production of evidence, a court has broad discretion to determine the appropriate sanction. . . .

It is well accepted that a court should always impose the least harsh sanction that can provide an adequate remedy. The choices include—from least harsh to most harsh—further discovery, cost-shifting, fines, special jury instructions, preclusion, and the entry of default judgment or dismissal (terminating sanctions). The selection of the appropriate remedy is a delicate matter requiring a great deal of time and attention by a court.

The Citco Defendants request dismissal—the most extreme sanction. However, a terminating sanction is justified in only the most egregious cases, such as where a party has engaged in perjury, tampering with evidence, or intentionally destroying evidence by burning, shredding, or wiping out computer hard drives. As described below, there is no evidence of such misconduct in this case.

Instead, the appropriate sanction here is some form of an adverse inference instruction that is intended to alleviate the harm suffered by the Citco Defendants. Like many other sanctions, an adverse inference instruction can take many forms, again ranging in degrees of harshness. The harshness of the instruction should be determined based on the nature of the spoliating party's conduct—the more egregious the conduct, the more harsh the instruction.

In its most harsh form, when a spoliating party has acted willfully or in bad faith, a jury can be instructed that certain facts are deemed admitted and must be accepted as true. At the next level, when a spoliating party has acted willfully or recklessly, a court may impose a mandatory presumption. Even a mandatory presumption, however, is considered to be rebuttable.

The least harsh instruction permits (but does not require) a jury to presume that the lost evidence is both relevant and favorable to the innocent party. If it makes this presumption, the spoliating party's rebuttal evidence must then be considered by the jury, which must then decide whether to draw an adverse inference against the spoliating party. This sanction still benefits the innocent party in that it allows the jury to consider both the misconduct of the spoliating party as well as proof of prejudice to the innocent party. Such a charge should be termed a "spoliation charge" to distinguish it from a charge where the jury is directed to presume, albeit still subject to rebuttal, that the missing evidence would have been favorable to the innocent party, and from a charge where the jury is directed to deem certain facts admitted.

Monetary sanctions are also appropriate in this case. . . . Awarding monetary sanctions "serves the remedial purpose of compensating [the movant] for the reasonable costs it incurred in bringing [a motion for sanctions]." This sanction is imposed in order to compensate the Citco Defendants for reviewing the declarations, conducting the additional depositions, and bringing this motion.

Three final notes. First, I stress that at the end of the day the judgment call of whether to award sanctions is inherently subjective. A court has a "gut reaction" based on years of experience as to whether a litigant has complied with its discovery obligations and how hard it worked to comply. Second, while it would be helpful to develop a list of relevant criteria a court should review in evaluating discovery conduct, these inquiries are inherently fact intensive and must be reviewed case by case. Nonetheless, I offer the following guidance.

After a discovery duty is well established, the failure to adhere to contemporary standards can be considered gross negligence. Thus, after the final relevant *Zubulake* opinion in July, 2004, the following failures support a finding of gross negligence, when the duty to preserve has attached: to issue a written litigation hold; to identify all of the key players and to ensure that their electronic and paper records are preserved; to cease the deletion of email or to preserve the records of former employees that are in a party's possession, custody, or control; and to preserve backup tapes when they are the sole source of relevant information or when they relate to key players, if the relevant information maintained by those players is not obtainable from readily accessible sources.

Finally, I note the risk that sanctions motions, which are very, very time consuming, distracting, and expensive for the parties and the court, will be increasingly sought by litigants. This, too, is not a good thing. For this reason alone, the most careful consideration should be given before a court finds that a party has violated its duty to comply with discovery obligations and deserves to be sanctioned. Likewise, parties need to anticipate and undertake document preservation with the most serious and thorough care, if for no other reason than to avoid the detour of sanctions.

. . .

E. Sanctions

The Citco Defendants have demonstrated that most plaintiffs conducted discovery in an ignorant and indifferent fashion. With respect to the grossly negligent plaintiffs—2M, Hunnicutt, Coronation, the Chagnon Plaintiffs, Bombardier Trusts, and the Bombardier Foundation—I will give the following jury charge:

The Citco Defendants have argued that 2M, Hunnicutt, Coronation, the Chagnon Plaintiffs, Bombardier Trusts, and the Bombardier Foundation destroyed relevant evidence, or failed to prevent the destruction of relevant evidence. This is known as the "spoliation of evidence."

Spoliation is the destruction of evidence or the failure to preserve property for another's use as evidence in pending or reasonably foreseeable litigation. To demonstrate that spoliation occurred, the Citco Defendants bear the burden of proving the following two elements by a preponderance of the evidence:

First, that relevant evidence was destroyed after the duty to preserve arose. Evidence is relevant if it would have clarified a fact at issue in the trial and otherwise would naturally have been introduced into evidence; and Second, that if relevant evidence was destroyed after the duty to preserve arose, the loss of such evidence would have been favorable to the Citco Defendants.

I instruct you, as a matter of law, that each of these plaintiffs failed to preserve evidence after its duty to preserve arose. This failure resulted from their gross negligence in performing their discovery obligations. As a result, you may presume, if you so choose, that such lost evidence was relevant, and that it would have been favorable to the Citco Defendants. In deciding whether to adopt this presumption, you may take into account the egregiousness of the plaintiffs' conduct in failing to preserve the evidence.

However, each of these plaintiffs has offered evidence that (1) no evidence was lost; (2) if evidence was lost, it was not relevant; and (3) if evidence was lost and it was relevant, it would not have been favorable to the Citco Defendants.

If you decline to presume that the lost evidence was relevant or would have been favorable to the Citco Defendants, then your consideration of the lost evidence is at an end, and you will not draw any inference arising from the lost evidence.

However, if you decide to presume that the lost evidence was relevant and would have been unfavorable to the Citco Defendants, you must next decide whether any of the following plaintiffs have rebutted that presumption: 2M, Hunnicutt, Coronation, the Chagnon Plaintiffs, Bombardier Trusts, or the Bombardier Foundation. If you determine that a plaintiff has rebutted the presumption that the lost evidence was either relevant or favorable to the Citco Defendants, you will not draw any inference arising from the lost evidence against that plaintiff. If, on the other hand, you determine that a plaintiff has not rebutted the presumption that the lost evidence was both relevant and favorable to the Citco Defendants, you may draw an inference against that plaintiff and in favor of the Citco Defendants—namely that the lost evidence would have been favorable to the Citco Defendants.

Each plaintiff is entitled to your separate consideration. The question as to whether the Citco Defendants have proven spoliation is personal to each plaintiff and must be decided by you as to each plaintiff individually.

In addition, all plaintiffs are subject to monetary sanctions. The Citco Defendants are entitled to an award of reasonable costs, including attorneys' fees, associated with reviewing the declarations submitted, deposing these declarants and their substitutes where applicable, and bringing this motion. The Citco Defendants shall submit a reasonable fee application to this Court for approval. Once approved, the costs are to be allocated among these plaintiffs.

I have also considered whether the Citco Defendants should be entitled to additional discovery. If a lesser sanction is appropriate that is always a better course. With regard to Coronation and Okabena, plaintiffs admit that backup tapes exist and have not been searched. They do not explain why such a search cannot still be conducted. The goal of discovery is to obtain evidence, not to issue sanctions. Thus, Coronation and Okabena are ordered to search their backup tapes for the relevant period at their expense, or demonstrate why such backup tapes cannot be searched, within thirty days.

Further discovery is not necessary for the remaining plaintiffs. Given the number of submitted declarations and numerous depositions that have already occurred in this action, more discovery of the remaining plaintiffs would not be fruitful. At this stage, the costs of conducting further discovery would far outweigh the benefit of any results. Therefore, no further discovery is warranted.

VI. CONCLUSION

For the reasons discussed above, the Citco Defendant's motion for sanctions is granted in part. While litigants are not required to execute document productions with absolute precision, at a minimum they must act diligently and search thoroughly at the time they reasonably anticipate litigation. All of the plaintiffs in this motion failed to do so and have been sanctioned accordingly.

The Clerk of the Court is directed to close this motion (Docket No. 248).

SO ORDERED.

Notes

1. Judge Scheindlin, in a 2013 ruling on the implications of spoliation for an adverse inference, held that the plaintiff (1) had a duty to place a litigation hold on documents that were of likely interest, and (2) an employee of the plaintiff, who made print copies of e-mails of likely import of key persons, including an individual defendant, but then ordered the permanent deletion of the computer file was at the least grossly negligent, if not willfully. The court found there was a clear duty to preserve these relevant documents and prejudice could be presumed. It followed that an adverse inference instruction to the jury that favored the defense could be given. *Sekisui America Corp. v. Hart*, 2013 WL 4116322 (S.D.N.Y. Aug. 15, 2013).

2. Recognizing that lower courts are well equipped to determine appropriate sanctions, appellate courts generally review rulings regarding spoliation sanctions using an abuse of discretion standard of review. *See Helget v. City of Hays*, 844 F.3d 1216 (10th Cir. 2017).

F. International Discovery

1. Obtaining Discovery Outside the United States to Support Litigation in an American Court

> *No aspect of the extension of the American legal system beyond the territorial frontiers of the United States has given rise to so much friction as the request for documents associated with investigation and litigation in the United States.*

Restatement of Foreign Relations Law of the United States (Revised) § 420, Reporters' Note 1 (Tent. Draft No. 3, 1982).

The American litigation system is unique. Our discovery process differs from that of most countries in two ways. First, though it is conducted under the managerial eye of the judge, it is party-driven. That is, the parties decide when and how they will take discovery—whom to depose, what interrogatories to send, what documents and ESI to request, etc. Second, the scope of discovery is very broad. As we have seen, information can be discoverable even though it will not be admitted into evidence at trial. As long as the request is relevant and proportional to the needs of the case (and does not intrude upon privilege or work product protection), it is proper.

Civil law countries, including those of most of continental Europe, approach discovery far differently. First, the process is run by the court. The judge actually engages in gathering the information. Second, depositions are largely unknown. Instead, the judge or someone under the judge's authority makes a resume—essentially a summary—of the witness's statement for use at trial. Third, the scope of discovery is far less intrusive than in American courts.

Suppose a case is pending in an American court. One of the parties, assume the defendant, is a citizen of another country. Assuming that party is subject to the personal jurisdiction of the American court, the defendant can be ordered to submit to discovery. For example, if a Spanish defendant refuses to attend his deposition, he can be sanctioned by the American court.

But what about production of documents and ESI that may be housed in Spain? Or suppose the defendant was a Spanish corporation and the plaintiff wanted to take the deposition of a relevant officer, who is in Spain. Can the American court require the foreign company to produce documents and ESI or to make the officer available for a deposition?

There are two principal methods to attempt discovery abroad for a proceeding in the United States. The first is through the Federal Rules of Civil Procedure and their counterparts at the state level. These court rules, however, have their limitations abroad, and sometimes can put parties in difficult positions. Some nations, through "blocking statutes," forbid their citizens from participating in the broad discovery process of the United States. Thus, a party may be forced to choose between violating the law of one nation or of the other.

The second method for discovery abroad uses procedures outlined under the Hague Convention on the Taking of Evidence Abroad in Civil or Commercial Matters. (This is not to be confused with various other Hague Conventions, one of which deals with service of process in foreign countries.) Not all countries are party to the Hague Evidence Convention. The United States, Australia, and most of the countries of western Europe are signatories.

The Hague Evidence Convention establishes three procedures that may be used in a court proceeding in a signatory country as an aid to retrieving evidence found in a foreign territory. First is the letter of request, traditionally called a "letter rogatory." It is correspondence sent by the American court to the appropriate official (usually a court) in the relevant foreign country. It asks the foreign official to permit discovery in the foreign country. Letters of request, even when they are effective, are notoriously slow; it is not uncommon to wait a year to get a response. If the foreign tribunal honors the letter, it will issue compulsory process for production of material. Some countries do not issue compulsory process to summon a witness to give a deposition, however, even in response to a letter of request.

Second is the use of a diplomat or consular agent to obtain the requested evidence. Here, a party may ask a consular officer or other person authorized to administer oaths to order discovery. This avenue rarely permits the use of compulsory process—meaning that if the foreign party refuses to give discovery, it likely will not be ordered.

The third method is the appointment of a commissioner, who need not be a public official, to take evidence. This route requires the consent of the appropriate foreign authority, however, so is rarely useful.

In *Societe Nationale Industrielle Aerospatiale v. U.S. District Court*, 482 U.S. 522 (1987), plaintiffs sued two French corporations responsible for the manufacture and marketing of an airplane. Plaintiffs were injured in a crash of such a plane in Iowa. They sued the French companies in federal court in Iowa, invoking alienage jurisdiction. The plaintiffs served requests to produce on the defendants under Federal Rule 34. The defendants argued that the plaintiffs were required to seek discovery through a letter of request under the Hague Convention. (No doubt, they realized that such a route, if effective at all, would take a great deal of time.)

The Supreme Court rejected the argument. The Hague Convention is not mandatory, and the plaintiffs were not required to try to use it first. The Federal Rules and the Hague Convention are alternatives, and the party seeking discovery may proceed with discovery under the Federal Rules if he desires. On the other hand, the Court recognized the need to protect foreign litigants from undue burden in discovery. So, it established a balancing test, based upon "scrutiny in each case of the [1] particular facts, [2] sovereign interests, and [3] likelihood that resort to those procedures will prove effective." The burden is on the foreign litigant to demonstrate that the balance requires application of the Hague Convention rather than the

Federal Rules. This approach allows the court to consider the intrusiveness of the particular discovery sought and the interests of the other country.

In the next case, foreign litigants contend that *Societe Nationale Aerospatiale* should not apply when the discovery sought concerned whether they were subject to personal jurisdiction in the American court.

In re Automotive Refinishing Paint Antitrust Litigation

United States Court of Appeals, Third Circuit
358 F.3d 288 (2004)

Rosenn, Circuit Judge.

This certified interlocutory appeal, arising out of alleged unlawful price-fixing by both domestic and foreign corporations, raises questions of considerable importance in antitrust litigation involving foreign nationals. Three of the issues are of first impression to this Court. [The first two issues do not concern us.] The final issue is whether jurisdictional discovery from foreign nationals may proceed under the Federal Rules of Civil Procedure without first resorting to the Hague Convention on the Taking of Evidence Abroad in Civil or Commercial Matters (Hague Convention or Convention).

The District Court . . . rejected a rule favoring first resort to Hague Convention procedures for jurisdictional discovery of foreign defendants. BASF AG and BASF Coatings timely appealed. We affirm.

I

The underlying federal antitrust class litigation involves sixty-three actions filed in five states, Pennsylvania, New Jersey, Ohio, Kentucky, and Delaware, by private parties. Those actions were transferred to, and consolidated in, the United States District Court for the Eastern District of Pennsylvania for pre-trial purposes by the Judicial Panel on Multidistrict Litigation. The class action complaint alleges that from 1993 to at least December 31, 2000, the foreign and domestic defendants conspired to raise and maintain the prices of automotive refinish paint throughout the United States. All defendants, except the appellants, have stipulated to certification of a national class consisting of all direct purchasers of automotive refinishes from the defendants.

The appellants filed motions to dismiss pursuant to Federal Rule of Civil Procedure 12(b)(2) for lack of personal jurisdiction. In support of their motions to dismiss, the appellants submitted affidavits stating that they did not have presence in the state of Pennsylvania and never sold any automotive refinish paint to any customers in Pennsylvania. . . .

The plaintiffs submitted publicly available information to show a threshold case of personal jurisdiction based on the appellants' contacts with the United States and support their request for jurisdictional discovery. In response to the plaintiffs' request for jurisdictional discovery, the appellants filed a joint motion for a protective order, contending that the plaintiffs' discovery request was overly broad and burdensome. They argued also that any jurisdictional discovery should proceed first under the Hague Convention, of which the United States and Germany are signatories.

The reasons proffered by the appellants' expert, Martin Reufels, were that Germany, unlike the United States, viewed the gathering of evidence as a judicial, rather than private, function. Therefore, Germany had a sovereign interest in keeping discovery conducted within its borders in conformity with its laws. According to Reufels, compelling the appellants to produce documents pursuant to the Federal Rules of Civil Procedures would offend Germany's sovereign interests. . . .

. . .

III

. . . The appellants argue that jurisdictional discovery in Germany, a Convention signatory nation, should first proceed under the Convention procedures, rather than the Federal Rules. The Convention prescribes certain procedures by which a judicial authority in one contracting nation may request evidence located in another nation. Our Supreme Court rejected a first resort rule in favor of the Convention in a case where personal jurisdiction was not contested and the discovery sought involved only the merits of the case. Societe Nationale Industrielle Aerospatiale v. United States Dist. Court for the S. Dist. of Iowa, [482 U.S. 522] (1987). The appellants argue specifically that we should carve out a narrow exception to the *Aerospatiale* decision where, as here, personal jurisdiction has yet to be established and the discovery sought is limited to proof of jurisdiction.

A

Aerospatiale holds that the Hague Convention does not provide exclusive procedures for obtaining documents and information located in a foreign signatory nation's territory. . . . *Aerospatiale* holds that the Convention's plain language, as well as the history of its proposal and ratification by the United States, unambiguously supports the conclusion that it was "intended as a *permissive supplement*, not a preemptive replacement, for other means of obtaining evidence located abroad." . . . Accordingly, the Convention does not deprive the District Court of its jurisdiction to order, under the Federal Rules of Civil Procedure, a foreign national party to the proceeding to produce evidence physically located within its territory.

Aerospatiale rejects next a rule of first resort favoring the Convention on grounds of international comity and respect for the "judicial sovereignty" of the signatory nation in which evidence sought is located. International comity does not require in all instances that American litigants first resort to the Convention procedures before initiating discovery pursuant to our Federal Rules. The concept of comity requires in this context "a more particularized analysis" of the respective interests of the foreign host nation and the requesting nation than a blanket first resort rule would generate. *Aerospatiale* notes that in many situations, the Convention procedures would be unduly time-consuming and expensive, and less likely to produce needed evidence than direct use of the Federal Rules. . . .

Notwithstanding its rejection of the first resort rule, *Aerospatiale* instructs the American courts to "exercise special vigilance to protect foreign litigants from the danger that unnecessary, or unduly burdensome, discovery may place them in a disadvantageous position." . . . "Judicial supervision of discovery should always seek to minimize its costs and inconvenience and to prevent improper uses of discovery requests. When it is necessary to seek evidence abroad, however, the district court must supervise pretrial proceedings particularly closely to prevent discovery abuses." *Id.*

. . .

B

The appellants argue that the District Court erred in extending the *Aerospatiale* holding to the underlying litigation where they have contested jurisdiction and the discovery sought is limited to proof of jurisdiction. The appellants seek our review of only the District Court's legal conclusion that the *Aerospatiale* holding applies equally to jurisdictional discovery. This certified issue involves a pure question of law, subject to our plenary and *de novo* review.

Specifically, the appellants argue that *Aerospatiale* is not applicable to jurisdictional discovery and that this Court should adopt a first resort rule in favor of the Hague Convention procedures based on considerations of international comity and respect for the German sovereignty, the host signatory nation where discovery is to be conducted. They argue that the *Aerospatiale* balancing approach is premised expressly on the existence of personal jurisdiction in that case. Where jurisdiction is disputed and not yet established, they assert the balancing approach must yield to a rule of first resort.

The appellants stress the split of authorities among federal district courts and state courts regarding the extension of *Aerospatiale* to jurisdictional discovery. . . .

. . .

The appellants are correct that *Aerospatiale* makes numerous references to the existence of personal jurisdiction in that case. We disagree, however, that the *Aerospatiale* holding is dependent on personal jurisdiction. . . .

The appellants also relied on the Federal Rules to challenge the District Court's personal jurisdiction. As we have stated above, it is well established that the trial court has inherent power and jurisdiction to decide whether it has jurisdiction. *Ins. Corp. of Ireland*, [456 U.S. at 706]. The appellants' arguments are also premised on the assumption that there is no personal jurisdiction in this case. Such an assumption is premature and unwarranted unless the result of the pending jurisdictional discovery shows otherwise. At this stage, where the appellants have voluntarily appeared in the court to challenge jurisdiction and jurisdictional discovery is pending, the District Court indisputably has jurisdiction to determine whether there is personal jurisdiction upon completion of jurisdictional discovery. Moreover, the denial of resort to Hague convention procedures for jurisdictional discovery is not unfair to the appellants because they "[had] taken advantage of the [Federal] [R]ule allowing them a preliminary hearing and determination of the issues raised in their motion."

Accordingly, the distinction drawn by the appellants between "merits" discovery and "jurisdictional" discovery, predicated on a false dichotomy of having and not having jurisdiction, amounts to no real difference because the court has jurisdiction for either type of discovery. The undisputed presence of personal jurisdiction in *Aerospatiale* is, therefore, tangential to its holding and irrelevant to the issue of whether *Aerospatiale* applies also to jurisdictional discovery.

There are other reasons supporting our conclusion that the *Aerospatiale* balancing approach applies equally to the determination of whether the Hague Convention procedures should be used initially for jurisdictional discovery. First, where *Aerospatiale* has categorically rejected a first resort rule for "merits" discovery, which we can expect to be more comprehensive or burdensome than jurisdictional discovery, there is more justification to reject a first resort rule for the more limited and less intrusive jurisdictional discovery. . . .

Second, where *Aerospatiale* has rejected the first resort rule even though the French defendants there may have faced possible penal sanction under France's "blocking statute," there is less justification for us to adopt a first resort rule where the appellants here face no such sanction because Germany has no "blocking statute." . . .

Third, where *Aerospatiale* has rejected the adoption of a blanket first resort rule based on the proffered reasons of respecting the "judicial sovereignty" of the signatory host nation and preventing discovery abuse, the same reasons proffered by the appellants here must fail as well. . . .

The appellants and their supporters argue generally that Germany is a civil law country where the gathering of evidence is a judicial function and that pursuing discovery without resort to the Convention may be deemed an affront to Germany's sovereignty. The *Aerospatiale* Court, as well as other courts, has found such argument "unpersuasive." . . . [T]here is no reason to assume that discovery under the Federal Rules would inevitably offend Germany's sovereign interest because presumably Germany, like the United States, would prohibit the alleged price-fixing conspiracy and would welcome investigation of such antitrust violation to the fullest extent. . . .

Similarly, following the *Aerospatiale* holding, we also find unpersuasive the appellants' argument that a first resort to the Hague Convention is required to avoid possible burdensome or intrusive discovery practice under United States law. *Aerospatiale*, [482 U.S. at 545–46]. Discovery abuse is an insufficient reason to avoid the Federal Rules because the appellants have remedies in the District Court to restrict discovery abuse. We expect that the District Court will follow *Aerospatiale's* instruction and "exercise special vigilance" to protect appellants from unduly burdensome or abusive discovery.

We agree with the District Court's legal conclusion that the *Aerospatiale* balancing test applies equally to jurisdictional discovery and that there is no first resort rule in favor of the Hague Convention procedures for jurisdictional discovery.

C

The appellants also argue alternatively that even if the *Aerospatiale* balancing approach applies to jurisdictional discovery, the three-prong test would favor first use of the Convention procedures in this case. The District Court rejected that argument, ruling that the appellants bore the burden of persuasion under the balancing test and that they failed to satisfy the burden. The court concluded alternatively that even if the plaintiffs bore the burden of persuasion, they had submitted adequate evidence to show that the balancing test disfavored first use of the Convention procedures for jurisdictional discovery in this case.

We agree first with the District Court's conclusion of law that the appellants bear the burden of persuasion as to the optional use of the Convention procedures. . . .

We also agree with the District Court's conclusions that the appellants have failed to satisfy their burden of persuasion under the *Aerospatiale* balancing test and that the evidence on record disfavors the first use of the Convention procedures for jurisdictional discovery. The court's conclusions in these two instances are reviewed only for abuse of discretion, and we find none.

Notes and Questions

1. How did the court distinguish between "jurisdictional" discovery and "merits" discovery?

2. In what circumstances might an American court require an American plaintiff to use a Hague Convention method of discovery rather than the Federal Rules?

2. Domestic Discovery in Aid of Foreign Proceedings

Here, we consider the converse of what we just studied: can American courts be used to get discovery to support litigation in another country? Section 1782 of the Judicial Code governs the involvement of federal courts in international discovery. In relevant part, § 1782 provides:

> The district court of the district in which a person resides or is found may order him to give his testimony or statement or to produce a document or other thing for use in a proceeding in a foreign or international tribunal. The order may be made pursuant to a letter rogatory issued, or request made, by a foreign or international tribunal or upon the application of any interested person and may direct that the testimony or statement be given,

> or the document or other thing be produced, before a person appointed by the court.

The Supreme Court has interpreted § 1782 broadly. In *Intel Corp. v. Advanced Micro Devices, Inc.*, 542 U.S. 241 (2004), one American company (AMD) complained to the appropriate administrator in the European Union (EU) that another American company (Intel) was violating EU antitrust law. AMD did not sue Intel, but hoped that the EU would proceed against Intel. To support the potential case by the EU against Intel, AMD brought a § 1782 proceeding in federal court where Intel is headquartered, asking that court to order Intel to produce discovery from an antitrust case against Intel in another federal court.

Despite the fact that the EU had not filed suit against Intel and that AMD was not asserting a claim against Intel, the Supreme Court held that § 1782 authorized (but did not require) the district court to order Intel to produce the materials. AMD was an "interested person" under the statute, and the EU antitrust enforcement mechanism constituted a "foreign or international tribunal" because its decision could be reviewed. The Court remanded to allow the district judge to weigh the relevant factors to determine whether to grant the discovery request.

The Court also rejected the argument that an American court cannot require production of materials that would not be discoverable in the foreign country. It found no support in § 1782 for such a "foreign discoverability" rule.

Without doubt, *Intel* has led to an increase in the amount of "§ 1782 litigation" in the federal courts. This increase has led, in turn, to more appellate pronouncements regarding the statute. An emerging trend recognizes that evidence produced in a § 1782 proceeding may be used not only in the foreign litigation *but in domestic litigation as well.* The Eleventh Circuit has been a leading voice in this regard. In *Glock v. Glock, Inc.*, 797 F.3d 1002 (11th Cir. 2015), it explained:

> Though it is clear from the statutory language that the law does not also establish a method for procuring discovery for use in a domestic proceeding, we find nothing in the language of § 1782 that purports to limit later uses of evidence that have been properly obtained under § 1782 . . .
>
> Instead, the statute is entirely silent on the issue of whether material procured under § 1782 may be used after it is lawfully obtained and used for the purpose for which it was obtained. This is not surprising because, throughout the history of the law, Congress was not focused on addressing what, if anything, could be done with documents that were previously lawfully obtained under the statute. Rather, "Section 1782 is the product of congressional efforts, over the span of nearly 150 years, to provide federal-court assistance in gathering evidence for use in foreign tribunals." *Intel Corp. v. Advanced Micro Devices, Inc.*, 542 U.S. 241, 247 (2004). . . .
>
> As the Federal Rules of Civil Procedure suggest, goals of our system of civil litigation include "securing the just, speedy, and inexpensive determination" of the proceeding. Fed. R. Civ. P. 1. Allowing parties to use, for

> purposes of litigation, documents they have lawfully obtained, regardless of whether they could have obtained them through discovery in the case in which they use them, furthers these goals. We see no reason why a different rule should apply to the use, in United States litigation, of documents that were previously lawfully obtained under § 1782. . . .
>
> [W]e find that § 1782 does not preclude, as a matter of law, the use of evidence procured pursuant to it in subsequent United States civil litigation.

The Second Circuit has reached the same conclusion. *In re Accent Delight International Ltd.*, 869 F.3d 121 (2d Cir. 2017).

Chapter 9

Streamlining Complex Cases

A. Introduction

A distinguishing characteristic of complex cases is the immense cost and burden that typically attend discovery and preparation for trial. Complex cases also pose daunting difficulties in organizing, presenting, and managing the trial itself, as well as the risk of a potentially devastating "all or nothing" verdict. These dynamics create considerable pressure to resolve complex cases short of trial. This Chapter explores some of the streamlining methods.

B. Dismissal on the Pleadings

1. Heightened Pleading Standards in Complex Cases

It used to be that a central feature of the Federal Rules of Civil Procedure was their adoption of a liberal system of "notice pleading," under which a complaint was sufficient if it gave the defendant general notice of the nature of plaintiff's claim and the grounds on which it rested. *See* Fed. R. Civ. P. 8(a)(2).

In *Swierkiewicz v. Sorema N.A.*, 534 U.S. 506, 512–15 (2002), the Supreme Court stated:

> [I]mposing the Court of Appeals' heightened pleading standard in employment discrimination cases conflicts with Federal Rule of Civil Procedure 8(a)(2), which provides that a complaint must include only "a short and plain statement of the claim showing that the pleader is entitled to relief." Such a statement must simply "give the defendant fair notice of what the plaintiff's claim is and the grounds upon which it rests." *Conley v. Gibson*, 355 U.S. 41, 47 (1957). This simplified notice pleading standard relies on liberal discovery rules and summary judgment motions to define disputed facts and issues and to dispose of unmeritorious claims. *See Leatherman v. Tarrant County Narcotics Intelligence and Coordination Unit*, 507 U.S. 163, 168–169 (1993). . . .
>
> Rule 8(a)'s simplified pleading standard applies to all civil actions, with limited exceptions. Rule 9(b), for example, provides for greater particularity in all averments of fraud or mistake. This Court, however, has declined to extend such exceptions to other contexts. In *Leatherman* we stated: "[T]he Federal Rules do address in Rule 9(b) the question of the need for

greater particularity in pleading certain actions, but do not include among the enumerated actions any reference to complaints alleging municipal liability under § 1983. *Expressio unius est exclusio alterius*." Just as Rule 9(b) makes no mention of municipal liability, neither does it refer to employment discrimination. Thus, complaints in these cases, as in most others, must satisfy only the simple requirements of Rule 8(a).[1]

. . . The liberal notice pleading of Rule 8(a) is the starting point of a simplified pleading system, which was adopted to focus litigation on the merits of a claim. *See Conley, supra*, at 48 ("The Federal Rules reject the approach that pleading is a game of skill in which one misstep by counsel may be decisive to the outcome and accept the principle that the purpose of pleading is to facilitate a proper decision on the merits").

. . . .

Respondent argues that allowing lawsuits based on conclusory allegations of discrimination to go forward will burden the courts and encourage disgruntled employees to bring unsubstantiated suits. Whatever the practical merits of this argument, the Federal Rules do not contain a heightened pleading standard for employment discrimination suits. A requirement of greater specificity for particular claims is a result that "must be obtained by the process of amending the Federal Rules, and not by judicial interpretation." *Leatherman, supra*, at 168. . . .

But then came *Twombly.*

Bell Atlantic Corp. v. Twombly

Supreme Court of the United States
550 U.S. 544 (2007)

JUSTICE SOUTER delivered the opinion of the Court.

Liability under § 1 of the Sherman Act, 15 U.S.C. § 1, requires a "contract, combination . . . , or conspiracy, in restraint of trade or commerce." The question in this putative class action is whether a § 1 complaint can survive a motion to dismiss when it alleges that major telecommunications providers engaged in certain parallel conduct unfavorable to competition, absent some factual context suggesting agreement, as distinct from identical, independent action. We hold that such a complaint should be dismissed.

---

1. [Court's footnote #4] These requirements are exemplified by the Federal Rules of Civil Procedure Forms, which "are sufficient under the rules and are intended to indicate the simplicity and brevity of statement which the rules contemplate." Fed. Rule Civ. Proc. 84. For example, Form 9 sets forth a complaint for negligence in which plaintiff simply states in relevant part: "On June 1, 1936, in a public highway called Boylston Street in Boston, Massachusetts, defendant negligently drove a motor vehicle against plaintiff who was then crossing said highway."

I

The upshot of the 1984 divestiture of the American Telephone & Telegraph Company's (AT & T) local telephone business was a system of regional service monopolies (variously called "Regional Bell Operating Companies," "Baby Bells," or "Incumbent Local Exchange Carriers" (ILECs)), and a separate, competitive market for long-distance service from which the ILECs were excluded. More than a decade later, Congress withdrew approval of the ILECs' monopolies by enacting the Telecommunications Act of 1996 (1996 Act), 110 Stat. 56, which "fundamentally restructure[d] local telephone markets" and "subject[ed] [ILECs] to a host of duties intended to facilitate market entry." *AT&T Corp. v. Iowa Utilities Bd.*, 525 U.S. 366, 371 (1999). In recompense, the 1996 Act set conditions for authorizing ILECs to enter the long-distance market....

"Central to the [new] scheme [was each ILEC's] obligation ... to share its network with competitors," *Verizon Communications Inc. v. Law Offices of Curtis V. Trinko, LLP*, 549 U.S. 398, 402 (2004), which came to be known as "competitive local exchange carriers" (CLECs). A CLEC could make use of an ILEC's network in any of three ways: by (1) "purchas[ing] local telephone services at wholesale rates for resale to end users," (2) "leas[ing] elements of the [ILEC's] network 'on an unbundled basis,'" or (3) "interconnect[ing] its own facilities with the [ILEC's] network." Owing to the "considerable expense and effort" required to make unbundled network elements available to rivals at wholesale prices, *Trinko, supra*, at 410, the ILECs vigorously litigated the scope of the sharing obligation imposed by the 1996 Act, with the result that the Federal Communications Commission (FCC) three times revised its regulations to narrow the range of network elements to be shared with the CLECs....

Respondents William Twombly and Lawrence Marcus (hereinafter plaintiffs) represent a putative class consisting of all "subscribers of local telephone and/or high speed internet services ... from February 8, 1996 to present." In this action against petitioners, a group of ILECs, plaintiffs seek treble damages and declaratory and injunctive relief for claimed violations of § 1 of the Sherman Act, which prohibits "[e]very contract, combination in the form of trust or otherwise, or conspiracy, in restraint of trade or commerce among the several States, or with foreign nations."

The complaint alleges that the ILECs conspired to restrain trade in two ways, each supposedly inflating charges for local telephone and high-speed Internet services. Plaintiffs say, first, that the ILECs "engaged in parallel conduct" in their respective service areas to inhibit the growth of upstart CLECs. Their actions allegedly included making unfair agreements with the CLECs for access to ILEC networks, providing inferior connections to the networks, overcharging, and billing in ways designed to sabotage the CLECs' relations with their own customers....

Second, the complaint charges agreements by the ILECs to refrain from competing against one another. These are to be inferred from the ILECs' common failure "meaningfully [to] pursu[e]" "attractive business opportunit[ies]" in contiguous markets where they possessed "substantial competitive advantages," and from a statement of Richard Notebaert, chief executive officer (CEO) of the ILEC Qwest, that competing in the territory of another ILEC "'might be a good way to turn a quick dollar but that doesn't make it right.'"

The complaint couches its ultimate allegations this way:

> "In the absence of any meaningful competition between the [ILECs] in one another's markets, and in light of the parallel course of conduct that each engaged in to prevent competition from CLECs within their respective local telephone and/or high speed internet services markets and the other facts and market circumstances alleged above, Plaintiffs allege upon information and belief that [the ILECs] have entered into a contract, combination or conspiracy to prevent competitive entry in their respective local telephone and/or high speed internet services markets and have agreed not to compete with one another and otherwise allocated customers and markets to one another."

The United States District Court for the Southern District of New York dismissed the complaint for failure to state a claim upon which relief can be granted. . . . The Court of Appeals for the Second Circuit reversed . . . .

We granted certiorari to address the proper standard for pleading an antitrust conspiracy through allegations of parallel conduct, and now reverse.

II

A

Because § 1 of the Sherman Act "does not prohibit [all] unreasonable restraints of trade . . . but only restraints effected by a contract, combination, or conspiracy," *Copperweld Corp. v. Independence Tube Corp.*, 467 U.S. 752, 775 (1984), "[t]he crucial question" is whether the challenged anticompetitive conduct "stem[s] from independent decision or from an agreement, tacit or express," *Theatre Enterprises*[, *Inc. v. Paramount Film Distributing Corp.*, 346 U.S. 537, 540 (1954)]. While a showing of parallel "business behavior is admissible circumstantial evidence from which the fact finder may infer agreement," it falls short of "conclusively establish[ing] agreement or . . . itself constitut[ing] a Sherman Act offense." Even "conscious parallelism," a common reaction of "firms in a concentrated market [that] recogniz[e] their shared economic interests and their interdependence with respect to price and output decisions" is "not in itself unlawful." *Brooke Group Ltd. v. Brown & Williamson Tobacco Corp.*, 509 U.S. 209, 227 (1993). . . .

. . . .

B

This case presents the antecedent question of what a plaintiff must plead in order to state a claim under § 1 of the Sherman Act. Federal Rule of Civil Procedure 8(a)(2) requires only "a short and plain statement of the claim showing that the pleader is entitled to relief," in order to "give the defendant fair notice of what the . . . claim is and the grounds upon which it rests," *Conley v. Gibson*, 355 U.S. 41, 47 (1957). While a complaint attacked by a Rule 12(b)(6) motion to dismiss does not need detailed factual allegations, a plaintiff's obligation to provide the "grounds" of his "entitle[ment] to relief" requires more than labels and conclusions, and a formulaic recitation of the elements of a cause of action will not do, see *Papasan v. Allain*, 478 U.S. 265, 286 (1986) (on a motion to dismiss, courts "are not bound to accept as true a legal conclusion couched as a factual allegation"). Factual allegations must be enough to raise a right to relief above the speculative level, see 5 C. Wright & A. Miller, Federal Practice and Procedure § 1216, pp. 235–236 (3d ed. 2004) (herein after Wright & Miller) ("[T]he pleading must contain something more . . . than . . . a statement of facts that merely creates a suspicion [of] a legally cognizable right of action"),[2] on the assumption that all the allegations in the complaint are true (even if doubtful in fact). . . .

In applying these general standards to a § 1 claim, we hold that stating such a claim requires a complaint with enough factual matter (taken as true) to suggest that an agreement was made. Asking for plausible grounds to infer an agreement does not impose a probability requirement at the pleading stage; it simply calls for enough fact to raise a reasonable expectation that discovery will reveal evidence of illegal agreement. . . . Hence, when allegations of parallel conduct are set out in order to make a § 1 claim, they must be placed in a context that raises a suggestion of a preceding agreement, not merely parallel conduct that could just as well be independent action.

The need at the pleading stage for allegations plausibly suggesting (not merely consistent with) agreement reflects the threshold requirement of Rule 8(a)(2) that the "plain statement" possess enough heft to "sho[w] that the pleader is entitled to relief." A statement of parallel conduct, even conduct consciously undertaken, needs some setting suggesting the agreement necessary to make out a § 1 claim; without that further circumstance pointing toward a meeting of the minds, an account of a defendant's commercial efforts stays in neutral territory. An allegation of parallel conduct is thus much like a naked assertion of conspiracy in a § 1 complaint: it gets the complaint close to stating a claim, but without some further factual enhancement it stops short of the line between possibility and plausibility of "entitle[ment] to relief."

. . . .

---

2. [Court's footnote #3] The dissent greatly oversimplifies matters by suggesting that the Federal Rules somehow dispensed with the pleading of facts altogether. . . . While, for most types of cases, the Federal Rules eliminated the cumbersome requirement that a claimant "set out *in detail* the facts upon which he bases his claim," *Conley v. Gibson*, 355 U.S. 41, 47 (1957) (emphasis added), Rule 8(a)(2) still requires a "showing," rather than a blanket assertion, of entitlement to relief. Without some factual allegation in the complaint, it is hard to see how a claimant could satisfy the requirement of providing not only "fair notice" of the nature of the claim, but also "grounds" on which the claim rests. . . .

. . . [I]t is one thing to be cautious before dismissing an antitrust complaint in advance of discovery . . . but quite another to forget that proceeding to antitrust discovery can be expensive. As we indicated over 20 years ago in *Associated Gen. Contractors of Cal., Inc. v. Carpenters*, 459 U.S. 519, 528, n. 17 (1983), "a district court must retain the power to insist upon some specificity in pleading before allowing a potentially massive factual controversy to proceed." . . .

. . . [Plaintiffs'] main argument against the plausibility standard at the pleading stage is its ostensible conflict with an early statement of ours construing Rule 8. Justice Black's opinion for the Court in *Conley v. Gibson* spoke not only of the need for fair notice of the grounds for entitlement to relief but of "the accepted rule that a complaint should not be dismissed for failure to state a claim unless it appears beyond doubt that the plaintiff can prove no set of facts in support of his claim which would entitle him to relief. . . ."

The phrase is best forgotten as an incomplete, negative gloss on an accepted pleading standard: once a claim has been stated adequately, it may be supported by showing any set of facts consistent with the allegations in the complaint. . . . *Conley* then, described the breadth of opportunity to prove what an adequate complaint claims, not the minimum standard of adequate pleading to govern a complaint's survival.

III

When we look for plausibility in this complaint, we agree with the District Court that plaintiffs' claim of conspiracy in restraint of trade comes up short. To begin with, the complaint leaves no doubt that plaintiffs rest their § 1 claim on descriptions of parallel conduct and not on any independent allegation of actual agreement among the ILECs.

The complaint makes its closest pass at a predicate for conspiracy with the claim that collusion was necessary because success by even one CLEC in an ILEC's territory "would have revealed the degree to which competitive entry by CLECs would have been successful in the other territories." But, its logic aside, this general premise still fails to answer the point that there was just no need for joint encouragement to resist the 1996 Act; as the District Court said, "each ILEC has reason to want to avoid dealing with CLECs" and "each ILEC would attempt to keep CLECs out, regardless of the actions of the other ILECs. . . ."

Plaintiffs' second conspiracy theory rests on the competitive reticence among the ILECs themselves in the wake of the 1996 Act, which was supposedly passed in the "'hop[e] that the large incumbent local monopoly companies . . . might attack their neighbors' service areas, as they are the best situated to do so.'" Contrary to hope, the ILECs declined "'to enter each other's service territories in any significant way,'" and the local telephone and high speed Internet market remains highly compartmentalized geographically, with minimal competition. Based on this state of affairs, and perceiving the ILECs to be blessed with "especially attractive business opportunities" in surrounding markets dominated by other ILECs, the plaintiffs assert that the ILECs' parallel conduct was "strongly suggestive of conspiracy."

But it was not suggestive of conspiracy, not if history teaches anything. In a traditionally unregulated industry with low barriers to entry, sparse competition among large firms dominating separate geographical segments of the market could very well signify illegal agreement, but here we have an obvious alternative explanation. In the decade preceding the 1996 Act and well before that, monopoly was the norm in telecommunications, not the exception. . . . The ILECs were born in that world, doubtless liked the world the way it was, and surely knew the adage about him who lives by the sword. Hence, a natural explanation for the noncompetition alleged is that the former Government-sanctioned monopolists were sitting tight, expecting their neighbors to do the same thing.

. . . We agree with the District Court's assessment that antitrust conspiracy was not suggested by the facts adduced under either theory of the complaint, which thus fails to state a valid § 1 claim.[3]

Plaintiffs say that our analysis runs counter to *Swierkiewicz v. Sorema N.A.*, 534 U.S. 506, 508 (2002), which held that "a complaint in an employment discrimination lawsuit [need] not contain specific facts establishing a prima facie case of discrimination under the framework set forth in *McDonnell Douglas Corp. v. Green*, 411 U.S. 792 (1973). . . ." As the District Court correctly understood, however, "*Swierkiewicz* did not change the law of pleading, but simply re-emphasized . . . that the Second Circuit's use of a heightened pleading standard for Title VII cases was contrary to the Federal Rules' structure of liberal pleading requirements. . . ." Even though Swierkiewicz's pleadings "detailed the events leading to his termination, provided relevant dates, and included the ages and nationalities of at least some of the relevant persons involved with his termination," the Court of Appeals dismissed his complaint for failing to allege certain additional facts that Swierkiewicz would need at the trial stage to support his claim in the absence of direct evidence of discrimination. . . . We reversed on the ground that the Court of Appeals had impermissibly applied what amounted to a heightened pleading requirement by insisting that Swierkiewicz allege "specific facts" beyond those necessary to state his claim and the grounds showing entitlement to relief.

Here, in contrast, we do not require heightened fact pleading of specifics, but only enough facts to state a claim to relief that is plausible on its face. Because the plaintiffs here have not nudged their claims across the line from conceivable to plausible, their complaint must be dismissed.

---

3. [Court's footnote #14] In reaching this conclusion, we do not apply any "heightened" pleading standard, nor do we seek to broaden the scope of Federal Rule of Civil Procedure 9, which can only be accomplished "'by the process of amending the Federal Rules, and not by judicial interpretation.'" *Swierkiewicz v. Sorema N. A.*, 534 U.S. 506, 515 (2002) (quoting *Leatherman v. Tarrant County Narcotics Intelligence and Coordination Unit*, 507 U.S. 163, 168 (1993)). On certain subjects understood to raise a high risk of abusive litigation, a plaintiff must state factual allegations with greater particularity than Rule 8 requires. Fed. Rules Civ. Proc. 9(b)–(c). Here, our concern is not that the allegations in the complaint were insufficiently "particular[ized]"; rather, the complaint warranted dismissal because it failed *in toto* to render plaintiffs' entitlement to relief plausible.

. . . .

Justice Stevens, with whom Justice Ginsburg joins except as to Part IV, dissenting.

. . . .

[T]his is a case in which there is no dispute about the substantive law. If the defendants acted independently, their conduct was perfectly lawful. If, however, that conduct is the product of a horizontal agreement among potential competitors, it was unlawful. Plaintiffs have alleged such an agreement and, because the complaint was dismissed in advance of answer, the allegation has not even been denied. Why, then, does the case not proceed? Does a judicial opinion that the charge is not "plausible" provide a legally acceptable reason for dismissing the complaint? I think not.

Respondents' amended complaint describes a variety of circumstantial evidence and makes the straightforward allegation that petitioners

> "entered into a contract, combination or conspiracy to prevent competitive entry in their respective local telephone and/or high speed internet services markets and have agreed not to compete with one another and otherwise allocated customers and markets to one another." Amended Complaint ¶ 51.

The complaint explains that, contrary to Congress' expectation when it enacted the 1996 Telecommunications Act, and consistent with their own economic self-interests, petitioner Incumbent Local Exchange Carriers (ILECs) have assiduously avoided infringing upon each other's markets and have refused to permit nonincumbent competitors to access their networks. The complaint quotes Richard Notebaert, the former CEO of one such ILEC, as saying that competing in a neighboring ILEC's territory "might be a good way to turn a quick dollar but that doesn't make it right." Moreover, respondents allege that petitioners "communicate amongst themselves" through numerous industry associations. In sum, respondents allege that petitioners entered into an agreement that has long been recognized as a classic *per se* violation of the Sherman Act. . . .

Under rules of procedure that have been well settled since well before our decision in *Theatre Enterprises*, a judge ruling on a defendant's motion to dismiss a complaint, "must accept as true all of the factual allegations contained in the complaint." *Swierkiewicz v. Sorema N.A.*, 534 U.S. 506, 508, n. 1 (2002). . . . But instead of requiring knowledgeable executives such as Notebaert to respond to these allegations by way of sworn depositions or other limited discovery—and indeed without so much as requiring petitioners to file an answer denying that they entered into any agreement—the majority permits immediate dismissal based on the assurances of company lawyers that nothing untoward was afoot. . . .

. . . .

Two practical concerns presumably explain the Court's dramatic departure from settled procedural law. Private antitrust litigation can be enormously expensive, and there is a risk that jurors may mistakenly conclude that evidence of parallel conduct has proved that the parties acted pursuant to an agreement when they in fact merely made similar independent decisions. Those concerns merit careful case management, including strict control of discovery, careful scrutiny of evidence at the summary judgment stage, and lucid instructions to juries; they do not, however, justify the dismissal of an adequately pleaded complaint without even requiring the defendants to file answers denying a charge that they in fact engaged in collective decisionmaking. More importantly, they do not justify an interpretation of Federal Rule of Civil Procedure 12(b)(6) that seems to be driven by the majority's appraisal of the plausibility of the ultimate factual allegation rather than its legal sufficiency.

I

. . . .

Under the relaxed pleading standards of the Federal Rules, the idea was not to keep litigants out of court but rather to keep them in. The merits of a claim would be sorted out during a flexible pretrial process and, as appropriate, through the crucible of trial. . . .

II

It is in the context of this history that *Conley v. Gibson*, 355 U.S. 41 (1957), must be understood. . . .

Consistent with the design of the Federal Rules, *Conley's* "no set of facts" formulation permits outright dismissal only when proceeding to discovery or beyond would be futile. Once it is clear that a plaintiff has stated a claim that, if true, would entitle him to relief, matters of proof are appropriately relegated to other stages of the trial process. Today, however, in its explanation of a decision to dismiss a complaint that it regards as a fishing expedition, the Court scraps *Conley's* "no set of facts" language. . . .

Everything today's majority says would . . . make perfect sense if it were ruling on a Rule 56 motion for summary judgment and the evidence included nothing more than the Court has described. But it should go without saying in the wake of *Swierkiewicz* that a heightened production burden at the summary judgment stage does not translate into a heightened pleading burden at the complaint stage. The majority rejects the complaint in this case because—in light of the fact that the parallel conduct alleged is consistent with ordinary market behavior—the claimed conspiracy is "conceivable" but not "plausible." I have my doubts about the majority's assessment of the plausibility of this alleged conspiracy. But even if the majority's speculation is correct, its "plausibility" standard is irreconcilable with Rule 8 and with our governing precedents. As we made clear in *Swierkiewicz* and *Leatherman*, fear of the burdens of litigation does not justify factual conclusions supported only by lawyers' arguments rather than sworn denials or admissible evidence.

. . . .

III

The Court does not suggest that an agreement to do what the plaintiffs allege would be permissible under the antitrust laws. . . . Rather, the theory on which the

Court permits dismissal is that, so far as the Federal Rules are concerned, no agreement has been alleged at all. This is a mind-boggling conclusion.

....

[T]he plaintiffs allege in three places in their complaint, ¶¶ 4, 51, 64, that the ILECs did in fact agree both to prevent competitors from entering into their local markets and to forgo competition with each other. And as the Court recognizes, at the motion to dismiss stage, a judge assumes "that all the allegations in the complaint are true (even if doubtful in fact)."

The majority circumvents this obvious obstacle to dismissal by pretending that it does not exist. The Court admits that "in form a few stray statements in the complaint speak directly of agreement," but disregards those allegations by saying that "on fair reading these are merely legal conclusions resting on the prior allegations" of parallel conduct. The Court's dichotomy between factual allegations and "legal conclusions" is the stuff of a bygone era. That distinction was a defining feature of code pleading, see generally Clark, The Complaint in Code Pleading, 35 Yale L.J. 259 (1925–1926), but was conspicuously abolished when the Federal Rules were enacted in 1938....

Respondents in this case proposed a plan of "'phased discovery'" limited to the existence of the alleged conspiracy and class certification. Two petitioners rejected the plan. Whether or not respondents' proposed plan was sensible, it was an appropriate subject for negotiation.[4] Given the charge in the complaint—buttressed by

4. [Court's footnote #13] The potential for "sprawling, costly, and hugely time-consuming" discovery [quoting n. 6 of the majority opinion which is omitted here] is no reason to throw the baby out with the bathwater. The Court vastly underestimates a district court's case-management arsenal. Before discovery even begins, the court may grant a defendant's Rule 12(e) motion; Rule 7(a) permits a trial court to order a plaintiff to reply to a defendant's answer, see *Crawford-El v. Britton*, 523 U.S. 574, 598 (1998); and Rule 23 requires "rigorous analysis" to ensure that class certification is appropriate, *General Telephone Co. of Southwest v. Falcon*, 457 U.S. 147, 160 (1982).... Rule 16 invests a trial judge with the power, backed by sanctions, to regulate pretrial proceedings via conferences and scheduling orders, at which the parties may discuss, *inter alia*, "the elimination of frivolous claims or defenses," Rule 16(c)(1); "the necessity or desirability of amendments to the pleadings," Rule 16(c)(2); "the control and scheduling of discovery," Rule 16(c)(6); and "the need for adopting special procedures for managing potentially difficult or protracted actions that may involve complex issues, multiple parties, difficult legal questions, or unusual proof problems," Rule 16(c)(12). Subsequently, Rule 26 confers broad discretion to control the combination of interrogatories, requests for admissions, production requests, and depositions permitted in a given case; the sequence in which such discovery devices may be deployed; and the limitations imposed upon them.... Indeed, Rule 26(c) specifically permits a court to take actions "to protect a party or person from annoyance, embarrassment, oppression, or undue burden or expense" by, for example, disallowing a particular discovery request, setting appropriate terms and conditions, or limiting its scope.... In short, the Federal Rules contemplate that pretrial matters will be settled through a flexible process of give and take, of proffers, stipulations, and stonewalls, not by having trial judges screen allegations for their plausibility *vel non* without requiring an answer from the defendant.... And should it become apparent over the course of litigation that a plaintiff's filings bespeak an *in terrorem* suit, the district court has at its call its own *in terrorem* device, in the form

the common sense of Adam Smith I cannot say that the possibility that joint discussions and perhaps some agreements played a role in petitioners' decisionmaking process is so implausible that dismissing the complaint before any defendant has denied the charge is preferable to granting respondents even a minimal opportunity to prove their claims. . . .

Notes and Questions

Note the *Twombly* majority's distinction between inferences that are merely "possible" (insufficient), "plausible" (sufficient), and "probable" (not required). Consider also the Court's statement that "[f]actual allegations must be enough to raise a right to relief above the speculative level." *Twombly*, 550 U.S. at 555. Does this suggest that the district court must "weigh" the strength of inferences from facts alleged in the complaint rather than on the basis of actual evidence and before discovery has occurred? If *Twombly* does not require the court to weigh the strength of inferences based on the allegations in the pleadings, what does this language mean?

Twombly's Aftermath

1. Only two weeks after *Twombly*, the Supreme Court decided *Erickson v. Pardus*, 551 U.S. 89 (2007). The plaintiff in *Erickson* was a prisoner who alleged that prison officials had violated his Eight Amendment rights by removing him from a treatment program for hepatitis C after he became suspected of using one of the syringes provided to him to inject illegal drugs. The Tenth Circuit upheld the dismissal of the complaint, on the ground that an Eighth Amendment claim for cruel and unusual punishment as a result of "deliberate indifference" to needed medical treatment required an allegation of substantial harm, and that petitioner had made "only conclusory allegations to the effect that he has suffered a cognizable independent harm" (beyond that he already faced from hepatitis C itself) as a result of his removal from the treatment program. In an opinion joined by seven Justices, the Supreme Court reversed, noting that the "liberal pleading standards set forth by Rule 8(a)(2)" were "even more pronounced in this particular case because petitioner has been proceeding . . . without counsel." *Id.* at 93–94. The Court stated:

> Federal Rule of Civil Procedure 8(a)(2) requires only "a short and plain statement of the claim showing that the pleader is entitled to relief." Specific facts are not necessary; the statement need only "'give the defendant fair notice of what the . . . claim is and the grounds upon which it rests.'" *Bell Atlantic Corp. v. Twombly*, 550 U.S. 544, 555 (2007) (quoting *Conley v. Gibson*, 355 U.S. 41 (1957)). In addition, when ruling on a defendant's motion to dismiss, a judge must accept as true all of the factual allegations contained in the

---

of a wide array of Rule 11 sanctions. See Rules 11(b), (c) (authorizing sanctions if a suit is presented "for any improper purpose, such as to harass or to cause unnecessary delay or needless increase in the cost of litigation"). . . .

> complaint. *Bell Atlantic Corp., supra* (citing *Swierkiewicz v. Sorema N. A.*, 534 U.S. 506, 508 n. 1 (2002). . . .

Id.

2. Despite *Erickson*, a 5-to-4 majority of the Supreme Court strongly reaffirmed and expanded on *Twombly's* main themes in *Ashcroft v. Iqbal*, 556 U.S. 662 (2009). The plaintiff in *Iqbal* was a Muslim citizen of Pakistan. He alleged that after the September 11, 2001, terrorist attacks, federal officials arrested and detained him under restrictive conditions. Two of the defendants named in the complaint were John Ashcroft, the former Attorney General of the United States, and Robert Mueller, the Director of the FBI. Iqbal's complaint[5] alleged that their conduct violated the First and Fifth Amendments to the Constitution of the United States because they had adopted policies that led to his designation as a person "of high interest" and subjected him to harsh conditions of confinement on account of his race, religion, or national origin. Ashcroft and Mueller moved to dismiss the complaint on the ground that it failed sufficiently to allege that their conduct violated Iqbal's clearly established constitutional rights, and they therefore enjoyed qualified immunity from suit. The district court and the Second Circuit upheld the sufficiency of the complaint. The Supreme Court granted Ashcroft and Mueller's petition for certiorari and reversed. Justice Kennedy authored the majority opinion, joined by Chief Justice Roberts and Justices Scalia, Thomas, and Alito. The majority held that in applying *Twombly*, a court must first identify the elements of a viable claim for relief. It concluded that in actions alleging unconstitutional discrimination by government officials, those officials may not be held liable for the unconstitutional conduct of their subordinates under a theory of *respondeat superior*. Rather, the plaintiff must allege that each defendant official's own actions violated the Constitution. . . .

The majority then concluded that Iqbal's allegations against petitioners Ashcroft and Mueller were insufficient under *Twombly*:

> Two working principles underlie our decision in *Twombly*. First, the tenet that a court must accept as true all of the allegations contained in a complaint is inapplicable to legal conclusions. Threadbare recitals of the elements of a cause of action, supported by mere conclusory statements, do not suffice. . . . Rule 8 marks a notable and generous departure from the hyper-technical, code-pleading regime of a prior era, but it does not unlock the doors of discovery for a plaintiff armed with nothing more than conclusions. Second, only a complaint that states a plausible claim for relief survives a motion to dismiss. Determining whether a complaint states a plausible claim for relief will, as the Court of Appeals observed, be a context-specific task that requires the reviewing court to draw on its judicial experience and common sense. . . .

---

5. The complaint alleged an implied cause of action for violation of Iqbal's constitutional rights under *Bivens v. Six Unknown Fed. Narcotics Agents*, 403 U.S. 388 (1971).

. . . .

We begin our analysis by identifying the allegations in the complaint that are not entitled to the assumption of truth. Respondent pleads that petitioners "knew of, condoned, and willfully and maliciously agreed to subject [him]" to harsh conditions of confinement "as a matter of policy, solely on account of [his] religion, race, and/or national origin and for no legitimate penological interest." The complaint alleges that Ashcroft was the "principal architect" of this invidious policy, and that Mueller was "instrumental" in adopting and executing it. These bare assertions, much like the pleading of conspiracy in *Twombly*, amount to nothing more than a "formulaic recitation of the elements" of a constitutional discrimination claim, namely, that petitioners adopted a policy "'because of,' not merely 'in spite of,' its adverse effects upon an identifiable group." As such, the allegations are conclusory and not entitled to be assumed true. To be clear, we do not reject these bald allegations on the ground that they are unrealistic or nonsensical. . . . It is the conclusory nature of respondent's allegations, rather than their extravagantly fanciful nature, that disentitles them to the presumption of truth.

We next consider the factual allegations in respondent's complaint to determine if they plausibly suggest an entitlement to relief. The complaint alleges that "the [FBI], under the direction of Defendant MUELLER, arrested and detained thousands of Arab Muslim men . . . as part of its investigation of the events of September 11." It further claims that "[t]he policy of holding post-September-11th detainees in highly restrictive conditions of confinement until they were 'cleared' by the FBI was approved by Defendants ASHCROFT and MUELLER in discussions in the weeks after September 11, 2001." Taken as true, these allegations are consistent with petitioners' purposefully designating detainees "of high interest" because of their race, religion, or national origin. But given more likely explanations, they do not plausibly establish this purpose.

The September 11 attacks were perpetrated by 19 Arab Muslim hijackers who counted themselves members in good standing of al Qaeda, an Islamic fundamentalist group. Al Qaeda was headed by another Arab Muslim—Osama bin Laden—and composed in large part of his Arab Muslim disciples. It should come as no surprise that a legitimate policy directing law enforcement to arrest and detain individuals because of their suspected link to the attacks would produce a disparate, incidental impact on Arab Muslims, even though the purpose of the policy was to target neither Arabs nor Muslims. On the facts respondent alleges the arrests Mueller oversaw were likely lawful and justified by his nondiscriminatory intent to detain aliens who were illegally present in the United States and who had potential connections to those who committed terrorist acts. As between that "obvious alternative explanation" for the arrests, *Twombly*, and the purposeful, invidious discrimination respondent asks us to infer, discrimination is not a plausible conclusion.

. . . .

Respondent offers three arguments that bear on our disposition of his case, but none is persuasive.

. . . .

Respondent first says that our decision in *Twombly* should be limited to pleadings made in the context of an antitrust dispute. This argument is not supported by *Twombly* and is incompatible with the Federal Rules of Civil Procedure.

. . . .

Respondent next implies that our construction of Rule 8 should be tempered where, as here, the Court of Appeals has "instructed the district court to cabin discovery in such a way as to preserve" petitioners' defense of qualified immunity "as much as possible in anticipation of a summary judgment motion." We have held, however, that the question presented by a motion to dismiss a complaint for insufficient pleadings does not turn on the controls placed upon the discovery process.

. . . .

Respondent finally maintains that the Federal Rules expressly allow him to allege petitioners' discriminatory intent "generally," which he equates with a conclusory allegation. Iqbal Brief 32 (citing Fed. Rule Civ. Proc. 9). It follows, respondent says, that his complaint is sufficiently well pleaded because it claims that petitioners discriminated against him "on account of [his] religion, race, and/or national origin and for no legitimate penological interest." Were we required to accept this allegation as true, respondent's complaint would survive petitioners' motion to dismiss. But the Federal Rules do not require courts to credit a complaint's conclusory statements without reference to its factual context.

It is true that Rule 9(b) requires particularity when pleading "fraud or mistake," while allowing "[m]alice, intent, knowledge, and other conditions of a person's mind [to] be alleged generally." But "generally" is a relative term. In the context of Rule 9, it is to be compared to the particularity requirement applicable to fraud or mistake. Rule 9 merely excuses a party from pleading discriminatory intent under an elevated pleading standard. It does not give him license to evade the less rigid—though still operative—strictures of Rule 8. . . .

Id. at 678–87.

Commentators have debated the actual impact of *Twombly* and *Iqbal* on dismissal rates. *See, e.g.*, Patricia W. Hatamyar, *The Tao of Pleading: Do* Twombly *and*

Iqbal *Matter Empirically?*, 59 AM. U. L. REV. 553, 556 (2010) (presenting a statistical analysis of the effects on grants of motions to dismiss of *Twombly* and *Iqbal* in comparison with those under *Conley*. Hatamyar concludes, based on the results of a multinomial logistic regression analysis of a randomly selected sample of cases, that although the "notice pleading" ideal of *Conley* had in fact been seriously eroded by the time of *Twombly*, those decisions, particularly *Iqbal*, have significantly increased the odds that a motion to dismiss will be granted with leave to amend, rather than denied. Additionally, in civil rights cases, "motions to dismiss were granted at a higher rate (53%) than in all cases combined (49%), and the rate 12(b)(6) motions were granted in those cases increased from *Conley* (50%) to *Twombly* (55%) to *Iqbal* (60%)."); Elizabeth M. Schneider, *The Changing Shape of Federal Civil Pretrial Practice: The Disparate Impact on Civil Rights and Employment Discrimination Cases*, 158 U. PA. L. REV. 517 (2010) (arguing that *Twomby* and *Iqbal* have, in effect advanced the summary judgment fact-screening of cases to the pleading stage and have had a disproportionate impact on the dismissal of civil rights and employment discrimination cases, which may reflect judges' subjective impressions and unconscious bias against such litigation); Joseph A. Seiner, *The Trouble with* Twombly: *A Proposed Pleading Standard for Employment Discrimination Cases*, 2009 ILL. L. REV. 1011 (2009) (presenting data and analysis suggesting that *Twombly* has increased the rate at which motions to dismiss are granted in Title VII employment discrimination cases). *See also* Patricia Hatamyar Moore, *An Updated Quantitative Study of* Iqbal*'s Impact on Rule 12(b)(6) Motions*, 46 U. RICHMOND L. REV. 603 (2012). In this updated study based on an expanded data base, Professor Moore concludes that "the impact of *Iqbal* has intensified since my earlier study." *Id.* at 605. In particular, "[t]he updated results indicate that the relative risk of a 12(b)(6) motion being granted *without* leave to amend, compared to being denied, was expected to be 1.75 times greater under *Iqbal* than under *Conley*, holding all other variables constant, and this increase is statistically significant." Further, "the odds of the case being entirely dismissed upon the grant of a 12(b)(6) motion without leave to amend were 1.71 times greater under *Iqbal* than under *Conley*." Finally, "the updated study continues to indicate that constitutional civil rights cases in particular were dismissed at a higher rate post-*Iqbal* than pre-*Twombly*." *Id.*

Compare Joe S. Cecil, George W. Cort, Margaret S. Williams & Jared J. Battaillon, *Motions to Dismiss for Failure to State a Claim After* Iqbal, *Report to the Judicial Conference Advisory Committee on Civil Rules* (Federal Judicial Center, March 2011). This study examines whether there was an increase in the rate of grants (with or without leave to amend) of motions to dismiss in 23 federal districts accounting for 51% of all civil filings between two nine month periods ending in June 2006 (pre-*Twombly*) and June 2010 (post-*Iqbal*), respectively, excluding prisoner and pro se actions. Contrary to the articles previously reviewed, which were primarily based on decisions published in computerized legal reference systems, the study considered both published and unpublished decisions. After adjusting for factors that the authors deemed to be unrelated to *Twombly* and *Iqbal*, such as differences among types of filings and across districts, and whether the motion was in response to an amended complaint, the study concludes that although there was a significant increase in the rate of *filing* motions to dismiss following *Iqbal* (from 4.0% to 6.2%), there was no statistically significant increase in the adjusted *grant rates* for such motions except in cases involving financial instruments. In particular, the authors conclude that there was no statistically significant increase in the grant rates in cases involving employment discrimination and civil rights. (A follow-on study tracked cases in which motions to dismiss were granted with leave to amend through to their ultimate disposition, and concluded that no change in the conclusions of the original study was indicated. Joe S. Cecil, George W. Cort, Margaret S. Williams, Jared J. Bataillon, & Jacqueline G. Campbell, *Update on Resolution of Rule 12(b)(6) Motions Granted with Leave to Amend, Report to the Judicial Conference Advisory Committee on Civil Rules* (Federal Judicial Center, November 2011).)

The implications of the FJC study no doubt will continue to be debated, because it also showed that there was in fact an increase between 2006 and 2010 from 66% to 75% in the rate at which some or all of the relief sought by the motion was granted. The conclusion that this did not show a statistically significant increase turned on the "adjustments" that the authors made for factors deemed unrelated to *Twombly* and *Iqbal*, including differing grant rates in differing districts, differences in the composition of cases, and whether the motion was made in response to a previously amended complaint. For a critical analysis of the Federal Judicial Center Study, see Lonny Hoffman, Twombly *and* Iqbal's *Measure: An Assessment of the Federal Judicial Center's Study of Motions to Dismiss*, 6 FED. CTS. L. REV. 1 (2011). An important shortcoming of the FJC's approach may be that it focused on changes in grant rates for motions to dismiss in the periods before *Twombly* and after *Iqbal. See* Jonah B. Gelbach, *Locking the Doors to Discovery? Assessing the Effects of* Twombly *and* Iqbal *on Access to Discovery*, 121 YALE L.J. 2270 (2012). Gelbach argues that the FJC and other studies focusing on changes in grant rates for motions to dismiss fail to capture the full effect of those decisions, because they do not take account of party behavior ("selection") in determining whether to institute litigation, to file a motion to dismiss, or to settle. (For example, stricter pleading standards may cause defendants to file more motions to dismiss than they otherwise would have, leading to an increase in the number of dismissals.) As a result, stricter pleading requirements may have a significant adverse impact on plaintiffs even if the grant rate remains the same. Gelbach develops a model designed to establish the "lower bound" for such negative effects. Applying that analysis to the data used in the FJC studies, he concludes that "*Twombly* and *Iqbal* have negatively affected plaintiffs in at least 15% to 21% of cases that faced a Rule 12(b)(6) motion in the post *Iqbal* data window.... [D]epending on the nature of the suit, these figures represent between one-fourth and two-fifths of the cases that fail to reach discovery on at least some claims in [that period]." *Id.*

Federal trial judges, under the guidance of the MANUAL FOR COMPLEX LITIGATION (FOURTH), have exercised this authority to require particularization of the plaintiff's case and to control discovery, using such devices as requirements for detailed "statements of contentions and proof," without imposing heightened pleading requirements to determine the legal sufficiency of the complaint at the outset. *See, e.g.*, *United States v. Am. Tel. & Tel. Co.*, 461 F. Supp. 1314 (D.D.C. 1978) (requiring the government in an antitrust action to file successive Statements of Contentions and Proof, each to become more specific than the last, "in which it shall describe, with specificity, each of the government's legal and factual contentions, including the activities of the defendants it expects to rely upon to prove its charges of violation of Section 2 of the Sherman Act."). Is this approach preferable, or does it open the door to the burdens and costs imposed by claims of dubious merit that are not screened out by a more rigorous pleading "gateway"? Are the burdens of such procedures themselves, which presuppose an opportunity for discovery, excessive?

2. The Heightened Pleading Requirements of the Private Securities Litigation Reform Act of 1995

The most prominent provision of the Federal Rules imposing a heightened pleading requirement is Rule 9(b), which provides that "a party must state with particularity the circumstances constituting fraud or mistake." The rule appears to be based on the view that allegations of fraud, although easily made, may be difficult to refute and may be particularly damaging to the reputation of the defendant, and on the idea that such actions frequently may be filed for the nuisance or settlement value without regard to their merit. *See* RICHARD D. FREER, CIVIL PROCEDURE § 7.3 (4th ed. 2017) (noting in addition that "fraud comes in a huge variety of fact patterns, meaning that the party accused of it should be given a detailed charge to enable her to respond and defend.").

Rule 9(b) generally has been interpreted to require particular allegations regarding the time, place and contents of the allegedly false representations, as well as the identity of the person by whom they were made. *Id.* Plaintiffs generally must specify "the who, what, when, where, and how: the first paragraph of any newspaper story." *DiLeo v. Ernst & Young*, 901 F.2d 624, 627 (7th Cir. 1990). But see *Santana v. Cook County Bd. of Review*, 270 F.R.D. 388, 389 (N.D. Ill. 2010): "That prescription really does not fit where the charged fraudulent conduct (whether RICO-violative or otherwise) is an entire pattern of activity over a period of time. . . . [H]eed must be given to [Rule 9(b)'s] directive that what must be pleaded with particularity are the '*circumstances* constituting fraud,' rather than a laundry-list recital itemizing the particulars of each individual fraudulent statement." Also, the Rule itself expressly provides that, notwithstanding its particularity requirement, "[m]alice, intent, knowledge, and other conditions of a person's mind may be alleged generally."

Against this background, Congress enacted the Private Securities Litigation Reform Act of 1995 ("PSLRA") over a veto by President Clinton. Congress acted in response to a perceived increase in frivolous securities class action lawsuits that were filed for the purpose of uncovering evidence of fraud through the discovery process or to coerce a settlement. The Act amends both the Securities Act of 1933 and the Securities Exchange Act of 1934. In 1998, Congress, concerned that litigants were avoiding the effects of its legislation by suing in state courts, also enacted the Securities Litigation Uniform Standards Act of 1998, Pub. L. 105-353, 112 Stat. 3227 (1998). That Act bars class action securities fraud lawsuits in state courts involving securities traded on national markets. As a result, most securities fraud class actions must be maintained in federal courts and are subject to PSLRA requirements.

The PSLRA contains many requirements that its proponents claimed would improve the handling of private class actions alleging securities fraud. One of these requirements is the use of heightened pleading standards in private securities fraud cases under the anti-fraud provisions of the Securities Exchange Act of 1934.[6] The Act reads in relevant part:

> (b) Requirements for securities fraud actions
>
> (1) Misleading statements and omissions
>
> In any private action arising under this chapter in which the plaintiff alleges that the defendant—
>
> (A) made an untrue statement of a material fact; or
>
> (B) omitted to state a material fact necessary in order to make the statements made, in the light of the circumstances in which they were made, not misleading;
>
> the complaint shall specify each statement alleged to have been misleading, the reason or reasons why the statement is misleading, and, if an allegation regarding the statement or omission is made on information and belief, the complaint shall state with particularity all facts on which that belief is formed.
>
> (2) Required state of mind
>
> In any private action arising under this chapter in which the plaintiff may recover money damages only on proof that the defendant acted with a particular state of mind, the complaint shall, with respect to each act or omission alleged to violate this chapter, state with particularity facts giving rise to a strong inference that the defendant acted with the required state of mind.
>
> (3) Motion to dismiss; stay of discovery
>
> (A) Dismissal for failure to meet pleading requirements

6. The particularity requirement of FRCP 9(b) continues to apply to actions under the Securities Act of 1933 that "sound in fraud." *See California Public Employees Retirement System v. The Chubb Corp.*, 394 F.3d 126, 160–63 (3d Cir. 2004).

> In any private action arising under this chapter, the court shall, on the motion of any defendant, dismiss the complaint if the requirements of paragraphs (1) and (2) are not met.
>
> (B) Stay of discovery
>
> In any private action arising under this chapter, all discovery and other proceedings shall be stayed during the pendency of any motion to dismiss, unless the court finds upon the motion of any party that particularized discovery is necessary to preserve evidence or to prevent undue prejudice to that party. . . .

15 U.S.C.A. §§ 78u-4(b)(1)–(3)(B).

The pleading requirements of the PSLRA supplement, but do not supersede, the specificity requirements of Rule 9(b). Before enactment of the PSLRA, the courts of appeals disagreed over the level of particularity with which plaintiffs were required to plead the defendant's degree of awareness of the fraud, or "scienter," for the purpose of stating a securities fraud claim. *See, e.g., In re GlenFed, Inc. Securities. Litig.*, 42 F.3d 1541 (9th Cir. 1994). The legislative history of the PSLRA indicates that the Act was based in part on previous decisions in the Second Circuit, which, despite Rule 9(b)'s express authorization to plead state of mind generally, had required litigants in securities fraud actions to plead particularized facts giving rise to a "strong inference" of fraudulent intent. *See, e.g., Powers v. British Vita, P.L.C.*, 57 F.3d 176 (2d Cir. 1995). However, the PSLRA did not resolve the disagreements among the circuits over the level of particularity that was required.

In particular, in interpreting the Act, the courts of appeals have divided on at least three distinct points: First, the Act requires that the complaint contain particularized allegations supporting a strong inference that the defendant acted with the "required state of mind." Before the PSLRA, it was settled that recklessness as well as a deliberate intent to mislead could satisfy the scienter requirement of certain provisions of the federal securities laws. In *In re Silicon Graphics Inc. Sec. Litig.*, 183 F.3d 970 (9th Cir. 1999), however, the Ninth Circuit concluded that Congress, in the PSLRA, had intended to require that the defendant's acts, if they were not deliberately intended to mislead, be such an extreme departure from ordinary standards of care that they were equivalent to intentional misconduct—a state of mind which it characterized as "deliberate recklessness." *Id.* at 977. By contrast, other courts of appeals held that the Act did not alter the level of scienter required by previous decisions, and that allegations of simple recklessness would suffice. *See, e.g., Ottmann v. Hanger Orthopedic Group, Inc.*, 353 F.3d 338 (4th Cir. 2003); *SEC v. Jakubowski*, 150 F.3d 675, 681–82 (7th Cir. 1998).

Second, the courts of appeals divided on what sort of circumstantial evidence might be relied upon to create a strong inference of scienter. Before the enactment of the PSLRA, the Second Circuit had "recognized two distinct ways in which a plaintiff might plead scienter without direct knowledge of the defendant's state of mind. The first approach is to allege facts establishing a motive to commit fraud and an opportunity to do so. The second approach is to allege facts constituting circumstantial evidence of either reckless or conscious behavior." *In re Time Warner Inc. Sec. Litig.*, 9 F.3d 259, 268 (2d Cir. 1993). Despite considerable legislative history showing that Congress intended to adopt the Second Circuit's "strong inference" standard without also incorporating its two-pronged approach to the kinds of circumstantial evidence sufficient to support such an inference, the Second Circuit continued to adhere to its previous approach after the enactment of the PSLRA. *See, e.g., Press v. Chemical Investment Services Corp.*, 166 F.3d 529 (2d Cir. 1999). By contrast, the Ninth Circuit rejected the "motive and opportunity" prong of the Second Circuit's approach in *In re Silicon Graphics, supra*, 183 F.3d at 974.

Yet a third conflict arose in determining when the facts alleged in the complaint were sufficient to create a "strong inference" of whatever level of scienter was required. The Supreme Court undertook to resolve that issue in the following case.

Tellabs, Inc. v. Makor Issues & Rights, Ltd.

Supreme Court of the United States
551 U.S. 308 (2007)

JUSTICE GINSBURG delivered the opinion of the Court.

This Court has long recognized that meritorious private actions to enforce federal antifraud securities laws are an essential supplement to criminal prosecutions and civil enforcement actions brought, respectively, by the Department of Justice and the Securities and Exchange Commission (SEC).... Private securities fraud actions, however, if not adequately contained, can be employed abusively to impose substantial costs on companies and individuals whose conduct conforms to the law.... As a check against abusive litigation by private parties, Congress enacted the Private Securities Litigation Reform Act of 1995 (PSLRA), 109 Stat. 737.

Exacting pleading requirements are among the control measures Congress included in the PSLRA. The Act requires plaintiffs to state with particularity both the facts constituting the alleged violation, and the facts evidencing scienter, *i.e.*, the defendant's intention "to deceive, manipulate, or defraud." *Ernst & Ernst v. Hochfelder*, 425 U.S. 185, 194, and n. 12 (1976). This case concerns the latter requirement. As set out in §21D(b)(2) of the PSLRA, plaintiffs must "state with particularity facts giving rise to a strong inference that the defendant acted with the required state of mind." 15 U.S.C. §78u-4(b)(2).

Congress left the key term "strong inference" undefined, and Courts of Appeals have divided on its meaning. In the case before us, the Court of Appeals for the Seventh Circuit held that the "strong inference" standard would be met if the complaint "allege[d] facts from which, if true, a reasonable person could infer that the defendant acted with the required intent...." That formulation, we conclude, does not capture the stricter demand Congress sought to convey in §21D(b)(2). It does not suffice that a reasonable factfinder plausibly could infer from the complaint's allegations the requisite state of mind. Rather, to determine whether a complaint's scienter allegations can survive threshold inspection for sufficiency, a court governed by § 21D(b)(2) must engage in a comparative evaluation; it must consider, not only inferences urged by the plaintiff, as the Seventh Circuit did, but also competing inferences rationally drawn from the facts alleged. An inference of fraudulent intent may be plausible, yet less cogent than other, nonculpable explanations for the defendant's conduct. To qualify as "strong" within the intendment of § 21D(b)(2), we hold, an inference of scienter must be more than merely plausible or reasonable—it must be cogent and at least as compelling as any opposing inference of nonfraudulent intent.

I

Petitioner Tellabs, Inc., manufactures specialized equipment used in fiber optic networks. During the time period relevant to this case, petitioner Richard Notebaert was Tellabs' chief executive officer and president. Respondents (Shareholders) are persons who purchased Tellabs stock between December 11, 2000, and June 19, 2001. They accuse Tellabs and Notebaert (as well as several other Tellabs executives) of engaging in a scheme to deceive the investing public about the true value of Tellabs' stock.

Beginning on December 11, 2000, the Shareholders allege, Notebaert (and by imputation Tellabs) "falsely reassured public investors, in a series of statements . . . that Tellabs was continuing to enjoy strong demand for its products and earning record revenues," when, in fact, Notebaert knew the opposite was true. . . .

The first public glimmer that business was not so healthy came in March 2001 when Tellabs modestly reduced its first quarter sales projections. In the next months, Tellabs made progressively more cautious statements about its projected sales. On June 19, 2001, the last day of the class period, Tellabs disclosed that demand for the TITAN 5500 had significantly dropped. Simultaneously, the company substantially lowered its revenue projections for the second quarter of 2001. The next day, the price of Tellabs stock, which had reached a high of $67 during the period, plunged to a low of $15.87.

On December 3, 2002, the Shareholders filed a class action in the District Court for the Northern District of Illinois. Their complaint stated, *inter alia*, that Tellabs and Notebaert had engaged in securities fraud in violation of § 10(b) of the Securities Exchange Act of 1934, and SEC Rule 10b-5, also that Notebaert was a "controlling person" under § 20(a) of the 1934 Act, and therefore derivatively liable for the company's fraudulent acts. Tellabs moved to dismiss the complaint on the ground that the Shareholders had failed to plead their case with the particularity the PSLRA requires. . . .

. . . .

[The district court dismissed plaintiffs' amended complaint with prejudice.] The Court of Appeals for the Seventh Circuit reversed in relevant part. . . . Like the

District Court, the Court of Appeals found that the Shareholders had pleaded the misleading character of Notebaert's statements with sufficient particularity. Unlike the District Court, however, the Seventh Circuit concluded that the Shareholders had sufficiently alleged that Notebaert acted with the requisite state of mind.

. . . .

. . . We granted certiorari to resolve the disagreement among the Circuits on whether, and to what extent, a court must consider competing inferences in determining whether a securities fraud complaint gives rise to a "strong inference" of scienter.

II

. . . .

Setting a uniform pleading standard for § 10(b) actions was among Congress' objectives when it enacted the PSLRA. Designed to curb perceived abuses of the § 10(b) private action—"nuisance filings, targeting of deep-pocket defendants, vexatious discovery requests and manipulation by class action lawyers . . ."—the PSLRA installed both substantive and procedural controls. . . .

Under the PSLRA's heightened pleading instructions, any private securities complaint alleging that the defendant made a false or misleading statement must: (1) "specify each statement alleged to have been misleading [and] the reason or reasons why the statement is misleading," 15 U.S.C. § 78u-4(b)(1); and (2) "state with particularity facts giving rise to a strong inference that the defendant acted with the required state of mind," § 78u-4(b)(2). . . .

[O]ur task is to prescribe a workable construction of the "strong inference" standard, a reading geared to the PSLRA's twin goals: to curb frivolous, lawyer-driven litigation, while preserving investors' ability to recover on meritorious claims.

III

A

We establish the following prescriptions: *First*, faced with a Rule 12(b)(6) motion to dismiss a § 10(b) action, courts must, as with any motion to dismiss for failure to plead a claim on which relief can be granted, accept all factual allegations in the complaint as true. . . .

Second, courts must consider the complaint in its entirety, as well as other sources courts ordinarily examine when ruling on Rule 12(b)(6) motions to dismiss, in particular, documents incorporated into the complaint by reference, and matters of which a court may take judicial notice. . . . The inquiry, as several Courts of Appeals have recognized, is whether *all* of the facts alleged, taken collectively, give rise to a strong inference of scienter, not whether any individual allegation, scrutinized in isolation, meets that standard. . . .

Third, in determining whether the pleaded facts give rise to a "strong" inference of scienter, the court must take into account plausible opposing inferences. The Seventh Circuit expressly declined to engage in such a comparative inquiry.

The strength of an inference cannot be decided in a vacuum. The inquiry is inherently comparative: How likely is it that one conclusion, as compared to others, follows from the underlying facts? To determine whether the plaintiff has alleged facts that give rise to the requisite "strong inference" of scienter, a court must consider plausible nonculpable explanations for the defendant's conduct, as well as inferences favoring the plaintiff. The inference that the defendant acted with scienter need not be irrefutable, *i.e.*, of the "smoking-gun" genre, or even the "most plausible of competing inferences," *Fidel*, 392 F.3d, at 227 (quoting *Helwig v. Vencor, Inc.*, 251 F.3d 540, 553 (C.A.6 2001) (en banc)). Recall in this regard that § 21D(b)'s pleading requirements are but one constraint among many the PSLRA installed to screen out frivolous suits, while allowing meritorious actions to move forward. Yet the inference of scienter must be more than merely "reasonable" or "permissible"—it must be cogent and compelling, thus strong in light of other explanations. A complaint will survive, we hold, only if a reasonable person would deem the inference of scienter cogent and at least as compelling as any opposing inference one could draw from the facts alleged.[7]

. . . .

IV

. . . We emphasize, as well, that under our construction of the "strong inference" standard, a plaintiff is not forced to plead more than she would be required to prove at trial. A plaintiff alleging fraud in a § 10(b) action, we hold today, must plead facts rendering an inference of scienter *at least as likely as* any plausible opposing inference. At trial, she must then prove her case by a "preponderance of the evidence." Stated otherwise, she must demonstrate that it is *more likely* than not that the defendant acted with scienter. . . .

. . . .

Justice Scalia, concurring in the judgment.

I fail to see how an inference that is merely "at least as compelling as any opposing inference," can conceivably be called what the statute here at issue requires: a "strong inference. . . ." If a jade falcon were stolen from a room to which only A and B had access, could it *possibly* be said there was a "strong inference" that B was the thief? I think not, and I therefore think that the Court's test must fail. In my view,

7. [Court's footnote #5] Justice Scalia objects to this standard on the ground that "[i]f a jade falcon were stolen from a room to which only A and B had access," it could not "*possibly* be said there was a 'strong inference' that B was the thief. . . ." I suspect, however, that law enforcement officials as well as the owner of the precious falcon would find the inference of guilt as to B quite strong—certainly strong enough to warrant further investigation. Indeed, an inference at least as likely as competing inferences can, in some cases, warrant recovery. See *Summers v. Tice*, 33 Cal.2d 80, 84–87, (1948) (in bank) (plaintiff wounded by gunshot could recover from two defendants, even though the most he could prove was that each defendant was at least as likely to have injured him as the other). . . . In any event, we disagree with Justice Scalia that the hardly stock term "strong inference" has only one invariably right ("natural" or "normal") reading—his.

the test should be whether the inference of scienter (if any) is *more plausible* than the inference of innocence.

. . . .

[The opinion of Justice Alito concurring in the judgment and the dissenting opinion of Justice Stevens are omitted.]

Notes and Questions

1. What precisely is the pleading standard articulated in *Tellabs* for securities fraud claims alleged under the Securities Exchange Act of 1934? How does it relate to the pleading standard announced by the Court in *Twombly*?

2. Does *Tellabs* require the court to weigh competing inferences based on pleading allegations, rather than actual evidence? Does it carry the potential of denying plaintiffs the opportunity for discovery of information within the exclusive control of defendants to support good faith allegations of corporate wrongdoing, significantly increasing the likelihood for dismissal of ultimately meritorious claims? If so, who bears responsibility for that result?

3. Many securities fraud complaints base their "particularized" allegations of falsity and scienter on information obtained from confidential sources. (For example, the complaint might allege that senior officers knew that reported profits were overstated based on statements by an unidentified corporate officer that an internal company report explicitly recognizing such an overstatement had been brought to their attention and discussed at a board meeting before the misleading reports were issued.) Why might such sources wish to remain confidential? Should courts require that their identities be revealed before the information they provide can satisfy the "particularity" requirement of the PSLRA? Before *Tellabs* the prevailing (though not universal) view among the circuits was that the names of confidential sources for securities fraud complaints need not be revealed so long as the information they provided contained sufficient indicia of reliability. After *Tellabs*, there was some indication that the "strong inference" standard as interpreted by the Supreme Court might require securities fraud plaintiffs to name their confidential sources. In *Higginbotham v. Baxter International, Inc.*, 495 F.3d 753 (7th Cir. 2007) (Easterbrook, C.J.), the Seventh Circuit concluded that, in light of *Tellabs*, information provided by unnamed sources must ordinarily be "discounted" and "[u]sually that discount will be steep." The court of appeals reasoned: "It is hard to see how information from anonymous sources could be deemed 'compelling' or how we could take account of plausible opposing inferences. Perhaps these confidential sources have axes to grind. Perhaps they are lying. Perhaps they don't even exist." Is this reasoning persuasive? The Seventh Circuit itself appeared to backtrack from (if not entirely repudiate) it on remand in *Tellabs*. *Makor Issues & Rights, Ltd. v. Tellabs Inc.*, 513 F.3d 702, 711–712 (7th Cir. 2008) (Posner, J.).

C. Summary Judgment

1. Introductory Note on the Importance of Summary Judgment in Complex Cases

For many years, courts discouraged the use of summary judgment under Federal Rule 56 as a means of disposing of cases without trial. *See, e.g., Poller v. Columbia Broadcasting System, Inc.*, 368 U.S. 464, 473 (1962) ("summary procedures should be used sparingly in complex antitrust litigation where motive an intent play leading roles [and] the proof is largely in the hands of the alleged conspirators"), and *Arnstein v. Porter*, 154 F.2d 464, 468 (2d Cir. 1946) (summary judgment should be denied when "there is the slightest doubt as to the facts").

This restrictive review was superseded by the Supreme Court's important 1986 "trilogy" of summary judgment decisions in *Anderson v. Liberty Lobby, Inc.*, 477 U.S. 242 (1986), *Celotex Corp. v. Catrett*, 477 U.S. 317 (1986), and *Matsushita Elec. Indus. Co. v. Zenith Radio Corp.*, 475 U.S. 574 (1986). Far from viewing summary judgment as a "disfavored procedure" in those decisions, the Supreme Court took precisely the opposite view. "Summary judgment procedure is properly regarded not as a disfavored procedural shortcut, but rather as an integral part of the Federal Rules as a whole, which are designed 'to secure the just, speedy and inexpensive determination of every action.'" *Celotex*, 477 U.S. at 327 (quoting Fed. R. Civ. P. 1).

In the wake of those decisions, summary judgment has become an increasingly important tool permitting the disposition of all types of cases before trial. However, the potential for avoiding the burdens that the trial of complex cases imposes on courts, parties, and jurors may create a special impetus for summary disposition in that context. *See* Arthur R. Miller, *The Pretrial Rush to Judgment: Are the "Litigation Explosion," "Liability Crisis," and Efficiency Clichés Eroding Our Day in Court and Jury Trial Commitments?*, 78 N.Y.U. L. Rev. 982, 1108 (2003). This raises the question whether special summary judgment standards making it more difficult for plaintiffs to defeat summary judgment have been or should be applied in complex cases.

2. Summary Judgment Basics

Federal Rule 56 authorizes the trial court to render judgment upon all or a part of a claim or defense, based on the court's determination that the party moving for summary judgment has demonstrated that "there is no genuine dispute as to any material fact and the movant is entitled to judgment as a matter of law." Fed. R. Civ. P. 56(a). Summary judgment is entered before trial, and is based upon the depositions, other discovery materials and affidavits submitted in support of and in opposition to the motion, rather than on oral trial testimony. Summary judgment is a tool for ferreting out cases in which there is no genuine dispute of fact, and thus no need for trial. To make this determination, the court goes beyond the pleadings to look at evidence. The parties proffer the evidence in various forms, including affidavits (which are sworn statements), depositions, and answers to interrogatories. The court then evaluates the evidence to determine whether there is a "genuine dispute as to any material fact" that requires a trial.

3. Summary Judgment in Complex Cases

Matsushita Elec. Indus. Co. v. Zenith Radio Corp.

Supreme Court of the United States
475 U.S. 574 (1986)

JUSTICE POWELL delivered the opinion of the Court.

This case requires that we again consider the standard district courts must apply when deciding whether to grant summary judgment in an antitrust conspiracy case.

I

....

A

Petitioners, defendants below, are 21 corporations that manufacture or sell "consumer electronic products" (CEPs)—for the most part, television sets. Petitioners include both Japanese manufacturers of CEPs and American firms, controlled by Japanese parents, that sell the Japanese-manufactured products. Respondents, plaintiffs below, are Zenith Radio Corporation (Zenith) and National Union Electric Corporation (NUE). Zenith is an American firm that manufactures and sells television sets. NUE is the corporate successor to Emerson Radio Company, an American firm that manufactured and sold television sets until 1970, when it withdrew from the market after sustaining substantial losses. Zenith and NUE began this lawsuit in 1974, claiming that petitioners had illegally conspired to drive American firms from the American CEP market. According to respondents, the gist of this conspiracy was a "'scheme to raise, fix and maintain artificially *high* prices for television receivers sold by [petitioners] in Japan and, at the same time, to fix and maintain *low* prices for television receivers exported to and sold in the United States.'" These "low prices" were allegedly at levels that produced substantial losses for petitioners. The conspiracy allegedly began as early as 1953, and according to respondents was in full operation by sometime in the late 1960's. Respondents claimed that various portions of this scheme violated §§ 1 and 2 of the Sherman Act, § 2(a) of the Robinson-Patman Act, § 73 of the Wilson Tariff Act, and the Antidumping Act of 1916.

After several years of detailed discovery, petitioners filed motions for summary judgment on all claims against them. The District Court directed the parties to file, with preclusive effect, "Final Pretrial Statements" listing all the documentary evidence that would be offered if the case proceeded to trial. Respondents filed such a statement, and petitioners responded with a series of motions challenging the admissibility of respondents' evidence. In three detailed opinions, the District Court found the bulk of the evidence on which Zenith and NUE relied inadmissible.

The District Court then turned to petitioners' motions for summary judgment. In an opinion spanning 217 pages, the court found that the admissible evidence did not raise a genuine issue of material fact as to the existence of the alleged conspiracy. . . .

B

The Court of Appeals for the Third Circuit reversed.

On the merits, and based on the newly enlarged record, the court found that the District Court's summary judgment decision was improper. . . . Turning to the evidence, the court determined that a factfinder reasonably could draw the following conclusions:

> 1. The Japanese market for CEPs was characterized by oligopolistic behavior, with a small number of producers meeting regularly and exchanging information on price and other matters. This created the opportunity for a stable combination to raise both prices and profits in Japan. American firms could not attack such a combination because the Japanese Government imposed significant barriers to entry.
>
> 2. Petitioners had relatively higher fixed costs than their American counterparts, and therefore needed to operate at something approaching full capacity in order to make a profit.
>
> 3. Petitioners' plant capacity exceeded the needs of the Japanese market.
>
> 4. By formal agreements arranged in cooperation with Japan's Ministry of International Trade and Industry (MITI), petitioners fixed minimum prices for CEPs exported to the American market. The parties refer to these prices as the "check prices," and to the agreements that require them as the "check price agreements."
>
> 5. Petitioners agreed to distribute their products in the United States according to a "five company rule": each Japanese producer was permitted to sell only to five American distributors.
>
> 6. Petitioners undercut their own check prices by a variety of rebate schemes. Petitioners sought to conceal these rebate schemes both from the United States Customs Service and from MITI, the former to avoid various customs regulations as well as action under the antidumping laws, and the latter to cover up petitioners' violations of the check-price agreements.

Based on inferences from the foregoing conclusions,[8] the Court of Appeals concluded that a reasonable factfinder could find a conspiracy to depress prices in the American market in order to drive out American competitors, which conspiracy was funded by excess profits obtained in the Japanese market. The court apparently

---

8. [Court's footnote #5] In addition to these inferences, the court noted that there was expert opinion evidence that petitioners' export sales "generally were at prices which produced losses, often as high as twenty-five percent on sales." The court did not identify any direct evidence of below-cost pricing; nor did it place particularly heavy reliance on this aspect of the expert evidence. . . .

did not consider whether it was as plausible to conclude that petitioners' price-cutting behavior was independent and not conspiratorial.

. . . .

II

We begin by emphasizing what respondents' claim is *not*. Respondents cannot recover antitrust damages based solely on an alleged cartelization of the Japanese market, because American antitrust laws do not regulate the competitive conditions of other nations' economies. . . . Nor can respondents recover damages for any conspiracy by petitioners to charge higher than competitive prices in the American market. Such conduct would indeed violate the Sherman Act . . . but it could not injure respondents: as petitioners' competitors, respondents stand to gain from any conspiracy to raise the market price in CEPs. . . . Finally, for the same reason, respondents cannot recover for a conspiracy to impose nonprice restraints that have the effect of either raising market price or limiting output. Such restrictions, though harmful to competition, actually *benefit* competitors by making supracompetitive pricing more attractive. Thus, neither petitioners' alleged supracompetitive pricing in Japan, nor the five-company rule that limited distribution in this country, nor the check prices insofar as they established minimum prices in this country, can by themselves give respondents a cognizable claim against petitioners for antitrust damages. The Court of Appeals therefore erred to the extent that it found evidence of these alleged conspiracies to be "direct evidence" of a conspiracy that injured respondents.

Respondents nevertheless argue that these supposed conspiracies, if not themselves grounds for recovery of antitrust damages, are circumstantial evidence of another conspiracy that *is* cognizable: a conspiracy to monopolize the American market by means of pricing below the market level. The thrust of respondents' argument is that petitioners used their monopoly profits from the Japanese market to fund a concerted campaign to price predatorily and thereby drive respondents and other American manufacturers of CEPs out of business. Once successful, according to respondents, petitioners would cartelize the American CEP market, restricting output and raising prices above the level that fair competition would produce. The resulting monopoly profits, respondents contend, would more than compensate petitioners for the losses they incurred through years of pricing below market level.

The Court of Appeals found that respondents' allegation of a horizontal conspiracy to engage in predatory pricing,[9] if proved, would be a *per se* violation of § 1 of

9. [Court's footnote #8] . . . For purposes of this case, it is enough to note that respondents have not suffered an antitrust injury unless petitioners conspired to drive respondents out of the relevant markets by (i) pricing below the level necessary to sell their products, or (ii) pricing below some appropriate measure of cost. An agreement without these features would either leave respondents in the same position as would market forces or would actually benefit respondents by raising market prices. Respondents therefore may not complain of conspiracies that, for example, set maximum prices above market levels, or that set minimum prices at *any* level.

the Sherman Act. Petitioners did not appeal from that conclusion. The issue in this case thus becomes whether respondents adduced sufficient evidence in support of their theory to survive summary judgment. We therefore examine the principles that govern the summary judgment determination.

III

To survive petitioners' motion for summary judgment, respondents must establish that there is a genuine issue of material fact as to whether petitioners entered into an illegal conspiracy that caused respondents to suffer a cognizable injury.... Respondents charge petitioners with a whole host of conspiracies in restraint of trade. Except for the alleged conspiracy to monopolize the American market through predatory pricing, these alleged conspiracies could not have caused respondents to suffer an "antitrust injury..." because they actually tended to benefit respondents....

Second, the issue of fact must be "genuine." Fed. Rules Civ. Proc. 56(c), (e). When the moving party has carried its burden under Rule 56(c), its opponent must do more than simply show that there is some metaphysical doubt as to the material facts.... Where the record taken as a whole could not lead a rational trier of fact to find for the non-moving party, there is no "genuine issue for trial."

It follows from these settled principles that if the factual context renders respondents' claim implausible—if the claim is one that simply makes no economic sense—respondents must come forward with more persuasive evidence to support their claim than would otherwise be necessary....

Respondents correctly note that "[o]n summary judgment the inferences to be drawn from the underlying facts... must be viewed in the light most favorable to the party opposing the motion...." But antitrust law limits the range of permissible inferences from ambiguous evidence in a § 1 case. Thus, in *Monsanto Co. v. Spray-Rite Service Corp.*, 465 U.S. 752 (1984), we held that conduct as consistent with permissible competition as with illegal conspiracy does not, standing alone, support an inference of antitrust conspiracy. To survive a motion for summary judgment or for a directed verdict, a plaintiff seeking damages for a violation of § 1 must present evidence "that tends to exclude the possibility" that the alleged conspirators acted independently. 465 U.S., at 764. Respondents in this case, in other words, must show that the inference of conspiracy is reasonable in light of the competing inferences of independent action or collusive action that could not have harmed respondents.

Petitioners argue that these principles apply fully to this case. According to petitioners, the alleged conspiracy is one that is economically irrational and practically infeasible. Consequently, petitioners contend, they had no motive to engage in the alleged predatory pricing conspiracy; indeed, they had a strong motive *not* to conspire in the manner respondents allege. Petitioners argue that, in light of the absence of any apparent motive and the ambiguous nature of the evidence of conspiracy, no trier of fact reasonably could find that the conspiracy with which petitioners are charged actually existed. This argument requires us to consider the nature of the alleged conspiracy and the practical obstacles to its implementation.

IV

A

A predatory pricing conspiracy is by nature speculative. Any agreement to price below the competitive level requires the conspirators to forgo profits that free competition would offer them. The forgone profits may be considered an investment in the future. For the investment to be rational, the conspirators must have a reasonable expectation of recovering, in the form of later monopoly profits, more than the losses suffered. . . . [T]he success of such schemes is inherently uncertain: the short-run loss is definite, but the long-run gain depends on successfully neutralizing the competition. Moreover, it is not enough simply to achieve monopoly power, as monopoly pricing may breed quick entry by new competitors eager to share in the excess profits. The success of any predatory scheme depends on *maintaining* monopoly power for long enough both to recoup the predator's losses and to harvest some additional gain. . . . For this reason, there is a consensus among commentators that predatory pricing schemes are rarely tried, and even more rarely successful. See, *e.g.*, Bork, [The Antitrust Paradox, pp. 149–55 (1978)]; Areeda & Turner, Predatory Pricing and Related Practices Under Section 2 of the Sherman Act, 88 Harv.L.Rev. 697, 699 (1975); Easterbrook, [*Predatory Strategies and Counterstrategies*, 48 U. Chi. L. Rev. 263, 268 (1981)]; Koller, *The Myth of Predatory Pricing—An Empirical Study*, 4 Antitrust Law & Econ.Rev. 105 (1971); McGee, *Predatory Price Cutting: The Standard Oil (N.J.) Case*, 1 J.Law & Econ. 137 (1958); McGee, *Predatory Pricing Revisited*, 23 J.Law & Econ., at 292–294. . . .

These observations apply even to predatory pricing by a *single firm* seeking monopoly power. In this case, respondents allege that a large number of firms have conspired over a period of many years to charge below-market prices in order to stifle competition. Such a conspiracy is incalculably more difficult to execute than an analogous plan undertaken by a single predator. The conspirators must allocate the losses to be sustained during the conspiracy's operation, and must also allocate any gains to be realized from its success. Precisely because success is speculative and depends on a willingness to endure losses for an indefinite period, each conspirator has a strong incentive to cheat, letting its partners suffer the losses necessary to destroy the competition while sharing in any gains if the conspiracy succeeds. . . .

Finally, if predatory pricing conspiracies are generally unlikely to occur, they are especially so where, as here, the prospects of attaining monopoly power seem slight. In order to recoup their losses, petitioners must obtain enough market power to set higher than competitive prices, and then must sustain those prices long enough to earn in excess profits what they earlier gave up in below-cost prices. . . . Two decades after their conspiracy is alleged to have commenced, petitioners appear to be far from achieving this goal: the two largest shares of the retail market in television sets are held by RCA and respondent Zenith, not by any of petitioners. . . .

The alleged conspiracy's failure to achieve its ends in the two decades of its asserted operation is strong evidence that the conspiracy does not in fact exist. . . .

. . . .

V

As our discussion in Part IV-A shows, petitioners had no motive to enter into the alleged conspiracy. To the contrary, as presumably rational businesses, petitioners had every incentive *not* to engage in the conduct with which they are charged, for its likely effect would be to generate losses for petitioners with no corresponding gains. The Court of Appeals did not take account of the absence of a plausible motive to enter into the alleged predatory pricing conspiracy. . . .

[L]ack of motive bears on the range of permissible conclusions that might be drawn from ambiguous evidence: if petitioners had no rational economic motive to conspire, and if their conduct is consistent with other, equally plausible explanations, the conduct does not give rise to an inference of conspiracy. . . . [T]he predatory pricing scheme that this conduct is said to prove is one that makes no practical sense: it calls for petitioners to destroy companies larger and better established than themselves, a goal that remains far distant more than two decades after the conspiracy's birth. Even had they succeeded in obtaining their monopoly, there is nothing in the record to suggest that they could recover the losses they would need to sustain along the way. In sum, in light of the absence of any rational motive to conspire, neither petitioners' pricing practices, nor their conduct in the Japanese market, nor their agreements respecting prices and distribution in the American market, suffice to create a "genuine issue for trial."[10]

. . . .

Justice White, with whom Justice Brennan, Justice Blackmun, and Justice Stevens join, dissenting.

. . . .

III

In reversing the Third Circuit's judgment, the Court identifies two alleged errors: "(i) [T]he 'direct evidence' on which the [Court of Appeals] relied had little, if any, relevance to the alleged predatory pricing conspiracy; and (ii) the court failed to consider the absence of a plausible motive to engage in predatory pricing." The Court's position is without substance.

A

The first claim of error is that the Third Circuit treated evidence regarding price fixing in Japan and the so-called five company rule and check prices as "'direct

10. [Court's footnote #21] We do not imply that, if petitioners had had a plausible reason to conspire, ambiguous conduct could suffice to create a triable issue of conspiracy. Our decision in *Monsanto Co. v. Spray-Rite Service Corp.*, 465 U.S. 752 (1984), establishes that conduct that is as consistent with permissible competition as with illegal conspiracy does not, without more, support even an inference of conspiracy.

evidence' of a conspiracy that injured respondents." . . . [A]fter reviewing evidence of cartel activity in Japan, collusive establishment of dumping prices in this country, and long-term, below-cost sales, the Third Circuit held that a factfinder could reasonably conclude that the five company rule was not a simple price-raising device:

> "[A] factfinder might reasonably infer that the allocation of customers in the United States, combined with price-fixing in Japan, was intended to permit concentration of the effects of dumping upon American competitors while eliminating competition among the Japanese manufacturers in either market."

I see nothing erroneous in this reasoning.

B

The Court's second charge of error is that the Third Circuit was not sufficiently skeptical of respondents' allegation that petitioners engaged in predatory pricing conspiracy. But the Third Circuit is not required to engage in academic discussions about predation; it is required to decide whether respondents' evidence creates a genuine issue of material fact. . . .

The Third Circuit indicated that it considers respondents' evidence sufficient to create a genuine factual issue regarding long-term, below-cost sales by petitioners. The Court tries to whittle away at this conclusion by suggesting that the "expert opinion evidence of below-cost pricing has little probative value in comparison with the economic factors . . . that suggest that such conduct is irrational." But the question is not whether the Court finds respondents' experts persuasive, or prefers the District Court's analysis; it is whether, viewing the evidence in the light most favorable to respondents, a jury or other factfinder could reasonably conclude that petitioners engaged in long-term, below-cost sales. I agree with the Third Circuit that the answer to this question is "yes."

. . . .

Notes and Questions

1. *Matsushita* articulated two central summary judgment principles: First, "if the factual context renders [plaintiffs'] claim implausible—if the claim is one that simply makes no economic sense—[plaintiffs] must come forward with more persuasive evidence to support their claim than would otherwise be necessary." 475 U.S. at 587. Second, the Court cited its decision in *Monsanto Co. v. Spray-Rite Service Corp.*, 465 U.S. 752 (1984), for the proposition that "conduct as consistent with permissible competition as with illegal conspiracy does not, standing alone, support an inference of antitrust conspiracy." 475 U.S. at 588. In a footnote, the Court suggested that the latter limitation is distinct and applies regardless of the plausibility of the alleged conspiracy. *See id.* at 597 n. 21.

2. *Eastman Kodak Co. v. Image Technical Services, Inc.*, 504 U.S. 451 (1992), supports the view that *Matsushita* did not change the standard for granting summary judgment. That case involved an antitrust claim against Kodak alleging that it had unlawfully tied the provision of service for its copiers to the sale of its parts by refusing to make parts available to independent service organizations. To establish their claim, plaintiffs were required to demonstrate that Kodak had "market power" in the parts aftermarket. Kodak contended that such power could not, as a matter of law, be found to exist because it was undisputed that it lacked market power in the original equipment copier market. Kodak argued that, as a result, any attempt to exercise such power in the derivative parts aftermarket would have failed because purchasers of new copiers would have taken account of that fact by purchasing their copiers from other suppliers. The Supreme Court rejected the argument on the ground that evidence of various market imperfections such as purchaser "lock in" and imperfect "life cycle pricing" supported plaintiffs theory, as did actual evidence that Kodak had in fact exercised power in the derivative aftermarket by charging supra-competitive prices for its service and providing service of lower quality than that offered by the ISOs. In this context, the Supreme Court held that summary judgment had improperly been granted, stating:

> The Court's requirement in *Matsushita* that the plaintiffs' claims make economic sense did not introduce a special burden on plaintiffs facing summary judgment in antitrust cases. The Court did not hold that if the moving party enunciates any economic theory supporting its behavior, regardless of its accuracy in reflecting the actual market, it is entitled to summary judgment. *Matsushita* demands only that the nonmoving party's inferences be reasonable in order to reach the jury, a requirement that was not invented, but merely articulated, in that decision. If the plaintiff's theory is economically senseless, no reasonable jury could find in its favor, and summary judgment should be granted.
>
> Kodak, then, bears a substantial burden in showing that it is entitled to summary judgment. It must show that despite evidence of increased prices and excluded competition, an inference of market power is unreasonable.

504 U.S. at 468–69 (citations omitted). This statement obviously stands in uneasy tension with *Matsushita* and *Monsanto*, a tension that the Court did not attempt to resolve.

D. Early Settlement

1. Excerpts from the Manual for Complex Litigation

The discussion of settlement in the Manual for Complex Litigation is particularly helpful in describing the realities and dynamics of the settlement process.

Substantial excerpts from that discussion accordingly are set forth below, including the MANUAL's section headings indicating the topics of discussion.

13. Settlement

13.1 Trial Judge's Role

§ 13.11 General Principles

Some cases involve important questions of law or public policy that are best resolved by public, official adjudication. Other times, however, resistance to settlement arises from unreasonable or unrealistic attitudes of parties and counsel, in which case the judge can help them reexamine their premises and assess their cases realistically. The judge can encourage the settlement process by asking at the first pretrial conference whether settlement discussions have occurred or might be scheduled. As the case progresses, the judge occasionally can suggest that the parties reexamine their positions in light of current or anticipated developments.

The judge can then facilitate negotiations by removing obstacles to compromise and can help overcome the intransigence or militance of clients. Without touching on the merits, the judge can focus the parties' attention on the likely cost of litigating the case to conclusion, in fees, expenses, time, and other resources. Other helpful measures include scheduling settlement conferences, directing or encouraging reluctant parties, insurers, and other potential contributors to participate, suggesting and arranging for a neutral person to assist negotiations, targeting discovery at information needed for settlement, and promptly deciding motions whose resolution will lay the groundwork for settlement.

Judges may be particularly helpful in identifying and encouraging consideration of nonmonetary solutions. Where, for example, the parties contemplate a continuing relationship, the court can stimulate thought about innovative and mutually beneficial arrangements for the future that may pave the way for agreement on monetary terms. . . .

Settlement efforts, however, should not delay or divert the pretrial process; both can and should operate effectively on parallel tracks. Nor should settlement efforts be permitted to impair the parties' perception of judicial fairness and impartiality. Some judges participate actively in settlement discussions of a case, as well as handling pretrial activity and trial if the case does not settle. Others are uncomfortable in what they view as a dual role. Occasionally, the parties request that the assigned judge participate in settlement discussions, waiving the right to seek recusal. Such involvement, however, might affect the parties' confidence in the judge's ability to try the case impartially. Thus, many judges rarely engage in substantive settlement negotiations in cases they are expected to try, particularly by bench trial. Instead, they bring in another judge or other neutral person for settlement purposes. . . .

§ 13.12 Timing/Relationship to Discovery

Many judges broach settlement at the initial scheduling conference. Counsel should prepare by discussing the possibility of settlement during the Federal Rule of Civil Procedure 26(f) conference, as the rule requires, and becoming familiar with their clients' positions. . . . Counsel should attend settlement conferences with full settlement authority or with immediate access to their client. Any impending or finalized settlement should be disclosed to the court promptly.

Although settlement should be explored early in the case, the parties may be unwilling or unable to settle until they have conducted some discovery. The benefits of settlement are diminished, however, if it is postponed until discovery is completed. A better approach may be to target early discovery at information needed for settlement negotiations. . . .

§ 13.13 Specific Techniques to Promote Settlement

A number of techniques have proven successful in promoting settlement. The list below is not exhaustive, and creativity in this aspect of the litigation has few risks. The following techniques may be productive:

- *Firm trial date.* Setting a firm trial date is generally the most effective means to motivate parties to settle. . . .
- *Reference to another judge or magistrate judge.* One way to avoid the appearance of partiality is to refer the parties to another judge or magistrate judge for settlement negotiations. . . .
- *Participation by parties.* Requesting or requiring that the parties or representatives attend settlement conferences may expedite negotiations and help avoid the delays involved in seeking authority. In any event, the attending parties will become better informed of the strengths and weaknesses of each side's case and the costs and risks of pursuing the litigation. The parties' presence can, however, inhibit frank discussion by counsel, who may feel obliged to keep up appearances for the benefit of their clients.
- *Confidential discussions with judge.* A judicial meeting with each party (or side) separately for confidential discussions, with their mutual consent, may help the parties find common ground. . . .
- *Settlement counsel, special masters, or experts.* The litigating attorneys may not be suited to conduct settlement discussions and may be hampered by personal antagonisms developed in the course of the litigation. In such cases, consider suggesting that one or more of the parties engage or designate special settlement counsel separate from lead and liaison counsel. Judges have also used special masters to assist in settlement of complex litigation and in post-settlement claims-resolution proceedings. . . .

- *Contribution bar orders.* To facilitate partial settlements in multiparty cases, the court may (unless prohibited by the underlying statute) approve as a term of the settlement an order barring claims for contribution or indemnification by nonsettling defendants. . . .
- *Offer of judgment.* Federal Rule of Civil Procedure 68 allows a party defending against a claim to serve an offer of judgment on the adverse party at any time up to ten days before trial (or proceedings to determine damages if liability has already been adjudged). The party served has ten days to accept or be liable for all costs incurred after the offer is made, unless it obtains a more favorable judgment. The court's invoking this procedure can create an added incentive to accept a reasonable offer in litigation (such as antitrust) where taxable costs may be high, particularly where the underlying statute defines costs to include attorneys' fees. . . .
- *Representative case(s).* The results of a trial of one or a few representative lead cases can provide information and motivation helpful to settlement of related cases.
- *Severance.* The early resolution of one or more issues by separate trial may provide a basis for settlement of others. The resolution of liability, damages, or other pivotal issues can provide the parties with the information or incentive needed for a comprehensive settlement. . . .

§ 13.14 Review and Approval

Ordinarily, settlement does not require judicial review and approval. Many of the exceptions to this rule, however, are of particular relevance to complex litigation. The Federal Rules require court approval of settlements in class actions (including actions brought by or against an unincorporated association as a class), shareholder derivative actions, and actions in which a receiver has been appointed. The antitrust laws require court approval of consent judgments proposed by the United States in actions it has instituted. . . .

. . . .

The judge must guard against the temptation to become an advocate—either in favor of the settlement because of a desire to conclude the litigation, or against the settlement because of the responsibility to protect the rights of those not party to it. . . .

The trial court may not rewrite a settlement agreement; if it is unacceptable the court must disapprove it, but it may suggest changes. . . .

. . . .

§ 13.23 Side Agreements

Agreements allocating financial responsibility among persons or entities are common—contracts of insurance and indemnification are prime examples. Occasionally, however, litigants try to apportion damages through side agreements that supplement their formal settlement agreements but are not intended to be disclosed to others. These agreements may not of themselves be unlawful or unethical, and on occasion there may be legitimate reasons for not disclosing them to other parties. In presenting settlement agreements for judicial approval, however, the parties are obliged to make full disclosure of all terms and understandings, including any side agreements. The settling parties may request that certain terms not be disclosed to other parties, but must justify this to the court.

Common types of side agreements include the following:

- *"Mary Carter" agreements.* In return for a settlement payment, the plaintiff may agree to release a particular defendant from liability, even though the defendant remains party to the suit, with the further provision that the defendant will be reimbursed in some specified manner out of any recovery against other defendants. . . . These agreements have been criticized as unfair to nonsettling defendants, because they align the interests of the "settling" defendant, who remains in the litigation, with those of the plaintiff (usually covertly), eliminating their normal adversarial relationship. Nevertheless, courts have rarely rejected a settlement on this basis, although it is advisable for the court to give such agreements particular scrutiny.

  The primary problem raised by Mary Carter agreements is disclosure. Typically, parties enter them secretly or request that the court not disclose the terms of the agreement. Nondisclosure, however, magnifies the prejudice to other parties, since neither the jury nor the defense can take the agreement into account when considering the testimony of the settling defendant; the agreement may therefore be ground for a new trial. For this reason, case law favors requiring disclosure of such agreements to the court, parties, and jury. . . .

- *Sharing agreements.* Defendants sometimes agree in advance to allocate responsibility for damages among themselves according to an agreed formula (often based on market share). These agreements serve the legitimate purposes of controlling parties' exposure and preventing plaintiffs from forcing an unfair settlement by threats to show favoritism in the collection of any judgment that may be recovered. They may, however, expressly prohibit or indirectly discourage individual settlements. They also create a disincentive for defendants to make available evidence indicating liability on the part of codefendants. Therefore, although they are generally appropriate, the court may refuse to approve or enforce agreements that violate public policy or unfairly prejudice other parties.

Sharing agreements should be discoverable. Once the agreement is made known, it may be possible to structure partial settlements to take its terms into account. . . .

- *"Most-favored nation" clauses.* Settlement agreements proposed early in the litigation often contain a "most-favored nation" clause to encourage early settlement by protecting all parties against being prejudiced by later, more favorable settlements with others. Such clauses typically obligate a signatory plaintiff to give signatory defendants a proportionate refund if the former settles with other defendants for less, or a signatory defendant to make additional payments to signatory plaintiffs if the former settles with other plaintiffs for more.

  Such clauses have several drawbacks: (1) the potential liability under them is indeterminate, making them risky; (2) the additional recovery they may produce for some plaintiffs without any effort by their attorneys makes it difficult to fix fees; and (3) the factors that induce parties to settle with different parties for different amounts, such as the time of settlement and the relative strength of claims, are nullified. Such clauses can provide an incentive for early settlement as well as an obstacle to later settlements. . . .

  . . . .

§ 22.91 Judicial Role and Settlement

In mass torts, as in other types of complex litigation, questions regarding the appropriate extent of judicial involvement in settlement negotiations are important because the costs associated with recusing a judge familiar with the litigation are high. Although some judges participate actively in settlement negotiations, others insulate themselves from the negotiations, leaving this activity to a magistrate judge, a special master, or a settlement judge. Judges who have been involved in unsuccessful settlement negotiations sometimes turn over to another judge the responsibility for trying the case because they have been privy to information on the merits of the case or on issues that would otherwise not have been revealed. Judges who have been involved in successful settlement negotiations may transfer to another judge judicial review of the settlement to avoid having to rule on the fairness, reasonableness, and adequacy of a settlement they helped to craft.

In some cases, a judge can facilitate settlement negotiations by establishing a system to collect information about past, pending, and likely future claims. In some MDL mass tort centralizations, courts have ordered claimants to complete questionnaires eliciting a wide range of information, such as the circumstances of their exposures and the severity of their injuries, to facilitate settlement negotiations or improve claim administration following settlement. . . . Judges have occasionally appointed special masters to assemble databases documenting essential information concerning the

> thousands of personal injury claims that may be pending. Special masters have sometimes used electronic data to compare individual pending cases against closed cases having similar characteristics to produce a range of settlement values.
>
> ....
>
> Parties that are unable to agree on a global settlement may still be able to agree on a process for resolving the litigation. For example, in cases involving immature torts, the parties may agree to use test-case trials to establish a range of values for resolving similar claims. Alternatively, they may agree to draw a representative sample of claims and resolve the sample through mediation, arbitration, or another form of alternative dispute resolution. Information generated through trials or ADR processes might enable the parties to arrive at a reasonable estimate of the value of the aggregate claims from which they drew the sample. Alternative dispute resolution techniques (e.g., summary jury trials) may assist the parties in valuing cases for settlement purposes and give the court and parties information about the viability of various trial options. Yet another approach is to appoint a special master to facilitate settlement by reviewing information on liability and damages and placing an estimated value on each claim. Judges have used this approach with considerable success in both single-incident and dispersed mass tort litigation.

MANUAL FOR COMPLEX LITIGATION §§ 13.1–13.23, 22.91 (2004) (footnotes omitted) (4th ed. 2007).

Notes and Questions

1. The MANUAL clearly contemplates the active involvement of the trial judge in promoting settlement of complex cases. Is this desirable? What dangers does it pose? Does a judge's engagement in settlement discussions increase the possibility of recusal?

2. In its discussion of the settlement of mass tort cases in § 22.91, the MANUAL notes various techniques including resolution of cases through ADR or the trial of test cases by which judges can collect information about the settlement value of pending claims. A large body of literature has discussed the importance of the "maturity" of mass torts in achieving their fair and efficient global resolution. Professor McGovern has written a number of leading articles on the concept of "maturity" in mass tort litigation. *See, e.g.*, Francis E. McGovern, *An Analysis of Mass Torts for Judges*, 73 TEX. L. REV. 1821 (1995). Professor McGovern explains that "maturity" of a mass tort occurs when relevant evidence has been fully developed in discovery, multiple verdicts or settlements have been reached, and novel legal issues have been resolved on appeal. At that point, sufficient information is available to make an acceptable global resolution possible. *Id.* at 1843. *See also* Francis E. McGovern, *The*

Tragedy of the Asbestos Commons, 88 VA. L. REV. 1721, 1739 n.42 (2002) (concluding that with the passage of time, multiple trials and settlements will establish a "marketplace of consistent values.").

E. Other Alternatives to Litigation

1. Overview of Methods of Alternative Dispute Resolution

The expense and delay of litigation in general, and of complex cases in particular, has led parties and courts to explore possibly more efficient and less burdensome alternatives to the judicial forum. In depth treatment of this development is the subject matter of law school courses in alternative dispute resolution and an enormous volume of literature. The American Bar Association Section of Litigation has published an excellent summary of the characteristics, advantages, and disadvantages of the most prevalent forms of alternative dispute resolution. *See* ALTERNATIVE DISPUTE RESOLUTION: THE LITIGATOR'S HANDBOOK 3–16 (Nancy F. Atlas, et al. eds., American Bar Association 2000). It canvases the characteristics, advantages, and disadvantages of common techniques such as neutral fact-finding, early neutral evaluation, mediation, summary jury trials, mini-trials, and arbitration as a means of obtaining a non-judicial resolution of a dispute. (Mediation and arbitration also are discussed in Chapter 5, section B of this text.)

Except for arbitration discussed separately below, these alternative dispute resolution techniques do not lead to a binding determination of the dispute. Rather, they seek to establish a process that will facilitate settlement of the action through use of a negotiation intermediary (mediation), or by obtaining a non-binding evaluation of the facts (neutral fact finding), or a determination by a neutral third-party decision-maker based on an abbreviated presentation of the evidence (early neutral evaluation, summary jury trials, and mini-trials). The precise details of these procedures are created by agreement of the parties, and accordingly vary from case to case.

2. Arbitration Under the Federal Arbitration Act

Arbitration under the Federal Arbitration Act is being employed with increasing frequency to obtain a binding resolution of complex commercial, antitrust, and securities disputes, as well as employment discrimination and consumer claims that previously have been the grist of class action and other aggregate litigation. The FAA was originally enacted in 1925. Congress later reenacted and codified the Act in 1947 as Title 9 of the United States Code. 9 U.S.C. §§ 1–16 (2000). Section 2 of the Act provides that "[a] written provision in any maritime transaction or a contract evidencing a transaction involving commerce to settle by arbitration a controversy thereafter arising out of such contract or transaction . . . shall be valid, irrevocable, and enforceable, save upon such grounds as exist at law or in equity for the revocation of any contract." Section 4 of the Act provides that a federal court should order compliance with an arbitration agreement if the court is "satisfied that the making of the agreement for arbitration or the failure to comply therewith is not in issue." The Act also provides for a stay of proceedings in federal district courts when an issue in the proceeding is referable to arbitration. *See id.* at § 3.

The Act was intended to "reverse the longstanding judicial hostility to arbitration agreements that had existed at English common law and had been adopted by American courts, and to place arbitration agreements upon the same footing as other contracts." *Gilmer v. Interstate/Johnson Lane Corp.*, 500 U.S. 20, 24 (1991). In *Southland Corp. v. Keating*, 465 U.S. 1, 10–11 (1984), the Supreme Court described the background and purpose of the Act as follows in the course of an opinion holding that the Act preempted California law prohibiting the arbitration of claims under that State's Franchise Investment Law:

> In enacting § 2 of the federal Act, Congress declared a national policy favoring arbitration and withdrew the power of the states to require a judicial forum for the resolution of claims which the contacting parties agreed to resolve by arbitration. . . .
>
> We discern only two limitations on the enforceability of arbitration provisions governed by the Federal Arbitration Act: they must be part of a written maritime contract or a contract "evidencing a transaction involving commerce" and such clauses may be revoked upon "grounds as exist at law or in equity for the revocation of any contract." We see nothing in the Act indicating that the broad principle of enforceability is subject to any additional limitations under State law.

The Court made clear that the substantive arbitration law created by and under the Act was applicable in both federal and state court and that "the purpose of the act was to assure those who desired arbitration and whose contracts related to interstate commerce that their expectations would not be undermined by federal judges, or . . . by state courts or legislatures." *Id.* at 13 (quoting *Metro Industrial Painting Corp. v. Terminal Construction Co.*, 287 F.2d 382, 387 (2d Cir. 1961) (Lumbard, C.J., concurring)).

Despite its apparent simplicity, the Act raises a host of complex issues. As arbitration agreements have spread beyond international and commercial contractual disputes in recent years to encompass a vast array of statutory and non-statutory claims in the antitrust, securities, employment, and consumer fields, federal and state courts have issued an impressive body of opinions addressing a wide range of questions under the Act.

The Supreme Court has made clear that whether a claim is arbitrable depends upon the agreement of the parties. The court must perform the "gateway" function of determining such matters as "whether the parties have a valid arbitration agreement at all or whether a concededly binding arbitration clause applies to a certain type of controversy." *Green Tree Financial Corp. v. Bazzle*, 539 U.S. 444, 452 (2003).

On the other hand, recent decisions have suggested that "procedural" issues relating not to whether the parties have agreed to arbitrate a matter, but rather to what kind of arbitration proceeding they have agreed to, are, absent clear resolution in the arbitration agreement itself, to be resolved by the arbitrators rather than the court. *Id* at 452–53. In *Green Tree Financial*, for example, a plurality opinion, joined by Justice Stevens concurring in the result, concluded that the question whether the arbitration agreement prohibited class arbitration was for the arbitrator, rather than the court, to decide. (The question of class arbitration is explored in more depth below and in Chapter 6.G.) The plurality stated:

> At the same time, we cannot automatically accept the South Carolina Supreme Court's resolution of this contract-interpretation question. Under the terms of the parties' contracts, the question—whether the agreement forbids class arbitration—is for the arbitrator to decide. The parties agreed to submit to the arbitrator "[*a*]*ll* disputes, claims, or controversies arising from or relating to this contract or the relationships which result from this contract." *Ibid.* (emphasis added). And the dispute about what the arbitration contract in each case means (*i.e.*, whether it forbids the use of class arbitration procedures) is a dispute "relating to this contract" and the resulting "relationships." Hence the parties seem to have agreed that an arbitrator, not a judge, would answer the relevant question. . . . And if there is doubt about that matter—about the "'scope of arbitrable issues'"—we should resolve that doubt "'in favor of arbitration.'" *Mitsubishi Motors Corp. v. Soler Chrysler-Plymouth, Inc.*, 473 U.S. 614, 626 (1985).

Green Tree Financial Corp., 539 U.S. at 451–53.

Even if a dispute is determined to be arbitrable under the terms of the parties' agreement, however, there may be a defense to arbitration. One defense is that Congress intended to preclude a waiver of federal judicial remedies for enforcement of a statutory right, based on appraisal of the text, legislative history, and policies underlying the particular statutory scheme at issue. *See Shearson/American Express, Inc. v. McMahon*, 482 U.S. 220, 226–27 (1987). For example, in earlier years, the Supreme Court and lower courts held that requiring arbitration of claims under the federal antitrust and securities acts would be contrary to the policies underlying those statutes. *See, e.g., Wilko v. Swan*, 346 U.S. 427 (1953) (claims under the Securities Act of 1933); *American Safety Equipment Corp. v. J.P. Maguire & Co.*, 391 F.2d 821 (2d Cir. 1968) (precluding arbitration of federal antitrust claims). Since 1980, however, the Supreme Court consistently has concluded that the arbitration of these and other statutory claims is not contrary to the policies of the underlying statutes. In *Gilmer v. Interstate/Johnson Lane Corp.*, 500 U.S. 20, 26 (1991), the Court stated, "[a]lthough all statutory claims may not be appropriate for arbitration, 'having made the bargain to arbitrate, the party should be held to it unless Congress itself has evinced an intention to preclude a waiver of judicial remedies for the statutory rights at issue.'" *Id.* Additionally, the Court explained that the burden was on Gilmer, the party seeking to avoid arbitration, "to show that Congress intended to preclude a waiver of a judicial forum for ADEA claims." *Id.* Further, such questions "must be addressed with a healthy regard for the federal policy favoring arbitration." *Id.* (quoting *Moses H. Cone Memorial Hosp. v. Mercury Const. Corp.*, 460 U.S. 1, 24 (1983)).

The conclusion that agreements to arbitrate federal statutory claims generally are enforceable does not resolve all issues arising from the need to protect federal statutory policies. In theory, a court might find specific provisions of an arbitration agreement regarding the arbitration of statutory claims to be in conflict with the Congressional objectives embodied in the statutory scheme, and so might strike them from the arbitration agreement if they are found to be severable, or, if not, strike down the agreement to arbitrate itself. . . . [H]owever, this "vindication of statutory rights" doctrine as a basis for modifying or invalidating arbitration agreements has been severely limited by the Supreme Court's decision in *American Express Co. v. Italian Colors Restaurant*, 133 S. Ct. 2304 (2013). In that decision, the Court rejected the doctrine as a basis for invalidating class action waivers in arbitration agreements in so far as the theory was that, absent the ability to maintain class proceedings, the litigation of plaintiff's claims would not be economically viable because the cost would exceed the potential recovery.

The Act also makes clear that generally applicable contract defenses may be raised to the enforcement of arbitration agreements. Section 2 of the Act expressly provides that written arbitration agreements subject to its provisions "shall be valid, irrevocable, and enforceable, *save upon such grounds as exist at law or in equity for the revocation of any contract.*" 9 U.S.C. § 2 (emphasis added). The purpose of the Act was to place arbitration agreements on the "same footing" as other contracts, not a superior footing. Accordingly, the Supreme Court has made clear that "[g]enerally applicable contract defenses, such as fraud, duress, or unconscionability, may be applied to invalidate arbitration agreements without contravening § 2." *Doctor's Associates, Inc. v. Casarotto*, 517 U.S. 681, 682 (1996).

Particularly since the Supreme Court's decision in *Gilmer, supra*, holding that federal employment discrimination claims may be subjected to binding arbitration agreements, claims of state law unconscionability have been raised with increasing frequency, on the grounds that arbitration agreements in the employment context usually are adhesive contracts with no opportunity for negotiation, and often contain one-sided provisions that apply unevenly to employers and employees and impose severe limitations on the remedies available to employees. For example, in *Ingle v. Circuit City Stores, Inc.*, 328 F.3d 1165, 1171–72 (9th Cir. 2003), the Ninth Circuit invalidated Circuit City's arbitration agreement with its employees on the grounds that the employees' unequal bargaining position precluded them from enjoying a meaningful opportunity to negotiate the terms of the contract ("procedural unconscionability"), coupled with the fact that the terms of the agreement were "so one-sided as to shock the conscience" ("substantive unconscionability"). The court noted that the agreement (1) was limited only to claims of employees, not those of the employer against its employees, (2) imposed a statute of limitations significantly shorter than the statutory period, (3) prohibited class arbitration, (4) required a filing fee that would not apply in a court action, (5) required the parties to split the often substantial costs of arbitration and authorized the arbitration panel to order the losing party to bear all of the costs of arbitration, (6) failed to authorize all of the relief that would be available in court by limiting, inter alia, the amount of front and back pay and punitive damages, and (7) permitted Circuit City, but not its employees, unilaterally to terminate the agreement. *See id.* at 1171–79. Similar provisions have generated a substantial volume of litigation in the federal courts of appeals. Such decisions have now been significantly limited by the Supreme Court's important decision in *AT&T Mobility LLC v. Concepcion*, 131 S. Ct. 1740 (2011), holding that state unconscionability doctrine is preempted by the FAA to the extent it is invoked to invalidate class action waivers in arbitration agreements.

Indeed, the Supreme Court has extended its preemption thinking to a potential conflict between the FAA and the National Labor Relations Act (NLRA). Section 7 of the NLRA provides that workers have the right to "self-organization, to form, join, or assist labor organizations, to bargain collectively . . . , *and to engage in other concerted activities for the purpose of collective bargaining or other mutual aid or protection.*" 29 U.S.C. § 157 (emphasis added). Some federal circuits used to interpret this language to mean that workers have a substantive right to sue their employers collectively, thus prohibiting mandatory arbitration provisions that purport to bar class actions. The Supreme Court in *Epic Systems Corp. v. Lewis*, 138 S. Ct. 1612 (2018), held that Congress did not intend by the NLRA language to allow workers to pursue employment rights through class actions. Therefore, said the Court, class action bans in arbitration clauses in collective bargaining agreements are not unlawful. The majority in *Epic Systems* also reaffirmed that the "Saving Clause" in the FAA only "allows courts to refuse to enforce arbitration agreements 'upon such grounds as exist at law or in equity for the revocation of any contract,'" *id.* at 1622, which in turn means "generally applicable contract defenses, such as fraud, duress, or unconscionability." *Id.*

Unlike consumer contracts and employment agreements, arbitration agreements between sophisticated parties will not be likely be held unconscionable, and might at first blush appear to present an attractive opportunity to reduce the costs and delays of litigation. This is particularly true in light of the fact that the discovery authorized by arbitration agreements and rules typically is more limited than that under the Federal Rules of Civil Procedure and their state counterparts, because strict rules of evidence do not apply, and because only limited judicial review of arbitration awards is permitted. *See* 1 Martin Domke & Larry E. Edmondson, Domke on Commercial Arbitration §§ 1:6, 32:1, 38:9 (3d ed. 2003).

In reality, however, the resolution of complex cases can be extremely time consuming and expensive even in the arbitral forum. The fact that discovery may be somewhat more limited and evidentiary rules somewhat relaxed does not mean that substantial discovery burdens will not exist or that the presentation of cases will not be difficult, time consuming, and expensive. Unlike court processes, which are provided at public expense, parties to the arbitration must defray all of its costs, including the fees of the arbitration panel, which can be very substantial, and the costs of facilities, travel, and administration. Moreover, arbitration agreements frequently provide for the appointment by each party of a "party" arbitrator, and their joint agreement on a "neutral" arbitrator, who presides. *See* 1 Domke on Commercial Arbitration § 24:4. This format may lend itself to "compromise" decisions that satisfy neither party and which are not subject to meaningful appellate review. *See id.* (noting that the "neutral" arbitrator on a three-person panel "may have to compromise in order to come to a majority award," and therefore concluding that "[t]he use of tripartite boards should be discouraged in commercial arbitration in the interest of the parties themselves in obtaining a fair decision"). In sum, the advantages of arbitration over court proceedings often are less than they initially might seem.

F. Streamlining the Trial Process

1. Is There a Complexity Exception to the Seventh Amendment?

The core of the American judicial system is the trial. Central to the trial is the jury, a neutral fact-finder comprised of the parties' peers. Complex cases, however, pose special problems for juries. The length of the trials and the number of parties, along with the complexity of the legal theories and factual issues presented, can make serving on a jury difficult and rendering a rational verdict even harder. This has led litigants, judges, and academics to wonder whether certain complex cases could be removed from jury decision-making.

Parties seeking to avoid the risks and uncertainties of juries, and judges wanting to streamline the judicial process through the elimination of juries, have many possible paths, but they face one chief obstacle, the Seventh Amendment to the United States Constitution. It provides that "In Suits at common law, where the value in controversy shall exceed twenty dollars, the right of a trial by jury shall be preserved." The Supreme Court has ruled that:

> The "right to a jury trial includes more than the common-law forms of action recognized in 1791 [when the 7th Amendment was ratified]; the phrase "Suits at common law" refers to "suits in which legal rights [are] to be ascertained and determined, in contradistinction to those where equitable rights alone [are] recognized, and equitable remedies [are] administered. . . ."
>
> To determine whether a particular action will resolve legal rights, we examine both the nature of the issues involved and the remedy sought. "First, we compare the statutory action to 18th-century actions brought in the courts of England prior to the merger of the courts of law and equity. Second, we examine the remedy sought and determine whether it is legal or equitable in nature." The second inquiry is the more important in our analysis.

Chauffeurs, Teamsters & Helpers, Local No. 391 v. Terry, 494 U.S. 558, 564–65 (1990).

The adoption of the Federal Rules of Civil Procedure and the merger of law and equity did not diminish the importance of the right to a jury trial for legal claims. Rule 38(a) provides that "The right of trial by jury as declared by the Seventh Amendment to the Constitution—or as provided by a federal statute—is preserved to the parties inviolate." The Supreme Court traditionally has taken great care to protect the right. "Maintenance of the jury as a fact-finding body is of such importance and occupies so firm a place in our history and jurisprudence that any seeming curtailment of the right to a jury trial should be scrutinized with the utmost care." *Dimick v. Schiedt*, 293 U.S. 474, 486 (1935).

Thus, in a suit containing both equitable and legal claims, the treatment of the former cannot infringe upon the right to have a jury resolve the latter. *See Beacon Theatres, Inc. v. Westover*, 359 U.S. 500 (1959) (holding that the defendant was entitled to a jury trial on its legal counterclaims and crossclaims filed in response to what the plaintiff styled as an equitable action before the trial court resolved common federal issues underlying plaintiff's claim for equitable relief); *Dairy Queen, Inc. v. Wood*, 369 U.S. 469, 473 (1962) (noting the applicability of *Beacon Theatres* regardless of "whether the trial judge chooses to characterize the legal issues presented as 'incidental' to equitable issues or not.").

A relevant question at this point is whether there is something about the nature of complex cases that renders them equitable rather than legal in character, perhaps because a jury's decision would offer an inadequate remedy. A partial response was given in *Ross v. Bernhard*, 396 U.S. 531, 538 n.10 (1970). After noting that Seventh Amendment analysis depends on the nature of the issue before the court and not the character of the overall action, the Supreme Court added, in a famous footnote:

> As our cases indicate, the "legal" nature of an issue is determined by considering, first, the pre-merger [of law and equity] custom with reference to such questions; second, the remedy sought; and, third, *the practical abilities and limitations of juries*. Of these factors, the first, requiring extensive and possibly abstruse historical inquiry, is obviously the most difficult to apply. See James, Right to a Jury Trial in Civil Actions, 72 Yale L.J. 655 (1963). (Emphasis added).

The first two considerations are well-established. The third is not. Did the Court cut from whole cloth a new test for determining the scope of the right to a jury trial preserved by the Seventh Amendment? Was the court simply acknowledging that at some point practical considerations may overcome our most strongly held principles? Could the third factor be treated as simply rephrasing the traditional scope of equitable relief, i.e. inadequate remedy at law? Finally, can the third factor be read as expressing the idea that at some point a trial may become so complex that a jury cannot render an adequate judgment? In so doing, does it violate another constitutional protection, that of due process? How do you frame the due process argument? Can you think of any other way to interpret this puzzling statement?

Suppose the capability of juries is a relevant factor in Seventh Amendment analysis. When might the practical abilities and limitations of juries actually justify foregoing a jury trial? *In re Japanese Electronic Products Antitrust Litigation*, 631 F.2d 1069, 1079 (3d Cir. 1980), described the complexity of a case as one situation where the limitations of juries would be exposed and the case should be taken from them:

> A suit is too complex for a jury when circumstances render the jury unable to decide in a proper manner. The law presumes that a jury will find facts and reach a verdict by rational means. It does not contemplate scientific precision but does contemplate a resolution of each issue on the basis of a fair and reasonable assessment of the evidence and a fair and reasonable application of the relevant legal rules. A suit might be excessively complex as a result of any set of circumstances which singly or in combination render a jury unable to decide in the foregoing rational manner. Examples of such circumstances are an exceptionally long trial period and conceptually difficult factual issues.

Likewise, in *In re Boise Cascade Securities Litigation*, 420 F. Supp. 99, 104 (W.D. Wash. 1976), the trial court noted the centrality of fairness in our adjudicatory system, especially under the Fifth and Fourteenth Amendments. The court observed:

> [A]t some point, it must be recognized that the complexity of a case may exceed the ability of a jury to decide the facts in an informed and capable manner. When that occurs, the question arises as to whether the right and necessity of fairness is defeated by relegating fact finding to a body not qualified to determine the facts. The third part of the analysis in footnote 10 to the majority opinion in *Ross v. Bernard, supra*, directly recognizes this.

The third factor from *Ross v. Bernard* suggests that the right to a jury trial may be limited in heretofore unrecognized ways. In *Beacon Theatres*, the Court wrote, "only under the most imperative circumstances, circumstances which in view of the flexible procedures of the Federal Rules *we cannot now anticipate*, can the right to a jury trial of legal issues be lost through prior determination of equitable claims." 359 U.S. at 510–11 (emphasis added). And in *Dairy Queen v. Wood*, the Court said:

> [I]n order to maintain such a suit [an equitable "accounting," which would not be tried to a jury] on a cause of action cognizable at law . . . the plaintiff must be able to show that the "accounts between the parties" are of such a "complicated nature" that only a court of equity can satisfactorily unravel them. . . . In view of the powers given to District Courts by Federal Rule of Civil Procedure 53(b) to appoint masters to assist the jury in those exceptional cases where the legal issues are too complicated for the jury adequately to handle alone, the burden of such a showing is considerably increased and *it will indeed be a rare case in which it can be met.*

369 U.S. at 478 (emphasis added). Despite these suggestions and attempts by litigants, this approach was rejected both by courts that found a complexity exception, *see, e.g., In re Japanese Electronic Products Antitrust Litigation*, 631 F.2d at 1080–83;

but see ILC Peripherals v. International Business Machines, 458 F. Supp. 423, 445, 447 (N.D. Cal. 1978), and those that did not, *see, e.g., In re U.S. Financial Securities Litigation*, 609 F.2d 411, 419, 423–26 (9th Cir. 1979).

In re Japanese Electronic Products Antitrust Litigation, 631 F.2d, at 1084–86, provides one of the most thorough treatments of the legal foundations for a complexity exception:

> Although no specific precedent exists for a finding a due process violation in the trial of any case to a jury, the principles that define the procedural requirements of due process would seem to impose some limitations on the range of cases that may be submitted to a jury. The primary value promoted by due process in factfinding procedures is "to minimize the risk of erroneous decisions." A jury that cannot understand the evidence and the legal rules to be applied provides no reliable safeguard against erroneous decisions. Moreover, in the context of a completely adversary proceeding, like a civil trial, due process requires that "the decisionmaker's conclusion . . . rest solely on the legal rules and evidence adduced at the hearing." Unless the jury can understand the legal rules and evidence, we cannot realistically expect that the jury will rest its decision on them.
>
> . . .
>
> If a particular lawsuit is so complex that a jury cannot satisfy this requirement of due process but is nonetheless an action at law, we face a conflict between the requirements of the fifth and seventh amendments. In this situation, we must balance the constitutionally protected interests, as they are implicated in this particular context, and reach the most reasonable accommodation between the two constitutional provisions.
>
> The due process objections to jury trial of a complex case implicate values of fundamental importance. If judicial decisions are not based on factual determinations bearing some reliable degree of accuracy, legal remedies will not be applied consistently with the purposes of the laws. There is a danger that jury verdicts will be erratic and completely unpredictable, which would be inconsistent with evenhanded justice. Finally, unless the jury can understand the evidence and the legal rules sufficiently to rest its decision on them, the objective of most rules of evidence and procedure in promoting a fair trial will be lost entirely. We believe that when a jury is unable to perform its decisionmaking task with a reasonable understanding of the evidence and legal rules, it undermines the ability of a district court to render basic justice.
>
> The loss of the right to jury trial in a suit found too complex for a jury does not implicate the same fundamental concerns. The absence of a jury trial requirement in equitable and maritime actions indicates that federal courts can provide fair trials and can grant relief in accordance with the principles of basic justice without the aid of a jury. Moreover, the Supreme

> Court has consistently refused to rule that preservation of civil jury trial is an essential element of ordered liberty required of the states by the due process clause of the fourteenth amendment.
>
> . . . .
>
> Therefore, we find the most reasonable accommodation between the requirements of the fifth and seventh amendments to be a denial of jury trial when a jury will not be able to perform its task of rational decision-making with a reasonable understanding of the evidence and the relevant legal standards. In lawsuits of this complexity, the interests protected by this procedural rule of due process carry greater weight than the interests served by the constitutional guarantee of jury trial. Consequently, we shall not read the seventh amendment to guarantee the right to jury trial in these suits.

Grounding a complexity exception in due process takes two steps. First, it must be shown that due process is violated when a jury decides a case that is so complex as to be beyond its capabilities. Second, the due process protection must override the Seventh Amendment right to a jury. (Recall the rule of construction that a specific provision—in this case the Seventh Amendment—normally prevails over a general protection—in this case due process.) The first step actually has two parts: one legal (does due process offer the protections claimed?) and one factual (are there cases that exceed the comprehension of juries?). With regard to the legal question, does due process in fact guarantee the right to a "comprehending factfinder?" Implicit in the factual question is the assumption that whatever virtues juries may have, *see id.* at 1085, judges are superior factfinders. With regard to the factual question, the court in *Japanese Electronics* reasoned as follows:

> First, the district court challenged the premise that a case could exceed a jury's ability to decide rationally and asserted that a jury was at least as able as a judge, the only alternative factfinder, to decide complex cases. The court noted that a jury possesses the wisdom, experience, and common sense of twelve persons. It has a greater effect than a judge in disciplining attorneys to present their cases clearly and concisely. Furthermore, its capabilities can be enhanced by special trial techniques like the preliminary charge and interim charges on the law contemplated by the district court in this case. On the basis of these observations, the court concluded that a jury "is brighter, more astute, and more perceptive than a single judge, even in a complex or technical case; at least it is not less so."
>
> Any assessment of a jury's ability to decide complex cases should include consideration not only of a jury's particular strengths and the possible enhancement of its capabilities but also of the particular constraints that operate on a jury in complex cases. The long time periods required for most complex cases are especially disabling for a jury. A long trial can interrupt the career and personal life of a jury member and thereby strain his commitment to the jury's task. The prospect of a long trial can also weed out

> many veniremen whose professional backgrounds qualify them for deciding a complex case but also prohibit them from lengthy jury service. Furthermore, a jury is likely to be unfamiliar with both the technical subject matter of a complex case and the process of civil litigation. The probability is not remote that a jury will become overwhelmed and confused by a mass of evidence and issues and will reach erroneous decisions. . . .
>
> Given that a jury has both particular strengths and weaknesses in deciding complex cases, we cannot conclude a priori that a jury is capable of deciding a suit of any degree of complexity. A litigant might prove that a particular suit is too complex for a jury. Because of the important due process rights implicated, a litigant should have the opportunity to make that showing.
>
> A general presumption that a judge is capable of deciding an extraordinarily complex case, by contrast, is reasonable. A long trial would not greatly disrupt the professional and personal life of a judge and should not be significantly disabling. In fact, the judge's greater ability to allocate time to the task of deciding a complex case can be a major advantage in surmounting the difficulties posed by the suit. Although we cannot presume that a judge will be more intelligent than a jury or more familiar with technical subject matters, a judge will almost surely have substantial familiarity with the process of civil litigation, as a result of experience on the bench or in practice. This experience can enable him to digest a large amount of evidence and legal argument, segregate distinct issues and the portions of evidence relevant to each issue, assess the opinions of expert witnesses, and apply highly complex legal standards to the facts of the case. The judge's experience also can enable him to make better use of special trial techniques designed to help the factfinder in complex cases, like colloquies with expert witnesses. The requirement that a judge issue findings of fact and conclusions of law offsets the substantial tendency to overlook issues in order that a verdict might be reached in these difficult cases. Fed. R. Civ. P. 52(a). Finally, if after trial and during deliberation a judge finds himself confused on certain matters or unable to decide certain issues, he can reopen the trial for the purpose of obtaining clarification or additional evidence. Fed. R. Civ. P. 59(a).

Id. at 1086–87.

In re U.S. Financial Securities Litigation, 609 F.2d 411 (9th Cir. 1979), appears to be more typical, however. Rather than analyzing the legal merits of a due process claim vis-à-vis a competent factfinder and its relative weight as compared to the Seventh Amendment, the court rejected a complexity exception for two main factual reasons. First, complex cases often are not in fact so complex. Second, juries are able to understand complex cases. With regard to the first point, the court advanced the logic:

> Many cases appear overwhelmingly complicated in their early stages. Nevertheless, by the time such cases go to trial, what had initially appeared

> as an impossible array of facts and issues has been synthesized into a coherent theory by the efforts of counsel. Moreover, in answering the Seventh Amendment question, courts should take into consideration the various procedural developments which serve to simplify and facilitate the trial of a "complex" case to a jury.
>
> The assumption that attorneys cannot develop and present complex cases to a jury underestimates the abilities of the bar, especially the experienced and capable counsel associated with the present litigation. . . .
>
> Also, the trial judge has the power and the authority to control, manage and direct the course of complex cases. The Federal Judicial Center developed the *Manual for Complex Litigation* for just such cases. . . .
>
> Various occurrences prior to trial may assist in simplifying the overwhelmingly complex case. A motion under Fed. R. Civ. P. 12 may be used to test the sufficiency of an adversary's pleadings. The facts may become sufficiently clear on some issues to entitle a party to have judgment entered as a matter of law under Fed. R. Civ. P. 56. The parties may stipulate to the admissibility of evidence, or to the facts themselves, thus reducing the time necessary to present a case at trial. The trial court could also order separate trials on some of the claims or issues under Fed. R. Civ. P. 42(b). And, as it is apparent from the present case, many cases or issues may be settled prior to trial.
>
> When a case involves complicated issues, the trial judge may appoint a master under Fed. R. Civ. P. 53(b) to assist the jury. In referring matters, the court has considerable discretion in deciding what the master should undertake to report upon. Fed. R. Civ. P. 53(c). We recognize that use of masters in jury cases is ". . . the exception and not the rule . . . ," because they do represent a limited inroad on the jury's traditional sphere. Fed. R. Civ. P. 53(b). Nevertheless, the use of a master is constitutional, and certainly is preferable to a denial of the Seventh Amendment right altogether.

Id. at 427–28. With regard to challenges to the competence of jurors, the court commented:

> The jury system has never been without its critics. . . . The opponents of the use of juries in complex civil cases generally assume that jurors are incapable of understanding complicated matters. This argument unnecessarily and improperly demeans the intelligence of the citizens of this Nation. We do not accept such an assertion. Jurors, if properly instructed and treated with deserved respect, bring collective intelligence, wisdom, and dedication to their tasks, which is rarely equaled in other areas of public service.
>
> . . . .
>
> . . . While we express great confidence in the abilities of judges, no one has yet demonstrated how one judge can be a superior fact-finder to the

> knowledge and experience that citizen-jurors bring to bear on a case. We do not accept the underlying premise of appellees' argument, "that a single judge is brighter than the jurors collectively functioning together."
>
> ... [E]xperience demonstrates that juries are capable of sorting out complex factual issues and applying the law to them.... Not only do we refuse to read a complexity exception into the Seventh Amendment, but we also express grave reservations about whether a meaningful test could be developed were we to find such an exception. Where would the courts draw the line between those cases which are, and those which are not, too complex for a jury? ... And we do not believe any case is so overwhelmingly complex that it is beyond the abilities of a jury.

Id. at 429–31. *See also Haynes Trane Service Agency, Inc. v. American Standard, Inc.*, 573 F.3d 947, 964–66 (10th Cir. 2009) (concluding that "[t]he right to a jury trial is not to be lightly denied; and before deeming a remedy at law inadequate, we must consider whether techniques are available to assist a jury in completing difficult tasks.").

Notes and Questions

1. One reason that *In re U.S. Financial Securities Litigation* declined to recognize a complexity exception is that courts have a variety of tools to minimize the complexity of cases presented to a jury. In fact, early post-merger Supreme Court cases noted that many claims with legal elements that might have been treated previously as equitable because of their complexity could now be considered purely legal because of the flexible procedures provided for by the Federal Rules. *See, e.g., Dairy Queen, Inc. v. Wood*, 369 U.S. 469, 478 n.19 (1962) ("It was settled in *Beacon Theatres* that procedural changes which remove the inadequacy of a remedy at law may sharply diminish the scope of traditional equitable remedies by making them unnecessary in many cases."). Nor does the list of tools in *U.S. Financial* exhaust the possibilities. For example, Federal Rule of Civil Procedure 16 gives the court broad power to take steps to improve "the quality of the trial," simplify and narrow issues, avoid unnecessary evidence, and order the presentation of evidence so that manageable and potentially dispositive issues may be decided first. It also allows courts to adopt "special procedures for managing potentially difficult or protracted actions that may involve complex issues, multiple parties, difficult legal questions, or unusual proof problems." Additionally, Rule 49 authorizes the use of special verdicts. Fed. R. Civ. P. 49(a)(1). Do you think these tools are sufficient to minimize the problems complexity poses? If not, what else could be done? *See* Katherine W. Wittenberg & Jeffrey R. Teeters, *Jury Project Confirms Best Practices of ABA's Jury Innovations*, A.B.A. SEC. LIT., Winter 2009, at 6–7 (describing the recommendations of the Seventh Circuit Bar Association American Jury Project Commission, including issuing early and specific instructions to the jury, allowing jurors to submit questions for witnesses to

the judge and attorneys for approval, and giving attorneys the opportunity to frame different aspects of the trial as it progresses by speaking directly to the jury).

2. The Supreme Court has not been quick to expand upon its complexity exception footnote in *Ross v. Bernhard*. The significance of the third factor of *Ross v. Bernhard's* footnote ten has been confined to public rights cases and administrative adjudication. In *Atlas Roofing Co. v. Occupational Safety and Health Review Comm'n*, 430 U.S. 442, 454–55 (1977), the Court wrote, "where jury trials would be incompatible with the whole concept of administrative adjudication," Congress may decline to make such a fact finder available without violating the Seventh Amendment. *Tull v. United States*, 481 U.S. 412, 418 n.4 (1987), picked up on this language as a way of limiting the Court's third factor:

> The Court has also considered the practical limitations of a jury trial and its functional compatibility with proceedings outside of traditional courts of law in holding that the Seventh Amendment is not applicable to administrative proceedings. But the Court has not used these considerations as an independent basis for extending the right to a jury trial under the Seventh Amendment.

In *Granfinanciera, S.A. v. Nordberg*, 492 U.S. 33, 42 (1989), the Court held in the context of bankruptcy proceedings that if the two-factor historical test indicated that the claim was legal, then the analysis must proceed to determine "whether Congress may assign and has assigned resolution of the relevant claim to a non-Article III adjudicative body that does not use a jury as factfinder." The Court then added:

> This quite distinct inquiry into whether Congress has permissibly entrusted the resolution of certain disputes to an administrative agency or specialized court of equity, and whether jury trials would impair the functioning of the legislative scheme, appears to be what the Court contemplated when, in *Ross v. Bernhard*, 396 U.S. 531, 538, n.10 (1970), it identified "the practical abilities and limitations of juries" as an additional factor to be consulted in determining whether the Seventh Amendment confers a jury trial right.... If a claim that is legal in nature asserts a "public right" ... then the Seventh Amendment does not entitle the parties to a jury trial if Congress assigns its adjudication to an administrative agency or specialized court of equity. The Seventh Amendment protects a litigant's right to a jury trial only if a cause of action is legal in nature and it involves a matter of "private right."

Id. at n.4. Note that while *Ross v. Bernhard's* third factor seems to have provided the invitation for finding a complexity exception, limiting it in this way does not foreclose the viability of the due process rationale for a complexity exception. Nevertheless, the possible existence of a complexity exception appears to be largely a thing of the past.

3. Although the Supreme Court does not appear to have adopted an expansive approach to a complexity exception, it showed a willingness to reserve complex

issues and trial decisions for the court in a suit otherwise requiring a jury determination by classifying the issue as one of law rather than fact. *See Markman v. Westview Instruments, Inc.*, 517 U.S. 370 (1996) (holding that the scope of a patent claim, i.e., the rights protected by the patent, is a matter of law for the courts to decide). There was no dispute in *Markman* that patent infringement cases required a jury trial. At issue was "whether the particular trial decision must fall to the jury in order to preserve the substance of the common-law right as it existed in 1791." *Id.* at 376. The Court first surveyed both history and precedent. Finding that neither provided a clear answer, it explained:

> [F]unctional considerations also play their part in the choice between judge and jury to define terms of art. . . . [T]he fact/law distinction at times has turned on a determination that, as a matter of the sound administration of justice, one judicial actor is better positioned than another to decide the issue in question.

Id. at 388 (internal quotations omitted). The Court concluded, "[J]udges, not juries, are the better suited to find the acquired meaning of patent terms." *Id.* In reaching this conclusion, the Court reasoned:

> The construction of written instruments is one of those things that judges often do and are likely to do better than jurors unburdened by training in exegesis. Patent construction in particular is a special occupation, requiring, like all others, special training and practice. The judge, from his training and discipline, is more likely to give a proper interpretation to such instruments than a jury; and he is, therefore, more likely to be right, in performing such a duty, than a jury can be expected to be.

Id. at 388–89 (internal quotations omitted). *Markman* does not allow for a wholesale complexity exception, but it does appear to make it easier for courts to re-describe as a question of law what at first blush might appear to be a factual matter, and so reserve the issue for court determination.

2. Bifurcation

Bifurcation is the process by which a judge orders multiple trials for issues presented in one suit. It is the obverse to consolidation under FED. R. CIV. P. 42(a), in which multiple cases are treated together for the purpose of pre-trial or trial. *See* Chapter 3, *supra*. Bifurcation refers to the general process of splitting, but as a technical term it designates a split into two trials. Trifurcation denotes a split into three trials, and a split into four or more trials is called polyfurcation. In federal court, judges derive the authority to bifurcate from FED. R. CIV. P. 42(b): "For convenience, to avoid prejudice, or to expedite and economize, the court may order a separate trial of one or more separate issues, claims, crossclaims, counterclaims, or third-party claims. When ordering a separate trial, the court must preserve any federal right to a jury trial."

Efficiency is the chief justification for bifurcation. The most common bifurcation is between the issues of liability and damages. "In the traditional form of trial, the damage issue must be litigated even where the verdict will ultimately reject liability; separation would eliminate the need for trying the damage issue in those cases . . ." Hans Zeisel & Thomas Callahan, *Split Trials and Time Saving: A Statistical Analysis*, 76 Harv. L. Rev. 1606, 1607 (1963). Such bifurcation will not result always in a more efficient process; if liability is found in the first trial, then a second trial for damages will often have to proceed (assuming a settlement is not reached), and in the end more time and resources may be spent than would have been in a single trial on both issues. However, in those cases where liability is not found, the process will be significantly more efficient than a longer trial on both issues. Likewise, a settlement often becomes more likely after the bifurcated trial on liability, so even where liability is found the process may end up more efficient. *See id.* at 1607–08. In short, separation of issues can result in a substantial average savings of time (perhaps 20%) because separation may make "the litigation of damages unnecessary." *Id.* at 1624. Despite efficiency, however, bifurcation is not without its problems, as discussed below.

Notes and Questions

1. The Ninth Circuit has explained: "Bifurcation of issues is an important device for trial efficiency, and we do not mean to foreclose its use, but the procedure which is adopted must not bar effective review or produce findings that are illogical or circular." *Symbolic Control, Inc. v. Int'l Bus. Machs Corp.*, 643 F.2d 1339, 1342 (9th Cir. 1980). In *Symbolic*, the district court ordered a bifurcated trial to first consider the issue of causation, which required an assumption that a violation had occurred in the first place. The Ninth Circuit frowned on this bifurcation, at least as applied to the specific facts:

> Assuming a violation, without evidence on the issue, in order to confine initial inquiry to the question of causation may not always foreclose an adequate causation analysis, but if the definition of the assumed violation remains amorphous, the causation inquiry can become both abstract and incomplete. That is what occurred here.

Id. at 1341.

2. Bifurcation also presents constitutional concerns. As the Fifth Circuit noted:

> This Court has approved bifurcation procedures on several occasions. However, this Court has cautioned that separation of issues is not the usual course that should be followed, and that the issue to be tried must be so distinct and separable from the others that a trial of it alone may be had without injustice. This limitation on the use of bifurcation is a recognition of the fact that inherent in the Seventh Amendment guarantee of a trial by jury is the general right of a litigant to have only one jury pass on a common issue of fact. The Supreme Court recognized this principle in *Gasoline*

> *Products Co., Inc. v. Champlin Refining Co.*, [283 U.S. 494] (1931) wherein it held that no Seventh Amendment violation occurs when an appellate court orders a new trial on the issue of damages, but lets stand the original jury's findings on liability. The Court explained, however, that a partial new trial may not be "properly resorted to unless it clearly appears that the issue to be retried is so distinct and separable from the others that a trial of it alone may be had without injustice." Id. at 500. Such a rule is dictated for the very practical reason that if separate juries are allowed to pass on issues involving overlapping legal and factual questions the verdicts rendered by each jury could be inconsistent.

State of Alabama v. Blue Bird Body Co., 573 F.2d 309, 318 (5th Cir. 1978). In *In the Matter of Rhone-Poulenc Rorer Inc.*, 51 F.3d 1293 (7th Cir. 1995), the Seventh Circuit reversed bifurcation when the same issue was decided by one jury and reexamined by another. Do you see how a judge must consider any split carefully to protect the Seventh Amendment rights of the parties?

3. One use of bifurcation is to consider affirmative defenses separately, particularly where an affirmative defense will be dispositive for the case. This form of split also has drawbacks. Sometimes the resolution of affirmative defenses requires addressing the merits of the plaintiff's claims, and the separation thus becomes a hindrance to that end. Richard L. Marcus, *Fraudulent Concealment in Federal Court: Toward a More Disparate Standard?*, 71 GEO. L.J. 829, 910–12 (1983).

4. The term bifurcation also may be used to describe the separation of issues at the pretrial level. Pretrial bifurcation actually may be the most common type of bifurcation, but since most pretrial orders are not published it is difficult to know the extent to which it enters into pretrial proceedings. Pretrial bifurcation essentially entails organizing pretrial issues in a sequential order, taking them one at a time for the purpose of discovery and dispositive motions. For a case where a court considers bifurcation both at the pretrial and trial levels, see *In re "Agent Orange" Product Liability Litigation*, 506 F. Supp. 762 (E.D.N.Y. 1980). For a case in which the pretrial is bifurcated without necessarily bifurcating trial, see *In re Love Canal Actions*, 547 N.Y.S.2d 174 (N.Y. Sup. Ct. 1989), *modified* 161 A.D. 2d 1169, 555 N.Y.S.2d 519 (A.D. 1990). For a case exploring bifurcation in the context of various class issues, see *In re Copley Pharmaceutical, Inc.*, 161 F.R.D. 456, 460 (D. Wyo. 1995).

5. Consider *In re Bendectin Litigation*, 857 F.2d 290 (6th Cir. 1988), in which the Sixth Circuit affirmed trifurcation (a three-way trial split) in a personal injury action where the district court decided to try separately the issue of proximate cause.

> In reviewing the district court's decision to trifurcate we further note Rule 42 which "giv[es] the court virtually unlimited freedom to try the issues in whatever way trial convenience requires." Thus, a court may try an issue separately if "in the exercise of reasonable discretion [it] thinks that course would save trial time or effort or make the trial of other issues unnecessary." Richmond v. Weiner, 353 F.2d 41, 44 (9th Cir. 1965). In this case, the

district judge considered the time savings in trying this case in this fashion, and surmised that if the plaintiffs won on this issue, another eight weeks of trial would be necessary to resolve the other questions.

Many courts have in fact permitted separate issue trials when the issue first tried would be dispositive of the litigation. The courts do so because the efficiency of the trial proceedings is greatly enhanced when a small part of the case can be tried separately and resolve the case completely. For example, in *Yung v. Raymark*, 789 F.2d at 401, we recently approved the separate trial of the issue of statute of limitations because if that issue were resolved to bar recovery, the court would be spared the necessity of trying liability and damages. "Whether resolution of a single issue would likely dispose of an entire claim is extremely relevant in determining the usefulness of a separate trial on the issue.... This procedure should be encouraged because court time and litigation expenses are minimized." *Id.* The defendant relies heavily on language like this. As the defense correctly observed: "[T]he plaintiffs can never win a case if they can't prove the drug caused the problem. That is the central issue in this case." And later, "[a]ll claims depended upon the answer to a single question. Does Bendectin, taken in therapeutic doses cause birth defects?" Plainly, Judge Rubin had a massive case management problem to resolve, and chose to do so by trying the case on a separate issue that would be dispositive.

857 F.2d at 316–17. But note Judge Jones' opinion, concurring in part and dissenting in part:

In conclusion, trifurcation orders present fundamental problems of fairness simply because the typical procedure in litigation does not involve the splitting up of a case, element by element, and trying each point to the jury separately. Rather, the plaintiff's entire case is presented to the jury at once, thereby preventing the isolation of issues in a sterile atmosphere. Simply because a litigant shares his complaint with eight hundred other claimants is not a reason to deprive him of the day in court he would have enjoyed had he been the sole plaintiff. However, as the majority points out, a trifurcation order is authorized and *necessitated* at some point so as to allow a district court to manage and control the complexities and massive size of a case. The duty of this court, however, is to prevent such a case-management tool from becoming a penalty to injured plaintiffs seeking relief via the legal system.

Id. at 328.

3. Summaries of Evidence as a Trial Simplification Device

One way to shorten complex trials is to shorten the process of actually introducing evidence. The presentation of evidence, whether by live witness testimony, or presentation of exhibits, takes time. Some of this time is taken up with the actual core of the testimony—the substance of what a party wishes to tell the judge or jury. However, much of it is also taken up with questions, background, evidentiary objections, argument, and rulings. Some judges have tried to advance this process by requiring parties to summarize evidence. There are several approaches to this technique. Some judges will require summary of deposition testimony only, while others will require summary of all direct examination testimony.

Summaries of Depositions

Federal Rule of Civil Procedure 43(a) provides that "[a]t trial, the witnesses' testimony must be taken in open court unless a federal statute, the Federal Rules of Evidence, these rules, or other rules . . . provide otherwise." However, Rule 32 provides a broad range of circumstances under which depositions, rather than testimony in open court, may be used to present testimony. FED. R. CIV. P. 32(a)(1)(B). One of the most basic ways to shorten the presentation of evidence is to find ways to shorten the amount of deposition testimony that needs to be presented. Federal Rule of Evidence 611(a) gives the judge the power, and the responsibility, to "exercise reasonable control over the mode and order of interrogating witnesses and presenting evidence so as to (1) make the interrogation and presentation effective for the ascertainment of the truth [and] (2) avoid needless consumption of time." Pursuant to this authority, some judges have required lawyers to summarize any testimony that they intended to introduce by deposition. In *In re Air Crash Disaster at Stapleton International Airport, Denver, Colorado, on November 15, 1987*, 720 F. Supp. 1493 (D. Colo. 1989), the court utilized two methods of summary testimony.

> Rather than limit the time available for the presentation of evidence, two modes of summary testimony were utilized. Attorneys agreed to summary presentation of the testimony and depositions of several witnesses. The primary method of summary testimony involves summarization of the relevant portions of a deposition in a one or two page narrative, prepared by the offering attorney. Opposing counsel is given an opportunity to review the summary and the deposition for accuracy. The offering attorney then reads a stipulated narrative summary to the jury.
>
> During the course of trial, disagreements as to the contents of certain deposition summaries arose. Some disputes were resolved either by presentation of the transcript and proposed summaries to the court for in camera review. At other times, opposing counsel was allowed to supplement the summary by reading limited portions of the deposition transcript to the jury. The summary deposition approach was particularly useful in presenting testimony of plaintiff Karen Johnson's rehabilitation practitioners whose professional commitments prevented travel from Boise, Idaho to Denver, Colorado for trial. The approach was also useful in presenting corroborative testimony on various issues, lessening the delay of repetitive testimony. Because the applicability of summary testimony is tempered by the court's preference for oral testimony in court, the parties were neither

> requested nor allowed to present the testimony of key witnesses in summary form. The use of summary deposition testimony in narrative form is a legitimate exercise of the court's inherent powers and authority under Rule 611.
>
> The second method of summary testimony involves the reading of a narrative statement of a witness's direct testimony while the witness is in court, under oath. The presenting attorney reads a summary of direct examination. The witness is then asked to supplement or correct the attorney's statement, under oath, again in narrative form. Testimony then proceeds through traditional cross and redirect examination. This method of presenting evidence is most useful in presenting the testimony of witnesses who appear to corroborate the testimony of key witnesses. In this trial for example, two of several passengers testified to their observations of the aircraft, events and weather conditions through the modified summary form.
>
> ....

Stapleton, 720 F. Supp. at 1503. The *Stapleton* court allowed summarized deposition testimony only when the actual deposition was otherwise admissible into evidence under Federal Rule of Civil Procedure 32. The court excluded a deposition summary of a witness who was not technically unavailable to testify at trial under the evidence rules. *Id.* at 1502–03. Also, the court noted that the summary approach worked best when the witness's summary corroborated that of a key witness. For key witnesses, the preference was still traditional live direct and cross examination. *Stapleton* notes that Rule 32 "does not alter the judicial preference for direct and cross-examination of a witness at trial." *Id.* at 1501.

The Seventh Circuit endorsed summarization of deposition testimony in *Oostendorp v. Khanna*, 937 F.2d 1177, 1179–80 (7th Cir. 1991). Summarized testimony was only required for those witnesses whom counsel wanted to testify via depositions—summary of the testimony of corroborative witnesses was not required. The court stated that "neither the due process clause nor the seventh amendment *requires* courts to admit deposition testimony; indeed the more common argument is that the Constitution forbids the substitution of depositions for the live testimony of witnesses." *Id.*

Summaries of Direct Testimony

The *Oostendorp* court held that mandatory summarization of deposition testimony did not violate due process. The plaintiff "was not denied the right to call witnesses." *Id.* The court noted that "due process gives parties to litigation the right to present evidence; the seventh amendment gives them the right to do so in front of a jury . . . as long as the procedures utilized by the trial courts are fair, there is no conflict with either constitutional provision." *Id.*

How far can this provision be taken? *Oostendorp* and *Stapleton* established that courts may require parties to submit whatever testimony they wish to present by deposition in summary form. May courts also require parties to summarize testimony for those witnesses who will appear in the courtroom? *See* Michael S. Horne, *Presenting Direct Testimony in Writing*, 3 Litigation 30 (1976). The practice originated with administrative agencies, which "encouraged presiding officers to require direct testimony in writing." *Id.* This practice spread to non-jury cases in federal courts. *Id.* In its most basic form, this can look like the second approach taken in *Stapleton*, with written summaries being used for direct testimony of non-key information.

Saverson v. Levitt, 162 F.R.D. 407 (D.D.C. 1995), is an example of how courts have expanded the *Stapleton* approach. In a jury trial, the judge directed in his scheduling order that

> [I]n preparation for trial and pursuant to Rule 16 of the Federal Rules of Civil Procedure, Federal Rule of Evidence 611(a), and Local Rule 209, counsel for the Plaintiff and the Defendant shall prepare all of the direct testimony of the witnesses they intend to call in their case-in-chief that are in their control in written narrative form and shall serve the same upon opposing counsel . . . that counsel shall confer in person and discuss and resolve any evidentiary objections, and then file the final versions, on three-hole punched paper, together with a witness list, with the Clerk of the Court and with Chambers . . . [that] any portion of the direct testimony which remains in dispute shall be filed separately, and the Court shall resolve these disputes, if any, prior to the trial . . . that the above-ordered direct testimony shall be by way of declaration, pursuant to 28 U.S.C. § 1746, or sworn written affidavit . . . [and] in lieu of the usual question-and-answer form of direct examination [read to the jury], although full cross examination shall be permitted at trial. . . .

Id. The plaintiff objected on the basis that the order was contrary to Federal Rule of Civil Procedure 43(a) and Federal Rule of Evidence 611(c), and would deprive the jury of the ability to observe the demeanor and make credibility determinations. *Id.* The court found that the Ninth Circuit had endorsed explicitly the practice in *Adair v. Sunwest Bank*, 965 F.2d 777, 780 (9th Cir. 1992). *Saverson*, 162 F.R.D. at 408. *Adair* held that the technique was a permissible mode of presenting direct testimony under Rule 611(a), and that the purpose of Rule 43(a)—to ensure the accuracy of a witness's statement by allowing the trier of fact to observe their appearance and demeanor—was fulfilled by written direct testimony, combined with oral cross and redirect. The *Saverson* court, therefore, concluded that "requiring parties to submit their direct testimony in writing in lieu of the usual question-and-answer form is sanctioned under the inherent powers of the Court, the Federal Rules of Civil Procedure and the Federal Rules of Evidence." 162 F.R.D. at 410. Central to the *Saverson* decision, as well as *Adair* though, was the fact that witnesses were subject to cross and redirect. *Id.* at 408.

These techniques can save time. In *Stapleton*, the trial took half the time that was projected. In bench trials, where the statements do not need to be read into evidence, such techniques can shorten a trial dramatically. *See* Gus J. Solomon, *Techniques for Shortening Trials*, 65 F.R.D. 485, 489 (1975) (describing how this technique has shortened potentially week-long trials to a day). Even when the testimony is read into the record, as in jury trials, time is still saved. Removal of objections, questions, and cumulative material all saves time.

Written direct also can deliver information in a much more easily understood manner. "The question and answer method is a strained device for obtaining information in an orderly fashion." James W. McElhany, *An Introduction to Direct Examination*, 2 LITIGATION 37 (1976). Complex information involving calculation or scientific data may be much more easily presented in writing. Written direct also avoids the charade of presenting information apparently from memory in response to questions. Horne, *supra*, at 31. Also, it allows the introduction of much more background information, simply because it will not take up the same amount of time. This will assist the jury in understanding the subject matter of the presentation. *Id.*

Summaries may be particularly useful for expert testimony. Expert qualifications may be summarized very briefly, for the benefit of the jury, when the person's status as an expert will not be seriously questioned by the other side. Solomon, *supra*, at 490. This saves yet more time. Judge Solomon states that "Oftentimes a witness who would have testified for three or four hours, or even longer, under traditional methods of examination, will complete his entire testimony, both direct and cross, in less than an hour." *Id.*

Summaries of Non-Testimonial Evidence

"Whenever possible, voluminous or complicated data at trial should be presented by counsel through summaries, including compilations . . . ." KLIMPFLEN ET AL., 10A FED. PROC., L. ED. § 26.893 (2008). Under Federal Rule of Evidence 1006, the underlying materials must be made available for examination. Also, summaries must be grounded in admissible evidence. *United States v. Davis*, 261 F.3d 1 (1st Cir. 2001). However, under these conditions, the summary may be admitted as evidence of the data it contains. *Id.* Even if these conditions are not met, the trial judge has discretion under Federal Rule of Evidence 611 to admit summaries, along with the underlying information.

Courts also have used this technique to make the presentation of evidence more effective. In *Nigh v. Dow Chemical*, 634 F. Supp. 1513 (W.D. Wis. 1986), the court required the use of summary evidence, refusing to allow the parties to read the full text of the exhibits into evidence.

> [The plaintiff objected to] the Court's decision to bar the reading of exhibits and extensive statements summarizing their contents by witnesses. Since exhibits are evidence, the recitation of the contents is cumulative and

> imposes on the Court and jury a significant waste of time. This is especially true in a case of this nature where the reading of exhibits could have added days to a lengthy trial. The Court has the inherent power to develop tools to promote the efficient presentation of cases. *See*, for example, *Eash v. Riggins Trucking Inc.*, 757 F.2d 557, 564 (3d Cir. 1985) (inherent power to impose monetary sanctions for activities short of contempt). The Court would also note that thoughtful consideration of such evidence as well as efficiency are promoted by the Court's practice. Rulings on the admissibility of exhibits generally precede the beginning of the trial. Counsel are freely allowed to read from exhibits in closing argument so that consideration of the evidence can be integrated into the context of the case in a manner consistent with the party's theories. The parties can, of course, freely designate those exhibits that they wish to be available to the jury during its deliberations, and can even have them shown to the jury during the course of their initial presentation. Finally, the Court carefully allowed quotation and summarization when it was necessary to understand the witness' comments concerning the exhibits.
>
> The Court discerns no prejudice to anyone from this practice, and is convinced that it is much more likely to produce a thoughtful verdict and thereby promote the ends of justice. Rule 611(a) of the Federal Rules of Evidence provides ample authority.

Nigh, 634 F. Supp. at 1518.

Notes and Questions

How far can these suggestions be pushed? Professors Tidmarsh and Trangsrud suggest "requir[ing] the lawyers to provide the jurors with the relevant portions of the depositions transcripts, and to let the jurors read them on their own time." Jay Tidmarsh & Roger H. Trangsrud, Modern Complex Litigation 1099 (2d ed. 2010). But they also note disapproval of such an approach. *Stine v. Marathon Oil Co.*, 976 F.2d 254, 267 (5th Cir. 1992) explains:

> We view with considerably greater concern, however, the district court's practice in this case of requiring the parties to provide excerpts of depositions to the jury, rather than allowing this testimony to be read in open court. Such a practice requires the jury to spend time outside the courtroom, over and above a full day in the courtroom. The jury's reading of the deposition excerpts was thus totally outside the supervision of the trial judge. Indeed, the procedure followed incurs a real risk that the jurors merely took the excerpts home and brought them back the next day unread and, thus, reached a verdict without having considered all the evidence. Marathon argues that this procedure violates Fed. R. Civ. P. 43(a) ("In all trials the testimony of witnesses shall be taken orally in open court, unless otherwise

> provided . . . by these rules.") and 77(b) ("All trials upon the merits shall be conducted in open court."). Marathon, however, overlooks the provisions of Fed. R. Civ. P. 32, "Use of Depositions in Court Proceedings," which allows the restricted use of depositions as evidence. There is no explicit requirement in Rule 32 that depositions be read in open court. Nevertheless, we believe that the practice of providing "evidence to go" or "takeout evidence" is generally inappropriate.

However, in the absence of an objection, and in view of the "almost invariable assumption of the law that jurors follow their instructions," the court declined to find error on the part of the court. *Id.*

4. Judicial Time Limits on Trials

Courts have broad discretion to set time limits on trials. Federal Rule of Civil Procedure 16(c)(2)(O) states that at the scheduling conference, the court may "establish[] a reasonable limit on the time allowed to present evidence." The advisory committee notes to that rule suggest, however, that "such limits must be reasonable under the circumstances, and ordinarily the court should impose them only after receiving appropriate submissions from the parties outlining the nature of the testimony expected to be presented through various witnesses, and the expected duration of direct and cross-examination."

Nevertheless, courts have broad discretion to set rather stringent limits. In *MCI Communications v. American Tel. & Tel. Co.*, 708 F.2d 1081 (7th Cir. 1983), for example, the court ruled it was not an abuse of discretion for the district court to limit a major antitrust trial to just 26 days when the parties expected an eight to nine month trial. *Id.* at 1172–73. Helping the Seventh Circuit to reach this conclusion, however, was the fact that, "The limits set by the district court were not absolute . . . . We cannot say that the district court was prepared to adhere strictly to its preliminary time limits without regard to possible prejudice to either party." *Id.* at 1172.

As the Eighth Circuit stated in *Johnson v. Ashby*, 808 F.2d 676, 678 (8th Cir. 1987):

> Trial courts have discretion to place reasonable limits on the presentation of evidence to prevent undue delay, waste of time or needless presentation of cumulative evidence. . . . In this era of crowded district court dockets federal district court judges not only may but must exercise strict control over the length of trials. Nonetheless, it may be an abuse of the trial court's discretion to exclude probative, non-cumulative evidence simply because its introduction will cause delay, and any time limits formulated in advance of trial must be fashioned with this in mind. Such limits should be sufficiently flexible to accommodate adjustment if it appears during trial that the court's initial assessment was too restrictive.

The Eighth Circuit went on to disapprove of exclusively complex or rigid methods of time-keeping, and held that adhering to "a rigid hour limitation involving a time-keeping method almost as complicated as in a professional football game" would have been an abuse of discretion. *Id.* Similarly Judge Posner stated in *McKnight v. General Motors Corp*, 908 F.2d 104, 115 (7th Cir. 1990) "to impose arbitrary limitations, enforce them inflexibly and by these means turn a federal trial into a relay race is to sacrifice too much of one good—accuracy of factual determination—to obtain another—minimization of the time and expense of litigation."

Since the judge has broad discretion to time trials, it is in the best interest of the attorneys to work together to set a realistic schedule for the litigation. Judges generally will be more willing to set limits amenable to the parties if the parties cooperate and make reasonable estimates and requests for time. Judges also are more likely to grant an extension of time if initial requests were reasonable and made in good faith. For more discussion of how to handle time limits in a complex case, see Martha Gooding, *Tempus Fugit: Trying a Case Against the Clock*, 53-JAN Fed. Law. 42 (2006).

---

5. *In re Fibreboard* and Trial by Statistics

Trying complex cases poses numerous practical problems implicating often conflicting policy considerations. Mass torts, in which a single or limited number of defendants inflict harm on a disproportionately large class of potential plaintiffs, create their own unique problems. Because many of the legal and factual issues will be the same for each plaintiff's claim, it is inefficient to try the cases separately. Moreover, the number of plaintiffs and the need for individual trials actually may prevent litigants from ever getting their day in court, at least in a timely fashion. Additionally, the commonality of claims against a defendant and the role this can play in preclusion and settlement negotiations mean that any given suit is potentially worth significantly more to the defendant than the plaintiff. Coupling this last fact with the resource asymmetry between a corporate defendant and an individual plaintiff diminishes the prospects for recovery.

Trial by statistics, which is explored in the following case and notes, is one way to solve some of these problems. After reading the case, ask yourself if you find the solution effective. Does it create new problems greater than those it purports to solve?

In re Fibreboard Corporation

United States Court of Appeals, Fifth Circuit
893 F.2d 706 (1990)

Patrick E. Higginbottham, Circuit Judge:

Defendants Fibreboard Corporation and Pittsburgh Corning Corporation, joined by other defendants, petition for writ of mandamus, asking that we vacate pretrial orders consolidating 3,031 asbestos cases for trial entered by Judge Robert Parker, Eastern District of Texas.

In 1986 there were at least 5,000 asbestos-related cases pending in this circuit. We then observed that "because asbestos-related diseases will continue to manifest themselves for the next fifteen years, filings will continue at a steady rate until the year 2000."[11] *Id.* at 470. That observation is proving to be accurate. In *Jenkins v. Raymark*, we affirmed Judge Parker's certification of a class of some 900 asbestos claimants, persuaded that the requirements of Rule 23(b)(3) were met for the trial of certain common questions including the "state of the art" defense. After that order and certain settlements, approximately 3,031 asbestos personal injury cases accumulated in the Eastern District of Texas.

The petitions for mandamus attack the district court's effort to try these cases in a common trial. In summary, and we will explain later in more detail, the district court has set these 3,031 cases for trial commencing February 5, 1990. The trial will proceed in three phases. Phase I is similar to the procedure approved in *Raymark* in which common defenses and punitive damages will be tried. In Phase II, and before the same jury, certain representative cases will be fully tried and the jury will decide the total, or "omnibus" liability to the class. In Phase III, any awarded damages will be distributed utilizing various techniques. Petitioners grumble over Phase I, conceding that it is no more than we have approved in *Raymark*, and focus their fire upon Phase II. Petitioners also attack limits placed on discovery from class members as well as the intense schedule for their oral depositions.

The standard of review is familiar. We are to issue a writ of mandamus only "to remedy a clear usurpation of power or abuse of discretion" when "no other adequate means of obtaining relief is available." *In re Paradyne Corp.*, 803 F.2d 604, 612 (11th Cir. 1986) (quoting *In re Extradition of Ghandtchi*, 697 F.2d 1037, 1038 (11th Cir. 1983) and *United States v. Fernandez-Toledo*, 737 F.2d 912, 919 (11th Cir. 1984)). As we stated in *In re Willy*, 831 F.2d 545, 549 (5th Cir. 1987):

> Mandamus cannot be used as a substitute for appeal even when hardship may result from delay or from an unnecessary trial. *Schlagenhauf v. Holder*, 379 U.S. 104, 110 (1964). Mandamus is an extraordinary remedy that should be granted only in the clearest and most compelling cases. *Kerr v. United States District Court*, 426 U.S. 394, 402–03 (1976); *In re Davis*, 730 F.2d 176,

11. [1] *See Jenkins v. Raymark Industries, Inc.*, 782 F.2d 468, 470 (5th Cir. 1986).

> 181 (5th Cir. 1984). A party seeking mandamus must show that no other adequate means exist to attain the requested relief and that his right to the issuance of the writ is 'clear and indisputable.' *Kerr v. United States*, 426 U.S. at 403 (quoting *Banker's Life & Cas. Co. v. Holland*, 346 U.S. 379, 384 (1953)).

Finally, mandamus relief is ordinarily inappropriate when review is obtainable on direct appeal. After a brief look at the background of these cases, we will return to the question of whether petitioners have met this extraordinary burden.

I

On September 20, 1989, Professor Jack Ratliff of the University of Texas Law School filed his special master's report in *Cimino v. Raymark*. The special master concluded that it was "self-evident that the use of one-by-one individual trials is not an option in the asbestos cases." The master recommended four trial phases: I (classwide liability, class representatives' cases), II (classwide damages), III (apportionment) and IV (distribution). On October 26, the district court entered the first of the orders now at issue....

Phase I is to be a single consolidated trial proceeding under Rule 42(a). It will decide the state of the art and punitive damages issues. The district court explained that:

> the jury will be asked to decide issues such as (a) which products, if any, were asbestos-containing insulation products capable of producing dust that contained asbestos fibers sufficient to cause harm in its application, use, or removal; (b) which of the Defendants' products, if any, were defective as marketed and unreasonably dangerous; (c) when each Defendant knew or should have known that insulators or construction workers and their household members were at risk of contracting an asbestos-related injury or disease from the application, use, or removal of asbestos-containing insulation products; and (d) whether each Defendant's marketing of a defective and unreasonably dangerous product constituted gross negligence. In answering issue (d), the Jury will hear evidence of punitive conduct including any conspiracy among the Defendants to conceal the dangers (if any) of asbestos. The wording of issues (c) and (d) will depend on the applicability of the 1987 Texas Tort Reform legislation to a particular class member's individual case.

....

The district court also described the proceedings for Phase II in its October 26 order. In Phase II the jury is to decide the percentage of plaintiffs exposed to each defendant's products, the percentage of claims barred by statutes of limitation, adequate warnings, and other affirmative defenses. The jury is to determine actual damages in a lump sum for each disease category for all plaintiffs in the class. Phase II will include a full trial of liability and damages for 11 class representatives and such evidence as the parties wish to offer from 30 illustrative plaintiffs. Defendants will choose 15 and plaintiffs will choose 15 illustrative plaintiffs, for a total of 41 plaintiffs. The jury will hear opinions of experts from plaintiffs and defendants regarding the total damage award. The basis for the jury's judgment is said to be the 41 cases plus the data supporting the calculation of the experts regarding total damages suffered by the remaining 2,990 class members.

Class members have answered questionnaires and are testifying in scheduled oral depositions now in progress. Petitioners attack the limits of discovery from the class members, but we will not reach this issue. It is sufficient to explain that defendants are allowed a total of 45 minutes to interrogate each class member in an oral deposition. These depositions will not be directly used at the trial in Phase II. Rather, the oral depositions, with the other discovery from class members, provide information for experts engaged to measure the damages suffered by the class.

II

Defendants find numerous flaws in the procedures set for Phase II of the trial. They argue with considerable force that such a trial would effectively deny defendants' rights to a jury under the seventh amendment, would work an impermissible change in the controlling substantive law of Texas, would deny procedural due process under the fifth amendment of the United States Constitution, and would effectively amend the rules of civil procedure contrary to the strictures of the enabling acts.

Plaintiffs deny that Phase II would deny defendants any right. Plaintiffs argue that every plaintiff is effectively before the court; that the evidence to be offered by their experts is more the use of summary evidence under Rule 1006 of the Federal Rules of Evidence than the use of math models to extrapolate total damages from sample plaintiffs. Plaintiffs concede that the contemplated trial is extraordinary, but argue that extraordinary measures are necessary if these cases are to be tried at all. While extraordinary, the measures are no more than a change in the mode of proof, plaintiffs say. The argument continues that Rule 23 is not the necessary vehicle for the ordered trial, but will sustain it, if the "consolidation" is viewed as a class. We turn to these arguments.

A

The contentions that due process would be denied, the purposes of *Erie* would be frustrated, and the seventh amendment circumvented are variations of a common concern of defendants. Defendants insist that one-to-one adversarial engagement or its proximate, the traditional trial, is secured by the seventh amendment and certainly contemplated by Article III of the Constitution itself. Defendants point out, and plaintiffs quickly concede, that under Phase II there will inevitably be individual class members whose recovery will be greater or lesser than it would have been if tried alone. Indeed, with the focus in Phase II upon the "total picture", with arrays of data that will attend the statistical presentation, persons who would have had their claims rejected may recover. Plaintiffs say that "such discontinuities" would be reflected in the overall omnibus figure. Stated another way, plaintiffs say that so long as their mode of proof enables the jury to decide the total liability of defendants with reasonable accuracy, the loss of one-to-one engagement infringes no right of defendants. Such unevenness, plaintiffs say, will be visited upon them, not the defendants.

With the procedures described at such a level of abstraction, it is difficult to describe concretely any deprivation of defendants' rights. Of course, there will be a jury, and each plaintiff will be present in a theoretical, if not practical, sense. Having said this, however, we are left with a profound disquiet. First, the assumption of plaintiffs' argument is that its proof of omnibus damages is in fact achievable; that statistical measures of representativeness and commonality will be sufficient for the jury to make informed judgments concerning damages. We are pointed to our experience in the trial of Title VII cases and securities cases involving use of fraud on the market concepts and mathematical constructs for examples of workable trials of large numbers of claims. We find little comfort in such cases. It is true that there is considerable judicial experience with such techniques, but it is also true we have remained cautious in their use.

The plaintiffs' answers to interrogatories and the depositions already conducted have provided enough information to show that if, as plaintiffs contend, the representative plaintiffs accurately reflect the class, it is a diverse group. The plaintiffs' "class" consists of persons claiming different diseases, different exposure periods, and different occupations. The depositions of ten tentative class representatives indicate that their diseases break down into three categories: asbestosis (plural and pulmonary)—eight representatives; lung cancer-three—representatives; and Mesothelioma—one representative.

In addition, plaintiffs' admissions of fact show the following disparities among class members.

a. The class includes persons who do not have legal claims against Defendant ACandS, Inc.

b. One or more members of the class may be barred from prosecuting claims against ACandS by virtue of their prior employment with ACandS.

c. The severity and type of physical or mental injuries varies among class members.

d. The nature and type of damage varies among class members.

e. Not all of the Plaintiffs have been injured by the acts, omissions, conduct or fault of all of the Defendants.

f. The dates of exposure to asbestos-containing products varies among class members.

g. The types of products to which class members were exposed varies among class members.

h. The dates that class members knew or should have known of their exposure to asbestos-containing products is not identical among class members. . . .

B

. . . .

We are told that Phase II is the only realistic way of trying these cases; that the difficulties faced by the courts as well as the rights of the class members to have their cases tried cry powerfully for innovation and judicial creativity. The arguments are compelling, but they are better addressed to the representative branches—Congress and the State Legislature. The Judicial Branch can offer the trial of lawsuits. It has no power or competence to do more. We are persuaded on reflection that the procedures here called for comprise something other than a trial within our authority. It is called a trial, but it is not.

The 2,990 class members cannot be certified for trial as proposed under Rule 23(b)(3). [Fed. R. Civ. P. 23(b)(3)] requires that "the questions of law or fact common to the members of the class predominate over any questions affecting individual members." There are too many disparities among the various plaintiffs for their common concerns to predominate. The plaintiffs suffer from different diseases, some of which are more likely to have been caused by asbestos than others. The plaintiffs were exposed to asbestos in various manners and to varying degrees. The plaintiffs' lifestyles differed in material respects. To create the requisite commonality for trial, the discrete components of the class members' claims and the asbestos manufacturers' defenses must be submerged. The procedures for Phase II do precisely that, but, as we have explained, do so only by reworking the substantive duty owed by the manufacturers. At the least, the enabling acts prevent that reading.

Finally, it is questionable whether defendants' right to trial by jury is being faithfully honored, but we need not explore this issue. It is sufficient now to conclude that Phase II cannot go forward without changing Texas law and usurping legislative prerogatives, a step federal courts lack authority to take.

III

We admire the work of our colleague, Judge Robert Parker, and are sympathetic with the difficulties he faces. This grant of the petition for writ of mandamus should not be taken as a rebuke of an able judge, but rather as another chapter in an ongoing struggle with the problems presented by the phenomenon of mass torts. The petitions for writ of mandamus are granted. The order for Phase II trial is vacated and the cases are remanded to the district court for further proceedings. We find no impediment to the trial of Phase I should the district court wish to proceed with that trial. We encourage the district court to continue its imaginative and innovative efforts to confront these cases. We also caution that defendants are obligated to cooperate in the common enterprise of obtaining a fair trial.

Notes and Questions

1. On what grounds did the court in *In re Fibreboard* issue the writ of mandamus? In formulating the new trial plan after the case had been returned to it, the district court explained that it had taken care "to avoid once again being sacrificed on the altar of due process." Is that an accurate characterization of the reasoning in *In re Fibreboard*? Despite expressions of concern about due process and the Seventh Amendment, did the appellate court decide the writ petition on narrower grounds—under *Erie* and by appeal to Texas tort law?

2. The District Court described its new trial plan in *Cimino v. Raymark Indus.*, 751 F. Supp. 649 (E.D. Tex. 1990). Once again, the trial was split into three phases. Phase I did not differ from its counterpart in *In re Fibreboard*. Phase II concerned worksite exposure and apportioned causation, but ultimately "the parties agreed to stipulate as to what the jury finding would have been." *Id.* at 654. That left Phase III.

> Phase III is the damage issue. The 2,298 class members were divided into five disease categories based on the plaintiff's injury claims. The Court selected a random sample from each disease category. . . . The damage case of each trial sample class member randomly drawn was then submitted to a jury. Each plaintiff whose damage case was submitted to the jury was to be awarded his individual verdict and the average verdict for each disease category would constitute the damage award for each non-sample class member.

Id. at 653. In justifying this approach, the court wrote:

> The post-trial hearing held November 6, 1990, has persuaded the Court that the samples used were, in fact, representative. When setting the sample size for each disease category, the Court sought a confidence level of 95%, in other words +/− 2.00 standard deviations. The testimony adduced at the post-trial hearing indicates that the actual precision level achieved by the samples exceeds that sought by the Court. . . .
>
> The Court is of the opinion that the distribution of variables between the samples and their respective subclasses is comparable. The Court finds that this procedure has proved to be a valid statistical exercise. The goodness-of-fit exceeded the acceptable limits articulated by the Court, and the Court perceives no need to try any more cases prior to extrapolation.
>
> The Court finds no persuasive evidence why the average damage verdicts in each disease category should not be applied to the non-sample members. . . . Individual members of a disease category who will receive an award that might be different from one they would have received had their individual case been decided by a jury have waived any objections, and the defendants cannot show that the total amount of damages would be greater under the Court's method compared to individual trials of these

> cases. Indeed, the millions of dollars saved in reduced transaction costs inure to defendants' benefit.
>
> ... Careful scrutiny has persuaded this Court that, in this case, science has assumed its proper role, a role that is in aid of the court and not in replacement of it.

Id. at 664–65.

3. Do you agree with the court's conclusion? Do you think this plan avoids the missteps that doomed its effort in *In re Fibreboard*? *See Cimino v. Raymark Indus., Inc.*, 151 F.3d 297 (5th Cir. 1998). Once again, the Fifth Circuit struck down the trial plan.

> In sum, as *Fibreboard* held, under Texas law causation must be determined as to "individuals, not groups." And, the Seventh Amendment gives the right to a jury trial to make that determination. There was no such trial determination made, and no jury determined, that exposure to Pittsburgh Corning's products was a cause of the asbestos disease of any of the one hundred sixty phase III plaintiffs. Nor does the stipulation determine or establish that. Accordingly, the judgments in all the one hundred forty-three phase III cases before us must be reversed and remanded.
>
> We turn now to the extrapolation cases. As to the matter of individual causation, it is obvious that the conclusion we have reached in respect to the phase III cases applies a fortiori to the extrapolation cases. In the extrapolation cases there was no trial and no jury determination that any individual plaintiff suffered an asbestos-related disease. Indeed, in the extrapolation cases there was no trial at all—by jury or otherwise—and there was no evidence presented. So, our holding as to the phase III cases necessarily requires reversal of the judgments in the five extrapolation cases before us.
>
> ....
>
> As to the matter of actual damages, the extrapolation cases are likewise fatally defective. Unlike the phase III cases, in the extrapolation cases there was neither any sort of trial determination, let alone a jury determination, nor even any evidence, of damages. The district court considered that these deficiencies were adequately compensated for by awarding each extrapolation case plaintiff who alleged an asbestos-related disease an amount of actual damages equal to the average of the awards made in the phase III cases for plaintiffs claiming the same category of disease. This plainly contravenes *Fibreboard's* holding that under the substantive law of Texas recoverable damages are the "wage losses, pain and suffering, and other elements of compensation" suffered by each of the several particular plaintiffs as "individuals, not groups." We also observe in this connection that none of the experts at the extrapolation hearing purported to say that the damages suffered by the phase III plaintiffs in a given disease category (whether

> as disclosed by the phase III evidence or as found by the jury) were to any extent representative of the damages suffered by the extrapolation plaintiffs in the same disease category. The procedure also violates Pittsburgh Corning's Seventh Amendment right to have the amount of the legally recoverable damages fixed and determined by a jury. The only juries that spoke to actual damages, the phase I and III juries, received evidence only of the damages to the particular plaintiffs before them, were called on to determine only, and only determined, each of those some one hundred seventy particular plaintiffs' actual damages individually and severally (not on any kind of a group basis), and were not called on to determine, and did not determine or purport to determine, the damages of any other plaintiffs or group of plaintiffs. We have held that "inherent in the Seventh Amendment guarantee of a trial by jury is the general right of a litigant to have only one jury pass on a common issue of fact." *Blue Bird Body Co.*, 573 F.2d at 318. This requires that if separate trials are ordered, the separately tried issues must be "distinct and separable from the others." *Id. See also Matter of Rhone Poulenc*, 51 F.3d 1293 (7th Cir. 1995). By the same token, where the issues to be separately tried are separable and distinct, the Seventh Amendment rights of the parties are preserved as to both sets of issues. *Blue Bird Body Co.*, 573 F.2d at 318. As the cited cases demonstrate, these principles are fully applicable in class actions for damages. It necessarily follows from these principles that the jury's phase III findings of the actual damages of each of the individual phase III plaintiffs cannot control the determination of, or afford any basis for denial of Pittsburgh-Corning's Seventh Amendment rights to have a jury determine, the distinct and separable issues of the actual damages of each of the extrapolation plaintiffs.
>
> We conclude that the extrapolation case judgments, as well as the phase III judgments, are fatally flawed, are contrary to the dictates of *Fibreboard*, and contravene Pittsburgh-Corning's Seventh Amendment rights.

Id. at 319–21.

4. This is a frustrating end to the *Fibreboard* saga. As the trial court observed:

> Transaction costs consumed $.61 of each asbestos-litigation dollar with $.37 going to defendants litigation costs; the plaintiffs receive only $.39 from each litigation dollar.... If the Court could somehow close thirty cases a month, it would take six and one-half years to try these cases and there would be pending over 5,000 untouched cases at the present rate of filing. Transaction costs would be astronomical.... The litigants and the public rightfully expect the courts to be problem solvers.

Cimino v. Raymark Indus., 751 F. Supp. 649, 650–52 (E.D. Tex. 1990).

5. *The Use of Statistics in Judicial Proceedings.* As *In re Fibreboard* shows, the use of statistical sampling to prove damages for a class of plaintiffs often runs into legal barriers. This does not mean that the use of statistical evidence at trial is always

problematic. In fact, statistical analysis is now used in a variety of courtroom proceedings. In making the case that trial by statistics, the subject of *In re Fibreboard* and the remaining notes, was simply an extension of accepted practices, one court surveyed the different ways in which courts had used statistics.

> Acceptance of statistical evidence is now commonplace in the Courts. The following illustrations demonstrate the diverse legal contexts in which statistics, particularly random sampling, has been used. Statistical evidence occurs frequently in Title VII employment discrimination cases, most often demonstrating a pattern or practice of discrimination on the part of the employer. Although noting that statistical proof is not irrefutable, the United States Supreme Court approved the use of statistical evidence to establish the plaintiff's prima facie case in *International Brotherhood of Teamsters v. United States*, 431 U.S. 324, 334–40 (1977). *See also Hazelwood School Dist. v. United States*, 433 U.S. 299, 307–13 (1977) (remanded to trial court to allow employer to present statistical evidence as to its hiring after it became subject to Title VII); *Capaci v. Katz & Besthoff, Inc.*, 711 F.2d 647, 653–57 (5th Cir. 1983) (court approved use of census data in gender discrimination case); *Vuyanich v. Republic Nat. Bank*, 505 F. Supp. 224 (N.D. Tex. 1980), *vacated on other grounds*, 723 F.2d 1195 (5th Cir. 1984) (extensive use of statistical studies of bank's personnel; some data rejected, but general statistical approach recognized including detailed description of regression analysis).
>
> Statistical evidence has been used in anti-trust cases to project pre and post merger market share and market concentration. *See State of Cal. v. American Stores Co.*, 872 F.2d 837, 841–42 (9th Cir. 1989); *Monfort of Colorado, Inc. v. Cargill, Inc.*, 591 F. Supp. 683, 705 (D. Colo. 1983) (although not conclusive, sufficiently high concentration and market share statistics can result in a prima facie showing of a violation of the Clayton Act). In trademark infringement suits, statistical sampling is useful in determining consumer product identification and confusion regarding trademarks. [*See Processed Plastic Co. v. Warner Communications, Inc.*, 675 F.2d 852, 854–58 (7th Cir. 1982) (survey of children between the ages of 6 and 12 in order to determine if Plaintiff's toy car was confused with Defendant's "Dukes of Hazzard" toy car); *Exxon Corp. v. Texas Motor Exchange, Inc.*, 628 F.2d 500 (5th Cir. 1980) (survey of 515 licensed drivers indicated high possibility of confusion between "Texon" and "Exxon"); *Zippo Manufacturing Co. v. Rogers Imports, Inc.*, 216 F. Supp. 670 (S.D.N.Y. 1963) (sample of 1,500 adult smokers to assess product identification of cigarette lighters).] In *R.J. Reynolds Tobacco Co. v. Loew's Theatres, Inc.*, 511 F. Supp. 867 (S.D.N.Y. 1980), the court permitted evidence of a professionally conducted consumer preference survey demonstrating the effect of an advertisement on consumers as a means of proving irreparable harm.

Statistical evidence frequently comes into play in civil rights cases. A class of Haitian refugees claiming discrimination in exclusion procedures was allowed to present a binomial analysis showing the number of Haitian versus non-Haitian refugees detained and paroled in *Jean v. Nelson*, 711 F.2d 1455, 1487–90, 1494–99 (11th Cir. 1983). In *Johnson v. City of Arcadia, Fla.*, 450 F. Supp. 1363 (M.D. Fla. 1978), the court inferred de facto discrimination from extensive historical statistical data presented by African-American citizens claiming deprivation of equal municipal services. Statistical data has also been used to prove up discrimination in jury selection cases. *See Castaneda v. Partida*, [430 U.S. 482 (1977)] (statistical evidence drawn from census data and grand jury records established prima facie case for discrimination against Hispanics in the Texas "key-man" selection system for grand juries); *Machetti v. Linahan*, 679 F.2d 236 (11th Cir. 1982) (statistical evidence showing disparity between percentage of females in adult populations and percentage of females on jury lists indicated unfair representation). Moreover, public opinion polls have been allowed in some state courts as evidence of community standards in obscenity cases. *See Carlock v. State*, 609 S.W.2d 787 (Tex. Cr. App. 1980); *Saliba v. State*, 475 N.E.2d 1181 (Ind. App. 2d Dist. 1985).

Evidence based upon statistical sampling has particularly received court approval in cases involving government inspection of large quantities of goods. *See United States v. 449 Cases Containing Tomato Paste*, 212 F.2d 567 (2d Cir. 1954) (court approved inspector's testing of samples, rather than requiring the opening of all cases); *E.K. Hardison Seed Co. v. Jones*, 149 F.2d 252 (6th Cir. 1945); *United States v. 43 1/2 Gross Rubber Prophylactics*, 65 F. Supp. 534 (D. Minn. 1946), *aff'd*, 159 F.2d 881 (8th Cir. 1947) (court determined that shipment was misbranded based upon evidence of a sample which indicated a potential of 1,500 defective prophylactics in shipment).

In the area of torts, statistics have been used to prove both liability and damages. The New Jersey Supreme Court has, in at least two cases, relied upon statistics showing the correlation between the theft of cars with keys left in the ignition and automobile accidents in the liability phase of a trial. *See Hill v. Yaskin*, 380 A.2d 1107 (N.J. 1977); *Zinck v. Whelan*, 294 A.2d 727 (N.J. 1972). Courts frequently permit evidence of life-expectancy or mortality tables when determining damages. *See Ageloff v. Delta Airlines, Inc.*, 860 F.2d 379 (11th Cir. 1988); *Espana v. United States*, 616 F.2d 41 (2d Cir. 1980); *Larsen v. International Business Machines Corp.*, 87 F.R.D. 602 (E.D.Pa. 1980) (use of work-life tables). Statistical evidence has proven to be particularly useful in the determination of lost or future revenues, profits or earnings. *See In re Knickerbocker*, 827 F.2d 281, 288–89 (8th Cir. 1987) (court allowed expert to testify as to future revenues, based upon historical analysis and price predictions); *G.M. Brod & Co. v. U.S. Home Corp.*, 759 F.2d 1526, 1538–40 (11th Cir. 1985) (expert testified as to profit projections based on industry norms); *Contemporary Mission, Inc. v. Famous Music Corp.*, 557 F.2d 918, 926–28 (2d Cir. 1977) (court allowed statistical analysis to predict future success of record which reached No. 61 on Billboard's "Hot Soul Singles" chart; analysis included every song that had reached No. 61 on the chart); *Thomas v. American Cystoscope Makers, Inc.*, 414 F. Supp. 255, 270 (E.D. Pa. 1976) (court allowed statistical evidence regarding income of medical partnerships to predict future income of a medical partnership).

> The reasons the courts have come to rely on statistics are the same reasons that society embraces the science. It has been proved to provide information with an acceptable degree of accuracy and economy.

Cimino v. Raymark Indus., 751 F. Supp. 649, 661–63 (E.D. Tex. 1990). Having read through these various uses of statistics, do you think the district court's trial plan in *In re Fibreboard* is more defensible? Less defensible? Is it a reasonable extension of accepted practices or an unjustified leap?

6. *Bellwether Trials.* The goal of the procedures used in *In re Fibreboard* and *Cimino* is to resolve the claims of many plaintiffs through the resolution of some subset of those claims. The latter is supposed to provide a sufficient basis for efficiently resolving the former. Various sorts of statistical analysis accomplish this. But there are other approaches. Bellwether trials are an example.

> [T]he trial of some members of a large group of claimants may provide a basis for enhancing prospects of settlement or for resolving common issues or claims is a sound one that has achieved general acceptance by both bench and bar. . . . The reasons for acceptance by bench and bar are apparent. If a representative group of claimants are tried to verdict, the results of such trials can be beneficial for litigants who desire to settle such claims by providing information on the value of the cases as reflected by the jury verdicts. . . .
>
> A bellwether trial designed to achieve its value ascertainment function for settlement purposes or to answer troubling causation or liability issues common to the universe of claimants has as a core element representativeness—that is, the sample must be a randomly selected one of sufficient size so as to achieve statistical significance to the desired level of confidence in the result obtained. Such samples are selected by the application of the science of inferential statistics. The essence of the science of inferential statistics is that one may confidently draw inferences about the whole from a representative sample of the whole.

In re Chevron U.S.A., Inc., 109 F.3d 1016, 1019 (5th Cir. 1997) (concluding that selected cases were not representative, however). *Compare Chevron with Cimino v. Raymark Indus.*, 751 F. Supp. 649, 652 (E.D. Tex. 1990) (the defendants "have adopted a 'fortress mentality' and are attempting to avoid liability by obstructing the Court's ability to provide a forum in these cases. . . . They assert a right to individual trials in each case and assert the right to repeatedly contest in each case every contestable issue involving the same products, the same warnings, and the same conduct.").

One court opinion strongly in favor of bellwether cases is *In re Methyl Tertiary Buthyl Ether (MTBE) Products*, 2007 WL 1791258 at *1–2 (S.D.N.Y. 2007): "Over the last decade, bellwether trials have become more common in large actions, and in particular, mass tort actions .... 'It is a fundamental principle of American law that every person is entitled to his or her day in court.' However, if plaintiffs file hundreds or thousands of individual actions, the sheer volume of the proceeding may overwhelm a court's ability to provide *any* plaintiff with relief in a timely and efficient manner." The court quotes *Chevron* for the view that bellwether cases are an acceptable device when the bellwether plaintiffs are selected on a statistically valid, random basis. Not all courts agree on the desirability of the bellwether device.

7. *Trial by Statistics.* Generally speaking, trial by statistics is the resolution of common issues of liability and damages through statistical sampling. Sampling generates a body of representative data from which individual claims can be inferentially resolved.

Trial by statistics is most useful when there are many similarly situated plaintiffs.

8. *The Importance of a Representative Sample.* One problem with the procedure struck down in *In re Fibreboard* was that the sample cases from which the lump sum damages amount was to be determined were not sufficiently representative of the class of plaintiffs as a whole. *In re Chevron U.S.A., Inc.* explained that "prior to any extrapolation" from sample trials, a court must "find that the cases tried are representative of the larger group of cases or claims." 109 F.3d 1016, 1020 (5th Cir. 1997) (representativeness lacking). The court in *Hilao v. Estate of Ferdinand Marcos* made such a finding of representativeness and approved a determination of compensatory damages based on statistical sampling:

> The district court allowed the use of a statistical sample of the class claims in determining compensatory damages. In all, 10,059 claims were received. The district court ruled 518 of these claims to be facially invalid, leaving 9,541 claims. From these, a list of 137 claims was randomly selected by computer. This number of randomly selected claims was chosen on the basis of the testimony of James Dannemiller, an expert on statistics, who testified that the examination of a random sample of 137 claims would achieve "a 95 percent statistical probability that the same percentage determined to be valid among the examined claims would be applicable to the totality of claims filed". Of the claims selected, 67 were for torture, 52 were for summary execution, and 18 were for "disappearance".

103 F.3d 767, 782 (9th Cir. 1996).

A representative sample certainly makes the results of a trial by statistics more accurate, but does it adequately address the problems found in *In re Fibreboard*? Also, how is representativeness to be determined? *Compare Watson*, 979 F.2d at 1018 (approving a plan where "the district court would select a group of 100 claimants at random. The three parties would then designate claimants they would accept as having 'representative claims.' The first 20 three-way matches would serve as plaintiffs in the punitive damages trials."), *with In re Chevron U.S.A.*, 109 F.3d at 1018–21 (rejecting a plan that "provided for a unitary trial on the issues of 'general liability or causation' on behalf of the remaining plaintiffs, as well as the individual causation and damage issues of the selected plaintiffs, and ordered the selection of a bellwether group of thirty (30) claimants, fifteen (15) to be chosen by the plaintiffs and fifteen (15) to be chosen by Chevron.").

9. *Punitive vs. Compensatory Damages.* Compensatory damages depend on the unique features, if there are any, of each plaintiff's claim. This is what makes the homogeneity of the class and the representativeness of the sample important. Some courts have found these concerns less pressing when punitive damages are at issue because the relevant focus is on defendant's conduct and not on the individual circumstances of each class member. *See Watson*, 979 F.2d at 1018–19.

> Based on the findings in [20 fully-tried plaintiff sample cases], the jury would then establish the ratio of punitive damages to compensatory damages for each class member. . . . Because of this minimal variance [with regard to the culpability of defendant's conduct], assessing the propriety of punitive damages on the basis of the claims of a cross-section of the plaintiff class should not, in the words of *Fibreboard*, require "lifting the description of the claims to a level of generality that tears them from their substantively required moorings." That the . . . jury will consider only punitive damages in a mass tort case materially distinguishes this case from *Fibreboard*. . . . More importantly, the Phase 2 jury is not to extrapolate punitive damages but, rather, is to determine a basis for assessment of punitive damages in the form of a ratio.

6. Due Process Problems with Trial by Statistics

Attempts to use statistical sampling in mass tort and disaster cases face three main barriers, each of which was identified by *In re Fibreboard*: (1) *Erie*/state law concerns; (2) Seventh Amendment concerns; and (3) due process concerns. The first two problems are addressed in detail by *In re Fibreboard* and *Cimino*. Turning to the third potential problem, courts have struggled to formulate an adequate way of analyzing the due process concerns. In *Blue Cross and Blue Shield of New Jersey, Inc. v. Philip Morris USA Inc.*, 344 F.3d 211, 227 (2d Cir.), *modified on other grounds*, 393 F.3d 312 (2d Cir. 2004), for example, the Second Circuit rejected a defense argument that aggregate proof violated the defendants' due process right to question every witness at trial. There is a sense, as *In re Fibreboard* shows, that statistical sampling as a way of proving damages somehow affronts due process, but what, exactly, apart from "a profound disquiet," is the problem?

Hilao v. Estate of Ferdinand Marcos analyzed the due process objection and concluded that there was not one:

> While the district court's methodology in determining valid claims is unorthodox, it can be justified by the extraordinarily unusual nature of this case. "'Due process,' unlike some legal rules, is not a technical conception with a fixed content unrelated to time, place and circumstances". *Cafeteria Works v. McElroy*, 367 U.S. 886, 895 (1961.) In *Connecticut v. Doehr*, 501 U.S. 1, 10 (1991), a case involving prejudgment attachment, the Supreme Court set forth a test, based on the test of *Mathews v. Eldridge*, 424 U.S. 319 (1976), for determining whether a procedure by which a private party invokes state power to deprive another person of property satisfies due process:
>
> First, consideration of the private interest that will be affected by the [procedure]; second, an examination of the risk of erroneous deprivation through the procedures under attack and the probable value of additional or alternative safeguards; and third, . . . principal attention to the interest of the party seeking the [procedure], with, nonetheless, due regard for any ancillary interest the government may have in providing the procedure or forgoing the added burden of providing greater protections.
>
> . . .
>
> Under the balancing test set forth in *Mathews* and *Doehr*, the procedure used by the district court did not violate due process.

103 F.3d at 786–87. *Hilao* applies a very specific sort of balancing test to weigh the due process interests of the parties. *Cimino v. Raymark Industries* also used a balancing test, but it was less formalized. Indeed, the trial court's (rejected) analysis in *Cimino* actually made due process considerations a justification for statistical sampling.

> However, a due process concern remains that is very troubling to the Court. It is apparent from the effort and time required to try these 160 cases, that unless this plan or some other procedure that permits damages to be adjudicated in the aggregate is approved, these cases cannot be tried. Defendants complain about the 1% likelihood that the result would be significantly different. However, plaintiffs are facing a 100% confidence level of being denied access to the courts. The Court will leave it to the academicians and legal scholars to debate whether our notion of due process has room for balancing these competing interests.

Cimino, 751 F. Supp. at 666. How strong do you find the due process objections? Are these responses sufficiently compelling?

Consider this excerpt, for example, from the Supreme Court's decision in *Wal-Mart Stores, Inc.* v. Dukes, 564 U.S. 338 (2011), which appears expressly to disapprove of Trial by Formula, at least in employment law pattern-or-practice cases:

> We have established a procedure for trying [employment] pattern-or-practice cases . . . . When the plaintiff seeks individual relief such as reinstatement or backpay after establishing a pattern or practice of discrimination, "a district court must usually conduct additional proceedings . . . to determine the scope of individual relief." [Citation omitted] At this phase, the burden of proof will shift to the company, but it will have the right to raise any individual affirmative defenses it may have, and to "demonstrate that the individual applicant was denied an employment opportunity for lawful reasons."
>
> The Court of Appeals believed that it was possible to replace such proceedings with Trial by Formula. A sample set of the class members would be selected, as to whom liability for sex discrimination and the backpay owing as a result would be determined in depositions supervised by a master. The percentage of claims determined to be valid would then be applied to the entire remaining class, and the number of (presumptively) valid claims thus derived would be multiplied by the average backpay award in the sample set to arrive at the entire class recovery—without further individualized proceedings. [Citation omitted] We disapprove that novel project. Because the Rules Enabling Act forbids interpreting Rule 23 to "abridge, enlarge or modify any substantive right," 28 U.S.C. § 2072(b) . . . ; a class cannot be certified on the premise that Wal-Mart will not be entitled to litigate its statutory defenses to individual claims.

564 U.S. at 366–367.

Is the Supreme Court signaling that there are significant due process issues with formulaic approaches to resolving complex litigation issues? Compare the Court's opinion in *Tyson Foods, Inc. v. Bouaphakeo*, 136 S. Ct. 1036 (2016). In that case, employees sued to recover compensation for time spent donning and doffing protective gear (they worked in a meat processing plant). The defendant had failed to keep relevant records, so the class representative relied upon expert testimony, which was based upon averages for various types of workers. The Court distinguished *Wal-Mart*: "While the experiences of the employees in *Wal-Mart* bore little relationship to one another, in this case each employee worked in the same facility, did similar work, and was paid under the same policy." *Id.* at 1048. Because an individual employee in *Tyson Foods*, suing individually, would be permitted to rely on the expert opinion, so could the class.

Contrast in turn the following language from the majority opinion in *AT&T Mobility LLC v. Concepcion*, 563 U.S. 333 (2011), in which the Supreme Court, in a narrowly divided 5-to-4 decision, held that the rule from *Discover Bank v. Superior Court*, 30 Cal.Rptr.3d 76 (2005), invalidating class arbitration waivers in certain consumer contracts, was preempted by the Federal Arbitration Act. "[C]lass arbitration greatly increases risks to defendants . . . . [W]hen damages allegedly owed to tens of thousands of potential claimants are aggregated and decided at once, the risk of error will often become unacceptable. Faced with even a small chance of a devastating loss, defendants will be pressured into settling questionable claims." 563 U.S. at 350. Do you think the Supreme Court agrees with the defense view that aggregation of damages will often present unacceptable risk of error?

For an interesting discussion of some of the issues involved in trial-by-formula in the class action context, see Frank Burt & Ramiro Areces, *'A Profound Disquiet': Losing Sight of Defendants' Rights in Rule 23 Class Certification Analysis*, 79 U.S.L.W. 1575 (2010); consider also Alexandra D. Lahav, *The Case for "Trial By Formula*," 90 Tex. L. Rev. 571 (2012). This latter article argues that there is a tension in current civil litigation (in particular current mass tort litigation) between the principle of liberty and the principle of equality. The author argues that recent Supreme Court jurisprudence has favored liberty, but that lower courts appropriately have been trying out procedures designed to promote "litigant equality" and "consistent outcomes." *Id.* at 577.

Chapter 10

Preclusion

A. Introduction

Consideration of preclusion doctrine in the context of complex litigation may be facilitated by a brief review of the "basics" of preclusion developed in introductory courses on Civil Procedure.

Preclusion doctrine promotes judicial and litigant economy by precluding relitigation of matters finally resolved by judicial decree. Preclusion also facilitates reliance on judicial decisions and enhances public confidence in the courts. As the Supreme Court observed in *Federated Dept. Stores v. Moitie*, 452 U.S. 394 (1981):

> This Court has long recognized that "[p]ublic policy dictates that there be an end to litigation; that those who have contested an issue shall be bound by the result of the contest, and that matters once tried shall be considered forever settled as between the parties." We have stressed that "[t]he doctrine of *res judicata* is not a mere matter of practice or procedure inherited from a more technical time than ours. It is a rule of fundamental and substantial justice, 'of public policy and private peace,' which should be cordially regarded and enforced by the courts."

Id. at 401 (citations omitted).

For an instructive general review of preclusion doctrine, *see* Richard D. Freer, Civil Procedure ch. 11 (4th ed. 2017). The historic doctrine of preclusion was divided into two branches, commonly referred to as "res judicata" and "collateral estoppel." In modern terminology, these are referred to as "claim preclusion" and "issue preclusion." Under the doctrine of claim preclusion, (1) a final judgment (2) "on the merits"[1] (3) precludes litigation by the same claimant against the same defendant (4) of any matter that was or might have been asserted (5) in support of the same "claim for relief." The prevailing, but not universal,[2] view in federal and most state courts treats all demands for judicial relief arising from the "same

1. Thus, for example, dismissals for lack of jurisdiction, improper venue, or failure to join an indispensable party do not have preclusive effect in subsequent litigation. *See* Fed. R. Civ. P. 41(b).

2. Some states have adopted narrower definitions. For example, California defines a "claim for relief" in terms of the "primary right" being asserted by the plaintiff, rather than with reference to whether the claims arise out of the same transaction. Under that definition, more than one claim for relief can arise from the same transaction depending on whether the successive actions seek to enforce the same "primary right" of the plaintiff.

transaction or occurrence" as presenting the same "claim for relief" for claim preclusion purposes. *See* RESTATEMENT (SECOND) OF JUDGMENTS § 24(1) (1982). As a result, once a final judgment on the merits has been rendered in an earlier action, the claimant in that action may not advance any legal or factual contention that it did assert or might have asserted in the earlier action in a subsequent action against the same defendant arising from the same transaction as the earlier action. This very broad application of the doctrine of claim preclusion has the effect of requiring parties to advance all factual and legal contentions in support of relief based on transactionally related events in the first judicial proceeding between them, even though procedural rules governing the joinder of claims ostensibly are permissive rather than mandatory. *See* FED. R. CIV. P. 18(a) and advisory committee's note (1966) (permitting but not requiring a party asserting a claim for relief to join as many claims as the party has against an opposing party).

By contrast, under the doctrine of "issue preclusion," (1) a final judicial decision of an issue of law or fact (2) precludes a party to the first action (3) from relitigating the "identical" issue in subsequent litigation, (4) provided that the issue was actually litigated and decided in the first case, and (5) was necessary to the decision of that case. Thus, issue preclusion (collateral estoppel) sweeps more broadly than claim preclusion by precluding relitigation of matters once decided even in subsequent litigation that does not arise from the same transaction or occurrence as the first action and therefore does not assert the same "claim for relief." At the same time, it operates more narrowly than claim preclusion by precluding only identical matters that were actually litigated and decided, and were necessary to the decision, rather than all matters that were or might have been advanced in support of the claim in the first action.

To the extent that complex litigation involves actions in which claims between the same parties have been voluntarily or mandatorily joined in successive actions under procedural rules permitting or requiring the joinder of parties and claims, application of the doctrines of claim and issue preclusion presents no special problems and well serves its historic purposes of judicial and litigant economy, finality, and repose. As discussed in more depth below, this also is true in class actions, in which members of a properly certified class action are treated as parties to the action for the purpose of claim and issue preclusion. However, some additional complexities relating to the scope of preclusion and adequacy of representation are present in the class action context.

Historically, however, the doctrines of claim and issue preclusion were not effective in encouraging comprehensive disposition of factually related claims asserted by or against different parties not joined in the initial action. With respect to claim preclusion, that is because factually related claims between different parties do not present the "same claim" for purposes of claim preclusion (unless the parties are found to be in "privity" with each other).

Issue preclusion also was ineffective in litigation against or by non-parties to the previous action for two reasons. First, a fundamental principle of due process of law is that preclusion cannot be asserted *against* a person who was not a party to the previous action. Second, issue preclusion asserted *by* non-parties to a previous action against persons who were parties to that action was prevented by the doctrine of "mutuality." Under the doctrine of mutuality, issue preclusion could not be asserted by a non-party to a previous action against a person who had lost on an issue in that action involving a different party because the non-party would not have been bound by the result had the judgment been in favor of rather than adverse to the losing party in the previous action. Courts thought it unfair that a party could take advantage of a favorable judgment by which it would not have been bound had the judgment been adverse.

As a result of the doctrine of mutuality, a party who had litigated and lost on one or more issues identical to those presented in subsequent actions by or against that same party arising from the same basic wrong or course of conduct, but in which the opposing parties differed, was not precluded from relitigating those same issues over and over again, imposing potentially large and unjustified costs on the parties and the legal system as a whole. (Consider, for example, the issue of product defect in the thousands of federal and state court actions arising from use of or exposure to toxic or hazardous products or substances such as tobacco or asbestos.) Thus, the utility of preclusion doctrine as a vehicle facilitating the comprehensive disposition of complex litigation in the absence of party joinder was significantly limited.

In *Blonder-Tongue Laboratories, Inc. v. Univ. of Illinois Found.*, 402 U.S. 313 (1971), and *Parklane Hosiery Co. v. Shore*, 439 U.S. 322 (1979), the Supreme Court held that mutuality was no longer a requirement for the application of issue preclusion in cases governed by federal preclusion law. These important holdings carried significant potential implications for complex litigation, which will be explored in the notes following *Parklane Hosiery.*

B. Non-Mutual Issue Preclusion

Parklane Hosiery Co. v. Shore

Supreme Court of the United States
439 U.S. 322 (1979)

MR. JUSTICE STEWART delivered the opinion of the Court.

This case presents the question whether a party who has had issues of fact adjudicated adversely to it in an equitable action may be collaterally estopped from relitigating the same issues before a jury in a subsequent legal action brought against it by a new party.

The respondent brought this stockholder's class action against the petitioners in a Federal District Court. The complaint alleged that the petitioners, Parklane Hosiery Co., Inc. (Parklane), and 13 of its officers, directors, and stockholders, had issued a materially false and misleading proxy statement in connection with a merger. The proxy statement, according to the complaint, had violated §§ 14(a), 10(b), and 20(a) of the Securities Exchange Act of 1934, 48 Stat. 895, 891, 899, as amended, 15 U.S.C. §§ 78n(a), 78j(b), and 78t(a), as well as various rules and regulations promulgated by the Securities and Exchange Commission (SEC). The complaint sought damages, rescission of the merger, and recovery of costs.

Before this action came to trial, the SEC filed suit against the same defendants in the Federal District Court, alleging that the proxy statement that had been issued by Parklane was materially false and misleading in essentially the same respects as those that had been alleged in the respondent's complaint. Injunctive relief was requested. After a 4-day trial, the District Court found that the proxy statement was materially false and misleading in the respects alleged, and entered a declaratory judgment to that effect. . . . The Court of Appeals for the Second Circuit affirmed this judgment. . . .

The respondent in the present case then moved for partial summary judgment against the petitioners, asserting that the petitioners were collaterally estopped from relitigating the issues that had been resolved against them in the action brought by the SEC.[3] The District Court denied the motion on the ground that such an application of collateral estoppel would deny the petitioners their Seventh Amendment right to a jury trial. The Court of Appeals for the Second Circuit reversed, holding that a party who has had issues of fact determined against him after a full and fair opportunity to litigate in a nonjury trial is collaterally estopped from obtaining a subsequent jury trial of these same issues of fact. . . . Because of an inter-circuit conflict, we granted certiorari. . . .

I

The threshold question to be considered is whether, quite apart from the right to a jury trial under the Seventh Amendment, the petitioners can be precluded from relitigating facts resolved adversely to them in a prior equitable proceeding with another party under the general law of collateral estoppel. Specifically, we must determine whether a litigant who was not a party to a prior judgment may nevertheless use that judgment "offensively" to prevent a defendant from relitigating issues resolved in the earlier proceeding.[4]

---

3. [Court's footnote #2] A private plaintiff in an action under the proxy rules is not entitled to relief simply by demonstrating that the proxy solicitation was materially false and misleading. The plaintiff must also show that he was injured and prove damages. . . . Since the SEC action was limited to a determination of whether the proxy statement contained materially false and misleading information, the respondent conceded that he would still have to prove these other elements of his prima facie case in the private action. The petitioners' right to a jury trial on those remaining issues is not contested.

4. [Court's footnote #4] In this context, offensive use of collateral estoppel occurs when the plaintiff seeks to foreclose the defendant from litigating an issue the defendant has previously litigated unsuccessfully in an action with another party. Defensive use occurs when a defendant seeks to prevent a plaintiff from asserting a claim the plaintiff has previously litigated and lost against another defendant.

A

Collateral estoppel, like the related doctrine of res judicata,[5] has the dual purpose of protecting litigants from the burden of relitigating an identical issue with the same party or his privy and of promoting judicial economy by preventing needless litigation. . . . Until relatively recently, however, the scope of collateral estoppel was limited by the doctrine of mutuality of parties. Under this mutuality doctrine, neither party could use a prior judgment as an estoppel against the other unless both parties were bound by the judgment. Based on the premise that it is somehow unfair to allow a party to use a prior judgment when he himself would not be so bound, the mutuality requirement provided a party who had litigated and lost in a previous action an opportunity to relitigate identical issues with new parties.

By failing to recognize the obvious difference in position between a party who has never litigated an issue and one who has fully litigated and lost, the mutuality requirement was criticized almost from its inception. Recognizing the validity of this criticism, the Court in *Blonder-Tongue Laboratories, Inc. v. University of Illinois Foundation*, [402 U.S. 313 (1971)] abandoned the mutuality requirement, at least in cases where a patentee seeks to relitigate the validity of a patent after a federal court in a previous lawsuit has already declared it invalid. . . .

B

The *Blonder-Tongue* case involved defensive use of collateral estoppel—a plaintiff was estopped from asserting a claim that the plaintiff had previously litigated and lost against another defendant. The present case, by contrast, involves offensive use of collateral estoppel—a plaintiff is seeking to estop a defendant from relitigating the issues which the defendant previously litigated and lost against another plaintiff. In both the offensive and defensive use situations, the party against whom estoppel is asserted has litigated and lost in an earlier action. Nevertheless, several reasons have been advanced why the two situations should be treated differently.[6]

First, offensive use of collateral estoppel does not promote judicial economy in the same manner as defensive use does. Defensive use of collateral estoppel precludes a plaintiff from relitigating identical issues by merely "switching adversaries. . . ." Thus defensive collateral estoppel gives a plaintiff a strong incentive to join all potential defendants in the first action if possible. Offensive use of collateral estoppel, on the

---

5. [Court's footnote #5] Under the doctrine of res judicata, a judgment on the merits in a prior suit bars a second suit involving the same parties or their privies based on the same cause of action. Under the doctrine of collateral estoppel, on the other hand, the second action is upon a different cause of action and the judgment in the prior suit precludes relitigation of issues actually litigated and necessary to the outcome of the first action. . . .

6. [Court's footnote #11] Various commentators have expressed reservations regarding the application of offensive collateral estoppel. Currie, Mutuality of Estoppel: Limits of the *Bernhard* Doctrine, 9 Stan. L. Rev. 281 (1957); Semmel, Collateral Estoppel, Mutuality and Joinder of Parties, 68 Colum. L. Rev. 1457 (1968); Note, The Impacts of Defensive and Offensive Assertion of Collateral Estoppel by a Nonparty, 35 Geo. Wash. L. Rev. 1010 (1967). Professor Currie later tempered his reservations. Civil Procedure: The Tempest Brews, 53 Calif. L. Rev. 25 (1965).

other hand, creates precisely the opposite incentive. Since a plaintiff will be able to rely on a previous judgment against a defendant but will not be bound by that judgment if the defendant wins, the plaintiff has every incentive to adopt a "wait and see" attitude, in the hope that the first action by another plaintiff will result in a favorable judgment.... Thus offensive use of collateral estoppel will likely increase rather than decrease the total amount of litigation, since potential plaintiffs will have everything to gain and nothing to lose by not intervening in the first action.

A second argument against offensive use of collateral estoppel is that it may be unfair to a defendant. If a defendant in the first action is sued for small or nominal damages, he may have little incentive to defend vigorously, particularly if future suits are not foreseeable.... Allowing offensive collateral estoppel may also be unfair to a defendant if the judgment relied upon as a basis for the estoppel is itself inconsistent with one or more previous judgments in favor of the defendant.[7] Still another situation where it might be unfair to apply offensive estoppel is where the second action affords the defendant procedural opportunities unavailable in the first action that could readily cause a different result.[8]

C

We have concluded that the preferable approach for dealing with these problems in the federal courts is not to preclude the use of offensive collateral estoppel, but to grant trial courts broad discretion to determine when it should be applied. The general rule should be that in cases where a plaintiff could easily have joined in the earlier action or where, either for the reasons discussed above or for other reasons, the application of offensive estoppel would be unfair to a defendant, a trial judge should not allow the use of offensive collateral estoppel.

In the present case, however, none of the circumstances that might justify reluctance to allow the offensive use of collateral estoppel is present. The application of offensive collateral estoppel will not here reward a private plaintiff who could have joined in the previous action, since the respondent probably could not have joined in the injunctive action brought by the SEC even had he so desired. Similarly, there is no unfairness to the petitioners in applying offensive collateral estoppel in this

7. [Court's footnote #14] In Professor Currie's familiar example, a railroad collision injures 50 passengers all of whom bring separate actions against the railroad. After the railroad wins the first 25 suits, a plaintiff wins in suit 26. Professor Currie argues that offensive use of collateral estoppel should not be applied so as to allow plaintiffs 27 through 50 automatically to recover. Currie, *supra*, 9 Stan. L. Rev., at 304. See Restatement (Second) of Judgments § 88(4), *supra*.

8. [Court's footnote #15] If, for example, the defendant in the first action was forced to defend in an inconvenient forum and therefore was unable to engage in full scale discovery or call witnesses, application of offensive collateral estoppel may be unwarranted. Indeed, differences in available procedures may sometimes justify not allowing a prior judgment to have estoppel effect in a subsequent action even between the same parties, or where defensive estoppel is asserted against a plaintiff who has litigated and lost. The problem of unfairness is particularly acute in cases of offensive estoppel, however, because the defendant against whom estoppel is asserted typically will not have chosen the forum in the first action.

case. First, in light of the serious allegations made in the SEC's complaint against the petitioners, as well as the foreseeability of subsequent private suits that typically follow a successful Government judgment, the petitioners had every incentive to litigate the SEC lawsuit fully and vigorously. Second, the judgment in the SEC action was not inconsistent with any previous decision. Finally, there will in the respondent's action be no procedural opportunities available to the petitioners that were unavailable in the first action of a kind that might be likely to cause a different result.[9]

We conclude, therefore, that none of the considerations that would justify a refusal to allow the use of offensive collateral estoppel is present in this case. Since the petitioners received a "full and fair" opportunity to litigate their claims in the SEC action, the contemporary law of collateral estoppel leads inescapably to the conclusion that the petitioners are collaterally estopped from relitigating the question of whether the proxy statement was materially false and misleading.

II

[The Court held that the Seventh Amendment was not violated by the application of non-mutual offensive issue preclusion.]

The judgment of the Court of Appeals is *Affirmed.*

MR. JUSTICE REHNQUIST, dissenting.

[The portion of Justice Rehnquist's opinion concluding that the use of offensive non-mutual collateral estoppel would violate the Seventh Amendment is omitted.]

II

Even accepting, *arguendo*, the majority's position that there is no violation of the Seventh Amendment here, I nonetheless would not sanction the use of collateral estoppel in this case. . . . In my view, it is "unfair" to apply offensive collateral estoppel where the party who is sought to be estopped has not had an opportunity to have the facts of his case determined by a jury. Since in this case petitioners were not entitled to a jury trial in the Securities and Exchange Commission (SEC) lawsuit, I would not estop them from relitigating the issues determined in the SEC suit before a jury in the private action. I believe that several factors militate in favor of this result.

First, the use of offensive collateral estoppel in this case runs counter to the strong federal policy favoring jury trials, even if it does not, as the majority holds, violate the Seventh Amendment. . . .

Second, I believe that the opportunity for a jury trial in the second action could easily lead to a different result from that obtained in the first action before the court and therefore that it is unfair to estop petitioners from relitigating the issues before

9. [Court's footnote #19] It is true, of course, that the petitioners in the present action would be entitled to a jury trial of the issues bearing on whether the proxy statement was materially false and misleading had the SEC action never been brought—a matter to be discussed in Part II of this opinion. But the presence or absence of a jury as factfinder is basically neutral, quite unlike, for example, the necessity of defending the first lawsuit in an inconvenient forum.

a jury. . . . The Court accepts the proposition that it is unfair to apply offensive collateral estoppel "where the second action affords the defendant procedural opportunities unavailable in the first action that could readily cause a different result." Differences in discovery opportunities between the two actions are cited as examples of situations where it would be unfair to permit offensive collateral estoppel. But in the Court's view, the fact that petitioners would have been entitled to a jury trial in the present action is not such a "procedural opportunit[y]" because "the presence or absence of a jury as factfinder is basically *neutral*, quite unlike, for example, the necessity of defending the first lawsuit in an inconvenient forum." [Emphasis added.]

. . . [T]hose who drafted the Declaration of Independence and debated so passionately the proposed Constitution during the ratification period, would indeed be astounded to learn that the presence or absence of a jury is merely "neutral," whereas the availability of discovery, a device unmentioned in the Constitution, may be controlling. It is precisely because the Framers believed that they might receive a different result at the hands of a jury of their peers than at the mercy of the sovereign's judges, that the Seventh Amendment was adopted. And I suspect that anyone who litigates cases before juries in the 1970's would be equally amazed to hear of the supposed lack of distinction between trial by court and trial by jury . . . .

Notes and Questions

Although *Blonder-Tongue Laboratories* and *Parklane Hosiery* expanded the group of persons *by whom* issue preclusion may be invoked, they did nothing to alter universe of persons *against whom* issue preclusion applies. Even in successive cases by multiple plaintiffs against a single defendant involving identical legal and factual issues, non-mutual preclusion is limited by the basic due process principle that a person may not be bound by the result of litigation to which she is not a party. Thus, for example, the fact that a defendant may be precluded from relitigating certain issues that it lost in an earlier action by one plaintiff in later actions by other plaintiffs does not imply that the plaintiffs in those later actions may not relitigate identical issues of law or fact on which the defendant prevailed against a different plaintiff in an earlier action.

1. Application of the *Parklane Hosiery* Doctrine in Complex Cases

Hardy v. Johns-Manville Sales Corp.

United States Court of Appeals, Fifth Circuit
681 F.2d 334 (1982)

GEE, CIRCUIT JUDGE:

This appeal arises out of a diversity action brought by various plaintiffs—insulators, pipefitters, carpenters, and other factory workers—against various manufacturers, sellers, and distributors of asbestos containing products. The plaintiffs, alleging exposure to the products and consequent disease, assert various causes of action, including negligence, breach of implied warranty, and strict liability. The pleadings in each of the cases are substantially the same. No plaintiff names a particular defendant on a case-by-case basis but, instead, includes several—often as many as twenty asbestos manufacturers—in his individual complaint. The rationale offered for this unusual pleading practice is that, given the long latent period of the diseases in question, it is impossible for plaintiffs to isolate the precise exposure period or to identify the particular manufacturer's product responsible. The trial court accepted this rationale and opted for a theory of enterprise- or industry-wide liability used in, for example, *Sindell v. Abbott Laboratories*, 26 Cal.3d 588, 163 Cal. Rptr. 132, 607 P.2d 924 (1980) (on proof that plaintiffs contracted a DES-related cancer and that their mothers took DES during pregnancy, market share apportionment determines a manufacturer's liability unless a given manufacturer exculpates itself by proving that its product could not have caused the injury). The trial court held that Texas courts, faced with the impossibility of identifying a precise causative agent in these asbestos cases, would adopt a form of *Sindell* liability, described as a "hybrid, drawing from concepts of alternative and/or concurrent liability and the law of products liability to form a type of absolute liability. . . ."

Defendants' interlocutory appeal under 28 U.S.C. § 1292(b) is directed . . . at the district court's amended omnibus order dated March 13, 1981, which applies collateral estoppel to this mass tort. . . . The omnibus order is, in effect, a partial summary judgment for plaintiffs based on nonmutual offensive collateral estoppel and judicial notice derived from this court's opinion in *Borel v. Fibreboard Paper Products Corp.*, 493 F.2d 1076 (5th Cir. 1973) (henceforth *Borel*). *Borel* was a diversity lawsuit in which manufacturers of insulation products containing asbestos were held strictly liable to an insulation worker who developed asbestosis and mesothelioma and ultimately died. The trial court construed *Borel* as establishing as a matter of law and/or of fact that: (1) insulation products containing asbestos as a generic ingredient are "unavoidably unsafe products," (2) asbestos is a competent producing cause of mesothelioma and asbestosis, (3) no warnings were issued by any asbestos insulation manufacturers prior to 1964, and (4) the "warning standard" was not met by the *Borel* defendants in the period from 1964 through 1969. Insofar as the trial court based its omnibus order on the res judicata effect of *Borel*, this aspect of the order is no longer valid. *Migues v. Fibreboard Corp.*, 662 F.2d 1183 (5th Cir. 1981). The sole issue on appeal is the validity of the order on grounds of collateral estoppel or judicial notice.

In *Flatt v. Johns-Manville Sales Corp.*, 488 F.Supp. 836 (E.D.Tex.1980), the same court outlined the elements of proof for plaintiffs in asbestos-related cases. There the court stated that the plaintiff must prove by a preponderance of the evidence that

1. Defendants manufactured, marketed, sold, distributed, or placed in the stream of commerce products containing asbestos.

2. Products containing asbestos are unreasonably dangerous.
3. Asbestos dust is a competent producing cause of mesothelioma.
4. Decedent was exposed to defendant's products.
5. The exposure was sufficient to be a producing cause of mesothelioma.
6. Decedent contracted mesothelioma.
7. Plaintiffs suffered damages.

Id. at 838, *citing Restatement (Second) of Torts* §402A(1) (1965). The parties agree that the effect of the trial court's collateral estoppel order in this case is to foreclose elements 2 and 3 above. Under the terms of the omnibus order, both parties are precluded from presenting evidence on the "state of the art"—evidence that, under Texas law of strict liability, is considered by a jury along with other evidence in order to determine whether as of a given time warning should have been given of the dangers associated with a product placed in the stream of commerce. Under the terms of the order, the plaintiffs need not prove that the defendants either knew or should have known of the dangerous propensities of their products and therefore should have warned consumers of these dangers, defendants being precluded from showing otherwise. On appeal, the defendants contend that the order violates their rights to due process and to trial by jury. Because we conclude that the trial court abused its discretion in applying collateral estoppel and judicial notice, we reverse.

CHOICE OF LAW

. . . .

Having determined that federal law of collateral estoppel governs, we next turn to an examination of just what that law is. . . .

In the wake of *Parklane*, it is clear that a right, question, or fact distinctly put in issue and directly determined as a ground of recovery by a court of competent jurisdiction collaterally estops a party or his privy from relitigating the issue in a subsequent action. So stated, the doctrine recognizes that a person "cannot be bound by a judgment unless he has had reasonable notice of the claim against him and opportunity to be heard in opposition to that claim." 1B J. Moore, *Moore's Federal Practice* ¶ 0.411 at 1252 (2d ed. 1982) (henceforth *Moore's*). The right to a full and fair opportunity to litigate an issue is, of course, protected by the due process clause of the United States Constitution. . . . While *Parklane* made the doctrine of mutuality effectively a dead letter under federal law, the case left undisturbed the requisite of privity, *i.e.*, that collateral estoppel can only be applied against parties who have had a prior "'full and fair' opportunity to litigate their claims. . . ." The requirement that a person against whom the conclusive effect of a judgment is invoked must be a party or a privy to the prior judgment retains its full vigor after *Parklane* and has been repeatedly affirmed by our court. . . .

THE NON-*BOREL* DEFENDANTS

This is the first and, in our view, insurmountable problem with the trial court's application of collateral estoppel in the case *sub judice*. The omnibus order under review here does not distinguish between defendants who were parties to *Borel* and those who were not; it purports to estop all defendants because all purportedly share an "identity of interests" sufficient to constitute privity. The trial court's action stretches "privity" beyond meaningful limits. While we acknowledge the manipulability of the notion of "privity," *see, e.g., Collateral Estoppel of Nonparties*, 87 Harv.L.Rev. 1485, 1490, 1494–95 & n.66 (1974), this has not prevented courts from establishing guidelines on the permissibility of binding nonparties through res judicata or collateral estoppel. Without such guidelines . . . opportunity to litigate disappears. Thus, we noted in *Southwest Airlines Co. v. Texas International Airlines*, 546 F.2d 84, 95 (5th Cir. 1977):

> Federal courts have deemed several types of relationships "sufficiently close" to justify preclusion. First, a nonparty who has succeeded to a party's interest in property is bound by any prior judgments against that party. . . . Second, a nonparty who controlled the original suit will be bound by the resulting judgment. . . . Third, federal courts will bind a nonparty whose interests were represented adequately by a party in the original suit.

(citations omitted). The rationale for these exceptions—all derived from *Restatement (Second) of Judgments* §§ 30, 31, 34, 39–41 (1982)—is obviously that in these instances the nonparty has in effect had his day in court. In this case, the exceptions elaborated in *Southwest Airlines* and in the *Restatement* are inapplicable. First, the *Borel* litigation did not involve any property interests. Second, none of the non-*Borel* defendants have succeeded to any property interest held by the *Borel* defendants. Finally, the plaintiffs did not show that any non-*Borel* defendant had any control whatever over the *Borel* litigation. . . .

The fact that all the non-*Borel* defendants, like the *Borel* defendants, are engaged in the manufacture of asbestos-containing products does not evince privity among the parties. The plaintiffs did not demonstrate that any of the non-*Borel* defendants participated in any capacity in the *Borel* litigation—whether directly or even through a trade representative—or were even part of a trustee-beneficiary relationship with any *Borel* defendant. On the contrary, several of the defendants indicate on appeal that they were not even aware of the *Borel* litigation until those proceedings were over and that they were not even members of industry or trade associations composed of asbestos product manufacturers.

[The court also rejected application of the doctrine of "virtual representation," discussed *infra* in this chapter.]

THE *BOREL* DEFENDANTS

The propriety of estopping the six defendants in this case who were parties to *Borel* poses more difficult questions. . . . The party asserting the estoppel must show that: (1) the issue to be concluded is identical to that involved in the prior action; (2) in the prior action the issue was "actually litigated"; and (3) the determination made of the issue in the prior action must have been necessary and essential to the resulting judgment.

> If it appears that a judgment may have been based on more than one of several distinctive matters in litigation and there is no indication which issue it was based on or which issue was fully litigated, such judgment will not preclude, under the doctrine of collateral estoppel, relitigation of any of the issues.

Federal Procedure, Lawyers Ed. § 51.218 at 151 (1981) (citations omitted). *See also, e.g., Moore's* ¶ 0.442; *Restatement (Second)—Judgments* § 29, comment a (1982).

Appellants argue that *Borel* did not necessarily decide that asbestos-containing insulation products were unreasonably dangerous because of failure to warn. According to appellants, the general *Borel* verdict, based on general instructions and special interrogatories, permitted the jury to ground strict liability on the bases of failures to test, of unsafeness for intended use, of failures to inspect, or of unsafeness of the product. Strict liability on the basis of failure to warn, although argued to the jury by trial counsel for the plaintiff in *Borel*, was, in the view of the appellants, never formally presented in the jury instructions and therefore was not essential to the *Borel* jury verdict.

Appellants' view has some plausibility. The special interrogatories answered by the *Borel* jury were general and not specifically directed to failure to warn. Indeed, as we discussed at length in our review of the *Borel* judgment, the jury was instructed in terms of "breach of warranty." 493 F.2d at 1091. Although the jury was accurately instructed as to "strict liability in tort" as defined in section 402A of the *Restatement (Second) of Torts*, that phrase was never specifically mentioned in the jury's interrogatories. It is also true that the general instructions to the *Borel* jury on the plaintiff's causes of action did not charge on failure to warn, except in connection with negligence. Yet appellants' argument in its broadest form must ultimately fail. We concluded in *Borel*:

> The jury found that the unreasonably dangerous condition of the defendants' product was the proximate cause of Borel's injury. This necessarily included a finding that, had adequate warnings been provided, Borel would have chosen to avoid the danger.

493 F.2d at 1093. As the appellants at times concede in their briefs, "if *Borel* stands for any rule at all, it is that defendants have a duty to warn the users of their products of the long-term dangers attendant upon its use, including the danger of an occupational disease." Indeed, the first sentence in our *Borel* opinion states that that case involved "the scope of an asbestos manufacturer's duty to warn industrial insulation workers of dangers associated with the use of asbestos." *Id.* at 1081. *See also* 493 F.2d at 1105 (on rehearing).... Nonetheless, we must ultimately conclude that the judgment in *Borel* cannot estop even the *Borel* defendants in this case for three interrelated reasons.

First, after review of the issues decided in *Borel*, we conclude that *Borel*, while conclusive as to the general matter of a duty to warn on the part of manufacturers of asbestos-containing insulation products, is ultimately ambiguous as to certain key issues.

. . . Like *stare decisis*, collateral estoppel applies only to issues of fact or law necessarily decided by a prior court. Since we cannot say that *Borel* necessarily decided, as a matter of fact, that all manufacturers of asbestos-containing insulation products knew or should have known of the dangers of their particular products at all relevant times, we cannot justify the trial court's collaterally estopping the defendants from presenting evidence as to the state of the art.

Even if we are wrong as to the ambiguities of the *Borel* judgment, there is a second, equally important, reason to deny collateral estoppel effect to it: the presence of inconsistent verdicts. In *Parklane Hosiery v. Shore* . . . the Court noted that collateral estoppel is improper and "unfair" to a defendant "if the judgment relied upon as a basis for the estoppel is itself inconsistent with one or more previous judgments in favor of the defendant." *Accord Restatement (Second)—Judgments* § 29(4) (1982). . . . On appeal, the parties inform us that there have been approximately 70 similar asbestos cases thus far tried around the country. Approximately half of these seem to have been decided in favor of the defendants.[10] A court able to say that the approximately 35 suits decided in favor of asbestos manufacturers were all decided on the basis of insufficient exposure on the part of the plaintiff or failure to demonstrate an asbestos-related disease would be clairvoyant. Indeed, the appellants inform us of several products liability cases in which the state of the art question was fully litigated, yet the asbestos manufacturers were found not liable. Although it is usually not possible to say with certainty what these juries based their verdicts on, in at least some of the cases the verdict for the defendant was not based on failure to prove exposure or failure to show an asbestos-related disease. . . . We conclude that the court erred in arbitrarily choosing one of these verdicts, that in *Borel*, as the bellwether.

Finally, we conclude that even if the *Borel* verdict had been unambiguous and the sole verdict issued on point, application of collateral estoppel would still be unfair with regard to the *Borel* defendants because it is very doubtful that these defendants could have foreseen that their $68,000 liability to plaintiff Borel would foreshadow multimillion dollar asbestos liability.

. . . .

Reversed.

---

10. [Court's footnote #14] The parties also inform us that there are at least seven judgments in favor of several of the defendants in this case alone.

2. The Scope of the *Parklane Hosiery* "Exceptions"

1. Courts have noted a wide range of circumstances making the application of offensive non-mutual offensive preclusion "unfair." A leading treatise notes the following: erroneous evidentiary exclusions (*Jack Faucett Assoc., Inc. v. AT&T*, 744 F.2d 118, 127 (D.C. Cir. 1984)); reliance on stipulations rather than evidentiary determinations (*id.* at 132); inconsistent findings in other litigation (*id.* at 129–30); reliance on findings made before a state court altered controlling state law (*Nations v. Sun Oil Co.*, 705 F.2d 742, 744–45 (5th Cir. 1983)); and the foreclosure of the admission of distinctive evidence arising from separate transactions between various plaintiffs and a common defendant (*Rufenacht v. Iowa Beef Processors, Inc.*, 656 F.2d 198, 202–03 & n. 1 (5th Cir. 1981)). *See* 18A WRIGHT, MILLER & COOPER, FEDERAL PRACTICE & PROCEDURE § 4465, at 733–34 n.12 (2d ed. 2002 & Supp. April 2018); *see also* RESTATEMENT (SECOND) OF JUDGMENTS § 29 (enumerating factors to consider when determining whether to grant non-mutual preclusion).

2. Should arbitration decisions carry non-mutual issue preclusive effect? Is it relevant that the scope of discovery in arbitration may not sweep as broadly as that authorized by the Federal Rules of Civil Procedure, that evidentiary rules for arbitration may be less rigorous than those prescribed by the Federal Rules of Evidence, that the scope of judicial review of arbitration decisions is severely limited, and that arbitration decisions frequently reflect a compromise of competing interests? *See* Joseph L. Daly, *Arbitration: The Basics*, 5 J. AM. ARB. 1, 61, 68 (2006). Despite such reservations arbitral awards have been used as the basis for asserting non-mutual preclusion in a number of cases. *See, e.g., Boguslavsky v. South Richmond Sec.*, 225 F.3d 127, 130 n.4 (2d Cir. 2000) (upholding the non-mutual preclusive effect of an NASD arbitral award in spite of "the fact that the [defendant] was not a party to the NASD proceeding"); *Norris v. Grosvenor Marketing Ltd.*, 803 F.2d 1281, 1285 (2d Cir. 1986) (upholding the application of nonmutual preclusion to issues adjudicated in an arbitration).

3. Should the fact that a previous decision was not appealable prevent it from receiving non-mutual offensive collateral estoppel effect? *See Winters v. Diamond Shamrock Chemical Co.*, 149 F.3d 387 (5th Cir. 1998) (upholding a refusal to give collateral estoppel effect to a previous decision remanding a case to state court for lack of jurisdiction on the ground that the previous decision was not appealable). The Fifth Circuit stated that "the availability of review is of paramount importance to the issue of preclusion." *Id.* at 395.

4. Some decisions have not confined themselves to the categories of "exceptions" specifically identified in *Parklane Hosiery* as justifying a refusal to apply non-mutual offensive collateral estoppel. Rather, some courts have taken the broader view that errors in the initial proceeding (even those not sufficient to warrant reversal on direct appeal), newly discovered evidence that could likely lead to a different result, or simple lack of confidence in the correctness of the earlier decision, may justify the denial of non-mutual preclusive effect. This approach accords with that suggested in the RESTATEMENT (SECOND) OF JUDGMENTS, explaining that relitigation may be

appropriate where "the prior determination was plainly wrong or . . . new evidence has become available that could likely lead to a different result." *Id.* § 29(8), cmt. j (1980). Is this open ended approach correct? Is the idea that doubts (or even certainties) about the correctness of an earlier decision justify denying preclusive effect inconsistent with the essential core of preclusion doctrine?

5. As illustrated by *Hardy*, courts considering complex cases have evidenced considerable caution in applying the *Parklane* doctrine. As a leading decision observed, application of non-mutual offensive collateral estoppel is "detailed, difficult, and potentially dangerous" and that "'fairness to the defendant' . . . is a critical finding necessary for the application of offensive estoppel." *Jack Faucett Assoc., Inc. v. AT&T*, 744 F.2d 118, 125 (D.C. Cir. 1984).

6. How should non-mutual preclusion apply to plaintiffs who have opted out of a class action? Should they be bound by an adverse result? *See In re Corrugated Container Antitrust Litig.*, 756 F.2d 411, 418–19 (5th Cir. 1985) ("A class action judgment cannot be used to collaterally estop an opt-out plaintiffs' action against a defendant in a separate action. An opt-out plaintiff is not a party to the class action and is not bound by the class action judgment."). Conversely, should they be able to take advantage of issues resolved adversely to the defendant if they subsequently commence individual actions? *See, e.g., Premier Elec. Const. Co. v. Nat'l Elec. Contractors Assoc., Inc.*, 814 F.2d 358, 361–67 (7th Cir. 1987) (denying the benefits of non-mutual issue preclusion to opt-out class members on the ground that it would be inconsistent with the intent of Rule 23 to eliminate "one-way intervention," and because allowing such preclusion would promote a multiplicity of actions).

C. Preclusion in Class Actions

1. Limits of Claim and Issue Preclusion in Class Actions

Cooper v. Federal Reserve Bank of Richmond

Supreme Court of the United States
467 U.S. 867 (1984)

Justice Stevens delivered the opinion of the Court.

The question to be decided is whether a judgment in a class action determining that an employer did not engage in a general pattern or practice of racial discrimination against the certified class of employees precludes a class member from maintaining a subsequent civil action alleging an individual claim of racial discrimination against the employer.

I

On March 22, 1977, the Equal Employment Opportunity Commission commenced a civil action against respondent, the Federal Reserve Bank of Richmond. Respondent operates a branch in Charlotte, N.C. (the Bank), where during the years

1974–1978 it employed about 350–450 employees in several departments. The EEOC complaint alleged that the Bank was violating § 703(a) of Title VII of the Civil Rights Act of 1964 by engaging in "policies and practices" that included "failing and refusing to promote *blacks* because of race."

Six months after the EEOC filed its complaint, four individual employees[11] were allowed to intervene as plaintiffs. In their "complaint in intervention," these plaintiffs alleged that the Bank's employment practices violated 42 U.S.C. § 1981, as well as Title VII; that each of them was the victim of employment discrimination based on race; and that they could adequately represent a class of black employees against whom the Bank had discriminated because of their race. In due course, the District Court entered an order conditionally certifying the following class pursuant to Federal Rules of Civil Procedure 23(b)(2) and (3):

> "All black persons who have been employed by the defendant at its Charlotte Branch Office at any time since January 3, 1974 [6 months prior to the first charge filed by the intervenors with EEOC], who have been discriminated against in promotion, wages, job assignments and terms and conditions of employment because of their race."

After certifying the class, the District Court ordered that notice be published in the Charlotte newspapers and mailed to each individual member of the class. The notice described the status of the litigation, and plainly stated that members of the class "will be bound by the judgment or other determination" if they did not exclude themselves by sending a written notice to the Clerk. Among the recipients of the notice were Phyllis Baxter and five other individuals employed by the Bank.[12] It is undisputed that these individuals—the Baxter petitioners—are members of the class represented by the intervening plaintiffs and that they made no attempt to exclude themselves from the class.

At the trial the intervening plaintiffs, as well as the Baxter petitioners, testified. The District Court found that the Bank had engaged in a pattern and practice of discrimination from 1974 through 1978 by failing to afford black employees opportunities for advancement and assignment equal to opportunities afforded white employees in pay grades 4 and 5. Except as so specified, however, the District Court found that "there does not appear to be a pattern and practice of discrimination pervasive enough for the court to order relief." With respect to the claims of the four intervening plaintiffs, the court found that the Bank had discriminated against Cooper and Russell, but not against Moore and Hannah. Finally, the court somewhat cryptically stated that although it had an opinion about "the entitlement to

11. [Court's footnote #2] Sylvia Cooper, Constance Russell, Helen Moore, and Elmore Hannah, Jr., sometimes referred to by the District Court as the "intervening plaintiffs" and by the parties as the "Cooper petitioners." . . .

12. [Court's footnote #5] In addition to Baxter, they were Brenda Gilliam, Glenda Knott, Emma Ruffin, Alfred Harrison, and Sherri McCorkle. All of these individuals, sometimes referred to as the "Baxter petitioners," stipulated that they received the notice.

relief of some of the class members who testified at trial," it would defer decision of such matters to a further proceeding.

Thereafter, on March 24, 1981, the Baxter petitioners moved to intervene, alleging that each had been denied a promotion for discriminatory reasons. With respect to Emma Ruffin, the court denied the motion because she was a member of the class for which relief had been ordered and therefore her rights would be protected in the Stage II proceedings to be held on the question of relief. With respect to the other five Baxter petitioners, the court also denied the motion, but for a different reason. It held that because all of them were employed in jobs above the grade 5 category, they were not entitled to any benefit from the court's ruling with respect to discrimination in grades 4 and 5. The District Court stated: "The court has found no proof of any classwide discrimination above grade 5 and, therefore, they are not entitled to participate in any Stage II proceedings in this case." The court added that it could "see no reason why, if any of the would be intervenors are actively interested in pursuing their claims, they cannot file a Section 1981 suit next week. . . ."

A few days later the Baxter petitioners filed a separate action against the Bank alleging that each of them had been denied a promotion because of their race in violation of 42 U.S.C. § 1981. The Bank moved to dismiss the complaint on the ground that each of them was a member of the class that had been certified in the Cooper litigation, that each was employed in a grade other than 4 or 5, and that they were bound by the determination that there was no proof of any classwide discrimination above grade 5. The District Court denied the motion to dismiss, but certified its order for interlocutory appeal under 28 U.S.C. § 1292(b). The Bank's interlocutory appeal from the order was then consolidated with the Bank's pending appeal in the Cooper litigation.

The United States Court of Appeals for the Fourth Circuit reversed the District Court's judgment on the merits in the Cooper litigation, concluding that (1) there was insufficient evidence to establish a pattern or practice of racial discrimination in grades 4 and 5, and (2) two of the intervening plaintiffs had not been discriminated against on account of race. . . . The court further held that under the doctrine of res judicata, the judgment in the Cooper class action precluded the Baxter petitioners from maintaining their individual race discrimination claims against the Bank. The court thus reversed the order denying the Bank's motion to dismiss in the Baxter action, and remanded for dismissal of the Baxter complaint. We granted certiorari to review that judgment . . . and we now reverse.

II

Claims of two types were adjudicated in the Cooper litigation. First, the individual claims of each of the four intervening plaintiffs have been finally decided in the Bank's favor.[13] Those individual decisions do not, of course, foreclose any

13. [Court's footnote #7] Two of those claims were rejected by the District Court and two by the Court of Appeals; all four of those determinations are now equally final.

other individual claims. Second, the class claim that the Bank followed "policies and practices" of discriminating against its employees has also been decided.[14] It is that decision on which the Court of Appeals based its res judicata analysis.

There is of course no dispute that under elementary principles of prior adjudication a judgment in a properly entertained class action is binding on class members in any subsequent litigation. See, *e.g., Supreme Tribe of Ben-Hur v. Cauble*, 255 U.S. 356 (1921); Restatement of Judgments § 86 (1942); Restatement (Second) of Judgments § 41(1)(e) (1982); see also Fed. Rule Civ. Proc. 23(c)(3); see generally Moore & Cohn, Federal Class Actions—Jurisdiction and Effect of Judgments, 32 Ill.L.Rev. 555 (1938). Basic principles of res judicata (merger and bar or claim preclusion) and collateral estoppel (issue preclusion) apply. A judgment in favor of the plaintiff class extinguishes their claim, which merges into the judgment granting relief. A judgment in favor of the defendant extinguishes the claim, barring a subsequent action on that claim. A judgment in favor of either side is conclusive in a subsequent action between them on any issue actually litigated and determined, if its determination was essential to that judgment.

III

A plaintiff bringing a civil action for a violation of § 703(a) of Title VII of the Civil Rights Act of 1964 has the initial burden of establishing a prima facie case that his employer discriminated against him on account of his race, color, religion, sex, or national origin. A plaintiff meets this initial burden by offering evidence adequate to create an inference that he was denied an employment opportunity on the basis of a discriminatory criterion enumerated in Title VII.

A plaintiff alleging one instance of discrimination establishes a prima facie case justifying an inference of individual racial discrimination by showing that he (1) belongs to a racial minority, (2) applied and was qualified for a vacant position the employer was attempting to fill, (3) was rejected for the position, and (4) after his rejection, the position remained open and the employer continued to seek applicants of the plaintiff's qualifications. *McDonnell Douglas Corp. v. Green*, 411 U.S. 792, 802 (1973). Once these facts are established, the employer must produce "evidence that the plaintiff was rejected, or someone else was preferred, for a legitimate, nondiscriminatory reason." *Texas Dept. of Community Affairs v. Burdine*, 450 U.S. 248, 254 (1981). At that point, the presumption of discrimination "drops from the case," and the district court is in a position to decide the ultimate question in such a suit: whether the particular employment decision at issue was made on the basis of race. . . .

14. [Court's footnote #8] The District Court rejected all of the class claims except that pertaining to grades 4 and 5; the claim on behalf of that subclass was rejected by the Court of Appeals. Again, that distinction between subclasses is no longer significant for the entire class claim has now been decided.

In *Franks v. Bowman Transportation Co*, 424 U.S. 747 (1976), the plaintiff, on behalf of himself and all others similarly situated, alleged that the employer had engaged in a pervasive pattern of racial discrimination in various company policies, including the hiring, transfer, and discharge of employees. In that class action we held that demonstrating the existence of a discriminatory pattern or practice established a presumption that the individual class members had been discriminated against on account of race. Proving isolated or sporadic discriminatory acts by the employer is insufficient to establish a prima facie case of a pattern or practice of discrimination; rather it must be established by a preponderance of the evidence that "racial discrimination was the company's standard operating procedure—the regular rather than the unusual practice." *Teamsters v. United States*, 431 U.S. 324, 336 (1977) (footnote omitted). While a finding of a pattern or practice of discrimination itself justifies an award of prospective relief to the class, additional proceedings are ordinarily required to determine the scope of individual relief for the members of the class.

The crucial difference between an individual's claim of discrimination and a class action alleging a general pattern or practice of discrimination is manifest. The inquiry regarding an individual's claim is the reason for a particular employment decision, while "at the liability stage of a pattern-or-practice trial the focus often will not be on individual hiring decisions, but on a pattern of discriminatory decisionmaking." *Id.*, at 360, n.46.

....

[T]he existence of a valid individual claim does not necessarily warrant the conclusion that the individual plaintiff may successfully maintain a class action. It is equally clear that a class plaintiff's attempt to prove the existence of a companywide policy, or even a consistent practice within a given department, may fail even though discrimination against one or two individuals has been proved. The facts of this case illustrate the point.

The District Court found that two of the intervening plaintiffs, Cooper and Russell, had both established that they were the victims of racial discrimination but, as the Court of Appeals noted, they were employed in grades higher than grade 5 and therefore their testimony provided no support for the conclusion that there was a practice of discrimination in grades 4 and 5. Given the burden of establishing a prima facie case of a pattern or practice of discrimination, it was entirely consistent for the District Court simultaneously to conclude that Cooper and Russell had valid individual claims even though it had expressly found no proof of any classwide discrimination above grade 5. It could not be more plain that the rejection of a claim of classwide discrimination does not warrant the conclusion that no member of the class could have a valid individual claim....

The Court of Appeals was correct in generally concluding that the Baxter petitioners, as members of the class represented by the intervening plaintiffs in the Cooper litigation, are bound by the adverse judgment in that case. The court erred, however, in the preclusive effect it attached to that prior adjudication. That judgment (1) bars the class members from bringing another class action against the Bank alleging a pattern or practice of discrimination for the relevant time period and (2) precludes the class members in any other litigation with the Bank from relitigating the question whether the Bank engaged in a pattern and practice of discrimination against black employees during the relevant time period. The judgment is not, however, dispositive of the individual claims the Baxter petitioners have alleged in their separate action. Assuming they establish a prima facie case of discrimination under *McDonnell Douglas*, the Bank will be required to articulate a legitimate reason for each of the challenged decisions, and if it meets that burden, the ultimate questions regarding motivation in their individual cases will be resolved by the District Court. Moreover, the prior adjudication may well prove beneficial to the Bank in the Baxter action: the determination in the Cooper action that the Bank had not engaged in a general pattern or practice of discrimination would be relevant on the issue of pretext. . . .

The Bank argues that permitting the Baxter petitioners to bring separate actions would frustrate the purposes of Rule 23. We think the converse is true. The class-action device was intended to establish a procedure for the adjudication of common questions of law or fact. If the Bank's theory were adopted, it would be tantamount to requiring that every member of the class be permitted to intervene to litigate the merits of his individual claim.

It is also suggested that the District Court had a duty to decide the merits of the individual claims of class members, at least insofar as the individual claimants became witnesses in the joint proceeding and subjected their individual employment histories to scrutiny at trial. Unless these claims are decided in the main proceeding, the Bank argues that the duplicative litigation that Rule 23 was designed to avoid will be encouraged, and that defendants will be subjected to the risks of liability without the offsetting benefit of a favorable termination of exposure through a final judgment.

This argument fails to differentiate between what the District Court might have done and what it actually did. The District Court did actually adjudicate the individual claims of Cooper and the other intervening plaintiffs, as well as the class claims, but it pointedly refused to decide the individual claims of the Baxter petitioners. Whether the issues framed by the named parties before the court should be expanded to encompass the individual claims of additional class members is a matter of judicial administration that should be decided in the first instance by the District Court. Nothing in Rule 23 requires as a matter of law that the District Court make a finding with respect to each and every matter on which there is testimony in the class action. Indeed, Rule 23 is carefully drafted to provide a mechanism for the expeditious decision of *common* questions. Its purposes might well be defeated by an attempt to decide a host of individual claims before any common question relating to liability has been resolved adversely to the defendant. We do not find the

District Court's denial of the Baxter petitioners' motion for leave to intervene in the Cooper litigation, or its decision not to make findings regarding the Baxter petitioners' testimony in the Cooper litigation, to be inconsistent with Rule 23.

The judgment of the Court of Appeals is reversed, and the case is remanded for further proceedings consistent with this opinion.

Notes and Questions

1. *Cooper* broadly states that "basic principles" of claim and issue preclusion apply in class actions. But the Supreme Court's opinion suggests that they may not apply in precisely the same way as in individual litigation. More particularly, the doctrine of claim preclusion generally precludes relitigation, between the same parties, not only of all matters that actually were, but also those that "might have been" litigated in support of the same "cause of action" or "claim for relief." Moreover, the prevailing modern view embraces an expansive definition of what constitutes the same "claim for relief" for this purpose as embracing "all rights of the plaintiff to remedies against the defendant with respect to all or any part of the transaction, or series of connected transactions, out of which the action arose." RESTATEMENT (SECOND) OF JUDGMENTS § 24(1).

2. Is *Cooper* consistent with this approach? Consider the claims that the Court held not to be precluded by the judgment in *Cooper.* These were the claims of individual discrimination against the Baxter plaintiffs. The Supreme Court based its holding in this respect on the "crucial difference" it perceived between "two types of claims" that might be advanced in Title VII litigation: (1) claims alleging a "pattern or practice" of discrimination that affected the class as a whole; and (2) claims of individual discrimination against particular members of the class. The invalidity of the former did not necessarily imply the invalidity of the latter, nor, conversely, did the validity of an individual claim or claims of discrimination necessarily imply the existence of a class wide pattern or practice of discrimination. Thus, the ultimate rejection of all "pattern or practice" claims of the class in *Cooper* did not necessarily imply the invalidity of the Baxter plaintiffs' claims of individual discrimination.

Is this holding consistent with the view that claim preclusion forecloses all theories of recovery and arguments that might have supported recovery based on the same transactions or occurrences as were involved in the first action? Consider, for example, whether, despite the fact that only a "disparate treatment" (*i.e.*, a claim based on intentional discrimination) pattern or practice claim was advanced on behalf of the class in *Cooper* (in n. 11 of its opinion, the Supreme Court quoted the District Court's statement that "The claim here . . . is the typical disparate treatment case."), a later attempt by one or more class members to maintain a "disparate impact" claim, either individually or on behalf of the same class, would have been precluded. If so, why were the individual claims of the Baxter plaintiffs different?

2. Relitigation of the Issue of Adequate Representation

The bedrock due process requirement of adequate representation provides the irreducible minimum requirement for binding the class. *See* Chapter 6, *supra*. The implications of the adequate representation requirement are uncertain, however. In particular, a conflict has arisen over the procedural mechanisms that are required to assure that the interests of the class have in fact been adequately represented.

Consider the following decision in the Second Circuit.

Stephenson v. Dow Chemical Co.

United States Court of Appeals, Second Circuit
273 F.3d 249 (2001)

PARKER, CIRCUIT JUDGE.

This appeal requires us to determine the effect of the Supreme Court's landmark class action decisions in *Amchem Products, Inc. v. Windsor*, 521 U.S. 591 (1997), and *Ortiz v. Fibreboard Corp.*, 527 U.S. 815 (1999), on a previously settled class action concerning exposure to Agent Orange during the Vietnam War. Daniel Stephenson and Joe Isaacson are two Vietnam War veterans who allege that they were injured by exposure to Agent Orange while serving in the military in Vietnam. In the late 1990s, Stephenson and Isaacson (along with their families) filed separate lawsuits against manufacturers of Agent Orange. These lawsuits were eventually transferred to Judge Jack B. Weinstein in the Eastern District of New York by the Judicial Panel on Multidistrict Litigation ("MDL Panel").

In 1984, however, some twelve years before these suits, virtually identical claims against these defendants, brought by a class of military personnel who were exposed to Agent Orange while in Vietnam between 1961 and 1972, were globally settled. The Isaacson and Stephenson actions were brought in 1998 and 1999 respectively. Judge Weinstein, who presided over the 1984 settlement, dismissed the claims of Stephenson and Isaacson, concluding that the prior settlement barred their suits. On appeal, plaintiffs chiefly contend, citing *Amchem* and *Ortiz*, that they were inadequately represented and, therefore, due process considerations prevent the earlier class action settlement from precluding their claims. Because we agree that *Amchem* and *Ortiz* prevent applying res judicata to bar plaintiffs' claim, we vacate the district court's dismissal and remand for further proceedings.

I. BACKGROUND

A. *Prior Agent Orange Litigation*

The Agent Orange class action litigation has a lengthy and complicated history, which we set forth in some detail below in order to convey the magnitude of this decision.

The first Agent Orange litigation began in the late 1970s, when individual veterans and their families filed class action suits in the Northern District of Illinois and Southern and Eastern Districts of New York, alleging that exposure to Agent Orange caused them injury. . . . By order of the MDL Panel, these actions were transferred to the Eastern District of New York and consolidated for pretrial purposes. Plaintiffs asserted claims of negligent manufacture, strict liability, breach of warranty, intentional tort and nuisance. . . .

In 1983, the district court certified the following class under Federal Rule of Civil Procedure 23(b)(3):

> those persons who were in the United States, New Zealand or Australian Armed Forces at any time from 1961 to 1972 who were injured while in or near Vietnam by exposure to Agent Orange or other phenoxy herbicides, including those composed in whole or in part of 2, 4, 5-trichlorophenoxyacetic acid or containing some amount of 2, 3, 7, 8-tetrachlorodibenzo-p-dioxin. The class also includes spouses, parents, and children of the veterans born before January 1, 1984, directly or derivatively injured as a result of the exposure. . . .

The court also ordered notice by mail, print media, radio and television to be provided to class members, providing in part that persons who wished to opt out must do so by May 1, 1984.

Trial of the class claims was to begin on May 7, 1984. . . . On the eve of trial, the parties reached a settlement. . . .

We affirmed class certification, settlement approval and much of the distribution plan. [*In re Agent Orange Product Liability Litig.*, 818 F.2d 145, 163–74 (2d Cir. 1987)]. . . . We rejected challenges to class certification, concluding that "class certification was justified under Rule 23(b)(3) due to the centrality of the military contractor defense. . . ." We specifically rejected an attack based on adequacy of representation, again based on the military contractor defense which, we reasoned, "would have precluded recovery by all plaintiffs, irrespective of the strengths, weaknesses, or idiosyncrasies of their claims." . . .

In 1989 and 1990, two purported class actions, *Ivy v. Diamond Shamrock Chemicals Co.* and *Hartman v. Diamond Shamrock Chemicals Co.*, were filed in Texas state courts. . . . These suits, on behalf of Vietnam veterans exposed to Agent Orange, sought compensatory and punitive damages against the same companies as in the settled suit. The plaintiffs alleged that their injuries manifested only after the May 7, 1984 settlement. Additionally, the Ivy/Hartman plaintiffs expressly disclaimed any reliance on federal law, asserting only state law claims. Nonetheless, the defendants removed the actions to federal court on the grounds that these claims had already been asserted and litigated in federal court. The MDL Panel transferred the actions to Judge Weinstein in the Eastern District of New York.

The district court rejected plaintiffs' motion to remand. . . .

The district court then turned to the plaintiffs' substantive arguments that it was unfair to bind them to the settlement when their injuries were not manifested until after the settlement had been reached. The district court rejected this argument, based on the following reasoning:

> All of the courts which considered the *Agent Orange* Settlement were fully cognizant of the conflict arguments now hypothesized by the plaintiffs and took steps to minimize the problem in the way they arranged for long-term administration of the Settlement Fund.
>
> In many cases the conflict between the interests of present and future claimants is more imagined than real. In the instant case, for example, the injustice wrought upon the plaintiffs is nonexistent. *These plaintiffs, like all class members who suffer death or disability before the end of 1994, are eligible for compensation from the Agent Orange Payment Fund.* The relevant latency periods and the age of the veterans ensure that almost all valid claims will be revealed before that time.
>
> Even when it is proper and necessary for the courts to be solicitous of the interests of future claimants, the courts cannot ignore the interests of presently injured plaintiffs as well as defendants in achieving a settlement. Class action settlements simply will not occur if the parties cannot set definitive limits on defendants' liability. Making settlement of Rule 23 suits too difficult will work harms upon plaintiffs, defendants, the courts, and the general public. [Emphasis added.]

The district court therefore dismissed the *Ivy/Hartman* litigation.

We affirmed the district court's dismissal. [*In re Agent Orange Product Liability Litig.*, 996 F.2d 1425, 1439 (2d Cir. 1993)]. . . .

. . . .

We . . . rejected plaintiffs' argument that their due process rights were violated because they were denied adequate representation and adequate notice in the prior action. We reasoned that "providing individual notice and opt-out rights to persons who are unaware of an injury would probably do little good." We concluded that the plaintiffs were adequately represented in the prior action, and that a subclass of future claimants was unnecessary "'because of the way [the settlement] was structured to cover future claimants.'"

. . . .

B. *The Instant Litigation*

1. *The Parties*

Daniel Stephenson served in Vietnam from 1965 to 1970, serving both on the ground in Vietnam and as a helicopter pilot in Vietnam. He alleges that he was in regular contact with Agent Orange during that time. On February 19, 1998, he was diagnosed with multiple myeloma, a bone marrow cancer, and has undergone a bone marrow transplant.

Joe Isaacson served in Vietnam from 1968 to 1969 as a crew chief in the Air Force, and worked at a base for airplanes which sprayed various herbicides, including Agent Orange. In 1996, Isaacson was diagnosed with non-Hodgkins lymphoma.

Defendants are chemical manufacturers who produced and sold to the United States Government the herbicide Agent Orange during the Vietnam War.

2. *Proceedings Below*

In August 1998, Isaacson filed suit in New Jersey state court, asserting claims only under state law. Defendants quickly removed the case to federal court and Isaacson's subsequent motion to remand was denied by Chief Judge Anne Thompson in the District of New Jersey. Thereafter, Isaacson's case was transferred to Judge Weinstein by the MDL Panel.

Stephenson filed his suit *pro se* in the Western District of Louisiana in February 1999, but he soon retained his current counsel. In April 1999, defendants moved for and were granted a Conditional Transfer Order by the MDL Panel, transferring this action to Judge Weinstein. After Stephenson's case was transferred, it was consolidated with the Isaacson case.

Defendants moved to dismiss under Federal Rule of Civil Procedure 12(b)(6), asserting that plaintiffs' claims were barred by the 1984 class action settlement and subsequent final judgment. Judge Weinstein granted this motion from the bench following argument, rejecting plaintiffs' argument that they were inadequately represented and concluding that plaintiffs' suit was an impermissible collateral attack on the prior settlement.

Because we disagree with this conclusion, based on the Supreme Court's holdings in *Amchem* and *Ortiz*, we must vacate the district court's dismissal and remand for further proceedings.

II. DISCUSSION

. . . .

A. *Removal Jurisdiction*

[The court sustained removal under the All Writs Act, 28 U.S.C. § 1651 on the ground that it was necessary to prevent frustration of the MDL court's previous settlement orders. The Supreme Court subsequently disapproved use of the All Writs Act as a basis for removal of an otherwise unremovable case. See *Syngenta Crop Protection, Inc. v. Henson*, 537 U.S. 28 (2002).]

B. *Collateral Attack*

The parties devote much energy to debating the permissibility of a collateral attack in this case. Plaintiffs assert that, since the Supreme Court's decision in *Hansberry v. Lee*, 311 U.S. 32 (1940), courts have allowed collateral attacks on class action judgments based upon due process concerns. Defendants strenuously disagree and contend that to allow plaintiffs' suit to go forward, in the face of the 1984 global settlement, would "violate defendants' right to due process of law. . . ."

Defendants contend that Supreme Court precedent permits a collateral attack on a class action judgment "only where there has been no prior determination of absent class members' due process rights." According to defendants, because the "due process rights of absent class members have been extensively litigated in the *Agent Orange* litigation," these plaintiffs cannot now attack those prior determinations. We reject defendants' arguments and conclude that plaintiffs' collateral attack, which seeks only to prevent the prior settlement from operating as res judicata to their claims, is permissible.

First, even if, as defendants contend, collateral attack is only permitted where there has been no prior determination of the absent class members' rights, plaintiffs' collateral attack is allowed. It is true that, on direct appeal and in the *Ivy/ Hartman* litigation, we previously concluded that there was adequate representation of all class members in the original *Agent Orange* settlement. However, neither this Court nor the district court has addressed specifically the adequacy of representation for those members of the class whose injuries manifested after depletion of the settlements funds. . . . Therefore, even accepting defendants' argument, plaintiffs' suit can go forward because there has been no prior adequacy of representation determination with respect to individuals whose claims arise after the depletion of the settlement fund.[15]

Second, the propriety of a collateral attack such as this is amply supported by precedent. In *Hansberry v. Lee*, 311 U.S. 32 (1940), the Supreme Court entertained a collateral attack on an Illinois state court class action judgment that purported to bind the plaintiffs. The Court held that class action judgments can only bind absent class members where "the interests of those not joined are of the same class as the interests of those who are, and where it is considered that the latter fairly represent the former in the prosecution of the litigation." *[C]f. Phillips Petroleum Co. v. Shutts*, 472 U.S. 797, 805 (1985) ("[I]t is true that a court adjudicating a dispute may not be able to predetermine the res judicata effect of its own judgment."). Additionally, we have previously stated that a "[j]udgment in a class action is not secure from collateral attack unless the absentees were adequately and vigorously

---

15. [Court's footnote #6] Defendants rely heavily on a recent Ninth Circuit decision, *Epstein v. MCA, Inc.*, 179 F.3d 641 (9th Cir. 1999), in support of their limited collateral review theory. *Epstein* held that a collateral attack is available only "to consider whether the procedures in the prior litigation afforded the party against whom the earlier judgment is asserted a 'full and fair opportunity' to litigate the claim or issue." According to the Ninth Circuit,

> Due process requires that an absent class member's right to adequate representation be protected by the adoption of the appropriate procedures by the certifying court and by the courts that review its determinations; due process does not require collateral second-guessing of those determinations and that review.

Id. at 648. Here, neither the district court nor this Court has determined the adequacy of representation *with respect to these plaintiffs* whose injuries did not arise until after the settlement expired. Without adopting the Ninth Circuit's decision in *Epstein*, we conclude that plaintiffs' collateral attack is proper even under its standard.

represented." *Van Gemert v. Boeing Co.*, 590 F.2d 433, 440 n. 15 (2d Cir. 1978); *aff'd* 444 U.S. 472 (1980).

Allowing plaintiffs' suit would be consistent with many other circuit decisions recognizing the ability of later plaintiffs to attack the adequacy of representation in an earlier class action. . . .

. . . .

We therefore hold that a collateral attack to contest the application of res judicata is available. We turn next to the merits of this attack.

C. *Due Process Considerations and Res Judicata*

. . . .

Res judicata generally applies to bind absent class members except where to do so would violate due process. Due process requires adequate representation "at all times" throughout the litigation, notice "reasonably calculated . . . to apprise interested parties of the pendency of the action," and an opportunity to opt out. *Shutts*, 472 U.S. at 811–12.

Both Stephenson and Isaacson fall within the class definition of the prior litigation: they served in the United States military, stationed in Vietnam, between 1961 and 1972, and were allegedly injured by exposure to Agent Orange. However, they both learned of their allegedly Agent Orange-related injuries only after the 1984 settlement fund had expired in 1994. Because the prior litigation purported to settle all future claims, but only provided for recovery for those whose death or disability was discovered prior to 1994, the conflict between Stephenson and Isaacson and the class representatives becomes apparent.[16] No provision was made for post-1994 claimants, and the settlement fund was permitted to terminate in 1994. *Amchem* and *Ortiz* suggest that Stephenson and Isaacson were not adequately represented in the prior Agent Orange litigation.[17] Those cases indicate that a class which purports to represent both present and future claimants may encounter internal conflicts.

. . . .

---

16. [Court's footnote #7] Again, we distinguish the *Ivy/Hartman* cases, which held that pre 1994 claimants were adequately represented in the prior Agent Orange litigation. This conclusion was based, at least in part, on those claimants' eligibility for compensation from the settlement fund. See *Ivy/Hartman I*, 781 F. Supp. at 919; *Ivy/Hartman II*, 996 F.2d at 1435–36.

17. [Court's footnote #8] We also note that plaintiffs likely received inadequate notice. *Shutts* provides that adequate notice is necessary to bind absent class members. *Shutts*, 472 U.S. at 812. As described earlier, *Amchem* indicates that effective notice could likely not ever be given to exposure-only class members. *Amchem*, 521 U.S. at 628. Because we have already concluded that these plaintiffs were inadequately represented, and thus were not proper parties to the prior litigation, we need not definitively decide whether notice was adequate.

Because these plaintiffs were inadequately represented in the prior litigation, they were not proper parties and cannot be bound by the settlement. We therefore must vacate the district court's dismissal and remand for further proceedings. . . .

Notes and Questions

1. The Supreme Court granted *certiorari* to review the Second Circuit's decision in *Stephenson*, but ultimately affirmed by an evenly divided Court (a disposition that has no precedential effect). *Stephenson v. Dow Chemical Co.*, 273 F.3d 249 (2d Cir. 2001), *aff'd by an equally divided court*, 539 U.S. 111 (2003) (per curiam). The force of the court of appeals' opinion may be undermined by the fact that it rested on alternative grounds: First, the issue of adequate representation of class members whose injuries first manifested themselves after the depletion of the settlement funds in the original *Agent Orange* class action had not been determined in that action, thus distinguishing the holding in *Epstein v. MCA, Inc.*, which was discussed in the Court's footnote 6 in *Stephenson*. *See* 273 F.3d at 258 n. 6.

Second, and in the alternative, the Second Circuit—relying on *Hansberry* and a host of authority in the courts of appeals—strongly suggested that in any event, the issue of adequate representation always provides a basis for collateral attack on the binding effect of a class action judgment.

2. Is it circular to say that class members are not bound by a class judgment unless they are adequately represented in the action, but then to conclude that they are bound by the judgment if the question of adequate representation was litigated and determined in an action in which they were members of the purported class? Is the judgment-rendering court in as good a position to determine adequacy of representation in making an initial class certification decision as the court in which enforcement of the judgment is later sought? Is there a difference between a class settlement judgment and a litigated judgment in this regard?

3. If the members of a purported class receive notice of the original action, should they be obligated to opt out to avoid the preclusive effect of the judgment if their interests were not in fact adequately represented? If they are not accorded an opportunity to opt out, should they be obligated to make an appearance in the original action to contest the adequacy of representation if they are to contest it at all?

4. The American Law Institute's Principles of the Law of Aggregate Litigation (2010) strongly endorses an approach that would limit the availability of collateral attacks on class action settlements. Section 3.01(c) provides that post-judgment challenges are "disfavored unless no proper procedure for contemporaneous challenge was available . . ." *Id.* To promote the finality of settlements, section 3.14 of the Principles provides that apart from a direct appeal, a class action settlement may not be challenged (other than on the grounds generally applicable to the vacation of final judgments) in the judgment-rendering court or a different court

except on the grounds that "the settlement court lacked personal or subject-matter jurisdiction, failed to make the necessary findings of adequate representation, or failed to afford class members reasonable notice and an opportunity to be heard as required by applicable law." *Id.*, § 3.14(a)(2). (This would not affect existing law governing malpractice or breach of fiduciary duty claims against class counsel. *Id.* § 3.14(b).) The comments explain that the purpose of a class action settlement is to achieve finality, and if collateral challenges to a settlement are allowed on grounds that could have been raised during the settlement approval process, the "integrity" of the process is diminished. *Id.* cmt. a. The comments also make clear that § 3.14 does not contemplate later relitigation of findings of adequate representation by the judgment rendering court.

Query: Given that the very debate about the availability of collateral attacks on class action judgments focuses on the meaning of *Shutts*' statement that the exercise of personal jurisdiction over absent class members lacking minimum contacts with the forum depends on notice, the right to opt out, and findings of adequate representation "at all times," and given the proposal's exception for cases in which the judgment rendering court lacks personal jurisdiction over absent class members, is section 3.14 entirely circular?

5. If a federal court declines to certify a class action under Rule 23, should class members be free to seek certification of an identical class in subsequent federal or state proceedings? In *In re Bridgestone/Firestone, Inc. Products Liability Litig.*, 333 F.3d 763 (7th Cir. 2003), the Seventh Circuit held that a federal court that had previously refused to certify a nationwide class action in a products liability action involving Ford vehicles and Firestone tires properly enjoined any class member from seeking certification of the same class in state court. In *Smith v. Bayer Corp.*, 131 S. Ct. 2368 (2011), the Supreme Court unanimously rejected the result in *In re Bridgestone/Firestone*. In *Smith*, the Court held a similar injunction was improper on two grounds. First, issue preclusion was inapplicable because defendant had not demonstrated that the legal standard governing class certification under Federal Rule 23 in the first action was identical to the standard governing class certification under the West Virginia counterpart of Rule 23, which might be more liberally construed. The issues in the two actions therefore had not been shown to be the same. Second, the injunction was improper because the unnamed members of the uncertified putative class in the first action were not "parties" to that action as is required for issue preclusion to apply, and no exception permitting the preclusion of non-parties (*see infra*, section D) was applicable. "The definition of the term 'party' can on no account be stretched so far as to cover a person like Smith, whom the plaintiff in a lawsuit was denied leave to represent." *Id.* at 2379. Further, the rule permitting absent members of a certified class to be bound by the judgment was inapplicable, because the first action was not a properly certified class action. The Court recognized the force of defendant's policy argument that its ruling would permit seriatim attempts at certifying identical classes by different members of a putative class, but found that argument insufficient to override settled principles of preclusion law. Instead, the remedy

lay in principles of *stare decisis* and comity among courts, which it expected would be applied with particular force in view of the broad availability of removal under CAFA (which was inapplicable in *Smith* itself).

Note, however, the Supreme Court's opinion in *China Agritech, Inc. v. Resh*, 138 S. Ct. 1800 (2018). In that case, shareholders of China Agritech had filed suit alleging securities fraud. The first complaint (*Dean*) was timely. The district court denied class certification. The action thereupon settled, and the suit was dismissed. A new set of plaintiffs who would have been members of the *Dean* class then filed a new complaint. This second complaint (*Smyth*) was timely. The district court again denied class certification. The plaintiffs settled, and the suit was dismissed. Subsequently a new group of plaintiffs who would have been members of the *Dean* and *Smyth* classes filed a third complaint. This complaint (*Resh*) was not timely within the basic statute of limitations. So, the *Resh* plaintiffs relied upon the pendency of the prior class actions as tolling the statute of limitations on behalf of the *Resh* class, citing *American Pipe & Constr. Co. v. Utah*, 414 U.S. 538 (1974) The Supreme Court rejected the tolling argument. 138 S. Ct. at 1804. *Class* claims filed by plaintiffs of a previously denied class cannot be brought if they are otherwise untimely. Only individual claims can benefit from tolling under *American Pipe*. *Id.* at 1806. In footnote 4 of the opinion, the Court referenced the *Smith v. Bayer* case, and distinguished it: "The state-court plaintiffs [in *Smith*] were not parties to the federal-court litigation, hence they could not be bound by its holding .... No such countervailing presumption favors Resh's untimely third federal class suit." *Id.* at 1808, n. 4. Is that a valid distinction? If no class was certified in *Smith*, and no class was certified in *Dean* or *Smyth*, how is Resh a party?

D. Preclusion of Nonparties to a Previous Action

1. Basic Principles

Martin v. Wilks

Supreme Court of the United States
490 U.S. 755 (1989)

Chief Justice Rehnquist delivered the opinion of the Court.

A group of white firefighters sued the city of Birmingham, Alabama (City), and the Jefferson County Personnel Board (Board) alleging that they were being denied promotions in favor of less qualified black firefighters. They claimed that the City and the Board were making promotion decisions on the basis of race in reliance on certain consent decrees, and that these decisions constituted impermissible racial discrimination in violation of the Constitution and federal statutes. The District Court held that the white firefighters were precluded from challenging employment decisions taken pursuant to the decrees, even though these firefighters had not been parties to the proceedings in which the decrees were entered. We think this holding contravenes the general rule that a person cannot be deprived of his legal rights in a proceeding to which he is not a party.

The litigation in which the consent decrees were entered began in 1974, when the Ensley Branch of the National Association for the Advancement of Colored People and seven black individuals filed separate class-action complaints against the City and the Board. They alleged that both had engaged in racially discriminatory hiring and promotion practices in various public service jobs in violation of Title VII of the Civil Rights Act of 1964, 42 U.S.C. § 2000e *et seq.*, and other federal law. After a bench trial on some issues, but before judgment, the parties entered into two consent decrees, one between the black individuals and the City and the other between them and the Board. These proposed decrees set forth an extensive remedial scheme, including long-term and interim annual goals for the hiring of blacks as firefighters. The decrees also provided for goals for promotion of blacks within the fire department.

The District Court entered an order provisionally approving the decrees and directing publication of notice of the upcoming fairness hearings. Notice of the hearings, with a reference to the general nature of the decrees, was published in two local newspapers. At that hearing, the Birmingham Firefighters Association (BFA) appeared and filed objections as amicus curiae. After the hearing, but before final approval of the decrees, the BFA and two of its members also moved to intervene on the ground that the decrees would adversely affect their rights. The District Court denied the motions as untimely and approved the decrees. . . . Seven white firefighters, all members of the BFA, then filed a complaint against the City and the Board seeking injunctive relief against enforcement of the decrees. The seven argued that the decrees would operate to illegally discriminate against them; the District Court denied relief.

Both the denial of intervention and the denial of injunctive relief were affirmed on appeal. . . . The District Court had not abused its discretion in refusing to let the BFA intervene, thought the Eleventh Circuit, in part because the firefighters could "institut[e] an independent Title VII suit, asserting specific violations of their rights." And, for the same reason, petitioners had not adequately shown the potential for irreparable harm from the operation of the decrees necessary to obtain injunctive relief.

A new group of white firefighters, the *Wilks* respondents, then brought suit against the City and the Board in District Court. They too alleged that, because of their race, they were being denied promotions in favor of less qualified blacks in violation of federal law. The Board and the City admitted to making race-conscious employment decisions, but argued that the decisions were unassailable because they were made pursuant to the consent decrees. A group of black individuals, the *Martin* petitioners, were allowed to intervene in their individual capacities to defend the decrees.

The defendants moved to dismiss the reverse discrimination cases as impermissible collateral attacks on the consent decrees. The District Court denied the motions, ruling that the decrees would provide a defense to claims of discrimination for employment decisions "mandated" by the decrees, leaving the principal issue for trial whether the challenged promotions were indeed required by the decrees. After trial the District Court granted the motion to dismiss. The court concluded that "if in fact the City was required to [make promotions of blacks] by the consent decree, then they would not be guilty of [illegal] racial discrimination" and that the defendants had "establish[ed] that the promotions of the black individuals . . . were in fact required by the terms of the consent decree."

On appeal, the Eleventh Circuit reversed. It held that, "[b]ecause . . . [the *Wilks* respondents] were neither parties nor privies to the consent decrees, . . . their independent claims of unlawful discrimination are not precluded. . . ." The court explicitly rejected the doctrine of "impermissible collateral attack" espoused by other Courts of Appeals to immunize parties to a consent decree from charges of discrimination by nonparties for actions taken pursuant to the decree. Although it recognized a "strong public policy in favor of voluntary affirmative action plans," the panel acknowledged that this interest "must yield to the policy against requiring third parties to submit to bargains in which their interests were either ignored or sacrificed." The court remanded the case for trial of the discrimination claims, suggesting that the operative law for judging the consent decrees was that governing voluntary affirmative-action plans.

We granted certiorari . . . and now affirm the Eleventh Circuit's judgment. All agree that "[i]t is a principle of general application in Anglo-American jurisprudence that one is not bound by a judgment *in personam* in a litigation in which he is not designated as a party or to which he has not been made a party by service of process." *Hansberry v. Lee*, 311 U.S. 32, 40 (1940). . . . This rule is part of our "deep-rooted historic tradition that everyone should have his own day in court." 18 C. Wright, A. Miller, & E. Cooper, Federal Practice and Procedure § 4449, p. 417 (1981). A judgment or decree among parties to a lawsuit resolves issues as among them, but it does not conclude the rights of strangers to those proceedings.[18]

Petitioners argue that, because respondents failed to timely intervene in the initial proceedings, their current challenge to actions taken under the consent decree

---

18. [Court's footnote #2] We have recognized an exception to the general rule when, in certain limited circumstances, a person, although not a party, has his interests adequately represented by someone with the same interests who is a party. See *Hansberry v. Lee*, 311 U.S. 32, 41–42 (1940) ("class" or "representative" suits); Fed. Rule Civ. Proc. 23 (same); *Montana v. United States*, 440 U.S. 147, 154–155 (1979) (control of litigation on behalf of one of the parties in the litigation). Additionally, where a special remedial scheme exists expressly foreclosing successive litigation by nonlitigants, as for example in bankruptcy or probate, legal proceedings may terminate preexisting rights if the scheme is otherwise consistent with due process. See *NLRB v. Bildisco & Bildisco*, 465 U.S. 513, 529–530, n.10 (1984) ("[P]roof of claim must be presented to the Bankruptcy Court . . . or be lost"); *Tulsa Professional Collection Services, Inc. v. Pope*, 485 U.S. 478 (1988) (nonclaim statute terminating unsubmitted claims against the estate). Neither of these exceptions, however, applies in these cases.

constitutes an impermissible "collateral attack." They argue that respondents were aware that the underlying suit might affect them, and if they chose to pass up an opportunity to intervene, they should not be permitted to later litigate the issues in a new action. The position has sufficient appeal to have commanded the approval of the great majority of the Federal Courts of Appeals, but we agree with the contrary view expressed by the Court of Appeals for the Eleventh Circuit in these cases.

We begin with the words of Justice Brandeis in *Chase National Bank v. Norwalk*, 291 U.S. 431 (1934):

> "The law does not impose upon any person absolutely entitled to a hearing the burden of voluntary intervention in a suit to which he is a stranger. . . . Unless duly summoned to appear in a legal proceeding, a person not a privy may rest assured that a judgment recovered therein will not affect his legal rights." *Id.*, at 441.

While these words were written before the adoption of the Federal Rules of Civil Procedure, we think the Rules incorporate the same principle; a party seeking a judgment binding on another cannot obligate that person to intervene; he must be joined. . . . Against the background of permissive intervention set forth in *Chase National Bank*, the drafters cast Rule 24, governing intervention, in permissive terms. See Fed. Rule Civ. Proc. 24(a) (intervention as of right) ("Upon timely application anyone shall be permitted to intervene"); Fed. Rule Civ. Proc. 24(b) (permissive intervention) ("Upon timely application anyone may be permitted to intervene"). They determined that the concern for finality and completeness of judgments would be "better [served] by mandatory joinder procedures." 18 Wright § 4452, p. 453. Accordingly, Rule 19(a) provides for mandatory joinder in circumstances where a judgment rendered in the absence of a person may "leave . . . persons already parties subject to a substantial risk of incurring . . . inconsistent obligations. . . ." Rule 19(b) sets forth the factors to be considered by a court in deciding whether to allow an action to proceed in the absence of an interested party.

Joinder as a party, rather than knowledge of a lawsuit and an opportunity to intervene, is the method by which potential parties are subjected to the jurisdiction of the court and bound by a judgment or decree. The parties to a lawsuit presumably know better than anyone else the nature and scope of relief sought in the action, and at whose expense such relief might be granted. It makes sense, therefore, to place on them a burden of bringing in additional parties where such a step is indicated, rather than placing on potential additional parties a duty to intervene when they acquire knowledge of the lawsuit. The linchpin of the "impermissible collateral attack" doctrine—the attribution of preclusive effect to a failure to intervene—is therefore quite inconsistent with Rule 19 and Rule 24.

. . . .

Affirmed.

[The dissenting opinion of Justice Stevens, with whom Justice Brennan, Justice Marshall, and Justice Blackmun join, is omitted.]

Note

Martin v. Wilks is the leading authority reaffirming the traditional principle that only parties to litigation are bound by the judgment. The Supreme Court rejected five-to-four the argument that non-parties with notice of a pending action that might affect their interests were obligated to seek to intervene in that action to avoid preclusion.

2. Circumstances in which Non-Parties May Be Precluded

a. Traditional Exceptions

The basic principle embraced by *Martin v. Wilks*—that only persons formally joined as parties to litigation are bound by the judgment—is subject to exceptions. An important example in the complex litigation context is the binding effect of a class action judgment where the requirements of due process—most notably, that the absent class members have been adequately represented—are satisfied. (Others, including preclusion based on relationships sometimes described as "privity," are summarized in the next principal case, *Taylor v. Sturgell*, 553 U.S. 880 (2008), *infra.*)

Particularly complex questions arise in the context of litigation by governmental entities, which may or may not bind other agencies or political subdivisions of the same federal or state government, and which may or may not bar subsequent litigation by private individuals. *See generally* 18A WRIGHT, MILLER & COOPER, FEDERAL PRACTICE AND PROCEDURE §§ 4458–58.1 (2d ed. 2002 & Supp. April 2018) (discussing the various aspects and difficulties of applying preclusive doctrines where government entities are parties). On the other hand, private litigation, even litigation seeking to protect the public at large (consider, for example, challenges to actions affecting the environment) generally does not preclude subsequent litigation by public agencies charged with enforcing the laws in question. *See generally id.* § 4458.1. Is this the proper result?

b. "Virtual Representation"

Outside the context of class actions properly maintained under applicable federal or state rules, a finding, without more, that absent persons were "adequately represented" by the parties in a previous case did not historically provide a basis for a finding that they were "in privity" for the purpose of preclusion.

However, before the Supreme Court's decision in *Taylor v. Sturgell, infra*, decisions of some courts had eroded this traditional view by holding that in some circumstances, the interests of absent non-parties were so aligned with those of the parties before the court that the latter were their "virtual representatives," with the consequence that the non-parties were bound by a judgment against the virtual representative. Expansive application of the "virtual representation" concept could significantly erode the principle embraced by *Martin v. Wilks* that only the parties to litigation are bound by the judgment, and could have a major impact in restricting relitigation of identical claims or issues in mass tort and other complex litigation settings.

Taylor v. Sturgell

Supreme Court of the United States
553 U.S. 880 (2008)

JUSTICE GINSBURG delivered the opinion of the Court.

"It is a principle of general application in Anglo American jurisprudence that one is not bound by a judgment *in personam* in a litigation in which he is not designated as a party or to which he has not been made a party by service of process." *Hansberry v. Lee*, 311 U.S. 32, 40 (1940). Several exceptions, recognized in this Court's decisions, temper this basic rule. In a class action, for example, a person not named as a party may be bound by a judgment on the merits of the action, if she was adequately represented by a party who actively participated in the litigation. In this case, we consider for the first time whether there is a "virtual representation" exception to the general rule against precluding nonparties. Adopted by a number of courts, including the courts below in the case now before us, the exception so styled is broader than any we have so far approved.

The virtual representation question we examine in this opinion arises in the following context. Petitioner Brent Taylor filed a lawsuit under the Freedom of Information Act seeking certain documents from the Federal Aviation Administration. Greg Herrick, Taylor's friend, had previously brought an unsuccessful suit seeking the same records. The two men have no legal relationship, and there is no evidence that Taylor controlled, financed, participated in, or even had notice of Herrick's earlier suit. Nevertheless, the D.C. Circuit held Taylor's suit precluded by the judgment against Herrick because, in that court's assessment, Herrick qualified as Taylor's "virtual representative."

. . . .

I

. . . .

A

The first suit was filed by Greg Herrick, an antique aircraft enthusiast and the owner of an F-45 airplane, a vintage model manufactured by the Fairchild Engine and Airplane Corporation (FEAC) in the 1930's. In 1997, seeking information that would help him restore his plane to its original condition, Herrick filed a FOIA request asking the Federal Aviation Administration (FAA) for copies of any technical documents about the F-45 contained in the agency's records.

To gain a certificate authorizing the manufacture and sale of the F-45, FEAC had submitted to the FAA's predecessor, the Civil Aeronautics Authority, detailed specifications and other technical data about the plane. Hundreds of pages of documents produced by FEAC in the certification process remain in the FAA's records.

The FAA denied Herrick's request, however, upon finding that the documents he sought are subject to FOIA's exemption for "trade secrets and commercial or financial information obtained from a person and privileged or confidential," 5 U.S.C. § 552(b)(4) (2006 ed.). In an administrative appeal, Herrick urged that FEAC and its successors had waived any trade-secret protection. The FAA thereupon contacted FEAC's corporate successor, respondent Fairchild Corporation (Fairchild). Because Fairchild objected to release of the documents, the agency adhered to its original decision.

Herrick then filed suit in the U.S. District Court for the District of Wyoming. Challenging the FAA's invocation of the trade-secret exemption, Herrick placed heavy weight on a 1955 letter from FEAC to the Civil Aeronautics Authority. The letter authorized the agency to lend any documents in its files to the public "for use in making repairs or replacement parts for aircraft produced by Fairchild. . . ." (internal quotation marks omitted). This broad authorization, Herrick maintained, showed that the F-45 certification records held by the FAA could not be regarded as "secre[t]" or "confidential" within the meaning of § 552(b)(4).

Rejecting Herrick's argument, the District Court granted summary judgment to the FAA. . . . The 1955 letter, the court reasoned, did not deprive the F-45 certification documents of trade-secret status, for those documents were never in fact released pursuant to the letter's blanket authorization. The court also stated that even if the 1955 letter had waived trade-secret protection, Fairchild had successfully "reversed" the waiver by objecting to the FAA's release of the records to Herrick. *Ibid.*

On appeal, the Tenth Circuit agreed with Herrick that the 1955 letter had stripped the requested documents of trade-secret protection. . . . But the Court of Appeals upheld the District Court's alternative determination—*i.e.*, that Fairchild had restored trade-secret status by objecting to Herrick's FOIA request. On that ground, the appeals court affirmed the entry of summary judgment for the FAA.

. . . .

B

The Tenth Circuit's decision issued on July 24, 2002. Less than a month later, on August 22, petitioner Brent Taylor—a friend of Herrick's and an antique aircraft enthusiast in his own right—submitted a FOIA request seeking the same documents Herrick had unsuccessfully sued to obtain. When the FAA failed to respond, Taylor filed a complaint in the U.S. District Court for the District of Columbia. . . .

After Fairchild intervened as a defendant, the District Court in D.C. concluded that Taylor's suit was barred by claim preclusion; accordingly, it granted summary judgment to Fairchild and the FAA. . . . [The District of Columbia Circuit affirmed.]

. . . .

We granted certiorari . . . to resolve the disagreement among the Circuits over the permissibility and scope of preclusion based on "virtual representation."

II

. . . .

A person who was not a party to a suit generally has not had a "full and fair opportunity to litigate" the claims and issues settled in that suit. The application of claim and issue preclusion to nonparties thus runs up against the "deep-rooted historic tradition that everyone should have his own day in court." [*Richards v. Jefferson County*, 517 U.S. 793, 798 (1996).] Indicating the strength of that tradition, we have often repeated the general rule that "one is not bound by a judgment *in personam* in a litigation in which he is not designated as a party or to which he has not been made a party by service of process." *Hansberry*, 311 U.S., at 40. See also, *e.g.*, *Richards*, 517 U.S., at 798; *Martin v. Wilks*, 490 U.S. 755, 761 (1989); *Zenith Radio Corp. v. Hazeltine Research, Inc.*, 395 U.S. 100, 110 (1969).

B

Though hardly in doubt, the rule against nonparty preclusion is subject to exceptions. For present purposes, the recognized exceptions can be grouped into six categories.

First, "[a] person who agrees to be bound by the determination of issues in an action between others is bound in accordance with the terms of his agreement." 1 Restatement (Second) of Judgments § 40, p. 390 (1980) (hereinafter Restatement). . . .

Second, nonparty preclusion may be justified based on a variety of pre-existing "substantive legal relationship[s]" between the person to be bound and a party to the judgment. . . . Qualifying relationships include, but are not limited to, preceding and succeeding owners of property, bailee and bailor, and assignee and assignor. See 2 Restatement §§ 43–44, 52, 55. These exceptions originated "as much from the needs of property law as from the values of preclusion by judgment." 18A C. Wright, A. Miller, & E. Cooper, Federal Practice and Procedure § 4448, p. 329 (2d ed. 2002) (hereinafter Wright & Miller).[19]

Third, we have confirmed that, "in certain limited circumstances," a nonparty may be bound by a judgment because she was "adequately represented by someone with the same interests who [wa]s a party" to the suit. *Richards*, 517 U.S., at 798 (internal quotation marks omitted). Representative suits with preclusive effect on nonparties include properly conducted class actions, see *Martin*, 490 U.S., at 762, n. 2 (citing Fed. Rule Civ. Proc. 23), and suits brought by trustees, guardians, and other fiduciaries. . . .

---

19. [Court's footnote #8] The substantive legal relationships justifying preclusion are sometimes collectively referred to as "privity." See, *e.g.*, *Richards v. Jefferson County*, 517 U.S. 793, 798 (1996); 2 Restatement § 62, Comment *a*. The term "privity," however, has also come to be used more broadly, as a way to express the conclusion that nonparty preclusion is appropriate on any ground. See 18A Wright & Miller § 4449, pp. 351–353, and n. 33 (collecting cases). To ward off confusion, we avoid using the term "privity" in this opinion.

Fourth, a nonparty is bound by a judgment if she "assume[d] control" over the litigation in which that judgment was rendered. . . . 1 Restatement §39. Because such a person has had "the opportunity to present proofs and argument," he has already "had his day in court" even though he was not a formal party to the litigation. *Id.*, Comment *a*, p. 382.

Fifth, a party bound by a judgment may not avoid its preclusive force by relitigating through a proxy. Preclusion is thus in order when a person who did not participate in a litigation later brings suit as the designated representative of a person who was a party to the prior adjudication. . . . And although our decisions have not addressed the issue directly, it also seems clear that preclusion is appropriate when a nonparty later brings suit as an agent for a party who is bound by a judgment.

Sixth, in certain circumstances a special statutory scheme may "expressly foreclos[e] successive litigation by nonlitigants . . . if the scheme is otherwise consistent with due process." *Martin*, 490 U.S., at 762, n. 2. Examples of such schemes include bankruptcy and probate proceedings, see *ibid.*, and *quo warranto* actions or other suits that, "under [the governing] law, [may] be brought only on behalf of the public at large," *Richards*, 517 U.S., at 804.

III

Reaching beyond these six established categories, some lower courts have recognized a "virtual representation" exception to the rule against nonparty preclusion. Decisions of these courts, however, have been far from consistent. See 18A Wright & Miller §4457, p. 513 (virtual representation lacks a "clear or coherent theory"; decisions applying it have "an episodic quality"). Some Circuits use the label, but define "virtual representation" so that it is no broader than the recognized exception for adequate representation. . . . But other courts, including the Eighth, Ninth, and D.C. Circuits, apply multifactor tests for virtual representation that permit nonparty preclusion in cases that do not fit within any of the established exceptions.

The D.C. Circuit, the FAA, and Fairchild have presented three arguments in support of an expansive doctrine of virtual representation. We find none of them persuasive.

A

The D.C. Circuit purported to ground its virtual representation doctrine in this Court's decisions stating that, in some circumstances, a person may be bound by a judgment if she was adequately represented by a party to the proceeding yielding that judgment. . . . But the D.C. Circuit's definition of "adequate representation" strayed from the meaning our decisions have attributed to that term.

In *Richards*, we reviewed a decision by the Alabama Supreme Court holding that a challenge to a tax was barred by a judgment upholding the same tax in a suit filed by different taxpayers. . . . The plaintiffs in the first suit "did not sue on behalf of a class," their complaint "did not purport to assert any claim against or on behalf of any nonparties," and the judgment "did not purport to bind" nonparties. There was no indication, we emphasized, that the court in the first suit "took care to protect the interests" of absent parties, or that the parties to that litigation "understood their suit to be on behalf of absent [parties]." In these circumstances, we held, the application of claim preclusion was inconsistent with "the due process of law guaranteed by the Fourteenth Amendment."

The D.C. Circuit stated, without elaboration, that it did not "read *Richards* to hold a nonparty . . . adequately represented only if special procedures were followed [to protect the nonparty] or the party to the prior suit understood it was representing the nonparty. . . ." As the D.C. Circuit saw this case, Herrick adequately represented Taylor for two principal reasons: Herrick had a strong incentive to litigate; and Taylor later hired Herrick's lawyer, suggesting Taylor's "satisfaction with the attorney's performance in the prior case."

The D.C. Circuit misapprehended *Richards*. As just recounted, our holding that the Alabama Supreme Court's application of res judicata to nonparties violated due process turned on the lack of either special procedures to protect the nonparties' interests or an understanding by the concerned parties that the first suit was brought in a representative capacity. . . . *Richards* thus established that representation is "adequate" for purposes of nonparty preclusion only if (at a minimum) one of these two circumstances is present.

. . . .

B

Fairchild and the FAA do not argue that the D.C. Circuit's virtual representation doctrine fits within any of the recognized grounds for nonparty preclusion. Rather, they ask us to abandon the attempt to delineate discrete grounds and clear rules altogether. Preclusion is in order, they contend, whenever "the relationship between a party and a non-party is 'close enough' to bring the second litigant within the judgment. . . ." Courts should make the "close enough" determination, they urge, through a "heavily fact-driven" and "equitable" inquiry. . . .

We reject this argument for three reasons. First, our decisions emphasize the fundamental nature of the general rule that a litigant is not bound by a judgment to which she was not a party. . . . Accordingly, we have endeavored to delineate discrete exceptions that apply in "limited circumstances." Respondents' amorphous balancing test is at odds with the constrained approach to nonparty preclusion our decisions advance.

. . . .

Our second reason for rejecting a broad doctrine of virtual representation rests on the limitations attending nonparty preclusion based on adequate representation. A party's representation of a nonparty is "adequate" for preclusion purposes only if, at a minimum: (1) the interests of the nonparty and her representative are aligned . . . and (2) either the party understood herself to be acting in a representative capacity or the original court took care to protect the interests of the nonparty. . . . In addition, adequate representation sometimes requires (3) notice of the original suit to the persons alleged to have been represented, see *Richards*, 517 U.S., at 801.[20] In the class-action context, these limitations are implemented by the procedural safeguards contained in Federal Rule of Civil Procedure 23.

An expansive doctrine of virtual representation, however, would "recogniz[e], in effect, a common-law kind of class action." *Tice* [*v. American Airlines, Inc.*, 162 F.3d 966, 972 (7th Cir. 1998)] (internal quotation marks omitted). That is, virtual representation would authorize preclusion based on identity of interests and some kind of relationship between parties and nonparties, shorn of the procedural protections prescribed in *Hansberry, Richards*, and Rule 23. These protections, grounded in due process, could be circumvented were we to approve a virtual representation doctrine that allowed courts to "create *de facto* class actions at will." *Id.* at 973.

Third, a diffuse balancing approach to nonparty preclusion would likely create more headaches than it relieves. Most obviously, it could significantly complicate the task of district courts faced in the first instance with preclusion questions. An all-things-considered balancing approach might spark wide-ranging, time-consuming, and expensive discovery tracking factors potentially relevant under seven- or five-prong tests. And after the relevant facts are established, district judges would be called upon to evaluate them under a standard that provides no firm guidance.... Preclusion doctrine, it should be recalled, is intended to reduce the burden of litigation on courts and parties. "In this area of the law," we agree, "'crisp rules with sharp corners' are preferable to a round-about doctrine of opaque standards." *Bittinger v. Tecumseh Products Co.*, 123 F.3d 877, 881 (C.A.6 1997).

C

....

The FAA next argues that "the threat of vexatious litigation is heightened" in public-law cases because "the number of plaintiffs with standing is potentially limitless." FOIA does allow "any person" whose request is denied to resort to federal court for review of the agency's determination. 5 U.S.C. § 552(a)(3)(A), (4)(B) (2006 ed.). Thus it is theoretically possible that several persons could coordinate to mount a series of repetitive lawsuits.

But we are not convinced that this risk justifies departure from the usual rules governing nonparty preclusion. First, *stare decisis* will allow courts swiftly to dispose of repetitive suits brought in the same circuit. Second, even when *stare decisis* is not dispositive, "the human tendency not to waste money will deter the bringing of suits based on claims or issues that have already been adversely determined

20. [Court's footnote #11] *Richards* suggested that notice is required in some representative suits, *e.g.*, class actions seeking monetary relief. See 517 U.S., at 801 (citing *Hansberry v. Lee*, 311 U.S. 32, 40 (1940), *Eisen v. Carlisle & Jacquelin*, 417 U.S. 156, 177 (1974), and *Mullane v. Central Hanover Bank & Trust Co.*, 339 U.S. 306, 319 (1950)). But we assumed without deciding that a lack of notice might be overcome in some circumstances. See *Richards*, 517 U.S., at 801.

against others." [D. SHAPIRO, CIVIL PROCEDURE: PRECLUSION IN CIVIL ACTIONS 97 (2001)]. This intuition seems to be borne out by experience: The FAA has not called our attention to any instances of abusive FOIA suits in the Circuits that reject the virtual-representation theory respondents advocate here.

IV

For the foregoing reasons, we disapprove the theory of virtual representation on which the decision below rested. The preclusive effects of a judgment in a federal-question case decided by a federal court should instead be determined according to the established grounds for nonparty preclusion described in this opinion.

. . . .

E. Interjurisdictional Preclusion

Complex litigation frequently involves overlapping federal and state cases arising from the same or related transactions and involving many of the same parties. As a result, problems of "interjurisdictional preclusion" arise. Where a state action goes to judgment first, litigants may seek to invoke the claim or issue preclusive effect of that judgment in still-pending federal proceedings. Conversely, where a federal judgment is rendered before the state proceedings are concluded, litigants may invoke the preclusive effect of the federal judgment in the state proceedings. These problems have particular significance in the context of complex litigation because the preclusive effect that state judgments will have in federal court or that federal judgments will have in state court may significantly affect the ability of the parties to class actions and other multi-party cases conclusively to resolve the disputes between them by litigation or settlement.

The Full Faith and Credit Clause of the Constitution (Art. IV, § 1) prescribes the preclusive effect of state court judgments in the courts of other states, but does not address the effect of state court judgments in federal court. By contrast, the preclusive effect of state court judgments in federal court is expressly addressed by the full faith and credit statute (28 U.S.C. § 1738). It provides that the "judicial proceedings of any court of any . . . State, Territory or Possession . . . shall have the same full faith and credit in every court within the United States and its Territories and Possessions as they have by law or usage in the courts of such State, Territory or Possession from which they are taken." *Id.* Thus, the preclusive effect of a state court judgment in federal court is determined, in the first instance, by the law of the judgment-rendering state.

Neither the Full Faith and Credit Clause nor the full faith and credit statute refers to the preclusive effect of federal judgments in state court. However, the Supreme Court has long held that federal judgments are entitled to the same preclusive effect in state court as they would have in federal courts. This principle is grounded in the Supremacy Clause (U.S. Const., Art. VI).

These general principles present a number of difficulties in application, as illustrated by the next two principal cases.

1. Preclusive Effect of State Judgments in Federal Court

Matsushita Electric Industrial Co. v. Epstein

Supreme Court of the United States
516 U.S. 367 (1996)

JUSTICE THOMAS delivered the opinion of the Court.

This case presents the question whether a federal court may withhold full faith and credit from a state-court judgment approving a class-action settlement simply because the settlement releases claims within the exclusive jurisdiction of the federal courts. The answer is no. Absent a partial repeal of the Full Faith and Credit Act, 28 U.S.C. § 1738, by another federal statute, a federal court must give the judgment the same effect that it would have in the courts of the State in which it was rendered.

I

In 1990, petitioner Matsushita Electric Industrial Co. made a tender offer for the common stock of MCA, Inc., a Delaware corporation. The tender offer not only resulted in Matsushita's acquisition of MCA, but also precipitated two lawsuits on behalf of the holders of MCA's common stock. First, a class action was filed in the Delaware Court of Chancery against MCA and its directors for breach of fiduciary duty in failing to maximize shareholder value. The complaint was later amended to state additional claims against MCA's directors for, *inter alia*, waste of corporate assets by exposing MCA to liability under the federal securities laws. In addition, Matsushita was added as a defendant and was accused of conspiring with MCA's directors to violate Delaware law. The Delaware suit was based purely on state-law claims.

While the state class action was pending, the instant suit was filed in Federal District Court in California. The complaint named Matsushita as a defendant and alleged that Matsushita's tender offer violated Securities Exchange Commission (SEC) Rules 10b-3 and 14d-10. These Rules were created by the SEC pursuant to the 1968 Williams Act Amendments to the Securities Exchange Act of 1934 (Exchange Act), 48 Stat. 881, as amended, 15 U.S.C. § 78a *et seq*. Section 27 of the Exchange Act confers exclusive jurisdiction upon the federal courts for suits brought to enforce the Act or rules and regulations promulgated thereunder.... The District Court declined to certify the class, entered summary judgment for Matsushita, and dismissed the case. The plaintiffs appealed to the Court of Appeals for the Ninth Circuit.

After the federal plaintiffs filed their notice of appeal but before the Ninth Circuit handed down a decision, the parties to the Delaware suit negotiated a settlement.[21] In

21. [Court's footnote #2] A previous settlement was rejected by the Court of Chancery as unfair to the class. See *In re MCA, Inc. Shareholders Litigation*, 598 A.2d 687 (1991).

exchange for a global release of all claims arising out of the Matsushita-MCA acquisition, the defendants would deposit $2 million into a settlement fund to be distributed pro rata to the members of the class. As required by Delaware Chancery Rule 23, which is modeled on Federal Rule of Civil Procedure 23, the Chancery Court certified the class for purposes of settlement and approved a notice of the proposed settlement. The notice informed the class members of their right to request exclusion from the settlement class and to appear and present argument at a scheduled hearing to determine the fairness of the settlement. In particular, the notice stated that "[b]y filing a valid Request for Exclusion, a member of the Settlement Class will not be precluded by the Settlement from individually seeking to pursue the claims alleged in the . . . California Federal Actions, . . . or any other claim relating to the events at issue in the Delaware Actions." Two such notices were mailed to the class members and the notice was also published in the national edition of the Wall Street Journal. The Chancery Court then held a hearing. After argument from several objectors, the Court found the class representation adequate and the settlement fair.

The order and final judgment of the Chancery Court incorporated the terms of the settlement agreement, providing:

> All claims, rights and causes of action (state or federal, including but not limited to claims arising under the federal securities law, any rules or regulations promulgated thereunder, or otherwise), whether known or unknown that are, could have been or might in the future be asserted by any of the plaintiffs or any member of the Settlement Class (*other than those who have validly requested exclusion therefrom*), . . . in connection with or that arise now or hereafter out of the Merger Agreement, the Tender Offer, the Distribution Agreement, the Capital Contribution Agreement, the employee compensation arrangements, the Tender Agreements, the Initial Proposed Settlement, this Settlement . . . *and including without limitation the claims asserted in the California Federal Actions* . . . are hereby compromised, settled, released and discharged with prejudice by virtue of the proceedings herein and this Order and Final Judgment. . . . (emphasis added).

The judgment also stated that the notice met all the requirements of due process. The Delaware Supreme Court affirmed. . . .

Respondents were members of both the state and federal plaintiff classes. Following issuance of the notice of proposed settlement of the Delaware litigation, respondents neither opted out of the settlement class nor appeared at the hearing to contest the settlement or the representation of the class. On appeal in the Ninth Circuit, petitioner Matsushita invoked the Delaware judgment as a bar to further prosecution of that action under the Full Faith and Credit Act, 28 U.S.C. § 1738.

The Ninth Circuit rejected petitioner's argument, ruling that § 1738 did not apply. . . . Instead, the Court of Appeals fashioned a test under which the preclusive force of a state court settlement judgment is limited to those claims that "could . . .

have been extinguished by the issue preclusive effect of an adjudication of the state claims." The lower courts have taken varying approaches to determining the preclusive effect of a state court judgment, entered in a class or derivative action, that provides for the release of exclusively federal claims. We granted certiorari to clarify this important area of federal law. . . .

II

The Full Faith and Credit Act mandates that the "judicial proceedings" of any State "shall have the same full faith and credit in every court within the United States . . . as they have by law or usage in the courts of such State . . . from which they are taken." 28 U.S.C. § 1738. The Act thus directs all courts to treat a state court judgment with the same respect that it would receive in the courts of the rendering state. Federal courts may not "employ their own rules . . . in determining the effect of state judgments," but must "accept the rules chosen by the State from which the judgment is taken." *Kremer v. Chemical Constr. Corp.*, 456 U.S. 461, 481–482 (1982). Because the Court of Appeals failed to follow the dictates of the Act, we reverse.

A

The state court judgment in this case differs in two respects from the judgments that we have previously considered in our cases under the Full Faith and Credit Act. As respondents and the Court of Appeals stressed, the judgment was the product of a class action and incorporated a settlement agreement releasing claims within the exclusive jurisdiction of the federal courts. Though respondents urge "the irrelevance of section 1738 to this litigation," we do not think that either of these features exempts the judgment from the operation of § 1738.

That the judgment at issue is the result of a class action, rather than a suit brought by an individual, does not undermine the initial applicability of § 1738. The judgment of a state court in a class action is plainly the product of a "judicial proceeding" within the meaning of § 1738. . . .

Further, § 1738 is not irrelevant simply because the judgment in question might work to bar the litigation of exclusively federal claims. Our decision in *Marrese v. American Academy of Orthopaedic Surgeons*, 470 U.S. 373 (1985), made clear that where § 1738 is raised as a defense in a subsequent suit, the fact that an allegedly precluded "claim is within the exclusive jurisdiction of the federal courts *does not necessarily make § 1738 inapplicable*." [Emphasis added.] In so holding, we relied primarily on *Kremer v. Chemical Constr. Corp.*, *supra*, which held, without deciding whether Title VII claims are exclusively federal, that state court proceedings may be issue preclusive in Title VII suits in federal court. *Kremer*, we said, "implies that absent an exception to § 1738, state law determines at least the . . . preclusive effect of a prior state judgment in a subsequent action involving a claim within the exclusive jurisdiction of the federal courts." *Marrese*, 470 U.S., at 381. Accordingly, we decided that "a state court judgment may in some circumstances have preclusive effect in a subsequent action within the exclusive jurisdiction of the federal courts." *Id.*, at 380.

... [I]n accord with these precedents, we conclude that § 1738 is generally applicable in cases in which the state court judgment at issue incorporates a class action settlement releasing claims solely within the jurisdiction of the federal courts.

B

Marrese provides the analytical framework for deciding whether the Delaware court's judgment precludes this exclusively federal action. When faced with a state court judgment relating to an exclusively federal claim, a federal court must first look to the law of the rendering State to ascertain the effect of the judgment. If state law indicates that the particular claim or issue would be barred from litigation in a court of that state, then the federal court must next decide whether, "as an exception to § 1738," it "should refuse to give preclusive effect to [the] state court judgment."....

1

We observed in *Marrese* that the inquiry into state law would not always yield a direct answer. Usually, "a state court will not have occasion to address the specific question whether a state judgment has issue or claim preclusive effect in a later action that can be brought only in federal court...." Where a judicially approved settlement is under consideration, a federal court may consequently find guidance from general state law on the preclusive force of settlement judgments.... Here, in addition to providing rules regarding the preclusive force of class-action settlement judgments in subsequent suits in state court, the Delaware courts have also spoken to the particular effect of such judgments in federal court.

Delaware has traditionally treated the impact of settlement judgments on subsequent litigation in state court as a question of claim preclusion. Early cases suggested that Delaware courts would not afford claim preclusive effect to a settlement releasing claims that could not have been presented in the trial court. See *Ezzes v. Ackerman*, 234 A.2d 444, 445–446 (Del. 1967).... As the Court of Chancery has perceived, however, "the *Ezzes* inquiry [was] modified in regard to class actions," *In re Union Square Associates Securities Litigation*, C.A. No. 11028, 1993 WL 220528, (June 16, 1993), by the Delaware Supreme Court's decision in *Nottingham Partners v. Dana*, 564 A.2d 1089 (1989).

....

... In *Nottingham*, the Court stated that: "When a state court settlement of a class action releases all claims which arise out of the challenged transaction and is determined to be fair and to have met all due process requirements, the class members are bound by the release or the doctrine of issue preclusion. Class members cannot subsequently relitigate the claims barred by the settlement in a federal court." *In re MCA, Inc. Shareholders Litigation*, 598 A.2d 687, 691 (1991).[22] We are aware of no Delaware case that suggests otherwise.

---

22. [Court's footnote #4] In fact, the Chancery Court rejected the first settlement, which contained no opt-out provision, as unfair to the class precisely because it believed that the settlement

Given these statements of Delaware law, we think that a Delaware court would afford preclusive effect to the settlement judgment in this case, notwithstanding the fact that respondents could not have pressed their Exchange Act claims in the Court of Chancery. The claims are clearly within the scope of the release in the judgment, since the judgment specifically refers to this lawsuit. . . .[23]

. . . Respondents do not deny that, as shareholders of MCA's common stock, they were part of the plaintiff class and that they never opted out; they are bound, then, by the judgment.[24]

2

Because it appears that the settlement judgment would be res judicata under Delaware law, we proceed to the second step of the *Marrese* analysis and ask whether § 27 of the Exchange Act, which confers exclusive jurisdiction upon the federal courts for suits arising under the Act, partially repealed § 1738. Section 27 contains no express language regarding its relationship with § 1738 or the preclusive effect of related state court proceedings. Thus, any modification of § 1738 by § 27 must be implied. In deciding whether § 27 impliedly created an exception to § 1738, the "general question is whether the concerns underlying a particular grant of exclusive jurisdiction justify a finding of an implied partial repeal of § 1738." *Marrese*, 470 U.S., at 386. "Resolution of this question will depend on the particular federal statute as well as the nature of the claim or issue involved in the subsequent federal action. . . . [T]he primary consideration must be the intent of Congress."

As an historical matter, we have seldom, if ever, held that a federal statute impliedly repealed § 1738. . . . The rarity with which we have discovered implied repeals is due to the relatively stringent standard for such findings, namely, that there be an "'irreconcilable conflict'" between the two federal statutes at issue. . . .

---

would preclude the class from pursuing their exclusively federal claims in federal court. See *In re MCA Inc. Shareholders Litigation*, 598 A.2d 687, 692 (1991) ("[I]f this Court provides for the release of all the claims arising out of the challenged transaction, the claims which the Objectors have asserted in the federal suit will likely be forever barred").

23. [Court's footnote #5] Apart from any discussion of Delaware law, respondents contend that the settlement proceedings did not satisfy due process because the class was inadequately represented. Respondents make this claim in spite of the Chancery Court's express ruling, following argument on the issue, that the class representatives fairly and adequately protected the interests of the class. . . . We need not address the due process claim, however, because it is outside the scope of the question presented in this Court. . . . While it is true that a respondent may defend a judgment on alternative grounds, we generally do not address arguments that were not the basis for the decision below. . . .

24. [Court's footnote #6] Respondents argue that their failure to opt out of the settlement class does not constitute consent to the terms of the settlement under traditional contract principles. Again, the issue raised by respondents—whether the settlement could bar this suit as a matter of contract law, as distinguished from § 1738 law—is outside the scope of the question on which we granted certiorari. We note, however, that if a State chooses to approach the preclusive effect of a judgment embodying the terms of a settlement agreement as a question of pure contract law, a federal court must adhere to that approach under § 1738. . . .

Section 27 provides that "[t]he district courts of the United States . . . shall have exclusive jurisdiction . . . of all suits in equity and actions at law brought to enforce any liability or duty created by this chapter or the rules and regulations thereunder." 15 U.S.C. § 78aa. There is no suggestion in § 27 that Congress meant for plaintiffs with Exchange Act claims to have more than one day in court to challenge the legality of a securities transaction. Though the statute plainly mandates that suits alleging violations of the Exchange Act may be maintained only in federal court, nothing in the language of § 27 "remotely expresses any congressional intent to contravene the common-law rules of preclusion or to repeal the express statutory requirements of 28 U.S.C. § 1738." *Allen v. McCurry*, [449 U.S. 90, 97–98 (1980).]

Nor does § 27 evince any intent to prevent litigants in state court—whether suing as individuals or as part of a class—from voluntarily releasing Exchange Act claims in judicially approved settlements. While § 27 prohibits state courts from adjudicating claims arising under the Exchange Act, it does not prohibit state courts from approving the release of Exchange Act claims in the settlement of suits over which they have properly exercised jurisdiction, *i.e.*, suits arising under state law or under federal law for which there is concurrent jurisdiction. In this case, for example, the Delaware action was not "brought to enforce" any rights or obligations under the Act. The Delaware court asserted judicial power over a complaint asserting purely state law causes of action and, after the parties agreed to settle, certified the class and approved the settlement pursuant to the requirements of Delaware Rule of Chancery 23 and the Due Process Clause. Thus, the Delaware court never trespassed upon the exclusive territory of the federal courts, but merely approved the settlement of a common-law suit pursuant to state and nonexclusive federal law. . . . While it is true that the state court assessed the general worth of the federal claims in determining the fairness of the settlement, such assessment does not amount to a judgment on the merits of the claims. . . .

The legislative history of the Exchange Act elucidates no specific purpose on the part of Congress in enacting § 27. . . . We may presume, however, that Congress intended § 27 to serve at least the general purposes underlying most grants of exclusive jurisdiction: "to achieve greater uniformity of construction and more effective and expert application of that law." When a state court upholds a settlement that releases claims under the Exchange Act, it threatens neither of these policies. There is no danger that state court judges who are not fully expert in federal securities law will say definitively what the Exchange Act means and enforce legal liabilities and duties thereunder. And the uniform construction of the Act is unaffected by a state court's approval of a proposed settlement because the state court does not adjudicate the Exchange Act claims but only evaluates the overall fairness of the settlement, generally by applying its own business judgment to the facts of the case. . . .

. . . .

Finally, precedent supports the conclusion that the concerns underlying the grant of exclusive jurisdiction in § 27 are not undermined by state-court approval of settlements releasing Exchange Act claims. We have held that state court proceedings may, in various ways, subsequently affect the litigation of exclusively federal claims without running afoul of the federal jurisdictional grant in question. In *Becher v. Contoure Laboratories, Inc.*, 279 U.S. 388 (1929) (cited in *Marrese*, 470 U.S., at 381), we held that state court findings of fact were issue preclusive in federal patent suits. We did so with full recognition that "the logical conclusion from the establishing of [the state law] claim is that Becher's patent is void." *Becher* reasoned that although "decrees validating or invalidating patents belong to the Courts of the United States," that "does not give sacrosanctity to facts that may be conclusive upon the question in issue." Similarly, while binding legal determinations of rights and liabilities under the Exchange Act are for federal courts only, there is nothing sacred about the approval of settlements of suits arising under state law, even where the parties agree to release exclusively federal claims. . . .

We have also held that Exchange Act claims may be resolved by arbitration rather than litigation in federal court. In *Shearson/American Express Inc. v. McMahon*, 482 U.S. 220 (1987), we found that parties to an arbitration agreement could waive the right to have their Exchange Act claims tried in federal court and agree to arbitrate the claims. It follows that state court litigants ought also to be able to waive, or "release," the right to litigate Exchange Act claims in a federal forum as part of a settlement agreement. As *Shearson/American Express Inc.* demonstrates, a statute conferring exclusive federal jurisdiction for a certain class of claims does not necessarily require resolution of those claims in a federal court.

Taken together, these cases stand for the general proposition that even when exclusively federal claims are at stake, there is no "universal right to litigate a federal claim in a federal district court." *Allen v. McCurry*, 449 U.S., at 105. If class action plaintiffs wish to preserve absolutely their right to litigate exclusively federal claims in federal court, they should either opt out of the settlement class or object to the release of any exclusively federal claims. In fact, some of the plaintiffs in the Delaware class action requested exclusion from the settlement class. They are now proceeding in federal court with their federal claims, unimpeded by the Delaware judgment.

. . . .

C

The Court of Appeals did not engage in any analysis of Delaware law pursuant to § 1738. Rather, the Court of Appeals declined to apply § 1738 on the ground that where the rendering forum lacked jurisdiction over the subject matter or the parties, full faith and credit is not required. . . .

As explained above, the state court in this case clearly possessed jurisdiction over the subject matter of the underlying suit and over the defendants. Only if this were not so—for instance, if the complaint alleged violations of the Exchange Act and the Delaware court rendered a judgment on the merits of those claims—would the exception to § 1738 for lack of subject-matter jurisdiction apply. Where, as here, the rendering court in fact had subject-matter jurisdiction, the subject-matter jurisdiction exception to full faith and credit is simply inapposite. In such a case, the relevance of a federal statute that provides for exclusive federal jurisdiction is not to the state court's possession of jurisdiction per se, but to the existence of a partial repeal of § 1738.

The judgment of the Court of Appeals is reversed and remanded for proceedings consistent with this opinion.

[The opinion of JUSTICE STEVENS, concurring in part and dissenting in part, is omitted.]

[The opinion of JUSTICE GINSBURG, with whom JUSTICE STEVENS joined, and with whom JUSTICE SOUTER joined as to Part II-B, concurring in part and dissenting in part, is omitted.]

Notes and Questions

1. What factors should be determinative of the implied partial repeal question? The usual reasons for a Congressional grant of exclusive subject matter jurisdiction to the federal courts are to ensure the uniform, expert, and sympathetic interpretation of federal law. Congress has done so in a number of areas, including federal antitrust law, 15 U.S.C. §§ 15, 26; cases under the Securities Exchange Act of 1934, 15 U.S.C. § 78aa; bankruptcy proceedings, 28 U.S.C. § 1334; patent and copyright cases, 28 U.S.C. § 1338(a); and crimes against the United States, 18 U.S.C. § 3231. Can these purposes adequately be served if state court judgments are allowed to preclude subsequent federal litigation of exclusively federal claims arising out of the same facts as a previous state judgment on purely state law claims? *See also In re Lease Oil Antitrust Litig.*, 200 F.3d 317, 320–21 (5th Cir. 2000); *Valley Disposal, Inc. v. Central Vermont Solid Waste Mgmt. Dist.*, 31 F.3d 89, 97–99 (2d Cir. 1994) (denying preclusion of exclusively federal claims).

2. Should a distinction on the implied repeal issue be drawn between claim and issue preclusion? On what grounds? In the *Marrese* case (discussed in *Matsushita*), the Court stated that "[o]ur decisions indicate that a state court judgment may in some circumstances have preclusive effect in a subsequent action within the exclusive jurisdiction of the federal courts." 470 U.S. at 380. The Court cited *Becher v. Contoure Laboratories, Inc.*, 279 U.S. 388 (1929), and *Kremer v. Chemical Const. Corp.*, 456 U.S. 461 (1982), as examples.

3. The *Matsushita* majority was unimpressed by the argument that preclusive effect should be denied because the judgment before it was rendered in a class action. Was this conclusion unduly facile, particularly in light of the claim that the class members had been inadequately represented and their federal claims undervalued by the Delaware trial court in approving the settlement? As previously discussed, the issue of adequate representation presented considerable difficulty on remand in *Matsushita*.

2. Preclusive Effect of Federal Judgments in State Court

Semtek Int'l Inc. v. Lockheed Martin Corp.

Supreme Court of the United States
531 U.S. 497 (2001)

JUSTICE SCALIA delivered the opinion of the Court.

This case presents the question whether the claim-preclusive effect of a federal judgment dismissing a diversity action on statute-of-limitations grounds is determined by the law of the State in which the federal court sits.

I

Petitioner filed a complaint against respondent in California state court, alleging inducement of breach of contract and various business torts. Respondent removed the case to the United States District Court for the Central District of California on the basis of diversity of citizenship, and successfully moved to dismiss petitioner's claims as barred by California's 2-year statute of limitations. In its order of dismissal, the District Court, adopting language suggested by respondent, dismissed petitioner's claims "in [their] entirety on the merits and with prejudice." Without contesting the District Court's designation of its dismissal as "on the merits," petitioner appealed to the Court of Appeals for the Ninth Circuit, which affirmed the District Court's order.... Petitioner also brought suit against respondent in the State Circuit Court for Baltimore City, Maryland, alleging the same causes of action, which were not time barred under Maryland's 3-year statute of limitations. Respondent sought injunctive relief against this action from the California federal court under the All Writs Act, 28 U.S.C. § 1651, and removed the action to the United States District Court for the District of Maryland on federal-question grounds.... The California federal court denied the relief requested, and the Maryland federal court remanded the case to state court because the federal question arose only by way of defense. Following a hearing, the Maryland state court granted respondent's motion to dismiss on the ground of res judicata. Petitioner then returned to the California federal court and the Ninth Circuit, unsuccessfully moving both courts to amend the former's earlier order so as to indicate that the dismissal was not "on the merits." Petitioner also appealed the Maryland trial court's order of dismissal to the Maryland Court of Special Appeals. The Court of Special Appeals affirmed, holding that, regardless of whether California would have accorded claim-preclusive effect to a statute-of-limitations dismissal by one of its own courts, the dismissal by the California federal court barred the complaint filed in Maryland, since the res judicata effect of federal diversity judgments is prescribed by federal law, under which the earlier dismissal was on the merits and claim preclusive.... After the Maryland Court of Appeals declined to review the case, we granted certiorari....

II

Petitioner contends that the outcome of this case is controlled by *Dupasseur v. Rochereau*, 21 Wall. 130, 135 (1875), which held that the res judicata effect of a federal diversity judgment "is such as would belong to judgments of the State courts rendered under similar circumstances," and may not be accorded any "higher sanctity or effect." Since, petitioner argues, the dismissal of an action on statute-of-limitations grounds by a California state court would not be claim preclusive, it follows that the similar dismissal of this diversity action by the California federal court cannot be claim preclusive. While we agree that this would be the result demanded by *Dupasseur*, the case is not dispositive because it was decided under the Conformity Act of 1872, 17 Stat. 196, which required federal courts to apply the procedural law of the forum State in nonequity cases. That arguably affected the outcome of the case. See *Dupasseur, supra*, at 135. See also Restatement (Second) of Judgments § 87, Comment *a*, p. 315 (1980) (hereinafter Restatement) ("Since procedural law largely determines the matters that may be adjudicated in an action, state law had to be considered in ascertaining the effect of a federal judgment").

Respondent, for its part, contends that the outcome of this case is controlled by Federal Rule of Civil Procedure 41(b), which provides as follows:

> "Involuntary Dismissal: Effect Thereof. For failure of the plaintiff to prosecute or to comply with these rules or any order of court, a defendant may move for dismissal of an action or of any claim against the defendant. Unless the court in its order for dismissal otherwise specifies, a dismissal under this subdivision and any dismissal not provided for in this rule, other than a dismissal for lack of jurisdiction, for improper venue, or for failure to join a party under Rule 19, operates as an adjudication upon the merits."

Since the dismissal here did not "otherwise specif[y]" (indeed, it specifically stated that it *was* "on the merits"), and did not pertain to the excepted subjects of jurisdiction, venue, or joinder, it follows, respondent contends, that the dismissal "is entitled to claim preclusive effect."

Implicit in this reasoning is the unstated minor premise that all judgments denominated "on the merits" are entitled to claim-preclusive effect. That premise is not necessarily valid. The original connotation of an "on the merits" adjudication is one that actually "pass[es] directly on the substance of [a particular] claim" before the court. Restatement § 19, Comment *a*, at 161. That connotation remains common to every jurisdiction of which we are aware. And it is, we think, the meaning intended in those many statements to the effect that a judgment "on the merits" triggers the doctrine of res judicata or claim preclusion....

But over the years the meaning of the term "judgment on the merits" "has gradually undergone change," R. Marcus, M. Redish, & E. Sherman, Civil Procedure: A Modern Approach 1140–1141 (3d ed. 2000), and it has come to be applied to some judgments (such as the one involved here) that do not pass upon the substantive merits of a claim and hence do not (in many jurisdictions) entail claim-preclusive effect.... That is why the Restatement of Judgments has abandoned the use of the term "—because of its possibly misleading connotations," Restatement § 19, Comment *a*, at 161.

In short, it is no longer true that a judgment "on the merits" is necessarily a judgment entitled to claim-preclusive effect; and there are a number of reasons for believing that the phrase "adjudication upon the merits" does not bear that meaning in Rule 41(b). To begin with, Rule 41(b) sets forth nothing more than a default rule for determining the import of a dismissal (a dismissal is "upon the merits," with the three stated exceptions, unless the court "otherwise specifies"). This would be a highly peculiar context in which to announce a federally prescribed rule on the complex question of claim preclusion, saying in effect, "All federal dismissals (with three specified exceptions) preclude suit elsewhere, unless the court otherwise specifies."

And even apart from the purely default character of Rule 41(b), it would be peculiar to find a rule governing the effect that must be accorded federal judgments by other courts ensconced in rules governing the internal procedures of the rendering court itself. Indeed, such a rule would arguably violate the jurisdictional limitation of the Rules Enabling Act: that the Rules "shall not abridge, enlarge or modify any substantive right," 28 U.S.C. § 2072(b).... In the present case, for example, if California law left petitioner free to sue on this claim in Maryland even after the California statute of limitations had expired, the federal court's extinguishment of that right (through Rule 41(b)'s mandated claim-preclusive effect of its judgment) would seem to violate this limitation.

Moreover, as so interpreted, the Rule would in many cases violate the federalism principle of *Erie R. Co. v. Tompkins*, 304 U.S. 64, 78–80 (1938), by engendering "'substantial' variations [in outcomes] between state and federal litigation" which would "[l]ikely ... influence the choice of a forum," *Hanna v. Plumer*, 380 U.S. 460, 467–468 (1965)....

....

We think the key to a more reasonable interpretation of the meaning of "operates as an adjudication upon the merits" in Rule 41(b) is to be found in Rule 41(a), which, in discussing the effect of voluntary dismissal by the plaintiff, makes clear that an "adjudication upon the merits" is the opposite of a "dismissal without prejudice":

> "Unless otherwise stated in the notice of dismissal or stipulation, the dismissal is without prejudice, except that a notice of dismissal operates as an adjudication upon the merits when filed by a plaintiff who has once dismissed in any court of the United States or of any state an action based on or including the same claim."

... [T]he primary meaning of "dismissal without prejudice," we think, is dismissal without barring the plaintiff from returning later, to the same court, with the same underlying claim. That will also ordinarily (though not always) have the consequence of not barring the claim from *other* courts, but its primary meaning relates to the dismissing court itself....

We think, then, that the effect of the "adjudication upon the merits" default provision of Rule 41(b)—and, presumably, of the explicit order in the present case that used the language of that default provision—is simply that, unlike a dismissal "without prejudice," the dismissal in the present case barred refiling of the same claim in the United States District Court for the Central District of California. That is undoubtedly a necessary condition, but it is not a sufficient one, for claim-preclusive effect in other courts.

III

Having concluded that the claim-preclusive effect, in Maryland, of this California federal diversity judgment is dictated neither by *Dupasseur v. Rochereau*, as petitioner contends, nor by Rule 41(b), as respondent contends, we turn to consideration of what determines the issue. Neither the Full Faith and Credit Clause, U.S. Const., Art. IV, § 1, nor the full faith and credit statute, 28 U.S.C. § 1738, addresses the question. By their terms they govern the effects to be given only to state-court judgments (and, in the case of the statute, to judgments by courts of territories and possessions). And no other federal textual provision, neither of the Constitution nor of any statute, addresses the claim-preclusive effect of a judgment in a federal diversity action.

It is also true, however, that no federal textual provision addresses the claim-preclusive effect of a federal-court judgment in a federal-question case, yet we have long held that States cannot give those judgments merely whatever effect they would give their own judgments, but must accord them the effect that this Court prescribes. . . . The reasoning of that line of cases suggests, moreover, that even when States are allowed to give federal judgments (notably, judgments in diversity cases) no more than the effect accorded to state judgments, that disposition is by direction of *this* Court, which has the last word on the claim-preclusive effect of *all* federal judgments. . . .

In other words, in *Dupasseur* the State was allowed (indeed, required) to give a federal diversity judgment no more effect than it would accord one of its own judgments only because reference to state law was *the federal rule that this Court deemed appropriate*. In short, federal common law governs the claim-preclusive effect of a dismissal by a federal court sitting in diversity. See generally R. Fallon, D. Meltzer, & D. Shapiro, Hart and Wechsler's The Federal Courts and the Federal System 1473 (4th ed. 1996); Degnan, Federalized Res Judicata, 85 Yale L.J. 741 (1976).

It is left to us, then, to determine the appropriate federal rule. And despite the sea change that has occurred in the background law since *Dupasseur* was decided—not only repeal of the Conformity Act but also the watershed decision of this Court in *Erie*—we think the result decreed by *Dupasseur* continues to be correct for diversity cases. Since state, rather than federal, substantive law is at issue there is no need for a uniform federal rule. And indeed, nationwide uniformity in the substance of the matter is better served by having the same claim-preclusive rule (the state rule) apply whether the dismissal has been ordered by a state or a federal court. This is, it seems to us, a classic case for adopting, as the federally prescribed rule of decision, the law that would be applied by state courts in the State in which the federal diversity court sits. . . . As we have alluded to above, any other rule would produce the sort of "forum-shopping . . . and . . . inequitable administration of the laws" that *Erie* seeks to avoid . . . since filing in, or removing to, federal court would be encouraged by the divergent effects that the litigants would anticipate from likely grounds of dismissal. . . .

This federal reference to state law will not obtain, of course, in situations in which the state law is incompatible with federal interests. If, for example, state law did not accord claim-preclusive effect to dismissals for willful violation of discovery orders, federal courts' interest in the integrity of their own processes might justify a contrary federal rule. No such conflict with potential federal interests exists in the present case. Dismissal of this state cause of action was decreed by the California federal court only because the California statute of limitations so required; and there is no conceivable federal interest in giving that time bar more effect in other courts than the California courts themselves would impose.

. . . .

Because the claim-preclusive effect of the California federal court's dismissal "upon the merits" of petitioner's action on statute-of-limitations grounds is governed by a federal rule that in turn incorporates California's law of claim preclusion (the content of which we do not pass upon today), the Maryland Court of Special Appeals erred in holding that the dismissal necessarily precluded the bringing of this action in the Maryland courts. The judgment is reversed, and the case remanded for further proceedings not inconsistent with this opinion.

Notes and Questions

1. What is the point of deciding that federal common law governs the preclusive effect of a federal diversity judgment in state court if that law in turn "adopts" the preclusion law of the state in which the federal court sits?

2. Does the logic of *Semtek*, coupled with the principles of *Erie*, suggest that the preclusion law that would be applied by the state in which the transferor court sits should control? If so, does that mean that in federal multidistrict proceedings consolidating multiple cases from many different district courts, as many different preclusion regimes as there are transferor courts may determine the preclusive effect of the multidistrict court's judgment? Would or should the answer to that question change if one or more of the cases before the multidistrict court were a nationwide class action with class members residing in multiple states, as opposed to individual actions filed by plaintiffs residing in those states? Would it matter if, following transfer of multiple individual and perhaps less than comprehensive class actions to the multidistrict court, an amended class action complaint were filed that included all of the previously asserted claims?

3. Entirely apart from multidistrict litigation, is the preclusive effect of a federal court's judgment in a state-law class action determined by the preclusion law of the

state in which the federal court sits or by the preclusion law of the state whose substantive law applies to the claims of the class? Does that depend on what preclusion law the state in which the federal class action court sits would apply to those claims? What preclusion law applies if subclasses from various states whose claims are governed by differing state laws are formed?

4. Given Justice Scalia's conclusion that federal common law must govern the preclusive effect of a federal court's judgment in a diversity action, it is clear that, as the Court recognized, state preclusion principles need not be adopted, "in situations in which the state law is incompatible with federal interests." *Semtek*, 531 U.S. at 509. The Court cited as a possible example, a federal court's dismissal for "willful violations of [a federal court's] discovery orders." *Id.* Do the complexities arising in federal multidistrict proceedings reviewed in the previous paragraphs suggest that in such proceedings, federal, rather than state, preclusion principles, should govern the preclusive effect of all final judgments of a federal multidistrict court, even in cases governed by state substantive law?

Index

[References are to sections.]

D

E

F

I

J

W